# Philosophy of Economics

# Handbook of the Philosophy of Science

*General Editors*

Dov M. Gabbay
Paul Thagard
John Woods

# Handbook of the Philosophy of Science
# Volume 13
# Philosophy of Economics

*Edited by*

**Uskali Mäki**

Director, Academy of Finland Centre of Excellence
in the Philosophy of the Social Sciences
University of Helsinki, Finland
Department of Political and Economic Studies

ELSEVIER

AMSTERDAM • BOSTON • HEIDELBERG • LONDON • NEW YORK • OXFORD
PARIS • SAN DIEGO • SAN FRANCISCO • SINGAPORE • SYDNEY • TOKYO
North Holland is an imprint of Elsevier

N·H

North Holland is an imprint of Elsevier
The Boulevard, Langford lane, Kidlington, Oxford, OX5 1GB, UK
Radarweg 29, PO Box 211, 1000 AE Amsterdam, The Netherlands

First edition 2012



**British Library Cataloguing in Publication Data**
A catalogue record for this book is available from the British Library

**Library of Congress Cataloging-in-Publication Data**
A catalog record for this book is available from the Library of Congress

ISBN: 978-0-444-51676-3

For information on all North Holland publications
visit our web site at elsevierdirect.com

Printed and bound by CPI Group (UK) Ltd, Croydon, CR0 4YY
Transferred to Digital Print 2012

For TINT

# GENERAL PREFACE

Dov Gabbay, Paul Thagard, and John Woods

Whenever science operates at the cutting edge of what is known, it invariably runs into philosophical issues about the nature of knowledge and reality. Scientific controversies raise such questions as the relation of theory and experiment, the nature of explanation, and the extent to which science can approximate to the truth. Within particular sciences, special concerns arise about what exists and how it can be known, for example in physics about the nature of space and time, and in psychology about the nature of consciousness. Hence the philosophy of science is an essential part of the scientific investigation of the world.

In recent decades, philosophy of science has become an increasingly central part of philosophy in general. Although there are still philosophers who think that theories of knowledge and reality can be developed by pure reflection, much current philosophical work finds it necessary and valuable to take into account relevant scientific findings. For example, the philosophy of mind is now closely tied to empirical psychology, and political theory often intersects with economics. Thus philosophy of science provides a valuable bridge between philosophical and scientific inquiry.

More and more, the philosophy of science concerns itself not just with general issues about the nature and validity of science, but especially with particular issues that arise in specific sciences. Accordingly, we have organized this Handbook into many volumes reflecting the full range of current research in the philosophy of science. We invited volume editors who are fully involved in the specific sciences, and are delighted that they have solicited contributions by scientifically-informed philosophers and (in a few cases) philosophically-informed scientists. The result is the most comprehensive review ever provided of the philosophy of science.

Here are the volumes in the Handbook:

Philosophy of Science: Focal Issues, edited by Theo Kuipers.

Philosophy of Physics, edited by Jeremy Butterfield and John Earman.

Philosophy of Biology, edited by Mohan Matthen and Christopher Stephens.

Philosophy of Mathematics, edited by Andrew Irvine.

Philosophy of Logic, edited by Dale Jacquette.

Philosophy of Chemistry, edited by Andrea Woody, Robin Hendry and Paul Needham.

Philosophy of Statistics, edited by Prasanta S. Bandyopadhyay and Malcolm Forster.

Philosophy of Information, edited by Pieter Adriaans and Johan van Benthem.

Philosophy of Technology and Engineering Sciences, edited by Anthonie Meijers.

Philosophy of Complex Systems, edited by Cliff Hooker.

Philosophy of Ecology, edited by Bryson Brown, Kent Peacock and Kevin de Laplante.

Philosophy of Psychology and Cognitive Science, edited by Paul Thagard.

Philosophy of Economics, edited by Uskali Mäki.

Philosophy of Linguistics, edited by Ruth Kempson, Tim Fernando and Nicholas Asher.

Philosophy of Anthropology and Sociology, edited by Stephen Turner and Mark Risjord.

Philosophy of Medicine, edited by Fred Gifford.

Details about the contents and publishing schedule of the volumes can be found at http://www.elsevier.com/wps/find/bookseriesdescription.cws_ home/BS_ HPHS/ description

As general editors, we are extremely grateful to the volume editors for arranging such a distinguished array of contributors and for managing their contributions. Production of these volumes has been a huge enterprise, and our warmest thanks go to Jane Spurr and Carol Woods for putting them together. Thanks also to Lauren Schulz and Derek Coleman at Elsevier for their support and direction.

# CONTENTS

## B. Specific Methods, Theories, Approaches, Paradigms, Schools, Traditions

# PREFACE

Uskali Mäki

In the course of its history, economics has been variously defined, including as the study of the consequences of actors' selfish pursuit of maximum wealth; and more abstractly in terms of 'economizing' or 'getting the most for the least'; in terms of exchange in the market; in terms of whatever can be identified by 'the measuring rod of money'; and in terms of rational choice faced with the scarcity of means in relation to the multiplicity of ends.

Even if conceived as a science of choice, only a small proportion of economic explanation is designed to explain episodes of individual behaviour. Most of it seeks to account for aggregate or social level phenomena, patterns, or regularities that have been observed statistically or through ordinary experience. The highly idealized and formalized models built for this purpose depict various kinds of social — typically market-like — "invisible hand" mechanisms that mediate between individual choices and collective outcomes as their unintended consequences. Such outcomes are represented as equilibrium positions, and their explanation or prediction often does not describe the process whereby the equilibria are attained. Adding a normative dimension to the explanatory use of social mechanisms, these outcomes have been portrayed either as generous such as in the Mandevillean idea of "private vices, public virtues" and in contemporary welfare theorems, or else as undesirable products of "invisible backhand" mechanisms of prisoner's dilemma type.

Economics has characteristics that make it a particularly inviting target and playground for philosophical argument and analysis. Economics is, and throughout its history has been, a chronically contested discipline. For some, it is *the queen of the social sciences*, characterized by uncompromised formal rigour and indispensable cognitive authority in social engineering — perhaps the only social science worth the name 'science'. For others, it is *the dismal science* in the special sense of being an empirical failure and of promoting dubious cultural values and group interests in society — a discipline that is only pretentiously scientific. (See [Mäki, 2002].)

There are many things that contribute to the controversial nature of economics. It is an academic discipline with broad public dimensions. Its concerns are connected to the most basic aspects of people's daily lives. The ideological and political stakes are obvious. As an epistemic institution, economics enjoys a strong position in contemporary society, with an institutionalized authority unquestioned by many. Yet it deals with a subject matter that is very complex and hard to get under epistemic control, so the chances of error are considerable. At the same time,

Handbook of the Philosophy of Science. Volume 13: Philosophy of Economics.
Volume editor: Uskali Mäki. General editors: Dov M. Gabbay, Paul Thagard and John Woods.

its subject matter is close to commonsense experience and beliefs, but economic theory violates them in two recognizable ways: through its theoretical idealizations, and through the corrections it suggests to make of commonsense beliefs by replacing them with allegedly deeper but counter-intuitive theories. Finally, an important source of controversy is a chronic mismatch between expectations and actual performance in relation to whatever goals economics is supposed to pursue.

Indeed, the proper goals or appropriate ambitions of economics are far from unambiguous. Some take it as an important task of economics to provide reliable predictions that will support its authoritative role in guiding economic policy. Repeated predictive failures have given rise both to ridicule among the critics and to more modest goal setting among practitioners. Such more modest goals can include some sort of explanatory understanding of how phenomena in the world might come about, or pointing out the various unavoidable tradeoffs in life, reminding the uninformed of the unpleasant fact of scarcity of resources in relation to people's wants (in doing the latter, economics would be a dismal science in an authentic sense while having some limited policy relevance). Yet, whatever view is adopted about the ambitions of economics, there will always remain some room for the critic to be dissatisfied with its performance.

Explicit controversy is typically prompted by an actual or alleged failure by economics, often at times of a crisis in the economy itself. Under the pressure of criticism and skepticism, some economists set out to defend their discipline. On both sides, arguments often ascend to metatheoretical and philosophical heights and become claims about the proper method and appropriate understanding of the nature of theory and of the goals of inquiry. Such debates, instigated by economic crises, have understandably followed a somewhat cyclical pattern.

Another possible source of philosophical reflection and debate is the emergence of new theories or research techniques that challenge more established ways of doing economics. The *Methodenstreit* of the 1880s was launched by Carl Menger's attempt to create space and justification for his new marginalist theory in the German-speaking world that was dominated by the historical school. More recently, the initiatives of experimental, behavioural and neuroeconomics have launched methodological debate and research, with philosophical arguments designed and used either to justify the new approaches or to question them.

During the $19^{th}$ century and for the most part of the $20^{th}$, philosophical and methodological arguments were designed and presented by thinkers who were also practitioners in economic inquiry. Not only were they practitioners, but many of them were among the leading economists of their time. These have included Nassay Senior, John Stuart Mill, Karl Marx, Wilhelm Roscher, William Stanley Jevons, Carl Menger, Alfred Marshall, Vilredo Pareto, Frank Knight, Lionel Robbins, Friedrich Hayek, Milton Friedman, Paul Samuelson, to name a few. At that time, there was no separate field of research for philosophical reflection on economics. On certain occasions, practitioners responded to the felt need for such reflection, but this did not lead to a collective and cumulative research characteristic of a field of specialized inquiry. Recognizable traditions were created, but there was little cumulative progress across generations concerning the details of the arguments.

This started changing in the late 1970s as a *field* of specialization started taking shape, known as the 'philosophy of economics' or 'economic methodology' depending on the primary disciplinary context of the activity. The usual indicators of an institutionalized research field could soon be identified, such as a growing number of specialists identifying themselves with the activity; development of an intensive and extensive network of communication between them; conferences and conference sessions focusing on shared research topics; growing number of publications, both books and journal articles; founding of specialized journals in the field (*Economics and Philosophy* since 1985 and the *Journal of Economic Methodology* since 1994); a loosely defined shared research agenda, or an interconnected set of (rival and complementary) agendas; a more formalized international organization (the International Network for Economic Method [INEM] since 1989); international graduate programmes (e.g., Erasmus Institute for Philosophy and Economics [EIPE] since 1997). As unmistakable indicators of an established field, there are handbooks such as the present one, and before it, *The Handbook of Economic Methodology* [Davis *et al.*, 1998] and *The Oxford Handbook of Philosophy of Economics* [Kincaid and Ross, 2009]. There are also many anthologies that jointly cover a great deal of ground in the expanding area (e.g., [Caldwell, 1993; Davis, 2006; Hausman, 2007]).

The early stages of the field in the 1970s and the 1980s were largely shaped by an alliance with the history of economic thought that was itself experiencing a similar growth. Most participants had a background in economics rather than philosophy. Karl Popper and Imre Lakatos were the authors whose then popular and easily accessible ideas in the philosophy of science were consulted and put in use in addressing questions such as: Are economic theories falsifiable or in general empirically testable? Does (this or that theory or field in) economics make progress? Given that these and other related questions had to be largely answered in the negative, the conclusion was drawn that Popperian and Lakatosian frameworks, strictly interpreted, had better be abandoned.

The situation is now very different. Philosophy and methodology of economics has in many respects a much closer connection with frontline philosophy of science. It not only critically employs a larger range of up-to-date ideas and tools developed elsewhere in philosophy, but it also contributes to the rest of philosophy of science, based on new ideas and results developed when examining economics. While large parts of the work are still done as history and methodology of economics by economists within economics departments, an increasing proportion is done within philosophy departments as contributions to the philosophy of science.

The topics and issues of inquiry still mostly derive from the practice of economic research and debate, but the ways in which they are portrayed and resolved are increasingly dependent on contemporary developments in the philosophy of science. The (un)realisticness of assumptions in what are nowadays called models is an old and central issue, and now the philosophical analysis of economic models is in close contact with the new work on models and modeling in the rest of the philosophy of science. Issues of causation are central for understanding economic reasoning, and the systematic utilization of philosophical work on causation has started recently. The newly launched analysis of economic explanation is connected to the ongoing philosophical work on mechanisms, unification, and contrastive questions. Many of the contributions to the philosophy of economics address issues in emerging subfields of economics, such as experimental, evolutionary, computational, institutional, behavioural, geographical as well as neuro economics. In these areas the philosophical issues are fresh and hot, providing philosophers the opportunity to watch closely and perhaps to intervene.

Much of this work is done and presented without waving flags with philosophical "isms" printed on them. Yet such labels are used and can be applied. Among the available positions we find Milton Friedman's alleged "instrumentalism" which is supposedly the position held by many practitioners. Other practitioners (but few if any philosophers of economics) may still find Popper's and Lakatos's "falsificationist" frameworks attractive, especially in their metatheoretical rhetoric. Variants of "neo-Millian" realism have been formulated by philosophers (such as Daniel Hausman, Nancy Cartwright, and myself). "Critical realism" inspired by Roy Bhaskar's work has won some souls just as in some other social sciences. There are also those — including some who pursue the rhetoric of inquiry project — who identify themselves as proponents of relativism, social constructivism or postmodernism.

The chapters of this volume are divided into two groups. Chapters in the first group deal with various philosophical issues characteristic of economics in general, from realism and Lakatos to explanation and testing, from modelling and mathematics to political ideology and feminist epistemology. Those in the second group discuss particular methods, theories and branches of economics, from forecasting and measurement to econometrics and experimentation, from rational choice and agency issues to game theory and social choice, from behavioural economics and public choice to geographical economics and evolutionary economics, and finally the economics of scientific knowledge.

The philosophy of economics is increasing in importance. First, in society at large, strong "economistic" trends (of marketization, commercialization, commodification, monetization) increasingly shape our cultural and mental landscape, and the discipline of economics relates to these processes both as a spectator and as a contributor. The performance of economics in these roles calls for philosophical scrutiny. Second, science is part of the social world and thereby also subject to these very same trends. "Naturalizing" the philosophy of science by utilizing the resources of economics therefore seems only natural. But the credibility and reliability of economics in that higher-order role is an open issue, again calling for philosophical reflection.

The undertaking ending up with this volume has taken time and effort. I warmly thank the contributors for agreeing to participate and for doing their share so excellently. Coordinating such a large group of authors has been a rewarding challenge. My thanks also go to Jane Spurr and Carol Woods for their help and encouragement as well as to the series editors, Dov Gabbay, Paul Thagard and John Woods. I am also grateful to Ilmari Hirvonen and Päivi Seppälä for preparing the Index.

## BIBLIOGRAPHY

[Caldwell, 1993] B. Caldwell, ed. *The Philosophy and Methodology of Economics.* Volumes I-III. Aldershot: Elgar, 1993.

[Davis *et al.*, 1998] J. B. Davis, D. W. Hands, and U. Mäki, eds. *The Handbook of Economic Methodology.* Cheltenham: Edward Elgar, 1998.

[Davis, 2006] J. B. Davis, ed. *Recent Developments in Economic Methodology.* Volumes I-III. Cheltenham: Elgar, 2006.

[Hausman, 2007] D. M. Hausman, ed. *Philosophy of Economics. An Anthology.* Cambridge: Cambridge University Press, 2007.

[Kincaid and Ross, 2009] H. Kincaid and D. Ross, eds. *The Oxford Handbook of the Philosophy of Economics.* Oxford: Oxford University Press, 2009.

[Mäki, 2002] U. Mäki. The dismal queen of the social sciences. In *Fact and Fiction in Economics. Realism, Models, and Social Construction*, pp. 3–34, U. Mäki, ed. Cambridge: Cambridge University Press, 2002.

# CONTRIBUTORS

**Paul Anand**
The Open University, UK.
p.anand@open.ac.uk
**Erik Angner**
University of Alabama at Birmingham, USA.
angner@uab.edu
**Roger E. Backhouse**
University of Birmingham, UK and Erasmus University Rotterdam, The Netherlands.
r.e.backhouse@bham.ac.uk
**Cristina Bicchieri**
Univeristy of Pennsylvania, USA.
cb36@sas.upenn.edu
**Marcel Boumans**
University of Amsterdam, The Netherlands.
m.j.boumans@uva.nl
**John Davis**
Marquette University, USA and University of Amsterdam, The Netherlands.
john.davis@marquette.edu
**Clive W. J. Granger**
University of California at San Diego, USA.
cgranger@ucsd.edu
**Til Grüne-Yanoff**
Helsinki Collegium of Advanced Study, Finland.
till.grune@helsinki.fi
**Francesco Guala**
University of Milan, Italy.
francesco.guala@unimi.it
**D. Wade Hands**
University of Puget Sound, USA.
hands@pugetsound.edu
**Daniel Hausman**
University of Wisconsin at Madison, USA.
dhausman@wisc.edu

**Kevin Hoover**
Duke University, USA.
kd.hoover@duke.edu
**Harold Kincaid**
University of Alabama at Birmingham, USA.
kincaid@uab.edu
**Hartmut Kliemt**
Frankfurt School of Finance and Management, Germany.
h.kliemt@frankfurt-school.de
**Tarja Knuuttila**
University of Helsinki, Finland.
tarja.knuuttila@helsinki.fi
**Aki Lehtinen**
University of Helsinki, Finland.
aki.lehtinen@helsinki.fi
**Christian List**
London School of Economics, UK.
C.List@lse.ac.uk
**George Loewenstein**
Carnegie Mellon University, USA.
gl20@andrew.cmu.edu
**Uskali Mäki**
University of Helsinki, Finland.
uskali.maki@helsinki.fi
**Caterina Marchionni**
University of Helsinki, Finland.
caterina.marchionni@helsinki.fi
**Philip Mirowski**
University of Notre Dame, USA.
Philip.E.Mirowski.1@nd.edu
**Mary S. Morgan**
London School of Economics, UK.
M.Morgan@lse.ac.uk
**Kristina Rolin**
Aalto University, Finland.
kristina.rolin@hse.fi
**Don Ross**
University of Cape Town, South Africa.
don.ross@uct.ac.za
**Aris Spanos**
Virginia Tech, Blacksburgh, USA.
aris@vt.edu

**Viktor J. Vanberg**
University of Freiburg, Germany.
vvanberg@vwl.uni-freiburg.de
**Jack Vromen**
Erasmus University of Rotterdam, The Netherlands.
vromen@fwb.eur.nl
**Jesus Zamora Bonilla**
UNED, Spain
jpzb@fsof.uned.es
**Jiji Zhang**
California Institute of Technology, USA.
jiji@hss.caltech.edu

Part A

# General Philosophical Themes

# REALISM AND ANTIREALISM ABOUT ECONOMICS

Uskali Mäki

## 1 INTRODUCTION

Economics is a controversial scientific discipline. One of the traditional issues that has kept economists and their critics busy is about whether economic theories and models are about anything real at all. The critics have argued that economic models are based on assumptions that are so utterly unrealistic that those models become purely fictional and have nothing informative to say about the real world. Many also claim that an antirealist instrumentalism (allegedly outlined by Milton Friedman in 1953) justifying such unrealistic models has become established as the semi-official practitioners' philosophy of conventional economics. Others argue that what is the case in the economy and the way economics relates to it are socially constructed such that there is no economics-independent way the world works or truths about it. On both of these pictures, realism would seem to have little to do with economics.

These pictures are too simplistic. There is more realism in and about economics than first would appear. To see this requires not just looking more closely, but also adjusting one's conception of scientific realism. It also requires taking a critical stance on much of what economists themselves and other commentators have claimed. Yet, historically, there is much wisdom available in the philosophical self-image of the discipline.

## 2 SCIENTIFIC REALISM IN CONVENTIONAL PHILOSOPHY OF SCIENCE

Conventional versions of scientific realism characteristically celebrate science for its achievements in penetrating into the secrets of nature and manipulating it [Psillos, 1999]. Indeed, much of the philosophy of science literature on scientific realism seems tailored for discussing issues around successful physical sciences. Given that economics does not deal with physical subject matter, that it does not obviously exhibit the sort of predictive and technological success usually attributed to the physical sciences, and that chronic controversy seems constitutive of economics, there is reason for some rethinking. One might simply conclude that scientific

Handbook of the Philosophy of Science. Volume 13: Philosophy of Economics.
Volume editor: Uskali Mäki. General editors: Dov M. Gabbay, Paul Thagard and John Woods.

realism is not a relevant issue for economics and its philosophy [Hausman, 1999; 2000; 2009]. Or one could conclude that formulations of scientific realism need to be adjusted so as to bring them closer to the concerns of a larger variety of disciplines such as economics [Mäki, 1996; 2000; 2005].

That these two indeed are the major options becomes obvious as we cite some of the representative formulations of scientific realism in the philosophy of science. Michael Devitt puts his version in primarily ontological terms: according to scientific realism "[t]okens of most current unobservable scientific physical types objectively exist independently of the mental." [Devitt, 1991, 24] Among the troubling elements here are 'unobservable', 'physical' and 'exist independently of the mental'. Economics does not deal with entities that are unobservable in the same way as paradigm cases in physics are, such as electrons and electromagnetic fields and ions. And the entities that economics does deal with do not exist independently of the mental. Just think of preferences and expectations, money and prices, households and business firms: they depend on human minds for their existence.

The famous Boyd-Putnam formulation was suggested as part of an argument for scientific realism: "terms in a mature science typically refer" and "the laws of a theory belonging to a mature science are typically approximately true" [Putnam, 1975-76, 179]. These claims are proposed to define scientific realism and are then supposed to provide the best explanation for the uncontroversial predictive and technological success of science: if scientific realism were not true, the success of science would be an inexplicable miracle. However, in the case of economics, there is no such similar obvious fact of success to be explained. Given that it is not clear whether there is any other sense in which economics might be a "mature science" whose "laws" are "approximately true", it is also not clear whether the Boyd-Putnam formulation is relevant to economics.

Rather strong epistemological formulations are popular in the philosophy of science. Instead of just suggesting that the world is knowable — that justifiable truths about it are attainable — scientific realism is taken to make the empirical claim that quite a bit of it is already known — that we are entitled to believe that many extant theories are true about it. Here is a characteristic formulation that stresses epistemic achievements: "Scientific realists suggest we have good reasons to believe that our best current scientific theories offer us literally true (or probably true, or approximately true, or probably approximately true) descriptions of how things stand in otherwise inaccessible domains of nature" [Stanford, 2003, 553]. Economists are typically very cautious in attributing literal truth to their theories and models (yet they tend to be more relaxed when talking about approximate truth), while they are far more prepared to attribute literal falsehood to models and their parts. But whatever beliefs and reasons about the truth of theories individual economists and their groups may have, they do not collectively share those beliefs and reasons to the extent of warranting the claim that as a disciplinary community of economists "*we* have good reasons" to have any, or at least very many, such beliefs.

The above selective summary suggests that the two options mentioned indeed seek to resolve a real discrepancy between standard formulations of scientific realism and the disciplinary reality of economics. One option is to put scientific realism aside as irrelevant; the other is to adjust those formulations so as to improve its relevance to economics and its philosophy. By taking the latter line we can see that much of the apparent antirealism in and about economics is just that, apparent only.

## 3 INGREDIENTS OF A MINIMAL SCIENTIFIC REALISM

The received conception of scientific realism has become an empirical thesis suggesting that good science (or most of current mature science) is justifiably believed to have gotten its theories (approximately) true about (mind-independently existing) unobservables, and this is why science is (explanatorily, predictively, and technologically) successful. In order not to drop economics from the realm of realism, we should see that we can instead drop all these elements and still keep our membership in the scientific realist club. What the members of the club share is a weaker version of realism: minimal scientific realism [Mäki, 2005; 2008].

Scientific realists should insist — as they have actually done — that being unobservable (a la electrons) is not an obstacle to existing in some required realist sense. But they should not insist that not being unobservable is an obstacle to being recognized as a philosophical issue to scientific realism. This is why minimal scientific realism does not include the notion of unobservability in its definition of scientific realism. It is enough to suppose that an item of interest to science may exist regardless of how that item is related to human perceptual faculties. This is important for accommodating many scientific disciplines that do not postulate electron-like unobservables.

Minimal realism should also avoid being specific about the kinds of thing that are considered for their existence. It should not take a restrictive stance on whether the existents are objects, properties, relations, structures, processes, events, powers, and so on. So minimal realism is uncommittal in the debates, say, over various versions of ontic structural realism as well as over the issue of dispositional and categorical properties. Closer scrutiny of research fields and specific theories is required in developing more local versions of scientific realism that include specific ideas about more specific sorts of thing that qualify as candidates for existing things. To flag this neutral attitude I use 'item' as a generic name for all conceivable existents.

Scientific realists should insist that many items in the world have a chance of existing mind-independently. The existence of electrons and solar systems, of mountains and monkeys is in no way dependent on the contents of human minds: what beliefs people have about them, what concepts and theories are held when talking about them. But minimal scientific realism does not include the notion of mind-independence in its definition of *scientific* realism. It is enough and appropriate to suggest that the items in the world exist *science-independently*. How exactly this will be cashed out in more detail depends on the further characteristics of the scientific discipline that is being considered.

A further important move is to set scientific realism free from established achievements by actual science. Instead of requiring that an item examined or postulated by science exists, it is enough to suppose that there is a chance that the item exists. Another way of putting this is to say that there is a fact of the matter as to whether an item does or does not exist science-independently. Nothing more is required by minimal scientific realism. This implies that one can be a realist about items that are only conjectured to exist. The insight behind this is that it takes a realist attitude for scientists to conjecture, and then conclude, perhaps after persistent inquiries, that an item does not exist after all — or else that it does. It is also no violation of realism not to draw either of these conclusions, but rather to suspend judgement, even indefinitely. Skepticism of this sort is compatible with minimal realism.

The same applies to truth. Instead of requiring that a theory is (approximately) true, it is enough to suppose that there is a chance that it is. In other words, there is a fact of the matter as to whether, and in what way, a theory is or is not true of the world, and this is independent of the beliefs scientists hold, of the evidence they have for or against the theory, of the persuasiveness of the arguments presented, and so on. For whatever reason, scientists can change their views about the truth of a theory, but this does not imply a change in its truth. Again, it takes a realist attitude to have such views as well as to change them. And it is no violation of this attitude if scientists suspend judgement as to whether a theory is true and remain agnostic, for however long. Scientists believing in the truth of theories with good reasons is too much to ask as a mark of scientific realism. A weaker sort of belief will do.

Minimal scientific realism does not require that science be portrayed as an uncontroversial success story. It is possible to be a realist about science without requiring that science has established its postulated entities as real and its theories as true, and it is not required that science exhibits triumphal predictive and technological achievements. Minimal scientific realism therefore is not set for offering a philosophical explanation of such achievements.

The minimalism suggested here enables accommodating scientific disciplines and episodes of scientific inquiry that are strongly hypothetical (speculative, conjectural, tentative) or erratic and uncertain, or predictively and technologically unsuccessful, or subject to chronic controversy and internal divisions. Perhaps they are like this because they are at their early or transitional stages of development; or because they are stuck on mistaken tracks of inquiry; or because they are subject to distorting political, ideological or commercial pressures; or because they deal with hard-to-access, epistemically recalcitrant materials. None of this as such rules out the possibility that theoretically postulated and examined things might exist in the world and that theories might be true about them; and that scientists, collectively and in the course of sufficiently long time spans, are interested in finding out the science-independent matters of fact about existence and truth; and that, prescriptively, scientists are to be urged to be so interested. And this — with qualifications — is all minimal realism is asking for.

One motive for formulating a minimal version of scientific realism is the recognition of diversity among scientific disciplines and research fields — not just any diversity, but one that has consequences for issues of realism and antirealism. While standard formulations of scientific realism fail to accommodate this diversity and therefore have limited scope, minimal realism is suitably undemanding and abstract to have a maximum reach or "applicability" across branches of science by depicting what they minimally share in common. Particular disciplines or research fields or even theories (or perhaps sufficiently uniform families of these) have special characteristics that can be captured by more specific local versions of realism.

Consider the role of epistemic confidence. Some disciplines are in a better position than others in determining whether a postulated item is real and whether a proposed theory is true. This difference may be due to the properties of the subject matter examined or to the stage or special trajectory of a discipline's development. The epistemically unlucky or immature disciplines should appropriately avoid excessive confidence and suspend definite epistemic judgement without violating realist principles.

Economics deals with a complex subject matter and is charged by its critics to have stuck on misguided tracks of inquiry and erroneous theoretical frameworks, but this does not appear to shake the confidence among many economists that they are doing the right thing. There is confidence on both sides, but this should not result in, respectively, antirealism and realism about economic theory. Both of them, as well as the various epistemic attitudes that reflect higher degrees of uncertainty, can be construed as attitudes compatible with, even presupposing, realism. So instead of implying a *philosophical* conflict between a realist and antirealist interpretation of (the success of) economics, we should construe the situation as a *scientific* conflict between two or more conceptions of whether economics has been successful. Grounds for confidence vary from discipline to discipline as well as within disciplines.

Consider then the issue of unobservables. Some disciplines face the issue of whether electron-like unobservables exist. Others don't. Economics deals with households and business firms, governments and central banks, preferences and expectations, money and prices, costs and revenues, wages and taxes, contracts and conventions. These are ordinary items that are recognizable experientially, and this is what distinguishes economics from physics. What economics and physics share in common is that they build models that are based on the heavy use of idealizations that are taken to be literally false about the world. Scientific realism faces special challenges in dealing with such falsehood. I will discuss these issues in the next section.

Then consider the issue of independence. Electrons and viruses and galaxies exist — if they do — mind-independently. Many central items in the domain of economics don't so exist. Their existence is essentially dependent on human minds. So we need to check if we can resort to the idea of science-independence in minimal scientific realism. Might the entities of economics and their properties exist economics-independently? This idea is challenged by the easy observation that ideas developed and promoted by academic economists at least occasionally appear to have consequences for the economy. Does scientific realism have a way of accommodating this observation? The literature on social constructivism and "performativity" prompts issues that I will discuss in the final section.

## 4 COMMONSENSIBLES AND THEIR MODIFICATIONS IN ECONOMIC MODELLING

### *Economics: science of commonsensibles*

Land, labour, and capital. Markets, money, prices. Private good, public good, merit good. Demand and supply. Individuals, households, business firms, central banks, government bureaus. Preferences, expectations, greed and fear. Cost and choice, budget and benefit. Competition, contract, convention. Auction, arbitrage, alertness. Risk, uncertainty, learning. Exchange and externality, property right and moral hazard. Wages, profits, taxes, subsidies, fairness. Saving and investment. Debt, mortgage, interest, trust. Unemployment, inflation, growth, recession. Trade, exports, imports. Competitiveness, comparative advantage, exchange rate. Gross Domestic Product, Sustainable Economic Welfare.

None of these look like electrons and their properties and behaviour. Indeed, there is a long tradition in economics of viewing the basic constituents of its subject matter as being familiar to us through commonsense experience. This has often been presented as a source of an epistemic advantage enjoyed by economics compared to physics. There is no direct access to the ultimate constituents of physical subject matter, so physics must infer to them from their effects, while economics deals with a domain that is more directly accessible through ordinary experience [Cairnes, 1888, 84]. This has implications for realism: "... the ultimate constituents of our fundamental generalizations are known to us by immediate acquaintance. In the natural sciences they are known only inferentially. There is much less reason to doubt the counterpart in reality of the assumption of individual preferences than that of the assumption of the electron" [Robbins, 1935, 105; see also 78-79]. Note that this optimism goes beyond mere minimal realism.

The idea should not be that economics deals with things of which we can have direct sense perception. The preferences and expectations of economic agents are unobservable in the sense of being inaccessible directly by senses. So are, say, multinational companies and the revenues they make and the institutional constraints they face. But they, just as money and prices, salaries and taxes, are familiar parts of our commonsense view of the social world within which we live our daily lives. These are *commonsensibles* rather than perceptibles or observables in any strict or pure sense. Commonsensibles involve concepts and inference, cultural meanings and shared interpretations - they involve the unavoidable hermeneutic moment of economics.

A further remove from being directly observable is due to the various modifications that the economically relevant commonsensibles undergo when theorized and modelled by economists. Goods exchanged in markets may become perfectly divisible in theoretical models. The messy local preferences familiar to us become transformed into the transitive and complete preferences of expected utility theory. Our local and flawed expectations become transformed into comprehensive rational expectations. Ordinary mortal people like us become infinitely lived agents in some models. Time-consuming and otherwise costly transactions become free and instantaneous. Internally structured business organizations with multiple goals become modelled as devoid of internal structure and pursuing nothing but maximum profits. Strategic rivalry between powerful price-making firms becomes non-strategic perfect competition among powerless price-taking firms. The (institutionally, culturally, politically and otherwise) complex structures of international trade of multiple goods between multiple countries become modeled as perfectly free trade of two goods between two countries with same technologies and same consumer tastes. Mathematical techniques of representation often make the items in such models even more poorly recognizable from the point of view of commonsense experience.

Given such theoretical transformations, one may wonder whether economics is really about commonsensibles after all. A natural doubt is that the items that appear to be talked about in economic theories and models are too far removed from ordinary experience and commonsense frameworks to qualify as commonsensibles, so it would be better to liken them with unobservables akin to electrons and viruses. In response to this doubt, one can argue that in modifying commonsensibles by various simplifications and idealizations the theorist does not thereby introduce entirely new kinds of entities and properties. There is no radical ontological departure from the realm of commonsense items when moving from boundedly rational to perfectly rational agents, or from messy preferences to well defined preferences, or from costly transactions to free transactions, or from time-consuming and permanently out-of-equilibrium processes to instant adjustments to market equilibria, or from particular market prices to inflation rates. Commonsensibles are modified by cognitive operations such as selection, omission, abstraction, idealization, simplification, aggregation, averaging. None of these amount to postulating new kinds of unobservable entities (but see the queries about macroeconomic entities by Hoover [2001]).

It is also possible to turn the above doubts about commonsensibles into doubts about existence. Not only do the idealizing modifications of ordinary items take them away from the commonsense realm, but they are taken away also from the realm of existents. Those idealized entities are fictions rather than candidates for real things. The philosophically minded economist Fritz Machlup has suggested just this idea. His prime example was the neoclassical or marginalist theory of the perfectly competitive firm [Machlup, 1967]. The theory depicts firms [1] as devoid of internal structure; [2] as perfectly informed; [3] as taking price signals as the only source of information; [4] as not interacting through rivalry; [5] as price takers rather than price makers; [6] as pursuing maximum profits as their only goal.

Machlup's reasoning is straightforward in concluding that in the neoclassical theory of the competitive firm, "all firms are pure fictions" [1967, 30], that the theory postulates "this purely fictitious single-minded firm" [1967, 10]. He warns against failing to keep apart these fictional theoretical firms and the familiar real organizations also called 'firms'. This may be interpreted as a claim about reference, implying that the term 'firm' in the neoclassical theory of the competitive firm fails to refer to real firms; and not only does it fail to so refer, but it is not even purported to refer. In the old-style instrumentalist manner, it is just an "intermediate variable" that serves useful functions in scientific inference without itself being connected to any real entities.

This conclusion derives from an implicit premise, the description theory of reference [Mäki, 1998]. According to this theory, the factual reference of a term is determined by the associated descriptions. Whenever those descriptions do not fit with anything in the world, the term fails to refer. So, the term 'firm' in the neoclassical theory of the competitive firm fails to refer to real firms simply because the assumptions of the theory [1]–[5] are not true of any real entities in the social world. This is why the assumptions cannot be used for identifying any real objects of reference.

There is no established account of reference to social objects that could here be appealed to in response to Machlup's fictionalism, but an obvious point of departure would be Donnellan's [1966] distinction between the attributive and referential uses of definite descriptions, the latter enabling the use of false descriptions referentially. We could generalise on this idea and suggest an analogous distinction for general descriptive terms such as 'firm': the assumptions associated to the term in neoclassical theory can be used both referentially and attributively. Machlup's suggested primary use of 'firm' is attributive. This enables him to infer to the conclusion that because nothing in the world satisfies the description provided by neoclassical assumptions, the term in this theoretical context is not to be used to refer to any things in the world. The alternative is to use the term referentially. In this case we hold that even if nothing in the social world satisfies the attribute of being a perfectly informed atomistic price-taking maximizer, it is not out of the question that the description can be used to pick out a class of non-fictional entities, namely real business firms. Just as I can be mistaken about your age and shoe size and still be talking about you, economists may employ false assumptions about firms and yet talk about them.

Once reference to real things is secured, we are ready to ask for the rationale for false descriptions. The literature in the theory of reference usually cites error, ignorance, and incompleteness as sources of falsehood. However, when an economist makes unrealistic assumptions, she is often not making an error or being ignorant. She is instead deliberately employing strategic falsehoods in order to attain some epistemic and pragmatic gains. This is the point of idealization.

## *Isolation by idealization*

In $19^{th}$ century economics, it was popular to think of economic theory as focusing on just a limited set of causally relevant factors and to examine the consequences of their functioning in the absence of other factors, that is, in the abstract. A more concrete account of the empirical world would require incorporating further causes that also contribute to the shaping of phenomena. Emphasizing different aspects of variations of this overall image of economic theorizing, J.S. Mill [1832] had ideas about the decomposition and composition of causes, Karl Marx [1858] entertained a Hegelian dialectics of the abstract and the concrete, Carl Menger [1883] pursued economics as what he called an exact science, Alfred Marshall [1890] explicitly employed the ceteris paribus clause, and so on.

Economic theories were often conceived in terms of their "premises" that were believed to be true even if incomplete. In these premises, agents were described as selfish and seeking nothing but maximum wealth, and returns in agriculture were described as diminishing. So on the one hand, it is

> "positively true ... to assert that men desire wealth, that they seek, according to their lights, the easiest and shortest means by which to attain their ends, and that consequently they desire to obtain wealth with the least exertion of labor possible". [Cairnes, 1888, 62]

On the other hand, it is

> "surely possible that the premises should be true, and yet incomplete — true so far as the facts which they assert go, and yet not including all the conditions which affect the actual course of events". [Cairnes 1888, 68]

Since not all causally influential factors are covered by a theory, its *implications* cannot be expected to match the phenomena. The factors covered by the theory in the real world combine with others not included in the theory. Therefore, its implications are true "hypothetically" only. As Cairnes writes, the conclusions of economics (but also of mechanics and astronomy)

> "when applied to facts, can only be said to be true in the absence of disturbing causes; which is, in other words, to say that they are true on the hypothesis that the premises include all the causes affecting the result". [Cairnes, 1888, p. 61]

A set of premises can be incomplete in two senses: first, in not listing all relevant causes (thus violating the whole truth); second, in not explicitly listing all the implicitly required idealizations (thus hiding its violation of nothing but truths). The first is the sense we find in Cairnes in the passages above. It enables Cairnes to claim that the premises can be true even if incomplete. The second can be understood as we notice that not listing all relevant causes – incompleteness in the first sense — can be implemented by way of formulating idealizing premises that neutralize some causes and so exclude them from theory or model. In the modellig style characteristic of $19^{th}$ century economics, such idealizations (or many of them) typically are not explicitly listed. Such idealizations are typically false if taken as claims about the world.

A strikingly modern approach was pursued by J.H. von Thünen [1826] who formulated a model of agricultural land use that has many characteristics of the $20^{th}$ century idea of economic model. He shared the idea that a model would only include a small set of causally relevant factors, but he also formulated his model using a number of explicitly stated idealizing assumptions of which he knew they are false — such as the region being of homogeneous fertility and climate, devoid of mountains and valleys, rivers and canals, with just one town in the middle, and no connections with the outer world. The point of the model was to isolate the causal role of distance from the town (mediated by transportation costs and land rents) in shaping the land-use structure in the region. The ensuing pattern in the model, that of concentric rings, is empirically inaccurate about any actual land-use structure, often by wide margins. This is unsurprising given the many causally relevant factors that the model excludes by its idealizations. Yet, von Thünen believed that his model managed to provide a true account of the functioning of the economic mechanism of distance. (See [Mäki, 2011].)

This work anticipated later styles of economic modelling, in which assumptions were formulated explicitly and more completely (but never fully) so as to make clear which potentially efficacious factors are being excluded. These assumptions state that some factors are absent or that some variables have the value of zero, while some others remain constant or within some normal intervals, and so on. Now *these* assumptions often are not true, and some of them never are. They are the idealizations that help neutralize the impact of many factors so as to enable focusing on the behaviour of and relationships between just a few at a time. The latter are thereby theoretically isolated from the former.

Given that one cannot guarantee that either those idealizations be true or that they are relaxed and replaced by other assumptions that jointly capture all relevant causal factors contributing to the occurrence of the phenomena of interest, predictive testing becomes particularly difficult. Indeed, the mainstream view in $19^{th}$ century economics was that theories cannot be expected to exhibit remarkable predictive successes and so are not to be tested by their predictions. Yet theories and models can be true of (fragments of) the world. This is in line with minimal scientific realism.

## *Friedman's 1953 essay*

The realist tradition has been supposed to be discontinued with Milton Friedman's and Fritz Machlup's statements in the early 1950s. The received interpretation of Friedman's 1953 essay portrays it as an antirealist and instrumentalist manifesto [Wong, 1971; Boland, 1979; Caldwell, 1990]. And given that Friedman's statement is typically taken to correctly characterize the theories, practices and attitudes of ("mainstream") economists, these practices and attitudes themselves are then taken to be antirealist rather than realist.

One can argue that this is not quite accurate and that Friedman's essay can be read as a realist statement and therefore not at all entirely out of phase with the earlier traditions (see e.g. [Mäki, 1990; 2009]; on realism in Friedman's economics, see [Hoover, 2009]).

Friedman had set out to defend conventional theory — in particular, the model of perfect competition and the assumption of profit maximization — against the criticisms that had been made against their unrealisticness. Friedman granted that many such assumptions are indeed unrealistic, but that this is irrelevant to their scientific value, or more strongly, a virtue in that "[t]ruly important and significant hypotheses will be found to have 'assumptions' that are wildly inaccurate descriptive representations of reality" [1953, 13]. All that matters — and this is a major deviation from the $19^{th}$ century tradition — is whether a theory or model predicts well, or predicts better than its rivals for a given purpose. From this many commentators have concluded that Friedman is committed to an instrumentalist conception of scientific theory that is uninterested in having true theories about the world.

While very insightful, Friedman's essay is also terribly confused and ambiguous, so readers can take liberties to provide their own favourite interpretations. A realist reading would appeal to passages like this: "the relevant question to ask about the 'assumptions' of a theory is ... whether they are sufficiently good approximations for the purpose at hand" [Friedman, 1953, 15]. So there is a fact of the matter as to how the assumptions relate to the world — and whether this is "sufficiently good" depends on the pragmatics of their use. Prediction fits in this picture in a non-instrumentalist manner, as a criterion of sufficient realisticness:

> the question whether a theory is realistic 'enough' can be settled only by seeing whether it yields predictions that are good enough for the purpose in hand or that are better than predictions from alternative theories. [1953, 41]

In other words, the unrealisticness of assumptions is not irrelevant after all. The task is to pay attention to their actual degree of realisticness and to judge whether it is sufficient for a given purpose.

Among the purposes or functions served by false idealizing assumptions is to help implement theoretical isolations in a controlled manner. One of Friedman's examples is Galileo's law of freely falling bodies and the associated assumption that air pressure is zero, so that bodies fall in a vacuum. To this we must add other idealizing assumptions, such as no magnetic forces and no other kinds of pushes and pulls such as the pull of the Moon and the other planets. These are mostly false assumptions that play the role of helping to isolate the impact of the Earth's gravity from other causal influences on the falling body. In analogy (that Friedman himself missed in his essay), one can construe the profit maximization assumption as involving the composite idealization that all other motives except the maximization motive have zero strength. The general realist principle is that theory construction is a matter of theoretical isolation whereby economists "abstract essential features of complex reality" (7).

This helps see why it is also a mistake to link Friedman's favourite as-if formulation of theory to instrumentalism. The as-if locution as such is a philosophically neutral tool that can be used for expressing a number of different ideas. A realist can use it for modelling phenomena in isolation, saying, "phenomena behave *as if* certain ideal conditions were met, viz. conditions under which only the theoretically isolated real forces are active (and we know those conditions are not actually met)", while an instrumentalist version suggests that "phenomena behave *as if* those forces were real (and we know those forces are not real)". Friedman uses the as-if in both ways, but here is a passage exhibiting his realist inclinations:

> A meaningful scientific hypothesis or theory typically asserts that certain forces are, and other forces are not, important in understanding a particular class of phenomena. It is frequently convenient to present such a hypothesis by stating that the phenomena it is desired to predict behave in the world of observation *as if* they occurred in a hypothetical and highly simplified world containing only the forces that the hypothesis asserts to be important. (40)

A major mistake by the proponents of the instrumentalist reading of Friedman's essay is to believe that the truth-value of a theory or model derives directly from the truth-values of its assumptions: false assumptions, therefore false theory, therefore instrumentalism. A minimal realist would argue that a theory or model with false assumptions is in principle capable of conveying true information about the world; or more strongly, that those idealizations are necessary strategic falsehoods for effecting theoretical isolation and thereby for acquiring true information about bits and pieces of the complex world.

## *Closed systems: Ontology vs methodology*

The above observations aspire to show how isolative theories and models based on idealizing assumptions are in line with scientific realism. This is not the only account available under the label of 'realism' in the philosophy of economics. There is a different understanding of realism whose proponents have argued otherwise, drawing their inspiration from Roy Bhaskar's work [Bhaskar, 1975; Lawson, 1997; 1999]. Their claim is that in its modelling practices "mainstream economics" depicts the economy as consisting of closed systems within which regular connections obtain between observable events. Economics is thereby committed to a "closed systems ontology" and an associated "Humean ontology of event regularities" while the underlying real causal mechanisms are not accessed by this method. This "positivist" and "deductivist" package essentially includes the extensive use of mathematics in creating and examining such closed system phenomena: "... the generalized use of formalistic economic methods presupposes that the social world is everywhere closed" [Lawson, 1999, 273]. Given that the real social world is open rather than closed, and given that causal mechanisms rather than event regularities are the real basis of social phenomena, mainstream economics is non-realist.

This account is questionable. The correct observation is that economists use methods of isolation, those of building and examining models that depict closed systems in some obvious sense, and that they use formal techniques in doing this. It is incorrect to infer from this observation that this practice is somehow committed to the ontology of closed systems and event regularities. To do so is to conflate methodology and ontology — to commit a fallacy of mistaking closed systems methods for a closed systems ontology. Instead of "economists use closed systems methods" implying "economists are committed to a closed systems ontology" the more likely correct inference would be from "economists believe the social world to be a very complex open system" to "economists use closed system methods as a way of addressing the complexity of the open social world" or some such. At any rate the latter is close to the spirit of the long methodological tradition in economics as outlined above – a spirit that I would characterize as realist. It is a different issue whether the methods actually used by economists – and the way they are used - are successful in accessing the complex subject matter (for example, whether the Millian tradition of composition of causes does justice to that complexity, see e.g. [Hausman, 2001]; or what roles econometrics can play in meeting the challenge, see e.g. [Hoover, 2001]).

## *Modelling invisible-hand mechanisms*

'Mechanism' is one of the most popular words used by economists. Indeed, economists believe to be modelling mechanisms of a variety of different kinds. Many of these mechanisms have an invisible-hand structure. Individuals with behavioural dispositions and powers act in pursuit of their individual goals; these are coordinated by some social structure, such as some market or market-like mechanism; and some aggregate level outcome will be produced, but not in virtue of individuals aiming at it. The invisible hand can generate welfare-enhancing outcomes in the spirit of Mandeville's "private vices, public virtues" as well as suboptimal outcomes of prisoner's dilemma type, mediated by the "invisible back-hand" [Aydinonat, 2008].

Invisible-hand mechanisms often produce "counter-intuitive" outcomes in the sense that they appear surprising or paradoxical from the point of view of ordinary uneducated points of view. Indeed, there is often a conflict between economic theory and the commonsense understanding of how the economy works — manifesting in conflicting perceptions such as free trade vs protectionism or growing government budget deficit vs spending cuts during recession. This might be taken to speak against the idea that economics is about commonsensibles.

One way of resolving the conflict is to recognize that the components of invisible-hand mechanisms are commonsensibles and that the way their mutual connections in causal structures are described in economic models departs from ordinary conceptions. In this sense, the familiar commonsensibles are both modified (by idealization etc.) and rearranged in theoretical economics. Given that economists believe that the causal rearrangement (possibly) gets the way the world works right, they thereby come to subscribe to more than just commonsense realism, namely scientific realism [Mäki, 1990; 1996].

Economists often initially only believe that the model they have built captures a mechanism that might be responsible for some phenomenon or pattern — rather than asserting that this is the mechanism actually responsible. So they use the model in offering a how-possibly explanation rather than a how-actually explanation. The abductive reasoning characteristic of much of theoretical modelling in economics is not inference to the best explanation but rather inference to a possible explanation. This feature of economic modelling fits very nicely with the stress in minimal realism on models and theories having a chance of being true (rather than having been established as true or being justifiably believed to be true of actual causation).

## 5 SOCIAL CONSTRUCTION (WHAT?) OF WHAT?

As economists in the $19^{th}$ century understood so well, it follows from the open systems character of the economy that theories and models are hard or impossible to test conclusively by their predictive implications. Later, Friedman exhibited awareness of these issues, downplaying his own emphasis on prediction as the goal and criterion of theorizing, and paying attention to its subjective and social aspects. In passages mostly neglected by commentators, Friedman stresses the roles of subjective judgement, disciplinary tradition and institutions, and consensus among economists, in shaping theory choice. These statements reinforce the admission that objectively decisive predictive tests are unavailable in economics. Here is a representative passage:

> Of course, neither the evidence of the economist nor that of the sociologist is conclusive. The decisive test is whether the hypothesis works for the phenomena it purports to explain. But a *judgment* may be required before any satisfactory test of this kind has been made, and, perhaps, when it cannot be made in the near future, in which case, the judgment will have to be based on the inadequate evidence available. In addition, even when a test can be made, *the background of the scientists* is not irrelevant to the judgments they reach. There is never certainty in science, and the weight of evidence for or against a hypothesis *can never be assessed completely "objectively."* The economist will be *more tolerant* than the sociologist in judging conformity of the implications of the hypothesis with experience, and he will be *persuaded* to accept the hypothesis tentatively by fewer instances of "conformity". (30; emphases added)

So complete objectivity in testing a theory is unattainable since *judgment* and *persuasion* are involved, and these are shaped by the *background* of the scientist and the degree of *tolerance* characteristic of a disciplinary culture. Another key passage recognizes the *tenacity* with which hypotheses are held against negative evidence and the powerful role of disciplinary *folklore* and *tradition* as well as *continued use* in creating the image of an acceptable hypothesis:

> [The evidence for the maximization-of-returns hypothesis] is extremely hard to document: it is scattered in numerous memorandums, articles, and monographs concerned primarily with specific concrete problems *rather than with submitting the hypothesis to test.* Yet the *continued use and acceptance* of the hypothesis over a long period, and the failure of any coherent, self-consistent alternative *to be developed and be widely accepted,* is strong indirect testimony to its worth. The evidence for a hypothesis always consists of its repeated failure to be contradicted, continues to accumulate so long as the hypothesis is used, and by its very nature is difficult to document at all comprehensively. It tends to become part of *the tradition and folklore of a science* revealed in the *tenacity* with which hypotheses are held rather than in any textbook list of instances in which the hypothesis has failed to be contradicted. (22-23; emphases added)

So Friedman's views in his 1953 essay were connected backwards to the $19^{th}$ century realist tradition as well as forward to later Kuhnian and social constructivist ideas about science [Mäki, 2009]. But social constructivism is usually considered an antirealist idea. Again, things are more complex and not always quite as they might first appear. We must ask: how much and what kinds of social construction can realism accommodate? Economics has been claimed to be rhetorical and "performative" with apparently antirealist implications, and it is by discussing these claims that we can set out to answer the question.

## *Rhetorical construction of world and truth?*

As an important part of a larger rhetoric of inquiry movement, the rhetorical aspects of economics started being highlighted in the emerging literature and debate from the early 1980s onwards (e.g., [McCloskey, 1985; McCloskey *et al.*, 1988; Mäki, 1995]). The general idea of rhetoric is that in writing and talking, people attempt to persuade their audiences by influencing the intensity of their beliefs. Scientific writing and talking is no exception: much of what scientists do is to try to persuade their various audiences (such as colleagues in their own and other fields, students, administrators, funding agencies, political decision makers, lay audiences).

Much of the literature on the rhetoric of economics has been preoccupied with the identification of various rhetorical ploys and textual strategies used by economists in their attempts to persuade. These include the use of metaphors (many of them having sources in physics and medicine), appeals to academic authority, intuition and introspection, and exhibiting mathematical brilliance. The rhetorical image of economics entertained by Deirdre McCloskey and Arjo Klamer has employed a "conversational model" of rhetoric: economics is conversation, and persuasion takes place within a conversation. McCloskey has enriched this into the notion of "honest conversation" by incorporating the idea of *Sprachethik*, defined in terms of principles such as, "Don't lie; pay attention; don't sneer; cooperate; don't shout; let other people talk; be open-minded; explain yourself when asked; don't resort to violence or conspiracy in aid of your ideas." (For the ethics of conversation about rhetoric, see [McCloskey, 1995; Mäki, 2000]).

None of the above as such has antirealist implications, but a central feature of the rhetoric of economics project (as pursued by McCloskey and Klamer) has been its outright antirealism, variously self-identified as relativism, pragmatism, social constructivism, or postmodernism. On this image of economics, whatever there is in the world and whatever is true about it, become just a result of rhetorical persuasion, a variant of social construction. Truth is nothing but persuasiveness, so truths are not something to be discovered, but rather to be constructed by way of rhetorical efforts. Truths are made in the conversations among those who are eligible of participation – the well-educated and well-behaved economists, as McCloskey has it. This sort of antirealism has been marketed as part of the package of economics as rhetorical.

However, it is obvious that one may acknowledge the reality and efficacy of rhetoric in scientific practice without implying such radically constructivist conclusions. The presence of rhetorical persuasion alone in no way rules out the possibility of attaining and communicating persuasion-independent truths about economic reality. While beliefs can be manipulated by rhetoric, truths cannot. A realist rhetoric, or rhetorical realism, is an option [Mäki, 1995]. Rather than taking reality and truth as outcomes of successful persuasive efforts, they can be viewed as independent of any such efforts, whether successful or unsuccessful, whether addressing some local audience or the "universal" audience, whether morally appropriate or inappropriate from the point of view of any formulation of the *Sprachethik*. The statements made by using economic models are true or false regardless of the successes and failures of the proponents of those statements in their attempts to persuade others to accept them. A model or a statement made in using the model is not true or false in virtue of being found persuasive or unpersuasive by a cohort of economists with a certain educational background, academic incentive structure, and moral standards.

This is not to say those factors are unimportant, on the contrary. It is obvious that various background beliefs and the institutional structure of economic research shape what is found persuasive and what counts as true at any given time. They also shape the likelihood of discovering persuasiveness-independent truths about the world by a community of inquirers. Admitting this much is to accept a modest social constructivism without radical antirealist implications. Yet in general, the recognition that rhetoric is real and consequential in scientific practice does not alone commit one to either antirealism or realism: such a recognition is relatively neutral regarding its philosophical implications and presuppositions.

## *"Performativity" and the economics-dependence of the economy*

While electrons and their kin exist — if they do — mind-independently, many central things in the domain of economics don't. Their existence is essentially dependent on human minds. What about the idea of science-independence in our minimal scientific realism? Might the entities of economics, their properties and behaviour exist economics-independently? Or might they and truths about them be dependent on economic theories and economists' beliefs? We have just discussed these issues in relation to the rhetoric of economics. Now we focus on the idea that economics is "performative" and thus shapes the social world — which implies that the world does not exist economics-independently after all.

There is a sense in which many things in society depend on science for their existence. Indeed, our social institutions and practices, beliefs and norms are deeply shaped by the products of science, from physics and biochemistry to epidemiology and psychology. Evidently, economics can be added to this list. There is a connection between the science of economics and the economic world that flows from the former to the latter. Economic theories and research results somehow directly shape people's beliefs and worldviews in ways that are relevant to their economic behaviour. Policy advice based on economic theories and research results shapes economic policies, and these in turn shape the economy. Moreover, economic theories, people's beliefs and economic facts are often connected through mechanisms of self-fulfillment and self-defeat. So there is no doubt that the economy is dependent on economics. One might conclude that the idea of science-independence does not serve scientific realism at all well in the case of economics.

To examine the issue, it will be useful to look more closely at the thesis of "performativity" — the idea that economics "performs" facts in the economy (e.g. [MacKenzie, 2006]). And in order to examine this performativity thesis, it will be useful to begin with a brief look at the original idea. On Austin's [1962] account of performativity, one performs an action by uttering some string of words, a performative sentence. If I say "I promise to deliver the paper by the deadline" I am thereby promising to deliver the paper by the deadline. To utter a performative sentence is not to describe a pre-existing action (e.g. of promising), it is to perform that action. *Saying so makes it so.* The connection between speaking words and doing things is one of *constitution* rather than causation. Saying "I apologize" constitutes the act of apologizing. Saying "I agree" constitutes the act of agreeing. Those utterings do not cause those acts, rather those acts are constituted by those utterings. To utter those sentences *is* to take those actions.

This authentic meaning of performativity has been obscured by the recent literature on how economic theory can have consequences for economic reality. MacKenzie recognizes the Austinian use of the term in characterizing certain speech acts in the world of finance such as when agreements and contracts are made. When, in response to an offer to sell or buy an asset at a particular price, someone says "done" or "agreed", then a deal is agreed [MacKenzie, 2006, 16]. Indeed, uttering such words performs the act of agreement, or in other words, constitutes it in a non-causal manner.

However, right thereafter the word 'performativity' is given three meanings that as such seem unrelated to the authentic meaning: an aspect of economics, such as an economic model, is performed in the sense of being used by economic agents ("generic performativity"); its use has consequences, it makes a difference ("effective performativity"); and its use makes the model more true ("Barnesian performativity") (17-19). MacKenzie's prime example is finance, so this gives three (or at least two) kinds of dependence of certain practices of finance in the real world on certain theories of finance – such as the Black–Scholes–Merton formula for option pricing.

In none of these three types of case is the relationship between an aspect of economics and some aspect of the economy constitutive. A constitutive relationship would require that uttering or writing down an economic model for an audience (that understands the model and perceives the uttering as genuine) establishes the model world as part of the real world. What is important is that in McKenzie's three kinds of case, the connection between economics and the economy is supposed to be implemented by the "use" of economics by economic actors. But using an economic model goes well beyond just recognizing it uttered or written down. Use involves taking further action. This undermines the idea that saying so non-causally makes it so.

Whatever one thinks of using the terms 'perform' and 'performativity' in novel (and somewhat obscure) ways, the important observation here is that a distinction must be drawn between constitution and causation, between an economic theory or model being connected to economic reality constitutively and causally. This is an important distinction because these two types of relationship have different implications for scientific realism.

The distinction has no such implications when applied to the subject matter of economics. The social world contains both causal and constitutive relationships, and realism is comfortable with both, simply because they are part of social reality. There is a formal contract between two economic actors provided these actors believe it is there and they — sometimes together with third parties – have performed the right sorts of speech acts indicating agreement. Such contracts belong to the subject matter of the economic theory of contracts. They are science-independent in that they are not created by acts of economic theorizing. Facts about such contracts are constituted by the beliefs and performative speech acts by the contracting parties, but they are not constituted (let alone "performed") by acts of scientific theorizing (let alone theories) about them. This is performativity within the economy, but not between economics and the economy.

Naturally economic theorizing can have consequences for the economy. But these consequences flow through indirect causal rather than direct constitutive connections. The popular phrase used is that the economy is "shaped" by economics. Literally speaking, economic theories do not shape the economy. Nor does economic inquiry. People do. In their various roles (as policymakers, students, investors, entrepreneurs, workers, consumers) people are exposed to the results of economic inquiry and learn, directly or indirectly, about the contents of economic theories, explanations and predictions, and are inspired by them, perhaps by being persuaded by the proponents, so as to modify their beliefs and perhaps their motives. These modified beliefs and motives make a difference for their behaviour, and this has consequences for the economy. The flow of these connections is a matter of causal influence rather than direct constitution. Hence the admission that some economic facts can be causally economics-dependent.

The same holds for MacKenzie's strongest form of "performativity" whereby the use of a model makes it more true, makes it more closely correspond to the world. If it happens that certain practices in real world finance are in line with the Black–Scholes–Merton formula for option pricing, this does not mean that the theoretical formula or its uttering by those three and other academic scholars "performs" those practices, making them occur by constitution. They may occur because the theoretical formula has managed to travel from academic research to economic practice in the manner outlined above. The connections are causal.

The possible causal connections between a theory and economic reality are limited in their powers to alter reality. Many of the idealizations of finance theory or particular models such as Black-Scholes-Merton are not made true by becoming known or found inspiring among market agents. Many of them just cannot be made true. Agents won't become omniscient or hyperrational even if they were to become increasingly calculative and self-seeking by being exposed to economic models in which agents are so portrayed. Transaction costs may diminish but not all the way to zero in consequence of using models that assume they are zero.

It is no threat to scientific realism about economics to acknowledge the possibility of causal economics-dependence of some items in the real-world economy. After all, economics as an academic discipline is itself social activity exercised within society, so such connections are a natural feature of social reality. Good social science will investigate such connections together with other causal connections in society at large.

What scientific realism about a fragment of science insists is the non-causal science-independence of the objects examined by that fragment (where 'science-independence' means independence of that fragment). This also suggests how to identify some of the opponents of scientific realism. Some versions of scientific antirealism hold that matters of fact in the (social) world are non-causally science-dependent, so can be created just by creating theoretical models of them. This would be a version of social constructivism too radical for scientific realism to accommodate.

## 6 CONCLUSION

Many further issues would have to be discussed in order to provide anything close to a comprehensive treatment of the issue of realism about economics. And many of the issues that have been discussed could be framed differently (for example in terms of more refined ideas about theoretical models). The foregoing remarks merely try to give a flavour of the sorts of special issues that need to be addressed in the case of economics, by general philosophers of science interested in scientific realism as well as those concerned about how economics performs and compares as a scientific discipline.

Philosophers of science should see that a narrow focus on a limited set of disciplines (such as physics) in developing generalized ideas about scientific realism (or just any philosophical account of science) will easily result in distorted images of some other disciplines or in dropping them from the realm of realism, thereby expelling them to the antirealist camp. Practicing economists and their critics should see that characteristics such as employing unrealistic assumptions, not postulating electron-like new unobservables, and the occasional economics-dependence of the economy are no obstacles to entertaining a scientific realist philosophy about economics.

One important lesson to draw is that formulating and using versions of scientific realism at different levels of abstraction and specificity (such as the most abstract minimal version and thicker versions tailored for particular disciplines or their parts) is useful in recognizing and examining what scientific disciplines share in common and how they differ from one another.

## BIBLIOGRAPHY

[Austin, 1962] J. L. Austin. *How to Do Things with Words.* Cambridge MA: Harvard University Press, 1962.

[Aydinot, 2008] E. Aydinonat. *The Invisible Hand in Economics.* London: Routledge, 2008.

[Bhaskar, 1975] R. Bhaskar. *A Realist Theory of Science.* Harvester, 1975.

[Boland, 1979] L. Boland. A critique of Friedman's critics, *Journal of Economic Literature* 17, 503-522, 1979.

[Cairnes, 1888] J. E. Cairnes. *The Character and Logical Method of Political Economy.* $2^{nd}$ ed. London. Macmillan, 1888.

[Caldwell, 1992] B. Caldwell. Friedman's methodological instrumentalism: A Correction, *Research in the History of Economic Thought and Methodology* 10, 119-128, 1992.

[Cartwright, 2001] N. Cartwright. Ceteris paribus laws and socio-economic machines. In *The Economic World View. Studies in the Ontology of Economics*, pp. 275–292, U. Mäki, ed. Cambridge: Cambridge University Press, 2001.

[Devitt, 1991] M. Devitt. *Realism and Truth.* Oxford: Blackwell, 1991.

[Donnellan, 1966] K. S. Donnellan. Reference and definite descriptions, *Philosophical Review* 75, 281-304, 1966.

[Friedman, 1953] M. Friedman. The methodology of positive economics. In his *Essays in Positive Economics.* Chicago: Chicago University Press, 1953. (Reprinted in [Mäki, 2009].)

[Hausman, 1998] D. M. Hausman. Problems with realism in economics, *Economics and Philosophy* 14, 185-213, 1998.

[Hausman, 2000] D. M. Hausman. Realist philosophy and methodology of economics: What is it? *Journal of Economic Methodology*, 7, 127-133, 2000.

[Hausman, 2001] D. M. Hausman. Tendencies, laws, and the composition of economic causes. In *The Economic World View. Studies in the Ontology of Economics*, pp. 293–307, U. Mäki, ed. Cambridge: Cambridge University Press, 2001.

[Hausman, 2009] D. M. Hausman. Laws, causation and economic methodology. In *The Oxford Handbook of Philosophy of Economics*, pp. 35–54, H. Kincaid and D. Ross, eds. Oxford: Oxford University Press, 2009.

[Hoover, 2001] K. D. Hoover. Is macroeconomics for real? in *The Economic World View. Studies in the Ontology of Economics*, pp. 225–245, U. Mäki, ed. Cambridge: Cambridge University Press, 2001.

[Hoover, 2002] K. D. Hoover. Econometrics and reality. In *Fact and Fiction in Economics. Models, Realism and Social Contsruction*, pp. 152–177, U. Mäki, ed. Cambridge: Cambridge University Press, 2002.

[Hoover, 2009] K. D. Hoover. Milton Friedman's stance: the methodology of causal realism. In *The Methodology of Positive Economics. Reflections on the Milton Friedman Legacy*, pp. 303–320, U. Mäki, ed. Cambridge University Press, 2009.

[Lawson, 1997] T. Lawson. *Economics and Reality.* London: Routledge, 1997.

[Lawson, 1999] T. Lawson. What has realism got to do with it? *Economics and Philosophy* 15, 269-282, 1999.

[Machlup, 1967] F. Machlup. Theories of the firm: marginalist, behavioral, managerial, *American Economic Review* 57, 1-33, 1967

[McCloskey, 1985] D. N. McCloskey. *The Rhetoric of Economics.* Madison: University of Wisconsin Press, 1985.

[McCloskey *et al.*, 1989] D. N. McCloskey, A. Klamer, and R. Solow, eds. *The Consequences of Economic Rhetoric.* Cambridge: Cambridge University Press, 1989.

[McCloskey, 1995] D. N. McCloskey. Modern epistemology against analytic philosophy: A reply to Mäki, *Journal of Economic Literature* 33, 1319-1323, 1995.

[MacKenzie, 2006] D. MacKenzie. *An Engine, Not a Camera. How Financial Models Shape Markets.* Cambridge, MA: MIT Press, 2006.

[Mäki, 1990] U. Mäki. Scientific realism and Austrian explanation, *Review of Political Economy*, 2, 310-344, 1990.

[Mäki, 1995] U. Mäki. Diagnosing McCloskey, *Journal of Economic Literature*, 33, 1300-1318, 1995.

[Mäki, 1996] U. Mäki. Scientific realism and some peculiarities of economics. In *Realism and Anti-Realism in the Philosophy of Science*, pp. 425–445, R. S. Cohen *et al.*, eds. *Boston Studies in the Philosophy of Science*, Vol. 169. Dordrecht: Kluwer, 1996.

[Mäki, 1999] U. Mäki. Representation repressed: Two kinds of semantic scepticism in economics. In *Incommensurability and Translation. Kuhnian Perspectives on Scientific Communication and Theory Change*, pp. 307–321, R. Scazzieri, R. Rossini Favretti, and G. Sandri, eds. Edward Elgar, 1999.

[Mäki, 2000a] U. Mäki. Reclaiming relevant realism, *Journal of Economic Methodology*, 7, 109-125, 2000.

[Mäki, 2000b] U. Mäki. Performance against dialogue, or answering and really answering: A participant observer's reflections on the McCloskey conversation, *Journal of Economic Issues*, 34, 43-59, 2000.

[Mäki, 2005] U. Mäki. Reglobalising realism by going local, or (how) should our formulations of scientific realism be informed about the sciences, *Erkenntnis*, 63, 231-251, 2005.

[Mäki, 2008] U. Mäki. Scientific realism and ontology. In *The New Palgrave Dictionary of Economics*, $2^{nd}$ edition. London: Palgrave Macmillan, 2008.

[Mäki, 2009] U. Mäki. Unrealistic assumptions and unnecessary confusions: Rereading and rewriting F53 as a realist statement. In *The Methodology of Positive Economics. Reflections on the Milton Friedman Legacy*, pp. 90–116, U. Mäki, ed. Cambridge University Press, 2009.

[Mäki, 2011] U. Mäki. Models and the locus of their truth, *Synthese*, 180, 47–63, 2011.

[Putnam, 1975-76] H. Putnam. What is 'realism'? *Proceedings of the Aristotelian Society*, New Series, 76, 177-194, 1975-76.

[Psillos, 1999] S. Psillos. *Scientific Realism. How Science Tracks Truth.* London: Routledge, 1999.

[Robbins, 1935] L. Robbins. *An Essay on the Nature and Significance of Economic Science.* $2^{nd}$ ed. London: Macmillan, 1935.

[Stanford, 2003] K. Stanford. Pyrrhic victories for scientific realism, *The Journal of Philosophy*, 100, 553-572, 2003.

[Wong, 1973] S. Wong. The F-Twist and the methodology of Paul Samuelson, *American Economic Review*, 63, 312-325, 1973.

# THE RISE AND FALL OF POPPER AND LAKATOS IN ECONOMICS

Roger E. Backhouse

## 1 INTRODUCTION

The rise and fall of Popper and Lakatos in economics are intimately connected with the sociology of the field of economic methodology. In the 1960s and before, the main discussions of economic methodology were, with some notable exceptions, either statements by leading practitioners about how economic inquiries should be undertaken, or discussions of those statements, either by other economists or by philosophers whose main concerns lay outside economics. Starting around the 1970s, a change took place, with economic methodology emerging as a field, mostly within economics, but partly outside it, characterised by the paraphenalia one would expect to find in an organised field: specialized journals, conferences, societies and textbooks. A major factor in this rise was interest in the work of Popper and Lakatos (though arguably not in that order). As the field began to be established, interest moved towards different questions which took it in different directions. Popper and Lakatos lost their central place.

## 2 EARLY ENGAGEMENTS WITH POPPER

Popper's work on scientific method was barely noticed in economics until his *Logik der Forschung,* published in 1934 , was translated as *The Logic of Scientific Discovery* (1959), as is illustrated by Table 1. His views on scientific method entered the journal literature almost immediately after the *Logik der Forschung* appeared, cited by Paul Rosenstein-Rodan and Friedrich Hayek, and were published in *Economica,* the journal published by the London School of Economics, where Hayek and Popper were professors. In the 1940s the only mention of Popper's work was by Hayek, and in the 1950s, most references to his work were to his critique of historicism, only two being to the ideas on scientific method that later became associated so firmly with his name. Of those, one was by his colleagues at LSE, Kurt Klappholz and Joseph Agassi [1959], and published in *Economica,* who stated categorically that their work was based on his.

After the *Logic of Scientific Discovery* was published in English, the situation changed. The first citation was by Kenneth Arrow, who bracketed his ideas with

Handbook of the Philosophy of Science. Volume 13: Philosophy of Economics.
Volume editor: Uskali Mäki. General editors: Dov M. Gabbay, Paul Thagard and John Woods.

Table 1. References to Popper in articles in English-language economics journals, 1930-1969

| | *Falsificationism* | *Historicism* | *Other* |
|---|---|---|---|
| 1930-9 | 2 | | |
| 1940-9 | | 1 | |
| 1950-9 | 2 | 4 | 3 |
| 1960-9 | 12 | 2 | 4 |

*Note*: This counts references to Popper in the 41 journals listed in JSTOR, excluding those specialist journals in separate fields (Economic history, Geography and Agricultural Economics). With interdisciplinary journals, economic articles were counted but articles in other fields (e.g. political science) were not. 'Other' covers his defense of the liberal tradition, the idea of probabilities as propensities, and his analysis of Platonism. Popper's own articles (1944-5) are excluded.

those of Milton Friedman when he wrote that 'sharpness of the implications of a hypothesis are a virtue, not a vice, provided of course the implications are not refuted by evidence' [Arrow, 1960, p. 177].[1] It is interesting that this equation of Friedman and Popper contrasted with one of the two assessments published in the 1950s [Day, 1955, p. 67] who had used Popper's work to criticise Friedman's views of scientific inference. The following year, Chris Archibald [1961] also used Popper to criticise Friedman, interpreting Friedman as a verificationist who believed that theories could be verified on the basis of successful predictions, even if some predictions were not successful. As economists cited Popper with greater frequency, they cited his emphasis on critical procedures, predictions as the test of a theory, rejection/criticisability not truth/falsity as the relevant demarcation criterion, the notion of empirical content and the contrast between empirical and mathematical sciences. By the late 1960s, it was being claimed that Popper's views had become dominant.

> Largely because of the influential work by Karl Popper [1934; 1959] broad-scale and persistent attempts at falsification are widely, though not universally, accepted as the key to the development of economic theory. [Bear and Orr, 1967, p. 192]

This remark is interesting because the most prominent methodological debates of the preceding two decades, that one might expect to have been crucial in determining the dominant methodological thinking, had not focused on Popper. An influential work was Friedman's 'The methodology of positive economics' [1953]. His emphasis on testing hypotheses on the basis of their predictions had, as has been explained, been seen as Popperian. Friedman had met Popper at the Mont

[1]Note that book reviews were not included in Table 1.

Pelerin Society, but the links between their ideas are uncertain, so would be problematic to claim that Friedman was propagating Popperian ideas.[2] Given the importance of the issue, it is worth quoting from an interview Friedman gave, in 1988, to Daniel Hammond [1993, p. 223]:

> **J.D.H.** [Did you read] Any philosophy when you were a graduate student?
>
> **M.F.** None that I recall. ... Certainly about the only methodology philosophy I've read is Popper. I have read his *Conjectures and Refutations* as well as ... *The Open Society and Its Enemies.* I think those are the two main things of Popper's that I've read. ...
>
> **J.D.H.** I noticed that in the *New Palgrave* [1987] Alan Walters says that in your 1953 methodology essay you introduced Popper's philosophy of science to economics. Would that be an overstatement, then?
>
> **M.F.** No. My introduction to Popper did not come from writings. I met him in person in 1947 at the first meeting of the Mont Pelerin Society ... I was very much impressed with him, and I spent a long time talking to him there. ... I didn't read his *Logic der Forschung*, but I knew the basic ideas from my contact with him, and I have no doubt that contact with him did have a good deal of influence on me.

Despite this, there is strong evidence that Friedman's arguments stemmed as much from ideas he had worked out as a practicing economist, before he met Popper.[3] The result was that, even if he was influenced by discussions with Popper, his methodology was distinctive, to the extent that it is misleading to see it as simply Popperian. In the 1950s and 1960s, it was Friedman whose work on methodology had the greatest influence, Popper being cited *far* less frequently. To place the citations in Table 1 in perspective, the combination "Friedman" plus "positive economics" occurs in 157 articles between 1952 and 1969 (excluding articles by Friedman).[4]

Further evidence that if Popperian ideas were being advanced during this period, they were doing so indirectly, behind the scenes, is provided by the methodological debates that took place in the prominent economics journals, notably the *American Economic Review.* It was Friedman whose ideas represented one side in the debate over marginalist theories of the firm. There was a debate over the role of assumptions in economic theory, centred on Friedman. In the course of this Paul Samuelson, arguably the leading economic theorist of the time, argued that assumptions should be realistic, a claim denounced by Fritz Machlup. The dominant framework taken from philosophy of science, *if there was one*, was logical empiricism. Nagel [1963], a leading logical empiricist, entered the debate over the realism

[2]For the most comprehensive discussion of Friedman's essay, approaching it from many angles, see Mäki [2009]. On the relation between Friedman and Popper see Hammond [1992].

[3]See [Hirsch and de Marchi, 1990].

[4]Given the dramatic difference in numbers, these have not been adjusted as have the figures in Table 1. Doing so would not alter the comparison significantly.

of assumptions. Machlup [1964] drew on such ideas in arguing against Samuelson. However, it is wrong to claim that there was a single dominant view. Rather, there was a range of approaches to methodology underlying the 'pragmatic' packages of styles of economics that came to dominate the literature.[5]

One influential approach was articulated in Tjalling Koopmans's *Three Essays on the State of Economic Science* (1957). He proposed that economic theories formed a sequence, each unrealistic, but the prelude to more realistic theories. This represented the approach of the Cowles Commission, central to the emergence of modern econometrics, and implied integrating rigorous, mathematical theory with formal statistical modelling to test such theories against data. Also emanating from Chicago, though from the Economics Department rather than the Cowles Commission, was Friedman's claim that theories should be tested according to their ability successfully to predict phenomena that they were designed to explain. Friedman spurned both the formal economic theory and econometric methods of the Cowles Commission. A third strand was Samuelson's operationalism, drawing on Percy Bridgman. The logical empiricism brought into the debate by such as Nagel and Machlup was a fourth strand.

The only economists who were consciously and openly drawing on Popper were those at LSE. The first to do this was Terence Hutchison. His *Significance and Basic Postulates of Economic Theory* (1938) had been written before his arrival at LSE, and was a plea for testability. He had read, and cited, the *Logic der Forschung*, but his arguments arguably reflected the logical positivism that was prevalent in the late 1930s as much as Popper. However, this book did not significantly influence economists' thinking, for it was too negative in its implications. A major part of Hutchison's argument (reminiscent of [Hayek, 1937]) was his attack on the idea of perfect knowledge, which had potentially destructive implications for the type of mathematical economic theory that was becoming fashionable. It met a hostile reception from Frank Knight, a leading figure at Chicago, and Machlup. Knight [1940] argued that the important facts in economics were subjective, and not testable. Machlup [1955] lambasted Hutchison as an 'ultra-empiricist', denying that it was necessary to test assumptions. Though he was one of the first to introduce Popper into economists' methodological discussions, it is hard to see him as having much influence.

A younger generation of LSE economists, strongly influenced by Popper, had much more influence.[6] The tradition, associated with Lionel Robbins, was that opportunities for testing economic theories arose only rarely, and that economics had to be largely based on *a priori* theorising. The challenge to Robbins came from the "LSE Staff Seminar in Methodology, Measurement and Testing" ($M^2T$), centred around Richard Lipsey and Chris Archibald. In the early 1960s, Archibald

[5]Pragmatic is used cautiously here, simply to denote that economists chose methods that they considered appropriate, without regard for formal methodological considerations. Appropriateness might be judged by any number of criteria – possibly, a critic might suggest, the ability to produce ideologically convenient conclusions (c.f. [Robinson, 1962]).

[6]This episode is discussed in detail in [de Marchi, 1988].

entered into a dispute with Friedman and Chicago over the theory of the firm. He started from the premiss that,

> in the last few years we have had something of a revolution in methodology, and the economists who have advocated the 'new methodology' have found that it gives them a powerful position from which to criticise Professor Chamberlin's theory of Monopolistic Competition. [Archibald, 1961, p. 2]

In the course of criticising Chamberlin, he also offered a critique of Chicago, that was taken up by Stigler [1963] and Friedman [1963]. He cited Klappholz and Agassi in support.[7] What Archibald was doing was offering a methodological critique that was clearly inspired by Popperian methodology. As was noted above, it was presented as an *alternative* to Friedman's methodology, not as reinforcing it.

The other major methodological product of the $M^2T$ group was Lipsey's *Introduction to Positive Economics* (1963). Though an introductory textbook, it was a manifesto for Popperian methodology. The title page was followed by a two-page collections of extracts from William Beveridge's farewell address as Director of LSE, entitled 'Fact and theory in economics', that attacked the notion that theory could be pursued without being constrained by data, concluding with the remark, 'It matters little how wrong we are with our existing theories, if we are honest and careful with our observations' [Lispey, 1963, p. vi]. In the opening remarks to the student on how the book should be used, he identified two main themes: that it was about 'being intelligently and constructively critical of the existing body of economic theory' and that theory must be tested against empirical observation [Lipsey, 1963, pp. xi-xii]. The first chapter, therefore, was a discussion of scientific method that referred the reader to Popper's *Logic of Scientific Discovery* for a more detailed account of how hypotheses might be refuted. The flowchart that illustrated scientific method ran from Definitions and hypotheses through logical deduction to Predictions. Empirical observation then led to the conclusion that either the hypothesis was refuted by the facts or was consistent with them.

What had happened by the late 1960s was that the notion of testability had come to permeate economics, as the most widespread methodology, but this was only partially Popperian in inspiration. $M^2T$ was explicitly Popperian in its approach, but it was but one among many approaches that emphasised testing. Friedman may have been influenced by Popper, but whilst some saw his methodology as Popperian, others argued explicitly that it was not. Other empiricist methodologies, such as that of Cowles, owed little if anything to Popper. In most quarters, Popperian ideas were blended with a broader empiricism, owing as much to logical empiricism as to Popper. Whilst it may have served economists, later, to

[7] He cites a forthcoming article by Klappholz and Agassi, but it is not clear which this is. Possibly it was their 1959 article, and that Archibald's article was drafted before that was published.

present their methodology as Popperian, the relations between economic methodology and Popper were far from straightforward.

## 3 LAKATOS AND THE EMERGENCE OF ECONOMIC METHODOLOGY

As, noted above, there was a spate of methodological discussions within economics during the 1960s, in which Popperian themes were never far from the surface. Mathematical economic theory and econometric (statistical) methods had advanced greatly since the Second World War, but without the dramatic successes that their earliest supporters had hoped for. The question of how theory and evidence related were topical. As information technology and data-collection improved, these questions became more urgent. It was against this background that Popperian methodology was augmented with those of Imre Lakatos. His 'Falsification and the methodology of scientific research programmes' was first published in a volume, *Criticism and the Growth of Knowledge* (1970) that was focused on comparing the ideas of Popper with those of Thomas Kuhn. To understand the way economists responded, it is necessary to go back to consider something of the early reception of Kuhn's ideas in economics.

The first person to bring Kuhn's ideas into economics was Bob Coats [1969], who asked 'Is there a structure of scientific revolutions in economics?' In asking this question, he was able to draw on the established view that economics had seen a number of revolutions, asking whether these could be interpreted as revolutions in the Kuhnian sense. That the ground was already prepared may not have been coincidental, for a major figure in the history of economic ideas had been the economist, Joseph Schumpeter, who had been at Harvard in the 1940s, and very much part of the milieu out of which Kuhn's ideas emerged. Schumpeter's analysis of the progress of economic thought was based on the notion that science was a professional activity, its practitioners sharing sets of standards. It ran in terms of 'classical situations' in which broad consensus prevailed, and periods of decay, out of which came revolutions (see [Backhouse, 1998, chapter 14]). It was but a short step to Kuhn. In economics, therefore, when Lakatosian ideas emerged as a Popperian response to Kuhn, they were rapidly taken up by historians of the subject.

In 1974, there took place the Napflion Colloquium on Research Programmes in Physics and Economics, out of which two volumes emerged, one on physics [Howson, 1976], the other on economics. The latter, *Method and Appraisal in Economics* [Latsis, 1976], was organised by Lakatos and one of his students, Spiro Latsis, and after his death was edited by Latsis. It offered a series of case studies, and some broad appraisals of Lakatosian methodology in relation to Kuhn and Popper. There was a strong historical dimension to the volume, in two senses. The case studies were inevitably historical, for this was the Lakatosian method: to compare rational reconstructions, written as though science progressed in accordance with his methodology, with the actual history. More than that, the volume involved several economists with reputation in the history of economic thought

(Coats, De Marchi, Blaug and Hutchison) with the result that methodology and history of economic thought, hitherto largely separate, began to be considered together. Even the eminent practitioners involved (Axel Leijonhufvud, Herbert Simon, and John Hicks) were adopting the role of observers of economics, rather than participants. The book thus marked a radical break with the tone of earlier methodological debates between Friedman, Samuelson, Archibald and others.

One type of paper in this volume appraised 'Kuhn versus Lakatos', as exemplified in the title of Blaug's chapter, or discussed whether there were 'Revolutions' in economics (Hicks and Hutchison). Another explored specific episodes in much more detail. Coats told the story of the relationship between economics and psychology as 'the death and resurrection of a research programme', whilst de Marchi analysed the case of the Leontief paradox in international trade theory, and economists' responses to it in terms of Lakatos's criteria. Latsis himself developed the idea that 'situational determinism could be seen as defining the hard core of a research programme in Lakatos's sense. Axel Leijonhufvud covered both types of inquiry, exploring the relevance of Lakatosian ideas in general, and then applying them to the specific problem of Keynesian economics. As he put it, economists found the 'Growth of Knowledge' literature fascinating. Perhaps of more significance, this provided a new way to think about and to test philosophical theories about method.

After the *Method and Appraisal in Economics*, the most significant development in the field of methodology was Mark Blaug's survey, *The Methodology of Economics* (1980). This was not the first textbook on economic methodology, Ian Stewart's *Reasoning and Method in Economics* (1979) having been published the previous year. Stewart's book reflected what had come to be known as 'the Received View' in philosophy of science: chapters on deduction, induction and the hypothetico-deductive method were followed by ones on distinctive features of economic data, economic theory and reality, applied economics and statistical methods. Arising out of years spent teaching a course in methodology, it was aimed at students of economics who were being trained to understand what they were (or would shortly) be doing. In contrast, Blaug parcelled most of this material off in an opening chapter, 'From the received view to the views of Popper'. The logical structure of economic theories was not what interested him. This was followed by a chapter 'From Popper to the new heterodoxy', the new heterodoxy covering Kuhn, Lakatos, and Feyerabend's methodological anarchism. Economic methodology was not settled, but was in a state of flux, the action being centred on Lakatos. Blaug reinforced this message, after a section on the history of economic methodology, with nine chapter-length case studies that constituted 'A methodological appraisal of the neoclassical research programme'. The method was defined by Lakatos, whose ideas were presented as a variant of Popperian falsificationism, and its relevance was to be assessed through case studies. His concern was engaged not to explicate the structure of economic theory, in the manner of logical empiricism, but to appraise it, his criterion being whether or not economists practiced the empiricism that they preached. His conclusion was that, much of the time, they did not:

> For the most part, the battle for falsificationism has been won in modern economics (would that we could say as much about some of the other social sciences). The problem is now to persuade economists to take falsificationism seriously. [Blaug, 1980, p. 260]

The appropriate strategy was not for economists to abandon attempts to test theory, but to find ways of making testing more effective. His case studies showed, so he argued, that where serious attempts had been made to test theories against data, the result had been progress, even if the outcome of testing had not always been conclusive. He ended up with a thoroughly Lakatosian assessment of the role of methodology.

> What methodology can do is to provide criteria for the acceptance and rejection of research programmes, setting standards that will help us to discriminate between wheat and chaff. These standards, we have seen, are hierarchical, relative, dynamic, and by no means unambiguous in the practical advice they offer to working economists. Nevertheless, the ultimate question we can and indeed must pose about any research programme is the one made familiar by Popper: what events, if they materialized, would lead us to reject that programme? A programme that cannot meet that question has fallen short of the highest standards that scientific knowledge can attain. [Blaug, 1980, p. 264]

This defined a role for the methodologist, as distinct from the economist, which involved establishing appropriate appraisal criteria through investigating, in a manner inspired by Lakatos, the history of the subject, to find out what had worked and what had not. Blaug thus used Lakatos to stake out economic methodology as a field with a distinct identity in a way that earlier writers had not.

In the 1980s, though other lines of inquiry were still pursued, debates over Popper and Lakatos arguably attracted the most attention. Rather than survey the list of Lakatosian case studies,[8] some of its key features can be identified by focusing on some examples.

Weintraub came to the field as a general equilibrium theorist who was invited, by Mark Perlman, editor of the *Journal of Economic Literature*, to write a survey article on the search for microfoundations of Keynesian macroeconomics, a literature that had developed rapidly in the mid 1970s. The resulting survey [Weintraub, 1977] made no reference to Lakatos or Popper. However, in when he expanded the article into a book, *Microfoundations: The Compatibility of Microeconomics and Macroeconomics* (1979), he presented his account as 'an imperfect attempt to trace the development and interlocking nature of two scientific research programmes (in the sense of Lakatos), macroeconomic theory and (general equilibrium) neo-Walrasian theory' [Weintraub, 1979, p. 1].[9] The collapse of Marshallian

[8]De Marchi [1991] provides a long list.

[9]He acknowledges the advice of Neil de Marchi, one of those involved in Latsis [1976].

economics, he argued, had spawned these two research programmes: to understand the microfoundations literature of the 1970s, it was necessary to understand the relationship between these two research programmes. He used Lakatosian ideas to argue, on methodological grounds, against some of the conclusions that critics of general equilibrium theory were drawing. In particular, Lakatos's idea of a hard core was used to defend general equilibrium theory against critics. It is only propositions in the protective belt, to which researchers are guided by the hard core, that should be tested: general equilibrium analysis lies in the hard core, so to complain that it is based on counter-factual assumptions is beside the point.

*Microfoundations* was followed six years later by *General Equilibrium Analysis: Studies in Appraisal* (1985). This left macroeconomics, and sought to explore more fully the 'neo-Walrasian' research programme that had made its appearance in the earlier book. In place of the hesitant use of Lakatos, replete with apologies for its naïve use, this was a much more confident use of Lakatos to argue against alternative appraisal criteria. More conventional chapters were interspersed with 'Classroom interludes', recounting exchanges between a teacher and students $\alpha, \beta, \gamma, \delta$, and $\varepsilon$ in the manner of Lakatos's *Proofs and Refutations* (1976). When it came to appraisal, he offered detailed list of hard-core propositions and positive and negative heuristics, providing a precise definition of the programme. Having done that he argued, in far more detail than in the earlier book, his case for arguing that the Arrow-Debreu-Mackenzie model was an instantiation of the hard core, that could be used for analysing the core, but was distinct from it. To place it alongside applied fields, such as human capital theory or monetary theory, as Blaug [1980] had done, was a mistake.

In responding to Lakatos, one of the puzzles was that the concept of a research programme was being applied to phenomena that seemed very different in scope: macroeconomic theory and general equilibrium analysis, the two programmes picked out by Weintraub, encompass large parts of economics. In contrast, Monetarism, human capital, or the new economics of the family, all picked out by Blaug [1980] were much narrower.[10] One response to do this is to see research programmes as differentiated structures, large programmes encompassing sub-programmes. Thus human capital theory might be a sub-programme within a broader neo-classical programme. At attempt was made to formalise this by Remenyi (1979), who argued that the distinction between core and protective belt had to be complicated by the introduction of 'demi-cores' that served as a core for sub-programmes within the main programme. Interaction between the protective belt, such demi-cores and the hard core opened up new possibilities for analysing the apparently complex structure of economic theories.

[10]De Marchi and Blaug [1991, pp. 29-30] use this as one way of classifying applications of Lakatosian methodology.

## 4 THE MOVEMENT FROM POPPER AND LAKATOS

The mid 1980s marked the high-point of interest in Lakatosian methodology, Weintraub's *Appraising Economic Theories*, published in 1985, being symbolic of this. However, some of those writing on economic methodology continued to adopt Popperian positions, little influenced by Lakatos. Two important examples are Lawrence Boland [1982] and Johannes Klant [1984]. Boland interpreted Popper, not as prescribing a particular methodology (falsificationism) but as deriving methods that were dependent on the problems to which they were to be applied. His book, therefore, focused on specific problems of economics and economic model-building. Klant, in contrast, offered a wide-ranging account of the philosophy of science, drawing far more than was conventional in the English-language literature, on continental philosophy and writing on economics. However, his conclusion, reflected in his title *The Rules of the Game: The Logical Structure of Economic Theories*, was a set of rules that should govern economic research. These contained many observations specific to economic theories, that reflected his wide studies outside the Popperian literature, but his core rules (that came first and without which the others would lose their significance) were couched in explicitly Popperian terms: theories were fallible and could be falsified, not confirmed; general economic theories are unfalsifiable ideal types, whereas empirical scientists should strive to achieve falsifiable theories [Klant, 1984, pp. 184-6].

At the end of 1985, a symposium was held in Amsterdam to mark Klant's retirement, the proceedings of which were eventually published as *The Popperian Legacy in Economics* [de Marchi, 1988]. The aim of the conference was to take a critical look at the role played by Popper's falsification criterion in economics, but it ranged very widely. The need for a demarcation criterion such as falsificationism (though not necessarily falsificationism) was defended by Blaug and Hutchison. Others, including Weintraub, explored the problem of how theory and evidence interacted in specific contexts, whilst others adopted a much more critical stance towards the entire Popper-Lakatos programme. During the rest of the decade these voices were to grow louder, to the extent that when de Marchi and Blaug organised a 'second' Lakatos conference in Capri, in 1989,[11] to establish what had been learned since the Napflion colloquium fifteen years earlier, the general attitude towards Lakatos's MSRP was one of widespread hostility. Some of strands in this reaction against Popper and Lakatos that emerged in Amsterdam need to be identified.

Daniel Hausman, a philosopher, opened by arguing that Popper's philosophy of science was a mess, confusing logical falsifiability with falsifiability as a methodology, or set of norms that should govern scientific practice. Scientific theories formed parts of larger systems comprising numerous auxiliary assumptions that made logical falsifiability inapplicable. As for the set of norms that Popper proposed should govern science, Hausman claimed that these were largely arbitrary. This critique of Popper was along similar lines to the criticism of Lakatos's ap-

[11] Like the first, it was supported by the Latsis Foundation.

praisal criterion, the prediction of novel facts, by Wade Hands. Earlier, Hands had claimed that 'Keynesian economics and Walrasian general equilibrium theory are more clearly best gambits than any of the other research programs to which the MSRP has been applied' [Hands, 1993/1985, p. 48], but they had failed to predict novel facts, or had done so only after the idea of a novel fact had been distorted beyond recognition. The only successful Lakatosian appraisal to date was the one by de Marchi, in Latsis [1976], which served to demonstrate how ill-suited to economics Lakatosian methodology was. In Amsterdam he sought to go beyond this, arguing that the notion of ad hoc-ness, central to Popperian and Lakatosian methodology, was ambiguous and that none of its definitions was satisfactory. The reason this was important for Popper and Lakatos was that their normative conclusions depended on it: Popper's main normative rule was to avoid ad hoc modications to theories, for to do so rendered them unfalsifiable; for Lakatos, ad hoc-ness involved modifying theories in ways that were inconsistent with the heuristics of a programme. These bore no necessary relation to the ways in which economists used the term.

Another line of attack was offered by Bruce Caldwell. Three years earlier, his *Beyond Positivism* (1982), arising out of an earlier doctoral thesis, had surveyed the field. As with Blaug's book, his starting point was the demise of the received view or logical empiricism. However, where Blaug had seen the Lakatos as the answer, Caldwell did not. In his chapter in [De Marchi, 1988], he confessed to having been naïve in his initial beliefs that methodology would explain what economists did, what it meant to do economics scientifically and that it would solve the problem of how to choose between theories [Caldwell, 1988, pp. 231-2]. What he found more persuasive was Kuhn's argument that there was no universally applicable, objective method for choosing between theories. This led him to advocate a form of pluralism, whereby the role of the methodologist is not those just listed, but the more general one of 'reveal[ing] the strengths and weaknesses of various research programmes in economics' [Caldwell, 1988, p. 243]. Though he denied that this was simply a provisional position, pending further advances in economic methodology, it was a modest one, but which might help set the agenda for further work. It is worth noting, however, that though critical of Lakatos, attaching greater weight to lessons drawn from Kuhn and Feyerabend, Caldwell chose to define the task of the methodologist in relation to research programmes: though he may not have intended it that way, this could be seen as a weakened Lakatosian position, shorn of any specific appraisal criterion.

However, the most radical critique came from Donald McCloskey and Arjo Klamer Their target was not Popperian or Lakatosian falsificationism so much as any prescriptive methodology, a stance first articulated in McCloskey's influential article, 'The rhetoric of economics' (1983). There he had opened with a broadside against economic methodology, or rather Methodology, with a capital-M, as he preferred to call it:

> Economists do not follow the laws of enquiry their methodologies lay down. A good thing too. If they did they would stand silent on human

> capital, the law of demand, random walks down Wall Street, the elasticity of demand for gasoline, and most other matters about which they commonly speak. In view of the volubility of economists the many official methodologies are apparently not the grounds for their scientific conviction. [McCloskey, 1983, p. 482]

Instead of turning to philosophy, 'as a set of narrowing rules of evidence', economists should turn to rhetoric — to the study of 'disciplined conversation', his approach drawing on Wayne Booth and Richard Rorty among others. The strategy he used to develop this argument was to list eleven characteristics of modernism [McCloskey, 1983, pp. 484-5], starting with the statement that prediction is the goal of science and ending with 'Hume's fork' that anything that does not contain either abstract reasoning concerning quantity or number, or experimental reasoning, should be committed to flames as 'sophistry and illusion'. Whereas philosophers believed few of these, 'a large majority in economics', he claimed, believed them all. The official methodology of economics was a modernist 'revealed, not a reasoned, religion' [McCloskey, 1983, pp. 486]. Instead of the arrogance and pretentiousness of Methodology, McCloskey argued, we should turn to the analysis of rhetoric, recognizing that economists used rhetorical devices just as much as did writers of literature.

The effects of McCloskey's article and subsequent book. It brought him a wide audience amongst economists who did not write, and generally did not read much, on methodology. Though there were attempts to analyse economics as discourse, it is not clear how far these were influenced specifically by McCloskey: his appeal to analyse economists' conversations formed part of a much wider movement. Within the emerging field of methodology, the part of his argument that was taken most seriously was that which overlapped with what those working on the sociology of science and science studies had been arguing. The emphasis in this literature was not so much on science (or economics) as a conversation but the idea that the testing of theories and hence the construction of knowledge was a social phenomenon. For example, Harry Collins [1985] had argued that, where the science in question was not yet decided, experimenters had simultaneously to decide on the validity of the theory and whether or not experiments were working properly. Little light was shed on this process, or so it was argued, by the rules for accepting or rejecting theories found in Popperian or Lakatosian methodology.

Early reactions to this challenge to Popperian and Lakatosian ideas is shown clearly in *The Popperian Legacy in Economics*, the papers are preceded with a detailed record of the discussions that took place at the 1985 conference in Amsterdam. Weintraub had presented a Lakatosian analysis of general equilibrium theory, but in the discussion was exposed to criticism from McCloskey and Klamer, who contended that such accounts were too 'thin' to be interesting He came to be persuaded that they were right: that the Lakatosian reconstructions that formed the basis for his analysis of the history of general equilibrium theory were not wrong, but they failed to reveal why the theory developed as it did. To explain that, a 'thicker' history, was required. However, though McCloskey and Klamer had been influential in his change of direction, it is significant that this shift of direction took him in the direction of English scholars, Stanley Fish, and Barbara Herrnstein-Smith, and the sociologist Karin Knorr-Centina. The next stage in his investigation of general quilibrium analysis was entitled *Stabilizing Dynamics: The Construction of Economic Knowledge* (1991), a long way from the Lakatosian perspective of his earlier book. As he proclaimed in the title of a forthright article, 'Methodology doesn't matter' [Weintraub, 1989].

During the 1980s the growth of work on economic methodology increased to such an extent, with sufficient interaction between contributors, that it became reasonable to consider that an organised field was emerging. Strongly influenced by Latsis [1976] and Blaug [1980], discussions of Lakatos's methodology of scientific research programmes and Popperian falsificationism provided themes with which many of those specialising in the subject chose to engage. Beyond the group of specialists, many economists were taking an interest in methodological questions, stimulated by the profound changes that had taken place in economics in the 1970s and after, notably the move from the 1960s Keynesian consensus to the new classical macroeconomics. "Austrian" economics had gained momentum, Radical economics of various types and Feminist critiques of economics were being developed, all of which had clear methodological dimensions. There was even discussion of the directions in which economic methodology should be moving, informed by philosophical perspectives outside both the older Received View and Popperianism (e.g. [Mäki, 1990]). The change that had taken place in the fifteen years since the conference organised by Lakatos in 1974 is shown by the programme of what has been called the 'second Lakatos conference', held in Capri in 1989, the papers from which were published in *Appraising Economic Theories* [De Marchi and Blaug, 1991], with thirty one contributors, and as three papers in *History of Political Economy* in 1991.[12]

## 5 APPRAISING ECONOMIC THEORIES

The Capri conference was organised to achieve three objectives: to elicit further Lakatosian case studies, to re-examine the coherence of the methodology of scientific research programmes (both in general and in relation to economics) and to have economists discuss these issues alongside physicists, sociologists and philosophers of science (Blaug in [De Marchi and Blaug, 1991, p. 499]). However, though the aim had from the start been to bring together both supporters and critics of Lakatos, the overall mood turned out to be one of general hostility to Lakatos's MSRP. Blaug estimated that only 12 out of 37 participants were 'willing to give Lakatos a further run for his money' and of those only five were unambigously positive about the value of his methodology. What concerned Blaug was not so much detailed criticisms, such as the difficulties with unambiguously defining re-

[12]These two papers are significant, for although they deal with broader issues, they show that two sociologists of science were present and were influential in discussions.

search programmes, or technical problems relating to the definition of novel facts. Rather it was what he described as 'a general attitude not just to methodology but also to economics as a whole' (Blaug in [De Marchi and Blaug, 1991, p. 500]).

*Appraising Economic Theories* offered a range of analyses that would have been difficult to imagine a decade earlier. It opened with detailed discussions, involving five authors, of the notions of theoretical progress and excess content.[13] There were discussions of testing theories, taking as examples job-search theory, demand analysis, game theory and experimental economics. There were explorations of how lines of inquiry had been either established or discarded, in econometrics, general equilibrium theory and unemployment. The question of how to delineate a research programme was explored, in three separate papers, in relation to macroeconomics, the field of economics where change had arguably been most dramatic during the 1970s. There were also appraisals of two heterodox traditions: that inspired by Sraffa and Austrian economics. What is remarkable about the volume is not simply the range of topics and contributors, but the fact that, subject to certain provisos, it offered a systematic discussion of economics across the board: microeconomics, macroeconomics, econometrics and experimental methods. Obviously, there were missing appraisals of other heterodox traditions. Perhaps more significant, because of what it implies about the focus of the methodological literature more generally, was the paucity of papers on applied fields, except where this formed a part of what economists had come to consider the "core" of the subject.

Blaug's reaction, expressed in the 'Afterword', to what he felt was a dismissive attitude to Lakatos and an unwillingness to take the MSRP seriously was to engage in a robust defense of falsificationism. In their meticulous analysis of the details of the MSRP, critics were, he contended missing the bigger, more important points. The relevant question was not whether there was a rigid distinction between 'hard core' and 'protective belt', for such a distinction was logically implied by the existence of evolving research programmes, but whether thinking in these terms served to focus attention on important questions. Similarly, to rail against 'novel fact fetishism' was to miss the important distinction between prediction of novel facts as a positive theory about what economists actually did (Lakatos's methodology of historical research programmes, MHRP) and as a theory about what they ought to do (MSRP). Criticism the latter was, he claimed, part of a general tendency to play down the importance of empirical testing in general, which he related to excessive concern with general equilibrium theory, a body of ideas that was highly vulnerable on this score. He was prepared to adopt a much looser, more pragmatic, interpretation of Lakatosian methodology.[14]

De Marchi shared many of Blaug's concerns, yet developed them in a radically different way. He opened with a wide-ranging survey of applications of MSRP to

[13]This totals include discussants' comments which were substantial and written by people who had previously published on the subject.

[14]The term pragmatic is used with deliberate ambiguity. On the one hand it denotes a willingness to be flexible in order to achieve bigger goals. On the other hand, Blaug's focus on whether or not Lakatosian methodology leads to the asking of interesting questions, though not pragmatism in the strict sense, resonates with Peirce's focus on the importance of questions.

economics prior to the Capri conference, making clear the breadth of the studies that had been undertaken.[15] This was the prelude to a critical review of that literature. It had achieved much, identifying the scale on which research programmes should be sought, identifying problem shifts in research programmes, defining and identifying novel facts, and analysing theoretical progress. Less work, however, had been done on testing whether economists did in fact behave rationally. He then moved on to arguing that greater attention should be paid to the process of discovery, and the interaction that could take place between hard core and heurisics. However, perhaps his most critical point was that the research programmes identified according to the Lakatosian schema seemed 'extraordinarily familiar'

> It looks like an exercise in re-naming ... We are given almost no help in the studies themselves ... for identifying RPs. Rather it looks as if existing, well recognized sub-disciplines and traditions have been taken and the label 'Research Program' appended. In other words, whatever economists themselves have identified as a distinct line of inquiry has been graced with the R designation. (De Marchi in [De Marchi and Blaug, 1991, p. 17])

Approaching this as a historian, de Marchi observed that this made it difficult to escape from Whiggish history. This criticism tied up with other major observation, that economists had what he called a 'Lakatosian self-image' (De Marchi in de Marchi and Blaug 1991: 2). It was because of this self-image, that those seeking to apply Lakatos's MSRP had such an easy task: economists were already thinking in terms that were substantially Lakatosian.

This similarity was sought not in economists' methodological statements about the importance of predicting novel facts but in a much more general vision of what science involved. De Marchi picked out several themes, centred on economists identification with mathematical and physical science. At the most basic level was the tendency to adopt Popper's 'three worlds' view, seeing a hierarchy between a world of physical phenomena, a world of beliefs and a world of objective rational knowledge, a perspective he traced back to John Stuart Mill (De Marchi in [De Marchi and Blaug, 1991, p. 3]). Related to that was seeing rationality and progress in science as being very closely linked. De Marchi's critique of methodologists use of Lakatos's MSRP was based on the premise that there was a gap between economists' self-perception and the reality of their situation (De Marchi in [De Marchi and Blaug, 1991, p. 6]).[16]

The tone of De Marchi's Introduction and Blaug's Afterword were clearly very different. There were clearly significant differences between them, but their belief in the value of further explicitly Lakatosian studies, though the most obvious, was

[15] At the risk of injustice to the authors writing after 1989, readers wanting a survey are simply referred to De Marchi's.

[16] I describe this reality gap as a premise, though it should be pointed out that he cited work by Latsis and Rosenberg as evidence.

perhaps not the most significant. Blaug wanted methodology to remain the ability to appraise, whether that was via MSRP or a simpler Popperian falsificationism. De Marchi, on the other hand, focused more on MSRP as a tool for historical understanding with his shift towards emphasizing discovery and his concerns about the Whiggishness of Lakatosian reconstructions of history. However, both Blaug, with his flexible attitude towards the details of Lakatos's MSRP and De Marchi, with his sympathetic attitude towards the Lakatos's critics, were moving on from the over-optimistic attitude towards MSRP as a simple tool with which the mysteries of economics could be unlocked. The Lakatosian era (and with it the Popperian, if that designation was ever appropriate) was at an end.

## 6 METHODOLOGY AFTER LAKATOS

Though work on economic methodology during the 1980s was dominated by discussions of Lakatos's MSRP, it had consistent opponents among philosophers. Two of these published widely read books in 1992. Though not Popperian, Alexander Rosenberg (*Economics – Mathematical Politics or Science of Diminishing Returns,* 1992), came to economics from the study of biology, drawing parallels with psychology to question whether economics would ever be able to predict successfully given its theoretical orientation. He raised the question of whether in fact, economics should be seen alongside political philosophy rather than as a science. Daniel Hausman (*The Inexact and Separate Science of Economics*, 1992) was arguably important not so much for its anti-Popperian and anti-Lakatosian arguments but for two other reasons. It shifted the focus of attention to issues such as how economic models should be understood, and it sought to identify possible reasons for economists' practices – what he termed 'empirical philosophy of science'. Hausman's book was widely discussed during the 1990s, this discussion marking a shift to a broader range of methodological issues, away from the questions of rationality and progress that were the main concern of Popper and Lakatos.[17]

Alongside from Blaug [1992] and Hutchison [1992], who sought to defend what they considered the essential Popperian insight — the emphasis on testability and testing — the Popperian tradition was defended by Lawrence Boland, by the mid-1980s possibly the most published Popperian methodologist [Boland, 1997, p. 249], but viewed that tradition very differently. For him, Popper was emphatically *not* about prescribing rules. Instead of a Popper seen through the distorting lens of Lakatos, Boland argued for the Socratic Popper, for whom the only rule was relentless criticism. If there were rules, they were very general: that one must make all possible improvements to a theory before attacking it, so that when one does so one is attacking the strongest possible version; and that nothing should be above criticism[18] Boland conceded that the emphasis on criticism was not as prominent

[17]If this were a broader account of economic methodology at this time, rather than simply an account of the changing attitude towards Lakatos and Popper, a broader range of figures and ideas would have to be considered.

[18]Some critics, it is admitted, felt that Popper, in practice, did not always extend this to his

in Popper's published work as it might have been, but that the place where, by most accounts, it was clearest was in his seminars. In those, criticism was part of a Socratic dialogue: learning took place through criticism, in a dialectical process (though Boland cited Plato's *Euthyphro* rather than Hegel):

> The dialogue proceeds by Socrates presenting his understanding of piety and impiety and inviting Euthyphro to point out where Socrates is in error ... Socrates wishes to learn where he is in error and thus lays out his understanding step by step. Unfortunately, at each step Euthyphro agrees with Socrates – consequently, if there is an error in Socrates' understanding, Euthyphro failed to find it. At the end, Socrates invites Euthyphro to restart at the beginning but Euthyphro declines. Thus, while there was the perfect opportunity to learn — discovering one's error — Socrates failed to learn anything. For my purposes, Plato's *Euthyphro* illustrates all of the major ingredients of Popper's theory of learning: trying to learn by discovering error, inviting criticism in order to learn, putting one's own knowledge at the maximum risk in doing so, and demonstrating the absence of guarantees. Of course, it is important to emphasise that the person who wishes to learn asks the questions. [Boland, 1997, p. 266]

The result was that Boland's Popperianism led him to write on methodology in a way that was dramatically different from his fellow Popperians, Blaug, Hutchison or Klant. He engaged in debate with other methodologists, arguing for his interpretation of Popper, but what justified his critical stance was his detailed engagement with economic theory. He explored issues such as maximizing behaviour, satisficing, equlibrium, individualism, equilibrium, time, dynamics, testability and the alleged value-neutrality of economic theory. Those coming to the subject either from philosophy or via Lakatos did address all these, but arguably none covered such a comprehensive list of topics foundational to economics (see [Boland, 1982; 1992; 1997; 2003]).

Another attempt at maintaining a Popperian position was made by Caldwell [1991]. Drawing on his earlier book, he rehearsed the reasons why falsificationism was not cogent and could not be followed in economics as well as explaining why the Lakatosian variant of Popper was also unsatisfactory. However, rather than abandon Popper, he argued that what Popper had called 'situational logic' was an appropriate method for the social sciences. The aim of the theoretical social sciences was, Caldwell [1991, p. 13] claimed, quoting Popper [1965, p. 342], 'to trace the unintended social repercussions of intentional human actions'. Thus rather than test the principle pf rationality, economist should test the model of the situation faced by individuals. 'It is sound methodological policy to decide not to make the rationality principle accountable but the rest of the theory; that is, the model' [1985, p. 362]. Though he advocated qualifying Popper's situational analysis, notably abandoning any claim that it was the *only* method appropriate

own views.

to the social sciences, Caldwell was more sympathetic towards it than Blaug [1985, p. 287] who, in a passage quoted by Caldwell, objected that situational analysis was 'very permissive of economic practice as interpreted in the orthodox manner'.

This led to the problem of how to reconcile situational analysis with Popper's falsificationism. Caldwell pointed out that Popper's own writings could provide no guidance, with the result that those who wished to follow him had to find their own route out of the apparent contradiction between them. One possibility (Blaug's) was to see rationality as part of the hard core of a Lakatosian research programme. However, Caldwell [1991, p. 22], here echoing perhaps, the methodological pluralism advocated in his earlier book, preferred a different route, namely 'positing an alternative and broader conception of acceptable scientific practice, one that would allow the use of *both* falsificationism and situational logic, each within the contexts in which it is most appropriate'. Critical rationalism provided a framework in which both falsificationism and critical rationalism could be accommodated, a position not dissimilar to Boland's.

Others moved towards a perspective that paid more attention to the social dimension of knowledge. De Marchi, one of those most heavily involved in the sequence of conferences on Popper and Lakatos, argued that Popper's ideas had been misapplied when methodologists had claimed that knowledge could be progressive. Instead, he took up the claim, long made by Lawrence Boland, that economists were generally conventionalists and problem solvers, not seeking the best theories. De Marchi juxtaposed Boland's argument with Rorty's argument that the singular statements rested, were not possible without 'prior knowledge of the whole fabric within which those elements occur' ([Rorty, 1980, p. 319]; quoted [De Marchi, 1992, p. 2]). For Boland, science was about learning and eliminating error, wheras for Rorty it was about a set of conversational conventions and practices. De Marchi [1992,. p. 3] observed that 'It is is precisely at this point that methodological debate in economics is joined today'. His solution was 'recovering practice', the subtitle of *Post-Popperian Methodology of Economics* (1992). This involved paying close attention to what economists actually did and, in the course of that, paying attention to the context of discovery as well as that of justification.

Where De Marchi can be seen as moving towards the view that science should be considered in its social context, but not committing himself to that, Hands, during the 1990s, moved decisively in that direction. In the 1980s he was what Boland [1997, p. 158] justifiably described as a 'reluctant Popperian'. Hands had been critical of Popper's and Lakatos's appraisal criteria, yet his research was framed by the agenda they set. However, by the time his essays were brought together as *Testing, Rationality and Progress: Essays on the Popperian Tradition in Economic Methodology* (1993) he had begun to move significantly away from this tradition towards an approach informed by the sociology of science. The title of his next book, *Reflection without Rules: Economic Methodology and Contemporary Science Theory* (2001), a systematic critical survey rather than a collection of essays, accurately shows both how far he had moved away from the Popperian tradition by the end of the decade and where he believed a superior approach could be found. The Popperian legacy was, for Hands, about rules for the conduct of science, an approach that he had come to believe was misconceived. There simply were no general rules. Though he considered pragmatist, discursive and Feminist turns in economic methodology, what clearly engaged him most were the sociological, naturalist and economic turns (the latter involving the application of economic arguments to science studies).[19] Though different in timing, and hence significantly different in execution, this echoed Weintraub's earlier move away from Lakatos.

It was also possible to move in the same direction, but to present this as evolving out of Lakatos's MSRP rather than a rejection of it, as is illustrated by a series of essays reflecting on the Capri conference and responding to Weintraub's emphasis on the social construction of knowledge, brought together in a volume with the subtitle, 'From Lakatos to empirical philosophy of science' [Backhouse, 1998]. Lakatos's MHRP, which involved comparison of a history reconstructed as if it had developed in accordance with MSRP with the actual history in order to test the latter, could be seen as a prefiguring the analysis of practice found in Hausman, De Marchi or Boland. However, whereas interest in scientific progress was one of the main casualties of the hostilities against Lakatos, Backhouse pursued this theme in *Truth and Progress in Economic Knowledge* (1997). However, despite its seemingly Popperian title, and its use of Lakatosian ideas about theoretical and empirical progress to frame the question, it moved away, in two directions. One was into pragmatism, though towards the emphasis on questions and problem-solving found in C. S. Peirce and Larry Laudan, rather than to Rorty's focus on conversation. The second was towards sociology of science. However, rather than focusing on the more general epistemological arguments against rule-making (represented most clearly by Weintraub and Hands), the book took up Harry Collins's analysis of natural-science experiments as providing a framework for thinking about econometric practices. This led, influenced also by Hausman's analysis of reactions to experimental evidence on preference reversals (in which the empirical dimension of his philosophy of science arguably stood out most clearly), into an exploration of how economists actually used evidence.

As was argued in Backhouse [1997], Lakatos's MSRP, helped focus attention on difference between empirical and theoretical progress. Consideration of empirical progress led into questions concerning econometrics, applied economics and the use of evidence by economic theorists. For such inquiries, the sociology of science, including Collins's studies of replication in natural science, were useful. However, theoretical progress had to be thought of differently. There had been attempts to apply MSRP to theoretical questions, but these were problematic (see, for example, [Weintraub, 1985; Backhouse, 1998]). Backhouse [1999] approached the problem by reverting to the Lakatos of *Proofs and Refutations* (1976), arguing that economic theory could be analyzed as mathematics, focusing on the role played by intuitive understanding of economic concepts in regulating theoretical

[19]This language of 'turns', the number of which might make one wonder whether 'spinning' would be a better metaphor, in itself indicates a change.

activity. This was very different from the comparatively direct relation between empirical and theoretical progress found in the MSRP, the context in which reference had previously been made to Lakatos's work on mathematics [Weintraub, 1985; De Marchi, 1991]. Evidence from empirical work might influence theory, but indirectly, though influencing intuitions and assumptions, not through direct testing.

The significance of the distinction between economic theory and applied economics was taken up by the two methodologists who, along with Boland, remained closest to Popper. Hutchison [1992] argued that the aims of economics had changed: whereas it had been an empirical science, concerned primarily with prediction, that was no longer the case: there had been a formalist revolution since 1945, in which economists had adopted aims that were purely internal to the discipline. He remained Popperian in that he retained his emphasis on appraisal, insisting that demarcations were essential to clear thinking. Blaug also took up the idea of the formalist revolution, emphasising the importance of testing theories against evidence (and subjecting them to severe tests).

It was, however, Blaug who chose, in the 1990s, to describe himself as 'an unrepentent Popperian' [1997, chapter 11]. In the second edition of *The Methodology of Economics* (1992) he left the book substantially unchanged, using the occasion to reiterate his position. He remained a falsificationist. Situational analysis, though advocated by Popper, was inconsistent with falsificationism. Critical rationalism, another idea taken from Popper, was too imprecise to be usable. Critics of falsificationism, he contended, sought to defend economics rather than to criticise it: 'the fundamental bone of contention is not about philosophy of science as applied to economics, but simply the kind of economics we are going to have' [1997, p. 175]. Blaug wanted economics to be an empirical science. Others (he cited Thomas Mayer) might be happy to derive their views of what constituted best practice from years of experience in economics, but Blaug (ibid.) felt the need 'to support my faith in an empirical science of economics by some meta-theoretical philosophical arguments', hence his appeal to Popperianism. He found it a mystery how people could study what went on in economics without any criterion for distinguishing between between good and bad practices. As far as he was concerned,

> The methodology which best supports the economist's striving for substantive knowledge of economic relationships is the philosophy of science associated with names of Karl Popper and Imre Lakatos. To fully attain the ideal of falsifiability is, I still believe, the prime desideratum in economics. [Blaug, 1992, p. xxiii]

## 7 CONCLUSIONS

How should this episode be interpreted? The argument presented here is that it represents a peculiar stage in the development of economic methodology as a field of study. Up to the 1960s, much work on economic methodology was undertaken, but with a few notable exceptions, this was largely by established figures whose main activities were elsewhere. In the 1970s, a generation arose that chose to specialize in economic methodology, this including both philosophers and economists. The reasons for this are beyond the scope of this essay, but presumably include the doubts about economics that surfaced in the 1970s, the rise of heterodox schools, and the proliferation of fields within economics (cf. [Backhouse, 2002] for a general discussion of this period). Not only did this group augment a significant number of established economists that wanted to explore methodological questions, but Blaug's textbook provided an agenda and identified the field. The existence of a group of specialists, together with an influential series of conferences, in which De Marchi was a crucial figure, gave the literature a momentum that had previously been lacking, when individuals were working much more on their own.

For this group, Popper and Lakatos provided an agenda. Not only that, but for many of those coming from economics, engaging with Popperian and Lakatosian ideas was the route through which they entered seriously into the philosophy of science. The result was, perhaps, an exaggerated emphasis on their work in relation to that of philosophers of science whose work might also have provided a way forward from the philosophical perspectives of the 1950s. Some engaged with Popper and Lakatos without accepting their methodologies;[20] others became Lakatosian in their methodology (there were few if any Popperians in this category), but later moved away, in a spectrum ranging from outright rejection of 'Methodology' as misconceived, to attempting to build on Lakatos, minimizing the extent of their movement away. At the former end were Weintraub, followed by Hands; at the other De Marchi and Backhouse.[21] Several remained Popperian throughout, but interpreted their Popper in radically different ways (Boland, Klant, Blaug, Hutchison, Caldwell).

Though Popper was continually in the background, it was Lakatos who attracted most attention, for it was his work that opened up the possibility of moving beyond previous discussions by bringing in history. It is no coincidence that Lakatos's MSRP became strongly associated with the history of economic thought: not only did his MHRP offer a clear role for the history of economic thought, but it opened up the prospect of a new way to think systematically about history. The latter promise may, in the end, have proved problematic, but it was arguably significant in opening up new perspectives in a field still dominated by the study of the classics (though many of the studies in Latsis 1976 and De Marchi and Blaug 1991 were historical, it is notable that they avoided the then-standard fare of Smith-Ricardo-Marx).

[20]No list of names is provided here, for it would be too long, including all those who argued against Popper and Lakatos, from philosophers such as Hausman and Mäki to students of rhetoric such as McCloskey. There are also many authors of case studies where it is hard to say how far they accepted the methodology, and how far they simply explored it for the purposes of a case study.

[21]In writing this paper, I have become embarassingly conscious of the extent to which the development of my own ideas on Lakatos owed far more to De Marchi's writing than I realised at the time.

This setting perhaps explains why the take-up of Popper and Lakatos amongst economic methodologists, and the subsequent movement away were so marked. The episode recounted here was far from being the whole of economic methodology during this period, for many people were pursuing methodological inquires from other perspectives. But this work, because it caused so many students of methodology to engage with each other, was particularly significant.

De Marchi [1991] pays great attention to what he calls the Lakatosian self-image of economists. This, of course, cuts two ways. On the one hand, adopting the criteria of Lakatos's MHRP, it can be seen as evidence for the appropriateness of MSRP (or at least components of it) to economics. On the other hand, it can be seen as explaining why economists are vulnerable to being seduced by MSRP. But what it succeeded in doing was focusing attention on the interplay, or lack of it, between theory and evidence, to an extent that the earlier literature had not achieved. One of the criticisms of MSRP to economics was that it failed to recognise the complexity of economic reasoning, finding it hard to accommodate the spectrum from abstract general equilibrium theory to applied econometric research. It sought to understand through exploring the applicability of simple appraisal criteria when, perhaps, the problem would ideally have gone the other way round, from building up a picture of how theory and application were related (something still not understood), progressing from there to appraisal. However, not only does that take a stance on the question of whether methodology should be concerned with criticizing or defending economic practices, but it is to adopt an un-Popperian inductive approach to the problem of economic methodology.

## ACKNOWLEDGEMENTS

This paper was completed while I was holding a Lachmann Research Fellowship at the London School of Economics. I am grateful for this support.

## BIBLIOGRAPHY

[Archibald, 1961] G. C. Archibald. Chamberlin versus Chicago. *Review of Economic Studies* 29:2-28, 1961.

[Arrow, 1960] K. J. Arrow. The work of Ragnar Frisch, econometrician. *Econometrica* 28:175-92, 1960.

[Backhouse, 1997] R. E. Backhouse. *Truth and Progress in Economic Knowledge.* Cheltenham: Edward Elgar, 1997.

[Backhouse, 1998b] R. E. Backhouse. *Explorations in Economic Methodology: From Lakatos to Empirical Philosophy of Science.* London: Routledge, 1998.

[Backhouse, 1998b] R. E. Backhouse. If mathematics is informal, perhaps we should accept that economics must be informal too. *Economic Journal* 108:1848-58, 1998.

[Bear and Orr, 1967] D. V. T. Bear and D. Orr. Logic and expediency in economic theorizing. *Journal of Political Economy* 75 (2):188-96, 1967.

[Blaug, 1980] M. Blaug. *The Methodology of Economics: How Economists Explain.* Cambridge: Cambridge University Press, 1980.

[Blaug, 1992] M. Blaug. *The Methodology of Economics.* 2nd ed. Cambridge: Cambridge University Press, 1992.

[Blaug, 1997] M. Blaug. *Not Only an Economist.* Cheltenham: Edward Elgar, 1997.
[Boland, 1982] L. A. Boland. *The Methodology of Economic Model Building: Methodology after Samuelson.* London: Routledge, 1982.
[Boland, 1992] L. A. Boland. *The Principles of Economics: Some Lies my Teachers told Me.* London: Routledge, 1992.
[Boland, 1997] L. A. Boland. *Critical Economic Methodology: A Personal Odyssey.* London: Routledge, 1997.
[Boland, 2003] L. A. Boland. *The Foundations of Economic Method: A Popperian Perspective.* London: Routledge, 2003.
[Caldwell, 1982] B. Caldwell. *Beyond Positivism: Economic Methodology in the Twentieth Century.* London: George Allen and Unwin, 1982.
[Caldwell, 1988] B. Caldwell. The case for pluralism. In *The Popperian Legacy in Economics*, ed. N. B. De Marchi, 231-44. Cambridge: Cambridge University Press, 1988.
[Caldwell, 1991] B. Caldwell. Clarifying Popper. *Journal of Economic Literature* 29:1-33, 1991.
[Coats, 1969] A. W. Coats. Is there a structure of scientific revolutions in economics? *Kyklos* 22:289-96, 1969.
[Collins, 1985] H. Collins. *Changing Order: Replication and Induction in Scientific Practice.* Beverley Hills: Sage, 1985.
[Day, 1955] A. C. L. Day. The taxonomic approach to the study of economic policies. *American Economic Review* 45 (1):64-78, 1955.
[De Marchi, 1988] N. B. De Marchi, ed. *The Popperian Legacy in Economics.* Cambridge: Cambridge University Press, 1988.
[De Marchi, 1991] N. B. De Marchi. Introduction. In *Appraising Economic Theories: Studies in the Methodology of Research Programmes*, ed. N. B. De Marchi and M. Blaug, 1-30. Cheltenham: Edward Elgar, 1991.
[De Marchi, 1992] N. B. De Marchi, ed. *Post-Popperian Methodology of Economics: Recovering Practice.* Dordrecht: Kluwer, 1992.
[De Marchi and Blaug, 1991] N. B. De Marchi and M. Blaug, eds. *Appraising Economic Theories: Studies in the Methodology of Research Programmes.* Aldershot: Edward Elgar, 1991.
[Friedman, 1963] M. Friedman. More on Archibald versus Chicago. *Review of Economic Studies* 30:65-67, 1963.
[M. Friedman, 1953] M. Friedman. The methodology of positive economics. In *Essays in Positive Economics*, ed. M. Friedman. Chicago, Il: Chicago University Press, 1953.
[Hammond, 1993] J. D. Hammond. An interview with Milton Friedman on methodology. In *The Philosophy and Method of Economics*, ed. B. Caldwell, 216-38. Vol. 1. Cheltenham: Edward Elgar, 1993.
[Hands, 1993] D. W. Hands. *Testing, Rationality and Progress: Essays on the Popperian Tradition in Economic Methodology.* Lanham, MD: Rowman and Littlefield, 1993.
[Hands, 2001] D. W. Hands. *Reflection without Rules: Economic Methodology and Contemporary Science Theory.* Cambridge: Cambridge University Press, 2001.
[Hausman, 1992] Hausman, D. M. 1992. *The Inexact and Separate Science of Economics.* Cambridge: Cambridge University Press, 1992.
[Hayek, 1937] F. A. Hayek. Economics and knowledge. *Economica* 4:33-54, 1937.
[Howson, 1976] C. Howson, ed. *Method and Appraisal in the Physical Sciences: The critical background to modern science, 1800-1905.* Cambridge: Cambridge University Press, 1976.
[Hutchison, 1938] T. W. Hutchison. *Significance and Basic Postulates of Economic Theory.* London: Macmillan, 1938.
[Hutchison, 1992] T. W. Hutchison. *Changing Aims in Economics.* Oxford: Basil Blackwell.
[Klant, 1984] J. J. Klant. *The Rules of the Game: The Logical Structure of Economic Theories.* Cambridge University Press: Cambridge. Translated by Ina Swart, 1984.
[Klappholz and Agassi, 1959] K. Klappholz and J. Agassi. Methodological prescriptions in economics. *Economica* 25:246-54, 1959.
[Knight, 1940] F. H. Knight. "What is truth" in economics. *Journal of Political Economy* 48 (1):1-32, 1940.
[Koopmans, 1957] T. C. Koopmans. *Three Essays on the State of Economic Science.* New York: McGraw Hill, 1957.
[Lakatos, 1976] I. Lakatos. *Proofs and Refutations: The Logic of Mathematical Discovery.* Cambridge: Cambridge University Press, 1976.

[Lakatos and Musgrave, 1970] I. Lakatos and A. Musgrave, eds. *Criticism and the Growth of Knowledge*. Cambridge University Press: Cambridge, 1970.

[Latsis, 1976] S. J. Latsis. *Method and Appraisal in Economics*. Cambridge: Cambridge University Press, 1976.

[Lipsey, 1963] R. G. Lipsey. *An Introduction to Positive Economics*. London: Weidenfeld and Nicolson, 1963.

[Machlup, 1955] F. Machlup. The problem of verification in economics. *Southern Economic Journal* 22 (1):1-21, 1955.

[Machlup, 1964] F. Machlup. Professor Samuelson on theory and realism. *American Economic Review* 54 (3):733-36, 1964.

[Mäki, 1990] U. Mäki. Methodology of economics: Complaints and guidelines. *Finnish Economic Papers* 3: 77-84, 1990.

[McCloskey, 1983] D. N. McCloskey. The rhetoric of economics. *Journal of Economic Literature* 21:481-517, 1983.

[Ngel, 1963] E. Nagel. Assumptions in economic theory. *American Economic Review* 53 (2):211-19, 1963.

[Popper, 1965] K. R. Popper. *Conjectures and Refutations*. New York: Harper and Row, 1965.

[Popper, 1959] K. R. Popper. *The Logic of Scientific Discovery*. London: Unwin Hyman, 1959.

[Remenyi, 1979] J. V. Remenyi. Core-demi-core interaction: towards a general theory of disciplinary and sub-disciplinary growth. *History of Political Economy* 11:30-63, 1979.

[Rorty, 1980] R. Rorty. *Philosophy and the Mirror of Nature*. Oxford: Basil Blackwell, 1980.

[Rosenberg, 1992] A. Rosenberg. *Economics - Mathematical Politics or Science of Diminishing Returns*. Chicago: Chicago University Press, 1992.

[Stewart, 1979] I. Stewart. *Reasoning and Method in Economics*. London: McGraw Hill, 1979.

[Stigler, 1963] G. J. Stigler. Archibald versus Chicago. *Review of Economic Studies* 30:63-64, 1963.

[Weintraub, 1977] E. R. Weintraub. The microfoundations of macroeconomics: a critical survey. *Journal of Economic Literature* 15:1-23, 1977.

[Weintraub, 1979] E. R. Weintraub. *Microfoundations: the Compatibility of Microeconomics and Macroeconomics*. Cambridge: Cambridge University Press, 1979.

[Weintraub, 1985] E. R. Weintraub. *General Equilibrium Analysis: Studies in Appraisal*. Cambridge: Cambridge University Press, 1985.

[Weintraub, 1989] E. R. Weintraub. Methodology doesn't matter, but the history of thought might. *Scandinavian Journal of Economics* 91 (2):477-93, 1989.

[Weintraub, 1991] E. R. Weintraub. *Stabilizing Dynamics: Constructing Economic Knowledge*. Cambridge: Cambridge University Press, 1991.

# MODELS AND MODELLING IN ECONOMICS

Mary S. Morgan and Tarja Knuuttila

## 1 INTRODUCTION

Interest in modelling as a specific philosophical theme is both old and new. In the nineteenth century the word model usually referred to concrete objects, oftentimes to the so-called mechanical models, that were built in an effort to grasp the functioning of unobserved theoretical entities (e.g. [Bolzmann, 1911]). Since then, the kinds of things called models in science have multiplied: they can be physical three-dimensional things, diagrams, mathematical equations, computer programs, organisms and even laboratory populations. This heterogeneity of models in science is matched in the widely different philosophical accounts of them. Indeed, discussion of models in the philosophy of science testifies to a variety of theoretical, formal, and practical aspirations that appear to have different and even conflicting aims (e.g. [Bailer-Jones, 1999]). In addition to approaches concerned with the pragmatic and cognitive role of models in the scientific enterprise, attempts have been made to establish, within a formal framework, what scientific models are. The syntactic view of models, once the "received view", and the semantic approach to models, the prevailing model-theoretic approach until recently, were both attempts of this kind. Yet the discussion of models was originally motivated by practice-oriented considerations, guided by an interest in scientific reasoning. This is perhaps one reason why the general philosophy of science has tended to downplay models relative to theories, conceiving them merely as — for example — heuristic tools, interpretations of theories, or means of prediction. Recently, however, this situation has changed as models have come to occupy an ever more central epistemological role in the present practice of many different sciences.

Models and modelling became the predominant epistemic genre in economic science only in the latter part of the twentieth century. The term "model" appeared in economics during the 1930s, introduced by the early econometricians, even though objects we would now call models were developed and used before then, for example, Marshall's [1890] supply-demand scissor diagrams (see [Morgan, 2011]). Yet, it was only after the 1950s that modelling became a widely recognised way of doing economic science, both for statistical and empirical work in econometrics, for theory building using mathematics, and in policy advice. Indeed, it became conventional then to think of models in modern economics as either mathematical objects or statistical objects thus dividing the economics community for

Handbook of the Philosophy of Science. Volume 13: Philosophy of Economics.
Volume editor: Uskali Mäki. General Editors: Dov M. Gabbay, Paul Thagard and John Woods.

the last half-century into those who were mainly practising econometric (statistically based) modelling and those who engaged in mathematical modelling. This community division is reflected in parallel bodies of commentary by philosophers of economics, analysing mathematical models in relation to economic theories and econometric models in relation to statistical theories and statistical data. Consequently, these have usually been viewed as different sorts of models, with different characteristics, different roles, and requiring different philosophical analysis.

This account deals with both so-called theoretical and empirical models of economics without assuming any principled difference between the two and in contrast to the general philosophy of science which has typically concentrated on mathematical modelling. We cover various perspectives on the philosophical status and different roles of models in economics and discuss how these approaches fit into the modern science of economics. Section 2 spells out some main accounts on the kind of entities economic models are thought to be, although, in order to categorise them in a general way, it is inevitable that the original accounts given by the different philosophers and economists presented below are certainly more subtle and versatile than our classification suggests. Section 3 in turn focuses on how models are used in economics. Since the status and function of models are not separable issues, there is some overlap between the two sections: the various accounts of the nature of models imply more often than not specific views on how models are supposed to be constructed, used and justified in scientific practice.

## 2 NATURE OF ECONOMIC MODELS

Modern economics does not differ from the other sciences, such as physics and biology, in its dependency on modelling, yet it lies in an interesting way between the natural and the social sciences in terms of its methods and the variety of models it utilizes. Core micro-economic theory has been axiomatized and economists use sophisticated mathematical methods in modelling economic phenomena. Macroeconomics relies in turn more on purpose-built models, often devised for policy advice. And a range of empirical and statistical models operate across the board in econometrics. Although the various model-based strategies of economics seem much like that of those of the natural sciences, at the same time economics shares an hermeneutic character with other social sciences. Economics is in part based on everyday concepts, and as economic agents ourselves we have a more or less good pre-understanding of various economic phenomena. Moreover, individuals' knowledge of economics feeds back into their economic behaviour, and that of economic scientists feeds in turn into economic policy advice, giving economics a reflexive character quite unlike the natural sciences. Recent literature has focussed on the various different kinds of "performativity" this creates for economics, particularly in the context of financial models (see [MacKenzie, 2006]), but the interactions between economic science and the economy have long been discussed amongst historians of economics and, indeed, economists themselves.

This very complexity of economic science has, without doubt, contributed to the fact that the status and role of economic models – being always apparently simpler than the economic behaviour that economists seek to understand — have been a constant concern for both philosophers and economists alike. In this situation, two major positions have been taken regarding the epistemic status of economic models. Firstly, economic models have been conceived of as idealized entities. From this perspective economists are seen to make use of stylized, simplifying, and even distorting assumptions as regards the real economies in their modelling activities. Secondly, it has been suggested that models in economics are various kinds of purpose built constructions: some are considered to have representational status, others are considered as purely fictional or artificial entities. Seeing models as constructions has been also been related to a functional account of models as autonomous objects that mediate between the theory and data, a perspective which conveniently brings together mathematical and econometric models.

## *2.1 Models as idealizations*

In the general philosophy of science, models and idealization are topics that tend to go together. The term 'idealization' is generically used, but it is very difficult to find a single or shared definition. A variety of usages of the term in economics appear in the rich collection of essays in Bert Hamminga and Neil De Marchi [1994], including their introduction, in which models are said, variously, to be the result of processes of generalizing, simplifying, abstracting, and isolating, following technical, substantive and conceptual aims or requirements (see also [Morgan, 1996; 2006; Mäki, 1992; 1994]). Idealization is typically potrayed as a process that starts with the complicated world with the aim of simplifying it and isolating a small part of it for model representation; as in the general analysis of the Poznan approach, where "idealization" is complemented with a reverse process of "concretization" [Nowak, 1994]. (This latter approach began to analyse idealization and modelling in the 1970s, but for some time was unrecognised by the mainstream of philosophy of science.) Three commentators particularly associated with questions of idealization in economic modelling, Nancy Cartwright, Daniel Hausman and Uskali Mäki, all draw on an old and venerable discussion going back in economics to John Stuart Mill [1843] whose account of how scientific theorizing could go ahead in economics relied on developing simple models in order to develop a deductive analysis (although of course he did not use the term model). However, because of the disturbing factors that always attended economic analysis in application to the world, he believed that economic laws could only be formulated and understood as tendency laws.

### *2.1.1 Idealization*

The basic idea that philosophers of economics have derived from Mill is to conceive of models as abstracting causally relevant capacities or factors of the real world for the purpose of working out deductively what effects those few isolated capacities or factors have in particular model (i.e. controlled) environments. However, the ways they have adapted the Millian ideas has varied.

Cartwright focusses on causal capacities that are supposed to work in the world, associating the aim of discovering them as being evident in and applicable to both mathematical and econometric modelling [1989; 1994]. According to her, despite the messiness of the economic world, there are sometimes found invariant associations between events. In these associations, causal capacities work together in particular configurations she calls "nomological machines" (e.g. [Cartwright, 1999, ch 3 and 6]). Mathematical models in economics are constructed as blueprints for those nomological machines, and may serve — in particular circumstances where those machines can be thought to operate without interference from the many other factors in the economy — to enable the scientist to study the way those capacities operate in the real world. Nevertheless, the conditions under which models can be used in econometrics to study such capacities are, she claims, particularly demanding and difficult. In contrast, Hoover [2002] and Boumans [2003] in reply, are more optimistic, arguing that econometric models can be used to help discover regularities, and invariant relations, of the economy even though economists do not know, *a priori*, the machines. So, models are rather to be thought of as working diagrams for the analysis of causal relations, rather than blueprints of already known machines. Indeed, Hoover discusses the difficult task of finding causal relationships in economics precisely in terms of "the mapping between theoretical and econometric models" [Hoover, this volume, p. 96].

Hausman [1990] discusses the process of figuring out the causal factors at work by the use of *ceteris paribus* clauses in theoretical models in a way that appears close to the Marshallian comparative static approach of a century earlier. For example, by an analysis of causal factors in the supply and demand diagram, he shows how economists argue using theoretical models by selecting additional factors from the *ceteris paribus* pound in order to explain, in casual rather than econometric terms, the simple observations of everyday economic life (such as "Why is the price of coffee high just now?"). Although Hausman's analysis does not go beyond casual application (see below), we can understand Boumans's [2005] dissection of the various kinds of ceteris paribus clauses that have to be fully labelled and accounted for in models as being relevant here. For Boumans, working with econometric models requires not just a commitment to decide which factors can be considered absent (*ceteris absentibus*), but to those which can be legitimately ignored because of their small effect (*ceteris neglictis*) as well as to those that are present but remain largely unchanged (*ceteris paribus*). This analysis extends and partly replaces an earlier typology of Musgrave [1981] for economic theory models by making a comparison of the use of such clauses in modelling, simulations and laboratory experiments in economics with economic models in economics (see [Boumans and Morgan; 2001; Mäki, 2000; Hindriks, 2006], for further developments of [Musgrave, 1981]).

Mäki's account, which builds on Nowak as well as on Mill, is, like Hausman's *ceteris paribus* discussion, dependent on "sealing off" the relations of interest from other influences. For Mäki a theoretical model is an outcome of the method of isolation, which he analyses as an operation in which a set of elements is theoretically removed from the influence of other elements in a given situation through the use of various kinds of often unrealistic assumptions [Mäki, 1992; 1994]. Thus in positing *unrealistic* assumptions economists need not adopt an *anti-realist* attitude towards the economic theory. Quite the contrary, unrealistic assumptions can even be the very means of striving for the truth, which Mäki puts as boldly as stating that "an isolating theory or statement is true if it correctly represents the isolated essence of the object" [1992, 344; 2011].

The authors mentioned above — Cartwright, Mäki, and to a more limited extent, Hausman — can be interpreted as proponents of a distinct strategy of idealization, one that we might refer to as one of isolation in the sense that the point is to capture only those core causal factors, capacities or the essentials of a causal mechanisms that bring about a certain target phenomenon. Weisberg [2007] suggests we characterise such models as products of "minimalist idealization" since they contain "only those factors that *make a difference* to the occurrence and essential character of the phenomenon in question" [p. 642, italics in the original]. This very Millian characterisation immediately raises a number of problems that arise in trying to separate out what those causal factors are. A convenient way — even an idealized case — to demonstrate what is at stake is to invoke the Galilean experiment [McMullin, 1985] as discussed by Cartwright [1999; 2006]. The aim of the Galilean experiment is to eliminate *all* other possible causes in order to establish the effect of one cause operating on its own [1999, p. 11]. From this analysis, Cartwright (in her more recent writings) has come to doubt whether the idea of looking at how one factor behaves in isolation works for economics remembering that her interest is in locating causal capacities in the world, while others, such as Boumans [2003; 2005], invoke the same ideal case to pose the question in terms of how to design econometric models which have sufficient statistical control features to locate invariant and autonomous relations in the data, while still others, like Mäki [2005], understand the issue in terms of how modellers use theoretical assumptions to seal off the effect of other factors. All these authors, explicitly or implicitly, appeal to the physical controls of laboratory experiments as a way to motivate their account of how models may be built to isolate elements of economic behaviour.

Terminology is important. The notion of 'idealization' does include more than a process to isolate causal factors, and no two commentators use the term in the same way. Mäki uses the term "isolation" as his central concept, under which he subsumes other related notions frequently dealt with in the discussions on modeling. Thus he treats for example, "abstraction" as a subspecies that isolates the universal from particular exemplifications; idealizations and omissions, in turn, are techniques for generating isolations: idealizations being deliberate falsehoods, which either understate or exaggerate to the absolute extremes. For Cartwright, in contrast, "idealization" and "abstraction" are the basic terms and categories involving two different operations. For her, too, idealization involves distortion, by which she means *changing* some particular features of the concrete object so that it becomes easier to think about and thus more tractable to model (Cartwright 1989). Abstraction in turn is a kind of omission, that of *subtracting* relevant features of the object and thus when it comes to abstraction it makes no sense to talk about the departure of the assumption from truth, a question that typically arises in the context of idealization (see [Cartwright, 1989 ch. 5; Jones and Cartwright, 2005]). But these views by no means exhaust the ways in which idealization is understood with respect to economic models. One interesting set of notions (found amongst the many others in Hamminga and De Marchi's [1994] collection), is Walliser's analysis of idealization as three different kinds of processes of generalisation: *extending* the domain of application (so as to transfer the model to other domains); *weakening* some of the assumptions to extend the set of applications; and *rooting*, providing stronger reasons for the model assumptions. For Hausman, the label is less important than the variety of things that it covers, though in his 1992 account of economic theorizing using models, we find an emphasis on the conceptual work that modelling plays and see this too in his account of the overlapping generations model, where idealization works through falsehoods and generalisations as much as through omissions and isolations. It is not difficult to find examples of such concept-related idealizations in economics, where assumptions such as perfect knowledge, zero transaction costs, full employment, perfectly divisible goods, and infinitely elastic demand curves are commonly made and taken by economists not as distortions, but as providing conceptual content in theoretical models, a point to which we return in section 3.3.2 below.

### *2.1.2 De-Idealization*

We have seen above that the term 'idealization' covers different strategies and, consequently, of ways of justifying them. One influential defence of idealization is the idea of de-idealization, according to which the advancement of science will correct the distortions effected by idealizations and add back the discarded elements, thus making the theoretical representations become more usefully concrete or particular. A classic formulation of this position was provided by Tjalling Koopmans who thought of models only as intermediary versions of theories which enabled the economist to reason his way through the relations between complicated sets of postulates. In the process of this discussion, in a much quoted comment, he portrayed "economic theory as a sequence of models":

> "Considerations of this order suggest that we look upon economic theory as a sequence of conceptional *models* that seek to express in simplified form different aspects of an always more complicated reality. At first these aspects are formalized as much as feasible in isolation, then in combinations of increasing realism." [Koopmans, 1957, p 142]

Nowak also thought that science should eventually remove the "counter-actual" idealizations in a process of "concretization" [Nowak, 1992]. But although economics may experience a process like this in locally temporal sequences of mathematical and econometric modelling (see, for example, the case discussed by Hindriks [2005]), it is difficult to characterise the more radical and noticeable changes in models as moves towards greater "realism" (to use Koopmans's term).

It is also possible to see the move to greater realism as a process of reversing idealizations. Considering such a project in economics gives us considerable insight into idealization and, indirectly, points to difficulties not just in Koopman's justification for idealization, but also in the other arguments made (above) about its usefulness. The potential processes of de-idealization, then, reveal a number of interesting and important points about the strategies of idealization.

First, idealization frequently involves particular kinds of *kinds of distortions* that often are motivated by *tractability considerations*, such as setting parameters or other factors in the model to a particular value, including extreme ones (such as zero or infinity). When such a model is de-idealized the importance of these assumptions to the model will become evident, though the particular problems they cause in the model are not likely to follow any standard pattern or share any obvious solution. So for example, Hausman's account of Samuelson's "overlapping generations model" refers to a paper which has been "carried away by fictions" [1992, p. 102]. By carefully unpacking Samuelson's various model assumptions — that is by informally attempting to de-idealize the model and by analysing the immediate critiques that offered similar analyses — Hausman shows how critical some of these idealizations are to the results of the model. He points out, for example, that: "The appeal of the overlapping-generations framework is that it provides a relatively tractable way to address the effects of the future on the present. It enables one to study an economy that is in competitive equilibrium with heterogeneous individuals who are changing over time. Yet the heterogeneity results from the effects of aging on an underlying homogeneity of tastes and ability." Hausman's deconstruction of the assumptions explores why some questions get left aside during the paper, and why such a well-used model nevertheless rests on some quite strange idealizing foundations.

Second, and more generally, the economist achieves computationally tractable models by *mathematical moulding* that will fit the pieces of the model together in such a way as to allow deductions with the model to go through (see [Boumans, 1999]). Once again, it is difficult to foresee in any general way what will happen when that twist is unravelled. While advances in mathematical techniques and computational power may change aspects of this problem, it seems unlikely to remove it altogether. Moreover, moving from a model which is analytical in mathematical terms to one that is tractable as a simulation does not in itself solve the problem, since each mode of using models requires a different idealization to make the model tractable. A related pragmatic move is found in idealizations that allow derivations to be made: it is often difficult to make sense of the very idea of relaxing those assumptions that are mainly aimed at facilitating the derivation of the results from the model. As Alexandrova [2006] asks of such assumptions:

> "In what sense is it more realistic for agents to have discretely as opposed to continuously distributed valuations? It is controversial enough to say that people form their beliefs about the value of a painting or the profit potential of an oil well by drawing a variable from a probability distribution. So the further question about whether this distribution is continuous or not is not a question that seems to make sense when asked about human bidders and their beliefs". [2006, 183]

As she argues, one simply does not know how statements concerning such "*derivation facilitators*" should be translated back into statements about the real entities and properties.

Third, taking Boumans' 2005 analysis of the *various ceteris paribus assumptions* seriously suggests that the difference between factors that can legitimately be assumed absent, those that are present but negligible, and those that are present, but within a range constant, may be critical in any de-idealization even before moving to an econometric model, yet economic modellers tend to lump these all into one bundle in the process of ideaslization.

Fourth, is the vexed question of de-idealizing with respect to the *causal structure*. If it really is the case that there are only a very few or one strong causal factor and the rest are negligible then the minimalistic strategy suggests that adding more detail to the model may in fact render the model worse from the epistemic point of view. It makes the explanatory models more complicated and diverts attention from the more relevant causal factors to the less relevant (see [Strevens, 2008]). More likely however, there are many causal factors operating, some of which have been idealized away for theoretical purposes, while simpler relations may have been assumed for the causal interactions. Yet, in econometric work, it is often found that the causes are not separable and so they should not have been be treated as independent of other previously included and omitted factors. De-idealization thus recreates a great deal of causal complexity in the model that may have been mistakenly assumed away in making the theoretical model. So, as soon as de-idealization begins — this notion of being able to study individual causal factors in isolation begins to crumble. All these problems may not appear so acute during a process of theorizing, but become immediately apparent for those concerned with models applied to the world, where far ranging idealizations about causal structures are likely to be invalid starting points in the attempts to map from economic to econometric models. The problem of unravelling causal claims in economic models has been the subject of much debate within economics in a literature that is well integrated into the general philosophical debates on causality (see [Heckman, 2000], on micro-economics models; [Hoover, 2001] on macro-economic models and more generally, [Hoover, 2008; this volume; Cartwright, 2006]).

Fifth, the *different levels of idealization* within a model may not be compatible with each other and this may become particularly evident if and when de-idealizations are made. Hoover [2008a] unpicks the idealizations of recent macroeconomic models to show how the reductionist idealizations embedded in their micro-foundations are not only individually problematic as separate idealizations (see [Kirman, 1992]), but problematic in that the various idealizations are either incompatible, or make seemingly contradictory assumptions in the model about the nature of the individuals with the aggregates.

Sixth, some idealisations in models are associated with concept formation. It is not at all clear what it means to de-idealize a concept within a mathematical model, though econometricians face this problem on a daily basis in their modelling (see below, section 2.1.3). This is self-evident in cases where well theorized concepts like "utility" are involved, but equally problematic in terms of concepts that might have empirical model counterparts such as the "natural rate of unemployment" or even with the more prosaic elements such as "prices" which still have to be de-idealized in particular ways for econometric models.

Lastly, of course, these *different kinds of idealizations are not independent* in the model, so that the effects of de-idealization are manifestly very difficult to predict. The assumptions needed to make the model mathematically tractable often threaten the very idea that causes can be isolated, since they frequently make the results derived from a model dependent on the model as a whole. And, if it is unclear which model assumptions "do the work", it is difficult to see how the model can isolate the behaviour of any specific causal factor or tendency and how the various other assumptions can be reversed satisfactorily. Consequently, de-idealization does not succeed in separating out what is negligible and thus irrelevant and what is not. All these problems must be acute in minimalist models because they are typically relatively thin and simple in order to isolate only a few causes, and must be constructed with the help of clearly purpose-built assumptions in order to provide a way to secure deductively certain results. As Cartwright [1999] has argued, the model economy has to be attributed very special characteristics so as to allow such mathematical representation that, given some minimal economic principles such as utility maximization, one can derive deductive consequences from it. Yet at the same time the model results are tied to the specific circumstances given in the model that has been created, making all the assumptions seem relevant for the results derived.

These difficulties all tend to water down the idea that as economic investigations proceed, one could achieve more realistic models through de-idealization. It also suggests that the notion of models as providing a forum for Galilean experiments sets too strict an ideal for economic modelling. Perhaps it provides a more useful philosophical basis in such a science as physics, where in many cases comprehensive and well-confirmed background theories exist giving the resources with which to estimate the effect of distortions introduced by specific idealizations, and provide guidance on how to attain particular levels of accuracy and precision. The method of modelling in economics should perhaps rather be compared with the use of models in sciences such as meteorology, ecology and population biology, sciences which do not so much lack comprehensive foundations as the relatively well behaved systems and well confirmed background theories that can be connected to specific knowledge of particular cases which allow idealizations and de-idealizations to be informative.

An alternative defence and interpretation of highly idealized models has been claimed in what several analysts, following Richard Levins [1966], have called "robustness analysis" [Wimsatt, 1987]. Robustness can be characterized as stability in a result that has been determined by various independent scientific activities, for instance through observation, experiment, and mathematical derivation. Applied just to modelling, where it has been taken to mean the search for predictions common to several independent models, the notion must however have a weaker epistemological power. Worse, in economics, such robustness claims are based on analysis carried out on models that are far from independent, usually being variations of a common "ancestor" and differing from each other only with respect to a couple of assumptions. While it is possible to claim that by constructing many slightly different models economists are in fact testing whether it is the common core mechanism of the group of models in question that is responsible for the result derived and not some auxiliary assumptions used [Kuorikoski *et al.*, 2007; Weisberg, 2006], this may not help in validating the model as stable and robust beyond the mathematical laboratory. In contrast, in the statistical laboratory of econometrics, robustness in model performance has been understood not in terms of core mechanisms, but as a relative quality of models in relation to data sets judged according to a set of statistical criteria applied within a modelling process (see [Spanos, this volume]), though there are cases where such tests have been carried out on related families of econometric models (see e.g. [Wallis, 1984]).

### *2.1.3 The Idealization vs. De-idealization Debate in Econometrics*

While the language of idealization and de-idealization is not so familiar in the philosophy of econometric models (with notable exceptions, for example, [Hoover, 1994]), these processes are endemic in the practises of econometrics at both grand and everyday levels. At a meta-level, though it has not been couched in these terms, the argument about the process of modelling in econometrics is exactly one as to whether it should proceed by processes of idealization or by ones of de-idealization. At a more everyday level however, we find that practical modelling in econometrics involves many processes of idealization and de-idealization at the same time.

At the practical level then, making and testing the validity of idealization decisions in econometrics covers a similar range of economic questions as those for mathematical models: Which variables should be included and omitted? What are the key causal relations between them? What simplifying assumptions can be made? What *ceteris paribus* clauses are involved? What tractability assumptions need to be made? What is the nature of their statistical and mathematical form? And so forth. But econometric modelling also includes making, and testing, idealizing assumptions about the nature of the economic data: about the probability distributions assumed, the nature of errors, the stochastic behaviours found in particular kinds of data, and so on.

However, in a significant difference with mathematical modelling, econometric modelling additionally involves a whole lot of de-idealizing decisions that are required to bring the requirements of the theory into some kind of coherence with the available data. Thus, for example, economic theory models rarely specify very clearly the details of time relations or the particular form of entities or relationships involved, and all these details have to be filled in the model. And from the data side, decisions must be made about which data set most closely resembles the economic entity being modelled, and so forth. This last activity reveals indeed how very deeply abstract and concept-ridden economists' economic terms are, even when they share the same name with every-day economic terms. Every modelling decision in econometrics involves a dilemma of how to measure the terms that economists use in their theories. Sometimes these measures are termed "proxies" because the theoretical term wanted is not one that is measured; other times it is a choice of what data best matched the conceptualised, abstract, terms of economists' models. Sometimes the model itself is used to derive the measurements needed within the model (see [Boumans, 2005; this volume], on the role of models in obtaining economic measurements). Modelling is carried out for many purposes in econometrics: to test theories, to measure relations, to explain events, to predict outcomes, to analyse policy choices, etc, each needing different statistical and economic resources and invoking different criteria in the modelling processes. All this activity means that econometric modelling — involving processes of both idealization and de-idealization — is very much an applied science: each model has to be crafted from particular materials for particular purposes, and such skills are learned through apprenticeship and experience as much as by book learning (see [Colander, 2008; Magnus and Morgan, 1997]).

At the meta-level, the argument over modelling is concerned with the relative role of theory and data in model making and goes on at both an abstract and specific level. Econometricians are more deeply engaged in thinking through the philosophical aspects of their modelling strategy compared to their mathematical modelling colleagues. These discussions indeed go back to the foundations of modelling in econometrics during the 1930s and 1940s. Thus, the infamous "measurement without theory debate" over the role of theory — both economic and statistical — in the making and using of econometric models, lead, in the post 1950s period, to an economics in which it was thought economists should provide mathematically expressed theoretical models while the econometrician should use statistics for model estimation and theory testing. Yet, in spite of this rhetoric, it is not possible simply to "confront theory with data", or "apply theory to data", for all the prosaic reasons mentioned above: economic theory does not provide all the resources needed to make econometric models that can be used for measurement or testing, or as Hoover so aptly puts it: "theories are rarely rich enough to do justice to the complexities of the data" [2000, p 221]. This is why those who developed econometrics introduced and developed the notion of model in the first place — namely as a necessary object in which the matching between theory and data could be accomplished. Whether, in this "new practice" of models, as

Boumans [2005] terms it, the notion of model was rather straightforward (as in Frisch and Tinbergen's work) or philosophically sophisticated (as in Haavelmo's work, below), models were conceived as a critical element in the scientific claims of economics (see [Morgan, 1990]).

Yet, despite these debates, there are no general agreed scientific rules for modelling, and there continue to be fierce arguments within the econometrics community over the principles for modelling and the associated criteria for satisfactory modelling (particularly given the variety of purposes to which such modelling is addressed). For the past two decades or so, the major question is no longer understood simply as to whether models should be theory driven or data driven; but as to whether the modelling process should be *"general to specific"* or *"simple to general"*, and given this, the relative roles of theory and data in these two different paths. (There are other positions and approaches, but we concentrate on just these two here.) That is, should econometric modelling proceed by starting with a most general model which incorporates all the possible influencing factors over the time frame that is then refined into one relevant for the specific case in hand; this is a kind of isolating process where the reducing or simplifying moves are validated by the given data resulting in a model with fewer factors (see [Cook and Hendry, 1994]). The alternative process starts with an already idealized model from economic theory that is then made more complex – or more general in the above sense — as factors are added back in to fit the data for the case at hand, i.e. a process of de-idealization. (That is, in this literature, "general" can not be equated to "simple".) However, the debate is not quite so simple as this because, associated with this main question, go issues of how statistical data are analysed and how statistical testing goes ahead. This current debate therefore can be well understood in terms of idealization and de-idealization, provided we include notions about the statistical aspects of models as well as the economic and mathematical in the resource base for modelling.

The "general-to-specific" school of modelling follows a practise (which is also embedded in computer software, and may even involve automatic model selection mechanisms) of beginning with the most general economic model relevant to the problem to decide which subset of its models are congruent with the data. At the same time, the econometrician conducts an extensive process of data analysis to ascertain the statistical and probability characteristics of the data. The choice of models within the subset is then made based on principles which include "encompassing" criteria: searching for the models which explain at least as much as other models explain and which do so most efficiently with respect to the data. In this process, the model gets leaner, as terms which play no statistical role *and* which have no economic rationale for inclusion are discarded. Thus, both economic elements and statistical criteria go into the modelling process and final choice of specific model. We might describe these joint statistical and economic modelling choices as a combination of different kinds of idealizations in the sense that the modelling seeks to extract — or isolate or discover — by using these processes the model that best characterises the economic behaviour represented in the specific data set.

Both data and theoretical aspects also go into the alternative "simple-to-general" approach, but here, in contrast, the process begins with a commitment to the already idealized mathematical model from theory, and aims to apply that to the data directly. A limited amount of adding back in relevant associated causal variables is carried out to obtain statistical fit. At the same time, the econometrician here makes assumptions about distributions, or fixes the particular statistical difficulties one by one, in processes that might be thought equivalent to the ways in which economic models are made tractable. So, on the economic side, such modelling is a process of de-idealizing, of adding back in previously omitted economic content. But on the statistical side, it looks more like a process of idealization, fixing the model up to the ideal statistical conditions that will validate inferences.

In this interpretation, we can see that when the general-to-specific modellers complain of the likely *in*validity of the inferences based on the statistical idealizations used by the theory-first modellers, they are in effect pointing to the implicit set of difficulties accompanying any de-idealization on the statistical side, which their own approach, because of its prior attention to those statistical issues, claims to minimize. On the other side, the theory-first modellers can be seen as complaining about data driven models and the lack of theoretical economic foundations in their rivals' approach, referring back (sometimes explicitly) to older philosophy of science arguments about the impossibility of theory-free observations and the dangers of empiricism. The arguments are complex and technical, but, as with those on causal modelling, well tuned into more general arguments in the philosophies of science and statistics (for recent discussions of the debate, see [Chao, 2007; Spanos, this volume]; and for a less technical discussion, see [Colander, 2008; Spanos, 2008]).

## *2.2 Models as constructions*

As an alternative to the idea that models idealize, isolate or abstract some causal factors, mechanisms or tendencies of actual economies it has been suggested that economic models are rather like pure constructions or fictional entities that nevertheless license different kinds of inferences. There are several variants of this option, which differ from each other in the extent to which they nevertheless are committed to the representational status of models and how much they pay attention to their actual construction processes. Moreover, the constructedness of models has been associated with a functional account of models as autonomous objects, rather than by characterizing them in relation to target systems as either theoretical models or models of data.

### *2.2.1 Ideal Types and Caricatures*

As we have seen idealization involves not just simplifications or omissions, but also distortion and the addition of false elements. When it comes to distortion in the social scientific context, Max Weber [1904] launched the famous idea of ideal types which present certain features in an exaggerated form, not just by accentuating those features left by the omission of others, but as a strategy to present the most ideal form of the type. Weber regards both individual economic behaviour and the market as viable subjects to consider as ideal types, in which a certain kind of pure economic behaviour might be defined. This kind of exaggeration, appears again in Gibbard and Varian's [1978] idea of economic theory modelling being one of creating caricatures, the purpose of which is to allow the economist to investigate a particular caricatured aspect of the model and thus to judge the robustness of the particular assumption that created such exaggeration. This has similarities to the idea of a robustness analysis of core causal features (as above).

Morgan [2006] interprets the caricaturing process as something more than the exaggeration of a particular feature, rather it involves the addition of features, pointing us to the constructed nature of the exaggeration rather than to it as an idealization, abstraction or isolation of causal factors. Take as an illustration, Frank Knight's 1921 assumption that economic man has perfect information: this can not be specified just as a lack of ignorance, for the model has to be fitted out with descriptions of what that means and this may be done in a variety of different positive ways. For example, one way to interpret the assumption of perfect knowledge is that such an economic man has no need of intelligence or power to reason, thus he could be re-interpreted as a mechanical device responding to stimuli, or, as Knight (later) suggested, as a slot-machine. At this point, the caricature is less clearly a representation of economic man as an idealization, isolation or abstraction, but rather his character was constructed as a positive figure of science fiction (see [Morgan, 2006]).

So, while idealizations can still be understood as representations of the system or man's behaviour (however unrealistic or positively false these might be), the more stylized models get, the less they can be considered as *models of* some specific systems or characters in the economy. As properties are *added* and attributed to the modelled entities and their behaviour, the model starts to look like an intricate, perhaps fictional, construction rather than an idealized representation of some real target system. Taking heed of these problems some economists and philosophers have preferred to approach models as pure constructions rather than as idealizations from real world systems.

### *2.2.2 Fictions and Artificial Systems*

A strong tradition in economics has understood economic models as fictions, able to give us some understanding of real economic mechanisms, even though they are not interpreted as representations of real target systems. This approach has also found adherents amongst philosophers of science (see [Suárez, 2008; Frigg, 2010]).

An early treatment of the role of fictions in economics is given by economist and philosopher Fritz Machlup, who has in his methodological writings considered the nature and role of economic agents in economic theory. He suggests that *homo oeconomicus* should be regarded along Weberian lines as an ideal type (above), by which he means that it is a mental construct, an "artificial device for use in economic theorizing", the name of which should rather be *homunculus oeconomicus,* thus indicating its man-made origins [Machlup, 1978, p. 298]. As an ideal type homo oeconomicus is to be distinguished from real types. Thus economic theory should be understood as a heuristic device for tracing the predicted actions of imagined agents to the imagined changes they face in their environment. Machlup treats neoclassical firms likewise: they should not be taken to refer to real enterprises either. According to traditional price theory, a firm — as conceptualized by economists — is only "a theoretical link" that is "designed to explain and predict changes in observed prices [...] as effects of particular changes in conditions (wage rates, interest rates, import duties, excise taxes, technology, etc)." [Machlup, 1967, p. 9]. To confuse such an heuristic fiction with any real organization (real firms) would be to commit "the fallacy of misplaced concreteness". The justification for modelling firms in the way neoclassical micro-theory does lies in the purpose for which the theory was constructed. In explaining and predicting price behaviour only minimal assumptions concerning the behaviour of the firm are needed if it is assumed to operate in an industry consisting of a large number of similar such enterprises. In such a situation there is no need to talk about any internal decision-making because a neoclassical firm, like a neoclassical consumer, just reacts to the constraints of the environment according to a pre-established behavioural — in other words, maximizing — principle.

The fictional account of economic modelling contrasts with the realist interpretation of economic modelling, which has been defended especially by Cartwright and Mäki (above). The fictionalists question the realist assumption that economists strive — in their actual practice and not in their *a posteriori* methodological statements — to make models represent the causally relevant factors of the real world and then use deductive reasoning to work out what effects these factors have. Robert Sugden, who is a theoretical economist himself, has claimed that this does not match the theorizing practice of economists. He uses Thomas Schelling's "checker board model" of racial sorting to launch his critique [2002] against the realist perspective which assumes that although the assumptions in economics are usually very unrealistic, the operations of the isolated factors may (and should) be described correctly. From this, Sugden claims that economic models should rather be regarded as constructions, which, instead of being abstractions from reality, are *parallel realities.*

Schelling [1978] suggests that it is unlikely that most Americans would like to live in strongly racially segregated areas, and that this pattern could be established only because they do not want to live in a district in which the overwhelming majority is of the other skin colour. He develops and uses a "checker board model" to explain this residential segregation. The model consists of an $8 \times 8$ grid of squares populated by dimes and pennies, with some squares left empty. In the next step, a condition is postulated that determines whether a coin is content with its neighbourhood. Whenever we find a coin that is not content we move it to the nearest empty square, despite the fact that the move might make other coins discontented. This continues until all the coins are content. As a result, strongly segregated distributions of dimes and pennies tend to appear — even if the conditions for contentedness were quite weak.

According to Sugden [2002], it seems rather dubious to assume that a model like the checkerboard model is built by presenting some key features of the real world and sealing them off from the potential influence of other factors at work: "Just what do we have to seal off to make a real city — say Norwich — become a checkerboard?" he asks (p. 127). Thus, "the model world is not constructed by starting from the real world and stripping out complicating factors: although the model world is *simpler* than the real world, the one is not a simplification of the other." (p. 131). Rather than considering models as representations he prefers to treat them as constructions, the checkerboard plan being something that "Schelling has *constructed* for himself" (p. 128).

Considering models as constructions is inherent in the fictional account of them. This is hardly surprising since constructedness gives the minimal criterion for what may be regarded as fictional: fictional worlds are constructed, and do not exist apart from having once been represented. Thus fiction contrasts at the outset with reality, which we take to exist quite apart from our representational endeavours. This also shows why it is misleading to associate fiction with falsehood. Fiction deals rather with the possible and the imaginary, with non-actual states in general, which is the reason why the fictional mode is not limited to the literary realm but can be extended to cover scientific accounts, too (see [Frigg, 2010]). However, while fictionalists can be considered as constructivists at the outset, they usually tend to stress the imaginary characteristics of models whereas other constructivists stress instead the artificiality of model systems that strive to *mimic*, at some level, some stylized features of the real systems. This is evident particularly in the macro-econometric field and often associated with Robert Lucas, who has famously written:

> "One of the functions of theoretical economics is to provide fully articulated, artificial economic systems that can serve as laboratories in which policies that would be prohibitively expensive to experiment with in actual economies can be tested out at much lower cost. To serve this function well, it is essential that the artificial "model" economy be distinguished as sharply as possible in discussion from actual economies [...]. A 'theory' is not a collection of assertions about the behaviour of the actual economy but rather an explicit set of instructions for building a parallel or analogue system — a mechanical, imitation economy. A 'good' model, from this point of view, will not be exactly more 'real' than a poor one, but will provide better imitations." [Lucas, 1980, p. 697]

So, whereas Cartwright has models as blueprints for nomological machines that might exist in the world, Lucas has theories as blueprints for building models that might mimic the world. This constructivist move transforms the relation between models and theory, for now the task of the theory is to produce models as analogues of the world, rather than to use them to understand how the world works (see [Boumans, 1997; 2006]. This move also transforms the sense of how theories or models are supposed to "fit" to the world, namely to the notion that such analogue world models can be fitted by calibration to particular data set characteristics rather than by parameter estimation and statistical inferences (see [Hoover, 1995]). Moreover, it parallels the post 1960s development of different kinds of purpose-built simulation models, which share the same mimicking aims though with a different mode of use, and which, contra Lucas, often claimed to be constructed as representational models — at some specified level — of a target system such as the operating structures of firms, the way people use economic information, or the basic behavioural functions of the macro economy (see [Morgan, 2004, and section 3.3.1]).

### *2.2.3 Constructed representations*

Many economists think of constructing their models expressly to represent certain, possibly stylized, aspects of economies (rather than getting to them via processes of idealization). Such constructivist accounts of models pay specific attention to the various elements of models as well as to the means of representation and the role of tractability. The problems of tractability suggests that increasing realisticness in some aspects of the representation will have to be traded off against simplification and distortion in other aspects, as Tinbergen recognised right from the start of modelling in economics:

> "In order to be realistic, it [the model] has to assume a great number of elementary equations and variables; in order to be workable it should assume a smaller number of them. It is the task of business cycle theory to pass between this Scylla and Charybdis. If possible at all the solution must be found in such simplifications of the detailed picture as do not invalidate its essential features." [Tinbergen, 1940, p 78]

From this perspective models feature as intricate constructions designed and assembled to answer specific questions, as in the early use of of business cycle models, where Boumans [1999] has shown how various ingredients can go into a single model: analogies, metaphors, theoretical notions, mathematical concepts, mathematical techniques, stylized facts, empirical data and finally relevant policy views. Striving to combine such diverse elements to one another tells us something interesting about modelling: it hints at the skill, experience, and hard work that are required to make a new model. Here, the image of a scientist as a modeller is very different from that of a theoretical thinker. Boumans, in fact, likens model construction to baking a cake without a recipe [1999, p. 67]. That econometric models are constructed from various ingredients including theoretical relations and statistical elements, is, as we have seen already, a reasonable description. But that mathematical economic models are also constructed in a similar manner may be a more surprising claim. Yet these mixtures are equally characteristic in mathematical models as Boumans' study shows, where mathematics plays the critical role of "moulding" these various different ingredients into one model. He argues that "new recipes" are created, then adapted and adopted to new circumstances and questions to form not a sequence of de-idealized or more realistic models as Koopmans suggests, but sequences of related models rather more like a kinship table (see [Hoover, 1991] for an example of such a kinship analysis of models). This account nicely captures the ways in which some models, such as the venerable IS-LM model in macroeconomics, experience an incredibly long life in which they are adapted to represent new theories, used to analyse new problems, and generally re-interpreted (see [De Vroey and Hoover, 2006]). The history of modelling strongly suggests that such constructed model sequences are as much driven by changes in the purposes of models as by the changes in theories.

This constructivist perspective on models goes against traditional views and philosophizing, even by economists themselves, probably because models have conventionally been approached as theoretical and abstract entities, whose seemingly simple and unified mathematical form disguises their very heterogeneity. Yet, in economists' own writings, we see discussions of how model construction takes place suggesting that it is more an intuitive and speculative activity than one of rule-following in which models are derived from theory via processes of idealization, though this does not mean that some idealizations are not involved (see for example [Krugman, 1993; Sugden, 2002]).

From the constructivist perspective, then, models are conceived as especially constructed concrete objects, in other words, as epistemic artefacts that economists make for a variety of different purposes. Knuuttila [2005] argues that, contrary to the philosophical tradition, one should take into account the media and representational means through which scientific models are materialized as concrete, inter-subjectively available objects. The use of representational media and different modelling methods provide an external scaffolding for the scientist's thinking, which also partly explains the heuristic value of modelling. It is already a cognitive achievement to be able to express any tentative mechanism, structure or phenomenon of interest in terms of some representational media, including assumptions concerning them that are often translated into a conventional mathematical form. While such articulation enables further development, it also imposes its own demands on how a model can be achieved and in doing so requires new kinds of expertise from the scientists. A nice example of this is provided by development of the Edgeworth-Bowley Box models. In discussing its cognitive aspects, Morgan [2004a; 2011] notes how its various representational features were initially a considerable cognitive step whereas today the Edgeworth-Bowley diagram is presented in the introductory courses of economics, but also how some of its early cognitive advantages were lost to later users as the model developed into its current stable form.

This artefactual character of models drawn in any media (including the abstract languages of mathematics) is enhanced by the way models typically also constrain the problem at hand, rendering the initial problem situation more intelligible and workable. So, in this sense, any representational media is double-faced in both enabling and limiting. This is easily seen in a case like the Phillips-Newlyn model, a real machine built to represent the aggregate economy in which red water circulated around the machine to show how the Keynesian economic system worked in hydraulic terms (see [Boumans and Morgan, 2004]). This material model enabled economists of the time to understand the arguments about stocks and flows in the macroeconomy, and enabled them to think about a wider set of possible functions at work in the economy, while at the same time, the media or representation created very specific limitations on the arrangements of the elements and their relation to each other. Another good example of how a model can both enable and constrain is provided by the IS-LM model, the most famous of several contemporary attempts to model the key assumptions of Keynes's *The General Theory of Employment, Interest and Money* (1936) (see [Darity and Young, 1995]). This model could be used to demonstrate some of Keynes's most important conclusions, yet at the same time it omitted many important features of his theory leading some economists to distinguish between the economics of Keynes and Keynesian economics (see [Backhouse, 2006; Leijonhufvud, 1968]).

Consequently, modellers typically proceed by turning these kinds of constraints built into models (due to its specific model assumptions and its medium of expression) into affordances. This is particularly evident in analogical modelling, where the artefactual constraints of both content and model language may hold inflexibly. Whether the model is an analogical one or not, scientists use their models in such a way that they can gain understanding and draw inferences from "manipulating" their models by using its constraints, not just its resources, to their advantage. It is this experimentable dimension of models that accounts for how models have the power, in use, to fulfill so many different epistemic functions as we discuss next and below (see [Morgan, 1999; 2002; 2011; Knuuttila and Voutilainen, 2003; Knuuttila, 2009]).

### *2.2.4 Models as Autonomous Objects*

From a naturalist philosophy of science viewpoint, the way that economists work with models suggests that they are regarded, and so may be understood, as autonomous working objects. Whereas the approaches mentioned above located the constructedness of models in relation to the assumed real or imaginary target systems, the independent nature of models can fruitfully be considered also from the perspectives of theory and data. Without doubt many models are rather renderings of theories than any target systems and some are considered as proto-theories not having yet the status of theory. On the other hand econometric models have at times been considered as versions of data.

In a more recent account, economic models are understood to be constructed out of elements of both theory and the world (or its data) and thus able to function with a certain degree of independence from both. The divide between theoretical models and econometric models seems misleading here since, from this perspective on model construction, both kinds of models are heterogeneous ensembles of diverse elements (see [Boumans, this volume]). This account understands models as autonomous objects within the "models as mediators" view of the role of models, which analyses them as means to carry out investigations on both the theoretical and the empirical sides of scientific work, particularly it treats them as instruments of investigation (see [Morrison and Morgan, 1999]). This power to act as instruments that enables the scientist to learn about the world or about their theories depends not only on their functional independence built in at the construction stage, but on another construction feature, namely models are devices made to represent something in the world, or some part of our theory, or perhaps both at once. These two features, function independence and representing quality — loosely defined, make it possible to use models as epistemic mediators (see section 3.3 below). Even the artificial world models of Lucas which are constructed as analogues to represent the outputs of the system, not the behaviour of the system, can be understood under this account, though their functions in investigations may be more limited. In this sense the models as mediators view takes also a mediating view in respect to the models as idealizations vs. the models as constructions divide — itself of course partly an idealization made up for expository reasons — since it takes a liberal attitude both as to what models are supposed to represent and also to the mode of their making via idealization and de-idealization or via a process of construction.

## 3 WORKING WITH MODELS

Looking at models as separately constructed objects pays specific attention to their workable aspects. Indeed, from the perspective of doing economics it is more useful to see that contemporary economics, like biology, uses a variety of different kinds of models for a variety of purposes, and that whether models are understood as idealizations or as constructions does not necessarily dictate *function*. Thus instead of trying to define models in terms of what they are, a focus could be directed on what they are used to do. This shifts also the unit of analysis from that of a model and its supposed target system to the very practice of modelling. Traditionally models are taken as representations and thus they are assumed to be useful to the extent that they succeed in representing their target systems correctly. In view of recent discussions on scientific representation this account of modelling is deemed problematic if only because representation seems such a tricky notion. One way to circumvent this problem is to proceed directly to the study the different roles models can take as instruments of investigation, but before this, we briefly consider the issue of representation.

## 3.1 Representation

The theme of representation has featured already at several points of this account. This is certainly no accident, since if we are to believe the philosophers of science, the primary epistemic task of models is to represent some target systems more or less accurately or truthfully (the idea of models as representations can be traced back to Heinrich Herz, see [Nordmann, 1998]). From this perspective, working with models amounts to using models to represent the world. According to the general philosophy of science the link between models and representation is as intimate as coming close to a conceptual one: philosophers have usually agreed that models are essentially representations and as such "models of" some real target systems. Moreover, the knowledge-bearing nature of models has been ascribed to representation. Whereas the representational nature of mathematical models in economics has been contested, this is certainly one way to read the debates about the status and functions of different kinds of models in econometrics where the notion that models represent is somehow taken for granted. The arguments are over how, and where, and with what success, econometric models, by representing the economy at different levels and with different aims, can be used to learn about measurements, patterns, regularities, causes, structures and so forth (see for example, [Backhouse, 2007]; and, for philosophical treatments, [Chao, 2007; 2008]).

Although there has been this consensus among the philosophers regarding the representational nature of models, the accounts given to the notion of representation have differed widely ranging from the structuralist conceptions to the more recent pragmatist ones (e.g. [Bailer-Jones, 2003; 2009; Suárez, 2004; 2010; Giere, 2004; 2009]). The pragmatist approaches to representation can be seen as a critique of the structuralist notions that are part and parcel of the semantic conception, which until recently has been the most widely held view on models in the philosophy of science (see [Hands, 2001, Chapter 7.4.1; Chao, 2008], for a discussion of structuralist notions applied to economics). The semantic conception provides a straightforward answer to the question of how models give us knowledge of the world: they specify structures that are posited as possible representations of either the observable phenomena or, even more ambitiously, the underlying structures of the real target systems. Thus, according to the semantic view, the structure specified by a model represents its target system if it is either structurally isomorphic or somehow similar to it (see [Brodbeck, 1968] on social science models, and more recently [van Fraassen, 1980; French and Ladyman, 1999; Giere, 1988]). The pragmatist critics of the semantic conception have argued, rather conclusively, that the structuralist notion of representation does not satisfy the formal and other criteria we might want in order to affirm representation (see e.g., [Suárez, 2003; Frigg, 2006]). The problem can be located in the attempt to find such properties both in the representational vehicle (the model) and the real object (the target system) by virtue of which a representational relationship can be established between a model and its target object.

So far, despite the numerous philosophical trials, no such solution to the general puzzle concerning representation has been presented. Hence the continued referral to representation does not seem to provide a reliable foundation to discuss the epistemic value of models. The alternative pragmatist accounts of representation seek to circumvent this traditional problem by making the representational relationship an accomplishment of representation-users. Consequently, it is common among pragmatist approaches to focus on the intentional activity of representation users and to deny that representation may be based only on the respective properties of the representing vehicle and its target object. However, if representation is primarily grounded in the specific goals and the representing activity of humans as opposed to the properties of the representing vehicle and its target, it is difficult to say anything very substantial and general about it from a philosophical point of view (cf. [Giere, 2004; Suárez, 2004]). Recently, Uskali Mäki has proposed a two-tiered notion of representation that attempts to overcome this problem by analysing the representational character of models into two parts. Thus, according to him, a model represents in two ways: Firstly, by being a *representative* of some target system for which it stands for as a surrogate system. Secondly, Mäki claims that our only hope to learn about the target by examining its surrogate is if they *resemble* one another in *suitable respects and sufficient degrees* [Mäki, 2009; 2011]. In conceiving of representation as jointly constrained by both the purposes of model users and the ontology of the real target Mäki's account mediates between the semantic and pragmatic notions of representation, remaining however open to the pragmatist criticisms concerning similarity as a basis of representation and simultaneously — perhaps — to the same difficulties of making general philosophical claims as pragmatists face.

One obvious way out of this problem is not to focus the discussion on the nature or properties of models and the initial representation, nor the representing aims of users, but to focus attention instead on the kinds of work that models do in economics. As we have already seen, economists (including of course econometricians) have used models for many different purposes: to explore the world, explain events, isolate causal capacities, test theories, predict outcomes, analyse policy choices, describe processes, and so forth; and philosophers of economics have tended to offer commentaries and analyses of how models may or may not fulfil these different particular purposes. Fulfilling such different functions can be gathered together under the broad notion that models operate as instruments of various kinds in science.

## *3.2 Instruments and Narratives*

Milton Friedman's "The Methodology of Positive Economics" (1953) has probably become the single most read work on the methodology of economics, its very fame testifying to its success in capturing some basic convictions held by economists. Most importantly, Friedman has been taken to claim that the "unrealism" of the *assumptions of economic theory* do not matter, the goal of science being the development of hypotheses that give "valid and meaningful" predictions about phenomena. Whereas this can be understood as a kind of naive instrumentalism, Friedman's famous essay can be read in many other ways (see the papers in [Mäki, 2009b]).

Friedman's remarks on the *nature of models* (as opposed to theories) are both less naive and more conventional in terms of the discussion of the idealized nature of models and their representational qualities. Indeed, in one interpretation of his words below, they seem close both to Mill's earlier arguments about isolating causes in economics (e.g. [Mäki, 1992]), as well as to later arguments about econometric models (see above). This latter congruence may reflect the fact that Friedman was also an empirical economist, as we see in his concern with the issue of the correspondence rules for working with models:

> "... a hypothesis or theory consists of an assertion that certain forces are, and by implication others are not, important for a particular class of phenomena and a specification of the manner of action of the forces it asserts to be important. We can regard the hypothesis as consisting of two parts: first, a conceptual world or abstract model simpler than the "real world" and containing only the forces that the hypothesis asserts to be important; second, a set of rules defining the class of phenomena for which the "model" can be taken to be an adequate representation of the "real world" and specifying the correspondence between the variables or entities in the model and observable phenomena". [Friedman, 1953, p. 24]

Friedman here suggests we think of a model as both a theory or hypothesis, and at the same time a representation of the real world. So, interpretations of his position could take us to the models as mediators route, or to the earlier and related simulacrum account of models in physics found in Cartwright [1983]. Of course, Friedman's terminology invokes the shadow of the notorious correspondence rules of logical positivism, yet, on the other hand one could argue that empirical modelling must depend upon the establishment of such rules in a practical sense (see [Hirsch and De Marchi, 1990, particularly Chapter 8], for an analysis of Friedman's empirical work with models).

Certainly developing correspondence rules has formed one of the major difficulties for economists seeking to defend the method of modelling, and for philosophers and methodologists seeking to account for the work done by economic models. This difficulty is immediately evident in the way that mathematical and other theoretical models are linked to the world in a way which seems quite ad hoc. Indeed, "casual application" is the term that Alan Gibbard and Hal Varian [1978] use to describe the way that economists use mathematical models to *approximately* describe economic phenomena of the world without undertaking any form of measurement or testing. In their account, mathematical models are connected to the world by "stories" which interpret the terms in the model in a way which is reflected in Hausman's [1990] argument that economists use such stories to explain particular real world events using ceteris paribus arguments (above). Morgan [2001; 2007] argues for taking a stronger position, suggesting that such narratives form an integral part not just in applying models to the world in both imagined and real cases, but constitute an integral element in the model's identity. For example, the prisoner's dilemma game is defined not just by its matrix, but by the rules of the game that are defined in the accompanying narrative text, and then it is the text that mediates the application of the game to various economic situations. Grüne-Yanoff and Schweinzer [2008] extend this argument to show how narratives also figure in the choice of solution concepts that are given by the theory of games. These accounts suggest that economists rely on experiential, intuitive and informal kinds of rules to establish correspondence for mathematical models and thus to make inferences from them.

In sharp contrast to this casual correspondence found in the use of mathematical models, the different econometric approaches to models (above) focussed seriously on what might be considered correspondence problems. That is, econometricians's arguments about model derivation and selection, along with their reliance on a battery of statistical tests, are really all about how to get a correspondence via models in fitting theory to the world: one might even say that econometrics could be broadly described as a project of developing the theory and practices of correspondence rules for economics. Certainly some of the most interesting conundrums of theoretical econometrics fall under this general label — such as the identification problem: an analysis of the statistical and data circumstances under which a model with relevant identifiable mathematical characteristics may be statistically identified, and so measured, using a particular data set. (There is a rich philosophically interesting literature on this fundamental problem from which we mention four examples — see [Fennell, 2007] for a recent contribution that relates to questions of mathematical form; [Aldrich, 1994; Boumans, 2005] for a discussion in terms of "autonomy"; and [Morgan, 1990] for an account of their early conceptualization.) From this perspective then, Friedman's position on models, in the quote above, is far from naïve – or philosophically dated.

More recently, a kind of sophisticated instrumentalism has been advanced by two philosophers of economics who specialise in econometrics — Kevin Hoover and Marcel Boumans. For them, models can function as instruments of observation and measurement in the process of identifying invariant economic phenomena. For Hoover [1994; 2000], this follows from recognising that economics is largely (and particularly at the macroeconomic or market level, rather than the individual level) a science of observation rather than one of experiment, so that he regards the many models generated within applied econometrics as instruments of observation that bring economic data into the economist's focus using both statistical and economic theories at various points in the modelling process.

Boumans [2005] follows Trygve Haavelmo, a contemporary of Friedman, whose less famous but more subtle philosophical tract of 1944, argued that the problem of econometrics be attacked not by thinking of models as matching devices, but by treating them as experimental designs. The link from models to experiment comes from statistical theory: the observed data set for any particular time and place being one single outcome from the passive experiments of Nature, so that the aim of econometric modelling is to design a model that will replicate Nature's (the Economy's) experiment. Then probability theory can be used to assess the model design given those experimental produced outcomes (the economic observations) (see [Morgan, 1990; Qin, 1993]). It should be noted that the notion of passive experiment here is that of any uncontrolled experiment carried out by the natural workings of the economy, whereas economists also work with the notion of "natural experiment": experiments that have occurred naturally but under conditions of such stability (nothing else changing) that they can count as controlled experiments.

Boumans develops this argument to show how models function as the primary instrument in this process, which enable measurement of the economic world. For Boumans, unlike Haavelmo, the task is not so much to advance theory testing, but to develop the relevant measuring instruments on which economics depends. This entails discussion of exactly how models are used to provide measurements, how to assess the reliability of such model instruments (via calibration, filtering etc), and how to understand precision and rigour in the econometric model context. For him, models are not just for observing the economy, but are complex scientific instruments that enable economists to produce measurements to match their concepts (see also [Boumans, 2007]).

## *3.3 Models and Their Epistemic Functions*

As Scott Gordon remarked of economic models "the purpose of any model is to serve as a tool or instrument of scientific investigation" [1991, p. 108]. That statement leaves a wide open field of possibilities (many ofwhich we have already discussed). Models have been used in a variety of functions within economics to:

- suggest explanations for certain specific or general phenomena observed or measured by using a model;
- carry out experiments to design, specify and even help execute policy based on a model;
- make predictions, ascertain counterfactual results, and conduct thought experiments using a model;
- derive solutions to theoretical problems that might be treated within a model;
- explore the limits and range of possible outcomes consistent with questions that can be answered using a model; and
- develop theory, concepts and classificatory systems with the model.

The very varied nature of these functions emphasizes how much models are the means for active work by economists rather than passive objects. A characteristic point is that such use generally involves some kind of manipulation and accompanying investigation into the model as an object. Whereas both Boumans and Hoover depict models as instruments to achieve something via an intervention elsewhere, in many of these uses of economic models, economists investigate the models as a way to investigate either the world for which it stands, or the theory that those models embed (see [Morgan, 2011]). When models are understood as a particular kind of tool or instrument, namely as investigative devices, their epistemic versatility is more fully revealed.

### *3.3.1 Experimental exploration*

Because experiments are seen has having a valid epistemic function within the philosophy of science, we begin with this notion as analogous for working with models. This also has the virtue of continuing the thread from Haavelmo's notions about the role of models in econometrics. Haavelmo [1944], recall, thought of models as designs for experiments that might replicate the activities within the economy. Probability reasoning was needed both because it provided a way to think about how observations were produced by those experiments of the economy, but also because it provided the basis for making valid inferences about how well the relations specified in the model matched those thrown up in the observations. Haavelmo was drawing on two traditions in statistical work: one that interpreted the measuring methods of statistics as a substitute for control in passive experiments; and another in which the design of real experiments relied on probability elements to obtain valid control. Such a combination confers a considerable advantage on those scientific fields that rely on statistically controlled experiments for it provides relevant rules for making valid inferences which are both more formal and more general when compared to the informal and purpose-specific practices that may be used to draw inferences from experiments in the laboratory and to extend such inferences beyond the laboratory in other sciences. The point here however is not the comparison with other scientific modes of experiment, but between the use of econometric models with other modes of modelling in economics.

Morgan [2002; 2003] has argued that we can also understand the habitual way that economists use mathematical models in economics as a form of experimental activity, while Mäki [1992; 2005] makes a somewhat different claim that models are experiments based upon his analogy between theoretical isolation and laboratory controls in making mathematical models. Such model experiments found in economics consist of posing questions and manipulating the model to answer them. Questions such as: "What will happen if a particular element in the model changes?" "Let us assume that a particular element has a particular value: what difference will this make?" and so forth. The final step in the model experiment is some kind of inference statement, inference about the world being modelled, or even inference about some theoretical puzzle. Of course, the inferences involved are clearly more informal than those in econometric models — recall the role of narratives (above) as one format in which economists may relate the work of model experiments to the world or to theory. And, in comparison with the possibilities of real experiments, Morgan [2005] suggests that model experiments have less epistemic power: model experiments have the power to surprise economists though these surprises can in principle be explained, but real experiments may confound them with findings that remain unexplainable.

How does work with models create surprising outcomes? Remember that models are not passive objects, but their usefulness as investigative instruments depends on them having sufficient internal resources for manipulation. Very simple models have few resources that can be made the subject of experiment. More complex models do have such resources, though very complex ones may become too complicated to experiment with. Models are of course built or made by the scientist, but, as we can learn from Koopmans's argument, it is not always obvious what kinds of economic behaviour a model implies. So, as Koopmans suggests, one of the uses of models is to enable the economist to understand the implications of taking several postulates together — and this may give surprising outcomes, as Hoover's discussion of the way micro and macro assumptions fit together (see earlier) examplifies. On the other hand, economic models are not made in the materials of the economy: hydraulic machines, diagrams, equations, are not economic actors and these artefacts of economic science are rarely directly performative as models. (There are, of course, some interesting exceptions: see [MacKenzie, 2006] on how models in finance made economic behaviour and outcomes more like the models of that behaviour.) This material difference limits the inferences that may be made from such models, just as it limits the possibilities of producing unexplainable outcomes (see [Morgan, 2005]). Despite these comparisons on inference and epistemic power which operate to the disadvantage of the mathematical models compared to the econometric ones, the experimental limitations of such models may be weighed against the variety of other epistemic functions that may be fulfilled when economists use mathematical models in investigative modes.

As an example of what is meant by a model experiment, consider the possibilities of simulation with models. While simulations in other sciences have often been used to produce numerical solutions where analytical solutions are problematic, in economics, simulation has more often been used to explore in a systematic fashion the range of outcomes consistent with a particular model structure. This experimental activity with a model — each simulation run constitutes an individual model experiment — provides information about the model. It may enable the economist to rule out certain values for the model because of the implausibility of the simulated behaviour, or it may offer support for particular versions of the model or for particular idealizations as a result of simulation experiments on closely related models (see [Morgan, 2004]). Simulation offers a form of experiment which is compatible with mimicking models, but also equally useful with representational constructions or idealized models. And in policy work, simulations with mathematical models are routinely used to help to frame the details of tax regimes, trade restrictions, and so forth, by varying the assumptions of the models to suggest answers to particular policy questions. Even econometric models may be subject to simulation: for example, the analysis of policy options on models that have already been validated for a specific country at a specific time.

### *3.3.2 Conceptual Exploration*

Perhaps because of the dominance of modelling in later twentieth century economics, models have come to be generally associated with functions that are more usually seen as the preserve of theory making. For example, the Edgeworth Box had a very long history in which economists from 1881 to the 1950s used it to derive solutions to various theoretical problems in several different domains of economics (see [Humphrey, 1996]). But not only was it used in the development of theory results, it was also critical in the development of new theoretical concepts — Edgeworth's contract curve and Pareto's optimal position were both framed within the Edgeworth Box (see also [Morgan, 2004a]). More broadly, Daniel Hausman, suggests that theoretical modelling is the main site in current economics in which concepts are formed and explored:

> "A theory must identify regularities in the world. But science does not proceed primarily by spotting correlations among various known properties of things. An absolutely crucial step is constructing new concepts — new ways of classifying and describing phenomena. Much of scientific theorizing consists of developing and thinking about such new concepts, relating them to other concepts and exploring their implications.
>
> This kind of endeavor is particularly prominent in economics, where theorists devote a great deal of effort to exploring the implications of perfect rationality, perfect information, and perfect competition. These explorations, which are separate from questions of application and assessment, are, I believe, what economists (but *not* econometricians) call "models"." [Hausman, 1984, p. 13]

We can see how this happens more generally by looking at the way in which the basic assumptions of micro-economics circa 1950 have been unpicked, reformed, and refined over the period since around 1970 as economists have used models as their preferred site to give content to, and explore notions of, concepts such as bounded rationality and imperfect information. This re-generation of theories has depended on working with models.

The classificatory functions of model using are almost a by-product of the modelling manipulations and experiments that go on in these processes of concept formation. Each run with a model, each slight change in the assumptions, each minor change in the set up, each substitution of a particular element, may give rise to a different result from the previous one with same or almost the same model. It is this variation in outcomes that leads to new classifications. An obvious example in modern economics is game theory, where minor changes in rule, and in matrix numbers, may lead to different outcomes. Each of these games can be thought of as a model in the sense that these games are treated by economists as models for economic situations (see [Morgan, 2007]). But as economists work on these models, they begin to classify their games along different dimensions: such as levels of co-operation, the number of times a game is played, and so forth, and thus develop conceptual labels within game theory: co-operative games, n-person games, etc. Similarly, the different forms and concepts of industrial competition were developed in industrial economics during the 1930s as models were used to develop the different cases and to classify them according to the number of firms and nature of competition. The proliferation of cases and the labelling activity suggests that we think of both these fields not as consisting of one general theory (of industry or of games) accompanied by an additional set of special cases, but as theoretical fields in which the main material consists of a carefully classified set of well defined models (see [Morgan, 2002]).

From an applied economics viewpoint, this makes the class of models the relevant space within which to "observe" stable regularities. The set of classes of models together make up the general theoretical field, such as game theory or industrial economics. That is, in such fields, the answer is not to seek complete homogeneity in economic life nor complete heterogeneity, but to use models to define the economic objects in the world within which a particular kind or class of behaviour can be isolated. This kind of vision underlies John Sutton's work and his "class of models" approach [2000] to applied economics where once again, models form investigative devices for finding out about the world, but the project depends on the classificatory and conceptual work of modelling that has gone beforehand.

### *3.3.3 Inferences from Models*

Thinking about the wide use of models in the experimental mode, picks up the practitioners' sense that working with models involves making inferences. These inferential relations are described under different terms ranging from deductive to inductive inference, and with forms of making inference that range from the stories of the casual application of mathematical model experiments to the formally rule-bound statistically-based inferences of econometric models. Both stories and econometric inference forms have been discussed at various points earlier in the essay (see particularly sections 3.2 and 2.1.3 with 3.3.1). Here we take the more traditional philosophers' puzzle, namely: how it is that by working with models, particularly the mathematical ones, and by using them in various modes, economists gain knowledge about the real world?

Traditionally, the form of inference invoked by economists for mathematical models has been *deductive inference.* The idea of models as a basis for deductive inference fits squarely with the conception of models as idealizations or isolations. From this perspective, such models are stand ins or surrogate systems that are used indirectly to study the causal workings of the real economies. Using models as stand ins or surrogates for real world systems, economists study the consequences of abstract, isolated facts, that is, what these factors or mechanisms would produce if unimpeded (e.g. [Cartwright, 1998]). This happens by way of studying the deductive consequences of the model assumptions, an idea formulated by Hausman as "the economists' inexact deductive method" [1992]. According to this, economists formulate, with the help of *ceteris paribus* clauses (other things being equal), plausible and useful generalizations concerning the functioning of relevant causal factors. Predictions are then deduced from these generalizations, certain initial conditions, and further simplifications. Although these predictions are supposed to be testable, they often are not that in practice, since, claims Hausman, the economic reality is so complex that the economists are not usually able to explicate the content of their ceteris paribus clauses, which takes us back to Mill's problem (and see [Cartwright, 2006]).

In an alternative argument to this view, Sugden [2002; 2009] has claimed that economists in fact infer inductively from their models. Studying examples from both economics and biology, Sugden notes that even though modellers are willing to make empirical claims about the real world based on their models, it is difficult to find from their texts any *explicit connections* made between the models and the real world. Their claims about the real world are typically not the ones they derive from their models, but something more general. Consequently, Sugden suggests that modellers are making *inductive inferences* on the basis of their models. One commonly infers inductively from one part of the world to another, for instance expecting that the housing markets of Cleveland resemble those of other large industrial cities in the northeastern USA, for instance. However, just as we can infer from real systems to other real systems, we can also infer from theoretical models to real systems. A modeler constructs "imaginary cities, whose workings he can easily understand" [Sugden, 2002, p. 130] in order to invite inferences concerning the causal processes that might apply to real cities. This possibility is based on our being able to see the relevant models as instances of some category, other instances of which might actually exist in the real world. Moreover, for inductive inference to work we have to accept that the model describes a state of affairs that is *credible* given our knowledge of the real world (see also [Mäki, 2009a]).

What is common to both views is the insight that models are typically valued for their results or output. However, the two perspectives diverge on the question of the extent to which some selected features of a given target system can be understood to be represented reasonably correctly in the model. Philosophically, it seems a more safe option to assume that this is the case, because then as a result of deductive inference one can assume that the results achieved depict at least one aspect of the total behaviour of the system under study. However, such an approach needs to assume that economic phenomena are separable, and that models provide us with some of the components, and that their arrangements are exhibited in the real world (see [Cartwright, 1989, p. 47], where she also discusses what else has to be assumed for a model to establish what she calls causal capacities). These are rather stringent conditions not met by many economic models as we discussed in the early sections of this essay. Thus while this option seems philosophically more straightforward, it is more difficult to see it working effectively in applying mathematical models casually to the world. Moreover, it is difficult to see how models as credible constructions can license inferences concerning the real world.

In this respect of model inferences the idea of models as investigative instruments does a lot of philosophical work. In this perspective economists are thought to gain knowledge from models by way of building them, manipulating them, and trying out their different alternative uses. Thus one can consider models as experimentable things, which through their different uses and interpretations facilitate many kinds of inferences: in helping researchers to systematically chart different theoretical options and their consequences thus enabling them to proceed in a more systematic manner in answering the questions of interest. The starting point of modelling may not be representing some real causal factors accurately but rather trying to make the model to produce certain kinds of results. In fact, modellers often proceed in a roundabout way, seeking to build hypothetical model systems in the light of the anticipated results or of certain features of the phenomena they are supposed to exhibit. If a model succeeds in producing the expected results or in replicating some features of the phenomenon, it provides an interesting starting point for further conjectures and inferences [Knuuttila, 2010]. These further investigations might be theory related or world related.

Reiss [2008], in a detailed study of how models are used by economists in drawing inferences, holds a middle position between that of Cartwright and Sugden. He argues that while both "models and thought experiments are representational devices, which sketch mechanisms that may be operative in an economy" (p. 124), investigations using them (such as Schelling's checkerboard model), offer only "prima facie, not valid (or sound) evidence" to support valid inference (about the reasons for segregated neighbourhoods), and, so that further empirical work would be needed to justify claims that such a model explains the observed phenomenon: that is, plausibility or credibility is not sufficient.

There is another sense in which Reiss's position can be taken as middle ground, for we might also consider the work done by economists with mathematical models as either thought experiments or the tracing out of counterfactuals. For thought experiments, we might look to the position taken by Steven Rappaport, who regards mathematical modellers as resolving "conceptual problems" by providing answers to such questions as Tiebout's [1956] problem "Is it *possible* for there to be a set of social institutions in which people will reveal their true preferences for public goods, and for the approximate quantities of these goods people want to be provided? The short version of the Tiebout's own answer to this problem is 'Yes', and his model explains and justifies this answer" [Rappaport, 1998, p. 133]. For Rappaport, mathematical models are used for learning about the structure and behaviour of possible economies which fulfil certain requirements or have certain characteristics, and they are answered by constructing models of the world in which those characteristics hold true, that is, in thought experiments. At the opposite side, we could point to the classic cliometric work of Robert Fogel [1970], whose counterfactual investigation of the historical claim that railways had been indispensable for the growth of the economy, depended upon investigations using mathematical models to construct a counterfactual world without railways for the American economy in 1890, that is to answer counterfactually a question about the real economy. This work was highly controversial partly because of the way that idealized mathematical models were used in answering the historical question. Both thought experiments and counterfactuals are traditional topics in philosophy, let alone philosophy of science and while there is some overlap with the modelling literature, models are not usually central to those discussions (see [McCloskey, 1990; Schabas, 2008]).

This orientation of modelling towards their results also accounts for why modellers frequently use the same cross-disciplinary *computational templates* [Humphreys, 2004], such as well-known general equation types, statistical distributions and computational methods. A good example of such a template is the logistic function, which applies to diverse dynamic phenomena across the disciplines, and has been used in economics amongst many other sciences. Sugden, following Schelling [2006], combines the idea of templates to that of social mechanisms. For Schelling the discovery of social mechanisms begins with previously observed empirical regularities, for which suitable often cross-disciplinary mathematical structures can be applied "inviting the explanation" in terms of underlying social mechanisms. This kind of reasoning that starts from conclusions, i.e. from previously observed empirical regularities to the tentative mechanisms that could have produced them, is abductive. Abduction starts from a set of accepted facts inferring their most likely explanations. Applying a well-defined tractable template to a new domain hardly qualifies as a most likely explanation but rather points at the element of opportunism present in modelling: the templates that have proven successful in some domain will be applied to other domains perhaps based on some similarity of behaviour or regularity. Certainly, the transporting of models between different domains of economics is relatively common, particularly in micro-economics, where, for example, models of consumer choice between goods were moved sideways to apply to other choices (which seem similar in the economists' way of thinking) such as that between leisure versus work, or to the number of children a family decides to have.

It is characteristic of modelling that a domain of interest is sometimes described (i.e. modelled) with the help of the terms, mechanisms and structures that are borrowed from another domain, which maybe familiar, or differently, or better, organised in certain respects [Black, 1962; Hesse, 1966]. Mary Hesse's work claims that many useful models represent the world in terms of analogies, and these enable scientists to infer various things about the domain of interest by making use of the analogy between it and another domain. In her account, the *positive* analogical features in common between the two domains afford support for making potential theoretical or conceptual developments based on the *neutral* analogical features of the comparison, and herein lies the possibilities for theory development from the comparison. In the context of economics, Morgan [1997] goes further in suggesting that even the negative features that come from such analogical comparison can be used as inference opportunities prompting theory development from using the model. She illustrates this with some work by Irving Fisher who used the mechanical balance as an analogical model to make new claims based on the aggregate level equation of exchange. The use of analogies from other fields has been quite common in the history of economics, with many and varied intersections between economics and physics and between economics and biology, and where metaphors, mechanisms, models and terms have been borrowed in both directions (see, for example, [Mirowski, 1994]). Indeed, modelling can be seen as a productive practice that uses as-if reasoning, analogies, familiar computational templates and other constructive techniques to probe the possible mechanisms underlying the phenomena of interest.

## 4 CONCLUSIONS: FROM MODELS TO MODELLING

The recent re-orientation of philosophy towards the practices of science offers an account very different from those earlier philosophy of science writings on the syntactic versus semantic accounts of models that dominated the field until recently. Whereas earlier philosophers worried about what models were and how to define them, particularly in relation to theory, over the last twenty years, as this essay has shown, philosophers of economics have aimed to analyse how economic scientists build models and what they do with models: how they use them, how they argue with them, and what they learn from using them. At the same time, commentaries by economists on their own practices are by no means a-philosophical as we have seen, and while they have not been particularly worried about defining models, they have taken up discussions, in their own terms, of classic philosophical questions such as idealization, correspondence rules, and so forth. At the intersection of these two positions, we have found philosophically-inclined economists and naturalistically-inclined philosophers engaged with economics, who together have opened up a rather new set of questions and agendas for philosophical commentary and analysis. This essay has examined a set of the issues that have emerged from this work and that in many respects beg for further analysis: the problems of de-idealization and what these say about idealization; the implications of models conceived of as fictions, artefacts and mediators; the different ways in which models are taken to represent and mimic; the importance of how models are used and thus their experimentable potential; the roles of content and materials in providing resources and constraints to modellers; the functions of stories, analogies, templates, credible world comparisons, and statistical rules in making and supporting different kinds and modes of inferences; and so forth. These various new foci are both distinctive in terms of topics, and thought provoking, if not challenging, to the older conventional philosophical positions. They follow, however, not just from a naturalistic turn towards the study of science, but also from a reframing of the basic object of study: from models to modelling, that is, to how economists construct models and work with them.

The analysis offered here reflects not only on the resources that a model-based discipline like economics offers to the philosopher of science interested in how scientific knowledge is established using models; but to a change going on in the current status of studies of modelling in philosophy. Whereas physics with its mathematical models was for long the base case for thinking about models and the benchmark for analysing modelling in all other fields, this is no longer the case. Biology, with its model organisms, and its reliance on them as experimental systems, now offers an alternative paradigmatic case, with very different characteristics, for the philosophical analysis of models [Creager *et al.*, 2007]. Economic modelling, as the evidence of this essay suggests, offers the kinds of rich and varied materials, ranging from the statistical models used by econometricians to the mathematical objects used by theorizers, providing an important third site for the serious philosophical study of models. Without benefit of the manipulable real objects, model organisms and experimental systems of biology, nor the well behaved and attested mathematical descriptions of physics, economics offers a scientific field in which models may look like the models of physics, but are used more like the experimental model systems of biology, and yet, whose inference regimes depend on modes of comparison that range from the heuristic to the statistical as befitting its social science domain.

## ACKNOWLEDGEMENTS

Tarja Knuuttila would like to thank the Academy of Finland for their financial support of this research.

## BIBLIOGRAPHY

[Aldrich, 1994] J. Aldrich. Haavelmo's identification theory. *Econometric Theory* 10, 198-219, 1994.

[Alexandrova, 2006] A. Alexandrova. Connecting economic models to the real world: game theory and the FCC spectrum auctions. *Philosophy of the Social Sciences* 36, 173-192, 2006.

[Backhouse, 2007] R. E. Backhouse. Representation in economics. In M. Boumans, ed., *Measurement in Economics: A Handbook*, pp. 35–52. London: Elsevier, 2006.

[Bailer-Jones, 1999] D. M. Bailer-Jones. Tracing the development of models in the philosophy of science. In Lorenzo Magnani, Nancy J. Nersessian and Paul Thagard, eds., *Model-Based Reasoning in Scientific Discovery*, pp 23–40. New York: Kluwer, 1999.

[Bailer-Jones, 2003] D. M. Bailer-Jones. When scientific models represent. *International Studies in the Philosophy of Science* 17, 59-74, 2003.

[Bailer-Jones, 2009] D. M. Bailer-Jones. *Scientific Models in Philosophy of Science.* Pittsburgh: University of Pittsburgh Press, 2009.

[Black, 1962] M. Black. *Models and Metaphors.* Ithaca: Cornell University Press, 1962.

[Boltzmann, 1911] L. Boltzmann. Models. In *Encyclopaedia Britannica*, $11^{th}$ ed., pp. 638-640. Cambridge: Cambridge University Press, 1911.

[Boumans, 1993] M. Boumans. Paul Ehrenfest and Jan Tinbergen: A case of limited physics transfer. In N. De Marchi, ed., *Non-natural Social Science: Reflecting on the Enterprise of More Heat than Light.* Durham: Duke University Press, 1993.

[Boumans, 1997] M. Boumans. Lucas and artificial worlds. In John B. Davis, ed., *New Economics and its History*, pp. 63-88. Durham: Duke University Press, 1997.

[Boumans, 1999] M. Boumans. Built-in justification. In Mary S. Morgan and Margaret Morrison, eds., *Models as Mediators*, pp. 66-96. Cambridge: Cambridge University Press, 1999.

[Boumans, 2003] M. Boumans. How to design Galileo fall experiments in economics. *Philosophy of Science*, 70, 2, 308-329, 2003.

[Boumans, 2005] M. Boumans. *How Economists Model the World to Numbers*. London, Routledge, 2005.

[Boumans, 2006] M. Boumans. The difference between answering a 'Why'-question and answering a 'How Much'-question. In Johannes Lenhard, Günther Küppers, and Terry Shinn, eds., *Simulation: Pragmatic Constructions of Reality, Sociology of the Sciences Yearbook*, pp. 107–124. New York: Springer, 2006.

[Boumans, 2007] M. Boumans, ed. *Measurement in Economics: A Handbook*. London: Elsevier, 2007.

[Boumans, 2011] M. Boumans. Measurement in economics. This volume.

[Boumans and Morgan, 2001] M. Boumans and M. S. Morgan. *Ceteris paribus* conditions: materiality and the application of economic theories. *Journal of Economic Methodology 8* (1), 11-26, 2001.

[Brodbeck, 1968/1959] M. Brodbeck. Models, meaning and theories. In N. Brodbeck, ed., *Readings in the Philosophy of the Social Sciences*, pp, 579–601. Macmillan, New York, 1968/1959.

[Cartwright, 1989] N. Cartwright. *Nature's capacities and their measurement*. Oxford: Clarendon Press, 1989.

[Cartwright, 1998] N. Cartwright. Capacities. In John B. Davis, D. Wade Hands and Uskali Mäki, eds., *The Handbook of Economic Methodology*. Cheltenham: Edgar Elgar, 1998.

[Cartwright, 1999] N. Cartwright. The vanity of rigour in economics: theoretical models and Galilean experiments. Centre for Philosophy of Natural and Social Science. Discussion paper series 43/99, 1999. (Published also in P. Fontaine and R. Leonard, eds., *The Experiment in the History of Economics*. Routledge, 2005.)

[Cartwright, 2002] N. Cartwright. The limits of causal order, from economics to physics. In U. Mäki, ed., *Fact and Fiction in Economics*, pp. 137-151, 2002.

[Cartwright, 2006] N. Cartwright. *Hunting Causes and Using Them: Approaches in Philosophy and Economics*. Cambridge: Cambridge University Press, 2006.

[Chao, 2007] H.-K. Chao. Structure. In *Measurement in Economics: A Handbook*, pp. 271–294. London: Elsevier, 2007.

[Chao, 2009] H.-K. Chao. *Representation and Structure: The Methodology of Econometric Models of the Consumption Function*, London: Routledge, 2009.

[Colander, 2008] D. Colander. Economists, incentives, judgment, and empirical work. Economics Discussion Papers, 2008-12, `http://www.economics-ejournals.org/economics/discussionpapers/2008-12`

[Cook and Hendry, 1994] S. Cook and D. Hendry. The theory of reduction in economics. In B. Hamminga and N. De Marchi, eds., *Idealization in economics*, pp. 71–100. Amsterdam: Rodopi, 1994.

[Creager *et al.*, 2007] A. Creager, M. N. Wise, and E. Lunbeck. *Science Without Laws: Model Systems, Cases, Exemplary Narratives*, Duke University Press, 2007.

[Darity and Young, 1995] W. Darity and W. Young. IS-LM: an inquest. *History of Political Economy*, 27, 1-41, 1995.

[De Vroey and Hoover, 2004] M. De Vroey and K. D. Hoover. *The IS-LM Model: Its Rise, Fall, and Strange Persistence* Duke University Press, 2004.

[Elgin, 2004] C. Elgin. True enough. *Philosophical Issues* 14, 113-131, 2004.

[Fennell, 2007] D. Fennell. Why functional form matters: revealing the structure in structural models in econometrics. *Philosophy of Science — Proceedings of the 2006 Biennial Meeting of the Philosophy of Science Association*, December 2007, 74(5), 1033-1045, 2007.

[Fogel, 1970] R. W. Fogel. *Railroads and American Economic Growth: Essays in Econometric History*. Baltimore: Johns Hopkins Press, 1970.

[French and Ladyman, 1999] S. French and J. Ladyman. Reinflating the semantic approach. *International Studies in the Philosophy of Science* 13, 103-121, 1999.

[Friedman, 1953] M. Friedman. *Essays in Positive Economics*. Chicago: University of Chicago Press, 1953.

[Frigg, 2006] R. Frigg. Scientific representation and the semantic view of theories. *Theoria* 55, 49-65, 2006.

[Frigg, 2010] R. Frigg. Models and fiction. *Synthese*, 172(2), 251–268, 2010.

[Gibbard and Varian, 1978] A. Gibbard and H. R. Varian. Economic models. *The Journal of Philosophy* 75(11), 664-677, 1978.

[Giere, 1988] R. N. Giere. *Explaining Science: A Cognitive Approach.* Chicago and London: The University of Chicago Press, 1988.

[Giere, 2004] R. N. Giere. How models are used to represent reality. *Philosophy of Science* 71, 742-752, 2004.

[Giere, 2010] R. N. Giere. An agent-based conception of models and scientific representation. *Synthese*, 172, 269–281, 2010.

[Gordon, 1991] S. Gordon. *The History and Philosophy of Social Science.* Routledge, New York, 1991.

[Grüne-Yanoff and Schweinzer, 2008] T. Grüne-Yanoff and P. Schweinzer. The role of stories in applying game theory. *Journal of Economic Methodology*, 15, 131-46, 2008.

[Haavelmo, 1944] T. Haavelmo. The probability approach in econometrics. *Econometrica*, 12(Supplement), iii-iv, 1-115, 1944.

[Hamminga and De Marchi, 1994] B. Hamminga and N. De Marchi, eds. *Idealization in Economics.* Amsterdam: Rodopi, 1994.

[Hausman, 1984] D. M. Hausman. *The Philosophy of Economics: An Anthology.* Cambridge: Cambridge University Press, 1984.

[Hausman, 1990] D. M. Hausman. Supply and demand explanations and their *ceteris paribus* clauses. *Review of Political Economy* 2 (2), 168-87, 1990.

[Hausman, 1992] D. M. Hausman. *The Inexact and Separate Science of Economics.* Cambridge: Cambridge University Press, 1992.

[Heckman, 2000] J. Heckman. Causal parameters and policy analysis in economics: A twentieth century retrospective. *Quarterly Journal of Economics*, 115, 1, 45-97, 2000.

[Hindriks, 2005] F. A. Hindriks. Unobservability, Tractability, and the Battle of Assumptions. *Journal of Economic Methodology* 12, 383-406, 2005.

[Hindriks, 2006] F. A. Hindriks. Tractability assumptions and the Musgrave-Mäki-typology. *Journal of Economic Methodology* 13, 401-423, 2006.

[Hirsch and de Marchi, 1990] A. Hirsch and N. de Marchi. *Milton Friedman: Economics in Theory and Practice*, New York: Harvester Wheatsheaf, 1990.

[Hoover, 1991] K. D. Hoover. Scientific research program or tribe? A joint appraisal of Lakatos and the new classical macroeconomics. In M. Blaug and N. De Marchi, eds., *Appraising Economic Theories: Studies in the Application of the Methodology of Research Programs*, pp. 364–394. Aldershot: Edward Elgar, 1991.

[Hoover, 1994] K. D. Hoover. Six queries about idealization in an empirical context. In B. Hamminga and N. De Marchi, eds., *Idealization in economics*, pp. 43–54. Amsterdam: Rodopi, 1994.

[Hoover, 1994a] K. D. Hoover. Econometrics as observation: the Lucas critique, causality and the nature of econometric inference. *Journal of Economic Methodology*, 1, 1, 65-80, 1994. (Reprinted in Daniel M. Hausman ed., *The Philosophy of Economics*, $3^{rd}$ ed, CUP, 2008.)

[Hoover, 1995] K. D. Hoover. Facts and artifacts: calibration and the empirical assessment of real-business-cycle models. *Oxford Economic Papers*, 47, 1, 24-44, 1995.

[Hoover, 2000] K. D. Hoover. Models all the way down. In R. E. Backhouse and A. Salanti, eds., *Macroeconomics and the Real World, Vol 1: Econometric Techniques and Macroeconomics*, pp, 219–224. Oxford University Press, 2000.

[Hoover, 2001] K. D. Hoover. *Causality in Macroeconomics*, Cambridge University Press, 2001.

[Hoover, 2002] K. D. Hoover. Econometrics and reality. In U. Mäki, ed., *Fact and Fiction in Economics*, pp. 152-77. Cambridge University Press, 2002.

[Hoover, 2008] K. D. Hoover. Causality in economics and econometrics. In S. Durlaf, ed., *The New Palgrave Dictionary of Economics.* Palgrave Macmillan, 2008.

[Hoover, 2008a] K. D. Hoover. Idealizing reduction: the microfoundations of macroeconomics. Working paper, Duke University, 2008.

[Hoover, 2011] K. D. Hoover. Economic theory and causal inference. This volume.

[Humphrey, 1996] T. M. Humphrey. The early history of the box diagram. Federal Reserve Board of Richmond. *Economic Review* 82 (1), 37-75, 1996.

[Humphreys, 2004] P. Humphreys. *Extending Ourselves. Computational Science, Empiricism and Scientific Method.* Oxford: Oxford University Press, 2004.

[Keynes, 1936] J. M. Keynes. *The General Theory of Employment, Interest and Money.* London: Macmillan, 1936, (reprinted 2007).

[Kirman, 1992] A. Kirman. Whom or what does the representative individual represent? *Journal of Economic Perspectives,* 6(2), 117-36, 1992.

[Knight, 1921] F. H. Knight. *Risk, Uncertainty and Profit.* Boston: Houghton Mifflin, 1921.

[Knuuttila, 2005] T. Knuuttila. Models, representation, and nediation. *Philosophy of Science* 72, 1260-1271, 2005.

[Knuuttila, 2006] T. Knuuttila. From representation to production: parsers and parsing in language technology. In Johannes Lenhard, Günther Küppers, and Terry Shinn, eds., *Simulation: Pragmatic Constructions of Reality. Sociology of the Sciences Yearbook*, pp. 41–55. New York: Springer, 2006.

[Knuuttila, 2008] T. Knuuttila. Representation, idealization, and fiction in economics: from the assumptions issue to the epistemology of modelling. In Mauricio Suárez, ed., *Fictions in Science: Philosophical Essays on Modeling and Idealization*, pp. 205–231. New York & London: Routledge, 2008.

[Knuuttila, 2009] T. Knuuttila. Isolating representations vs. credible constructions? Economic modelling in theory and pactice. *Erkenntnis*, 70, 59–80, 2009.

[Knuuttila, 2009a] T. Knuuttila. Some consequences of the pragmatic approach to representation. In M. Dorato, M Rèdei and M. Suárez, eds. *EPSA Launch of the European Philosophy of Science Association*, Vol I: Epistemology and Methodology of Science, pp. 139–148. Dordrecht, Springer, 2009.

[Knuuttila and Voutilainen, 2003] T. Knuuttila and A. Voutilainen. A parser as an epistemic artefact: a material view on models. *Philosophy of Science* 70, 1484–1495, 2003.

[Koopmans, 1957] T. Koopmans. *Three Essays on The State of Economic Science* McGraw Hill, New York, 1957.

[Krugman, 1993] P. Krugman. How I work. *The American Economist* 37 (2), 25-31, 1993.

[Kuorikoski *et al.*, forthcoming] J. Kuorikoski, A. Lehtinen, and C. Marchionni. Economics as robustness analysis. *The British Journal for the Philosophy of Science*, forthcoming.

[Leijonhufvud, 1968] A. Leijonhufvud. *On Keynesian Economics and the Economics of Keynes. A Study in Monetary Theory.* New York: Oxford University Press, 1968.

[Levins, 1966] R. Levins. The strategy of model-building in population biology. *American Scientist*, 54, 421-431, 1996.

[Lucas, 1980] R. E. Lucas. Methods and problems in business cycle theory. *Journal of Money, Credit and Banking*, 12, 696-715, 1980.

[Machlup, 1967] F. Machlup. Theories of the firm: marginalist, behavioral, managerial. *American Economic Review* Vol. LVII, 1-33, 1967.

[Machlup, 1978] F. Machlup. *Methodology of Economics and Other Social Sciences.* New York: Academic Press, 1978.

[MacKenzie, 2006] D. MacKenzie. *An Engine, Not a Camera.* MIT Press, 2006.

[Magnus and Morgan, 1999] J. Magnus and M. S. Morgan. *Methodology and Tacit Knowledge: Two Experiments in Econometrics.* Wiley, 1999.

[Mäki, 1992] U. Mäki. On the method of isolation in economics. In Craig Dilworth, ed., *Idealization IV: Intelligibility in Science*, pp. 317-351. Amsterdam: Rodopi, 1992.

[Mäki, 1994] U. Mäki. Reorienting the assumptions issue. In Roger Backhouse, ed., *New Directions in Economic Methodology*, pp. 236–256. London: Routledge, 1994.

[Mäki, 2000] U. Mäki. Kinds of assumptions and their truth: shaking an untwisted F-twist, *Kyklos* 53 - Fasc. 3, 317-336, 2000.

[Mäki, 2002] U. Mäki, ed. *Fact and Fiction in Economics.* Cambridge: Cambridge University Press, 2002.

[Mäki, 2004] U. Mäki. Realism and the nature of theory: A lesson from J.H. von Thünen for economists and geographers, *Environment and Planning A*, 36, 1719-1736, 2004.

[Mäki, 2005] U. Mäki. Models are experiments, experiments are models. *Journal of Economic Methodology* 12, 303-315, 2005.

[Mäki, 2006] U. Mäki. Remarks on models and their truth. *Storia del Pensiero Economico* 3, 7-19, 2006.

[Mäki, 2009] U. Mäki. Realistic realism about unrealistic models. To appear in H. Kincaid and D. Ross, eds., *Oxford Handbook of the Philosophy of Economics*, pp. 68–98. Oxford: Oxford University Press, 2009.

[Mäki, 2009a] U. Mäki. Missing the world: models as isolations and credible surrogate systems. *Erkenntnis*, 70, 29–43, 2009.

[Mäki, 2009b] U. Mäki, ed. *The Methodology of Positive Economics. Milton Friedman's Essay Fifty Years Later*. Cambridge University Press, 2009.
[Mäki, 2011] U. Mäki. Models and the locus of their truth. *Synthese*, 180, 470063, 2011.
[Mäki, 2011] U. Mäki. Realist and antirealist philosophies of economics, this volume.
[Marshall, 1890/1930] A. W. Marshall. *Principles of Economics* ($8^{th}$ edition). London: Macmillan, 1890/1930.
[McCloskey, 1990] D. N. McCloskey. *If You're So Smart. The Narrative of Economic Expertise.* Chicago: The University of Chicago Press, 1990.
[McMullin, 1985] E. McMullin. Galilean idealization. *Studies in History and Philosophy of Science*, 16 (3), 247-73, 1985.
[Mill, 1843] J. S. Mill. *A System of Logic*. London: Longman, Green, & co, 1943.
[Mirowski, 1994] P. Mirowski, ed. *Natural Images in Economic Thought: Markets Read in Tooth and Claw*. Cambridge University Press, 1994.
[Morgan, 1990] M. S. Morgan. *The History of Econometric Ideas*. Cambridge: Cambridge University Press, 1990.
[Morgan, 1996] M. S. Morgan. Idealization and modelling (a review essay). *Journal of Economic Methodology* 3, 1, 131-8, 1996.
[Morgan, 1997] M. S. Morgan. The technology of analogical models: Irving Fisher's monetary worlds. *Philosophy of Science* 64, S304-314, 1997.
[Morgan, 1999] M. S. Morgan. Learning from models. In M. S. Morgan and M. Morrison, eds., *Models as Mediators: Perspectives on Natural and Social Science*, pp. 347–388. Cambridge: Cambridge University Press, 1999.
[Morgan, 2001] M. S. Morgan. Models, stories and the economic world. *Journal of Economic Methodology*, 8(3) 361-84, 2001. (Also in [Mäki, 2002, pp 178-201].)
[Morgan, 2002] M. S. Morgan. Model experiments and models in experiments. In L. Magnani and N. Nersessian, eds., *Model-Based Reasoning: Science, Technology, Values*, pp. 41–58. Kluwer Academic/Plenum Press, 2002.
[Morgan, 2003] M. S. Morgan. Experiments without material intervention: model experiments, virtual experiments and virtually experiments. In H. Radde, ed., *The Philosophy of Scientific Experimentation*, pp. 216–235. University of Pittsburgh Press, 2003.
[Morgan, 2004] M. S. Morgan. Simulation: the birth of a technology to create evidence in economics. *Revue d'Histoire des Sciences*, 57, 2, 341-77, 2004.
[Morgan, 2004a] M. S. Morgan. Imagination and imaging in economic model-building. *Philosophy of Science*, 71, 5, 753-66, 2004.
[Morgan, 2005] M. S. Morgan. Experiments versus models: new phenomena, inference and surprise. *Journal of Economic Methodology,* 12, 2, 317-29, 2005.
[Morgan, 2006] M. S. Morgan. Economic man as model man: ideal types, idealization and caricatures. *Journal of the History of Economic Thought* 28, 1, 1-27, 2006.
[Morgan, 2007] M. S. Morgan. The curious case of the prisoner's dilemma: model situation? Exemplary narrative? In A. Creager, M. Norton Wise, and E. Lunbeck, eds., *Science Without Laws: Model Systems, Cases, Exemplary Narratives*, pp. 157–185. Duke University Press, 2007.
[Morgan, forthcoming] M. S. Morgan. *The World in the Model.* Cambridge University Press, forthcoming.
[Morgan and Boumans, 2004] M. S. Morgan and M. Boumans. Secrets hidden by two-dimensionality: the economy as a hydraulic machine. In S. de Chadarevian and N. Hopwood, eds., *Models: The Third Dimension of Science*, pp. 369–401. Stanford University Press, 2004.
[Morgan and Morrison, 1999] M. S. Morgan and M. Morrison, eds. *Models as Mediators: Perspectives on Natural and Social Science*, Cambridge: Cambridge University Press, 1999.
[Morrison and Morgan, 1999] M. Morrison and M. S. Morgan. Models as mediating instruments. In M. S. Morgan and M. Morrison, eds., *Models as Mediators: Perspectives on Natural and Social Science*, pp. 10–37. Cambridge: Cambridge University Press, 1999.
[Musgrave, 1981] A. Musgrave. 'Unreal assumptions' in economic theory: the F-Twist untwisted. *Kyklos*, 34, 377-87, 1981.
[Nordmann, 1998] A. Nordmann. Everything could be different: the *Principles of Mechanics* and the limits of physics. In D. Baird, R.I.G. Hughes and Alfred Nordmann, eds., *Heinrich-Hertz: Classical Physicist, Modern Philosopher*, pp. 155–171. Dordrecht: Kluwer, 1998.

[Nowak, 1992] L. Nowak. The idealizational approach to science: a survey. In J. Brezinski and L.Nowak, eds., *Idealization III: Approximation and Truth*, pp. 9–63. Vol. 25 of Poznán Studies in the Philosophy of Sciences and Humanities, Amsterdam & Atlanta, GA: Rodopi, 1992.

[Nowak, 1994] L. Nowak. The idealization methodology and econometrics. In B. Hamminga and N. De Marchi, eds., *Idealization in Economics*. Amsterdam: Rodopi, 1994.

[Qin, 1993] D. Qin. *The Formation of Econometrics*. Clarendon Press, Oxford, 1993.

[Rappaport, 1998] S. Rappaport. *Models and Reality in Economics*. Cheltenham: Edward Elgar, 1998.

[Reiss, 2008] J. Reiss. *Error in Economics: Towards a More Evidence-Based Methodology*. Routledge: London, 2008.

[Samuelson, 1958] P. Samuelson. An exact consumption-loan model of interest with or without the social contrivance of money. *Journal of Political Economy* 66, 467-82, 1958.

[Schabas, 2008] M. Schabas. Hume's monetary thought experiments. *Studies In History and Philosophy of Science*, A, 39, 2, 161-169, 2008

[Schelling, 2006] T. Schelling. *Strategies of Commitment and Other Essays*. Harvard: Harvard University Press, 2006.

[Spanos, 2008] A. Spanos. The 'Pre-Eminence of Theory' versus the 'General-to-Specific' cointegrated VAR perspectives in macro-econometric modelling economics. Discussion Papers, 2008-25: `http://www.economics-ejournals.org/economics/discussionpapers/2008-25`.

[Spanos, 2011] A. Spanos. Philosophy of econometrics. This volume.

[Strevens, 2008] M. Strevens. *Depth: An Account of Scientific Explanation*. Harvard: Harvard University Press, 2008.

[Suárez, 2003] M. Suárez. Scientific representation: against similarity and isomorphism. *International Studies in the Philosophy of Science* 17, 225-244, 2003.

[Suárez, 2004] M. Suárez. An inferential conception of scientific representation. *Philosophy of Science* (Symposia) 71, 767-779, 2004.

[Suárez, 2008] M. Suárez. Scientific fictions as rules of inference. In Mauricio Suárez, ed., *Fictions in Science: Philosophical Essays on Modeling and Idealization*, pp. 158–179. New York & London: Routledge, 2008.

[Suárez, 2008a] M. Suárez, ed. *Fictions in Science: Philosophical Essays on Modeling and Idealization*. New York & London: Routledge, 2008.

[Suárez, 2010] M. Suárez. Scientific representation. *Blackwell's Philosophy Compass*, 5, 91–101, 2010.

[Sugden, 2002] R. Sugden. Credible worlds: the status of the theoretical models in economics. In Uskali Mäki, ed., *Fact and Fiction in Economics: Models, Realism, and Social Construction*, pp. 107–136. Cambridge: Cambridge University Press, 2002.

[Sugden, 2009] R. Sugden. Credible worlds, capacities, and mechanisms. *Erkenntnis*, 70, 3–27, 2009.

[Sutton, 2000] J. Sutton. *Marshall's Tendencies. What Can Economists Know?* Gaston Eyskens Lecture, University of Leuven. Cambridge, Mass: MIT Press, 2000.

[Tinbergen, 1940] J. Tinbergen. Econometric business cycle research. *Review of Economic Studies*, 7, 73-90, 1940.

[van Fraassen, 1980] B. van Fraassen. *The Scientific Image*. Oxford: Oxford University Press. 1980.

[Wallis, 1984] K. F. Wallis. *Models of the U.K. Economy: A review of the ESRC Macroeconomic Modelling Bureau*, Oxford University Press, 1984.

[Walliser, 1994] B. Walliser. Three generalizations processes for economic models. B. Hamminga and N. De Marchi, eds. *Idealization in Economics*, pp. 55–70. Amsterdam: Rodopi, 1994.

[Weber, 1904] M. Weber. 'Objectivity' in social science and social policy. In E. A. Schils and Henry A. Finch, trans. and eds., *The Methodology of the Social Sciences*, New York: Free Press, 1904.

[Weisberg, 2006] M. Weisberg. Robustness analysis. *Philosophy of Science* 73, 730-742, 2006.

[Weisberg, 2007] M. Weisberg. Three kinds of idealization. *The Journal of Philosophy* 104, 12, 639-59, 2007.

[Wimsatt, 1987] W. C. Wimsatt. False models as means for truer theories. In Matthew H. Nitecki and Hoffman, Antoni, eds., *Neutral Models in Biology*, pp. 23–55. New York: Oxford University Press, 1987.

# ECONOMIC THEORY AND CAUSAL INFERENCE

Kevin D. Hoover

## 1 REDUCTIONIST AND STRUCTURALIST ACCOUNTS OF CAUSALITY

Economists have intermittently concerned themselves with causality at least since David Hume in the $18^{th}$ century. Hume is the touchstone for all subsequent philosophical analyses of causality. He is frequently regarded as a causal skeptic; yet, as an economist, he put a high priority on causal knowledge.[1] In "On Interest" [Hume, 1754, p. 304], one of his justly famous economic essays, he writes:

> it is of consequence to know the principle whence any phenomenon arises, and to distinguish between a cause and a concomitant effect ... nothing can be of more use than to improve, by practice, the method of reasoning on these subjects

The utility of causal knowledge in economics is captured in Hume's conception of what it is to be a cause: "we may define a cause to be *an object, followed by another, ... where, if the first had not been, the second never had existed*" [Hume, 1777, p. 62]. Causal knowledge lays the groundwork for counterfactual analyses that underwrite economic and political policy judgments.

At least two questions remain open: first, what exactly are causes "in the objects" [Hume, 1739. p. 165]? second, how can we infer them from experience? Hume answers the first question by observing that the idea of cause comprises *spatial contiguity* of cause to effect, *temporal precedence* of cause over effect, and *necessary connection* between cause and effect. Necessary connection "is of much greater importance" then the other two elements [Hume, 1739, p. 77]. Necessary connection is the basis for practical counterfactual analysis.

Hume answers the second question by pointing out that contiguity and temporal precedence are given in experience, but that no experience corresponds to the notion of necessary connection. Since Hume famously believed that all knowledge is either logical and mathematical or empirical, the failure to find an *a priori* or an empirical provenance for the idea of necessary connection provides the basis for the view that Hume is a causal skeptic.

[1] See Hoover [2001, ch. 1] for a fuller discussion of Hume's views on causality as a philosophical and economic problem.

Handbook of the Philosophy of Science. Volume 13: Philosophy of Economics.
Volume editor: Uskali Mäki. General editors: Dov M. Gabbay, Paul Thagard and John Woods.

According to Hume, the closest that we can come to an empirical provenance for the idea of necessary connection is the habit of mind that develops when two objects or events are constantly conjoined. Unfortunately, constant conjunction is too weak a reed to support a satisfactory account of the connection between causal knowledge and counterfactual analysis — however practically important Hume deemed the latter.

After Hume, the dominant strategy in the analysis of causality has been reductive. Its objects are, first, to define causes in terms of something less mysterious with the object of eliminating causality as a basic ontological category and, second, to provide a purely empirically grounded mode of causal inference. An important modern example is found in Patrick Suppes [1970] probabilistic theory of causality. For Suppes, $A$ *prima facie* causes $B$, if the probability of $B$ conditional on $A$ is higher than the unconditional probability of $B$ ($P(B|A) > P(B)$). The type of empirical evidence that warrants calling one thing the cause of another becomes, in this approach, the meaning of cause: the ontological collapses to the inferential.

Such approaches are not successful. As Suppes and others realized, the concept of cause must be elaborated in order to capture ordinary understandings of its meaning. For example, cause is asymmetrical: if $A$ causes $B$, $B$ does not (in general) cause $A$. It is easy to prove that if $A$ is a *prima facie* cause of $B$, then $B$ is a *prima facie* cause of $A$.[2] Asymmetry can be restored by the Humean device of requiring causes to occur before their effects: $P(B_{t+1}|A_t) > P(B_{t+1})$ does not imply $P(A_{t+1}|B_t) > P(A_{t+1})$.

Another standard counterexample to *prima facie* cause as an adequate rendering of cause *simpliciter* is found in the correlation between a falling barometer and the onset of a storm. Although these fulfill the conditions for *prima facie* cause, we are loath to say that the barometer causes the storm. The standard device for avoiding this conclusion is to say the barometer will not be regarded as a cause of the storm if some other variable — say, falling air pressure — screens off the correlation between the putative cause and effect. The probability of a storm conditional on a falling barometer *and* falling air pressure is the same as the probability of a storm conditional on falling air pressure alone. The falling barometer does not raise the probability of the storm once we know the air pressure. Such a screening variable is known either as a *common cause* (as in this example in which the falling air pressure causes both the falling barometer and the storm) or as an *intermediate cause* (when the variable is a more direct cause that stands between the effect and a less direct cause in a chain).

These are only two examples of the various additional conditions that have to be added to bring the simple notion of *prima facie* cause into line with our ordinary notions of causation. Such strategies suggest, however, that the reductive notion

---

[2]See Hoover [2001, p. 15]. The joint probability of $A$ and $B$ can be factored two ways into a conditional and a marginal distribution: $P(B,A) = P(B|A)P(A) = P(A|B)P(B)$. If $A$ is a *prima facie* cause of $B$, then $P(B|A) > P(B)$. Substituting for $P(B)$ in the joint probability distribution gives us $P(B|A)P(A) < P(A|B)P(B|A)$ or $P(A|B) > P(A)$ — that is, $B$ is a *prima facie* cause of $A$.

is haunted by the ghost of a more fundamental concept of causality and that we will not be satisfied until the reductive notion recapitulates this more fundamental notion.

Recognition of the specter of necessary connection suggests another possibility: simply give the reductive strategy up as a bad job and to embrace causality as a primitive category, admitting that no satisfactory reduction is possible. Such an approach once again distinguishes the ontology of causality from the conditions of causal inference that had been conflated in reductivist accounts. Such a non-reductive strategy implies that we can never step outside of the causal circle: to learn about particular causes requires some prior knowledge of other causes. Nancy Cartwright [1989, ch. 2] expresses this dependence in a slogan: "no causes in; no causes out." It is also the basis for James Woodward's [2003] "manipulability" account of causality (cf. [Holland, 1986]). Roughly, a relationship is causal if an *intervention* on $A$ can be used to alter $B$. The notion of a manipulation or an intervention may appear to be, but is not in fact, an anthropomorphic one, since it can be defined in terms of independent variations that may arise with or without human agency. Nor is the circularity implicit in this approach vicious. What is needed is that some causal relationship (say, $C$ causes $A$) permits manipulation of $A$, while what is demonstrated is the existence of a causal relationship between $A$ and $B$ — what is proved is not what is assumed.

Causal knowledge in a manipulability account is the knowledge of the structure of counterfactual dependence among variables — for example, how a clock works or how it will react to various interventions. Whereas in reductive accounts of causality, the connection between the structure of causes and counterfactual analysis was too weak to be satisfactory, here it is basic. Woodward's account is closely allied with the analyses of Pearl [2000] and Hoover [2001]. I prefer the term *structural* account to manipulability account, since manipulations are used to infer structures and structures are manipulated. Still, that preference is merely a matter of terminology — the underlying causal ontology is the same in all three accounts.

A structural account seems particularly suited to economics. Economics is distinguished from other social sciences in its dedication to a core theory that is shared, to one degree or another, by most economists. The core theory can be seen as articulating economic mechanisms or structures not unlike physical mechanisms that provide the classic illustrations of causal structure. While the very notion of an economic structure seems to favor the manipulability or structural account of causality, with its fundamentally causal ontology, the same tensions already evident in Hume's account of causality are recapitulated through the history of economics. These tensions are reflected in two problems: the *inferential problem* (how do we isolate causes or identify structure?) and *counterfactual problem* (how do we use a knowledge of causal structure to reason to unobserved outcomes?).

John Stuart Mill, one of a distinguished line of philosopher/economists, contributed answers to both questions. In his *System of Logic* (1851), he describes various canons for inferring causes from empirical data. But in his *Principles of*

*Political Economy* (1848) he denies that economic structures can be inferred from these or other inductive rules. For Mill, economics involves many considerations and many confounding causes, as well as human agency. While there may be some coarse regularities, it is implausible that any economic laws or any strict causal relationships could be inferred from data. But economics is not, therefore, hopeless as a counterfactual science. Rather it is "an inexact and separate science" [Hausman, 1992]. Economics is the science of wealth in which the choices of human actors, known to us by direct acquaintance, interact with the production possibilities given by nature and social organization. From our *a priori* understanding, we can deduce axiomatically the effects of causes in cases in which there are no interfering factors. When we compare our deductions to the data, however, we do not expect a perfect fit, because there are in fact interfering factors and our deductions must be thought of as, at best, tendencies. There is no simple mapping between the deductions of theory and any sort of empirical test or measurement. Implicitly at least, Mill's view has been highly influential in economics. Yet it gives rise to a perennial conundrum: if we know the true theory, we can dispense with empirical study; but how do we know that the theory is true?

I shall use the tension between the epistemological, inferential problem and the ontological, counterfactual problem as a background against which to situate four approaches to causality in economics. These four approaches are different, yet overlapping and sometimes complementary. The goal will not be to ask, which is right? Rather, what is right about each? They are 1) the notion of causal order implicit in the Cowles Commission [Koopmanns, 1950; Hood and Koopmanns, 1953] analysis of structural estimation, revived in, for example, Heckman [2000]; 2) Granger-causality [Granger, 1969; 1980; Sims, 1972]; 3) the structural account of causality that appeals to invariance under intervention as an inferential tool [Hoover, 2001]; and 4) the graph-theoretic approaches associated with Judea Pearl [2000] and Glymour, Spirtes, and Scheines [2000].

Both economic theory and econometrics have become sciences expressed in models. My approach will be to discuss causality in relationship to the mapping between theoretical and econometric models. This mapping is related in a complex way to the distinction between the inferential and the counterfactual problems. To keep things concrete, I will use macroeconomic models to illustrate the key points.

## 2 STRUCTUAL ESTIMATION AND CAUSALITY

Trygve Haavelmo's monograph "The Probability Approach in Econometrics" (1944) marks a watershed in the history of empirical economics. Appropriately defined, econometrics is an old discipline, going back perhaps to William Petty and the tradition of "political arithmetic." Some of the characteristic tools of econometrics are traceable to William Stanley Jevons if not to earlier economists (see [Morgan, 1990]). Yet, until Haavelmo there was considerable doubt whether classical statistics had any relevance for econometrics at all. Haavelmo's great innovation was to suggest how economic tendencies could be extracted from nonexperimental economic data — that is, to suggest how to do what Mill thought could not be done. The true interpretation of Haavelmo's monograph is highly disputed (see [Spanos, 1995]). On one interpretation, economic theory permits us to place enough structure on an empirical problem that the errors can be thought to conform to a probability model analyzable by standard statistical tools. On another interpretation (associated with the "LSE (London School of Economics) approach" in econometrics), analysis is possible only if the econometric model can deliver errors that in fact conform to standard probability models and the key issue is finding a structure that ensures such conformity [Mizon, 1995].

The Cowles Commission took the first approach. The problem, as they saw it, was how to identify and measure the strength of the true causal linkages between variables. To do this, one started with theory. Suppose, to take a textbook example, that theory told us that money ($m$) depended on GDP ($y$) and GDP on money as

(1) $m = \alpha y + \varepsilon_m$

(2) $y = \beta m + \varepsilon_y$,

where the variables should be thought of as the logarithms of the natural variables and $\varepsilon_m$ and $\varepsilon_y$ are error terms that indicate those factors that are irregular and cannot be explained. Following Haavelmo, the Cowles Commission program argues that if a model is structural then these error terms will follow a definite probability distribution and can be analyzed using standard statistical tools. Furthermore, if the structural model is complete, then the error terms will be independent of (and uncorrelated with) each other.

If we have a model like equations (1) and (2), including knowledge of $\alpha$ and $\beta$ and of the statistical properties of $\varepsilon_m$ and $\varepsilon_y$, then answering counterfactual questions (probabilistically) would be easy. The problem in the Cowles Commission view is that we do not know the values of the parameters or the properties of the errors. The real problem is the inferential one: given data on $y$ and $m$, can we infer the unknown values? As the problem is set out, the answer is clearly, "no."

The technique of multivariate regression, which chooses the coefficients of an equation in such a manner as to minimize the variance of the residual errors, implicitly places a directional arrow running from the right-hand to the left-hand side of an equation. The error terms are themselves estimated, not observed, and are chosen to be orthogonal to the left-hand side regressors — the implicit causes. Although if we knew the direction of causation, a regression run in that direction would quantify the relationship, we cannot use the regression itself to determine that direction. Any regression run in one direction can be reversed, and the coefficient estimates are just different normalizations of the correlations among the variables — here of the single correlation between $m$ and $y$.[3] We have

[3] If $\rho$ is the correlation between $y$ and $m$, then the regression estimate of $\alpha$ is $\hat{\alpha} = \rho\sqrt{\sigma_m^2/\sigma_y^2}$ and the estimate of $\beta$ is $\hat{\beta} = \rho\sqrt{\sigma_y^2/\sigma_m^2}$, where $\rho$ is the correlation coefficient between $y$ and $m, \sigma_m^2$ is the estimated variance of $m$, and $\sigma_y^2$ is the estimated variance of $y$.

no reason to prefer one normalization over another.

Of course, if we knew the values of $\varepsilon_m$ and $\varepsilon_y$, it would be easy to distinguish equation (1) from equation (2). But this is just what we do not know. Our best guesses of the values of $\varepsilon_m$ and $\varepsilon_y$ are determined by our estimates of $\alpha$ and $\beta$, and not the other way round.

The problem is made easier if equations (1) and (2) are influenced by other, and different, observable factors. Suppose the theoretical model is

$$(3) \quad m = \alpha y + \delta r + \varepsilon_m$$

$$(4) \quad y = \beta m + \gamma p + \varepsilon_y,$$

where $r$ is the interest rate and $p$ is the price level. Relative to the two-equation structure $y$ and $m$ are *endogenous* and $r$ and $p$ are *exogenous* variables. The values of the parameters can be inferred from regressions of the endogenous variables on the exogenous variables. First, eliminate the endogenous variables by substituting each equation into the other and simplifying to yield:

$$(3') \quad m = \tfrac{\alpha\gamma}{1-\alpha\beta} p + \tfrac{\delta}{1-\alpha\beta} r + \tfrac{\alpha}{1-\alpha\beta} \varepsilon_y + \tfrac{1}{1-\alpha\beta} \varepsilon_m$$

$$(4') \quad y = \tfrac{\beta\delta}{1-\alpha\beta} r + \tfrac{\gamma}{1-\alpha\beta} p + \tfrac{\beta}{1-\alpha\beta} \varepsilon_y + \tfrac{1}{1-\alpha\beta} \varepsilon_y.$$

Next estimate regressions of the form

$$(5) \quad m = \Pi_1 p + \Pi_2 r + \mathrm{E}_m$$

$$(6) \quad y = \Gamma_1 p + \Gamma_2 r + \mathrm{E}_y,$$

where $\Pi_1, \Pi_2$, $\Gamma_1$ and $\Gamma_2$ are estimated coefficients and $\mathrm{E}_m$ and $\mathrm{E}_y$ are regression residuals. Such a regression is known as a *reduced form* because it expresses the endogenous variables as functions of the exogenous variables and errors only.

The estimated coefficients of (5) and (6) can be matched with the coefficients on the corresponding variables in (3′) and (4′): $\Pi_1 = \frac{\alpha\gamma}{1-\alpha\beta}$, $\Pi_2 = \frac{\delta}{1-\alpha\beta}$, $\Gamma_1 = \frac{\beta\delta}{1-\alpha\beta}$, and $\Gamma_2 = \frac{\gamma}{1-\alpha\beta}$. Given this *identification* of the estimated coefficients with the theoretical coefficients, the parameters are easily recovered. A little calculation shows that $\alpha = \Pi_1/\Gamma_2$, $\beta = \Gamma_1/\Pi_2$, $\delta = \frac{\Pi_2^2\Gamma_2}{\Pi_2\Gamma_2 - \Pi_1\Gamma_1}$, and $\gamma = \frac{\Pi_2\Gamma_2^2}{\Pi_2\Gamma_2 - \Pi_1\Gamma_1}$. It is only the assumption that we know the theoretical structure of (3′) and (4′) that allows us to recover these parameter estimates. In the argot of econometrics, we have achieved identification through "exclusion restrictions": theory tells us that $p$ is excluded as a cause of $m$ and that $r$ is excluded as a cause of $y$.

It is easy to see why we need factors that are included in one equation and excluded from another simply by looking at the formulae that define the mapping between the theoretical and estimated coefficients. For example, if $r$ did not appear in (3′), we could interpret $\delta$ as equal to zero, so that (3′) would collapse to (3). Then $\Pi_2$ and $\Gamma_1$ would both equal zero, and $\beta$ (the causal strength of $m$ on $y$ in (4′), the other equation) would not be defined.

The Cowles Commission approach privileges economic theory in manner that is strikingly anti-empirical. We can use the strategy to measure a causal strength, such as $\beta$, only on the assumption that we have the form of the structure correct as in (3′) and (4′). Not only is that assumption untested, it is untestable. Only if the theory implies more restrictions than the minimum needed to recover the structural parameters — that is, only if it implies "over-identifying restrictions" — is a statistical test possible. What is more, the Neyman-Pearson statistical testing strategy adopted by Haavelmo and the Cowles Commission has been interpreted as implying one-shot tests, in which the theoretical implication to be tested must be designated in advance (see [Spanos, 1995]). Mutual adaptation between the empirical tests and the theory that generated the testable implications invalidates the statistical model.[4] While there is some possibility of adapting the Neyman-Pearson procedures to account for specification search, only the simplest cases can be analyzed. Mutual adaptation is certainly practiced, but it lacks a sound foundation given the statistical approach generally adopted in economics.

Herbert Simon [1953] clarified how identified structural models could be interpreted causally. If we know that the parameters $\alpha, \beta, \delta$, and $\gamma$ are mutually independent — that is, the values taken by one places no restrictions on the range of values open to the others — we can place the arrows of causation in a system like (3) and (4), say, as

$$(3'') \quad m \Leftarrow \alpha y + \delta r + \varepsilon_m$$

$$(4'') \quad y \Leftarrow \beta m + \gamma p + \varepsilon_y,$$

where the symbol "$\Leftarrow$" is interpreted as a directional equality. In this case, $m$ and $y$ are mutual causes. If $\alpha$ were zero under all circumstances – that is, if $y$ were omitted from equation (4″), then $m$ would cause $y$, but $y$ would not cause $m$. Such systems with a one-way causal order are called *recursive*.

Simon pointed out an inferential problem closely related to the identification problem. To keep things simple, consider a recursive system without error terms:

$$(7) \quad m = \delta r,$$

$$(8) \quad y = \beta m + \gamma p.$$

In this system, if $\beta, \delta$, and $\gamma$ are mutually independent parameters, $m$causes $y$. But can we infer the causal structure from data alone? Unfortunately not. Adding (7) and (8) yields

$$(7') \quad m = \tfrac{-1}{1-\beta} y + \tfrac{\gamma}{1-\beta} p + \tfrac{\delta}{1-\beta} r,$$

[4]In the simplest cases, this is obvious. If one adopts a rule of trying different regressors until one finds one that passes a $t$−test at a 5 percent critical value, then the probability of finding a "significant" relationship when the null hypothesis of no relationship is in fact true is much greater than one in twenty. For more complicated search procedures, the effect of search on the true size of statistical tests is hard to work out analytically. In can be shown, however, that some search procedures impose a large cost to search, while others impose quite small costs [Hoover and Perez, 1999; 2004].

While substituting (7) into (8) yields

$$(8')\quad y = \gamma p + \beta\delta r.$$

Every solution to (7) and (8) is also a solution to (7′) and (8′), yet in the first system $m$ appears to cause $y$, and in the second system $y$ appears to cause $m$. One might say, "yes, but the second system is clearly derived from the first." But this is not so clear. If we replace the second system with

$$(7'')\quad m = \phi y + \lambda p + \mu r,$$

$$(8'')\quad y = \theta p + \rho r,$$

then what appear to be coefficients that are functions of more basic parameters in (7′) and (8′) can be treated as themselves basic parameters. Taking an appropriate linear transformation of (7″) and (8″) will convert it to a system with a causal order like that of (7) and (8) in which the coefficients are functions of *its* parameters. The same set of values for $m$, $y$, $r$, and $p$ are consistent with this new system as with the three previous systems. The data alone do not seem to prefer one causal order over another. This is the problem of *observational equivalence.*

If we had some assurance that we knew which coefficients were true parameters and which were functions of more basic parameters, or even if we knew for certain which exogenous variables could be excluded from which equations, then we could recover the causal order.

At this point, the theoretical causal analyst is apt to turn to the economist and say, "we rely on you to supply the requisite subject matter knowledge." Surprisingly, economists have often been willing to oblige on the basis of *a priori* theory or detailed knowledge of the economy. But we are entitled to ask: "Where did such detailed knowledge come from? How was the theory validated? Was the validation done in a way that did not merely assume that the problem of observational equivalence had been solved at some earlier stage? And, if it were soluble, at the earlier stage, why is it a problem now?"

## 3 THE ASSAULT ON MACROECONOMETRIC MODELS

The epistemic problem of inferring causal strengths threatens to undermine the counterfactual uses of causal structure. Macroeconometric models are wanted in large part to conduct policy analysis. Without knowledge of the parameter values true policy analysis — that is, working out the effects of previously unobserved policy — is not possible (see [Marschak, 1953]). Despite the fact that the Cowles Commission program had clearly articulated the central difficulties in inferring causal structure, macromodeling in the 1950s and 1960s was undaunted. I believe that the main reason for ignoring the vast epistemic problems of structural modeling can be traced to the confidence in our direct, nonempirical acquaintance with true economic theory that many economists shared with (or inherited from) Mill. The Cowles Commission program pointed to the need for *a priori* theory.

Yet, this was not a problem, because what most distinguished economics from all other social sciences was, as Cartwright [1989, p. 14] later put it, "economics is a discipline with a theory."

But was it well enough articulated? The structural econometric models of Jan Tinbergen, starting in the 1930s, through Lawrence Klein in the 1950s were models of macroeconomic aggregate data reflecting commonsensical assumptions about their interrelationships. Deep economic theory typically referred to the decision problems of individual agents — it was microeconomic. Even Keynes's *General Theory* (1936), the bible of macroeconomics, had referred to individual behavior as a basis for aggregate relationships, such as the consumption function or the money-demand function. In his early review of the *General Theory*, Leontief [1936] called for grounding these relationships in a general-equilibrium framework in which the interactions of all agents had to be mutually consistent. Klein [1947] himself called for deriving each macroeconomic relationship from the optimization problems of individual economic actors. Together these quests formed the program of *microfoundations for macroeconomics.*

Klein's leg of the microfoundational program developed more rapidly than Leontief's. It was soon discovered that because decision-making is oriented toward the future, expectations are important. This was particularly clear in the investment literature of the late 1950s and early 1960s and led to a flowering of theoretical studies of expectation formation associated with the Carnegie Institute (now Carnegie-Mellon University). Because expectations must be grounded in past information and because the economic effects are slow to unfold, the current values of variables depend on past values. In other words, the quest for microfoundations underscored the dynamical character of economic relationships, reviving lines of inquiry that had begun in the interwar period.

The Leontief leg of the microfoundational program finally took off around 1970. Robert Lucas, in a series of papers that launched the *new classical macroeconomics*, insisted that models should respect the constraints of general equilibrium.[5] Lucas made two key assumptions. Up to this point, most economists had thought that macroeconomic phenomena arose in part because one market or other failed to clear. Modeling non-clearing markets is theoretically difficult. Lucas's first assumption is that markets in fact (at least to a first approximation) clear. His second assumption is that expectations are formed according to Muth's [1961] *rational expectations hypothesis.* The rational expectations hypothesis assumed that what economic actors expect is, up to a random error, what the economic model predicts. Rational expectations are appealing to economists because they do not imply an informational advantage on the part of the modeler. If models could actually outpredict economic actors, then there would be easy profit opportunities for the modeler. But the modelers are themselves economic actors (and inform other economic actors) who would themselves take advantage of the profit opportunities with the effect of changing prices in such a way that the opportunity disappeared (the process referred to as *arbitrage*). In effect, acting on non-rational

[5]See Hoover [1988; 1992a; 1992b].

expectations would help to make the economy conform to rational expectations.

Lucas's assumptions had strong implications for monetary policy as well. In a world in which markets clear, under conditions that many economists regard as reasonable, increases in the stock of money raise prices but do not change real quantities: there is pure inflation. In such a world, only an expectational error would allow a monetary-policy action to have a real (as opposed to a purely inflationary) effect. If people have rational expectations, then monetary policy actions can induce such errors at best randomly. *Systematic* monetary policy cannot, therefore, have real effects on the economy. This is the *policy-ineffectiveness proposition*, which was the most startling result of the early new classical macroeconomics [Sargent and Wallace, 1976].

We can see how Lucas's analysis relates to causality and the Cowles Commission program through a simple structural model (again the variables should be interpreted as the logarithms of natural variables):

$$(9)\quad y_t = \alpha(p_t - p_t^e) + \varepsilon_{yt},$$

$$(10)\quad p_t = m_t - y_t,$$

$$(11)\quad m_t = \gamma_1 m_{t-1} + \gamma_2 y_{t-1} + \varepsilon_{mt},$$

$$(12)\quad p_t^e = E(p_t|\Omega_{t-1}).$$

The variables are the same as those defined earlier, except that now the dynamic relationships are indicated by time subscripts. Equation (9) says that prices affect real GDP only if they differ from expectations formed a period earlier. Equation (10) shows that the level of prices is determined by the size of the money stock relative to real GDP. Equation (11) is the monetary-policy rule: the central bank sets the money supply in response to last period's levels of money and real GDP. Finally, (12) says that expected prices are formed according to the rational expectations hypothesis — i.e., they are the mathematical expectation of actual prices based on all the information available up to time $t-1$. The information set ($\Omega_{t-1}$) includes the structure of the model and the values of all variables and parameters known at $t-1$, but does not include the values of the current error terms.

The model is easily solved for an expression governing GDP,

$$(13)\quad y_t = \frac{\alpha}{1+\alpha} m_t - \frac{\alpha\gamma_1}{1+\alpha} m_{t-1} - \frac{\alpha\gamma_2}{1+\alpha} y_{t-1} + \frac{1}{1+\alpha} \varepsilon_{yt},$$

as well as one governing money that merely recapitulates the earlier equation

$$(11)\quad m_t = \gamma_1 m_{t-1} + \gamma_2 y_{t-1} + \varepsilon_{mt}.$$

The system (11) and (13) is identified. In some sense, it shows mutual causality: $m$ causes $y$, and $y$ causes $m$. Yet, if we restrict ourselves to current (time $t$) values, then contemporaneously $m_t$ causes $y_t$.

The coefficients in (13) are functions of the parameters of the model (9)–(12) because of the way expectations are formed: economic actors are seen as accounting for the structure of the model itself in forming expectations. Lucas [1976] criticized macromodelers for failing to incorporate expectations formation of this sort into their models. In his view, despite the claim that they were "structural," previous macromodelers had estimated forms such as

$$(14)\quad y_t = \Pi_1 m_t + \Pi_2 m_{t-1} + \Pi_3 y_{t-1} + \mathrm{E}_{yt},$$

$$(15)\quad m_t = \Gamma_1 m_t + \Gamma_2 m_{t-1} + \Gamma_3 y_{t-1} + E_{mt},$$

with enough exclusion restrictions to claim identification. He argued that these estimates were not grounded in theory — at least not in a theory that took dynamics, general equilibrium, and rational expectations seriously. In effect, Lucas argued that the coefficients in (14) and (15) were not casual, structural parameters but coefficients that were functions of deeper parameters. Mapping these coefficients onto those in (11) and (13) yields: $\Pi_1 = \frac{\alpha}{1+\alpha}$, $\Pi_2 = \frac{-\alpha\gamma_1}{1+\alpha}$, $\Pi_3 = \frac{-\alpha\gamma_2}{1+\alpha}$, $\Gamma_1 = 0$, $\Gamma_2 = \gamma_1$, and $\Gamma_3 = \gamma_2$.

Notice that $\Gamma_2$ and $\Gamma_3$just recapitulate the parameters of the policy function (11). In contrast $\Pi_1$, $\Pi_2$, and $\Pi_3$ are coefficients that shift with any change in one of the policy parameters. Equation (14) may have appeared to the macromodeler to be a structural relationship, but if Lucas's theory is correct it would not be invariant to policy manipulation, as Haavelmo and the Cowles Commission had insisted that a causal relationship should be. This is the *policy noninvariance proposition* or *Lucas critique.*

While the Lucas critique is a celebrated contribution to macroeconomic analysis, in this context it is secondary. It might be interpreted as little threat to the Cowles Commission program. Instead of identifying structure through exclusion restrictions, Lucas seems to show us that a more complicated, nonlinear identification is needed. The demands on *a priori* theoretical knowledge are higher, but they are of the same kind. Once the parameters are identified and estimated, counterfactual analysis can proceed using (11) and (13). In fact, the combination of the idea that only unexpected prices can have real effects (encapsulated in the "surprise-only" aggregate-supply function (9)) and rational expectations renders counterfactual analysis impossible. To see this, substitute (11) into (13) to yield

$$(16)\quad y_t = \left(\frac{1}{1+\alpha}\right)(\alpha\varepsilon_{mt} + \varepsilon_{yt}).$$

Equation (16) says that real GDP depends only on random shocks and on the shape of the aggregate-supply function (the parameter $\alpha$), but not in any way on the policy parameters $\gamma_1$ and $\gamma_2$. This is the formal derivation of the policy ineffectiveness proposition.

One might be inclined to dismiss policy-ineffectiveness as a very special and very likely non-robust result. In particular, economists typically place less confidence in dynamic theory than in equilibrium theory. But, as it turns out, policy ineffectiveness is a generic property of models with a surprise-only supply structure and rational expectations. Although there are alternatives, it characterizes a broad and attractive class of models.

The new classical approach can be seen as placing extreme faith in economic theory and, nevertheless, completely undermining the counterfactual analysis that causal analysis in the Cowles Commission framework was meant to support. Toward the end of the 1970s, macromodels were assaulted from the opposite extreme. Rejecting the typical identifying restrictions used in macromodels as literally "incredible" — not grounded in theory or other sure knowledge — Christopher Sims [1980] advocated the abandonment of the Cowles Commission program in favor of a nonstructural characterization of macroeconomic data, the so-called vector autoregression (VAR). A VAR might take a form such as

$$(17)\quad y_t = \Pi_1 y_{t-1} + \Pi_2 m_{t-1} + \Pi_3 p_{t-1} + \mathrm{E}_{yt},$$

$$(18)\quad m_t = \Gamma_1 y_{t-1} + \Gamma_2 m_{t-1} + \Gamma_3 p_{t-1} + \mathrm{E}_{mt},$$

$$(19)\quad p_t = \Lambda_1 y_{t-1} + \Lambda_2 m_{t-1} + \Lambda_3 p_{t-1} + \mathrm{E}_{pt}.$$

These equations should be understood as reduced forms. The coefficients are not structural and the error terms are not in general independent. While only a single lagged value of each variable is shown, in general these lags should be taken as standing for a set of longer (possibly infinite) lagged values.

Having eschewed structure, the Cowles Commission analysis of causal order is not available to the VAR modeler. VAR analysis, however, grew out of an older tradition in time-series statistics. Sims [1972] had introduced Granger's [1969] approach to causality into macroeconometric analysis. Granger's notion is temporal (causes must precede effects) and informational ($A$ causes $B$ if $A$ carries incremental information useful in predicting $B$). In (17), for instance, $m$ does not Granger-cause $y$ if the estimate of $\Pi_2$ is statistically insignificant.

Granger-causality does not suffer from the inferential problem: systems like (17)–(19) are easily estimated and the statistical tests are straightforward. But it is no help with the counterfactual problem, despite the ease with which many practicing economists have jumped from a finding of Granger-causality to an assumption of controllability. Just recalling that the reduced-form parameters of the VAR must be complicated functions of the underlying structure should convince us of the unsuitability of Granger-causal ordering to counterfactual analysis.

More specifically, Granger-causality is easily shown not to be necessary for counterfactual control. Imagine that structurally $m$ causes $y$, and that $m$ is chosen in such a way to offset any systematic (and, therefore, predictable) fluctuations in $y$, then $m$ will not be conditionally correlated with $y$ (i.e., $\Pi_2 = 0$). For example, suppose that the wheel of ship causes it to turn port or starboard, but that the helmsman tries to hold a perfectly steady course. The ship is buffeted by the waves and swells. Yet, if the helmsman is successful, the ship travels in straight line, while the wheel moves from side to side in an inverted counterpoint to the movements of the sea. There should be no observable correlation between the direction of the ship and that of the wheel along a single heading.

Granger-causality may not be sufficient in practice for counterfactual control. Suppose that *ceteris paribus* the higher the stock of money or the lower the demand for money, the higher the price level. Further suppose that the demand for money will be lower when people anticipate inflation (i.e., prices higher in future than today). If people know that the money stock will rise in future, then prices will rise in future, so that inflation is higher and the demand for money is lower today. In that case, prices will rise somewhat today as a fixed supply of money would otherwise exceed the lower demand. Now if people are better able to predict the future course of money than are econometricians, then the econometricians will find that prices today help to predict the future stock of money. In this case, prices Granger-cause money, even though money structurally causes prices *ex hypothesi* [Hoover, 1993, 2001, ch. 2].

One might counter this argument by saying that it simply shows that the econometrician has relied on incomplete information. It raises an important ontological issue for macroeconomics. Given the way that macroeconomic aggregates are formed, it is likely that there is *always* more information reflected in the behavior of people than is reflected in even an ideal aggregate. If that is so, then conflicts between structural and Granger-causality are inevitable.

A similar point applies to the assumption of time order implicit in Granger-causality: causes strictly precede effects. Practically, this is clearly not true. Contemporaneous Granger-causality easily shows up with data sampled at coarse intervals: months, quarters, years. But would it go away if we could take finer and finer cuts of the data? The existence of an aggregate such as real GDP as a stable, causally significant variable is threatened by taking too fine a cut. Real GDP measures the flow of goods and services — the amount of final products produced over a unit of time. While one could in principle add up such a quantity over intervals of an hour or a second, such an aggregate would fluctuate wildly with the time of day (think what happens to GDP at night or meal times) in a way that has no causal significance in macroeconomics. At any interval over which it is causally significant, the relationships may be contemporaneous rather than strictly time-ordered.

As already observed, the most developed theory is about static equilibrium or steady states. The relationships in such steady states are essentially timeless, yet this does not rule out a structural causal order (notice that there are no time subscripts in (3″) and (4″) above).

Economists have found it hard to get by with just Granger-causality and VARs. This is because they are not ready to abandon counterfactual analysis. The VAR program started at the nonstructural extreme. It has gradually added just enough structure to permit a minimal counterfactual analysis. A key feature of the VAR is that all variables are modeled as endogenous. Ultimately, it is only the errors (or "shocks") that cause movements in the variables. But the shocks in (17)–(19) are intercorrelated. What does it mean to evaluate, say, a money shock when any randomly selected value of $E_{mt}$ changes the probability distribution of $E_{yt}$ and $E_{pt}$ as well? In the wake of criticism from Cooley and LeRoy [1985], Leamer [1985] and others, Sims [1982; 1986] and other VAR analysts quickly admitted that contemporaneous structure was needed.

The preferred structures involved a linear transformations of the VAR that eliminated the correlation between the error terms. A typical structural VAR (or SVAR) takes the form:

$$(20)\quad y_t = \Pi_1 y_{t-1} + \Pi_2 m_{t-1} + \Pi_3 p_{t-1} + E_{yt},$$

$$(21)\quad m_t = \Gamma'_y y_t + \Gamma'_1 y_{t-1} + \Gamma'_2 m_{t-1} + \Gamma'_3 p_{t-1} + E'_{mt},$$

$$(22)\quad p_t = \Lambda'_m m_t + \Lambda'_y y_t + \Lambda'_1 y_{t-1} + \Lambda'_2 m_{t-1} + \Lambda'_3 p_{t-1} + E'_{pt}.$$

This system is recursively ordered with $y_t$ causing $m_t$, and $y_t$ and $m_t$ causing $p_t$. (The transformation of the VAR into an SVAR in which each variable is a direct cause of every variable below it in the recursive order is called *triangular* and is achieved through a *Choleski decomposition.*) At all other lags the system remains causally unstructured. But this minimal structure is enough to eliminate the correlations among the error terms. So now, a unique shock to the money equation or the price equation makes sense. The typical way of evaluating SVARs is to calculate the effects of a shock to a single equation, setting all other shocks to zero. These are called *impulse-response functions* and are usually displayed as a separate graph of the path of each variable in response to each shock.

Unfortunately, the Choleski transformation that generated the triangular ordering of the contemporaneous variables is not unique. There are six possible Choleski orderings. These are observationally equivalent in the sense that they are all transformations of the same reduced form. And with $n$ variables, as long as at least $n(n-1)/2$ restrictions are imposed to secure identification, there can be non-Choleski (i.e., not strictly recursive) orderings as well.

Not only does formal economic theory not often express a preference for a particular contemporaneous ordering, the founding sentiment of the VAR program was that theory was not to be trusted to provide structure. In practice macroeconomists have offered casual, often temporal, arguments to support particular orderings. For example, commodity prices are observed daily but the Federal Reserve's policy action must act slowly, so the commodity-price index must be ordered ahead of the Federal Reserve's targeted interest rate. These are mostly "Just So" stories and easily fall foul of some of the problems with temporal arguments that applied in the case of Granger-causality.

Structural VARs have become the dominant tool of empirical macroeconomics, often adopted by researchers who subscribe to the fundamental tenets of the new classical macroeconomics, even while distrusting the details of any theoretical model that could generate identifying restrictions. But the SVAR stands in an uneasy relationship with the new classical analysis.[6] If the Lucas critique is cor-

[6]On the tension within the new classical macroeconomics between the SVAR and structural approaches, see Hoover [2005].

rect, then are not the coefficients of the SVAR likely to shift with changes in economic policy, rendering the impulse-response functions inaccurate?

One response has been to admit the Lucas critique on principle but to argue that true changes in policy are rare [Sims, 1986]. Most monetary-policy actions are seen as realizations of particular processes. Impulse-response functions may prove to be accurate on this view; yet, once again, how is one to conduct counterfactual analysis? LeRoy [1995] has argued — unpersuasively in my view — that a policymaker can be seen as delivering a set of nonrandom shocks without violating rational expectations. Leeper and Zha [2003] do not go quite so far. They argue that there is a threshold of perceptibility for violations of randomness. Below that threshold (defined by the duration of the string and the size of the shocks), a policymaker can deliver a string of nonrandom shocks that do not trigger the Lucas critique and, yet, are economically significant.

The example of the new classical model in (9)–(13) demonstrates a generalizable point that in those cases in which the Lucas critique is relevant, policy is innocuous. Counterfactual analysis needs some structure, the SVAR does not provide enough. I return to this point in Section 5 below.

## 4 INFERRING CAUSES FROM INTERVENTIONS

The Cowles Commission approach put theory to the forefront in order to support counterfactual policy analysis. The skeptical SVAR program tried to do with as little theory as possible. The SVAR program sees the Lucas critique as a threat, since true changes in policy regime would vitiate the VAR estimates. My own approach in earlier work (summarized in Hoover 2001, chs. 8-10) is, in sense, to embrace the Lucas critique as a source of information about the underlying causal structure. The idea is an essential one for the structural or manipulability account: the causal relationship is defined as one that possesses a certain type of invariance. The previous equations used to illustrate Simon's account of causal order can be used to show this point.

Suppose that the system (7) and (8), in which $m$ causes $y$, reflect the true — but unknown — causal order. A policy intervention might be a change in the parameter $\delta$. The parameter may not be identified, and, so, the change will not be directly observed. Yet, we may know from, for example, institutional (or other nonstatistical) information that a policy change has occurred. Such a change would, however, not alter the parameters of (8). Now suppose that the system (7′) and (8′), which could be interpreted (incorrectly, of course) as reflecting $y$ causing $m$, is considered as an alternative. Again, if we know that a policy change has occurred, we see that *both* the coefficients of the $m$ equation (7′) and the $y$ equation (8′) have shifted. The stability of (7) and (8) against the instability of (7′) and (8′) argues in favor of the causal direction running from $m$ to $y$. There is no free lunch here. Where identification in structural models is achieved through *a priori* theoretical knowledge, identification of causal direction is achieved here through knowledge of *independent* interventions.

This invariance approach is closely related to the econometric notion of *superexogeneity* [Engle, Hendry, and Richard, 1983; Hendry 1995]. Superexogeneity is defined with reference to the stability of the statistical distribution in the face of interventions. My own approach emphasizes the importance of referring to the causal structure itself and is, in that sense, more fundamentally indebted to the Cowles Commission analysis of structure. The importance of this distinction can be seen in the new classical model whose solution is given in (11) and (13). On a superexogeneity standard, the instability of the coefficients of (13) in the face of a change in policy that (observable or not) changes $\gamma_1$ or $\gamma_2$, might be taken to count against $m_t$ contemporaneously causing $y_t$. Yet, on the Cowles Commission standard, the causal order clearly runs from $m_t$ to $y_t$. The important point is that the effects of interventions do not run against the arrow of causation. This is still true in this case, an intervention in the aggregate-supply process (a change in $\alpha$) does not result in any shift of the coefficients of (11).

Favero and Hendry [1992] and Ericsson and Hendry [1999] have used superexogeneity tests to check whether the Lucas critique matters in practice (see also [Ericsson and Irons, 1995]). This is exactly right. And if it does not — probably because expectations are not formed according to the rational-expectations hypothesis — then the inference of causal direction from invariance is easier. But if the Lucas critique in fact matters, then more subtlety is needed to tease causal direction out of information about invariance.

The key point is that it is not invariance but structure that defines causality; invariance only provides information that is often helpful in causal inference. There is always invariance at some level, but not always at the level of ordinary correlations or regression relationships.

## 5 GRAPH-THEORETIC ACCOUNTS OF CAUSAL STRUCTURE

Causal inference using invariance testing is easily overwhelmed by too much happening at once. It works best when one or, at most, a few causal arrows are in question, and it requires (in economic applications, at least) the good fortune to have a few — but not too many — interventions in the right parts of the structure. Over the past twenty years, a new analysis of causal structure based in graph theory has provided important theoretical and practical advances in causal analysis [Spirtes, Glymour, Scheines, 2000; Pearl, 2000]. These advances have, however, barely touched economics, yet they may help to overcome some of the limitations of the invariance approach.

In the Cowles Commission account an adequate econometric model has two distinct but related parts: the probability distribution of the variables and their causal structure. Spirtes *et al.*, [2000] and Pearl [2000] subscribe completely to this view of structure, but offer a more perspicacious way of keeping track of causal relations. Graphs have been used for more than a century to indicate causal structure, but only recently have the mathematical tools of graph theory given researchers a highly efficient way to express causal connections and to analyze and manipulate them in relations to the associated probability distributions.

The key idea of the graph-theoretic approach is related to Reichenbach's [1956] *principle of the common cause.* If $A$ and $B$ are probabilistically dependent, then either $A$ causes $B$ or $B$ causes $A$ or both have a common cause. The common cause might be a parent as in Figure 1 or a set of ancestors as in Figure 2. The *causal Markov condition* is closely related to Reichenbach's principle. Roughly, it says that if $\boldsymbol{C}$ is a set of ancestors to $A$ and $B$ and if $A$ and $B$ are not directly causally connected and are not probabilistically independent, then $A$ and $B$ are independent conditional on $\boldsymbol{C}$.

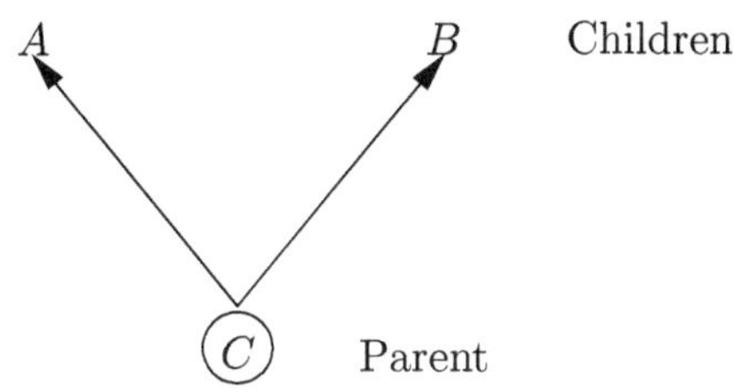


Figure 1. A Common Cause

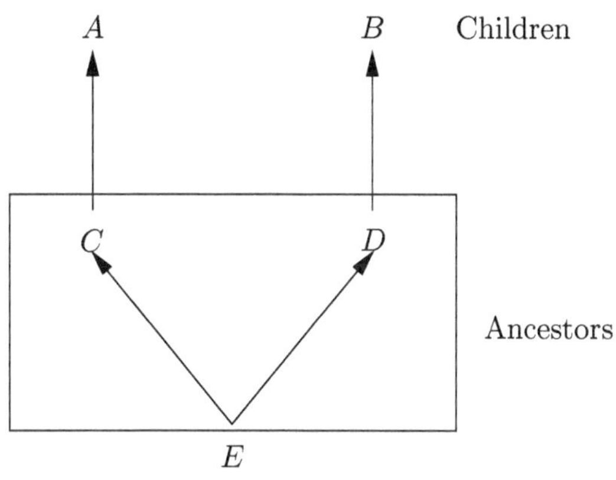


Figure 2. Common Ancestors

In practice, independence is usually judged by estimating (conditional) correlations among variables. This raises three issues. First, independence implies an absence of correlation, but an absence of correlation does not imply independence. (For an example, see Lindgren [1976, p. 136].)

Second, the independence relationships of interest are those of the population, and not the sample. Inference about sample correlations is statistical and thus reliable only subject to the usual caveats of statistical inference.

But, third, even measured correlations are meaningful only in the context of a maintained model of the probability distribution of the variables. This distinction becomes important when statistics that apply to *stationary* or *homogeneous* data interpreted as applying equally well to *nonstationary* or *inhomogeneous* data. For example, the well-known counterexample to Reichenbach's principle of the common causes due to Elliott Sober [1994; 2001] states that bread prices in England and sea levels in Venice, which *ex hypothesi*, are not causally connected are nonetheless correlated, violating Reichenbach's principle. Hoover [2003] shows that Sober implicitly assumes a stationary probability model when the best model would involve variables that either trend or follow a random walk. Time-series statisticians have known for a long time than ordinary measures of correlation fail to indicate probabilistic dependence in such models. Keeping these caveats in mind, we shall, for purposes of exposition, assume that correlations measure independence.

The idea of vanishing conditional correlation is also found in the notion of *screening*, familiar from the literature on probabilistic causation. If $\text{cor}(A, B) \neq 0$ and $\boldsymbol{C}$ is causally between $A$ and $B$ ($A \rightarrow \boldsymbol{C} \rightarrow B$ or $A \leftarrow \boldsymbol{C} \leftarrow B$), then $\text{cor}(A, B|\boldsymbol{C}) = 0$.

Conditioning can also induce correlation. The classic example if shown in Figure 3. Here $\text{cor}(A, B) = 0$, but $\text{cor}(A, B|C) \neq 0$. $C$ is called an *unshielded collider* on the path *ACB*. It is a "collider" because two causal arrows point into it, and it is "unshielded" because $A$ and $B$ are not directly causally connected. Figure 4 shows two shielded colliders. In each case $\text{cor}(A, B) \neq 0$.

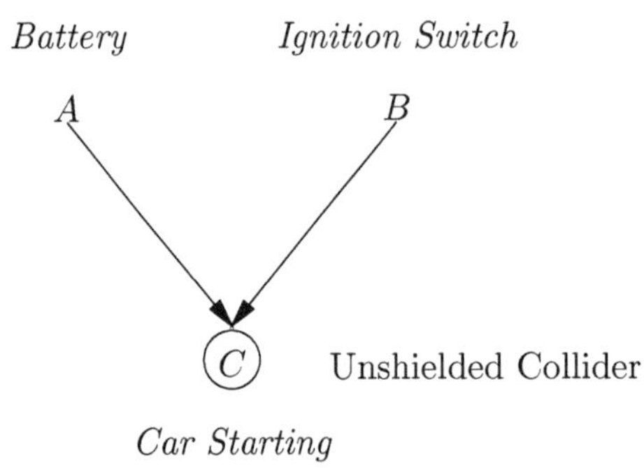


Figure 3. An Unshielded Collider

There is a number of algorithms that start with all the first-order correlations of a set of variables and search for patterns of unshielded colliders, common causes, and screens consistent with the observed correlations. The best known software for implementing these algorithms is the *Tetrad* program of Sprites *et al.* [1996].

The *Observational Equivalence Theorem* [Pearl, 2000, p. 19, Theorem 1.2.8; Sprites *et al.*, 2000, ch. 4] states that any probability distribution that can be faithfully represented in a causally sufficient, acyclical (or what econometricians would call a recursive) graph can equally well be represented by any other acycli-

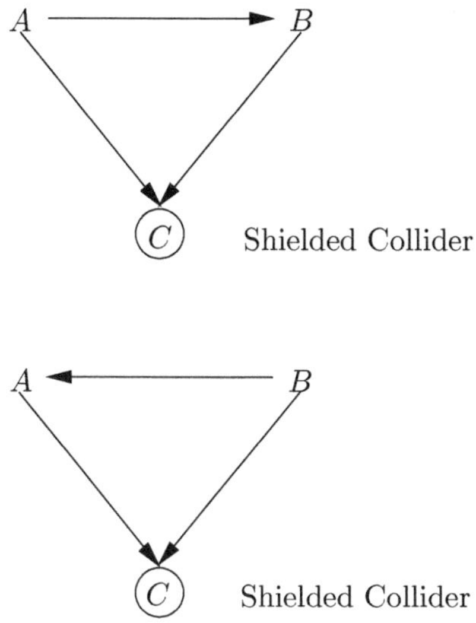


Figure 4. Shielded Colliders

cal graph that has the same skeleton (i.e., the same causal connections ignoring direction) and the same unshielded colliders. Such graphs form an observationally equivalent class. Figure 4 shows two observationally equivalent graphs. They have identical skeletons and no unshielded colliders. The following two graphs are also observationally equivalent:

(i) $A \rightarrow B \leftarrow C \rightarrow D$, and

(ii) $A \rightarrow B \leftarrow C \leftarrow D$

In each case, they have the same causal connections and an unshielded collider at $A$ on the path $ABC$ but differ in the direction of causation between $C$ and $D$. A program such as *Tetrad* can direct the arrows between $A$ and $B$ and between $B$ and $C$, it cannot direct the arrow between $C$ and $D$.

How can graph-theoretic ideas be applied to macroeconomics? One limitation is worth noting at the outset. Search algorithms based on the causal Markov condition can easily miss causal linkages in situations of optimal control (for example, the helmsman in section 3 who tries to steer on a constant heading) for exactly the same reason that Granger-causality tests failed: in the ideal case, the values of the control variable are chosen to minimize the variability of the controlled variable, and the correlation between them vanishes [Hoover, 2001, pp. 168–170]. Spirtes *et al.* [2000, p. 66] and Pearl [2000, p. 63] dismiss this as a "Lebesgue measure-zero" result. While this may do in some cases, it will not do in economics, because such cases arise naturally in economics when policies are chosen optimally to minimize the variability of a target. (Stabilizing GDP around its trend is much like stabilizing the movements of a ship around the preferred heading.) This, by no means, renders the approach or the algorithms useless, but it does serve remind us that it is the causal structure that is primary and not the tools that are used to uncover it. When tools do not work in some circumstances, other tools are needed.

Another problem in applying these tools to macroeconomic applications is that, in most cases, they have been developed with stationary, non-time-dependent data in mind. But macroeconomics works primarily with time-series and often with nonstationary time series. Swanson and Granger (1997) made a first pass at applying these methods to VARs. Their method can be explained with reference to the VAR in (17)-(19). Although the variables the variables themselves are time-dependent and possibly nonstationary, the error terms are not. If the VAR is correctly specified, then the residual errors are serially uncorrelated with a zero mean and constant variance. Instead of looking at the correlations among the primary variables, Swanson and Granger look at the correlations among their corresponding error terms, reinterpreted as the variables with their time-series dynamics filtered out.

Swanson and Granger limit themselves to causation in a line without considering common causes (e.g., $\tilde{Y}_t \rightarrow \tilde{M}_t \rightarrow \tilde{P}_t$, where the tildes over the variables indicate that they are filtered). They do not use the common algorithms available in *Tetrad*. Instead, they check for screening directly. This allows them to put the variables in order, but not to orient the arrows of causation. Like other VAR analysts, once they have selected an order, they rely on an argument of temporal priority to orient the chain of causation. Once they have determined the order among the filtered variables, they impose them on the original VAR and transform it into an SVAR.

## 6 A SYNTHETIC PROGRAM FOR UNCOVERING THE CAUSAL STRUCTURE OF VARS

I have been highlighting the tensions between causal inference and the counterfactual uses of causation and the parallel tensions between structural and nonstructural econometric models. But despite these tensions, my aim is essentially the irenic one of looking for the best in the various approaches. The best available account of causal order in economics is found in the Cowles Commission structural analysis. But as a strategy of causal inference it is infeasible. It provides no mechanism for effective feedback from empirical facts about the world to the theory that is used to structure the empirical measurement of causes. The VAR program has that much right. The identification assumptions of the Cowles Commission program *are* incredible. Unfortunately, the VAR program also needs structure to proceed. The questions are: how little structure can we get away with and still have something useful to say? and how are we to learn about structure? I want to conclude by briefly describing my research program on the causal orderings of VARs (joint work with Selva Demiralp and Stephen J. Perez). Our approach emphasizes the complementarity of various approaches to causation in macroeconomics.

We start where Swanson and Granger left off. Their useful idea is that the contemporaneous causal order of the SVARs can be determined by applying graph-theoretic methods to the filtered variables. Along with a small group of other researchers, we have extended their methods to consider recursive or acylical orderings more generally and not just simple causal chains (see [Demiralp and Hoover, 2003] and the references therein). For this we used the PC algorithm in *Tetrad*. What makes this a nontrivial exercise is that the algorithms in *Tetrad* are data search procedures in which the search path involves multiple sequential testing. Economists are famously wedded to a Neyman-Pearson statistical testing philosophy in which such "data mining" is viewed with the greatest skepticism. Previously, Hoover and Perez [1999; 2004] have investigated LSE search methodologies in Monte Carlo studies and have demonstrated that properly disciplined search algorithms can, despite economists fears, have extremely well-behaved statistical properties. Demiralp and Hoover [2003] demonstrate in a Monte Carlo study that the PC algorithm is very effective when applied to the SVAR at recovering the skeleton of underlying causal graphs and, provided that signal strengths are high enough, at oriented the edges as well.

The problem of whether or not (or to what degree) an algorithm identifies a causal order is not as straightforward as determining the distribution of a statistical test — the typical application of Monte Carlo studies. In particular, the effectiveness is likely to be highly dependent on the true underlying causal structure — something that cannot be known in advance in actual empirical applications. Demiralp, Hoover, and Perez [2008] have therefore developed a bootstrap method in which simulations can be adapted to actual data without knowing the true underlying structure. The bootstrap method starts by estimating a VAR, in the same way as one normally obtains the filtered variables, but then treats the error terms as a pool of random variates from which to construct a large number of simulated data sets. A causal search algorithm is then applied to each simulated data set and the chosen causal order is recorded. Statistics summarizing the frequency of occurrence of different causal structures are then used in the manner of Monte Carlo simulations in the earlier study to construct measures of the reliability of the causal identification for the specific case under study.

Graph-theoretic methods are attractive in the VAR context partly because they are well suited to handle relatively large numbers of variables. Nevertheless, as we have already seen, there may remain some observational equivalence, so that some causal links cannot be oriented. Macroeconomics quite commonly involves policy regime changes and structural breaks that can be exploited as in my own earlier approach to causal inference.

The impulse-response functions of VARs are known to be inaccurately estimated. In part, this arises because they include large numbers of lagged and often highly correlated regressors. Conditional on the contemporaneous causal order being held fixed, it should be possible to conduct systematic exclusion restrictions of variables and their lags from the different equations of the structure. These are effectively Granger-causality tests. The elimination of variables which are not

Granger-causal should help to sharpen the estimates.

This program of discovering the structure of the VAR from data helps to preserve the insight that *a priori* theory alone cannot get us too far. But let me end on a cautionary note. The discovery of the contemporaneous causal VAR through graph-theoretic methods supplemented by invariance-based methods and refined by Granger-causality tests may still not deliver enough structure to support counterfactual analysis.

To illustrate the problem, the structure in (11) and (13) is compatible with an SVAR in which contemporaneous money causes contemporaneous real GDP. And, as we have seen, it delivers policy ineffectiveness. It is a simple model, but policy ineffectiveness generalizes to complex models.

Since the 1970s, however, many — if not most — macroeconomists have come to believe that, in the short run, systematic monetary policy does have real effects. This might be because expectations are not formed rationally (or because economic actors follow rules of thumb that make no reference to expectations at all) or because slowly adjusting wages and prices undermine the surprise-only aggregate supply relationship. To make the point in a simple way, we can imagine that for either of these reasons (11) is replaced by

$$(23)\quad y_t = \beta m_t + \varepsilon_{yt},$$

which shows that money directly affects real GDP.

Notice that (11) and (23) form a system which is, again, consistent with an SVAR in which money is contemporaneously causally ordered ahead of real GDP. But the system (11) and (23) does not display policy ineffectiveness. Indeed, systematic monetary policy can be quite powerful in this system. Both the system (11) and (13) and the system (11) and (23) are compatible with the same SVAR. But the counterfactual experiment of what happens to real GDP when systematic monetary policy is changed (that is, what happens when $\gamma_1$ or $\gamma_2$) is changed are radically different: in the first case, nothing; in the second case, a great deal [Cochrane, 1998].

In a sense, we have come full circle. The initial problem was that we needed to assume that we already knew the causal structure in order to make measurements of causal strengths and to conduct counterfactual analysis. We argued that a variety of methods of causal inference may allow us to discover large parts of causal structure. And now we see that even if we are very successful, it still may not be enough for counterfactual analysis. None of our methods definitively resolves the initial tension.

It is, perhaps, not ultimately resolvable. Yet, I do not view the process as hopeless. Rather it is one of iterating between whichever pole is most immediately obstructing our progress. For example, in a more complicated version of the problem just set out Òscar Jordá and I [Hoover and Jordá, 2001] assume that the economy consists partly of agents who follow an analogue to (11) and (13) and partly agents who follow an analogue of (11) and (23). On the assumption that the shares of each type of agent is stable, we use changes in monetary policy regimes to recover the shares and to identify the underlying structure. This approach parallels closely the invariance-based methods of causal inference. But notice that it still relies on strong assumptions not only of the constancy of the shares, but also of the particular forms of the two aggregate-supply functions. We try to make these as generic and general as possible, but they cannot be perfectly general. So, we are again brought round to the conclusion that counterfactual analysis requires strong untestable, *a priori* assumptions, and to the open question: how do we know that they are true?

## BIBLIOGRAPHY

[Cartwright, 1989] N. Cartwright. *Nature's Capacities and Their Measurement.* Oxford: Clarendon Press, 1989.

[Cochrane, 1998] J. H. Cochrane. What Do the VARs Mean? Measuring the Output Effects of Monetary Policy, *Journal of Monetary Economics,* 41(7), 277-300, 1998.

[Cooley and LeRoy, 1985] T. F. Cooley and S. F. LeRoy. Atheoretical Macroeconometrics: A Critique, *Journal of Monetary Economics* 16(3), 283-308, 1985.

[Demiralp and Hoover, 2003] S. Demiralp and K. D. Hoover. Searching for the Causal Structure of a Vector Autoregression, *Oxford Bulletin of Economics and Statistics* 65(supplement), 2003, pp. 745-767, 2003.

[Demiralp *et al.*, 2008] S. Demiralp, K. D. Hoover, and S. J. Perez. A Bootstrap Method for Identifying and Evaluating a Structural Vector Autoregression, *Oxford Bulletin of Ecoomics and Statistics*, 70(4), 509–533, 2008.

[Engle *et al.*, 1983] R. F. Engle, D. F. Hendry and J.-F. Richard. Exogeneity, *Econometrica* 51(2), 277-304, 1983.

[Ericsson and Hendry, 1999] N. R. Ericsson and D. F. Hendry. Encompassing and Rational Expectations: How Sequential Corroboration Can Imply Refutation, *Empirical Economics* 24(1), pp. 1-21, 1999.

[Ericsson and Irons, 1995] N. R. Ericsson and J. Irons. The Lucas Critique in Practice: Theory Without Measurement, in Kevin D. Hoover (ed.) *Macroeconometrics: Developments, Tensions and Prospects.* Boston: Kluwer, pp. 263-312, 1995.

[Favero and Hendry, 1992] C. Favero and D. F. Hendry. Testing the Lucas Critique: A Review, *Econometric Reviews* 11(3), 265-306, 1992.

[Granger, 1969] C. W. J. Granger. Investigating Causal Relations by Econometric Models and Cross-Spectral Methods, *Econometrica*, 37(3), 424-438, 1969.

[Granger, 1980] C. W. J. Granger. Testing for Causality: A Personal Viewpoint, *Journal of Economic Dynamics and Control* 2(4), November, 329-352, 1980.

[Haavelmo, 1944] T. Haavelmo. The Probability Approach in Econometrics, *Econometrica* 12 (supplement), July, 1944.

[Hausman, 1992] D. M. Hausman. *The Inexact and Separate Science of Economics.* Cambridge: Cambridge University Press, 1992.

[Heckman, 2000] J. J. Heckman. Causal Parameters and Policy Analysis in Economics: A Twentieth Century Retrospective, *Quarterly Journal of Economics* 115(1), 45-97, 2000.

[Hendry, 1995] D. F. Hendry. *Dynamic Econometrics.* Oxford: Oxford University Press, 1995.

[Holland, 1986] P. W. Holland. Statistics and Causal Inference [with discussion], *Journal of the American Statistical Association* 81(396), 945-960, 1986.

[Hood and Koopmans, 1953] W. C. Hood and T. C. Koopmans, eds. *Studies in Econometric Method,* Cowles Commission Monograph 14. New York: Wiley, 1953.

[Hoover, 1988] K. D. Hoover. *The New Classical Macroeconomics: A Sceptical Inquiry.* Oxford: Basil Blackwell, 1988.

[Hoover, 1992a] K. D. Hoover. The Rational Expectations Revolution: An Assessment, *The Cato Journal* 12(1), 81-96, 1992.

[Hoover, 1992b] K. D. Hoover, ed. *The New Classical Macroeconomics* in 3 volumes. Aldershot: Edward Elgar, 1992.

[Hoover, 1993] K. D. Hoover. Causality and Temporal Order in Macroeconomics or Why Even Economists Don't Know How to Get Causes from Probabilities, *British Journal for the Philosophy of Science,* 44(4), 693-710, 1993.

[Hoover, 2001] K. D. Hoover. *Causality in Macroeconomics.* Cambridge: Cambridge University Press, 2001.

[Hoover, 2003] K. D. Hoover. Nonstationary time series, cointegration, and the principle of the common cause, *British Journal for the Philosophy of Science* 54(4), pp. 527-551, 2003.

[Hoover and Jordá, 2001] K. D. Hoover and Ò. Jordá. Measuring Systematic Monetary Policy, *Federal Reserve Bank of St. Louis Review* 83, 113-138, 2001.

[Hoover and Perez, 1999] K. D. Hoover and S. J. Perez. Data Mining Reconsidered: Encompassing and the General-to-Specific Approach to Specification Search, *Econometrics Journal* 2(2), 167-191, 1999.

[Hoover and Perez, 2004] K. D. Hoover and S. J. Perez. Truth and Robustness in Cross Country Growth Regressions, *Oxford Bulletin of Economics and Statistics* 66(5), 765-798, 2004.

[Hume, 1739] D. Hume. *A Treatise of Human Nature*, 1739. Page numbers refer to the edition edited by L.A. Selby-Bigge. Oxford: Clarendon Press, 1888.

[Hume, 1754] D. Hume. Of Money,' in *Essays: Moral, Political, and Literary*, 1754. Page references to the edition edited by Eugene F. Miller. Indianapolis: Liberty*Classics*, 1885.

[Hume, 1777] D. Hume. *An Enquiry Concerning Human Understanding*, 1777. Page numbers refer to L.A. Selby-Bigge, editor. *Enquiries Concerning Human Understanding and Concerning the Principles of Morals*, $2^{nd}$ edition. Oxford: Clarendon Press, 1902.

[Keynes, 1936] J. M. Keynes. *The General Theory of Money, Interest and Prices.* London: Macmillan, 1936.

[Klein, 1947] L. R. Klein. *The Keynesian Revolution.* New York: Macmillan, 1947.

[Koopmans, 1950] T. C. Koopmans. *Statistical Inference in Dynamic Economic Models*, Cowles Commission Monograph 10. New York: Wiley, 1950.

[Leamer, 1985] E. Leamer. Vector Autoregressions for Causal Inference? in Karl Brunner and Alan H. Meltzer (eds) *Understanding Monetary Regimes*, Carnegie-Rochester Conference Series on Public Policy, Vol. 22. North Holland, Amsterdam, pp. 225-304, 1985.

[Leeper and Zha, 2003] E. M. Leeper and Tao Zha. Modest Policy Interventions, *Journal of Monetary Economics* 50(8), pp. 1673-1700, 2003.

[Leontief, 1936] W. Leontief. The Fundamental Assumption of Mr. Keynes's Monetary Theory of Unemployment, *Quarterly Journal of Economics*, 51(1), 192-197, 1936.

[LeRoy, 1995] S. F. LeRoy. On Policy Regimes, in Kevin D. Hoover (ed.) *Macroeconometrics: Developments, Tensions and Prospects.* Boston: Kluwer, pp. 235-252, 1995.

[Lindgren, 1976] B. Lindgren. *Statistical Theory*, $3^{rd}$ ed., New York: Macmillan, 1976.

[Lucas, 1976] R. E. Lucas, Jr. Econometric Policy Evaluation: A Critique, in Karl Brunner and Allan H. Meltzer (eds.) *The Phillips Curve and Labor Markets.* Carnegie-Rochester Conference Series on Public Policy, vol. 11, Spring. Amsterdam: North-Holland, pp. 161-168, 1976.

[Marschak, 1953] J. Marschak. Economic Measurements for Policy and Predictions, in W. C. Hood and T. C. Koopmans (eds.) *Studies in Econometric Method,* Cowles Foundations Monograph no. 14. New York: Wiley, 1953.

[Mill, 1848] J. S. Mill. *Principles of Political Economy with Some of Their Applications to Social Philosophy*, 1948. Edited by. W.J. Ashley. London: Longman, Green, 1909.

[Mill, 1851] J. S. Mill. *A System of Logic, Ratiocinative and Deductive: Being a Connected View of the Principles of Evidence and the Methods of Scientific Investigation*, 3rd. ed., vol. I. London: John W. Parker, 1851.

[Mizon, 1995] G. E. Mizon. Progressive Modelling of Economic Time Series: The LSE Methodology, in Kevin D. Hoover (ed.) *Macroeconometrics: Developments, Tensions and Prospects.* Boston: Kluwer, pp. 107-170, 1995.

[Morgan, 1990] M. S. Morgan. *The History of Econometric Ideas.* Cambridge: Cambridge University Press, 1990.

[Murh, 1961] J. F. Muth. Rational Expectations and the Theory of Price Movements, *Econometrica* 29(3), 315-335, 1961.

[Pearl, 2000] J. Pearl. *Causality: Models, Reasoning, and Inference*, Cambridge University Press, Cambridge, 2000.

[Reichenbach, 1956] H. Reichenbach. *The Direction of Time*. Berkeley and Los Angeles: University of California Press, 1956.
[Sargent and Wallace, 1976] T. J. Sargent and N. Wallace. Rational Expectations and the Theory of Economic Policy, *Journal of Monetary Economics* 2(2), 169-183, 1976.
[Simon, 1953] H. A. Simon. Causal Ordering and Identifiability, in Herbert A. Simon, *Models of Man*. New York: Wiley 1957, ch. 1, 1953.
[Sims, 1972] C. Sims. Money, Income and Causality, reprinted in Robert E. Lucas, Jr. and Thomas J. Sargent (eds.) *Rational Expectations and Econometric Practice*. George Allen and Unwin, 1981, pp. 387-403, 1972.
[Sims, 1980] C. A. Sims. Macroeconomics and reality, *Econometrica*, Vol. 48, pp. 1-48, 1980.
[Sims, 1982] C. A. Sims. Policy Analysis with Econometric Models, *Brookings Papers on Economic Activity*, no. 1, 107-152, 1982.
[Sims, 1986] C. A. Sims. Are Forecasting Models Usable for Policy Analysis? *Federal Reserve Bank of Minneapolis Quarterly Review* 10(1), Winter, 2-15, 1986.
[Sober, 1994] E. Sober. The Principle of the Common Cause, in *From a Biological Point of View*, Cambridge: Cambridge University Press, pp. 158-74, 1994.
[Sober, 2001] E. Sober. Venetian Sea Levels, British Bread Prices, and the Principle of the Common Cause, *British Journal for the Philosophy of Science*, 52(2), pp. 331-46, 2001.
[Spanos, 1995] A. Spanos. On Theory Testing in Econometrics: Modeling with Nonexperimental Data, *Journal of Econometrics* 67(1), 189-226, 1995
[Spirtes *et al.*, 2000] P. Spirtes, C. Glymour, and R. Scheines. *Causation, Prediction, and Search*, $2^{nd}$ edition. Cambridge, MA: MIT Press, 2000.
[Spirtes *et al.*, 1996] P. Spirtes, R. Scheines, C. Meek, T. Richardson, C. Glymour, H. Hoijtink and A. Boomsma. *TETRAD 3: Tools for Causal Modeling*, program (beta version, October 1996) and user's manual on the worldwide web at `http://www.phil.cmu.edu/tetrad/tet3/master.htm`
[Suppes, 1970] P. Suppes. A Probabilistic Theory of Causality, *Acta Philosophica Fennica*, Fasc. XXIV, 1970.
[Swanson and Granger, 1997] N. R. Swanson and C. W. J. Granger. Impulse Response Functions Based on a Causal Approach to Residual Orthogonalization in Vector Autoregressions, *Journal of the American Statistical Association* 92(437), 357-367, 1997.
[Woodward, 2003] J. Woodward. *Making Things Happen*. Oxford: Oxford University Press, 2003.

# NATURALISM AND THE NATURE OF ECONOMIC EVIDENCE

Harold Kincaid

There has been much interesting work done in the philosophy and social studies of science on the role of evidence within science. That work tries to avoid the extremes of radical social constructivism and the logic of science ideal of the positivists. It also tries to look at evidence as it is actually used in the sciences. This chapter attempts to apply this general perspective to economics. Section 1 discusses general issues about evidence. Section 2 looks at those issues as they arise concerning observational evidence in economics. Section 3 then turns to a similar discussion about experimental economics. Section 4 applies the general perspective developed in the first three sections to questions about evaluating evidence for models with unrealistic or false assumptions.

## 1 NATURALISM AND EVIDENCE

In this section I sketch a general framework for thinking about evidence, viz. naturalism, that has widespread acceptance in the philosophy of science. I describe the basic idea, trace out some of its implications, and illustrate it by discussing two philosophy of science controversies—about the role of prediction vs. accommodation and the dispute between Bayesians and frequentists — that are particularly relevant to economics.

The dominant trend in current philosophy of science is naturalized epistemology. Naturalism has various interpretations, some logically weaker and some stronger. A weak version is the claim that

1. empirical evidence is relevant to philosophical accounts of epistemic concepts

A stronger version of naturalism claims that:

2. philosophical accounts of epistemic concepts are to be judged solely by the methods, standards and results of the sciences.

Of course,each of these is open to multiple interpretation and (2) in particular is a slogan summarizing numerous related but distinct ideas.

A good representative of the weak form of naturalism is found in reliablism as developed in traditional analytic epistemology. Reliablism of this form holds that a belief is justified iff it is produced by a reliable process, i.e. one producing truth.

Handbook of the Philosophy of Science. Volume 13: Philosophy of Economics.
Volume editor: Uskali Mäki. General editors: Dov M. Gabbay, Paul Thagard and John Woods.

Obviously on this view empirical evidence about which processes are reliable is essential. However, this view does not instantiate the second thesis. Why? The evidence for the reliablist account is the considered judgments of philosophers about what is and is not justified.[1] Typically these judgments are taken to provide a priori truths about our fundamental epistemic concepts. Strong naturalism denies that 1) there are any a priori truths about epistemology that do real work in telling us what to believe ($x$ is justified iff it is justified is perhaps an a priori truth but an unhelpful one) and 2) that the considered judgments of philosophers provides any very useful evidence about anything.[2]

Strong naturalism thus argues that developing accounts of good evidence and other epistemic notions is part and parcel of the scientific understanding of the world. This immediately makes psychology, the social sciences, and history of science fundamental to understanding the nature and role of evidence. This project undergirds much of the work in contemporary science studies. That research goes in a variety of different directions, some purely descriptive and others both descriptive and normative. I will not canvass all the various positions.[3] However, there are some general morals common to most of this work that I want to rely on in this chapter in analyzing issues about evidence in economics. They include:

1. looking for a logic of science — a universal, formal a priori set of inferences rules — is often misguided

2. claims about good inferences often depend on domain specific substantive assumptions — for example, "simplicity" is often not a purely logical notion but a substantive assertion about the world[4]

3. identifying the social processes involved in a given discipline can be an important part of understanding how evidence works in that field and can sometimes reveal that the rhetoric of a discipline does not match its practice

4. evidence claims are arguments in that they rest on a variety of background assumptions which are essential for their force

I want to flesh out this general perspective somewhat by applying it to two standard debates in the philosophy of science which are particularly relevant to controversies in economic methodology. My general argument will be that these debates turn on presuppositions that ought to be rejected on naturalist grounds.

There is a long standing dispute in statistics between Bayesian and frequentist approaches. General positions have emerged in the philosophy of science in the last two decades refining these stances [Howson and Urbach, 2005; Mayo, 1996]. Both are entirely accounts of confirmation and have little or nothing to say about

[1]Goldman [2001], a well-known advocate of reliablism and "scientific epistemology" (his term), nonetheless still clings to the tradition project of analytic epistemology of balancing principles against considered judgements in providing an account of justification.

[2]See Bishop and Trout [2005] for a good contemporary summary.

[3]See Hands [2002] for a good general survey.

[4]As Elliott Sober [1991] argues in his account of simplicity in phylogenetic inference.

other scientific virtues such as explanation. Both I will argue still embody the logic of science ideal.

The Bayesian approach of course starts from Bayes' theorem, perhaps best put as

$$p(H/E) = p(h) \times p(e/h)|p(h) \times p(e/h) + p(h_1) \times p(e/h_1) + \ldots + p(h_n) \times p(e/h_n)$$

which tells us that the probability of a hypothesis, given a set of data, depends on:

> prior probability of the hypothesis and its competing alternatives (the priors)

the probability of the data given the hypothesis and given its competing alternatives (the likelihoods)

Probability takes a value between 0 and 1, the likelihoods being equal to 1 when the hypothesis logically entails the evidence. Given this information, we can theoretically determine if the data supports the hypothesis by asking if $p(H/E) > p(H)$. We can determine how much the evidence supports the hypothesis over alternatives, measured as $p(E/H) \times p(h)|p(E/notH) \times p(\text{not } H)$ which is known as the likelihood ratio.

"Probability" can be read in different ways. In the starkest form probability is taken as "degree of belief" or "level of confidence, " producing what is known as (misleadingly I shall argue) subjective Bayesianism. Objective Bayesianism would eschew the degree of belief talk and apply Bayes' theorem using known relative frequencies such as prevalence in a given population.

The Bayesian approach has several things going for it. Bayes' theorem is a logical truth and violating it is inconsistent. Moreover, various intuitive judgments about evidence can seemingly be understood in a Bayesian framework. For example, it provides a natural explanation for why diverse evidence is to be preferred. Since the probability of getting the same result after one test goes up, further evidence of the same sort has a decreasing marginal effect. Getting positive evidence from an entirely different case does not have this problem.

There are various other issues about confirmation that can be illuminated by looking at them through the lens of Bayes' theorem [Howson and Urbach, 2005].

There are various criticisms of Bayesian approaches to confirmation, but the most fundamental one concerns the key difference between Bayesian and frequentists — the nature of probability. Frequentists want an account of confirmation based on objective error probabilities, where objective error probabilities are defined by the relative frequencies in indefinitely many repetitions of a testing procedure. Single hypotheses thus do not have probabilities, but we can be assured that a particular claim is warranted if it passes a test that has high probability in repeated uses of accepting the hypothesis when it is true and rejecting it when it is false [Mayo, 1996].[5] According to the frequentists, subjective Bayesian approaches make confirmation hopeless subjective, a problem their approach does not have.

[5]This is the charitable interpretation of Mayo based on the way she applies her idea of a

Related to the Bayesian vs. frequentist controversy is the important question whether hypotheses that have been designed to accommodate known data are less well confirmed than those that predict novel data. Those who deny there is a difference argue that all that matters is the content of the hypothesis and evidence — when the investigator came to know the evidence is irrelevant. A scientist who advances a hypothesis that predicts data he did not know about is in no different situation than one who advances the same hypothesis knowing the evidence. Either the evidence does or does not support the hypothesis.

The argument for a difference turns on the fact that accommodation seems much easier than prediction. A compelling example is curve fitting: one can find an hypothesis that predicts the data simply by drawing a line through all the data points. That is much easier and less informative, the idea, goes than predicting a new data point you do not yet have.

The naturalist response to these debates that I would favor is essentially to curse both houses. Implicit in arguments from either side is the logic of science ideal and much appeal to intuitions. Either accommodation is always inferior or it is always equivalent. Confirmation can be captured by logical rules — described by Bayes' theorem in one case and by the deductive asymptotic traits of sampling from a frequency distribution in the other. Naturalists deny that we can get so much work out of so little. Confirmation is a complex, contextual process that involves a host of factors that cannot be captured in simple rules such as "update beliefs according to Bayes' theorem" or "minimize Type I and Type II errors."

Not surprisingly advocates on both sides resort to some unhelpful rhetoric in the face of complexity. This is illustrated by the ironic fact that Bayesians [Howson and Urbach, 2005] typically deny that facts about psychological states are relevant in the accommodation vs. prediction debate but then want to relativize confirmation entirely to an individual's prior beliefs and that frequentists accuse Bayesians of subjectivism while advocating the view that psychological states can matter because they influence the characteristics of a test [Mayo, 1996].

Let's look first at the Bayesian vs. frequentist debate. The charge of "subjectivism" against the Bayesians is overplayed. Every use of "objective" statistical measures depends on a host of prior assumptions, not all of which can be evaluated by the favored measure of long run error characteristics. The most obvious such assumption is about the possible hypotheses to consider in the first place. Bayesians are in fact much more explicit about those assumptions and can report the effects they have on the inferences drawn. In that sense they are more "objective." Moreover, they can certainly use the "objective" facts about sampling from populations to estimate likelihoods.

Perhaps the most serious issue raised by Bayesians against the frequentists concerns the propriety of making decisions about what to believe in specific instances from long term error characteristics. The problem is that the asymptotic charac-

stringent test. Her actual formulation is that a stringent test is one which requires that (1) the hypothesis fit the data and (2) the the probability of passing the test when the hypothesis is false is low. So far as I can see this does not on its own say anything about the false positive rate.

teristics of a test are an uncertain guide to its use in a single instance. Long-run frequencies in infinite repetitions by themselves are consistent with finite samples entirely lacking the asymptotic characteristics. It is not clear that there is an adequate frequentist response to this problem.[6]

A second important problem is that deciding what to believe based on a stringent frequentist test can easily be shown to result in error because it embodies the fallacy of ignoring the base rate. Consider a diagnostic test that has both very low false negative rate and false positive rate. This means that $p(E/H)|p(E/\text{not } H)$ is very large and that the test is stringent. Yet if the disease in question is very rare in the population and no more is known than that the patient comes from this population (no other risk factors are known), the probability that the patient has the disease, given a positive result, is extremely small and thus not at all good evidence that they have the disease. The base rate has been ignored.

What is clear is that both the Bayesians and frequentists claim more than their methods warrant. For the frequentists that is fairly obvious from the problems mentioned above resulting from the need to assess the base rate, to specify the set of competing hypotheses, and to assure that the criteria (e.g. independent draws) of the frequentist tests are satisfied.[7] The urge to go beyond what your formalism can warrant is also strong in the Bayesian tradition. Something which has not generally been noted is that Bayes' theorem is silent on many fundamental methodological controversies. Inference to the best explanation [Day and Kincaid, 1994] is a prime example in this regard. It is commonly thought that explanatory power has some role to play in confirmation. If that is to mean anything more than the trivial claim the predictive power is important in confirmation, then some substantive notion of explanation needs to be invoked. Citing causes is a natural direction to go. However, factoring that kind of information requires considerable background knowledge, knowledge that will arguably be domain specific. Bayes' theorem is silent on these issues.

So the proper naturalist response is that the place of evidence in science is not going to be capatured by Bayes' theorem or by focusing on type I and II errors alone. Both of these elements must be incorporated in a complex argument employing contextual background knowledge.

Thus the naturalist approach to the accommodation/prediction debate is again to reject the terms in which it is framed. In its usual format, the debate assumes that there is one right answer to the question that holds in all epistemic situations and that the right way to decide the issues is by means of intuitions about examples and counter examples. Assuming one right answer implicitly presupposes the logic of science ideal. Deciding the issue by appeal to intuitions assumes the conceptual analysis approach that naturalism rejects in favor of an epistemol-

[6]There is work on finite samples that might be a partial to this problem, but mainstream statistical practice relies heavily on the asymptotic characteristics of statistics.

[7]Another, quite serious problem that establishes this is the "file draw problem. Journals frequently do not report null results. So if there is no effect, correlation, etc. in reality but twenty investigators do independent significance tests at the .05 level, one in twenty will find a positive result and get published.

ogy that is continuous with the sciences. Simply put, the naturalist stance on the prediction/accommodation debate is that it is an empirical issue, one that is unlikely to have a uniform answer. Some kinds of accommodating may produce reliable results, others not. Some kinds or instances of predicting unknown data may providing especially compelling evidence, some may not. It is easy enough to construct cases where the fact that the investigator knew the data in advance suggests bias and equally easy to find cases where it is irrelevant. Typically Bayesians deny that there is anything wrong with accommodation and frequentists believe there is [Howson and Urbach, 2005; Mayo, 1996]. However, in their more subtle moments, both acknowledge that context matters and that there is no universal answer to the question as generally framed.[8] This is in keeping with the general naturalist view sketched above about the Bayesian-frequentist debate. I will illustrate this approach in the concrete in the next section when we discuss data mining in econometrics.

## 2 NONEXPERIMENTAL EVIDENCE

The debates sketched above certainly show up in discussions of the force and proper role of nonexperimental evidence in economics. In this section I review some of the issues and argue for a naturalist inspired approach. I look at some standard econometric practices, particularly significance testing and data mining.

The logic of science ideal is heavily embodied in the widespread use and the common interpretation of significance tests in econometrics. There are both deep issues about the probability foundations of econometrics that are relevant here and more straight forward — if commonly missed — misrepresentations of what can be shown and how by significance testing. The naturalist stance throughout is that purely logical facts about probability have only a partial role and must be embedded in complex empirical arguments.

The most obvious overinterpretation of significance testing is that emphasized by McCloskey and others [McCloskey and Ziliak, 2004]. A statistically significant result may be an economically unimportant result; tiny correlations can be significant and will always be in large samples. McCloskey argues that the common practice is to focus on the size of p-values to the exclusion of the size of regression coefficients.[9]

Another use of statistical significance that has more serious consequences and is overwhelmingly common in economics is using statistical significance to separate hypotheses into those that should be believed and those that should be rejected and to rank believable hypothesis according to relative credibility (indicated by

[8] Mayo is a careful attempt to sort out different kinds of novel predictions that by itself goes some way in deconstructing the traditional debate.

[9] Hoover and Siegler [2007] raise serious doubts about the veracity of McCloskey's data. However, I think it is obvious that it is common to reject a variable on the grounds of no statistical significance regardless of the effect size, leading to situations where an apparent large effect that is significant at the .06 level being ignored.

the phrase "highly significant" which comes to "my $p$ value is smaller than yours"). This is a different issue from McCloskey's main complaint about ignoring effect size. This interpretation is firmly embedded in the practice of journals and econometric textbooks.

Why is this practice mistaken? For a conscientious frequentist like Mayo, it is a mistake because it does not report the result of a stringent test. Statistical significance tests tell us about the probability of rejecting the null when the null is in fact true. They tell us the false positive rate. But a stringent test not only rules out false positives but false negatives as well. The probability of this is measured by 1-minus the power of the test. Reporting a low false positive rate is entirely compatible with a test that has a very high false negative rate. However, the power of the statistical tests for economic hypotheses can be difficult to determine because one needs credible information on possible effect sizes before hand (another place frequentists seem to need priors). Most econometric studies, however, do not report power calculations. Introductory text books in econometrics [Barreto and Howland, 2006] can go without mentioning the concept; a standard advanced econometrics text provides one brief mention of power which is relegated to an appendix [Greene, 2003]. Ziliak and McCloskey find that about 60% of articles in their sample from American Economic Review do not mention power. So one is left with no measure of the false negative rate and thus still rather in the dark about what to believe when a hypothesis is rejected.

Problems resulting from the lack of power analyses are compounded by the fact that significance tests also ignore the base rate or prior plausibility. Sometimes background knowledge can be so at odds with a result that is statistically significant that it is rational to remain dubious. This goes some way in explaining economists conflicted attitude towards econometrics. They are officially committed to the logic of science ideal in the form of decision by statistical significance. Yet they inevitably use their background beliefs to evaluate econometric results, perhaps sometimes dogmatically and no doubt sometimes legitimately, though the rhetoric of significance testing gives them no explicit way to do so.

A much deeper question about the statistical significance criterion concerns the probability foundations of econometric evidence. This is a topic that has gotten surprisingly little discussion. Statistical inferences are easiest to understand when they involve a chance set up [Hacking, 1965]. The two standard types of chance set ups invoked by statisticians are random samples from a population and random assignment of treatments. It is these chance set ups that allow us to draw inferences about the probability of seeing particular outcomes, given a maintained hypothesis. Current microeconometric studies that depend on random samples to collect survey data do have a foundation in a chance set up and thus the probability foundations of their significance claims are clear. The problem, however, is that there is much econometric work that involves no random sample nor randomization.

This lack of either tool in much economic statistics discouraged the use of inferential statistics until the "Probability Revolution" of Haavelmo [1944]. Haavelmo suggested that we treat a set of economic data as a random draw from a hypothetical population consisting of other realizations of the main economic variables along with their respective measurement errors and minor unknown causes. However, he gives no detailed account of what this entails nor of what evidence would show it valid. The profession adopted the metaphor and began using the full apparatus of modern statistics without much concern for the question whether there is a real chance set up to ground inferences. The practice continues unabetted today.

One fairly drastic move made by some notable econometricians such as Leamer and commentators such as Kuezenkamp is to take a staunch antirealist position. Thus Leamer [Hendry *et al.*, 1990] doubts that there is a true data generating process. Kuezenkamp [2000], after surveying many of the issues mentioned here, concludes that econometric methods are tools to be used, not truths to be believed. If the goal of econometrics is not to infer the true nature of the economic realm but only to give a perspicuous rendering of the data according to various formal criteria, then worries about the chance set up are irrelevant. Obviously this is surrendering the idea of an economic science that tells us about causes and possible policy options. It is seems that when the logic of science ideal confronts difficulties in inferring successfully about the real world, the latter is being jettisoned in favor of the former.

The best defense given by those still interested in the real world probably comes from the practices of diagnostic testing in econometrics. The thought is that we can test to see if the data seem to be generated by a data generating process with a random component. So we look at the properties of the errors or residuals in the equations we estimate. If the errors are orthogonal to the variables and approximate a normal distribution, then we have evidence for a randomizing process. The work of Spanos [2000] and Hoover and Perez [1999], for example, can be seen as advocating a defense along these lines.

These issues are complicated and a real assessment would be a chapter in itself. But I can sketch some issues and naturalist themes. First, if tests of statistical significance on residuals are seen as decisive evidence that we have good reason to believe that we have a random draw from many different hypothetical realizations, then we confront all the problems about over interpreting significance tests. These tests have the same problem pointed out about using significance tests as an epistemic criterion. We do not have a grip on the prospects for error unless we have at least a power calculation and background knowledge about prior plausibility. So we do not know what to infer from a diagnostic test of this sort. Moreover, there is also the problem concerning what is the chance set up justifying this diagnostic test in the first place. Taken in frequentist terms, the test statistic must be some kind of random draw itself. So the problem seems to be pushed back one more step.

However, despite these problems, there is perhaps a way to take diagnostic testing as a valuable aid in justifying probability foundations if we are willing to make it one component in an overall empirical argument of the sort that naturalists think is essential. A significance test on residuals for normality or independence, for example, can be seen as telling us the probability of seeing the evidence in hand if it had been generated from a process with a random component. That does not ensure us that the hypothesis was plausible to begin with nor tell us what the prospects of false positives are, but it does give us evidence about $p(E/H =$randomly generated residuals). If that information is incorporated into an argument that provides these other components, then it can play an important role. In short, significance test is not telling us that we have a random element in the data generating process — it is telling us what the data would like if we did.

These issues have natural connections to debates over "data mining" and I want to turn to them next. A first point to note is that "data mining" is often left undefined. Let's thus begin by distinguishing the different activities that fall under this rubric:

### *Finding patterns in a given data set*

This is the sense of the term used by the various journals and societies that actively and positively describe their aim as data mining. "Finding patterns" has to be carefully distinguished from the commonly used phrase "getting all the information from the data" where the latter is sufficiently broad to include inferences about causation and about larger populations. Finding patterns in a data set can be done without using hypothesis testing . It thus does not raise issues of accommodation and prediction nor the debates over probability between the Bayesians and frequentists.

### *Specification searches*

Standard econometric practice involves running multiple regressions that drop or add variables based on statistical significance and other criteria. A final equation is thus produced that is claimed to be better on statistical grounds.

### *Diagnostic testing of statistical assumptions*

Testing models against data often requires making probability assumptions, e.g. that the residuals are independently distributed. As Spanos [2000] argues, this should not be lumped with the specification searches described above — there is no variable dropping and adding based on tests of significance.

Senses 1 and 3 I would argue are clearly unproblematic in principle (execution is always another issue). The first form is noninferential and thus uncontroversial. The third sense can be seen as instance of the type of argument for ruling out chance that I defended above for the use of significance tests. Given this interpretation — rather than one where the results all by themselves are thought to confirm a hypothesis — this form of data mining is not only defensible but essential.

The chief compelling complaint about data mining concerns the difficulties of interpreting the frequentist statistics of a final model of a *specification* search.

Such searches involve multiple significance tests. Because rejecting a null at a p value of .05 means that one in twenty times the null will be wrongly rejected, the multiple tests must be taken into account. For simple cases there are various ways to correct for such multiple tests whose reliability can be analytically verified; standard practice in biostatistics, for example, is to use Bonferroni correction [1935] which in effect imposes a penalty for multiple testing in terms of p values required. As Leamer points out, it is generally the case that there are no such analytic results to make sense of the very complex multiple hypothesis testing that goes on in adding and dropping variables based on statistical significance — the probability of a type I error is on repeated uses of the data mining procedure is unknown despite the fact that significance levels are reported.[10]

Mayer [2000] has argued that the problems with data mining can best be solved by simply reporting all the specifications tried. However, fully describing the procedure used and the models tested does not solve the problem. We simply do not know what to make of the final significance numbers (nor the power values either on the rare occasions when they are given) even if we are given them all.

Hoover and Perez [1999] provides an empirical defense that might seem at first glance a way around this problem. Perhaps we do not need a frequentist interpretation of the test statistics if we can show on empirical grounds that specific specification search methods,. e.g. Hendry's general to specific modelling, produce reliable results. Hoover, using Monte Carlo simulations to produce data where the true relationship is known, shows that various specification search strategies, particularly general to specific modeling, can do well in finding the right variables to include.

However, there is still reason to be skeptical. First, Hoover's simulations assume that the true model is in the set being tested (cf. [Ganger and Timmermann, 2000]). That would seem not to be the case for many econometric analyses where there are an enormous number of possible models because of the large number of possible variables and functional forms. There is no a priori reason this must always be the case, but once again, our inferences depend crucially on our background knowledge that allows us to make such judgments. These assumptions are particularly crucial when we want to get to the correct causal model, yet there is frequently no explicit causal model offered. Here is thus another case where the frequentist hope to eschew the use of priors will not work.

Moreover, Hoover's simulations beg important questions about the probabilistic foundations of the inferences. His simulations involve random sampling from a known distribution. Yet in practice distributions are not known and we need to provide evidence that we have random sample. These are apparently provided in Hoover's exercise by fiat since the simulations assume random samples [Spanos, 2000].

[10]There are sophisticated methods in the general statistical literature that can produce usable results in specification searches, e.g. leave one out estimators. These seem not to have made it into the econometric literature.

However, the problems identified here with specification searches have their roots in frequentist assumptions, above all the assumption that we ought to base our beliefs solely on the long run error characteristics of a test procedure. The Bayesians argue, rightly on my view, that one does not have to evaluate evidence in this fashion. They can grant that deciding what to believe on the basis of, say, repeated significance tests can lead to error. Yet they deny that one has to (and, more strongly and unnecessary to the point I am making here, can coherently) make inferences in such a way. Likelihoods can be inferred using multiple different assumptions about the distribution of the errors and a pdf calculated. What mistakes you would make if you based your beliefs solely on the long term error rates of a repeated significance testing procedure is irrelevant for such calculations. Of course, Bayes' theorem still is doing little work here; all the force comes from providing an argument establishing which hypotheses should be considered and what they entail about the evidence.

So data mining can be defended. By frequentists standards data mining in the form of specification searches cannot be defended. However, those standards ought to be rejected as decisive criterion in favor of giving a complex argument. When Hoover and others defend specification searches on the empirical grounds that they can work rather than on the grounds of their analytic asymptotic characteristics, they are implicitly providing one such argument.

## 3 EXPERIMENTAL EVIDENCE

I turn in this section to look at some issues concerning experimental evidence in economics. My framework is again the naturalist one outlined in Section 1. I begin by describing some further naturalist ideas that are particularly relevant to thinking about experimental evidence.

I take the following ideas about experimental science as reasonably well established:[11]

Experimental practices tend to take on a life of their own. Scientists, like everybody else, are plying their trade — looking to see how past successes can be turned into new but related projects. Past successful practices become part of the experimentalist's culture and often come to be "black boxed", i.e. taken for granted with the substantive assumptions becoming invisible. Methods are thus enshrined as fundamental and unassailable — -as following from the logic of science. New areas of experimentation will often borrow methods that have obtained this status from other disciplines. Experimental practice then becomes the process of looking for ways of applying those methods. A tight connection to testing theory in the relevant domain often is not paramount. The processes of deciding when experiments are successful is not a matter of pure scientific method and is generally social in nature. That does not mean that these decisions are

[11]Important discussions are Gooding *et. al*, [1999], Radder [2003], Gallison [1987], Collins [2004].

made without reason or evidence but rather that they are not entailed by either the general logic of science nor by the theories of the relevant disciplines. Decisions have to be made; they (1) usually require domain specific substantive principles and (2) are generally collective decisions. To evaluate a line of experimental work thus requires more than the tools of logic and theory; it requires an assessment of how those collective decisions are made and the empirical principles invoked.

I want to argue that these naturalist morals are useful for thinking about some aspects of experimental economics. Let me first sketch a standard story that experimental economists tell themselves about what they do. Borrowing from experimental psychology, they distinguish two different ways results might be valid: internally and externally. For experimental economists, internal validity typically means that the experimental treatment really did have the outcome observed. External validity concerns the question whether valid experimental results can be generalized to the world outside the lab.

Experimental economists, the story continues, have successfully identified a set of methodological tenets that help ensure internal validity, and that has been their primary goal. External validity is a different question and more difficult. That does not, however, detract from the value of experimental work for two reasons. Economic theory can still be tested if the experimental setup realizes the variables it describes, and experiments can do just that. Moreover, experiments can show that some phenomena are robust in the experimental situation, thus forcing theory to propose explanations. All of this can be done without worrying about external validity.[12]

This picture reflects my naturalist morals about experimentation in multiple ways. On the sociological plane, it provides a rationale for experimental practices that have definitely taken on a life of their own. The sharp internal/external distinction makes it possible to keep all the questions in the lab if need be. That distinction also provides a foundation for the claim that there are universal methods (such as randomization) that are available to control inferences, usually methods for inferring *internal* validity. Internal validity is seen as the domain of experimental control that allows for precision; external validity is much less discussed, though the ideal of formal, logical rules for evaluation is still strong (see [Samuelson, 2005]).

However, following the contextualist picture described above, I think this story misrepresents — in ways typical of experimental sciences in general — the actual situation. The universal inference rules are not really so universal and indefeasible. The internal/external distinction is not so sharp. The actual process of producing credible experimental results is much more complicated and contestable than is advertised in the official story experimentalists tell themselves. Seeing why this is can lead to some potentially useful reminders about the status of experimental economics and, I would also think, some useful ideas for analyzing the history of work in this area.

[12]Guala's excellent survey of the field and the philosophy of science issues it raises assumes such a picture.

In debunking the standard story I want to focus on first on three methodological tenets in experimental economics: randomization, monetary incentives, and scripting. Experimental economics has taken over the rationale for experimental design so popular in medicine and psychology. The claim is that on purely logical grounds we know that randomizing subjects to treatment vs. control group ensures that we have controlled for unknown factors: "This insidious problem [unknown factors] has an amazingly simple solution... assign the conditions in random order and your treatments will... become independent of all uncontrolled variables" [Friedman and Cassar, 2004]. The other common rationale for randomization is that randomization allows for statistical inference. In both cases logical facts about probability are claimed to tell us whether our experimental work is good. This is a paradigm case of treating experimental practice as embodying the formal logic of science, free from substantive and contingent assumptions.

However, randomization does not ensure that unknown factors are controlled for several reasons. In any single random assignment, differences between groups for unknown factors are likely — it is only in indefinitely many repetitions that factors will be balanced.[13] So we confront the problems again the Bayesians worry about, viz. how to infer to the single case from long run probabilities.

Moreover, treatments happen to groups after randomization, so anything associated with the treatment will be differentially assigned to groups. A humorous example illustrating that as a result this time lag randomization can produce spurious results comes from early experiments claiming to show that oat bran lowers serum cholesterol. Participants were randomly assigned either a treatment of multiple muffins a day to eat or to continue their normal diet. Serum cholesterol did indeed reduce in the treatment groups and the result was published. However, eating the muffins left the subjects with a full stomach and a decline in the regular uptake of fatter foods. The inference to oat bran as a direct cause of reduced cholesterol on the basis of these results was thus dubious.

In practice randomization might be doing a relatively good job of producing equal groups on important factors and there might be no factors associated with the treatment that are relevant. But it takes an argument to show that; logic won't do the trick. So sometimes in randomized clinical trials in medicine researchers check to see that balance has been achieved after randomization.

I should note that my cautions here were advanced by those who first developed the methodological principles involved in the internal/external distinction — Campbell and Cronbach [1957]. They made it clear that the internal validity (Campbell's term, Cronbach had a different terminology) brought by randomization did not show that the treatment was the cause of the observed effect. That required, in Campbell's terminology, showing construct validity — showing that the description of the treatment captured the relevant causal variable. The oat bran experiments lacked construct validity.

[13] It is sometimes claimed that a sufficiently large sample will solve the problem because of the law of large numbers. So far as I can see, that kind of justification would only work for a sufficiently large number of repetitions of the experiment.

Other standard methodological tenets beyond randomization suggest that economists implicitly know that randomization is not all that it is claimed to be. One obvious worry about experimental results is that subjects do not interpret the experimental setup as intended — in short, their understanding is a factor associated with the treatment that may be confounding. According, it has become de rigor in experimental economics to use monetary incentives and detailed scripts on the thought that this will control such confounding. These methods have become essential and it is very hard to get anything published that violates them.

These requirements are another instance of turning substantive, contingent claims about the world into unassailable norms, a standard move in all experimental sciences. That these assumptions are indeed domain specific, defeasible assumptions is illustrated by the fact that they are largely ignored in psychological research and that researchers can sometimes provide good empirical reason why they should be. Research shows that financial incentives can sometimes get in the way of following the script being used [Betsch and Haberstroh, 2001].

In this connection it is interesting to note a common rationale for scripting and other such tenets: they produce reliability, i.e. repeatable results in different replications of an experiment [Hertwig and Ortman, 2001]. Taking measures of reliability as an end in themselves without much concern for other experimental virtues such as external validity is a natural strategy for experimenters defending the autonomy of their enterprise. It produces a nice number that seems to measure validity and do so without getting into thorny questions of generalizability. However, high reliability can also simply be an indication of a very successful process of social construction, not of accurately measuring something. That is arguably the case in much psychological testing [Michell, 1999].

My last application of the naturalist morals will be to the internal/external distinction that is so crucial to the story experimental economists tell themselves. Recall that the distinction grounded the claim that experimental logic allows for inferring the effects of the treatment and that it does regardless of the external validity of the study. I argued above that we should be suspicious that experimental logic alone can do so much work. I now want to argue that we should also be sanguine about the internal/external distinction in the first place.

In many important instances I believe that a sharp internal/external validity distinction cannot be drawn in that assessments of internal validity must rely on judgments of external validity. This conclusion thus makes it clear that assessing the internal validity of an experiment is a still messier thing than experimental economists want to admit.

How can internal validity depend on judgments about external validity? In the abstract, this conclusion should follow from the holism of testing and the contextualism characteristic of naturalism. Inferences about causation in one situation (the experimental) ought sometimes to depend on what we know about that cause in other situations (the world outside the lab). Causal inference is made against background knowledge, and there is no reason that background knowledge might not in some cases be information about a causal factor in the experiment derived from knowledge about that causal factor in the world outside the experiment.

We can make this abstract argument more concrete. Recall what randomization allows you to do — it allows you to infer that *somehow* the treatment in the experimental situation influenced the outcome. You learn that intervention $X$ in the laboratory setting produced outcome $Y$. However, the *laboratory setting* is a fixed element, so by definition it does not vary in a single experiment and thus its effects are not controlled for. But tests of external validity provide one route to getting the evidence needed to evaluate the role of the experimental setting — by learning that the laboratory setting itself is a potential confounding cause. In short, asking whether the results are externally valid is one important route to determining if I really know what the treatment is in my experiment.

I suspect that this problem — not fully understanding what the laboratory setup really is in causal terms — is much wider than acknowledged in experimental economics. And failures to worry about external validity only make the situation worse. Issues involved in framing effects are a good case in point. Experimenters acknowledge that how subjects frame the experiment matter to outcomes. That is part of the reason for the insistence on explicit scripts, and varying those scripts is one way to look for factors influencing how subjects frame the experiment. However, these verbal cues are only part of the story. The experiment itself is a social situation where norms, expectations, etc. are involved; we can about that social the situation from background knowledge we may have or get from asking if the results are externally valid.

One piece of background knowledge we have is that differences in norms can matter and that individuals in repeated interactions may develop norms of strong reciprocity. These motivations lead Carpenter *et al.* [2005] to investigate what they call "social framing." They studied the ultimatum and dictator games in the typical laboratory setup — college students in a university environment — and then with blue collar workers on site in a warehouse field experiment. Proposers in the workplace made more generous offers. To rule out demographic differences of the individuals as the cause, a third experiment with college students at a junior college with the same demographics as the warehouse workers was conducted. These students did not make more generous offers. Social framing clearly seems to make a difference.

This data is thus relevant to determining the internal validity of many experiments involving the ultimatum and related games. Good experiments after the results of Carpenter et al need to find some way to control for the relevant social aspects of the experimental situation. Investigating internal validity and external validity go hand in hand thus go hand in hand.

I want now to continue my argument that the standard story that experimental economists tell themselves is illuminated by morals from the philosophy of science by looking in more detail at what is involved in the external validity. Here the question is the extent to which judgments of external validity are amenable to purely formal tests. The notion of external validity also raises issues in philosophy of science that are strangely mostly undiscussed.

First, let's consider some proposals on what external validity requires that seem not entirely satisfactory. Starmer [1999] in an interesting early philosophical discussion of experimental economics suggests that external validity requires predictive accuracy. He concludes, however, that there are likely to be unresolvable differences in such evaluations due to the holism of testing and underdetermination of theory by data.

These claims are implausible. Predictive accuracy by itself is neither necessary nor sufficient for external validity. I take this to be the obvious upshot from the fact that confounded models can predict correlations correctly and from the fact that models that do not predict well due to simplifications, idealizations, etc. may nonetheless pick out real causal processes. Starmer's skepticism about external validity also seems misplaced on naturalist grounds. Underdetermination, I would argue, is always a local and contingent affair, never inherent in the human epistemic situation. No doubt there is often plenty of room for maneuver when experimental results don't seem to reflect external reality. But blanket judgments that there will always be competing incompatible interpretations are implausible.

A much better account of external validity comes from Guala [2005]. On his view, showing external validity involves an analogical argument, with a good argument working by eliminative induction — by ruling out competing explanations to the analogy. I would affirm this picture but with two important caveats. First, I would argue that every experimental situation is essentially about a *causal* claim and that consequently every claim to external validity is a claim to know something about real world *causes.* So the analogies we want are causal ones and the competing explanations are competing causal stories.

Secondly, asking whether experimental economic systems are analogous to real world phenomena seems to me to be asking an unnecessarily misleading question. I would argue that we are never in the situation of comparing an experimental setup to the world simpliciter. Rather, we are always in the situation of asking whether the experimental setup under a description is analogous to real world phenomena under a description. This is a deeper point than pointing out that we always compare some aspect of the two [Guala, 2005]. Comparing aspects still suggests that we have unvarnished, atheoretical access. I take it that many developments in $20^{th}$ century philosophy (Quine being the prime instance) support this point.

While this may be a deep (or now trivially obvious) point, the place of descriptions in evaluating experimental work has quite direct practical implications. Evaluating external validity for experimental economics cannot be done without already having some theory, set of categories, etc. about the "external" social world and the experimental set up. For experimental economics, this means a set of assumptions about the nature of economic reality. In particular, I suggest that frequently assumptions are made that there is a distinct set of economic variables that the experimental setup can capture and that the external world is accurately described by them. "A distinct set of economic variables" requires that the social world either divides in some nontrivial way into economic processes as opposed to cultural, social, religious, ethnic, etc. ones or that the latter are fully amenable to economic analysis. A long tradition from Mill to Hausman takes that distinction as unproblematic. That seems to me as a general claim dubious, though it is plausible that there are specific domains where the distinction is relatively straightforward. But that has to be argued case by case.

Another related common assumption sometimes presupposed by claims of external validity is a certain kind of individualism. It is assumed that the entities we are generalizing to are individuals in at least this sense: there are basic units with well defined utility functions. That generally means internal structure is irrelevant. This raises questions when the units are aggregations of individuals.

To see why all of this matters to evaluating the external validity of experimental economics, let me cite two rather different sets of experimental work: work on auctions and on industrial organization. The experimental work on auctions seems to me a place where a strong case can be made that we can assume a sharp separation between the economic and the social, at least in some cases. So take the work nicely described by Guala on the spectrum auctions and on gas leases in the Gulf of Mexico. In the former case, the external world was literally constructed to match the experimental setup. In the latter case, there was a very careful attempt to show that the real world auctions were replicated in the experimental situation. In both cases there is arguably a quite meaningful sense in which there are separable economic variables describing the experiment and the world it is supposed to tell us about.

Moreover, the individualism assumptions may be relatively plausible as well. Many real world auctions just are bidding between persons and so there is no worry about treating a corporate actor as a unitary individual. Even when the actors are collective entities as they are in both the gas and spectrum auctions, the very nature of the auction may make it plausible that they act like one individual. The auctions in question were one time events involving a small set of decision variables. The conflicting goals of individuals or subunits making up the corporate entities involved could not surface at different times producing a nonunitary actor. However, the case has to be made.

If auctions can be a clear case where we can safely assume that there is a parallel between experimental variables and similar separable variables in the world outside, work on industrial organization is rather different. Typical experimental work consists of testing whether competition among experimental subjects fits a Bertrand, Cournot, or some other model. Yet work in industrial organizations where firms — not individuals — are the target make almost no use of results from experimental economics [Sutton, 1998]. There is good reason not to: The diversity of explanatory factors used in industrial organization find no easy parallel in the experiment situation.

The basic actors are firms, not individuals. While firms were long treated as individuals and still are for many modeling purposes, more sophisticated, recent work no longer takes firms as black boxes. Sutton, for example, in his concrete historical explanations appeals to competing interests inside the firm, a step reflected theoretically in the principal-agent and transaction costs accounts of the firm. So the parallel between the basic entities in experiments and the larger world is in question.

Moreover, there are other explanatory factors and phenomena in industrial organization that have no counterpart in the experimental work. Thus much work in IO has concerned the relation between R&D investment relative to size and market concentration ratios as well as life histories of industries as a whole. Coalitions and collusion are important factors. Market size matters as does government interventions in terms of subsidies, war-time purchases, etc. None of these things are captured in experimental work on industrial organization. Not surprisingly, these factors at bottom represent the need to bring more sociological and contingent factors into the usual maximizing under constraints perspective of economics.

So the moral of this section is the same of the last one on observational evidence. Providing evidence is giving a complex argument whose full structure is often not made explicit and one that cannot be made on purely formal grounds alone despite the natural tendency to treat them as if they could. This is why neither observational evidence or experimental evidence has any automatic priority — one can argue badly or well using either type of evidence.

## 4 EVIDENCE AND UNREALISTIC CAUSAL MODELS

I want to finish this chapter by considering a perennial issue in economic methodology, the realism of assumptions debate. Following my naturalist framework, I will be skeptical of any purported all-purpose solution. My positive thesis will be that providing evidence requires a complex argument involving essential contextual background information. I look at some specific uses of unrealistic models in economics to examine some ways that unrealistic assumptions can be dealt with. This will instantiate my general tenet that the crucial philosophy of science issues have to be evaluated in ways continuous with and mindful of the details of economic argumentation.

No doubt models serve many roles in economics and science in general. I want to focus on models that claim to identify causal relations, a use that I argue elsewhere (see the chapter on the nature of economic explanation in this volume) is the clearest case of how models explain. The key question then is when do models with unrealistic assumptions nonetheless identify causal relations. I want to argue that there are a variety of argument strategies that can successfully show that such models do sometimes succeed. I do so by looking at models and evidence in Sutton's work on market structure.

Sutton wants to explain, among other things, the relation between R&D spending, measured by the ratio of spending to industry sales, to the level of concentration in a given industry. Sutton's work describes three relevant causal mechanisms: price competition, externality effect (the effect of a new product entry on other products), and an escalation mechanism. It is the latter I want to concentrate on here.

An escalation mechanism refers to the process whereby firms increase spending on R&D to improve product quality and thereby attract a greater share of the market. Escalation in this sense is opposed to the opposite strategy of proliferation where spending is spread across different products. A firm will increase spending on improving a specific product only if it is profitable. A key factor determining profitability is the degree of substitutability in the market — fragmented markets are those with low substitutability between product types, homogeneous markets are those with high similarity between product types. In a fragmented market, the argument goes, R&D escalation will not be profitable, since increases in market share will only come from selling products in an individual, small product group. In a homogeneous market, however, escalation will be profitable when market shares are low. So we should see greater concentration in homogeneous markets than fragmented ones. Thus the escalation mechanism should place a lower bound on the one firm concentration ratio. Where that lower bound will fall also crucially involves the elasticity of the cost function for product quality which influences the strength of the escalation mechanism.

Sutton provides a diverse lot of evidence for the claims made in this model, including case studies and regression results on two samples of industry, one with high concentration and one with low. It is an interesting question to what extent the difficulties with observational evidence cited above confront this work. Sutton is weary of drawing causal conclusions from the regression data alone and believes case studies are essential to confirming his conclusions. I think a good case could be made that his work provides the kind of contextualized, fleshed out argument that is needed from the naturalist perspective. However, that is not my direct target here. Rather I want to look at the unrealistic assumptions in Sutton's model and the strategies he uses for dealing with them. Below I list the key unrealistic assumptions and why Sutton believes they do not prevent his model from getting at operative causes.

### *The nature of competition is not specified*

We know from game theory results that it makes a difference to equilibrium results if we model competition as Cornot or Bertrand. Shouldn't these be included and isn't his account dubious without doing so? Sutton in effect argues that these differences have no effect. He does that by defining an "equilibrium configuration" of product types (which are observable) that requires viability and stability. Viability is the assumption that the firms that survive are able to cover their fixed costs. Stability is the requirement that there be no room for arbitrage at equilibrium — no set of products can be added that will cover their fixed costs. He shows that the set of equilibrium configurations contains the set of Nash equilibriums for various different competition games that might be played. His empirical results only depend on the equilibrium configuration, so the form of competition is irrelevant.

## *Equal access to technology*

Sutton's models work from the assumption that all firms have equal access to the given technology. This is obviously not the case. The key variable derived from Sutton's model is the lower bound on concentration. More realistic models in the literature that allow differential access to technology show that this *increases* the concentration level. This complication is thus not directly relevant to the question of whether there is a lower bound.

## *Agents have perfect information about technology and demand*

Obviously this is not true. Sutton argues that it does not undermine his results by showing that the lower bounds on concentration would still be entailed by the model if certainty was replaced by high probability.

## *The escalation mechanism is not the only relevant causal factor*

That is certainly true. Two other obvious ones are how technical standards are set and is the effects of learning by doing. However, recall that Sutton's main claim is about lower bounds *across* industries. Sutton looks at models of bargaining over standards and of learning by doing and shows that they are very sensitive to details that are likely to be industry and institution specific. So the basic argument seems to be that while there is evidence for an escalation mechanism across industries, there is good reason to believe that other causes will not have a *systematic* effect across industries.

You need not find these arguments beyond doubt to see my general moral, viz. that it takes a concrete, model and problem-specific argument to deal with unrealistic models and that there are various ways that can be done. Discussing the problem at the abstract level, e.g. as in much of the massive literature on Friedman's original article, is unlikely to be helpful. Thus the broad naturalist position advocated here supports the efforts of those like Mäki and Morgan who argue there are many different kinds of assumptions in economics and that their status cannot be assessed in one fell swoop.

# CONCLUSION

Summing up the arguments of this chapter is not easily done. That is as it should be if the naturalist approach to evidence is correct, for it denies simple formal criterion for assessing evidence in favor of the view that every presentation of evidence in the sciences is a complex skein of arguments involving domain specific assumptions and domain specific interpretations of what general principles are invoked. There is a natural tendency to treat results as following from simple, general and more or less unchallengeable principles and I have shown that certainly holds true in the presentation of both observational and experimental evidence in economics. But in fact the arguments given are complex and various. I hope my attempt here to cash out some common evidence arguments help to attaining great clarity about how and how successfully economists argue.

## BIBLIOGRAPHY

[Barretto and Howland, 2006] H. Barretto and F. M. Howland. *Introductory Econometrics.* Oxford: Oxford University Press, 2006.

[Berk, 2004] R. Berk. *Regression Analysis: A Constructive Critique.* Thousand Oaks, CA: Sage, 2004.

[Bishop and Trout, 2005] M. Bishop and J. D. Trout. *Epistemology and the Psychology of Human Judgment.* Oxford: Oxford University Press, 2005.

[Bonferroni, 1935] C. E. Bonferroni. "Il calcolo delle assicurazioni su gruppi di teste." In *Studi in Onore del Professore Salvatore Ortu Carboni.* Rome: Italy, pp. 13-60, 1935.

[Campbell, 1957] D. Campbell. Factors Relevant to the Validity of Experiments in Social Settings, *Psychological Bulletin,* 54: 297-312, 1957.

[Carpenter *et al.*, 2005] J. Carpenter, S. Burks, and E. Verhoogen. Comparing Students to Workers. In Carpenter *et al.*, 26–291, 2005.

[Carpenter *et al.*, 2005] J. Carpenter, G. Harrison, and J. List, eds. *Field Experiments in Economics.* Amsterdam: Elsevier, 2005.

[Cohen, 1994] J. Cohen. The Earth is Round (p <.05), *American Psychologist,* 49(12), 997–1003, 1994.

[Collins, 2004] H. Collins. *Gravity's Shadow.* Chicago: University of Chicago Press, 2004.

[Day and Kincaid, 1994] T. Day and H. Kincaid. Putting Inference to the Best Explanation In Its Place, *Synthese,* 98: 271-295, 1994.

[McCloskey and Ziliak, 1996] D. N. McCloskey and S. T. Ziliak. The Standard Error of Regressions, *Journal of Economic Literature,* American Economic Association, 34(1), 97-114, 1996.

[Friedman and Cassar, 2004] D. Friedman and A. Cassar. *Economics Lab.* London: Routledge.

[Gallison, 1987] P. Gallison. *How Experiments End.* Chicago: University of Chicago Press, 1987.

[Goldman, 2001] A. Goldman. Replies to the contributors. *Philosophical Topics,* 29:461-511, 2001.

[Gooding *et al.*, 1999] D. Gooding, T. Pinch, and S. Schaffer. *The Uses of Experiment.* Cambridge: Cambridge University Press, 1999.

[Granger and Timmermann, 2000] C. Granger and A. Timmermann. Data mining with local model specification uncertainty: a discussion of Hoover and Perez, *Econometrics Journal,* 2:22-225, 2000.

[Green, 2003] Q. Green. *Econometric Analysis.* New Jersey: Prentice Hall, 2003.

[Guala, 2005] F. Guala. *The Methodology of Experimental Economics.* Cambridge: Cambridge University Press, 2005.

[Haavelmo, 1944] T. Haavelmo. The Probability Approach in Econometrics, *Econometrica,* 12, Supplement 1, 1944.

[Hacking, 1965] I. Hacking. *The Logic of Statistical Inference.* Cambridge: Cambridge University Press, 1965.

[Hands, 2002] W. Hands. *Reflection without Rules.* Cambridge: Cambridge University Press, 2002.

[Hendry *et al.*, 1990] D. Hendry, E. Leamer, and D. Poirier. The ET dialogue: a conversation on econometric methodology, *Econometric Theory,* 2:171-261, 1990

[Hertwig and Ortman, 2001] R. Hertwig and A. Ortman. Experimental Practices in Economics: A Methodological Challenge for Psychologists? *Behavior and Brain Sciences,* 24:383-451, 2001.

[Hoover and Siegler, 2008] K. Hoover and M. Siegler. Sound and Fury: McCloskey and Significance Testing in Economics, *Journal of Economic Methodology,* 15:1-39, 2008.

[Hoover and Perez, 1999] K. Hoover and S. Perez. Data Mining Reconsidered: Encompassing and the General-to-Specific Aproach to Specification Search, *Econometrics Journal,* 2:1-25, 1999.

[Howson and Urbach, 2005] C. Howson and P. Urbach. *Scientific Reasoning.* LaSalle, IL: Open Court, 2005.

[Kincaid, 2002] H. Kincaid. Scientific Realism and the Empirical Nature of Methodology: Bayesians vs. Frequentists. In in Clarke and Lyons, *Recent Themes in the Philosophy of Science*, pp. 39–62, Dordrecht: Kluwer, 2002.

[Keuzenkamp, 2006] H. Keuzenkamp. *Probability, Econometrics and Truth: The Methodology of Econometrics.* Cambridge: Cambridge University Press, 2006.

[Mayer, 2000] T. Mayer. Data Mining: A Reconsideration, *Journal of Economic Methodology*, 7:183-194, 2000.

[Mayo, 1996] D. Mayo. *Error and the Growth of Knowledge.* Chicago: University of Chicago Press, 1996.

[McCloskey and Ziliak, 2004] D. McCloskey and S. T. Ziliak. Size Matters, *Journal of Socio-economics*, 33:527-546, 2004.

[Radder, 2003] H. Radder. *The Philosophy of Scientific Experimentation.* Pittsburgh: University of Pittsburgh Press, 2003.

[Samuelson, 2005] L. Samuelson. Economic Theory and Experimental Economics, *Journal of Economic Literature*, 43:65-107, 2005.

[Sober, 1991] E. Sober. *Reconstructing the Past.* Cambridge: MIT Press, 1991.

[Spanos, 2000] A. Spanos. Data Mining Revisited: Hunting without a License, *Journal of Economic Methodology*, 7, 2000.

[Starmer, 1999] C. Starmer. Experiments in Economics: Should We Trust the Dismal Scientists in White Coats? *Journal of Economic Methodology*, 6(1):1–30, 1999.

[Sutton, 1998] J. Sutton. *Technology and Market Structure.* Cambridge: Cambridge University Press, 1998.

# SOME ISSUES CONCERNING THE NATURE OF ECONOMIC EXPLANATION

Harold Kincaid

There is a long and substantial body of literature in philosophy and philosophy of science about the nature of explanation. Those issues likewise show up in economics in various guises, though often not explicitly stated and discussed. In what follows I first outline some general issues about explanation and state what I take to be some general morals. I then look at various practices and disputes in economics, outline where the issues of explanation come up, and try to determine which claims are plausible which are not. Section 1 provides the background. Section II looks at attempts to provide purely formal accounts of explanation in economics. Section III looks at arguments given that economics does not seek explanations in terms of unobservables. Section IV looks at issues surrounding macro vs micro explanation. Section V discusses how models can explain while being unrealistic. Section VI looks at functional and selectionist explanations, especially evolutionary game theory. Section VII looks at some ontological assumptions about causation raised by standard regression models in economics.

## 1 SOME CONTROVERSIES ABOUT EXPLANATION

Work on explanation in philosophy of science is one area where progress has been made, albeit much of it negative. The nomological deductive model of explanation was dominant up through the sixties. It equated explanations with deductions of a description of the phenomena to be explained from premises essentially including scientific laws. There was some (and still is) controversy about what a scientific law involves, but generally speaking laws were thought to be nonaccidental generalizations that made no reference to particulars and supported counterfactual claims. Deriving Kepler's laws from Newton's laws of motion was a successful explanation; deriving the claim that I found a penny in my pocket from the generalization "all the coins in my pocket are pennies" is not a successful explanation. The latter, unlike the former, involves an accidental generalization about a particular that would not support counterfactuals.

This view was eventually rejected on multiple grounds, some more radical than others. The more moderate criticism was that derivation from a law was neither necessary nor sufficient to explain because clear counterexamples could be generated. All men who take birth control pills do not get pregnant and so John who

Handbook of the Philosophy of Science. Volume 13: Philosophy of Economics.
Volume editor: Uskali Mäki. General editors: Dov M. Gabbay, Paul Thagard and John Woods.

takes such pills did not get pregnant. There is derivation from a law, but the law is irrelevant. John also has now has paresis, which we can explain as resulting from his syphilis (and, earlier in the causal chain, to his mistaken belief that birth control pills prevent STDs), although we do not have a law on the books that subsumes the event in question. Not surprising, there have been multiple attempts to revise the account to get around these problems, which in turn led to a new round of counterexamples.

A related set of criticisms concerned distinguishing the scientific laws from the nonscientific. No reference to particulars as a criterion is doubtful because it is merely syntactic. References to a particular can be turned into references to predicate. So if the laws of evolution seem to refer to a particular–this planet–we can take them to be about "Darwinian systems." Some apparent accidental generalizations can support counterfactuals. If my pockets are designed such that only pennies can put in them, then if were try to place a quarter in them, I would fail. Again, various attempts to refine away such counterexamples resulted.

The more radical criticism came from the broad postpositivist movement in science. There are various ways to formulate its core commitments, but in rough terms they are a form of naturalism which holds that philosophy of science had to be sensitive to what scientists actually do. Taken seriously, this means rejecting conceptual analysis tested on philosophers intuitions as the final arbiter and thus giving up on Hempel's project. The goal then is to better understand how science works. With that as the goal, numerous historical, sociological and rational reconstructive accounts of the practice of explanation in science emerged. They extended the counterexamples: much of science explains in ways that are not well captured by deriving from laws.

Some general results followed. One was that explanation is often about citing of causes. Causes had been excluded by the positivist minded as too metaphysical, but scientists certainly seemed to talk of causes, at least those — like economists — not already in the grips of the dogma at issue. John's calamities have a natural causal explanation that grounds our sense that the derivation from laws is neither sufficient nor necessary. The citing of causes becomes a paradigm of explanation.

There have been some attempts to take the science seriously but to leave out the causation. The most developed tries to account for explanation in terms of unification. My suspicion is that such accounts are Hempel's project in new clothes. Derivation and other formal criterion are claimed to be the essence of explanation. While the goal of unification certainly is part of the practice of science and worthy of investigation, I doubt that there is any useful claim of the form "x explains if and only if x is unified in such and such a way." The most developed account is that of Kitcher [1989], who takes explanation to come from instantiating an argument pattern or schema, where Darwinian selectionist explanations are his prime examples.

A number of doubts about Kitcher's account have been raised [Kincaid, 1996]. Kitcher distinguishes multiple argument patterns in biology, for example, simple selection, directional selection, and so on. How do we determine that these are separate patterns rather than one more complex one? When is one pattern simpler than another? How do we weigh the scope of the pattern against its simplicity, something Kitcher's account requires us to do? What makes these decision an objective matter rather than simply a subjective sense of "seeing things fit together"? And why should we expect that there should be simple patterns in the first place? Don't the social and biological sciences show a diversity of processes, so that we can ask the same question that has been asked about simplicity — why think unified theories are better? Finally, it is quite clear that we can think of unification as a good thing for reasons unconnected to explanation—finding interconnections increases the possibilities for triangulation and boot strap testing, for example.

More careful and detailed looks at scientific practice led to the recognition that context plays an essential part in many explanations and that it is sometimes useful to think of explanations as the answers to specific kinds of questions [Garfinkel, 1981]. Questions and their answers have an inevitable contextual component. If I ask "why did Adam eat the apple?" the question is ambiguous until I specify the relevant contrast classes. Do I want to know why Adam rather then Eve ate the apple? Do I want to know what Adam ate the apple rather than throwing it? And so on. Furthermore, the background knowledge of scientists seeking explanations dictates what general kind of information is relevant. So, for example, in physics before the rise of quantum mechanics, no answer that involved action at a distance would be considered relevant. Keeping clear about these contextual elements allow for a more nuanced approach to explanation and we will see below that it can help dissolve some standard confusions.

One important implication of the above developments is that assessing explanations is unlikely to be a purely formal process. By a formal process I mean ones that rely on only logical properties rather than on substantive domain specific information (R squared is often thought to be a purely formal measure as we will see below). Given that the paradigm case of explanation is the citing of causes and that explanation involves context, we should expect that evaluating explanations requires a detailed argument invoking domain specific assumptions. Many different kinds of causes can be invoked: distal, structural, necessary, sufficient, important, and so on. Moreover, when identifying causes, decisions have to be made and justified about what to take as part of the causal field — the causal factors that are treated as background and irrelevant. Combining such variations will be part of the process of setting the contrast class and relevance relation as determined by the interests of those seeking explanations. We will see later that spelling out such complete set of elements in an explanation can sometimes clarify controversies over explanation in economics.

## 2 FORMAL CRITERIA FOR EXPLANATION IN ECONOMICS

The lure of formal criteria for explanatory success is still strong in contemporary economics. I want to look at two general instances which are fairly common in contemporary economics — the notion that explanation comes from providing a set of equations and that explanatory power is measured by the amount of explained variance, or R squared.

The nomonological deductive model of explanation still carries enormous weight within economics. This is obvious from a core practice of the profession: taking a set of equations as necessary and sufficient for producing an explanatory model. The equations of a given model are supposed to be the universal regularities that a nomological deductive explanation needs. The set of equations is used to show that the phenomena of interest can be derived from the model. There is of course sometimes a causal story lurking in the background, and the commonly used phrases "is a function of," "is associated with," and "is determined by" can have causal overtones. But the causal interpretation is usually in the background if present at all. Moreover, when it comes to testing the model, the causal interpretation frequently drops out altogether as regression equations are estimated without much pretense of showing causality.

Let me cite one example to illustrate my point — various models from growth theory.[1] The seminal Solow [1956] model dates from the mid1950s and versions of it have dominated neoclassical thinking about growth and development. Output is determined by an aggregate production function that makes output a function of the supply of capital and labor, where the size of the latter is determined by an exogenously given level of technology. The size of the capital stock is determined by the savings, population growth, depreciation, and technological growth rates, all of which are taken as exogenous.

There are two crucial implications of this model for development. First increases in savings and capital investments are central for growth and second, economies will converge toward a steady state where growth is constant. The level of growth in the steady state depends only on the exogenously given technological change.

However, the original Solow model had some unwelcome consequences. Among others it implies that new investment in the underdeveloped countries should have a much higher rate of return and thus we should see very heavy investment from the developed countries. That is not what the evidence shows.

This has resulted in what is called an "augmented Solow model" [Mankiew, 1995].

The augmented Solow model results from seeing that the unwanted predictions depend crucially on the relative share of capital. A higher share of capital implies greater effects on income of savings and that return to capital varies less with income. But if we add to the Solow model another capital variable — for human capital — we get a change of the relative share of capital (physical and human) and thus the troubling predictions go away. Since human capital theory was a major innovation in the period after Solow's account was proposed, this is a natural emendation.

Mankiew's model still leaves technological change exogenous. So further development has worked to make it endogenous. In Romer's [1990; 1994] models,

[1]For a much longer discussion of growth theories and issues in the philosophy of science, see [Kincaid, 2008].

on which I focus here, technological change becomes explained in that there is a knowledge producing sector that takes physical and human capital and existing knowledge as inputs and produces technological designs as output. This sector also introduces economies of scale and drops perfect competition in that part of the knowledge produced is proprietary and produced by monopolies and that part of the knowledge produced becomes a public good. So we have the promise of explaining technological progress and doing so with a more realistic model that breaks with some general equilibrium theory simplifications found in the augmented Solow model.

Finally, further developments tried to bring in social factors such as the rule of law. Barro [2001] is perhaps the best known advocate of this approach and he uses cross country regressions to test versions of the most extensive model that incorporates all the factors added to the original Solow model. Thus the final instantiation tested by Barro is described by the equation:

$$Y = f(K, L, s, n, H, \text{ and } I),$$

where $Y$ is GDP, $K$ and $L$ are capital and labor, $s$ and $n$ are savings rate and population size, $H$ is investment in human capital, and $I$ is set of institutional factors—rule of law, property rights, size of government, etc

What implicit assumptions about explanation does this body of work make? Its explanations come by showing that there are functional relations between variables — in short, universal regularities. Moreover, these models are committed to universal regularities in a very strong sense in that the assumption is that there is one production function which describes all economies.

Is growth theory then committed to a nomological-deductive model of explanation? The language used to describe these models is ambiguous in that there are clearly times when the implication is that there are more than universal regularities involved–the models are describing the causes of growth. However, there is no attempt here to develop an explicit causal model using structural equations that specify the details of the causal process. By the time this work is crystalized in Barro's empirical work, the implicit causal model is the simple shown in Figure 1.

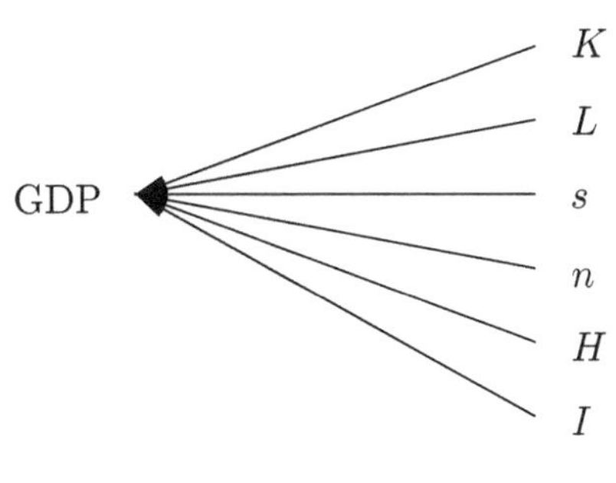


Figure 1. Causal model of cross country growth regressions

Obviously this is an entirely implausible causal model, for there is good reason to think there are causal influences from the independent variable GDP to the dependent variables and causal relations among the latter. So the causal model is really only gestured to and the real explanatory work is being done by the universal regularities. These explanations are thus through and through nomological deductive and thus perhaps suspect for that reason.

I have used growth theory to show that nomological-deductive models still hold sway in economics. Perhaps growth theory is unique in this regard? I do not think it is. The practice of writing down a set of equations without a causal interpretation and using that model to explain is standard fare in mainstream economics.

There is one route to defending this practice that has not been explicitly advanced in the case of economics but that is worth exploring. It turns on issues about dynamical systems. The argument is this: We may know that deduction from laws seems neither necessary nor sufficient for explanation, but our naturalist stance requires us to take scientific practice seriously, and surely deduction from laws is sometimes a crucial part of how scientists explain. To be more specific, a standard scientific practice is to identify a set of differential equations that suffice to trace the movement of variables through state space. When they have found models that can successfully do so, they claim to have explained the dynamics of the system. So if economists can do the same, then we have only bad a priori reasons to deny that they are explaining.

Applied to growth theory, the argument would then be that its practitioners are doing something similar, viz. trying to describe the value of GDP over time as a function of a key set of variables. If the available data are consistent with the growth models, they then have explained even if there is no plausible causal model being tested.

I am skeptical of this defense. It leaves economics without much policy relevance since we are explicitly eschewing causal notions. Also, if I claim that that my model of movement through state space allows me to tell governments what variables to manipulate, then I am claiming that intervening on a variable will lead to changes in GDP and I have invoked a classic conception of causality, viz, that an intervention on one factor produces a change in another (see [Woodward, 1997]).

Let me turn now to the other formalist notion of explanation common in economics (and elsewhere). It is standard practice to claim that one model has more explanatory power than another if it has a higher R squared. R squared is measure of goodness of it of data about a line showing the relation between changes in two or more variables. The closer the cloud of data the line, the greater the explained variance. This is a formal criterion in that it can be determined by calculation alone.

While appeal to R squared is a common rhetorical device, it is a very tenuous connection to any plausible explanatory virtues for many reasons.[2] Either it is

[2]The discussion that follows draws on Northcott [2005] discussion on causation, the extensive body of work pointing out the flaws in heritability measures in biology which rest on explained variance (see [Kaplan, 2000] and that in the social sciences debunking overinterpreting regression

meant to be merely a measure of predictability in a given data set or it is a measure of causal influence. In either case it does not tell us much about explanatory power. Taken as a measure of predictive power, it is limited in that it predicts variances only. But what we mostly want to predict is levels, about which it is silent. In fact, two models can have exactly the same R squared and yet describe regression lines with very different slopes, the natural predictive measure of levels. Furthermore even in predicting variance, it is entirely dependent on the variance in the sample — if a covariate shows no variation, then it cannot predict anything. This leads to getting very different measures of explanatory power across samples for reasons not having any obvious connection to explanation.

Taken as a measure of causal explanatory power, R squared does not fare any better. The problem of explaining variances rather than levels shows up here as well—if it measures causal influence, it has to be influences on variances. But we often do not care about the causes of variance in economic variables but instead about the causes of levels of those variables about which it is silent. Similarly, because the size of R squared varies with variance in the sample, it can find a large effect in one sample and none in another for arbitrary, noncausal reasons. So while there may be some useful epistemic roles for R squared, measuring explanatory power is not one of them.

## 3 THEORETICAL ENTITIES AND EXPLANATION

There have been long standing debates in the philosophy of science about the place of theoretical posits in science, most around epistemological issues concerning how belief in them is warranted. A related but distinct question that has been raised about economics is the extent to which economic theory is about unobservables. It has been argued by Mäki [2002] and Hausman [1998] that economics largely is unconcerned with theoretical nonobservational entities. Both, reasonably enough, note that the observable/nonobservable distinction can be drawn in various ways and that its epistemic importance is questionable. However, both think the entities postulated by economics are on the par with ordinary relative observables like tables and chairs — they are, in Mäki's terminology, commonsensibles. Mäki argues that unobservable entities are no major concern for social scientists. They are of no major concern because the posits of social theories are continuous with the common sense realm, and social scientists, as social actors themselves, have access to this realm. Hausman affirms the claim that most standard entities invoked by economics, e.g. expected utilities, are extrapolations from ordinary common sense notions such as belief and desire and adds that when they are not — such as Marxian labor values — they have turned out not to be important in economics.

Several lessons from postKuhnian naturalist philosophy of science are relevant here:

1. Scientific theories are not always unified, monolithic entities and they are

results [Berk, 2004]).

not the whole of science. From Kuhn [1962], work in the history and sociology of science [Beller, 1999], arguments developed by advocates of the semantic view of theories [Giere, 1988], and work on the role of models in science by Cartwright [1999], we have good reason to believe that "theories" have diverse interpretations across individuals and applications, are often not a single axiomatizable set of statements, and involve differing kinds of extratheoretical assumptions and devices in the process of explaining.

2. Our knowledge of the world is not divided into natural kinds such that we can evaluate the epistemic status of their tokens all at once and such that some kinds of knowledge have automatic epistemic privilege over others. These points are relevant because they should make us suspicious of quick pronouncement about what economics is about and of claims that there are certain kinds of knowledge — in this case "commonsensibles" — that share a common epistemic fate.

I would thus defend the view that there is no short story of what economics is about and in that telling the longer story we would find that it is often not about "commonsensibles" at all. No doubt, given the holism of meaning, our common sense economic concepts have *some* connection to the terms in which economic theory explains. Yet that connection is not enough, because the claim is that objects and processes described by economic theory are familiar everyday objects much like tables and chairs. I think economics traffics in objects and processes that have an everyday counterpart but themselves are not commonsensibles at all as well as objects and process that have no everyday counterpart, though the two kinds of case are bound to be arbitrary in some cases because what objects exist and what properties they have are interrelated.

An example from the first category is explaining price changes as due to changes in demand. Of course we take price and demand changes as occurrences observed in everyday life. However, the common sense observed notion of demand—"there is a big line at the gas station" — is worlds apart from the "demand" notion that is refined by theory into shifts in demand curves and moves along the curve, not to mention the full details defined by a Slutsky matrix. It is a truism in economics that these notions of demand are very difficult to observe because their component elements are hard to identify. It is very hard to see how it is that we have knowledge of them of the sort we have of tables and chairs. Hausman's claim that apparently unobservable aggregate quantities are really just averages of observable quantities seems mistaken in this fundamental case.

An example from the second category are the various equilibrium concepts in game theory. We explain the behavior of oligopolies as the result of strategies in some kind of equilibrium in some kind of game. A subgame perfect Bayesian equilibrium of a two stage Cournot game seems rather far from any common sense object we observe. In fact, a fundamental problem in industrial organization is to find any way to tie this entity to anything observable at all [Sutton, 1998]. There certainly seem to be unobservables in economics.

## 4 WHEN DO MODELS EXPLAIN?

The fact that economics is bound to posit entities and processes that are unobservable is closely connected to another standard issue in economic methodology, namely, how can models with false assumptions explain? Note that this is distinct from the question how we can have good *evidence* for models with false assumptions, though of course there are interconnections. It is the question about explanation that I turn to in this section.

One route to showing that unrealistic models in economics can explain is in effect to deny that there are falsehoods involved. We might hold that the general claims of economics such as price equals marginal product are really generalizations with an implicit clause saying "assuming other things are equal." Thus the laws used to explain are not false but qualified *ceteris paribus*. This view is sometimes supported by arguments that even in physics the fundamental laws are qualified ceteris paribus (see [Cartwright, 1984]) — the force on a body due to gravity is equal to mass times acceleration only assuming no other physical forces are present.

Several objections have been raised against this defense [Earman and Roberts, 1999; Earman *et al.*, 2002]. There is the worry that treating economic claims as qualified ceteris paribus renders them nonfalsifiable or makes them superfluous. Either we can specify what the "other things being equal" are or we cannot. If we cannot, then social claims qualified ceteris paribus seem unfalsifiable, for every failed prediction has an out — other things weren't equal. If in fact we can specify what those "other things" are and show that the model is accurate when they are present, then these conditions can just be added in and we do not need to think of social science claims as qualified ceteris paribus at all. Moreover, it is not clear that the basic laws of physics are qualified ceteris paribus. It is true that the fundamental laws describe different fundamental forces and that real explanations frequently have to combine those forces. However, in many cases it is possible to say how the forces combine.

Another objection, not commonly recognized, to the ceteris paribus defense is that all the attempts to spell out ceteris paribus laws implicitly presuppose the nomological-deductive account of explanation. It is assumed that to show that models explain is to show that they embody laws. However, as I argued above, that seems a misguided approach, for the connection between explanation and laws is neither obvious nor fundamental.

Perhaps a more defensible version of the other things being equal strategy is this. Traditionally philosophers have thought of theories as a set of sentences. However, there are various difficulties with this syntactic view of theories. In response to those difficulties some have proposed what is called the semantic view of theories. Putting complexities aside, the semantic view denies that theories are set of statements that are either true or false of the world. Theories instead are defining abstract entities–possible models. Thus the theory of evolution is defining an possible entity, namely, a Darwinian system. That system is one in which there is heritable variation and selection. On the semantic view of theories it is a separate and further empirical question whether there is anything in the world corresponding to the abstract entity described by the theory.

Viewing social science theories from the semantic view of theories certainly avoids the awkwardness of claiming that social science generalizations are true ceteris paribus. However, it may be that it does so simply by putting the problem elsewhere, for we still have the problem of which models actually describe the world and which do not–or put differently, how does a model of a possible reality explain the actual world if it makes assumptions not true of it?

These questions are pursued by a sizable literature in general philosophy of science on the role of models. That literature suggests a number of possible alleged ways that models might capture reality despite their unrealistic assumptions that have been proposed in the literature. Among them are that a model explains if:

1. it provides "insight". This is a common informal rational given by social scientists in defense of particular models.

2. it unifies, i.e. shows how different phenomena might be captured by the same model [Morgan and Morrison, 1999].

3. it serves as an instrument — we can do things with it [Morgan and Morrison, 1999].

4. it is isomorphic to the phenomena of interest [Giere, 1988].

5. it fits the phenomena into a model [Cartwright, 1984].

No doubt there is something to all these claims. Yet none of them by itself seems sufficient to help us tell the good unrealistic models from the bad. Insight threatens to be nothing more than a warm, fuzzy intellectual feeling — we need some kind of explanation of what insight is, how we tell when it is legitimate, and so on. Models that apply across diverse phenomena generally gain some kind of support from doing so. However, it is also possible to tell the same false story over and over again about different phenomena. Many have accused advocates of rational choice models with highly unrealistic assumptions (perfect foresight, etc) of doing just that. Likewise, it is surely right that models serve multiple functions, among them allowing manipulation of components to determine consequences. Still, we can manipulate an abstract model that applies to nothing at all — when does manipulation show that we are capturing real processes rather than imaginary?

The idea that good models are those that stand in some kind of one to one relationship with things in the world is also insufficient, though it is more promising than the previous criteria. However, how do the idealizations of a model stand in a one to one relation to the world exactly? Do the agents with perfect foresight in the market economy model stand in such a relation to real world agents? We can posit a relation, but the question still seems to remain whether doing so explains anything. Moreover, when models are based on abstractions — the leaving out of factors — there is presumably nothing in the model that represents them. How do I know that is not a problem?

One reasonable route around the problems cited above is to focus on finding causes. If we have evidence that a model with unrealistic assumptions is picking out the causes of certain effects, then we can to that extent use it to explain despite the irrealism. If I can show my "insight" is that a particular causal process is operative, then I am doing more than reporting a warm feeling. If I can show that the same causal processes is behind different phenomena, then unification is grounded in reality. If I can provide evidence that I use my model as an instrument because it allows me to describe real causes, then I can have confidence in it. Finally, if I can show that the causes postulated in the model are operative in the world, I can begin to provide evidence that the model really does explain.

How is it possible to show that a model picks out real causes even though it is unrealistic? Social scientists adopt a number of strategies to do so. Sometimes it is possible to show that as an idealization is made more realistic, the model in questions improves in its predictive power. Another strategy is doing what is known as a sensitivity analysis. Various possible complicating factors can be modeled to see their influence on outcomes. If the predictions of a model hold up regardless of which complicating factors are added in, then we have some reason to think the model captures the causal processes despite its idealizations or abstractions. There are a number of other such methods potentially available to social scientists. After all, the natural sciences use idealizations and abstractions on a regular basis with success, so there must be ways of dealing with them.

## 5 MACRO AND MICROEXPLANATION

A key longstanding methodological debate within economics has been about the proper role of microexplanations and macroexplanations. The official ideology of main stream economics is methodological individualism which gives some kind of priority to individuals in explaining the economic. However, that priority can take different forms, and in what follows I discuss some of them and their plausibility.

The standard short form slogan of methodological individualism is that all economic explanations should be in terms of individuals. However, this can mean multiple things with rather different implications. Some of the possible claims are:

1. Any well confirmed economic theory can be reduced to an account solely in terms of individuals.

2. Facts about individuals determine the facts about economic aggregates.

3. Reference to individualist mechanisms is necessary for successful explanations of economic phenomena.

4. Seeking individualist explanations is the most fruitful research strategy in economics.

There are of course interconnections between these claims and they too admit of multiple interpretations. I deal with both as I discuss each thesis.

Individualism as a claim about theory reduction can be fairly precisely delineated, since there is a fairly substantial literature in the history and philosophy of science to rely on. Newtonian mechanics can be reduced to general relativity in the limit case of low velocities and thermodynamics reduced to statistical mechanics.[3] To reduce one theory to another is to show that one theory can explain everything the other can and is in some sense more basic. Reduction is at issue only if two theories say apparently different things or describe the world in different categories. Thus if one theory is going to explain what another does, then there must be some way to capture the categories of the reduced theory in the reducing theories own terms. One standard way of doing so is by providing bridge laws of the form "Reducing theory term A is applicable if and only if reduced term B is applicable." The connection need not be shown to be conceptual or true by the meanings of the words; lawlike equivalence suffices. Thus temperature is lawfully coextensive with "mean kinetic energy" and that works for reduction even if we wouldn't equate them in ordinary language as synonyms. Furthermore, such bridge laws need not capture the reduced term exactly, for the reducing term may be shown to be vague in various ways in the process of reduction. What is needed is then is at least an analogue of the reduced term, and the further the analogue is away from the original term, the closer the reduction will be to a simple elimination and a denial that the reduced theory explains much of anything.

It is standard to argue that reduction is achieved if we can provide the bridge laws linking the two domains and then show that the generalizations of the reduced theory are captured as generalizations of the reducing theory as when we can derive the gas laws from statistical mechanics with the help of the bridge law relating temperature and mean kinectic energy. However, this is wrong. It is wrong because it assumes that the essence of explain is deriving generalizations, something that we saw earlier was problematic. Moreover, we can have bridge laws that beg the question for reduction — for example, emotions were sometimes translated by behaviorist reductions to emotion laden behavioral terms, e.g. anger behavior.

Given the above account of reduction, we can list two potential obstacles to reduction:

1. multiple realizations where the reduced theories' basic categories are brought about in indefinitely many ways by the reducing theory. In this case there is a many-one relation between the basic terms and thus no coextension bridge law is to be had.

2. presupposing the reduced theory in the reducing explanations as happens in explaining emotions in behavioral terms such as "anger behavior."

---

[3]In actual practice the latter is not as straightforward as typically presented. See [Sklar, 1995].

Whether these potential problems are real has to be shown empirically, case by case. There is evidence to think they are indeed sometimes real in economic explanation.

The multiple realizations problem is likely in the many cases where economics explains aggregate phenomena, though for several different reasons. One source of problems comes when we explain aggregate phenomena in terms of competitive selection between aggregates. Firms are a prime example. There is a long, largely informal tradition of arguing that the standard maximizing traits will be found in firms because those without them will not survive. There is a much more formal body of work applying evolutionary game theory to the strategies of firms. In both cases, the selection process does not "care," as it were, about how firms bring about their strategies in terms of organizing individual behavior. All that counts is that the strategy is played. This means that if firms hit on different ways of realizing the same organizational strategies in the behavior of individuals, it will make no difference to processes at the aggregate level.

However, we have good economic reasons for thinking that there are many ways to produce standard firm characteristics such as hierarchical structures, long term employment relations, etc. A variety of different individual level models have been offered in the literature for these practices, e.g. incentives not to shirk, transaction costs, and many other mechanisms can logically do the trick (see [Kincaid. 1995]).

Another area where we might expect multiple realizations to be real phenomena is in macroeconomics. There are several reasons for this. (1) Scale relativity: real causal patterns may be identified at one scale of measurement and not available at another. This is a common theme in the literature on complexity and has been used as an argument against reductionist programs by philosopher's of science [Ladyman and Ross, 2007] and specifically in the case of macroeconomics by Hoover [2001], though he does not use this terminology. Aggregate concepts like GDP lose any definite sense at some point if we look for finer and finer grained measures in terms of individual behavior. So multiple realizations are inevitable because the lower equivalent is indeterminate. (2) Even when we can make sense of translating aggregate macroeconomic concepts into individualist terms, it is quite likely that there are many different sets of individual behaviors that can bring about the aggregate phenomena like the rate of inflation because they describe aggregate averages where the averages do not determine the distribution from which they result.

A second likely obstacle to reduction comes from the fact that many so called individualist explanations are really individualist only in name. This occurs for two reasons. First, what is labelled an individual in economics is not always an individual human being. So firms are treated as individuals, for example. More drastically still, many economic models use "representative agents"–they treat aggregates of individuals as if there were individuals with well-defined utility functions, etc. There is an unrefuted literature showing that this methodology cannot be defended on the grounds that the behavior of individual human beings will aggregate in such a way that they will in total act like an individual with a well defined utility function. So representative agents do not fit well with methodological individualism.

There are also deep questions whether standard neoclassical economics is actually about individual human beings at all. Ross [2005] argues that neoclassical formalism is silent on what agents actually it covers — there is nothing in the formalism per se that have to make neoclassical theory about individual human beings. Moreover, the extensive and replicated results from experimental economics seems to show that individual human beings violate many of the assumptions of the neoclassical models of individual choice. That does not rule out a methodological individualism based on more realistic theories of individual behavior, but it is standard choice theory that is usually pointed to as an example of what a good individualist theory should look like. This point is telling also against versions individualism discussed later that require only individualist mechanisms.

Individualist theories in economics, even if they are plausible accounts of individual human behavior, can nonetheless fail to support the reductionist program. They can implicitly or explicitly presuppose accounts of nonindividual economic entities. Work in classical game theory is good illustration. Game theory accounts of particular phenomena begin with a set of strategies, payoffs, kinds of players, and shared knowledge. However, all these things arguably presuppose that institutions are already in place (Kincaid 2001). Common knowledge assumptions are a standard way to explain norms and conventions, so to assume them is to assume the conventions or norms are already in place. Differentiating players into types that are known assumes the social organization involved in establishing and reinforcing social statuses or roles. A constrained set of possible strategies from all the logically possible ones assumes the kind of shared understandings and social possibilities that come with a definite social organization as the do preset payoffs of actions. This does not mean there is necessarily anything wrong with these explanations, but it does mean they do not adhere to the strictures of methodological individualism.

Let's turn next to some of the logically weaker claims associated with methodological individualism that were listed at the beginning of this section. If full individualist reductions are not likely, might it still not be the case that economic explanations must supply individual *mechanisms* — must describe how individuals acting on their preferences under constraints bring about the phenomena to be explained?

This certainly does not follow from any *general* scientific demand for mechanisms for two reasons. While physics during much of its development required mechanisms in the sense of a continuous causal process, that was called into question by the development of quantum mechanics with its action at a distance. Furthermore, mechanisms can be described to different degrees and at different levels. Cosmology provides causal mechanism but at a very aggregate level. Every day life is full of causal explanations without molecular details. Such explanations can be as well confirmed as any. So there is no all-purpose demand for mechanisms in explanation.

A more useful way of thinking about the need for mechanisms is to consider three questions: how good is our evidence at the aggregate level? What do our explanations at the aggregate level assume about processes at the levels below? How good is our knowledge at the level of entities composing the aggregate? It is clear that the answers to these questions is an empirical matter and nothing a priori ensures that in some circumstances we might know much at the aggregate level, do so without presupposing anything specific at the microlevel, and have no good causal knowledge at the lower level. It then becomes a case by case empirical issue whether mechanisms are required.

## 6 FUNCTIONAL EXPLANATION AND EVOLUTIONARY ECONOMICS

There is a long-standing tradition in the social sciences in general of explaining social practices by the functions they serve. These explanations also occur in economics, though economics is generally more explicit that they are connected to competition and selection mechanisms. I want to discuss some general issues about such explanations, though I will not take up the full the set of issues about evolutionary economics that lie in the background.

The most commonly cited problem with functional explanations is that seem committed to an unscientific teleology. The general consensus is that explaining social phenomena by the functions they serve is legitimate only if there is a causal process tying useful effects to the existence of the practice in question. It is often claimed that doing so requires biological analogies that are only metaphorical and have no realistic social counterpart.

Elster provides one early account of what this involves. A functional explanation of the form $A$ exists in order to $B$ for group $C$ is valid only if:

1. $A$ causes $B$
2. $B$ is beneficial for $C$
3. $B$ is an unintended consequence and unrecognized for the actors in $C$
4. $B$ maintains $A$ by a causal feedback loop running through $C$

There are several problems with this account, however. For one, it makes it essential that functional explanations are in part about individuals, but this imposes are strong methodological individualism that is implausible in economics as I have already argued. One important strand of functional argument in economics is that which sees the behavior of firms as determined by a competitive process such that we can be sure that firm strategies exist in order to maximize profits. Another important strand of argument [Friedman, 1953; Nelson and Winter, 1982] is that these competitive processes can operate and be described independently of the motives of individuals. Elster would rule this out by fiat.

A second problem is that a mere positive feed back loop between effects and what is being explained is a much too broad a notion of functional explanation.

Processes where $A$ can cause $B$ and that effect in turn can reinforce As persistence describe a very wide variety of causal processes indeed. Any system in an equilibrium situation where the mutual interaction between variables keep each in a set range will be a functional explanation.

So I would argue that a more helpful account of functional explanation is the following [Kincaid, 2007]:

1. $A$ causes $B$
2. $A$ persists because it causes $B$
3. $A$ is causally prior to $B$, i.e. $B$ causes $A$'s persistence only when caused by $A$.

The first claim is straightforwardly causal. The second can be construed so as well. At $t_1$, $A$ causes $B$. That fact then causes $A$ to exist at $t_2$. In short, $A$'s causing $B$ causes $A$'s continued existence.[4]

The third requirement serves to distinguish functional explanations from explanations via mutual causality. If $A$ and $B$ interact in a mutually positive reinforcing feedback look, then $A$ causes $B$ and continues to exist because it does so. Yet the same holds for $B$ vis-à-vis $A$. Functional explanations do not generally have this symmetry. Thick animal coats exist in order to deal with cold temperatures, but when cold temperatures are present there is no guarantee that thick coats arise. And surely, even if they do, there is no reason that would they do not cause the cold to persist.

So functional explanations in economics can be perfectly legitimate if they satisfy these three explicit causal requirements. Could they do so without making false biological analogies? The most general description of a causal system describes a set of variables whose values evolve through state space. At this level of description we are told very little: current entities stand in some relation to past ones. Natural selection is inevitably an instance of this as a causal system satisfying the three conditions above. Functional explanations as causal are also an instance. Every causal system is analogous in being a dynamical system. The point here is that whether one set of causal relations is analogous or disanalogous to another depends on the level of description we are using.

So at the most abstract level it is a trivial truth that functional explanations are indeed analogous to Darwinian evolutionary systems in so far as they are causal systems. They are disanalogous in that social entities have no DNA that replicates. But then the HIV virus has no DNA either (it is an RNA virus). We find analogous processes in DNA and RNA organisms despite the differences because we abstract from the details to identify abstract causal patterns.

So do functional explanations commit us to some illegitimate analogy to natural selection? No, because natural selection explanations are just one realization of the

[4]Wright's [1973] account is a partial inspiration here, but it has to be stripped of its conceptual analysis pretensions. And the requirement here is explaining persistence rather than existence.

above schema which is thus the more general pattern [Kincaid, 1986; Harms, 2004]. $A$'s causing $B$ may result in $A$'s persistence by means that don't involve genetic inheritance, literal copying of identifiable replicators distinct from their vehicles or interactors, etc. In fact not all biological processes of natural selection require this level of analogy — differential survival can be caused by other processes (see [Godfrey-Smith, 2000]).

In this regard, Pettit [1996] notes that explanations of this general form do not even require a *past* history of selective processes. He argues that to establish a functional explanation we need only prove "virtual selection." Virtual selection refers to processes that would exist if some social practice with beneficial effects were to change. Suppose golfing may not be present now because of the positive benefits it had in the past, but if golfing were now challenged, then there would be pressures to maintain it. This virtual selection is just one way to make it true that $A$ persists because it causes $B$, where $B$ is a beneficial effect.

If differential selection processes can undergird functional explanations in economics, there still remain many unresolved issues about such explanations. Two I want to concentrate on here are the level at which selection acts and the relation of functional explanations to other kinds of explanations. Biologists and philosophers of biology have debated the prospects for group selection processes over and above selection on individuals. An emerging consensus on biological and social evolution [Sober and Wilson, 1998] sees natural selection as a multi-level process that can act at various levels. Group selection of a trait occurs when the trait is differently distributed in different groups in a population and those groups with a higher frequency of the trait are thereby more fit in that group size increases relative to other groups. In this situation the frequency of a trait can increase in the population as a whole, even though it may be less fit in each group. If the effects on group productivity are strong, the trait can evolve. Advocates of evolutionary game theory in economics have transported this consensus view into their analyses [Bowles, 2003].

However, there remains an important ambiguity in how group selection is understood that has consequences for evolutionary game theory in economics. Note two things about this notion of group selection. The fitness of the group is defined by ability to increase in size — to increase the number of *individuals* in the group. Thus the unit of measurement is individual organisms or economic actors specified by trait or strategy type. It is this choice of unit that makes an intergrated multilevel account possible: the effects of genic, individual, and group selection are compared in terms of differential survival of individual organisms of specified types.

However, there is another sense of group selection that sometimes is invoked without noting the difference. So group selection can occur when there are different kinds of groups that produce new groups that resemble them, when groups vary in their traits, and those traits have varying influences on the next generation. This is group selection where the units of measurement are groups, not individual organisms. If a trait leads to more groups of one kind, there can be group selection regardless of what happens to the number of individual organisms in them. Arguably this notion of group selection is what various biologists and social scientists have had in mind. It was explicitly contrasted with the current consensus notion in the mid 1980s [Kincaid, 1986; Damuth and Heissler, 1987].

The complications introduced by group selection in the second sense have not received sufficient attention. Group selection in the multilevel sense of Sober and Wilson studies a different dependent variable than that selectionist accounts based on the survival of groups. Thus, the claims of multilevel selection to integrate both group and individual processes. There are also complex issues surrounding the very idea of selection "acting at a level" that I cannot address here. But at the very least it is important to keep the two different senses of group selection — differential survival of individuals because of group membership and differential survival of types of groups — distinct.

The second complication mentioned above concerns how functional explanations in economics relate to other causal processes. While it is common to make claims such as "long term contracts exist in order to minimize transaction costs" as if the phenomena were fully explained, it is quite possible for functional causes to coexist with other nonfunctional causes. Game theory explanations are a nice case in point. When there are multiple equilibria, then when an equilibrium is reached, we can explain it as existing and persisting because it is optimal. However, this functional explanation has to be compatible with whatever explains why one equilibria exists rather than another. If we think of explanations as answering questions that can vary according to context, then game theory might answer the question "why is there some norm rather than none" while leaving the question "why this norm rather than that?" unanswered.

A final interesting question about functional explanations in economics as I have described them concerns the relation between models invoking differential survival and those involving learning. Vromen [1996] has argued that adaptive learning models are not consistent with evolutionary explanations. Selection processes require static individuals but adaptive learning prevents that. I think Vromen is right to the extent that the two factors have to be explicitly incorporated and that simply mentioning adaptive learning as a basis for evolutionary and hence functional accounts is insufficient. However, I think it is clear that learning can be combined with selection and in fact be described in selectionist terms. One key to seeing this is to recall that selection processes can be defined very abstractly and that learning is a kind of differential survival. Furthermore, there are existing models that show how both learning and differential survival of individuals can be combined [Boyd and Richerson, 2005].

## 7 THE NATURE OF ECONOMIC CAUSES

An interesting set of issues arises in connection with the ontological nature of causation in the economic realm. Recall the growth theories discussed earlier. I pointed out that these are frequently taken to provide nomological deductive explanations. However, they are not uniformly taken this way. They are also taken to describe the causes of economic growth. They are typical of much economics: a set of equations with some kind of causal interpretation is laid out and then tested by statistical means — usually by some form of regression analysis.

This general project relies on specific presuppositions about how economic causes work, something we should expect given general framework advocated above where claims about explanatory virtues are substantive empirical and often domain specific claims. These presuppositions come in the way the causal relationships are described and in the kind of data that is thought relevant. Let's take the simplest case illustrated by the current neoclassical growth theories. Growth is the dependent variable and is claimed to be causally influenced in either a negative or positive direct by a set of independent variables. A data set is obtained, sometimes cross sectional and sometimes panel data, with information about growth rates and their possible causal influences from many different countries. Regressions are then fitted to that data, with some possible independent variables being declared relevant and others irrelevant on the basis of significance tests.

As a vibrant literature on this paradigm in sociology and political science points out [Abbott, 2001], there are very strong causal assumptions lurking, ones that are often not true of the social world. The project represented by neoclassical growth theory makes these same kind of assumptions, namely:

1. Fixed entities with attributes. There is a universe of individuals and a fixed set of properties that are distributed among them. There is a fixed set of countries and a fixed batch of properties that are relevant to all

2. Constant causal relevance. There is one set of the causes of growth that are always part of the causal story.

3. Common time frame for causes and effects and for partial causes of the same effect. The measured fluctuations in the causal variables occur in the same time frame as each other and as the fluctuations in the effect variables. Changes in the determinants of growth occur over a one year period as do the changes in growth, precluding the duration of the causing event and the effect event from occurring at different time scales.

4. Uniform effects. The influence of a variable cannot vary according to context. There is one production function common to all countries. If the influence of a variable depends on the level of another variable, then the model is misspecified and a further variable representing the interaction effects of the two variables needs to be added. The resultant model then has every variable with a constant effect. In short, context can always be removed.

5. Independent effects. Each causal factor makes an independent contribution to the effect — their causal influence is separable.

6. Causal influence is found in variations of mean values.

7. Causation is not asymmetric. Increases in the value of a causal factor will increase the size of the effect and decreases will decrease the size of the effect.

The important point is not that these presuppositions cannot be true. They can be. But they are very strong assumptions when it comes to explaining complex economic and social phenomena. To return to our previous example, growth theory as pursued by development economics as opposed to neoclassical growth theory provides plenty of situations where these assumptions are highly implausible. Let me mention three.

Necessary causes are important in growth. Education, for example, seems not to suffice for growth (think of Cuba) but it may be a necessary requirement. Infrastructure of other sorts — e.g. roads — have a similar place. However the picture of causation in the equation and regressions approach has no place for necessary causes — all causes are individually sufficient to produce some effect. Causation is often conjunctural — it takes factors in combination to produce a given outcome. So the long standing idea of complementarities — which now has made it into rigorous models — describes exactly such a situation. Conjunctural causes do not fit easily with the regression and equations approach. Levels matter for how factors influence growth. There are probably "tipping points" in economic growth — situations where at a low level some factor has not effect but must reach some higher level to spur growth.

## 8 CONCLUSION

Naturalism in the philosophy of science suggests that philosophy of science has to be continuous with science itself and that it cannot produce useful a priori conceptual truths about explanation. Issues about the nature of explanation are scientific issues, albeit ones that certainly can gain from careful attention to clarifying the claims involved. Not surprisingly, the scientific issues surrounding explanation in economics vary according to the part of economics that is under scrutiny. Clarifying claims about economic explanation in the concrete can shed both light on the economics and on our philosophical understanding of explanation.

## BIBLIOGRAPHY

[Abbot, 2001] A. Abbott. *Time Matters.* Chicago: University of Chicago Press, 2001.

[Alchian, 1950] A. Alchian. Uncertainty, evolution and economic theory, *Journal of Political Economy* 58:211-221, 1950.

[Barro, 2001] R. Barro. *Determinants of Economic Growth.* Cambridge: MIT Press, 2001.

[Beller, 1999] M. Beller. *Quantum Dialogues.* Chicago: University of Chicago Press, 1999.

[Berk, 2004] R. Berk. *Regression Analysis: A Constructive Critique.* Thousand Oaks, CA: Sage, 2004.

[Bowles, 2003] S. Bowles. *Microeconomics: Behavior, Institutions, and Evolution.* Princeton: Princeton University Press, 2003.

[Boyd and Richardson, 2005] R. Boyd and P. Richerson. *The Origin and Evolution of Cultures.* Oxford: Oxford University Press, 2005.

[Cartwright, 1984] N. Cartwright. *How the Laws of Physic Lie.* New York: Oxford University Press, 1984.

[Cartwright, 1999] N. Cartwright. *The Dappled World.* New York: Cambridge University Press, 1999.

[Earman and Roberts, 1999] J. Earman and J. Roberts Ceteris Paribus, There Is No Problem of Privisoes, *Synthese* 118: 439-478, 1999.

[Earman *et al.*, 2002] J. Earman, J. Roberts, and S. Smith. Ceteris Paribus Lost. *Erkenntnis* 57: 281-301, 2002.

[Friedman, 1953] M. Friedman. The Methodology of Positive Economics. In *Essays in Positive Economics.* Chicago: University of Chicago Press, 1953.

[Garfinkle, 1981] A. Garfinkle. *Forms Of Explanation: Rethinking Questions In Social Theory.* New Haven: Yale University Press, 1981.

[Giere, 1988] R. Giere. *Explaining Science.* Chicago: University of Chicago Press 1988.

[Godfrey-Smith, 2000] P. Godfrey-Smith. The Replicator in Retrospect, *Biology and Philosophy,* 15: 403 – 423, 2000.

[Harms, 2004] W. Harms. *Information and Meaning in Evolutionary Processes.* Cambridge: Cambridge University Press, 2004.

[Hausman, 1998] D. Hausman. *Causal Asymmetries.* New York: Cambridge University Press, 1988.

[Heisler and Damuth, 1987] J. Heisler and H. Damuth. A method for analyzing selection in hierarchically struct[ured populations. *The American Naturalist,* 130(4): 582-602, 1987.

[Hoover, 2001] K. Hoover. *Causality in Macroeconomics.* Cambridge: Cambridge University Press, 2001.

[Kaplan, 2000] J. Kaplan. *The Limits and Lies of Human Genetic Research.* London: Routledge, 2000.

[Kincaid, 2008] H. Kincaid. Explaining Growth. In H. Kincaid and D. Ross, *The Oxford Handbook of Philosophy of Economics.* Oxford: Oxford University Press, 2008.

[Kincaid, 2006] H. Kincaid. Functional Explanation and Evolutionary Social Science. In Risjord and Turner, eds. Handbook of the Philosophy of Social Sciences, 2006.

[Kincaid, 1995] H. Kincaid. Optimality Arguments and the Theory of the Firm. In *The Reliability of Economic Models: Essays in the Epistemology of Economics,* ed. Daniel Little. Boston: Kluwer, 211-236, 1995.

[Kincaid, 1996] H. Kincaid. *Philosophical Foundations of the Social Sciences: Analyzing Controversies in Social Research.* Cambridge: Cambridge University Press, 1996.

[Kincaid, 2001] H. Kincaid. Assessing Game-Theoretic Accounts in the Social Sciences. In *Proceedings of the Congress on Logic, Methodology and the Philosophy of Science,* Dordrecht: Kluwer, 2001.

[Kitcher, 1989] P. Kitcher. Explanatory Unification and the Causal Structure of the World. In *Scientific Explanation.* Ed W. Salmon and P. Kitcher. Minneapolis: University of Minnesota Press, 1989.

[Ladyman and Ross, 2007] J. Ladyman and D. Ross. *Everything Must Go.* Oxford: Oxford University Press, 2007.

[Mäki, 2002] U. Mäki. Some non-reasons for non-realism about economics. In *Fact and Fiction in Economics. Realism, Models, and Social Construction,* ed. U. Mäki. Cambridge University Press, 90-104, 2002.

[Mankiew, 1995] N. Mankiew. The Growth of Nations, *Brookings Papers on Economic Activity* 25: 275-310, 1995.

[Morgan and Morrison, 1999] M. Morgan and M. Morrison. *Models as Mediators.* Cambridge: Cambridge University Press, 1999.

[Nelson and Winter, 1982] R. Nelson and S. Winter. *An Evolutionary Theory of Economic Change.* Cambridge: Harvard University Press, 1982.

[Northcott, 2005] R. Northcott. Pearson's Wrong Turning: Against Statistical Measures of Causal Efficacy, *Philosophy of Science* 72: 900–912, 2005.

[Pettit, 1996] P. Pettit. Functional explanation and virtual selection. *British Journal for the Philosophy of Science,* 44: 291-302, 1996.

[Romer, 1990] P. Romer. Endogenous Technological Change, *Journal of Political Economy,* 1990.

[Rober, 1994] P. Romer. The Origins of Endogenous Growth, *Journal of Economic Perspectives* 8: 3-22, 1994.

[Ross, 2005] D. Ross. *Economic Theory and Cognitive Science: Microexplanation*. Cambridge: MIT Press, 2005.

[Sklar, 1995] L. Sklar. *Physics and Chance*. Cambridge: Cambridge University Press, 1995.

[Sober and Wilson, 1998] E. Sober and D. Wilson. *Unto Others: The Evolution and Psychology of Unselfish Behavior*. Cambridge: Harvard University Press, 1998.

[Solow, 1956] R. Solow. A Contribution to the Theory of Economic Growth, *Quarterly Journal of Economics* 70: 65-94, 1956.

[Sutton, 1998] J. Sutton. *Technology and Market Structure: Theory and History*. Cambridge: MIT Press, 1998.

[Vromen, 1996] J. Vromen. *Economic Evolution*. London: Routledge, 1996.

[Woodward, 1997] J. Woodward. Explanation, Invariance, and Intervention, *Philosophy of Science* 64: S26-41, 1997.

[Wright, 1973] L. Wright. Functions. *Philosophical Review*, 82: 139-168, 1973.

# THE UNREASONABLE EFFICACY OF MATHEMATICS IN MODERN ECONOMICS

Philip Mirowski

"I came to the position that mathematical analysis is not one of many ways of doing economic theory. It is the only way. Economic theory *is* mathematical analysis. Everything else is just pictures and talk."

Robert Lucas (in [Warsh, 2006, p.168])

The purported identity of economics and mathematics is apparently taken for granted in the contemporary world. There was an era during the first century of the existence of neoclassical economic theory when the role of mathematics in economic reasoning and expression constituted a burning issue: mathematical models were taken to be a *subset* of all economic discourse, and consequently many of the major figures in the field would defend the efficacy of particular formalisms from various vantage points situated within economics. As Mirowski [1991] demonstrated, mathematical expression had only began to occupy an increasing proportion of pages of the major economics journals from the 1930s onwards, and this coincided with the initial rise to dominance of the neoclassical school in various individual cultural contexts. It was therefore to be expected that the discussions of the import and impact of mathematics intensified towards the middle of the $20^{th}$ century, although one notes a nascent tendency to conflate neoclassical economics with mathematical economics *tout court* (a synecdoche which would have distressed many economists from Alfred Marshall to Ronald Coase, and from Herbert Simon to Donald Katzner). Nevertheless, as the orthodoxy became consolidated in the postwar period, it transpired that: (a) the belief began to be expressed amongst economists that economic theory was simply equivalent to a generic mathematics, to such an extent that many otherwise sophisticated economists started to claim that it was the mathematical 'tools' themselves which were the primary driver of the development of modern economic theory; (b) a period of criticism of economists by mathematicians and sophisticated practitioners blossomed from the 1940s onwards, only to peter out by the 1980s; and (c) after the Fall of the Wall and the accession of American neoclassical economics to world dominance, the topic of the role and implications of mathematics fell into desuetude. The lapse into silence of economic methodologists has furthermore coincided with what some see as a relative relaxation of the self-conscious elevation

Handbook of the Philosophy of Science. Volume 13: Philosophy of Economics.
Volume editor: Uskali Mäki. General editors: Dov M. Gabbay, Paul Thagard and John Woods.

of levels of mathematical formalism in current issues of the 'top' economics journals. One consequence of this curious trajectory has been that, for decades now, there has been essentially no contact between the lively postwar debates over the philosophy of mathematics (covered in vol.9 of this *Handbook*) and the philosophy of economics. Hence neither the 'big three' foundational positions designated as logicism, intuitionism, and formalism (with one important exception discussed below), nor more subtle philosophical schools (such as Platonism, naturalism, or structuralism), have played any substantive role in modern economics; nor have philosophers attempted to deploy them in order to illuminate economic practice. The recent Elgar *Handbook of Economic Methodology,*[1] for instance, contains no entry for "Mathematics", nor for any philosophical school of meta-mathematics, nor indeed, for any other cognate term. Some philosophers [Rosenberg, 1992; McCloskey, 1994; Lawson, 2003; Blaug, 2003] have sought to indict modern economics as constituting little more than a minor outpost of the mathematics profession, but that merely reproduces the Lucas position above, while reversing the evaluative stance. The untutored conviction that modern economics is simply the inexorable playing out of a monolithic mathematical program has yet to be subjected to careful analytical scrutiny. In the midst of this general disinterest, any short article cannot seriously aspire to conjure an elaborate philosophical sensitivity on the part of economists, much less forge the possible but absent connections to the modern philosophy of mathematics.

However, it may be important to realize that some mathematicians who have cast their gaze in the direction of economics have taken the opposite position. Indeed, there have been mathematicians who have instead expressed profound skepticism towards the standard practices of economists. Their indictments range from technical criticisms of sloppy practices in the use of set theory[2] and ignorance of the theory of foliations [Saari, 1995; 1999] to misrepresenting the technical mathematical concept of "complexity" [Israel, 2005], to the tendency to "dress scientific brilliancies and scientific absurdities alike in the impressive uniform of formulae and theorems. Unfortunately, however, an absurdity in uniform is far more persuasive than an absurdity unclad. The very fact that a theory appears in mathematical form, for instance, that a theory has provided the occasion for the application of a fixed point theorem... somehow makes us more ready to take it more seriously" [Schwartz, 1986, p.22]. For these mathematicians, it most decidedly has *not* been mathematics alone that drives economics; yet, *qua* mathematicians, they also did not feel it was their duty to supply a list of causes that have brought about what they consider sub-optimal practices. Is it any wonder that when an economic theorist actually sets out to seriously discuss the effects of mathematics upon contemporary economics these days, his remarks are derided

[1][Davis *et al.*, 1998]. The closest it comes is an entry on "Axiomatization" by Vilks, which does not cover any of the topics we touch upon here. One observes the same relative dearth in such outlets as *Economics and Philosophy* and the *Journal of Economic Methodology*.

[2]See, for instance Thomas Kuczynski, quoted in [Fischer, 1993, p.129] and Vilks in [Davis *et al.*, 1998, p.32].

as a jejeune emotional outburst?[3]

In this entry, we shall avoid the common presumption that mathematics serves as an uncontested surrogate for logic and rationality in all scientific research, or a uniquely effective prophylactic against error in all its manifestations; but equally eschew the notion that mathematics and economics are identical; and instead approach the use of mathematics in economics as a particular set of practices with their own special characteristic modalities and justifications. This conforms to a subset of recent trends in the philosophy of mathematics which tend to stress quasi-empirical and historicist approaches to understanding science in action [Ferrieros and Gray, 2006; Tymoczko, 1998; Aspray and Kitcher, 1988]. There are a number of points where these modalities and justifications *might* intersect with current philosophical issues in mathematics, and we shall point these out along the way. However, the reader would be prudent to keep in mind that the modern economics profession has succeeded quite well by suppressing or otherwise ridiculing anyone who has sought to approach the question from a methodological direction.[4]

In order to lend some semblance of decorum to what has often appeared little more than unseemly brawls, we shall divide our survey into three distinct questions: (1) What types of defenses and forms of objections have been raised in the pre-1980 period to the generic use of mathematics in economics? (2) What have been the primary explanations of the types of mathematical practices prevalent specifically in Neoclassical economics since its inception? (3) What are some alternative arguments (both ontological and epistemic) for a philosophically appropriate approach to mathematics in economics in the future?

## 1 THE CLASSICAL ARGUMENTS

The possibility of serious mathematical formalization of economic theories began to be broached in the middle of the $19^{th}$ century, and various rationales for that project soon followed close on their heels. Some of the earliest proponents, such as Augustin Cournot, began their careers believing that the spread of markets would induce more "rational" behavior on the part of the general populace, and thus bring their behavior into closer correspondence with mathematics that had been developed within rational mechanics; however, in Cournot's case, he soon grew disenchanted with his subjects, and abandoned mathematical economics for the remainder of his career [de Ville and Menard, 1989]. Economists more stalwart in their advocacy of the necessity of mathematical expression as a generic imperative tended to break in one of two directions when rendering an account of their

[3]A nice recent example is [Rubenstein, 2006] which he reports a referee disparaged as "an outpouring from a therapist's couch" (p.865).

[4]See, for instance, [Samuelson, 1994; Maskin, 2004; Binmore, 2005]. The latter writes: 'I understand the temptation to dwell on game theory's dubious history: its stops and starts, its dead ends, and its failure to be a theory of everything. But surely the time has come to put aside these outmoded misgivings. The success of game theory is now an objective historical reality. Why not accept this simple fact?" (p.28)

program. The first class of defense tended to be ontological, insisting that something about the economy intrinsically dictates the use of mathematics, usually taking the form of an assertion that the economy is "naturally quantitative". This defense resembles the "Putnam-Quine" thesis concerning the 'indispensability' of mathematics for empirical science [Colyvan, 2001; 2004]. The second defense is usually phrased as "mathematics is a language", but of course a language of a particularly privileged type, which must have salutary effects upon the larger research program. This position veered closest to the formalist program in the philosophy of mathematics, especially during the brief postwar liaison between one subset of mathematical economics and the Bourbakist movement within mathematics. Sometimes, especially in earlier eras, both defenses were mixed and conflated, often on the very same page. A bellwether example can be taken from one of the progenitors of neoclassical economics, William Stanley Jevons, in his *Theory of Political Economy*:

> It is clear that economics, if it is to be a science at all, must be a mathematical science... simply because it deals in quantities.... The symbols in mathematical books are not different in nature from language... They do not constitute the mode of reasoning they embody; they merely facilitate its exhibition and comprehension. [1970, p.78]

The fact that these classical defenses were repeatedly conflated throughout the $20^{th}$ century perhaps reveals more about their common weaknesses than it does about any possible cogency or coherence. We shall briefly deal with each below.

## *1.1 The Ontological Move: The Economy as 'naturally quantitative'*

In a sense, this classical defense is merely a corollary of the early modern position that God had written the "Book of Nature" in mathematical language. As political economy shed its origins in moral philosophy, the theological foundations for the ontological defense also were progressively relinquished. Often, political economists attempted to piggyback squarely upon the shoulders of natural philosophers: Science had shown that Nature was mathematical; the Economy was a Natural process; ergo, the Economy was mathematical. This syllogism came to grief over time due to changing ontological commitments as to the fundamental nature of the Economy.

Although basic ontological issues are covered elsewhere in this *Handbook,* for our current purposes it is enough to note that as long as 'the economy' was conceptualized as coextensive with a discrete subset of physical existence, appeals to natural processes were less subject to challenge. However, the irony inherent in this situation was that this constituted the era of classical political economy and the relatively limited and unsuccessful mathematization of economics. It was only when economics became reoriented in a more mentalist direction, and hence away from its prior Classical grounding the economy in its physicalist dimension, that sustained mathematical research took hold. As this trend has continued, and after 1950 the economy was increasingly itself reconceptualized as an information processor, and thus simultaneously upgraded from a mere subset of human experience to potentially being able to encompass the entire universe of human and non-human activity [Mirowski, 2002], that an ontological appeal to the intrinsic quantitative character of the economy tended to lose whatever cogency it may have initially possessed.

Much of this curious trajectory left its wake in the economics literature in the format of endemic disputes over whether the entities postulated by the theory in question were in fact 'measurable' or not. If the economy had indeed been transparently naturally quantitative, then it is hard to understand why such controversies absorbed so much time and energy on the part of economists. The disputes which began in the later $19^{th}$ century were not confined to a single school: Marxists argued whether the labor values privileged in their theories were truly 'measurable', neoclassicals anguished over the 'measurability' of utility, while Institutionalists struggled over the measurability of the macroeconomy. Furthermore, the track record of success or failure with regard to measurement issues does not go very far in explaining why some schools of economics failed while others succeeded. Arguably, the Institutionalist invention of the National Income Accounts have enjoyed the longest track record of widespread practical implementation of useful quantitative techniques in the annals of the history of economics, but this did little to prevent the demise of the program in the later $20^{th}$ century. Professional accountants devoted prodigious efforts to building the social structures which would implement and stabilize quantification of the economy, as well as instituting double-entry algebras, but they were almost entirely ignored by the economic orthodoxy. Conversely, the neoclassical program rose to dominance by claiming that it had circumvented the conundrum by resort to 'ordinalist' rather than 'cardinalist' utility; but in fact there was much about this purported dispensation that did not actually solve the ontological problem of the rationalization of the mathematics.[5] Of course conventional measurability is no necessary prerequisite for mathematical discourse, but in the case of economics, when compared to other disciplines like psychology or physics, very little concern was ever expended to incorporate insights from the subset of mathematics which explored representation systems, homeomorphisms and semi-orders under the rubric of "measurement theory".[6]

Nevertheless, the man in the street might retort that "prices and quantities and money are numbers," and that settles the issue of the obvious mathematical character of the economy. However, economic historians such as Witold Kula [1986] have pointed out that prior to the Renaissance most economic entities lacked the algebraic structure and invariance which is required to subject them to rudimentary mathematical manipulation; it is well known that for aeons money in the form

[5]See [Hands, 2006a; 2006b], where it is argued that the move to ordinalism allowed economists to dissociate observability from mathematical quantification, only to then deny that preferences had any necessary mathematical structure.

[6]See [Krantz *et al.*, 1971; Roberts, 1979].

of coin similarly was compromised. Long ago Werner Sombart reminded us that medieval merchants did not keep accounts in such a way as to judge whether they were actually making a profit by modern standards. This has led historians like Hadden [1994] to suggest that the quantitative practices we associate both with natural science and the economy were introduced in Early Modern Europe simultaneously, through a series of beliefs and activities that *imposed* a mathematical character upon the phenomena. Whatever else one may think about this history, it is clear that there is no firm evidence that prices, commodity units and money were ever constituted as numbers in some pristine ontological sense: they were (and still are) contingent upon a whole range of other social practices, might be reorganized in a myriad of ways, and exhibit no 'natural' or stable mathematical character. Hence a defense of mathematical economics which points to the natural occurrence of numbers in the economy puts the cart before the horse.

Before one dismisses this point on the grounds that it refers to an era long dead and gone, and cannot possibly refer to the modern situation, let us consult the opinion of a modern Nobel Prize recipient:

> Having chosen a unit of measurement for each [commodity] and a sign convention to distinguish inputs from outputs, one can describe the action of an economic agent by a vector in the commodity space $\mathbb{R}^l$. The *fact* that the commodity space has a structure of a real vector space is a basic reason for the success of the mathematization of economic theory. [Debreu, 1984, p.267-8]

One observes this as a modern variant of the ontological defense; it is also based upon a false premise. No commodity units actually display the requisite phenomenological invariance of identity to physically underwrite the imposition of an algebra, much less a connected topological space, be it for either purposes of consumption or production. The demonstration of this principle for a mentalist doctrine like neoclassical theory is easy: invariance would depend upon subjective states which vary between items and observers. To every individual *qua* individual, each apple is different: some bigger, some stunted, some mottled, some McIntosh, some engineered to taste like tomatoes...[7] Consequently, for the purposes of economics, by contrast with Newtonian physics, there can be no legitimately independent Euclidean space. However, if one adopts a more objectivist vantage point with regard to physical production, perhaps even abjuring neoclassical theory, the point remains. Nicholas Georgescu-Roegen [1976] insisted that the imposition of cardinality always leaves a qualitative residual, which is why production functions cannot truly capture physical production activities. Indeed, commodity identities rarely map one-to-one into production efficacy (gasoline might be sold by the gallon, but its efficacy depends upon an array of variables, such as foot-pounds

[7] Indeed there was an attempt by Kelvin Lancaster in the 1960s to rewrite the 'commodity space' in terms of physical characteristics, but significantly, the innovation was ignored. The reason is that it inadvertently reveals the lack of invariance of the commodity space relative to subjective perception.

per BTU, sulfur content, Reynolds number, etc. etc.), and therefore commodity identities (such as they might be) have no fixed relationship to physical identities. Therefore, Debreu the Bourbakist (see below) has the situation backwards: the topological properties of commodities do not underwrite the legitimacy of his mathematics; rather, it is the operation of the economy which imposes some topology (perhaps Euclidean, perhaps not) as part and parcel of the institution of a certain set of mathematical practices deployed by the agents. If the topology of commodity space and the operation of the price system are functionally interdependent, then there is no fixed natural property of the world we can point to in order to justify the mathematical formalisms of neoclassical theory. Indeed, it would seem that commodities do not generally conform to a Euclidian vector space defined over the reals.

This brings us to the Putnam-Quine thesis [Putnam, 1979; Colyvan, 2001, 2004]. Philosophers of mathematics have interpreted this as a metaphysical thesis stating that the observed indispensability of mathematics to empirical science is sufficient warrant for us to believe in the existence of the mathematical entities posited by those eminently successful theories. As Putnam writes, "If the calculus had not been 'justified' Weierstrass style, it would have been 'justified' anyway. The point is that the real justification of the calculus is its *success* — its success in mathematics, and its success in physical science" [1979, pp.65-6]. More than one philosopher has noted that this might appear more plausible in the context of a philosophy like Quine's holism, but less than compelling in a vision where success is distributed rather more unevenly across propositions, theories, schools and even different sciences. For example, what is to prevent one science from appropriating a mathematical artifact which has previously proven effective in another unrelated science, on the grounds of a mistaken epistemic inductive inference? Alex Rosenberg [1992, pp.232-4] has noted that neoclassical economics has resort to the same sorts of mathematics as that found in mechanics and some fields of biology, but that one cannot infer from that the equivalence of 'success' in all three disciplines.

As it stands, modern economists have not been moved to make explicit appeal to the Putnam-Quine thesis, but do display a rather unsavory tendency to maintain that might makes right.[8] If there ever arose an occasion when they were forced to render a serious philosophical account of the nature of their 'success', then perhaps the Putnam-Quine thesis might then come into play.

## *1.2 The Linguistic Move: mathematics as a language*

Many economists have quoted the epigraph to Paul Samuelson's *Foundations of Economic Analysis* [1947] "Mathematics is a language"; relatively few, however, have been capable of illuminating more precisely why this should serve as a defense of mathematical expression in economics. Tjalling Koopmans, in his *Three Essays*, provides this gloss:

[8]Cf. fn. 3 above. See also, [Weintraub, 2005].

> That the mathematical method when correctly applied forces the investigator to give a complete statement of assuredly noncontradictory assumptions has generally been conceded as far as the relations of the assumptions to reasoning is concerned. To this may be added that the absence of any natural meaning of mathematical symbols, other than the meaning given to them by postulate or by definition, prevents the associations clinging to words from intruding upon the reasoning process. [1957, pp.172-3]

Another member of the Cowles commission and fellow Nobelist, Gerard Debreu, asserted that: "In its mathematical form, economic theory is open to efficient scrutiny for logical errors... [It assists in] removing all their economic interpretations and letting their mathematical infrastructure stand on its own. The greater logical solidity of more recent analyses has contributed to the rapid contemporary construction of economic theory" [1991, p.3].

The problem with such propositions is threefold: (a) the auxiliary claims made by Koopmans and Debreu can be easily refuted by counterexamples; (b) when divested of their misleading auxiliary hypotheses, their equation of mathematics with language runs the risk of emptiness; and (c), these and other economists have shown themselves uninterested in investing the comparison with real substance. Let us take each objection in turn.

When economists compare mathematics to a language, they do not generally mean that it is one among many languages in terms of strengths and drawbacks; rather, they intend it as a prelude to explain why mathematics constitutes a *superior* mode of discourse relative to the vernacular. This becomes obvious, even in the truncated quotes above. Yet while the superior virtues are confidently conjured, they are never actually demonstrated, mainly because as individual virtues, they can be readily challenged. Take Koopmans' evocation of the bracing discipline of mathematics upon the individual investigator. By the 1950s, when Gödel's theorems had become something of a topic outside the small circle of metamathematicians, Koopmans should have been aware that a "*complete* statement of assuredly noncontradictory assumptions" was by no means automatically guaranteed. Furthermore, the idea that mathematics stood wonderfully empty of allusion, metaphor, synecdoche and wordplay could be refuted from within the history of economics itself — this will be covered in Section 2 below. Likewise, Debreu's assertion that mathematics' refining fire sped up the evolution of modern economics could be countered by claims emanating from his colleagues such as Kenneth Arrow and David Kreps that very little truly novel took place in modern economics after the triumph of the Cowles program in the 1960s.[9] Or, one might

[9]David Kreps [1997, 73, 77], for instance, suggested that "the development of economics seems fairly moribund, at least compared with the late 1970s" and that there was a "decrease in the importance of deduction in economic [theory]." Joseph Stiglitz [2003, 572] complained, "Something was wrong — indeed, seriously wrong — with the competitive equilibrium models which represented the prevailing paradigm." Arrow, who was sometimes credited with seeking to encourage new departures at the Santa Fe Institute, mourned that "the Santa Fe Institute

point to more recent formal proofs with relatively negative consequences for the neoclassical program, such as the Milgrom-Stokey no-trade theorem, or the Sonnenschein/Mantel/Debreu results on the lack of restrictions placed upon excess demand functions within Walrasian general equilibrium (both from the 1970s), and ask why the profession still seems to have more or less ignored them. The trajectory of modern economic theory is full of contradictions and paradoxes that defy any notion of a central regulative principle or linguistic ukase holding economists' feet to the fire [Mirowski and Hands, 2006]. Thus one is left to wonder just how seriously the target audience for these confident pronouncements was supposed to take the virtues purportedly linked to the 'language' of mathematics.

The *aporia* surrounding the assertion that mathematics is a language are not confined to the precincts of economists, but are found throughout the sciences. Indeed, for many scientists, it has become an excuse for avoiding any detailed discussion of the role of efficacy of mathematics. As Brian Rotman has written:

> A conception of mathematics as... the transparent medium for conveying and transmitting [knowledge] has become, whatever insights and energy it might have once provided in the Cartesian tradition, explanatorily inert and passive. And it is precisely because nothing new issues from it — about mathematical practice or the constitution of its objects — that the conception is so easy to own and assent to as an unproblematic and obvious truism... In most cases they are, indeed, little more than a recognition of the extended symbolicity of a discipline. [1993, p.21]

If economists were to take this line of defense more seriously, one would have expected them to engage with issues of semantics and pragmatics of the use of mathematics in economics, and not to focus so very intently upon syntax, as has been suggested in philosophy by Tymoczko [1998, p.389]. There has, of course, been an isolated individual here and there who has proposed a semantic/syntactic clarification [Dennis, 2002], or seeking to treat the deployment of mathematics in specific instances from a rhetorical perspective [McCloskey, 1994]; but by and large, these have been ignored within the discipline.

Generally, it has been historians of mathematics who have proven more willing to explore the actual social implications of the characterization of mathematics as a language. One of the more controversial implications which resides very near the surface of most discussions of the escalation of the resort to more esoteric mathematics in economics is the fact that its spread has served more to *exclude* participation than it does to widen the circle of discourse.[10] A nice exploration of

has not developed a consistent economic program": "As I think more about complexity theory, I become more concerned that there is some sense in which we will never know how the economy operates" (quoted in [Colander *et al.*, 2004, 294, 298]).

[10] "The spread of mathematized economic theory was helped even by its esoteric character. Since its messages cannot be deciphered by economists who do not have the proper key, their evaluation is entrusted to those who have access to the code" [Debreu, 1991, p.6]. The same sorts of comments were made in physics almost three centuries ago [Gingras, 2001].

this proposition in the context of $19^{th}$ century mathematical physics is [Warwick, 2003], which argues that far from being an especially self-contained and transparent mode of expression, "it is the most esoteric and technical disciplines that are actually the most social" (p.45) because they require a prodigious complement of institutional structures simply to make the mathematical mode of research viable. Lacking the pedagogical and cultural apparatus, personal facility in abstract reasoning never suffices to produce plausible mathematical research. Warwick shows, for instance, that Maxwell's electrodynamical theory could not be dependably understood by contemporaries a stone's throw away in London, and that Einstein's theory of relativity was worse than Greek for the aether theorists ensconced on the banks of the Cam. He maintains these incidents "illustrate the doubly conservative role that training systems can play, initially by resisting and then by preserving and propagating a new theory" [2003, p.358].

Considerations of pedagogy should not be dismissed as bearing minimal importance for philosophical concerns within any field in which mathematics becomes a major criterion for success. Mathematics so happens to be a singular sphere of human discourse whereby insistence upon the self-contained discreteness of intellectual constructs is pushed to an extreme (whatever the actual course of events), resulting in rigidly inflexible claims that the manipulation of designated concepts is either unambiguously correct or incorrect. This skewed construction of knowledge is particularly serviceable in the classroom, where discipline and the hierarchical dominance of teacher over student can be then projected into the realm of knowledge itself. Once internalized, it promotes the impression that the subject matter of mathematics seems to police itself, sanctioning the correct application of its own rules. This fact goes some distance in explaining that most working mathematicians would rather adopt some vague form of Platonism rather than seriously entertain the idea that they themselves participate in the construction of mathematics as a body of thought. But more to the point, this quotidian Platonism then gets projected onto the world which is the subject matter of the field colonized by mathematical expression as well. A mathematized world — say, a mathematized *economy* — by extension then also seems capable of policing itself, since it is being portrayed as existing independently of the way any analyst might characterize it, puttering along on its own terms. In this way, everyday Platonism (based in classroom pedagogy) can actually *reinforce* the belief in something like *laissez-faire*. Of course, no model comes equipped an inevitable political orientation; but it does behoove us to stay aware of such subliminal messages potentially carried by this supposedly empty language.

Some sociologists of science have followed up on these propositions to suggest how they may have played out in modern economics. Marion Fourcade [2006, pp.159-60], for instance, has suggested that the stress upon mathematical expression in the training of economists serves both to extract tyros from the parochial vernacular of their youth as a prelude to rendering them willing recruits to a supposedly globalized technocratic elite; and further, it helps promulgate the unarticulated philosophical premise that, "economics relies upon abstract universal reasoning in terms of 'representative agents' and a 'representative economy'... Economic problems are detached from their local context, and are generally understood to be instances of some universal phenomena." When Gerard Debreu writes:

> An economy $E$ is defined by: for each $i = 1, \ldots, m$ a non-empty subset $x_i$ of $\mathbb{R}^l$ completely preordered by $\leq_i$; for each $j = 1, \ldots n$; a non-empty subset of $y_j$ of $\mathbb{R}^l$ ; a point $\omega$ of $\mathbb{R}^l$ . A state of $E$ is an $(m+n)$-tuple of points of $\mathbb{R}^l$ [1959,p.75],

his notation is freighted with all manner of ontological implications for the very meaning of what it is to gesture towards "an economy", the location of the analyst perched in his view from nowhere, and even deeper inarticulate notions about the ambitions of economics as a nomothetic science. These inarticulate presuppositions are not rendered transparent through the 'language' of mathematics; rather, they are conveyed through the attendant socialization required to endow them with significance, a socialization which is provided under the rubric of "provision of the tools of economics". This and more is obscured by the catchphrase, "mathematics is a language".

It seems that the postwar economists enamored of the proposition that "mathematics is a language" were not entirely philosophical naïfs, but may have been merely relaying garbled notions of the school of philosophy of science they were most familiar with at the time, namely, logical positivism [Mirowski, 2004b]. Especially due to their involvement with Operations Research, many economists most anxious to promote the use of mathematics in economics had come into contact with key positivist philosophers who had emigrated to America, such as Hans Reichenbach and Rudolf Carnap. Around that time, Carnap had been promoting a vision of philosophy as "the mathematics and physics of language" [Richardson, 2003, p.180], and had just published his *Logical Syntax of Language* (1934). Although the Vienna Circle generally was interested in the logicist program, Carnap had become attracted to the idea of providing a metalanguage for all of science. Philosophical analysis under this description would consist of the translation of key statements of a given science into a formal mode, as a prelude to the detection and banishment of metaphysical elements. By the time of his contribution to the *International Encyclopedia of Unified Science* (1938), Carnap was insisting that the philosophy of science should not be concerned with the actual activities of real scientists, but instead be the study of the content of the science as reduced to linguistic expressions, which he posited as an axiom system, a specific calculus and a system of semantical rules for interpretation of the calculus. For Carnap, formalization made it possible to forgo the need for an intuitive understanding of the theory in question; and it was frequently something very like this position that lay behind the $20^{th}$ century economist's claims that mathematics was just a language [Hands, 2007].

## 2 THE ROLE AND FUNCTIONS OF MATHEMATICS IN NEOCLASSICAL ECONOMICS

In this section, we turn our attention from attempts to provide generic foundations for the use of mathematics in economics to more focused attempts to discuss the role and significance of mathematics within neoclassical economics. Taking a cue from authors such as [Ferreiros and Gray, 2006], we shall proceed under the premise that these issues cannot be treated in isolation from the actual historical practices of economists and their relevant reference groups. Over the last few decades, a small group of scholars has begun to explore the mathematical activities of specific economists, with an eye towards explanation of the roles that mathematics has served in orthodox economics.[11] In lieu of a comprehensive survey, we shall cover a proper subset of that work, chosen according to topics which bear most directly upon salient controversies in the philosophy of mathematics. The issues touched upon here will encompass: (a) The origins of the neoclassical model in physics; (b) the impact of Bourbakism upon the Cowles program for Walrasian general equilibrium; (c) Weintraub on formalism in modern economics; and (d) the place of John von Neumann in the shaping of $20^{th}$ century mathematical economics.

### *2.1 The Physics Inspiration of Neoclassical Economics*

One can find numerous comments by neoclassical economists dropped *en passant* along the lines that, "A utility function of a consumer looks quite similar to a potential function in the theory of gravitation" [Koopmans, 1957, p.176], but only when they were followed up by historians, did the extent of the debt of orthodox economics to physics become clear. It is now commonly acknowledged that the origins of neoclassical theory were rooted in the imitation of the novel formalisms of energy physics which had been developed in the mid-$19^{th}$ century.[12] Indeed, key protagonists such as Leon Walras, William Stanley Jevons and Francis Edgeworth explicitly acknowledged that they were copying physics in the first instance in order to hasten along economics to attainment of the status of a mathematical science. Physics provided the specific formalisms, as well as the general approach to modeling deterministic systems. Components of the initial appropriation included equating "utility" with potential energy, 'commodity space' with n-dimensional Euclidean space, 'price' with force, and 'trade' with motion in space. The notion of "equilibrium" had not occupied pride of place in economic theory until after it was lifted wholesale from physics, as was the primacy of constrained maximization in its determination. Not every feature of the mathematical energy model

[11]A roll call would include [Weintraub, 1985; 1991; 2002; Weintraub and Mirowski, 1994; Kjeldsen, 2000; 2001; Sent, 1998; Wulwick, 1995; Bausor, 1995; Mirowski, 1989; 2002; 2004a; Rizvi, 1994; 1998; Guerraggio and Molho, 2004; Perona, 2005].

[12]The clearest statement of this thesis came in [Mirowski, 1989]. For critique and elaboration, see [De Marchi, 1993; White, 2004].

found an exact correlate in the novel economics;[13] but then perhaps complete isomorphism was not required for the purposes of sparking off a new research program in economics. What is more significant is to come to appreciate the sheer number of ontological and epistemological premises which were freighted over into economics under the pretence of simply adopting a few tools from their physical science brethren, without much in the way of conscious discrimination.

We can start with the elevation of the calculus to central mathematical technique within economics. Mathematical expression had been tentatively explored prior to the 1870s in political economy, but an insuperable obstacle had proven to be the inability to rally any substantial following around any single formalism. The expropriation of field theory solved many thorny problems at one fell swoop. The lowest common denominator of competence amongst the scientifically trained in the $19^{th}$ century was some familiarity with classical mechanics; and therefore settling upon pre-entropic energy physics as the template maximized the potential pool of recruits for a crusading mathematical economics. It is precisely for this reason that early neoclassical theorists were frequently called "marginalists" (a now obsolete designation): the imitation of classical mechanics of potentials practically imposed an obsession over 'small changes' in economic life, along with the elevation of such notions as 'diminishing marginal utility' and 'diminishing returns' to temporary status as 'laws' in their own right. Furthermore, $19^{th}$ century conceptions of rigor tended to root the particular target mathematical model in a physical analogue, so the imitation of physics simultaneously provided a high-quality mathematical warrant for the asserted lack of logical contradictions within the model. Insofar as opponents to mathematical economics had insisted upon the exceptional (and perhaps ineffable) character of human activity, the metaphorical overtones of Natural Motion and mental energies provided a strong retort concerning the relevance of the natural-science approach to the economy. It could also be used to mask the dogmatic tendencies inherent in the drive to displace previous classical political economy, as openly admitted by Alfred Marshall:

> The new analysis is endeavoring gradually and tentatively to bring over into economics, as far as the widely different nature of the material will allow, those methods of the science of small increments (commonly called the differential calculus) to which man owes directly or indirectly the greater part of the control he has obtained in recent times over physical nature. It is still in its infancy; it has no dogmas, no standards of orthodoxy....[yet] there is a remarkable harmony and agreement on essentials among those working constructively by the new method; and especially among such of them as have served an apprenticeship in the simpler and more definite, and therefore more advanced, problems of physics. [1920, pp.xvi-xvii]

Even more significantly, recourse to classical mechanics tended to impose what

[13]See, for instance, the argument that a conservative vector field would only be fully carried over into neoclassical theory in the case of 'compensated' prices, in (Hands in [De Marchi, 1993]).

has sometimes been called the 'norm of closure': the ontological portrayal of the economy as a system bounded in time and space, upon which is superimposed a tendency to atomism and the prohibition of the generation of novelty by any functional composition.[14] It effectively banished history as a serious source of inspiration for political economy, reducing time to the ontological status of just another indexical variable on a par with spatial orientation. Most of all, it is doubtful that any of these dramatic alterations of angle of approach to the problem of political economy were consciously intended by any of the progenitors; they said they were motivated by the fact that science dictated the use of this particular mathematics, but neglected to detect a mathematics loaded with unforeseen ontological consequences for economics, and then their heirs were left to explore all the ways their world picture had been stretched, shrunk and pressed by the bequest of their imitation of physics.

## *2.2 The Allure of Bourbakism for mid-20$^{th}$ century Neoclassicism*

However much the first few generations of neoclassical economists were concerned to trumpet their mathematical credentials, the actual influence of philosophical commitments originating in academic mathematics upon the economics discipline had to wait for roughly another 80 years. Direct contact with the mathematics profession finally was brought about by two semi-independent events: the rise to authority of Bourbakist-influenced cadre at the Cowles Commission in the 1950s, and the slow but steady infusion of von Neumann-inspired themes into the discipline beginning in the 1940s. Interestingly enough, these two streams correspond to what Amy Dahan Dalmedico [2001] claims were the two rival 'images' or foundational stances prevalent in the mathematics profession from the end of WWII to roughly the 1990s. We cover the former in this section, and the latter in the next.

It may seem incongruous to observe the austere French philosophical doctrines of Bourbakism, which notoriously championed the 'purity' of mathematics isolated from all application, gaining a foothold in an inescapably 'applied' context like American neoclassical economics; but such curious phenomena are precisely what one uncovers upon assuming a more naturalist/historicist approach to the philosophy of mathematics. Historians of mathematics are familiar with the way Bourbakist attitudes became quite popular in the American profession in the 1940s, and in particular at the University of Chicago. The Cowles Commission, located at Chicago from 1938-54, became the launching pad for those Bourbakist attitudes into the economics discipline.[15]

Most economists associate the Cowles Commission with the invention and development of structural econometrics, and therefore tend to think of it as a bastion

[14]One economist who insisted upon the dangers of these analytical prohibitions was Nicholas Georgescu-Roegen [1976].

[15]The accounts of Bourbakism and its relationship to economics herein are based upon [Corry, 1992, 2001; Dieudonné, 1982; Weintraub and Mirowski, 1994; Dalmedico, 2001].

of quantitative empiricism. While it may have started out that way in the 1930s, by the time that Tjalling Koopmans acceded to the research directorship in 1948, the Cowles researchers had more or less absolved themselves of empirical obligations in favor of mathematical elaboration of the Walrasian model of general equilibrium [Mirowski, 2002, ch.5]. Given the intrinsic impossibility of a comprehensive empirical implementation of a truly phenomenological general equilibrium, the Cowles staff was more or less forced to focus all their efforts upon building abstract mathematical models absolved of all empirical constraint. Thus, Cowles stood primed for a different set of philosophical justifications for its mathematical endeavors when Gerard Debreu joined the unit in 1949.

Debreu had been trained in France by Henri Cartan, one of the founders of the Bourbaki movement, and had been won over to their style, which has been described as an approach of uncompromising rigor, with no didactic or heuristic concessions to the reader. As André Weil, another Bourbaki member wrote, "Metaphysics had become mathematics, and is ready to form the topic of a treatise whose cold beauty would be incapable of moving us" (quoted in [Dalmedico, 2001, p.236]). The axiomatic method was married to an ideology which sought to free mathematics from all dependence upon physical necessity, the resulting axiomatic exercises which would reveal the "mother-structures" from which whole fields of mathematics could be derived. Bourbaki conceived of itself as elaborating one version of the 'formalist' program in the foundations of mathematics, but one which would push the imperatives of unity and "top down" approaches to formalization far beyond anything present in the Hilbertian origins of the program. The audacity of their joint enterprise of rewriting the whole of mathematics from the ground up promoted their notion of the preeminence of 'structure'. They dictated their mathematics be conducted around a 'tool,' rather than be prompted by a problem drawn from some applied science. Once the appropriate root mother-structure was agreed upon, then the fields of mathematical endeavor to discourage were extensive, in order to clear away what they called 'axiomatic trash'. Bourbaki tended to favor algebraic-, order- and topological-structures as their mother entities, while they tended to disparage classical analysis. Their object was not so much to encourage innovation as to inscribe truth in tablets of stone for the ages:

> It seemed very clear that no one was obliged to read Bourbaki... a bible in mathematics is not like a bible in other subjects. It's a very well arranged cemetery with a beautiful array of tombstones... There was something which oppressed us all: everything we wrote would be useless for teaching. [Guedj, 1985, p.20]

Inevitably, Debreu produced his version of the Bourbakist bible for the neoclassical economics profession in the guise of *The Theory of Value* [1959]. All the Bourbakist hallmarks were there in plain view: disdain for classical analysis and the calculus, an excessive fascination with topology, an elitist assertion that the Walrasian general equilibrium model was *the* mother-structure of all of economics without any serious justifications proffered, teeth-jarring abstraction, and genuflection before the axiomatic method. Furthermore, other than some hand-waving over redefining the commodity over states of the world (see below), there was very little really 'new'; and it was certainly useless for pedagogic purposes. Not unexpectedly, Debreu was concerned to simply deny the origins of neoclassical economics in the imitation of physics, if only to sever the Walrasian system from any semblance of dependence upon physical necessity as embodied in the original specifications of the field.[16] The Bourbakists at Cowles thus innovated the line now parroted by many orthodox economists, that whatever ambitions to imitate physics that may have been present at the creation of Walrasian general equilibrium, they have been superseded by adherence to the canons of rigor held dear by professional mathematicians.[17] As we observed at the outset of this chapter, for many the field of neoclassical economics thus came to be conflated with the field of mathematics *tout court*.

The Bourbakist ascendancy earned Nobels in economics for Debreu and his Cowles comrades, but it remains an open philosophical question whether or not the Bourbakist interlude was really all that successful. Leo Corry [1992; 2001] has explicitly argued that the Bourbakist program was a failure on its own terms: the vaunted 'structures' were not able to perform the omnipotent feats trumpeted by Bourbaki, and ended up more or less irrelevant for the concrete issues covered by the members of Bourbaki. The mother-structures *qua* structures proved barren: "Bourbaki's work did imply many important contributions to $20^{th}$ century mathematics, but the concept of *structure* is certainly not among them" [2001, p.184]. But more to the point, the Whig interpretation of the history of mathematics bandied about by Bourbaki has been falsified by subsequent events: the Bourbakist interlude is now regularly bemoaned as a disaster for the mathematics profession.[18] It transgresses beyond our present remit to describe why this has transpired; but it does behoove us to inquire whether a similar case might not be made for the Bourbakist interlude *within* neoclassical economics.

The case for the failure of Bourbakism in economics might start by pointing out that the Cowles program was more notable for providing mathematical proofs of what it could not achieve, than as a cornucopia of new departures within economics. Although the Arrow-Debreu proof of the existence of general equilibrium under relatively weak assumptions is rightly regarded as a triumph, Cowles found it could not prove uniqueness or stability of equilibrium under similarly weak circumstances. The literature on dynamics wandered into a sequence of *culs-de-sac*, with

---

[16]Debreu later wrote: "physics did not completely surrender to the embrace of mathematics... economic theory could not follow the role model offered by physical theory... Being denied a sufficiently secure experimental base, economic theory has to adhere to the rules of logical discourse and must renounce the facility of internal inconsistency" [1991, p.2].

[17]This has even been repeated by some historians who should know better, such as [Ingrao and Israel, 1990; Weintraub, 2002].

[18]Some meditations upon the modern revulsion against Bourbaki can be found in [Dalmedico, 2001; Galison, 2004; Rota, 1997]. "[T]he identification of mathematics with the axiomatic method for the presentation of mathematics was not yet [in the 1940s] thought to be a preposterous misunderstanding (only analytic philosophers pull such goofs today)" [Rota, 1997, p.15].

no consensus position ever coming to the fore. Even more disturbing to many participants, the Sonnenschein/ Mantel/Debreu results proved that Walrasian general equilibrium placed almost no empirical restrictions upon excess demand functions, cutting the theory of demand free from the entire tradition.[19] If the Walrasian system were indeed the mother-structure of all neoclassical economics, then it has proven to have been distressingly barren in the interim.

If one were to pursue the other parallels, one would rapidly discover many contemporary economists making similar statements about a withdrawal from excessive formalism and empty axiomatic exercises in the modern profession, much the same as their counterparts have done of late in the mathematics department. Yet if one casts one's glance over at physics in its hour of need, especially in the area of string theory, there seems to be a perfervid season of withdrawal from the world into a sort of mathematics-besotted solipsistic isolation [Galison, 2004; Smolin 2006; Holt, 2006]. Edward Witten, the guru of string theory, was awarded a Fields Medal by the mathematics community, but it is still unclear if he has made any lasting contribution to empirical physics. Gauging the extent of the truth of these assertions will have to be left to future historians and philosophers of science, as will the task of explaining why the near-religious fervour for Bourbaki was reversed so easily in the interim.

## *2.3 Weintraub on formalism*

Roy Weintraub has been the most important contemporary author to conduct sustained research into the meaning and significance of mathematical practice within economics, and has provided a consolidated statement of his views in *How Economics became a Mathematical Science* (2002). He began by building a Lakatos-inspired rational reconstruction of the Walrasian program in the years 1930-54 in his *General Equilibrium Analysis: studies in appraisal* (1985), (which includes a mean imitation of the style of *Proofs and Refutations*) asserting there that "it is a minor scandal that there is no comprehensive history of either the rise of econometrics or the mathematization of economics" (p.140). While he left the pre-WWII history to others, he did set about trying to rectify the omission with his *Stabilizing Dynamics* (1991), showing, amongst other things, that the very meaning of 'equilibrium' varied dramatically in a sequence of papers dating from the 1930s to 1950s. In the later 1980s, he attempted in various ways to defend the thesis that the Walrasian program was 'empirically progressive'. However, somewhere along the way he became disenchanted with the application of Lakatos, and indeed, with philosophy in general, when it came to writing the history of economics. Over time, he has become perhaps the premier supporter of bringing the perspective of the 'social studies of science' over into the history of economics, all the while maintaining his generally favorable stance towards the modern neoclassical program. Further, he insists that historians of economics should consult the history

[19]These assertions are discussed in detail in: [Weintraub, 1991; Mirowski and Hands, 2007; Rizvi, 1998], and in any good graduate-level microeconomics textbook.

of mathematics when setting out to engage the issue of the role of mathematics in economics. This has not won him followers in the profession: those who agree that the neoclassical program is progressive tend to be put off by the science studies and the insistence upon separate standards for historical scholarship (being satisfied with simple Whig fairy tales), and those who agree that neoclassical economics is the story of development of mathematical facility tend to quail at the notion that mathematics itself is an historical subject, while those who seek methodological insight tend to be put off by his hostility to philosophy.

The ways in which Weintraub negotiates these straddles is best exemplified by the latest book. There he attacks numerous methodologists who make the mistake (in his estimation) of starting off from the premise that formal=abstract=pure, and in particular objects to historians who start out by associating the $20^{th}$ century rise of the general equilibrium program with the 'formalist' program in metamathematics, only to claim that internal developments in mathematics from Gödel's theorems onwards have scuttled it for good. He correctly points out (citing the work of Leo Corry) that Hilbert regarded his formalist program not as a withdrawal into purity, but rather as a means of organizing and further developing research in physics. "The program was not a call for rigor as opposed to intuition in mathematics, nor did it call for a change in the way mathematics was henceforth to be done" [2002, p.88]. Rather, leaning on a distinction first proposed by Leo Corry on the difference between an "image" of mathematics – second-order questions concerning the methodology, history and sociology of a discipline, like standards for acceptance of proofs, notions of rigor, the goals of the mathematical enterprise — and the corpus of mathematics – presumably the collection of theorems, proofs and accompanying statements about them — Weintraub suggests it is the "image" that is the appropriate subject matter for the historian, while her job is to leave the corpus alone.

Weintraub's chapter 3 reveals how this position would play out with regard to the philosophy of mathematics. There he states that Hilbert's formalist program was only important for mathematical economics in its guise as an 'image', but not in its instantiation as a moment in the development of mathematical knowledge. In particular, he splits Hilbert's program into an 'Axiomatic Approach' (image) and a 'Finitistic Program for the Foundation of Arithmetic' (corpus). Gödel's 1930 proof did indeed show that the Finitistic Program could not succeed, but Weintraub claims this was of little consequence for economics, since it was the Axiomatic Approach that tended to instruct further generations as to the goals towards which they could strive.

> The image of mathematics shared by Volterra, Evans, Edgeworth and Pareto used mechanical reductionism [ie. Appropriating models from physics — P.M.] to make scientific arguments rigorous... In contrast, the emerging view of mathematical truth, Hilbert's AA, appeared to require a quite different conceptualization....for any system, truth as consistency was to be relative to the structure in which that system was embedded. So, for example, if two person game theory were to be formalized, it would be as true... as the logic itself could guarantee,

as true then as arithmetic... This new image of mathematics shaped an emergent mathematical economics." [20]

Weintraub admits that transient enthusiasms in mathematics could come to influence the content of economics; indeed, in the next chapter he turns to recount the story of Debreu and Bourbakism covered in the previous section above. However, he hesitates to follow it up into the question of the relative 'failure' of Bourbakism, either in mathematics, economics or elsewhere. He instead adopts the position that, "historians of economics cannot look to those communities of philosophers to help us understand the developing connection between mathematics and economics in the $20^{th}$ century. Mixing the connection between mathematics and economics with the idea of formalism is explosive for those who try to reconstruct the history of economics... The concept of a true scientific theory has changed over the $20^{th}$ century as the image of mathematical knowledge changed" [2002, p.99]. The historian is not warranted to pose large questions about the consequences of the interplay of the content of mathematics and economics, according to Weintraub; all he can do is notice that standards have changed over time.[21]

It is instructive to consider just how close Weintraub's position appears to that of, say, Debreu, even though it would seem that Bourbakism gets just about as far away from science studies as it is possible for two doctrines to be. Both come from backgrounds in applied mathematics. Both seek to deny the importance of either the 'external economy' or else the original provenance of the neoclassical model in physical mathematics in any evaluation of the neoclassical research program. Both imagine the relevant criteria for progress in science are entirely self-referential and self-generated in an elite community with well-policed boundaries. Both evaluate specific formalisms with the help of unmotivated aesthetic criteria. Debreu believes his Bourbakism protects him from cracks in the foundations of mathematics; Weintraub thinks the cracks are only there if you choose to see them. Both at various junctures took it for granted that Walrasian general equilibrium (and possibly even the Cowles program) constitutes the core doctrine around which mathematical research should be regarded as legitimate in economics; neither is impressed by alternative programs, or the qualms expressed by various orthodox neoclassicals in the course of their own research. Both apparently regard philosophy as a waste of time, and seem content that economics is thought to be making progress by those in charge. Debreu enjoyed a professorship in the mathematics department at Berkeley; Weintraub insists that one should approach the history of economics through the history of mathematics.

---

[20][Weintraub, 2002, p.98]. I have rearranged the order of some sentences in this quote to enhance clarity.

[21]This prescription is also extended to heterodox economists, who are enjoined not to criticize neoclassical economics in [Weintraub, 2005]. For a critique of Weintraub's understanding of the Hilbert Program in mathematics, see [Boylan and O'Gorman, 2007].

## *2.4 John von Neumann and the computational turn*

There have been very few first-class mathematicians who have turned their attention in any sustained way towards economics: John von Neumann was the premier example in the $20^{th}$ century. Perhaps because of that fact, the exact nature and character of his legacy is a topic of intense dispute, even a half-century after his death [Mirowski, 2002, chap. 3]. It would seem the inventor of game theory [1928] and the person who bequeathed both fixed-point proofs of equilibrium and separating hyperplane techniques to economics would enjoy an unchallenged place in the Pantheon; but in fact, the situation is far from settled. Indeed, one of the enduring sources of embarrassment for the modern economics orthodoxy has been the fact, never entirely acknowledged, that von Neumann explicitly rejected the twin pillars of postwar neoclassical mathematical economics, viz., Walrasian general equilibrium and the Nash solution in game theory. In the classic *Theory of Games and Economic Behavior* [1944, p.6], he called for a new mathematics to displace the Newtonian calculus in economics, because "it is unlikely that a mere repetition of the tricks which served us so well in physics will do for social phenomena too." Yet the version of the new mathematics proposed therein did not long satisfy the brooding Sampson, since after WWII he turned his back on his own creation, and instead spent the remainder of his days developing the modern digital computer and what we will call here for shorthand purposes the new computational approach to mathematics. Although he made numerous suggestions in correspondence and other unpublished sources concerning the implications of the new computationalism for the future of economics [Mirowski, 2002, chap.5], there was no parallel text to *The Theory of Games* left for his followers to contemplate. No wonder his legacy in economics has languished in so persistently an unclear state.

In post-war mathematics, John von Neumann was one of the leaders of the anti-Bourbaki faction [Dalmedico, 2001]. Losing faith in the Hilbert formalist program almost immediately on the heels of Gödel's theorems, he turned away from axiomatization as a source of inspiration for mathematical research, and instead became an advocate of the position that fruitful new directions in mathematics would come from immersion in the technical problems thrown up by the special sciences (with a bias towards the sciences most promoted by his military paymasters — nonlinear dynamics, meteorology, operations research, brain science, biological evolution, and most spectacularly, digital computation). He made profound contributions to all those fields, but the one which he himself believed would guarantee his fame down through the ages as a mathematician was the development of the electronic computer and its formal abstract analogue, the theory of automata. No one person 'invented' the digital electronic computer; but it was von Neumann who was most responsible for ushering us into what we now consider the Cybernetic Age.

Von Neumann pioneered (but did not live to complete) a logical theory of automata as abstract information processing entities exhibiting self-regulation during interaction with an environment. It was framed to address questions such as: [i]

What are the necessary prerequisites for the self-regulation of an automaton? (A: The von Neumann architecture for the computer.) [ii] What are the formal prerequisites for self-reconstruction of an abstract automaton with offspring of the same level of complexity? (A: The theory of cellular automata.) [iii] Does a universal automaton exist that can construct any other automaton? (A: Yes, the Universal Turing Machine.) [iv] What are the abstract preconditions for an automaton constructing a second automaton of complexity level greater than the parent — That is, what are the formal prerequisites for evolution? This series of questions and their answers has become the progenitor of the main line of formalization in computer science, as well as the preferred angle of approach in what have been called the modern sciences of complexity.[22]

There are very roughly two distinct camps who claim the mantle of von Neumann in modern mathematical economics. The first, which has garnered the lion's share of attention, are those who feel that the primary lesson of von Neumann's legacy is that economists should take to heart that existing orthodox neoclassical models should be rendered 'computable', or in more technical terms, recursively realizable. This position simply ignores the evidence of von Neumann's hostility to the Walrasian model, and indeed, to utility theory. The first, and sadly neglected, figure to make this case was Alain Lewis.[23] Other recent economists adopting a similar position are Marcel Richter and Vela Velupillai. The latter has made his philosophical position clear in a series of papers [2004, 2005a, 2007]:

> Classical real analysis is only one of at least four mathematical traditions within which economic questions can be formalized and discussed mathematically. Non-standard, constructive and computable analyses have been playing their own roles in the formalization and mathematization of economic entities — but mostly within the closure of neoclassical economic theory... [after listing a number of axioms and theorems from Debreu's *Theory of Value*] then it can be shown that *none* of the propositions, theorems and claims of a mathematical sort would retain their validity without drastic modifications of their economic content and implications. In particular, not a single formal proposition in the *Theory of Value* would have any numerical or computational content". [2005a, pp.852, 862]

The problem with analysis emanating from this first camp is that it is so unremittingly bleak and negative — undoubtedly one of the reasons why this form

[22]See, for instance, [Cowan, 1994]. For von Neumann's posthumous notes on automata theory, see [1966]. For some meditations upon possible modern approaches to 'complexity' in economics, see [Velupillai, 2005b; Rosser, 2008].

[23]See the letter from Lewis to Debreu dated December 12, 1985, reproduced in [Mirowski, 2002, pp.526-7]: "In exact analogy to the nonstandard models of arithmetic, the continuous models of Walrasian general equilibrium pay for the use of continuity... with a certain non-effectiveness, that can be made precise recursion-theoretically... When I first obtained the results for choice functions, I thought my next task would be the reformulation of *The Theory of Value* in the framework of recursive analysis."

of 'computational economics' has played so little role in the development of the modern orthodoxy. The second camp seeks to cut the Gordian knot by dispensing with attempts to either fortify or criticize neoclassical economics, and instead propose that von Neumann's theory of automata can serve as a template for an entirely new approach to the formalization of economic life. We turn to a brief discussion of their program in the following section.

## 3 POST-1980 DEVELOPMENTS IN ALTERNATIVE POSSIBILITIES FOR MATHEMATICAL FORMALIZATION IN ECONOMICS

I have argued in [Mirowski, 2002] that the trajectory of the orthodoxy began the $20^{th}$ century primarily as the oft-acknowledged theory of static allocation, patterned upon classical mechanics, but that during World War II its path got deflected by events and personalities (too numerous to recount here) towards an altogether different conception of its core doctrine, one that might be summarized as recasting the economic agent as an information processor, particularly in the area of game theory. It goes without saying that the wartime development of the computer and its subsequent diffusion into nearly every sphere of intellectual discourse had quite a bit to do with what has been the most significant reorientation of the economics discipline in the last century, one that has nowhere near yet exhausted its promise. So one portion of this transformation could be laid at the door of John von Neumann; but in fact there have been numerous independent causes of the transformation. Nevertheless, further developments in the computational and biological sciences portend another deflection of the central tendency of microeconomics, which, if it comes to dominate, will transmute once more the very quiddity of economics. Because we seem to be living in the early stages of the emergence of the new tradition, the most that can be accomplished here is an attempt to describe the stark outlines of the new analytic vision, and point out some ways in which it has become manifest in alternative mathematical formalisms.

The shift which is promoted by the second wave of inheritors of the mantle of von Neumann is a modern microeconomics which is becoming less and less interested in the 'correct' specification of the economic agent and her cognitive capacities, and is instead increasingly concerned with the formal specification of markets as evolving computational algorithms [Mirowski, 2007]. The reader may be tempted to reject this distinction out of hand: At minimum, the neoclassical tradition has always taken the nature of markets as the central province of economics, has it not?

### 3.1 *Mathematics shapes the content of economic theory*

In fact, a judicious and unbiased overview of the history of the first century of neoclassical economics would confirm that it had been much more fascinated with the status and nature of *agents* than with the structure and composition of markets.

Most of the time, the concept of the market was treated as a general synonym for the phenomenon of exchange itself, and hence rendered effectively redundant. Even in the few instances when key thinkers in the tradition felt they should discuss the actual sequence of bids and asks in their models of trade — say, for instance, Walras with his *tâtonnement* and his *bons*, or Edgeworth with his recontracting process – what jumps out at the economic historian is the extent to which the sequence of activities posited therein had little or no relationship to the operation of any actual contemporary market.[24] Mid-20$^{th}$ century attempts to develop accounts of price dynamics were, if anything, even further removed from the increasingly sophisticated diversity of market formats and structures and the actual sequence of what markets accomplish.[25] Whilst there would be many ways to account for this incongruous turn of events, the condition we shall opt to stress here was the strong dependence of the neoclassical tradition upon *physics* to provide the respected paradigm of scientific explanation. Not only had energy physics provided the original agent formalism of optimization over a utility field in commodity space [Mirowski, 1989]; it also supplied the background orientation to which law-governed explanations were presumed to conform. The strong reductionism inherent in modern physics suggested that all agents would of necessity exhibit some fundamental shared characteristics (viz., "rationality") and therefore, for modeling purposes, should be treated as all alike. Furthermore, any differences in market structures where the agents congregated would be treated as second-order complications (viz., perfect competition vs. monopoly) or else collapsible to commodity definitions ('the' labor market; 'the' fish market), and therefore "The Market" came to be modeled as a relatively homogeneous and undifferentiated entity. Whether justified as mere pragmatic modeling tactic (for reasons of mathematical tractability) or a deeper symmetry bound up with the very notion of the possibility of existence of "laws of economics," market diversity was effectively suppressed, as one can still observe from modern microeconomics textbooks.

One modern illustration of this thesis can be observed in the work of an avowed critic of neoclassical economics, Joseph McCauley [2005]. As a physicist, he takes his cue from more modern approaches that ideally begin with some set of symmetry principles imposed *a priori*, and then presuming that time series of a commodity price is the output of some unknown dynamical system, selects some functions (mostly taken from statistical mechanics) that tend to mirror the stochastic profile of some representative empirical samples. The object of the exercise appears to be to uncover the 'equations of motion' by imposing a physical conception of equilibrium, purportedly because of "the complete absence of a dynamical systems description of biological evolution" (p.77). However much he pleads he is on guard against crude imitation of physical models, and holds no allegiance to the

[24]A symptom of the general oblivion to market structures is the urban myth about Walras being inspired by the Paris Bourse. A good historian such as Walker [2001] makes short work of this fairy tale.

[25]The essential disconnect between theories of market dynamics and any empirical sensibility with regard to process is revealed by the historical discussions in Weintraub [1991] and Perona [2005].

neoclassical orthodoxy, much of the economic content is directly dictated by the peculiarities of the mathematical traditions of contemporary physics. For instance, the commodity definition is treated as fixed and independent of the equations of motion;[26] the time series is treated as though it were the readout of a single generic market (though frequently it is no such thing); invariance is smuggled in through a no-arbitrage condition; and all considerations of Turing computability are assumed away (p.74). Here we observe the physicist's notion of legitimate lawlike behavior being *imposed* through the theory-laden importation of certain mathematical formalisms. It is not the neoclassical tradition *per se*, but rather the scientific font of familiar mathematical formalisms, shaped by generations of physicists honing their mathematics to address what they conceive as the most salient problems within the physics community, that dictates real theoretical content of what markets are thought to be and do. Given that many underemployed physicists have sought refuge in economics and finance, this behavior is still rife in most modern economics journals.

Nevertheless, the post-1980 weakening of the cultural dominance of physics as the prime exemplar of scientific explanation, and its gradual displacement by the sciences of computation and evolutionary biology, have opened up the conceptual space for an economics which has become less fixated upon agency and more concerned to theorize the meaning and significance of a diversity of (small-m) markets. In the same way we now are more likely to appreciate that neither biology nor computation can be fully reduced to physics, the incipient vision of markets as evolving computational entities will not itself be reducible to the prior neoclassical tradition. Indeed, one objective of this chapter is to highlight the as-yet unacknowledged divergences of this literature from neoclassical precepts, and to elevate to consciousness the ways in which the novel orientation prompts heretofore unimagined questions to be broached and answered.

The abstract theory of computation seems suited to encompass the diverse (and open-ended) roster of functions performed by the range of extant market forms: data dissemination, order routing, order execution, price and quantity output, delivery, clearing and settlement. A half-century of experience with computers has taught us that they are not simply or solely calculators or language-recognition devices (although that is the idiom that has been prevalent in their formalization), but protean command-control-communication devices, the consequences of which often outstrip the intentions of their builders. Although experience with markets has extended back through incomparably more vast stretches of history, the realization that markets are equally command-control-communications prostheses has been stymied up until now by the century-old predilection to pattern market models upon physical machine systems [Mirowski, 1989]. This tendency within

[26] Here one can't help but notice that the incompatibility of general relativity with other major branches of physics is reprised in a lack of appreciation for one of the major lessons of relativity theory: "The geometry of space is not part of the laws of nature... This means that the laws of nature have to be expressed in a form that does not assume space has any fixed geometry" [Smolin, 2006, p.81].

economics has not only prompted recourse to physical mathematics (the calculus, field theory, Euclidean space, random walks), but also physics-envy aspirations to a Theory of Everything in which all markets were but minor variations on a canonical model of The Market occupied by The Agent. A theory of markets based upon automata codifies the fact that there is no ur-model or über-machine to which the blooming, buzzing profusion of phenomenological markets can be reduced. Furthermore, since the theory of automata is independent of the nature of the substrate upon which they may be physically realized, the program is amenable to portrayal of markets as composed solely of humans, or human-machine hybrids, or indeed, entirely of machines in the format of modern computers. Since this constitutes a major departure within the history of economic thought, we shall refer to these novel entities as "markomata".

What role is played by abstract mathematical theory in such a research program? First and foremost, it provides an analytical framework of permissions and prohibitions of what can and cannot be done by specified classes of markomata. Secondly, it reveals how diverse markomata can be arrayed in hierarchies for the purposes of further analysis: hierarchies of computational capacity, hierarchies of language recognition, and hierarchies of computational complexity. This insistence upon the diversity of markomata explains why mathematical expression starts off with the theory of automata, and does not immediately commence with the theory of Turing Machines, as the icon of the maximum degree of computational capacity, as suggested by the Church-Turing Thesis.[27] The economic rationale for the distinction is that the theory of Turing Machines ignores limitations of space and time in the process of calculation, whereas the theory of automata immediately takes them into account. Nevertheless, anything that cannot be computed on a Turing Machine (henceforth, 'Turing non-computable') will be treated as subsisting outside the realm of science from the vantage point of the theory of markomata.[28] Third, even though the theory of automata serves in the first instance as a taxonomizing device for markomata, we shall argue it also permits the postulation of certain abstract theoretical generalizations about the market system in its totality.

Where is "the model" which summarizes markomata theory? Old habits indeed die hard, even when one is unaware of their provenance. Modern biologists don't ask for "the model" of evolution any more; nor do computer scientists cite 'the model' of 'the computer'.[29] In order to deal with phenomena that are intrinsically diverse and always undergoing metamorphosis, they have renounced the Cold War ambition to find that Bourbakist mother structure to which all scientists within the disciplinary bailiwick must pledge their troth. Since the first commandment of

[27]The Church-Turing Thesis identifies effectively computable functions with recursive functions, or equivalently with functions computable by Turing Machines. For further explication, see Davis *et al.* [1994, pp.68-9]; and Cotogno [2003].

[28]This includes the mathematical specification of agent maximization over infinite preference sets or continuous utility functions. See Mirowski [2002, pp.427-435]. By implication, this rules out any welfare appeals to Pareto optimality as well.

[29]For the situation in biology, one might consult Depew and Weber [1995], Kay [2000]; for the situation in computer science, see Mahoney [1997].

this program is that "Thou shalt not reify The Market," then readers looking for a canonical model are bound to be disappointed. There are only specific formalisms intended to capture the salient features of specific markets, all couched in the mathematics of the theory of automata.

## 3.2 *Markets as automata*

The most rudimentary description of a market begins with the notion of a finite automaton. A finite automaton Ŧ defined over an alphabet $\alpha = \{\alpha_1 , \ldots \alpha_m \}$ with states $\theta = \{\theta_1 , \ldots \theta_n \}$ is given by a function $T$ called a transition function which maps each pair $(\theta_i , \alpha_j )$ into a state $\theta_k$ ; a subset of states $\Theta = \{ \theta_k \}$ called final accepting states causes Ŧ to halt. A finite automaton can be thought of as an extremely limited computing device with no external memory capacity but a single working tape, which it can read only once. After reading a symbol on the tape, it either accepts or rejects it, depending upon the state that the device is in; it then enters the next state prescribed by the transition function. If the transition function $T$ maps an existing state of Ŧ into more than one state, then it is called a nondeterministic finite automaton (NDF).

Suppose we set out to formalize one function of one simple market as an automaton. In one (arbitrary) initial economic example, the order execution function of a very rudimentary market, such as the posted- or fixed-price market, will be modeled as a nondeterministic finite automaton. A single unit of the commodity is offered at a single price, where the alphabet concerned is the rational numbers; order execution either matches that number as bid by the purchaser, or is rejected. At this early stage, it is important to note that it is merely the order execution function that is captured by this NDF, and not the entire range of functions potentially performed by any real-world instantiation of the posted-price market. Data dissemination, order routing, clearing, record-keeping, and all the rest might themselves be composed of automata of various degrees of computational capacity; any real-world market is formally characterized by the composition of these component automata; and this begins to reveal the true combinatorial explosion of forms inherent in the theory of markomata.

Even restricting ourselves solely to order matching and execution, the possibilities present in any real-life situation begin to outstrip our capacity to subject them to formal abstraction. Can buyers themselves bid, or only respond to the sellers' ask? Are there multiple buyers/sellers, and can they initiate/respond in real time? Can they react to one another, as well as to the opposing side of the market? Can they communicate through channels other than the order execution algorithm? The explosion is partially mitigated by subjecting markomata to the computational and complexity hierarchies propounded within automata theory. The first, and most important, computational hierarchy is known in computer science as the "Chomsky hierarchy" [Davis *et al.*, 1994, pp.327-9]. It relates the complexity of the language recognized to the memory capacity of the class of au-

Table 1. Markomata Hierarchy of order execution

| Automaton type | Recognizes lang. | Memory | Markomata |
|---|---|---|---|
| Finite | Regular | None | Posted-price |
| Pushdown | Context-free | Pushdown stack | Sealed bid |
| Linear bounded | Context sensitive | Finite tape | Double auction |
| Turing Machine | Recursively enumerable | Infinite tape | None |

tomata deployed.[30] It is summarized for the order execution function in Table I below.

One implication of the Chomsky hierarchy is that some problems, which are unsolvable at the lower levels of computational capacity, can be shown to be solvable at the higher levels. Furthermore, there exist some problems that cannot be solved even at the most powerful level of the hierarchy; some strings are Turing non-computable on the Turing Machine. However, the hierarchy is inclusive, in the sense that the more powerful automaton can perform all the calculations of the automaton lower down in the hierarchy, because it can *simulate* the operation of machines of lesser computational capacity. This leads to the important notion of 'markomata simulation'.

The idea of one markomata simulating the operation of another is quite familiar to market practitioners, even though it has been absent up until now in economic theory. For instance, the futures market for red no.6 wheat 'simulates' the spot market for red no.6 wheat, in the sense that it can perform the same operations, augmented by other related operations, in the course of 'tracking' the wheat market. Likewise, the dealer-organized wholesale market 'simulates' the posted-price markets of the retailer, while superimposing other functions. In an abstract computational sense, the futures market 'encapsulates' the model of the spot market within its own algorithms. This would be the case even if the futures markets were operated as a double auction, whereas the spot markets were operated as a sealed-bid auction. The theory of computation informs us that certain specific market forms can simulate other market forms *as long as* they are composed of markomata of greater or equal computational capacity. The reason that the markomata hierarchy does not collapse down to a single flat uniformity is that more computationally complex markets situated higher in the Chomsky hierarchy perform other functions over and above those performed by the markets that they simulate: for instance, futures markets may seek to arbitrage price discrepancies as well as track the spot markets in their purview.

Table I above suggests that some forms of automata may be mapped into different formats of order execution familiar from the literatures of experimental economics and market microstructure. While the posted price format possesses no

[30]More elaborate definitions of each class of automaton can be found in Mirowski [2002, pp. 88-92], Taylor [1998], and of course, Davis *et al.* [1994].

memory capacity and therefore qualifies as a finite automaton, a sealed bid auction requires the comparison of a submitted bid to an ordered array of previously entered bids stored in a memory, and therefore qualifies as one of a number of k-headed pushdown automata [Mirowski, 2002, p.571]. Sealed bid order execution requires an ordering of submitted bids, which can be captured by a first-in first-out memory stack: hence the 'pushdown'. The standard double auction requires even more prodigious memory capacity, given that sequences of bids and asks stored in different identifiable memory locations must be retrieved and compared, and therefore should exhibit the computational capacity of (at least) a linear bounded automaton. Table I also suggests that no extant markomata has the power of a Turing Machine.

Thus the system as a whole exhibits no tendency to move towards any 'equilibrium' (a term borrowed from physics in any event); rather, individual markomata do serve to achieve very specific local functions and objectives, often discussed in the experimental and microstructure literatures. The Dutch or descending clock auction promotes the clearing of a market in a fixed specific time frame. The posted price market reduces personal interaction in the marketplace to a relative minimum. Dealer-mediated markets often provide liquidity to a target clientele. The computerized limit order book provides a public record in real time in the form of an accessible order book. The double auction market helps reduce the immediate opportunities for profitable arbitrage of the commodities sold. The sealed-bid limits the transparency of the identities of prospective buyers to each other. The posted-price market leaves open vast opportunities for arbitrage, but manages to withstand most efforts on the part of buyers to 'game' the rules of the market to their own advantage. The roster of objectives served by markomata of differing stripes is effectively limitless.

Because the same physical commodity can be and often is sold through different markomata, sometimes even within the same spatiotemporal coordinates, and as experimental economics reveals, different markomata display different price and quantity profiles, it follows that there can be no such lemma as the 'law of one price' in computational economics. It follows that there can exist no 'law of supply and demand' at the aggregative level, although for pragmatic purposes it may be thought to exist for certain individual markomata. If there might be a universal terminus toward which all automata tend, it is toward their internally defined 'halting conditions'. But even here, one can easily overstate the predictable mechanical character of market automata. It is a theorem of computational theory that:

> There is no algorithm that, given a program in the language $L(\alpha)$ and an input to that program, can determine whether or not the given program will eventually halt on the given input. [Davis *et al.*, 1994, p.68]

The undecidability of the halting problem bears direct relevance for the ambitions of an evolutionary computational economics. The impossibility theorems of computational theory do not belie the construction of specific markomata for attainment of specific targeted functions (since this is the practitioner's notion of the 'predictability' of the market); they merely prohibit the economist from making any ironclad predictions about the inevitable outcomes of the price system as a whole. As individual markomata become increasingly networked, their computational powers become increasingly complex, and transcendental guarantees that a particular market format will continue to operate as it has done in the past are repeatedly falsified.

In markomata economics, the very notion of 'market failure' thus assumes an entirely different meaning. When a markomata fails, it appears unable to halt. Prices appear to have no floor (or ceiling, in the case of hyperinflation), and the communication/ coordination functions of the market break down. Hence there exists the phenomenon of 'circuit-breakers', which make eminent good sense in a computational economics (even as they are disparaged in neoclassical finance theory). Earlier generations of market engineers had apprehended the need for a manual override when there were 'bugs' in the system. And as any software engineer knows, one never entirely banishes all bugs from real-world programs. Markomata, therefore, never can become reified as the apotheosis of rationality.

## *3.3 The Mathematics of Evolution in Economics*

There is now a substantial literature that expresses deep discontent with the mathematical image of evolution as a process of search over an independently defined and given fitness surface. Since this image is essentially isomorphic to the neoclassical posit of a given objective function subject to search for extrema, this literature has direct consequence for commonplace notions of the congruence of optimization with evolution. For instance, it has recently been argued that, "Any attempt to introduce a unitary analogous concept of 'reproductive fitness' into dynamical models as a scalar ordinal, which will explain or predict quantitative changes in the frequency of types, must fail" [Ariew and Lewontin, 2004, p.348]. In biology, the attempt to equate fitness with frequency classes of reproduction has served to suppress ecological and demographic details of species that were empirically shown to be critical to understanding the survival and reproduction of demes, not to mention aspects of inter-species interactions. In game theory, 'replicator dynamics' has equally misrepresented the ways in which information processing is not effectively separable from the context in which it is taking place. Mathematical choices originally justified in the name of tractability often have served to suppress the very aspects of the problem that had caused the inquiry to be situated within the broad purview of evolution in the first place. One role of the computational tradition has been to isolate those aspects of mathematical models that were obstructing truly evolutionary theorizing.

One of the consequences of the rise to prominence within biology of the "information transmission" paradigm of evolution has been the wholesale re-evaluation of the conventional portrait of evolution as a dynamical system traversing an independently-constituted fitness surface. The "traditional theory of 'dynamical systems' is not equipped for dealing with constructive processes... it was precisely the elimination of [the transformation of] objects from the formalism that made dynamical systems approaches so successful" [Fontana and Buss, 1996, p.56]. When it came to modeling evolution after the fashion of dynamical systems, evolving entities were often treated as black boxes, with variation attributed to some external stochastic process inducing motion on an isotropic phenotype space, with a one-to-one correspondence to a putative additively decomposable genotype, usually motivated by considerations of mathematical tractability. Dissatisfaction with this reduction of change to stasis, especially at the Santa Fe Institute, led in the interim to a fascination with high dimensionality, chaos, determinism indistinguishable from randomness, and other mathematical phenomena all frequently lumped together under the broad tent of 'complexity theory'. The quest of these researchers was to try and capture real change as the qualitative transformation of entities arising out of quantitative dynamical interactions.

While it has proven much more difficult to abjure all dependence upon mathematical metaphors of motion than anyone had originally imagined, the biologist Walter Fontana and his collaborators have come up with some concrete proposals to explain why the mathematical presuppositions of dynamical systems have presented obstacles to the modeling of biological phenomena neglected by the Fisherian school and propounded by their opponents, the followers of the 'modern synthesis', such as punctuated equilibrium, path dependency, irreversibility, and the appearance of real novelty. Briefly, Fontana insists that evolution consists of (at least) two analytical phenomena, selection and development, which must be accorded equal attention in model construction. Selection can be modeled as motion on a space; but development must take into account the convoluted relationship of phenotypes to genotypes. Conventional treatments of fitness surfaces misconstrue the phenomena because phenotypes cannot be modified directly. The geometry of fitness surfaces "relates phenotypes without taking into account the indirection required to change them, an indirection which runs through the process by which phenotypes arise from genotypes... what is needed is a criterion of *accessibility* of one phenotype from another by means of mutations" [2003, p.13]. Hence, mutation has received insufficient appreciation within evolutionary theory because it is better conceived as a structural component of the topology of phenotypic space.

Fontana makes reference to topology in a sense not generally used in the literature on evolutionary computation. His contention is not simply the standard complaint that phenotypes are collapsed to genotypes in most fitness surfaces; it is that, without exception, these surfaces are portrayed as exhibiting a specific topology, that of a metric space. This means that there is presumed to exist a well-defined distance metric between any two points of the space, that every element can be reached from every other element, and that motion is reversible on these spaces, because the relation of "nearness" is presumed symmetrical. The evolutionary modelers rarely devote explicit consideration to the nature of the fitness space, however; mostly they just posit a Euclidean vector space for their dynamical systems as though they were second nature. To acquiesce in this practice essentially means subscribing to the doctrine that space has no built-in biases; that you can always get there from here. No wonder mutation comes to resemble a third wheel or an unnecessary appendage.

Fontana proposes that we replace this practice with the posit of a fitness space which possesses less topological structure than a metric space, but whose structure embodies the developmental constraints which link the genotype to the realized phenotype [Fontana, 2003]. Formally, he suggests an 'accessibility pretopology' based upon formal notions of asymmetry of neighborhoods and nearness. In such a pretopology, France can be considered to be 'near' Monaco since a large proportion of Monaco's boundary borders on France; but conversely, Monaco cannot be said to be 'near' France, since only a tiny fraction of France's boundary borders Monaco. Consequently, it will be easier to leave Monaco for France than it will be to leave France for Monaco. Translated back into biological terms, the pretopology of the fitness surface captures the amount of 'neutral' genetic mutation that is possible without showing up as phenotypic change, as well as incorporating an index of the extent of epistasis within the system. The implications of such a revision of fitness concepts has direct consequences for the conceptualization of evolution:

A population of replicating and mutating sequences under selection drifts on a neutral network of currently best shapes until it encounters a 'gateway' to a network that conveys some advantage or is fitness neutral. That encounter, however, is evidently *not* under the control of selection, for selection cannot distinguish between neutral sequences. While similar to the phenomenon of punctuated equilibrium recognized by Gould and Eldridge in the fossil record of species evolution, punctuation in evolving RNA populations occurs in the *absence* of externalities (such as meteorite impact or abrupt climate change), since it reflects the variational properties of the underlying developmental architecture (here: folding).

Fontana's fundamental point is that treating evolution purely on the paradigm of a physical dynamical system invests 'too much' plasticity in the population and too little in the fitness surface; and if the rate of change of the organism is roughly on a par with the rate of change of the environment, then there is no 'evolution' *per se*, only standard optimization. What permits true evolution is a reservoir of variability which is not immediately accessible to 'search' or selection, but is generated by principles specific to the structure of the phenomena in question — in molecular biology, it is the principles of DNA-RNA transcription and subsequent RNA folding; at the level of individual organic *bauplan* it could be the developmental constraints or 'spandrels' of Lewontin and Gould [1978]; at the population level it would be the phenomenon of co-evolution. The devil hides in the details of the very notion of 'continuity' built into the posit of the fitness surface: "What determines continuity is not the degree to which a modification is incremental, but the degree to which that modification is easy to achieve by virtue of the mechanism underlying the genotype-phenotype relation" [Stadler *et al.*, 2001]. Both development and mutation matter fundamentally to evolution because they govern these principles of ease or difficulty of change, and as such determine the pretopology of the fitness surface. They also help explain why it is frequently impossible to 'work backwards' to major evolutionary transitions: over time, the population drifts away from the critical point of accessibility at which there were major regime changes: novelty itself is context-specific.

Biology cannot be reduced to physics by means of the copying the formalisms of physical dynamics; computation will not be reducible to biology by copying the structural interactions of selection (dynamical systems) and development (genotype-phenotype pretopology) found there. The scientists concerned with each class of phenomenon will only begin to comprehend true change within the ambit of their studies when their models incorporate mathematical presumptions of the most basic sort – primitive notions of distance, nearness, continuity, symmetry, computability, and the like – which they have independent reasons to certify are characteristic of the phenomena which are the subject of their inquiries. The more we become concerned with the "sciences of the artificial", in Herbert Simon's telling phrase, the more this dictates that we must take the activities of the scientist more directly into account. Fontana seeks to make this point at an abstract level about scientific research:

When we wish to change the behavior of systems, we often have a spatial metaphor in mind, such as going from 'here to there', where 'here' and 'there' are positions in the space of behaviors. But what exactly is the nature of this space? Who brought it to the party? It is a popular fallacy to assume that the *space* of behaviors is there to begin with. This is a fallacy even when all possible behaviors are known in advance. How does this fallacy arise? When we are given a set of concrete or abstract entities of any kind, we almost always can cook up a way of comparing two such entities, thereby producing a definition of similarity (or distance). A measure of similarity makes those entities hang together naturally in a familiar metric space. The fallacy is to believe the so-constructed space is real. It isn't, because that measure of similarity is not based on available real-world operations, since we cannot act on behaviors directly. We have only system-editors, we don't have property-editors. Seen from this operational angle, that which structures the space of behaviors is not the degree of similarity among behaviors but a rather different relation: operational *accessibility* of one behavior from another in terms of system-reconfigurations. This brings the mapping from systems to behaviors into the picture. The structure of behavior-space is then induced by this mapping. It cannot exist independently of it. [2003, p.17]

Here is where the initial foundational connection between computational and evolutionary economics is forged. As section 1.1 suggested, there is no such thing as commodity space; and from the work of Fontana we can come to realize that the ubiquitous dependence upon the Euclidean metric of commodity space was the primary obstacle to the capture of truly *evolutionary* phenomena, such as the intrinsic irreversibility of economic activities, the significant role of mutation, the advent of real novelty, and the sustenance of true diversity in market operations. To put it starkly: belief in the myth of The Monolithic Market has been unwittingly predicated upon belief in the existence of an independent homogeneous commodity space, and enforced by the properties of symmetry and invariance embodied in that space. (In a phrase: You could always get there from here, so the vehicle didn't matter.) Computational economics demonstrates in an analytical fashion why no one had previously noticed that it was nevertheless logically entailed by the 'harmless' mathematical assumptions of neoclassical models. Evolution was neutralized by the assumed symmetry of the ontological space of the mathematized neoclassical economy.

## 4 A REVIVAL OF PHILOSOPHY OF MATHEMATICS FOR ECONOMICS?

It would be a mistake to read the results in section 3 above as counseling the trading of one master discourse (physics) for another (biology or computational science). It would also be an error to come away with the impression that if we just switched from classical analysis to discrete mathematics, or from dynamical systems theory to the theory of computation, that economics would finally be delivered unto the Promised Land. Although we have not surveyed them here, the history of economic thought is littered with abortive attempts to import quirky and idiosyncratic fields of mathematics into the discipline.[31] Indeed, enthusiasm for some branch of mathematics which lacks a distinguished pedigree of extended proof of itself within the precincts of some natural science is almost automatically regarded as a sure-fire ticket to crackpot status in economics. And even then, open and self-conscious admission of expropriation of mathematics from another field is viewed as something best kept private between consenting adults.

The lesson we extract here is rather that different mathematical traditions cannot be doffed and discarded indifferently and carelessly like some second-hand gladrags, while "the Economy" endures naked and pristine underneath. Mathematics bears implicit content, oftentimes freighted in below the waterline of consciousness. Mathematics also both fosters and telegraphs a conception of the place of economics in the ecology of academic disciplines, empowering some and erecting insuperable barriers for others. Adherence to a mathematical tradition can lock a whole school into a limited repertoire of research techniques for generations, for instance imposing a crude regimen of (linear stochastic) empirical practices in some cases, while banishing empiricism altogether in others. You might think this would render mathematically sophisticated practitioners eminently well-placed to reflect sagaciously upon the advantages and drawbacks of particular formalisms; but there has been little evidence in the history of economics to support such a view. Instead, most economists have treated mathematics as though it were a merciless monolithic taskmaster, ensconced in the campus department of mathematics, and the only options open to the tyro are to submit or despair of making

[31]See, for instance, the attempt of [Clower and Howitt, 1978] to introduce number theory (perhaps the branch of mathematics least associated with scientific applications); or else the spectacle of both Palomba [1968] and Ellerman [1995] attempting to introduce group theory with respect to the modeling of double entry accounts. Velupillai's [2005a; 2007] championing of Diophantine equations has sparked little interest or comment.

any contribution to the grand movement of economic thought. No one has noticed the theorists of rational choice preaching the absence of choice when it came to the core doctrines of the discipline.

One would like to believe that measured reflection could forestall the prospect of any future economics simply capitulating to the next culturally dominant science that came down the pike, latching onto its characteristic formalisms because it just seemed like the common-sense superior way to express cutting-edge laws of nature.[32] One would also feel gratified to be exposed to a better class of justifications for the specific mathematical formalisms favored by the profession; superior at least to the classical motives surveyed above in section 1. It would appear that this brand of philosophical reflection will not be nurtured within the existing framework of the economics profession in the foreseeable future. A marginally more likely scenario is that a separate philosophical conversation will need to take place to build and sustain a tradition of rational assessment of the role and functions of mathematics in economic research and discourse. Perhaps a glimpse of the sort of philosophy which might perform this function may be provided by the recent work of David Corfield [2003].

In a nutshell, Corfield suggests that professional philosophy of mathematics should wean itself away from the opinion that all the really foundational issues that concern philosophers were devised mostly before 1930, and that their consequences were more or less worked out in set theory, proof theory and model theory in subsequent generations. He calls upon philosophers to give up their self-imposed identities of "chroniclers of proto-rigorous mathematics" in the shadow of Frege, and pay attention to more of the things that concern modern practicing mathematicians, both basic and applied. As he puts it:

> If I define *snook* to be a set with three binary, one tertiary and a couple of quaternary operations, satisfying this that and the other equation, I may be able to demonstrate with unobjectionable logic that all finite snooks possess a certain property, and then proceed to develop snook theory right up to noetherian centralizing snook extensions. But, unless I am extraordinarily fortunate and find powerful links to other areas of mathematics, mathematicians will not think my work worth a jot. By contrast, my articles may well be in demand if I contribute to the understanding of Hopf algebras, perhaps via noetherian centralizing Hopf algebra extensions. Surely, the philosopher ought to be able to tell us something about the presuppositions operating in the mathematical community today which would account for the difference. [2003, p.11]

Corfield goes on to suggest a range of factors which would be relevant to shedding light upon such a question: logical concerns within some existing calculus

[32]The fad in evolutionary ethology to embrace the Nash equilibrium as an ideal instrument to describe the behavior of animals, and then its re-importation back into 'evolutionary game theory', shows this naïve infatuation can go in both directions.

and plausibility, to be sure, but also psychological factors, technological factors (including the state of play in relevant neighboring sciences), and sociological and institutional factors. He proceeds to show how this can be done in a number of fascinating cases, from automated theorem provers, and the treatment of Bayesianism in mathematics, to exploration of the strange trajectory of groupoids, and the resort to analogy across mathematical subspecialties. Although he never once considers economics in his case studies, he is especially illuminating on the role of analogies, favorably quoting Rota [1986, ix] that, "The enrapturing discoveries of our field systematically conceal, like footprints erased in sand, the analogical train of thought that is the authentic life of mathematics." It is here, for example, that the philosopher can engage the historian of economics in a fruitful dialogue. It certainly would fortify the sorts of case studies which we have briefly touched upon in sections 2 and 3 above.

A revival of the philosophy of mathematics for economics along these lines would range widely over the disciplines for comparative assessments, and would not acquiesce in proof techniques or appeals to authority from practitioners as anything more than empirical data for further consideration. Most significantly, it would not seek to rank practitioners according to their mathematical prowess, but rather according to their ability to integrate mathematical research with the cogency of their economic concepts. As Corfield writes, "Mathematicians today, aware of the volume of production of their colleagues, are far more concerned that their work be ignored through a lack of interest than through any fear that it will be found incorrect" [2003, p.170]. The real task is to comprehend what economists find 'interesting' about the mathematics that they propagate and promote, and just perhaps, how that interest can mutate through time.

## BIBLIOGRAPHY

[Ariew and Lewontin, 2004] A. Ariew and R. Lewontin. The Confusions of Fitness, *British Journal for the Philosophy of Science*, (55):347-63, 2004.

[Arrow and Intriligator, 1981] K. Arrow and M. Intriligator, eds. *Handbook of Mathematical Economics. Vol. 1* Amsterdam: North Holland, 1981.

[Aspray and Kitcher, 1988] W. Aspray and P. Kitcher. *History and Philosophy of Modern Mathematics.* Minneapolis: University of Minnesota Press, 1988.

[Bausor, 1995] R. Bausor. Liapunov Techniques in Economic Dynamics and Classical Thermodynamics, pp.396-405 in Ingrid Rima, ed., *Measurement, Quantification and Economic Analysis.* London: Routledge, 1995.

[Binmore, 2005] K. Binmore. Review of Nicola Giocoli's *Modeling Rational Agents. ESHET Newsletter*, Spring. Pp.26-28, 2005.

[Blaug, 2003] M. Blaug. The Formalist Revolution of the 1950s. *Journal of the History of Economic Thought* 25.2:145–56, 2003.

[Boylan and O'Gorman, 2007] T. Boylan and P. O'Gorman. Axiomatization and Formalism in Economics, *Journal of Economic Surveys*, (21):426-446, 2007.

[Carnap, 1936] R. Carnap. *Logical Syntax of Language.* London: Routledge Kegan Paul, 1936.

[Clower and Howitt, 1978] R. Clower and P. Howitt. The Transactions Theory of a Demand for Money, *Journal of Political Economy*, (86):449-465, 1978.

[Colander *et al.*, 2004] D. Colander, R. Holt, and J. B. Rosser. *The Changing Face of Economics: Conversations with Cutting Edge Economists.* Ann Arbor: University of Michigan, 2004.

[Colyvan, 2001] M. Colyvan. *The Indispensability of Mathematics.* New York: Oxford University Press, 2001.

[Colyvan, 2004] M. Colyvan. Indispensability Arguments in the Philosophy of Mathematics, *Stanford Encyclopedia of Philosophy*, `http://plato.stanford.edu/entries`, 2004.

[Corfield, 2003] D. Corfield. *Towards a Philosophy of Real Mathematics.* Cambridge: Cambridge University Press, 2003.

[Corry, 1989] L. Corry. Linearity and Reflexivity in the Growth of Mathematical Knowledge, *Science in Context*, (3):409-40, 1989.

[Corry, 1992] L. Corry. Nicolas Bourbaki and the Concept of Mathematical Structure, *Synthese*, (22):315-348, 1992.

[Corry, 1997] L. Corry. David Hilbert and the Axiomatization of Physics, *Archive for the History of the Exact Sciences*, (51):83-198, 1997.

[Corry, 1999] L. Corry. Hilbert and Physics in Jeremy Gray, ed., *The Symbolic Universe.* Oxford: Oxford University Press, 1999.

[Corry, 2001] L. Corry. Mathematical Structures from Hilbert to Bourbaki, pp. 167-185 in Dalmedico and Bottazzini, eds., *Changing Images in Mathematics.* London: Routledge, 2001.

[Cotogno, 2003] P. Cotogno. Hypercomputation and the Physical Church-Turing Thesis, *British Journal for the Philosophy of Science*, (54):181-223, 2003.

[Cowan *et al.*, 1994] G. Cowan, D. Pines, and D. Meltzer, eds. *Complexity: Metaphors, Models and Reality.* Reading, Mass: Addison-Wesley, 1994.

[Dalmedico, 2001] A. Dalmedico. An Image Conflict in Mathematics after 1945. In Dalmedico and Umberto Bottazzini, eds, *Changing Images in Mathematics.* London: Routledge, 2001.

[Davis *et al.*, 1998] J. Davis, D. W. Hands, and U. Mäki. *The Handbook of Economic Methodology.* Cheltenham: Elgar, 1998.

[Davis *et al.*, 1994] M. Davis, R. Sigal, and E. Weyuker, *Computability, Complexity and Languages.* $2^{nd}$ ed. San Diego: Morgan Kaufmann,1994.

[Debreu, 1959] G. Debreu. *The Theory of Value.* New Haven: Yale University Press, 1959.

[Debreu, 1984] G. Debreu. Economic Theory in the Mathematical Mode, *American Economic Review*, (74):267-278, 1984.

[Debreu, 1991] G. Debreu. The Mathematization of Economic Theory, *American Economic Review*, (81):1-7, 1991.

[De Marchi, 1993] N. De Marchi, ed. *Non-Natural Social Science.* Durham: Duke University Press, 1993.

[Dennis, 2002] K. Dennis. Nominalizing the Numeric, *Cambridge Journal of Economics*, (26):63-80, 2002.

[De Ville and Menard, 1989] P. De Ville and C. Menard. An Insolent Founding Father, *European Economic Review*, (33):494-502, 1989.

[Dieudonné, 1982] J. Dieudonné. *A Panorama of Pure Mathematics.* New York: Academic Press, 1982.

[Ellerman, 1984] D. Ellerman. Arbitrage Theory: A Mathematical Introduction, *SIAM Review*, (26):241-261, 1984.

[Ellerman, 1995] D. Ellerman. *Intellectual Trespassing as a Way of Life: Philosophy, Economics, Mathematics.* Lanham: Rowman and Littlefield, 1995.

[Ferreiros and Gray, 2006] J. Ferreiros and J. Gray, eds. *The Architecture of Modern Mathematics.* Oxford: Oxford University Press, 2006.

[Fischer, 1993] R. Fischer. Mathematics as a Means and as a System. In Sal Restivo, Jean Bendegem and Roland Fischer, eds. *Math Worlds.* Albany: SUNY Press, 1993.

[Fontana, 2003] W. Fontana. The Topology of the Possible. In A. Wimmer and R. Koessler, eds., *Paradigms of Change*, 2003.

[Fontana and Buss, 1996] W. Fontana and L. Buss. The Barrier of Objects. In John Casti and Anders Karlqvist, eds., *Boundaries and Barriers.* Reading: Perseus, 1996.

[Fourcade, 2006] M. Fourcade. The Construction of a Global Profession, *American Journal of Sociology*, (112):145-194, 2006.

[Galison, 2004] P. Galison. Mirror Symmetry. In M. N. Wise, ed. *Growing Explanations: Historical Perspectives on Recent Science*, pp. 23–63. . Durham: Duke University Press, 2004.

[Georgescu-Roegen, 1976] N. Georgescu-Roegen. *Energy and Economic Myths.* Elmsford: Pergamon Press, 1976.

[Gingras, 2001] Y. Gingras. What Did Mathematics Do to Physics? *History of Science*, (39): p.383-416, 2001.

[Guedj, 1985] D. Guedj. Nicolas Bourbaki, Collective Mathematician, *Mathematical Intelligencer*, (7:2):18-22, 1985.

[Guerraggio and Molho, 2004] A. Guerraggio and E. Molho. The Origins of Quasi-concavity: a development between mathematics and economics, *Historia Mathematica*, (31):62-75, 2004.

[Hadden, 1994] R. Hadden. *On the Shoulders of Merchants: exchange and the mathematical conception of nature.* Albany: SUNY Press, 1994.

[Hands, 2006a] D. W. Hands. Individual Psychology, Rational choice and Demand, *Revue de Philosophie Economique*, (13) 2006.

[Hands, 2006b] D. W. Hands. Integrability, Rationalizability and Path Dependency in Demand theory. In [Mirowski and Hands, 2006], 38(Suppl 1):153-185, 2006.

[Hands, 2007] D. W. Hands. A Tale of Two mainstreams, *Journal of the History of Economic Thought*, Volume 29, Issue 1, pp. 1–13, 2007.

[Holt, 2006] J. Holt. Unstrung, *New Yorker*, October 2, 2006.

[Ingrao and Israel, 1990] B. Ingrao and G. Israel. *The Invisible Hand.* Cambridge: MIT Press, 1990.

[Israel, 2005] G. Israel. The Science of Complexity: Epistemological Problems, *Science in Context*, (18):479-509, 2005.

[Jevons, 1970] W. S. Jevons. *The Theory of Political Economy.* Baltimore: Penguin, 1970.

[Kjeldsen, 2000] T. Kjeldsen. A Contextualized Historical Analysis of the Kuhn-Tucker Theorem in Nonlinear Programming, *Historia Mathematica*, (27):331-61, 2000.

[Kjeldsen, 2001] T. Kjeldsen. John von Neumann's Conception of the Minimax Theorem: a journey through different mathematical contexts, *Archive for the History of the Exact Sciences*, (56):39-68, 2001.

[Koopmans, 1957] T. Koopmans. *Three Essays on the State of Economic Science.* New York: McGraw Hill, 1957.

[Krantz *et al.*, 1971] D. Krantz, R. Lutz, P. Suppes, and A. Tversky. *Foundations of Measurement.* San Francisco: Academic, 1971.

[Kreps, 1997] D. Kreps. Economics — the Current Position. In Bender and Schorske, 1997.

[Kula, 1986] W. Kula. *Measures and Men.* Princeton: Princeton University Press, 1986.

[Lakatos, 1978] I. Lakatos. *Proofs and Refutations.* Cambridge: Cambridge University press, 1978.

[Lawson, 2003] T. Lawson. *Reorienting Economics.* London: Routledge, 2003.

[Mahoney, 1997] M. Mahoney. Computer Science. In John Krige and Dominique Pestre, eds., *Science in the $20^{th}$ Century.* Amsterdam: Harwood, 1997.

[Marshall, 1920] A. Marshall. *Principles of Economics.* $8^{th}$ ed. London: Macmillan, 1920.

[Maskin, 2004] E. Maskin. Review of Weintraub's *How Economics became a Mathematical Science. Journal of Economic Literature.* (42:1), 2004.

[McCauley, 2005] J. McCauley. Making Mathematics Effective in Economics, in K. Velupillai, ed., *Computability, Complexity and Constructivity in Economic Analysis.* Malden: Blackwell, 2005.

[McCloskey, 1994] D. N. McCloskey. *Knowledge and Persuasion in Economics.* New York: Cambridge University Press, 1994.

[Mirowski, 1991] P. Mirowski. The How, the When and the Why of Mathematics in Economics, *Journal of Economic Perspectives*, (5):145-158, 1991.

[Mirowski, 2002] P. Mirowski. *Machine Dreams.* New York: Cambridge University Press, 2002.

[Mirowski, 2004a] P. Mirowski. *The Effortless Economy of Science?* Durham: Duke University Press, 2004.

[Mirowski, 2004b] P. Mirowski. The Scientific Dimensions of Society and their Distant Echoes in American Philosophy of Science, *Studies in the History and Philosophy of Science A*, (35):283-326, 2004.

[Mirowski, 2007] P. Mirowski. Markets Come to Bits: Markomata and the future of computational evolutionary economics, *Journal of Economic Behavior and Organization*, (63):209-242, 2007.

[Mirowski and Weintraub, 1994] P. Mirowski and E. R. Weintraub. The Pure and the Applied: Bourbakism Comes to Mathematical Economics, *Science in Context*, Summer, 7:245-272, 1994.

[Mirowski and Hands, 2006] P. Mirowski and D. W. Hands. *Agreement on Demand.* Durham: Duke University Press, 2006.

[Palumba, 1960] G. Palomba. *A Mathematical Interpretation of the Balance Sheet.* Geneva: Droz, 1960.

[Perona, 2005] E. Perona. Birth and Early history of Nonlinear Dynamics in Economics, *Revista de Economia y Estatistica*, (43:2):29-60, 2005.

[Putnam, 1979] H. Putnam. *Mathematics, Matter and Method: Philosophical Papers, vol 1.* Cambridge: Cambridge University Press, 1979.

[Richardson, 2003] A. Richardson. The Geometry of Knowledge: Lewis, Becker, Carnap, *Studies in the History and Philosophy of Science.* (34):165-182, 2003.

[Rizvi, 1994] S. A. T. Rizvi. Game Theory to the Rescue? *Contributions to Political Economy* 13:1–20, 1994.

[Rizvi, 1998] S. A. T. Rizvi. Responses to Arbitrariness in Contemporary Economics. In *New Economics and Its History*, edited by John B. Davis. *History of Political Economy*_29 (supplement): 273, 1998.

[Roberts, 1979] F. Roberts. *Measurement Theory.* Reading: Addison Wesley, 1979.

[Rosenberg, 1992] A. Rosenberg. *Economics – Mathematical Politics or Science of Diminishing Returns?* Chicago: University of Chicago Press, 1992.

[Rosser, 2008] J. B. Rosser. Computational and Dynamic Complexity in Economics, James Madison working paper, 2008.

[Rota, 1997] G.-C. Rota. *Indiscrete thoughts.* Boston: Birkhauser, 1997.

[Rotman, 1993] B. Rotman. *Ad Infinitum: the ghost in Turing's machine.* Stanford: Stanford University Press, 1993.

[Rubinstein, 2006] A. Rubinstein. Dilemmas of an Economic Theorist, *Econometrica*, (74):865-883, 2006.

[Saari, 1995] D. Saari. Mathematical Complexity of Simple Economies, *Notices of the American Mathematical Society*, (42):222-230, 1995.

[Saari, 1999] D. Saari. Foliations Leaf through Economics, *Macroeconomic Dynamics*, (3):384-426, 1999.

[Samuelson, 1994] P. Samuelson. The To-be-expected Angst... *Eastern Economic Journal*, (20):267-273. 1994.

[Schwartz, 1986] J. Schwartz. The Pernicious Influence of Mathematics on Science. In M. Kac *et al.*, eds. *Discrete Thoughts*, pp. 19–25. Boston: Birkhauser, 1986.

[Sent, 1998] E.-M. Sent. *The Evolving Rationality of Rational Expectations.* New York: Cambridge University Press, 1998.

[Smolin, 2006] L. Smolin. *The Trouble with Physics.* New York: Harcourt, 2006.

[Stadler *et al.*, 2001] B. Stadler, P. Stadler, G. Wagner, and W. Fontana. The Topology of the Possible: formal spaces underlying patterns of evolutionary change, .*Journal of Theoretical Biology*, (213):241-274, 2001.

[Tymoczko, 1998] T. Tymoczko, ed. *New Directions in the Philosophy of Mathematics.* Rev. ed. Princeton: Princeton University press, 1998.

[Velupillai, 2004] K. V. Velupillai. Constructivity, Computability and Computers in Economic Theory, *Metroeconomica*, (55):121-140, 2004.

[Velupillai, 2005a] K. V. Velupillai. The Unreasonable Ineffectiveness of Mathematics in Economics, *Cambridge Journal of Economics*, (29):849-72, 2005a.

[Velupillai, 2005b] K. V. Velupillai, ed. *Computability, Complexity and Constructivity in Economic Analysis.* Oxford: Blackwell, 2005.

[Velupillai, 2007] K. V. Velupillai. Variations on the Theme of 'Conning' in Mathematical Economics, *Journal of Economic Surveys*, (21):466-505, 2007.

[von Neumann and Morgenstern, 1964/1944] J. Von Neumann and O. Morgenstern. *The Theory of Games and Economic Behavior.* New York: Wiley, 1944/1964.

[von Neumann, 1966] J. Von Neumann. *The Theory of self-Reproducing Automata.* Ed. Arthur Burks. Urbana: University of Illinois Press, 1966.

[Walker, 2001] D. Walker. A Factual Account of the Functioning of the $19^{th}$ Century Paris Bourse, *European Journal for the History of Economic Thought*, (8): 186-207, 2001.

[Warsh, 2006] D. Warsh. *Knowledge and the Wealth of Nations.* New York: Norton, 2006.

[Warwick, 2003] A. Warwick. *Masters of Theory.* Chicago: University of Chicago Press, 2003.

[Weintraub, 1985] E. R. Weintraub. *General Equilibrium Analysis: studies in appraisal.* New York: Cambridge University press. 1985.

[Weintraub, 1991] E. R. Weintraub. *Stabilizing Dynamics.* New York: Cambridge University Press, 1991.

[Weintraub, 2002] E. R. Weintraub. *How Economics became a Mathematical Science.* Durham: Duke University Press, 2002.
[Weintraub, 2005] E. R. Weintraub. Filing Formal Objections: a polemic paper delivered at University of Rome, May, 2005.
[White, 2004] M. White. In the Lobby of the Energy Hotel, *History of Political Economy,* 36(2):227-271, 2004.
[Wulwick, 1995] N. Wulwick. The Hamiltonian Formalism and Optimal Growth Theory. In Ingrid Rima, ed., *Measurement, Quantification and Economic Analysis*, pp. 406–435. London: Routledge, 1995.

# FEMINIST PHILOSOPHY OF ECONOMICS

Kristina Rolin

## INTRODUCTION

As a profession academic economics has been and still is outnumbered by men [Ferber and Nelson, 2003, 3]. In many countries, the proportion of women among academic economists is even lower than among academicians in general [Jacobsen *et al.*, 2006, 428].[1] Feminist philosophy of economics is concerned with the question of whether the under-representation of women in economics has influenced what is studied in economics, how it is studied, and what falls outside the scope of economics. Feminist philosophy of economics aims to understand what makes an economic inquiry *feminist* and how economists who identify themselves as feminists have contributed to economics. Since feminism is a moral and political stance which implies a commitment to egalitarian values, feminist philosophy of economics is bound to encounter the more general philosophical question of whether moral and political values are allowed to play a role in scientific inquiry. Whereas it is often granted that moral and political values have a legitimate role to play in debates about what research topics are worthy of pursuit and for what practical purposes scientific knowledge is sought, the contested issue is whether moral and social values are allowed to play a role in the epistemic justification of scientific knowledge. The latter question is of interest not only to feminist epistemology and philosophy of science; it has been addressed by a number of philosophers who are often identified with mainstream philosophy of science (e.g., [Hempel, 1965; Kuhn, 1977; Rudner, 1953]). Recent years have witnessed a reemergence of interest in the question of what the role of moral and political values is and should be in science (see e.g., [Douglas, 2000; Kincaid *et al.*, 2007; Lacey, 1999; Machamer and Wolters, 2004]). The on-going controversy over the role of moral and political values in science has challenged the simple and unexamined idea that scientific inquiry is objective insofar as it is fully free from moral and political values. Not surprisingly, feminist philosophy of economics has turned to feminist epistemology and philosophy of science for alternative conceptions of objectivity. In feminist philosophy of economics, the most influential conceptions

[1]See *Newsletter of the Committee on the Status of Women in the Economics Profession* for recent information on the status of women in economics in the USA and other countries. The Committee on the Status of Women in the Economics Profession (CSWEP) was founded in 1971 in the meeting of the American Economic Association.

Handbook of the Philosophy of Science. Volume 13: Philosophy of Economics.
Volume editor: Uskali Mäki. General editors: Dov M. Gabbay, Paul Thagard and John Woods.

of objectivity have been provided by Sandra Harding's [1991] feminist standpoint epistemology and Helen Longino's [1990] contextual empiricism.

Besides feminist epistemology and philosophy of science, feminist philosophy of economics has been inspired by feminist economics. The 1993 publication of *Beyond Economic Man: Feminist Theory and Economics* edited by Marianne A. Ferber and Julie A. Nelson was a landmark event in bringing together a group of scholars working on economics, feminist theory, and philosophy of science. *Beyond Economic Man* was soon followed by the publication of another collection of essays, *Out of the Margin: Feminist Perspectives on Economics* edited by Edith Kuiper and Jolande Sap in 1995, and the founding of the journal *Feminist Economics* in 1995.[2] In their introduction to a more recent collection of essays, *Feminist Economics Today* (2003), Ferber and Nelson set out to make an assessment of the impact of *Beyond Economic Man, Out of the Margin* and *Feminist Economics* on the profession. They regret that feminist work in economics has had little impact on textbooks and mainstream journals in economics even though feminist economics comprises a vital community of scholars. A similar observation can be made of feminist philosophy of economics. Contributions to feminist philosophy of economics are most likely to be found either in the journal *Feminist Economics* or in anthologies dedicated to the topic such as *Toward a Feminist Philosophy of Economics* (2003), edited by Drucilla K. Barker and Edith Kuiper.

In this essay I aim to give an overview of the central themes in feminist economics. First, I address the question of what makes an economic inquiry *feminist*. Second, I review a controversy over the question of whether rational choice theory is acceptable and useful for feminist economics. Third, I address the question of whether moral and political values are allowed to play a role in economics and what this role might be. I will also discuss feminist attempts to redefine the notion of objectivity. Fourth, I provide an introduction to a debate concerning the question of whether feminist philosophy of economics should embrace Tony Lawson's conception of critical realism.

## WHAT MAKES AN ECONOMIC INQUIRY *FEMINIST*?

Feminist research is often understood to be research which aims to provide knowledge "for women." However, there is a variety of views about what the commitment to do research for women actually means. Whereas some views do not require that economic methodology be revised in any way, others require that traditional concepts and methods of economic inquiry be challenged. Some views suggest that the very definition of economics as a discipline needs to be questioned. Sharon Crasnow [2007] identifies three different responses to the question of what makes a social science *feminist*: (1) feminist research focuses on research topics which are of particular interest to feminist politics; (2) feminist research is characterized

[2] *Feminist Economics* is the journal of the International Association for Feminist Economics (IAFFE) which was founded in 1992. *Feminist Economics* was rewarded as the best new journal by the Council of Editors of Learned Journals in 1997.

by the use of the concept of gender; (3) feminist research aims to reveal structures of power, especially those structures organized by gender. All of these three approaches can be found in feminist philosophy of economics. In this section I give a brief account of them.

As to the first approach, there is no doubt that "feminism" in feminist economics signals an interest in certain topics. A quick glance through the titles in the 2008 issues of *Feminist Economics* reveals that the following topics continue to be of interest to the community: gender gap in wages; multiple discrimination in the labor market; policies aiming to balance family and labor market work; sex differences in altruistic behavior; the role of unpaid market labor in families; the distribution of the costs of having children; gender differences in employment; women's part-time work penalties; and the division of household labor. There is, indeed, no shortage of research topics for those economists who are concerned with gender inequalities in the world. According to the World Economic Forum's *Global Gender Gap Report* (2007), no country in the world has eliminated the gender gap in all the main areas of social and economic life: economic participation and opportunity, political empowerment, educational attainment, health and survival. The smallest gender gap can be found in (1) Sweden, (2) Norway, (3) Finland, (4) Iceland, and (5) New Zealand [Hausmann *et al.*, 2007, 7].

However, it is unsatisfactory to characterize feminist economics merely in terms of its preference for certain research topics. This is evident if we consider feminist responses to Gary Becker's "new home economics" [Becker, 1981]. The division of labor among women and men is certainly a topic which is of interest to feminist politics. Yet, Becker's approach to the topic has been met with severe criticism in feminist economics. Many feminist economists argue that Becker's approach is biased because it represents the traditional division of labor among women and men mainly as an outcome of individual choice, and downplays the role of more and less subtle forms of gender-based discrimination in the labor market [Ferber and Nelson, 1993, 6-7].

The second and the third responses to the question of what makes an economic inquiry *feminist* are more promising than the first one. They attempt to characterize feminist economics not merely in terms of its subject matter of inquiry but in terms of an approach to a subject matter of inquiry. It is not easy to make a clear-cut distinction between the two approaches because most analyses of gender turn out to be analyses of power structures organized by gender. Therefore, I discuss the two approaches together.

The second and the third approach to understanding what makes an economic inquiry *feminist* appeal to the concept of gender as it has been developed in feminist theory. To make use of the concept of gender in research implies more than recognizing the obvious fact that most economic agents are male or female. The concept of gender refers to the many ways that differences between females and males are socially constructed and contested. Gender is constituted by gender ideologies, that is, beliefs or tacit assumptions of the form 'x is masculine' or 'x is feminine' where x can stand for a number of things, including bodily features, gestures, clothing, household tasks, tools, professions, virtues, and even philosophical concepts such as rationality and objectivity. To say that gender is constituted by gender ideologies means that the things understood to be masculine or feminine (or gender neutral) are not inherently masculine or feminine (or gender neutral). They are gendered (or gender neutral) for some people in some context insofar as those people in that context speak or behave as if those things are gendered (or gender neutral). Gender ideologies make it possible for human beings to "do gender" as they do other things [West and Zimmerman, 1987]. Gender ideologies also give content to social expectations, that is, normative beliefs about what behaviors are appropriate for women as women and men as men [Connell, 1985]. In feminist philosophy of economics, the concept of gender has inspired analyzes of gender ideologies in the rhetoric of economics [McCloskey, 1993] as well as in the criteria used to judge what counts as "good economics" [Nelson, 1995].

Androcentrism and sexism are other important concepts introduced by feminist theory to economics. By androcentrism is meant the practice of treating men's experiences and social roles as generic whereas women's experiences and social roles are invisible or treated as deviations from the norm. By sexism is meant a set of value judgments which state that females or the feminine are inferior to males or the masculine. In their introduction to *Beyond Economic Man*, Ferber and Nelson identify both androcentrism and sexism in traditional mainstream economics. An example of androcentrism is the tendency to efface gender by focusing on abstract individuals as the preferred units of analysis [Ferber and Nelson, 1993, 5]. Another example is the tendency to underestimate the role of women's unpaid labor in accounts of human capital formation as well as in accounts of GNP [Ferber and Nelson, 1993, 5]. An example of sexism is the assumption that social and economic inequalities are an outcome of women's choices [Ferber and Nelson, 1993, 6].

When the concepts of gender, androcentrism, and sexism are transported from other social sciences to economics, they give rise to two concerns. One concern is the lack of attention to gender in much of economic research. Another concern is the question of whether some assumptions in economics are gendered despite their apparent neutrality. Not surprisingly, many contributions to feminist philosophy of science address the question of whether the assumptions in rational choice theory are androcentric and whether they should be accepted. I will provide an overview of this debate in the next section.

Clearly, the latter concern constitutes a more fundamental challenge to economics than the former. Nelson [1993; 1996] and Strassman [1993] argue that the recognition of gender ideologies in economics will ultimately lead feminist philosophy of economics to question the tendency to define economics by its approach rather than by its subject matter of inquiry. By "economic approach" they mean the commitment to apply rational choice theory to various kinds of social phenomena. Nelson argues that gender ideologies underlie the practice of giving high prestige to esoteric mathematical modeling at the expense of other kind of theorizing in economics [1993, 25-28; see also Nelson, 1998, 191]. She suggests that behind the high prestige of mathematical modeling is its culture-wide association with masculinity [1993, 33]. Nelson recommends that economists adopt an alternative definition of economics. She suggests that economics be defined as a discipline which studies "how humans, in interaction with each other and the environment, provide for their own survival and health" [1993, 34]).

Both Joyce Jacobsen [2003] and Nelson [1998] argue that the feminist commitment to understand "how the world actually works" means that feminist economics is more faithful to "empiricism" than mainstream economics. By "empiricism" they refer to research where the emphasis is on the analysis of empirical data [Jacobsen, 2003, 95; Nelson, 1998, 191]. As Jacobsen explains, feminist economics aims to uncover "what economic agents actually do, rather than asserting that they act in particular ways that are consistent with economic theory" [2003, 93; see also Hands, 2001, 269].

In this section I have shown that feminist philosophy of economics is critical of the "add women and stir" approach to correcting the short-comings of traditional mainstream economics [Ferber and Nelson, 1993, 6]. *Feminism* in feminist economics is not just about paying more attention to women, families, and unpaid work; it is about challenging assumptions in widely used economic models. In the next section, I aim to specify what assumptions have been criticized in feminist philosophy of science.

## IS RATIONAL CHOICE THEORY ANDROCENTRIC?

Interestingly, there is no consensus among feminist philosophers of economics about what a feminist stance towards rational choice theory should be. Whereas some philosophers suggest that rational choice theory be abandoned, others see it as a useful tool for feminist research provided that it is interpreted in certain ways. In this section I provide an overview of the feminist controversy over rational choice theory.

At the radical end of feminist criticisms of rational choice theory is Paula England's contribution to *Beyond Economic Man*. England [1993] argues that rational choice theory is not acceptable because it reflects an androcentric bias. According to England, androcentrism is manifested in the following four assumptions: first, the assumption that interpersonal utility comparisons are impossible; second, the assumption that preferences are exogenous to economic models and unchanging; third, the assumption that agents are selfish (in the sense that their utility functions are independent from others' utility functions); and fourth, the assumption that these three assumptions do not apply to relations within families [1993, 37]. England argues that these four assumptions are androcentric because they "exaggerate both the atomistic, separative nature of behavior in markets and the connective empathy and altruism within families" [1993, 37]. In her view, these four assumptions are problematic because they render invisible women's contributions to production as well as men's power over women in markets and families [1993, 38]. One problem in England's argument is that not all applications of rational choice theory are committed to the assumptions she sees as androcentric (see also [Anderson, 2002; Cudd, 2002]).

Nelson's contribution to *Beyond Economic Man* (1993) is a representative of a moderate stand with respect to rational choice theory. Nelson does not suggest that feminist economists abandon rational choice theory. Instead, she recommends that feminists adopt a pluralistic approach to economic methodology. According to Nelson, the high prestige given to esoteric mathematical modeling in economics limits unnecessarily its scope of inquiry. As she explains: "Study of actual markets tends to give way to study of ideal abstract markets or hypothetical games" [1993, 26]. Nelson's contention is that economics would benefit from a richer definition of economics that is open to other approaches and methods (see also [Nelson, 1995; 1996]). As part of her attempt to redefine economics, she puts forward the following proposal: "Let us start by speaking of the mathematical theory of individual choice as 'the mathematical theory of individual choice' instead of as 'economic theory,' of the choice theoretic approach as 'the choice-theoretic approach' instead of as 'the economic approach"' [1993, 34].

Ann Cudd [2002] holds the view that rational choice theory is useful for feminist research provided that it is interpreted in certain ways. According to Cudd, the application of bargaining theory to household production and distribution is a good example of rational choice theory in the service of feminist research [2002, 407]. She argues that bargaining theory has served feminist ends because "the family is now seen as a primary site of injustice, and hence in need of a theory (and practice) of distributive justice, a task for which rational choice theory is well suited" [2002, 409].

Cudd [2002] takes issue with England's [1993] argument by claiming that it is based on a misunderstanding of rational choice theory. According to Cudd, rational choice theory assumes that agents are self-interested in the sense of "non-tuism," that is, they are not motivated by the preferences of those they are interacting with. As Cudd explains: "In assuming non-tuism, rational choice theory assumes only that the preferences of the agents are in principle statable apart from others' preferences" [2002, 399]. Cudd argues that non-tuism does not entail selfishness if by selfishness is understood choices where agents prefer their own well-being over that of others. Cudd argues further, contra England [1993, 45], that altruism is not precluded by the assumption that agents have mutually independent utility functions. As Cudd explains: "The well-being of others could enter a non-tuist's utility function, but not as another's utility function" [2002, 399]. Thus, Cudd concludes that non-tuism does not entail what England calls a "separative" self. According to Cudd, rational agents must order their preferences under the influence of social norms; otherwise, they would not consider all the consequences of their actions [2002, 405].

Unlike England [1993], Cudd [2002] does not recommend that feminists abandon rational choice theory. However, she suggests that rational choice theory be revised in order to serve feminist research better. According to Cudd, the real problem in rational choice theory is that its construal of individual autonomy as non-tuism does not provide a sufficiently strong conception of autonomy for feminist research.

She argues that the conception of autonomy as non-tuism is too weak because it leaves open the possibility that agents' preferences are non-autonomous in a more fundamental sense [2002, 411]. Non-autonomous preferences are a problem especially for the subordinate insofar as their subordination makes it difficult for them to form the kind of preferences that would express their basic human needs [2002, 409]. Cudd recommends that feminists revise rational choice theory so that it does not take individual preferences and beliefs about available options as given. She recommends also that rational choice theory is interpreted as a theory of structural incentives. A feminist interpretation of rational choice theory would acknowledge that the social environment systematically rewards and punishes behaviors by social groups and thereby induces a preference structure on their members [Cudd, 2002, 413].

Also Elizabeth Anderson [2002] holds the view that rational choice theory serves feminist research if it is revised in certain ways. Anderson argues that feminist philosophy of economics should interpret rational choice theory as a kind of "methodological rationalism" [Davidson, 1982] because this interpretation enables feminists to understand how moral and political values are relevant to rational choice theory. Insofar as rational choice theory is understood as methodological rationalism, it advises us to attribute those beliefs and desires to individuals that enable us to represent their choices as maximizing their expected utility. Thus, rational choice theory functions as a default assumption in explanations of human behavior; resort to alternative explanations would be warranted only when one cannot make sense of human behavior in terms of rational choice theory. Anderson claims that the justification for making a particular theory of rationality the default explanatory framework is that it is normatively correct [Anderson, 2002, 371]. Thus, she recommends that feminist philosophy of economics endorse "critical methodological rationalism," that is, a kind of methodological rationalism which includes a critical reflection on the conception of rationality that is accepted as a feminist ideal [Anderson, 2002, 393-394].

Following Deirdre McCloskey, Anderson suggests that we distinguish two different versions of rational choice theory, a formal and a rhetorical version [McCloskey, 1985]. A formal theory of rational choice says merely that an agent's preferences fit into a single, complete, and transitive ordering and that an agent tends to maximize her utility. A formal theory concerns the relative ranking of an agent's preferences and disregards the content of these preferences as well as the agent's reasons for having them [Anderson, 2002, 373-374]. Anderson argues that a formal theory of rational choice is of limited interest to feminist research because "it effaces the distinction between action on one's own autonomous preferences, and action governed by oppressive social norms" [2002, 392]. Thus, Anderson seems to agree with Cudd [2002] that the conception of individual autonomy implicit in a formal version of rational choice theory is too thin to serve the purposes of feminist research.

Anderson argues that a rhetorical version of rational choice theory is of interest to feminist research because it includes a thicker ideal of human agency than a formal version [Anderson, 2002, 374-375]. A rhetorical theory of rational choice suggests that the ideal economic agent is self-transparent, opportunistic, resourceful, enterprising, self-reliant, calculating, autonomous, and self-confident [2002, 375]. Anderson calls this ideal of economic agent a *rhetorical* theory of rational choice because it is based on a narrative about how people are likely to behave in a wide range of social settings [2002, 374]. As Anderson explains: "[I]t is the rhetorical aspects of rational choice theory rather than the formal axioms that bear the weight of most rational choice explanations of human events" [2002, 376]. The reason for this is that a rhetorical version of the rational choice theory describes those psychological conditions under which human beings are capable of fulfilling the otherwise hard to achieve conditions of formal rational choice theory. Without the psychological conditions described in a rhetorical version of rational choice theory, human beings are likely to be vulnerable to various social pressures which generate multiple, conflicting, incomplete, and intransitive preference orderings [2002, 377]. According to Anderson, the normative ideal of human agency embedded in a rhetorical theory of rational choice should be understood as an achievement rather than as a given condition [2002, 390-391].

A crucial question for feminist philosophy of economics is whether the normative ideal of human agency that is embedded in a rhetorical theory of rational choice is consistent with feminism. After all, the "rationality" in rational choice theory is contested in light of many philosophical theories of rationality. For example, rational choice theory tells individual agents to defect in one-shot prisoner's dilemma (because defection is more rational than cooperation from a purely self-interested point of view), whereas a Kantian theory of rationality tells individual agents to cooperate (because one cannot rationally will defection as a universal principle of action) [Anderson, 2002, 371]. Anderson recommends that feminist economists accept some aspects of a rhetorical theory of rational choice and reject others. She argues that feminists should accept the assumption that an ideal human agent is autonomous and self-confident because these two features are part of human dignity; whenever there is a deviation from these norms feminists can inquire whether it is due to oppressive conditions [Anderson, 2002, 393].

Despite her favorable appraisal of a rhetorical theory of rational choice, Anderson does not recommend that it is adopted as a universal model of explanation in social sciences. Anderson argues that a rhetorical theory of rational choice does not always provide good explanations of human behavior simply because "what counts as a good explanation of a phenomenon depends on what aspects of that phenomenon one wants to understand" [2002, 389]. One common defense of rational choice theory is that there is no alternative explanatory model of human behavior that has comparable scope. According to Anderson, this is a good argument in favor of rational choice theory only insofar as there is value in having one theory explain everything [2002, 389].

According to Helen Longino [1993], what is at stake in the feminist debate on rational choice theory is not only the question of what counts as a good explanation in feminist economics. Another equally important question is whether the epistemic goal of feminist economics should be prediction or explanation. In the former case, one test of the adequacy of rational choice theory is its ability to predict the phenomena we can observe, with the degree of accuracy that is thought to be sufficient for the purpose of inquiry. In the latter case, we assess the epistemic merits of rational choice theory on the basis of whether it is capable of giving an account of those factors that are causally significant in bringing about observed phenomena [Longino, 1993, 166].

To summarize, the feminist controversy over rational choice theory ranges over a variety of positions, at the one end the view that rational choice theory is thoroughly androcentric and at the other end the view that a particular version of rational choice theory is useful to feminist research. Despite their disagreements, feminist philosophers of economics seem to share the view that rational choice theory is an example of a scientific theory which is laden with moral and social values. As Anderson explains, moral and social values sometimes play the same role in social sciences as they do in medicine. Moral and social values set the norm and deviations from the norm are thought to require explanation [2002, 393]. Thus, the debate on the role of rational choice theory in feminist economics gives rise to the question of whether moral and social values can legitimately enter into the justification of economic theories and whether economic theories can be objective at all. This is the topic of the next section.

## VALUES AND OBJECTIVITY IN ECONOMICS

In feminist philosophy of economics we can find two slightly different ways to think about the role of moral and political values in scientific inquiry. A radical position is that scientific inquiry is inevitably laden with moral and political values. A moderate position is that moral and political values can enter into otherwise acceptable scientific inquiry but they do not necessarily do so. The two positions differ in what they recommend as an antidote to a value-laden scientific inquiry. If scientific inquiry is understood to be value-laden *necessarily*, then the cure is to detect androcentric and sexist assumptions and to replace them with feminist values. If scientific inquiry is understood to be value-laden *contingently*, then the cure is to introduce a diversity of perspectives into scientific communities with the expectation that a diverse community is capable of deciding whether value influence in research is acceptable in particular cases. Both of these two positions share the view that moral and political values do not necessarily corrupt scientific research. Whether they are "good" or "bad" for science depends on what kinds of value they are and what roles they play in scientific inquiry. In this section I provide an overview of the two feminist positions with respect to values and objectivity in science.

In her contribution to the first issue of *Feminist Economics*, Sandra Harding argues that moral and political values enter into economic inquiry inevitably because theories are underdetermined not just by the evidence that happens to have been collected for them, but by any possible evidence [1995, 12]. Harding claims that "neutrality, in the sense of freedom from all social values and interests, is neither possible nor desirable" [1995, 9]. Harding's argument has been criticized by Susan Haack [1996]. Haack points out that the argument includes a false premise, the claim that scientists have to accept some theory or hypothesis on the basis of moral or political values when the evidence is not sufficient [1996, 84]. This premise is false because scientists have other options. They can suspend a judgment and continue inquiry, or they can assign some degree of evidential warrant to a theory or a hypothesis [Haack, 1996, 84].

Indeed, it is difficult to see why feminist philosophy of economics should be committed to the thesis that moral and political values *inevitably* influence the acceptance of theories and hypotheses in economics. For the purpose of developing a feminist understanding of economics, it is sufficient to adopt a weaker thesis, the claim that moral and political values *can* influence the acceptance of a theory or a hypothesis in what by all other criteria counts as acceptable scientific inquiry. If one adopts the weaker thesis, then it is a matter of case by case analysis to determine whether moral or political values have actually entered into economic inquiry. The role of moral and political values in economic inquiry cannot be settled by means of a priori argumentation alone [Rolin, 2002, 237].

The weaker thesis is supported by Diana Strassmann's [1993] and Helen Longino's [1993] analysis of the partial nature of models in economics. Both Strassmann and Longino emphasize that partiality is an intrinsic feature of all models in science [Strassmann, 1993, 55; Longino, 1993, 166]. Models are designed to account for some aspects of reality thought to be significant and to some degree of precision thought to be sufficient for the purpose of inquiry. Sometimes the decision to count some aspects of reality as more significant than others is based on moral and political values but it does not necessarily have to be so. So, to claim, as Harding [1995] does, that economic inquiry is inevitably value-laden, is to make an overstatement.

Strassman [1993] and Longino [1993] suggest that analyzing the partiality of models is a key to understanding how economic inquiry can become value-laden. As Strassmann explains: "Models, like maps, highlight certain aspects of a situation while suppressing others. Since a model can never completely capture the phenomenon in its entirety, questions of the 'truth' or 'falsity' of a model are less relevant to judgments about its quality than are questions of its appropriateness, aptness, and helpfulness in a given context" [1993, 55]. Strassmann [1993] presents four case studies to illustrate how social values can underlie the partial nature of models in economics. She argues that the "story of the market place of ideas," the "story of the benevolent patriarch," the "story of the woman of leisure," and the "story of free choice" are tacit and value-laden narratives which have informed modeling in economics [1993, 56-63]. Longino holds the view that the partiality of models is not in and of itself a defect in economic inquiry [1993, 166]. The partiality of models is a problem only insofar as it is not informed by a self-reflective understanding of its partiality.

In her contribution to the first issue of *Feminist Economics*, Janet Seiz [1995] voices a view shared by many philosophers and economists who work on feminist philosophy of science. Seiz claims that feminist philosophy of economics needs a concept of objectivity that enables it to occupy a middle ground between an uncritical belief in the objectivity of mainstream economics and the epistemological relativism of postmodern science studies [1995, 113]. According to Seiz, such a concept of objectivity should enable feminist economists to embrace both fallibilism (the view that scientific knowledge is at best fallible, not certain) and the belief that it is, nevertheless, possible and desirable to pursue less false and less partial accounts of social reality [1995, 114]. Whereas many feminist economists and philosophers agree on this view, they disagree on the question of what conception of objectivity serves these ends best. The two most influential theories of objectivity are provided by Harding's feminist standpoint epistemology and Longino's contextual empiricism.

According to Harding, research is objective when it starts from the lives of unprivileged groups [1991, 150; see also page 142]. She calls this view "strong objectivity." In economics "strong objectivity" means that economists should actively seek to identify culture-wide assumptions "by starting off thought from outside those dominant frameworks" [Harding, 1995, 27]. By calling this conception of objectivity "strong" Harding intends to distinguish it from "weak objectivity." By "weak objectivity" she means the view that moral and political values can be kept in check by following the prevailing standards of scientific inquiry [1995, 15]. Harding argues that this conception of objectivity is weak because it is not able to identify culture-wide assumptions that have shaped economic inquiry. At best, it can identify idiosyncratic values held by individuals or research groups. Harding suggests that weak objectivity is not just useless; even worse, it is part of the problem [1995, 15]. As Harding explains: "It defends and legitimates the institutions and practices through which the distortions and their often exploitative consequences are generated" [1995, 15].

Harding's conception of "strong objectivity" is based on a contested view which I call the thesis of epistemic privilege [Rolin, 2006]. The thesis of epistemic privilege is the claim that those who are unprivileged with respect to their social positions are likely to be privileged with respect to gaining knowledge of social reality. According to Harding, unprivileged social positions are likely to generate perspectives which are "less partial and less distorted" than the perspectives generated by other social positions [Harding, 1991, 121; see also pages 138 and 141]. The thesis of epistemic privilege is sometimes believed to include two other assumptions, an assumption of *essentialism* and an assumption of *automatic* epistemic privilege [Wylie, 2004, 341]. Whereas the assumption of essentialism is that all women share the same socially grounded perspective in virtue of being women, the assumption of automatic epistemic privilege is that epistemic privilege accrues to the subordinate automatically, just in virtue of their occupying a particular social position. As Alison Wylie argues, it is not clear that anyone who has advocated feminist standpoint epistemology has ever endorsed either one of these two problematic views [2004, 341].

Nevertheless, the thesis of epistemic privilege remains problematic in its own right. One problem is that Harding's feminist standpoint epistemology does not provide any standards of epistemic justification which enable one to judge some socially grounded perspectives as better than others. As Louise Antony [2002] and Helen Longino [1999] argue, the thesis of epistemic privilege seems to be inconsistent with another thesis advanced by feminist standpoint epistemology, the situated knowledge thesis. The situated knowledge thesis is the claim that all scientific knowledge is socially situated [Harding, 1991, 11; see also pages 119 and 142]. Whereas the thesis of epistemic privilege relies on the assumption that there are *impartial* standards which allow one to judge some perspectives as better than others, the situated knowledge thesis seems to undermine this assumption by suggesting that all knowledge is *partial*. In other words, feminist standpoint epistemology contains the paradox that, on the one hand, it claims that the standpoint of the subordinate is epistemically privileged, while on the other hand, it denies that there are any epistemic standards which are independent of standpoints [Longino, 1999, 338].

Another objection to the thesis of epistemic privilege is that there is not sufficient evidence to support it [Pinnick, 1994]. Indeed, the two objections to the thesis of epistemic privilege are closely connected. As long as it is not clear by what standards one can judge some perspectives as better than others, it is not clear either what kind of evidence one can expect in support of the thesis of epistemic privilege [Rolin, 2006, 126]. Thus, one challenge for feminist standpoint epistemology is to translate the thesis of epistemic privilege into an empirical hypothesis and to present evidence in its support [Rolin, 2006, 127]. As Wylie explains: "It is only through the grounded analysis of concrete examples that we are likely to move beyond recurrent controversy about the viability of standpoint theory and delineate, with precision, its potential and limitations" [2004, 347].

Longino [1990] develops a social account of objectivity which is an alternative to Harding's conception of strong objectivity. Whereas Harding seems to understand objectivity as a standpoint that an individual scientist can adopt, Longino thinks that objectivity is achieved primarily by communities and only derivatively by individuals. As Longino explains: "Scientific communities will be objective to the degree that they satisfy four criteria necessary for achieving the transformative dimension of critical discourse: (1) there must be recognized avenues for the criticism of evidence, of methods, and of assumptions and reasoning; (2) there must exist shared standards that critics can evoke; (3) the community as a whole must be responsive to such criticism; (4) intellectual authority must be shared equally among qualified practitioners" [1990, 76; Longino, 2002, 128-135]. Longino's social account of objectivity escapes the paradox in feminist standpoint epistemology because it gives up the claim that some standpoints are epistemically privileged and it grounds the epistemic justification of scientific knowledge in the public and shared standards of scientific communities.

Nevertheless, Longino's social account of objectivity has been met with criticism in feminist philosophy of science. The criticisms fall into three categories. One criticism is that Longino's account is in danger of collapsing into a form of epistemic relativism because it relativizes objectivity to a community practice [Crasnow, 2003, 140; Clough, 1998, 91]. Crasnow suggests that feminist philosophy of science develop a conception of objectivity which transcends the conception of objectivity as a form of "intersubjectivity" [2003, 136]. What this account of objectivity could be is an open question for future research. Another criticism is that Longino does not provide a naturalistic justification for her account of objectivity. Miriam Solomon and Alan Richardson [2005] suggest that some case studies or some other kind of empirical evidence are needed to support the hypothesis that the four norms of public criticism, uptake of criticism, shared standards, and tempered equality of intellectual authority *actually* promote the epistemic goals of science, either truth or empirical success. Yet another criticism claims that Longino's social account of objectivity is too even-handed with respect to different moral and political values in science. Janet Kourany [2005] and Kristen Intemann [2008] suggest that Longino's ideal of "social value management" [Longino, 2002, 50] is not sufficiently normative to count as a *feminist* philosophy of science.

In summary, feminist philosophy of economics cannot be characterized in terms of a single position with respect to values and objectivity in science. Instead, it is characterized by a lively controversy over how moral and political values can enter into otherwise acceptable economic inquiry and what kind of objectivity should serve as an ideal for feminist economics. Feminist philosophy of economics does not entertain the view that scientific inquiry is objective insofar as it is fully free from moral and political values. It is recognized that moral and political values can enter into economic inquiry by determining what aspects of reality models are expected to represent and to what degree of accuracy they are expected to represent them. This said it is important to notice that feminist philosophy of economics rules out certain kinds of value influences in science as illegitimate. As Anderson explains, values are illegitimate insofar as they drive inquiry to a predetermined conclusion [2004, 1]. Thus, what is really at stake in the debate over values in science is dogmatism and not values as such [Anderson, 2004, 3]. Values are an epistemic problem for science insofar as they lead scientists to dogmatism. However, values do not always do so. We can present arguments against or in favor of certain values. Therefore, there is no need to be dogmatic about moral and political values in science (see also [Crasnow, 2007, 779]).

## "CRITICAL REALISM:" A CONTESTED VIEW IN FEMINIST PHILOSOPHY OF ECONOMICS

At the turn of the century, the journal *Feminist Economics* featured a debate on Tony Lawson's "critical realism" and its relation to feminist philosophy of economics. Lawson [1999] argues that feminist philosophy of economics should embrace his conception of critical realism for two reasons. First, critical realism would help feminists better analyze the limitations of mathematical modeling in economics. Second, it would help feminists better argue for the insights of feminist standpoint epistemology in economic inquiry. Lawson's 1999 contribution to *Feminist Economics* has elicited several critical responses [Barker, 2003; Harding, 1999; 2003; Nelson, 2003; Peter, 2003a; 2003b; Poutanen, 2007; Staveren, 2004; see also Lawson 2003a; 2003b]. In this section I give an overview of Lawson's contested arguments.

What is "critical realism"? According to Lawson, critical realism is mainly a view concerning the ontology of social reality. In critical realism, social reality is understood to be structured and dynamic, meaning that social structures condition human agency and human agency in turn depends upon social structures [1999, 32]. By social structures Lawson means such things as social rules, social relations, and social positions [1999, 33]. Lawson advances a transcendental argument in support of critical realism. He argues that "experimental activity and results, and the application of experimentally determined knowledge outside of experimental situations, can be made intelligible only through invoking something like an ontology of structures, powers, generative mechanisms, and their tendencies that lie behind and govern the flux of events in an essentially open world" [1999, 31].

Lawson's first argument begins with the observation that mathematical modeling is an attempt to relate one set of events or states of affairs to others. According to Lawson, modeling presupposes regularities of the form "whenever event or state of affairs x then event or state of affairs y" [1999, 29]. Lawson claims that such event regularities occur only in closed systems which are most likely to be found in laboratories where scientists are able to create well-controlled experimental situations [1999, 30]. In the social realm, however, scientists can rarely create closed systems, and hence, Lawson argues, it is very unlikely that they can find event regularities [1999, 32-35]. Lawson concludes that mathematical modeling is not capable of dealing with the social realm [1999, 35]. He claims also that the practice of mathematical modeling in economics is "masculinist" [1999, 29 and 36]. And he suggests that "those empirically-oriented feminists in economics insistent upon applying standard econometric methods in all contexts are proceeding wholly in the wrong direction" [1999, 35].

As we have seen, feminist philosophy of economics includes arguments in light of which Lawson's position is contested. Whereas many feminist economists are critical of the tendency to equate economics with a certain kind of mathematical modeling, they do not find sufficient reasons for its wholesale rejection [Nelson, 1993; Strassman, 1993]. Instead, they recommend that feminist economists understand such models to offer merely partial understanding of social reality [Longino, 1993; Strassman, 1993], and that they make room for alternative methodological approaches in economics [Jacobsen, 2003; Nelson, 1993]. Moreover, even if feminist economists are critical of the tendency to associate mathematical modeling with masculinity, they provide a different diagnosis of the real problem beneath this symptom than Lawson does. The real problem in their view is not so much in the methods themselves as it is in the stereotypes attached to the methods, and more generally, to mathematical sciences. Thus, the challenge is to reform not merely the methods of economics but also science education as well as the public understanding of science so that mathematical sciences such as economics are no longer seen as "masculine" disciplines.

Let me turn to Lawson's second argument, the claim that feminist philosophy of economics should embrace his conception of critical realism because it helps them argue for the thesis of epistemic privilege, that is, the claim that unprivileged social positions are likely to generate less false and less partial perspectives on social reality than other positions. Lawson argues that a theory of contrastive explanation helps feminists understand how marginal positions can generate epistemic advantages. A theory of contrastive explanation states that explanatory questions are contrastive. This means that whenever we pose an explanation question of the type "Why a certain state of affairs A is the case?" we need to provide a specification of the form: "Why a state of affairs A rather than B or C etc.?" A contrastive explanation question directs scientists to pick out certain kinds of causal factors from the causal history of A as explanatory factors. According to Lawson, a marginal position can provide an epistemic privilege because it enables one to recognize new and significant contrasts in need of explanation [1999, 41]. As Lawson explains: "The task of detecting and identifying previously unknown causal mechanisms seems to require the recognition of surprising or interesting contrasts, and the latter in turn presupposes people in positions of being able to detect relevant contrasts and to perceive them as surprising or otherwise of interest and to want to act on their surprise or aroused interest" [1999, 40-41]. According to Lawson, "It follows that science, or the knowledge process more generally, can benefit if undertaken by individuals who are predisposed in different ways, who are situated differently" [1999, 41].

The idea that a theory of contrastive explanation can serve feminist philosophy of economics, is certainly interesting and worthy of more explorations in feminist philosophy of economics. However, the idea in itself does not support the conclusion in Lawson's argument, the claim that feminist philosophy of economics should embrace his conception of critical realism. This is because a theory of contrastive explanation can be adopted independently of any commitment to critical realism.

The debate on the role of critical realism in feminist philosophy of economics seems to be stagnated (see also [Poutanen, 2007]). This may be due to lack of case studies or examples that would serve to ground general claims about the role of modeling and the role of contrastive explanation questions in feminist economics. One striking feature of the debate that has taken place in *Feminist Economics* between 1999 and 2003 is the absence of any references to feminist philosophers' work on the ontology of social reality. Feminist work on the ontology of social reality aims to understand the socially constructed and contested nature of gender and race (see e.g., [Haslanger, 2000]). It is difficult to see what new insights the arid concepts of critical realism, such as social rules and social positions, could bring to contemporary feminist work on the ontology of social reality. Much of the feminist work on the ontology of social reality has already moved beyond the simple notions of rules and positions to develop a more complex account of how identities, desires, and bodies shape and are shaped by discursive practices. To claim that social structures condition and depend upon human agency is just to state the obvious in a debate where the challenge is to understand where and how interventions can be made into hegemonic gender and racial ideologies.

## CONCLUSION

As we have seen feminist philosophy of economics has been inspired by feminist economics and feminist epistemology and philosophy of science. It addresses such questions as what makes an economic inquiry feminist, whether rational choice theory is androcentric, whether feminists should challenge the definition of the discipline by its approach rather than by its scope of inquiry, whether moral and political values are allowed to play a role in economic inquiry, how objectivity should be understood in economics, and whether feminist economics should be committed to a particular view on the ontology of social reality. The economists and philosophers who are engaged in these debates tend to disagree especially on two issues, on the role of rational choice theory in feminist economics and the conception of objectivity.

## BIBLIOGRAPHY

[Anderson, 2002] E. Anderson. Should Feminists Reject Rational Choice Theory? In Louise M. Antony and Charlotte E. Witt (eds.), *A Mind of One's Own: Feminist Essays on Reason and Objectivity.* Second Edition. Boulder: Westview Press, pp. 369-397, 2002.

[Anderson, 2004] E. Anderson. Use of Value Judgments in Science: A General Argument, with Lessons from a Case Study of Feminist Research on Divorce. *Hypatia* 19 (1), 1-24, 2004.

[Antony, 2002] L. Antony. Quine as Feminist: The Radical Import of Naturalized Epistemology. In Louise M. Antony and Charlotte E. Witt (eds.), *A Mind of One's Own: Feminist Essays on Reason and Objectivity.* Second Edition. Boulder: Westview Press, pp. 110-153, 2002.

[Barker, 2003] D. K. Barker. Emancipatory for Whom? A Comment on Critical Realism. *Feminist Economics* 9 (1), 103-108, 2003.

[Barker and Kuiper, 2003] D. K. Barker and E. Kuiper, eds. *Toward A Feminist Philosophy of Economics.* London and New York: Routledge, 2003.

[Becker, 1981] G. Becker. *A Treatise on the Family.* Cambridge: Harvard University Press, 1981.

[Clough, 1998] S. Clough. A Hasty Retreat from Evidence: The Recalcitrance of Relativism in Feminist Epistemology. *Hypatia* 13 (4), 88-111, 1998.

[Connell, 1985] R. W. Connell. Theorizing Gender. *Sociology* 19 (2), 260-272, 1985.

[Crasnow, 2003] S. Crasnow. Can Science Be Objective? Feminism, Relativism, and Objectivity. In Cassandra L. Pinnick, Noretta Koertge, and Robert F. Almeder (eds.), *Scrutinizing Feminist Epistemology: An Examination of Gender in Science.* New Brunswick and London: Rutgers University Press, pp. 130-141, 2003.

[Crasnow, 2007] S. Crasnow. Feminist Anthropology and Sociology: Issues for Social Science. In Stephen P. Turner and Mark W. Risjord (eds.), *Handbook of the Philosophy of Science: Philosophy of Anthropology and Sociology.* Amsterdam and Oxford: Elsevier, pp. 755-789, 2007.

[Cudd, 2002] A. E. Cudd. Rational Choice Theory and the Lessons of Feminism. In Louise M Antony and Charlotte E. Witt (eds.), *A Mind of One's Own: Feminist Essays on Reason and Objectivity.* Second Edition. Boulder: Westview Press, pp. 398-417, 2002.

[Davidson, 1982] D. Davidson. Psychology as Philosophy. In Donald Davidson, *Essays on Actions and Events.* Oxford: Oxford University Press, pp. 229-239, 1982.

[Douglas, 2000] H. Douglas. Inductive Risk and Values in Science. *Philosophy of Science* 67 (4), 559-579, 2000.

[England, 1993] P. England. The Separative Self. In Marianne A. Ferber and Julie A. Nelson (eds.), *Beyond Economic Man: Feminist Theory and Economics.* Chicago and London: The University of Chicago Press, pp. 37-53, 1993.

[Ferber and Nelson, 1993] M. A. Ferber and J. A. Nelson, eds.*Beyond Economic Man: Feminist Theory and Economics.* Chicago and London: The University of Chicago Press, 1993.

[Ferber and Nelson, 1993b] M. A. Ferber and J. A. Nelson. Introduction: The Social Construction of Economics and the Social Construction of Gender. In Marianne A. Ferber and Julie A. Nelson (eds.), *Beyond Economic Man: Feminist Theory and Economics.* Chicago and London: The University of Chicago Press, pp. 1-22, 1993.

[Ferber and Nelson, 2003] M. A. Ferber and J. A. Nelson. *Feminist Economics Today: Beyond Economic Man.* Chicago and London: The University of Chicago Press, 2003.

[Ferber and Nelson, 2003a] M. A. Ferber and J. A. Nelson. Introduction: Beyond Economic Man, Ten Years Later. In Marianne A. Ferber and Julie A. Nelson (eds.), *Feminist Economics Today: Beyond Economic Man.* Chicago and London: The University of Chicago Press, pp. 1-31, 2003.

[Haack, 1996] S. Haack. Science as Social – Yes and No. In Lynn Hankinson Nelson and Jack Nelson (eds.), *Feminism, Science, and the Philosophy of Science.* Dordrecht: Kluwer Academic Publishers, pp. 79-93, 1996.

[Hands, 2001] D. W. Hands. *Reflection without Rules: Economic Methodology and Contemporary Science Theory.* Cambridge: Cambridge University Press, 2001.

[Harding, 1991] S. Harding. *Whose Science? Whose Knowledge? Thinking from Women's Lives.* Ithaca: Cornell University Press, 1991.

[Harding, 1995] S. Harding. Can Feminist Thought Make Economics More Objective? *Feminist Economics* 1 (1), 7-32, 1995.

[Harding, 1999] S. Harding. The Case for Strategic Realism: A Response to Lawson. *Feminist Economics* 5 (3), 127-133, 1999.

[Harding, 2003] S. Harding. Representing Reality: The Critical Realism Project. *Feminist Economics* 9 (1), 151-159, 2003.

[Haslanger, 2000] S. Haslanger. Gender and Race: (What) Are They? (What) Do We Want Them To Be? *Noûs* 34 (1), 31-55, 2000.

[Hausmann *et al.*, 2007] R. Hausmann, L. D. Tyson, and S. Zahidi, eds. *The Global Gender Gap Report 2007.* Geneva: World Economic Forum, 2007.

[Hempel, 1965] C. G. Hempel. Science and Guman Values. in Carl G. Hempel, *Aspects of Scientific Explanation and other Essays in the Philosophy of Science.* New York: The Free Press, pp. 81-96, 1995.

[Intemann, 2008] K. Intemann. Increasing the Number of Feminist Scientists: Why Feminist Aims Are Not Served by the Underdetermination Thesis. *Science & Education* 17 (10), 2008.

[Jacobsen, 2003] J. P. Jacobsen. Some Implications of the Feminist Project in Economics for Empirical Methodology. In Drucilla K. Barker and Edith Kuiper (eds.), *Toward a Feminist Philosophy of Economics.* London and New York: Routledge, pp. 89-104, 2003.

[Jacobsen *et al.*, 2006] J. P. Jacobsen, R. E. Robb, J. Burton, D. H. Blackaby, J. Humphries, H. Joshi, X. Wang, and X.-Y. Dong. Explorations: The Status of Women Economists. *Feminist Economics* 12 (3), 427-474, 2006.

[Kincaid *et al.*, 2007] H. Kincaid, J. Dupré, and A. Wylie, eds. *Value-Free Science? Ideals and Illusions.* Oxford: Oxford University Press, 2007.

[Kourany, 2005] J. Kourany. A Feminist Primer for Philosophers of Science. In *Philosophy – Science – Scientific Philosophy*, edited by Christian Nimtz and Ansgar Beckermann. Paderborn: Mentis, pp. 287-305, 2005.

[Kuhn, 1977] T. Kuhn. Objectivity, Value Judgment, and Theory Choice. In Thomas Kuhn, *The Essential Tension: Selected Studies in Scientific Tradition and Change.* Chicago: The University of Chicago Press, pp. 320-339, 1977.

[Kuiper and Sap, 1995] E. Kuiper and J. Sap, eds., with S. Feiner, N. Ott, and Z. Tzannatos. *Out of the Margin: Feminist Perspectives on Economics.* London: Routledge, 1995.

[Lacey, 1999] H. Lacey. *Is Science Value Free? Values and Scientific Understanding.* London: Routledge. 1999.

[Lawson, 1999] T. Lawson. Feminism, Realism, and Universalism. *Feminist Economics* 5 (2), 25-59, 1999.

[Lawson, 2003a] T. Lawson. Ontology and Feminist Theorizing. *Feminist Economics* 9 (1), 119-150, 2003.

[Lawson, 2003b] T. Lawson. Theorizing Ontology. *Feminist Economics* 9 (1), 161-169, 2003.

[Longino, 1990] H. E. Longino. *Science as Social Knowledge: Values and Objectivity in Scientific Inquiry.* Princeton: Princeton University Press, 1990.

[Longino, 1993] H. E. Longino. Economics for Whom? In Marianne A. Ferber and Julie A. Nelson (eds.), *Beyond Economic Man: Feminist Theory and Economics.* Chicago and London: The University of Chicago Press, pp. 158-168, 1993.

[Longino, 1999] H. E. Longino. Feminist Epistemology. In John Greco and Ernest Sosa (eds.), *The Blackwell Guide to Epistemology.* Malden and Oxford: Blackwell Publishers, pp. 327-353, 1999.

[Longino, 2002] H. E. Longino. *The Fate of Knowledge.* Princeton: Princeton University Press, 2002.

[Machamer and Wolters, 2004] P. Machamer and G. Wolters, eds. *Science, Values, and Objectivity.* Pittsburgh: The University of Pittsburgh Press, 2004.

[McCloskey, 1985] D. N. McCloskey. *The Rhetoric of Economics.* Madison: University of Wisconsin Press, 1985.

[McCloskey, 1993] D. N. McCloskey. Some Consequences of a Conjective Economics. In Marianne A. Ferber and Julie A. Nelson (eds.), *Beyond Economic Man: Feminist Theory and Economics.* Chicago and London: The University of Chicago Press, pp. 69-93, 1993.

[Nelson, 1993] J. A. Nelson. The Study of Choice or the Study of Provisioning? Gender and the Definition of Economics. In Marianne A. Ferber and Julie A. Nelson (eds.), *Beyond Economic Man: Feminist Theory and Economics.* Chicago and London: The University of Chicago Press, pp. 23-36, 1993.

[Nelson, 1995] J. A. Nelson. Feminism and Economics. *Journal of Economic Perspectives* 9 (2), 131-148, 1995.

[Nelson, 1996] J. A. Nelson. *Feminism, Objectivity, and Economics.* London and New York: Routledge, 1996.

[Nelson, 1998] J. A. Nelson. Feminist Economic Methodology. In John B. Davis, D. Wade Hands, and Uskali Mäki (eds.), *The Handbook of Economic Methodology.* Cheltenhan and Northampton: Edwars Elgar, pp. 189-192, 1998.

[Nelson, 2003] J. A. Nelson. Once More, with Feeling: Feminist Economics and the Ontological Question. *Feminist Economics* 9 (1), 109-118, 2003.

[Peter, 2003a] F. Peter. Critical Realism, Feminist Epistemology, and the Emancipatory Potential of Science: A Comment on Lawson and Harding. *Feminist Economics* 9 (1), 93-101, 2003.

[Peter, 2003b] F. Peter. Foregrounding Practices: Feminist Philosophy of Economics Beyond Rhetoric and Realism. In Drucilla K. Barker and Edith Kuiper (eds.), *Toward a Feminist Philosophy of Economics.* London and New York: Routledge, pp. 105-121, 2003.

[Pinnick, 1994] C. Pinnick. Feminist Epistemology: Implications for Philosophy of Science. *Philosophy of Science* 61, 646-657, 1994.

[Poutanen, 2007] S. Poutanen. Critical Realism and Post-Structuralist Feminism: The Difficult Path to Mutual Understanding. *Journal of Critical Realism* 6 (1), 28-52, 2007.

[Rolin, 2002] K. Rolin. Is 'Science as Social' a Feminist Insight? *Social Epistemology* 16 (3), 233-249, 2002.

[Rolin, 2006] K. Rolin. The Bias Paradox in Feminist Standpoint Epistemology. *Episteme* 3 (1-2), 125-136, 2006.

[Rudner, 1953] R. Rudner. The Scientist qua Scientist Makes Value Judgments. *Philosophy of Science* 20 (1), 1-6, 1953.

[Seiz, 1995] J. A. Seiz. Epistemology and the Task of Feminist Economics. *Feminist Economics* 1 (3), 110-118, 1995.

[Solomon and Richardson, 2005] M. Solomon and A. Richardson. A Critical Context for Longino's Critical Contextual Empiricism. *Studies in the History and Philosophy of Science* 36, 211-222, 2005.

[van Staveren, 2004] I. van Staveren. Feminism and Realism: A Contested Relationship. *Post-Autistic Economics Review* 28, 25 October 2004, article 2, 2004.

[Strassmann, 1993] D. Strassmann. Not a Free Market: The Rhetoric of Disciplinary Authority in Economics. In Marianne A. Ferber and Julie A. Nelson (eds.), *Beyond Economic Man: Feminist Theory and Economics*. Chicago and London: The University of Chicago Press, pp. 54-68, 1993.

[West and Zimmerman, 1987] C. West and D. H. Zimmerman. Doing Gender. *Gender and Society* 1 (2), 125-151, 1987.

[Wylie, 2004] A. Wylie. Why Standpoint Matters. In Sandra Harding (ed.), *The Feminist Standpoint Theory Reader: Intellectual and Political Controversies*. New York and London: Routledge, pp. 339-351, 2004.

# THE POSITIVE-NORMATIVE DICHOTOMY AND ECONOMICS

D. Wade Hands

*Science is science and ethics is ethics; it takes both to make a whole man; but only confusion, misunderstanding and discord can come from not keeping them separate and distinct, from trying to impose the absolutes of ethics on the relatives of science.* [Friedman, 1955, p. 409]

*Morality, it could be argued, represents the way that people would like the world to work — whereas economics represents how it actually* does *work..* [Levitt and Dubner, *Freakonomics*, 2005, p. 13]

## 1 INTRODUCTION TO THE POSITIVE-NORMATIVE DICHOTOMY

There seems to be a clear distinction between the statement "I give to charity" (i.e. it *is* the case that I give) and the statement "I ought to give to charity" (i.e. it would be a good thing if I were to give). What *is* the case is one thing, a factual matter; and what *ought* to be the case is something else entirely, a matter of valuation, or of right and wrong. Perhaps one actually does what one ought to do, but then again, perhaps not. In either case, there does not appear to be any necessary relationship between the two types of statements; that something is the case does not imply that it should be that way, and that it should be that way does not imply that it is. The difference between "is" and "ought" seems substantive enough to be called a *dichotomy*: a distinction between two fundamentally different things. It is a dichotomy that we employ effortlessly in everyday life — and thus, may not appear to require philosophical analysis — but it is a dichotomy nonetheless. This is not to say of course that it is easy to determine what "is" in any particular case (What is the temperature at the center of the sun? or What is the most effective way to reduce unemployment?) nor is it always easy to know what one "ought" to do (What are the appropriate limits of tolerance? or Is lying ever the morally right thing to do?), but understanding the general conceptual difference seems to be straightforward. Even the family dog behaves as if she knows the difference between the shoe she (in fact) just chewed and the toy she ought to have chewed instead.

While the dichotomy between positive and normative — descriptive and prescriptive, facts and values, etc. — may appear straightforward, it has long been

Handbook of the Philosophy of Science. Volume 13: Philosophy of Economics.
Volume editor: Uskali Mäki. General editors: Dov M. Gabbay, Paul Thagard and John Woods.

the subject of philosophical debate. Although the is-ought distinction has ancient roots in Western philosophy, much of the contemporary discussion can be traced to David Hume. For this reason it has also been called "Hume's dichotomy," "Hume's fork," and "Hume's guillotine." Hume's primary concern was to block efforts to ground ethics in the facts of nature. In his own words:

> In every system of morality, which I have hitherto met with, I have always remark'd that the author proceeds for some time in the ordinary way of reasoning, and establishes the being of God, or makes observations concerning human affairs; when of a sudden I am supriz'd to find, that instead of the usual copulations of propositions, *is*, and, *is not*, I meet with no proposition that is not connected with an *ought*, or an *ought not*. This change is imperceptible; but is, however, of the last consequence. For as *ought*, or *ought not*, expresses some new relation of affirmation, 'tis necessary that it should be observ'd and explain'd; and at the same time that a reason should be given, for what seems altogether inconceivable, how this new relation can be a deduction from others, which are entirely different from it. [Hume, 1888, p. 469, emphasis in original]

The term "naturalistic fallacy" was introduced by G. E. Moore early in the 20th century for the related error of trying to (or believing that one can) derive/deduce an "ought" from an "is," and the imperative that "one cannot deduce an ought from an is" is often considered to be the positive-normative dichotomy's most enduring philosophical lesson. Although this interpretation has reduced some of the controversy surrounding the dichotomy, it has not eliminated it. Even in this rather narrow imperative form, the dichotomy has been, and continues to be, much debated within the philosophical literature (Searle 1965, 2001). But the focus here is not purely philosophical debates, it is on how the positive-normative dichotomy has been interpreted within the economics literature, and it is to that topic we now turn.

## 2 THE HISTORY OF THE POSITIVE-NORMATIVE DICHOTOMY IN ECONOMICS

Economics is a discipline that has traditionally maintained (or at least insisted that it is important to maintain) a strict dichotomy between the positive and the normative; economic science tells (or should tell) us what "is" the case, while normative and ethical inquires tell us what "ought to be."[1] One economist that

[1] It is quite common, and not unreasonable, for discussions of the positive-normative dichotomy in economics to be couched in terms of the related, but somewhat broader, distinction between facts and values (e.g. [Blaug, 1992, Ch.5; Dasgupta, 2005; Gordon, 1977; Mongin, 2006; Nagel, 1961, pp. 485-502; Weston, 1994]), but I have self-consciously resisted that temptation here. There are many reasons for this, but let me try to explain the most important one. The problem is that if one wants to seriously examine the fact-value distinction as it affects economic science

is frequently cited regarding the importance of separating positive and normative is John Neville Keynes. It is useful to quote him at length.

> As the terms are used here, a *positive science* may be defined as a body of systematized knowledge concerning what is, a *normative* or *regulative science* as a body of systematized knowledge relating to criteria of what ought to be, and concerned therefore with the ideal as distinguished from the actual; and *art* as a system of rules for the attainment of a given end. The object of a positive science is the establishment of *uniformities*, of a normative science the determination of *ideas*, of an art the formulation of *precepts*.
>
> The problem whether political economy is to be regarded as a positive science, or as a normative science, or as an art, or as some combination of these, is to a certain extent a question merely of nomenclature and classification. It is, nevertheless, important to distinguish economic enquiries according as they belong to the three departments respectively; and it is also important to make clear their mutual relations. [Keynes, 1917, pp. 34-5, emphasis in original]

Note that while Neville Keynes emphasized the distinction between positive and normative, he was not arguing that normative concepts have no place in economic science. Writing in the pre-positivist British context (the first edition was published in 1890), Keynes viewed the positive and the normative as different *kinds of sciences* — one descriptive and one prescriptive — thus leaving the door open for economists to pursue the material welfare economics [Cooter and Rappoport, 1984] endorsed by Keynes's colleague Alfred Marshall and other Cambridge neoclassicals such as Arthur Pigou [1920].

The importation of logical positivist ideas and other changes within the economics profession during the first few decades of the twentieth century led to the adoption of an even stronger version of the dichotomy than the one defended by Neville Keynes. The dichotomy — the strict separation of the positive and the normative — was replaced by an epistemic condemnation and *prohibition* of the normative; not only was it necessary to recognize that positive and normative statements were fundamentally different, in addition it was argued that the normative was scientifically illegitimate and should be prohibited from proper economic

it would be necessary to consider the debate over the theory- or social- "ladenness" of empirical observations — the question of whether, how, or to what extent, theoretical or social values determine/condition scientific facts (in economics and other sciences). This is a very important question that has played a major role in many contemporary methodological debates (see Blaug 1992 or Hands 2001), but as such it is a topic that would lead us too far away from the question of the *relationship* between the positive and the normative in economics and into the methodological jungle of properly characterizing "positive" economics. This is a discussion of the "Positive-Normative dichotomy and economics," not "major issues in economic methodology," and as such the decision was made to focus on the *relationship* between positive and normative within the economics literature and how the (implicit or explicit) definition/characterization of the *normative* has affected this relationship; and to try to steer around the broader methodological/philosophical question of the general relationship between values and empirical science.

science. According to logical positivism there were only two types of meaningful discourse — empirical science (synthetic knowledge) and logic/mathematics (analytic knowledge) — everything else was meaningless metaphysics. Since normative economics was based on presuppositions that were not derived from either of these two sources, normative economic science ceased to be any type of science at all, and was relegated to the epistemic dustbin along with religion, metaphysics, and other "meaningless" discourse. This positivist view of the normative was often combined with an emotivist view of ethics — that ethical statements were simply expression of attitude or emotion [Davis, 1990].

One of the most influential voices supporting the prohibition of the normative was Lionel Robbins [1935]. Like earlier authors, he demarcated "ought" from "is":

> Economics deals with ascertainable facts; ethics with valuations and obligations. The two fields of inquiry are not on the same plane of discourse. Between the generalisations of positive and normative studies there is a logical gulf fixed which no ingenuity can disguise and no juxtaposition in space or time bridge over. [Robbins, 1935, p. 148]

But Robbins went beyond merely claiming that "propositions involving 'ought' are on an entirely different plane from propositions involving "is"' (ibid., pp. 142-43) — he argued that separate was not epistemically equal — that normative propositions were "illegitimate" and had no place within economic science.

Robbins effectively employed his prohibition of the normative in his general argument against *interpersonal utility comparisons* and economic policies based on such comparisons. Comparing the satisfaction/utility two different people receive from a particular bundle of commodities or level of income

> ... is a comparison which necessarily falls outside the scope of any positive science. To state that A's preference stands above B's in order of importance is entirely different from stating that A prefers n to m and B prefers n and m in a different order. It involves an element of conventional valuation. Hence it is essentially normative. It has no place in pure science. (ibid., p. 139)

Robbins used the scientific illegitimacy of interpersonal utility comparisons to attack the utilitarian argument — endorsed by Marshall, Pigou, and others — that the diminishing marginal utility of money income provided economics with scientific grounds for redistributing income from the rich to the poor and progressive income taxes as a means for achieving such redistributions. Since interpersonal utility comparisons were normative and had no place in scientific economics, Robbins argued that any redistribution or progressive taxes based on economics analysis containing such assumptions was scientifically illegitimate.

> Hence the extension of the Law of Diminishing Marginal Utility, postulated in the propositions we are examining is illegitimate. And the arguments based upon it therefore are lacking in scientific foundations

> ... The conception of diminishing relative utility (the convexity downwards of the indifference curve) does not justify the inference that transferences from the rich to the poor will increase total satisfaction ... Indeed, all that part of the theory of public finance which deals with "Social Utility" must assume a different significance. Interesting as a development of an ethical postulate, it does not at all follow from the positive assumptions of pure theory. (ibid., p. 141)

Robbins fully admitted that we make interpersonal utility comparisons all the time in our daily lives (ibid., p. 140), but as in many other cases, usefulness in everyday life does not imply validity for scientific inquiry. He, like Max Weber [1949], was also willing to allow economic scientists the option of attributing moral, or otherwise value-laden, preferences to economic agents and examining the implications of such preferences, but if the normative values of the economists doing the research (as opposed to the agents being studied) leaked into the analysis, then it ceased to be science.

During the next few decades Robbins's view of the relationship between positive and normative economics was endorsed by a growing number of influential, and soon to be influential, economists. A good example of such support can be found in various statements by Milton Friedman. Although many of the methodological views Friedman presented in his famous 1953 paper on economic methodology differed from those Robbins endorsed, his view of the positive-normative dichotomy was essentially the same.

> Positive economics is in principle independent of any particular ethical position or normative judgments. As Keynes says, it deals with "what is," not with "what ought to be" ... Its performance is to be judged by the precision, scope, and conformity with experience of the predictions it yields. In short, positive economics is, or can be, an "objective" science, in precisely the same sense as any of the physical sciences. [Friedman, 1953, p. 4]

By the middle of the twentieth century, Robbins's view of the positive-normative dichotomy, reinforced by a number of other influential economists, had become essentially the conventional wisdom within the economics profession. This is not to suggest there were not critics of the dichotomy [Little, 1949; Souter, 1933] and/or Robbins's use of it to indict interpersonal utility comparisons [Robertson, 1952], but for the majority of English-language economists, including many of those writing on economic methodology, the profession's main goal was to produce positive economic *science*: science that tells us what *is* the case. As *science*, such positive inquiry should never be mixed up with normative or ethical concerns regarding how things ought to be. For many economists normative ideas had an important role to play in economic policy debates, but not in economic science strictly defined. Of course debate continued (and continues) about what exactly is required for the successful practice of positive economics — that has been the traditional subject matter of economic methodology [Hands, 2001] — but there is hardly any debate about whether scientific practice should be sharply distinguished from normative and ethical concerns; the relationship between is and ought is a strict *dichotomy* and everything on the normative side of the dichotomy should be *prohibited* from economic science. The profession's conventional wisdom on the matter is reflected nicely in Kurt Klappholz's remarks from the late 1950s:

> I have tried to show that the various claims, often advanced "... with an air of penetrating profundity," that economics is *necessarily* value-impregnated can easily be refuted. Why, then, should criticisms which so clearly miss the target continue to be urged so vociferously? And why should the defenders of the "orthodox" position respond to these criticisms by reiterating the principle of ethical neutrality rather as if present-day geographers continued to insist that the earth is not flat? [Klappholz, 1959. p. 111, emphasis in original]

The tone of this quote is as important as its content. Klappholz is not simply disagreeing with those like Gunner Myrdal [1958] who argued that normative values are inexorably intertwined with economic science — so intertwined that the most "objective" approach the economic scientist could possibly take was simply to state (self-consciously, openly, and explicitly), rather than eliminate, his or her normative presuppositions — he expresses a frustration that one *even needs to respond* to such flat-earth critics. The implication being that it is so obvious that the normative has no place in economic science that there is simply nothing to discuss.

One of many critical responses that have been made to economists' commitment to the positive-normative dichotomy is that while the profession may preach the importance of maintaining a strict dichotomy, it has not always been successful practicing what it preaches [Blaug, 1992]. One of the most commonly cited examples of the profession's failure to practice this dichotomization, involves the norm-ladenness of the concept of economic efficiency. As the profession turned away from interpersonal utility comparisons during the late 1930s and 1940s, the earlier utilitarian policy criterion (maximize total or average utility) was replaced by the Pareto criterion. According to the Pareto criterion a particular distribution of resources was Pareto Optimal (and thus efficient) if and only if any reallocation that would make one person better off would also make someone else worse off. Perhaps the most important result of Pareto-based welfare economics was the so called "First Fundamental Theorem of Welfare Economics," which proved that any competitive equilibrium is Pareto Optimal (see any standard microeconomics textbook). Economists embraced the change to the Pareto criteria in welfare economics primarily because it offered an evaluative standard that was devoid of all of the troublesome normative issues associated with interpersonal comparisons of utility and thus provided a strictly positive/scientific way of making judgments about social welfare and microeconomic policy. And yet, as many economists and philosophers have argued over the years, employing the Pareto criterion in welfare economics does not necessarily allow economists to avoid commitment to moral theory (see [Blaug, 1992; Hausman and McPherson, 2006]). There are a variety of such criticisms, but a relatively standard argument is that since the Pareto criterion is based entirely on satisfying the preferences of the relevant economic agents — making them better off or worse off — it is implicitly committed to an individual preference satisfaction view of the good. Of course it may be that most economists would accept that bringing about states of the world that increase the satisfaction of individual preferences should be the sole basis for good social policy, but even if it is professionally acceptable it is still a commitment that functions "as a Trojan horse smuggling ethical commitments into the theoretical citadel of positive mainstream economics" [Hausman and McPherson, 2006, pp. 67-68]. Armed with this ostensibly value-free definition of economic efficiency, the First Fundamental Theorem of Welfare Economics allows economists to "conclude that, *ceteris paribus*, perfectly competitive equilibria are morally desirable and market imperfections that interfere with the achievement of competitive equilibria are morally undesirable" (ibid., p. 66) — a conclusion that sounds very close to positive economics asserting what ought to be.

Although such criticism of economists' theoretical practice may be legitimate, the tensions between the profession's rhetoric and practice will not be the focus of this discussion. Whether the argument is that economists have traditionally endorsed the positive-normative dichotomy, or criticism of the profession for not living up to what it preaches, the discussion leaves in place the claim that facts and values constitute a strict *dichotomy*. It is this claim — a claim that is taken as a given in most debate about the positive and normative economics — that I wish to examine.

The remainder of the paper will be divided into two parts. The next section will start by emphasizing that not everything that is "normative" concerns ethics, and go on to draw out some of the implications of this (increasingly recognized) fact for economic theorizing. The second part makes the case that, even if one is only interested in ethical normativity, then there are still serious difficulties with the claim that the difference between positive and normative constitutes a strict dichotomy. There is obviously a useful everyday distinction between facts and values, but the two sets of concepts are far too entangled for us to be able to speak sensibly about the strict separation that economists have traditionally endorsed.

## 3 NORMATIVE AND ETHICALLY NORMATIVE

For many practicing economists trained in the post World War II era — the time when Friedman's essay was "the only essay on methodology that a large number, perhaps majority, of economists have ever read" [Hausman, 1992, p. 162] — the term "normative economics" meant the inclusion of "moral" or "ethical" concerns with economic analysis. Of course authors like Friedman and Robbins did not explicitly equate the normative and the ethical[2] — Friedman says positive statements are "independent of any particular ethical position or normative judgments" [Friedman, 1953, p. 4] — but one can also see how it would be easy to slide into the identification of normative exclusively with ethical. For example in his demarcation of "is" from "ought" Robbins says: "Economics deals with ascertainable facts; ethics with valuations and obligations" [Robbins, 1935. p. 148] and notice Friedman's sharp differentiation of science and ethics in the 1955 quote in the epigraph. The identification of normative exclusively with ethical was certainly clear in the welfare economics of the period where (Pareto) "efficiency" was frequently contrasted with considerations of "equity" in the distribution of income/resources; the former being viewed as a proper subject for economic science, and the latter being viewed as a purely ethical issue. The identification of the normative with the ethical is also implicit in many of the standard examples that economists used (and continue to use) as exemplars of economic analysis: the critique of both minimum wages and rent control (both economically inefficient, but supported by the public on ethical grounds) and the defense of perfectly price discriminating monopoly (economically efficient, but viewed as unfair). Finally, and perhaps most importantly for the culture of economics, the identification of the normative with the ethical is common in economics textbooks. For example, the seventeenth edition of the most famous introductory economic textbook of all time (Samuelson) explains "positive economics versus normative economics" in the following way:

> In thinking about economic questions, we must distinguish questions of fact from questions of fairness ...
>
> *Positive economics* deals with questions such as: Why do doctors earn more than janitors? Does free trade raise or lower the wage of most Americans ...
>
> *Normative Economics* involves ethical precepts and norms of fairness. Should poor people be required to work if they are to get government assistance? ... [Samuelson and Nordhaus, 2001, pp. 7-8]

Of course, outside of economics, it is clearly not the case that everything that is "normative" involves ethics. When someone says "you ought to get more exercise" they do not mean that you ought to get more exercise to be moral; they mean you ought to exercise to be healthy. It is norm, but a norm of good health, not an ethical norm. More relevant to economics and economic methodology, when a Popperian philosopher of science says "scientists ought to make bold conjectures and subject those conjectures to severe empirical tests" they are not saying that

[2]It is interesting that even though Robbins did not literally equate normative and ethical, that was a common interpretation of his position. For example in R. W. Souter's 1933 review of the first edition of Robbins's *Essay* one of his criticisms is that "the terms 'normative' and 'ethical' are not synonyms" [Souter, 1933, pp. 401-02]. If pointing out that normative and ethical were *not* synonymous was considered to be a serious critique of Robbins, it must have been possible to read him as suggesting they were in fact synonyms.

failing to live up to such methodological standards makes you an ethically bad person; they are saying that it makes you an epistemically bad scientist. Economic methodology has traditionally been *normative* in this sense — it explains what economists *ought* to do to be good scientists — and the relevant norms are the norms of proper scientific behavior, epistemologically-grounded norms, not the norms of proper moral conduct. In general normative terms are simply terms that are action-guiding or prescriptive, and normative statements are statements involving such terms. The relevant norms might be social, legal, epistemological, aesthetic, or a host of other types; ethical norms are just one very special case of such prescriptive terms. On this ground alone the way that economists have traditionally discussed positive and normative seems problematic. Even if, for the sake of argument, we accept the claim that there is a strict dichotomy between the positive and the normative, it still seems unreasonable to characterize the dichotomy in the way that economists traditionally have. What gets left out are all those things — all those aspects of economic theory and practice — that are normative, but not ethically normative.

So why is the profession's traditional conventional wisdom on this matter a problem? Why can't we just say that although there are other kinds of normative statements than ethical statements, economists traditionally have, perhaps for policy reasons, chosen to focus on the ethically normative? Why not just accept that the two most important categories *for economics* are "positive" (i.e. scientific and objective) and "ethically normative" (i.e. those involving individual/social values about what is ethically right or good) and go on thinking about such things as modern economists traditionally have? One problem is that a case can be made — and has been made — that the core economic theory, rational choice theory, falls into *neither one of these two categories*; it is *neither* a positive/descriptive theory of real economic agents, *nor* an ethical theory about what such agents ought to do. It is, many argue, *normative but not ethically normative.* Such a position implies that rational choice theory — the theoretical heart of microeconomics — may not be contained in either of the two categories that economists regularly use to classify economic theories. This is an important point that requires some elaboration.

Before embarking on the discussion of normative choice theory, it is useful to clarify how some of the key terms will be used and explain the emphasis on rational choice theory. Here, and throughout the rest of this discussion, I use the generic term "rational choice theory" for all of the various specific theories — decision theory, utility theory, expected utility theory, consumer choice theory, etc. — that start with agents having well-ordered preferences (or more abstractly, a choice function) defined over a choice space, and explain behavior as the result of acting in an instrumentally rational way (making the best, or optimal, choice) given those preferences. In the standard neoclassical theory of consumer choice, the economic agent has well-ordered preferences (a suitably concave ordinal utility function, or the equivalent complete, transitive, monotonic and convex preferences) defined over the relevant commodity space, a standard linear budget constraint that restricts the agent to an affordable set, and the agent's behavior (demand functions) is explained as the result of maximizing the utility function over (or choosing the most preferred bundle from) this budget set. In the more general case involving decision making under risk, the basic model is modified to include the probabilities of various outcomes, but the resulting expected utility theory is still an instantiation of generic theory of rational choice.

The following discussion will focus exclusively on rational choice theory even though there is obviously a lot more to economics than rational choice. There are two main reasons for this. First, debates about the positive-normative dichotomy in economics (either historically or within the recent literature) have focused much more on microeconomics than other areas of economics such as macroeconomics or econometrics, and second, rational choice theory is at the heart of microeconomics. This is not to say that other areas within economics are completely devoid of such debates, only that microeconomics has generally been at the center of the storm. This is exhibited both in the history of the positive-normative dichotomy in section two above, and in the discussion of contemporary controversies (e.g. [Caplin and Schotter, 2008]). Of course within microeconomics rational choice focuses exclusively on individual behavior (or the behavior of agents that can be modeled as if they were individuals: firms, governments, etc.) and there is more to the microeconomic theory of markets, prices, and strategic interaction than individual behavior. In general a microeconomic explanation/prediction of some phenomenon involves two (interrelated but separable) levels of theorizing: the behavior of the individual agents (which involves some version of rational choice theory) and the characterization of the institutional framework for the interaction of these individual agents (competitive markets, classical game theory, evolutionary game theory, etc.). Regardless of the specification of the second-level institutional framework, the specification of the individual agent is a necessary part of the story and is always given by some version rational choice theory. Rational choice is thus at the heart of microeconomics and microeconomics has been at the center of most debates about the positive-normative dichotomy in economics.

If economists started with systematic empirical observations of agent's preferences, constraints, and choices and then merely generalized those observations to obtain scientific laws of economic behavior, then it would certainly be legitimate to claim that rational choice theory is a *descriptive* theory of agent behavior (a positive theory about what "is" the case for all, or a certain class of, agents). But this is not how economic analysis has typically proceeded. The assumptions made on preferences or utility functions have not traditionally been generalizations based on systematic observations (i.e. descriptions) of the actual preferences of economic agents — the economic scientist does not have access to the mental states (preferences, beliefs, and desires) of agents — but rather they are assumptions — such as transitivity, completeness and convexity — that seem to be necessary for such preferences to be "rational." The standard approach imposes very specific structural restrictions on the preferences of agents — restrictions consistent with "rational" preferences — and then uses the agent striving to satisfy such rational preferences as the explanation of the relevant behavior. Of course just because key theoretical terms (such as preference) are not necessarily descriptive does not imply that the theory cannot contribute to our scientific understanding of economic behavior. There are many different approaches to economic methodology — including, but certainly not restricted to, Friedman [1953] and the Millian tradition (Hausman 1992) — that attempt to explain why an economic theory resting on assumptions that are not literally (or even approximately) descriptively true may still be an adequate scientific theory. The point here is not that there is necessarily something epistemically pernicious going on in the practice of rational choice theory, but to suggest that whatever rational choice theory is, it is not a scientific theory that fits neatly into the "positive" category as economists have traditionally defined it.

An alternative way of thinking about rational choice theory in economics — and the standard way that philosophers, particularly philosophers of decision theory, characterize rational choice theory — is as a specific type of *normative* theory, a normative theory of rationality (see [Davidson, 2001; 2004; Suppes, 1961] for example). According to this interpretation, rational choice theory is not a descriptive/positive theory (or even an attempt at such a theory), but rather a normative theory of what *an agent ought to do in order to be rational.* As Daniel Hausman and Michael McPherson explain:

> Utility theory lays down formal conditions that choices and preferences ought to satisfy. It is not a positive theory because it says nothing about the extent to which people are rational, and it is not merely a model or definition because rationality is itself a normative notion. To define what rational preference and choice are is ipso facto to say how one ought rationally to prefer and to choose. [Hausman and McPherson, 2006, p. 49]

While there are many different versions of this general interpretation of rational choice theory and substantive debate about the philosophical details, it is fair to say that during the second half of the 20th century this became the standard way of talking about rational choice theory among philosophers. As Robert Nozick explains:

> An elaborate theory of rational action has been developed by economists and statisticians, and put to widespread use in theoretical and policy studies. This is a powerful, mathematically precise, and tractable theory. Although its adequacy as a description of actual behavior has been widely questioned, it stands as the dominant view of the conditions that a rational decision should satisfy: it is the dominant normative view. [Nozick, 1993, p. 41]

Although this normative interpretation has not been the standard view of rational choice theory among economists — for most economists it is a positive/scientific theory of economic behavior — it does seem to be the way that rational choice theory has been interpreted by many behavioral economists, experimental economists, and experimental psychologists.[3] For example, Richard Thaler opened his much-cited 1980 paper on "a positive theory of consumer choice" with the following paragraph:

> Economists rarely draw the distinction between normative models of consumer choice and descriptive or positive models. Although the theory is normatively based (it describes what rational consumers *should* do) economists argue that it also serves well as a descriptive theory (it predicts what consumers in fact do). This paper argues that exclusive reliance on the normative theory leads economists to make systematic, predictable errors in describing and forecasting consumer choices. [Thaler, 1980, p. 39]

Daniel Kahneman and Amos Tversky introduced their *Choices, Values, and Frames* with similar remarks:

> The study of decisions addresses both normative and descriptive questions. The normative analysis is concerned with the nature of rationality and the logic of decision making. The descriptive analysis, in contrast, is concerned with people's beliefs and preferences as they are, not as they should be. The tension between normative and descriptive considerations characterizes much of the study of judgment and choice. [Kahneman and Tversky, 2000, p. 1]

For these behavioral economists rational choice theory is a normative theory even though most economists do not recognize it as such. They argue that it fails empirically as a descriptive theory of actual people — a job better done by more behavioral and psychological theories — but this is not surprising since it is normative; it only "describes what rational consumers *should* do" (Thaler above). Again, this does not necessarily mean that it cannot play an important role in economic science, simply that the role is normative and its relationship to the positive science of economics is far more complex than what is provided by the profession's traditional view of the positive-normative dichotomy.

Just to review, the argument often made is that rational choice theory is a normative theory — a theory of what one ought to do to be rational — but this in no way implies/suggests that the theory has anything to do with ethics (combining rational choice theory with a particular notion of the good makes an ethical commitment, but not rational choice theory alone). There is no reason to believe that having transitive preferences and acting rationally on those preferences makes one a morally good person. In fact one of the key features of "rationality" as defined by rational choice theory — having rational preferences and acting optimally on them — is that rational behavior has nothing whatsoever to do with

[3]See [Heukelom, 2008] for a detailed discussion of the way positive and descriptive are used in behavioral economics.

the *content* (particularly the moral content) of the agent's preferences. One could certainly have well-ordered — transitive and complete — preferences for murder and proceed to satisfy those preferences in an optimal way. Rationality in the sense of rational choice theory does not imply moral choice; it may be a normative theory, but it is not an ethically normative theory.

So most modern economists generally consider rational choice theory to be a positive, not a normative, theory; endorse the position that normative statements/concepts should be prohibited from scientific economics; and equate normative theories/presuppositions with ethics. On the other hand there is an extensive literature in the philosophy of decision theory, behavioral economics, and experimental psychology that considers the standard model of consumer choice and other rational choice-based parts of microeconomics to be normative (though not ethical) theories of *rational* choice and that contrasts such normative theories with various positive/descriptive approaches to predicting and explaining human behavior. So why is this a problem? Why is a divergence between what the majority of economists seem to think about the positive-normative dichotomy and the view of these other groups an issue of concern? There are at least three reasons why this divergence might be problematic.

First, there is an extensive philosophical literature on normative rationality — the theory of "practical" rationality — and since microeconomics is the field where rational choice has had it greatest impact (including policy impact), communication and cross-fertilization between philosophers and economists on these matters would be very useful and the divergence flies in the face of such endeavors. Although the normative characterization of rationality has increasingly come to be acknowledged by those writing on the philosophy of economics [Davis, 2003; Hausman and McPherson, 2006; Mongin, 2005; Ross, 2005], there is still a long way to go to have (even the possibility) recognized by most practicing economists. As Don Ross explains this leaves philosophers and economists (unnecessarily) wrestling with two separate, but quite interrelated, sets of questions.

> Generalizing very broadly, for philosophers rational choice theory is a branch of normative inquiry, part of the answer to questions about what an ideally rational agent *ought* to do. For economists, by comparison, rational choice theory is often viewed as contributing to *descriptive science*, offering analysis of what economic agents *in fact* do given the assumption that they are rational. Economists' use of rational choice theory is thus exposed to criticisms of a sort that philosophers can shrug off, namely, attacks based on evidence that people are not, as a matter of fact, rational in the way they assume. On the other hand, rational choice philosophers, but not economists, must answer worries about the normative appropriateness of being ideally rational, in the relevant sense, in the first place. [Ross, 2005, p. 91, emphasis in original]

Secondly, thinking of rational choice as a normative, but not ethical theory has the potential to redefine the relationship between "rational" and "actual" behavior. If rational choice tells us what agents ought to do to be rational and observed/experimental action is inconsistent with such behavior, then attention shifts from whether rational choice theory or the observation/experiment is wrong, to questions about the things that might cause, and therefore explain, such deviations from optimality and/or to questions about whether the given conception of rationality is appropriate. Although this is increasingly the way that behavioral economists [Camerer, and Loewenstein, 2004; Lichtenstein and Slovic, 2006], experimental economists [Guala, 2005; Starmer, 2005], and those doing research on neuroeconomics [Glimcher, 2003], view the relationship between rational choice theory and descriptive economics, particular authors and/or research programs have very different views of the implications of actual human behavior systematically deviating from that which rationally ought to be done. One approach, discussed above, is the critical stance of many behavioral economists; the implication of the evidence is simply that rational choice theory is not a very good descriptive theory and should be replaced by one that is (or those that are) better at predicting and explaining behavior. But an entirely different stance has been taken by others who recognize the discrepancy between observed/experimental behavior and the norms of rationality; it is that the norms of rationality "should" guide behavior and if actual agents do no behave in the way they "should" then the important question is why they are making such errors. For example, the neuroeconomist Paul Glimcher says:

> Economic models describe the task that animals and humans face in any decision-making situation. They define how a problem *should* be solved. Real animals and real people deviate from these solutions; they perform suboptimally. [Glimcher, 2003, p. 334]

Another approach — somewhere between putting the onus on rational choice theory and putting it on the agents — is the recent literature on "libertarian paternalism" [Sunstein and Thaler, 2003; 2008; Loewenstein and Haisley, 2008]. Here the fact that humans often fail to live up to the norms of rationality sets the stage for the design of choice architectures that "nudge" agents in the direction of making more rational choices — those associated with more effective satisfaction of their own individual preferences — while still maintaining the libertarian/Millian premise that people should be broadly free to do as they like as long as it does not impose costs on others. These topics are some of the most rapidly growing and hotly contested in contemporary economic theory and yet they all essentially start from the position that rational choice theory to some degree provides norms for rational behavior and that it is not a very good description of what individual economic agents actually do. There is much for philosophers, economists, and other behavioral scientists to sort out about these various positions and much work is currently underway (much of it discussed elsewhere in this Handbook), but notice that the traditional position of most economists — that rational choice theory is exclusively positive and that normative theories necessarily involve ethics — simply closes the door on this discussion and effectively prevents the economics profession from even addressing the serious issues raised within these recent debates.

The final issue concerns economics as a robust social science of human behavior. Humans are normative creatures — obligation matters to behavior – and often the norms have nothing explicitly to do with ethics (although sometimes they do — see below). Narrowly defining the normative and endorsing a strict separation between proper economic science and such normative issues, leaves economics unable to recognize, explain, or accommodate, many important aspects of human behavior (even economic behavior). This issue will be discussed in more detail below.

## 4 THE ENTANGLEMENT OF POSITIVE AND (ETHICALLY) NORMATIVE

Although there are clearly many other forms of normativity — including what one ought to do to be rational — let us turn away from these and focus on the ethically normative. This section will go through a few of the reasons why the traditional normative-positive dichotomy might not stand up to critical scrutiny even if one defines "normative" in this narrow (moral) way. Although taken alone, none of these reasons provides a knock-down argument that the positive-normative dichotomy really isn't a dichotomy; all of them, taken as an ensemble, do add up to a rather substantive criticism of the standard view. Some of the arguments in this section focus specifically on economics, while others are more general. It is perhaps best to think of the following as a (nonexhaustive) list of the ways that positive science and normative ethics are entangled: in general, as well as specifically within economics.

The standard reading of the dichotomy is that "one cannot deduce ought from is." Although, as noted above, there exists a philosophical literature contesting even this narrow view, I will make no attempt to challenge this deductive interpretation of the dichotomy. The argument in this section is simply that deduction is a very strong, and in many ways not the most interesting, relationship; even if one cannot deduce ought from is, the two categories do have many significant connections (weaker than deducibility). Positive and normative are *entangled,* and entangled in significant enough ways that the distinction, as common and useful as it is, cannot reasonably be considered a dichotomy. I will discuss three such relationships.

a. *Given certain moral presuppositions "is" does imply "ought"*: If one is committed to a *consequentialist* ethical system — utilitarianism being the most obvious — then the fact that certain consequences *do actually follow* from certain actions may imply that such actions *ought to be done.* For a classical utilitarian, what ought to be done depends on the pleasures and pains associated with the act — note the *fact* of the pleasures and pains associated with the act. Once one decides that act $A$ in fact causes more pleasure than act $B$ (it *is* the case that $A$ causes more pleasure than $B$) then $A$ *ought* to be done. This is of course not a violation of the argument that "is" (alone) cannot imply "ought" — there needs to be a moral antecedent along with the facts of the matter — but *given* that moral antecedent, then what is the case, the matter of fact, does imply what ought to be done.

This has at least two interesting (or perhaps ironic) implications for economics. First, during the 19th century, the profession of economics, benefited greatly from just this "fact" of utilitarian ethics. Within a utilitarian framework, what ought to be done with respect to public policy depends on what the results of various actions *will in fact be.* Policy makers thus *need a social science like economics* in order to be able to decide what ought to be done. In the earlier religion-dominated world, the right policy was the one that was right with God — in order to obtain that information one consulted god's representatives (i.e. the clergy); in a utilitarian-dominated world the right policy is one that gives the most benefit for the least cost — to obtain that information one needs social scientists (economists in particular). It thus seems rather ironic that economists would be so insistent about separating is and ought when the relationship between the two has played such an important role in the history of the profession.

There is also a second, closely related, irony associated with the profession's commitment to some version of a utilitarian or individual preference satisfaction view of the good. Since so many economists would accept such a definition of the good — at least in their professional roles — it means that such a moral presupposition is actually a *given* among economists. If it is a given among economists (and thus implicitly a normative premise), then *all that is required to obtain a statement about what ought to be* is information about what is (what is in fact) the case. Consider two policies $X$ and $Y$. And let us assume – an assumption that seems to stand up to empirical scrutiny — that most economists in their professional capacity would accept the following quite general (moral) commitment:

> The best (good) policy (ceteris paribus) is the one that makes people better off (that is, it leads to the highest level of utility or preference satisfaction among the relevant individuals).

Given this presupposition, if our economic analysis tells us that "policy $X$ (ceteris paribus) makes people better off than policy $Y$" then it immediately follows that the society *ought* to do $X$ (rather than $Y$). Again, this does not say that we can infer ought from (only) is, but if a community has a shared moral presupposition, as most economists do [Dasgupta, 2005], then *in practice* all that is required to know what ought to be done is to know what will actually happen [Davis, 1991]. This means that as a practical matter among economists, knowing (positively) what is, tells us exactly what (normatively) ought to be.

b. *Ought often causes/explains is* because moral norms exist in social life and matter to behavior. Consider the traditional sociological explanation of human behavior. In brief, sociologists argue that humans are members of social communities, and as members of such communities they share certain social norms and values, and these norms and values are the cause, and thus explain, the behavior of individuals within the society. While most economists consider this to be an over-socialized view of human behavior, the key point remains even if social values are not the sole determinant of individual behavior. One does not need complete social determinism to realize that a society where most people believe that it is wrong to murder, will (in fact) be a society where there is substantially fewer murders than in a society where the social norms encourage such behavior. What *is* the case in society is determined, at least in part, by what the community believes *ought* to be done. The "is" of human behavior is thus caused/explained by the "oughts" of the relevant social norms. Of course the reason the ought causes/explains behavior is because of the fact that the majority of the people in the society do what they ought to do — so the "is" is both what ought to be done and what is done — but it does point to the fact that ethical norms matter to human behavior and a successful behavioral/social science often needs to recognize that fact.

This argument has direct relevance to some of the recent critiques of rational choice theory originating from within experimental psychology and experimental economics [Kahneman, 2003; Kahneman and Tversky, 2000] for example). It is regularly observed that in experimental situations people do not do what is "rational" from a purely economic, rational choice, perspective. In the "ultimatum game" for instance, where a player's rational self-interested behavior would be to offer the smallest possible amount of the good in question, people systematically offer a larger, more "fair," distribution. Agents in experimental situations also systematically overcontribute to public goods [Guala, 2005]. These are just two of many such cases where positive economics — a science that ostensibly tells us what is the case — ends up not successfully predicting what "is" because of the influence of people's moral values and sense of fairness. In such cases "what ought to be" often tells us what will happen more accurately than positive economic theory that neglects such normative considerations. Ought again contributes to what is;

c) *Moral ought implies can (and can depends on what is the case)*: This third interaction of positive and (ethically) normative is more general and less specifically concerned with economics. If one ought to do A (in order to act morally) then it implies that one *could possibly do* A, and since what one can possibly do in turn depends on what is in fact the case, then what one ought to do depends on what is. Most ethical systems have some variant of "thou shall not kill" and no ethical system has any variant of "thou shall not be more than fifty feet tall." The reason is of course that it is possible to kill (and it is bad to do so); we know of no circumstances under which it is possible for people to be more than fifty feet tall. Since ought implies can, and can implies "is possible," then ought implies "is possible" (and "is possible" is about what "is" the case). Thus while one may not be able to deduce "ought" from "is," what is the case puts limitations on that which is possible, which in turn determines the boundaries of moral behavior. It is not a deductive relationship, but it is a fundamental relationship.

One of many cases where this relationship becomes important in contemporary life is in the area of medical ethics. When there was very little that physicians could do — when what was within their power was quite limited — then there was very little debate about what physicians should do to behave morally (do no harm seemed to be sufficient). But technology has changed things — what *is* possible has greatly expanded — and correspondingly so has the controversy about what ought to be done. In economics, one could tell a similar story about macroeconomic policy for alleviating unemployment. Prior to the 1940s it was not considered the responsibility of governments in even the most advanced economies to reduce unemployment — it was not something they *ought* to do. In some countries it was the government's responsibility to reduce the damage, the human suffering, caused by unemployment — in the same sense that it might be the government's responsibility to reduce the human suffering caused by a hurricane or volcano — but not to *prevent* unemployment (any more than to prevent a hurricane or volcano). Once the (Keynesian) tools existed to help governments reduce unemployment — once it became clear that reducing unemployment *is* possible — then it became something that *ought* to be done. Again, this is not deducing "ought" from "is," but it ties the two categories up in extremely important and often unrecognized ways.

## 5 CONCLUSION

This paper has investigated a number of different aspects of the positive-normative dichotomy and economics. Section one briefly reviewed the philosophical discussion of the topic and section two provided a more extensive discussion of the dichotomy in the history of modern economics. Section two concluded that by the second half of the twentieth century the majority of economists considered the relationship between positive and normative to be a strict dichotomy and agreed with Robbins and others that the normative had no place in, and should be prohibited from, economic science. Section three analyzed the current status of the positive-normative dichotomy in economics. It was argued that in addition to accepting the strict dichotomy and the prohibition of the normative, most practicing economists also identify the normative exclusively with ethics (although this may be changing). It was argued that this standard characterization was problematic for a number of reasons, most involving the idea that rational choice theory may itself be a normative theory: a normative theory of rational action. The final section moved away from economics and examined some of the more general concerns about the positive-normative dichotomy.

The bottom line seems to be that although there is obviously a useful distinction between "is" and "ought," that distinction should not be exaggerated. "Is" and "ought" (even morally "ought") are far too interconnected to justify the strict dichotomy and prohibition that economists have traditionally endorsed (if not always practiced). Following the advice of the philosopher Hilary Putnam, the dichotomy should be "disinflated":

> If we *disinflate* the fact/value dichotomy, what we get is this: there is a distinction to be drawn (one that is useful in some contexts) between ethical judgments and other sorts of judgments. This is undoubtedly the case, just as it is undoubtedly the case that there is a distinction to be drawn (and one that is useful in some contexts) between *chemical* judgments and judgments that do not belong to the field of chemistry. *But nothing metaphysical follows from the existence of a fact/value distinction in this (modest) sense.* [Putnam, 2002, p. 19, emphasis in original]

In some sense the strict fact/value dichotomy should have disappeared (or at least been disinflated) along with the hegemony of positivist philosophical ideas. Since all of the rigid dichotomies of the positivist era — meaningful-meaningless, theory-observation, *a priori-a posteriori*, analytic-synthetic, etc. — have, during the latter half of the 20th century, slowly but surely surrendered to more local and context-specific variants of these distinctions, it would seem that the fact-value dichotomy would have suffered (or perhaps benefited) from the same disinflation. One would also suspect that economics — a discipline that has seemed to have so much trouble staying on the science side of these positivist-inspired distinctions — would be the first to welcome this disinflation. Obviously that has not been the case; many economists continue to insist that the fact/value dichotomy is much more than a convenient distinction. Such insistence *is* a fact of professional life in economics, but I hope that have been able to demonstrate that it does not necessarily need (or *ought*) to be the case. The normative is involved (ethically and otherwise) in economic theorizing and one cannot even begin to assess these involvements until they are recognized, and recognition would be much easier if the economics profession were willing to disinflate the positive-normative dichotomy into a useful, but more flexible, distinction.

## ACKNOWLEDGEMENTS

I would like to thank John Davis and Uskali Mäki for helpful comments on earlier drafts of this chapter. Errors and omissions of course remain solely the author's responsibility.

## BIBLIOGRAPHY

[Balug, 1992] M. Blaug. *The Methodology of Economics: Or How Economists Explain*, 2nd edition, Cambridge: Cambridge University Press. 1992. [1st edition 1980].

[Camerer and Loewenstein, 2004] C. F. Camerer and G. Loewenstein. Behavioral Economics: Past, Present, Future. In *Advances in Behavioral Economics*, C. F. Camerer, G. Lowenstein, and M. Rabin. eds., Princeton: Princeton University Press, 3-51, 2004.

[Caplin and Schotter, 2008] A. Caplin and A. Schotter, eds. *The Foundations of Positive and Normative Economics: A Handbook*. Oxford: Oxford University Press, 2008.

[Cooter and Rappoport, 1984] R. Cooter and P. Rappoport. Were the Ordinalists Wrong About Economics? *Journal of Economic Literature*, 22, 507-30, 1984.

[Dasgupta, 2005] P. Dasgupta. What Do Economists Analyze and Why: Values or Facts? *Economics and Philosophy*, 21, 221-278, 2005.
[Davidson, 2001] D. Davidson. *Essays on Actions and Events.* 2nd Edition, Oxford: Clarendon Press, 2001. [1st Edition 1980].
[Davidson, 2004] D. Davidson. *Problems of Rationality.* Oxford: Clarendon Press, 2004.
[Davis, 1990] J. B. Davis. Cooter and Rappoport on the Normative, *Economics and Philosophy*, 6, 136-46, 1990.
[Davis, 1991] J. B. Davis. Interpretation of Interpersonal Utility Comparisons: Positive, Normative, or Descriptive. *Journal of Income Distribution*, 1, 73-90, 1991.
[Davis, 2003] J. B. Davis. *The Theory of the Individual in Economics.* London: Routledge, 2003.
[Friedman, 1953] M. Friedman. The Methodology of Positive Economics. In *Essays in Positive Economics.* Chicago: University of Chicago Press, 3-43, 1953.
[Friedman, 1955] M. Friedman. What All is Utility? *The Economic Journal*, 65, 405-09, 1955.
[Glimcher, 2003] P. W. Glimcher. *Decisions, Uncertainty, and the Brain: The Science of Neuroeconomics.* Cambridge, MA: MIT Press, 2003.
[Gordon, 1977] H. S. Gordon. Social Science and Value Judgments, *Canadian Journal of Economics*, 10, 529-46, 1977.
[Guala, 2005] F. Guala. *The Methodology of Experimental Economics.* Cambridge: Cambridge University Press, 2005.
[Hands, 2001] D. W. Hands. *Reflection Without Rules: Economic Methodology and Contemporary Science Theory.* Cambridge: Cambridge University Press, 2001.
[Hausman, 1992] D. M. Hausman. *The Inexact and Separate Science of Economics.* Cambridge: Cambridge University Press, 1992.
[Hausman and McPherson, 2006] D. M. Hausman and M. McPherson. *Economic Analysis, Moral Philosophy and Public Policy.* Cambridge: Cambridge University Press, 2006.
[Heukelom, 2008] F. Heukelom. Kahneman and Tversky and the Making of Behavioral Economics, PhD Thesis, University of Amsterdam, 2008.
[Hume, 1888] D. Hume. *A Treatise of Human Nature*, Reprinted from the Original Edition in Three Volumes, L. A. Selby-Bigge (ed.), Oxford: Oxford University Press, 1888 [originally published in 1739].
[Kahneman, 2003] D. Kahneman. Maps of Bounded Rationality. *American Economic Review*, 93, 1449-1475, 2003.
[Kahneman and Tversky, 2000] D. Kahneman and A. Tversky, eds. *Choices, Values, and Frames.* Cambridge: Cambridge University Press, 2000.
[Keynes, 1917] J. N. Keynes. *The Scope and Method of Political Economy.* 4th Edition, London: Macmillan & Co, 1917.
[Klappholz, 1964] K. Klappholz. Value Judgments and Economics. *The British Journal for the Philosophy of Science*, 15, 97-114, 1964.
[Levitt and Dubner, 2005] S. D. Levitt and S. J. Dubner. *Freakonomics: A Rogue Economist Explores the Hidden Side of Everything.* New York: Harper Collins, 2005.
[Lichtenstein and Slovic, 2006] S. Lichtenstein and P. Slovic, eds. *The Construction of Preference*, Cambridge University Press, 2006.
[Little, 1949] I. M. D. Little. The Foundations of Welfare Economics. *Oxford Economic Papers*, 1, 227-46, 1949.
[Loewenstein and Haisley, 2008] G. Loewenstein and E. Haisley. The Economist as Therapist: Methodological Ramifications of 'Light' Paternalism. In *The Foundations of Positive and Normative Economics.* A. Caplin and A. Schotter, eds., Oxford: Oxford University Press, 210-45, 2008.
[Mongin, 2006] P. Mongin. Value Judgments and Value Neutrality in Economics. *Economica*, 73, 257-86m 2006.
[Myrdal, 1958] G. Myrdal. *Value in Social Theory*, London: Routledge, 1958.
[Nagel, 1961] E. Nagel. *The Structure of Science: Problems in the Logic of Scientific Explanation.* New York: Harcourt, Brace & World, 1961.
[Nozick, 1993] R. Nozick. *The Nature of Rationality.* Princeton, NJ: Princeton University Press, 1993.
[Pigou, 1920] A. C. Pigou. *The Economics of Welfare*, $1^{st}$ Edition. London: Macmillan, 1920.
[Putnam, 2002] H. Putnam. *The Collapse of the Fact/Value Dichotomy and Other Essays.* Cambridge, MA: Harvard University Press, 2002.

[Robbins, 1935] L. Robbins. *An Essay on the Nature and Significance of Economic Science.* $2^{nd}$ Edition, London: Macmillan and Co, 1935. [1952 printing].

[Robertson, 1952] D. H. Robertson. *Utility and All That and Other Essays.* London: George Allen & Unwin, 1952.

[Ross, 2005] D. Ross. *Economic Theory and Cognitive Science.* Cambridge, MA: MIT Press, 2005.

[Samuelson and Nordhaus, 2001] P. A. Samuelson and W. D. Nordhaus. *Economics* $17^{th}$ Edition. New York: McGraw-Hill, 2001.

[Searle, 1964] J. R. Searle. How to Derive 'Ought' from 'Is'. *Philosophical Review*, 73, 43-58, 1964.

[Searle, 2001] J. R. Searle. *Rationality in Action.* Cambridge, MA: The MIT Press, 2001.

[Souter, 1933] R. W. Souter. ' The Nature and Significance of Economic Science' in Recent Discourse. *Quarterly Journal of Economics*, 47, 377-413, 1933.

[Starmer, 2005] C. Starmer. Normative Notions in Descriptive Dialogues. *Journal of Economic Methodology*, 12, 277-89, 2005.

[Sunstein and Thaler, 2003] C. R. Sunstein and R. Thaler. Libertarian Paternalism is Not an Oxymoron, *University of Chicago Law Review*, 70, 1159-1202, 2003.

[Sunstein and Thaler, 2008] C. R. Sunstein and R. Thaler. *Nudge: Improving Decisions About Health, Wealth, and Happiness.* New Haven, CT: Yale University Press, 2008.

[Suppes, 1961] P. Suppes. The Philosophical Relevance of Decision Theory,' *Philosophy of Science*, 58, 605-614, 1961.

[Thaler, 1980] R. Thaler. Toward a Positive Theory of Consumer Choice, *Journal of Economic Behavior and Organization*, 1, 39-60, 1980.

[Weber, 1949] M. Weber. *The Methodology of the Social Sciences*, Translated and edited by E. A. Shils and Henry A. Finch, New York: The Free Press, 1949.

[Weston, 1994] S. C. Weston. Toward a Better Understanding of the Positive/Normative Distinction in Economics. *Economics and Philosophy*, 10, 1-17, 1994.

# ECONOMIC THEORY, ANTI-ECONOMICS, AND POLITICAL IDEOLOGY

Don Ross

## 1 INTRODUCTION

Economics is the only established discipline that is regularly charged not just with including ideologically motivated research programs and hypotheses, but with actually *being* (at least in its institutionalized mainstream form) an ideology. As Coleman [2002] documents, this charge has followed economics since its modern inception as 'political economy' in the eighteenth century. There is a veritable *tradition* of what Coleman calls 'anti-economics', most famously populated by people such as Ruskin and Carlyle, and extending in the contemporary environment to include philosophers John Gray[1] and John Dupré,[2] numerous popular agitators associated with environmentalism and the self-styled 'anti-capitalist' and 'anti-globalization' movements, and no small number of disillusioned economists.[3] Of course all disciplinary establishments rightly attract critical literature; but as far as I know no one has ever published a book called 'The Death of Geology' featuring a hangman's noose on the cover.[4] Coleman's compendium of evidence shows conclusively, in case anyone hasn't been keeping their eyes and ears open, that economics is actively *hated* by a substantial number of people. There is no other discipline of which this is true, except insofar as some people hate all actual and would-be scientific disciplines from religious, green, or aesthetic motivations.[5]

[1]See various passages in Gray [1998] and elsewhere.

[2]See Dupré [2001] and elsewhere.

[3]See Heilbroner and Milberg [1995], Lawson [1997], Ormerod [1997], Hodgson [2001], Keen [2002], Fullbrook [2003]. It should be noted that not all of these authors accuse economists in general of ideologically motivated bad faith; Ormerod, in particular, doesn't even suggest this in tone or innuendo, or by gesturing at political associations. The others, however, all at least occasionally employ 'liberation language' which may or may not imply political / ideological motivations, but does signal to populist anti-economists that they ought to appreciate the services being rendered.

[4]I allude to Ormerod [1997]. As noted above, his *The Death of Economics* is in fact the most constructive and least ideological of the screeds cited in the previous note. One assumes that his publishers knew a promising sales angle when they saw one. That this *is* good marketing itself says something about the strange reputation of economics.

[5]Famously, influential American and Islamic religious fundamentalists express specific hatred for evolutionary biology. Given that there is no such thing as contemporary *non*-evolutionary biology, this amounts in point of fact to hatred of biology. However, and most relevantly in

Handbook of the Philosophy of Science. Volume 13: Philosophy of Economics.
Volume editor: Uskali Mäki. General editors: Dov M. Gabbay, Paul Thagard and John Woods.

My aim in this essay is to examine this situation as a philosopher of science. It is partly economists' claims to be doing science, rather than politics, that make the stakes so high when it is alleged that economics is ideology. The expertise and authority that economists claim are those accorded to science. This plays a key role in inflaming critics; economists present themselves not as merely bringing one among various possible sets of policy opinions to the democratic table for consideration, but as informing laypeople, from the necessarily non-democratic institutional precincts of science,[6] that certain policy ideas are factually impossible or so costly as to be implausible. It is the conjunction of a high enlightenment scientific stance and preoccupation with policy that makes economics so toxic to some. Although a fraction of economists concern themselves with questions of basic scientific interest,[7] most economic modeling and data analysis are directly motivated by social and political problems. This can be said of social sciences generally. However, a distinctive feature of economics, and the final one necessary for explaining the antagonistic passions it arouses, is that uniquely among the social sciences economists can claim to have a clearly dominant set of rigorous theoretical foundations, as a result of which they need not hedge their claims to epistemic authority in a way that a sociologist, forced to justify all her particular conceptual assumptions at every turn, cannot avoid. Uniquely among social scientists, economists are not forced by theoretical instability to be humble. (Hence the tireless efforts of debunkers of economics to exaggerate such pockets of disorder as can be found in economic theory. See [Dasgupta, 2002] for review and rebuttal.)

Let me be clear at the outset that I do not really believe that the charge that most (let alone all) economics is ideology is plausible. If such a belief were required to motivate the inquiry in this essay then I would not elect to undertake it. However, as I will explain, different economists answer the charge in divergent ways, partly because the content of the charge itself has varied, but also because economists have held different positions on both the actual and the appropriate relationships between economic theory and normative opinion (both as regards policy and political philosophy). Therefore, considering the charge in its various manifestations and evaluating its similarly various answers, is of value for light it sheds on both the nature of economics and on fact/value issues in the philosophy of science.

It would be impossible to say anything significant about the relationship between economics and ideology at less than monograph length without first delim-

the present context, American creationists don't feel they can oppose biology *in principle*, and so they go to great lengths to fabricate a heterodox biology. It seems clear that some of these creationists hate all science, but deem it politically unwise to say so before non-sympathetic audiences; Darwinian theory is used by them as a wedge. By contrast, few people do themselves harm in mass electoral politics by running down economics in general.

[6]By 'necessarily' here I allude to the claim that a democratic science would be ineffective as science. It would distract too much from present concerns to explain why I regard the alternative view, as expounded by (*inter alia*) Fuller [2001], to be deluded.

[7]For example: neuroeconomists modeling the capacity of the brain's reward system to commit to savings instead of consumption [Benhabib and Bisin, 2005]; or ethological economists modeling the market dynamics of parasite-cleaning services among fish [Bshary, 2001].

iting the scope of each. By 'economics' I refer to the establishment economics of the global academy. This is difficult to analytically define, but easy to pick out ostensively, thanks to the fact that there is a single standard undergraduate and postgraduate economics curriculum taught in the majority of the world's universities. Though many programs make room for optional units of heterodoxy, virtually *every* economist hired by national treasuries, reserve banks, large corporations, private investment banks, and policy analysis institutions has their core training in the standard curriculum. Like any living institutionalized tradition, mainstream economics is fuzzy on its boundaries. It includes elements of Marx as part of its 'inside' history, but interprets him as the second main figure in a Ricardo-Marx-Sraffa-Robinson historical sub-current, rather than as the prophet of the pathology and coming demise of capitalism. It is now clearly making room, after some resistance, for behavioral/experimental methods and much greater attentiveness to institutions and their evolutionary dynamics than it allowed during a strong anti-historicist phase that lasted from the 1930s through the 1970s. But it does not, in any precinct, accept verbal argument as a substitute for rigorous modeling, and it is therefore committed to an axiomatic style. Though it will entertain almost any secondary interest – including interest in justice – as legitimate, interest in efficiency is *always* the primary interest, and this is what makes something count as economics according to the mainstream. It treats microeconomics as more fundamental than macroeconomics, and this is reflected in curriculum requirements. The theoretical core of establishment microeconomics is neoclassical consumer theory and game-theoretic industrial organization, auction, bargaining and market microstructure theory, and the empirical core is analysis of household consumption data and dynamic pricing and production modeling. In macroeconomics the establishment recognizes considerable theoretical uncertainty, though its basic conceptual framework is still that established by Keynes and Hicks, albeit with emphasis on a much wider range of policy instruments and variables and no commitment to the Phillips curve. The economics of financial markets is a distinct specialization with its own foundational models. Law and economics is another optional specialization, but with less *sui generis* foundations that are based in core micro theory. Finally, all economists learn at least a basic set of econometric techniques.

The entire discussion in this essay applies to economic *theory*. A great deal of the activity carried out by economists is measurement, which it is silly to regard as ideology. Still more activity, foundational work in econometrics, is theory of (distinctively economic) measurement. This, likewise, cannot be ideology. Though some anti-economists, influenced by post-modern ambitions to show that every 'text' from plays to laundry lists can be deconstructed to yield ideological motivations and presuppositions, aim to find ideology in econometrics, their cause does not require them to try or to succeed at this. They need simply point out that it is economic theory in interaction with policy ends and means that determines the classes of events and types of processes econometricians seek to measure and to learn to measure better. Anti-economists can thus think that econometricians waste resources measuring poorly motivated classes of events and processes without having to argue that they are first-order peddlers of ideologies.[8] It is enough for their purposes if they can convict economic theorists and policy advisors of occupying that role.

On 'ideology' we must take our lead from sociologists and political scientists. Freeden [1996] is representative of the main prevailing conception among them. First, ideologies simplify, often with considerable distortion, models of causal relationships in political, social and economic domains that usually have some basis in intellectual work. But the primary function of an ideology is not explanation, prediction or understanding. Rather, it is coordination, for purposes of political behavior (including purely rhetorical behavior), on meanings for normatively freighted concepts such as 'liberty' and 'justice,' which the academy treats as essentially and permanently contestable. As Freeden puts it, "an ideology will link together a particular conception of human nature, a particular conception of social structure, of justice, of liberty, of authority, etc.. '*This* is what liberty means, and *that* is what justice means, it asserts ..." (p. 76). Furthermore, these conceptions are always made in more-or-less explicit contrast with alternative, also ideological, conceptions already in play. (The rise of a new ideology often, then, causes adjustment in prior ideologies with which it sets up oppositions, development with which the newer ideology may then feel a need to grapple, and so on recursively; ideologies are inherently dynamic even when, as with Soviet-style Marxism in Stalin's time, they are centrally and deliberately controlled.) Though some ideologies, such as most versions of socialism, aim to have universal scope, others, such as racist Shintoism in Japan and Islamic and American conservative versions of political-religious fundamentalism, are avowedly parochial. An economist is bound to note that, in light of the idea that ideologies are systems for coordinating action, evolutionary game theory is the obvious technology for modeling their dynamics. They plausibly have much in common with rituals, as recently modeled by Chwe [2003]. Many proponents of ideologies will typically indulge some degree of bad faith — from consciously or semi-consciously suppressing counter-ideological data and arguments to deliberately prevaricating — but it is crucial to the vigor of an ideology that most of its promoters believe themselves to be epistemically or morally conscientious or both; when this ceases to be the case, an ideology is on its way to death.

The fact that ideologues are roused to unusual excitement by economics is just one side of the discipline's peculiar relationship to ideology. The other side is that economics and ideology closely share their history and developed under one another's profound influence. Though there have long been bodies of religious thought that function politically and socially as ideologies do, the modern idea of secular ideology is exactly as old as political economy/economics, and arose in response to the same historical contingency: the rise of mass markets based on specialization of labor and on institutions for concentrating capital so as to

[8]They can consistently add, if they like, that econometric activity helps to shroud economics-as-ideology in forbidding technical armor that intimidates external critics.

efficiently allocate risk.

Modern ideologies are popularly conceived as lying along a one-dimensional spectrum from right to left. Since they are totalizing — this being part of what makes them ideologies — people who think by means of them tend to sort anything that contests them on this same spectrum. As a result, a prevailing 'ideology of ideologies' denies that there are comprehensive and coherent political views that have no assignable place on the spectrum. The spectrum itself arose in the context of the French Revolution, when it was used to order political agents according to the extent to which they were in favor of discarding, reforming or conserving traditional institutions. Almost from the start those on the left found their most salient and coherent criticism coming from the new, and then extremely fashionable, self-announced science of political economy, when Edmund Burke invoked its principles (as he interpreted them) to claim that all points left of a particular point on the spectrum were doomed to be self-undermining as a matter of scientific fact. Given the left's perfect record of political failure until the mid-nineteenth century, it was incumbent on left advocates to find theoretical grounds for denying Burke's claim – they could not answer him simply by pointing to experience. In the process left ideology developed its initial characteristic principles based around deliberate redistribution of property in the interests of greater equality; the institution of private property in the means of production came to be seen as *the* traditional institution on which other traditional institutions depend for their tenacity.[9] Marx's was of course the towering contribution here, and Marx chose theoretical political economy as the fundamental site for his dialectic.

Dominant ideological attitudes and prevailing paradigms in economics shadowed one another closely through the twentieth century. Before World War I, the governing ideology in the industrial societies stressed the imperative of leaving price setting to the interaction of supply and demand,[10] just as did high neoclassical economics. The left came to regard this as an apology for the status quo in property distribution, and even if this was unjustified as a generalization there is no doubt that wealthy interests often appealed to economic theory in defense of rents. In the1930s economists discovered, or thought they had discovered, the virtues of regulation and planning. Because of the popular linking of free markets with status quo property protection, this was taken to be a leftward shift on the spectrum, which governing political sentiment influenced by the Great Depression closely tracked. Within a few years Karl Polanyi [1944] had re-written the history of industrial society, to the satisfaction of most non-communist academic and journalistic opinion, so that the formerly triumphant rise of market-focused society had become the story of the tragic suffering of the working class along the rough road to the rationally managed welfare state. Galbraith [1960] rings the same theme with

[9]I mean 'traditional' here only in reference to the status quo that the left aimed to abolish or reform. Most left advocates have recognized that property institutions were massively transformed by the rise of capitalism and so are not traditional in any stronger sense.

[10]This remark is broadly true even of American Progressives and German social democrats, who tended to concentrate their fire on anti-market monopolists rather then the market itself.

more complacency and greater emphasis on practical policy. But by two decades later, the Lucas critique had re-convinced dominant policy opinion in economics that market processes are necessarily relatively autonomous, while on the popular level Thatcher and her imitators invoked Hayek to justify ideological celebration of the retreat of the state (even if the Thatcherite state did not actually retreat so much as re-allocate its resources from ownership of assets to regulation[11]). As of present writing, prominent voices advocating pragmatically judicious mixtures of private and public institutional governance scold yesterday's "extremists" of both sides, in economics [Stiglitz, 1996; 2003] and populist political economy [Frank, 2001] alike. In summary: left, right and centre have partly defined themselves for decades around the question of how much state regulation of markets is appropriate, with complete suppression of markets amounting to the limiting case on the extreme left. However, fascism and democratic forms of right communitarianism fit awkwardly into this scheme, since they favor subordination of market-driven motivations to nationalistic and civic virtue considerations respectively.

An economist of whiggish inclinations might read this familiar history as consistent with the idea that dominant popular ideology just simplifies and moralizes whatever policy perspectives scientific economists first discover by rational investigation to be best justified. On this interpretation, ideological economics is just pop economics, and is ultimately controlled, with lags, by professional economics. This view is not *nonsense* and should not be waved aside as *entirely* simplistic and self-flattering. For one thing, there *is* a reliably observable lag between academic and popular enthusiasms with respect to large-scale economic policy frameworks, and it would pay implausible tribute to economists' cultural and political prescience to imagine that they unerringly sniff the coming wind so as to position themselves in front of populist parades. It is more realistic to suppose that they often make genuine discoveries that others repeat subsequently, partly by reflecting on experience and partly by encountering and reacting to ideologically spun popularizations of professional economics. Still, we also know that ideologies coalesce gradually, and from many of the same forces that cause academic consensus to crystallize. The latter do so faster because academics form a tighter community of opinion and devote more resources to coordination of ideas than other people. To some extent, then, professional and popular policy fads are products of common historical causes. There surely can be no serious doubt that economics and ideology have been locked in a close dance, where neither side yields uncontested lead, for the entire short histories of both modern economics and secular ideology.

Let me now integrate this point with my opening one: while similar dancing might go on to a limited extent between popular philosophy and all scientific disciplines, the extent to which economics and ideology influence one another is qualitatively distinctive. No discipline is remotely as significant to ideological shifts as economics; and, as stressed at the outset, no discipline conducts its business under the relentless ideological scrutiny and pressure that economics does. The basic reason for this is plain: economics is the discipline most directly concerned with

[11]Vogel [1996].

the social distribution of resources, and secular ideologies are, first and foremost, devices by which people coordinate on norms for regulating flows of resources among social groups. Economics dances closely with ideology because they are, at any given time, listening to the same band, even if with different sensibilities and levels of appreciation.

I have now said enough by way of background framing to state the goal of this essay. I will offer grounds for accepting that economics is entitled to scientific status *despite* its close and unremitting dance with ideology. As noted earlier, I am less interested in this unsurprising conclusion *per se* than I am in what the details of the answer tell us about the nature of both professional economics and ideology. Let me also note that I do not intend my strategy for defense to apply to other social sciences, except insofar as they (or branches of them) have theoretical foundations that are as transparent to their users, and as practically powerful in framing empirical investigation and modeling, as those of economics. My view here is *not* that such foundations are necessary for objectivity, so I am *not* suggesting that a sociologist or anthropologist is necessarily trapped in ideology to a greater extent than an economist. My point is much more modest. Where there are relatively consensual foundations it is a great deal easier to identify disciplinary boundaries than where there are not. As a result, the philosophy of anthropology (for example) is harder than the philosophy of economics (or of physics, or of biology) and I disavow any attempt to address the former here. That is just to say, then, that this essay is not an exercise in philosophy of social sciences other than economics.

## 2 ANTI-ECONOMISTS AND MARKETS

As noted above, essential fuel for hatred of economics is the widespread view that economics pretends to be science while in fact being ideology – in particular, ideology produced for the benefit of the powerful, for which economists are paid in kind. Some anti-economists explicitly say that they regard economics as *being* ideology, while others insist that economics is essentially a tool that serves ideology. To still others we can *attribute* opinions about ideological dominance to economists on the basis of other things they claim. What is meant by such self-attribution and attribution, and what justifications for their views do anti-economists tend to offer?

Coleman [2002] concludes, on the basis of ample evidence he reviews, that "Anti-economics has commonly presented one supreme ground as to why economics is a bane: that is, that economics is sympathetic to the market. Anti-liberal anti-economics (both Right and Left), and their [sic] allies in nationalism, in the religion of love, and in the cults of nature and art, have all tried to show that economics is a bane on account of its sympathy towards the market" (p. 232). We will consider later how far it is correct for anti-economists to attribute 'sympathy towards the market' to economists generally; for the moment our concern is just with what unites anti-economists. They begin from the observation that market institutions are of great political and social importance in (at least) modern industrial and post-industrial culture, and that market-focused behavior is more reliably rewarded in this culture than any other generic type of behavior. On various grounds, sometimes radical and sometimes conservative, they deplore these facts. They then allege that the very purpose of economics is to help entrench them. Economics is generally held to do this by a combination or subset of four main activities:

(i) showing how market mechanisms may be made to work better in their own terms;

(ii) encouraging celebration of market institutions and market behavior by promoting the belief that societies in which production, and therefore capital resource allocation, is dominated by market-focused institutions[12] are systematically likely to be more efficient than other sorts of societies, and therefore tend to produce higher per capita welfare that leaves even poorer citizens materially better off than they would otherwise be;

(iii) encouraging celebration of market institutions and market behavior by promoting the belief that as market-focused institutions become more dominant in a society, this tends to widen the scope of liberty and/or democracy in the society in question;

(iv) promoting the belief that dominance of societies by market-focused institutions is natural and so ineradicable or uncontainable, by claiming scientific authority in offering theories and even 'laws' that purport to state objective truths about relationships between markets and other types of social structures and processes.

We will consider the extent to which it is reasonable to ascribe these ambitions to economics throughout the essay. For the moment, let us just note that it is easy to cite particular leading economists who engage in all of the activities above.

The reader may have noted the absence of reference to a value that has been crucially contested during the history of ideological responses to economics, viz., equality. Left anti-economists are suspicious of or hostile to markets mainly because they believe that markets amplify and perpetuate material and social inequalities; and some right anti-economists dislike markets because they believe that markets undermine differences in status they hold to be valuable. However, few anti-economists have attributed to economics the *first-order* goal of either reducing or promoting equality of outcomes. This is for the good reason that few economists have, in fact, supposed that any specifically and narrowly *economic* programme, by itself, tends necessarily to either undermine or enhance equality of

[12]By 'market-focused' institutions I refer not only to *direct* market institutions, such as private companies, stock exchanges and investment banks, but also to institutions structured so as to work in a market context. It is because this includes most large-scale institutions in contemporary industrial and post-industrial societies, and many powerful social norms, that it is appropriate to refer to such whole societies as 'market societies'.

outcomes. Many, though by no means all, economists over the years have believed that equality of outcomes is a *prima facie* good that is traded off against others, including aggregate and / or average and/or minimum welfare levels. Many have also supposed that there are in-principle trade-offs between equality of outcomes and liberty. (Equality of *opportunity* has often been partially equated with liberty.) Anti-economists have not *in general* disputed the second supposition, though they have of course defended (different) very strong views about where the trade-off between equality of outcomes and liberty ought to be struck. However, few on either side have taken this to be in itself an economic dispute; thus a view on it has not generally been *constitutive* of what is baleful about economics according to anti-economists; rather, they have generally maintained that economics helps to encourage libertarian stances on this trade-off as a causal product. As regards putative trade-offs between equality and welfare, left anti-economists have often denied that these are necessary. However, they have generally seen belief in such trade-offs as arising from commitment to market-focused institutions. Thus this aspect of economics has generally been treated by anti-economists as a second-order rather than a first-order bane. This explains its absence from the list above. We will return explicitly to issues around equality towards the end of the essay.

On the basis of the foregoing, we may distinguish between five stances on the relationship between economics and ideology, each of which contributes to a distinct grade of anti-economics:

**Stance 1:** Economics aims at goals (i) through (iv) and succeeds at none of them except insofar as it fashions and promotes an ideology.

This stance is equivalent to the strongest possible anti-economics, holding that economics is *all* or *mainly* promotion of 'pro-market' ideology. One might expect to find it maintained only by extreme ideologues. In fact, however, the main route to it by critics who do not rant is by way of sweeping methodological criticisms, often very sober ones whose motivation is not (or at least not mainly) ideological. Philosophers of science who are critical of what they take to be the general foundational edifice of economics belong in this sub-camp of anti-economists. Leading examples are Hollis and Nell [1975] and Hausman [1992].[13] Hausman, the most sophisticated proponent of the stance, sets up general equilibrium reasoning as the theoretical core of all of economics, and then argues for the more-or-less complete irrelevance of general equilibrium reasoning to empirical or policy problems. It is hard to see how this conjunction of opinions does not imply the strongest possible grade of anti-economics. On the other hand, if Hausman adopted the broader conception of mainstream economics in use here, it may be that this would lead him to endorse a weaker grade or to entitle him to say that he is not

[13] Hausman would likely protest that he is not an anti-economist, but a constructive critic of such economic theory as is, according to him, insufficiently sensitive to empirical testing. However, Hausman's identification of the core of economic theory with general equilibrium theory causes him, in my view, to underestimate both the extent and the power of empirical testing in day-to-day economics.

an anti-economist but just a critic of derivations of policy from general equilibrium reasoning. Because anti-economist philosophers of science are more likely than others to recognize the motivational warrant of epistemological and methodological conservatism within science generally, they are less inclined than other anti-economists to attribute ideologically motivated bad faith to economists. But, typically, neither do they explicitly disavow such attributions, at least as applied to many or most economists, and because they are legitimate scholarly authorities they provide powerful ammunition to more overtly ideological anti-economists. Some economists (e.g. [Heilbroner and Milburg, 1995; Ormerod, 1997; Lawson, 1997; Blaug, 2002]) echo the generic methodological criticisms of philosophers, and for polemical purposes their authority is even more useful. They are also, in general, less circumspect in their rhetoric than the philosophers.

**Stance 2:** Economics aims at all or some of goals (i) through (iv) but succeeds (sometimes or often) by means other than ideological construction and promotion only at goal (i).

This stance is equivalent to holding that activity in economics divides into two parts: (a) technical activity performed in service to market-promoted interests, and (b) promotion of 'pro-market' ideology. As Schumpeter [1950, p. 129] observes, anti-economists can concede that economists are often technically successful. The most influential anti-economist of all, Marx,[14] certainly allowed that Smith and Ricardo had gone far in achieving (i). In general, for anti-economists who insist that economics is ideologically committed to (rather than scientifically justified in pursuing) goal (ii), little is at stake over the question of whether they sometimes or often succeed at (i).

What crucially separates stronger from weaker forms of anti-economics are different views of economists' success with respect to goal (ii). Marx, of course, thought that communism would be even more productively powerful than capitalism, so he did not concede (ii) to mainstream economics except insofar as it criticized feudalism and agrarianism. A different route to entire rejection of (ii) while conceding (i) is taken by some environmentalists who define productive superiority in terms of what they call *sustainable* productivity, and who hold the very radical view that markets are incapable of that. Environmentalist E.F. Schumacher [1973] and his 21$^{st}$-century followers at least approximate this position, since the scope they leave for markets as compatible with sustainability is so pinched that it is no longer clear they are imagining markets, as most economists understand them, at

[14]Many readers will object here, pointing out that surely Marx was an economist himself. Yes; but as Coleman points out, there is no contradiction in someone's being both an economist and an anti-economist. Much of *Capital* is indeed economics according to the mainstream tradition, as I noted earlier. But as I also remarked, the Marxist system as a whole is not regarded as economics by the mainstream, and much in its corpus is fervid anti-economics. As Coleman [2002, p. 234] observes, when the severe problems with Marx's economics based on the labor theory of value came to be widely recognized among Marxists "Marx the materialistic (even positivistic) economist began to be replaced by a 'young' and philosophizing Marx. This is reflected in the greatly shrunken attention of Marxists to anything that could be described as economics ...".

all. (See [Brecher and Costello, 1994; Bello, 2004].)

Stance 2 is a strong form of anti-economics because, in denying that market-focused institutions are even a basis for productive superiority, it leaves little hope of explaining the institutional significance of economics except by recourse to the hypothesis that economists are, wittingly or unwittingly, stooges of the powerful.

Some anti-economists deny the *value*, rather than the achievability, of goal (ii), which then knocks back onto the justification of the intellectual and other resources lavished on goal (i). Most $19^{th}$-century romantic and many contemporary green anti-economists agree that economic analysis shows market mechanisms to be productively superior to alternatives, but deplore economics because, on moral grounds, they deplore increased material productivity. A major impediment to the popularity of this stance, at least on the left, is that it seems to entail the view that the world's poorer people and regions should refrain from attempting to catch up to rich ones, and that people in rich parts of the world are obliged not to help them to do so. There is of course nothing logically incoherent in such a position, but anyone who advocates it and is not herself poor must expect more ridicule and abuse than counter-argument. Meanwhile, defenders of the attitude are even scarcer in the third world than they are in the first. Note that an economist who points this out — and I think it morally dubious *not* to point it out, whenever the attitude emerges — thereby engages in direct normative argument with ideological critics of economics.

**Stance 3:** Economics aims (at least) at goals (i) through (iii), succeeds (sometimes or often) at goals (i) and (ii), but in seeking to show that market-focused institutions are more conducive to liberty or democracy economics becomes ideology.

Varieties of anti-economics that are motivated by imputing goal (iii) – as well as (iv) — to economics and then declaring them to be ideological will seem to many economists to simply be peddling populist confusion. Whatever particular economists might have believed and defended in their non-professional capacity, it will be said, *scientific* economics is not in the business of defending abstract political norms as in imputed goal (iii), or metaphysical claims as in imputed goal (iv). For reasons I will now explain, I will refer to this as the 'turtle defense'.

While it is certainly true that the vast majority of papers in economics never mention liberty, democracy or laws of markets (and many never mention even markets; see below), responding to popular anti-economic stances on the basis of this is hasty for several reasons. While no one should regard it as a proper scientific aim to *lobby for* freedom or democracy, economists certainly study, in a scientific spirit, the causal and/or equilibrium foundations of liberty and democracy/justice [Jackman, 1973; Przeworski *et al.*, 2000; Binmore, 1994; 1998]; and on the basis of such study a significant number of economists have indeed concluded that strong market-focused institutions are at least a necessary condition in a society for both [Usher, 1981; Friedman, 2005]. Given the irreducibly normative character of the concepts of liberty and democracy/justice, arguments for the truth of this proposition will inevitably be taken as advocacy for market-focused institutions. But few economists will agree that arguments for the propositions, whether ultimately successful or not, are *necessarily* ideological. Since anti-economists claim that they *are*, we here have a dispute between economists and their critics that should not simply be avoided by denying that economists harbor ambitions to comment professionally on grand normative questions. Economists' theses on these questions *might* be *true*; and we should not guarantee our own inability to discover this as a consequence of a tactic adopted for dodging often irresponsible anti-economists. In fact, I will argue later, the most convincing defenses economists have given of the importance of markets for welfare and productivity have tipped unavoidably into direct consideration of these questions; Schumpeter, I will maintain, remains the most impressive voice from the side of economics on imputed goals (i)–(iii) and their interrelationships. Finally, economists can completely retreat from goal (iv) only by embracing a degree of historicism and relativism that is not borne out by the practice of most of those who engage in theory at all. (To reiterate: I recognize that most economists do not.) The intellectual standards of most anti-economists — excluding serious methodological critics such as Hausman — are generally shoddy; but their imputations to economics of goals (iii) and (iv) are not *baseless*, and to try to ignore them by pretending that they are is at best to bypass interesting questions. At worst it is to enhance the cogency of their case by appearing to add hypocrisy and arrogance to their list of motivated grievances.

Stance 3 is virtually unoccupied. Those who *seem* to occupy it generally do so because they re-define 'liberty' so that it no longer means what it does in the versions of liberal theory with which many economists have been associated. It invites less confusion to understand such people as adopting the next stance.

**Stance 4:** Economics sometimes or often aims at goals (i) and (ii), succeeds in showing that there is a systematic relation of mutual reinforcement between dominance of societies by market-focused institutions and personal liberty in those societies, but in seeking to show that market-focused institutions are more conducive to democracy economics becomes ideology.

This grade of anti-economics is advocated by those who insist that libertarian conceptions of freedom are self-undermining, leading to Hobbesian anarchy and insecurity rather than genuine — typically, in some sense, Hegelian — freedom. Stance 4 is occupied by many conservative communitarians and so-called 'post-colonialist' social critics who regard the liberal-individualist ethos as a modern and peculiarly Western pathology, and who therefore insist that liberty requires redefinition if it is to be a consistent positive ideal. One sometime diagnostic feature of the stance (though not the feature that, *per se*, makes it a version of anti-economics) is emphasis on the idea that liberty and democracy are wholly distinct ideals. A recent systematic exposition and defense of the stance *as* a brand of anti-economics is Hamilton [2003]. Proponents can concede that markets promote individual liberty of the sort they reject as a norm, while arguing that what is traded off for it is something genuinely valuable, be this community cohesion and shared purpose or the welfare of the less well-off. The first charge typically used to come from the right and the second from the left (though not from Marx, who supposed that communism would promote everyone's freedom better than market-focused society), but recent left critics have been more inclined to echo the right on this point. This is explained by the fact that the populist left has over the past few decades appropriated environmentalism, which began as an aspect of right anti-economics.[15] It is plausible to suppose that the existence of establishment economics as a foil for the ideological left was crucial for this appropriation.

Some anti-economists have been willing to concede that economics succeeds in both aspects of (iii). Advocates of Soviet-style Marxist, fascist, or theocratic-fundamentalist anti-economics positions can all cheerfully[16] admit that market institutions promote democracy, either because they disapprove of democracy, or think that the kind of democracy in question is worthless because it is 'bourgeois' or individualist. However, none of these normative standpoints are currently taken seriously (as first-order standpoints) outside populist contexts. What about conservative communitarians? I would argue — though, because this would carry us at length into deep issues in political philosophy, I will not do so here — that to be a conservative communitarian *and* to admit that market institutions promote productivity and freedom and democracy *and* to nevertheless be against economic defense of market institutions would be tantamount to losing all perceptible distance from fascism.[17] Though I think there are in fact a non-trivial number of current fascists who don't realize that they endorse fascism, I will assume that a view's being (wittingly or unwittingly) fascist is sufficient to make it unacceptable. This is ultimately because all normative arguments so far advanced for fascism are easily shown to be unsound. I assert that the same can be said of Soviet-style Marxism. It is eventually reasonable to pronounce movements intellectually dead under such circumstances, even if they are not politically dead under different labels.[18]

**Stance 5:** Economics aims and sometimes or often succeeds at goal (i), with or without success at goals (ii) or (iii), but in seeking to show that dominance of societies by market-focused institutions is natural, economics becomes ideology.

---

[15]See [Bramwell, 1989].

[16]The mind strains somewhat trying to think of notable acolytes of any of these doctrines who were also cheerful. Stalin liked a joke, but his favorites seem to have been about people being executed.

[17]By 'fascism' I mean the approximate body of beliefs Mussolini professed to hold during his campaign for and early years in power. It confuses matters to regard Nazism as an ideology associated with fascism, since it was mostly just unprincipled and unrestrained thuggery, Hitler's sincere anti-Semitic delusions and the successful wooing of many fascists (including Mussolini) by the Nazis notwithstanding.

[18]Cuba is governed by Soviet-style Marxists, and Eritrea by fascists. Neither regime is intellectually defensible. Theocratic fundamentalism is obviously not politically dead, but it is equally devoid of intellectual merit.

This is well-worn theme in both academic [Dupré, 2001; Mirowski, 1989; 1994; 2002] and popular [Frank, 2001; Aune, 2002] criticism of mainstream economics. In the non-populist context, there are two routes to it. One is generic: extreme humanists who believe that *all* attempts to show that there are non-trivial natural limits on plausible norms of social organization that social science can discover[19] are disguised ideology apply this conclusion to putatively scientific economics along with other disciplines (especially cognitive and behavioral sciences). Dupré [2001] is a representative instance. The other route tries to isolate economics as making *special*, and deluded, assumptions about what is natural. Scholarly versions of this criticism are found in Mirowski [1988; 1994; 2002] and Ingrao and Israel [1990]. It should be noted that critics of the second route are less likely to emerge as *anti*-economists than as advocates of less (in their terms) megalomaniacal economics. That is, they tend to favor clear abandonment by economists of goal (iv). Critics of the first route are almost invariably anti-economists due to the conjunction of two things they believe: first, that there is no humbler station available for economics to retreat to in search of objectivity; and second that whereas other putatively objective human sciences are products of metaphysically confused *culture*, economics is attempted ideological hijacking that plays a first-order role in blocking that culture's path to self-understanding. These critics thus combine Stance 5 with Stance 1.

This form of anti-economics is the version with which philosophers of science (as opposed to political philosophers) have mainly dealt. Rebutting it requires two steps. The first is metaphysical: one must make the case against route 1 critics that social sciences can and do discover objectively true generalizations. There is a large philosophical literature on this matter to which I have no new contribution to make. Then one must show that economics is not a special failure in this regard. Part of this task consists in making the case that economics suffers from no systematic and endemic methodological or ontological pathologies. This also lies outside the scope of the present essay; the reader is referred to Dasgupta [2002] and Ross [2005]. Another part of the task consists in replying to the other versions of anti-economics, in order to defeat the stance 5 critic's contention that economics is disguised ideology. That *is* part of the objective here, but is pursued as an aspect of answering stances 1–4.

It should be noted that one logical possibility in the space of anti-economic stances remains unconsidered. In principle, someone could accept that economics aims and succeeds at goal (iv) while also claiming that it aims and fails at goals (ii) and/or (iii). For an anti-economist, this would amount to a position of romantic fatalism, involving regretting the truth. As Coleman [2002] documents, such fatalism has not actually been rare (especially among artists[20]), but it almost always

[19] I am thus not referring to limits on our, e.g., building better societies through telepathy or achievement of eternal youth.

[20] Keats, with his fussing about unwoven rainbows, is representative of the kind of position I have in mind here — though I make no pretense of appreciating whatever more subtle ironies of artistic purpose humanistic scholars might identify in great creators like Keats. It is not among my purposes here to defend economists from charges of philistinism (which is not to say that I

derives anti-economics from a more general anti-modernity, and it is the exclusive preserve of conservatives. Since it is typically wistful or theatrical rather than activist (either intellectually or politically), I will henceforth ignore it.

If we therefore set aside consideration of goal (iv) as a variable that depends partly on the values of the other goals, then the possible ways of not endorsing anti-economics are as follows:

E1: Economics aims at, and for non-ideological reasons often succeeds at, goal (i); but economics does not aim at goals (ii) or (iii).

E2: Economics aims at, and for non-ideological reasons often succeeds at, goals (i) and (ii); but economics does not aim at goal (iii).

E3: Economics aims at, and for non-ideological reasons often succeeds at, goals (i) and (ii); aims to show that market-focused institutions are superior to alternative types of institutions for allocating scarce resources at promoting personal liberty and often succeeds, for non-ideological reasons, in showing this; but economics does not aim at showing that market-focused institutions are superior to other institutions at promoting democracy.

E4: Economics aims at goals (i) through (iii) and often succeeds, for non-ideological reasons, at all three.

E5: Economics does not aim at any of goals (i) through (iii), but aims and succeeds at something else.

There are, to my knowledge, no defenses of economics based on claiming success at goal (iii) while denying it of goal (ii), since conclusions concerning (ii) always serve as essential premises in arguments for achievement of (iii). The same point applies on the relationships between goals (i) and (ii).

Many economists might jump to say at this point that E5 is the obviously sensible, and empirically best justified, position. The simple reason for this would be that (i)–(iii) all concern markets, and quite a lot of economics does not seem to be about markets. Economics is the science that studies relative efficiency in response to scarcity.[21] Then, famously, we are applying economics when we study Robinson Crusoe allocating his labor between harvesting breadfruit and making a fishing rod [Robertson, 1957], even though he faces no market. We are applying economics when we study games among small numbers of agents, bears foraging for food, and development agencies or governments parametrically choosing project investments. None of these activities involve attention to markets.

accept such charges). Theatrical stance 5 anti-economics in literary fiction remains common; for a perfect example of the type, see [Metcalf, 1980].

[21] Note that it would be redundant to suppose that we needed, like Robbins [1935, p. 16], to include reference to humans here, or to agents at all. Agency is indeed fundamental to economics. But this is because scarcity presupposes it — nothing is scarce to a rock. Then, also with reference to Robbins's famous definition: reference to efficiency builds in reference to means as opposed to ends. See Ross [2005] for details.

Therefore, it might be urged, all anti-economics makes a version of the mistake I attributed above to Hausman, of beginning from an overly narrow conception of economics' fundamental character. There can be scientific economics even if everything economists have ever said about markets is motivated by ideology.[22]

This response partly repeats the turtle defense discussed above, and so invites the same reply. But one might think that E5 should at least be *part of* a full response to anti-economics. Notice, however, that it engages the anti-economist as if hers were an exercise in analytic philosophy, in which the battle is about what to *mean* by 'economics'. No anti-economist — not even Hausman — means to *only* be attacking an *analysis* of economics. The anti-economist's target is the history of intellectual activity that, citing Hausman again (now with approval) establishes the tradition of economics as a *separate* science. If there had never been a tradition of seeking systematic generalizations about markets, then the examples of non-market-related topics for economists listed above would be grouped together as instances of study of optimization. Crusoe's would be parametric optimization. If we were not studying Crusoe in preparation for embedding him in social processes — specifically, markets — after Friday comes along, we would have no reason not to treat his parametric optimization as just another dimension of his psychology. Nowadays, we'd approach it using the methods of behavioral economics and neuroeconomics [McCabe, 2003]; but there would be no motivation for calling it any such thing. It is exciting, for example, that the model of asset pricing in markets has turned out to apply to the value predictions of the brain's dopaminergic reward system [Montague and Berns, 2002], because this means that we can draw benefit in neuroscience from decades of modeling of markets. Without relationships of this kind, the neuroeconomic model would be just another computational model of a particular neurotransmitter pathway. As for nonparametric optimization, in our other examples above, the context provided by two centuries of studying markets is relevant in a similar way. Where people in institutional settings are concerned, we typically take one crucial aspect of the rules of their games — the strategies available to them — as known by virtue of the fact that we know what sort of market is constituted by their interaction. As often with things taken for granted, there's seldom any need to explicitly mention this. To see that a situation is a game of a certain sort is to see that it instantiates a certain sort of imperfectly competitive micro-market.

If this argument seems fussy, this is just because the tempting quick leap to E5 in response to the anti-economist is an attempt to finesse her charge rather than respond to it on its own terms. Economics indeed goes beyond the study of markets. But the tradition that gives economics the distinctive character that it has, and that the anti-economist dislikes and regards as ideology in disguise, is a tradition derived from the study of markets. The tradition has been so derived because markets have been thought by almost all economists to be of central significance to optimization among groups of agents. Furthermore, economists

[22]The defender of E5 of course doesn't have to admit this; the point is just that she can allow it without risk to her view.

have overwhelmingly been motivated, in the policy contexts in which the issues over ideology are mainly interesting, by the conviction that existing markets could be improved, or markets established where they have not been operating, to good welfare effects; or that some useful properties of markets could be simulated by planners. In light of this real history of their disciplinary tradition, economists concede too much, and too much that matters a great deal, to anti-economists if they fail to defend one of E1–E4.

What of the possibility that economics (crucially) studies markets, but is not committed to any of goals (i)–(iii) because it might reach or has reached mainly pessimistic conclusions about markets? This suggests a response not included in E1–E5. However, no actual economist makes this response. Of course, some economists have been pessimistic about *free* or about *perfectly competitive* markets, but these are different claims (to be discussed at length below). Marx was pessimistic about (all) markets in one sense, but as we saw he accepted that economics succeeds at goal (i) and, up to a point, at goal (ii). (He is an anti-economist because he also thinks that economics necessarily aims higher and then fails.) Schumpeter was pessimistic about markets in a different sense. According to him economics is a success at goals (i) and (ii) but, because markets promote democracy but democracy doesn't promote (efficient) markets, markets undermine themselves in the long run. Thus, relative to the anti-economist, Schumpeter is simply an economist who responds by means of E3 — and happens to add a pessimistic sociological theory. Mirowski [1989; 2002] is about as skeptical concerning mainstream economics as it is possible to be without being an anti-economist. But even he doesn't steer clear of anti-economics *by* being too pessimistic about markets to be accommodated within E1–E4: Mirowski [2002] defends E1 (and might, for all he says about this, accept E2) but with the caveat that the markets in question are essentially historical, embedded in institutions, and structurally complex.

I will therefore now go on to analyze the relationship between economics and ideology in terms of the above set of anti-economist stances and economist's possible replies.

## 3 ECONOMIC THEORY AND THE NORMATIVE STATUS OF THE MARKET

As noted above, anti-economic criticism has generally been motivated by dislike or fear of the widening and deepening of markets, conjoined with the conviction that economics promotes such expansion. By expansion is generally meant: (1) relaxing regulations on production, distribution, or licensing requirements or eligibility, such that wider ranges of people are able to produce given goods or services for sale, and (2) relaxing regulations such that goods and services which could not formerly be legally traded for mutual gain, including monetary gain on at least one side, become available for such trade. Elimination of a state monopoly or group of exclusive licensees is an obvious instance of an expansion of type (1). Allowing people to subdivide land estates and sell off small parcels where formerly this was not permitted is an instance of (2). Elimination of legally protected craft guilds, and other labor market liberalizations, are simultaneously instances of both (1) and (2), since anyone who deems their skill at the craft adequate to find demand at the reserve selling price may then enter the relevant labor market, and labor services of a kind which could not formerly be sold become marketable.

In this section, I focus on the extent to which economic theory has indeed promoted market expansion, and on the theoretical bases on which it has done so when it has done so. I will consider these under two general classes of motivating arguments: (I) arguments from static efficiency and (II) arguments from conditions promoting technical innovation (dynamic efficiency). No argument for policy measures such as market expansion can follow only from premises reporting scientific discoveries. In the case of arguments for market expansion from (I) and (II), the background normative premise is that welfare efficiency is *prima facie* desirable. We will consider the status of that premise in the context of ideology in the next section.

## *3.1 Markets and static efficiency*

There can be no serious question that modern political economy *began* by placing great weight on efficiency, conceived in terms of what we would now characterize as comparative statics. Furthermore, it did so in a way that took a strong policy norm for granted. Adam Smith and his immediate successors assumed that the task of the political economist was to pick out a class of general policy regimes in which a nation's stock and flow of wealth are optimized (at least, relative to other policy regimes explicitly considered, including most importantly the status quo). Then Smith thought that markets should be expanded in the specific sense of eliminating tariffs for the equally specific purpose of improving efficiency by reducing the opportunities of what we would now call rent-seekers: inefficient producers and *rentiers* whose levels of profit depend on the existence of the market restrictions created by tariffs, and which accrue to them at the direct expense of greater achievable national wealth. Similar remarks about motivation apply to Ricardo.

Thus classical political economy before Marx was closely associated with goals (i) and (ii) as imputed by anti-economists. So were Smith and Ricardo advocates of an ideology? It would be premature to try to answer this question directly at this point — a verdict on whether or where ideology is to be found in economics is intended to emerge dialectically over the whole course of the paper. For now, let us just begin to sneak up on an answer. As Backhouse [2002, p. 184] points out, Smith in *The Wealth of Nations* was engaged in what we would now call welfare economics. In so doing, he produced the first analysis as such of the modern notion of comparative-static market-wide efficiency. It would be obtuse to try to make much argumentative weight against claims that he was an ideologue (to some extent) from the fact that he produced no *explicit* novel conception of justice by which to coordinate support for policy reform. He certainly *did* hope to contribute to coordination of policy reform, and regardless of what is or isn't explicit, he *implicitly* offered a conception of justice that conflicted directly with the prevailing, loosely Aristotelian, idea according to which there is natural justice in some people having special, purely positional, entitlements. So our ultimate verdict on ideology in economics will have to be consistent with their being at least an *incipient* ideology in Smith.

As many commentators have observed over the years — but especially recently (see [Rothschild, 2002]) — Smith's later appropriation as an ideological icon to be invoked specifically against the left typically involves historical ignorance. Smith's two most straightforward policy prescriptions, removal of tariffs and provision of universal state-sponsored education, were motivated by his concern to undermine established interests who owed their advantages merely to their being established. To this extent Smith's incipient ideology tends to the left. On the other hand, the later use of Smith against the left was not *merely* a case of expropriation.[23] Smith's great theme so far as the means to his favored ends was concerned was division of labor. Marx, of course, later equated this with alienation. *If* emancipating people from the division of labor is taken to lie at the core of left ideology, Smith cannot be a theorist of the left, and left ideology will tend to cast Smith's political economy as embodying a rival vision. This issue will be revisited near the end of the present essay.

As Muller [2002] shows, the ideal ideological foil for Smith, insofar as Smith is interpreted as advancing an ideology, comes from the right rather than the left. This foil is his contemporary Justus Möser. Möser, like Marx, objected to the division of labor, but on conservative rather than Marx's emancipatory grounds. He feared and called for resistance to all market expansion *because* he agreed that markets increase productive efficiency and material well-being. They thereby strongly tempt people to embrace the division of labor and in doing so to abandon the traditional social roles that are taken by Möser to appropriately define their whole beings in indissoluble relationships to their communities. Smith is often regarded as the economist's economist. On similar grounds, Möser is the anti-economist's anti-economist, since he doesn't merely oppose what he takes economics to be *despite* his believing that it achieves goals (i) through (iii); he opposes it *because* he thinks it achieves these goals, including promotion of democracy. Expansion of the market, he fears, will enable people to consume 'unnecessary' luxuries such as "leather gloves, wool stockings, metal buttons, mirrors, cotton caps, knives and needles" [Muller, 2002, p. 98]. It will allow for the funding of improved roads that will in turn allow traveling salesmen to get more easily and widely about (*ibid*, p. 97). A contemporary communitarian might be amazed to find that Möser opposes even weekly *local* markets *because* "they would draw women and children away from the 'bourgeois tranquility' ... of the home and into the marketplace, where

[23]Burke associated himself closely with Smith's ideas; but one might argue that Burke's conservatism was in spite of this and in tension with it, and that Burke was thus the first right advocate who expropriated Smith.

they would chat and waste money on snacks and pleasantries" (*ibid*, p. 99). Going beyond Smith in imagining what market expansion might achieve, Möser *worried* that poverty might be eradicated, in which case the virtue of the rich could no longer be aroused and activated by the suffering of the poor.

The degree to which these opinions and their justifications make a contemporary reader boggle suggests that, if economics is in part an ideology, it has successfully annihilated its *complete* opposition, at least from the right. Möser's is almost the only sophisticated written expression one can find of stance-5 anti-economics that doesn't concentrate critical attention on goal (iv). It is slightly poignant that this voice is heard at the very dawn of modern economics, and then never again.

The reason one must find a figure like Möser to present a clean ideological contrast to Smith is that the latter's advocacy of market expansion is tightly restricted by contemporary libertarian standards. And it is also for this reason that Smith's enlistment into more contemporary ideological conflicts has usually involved misrepresentation by both right and left. Ideologues egregiously disregard his writings in attributing to him the conviction that *unlimited* market expansion is normatively ideal. (For example, [Polanyi, 1944] implies such an attribution, though he is sly about it, produces no quotations which, if read in context, would support his insinuation, and ignores the copious counter-evidence in Smith's writings.) Smith famously thought that the invisible hand was superior to sympathetic intentions in allocating *some* kinds of goods — in particular those of the "butcher, brewer and baker" whose "self-love" leads them to contribute their services more reliably than would their benevolence [Smith, 1970/1776, 119]. However, there is no textual or biographical evidence, and much against it, for the claim that he thought this principle applied outside of a comparatively narrow sphere of material goods and quotidian services. This claim first appears in anti-economist tracts, then associated itself with the popular image of Smith as the 'father of capitalism' and *then* found its way into casual statements by some later economists who, one must infer, had never read past the first few pages of *The Wealth of Nations*.[24] By this mechanism a legend was invested with economists' authority and amplified.

Someone determined to construct a more ideologically provocative Smith might argue that the expansion of markets as Smith favored it, once embarked upon, is bound of its own natural accord to continue unchecked to embrace all social spheres, at least until people learn this consequence and a backlash occurs. (This is certainly what Polanyi maintains, though he asserts it rather than presents evidence for it.) If it were an economist rather than an anti-economist who advanced

[24]Economic *theorists* during the highest phase of ahistoricism in economics, roughly 1950–1973, were more likely to be unread in the disciplinary classics than contemporary theorists. I do not know whether the same point applies to economic practitioners who consult theory only as needed for practical purposes. On the one hand, practitioners are likely to be influenced to some extent by what their professors mentioned while they were in school, so things might have recently improved; on the other hand, the extent to which an economic practitioner can be atheoretical has progressively grown as a consequence of more efficiently refined employment markets for economists and new analytical technology that builds theoretical mechanisms into software designs and allows economists to forget about them. The second force might have overwhelmed the opposite-trending first force over the past few decades.

such an argument, and without the caveat about the backlash, this would be a way of trying to achieve goal (iv). But there is no sustainable evidence for the assertion that Smith wittingly promoted it.

Indeed, the idea that economics promotes goal (iv) on the basis of claims that markets are necessarily optimally efficient, though deployed with persistent rhetorical relish by anti-economists,[25] is almost grotesquely mistaken in light of the actual relationship between treatments of market efficiency and attitudes to policy in most of the history of the discipline. Walras of course generalized from the limited cases considered by Smith to conceptualize the perfectly competitive market, and argued that this represented a limiting case of static efficiency. However, as Backhouse [2002, p. 270] observes, citing standard evidence, none of the great early neoclassical economists, including Walras, were supporters of *laissez-faire* policy. Walras recognized that perfect competition is a logical/analytic rather than a normative ideal for actual markets, both because perfectly competitive markets cannot arise, and because it is unclear how to think evaluatively of a hypothetical institutional scenario in which there are market-determined rates of interest and private firms set prices, but there is no cost of capital and all profits converge to zero.

Certainly, there was an important period, following Walras's argument that perfect competition implies welfare maximization, when prevailing opinion among economists took perfectly competitive equilibrium to be a regulative ideal for *planners*.[26] The idea here was straightforward: if perfect-competition analysis identifies an economy's welfare frontier, and if welfare efficiency increases with approximation to perfectly competitive general equilibrium, then the planner can keep re-allocating inputs so as to get, by trial and error, as close as possible to the frontier. Note that this program required an assumption utterly incompatible with goal (iv) as so often imputed to economists by anti-economists. If markets are, in addition to being welfare-efficient, also natural, then any role for a planner is otiose at best and more likely to delay or impede achievement of the ideal equilibrium. The rationale for the view that planning is more likely than the market to carry an economy to its welfare frontier was, though already clear enough to a majority of economists in the 1930s and 1940s, given a significant boost by Samuelson's [1954] theory of pure public goods as fundamental market failures. This closely followed the Arrow-Debreu welfare theorems of 1951. These are often celebrated as the proper demonstration of Smith's inductive conviction about markets, though scholarly commentators generally recognize that it is really Walras who is vindicated. However, for the reason just indicated, Arrow-Debreu represented the high-tide achievement for welfare economics based on central planning. Perfect-competition economics as practiced was the *antithesis* of popularly so-called 'free market economics'.

[25]Dupré [2001, pp. 120–122] strongly suggests this common line without ever quite putting it directly. He is careful, though, to dissociate Smith from it.

[26]Backhouse [2002, pp. 279–282] provides an elegant summary.

The program for planning economies to welfare optima fell on hard times soon after this greatest moment. Standard explanations emphasize one or both of two routes to trouble. Most economists give priority to the Lipsey-Lancaster theory [1956] of the second-best, which shows that one cannot infer from an allocation's getting closer to the perfectly competitive equilibrium that the allocation in question is necessarily increasing in efficiency.[27] It is testimony to the depth of popular confusion in this area that one easily finds instances in public affairs journalism of this result being invoked as a "disappointment" for "free marketers" [Allen, 2004]. If anything, given the rationale for central planning that the result severely complicated, it is the reverse. Related problems for welfare economics based on planning stemmed from the fact that its most complete possible formulation occurs in the context of Arrow-Debreu general equilibrium theory, the policy relevance of which was called into question by the so-called excess demand literature of the 1970s.[28] If, in consequence of these developments, contemporary economists devote less attention to central planning than left anti-economists think they would were they not ideologues, then it must be emphasized that this part of the history of theory has absolutely nothing to do with goal (iv). Perfect competition was *never* thought by most economists to shed interesting light on the probable consequences of real (let alone 'natural') markets, and was eventually found not to shed policy-relevant light on the consequences of planned economies either.

To make her case in this area look at all plausible without introducing outright confusion, the anti-economist must emphasize the second trend in the literature that helped to discredit policy-focused economics built around planning. This builds on the famous Coase theorem [1960], according to which, in a world of zero transaction costs, private bargaining in isolated bargaining games will produce efficient allocations relative to those games alone regardless of legal allocations of rights. This idea probably comes as close to a (relatively[29]) rigorous articulation of goal (iv) as one finds in economics. I say an 'aspect' because it directly implies nothing about the social optimality of markets: the conjunction of a set of efficient solutions to isolated bargaining games is not necessarily equivalent to any social welfare optimum as this has been (variously) understood in economics if agents can link these games by forming coalitions (as, of course, they typically can and do). However, the Coase theorem plausibly captures the claim at the heart of goal (iv), which is that the workings of markets cannot be suppressed in a *principled* way by ordinances. (Of course they can be distorted in unprincipled ways by uses of physical force.) This does not show that goal (iv) is actually achieved by the Coase theorem. There is, after all, nothing 'natural' about zero transaction costs. Furthermore, the theorem has no applicability to real bargaining outcomes or contracts in the presence of asymmetries of information; but these are ubiquitous in 'natural' economies ([Stiglitz, 1996] and elsewhere).

[27]Though see Foster and Sonnenschein [1970].

[28]Sonnenschein [1972; 1973], Mantel [1974; 1976], Debreu [1974].

[29]The Coase theorem isn't literally a theorem, since it isn't proven from formal axioms.

Of course, the anti-economist is not surprised that goal (iv) isn't achieved; she insists that aiming at it constitutes ideology because it is unachievable. The relevant question in the present context is whether it is reasonable to attribute the goal to mainstream economics. The best case the anti-economist can make out for doing so requires her to identify mainstream economics with the so-called 'Chicago school,' to which Coase himself is a leading contributor. Certainly, some University of Chicago economists, notably George Stigler, Milton Friedman and Gary Becker, have been highly visible in economics since World War II, and (at least in Friedman's case) exercised influence on macroeconomic policy. One must concede that, at least in the cases of Stigler and Friedman, it is often (but far from always) difficult to cleanly disentangle scientific motives from political ones in their work as economists. Note that Friedman has consistently championed the idea that 'positive' and 'normative' economics are distinct but legitimate parts of economics; so although he would deny the verdict that they cannot always be pried apart in application to his own work, he would acknowledge no reason to apologize for the kinds of polemical activities that anti-economists would call ideological. In the concluding section of this essay, I will go some distance toward granting him his case here, for reasons I haven't yet introduced. For the moment, however, what must be pointed out is that the Chicago school has been far less influential in economic *theory* than it has been in economic policy or (especially) on popular economic *discourse*.

Where theory is concerned, there have been two 'Chicago schools': a macroeconomic policy school led by Friedman and Stigler, and a school focused on applications of economics to law, whose proximate originator was Coase and which is given its classic expression by Posner [1998]. Underlying Chicago law and economics is a sophisticated microeconomic model of human behavior developed mainly by Becker (e.g., [1976]), to which Stigler has also contributed [Stigler and Becker, 1977]. Unification of the schools is thus instantiated biographically in Stigler.

How persuasively can an anti-economist try to maintain that Stigler is a representative leader of post-war economics? Liner [2001] reviews citations of journal articles by economists in microeconomics, macroeconomics and econometrics textbooks used in American graduate school courses in the 1996-97 academic year. This provides a more interesting measure of an economist's status than publication counting, since it assesses his or her relative weight in the reproduction of a new generation of economists. Among leading contemporaries of Stigler, Paul Samuelson by this measure has overwhelmingly stronger claim to be regarded as influential: he is still the fifth most-frequently cited economist, decades after the end of his period of peak activity, while Stigler is not among the listed top 50. (Friedman is $42^{nd}$, with fewer than half as many citations as Samuelson.) None of the *distinctive* Chicago School properties that an anti-economist would emphasize are true of Samuelson: on macroeconomic policy he has been broadly Keynesian, and in microeconomics he initiated focus on market failures.

Where Coase's and Becker's respective levels of influence on theory are concerned, in neither case has the direction of development of their ideas been that which an anti-economist would have predicted. Economic analysis of law in the broadly Coasian tradition is increasingly preoccupied with applications of game theory[30] and behavioral economics,[31] reflecting the growing recognition of the importance of information asymmetries and incomplete contracts. The contemporary figure who can make the most persuasive claim to have inherited Coase's mantle as the most influential theorist of law and economics, Cass Sunstein, is indeed at Chicago; but by no stretch can the anti-economist depict him as a promoter of ever less regulated markets. As for Becker, his greatest (and enormous) domain of influence is in applications of economic analysis to micro-level phenomena dominated by shadow prices rather than monetary prices, such as family dynamics, criminal behavior and deterrence, addiction and much else. But this area is dominated by the new behavioral economics which, while acknowledging historical precedence to Becker, now almost uniformly applies game theory rather than deriving propositions from assumptions of market efficiency [Camerer, 2003]. In the vast majority of behavioral models the lifetime-consistent agent who maximizes a global utility function across a network of linked implicit markets promoted in, *inter alia*, Stigler and Becker [1977] has been replaced by the meliorating agent of Herrnstein [1997], who struggles to avoid being exploited in markets due to his natural disposition for hyperbolic discounting and cyclical preferences. What saves this economic agent from being money pumped is a combination of the absence of many consistently rational agents to do the pumping, plus the limits on feasible informational efficiency [Cubitt and Sugden, 2001] that have become the hallmark of post- general equilibrium modeling throughout the profession.

At this point the anti-economist is down to one last source of hope for showing that economics is committed to goal (iv) on the basis of static efficiency considerations. This is a source identified by Dasgupta [2005]. He cites a number of critics, mainly philosophers,[32] who accuse contemporary development economics of being an "ethical desert". Now, development economics is plausibly the current part of the discipline that has inherited the burden dropped by analytic welfare economics when it hit the three walls of the second-best theorem and the excess demand results mentioned above, plus Arrow's impossibility theorem; that is, it is the part of economics most directly motivated by concern to improve the plight of the less well off. Why, despite the fact that, as Dasgupta says "it is a concern with ethics that has prompted many of us to study the phenomenon in the first place" (*ibid*, p. 270), might development economics be deficient in its attentiveness to ethics? The answer, according to the critics Dasgupta answers, is that it focuses on efficiency (under one conceptualization or another) to the exclusion of morality. Since it is obvious that contemporary development economics accords constant attention to roles that can be played by governments and public institutions, and not just or

[30]Baird, Gertner and Picker [1994].

[31]See Sunstein [2000].

[32]Specifically, among others: Bernard Williams, Hilary Putnam and Martha Nussbaum. Dasgupta is not exactly dredging up obscure and non-influential philosophers with whom to quarrel here.

even mainly to markets, the charge is relevant to the imputed goals of economics only in a roundabout way. Perhaps the reason economists think we should ignore considerations of ethics in favor of considerations of efficiency is that efficiency equilibria, whatever combination of free markets and active public policies we use to reach them, are naturally stable in a way that ethical orders are not. Thus, the critic alleges, economists think they are being practical in ignoring ethics; but this causes them to value only what markets can value and pay no attention to central dimensions of good living.—index development economics

Dasgupta roundly rejects this conclusion. Current policy packages studied in development economics are uniformly based on a strong ethical consensus among economists that poverty is an evil we should aim to eradicate, and on which large expenditure of resources is appropriate. This consensus may not have clear intellectual, as opposed to merely intuitive, foundations. However, as Dasgupta documents in detail, it is *because* it is so strong in its content that economists can leave questions of its ultimate justification to philosophers, and devote themselves to the (extraordinarily difficult) *factual* questions concerning which policy mixes promote development and make inroads against poverty. Anti-economists, as noted, routinely imagine that development economists are too preoccupied with monetary indicators of well being because they suppose that the only real value is that measured by markets. They often cite Sen [1999] to try to demonstrate that mainstream economists have a pinched view of the ends of development, which (Sen argues) they inherit from the history of welfare-economic theory. As Dasgupta observes, this history as presented by Sen is a caricature (*ibid*, p. 224). Development economists usually measure changes in well being by measuring changes in household consumption expenditure [Revallion, 1994]. This is for the simple reason that HCE has empirically proved to be the most reliable proxy for every one of Sen's touted development goals that anyone has any clear and practical protocol for comparatively measuring at all.[33] The overwhelming majority of policy work in development economics is closely and regularly connected to fieldwork at the micro level, with constant and multi-sourced feedback from the project level. The idea that its agents are ethically insensitive, and that this is attributable to a tradition in economic theory of modeling bloodless utility-maximization, is literally nonsense.

All of the plausible routes by which an economist might get from a normative commitment to static efficiency to either of goals (ii) or (iv) have now been reviewed. In none of these instances has the anti-economist's case for accusing economists of being devoted to market expansion because of an ideological commitment to static efficiency as a pre-eminent value been sustained. The best evidence that could be found for the contention is that classical political economy

[33]For an example of the pragmatic considerations that guide choices of proxies by development economists in the field, see [Bhorat *et al.*, 2001]. Any attempt to make these researchers out as relying on market-priced indicators rather than shadow-priced estimates of non-tradable goods because they are blind to non-market values would have to ignore what they actually say about the matter.

incorporates an incipient ideological commitment to reducing rent-seeking. Except to the extent that division of labor is associated with Marxist alienation — about which more will be said in the concluding section of the current essay — this is a left-trending rather than a right-trending motivation in its original incarnation in Smith. However, it is true that the use of economic theory to crusade against rent-seeking is today more typically conceived as right-trending, both by those who pursue it and by their critics. The founders of the public choice literature, Buchanan and Tullock [1962], and the prolific American economist and policy advocate Thomas Sowell, come to mind here.[34] The reason for the reversal in ideological polarity where anti-rent-seeking is concerned is obvious: the most pervasive rent-seeking in both Smith's time and ours involves exploitation of the power of the state, but whereas the state in Smith's time was regarded as mainly protecting status-quo interests, in the twentieth century it came to be widely regarded as an agent for extending democracy and for redistributing wealth *against* the market. (Ironically, in the present context, this is a legacy of the shift that found its first consistent expression in so-called classical welfare economics and was later promoted to near-dogma in economics for a few decades by Keynes.) Thus those who view economics as primarily or secondarily a weapon against rent-seeking are likely to also see it, to that extent, as furnishing arguments against state encroachments on the operations of the market.

While there is little room for doubt that Sowell has become an ideologue, if he wasn't already one at the beginning of his public career,[35] it is far from obvious that opposition to rent-seeking on grounds of efficiency should be regarded as ideological in the contemporary setting. Regardless of what they think about rent-seeking by public officials, almost every economist agrees that *one* leading source of large-scale rent-seeking is big business. Economists' opposition to such rent-seeking is often motivated explicitly on behalf of less powerful members of society. Thus, to cite just one of thousands of possible examples, Bhagwati [2004, p. 127] objects to U.S. tariffs on clothing imports because, *inter alia*, these mainly apply to cheaper products that wealthier Americans don't consume. Opposition to rent-seeking in eighteenth- and nineteenth century Britain was plausibly ideological (in part) because it coordinated political action across a suite of attitudes that are reasonably well captured by the left-right ideological spectrum. Similar remarks do not seem justified in application to present concerns. Socially significant rents are today both defended and attacked from all over the political spectrum. In the United States, economists' expressed concerns about rents expropriated by labor unions are almost sure to be regarded as right advocacy; whereas in South Africa

[34]It is noteworthy in this regard that Sowell associates himself with the classical rather than the neoclassical tradition in economic theory [Sowell, 1977].

[35]Over the years, Sowell has increasingly shown strong support for American conservative positions that have nothing to do with defense of markets or limitations on rent-seeking, such as opposition to women's reproductive rights and gay marriage. I do not know whether Sowell always maintained these anti-libertarian views, or simply had less occasion to publicly expound them when he was regarded mainly as an expert in economics rather than as an all-purpose policy celebrity.

Nicoli Nattrass, a leading public economist who explicitly associates herself with the ideological left, criticizes union rent-seeking on grounds that it contributes to the immiseration of the unemployed.[36] (Nattrass also criticizes South African business for concentrating on capital-intensive rather than labor-intensive investment. Whatever the disputed economic rationale for this is, it does *not* seem to be an instance of rent-seeking). Arguably, then, where contemporary economists continue to uphold static efficiency as a policy norm, this is an instance in which they have *resisted* shifts of ideological motivation rather than contributed to them.

Economists' study and promotion of static efficiency thus lends provisional support to response E1 to the anti-economist who charges that economics is ideology. I do not think this should deeply trouble the anti-economist, because this ground is not the best one on which she can pursue her case (at least, since Möser's time). I have dealt with it at some length, however, because it has been, historically, the anti-economist's most frequently chosen battlefield. Anti-economists have kept returning to it, I suggest, because they often simply do not know about or understand the crucial technical developments in the history of welfare economics on which the issue turns. (Readers who find this charge implausible are referred to Coleman [2002, pp. 226–228].) Better ammunition for the allegation that economics is ideology comes to hand when we consider economists' normative appeals to dynamic efficiency.

## *3.2 Markets and dynamic efficiency*

Left anti-economists get good promotional traction whenever they can associate mainstream economics with the obviously ideological Thatcher government of the UK and the Reagan/first Bush administration in America.[37] Thus they have appreciated Thatcher's several invocations of F.A. Hayek as the intellectual inspiration behind her program, and the award of the Medal of Freedom to Hayek by Bush. It is uncomfortable for them that Hayek was for several decades written out of the mainstream history of recent economic theory by professional economists. However, this seems to be changing: in his emphasis on the importance of complexity in economics, his rejection of the strong ahistoricism and anti-institutionalism that characterized economics in the three postwar decades, and his pioneering efforts to link economics with cognitive science,[38] Hayek anticipated *all* of the main winds of change now blowing most strongly in economic theory. The recent intellectual biography by Caldwell [2004] helps to remind economists of this, and — a development of mixed portent for anti-economists — dissociates Hayek's thought to some extent from the ideologized stereotype that appealed to Thatcher and her circle.

[36]See Nattrass and Seekings [2004] and other work.

[37]If this administration was often more rhetorically than actively ideological, the situation seems to have been reversed in the government of the second President Bush. Few economists approved of the policies of the latter.

[38]I refer to Hayek [1952], which he intended to be relevant to his work in social science and which he indeed subsequently connected with it.

I have led off with Hayek here because he is obviously the pre-eminent theorist of the normative implications of free-market dynamics. Many readers will also simply take it as given that he was an ideologue. To the extent, then, that he ultimately wins his battle against Keynes and others to be regarded as the most profound economic theorist of the twentieth century — which is a serious possibility — perhaps the ideology of economics turns out to be the ideology of Hayek.

Hayek's first major idea, that the market is an irreplaceable transmitter of information about demand and prices, was first elaborated as a criticism of socialism by his mentor von Mises.[39] The soundness of the basic point is indicated by the fact that it led Lange and other leading socialists among economists to propound market socialism, the idea that the market as a register of demand and a price-setting mechanism could be dissociated from the wage labor system in which the capitalist and the worker are different people. This idea has had long legs, having been taken further by later generations of economists (e.g., [Bowles and Gintis, 1998]) when to the Austrian critique of planning was added the problems for perfectly competitive equilibrium as benchmark indicator discussed above.[40]

Hayek's position in the famous 'socialist calculation controversy' was distinctive. The fundamental problem with planning, he stressed, is not merely that the planner could not plausibly process all the information about demand she would need in order to allocate capital and other inputs. (Someone might imagine that this part of the problem merely awaited the development of contemporary computing technology.) Rather, the problem is that planning differs from the market in having no naturally efficient mechanism for *creating* new sites of economic activity — new products, new forms of productive organization, new consumption lifestyles. The crucial form of efficiency characteristic of markets, according to Hayek, is *dynamic*; and this dynamicism arises precisely in the aggregate consequences of market activity being spontaneous, and not constrained within the limitations of intentional human imagination.[41]

A number of points are important here, both as regards the normative and the positive aspects of this conception of Hayek's, which in various ways he spent his entire career promoting. Let us begin with the normative. First, it integrates the goals (i)–(iv) that anti-economists impute to economics to an extent that standard neoclassical thought does not approach. Concerning goal (i), it suggests that markets can be made to function best *with respect to their tendency to dynamically transform the economy*, to the extent that they are left alone after being furnished

[39]According to Backhouse [2002], the point originated with Gustav Cassel. Curiously, Caldwell [2004], who devotes substantial attention to Hayek's intellectual precursors, doesn't mention this. But then Cassel's role in the network of attribution tends to be generally curious, partly because he himself was extraordinarily stingy with citations.

[40]Moral philosophers who pay attention to economics have also found it attractive. See [Buchanan, 1985].

[41]'Intentional' is used here in the philosopher's sense rather than the everyday sense. Philosophical intentionality incorporates the everyday idea of deliberateness, but grounds it in something more basic, viz., the idea of explicit representation of a thought's or idea's full content. It services Hayek's thought better than the everyday notion.

with the basic legal foundations that Hayek, like Hobbes and Smith before him, recognized they required. Goal (iv) takes on a new and subtler meaning in Hayek's conception than in classicism or neoclassicism because in Hayek's treatment 'natural' tends to be assimilated to 'spontaneous' and contrasted with 'deliberately constructed'. Goals (ii) and (iii), at least with respect to the libertarian aspect of (iii), become not two separate goals but one unified one. This is because liberty, whatever intrinsic value one might or might not believe it to have (and Hayek clearly took it to have a good deal[42]), emerges as a necessary condition for the individual experimentation that, according to Hayek, is the basis for the diversity on which cultural and market selection operate to yield the welfare benefits of unplanned order. Democracy is defended on similar grounds, though not held to be as effective as liberty for spontaneous order, and very far from sufficient for it [Hayek, 1944, pp. 68–79; 1960, pp. 104–117]. But free markets are argued to be necessary to democracy, since planning undermines it by requiring all to converge on a synoptic view, Finally, productive efficiency comes to mean something special too: not merely use of resources with minimal opportunity costs, as in the neoclassical framework, but fruitfulness of generation. Thus goals (i)–(iv) effectively become a single interlocked package — just as the anti-economist alleges they are for economics in general.

Insofar as the great property of the market for Hayek is its generative creativity, it is hardly surprising that he rejects perfectly competitive equilibrium as a regulative ideal. A market at equilibrium would for Hayek be a *dead* market, incapable of producing its fundamental good. With this conviction Hayek cut himself off from the remaining part of the professional economics of the postwar period from which he had not already alienated himself when he declined to follow Keynes. Thus the anti-economist who wishes to credit (or discredit) Hayek with articulating the essential ideology of economics must suppose that what passed for mainstream economics wandered seriously off its normal course for at least forty or fifty years after the mid-1930s. I intend no argument by *reductio* in saying this, for it would at least not be an *outrageous* contention. Robbins, who embodied the institutional mainstream for a number if years, was Hayek's close ally until Keynes's *General Theory* along with the influence of Hicks won him over to the other side; and John Bates Clark issued pragmatist denunciations of the significance of the Walrasian general equilibrium project in the early twentieth century that are now echoed by methodological crusaders for behavioral economics such as Bowles and Camerer. In the previous section I presented grounds for doubting that anti-economists can plausibly spin the Chicago School leaders as representative economic theorists. In light of current trends, they may have a more hopeful case where Hayek is concerned.

[42]Hayek not infrequently asserts that liberty is an end in itself. See, for example p. 78 of *The Road to Serfdom* [Hayek, 1944], where he endorses Lord Acton's favorable contrast of liberty with democracy in this regard. However, in the most coherent and thorough statement of his political philosophy, Hayek [1960] argues for liberty based on premises concerning the conditions for spontaneous order, rather than assuming it as a primitive good.

To what extent is there objective evidence for Hayek's leading positive claims? His theory of what we would now, after several decades of systems theory, call 'distributed control', has been strongly vindicated in at least one of the domains to which Hayek himself argued for its application, behavioral/cognitive science. Across the many attempts to create environmentally responsive automated control systems, in a wide variety of design settings with different technologies, central decision bottlenecks have repeatedly proven inferior to models that spread control throughout information-processing architectures and allow specialist units with limited access to global perspectives or goals to exert temporarily exaggerated influence before being usurped by others as contingencies evolve. Selfridge's [1959] 'Pandemonium' model — developed seven years after Hayek's *Sensory Order* – was the pioneering design of this type. It has since spawned a host of more sophisticated successors in artificial intelligence, robotics, and operations management [Edelman, 1995; Kelso, 1995; Brooks, 1999; Kennedy and Eberhart, 2001]. By contrast, systems that must refer all or most decisions to fixed command units manipulating stacks of rules have generally proven brittle — that is, incapable of or too slow to respond to unpredictable shifts in environmental parameters and unable to sustain the degree of minor damage necessary for powerful learning by trial and error. Early AI and other control systems of this sort can accurately and evocatively be described as cybernetic Soviet Unions. This insight has been extensively applied in a new and increasingly influential style of economics associated most strongly with the Santa Fe Institute [Anderson *et al.*, 1988, Arthur *et al.*, 1997; Albin, 1998; Blume and Durlauf, 2005].

These developments indeed testify to the acuity of Hayek's conceptual insight. They constitute, I suggest, the strongest basis in the intellectual and historical record for thinking that groups of agents who want to prevent their productive capacities from degenerating will, if they are wise, use markets as computers. Note, however, that this recommendation falls well short of the full reach of Hayek's program in political economy. Since the individual agents in most successful distributed control models are deterministic units with no scope for individual creativity whatsoever, the argument from computational capacity provides no basis for Hayek's contention that liberty is essential for a productive market. It *is* important in distributed-control architectures that the robotic agents not be completely enslaved to a preconceived *top-down* plan, but this is a far more limited kind of liberty than the classical notion to which Hayek aspired. To see this, we may note that an Orwellian state might achieve Hayekian computational success by running a distributed-control simulation of its economy and directing assets about — including laborers — exactly as the simulation suggested. Such a state would indeed have to be willing to allow at least *part* of its productive economy to be unpredictable. However, it seems there would be nothing to preclude it from using non-invested portions of surplus from this economy to maintain unproductive infrastructure that had merely oppressive functions connected with preserving oligarchs in power. After all, Hayek's argument cannot possibly establish the fantastic result that *any* drag on the market by the state must cripple it, since it is precisely one of the strengths of distributed-control systems that they are *not* brittle in this way. Ironically, Hayek's political program is undermined by the very fact that the market on his dynamic conception *escapes* being subject to a counterpart of the theory of the second-best. This leaves no basis for the contention that 'Stalinism with a good Santa Fe model' would be too inefficient to perpetuate itself.

The extent to which Hayek over-reached in trying to fuse goals (i)–(iv) in promotion of market expansion is further suggested by the example of his more pessimistic compatriot Schumpeter. In the latter's great [1950] work on the relationship between economics and politics, he provides sustained argument for the claim that 'capitalism' — in which he includes relatively unregulated markets as partly constitutive, but follows Marxists in giving more weight to private control of returns from production — is productively superior to socialism as a matter of fact, *given a certain set of cultural habits and expectations.* In particular, Schumpeter argues that capitalist economies can be expected to out-produce socialist ones with equivalent starting endowments only if people believe their activities have some possibility of creating personal and family financial empires. Popular democracy, according to him, tends to undermine this expectation by replacing unregulated competition amongst families with bureaucratized corporate structures that break the direct connection between innovative business activity and personal returns. Because, for Schumpeter, what retards the creativity of the market is bureaucratization, and because corporate bureaucracies and public bureaucracies are much the same from this point of view, it is possible for socialism to evolve from capitalism incrementally and without legal or political discontinuities. Thus, he explicitly argues, socialism, as the replacement of market-focused institutions by planning-driven ones, need involve no threat to liberty, except the highly particular liberty of swashbuckling in business that only a tiny (though immensely influential) fraction of people ever enjoyed anyway.

Like Hayek, Schumpeter insists that perfect competition modeling is irrelevant to evaluating the relative productive capacities of actual economies.[43] His reasons for this view are also similar to Hayek's: the relevant sort of efficiency to be considered in real economies is dynamic, not static, and the special property that explains the productive superiority of classical markets over planned production infrastructure is the creativity of the former. However, whereas Hayek disconnects this creativity from the intentions even of individuals — and thereby ironically undermines his own contention that unregulated markets and political liberty are necessarily mutually reinforcing — Schumpeter locates the source of creativity in the intentional motivations of entrepreneurs. Since for him the origins of superior

[43] Anticipating game-theoretic reasoning about entry deterrence, he argues that even monopolies can be highly efficient. Nevertheless, "[P]erfect competition is not only impossible but inferior, and has no title to being set up as a model of ideal efficiency. It is hence a mistake to base the theory of government regulation of industry on the principle that big business should be made to work as the respective industry would work on perfect competition. And socialists should rely for their criticisms on the virtues of a socialist economy rather than on those of the competitive model" [Schumpeter, 1950, p. 106].

market productivity, during the historical epoch in which it is superior, are *cultural*, achievement of goal (ii) as imputed to economists by anti-economists cannot be accomplished by *economics*; it instead lies in the provinces of sociology and psychology. And obviously, in light of what we observed above, Schumpeter cannot assign either of the other aspects of goal (iii) to economics. Finally, Schumpeter is as clear a case as one could find of an economist favorably disposed to market expansion who denies goal (iv); far from being natural, organization of society around market-focused institutions is according him historically peculiar, not to be expected to persist insofar as it arises, and not achievable in the long run even if most people in a democracy could be persuaded to endorse it. "[W]hether favorable or unfavorable, value judgments about capitalist performance are of little interest," he announces (*ibid*, p. 129). "For mankind is not free to choose. This is not only because the mass of people are not in a position to compare alternatives rationally and always accept what they are being told. There is a much deeper reason for it. Things economic and social move by their own momentum and the ensuing situations compel individuals and groups to behave in certain ways whatever they may wish to do — not indeed by destroying their freedom of choice but by shaping the choosing mentalities and by narrowing the list of possibilities from which to choose. If this is the quintessence of Marxism then we have all of us got to be Marxists."

Review of the two great political economists who most emphasized dynamic efficiency, both positively and normatively, thus leads to the following conclusions. First, Schumpeter thought goal (ii) was defensible as a description of a historical period, but since he took economics to be an ahistorical science, he concluded that economics, properly speaking, could aim only at goal (i). But Schumpeter has no distinctive reason for thinking that economics must be ahistorical; here he was merely blinded by the near-consensus among methodologists and positivist philosophers who were his contemporaries. Furthermore, he thought it demonstrable that market-focused institutions are conducive to liberty (though he also thought, in disagreement with Hayek, that socialism, provided it arose from capitalism without interruption of legal continuity, need not threaten liberty). Thus although the 'official' Schumpetarian response to the anti-economist is E1, the rationally reconstructed response, at which we arrive by jettisoning unmotivated positivism, is E3.

Hayek is the anti-economist's economist, because he advocated an economics aimed at goals (i)–(iv). However, he is useful to the ultimate purpose of the anti-economist only to the extent that he can reasonably be found to be representative of economists in this respect. Obviously he is not representative of *historical* economists in his advocacy of goals (ii) and (especially) the libertarian aspect of goal (iii); and in maintaining the other aspect of goal (iii) he parts company even with Schumpeter, let alone with figures like Samuelson. But in light of his possible posthumous triumph as a methodologist, might he *turn out to be* representative? After all, Hayek's polemical books are more prescient in light of the experiences of the past few decades, both economic and political, than Schumpeter's comparable major work. Perhaps we will come to read Keynes, Hicks, Samuelson, Stiglitz and even Schumpeter as having made valuable contributions to goal (i), and as having been confused about goals (ii)–(iv); then we could go back and read what I called the 'incipient ideology' of the classical political economists as the anticipation of full Hayekian economics — which will then turn out to be either ideology or a basis for sound economic science with normative implications depending on whether Hayek's own unsuccessful defenses of goals (iii) and (iv) can be rescued. This possibility sets the stage for the concluding section of the essay.

## 4 NON-IDEOLOGICAL ECONOMICS

Let me open it by reminding the reader of a point made at the outset. The explicit question addressed here is whether economics is necessarily ideological.[44] This is asked in the Cartesian spirit, where doubt is entertained for methodological purposes rather than sincerely, since I take it that the answer is obviously 'no'. What is at stake in addressing the explicit question is a more serious underlying one: how, in detail, should economists most consistently reply to the charge that they are ideologues, and what do we learn about both economics and ideology by reflecting on this answer?

Most economists do not think they are promoting ideology. This in itself cuts little ice with critics because most economists never consider the issue at all, and blindness to ideological pressures is a characteristic consequence of ideology, according to at least those anti-economists influenced by Marxism. However, the experts who nurture and develop the theory of comparative static efficiency to which most unreflective economists defer also don't think they are promoting ideology, and I have argued that they are correct in this belief, both logically and historically. Here Milton Friedman [1953] would have us believe the matter ends: the theorists construct, and the practitioners apply, positive economics, which consists in building normatively neutral models. When they then go on to offer policy advice, this will of course be normative, and might or might not be influenced by ideology from case to case.

Few will now agree that the matter can be so simple. This is partly for philosophical reasons related to the famous 'failure of positivism'.[45] But, more importantly, it is because of changes in the beliefs and practices of economists. When

[44]Philosophers at ease, please. I use 'necessarily' here in the everyday sense, as meaning 'more or less bound to be, given the sorts of things people want economics to do and the matters they pay economists to concern themselves with'. I don't mean literally logically or metaphysically necessary. I take it that the answer to the question understood in the second way would obviously be 'no', but that this is of little interest.

[45]While acknowledging that positivism in the sense of *logical* positivism failed, let me add that this failure was technical, not profound. In disciplines outside of philosophy (and even within some precincts of philosophy), what people imagine by 'the failure of positivism' is absurdly overblown and deeply ignorant. For an economist who has written nonsense on this, see Addleson [1997] (and see criticism by Ross [1998]). Michael Friedman [1999] is recommended as an antidote. For implications of the point in the philosophy of economics, see Ross [2005].

Friedman wrote his 'Methodology of Positive Economics' it was plausible to suppose that economic analysis had itself established as *facts* that if 'market' is interpreted institutionally then goal (ii) is foolish, while if 'market' is interpreted purely technically then goal (ii) had (just) been achieved by Debreu and Arrow. It was then natural to insist on the technical reading, in which case goals (iii) and (iv) must immediately fall outside the scope of the positive economist's domain of comment. This left all of the reflections of Hayek and Schumpeter that are relevant to the evaluation of markets lying outside the boundaries of professional inquiry.

Few contemporary economists, including those who strongly disagree with one or both of them, would now consent to locking Hayek and Schumpeter out of the house. The reasons for this change are, once again, not philosophical, but rooted in the experience of economists. The majority of contemporary economists *do* in fact endorse goal (ii), now interpreted as a claim about real institutional markets, imputed to them by anti-economists.[46] The arguments for market expansion that now find favor with them are broadly Hayekian. In addition, Schumpeter's arguments for (ii) as holding under some historical conditions continue to appear sound, while the cultural considerations that led him to doubt their continuing institutional relevance seem overblown[47] — capitalists can be well motivated by more than the thrill of empire-building, which governments in any case have not generally proscribed as he forecast.

The proportion of economists who embrace goal (iii) is also far from trivial. Most likely take it as vindicated up to a point (different points in different cases, of course) because they think there is inductive evidence for the *fact* that relatively unregulated markets are favorable for liberty [Friedman, 2005]. (Some make this relationship tautologous, but then it is uninteresting.) Most of them will indicate much murkier evidence for a therefore more tentatively entertained *possible fact* that markets are good for democracy [Barro, 1997; Przeworski *et al.*, 2000]. They can point out that their normative interest in these putative possible facts is hardly parochial; the vast majority of contemporary people think that liberty is good to the extent that we don't have to — as yet another matter of fact — trade it off for other goods, and that democracy is either primitively good or almost primitively good. As for goal (iv), an opinion on it really must be a philosophical opinion, but most economists don't arrive at it philosophically; they are, like other scientists, turned into instinctive realists by their sheer familiarity with their domain as a zone of regularities that don't seem subject to voluntary manipulation. Where economists have been ambivalent about (iv), the main influence has been Milton Friedman's widely taught but philosophically muddled instrumentalism[48]

[46]Note that the words 'free' or 'unregulated' are not inserted in front of 'markets' in this statement. My claim here is intended to apply even to the most prominent current advocate of strong public-sector management of national and international capital, Stiglitz.

[47]As Muller [2002] stresses, this part of Schumpeter's argument was partly for ironic effect to begin with, part of his tactic for insinuating his argument into an ideologically hostile climate.

[48]As Mäki [1986; 1992] shows, Friedman advertises his position as instrumentalism when it is in fact a variety of common-sense *realism*. But, in my experience, most economists remember and

about models and theories. However, the increasing integration of economics with neighboring sciences through behavioral economics, and the emphasis in behavioral economics on grounding preference in cognitive and neural mechanisms, may be expected to erode this peculiar basis for irrealism.

When economists present evidence for claims about relationships between market institutions, on the one hand, and welfare, liberty and democracy on the other, the critic who insists that economics is ideology cannot *sincerely* dispute the matter by producing economic evidence for alternative claims. If she does so, she engages in economics and implicitly concedes that economics is not ideology. (She might *cynically* cite economic evidence, if she thinks that *sounding like* an economist is effective polemic.) What she is more likely to do if she understands what consistency demands is deny that 'welfare' or 'liberty' or 'democracy' can be given interpretations independent of ideology. Economists can respond to this in one of two ways. They can, following Dasgupta [2005], point out that what they measure are proxies for welfare, liberty and democracy that remain proxies on *all* conceptions of these ideas taken seriously by competing schools of thought in moral and political philosophy; thus economists abstract from moral controversies without ceasing to be morally motivated. Alternatively, they can follow Binmore [1994; 1998] in using economic modeling technology to make explicit arguments for conceiving of over-arching social-political objectives in a particular way, thereby shifting the burden of argument back to the critic. Dasgupta's and Binmore's strategies have something important in common: both try to transcend what they take to be parochial philosophical opinions using analytical tools that, they can each argue, are in no way fashioned from the motivations of any ideology.

It is important here that neither Dasgupta nor Binmore echo Friedman's claim to be ethically disinterested until the moment when they write 'Policy applications' as a chapter heading. Dasgupta argues that the development economist is motivated by the conviction that poverty, in every possible non-esoteric sense, is a bane. This is held to be a pre-theoretical commitment, not the consequence of a philosophical argument. Binmore says only half-jokingly that his reason for having written two thick volumes in promotion of a logical path to greater egalitarianism is that his brain has been colonized by a justice meme that, like all memes, selfishly aims to replicate itself. Thus instead of denying that they are ideologues on grounds that they are, as positive economists, simply barometers for objective facts, Dasgupta and Binmore claim to rise above ideological factionalism by simply assuming and declaring some common-and-garden moral convictions as motivations.

This is, I suggest, the most effective response to the anti-economist. Except when literally engaged in nothing but calculations, economists should admit to endorsing (which is not quite the same thing as *promoting*, in the sense of providing *new* motivations for) ideology on *one* interpretation. That is: if the critic who charges that economics is ideology takes the stance of Möser and says that nothing in economic fact or argument shows or can show that she should *approve*

repeat the advertisement rather than the substance after reading Friedman in graduate school.

*of* welfare improvements or increased liberty or widened democracy, on *any* non-esoteric interpretation of these objectives, then her logic should be admitted to be sound. Almost all contemporary economists believe in what I called the 'implicit ideology' of Adam Smith, and would not go on being interested in economics if they ceased to believe in it. But — and here lies the relevance of the distinction between ideological endorsement and ideological promotion — so does a clear majority of citizens in every society where the very conversation about what is and is not ideological has political significance in the first place. Allowing oneself to be 'ideological' in this sense makes philosophers suspicious because it indeed treats some norms as outside of consideration without giving extra-historical arguments for doing so. But this is not the sense of 'ideological' that has mattered to anti-economists.

In light of the discipline's history and current applications, economics should be recognized as part of the ideology of modernity and liberal democracy. Acknowledging this is consistent with *denying* the main intended content of the anti-economist's accusation, from right or left. The concession admits, I contend, only the philosopher's point: Möser, Carlyle, Mussolini, Lenin, theocratic fundamentalists, Marx when he is dreaming of communist utopia instead of analyzing something, are all excluded from the economic argument for no *timelessly* sound reason. Lest my point here be thought banal – no one but someone wearing the philosophical attitude, after all, minds throwing Mussolini out of the conversation, and no one *should* mind sending Carlyle or Lenin straight out behind him — philosophers following Macintyre [1981] or Nussbaum [1986] might point out that we'll be compelled to include Aristotle on the list too. I agree. This is a consequence of — is in fact partly constitutive of — what is meant in calling economics intrinsically modern.

The left-right ideological spectrum sorts secular ideologies by reference to how much we should be prepared to pay, in terms of dismantled institutions and discarded social customs, for mixtures of mass welfare improvement, liberty and democracy. Every ideology positioned on the spectrum — socialism, welfarism, libertarianism (both 'right' and 'left'[49]) — is broadly liberal in that they all recognize general welfare optimization, liberty and democracy as *prima facie* goods, even if some very conservative and very radical positions would trade off a great deal of one or more of them. (Specific modern ideologies add to this mix distinctive *prima facie* goods not recognized as such by the others: socialism adds equality and welfarist conservatism adds traditional family and community structures.) Mainstream economics is intrinsically liberal and modern because at every point in its historical evolution its concerns and its analytical tools have been shaped by commitment to this same attitude.

[49]This distinction has limited importance in the context of current ideologies because 'left libertarianism' is still largely a sophisticated political philosophy [van Parijs, 1995] that hasn't yet spawned a fully-fledged ideology, if it ever will. However, there are populist 'basic income' movements in Latin America and South Africa that constitute a germ.

When one sets out to place a particular view on the left-right spectrum, one may confront one of two kinds of indeterminacy. *Moderate* indeterminacy arises because both specific modern ideologies *and* rigorous analyses differ on the extent to which, and the precise respects in which, the *prima facie* modernist goods require trade-offs among one another in the first place.[50] This is to say: there is not one unambiguous spectrum that is independent of the very ideologies we use the spectrum to sort. *Radical* indeterminacy arises with respect to positions that deny that the trio of modernist goals is even valuable. Because of radical indeterminacy, the spectrum is unhelpful for understanding ideologies not descended from the same enlightenment tradition that spawned political economy, for example fascism and theocratic fundamentalism.

Consider fascism as the illustrative example. Most of Mussolini's followers in the 1920s and 1930s paid lip service to mass welfare improvement, so they weren't completely consistent in their anti-modernity. But it made little sense to regard them as conservatives, since they proposed to *smash* most of the institutional and moral status quo as they found it. The Marxist insistence on regarding them as capitalists in desperate straits was literally ridiculous, and damaging to the sophistication of Marxism itself because it implied a shallow analysis of capitalism as being essentially a doctrine about legal property ownership. Since fascists proposed to subject all capital allocations to the imperatives of state power, their anti-capitalism cut closer to the roots than Marx's, who looked forward to autonomous proletarians allocating capital from the bottom up — communes are small businesses of sorts, but Leviathan is not like a business at all. Most people will agree that it makes little sense to ask whether Genghis Khan or Emperor Claudius were rightists or leftists. Must it then make sense to ask this of fascists merely because they were aware of the spectrum, framed some of their rhetoric in terms their opponents drew from it, and ultimately compromised, like all ideologues who come near to power, with these opponents? The regime that administered South African apartheid was basically fascist, and it indeed regarded none of the modernist goals as even *prima facie* goods. Thus one creates only confusion if one tries to understand it by placing it on the modernist ideological spectrum. Furthermore, this example illustrates the extent to which economic logic is essentially entangled with liberal modernism. The apartheid regime's democratic rhetoric fitted out for the Cold War was accompanied, at least before the regime became entirely corrupt, by anti-capitalist diatribes for the consumption of its core domestic constituency, Afrikaners who sought protection from twin market forces of black labor and English capital [Lowenberg, 1989; Kenney, 1997]. This rhetoric was translated into action: the main economic agenda of the apartheid state consisted in throttling the free labor market and imposing sweeping industrial and import-substitution policies that the avowedly socialist African National Congress dismantled as soon

[50]Binmore [1994; 1998] argues that belief in these trade-offs is *generally* a function of insufficient analysis. What he defends as 'whiggery' amounts to abandonment of the basis for ideological conflict *within* the modern liberal normative perspective. His case is highly persuasive, especially in conjunction with arguments due to van Parijs [1995].

as it took office. It is not necessary to regard the ANC as thereby having betrayed its socialist orientation.[51] The apartheid economic policies were motivated by anti-modernism, anti-liberalism and anti-economics; democratic socialism is inconsistent with all of these things.

The extent of moderate indeterminacy we confront in real politics advises us that now, more than two centuries after the left-right spectrum came into use, it would be helpful construct an ideological topology more complex than a two-dimensional line. But this can readily be done in a principled way. (See, e.g., [Binmore, 1998, pp. 503–505].) The *reason* it can be done is that modern ideologies are all *based on* sophisticated packages of integrated policy principles that identify specific status quo institutions and customs as targets of first-order reform, and others as targets of first-order strengthening and promotion. Pointing this out is not inconsistent with the idea that all ideologies are, by their nature, incomplete in their visions and confused in their appreciations of what they really imply. Ideologies are simplifications of reality, typically drastic ones, and governments that try to literally implement ideologies in policy can expect to fail. But specific ideological policies with respect to status quo institutions and customs are specifiable.

Let me be clear that I am *not* suggesting that ideologies are *merely* populist simplifications of political philosophies. Ideologies distinctively add to policy preferences aspirational models of ideal social and political citizenship that sound political philosophies do well to avoid. To illustrate this point, consider, for example, Bottomore's criticism of Schumpeter in his introduction to a 1975 edition of *Capitalism, Socialism and Democracy*:

> [T]here is no place in his analysis for a consideration of socialism as a class movement which seeks to abolish or attenuate class differences, and so achieve greater social equality and a liberation of the mass of the people from the constraints imposed by ruling classes. Schumpeter is concerned only with the economic reorganization of society, and when he asks whether socialism can work, what he means is whether it can be economically efficient and productive. This is a very narrow view of the socialist movement, and one which exaggerates its cultural diversity. There is, unmistakably, in modern socialism, despite the variety of its forms, a central preoccupation with the related issues of social equality and individual autonomy and self-determination. On the other side, few socialists have equated socialism with centralized public ownership and planning of the economy, or to put the matter in broader terms, have conceived socialism only as a mode of production. If socialism had to be characterized in a single phrase it would be more appropriate to describe it as a movement of human liberation, in which the transformation of the economic system is only one element,

[51] Of course, someone might still contend that the ANC government has been insincere about socialism on the basis of other evidence.

> and itself gives rise to diverse choices in the construction of a different type of system (pp. *xi–xii*).

Then, in a refrain typical of anti-economists, Bottomore maintains that Schumpeter has a pinched notion of democracy, wherein citizens are "consumers" of administrative services and policies. This, he claims, goes with a proto- public choice view of politics attributed to Weber, which is contrasted with a "classical view" — broadly, what Pettit [1997] has more recently theorized as 'Republicanism', which in a wider context is a variety of 'deliberative', 'participatory' or 'liberation' democracy.[52]

Almost all economists are skeptical about such ideas. For one thing, they will wonder what kinds of policies might shape plausible incentives in such a way as to implement them and make them stable. Lest it be thought that Bottomore is merely using imprecise language in an effort to inspire his audience to aim at wider-ranging institutional policy reform, recall that the target of this criticism is, of all people, Schumpeter. That is, Bottomore's remarks are directed at the major economist *least* inclined to minimize the significance of broad cultural values in influencing economic phenomena. Consider the following remarks of Schumpeter's, all from the book Bottomore's comments introduce:

> As regards the economic performance, it does not follow that men are 'happier' or even 'better off' in the industrial society of today than they were in the medieval manor or village. As regards the cultural performance, one may accept every word I have written [in defense of the productive superiority of capitalism] and yet hate it — its utilitarianism and the wholesale destruction of Meanings incident in it — from the bottom of one's heart [1950, p. 129].
>
> [S]ocialism aims at higher goals than full bellies, exactly as Christianity means more than the somewhat hedonistic values of heaven and hell. First and foremost, socialism means a new cultural world. For the sake of it, one might conceivably be a fervent socialist even though believing that the socialist arrangement is likely to be inferior as to economic performance. Hence no merely economic argument for or against can ever be decisive, however successful in itself (*ibid*, 170).
>
> [C]apitalism does not merely mean that the housewife can influence production by her choice between peas and beans; or that the youngster may choose whether he wants to work in a factory or on a farm; or that plant managers have some voice in deciding what and how to produce: it means a scheme of values, a civilization, an attitude toward life — the civilization of inequality and of the family fortune (*ibid*, 419).

[52]To his credit Bottomore acknowledges that "[t]he difficulties of extending democracy in such ways are now all too evident". In 1975 they were evident to far fewer political theorists on the left than they are now. However, while attention is on the subject of prescience, let us note, following Muller [2002, p. 17], that the proto-economists Grotius and Hobbes were both crucially motivated by the conviction that Republicanism is naïve.

If these are the remarks of someone who is, according to the anti-economist, trapped in a narrow technocratic worldview, then almost all economists will blink in wonder at what the missing breadth of vision could possibly consist in. The answer is aspirational yearning to transcend scarcity and materiality altogether. This is a typical element of *ideology* essential to anti-economics, qualitatively different from the intuitive modern morality assumed by Dasgupta and Binmore, and foreign to economics. The economic attitude is consistent with policies drawn from anywhere on the left-right spectrum that acknowledge scarcity as fundamental to political and social organization. In this sense it is not ideology. The economic attitude is *inconsistent* with transcendence of materialism and scarcity, and it insists on directing attention to means rather than being captivated by ends — it is practical rather than aspirational. In this sense too economics is not political (as opposed to philosophical) ideology — it is indeed the antithesis of political ideology.

This is the main reason economics is hated by anti-economists. To those who find moral-political nobility only in transcendent aspirations, the economic must seem crass, brutally insisting on reminding reformers of the limits to possibility. This can easily seem like defense of the status quo; and it typically *will* be defense of the status quo if the only alternative presented is an aspirational fantasy, since as Binmore [1994; 1998] emphasizes, attempts to realize such fantasies can amount only to deliberate disruption of normative-institutional equilibria; and something Burke was right about is that far more such disequilibria are catastrophes for the modernist values, including welfare maximization, than improvements on them. Economists stress that progress must move along equilibrium paths, in which those with the power to veto improvement are incentivized not to do so.

Let us consider two examples of political values that are consistent with the economic attitude if considered with scarcity in view, and inconsistent with economics if aspired to transcendentally. As noted earlier, socialists distinguish themselves from other modernists by attaching special value to equality. And of course most socialists are then suspicious of unregulated markets because they think that these tend to amplify inequalities. No economist should have difficulty regarding such worries as based on plausible empirical hypotheses that must be tested under specific conditions, whether she shares the attachment to equality or not; as someone committed to goal (ii) she relies on markets as information-processors but not necessarily as ultimate arbiters of assets. And, of course, there has been much important analysis done by economists who do regard equality as valuable (e.g., [Roemer, 1996]), including those interested in the question of inequality's impact on the *prima facie* goods acknowledged along the spectrum (see [Eicher and Turnovsky, 2003]). The core result of Binmore's [1994; 1998] social bargaining model is that there is no theoretical trade-off between welfare efficiency and equality. However, no economist will agree that strict equality of outcomes through suppression of markets is a rationalizable policy; in the absence of the measurements that markets perform, it is not even clear that the ideal has any operational meaning. To an imagination captivated by transcendental aspirations, this will seem like hateful defeatism.

As a second example, consider the question deferred from section 3.1 as to whether the implicit ideology in Smith should be regarded as left-trending or right-trending. It was noted that the second interpretation, which has been pressed by both left and right ideologues, depends on following Marx in regarding division of labor as implying alienation. Neither Marx nor anyone else has ever indicated *how* abolition of division of labor would be made compatible with scarcity. To the extent that alienation is taken to be a consequence of exploitation, market socialists think they have an answer to this problem; but it will not satisfy orthodox dreamers. The main point, in any case, is that the only right-trending aspect that can be found in Smith's implicit ideology requires adoption of a prior anti-economic attitude.

Economics being 'ideological' in only what I have called the philosophical sense is consistent with its being scientific. The modern liberal-democratic political and social agenda exposes as problems a range of challenges to efficiency and alignment of incentives about which there are facts to be carefully discerned. Indeed, what prevents the philosophical ideology of economics from sliding towards political ideology is precisely the commitment to rigorous modeling in economic practice and axiomatic foundations in economic theory. These make it effectively impossible for economists to simply stake out positions *within* the modern spectrum and then wish away some inconvenient aspect of scarcity; an empirically adequate model will force its expression somewhere. Thus the socialist Lange was persuaded by the model-based arguments of the libertarian von Mises to prefer market socialism to state socialism; thus the socialist van Parijs appropriates models due to the libertarian Friedman of the effects of a basic income grant, adds additional features of his own consistent with the constraints respected by Friedman, and the result is a set of policy proposals that take up a hitherto unoccupied point on the spectrum (and which requires us to complicate the dimensionality of the spectrum). Dasgupta and Binmore are not shy with policy proposals, but it is pointless to try to identify them with the left or the right. This is because their analyses are sufficiently formal to have content that holds its anchor through any amount of rhetorical spin, whether offered by the authors themselves or by commentators.

Of course, economists are often prone, as people with political interests and preferences, to associate themselves with ideological labels. Some become political ideologues and to that extent cease to be, or to mainly be, economists. But, in general, economists commit to liberal-democratic modernism when they take up the economic project, and thereafter the formal technology in which they are required to set their analyses prevents them from being able to tie their conclusions to the agendas of more specifically ideological tribes.

In the end, then, which of the positions E1 through E5 do I recommend as the best response to the anti-economist who alleges that economics is ideology? The arguments from dynamic efficiency pioneered by Hayek get us at least as far as E2. Hayek tried to establish E4 on general theoretical grounds but, for reasons discussed in the previous section, did not succeed even in establishing E3. This does not mean that E3 and E4 are unreachable; but it is almost surely a mistake to try, as Hayek did, to reach them by a purely abstract route. If E3 and E4 can be established, this will need to be by means of inductive evidence that supports models of development in which market activities consistently emerge as positive causal factors for expansion of liberty and/or democracy and/or (if liberty and democracy involve trade-offs) some vector product of them. Though B. Friedman [2005] believes that the positive verdict is already in, Dasgupta [2005] argues that this is at present wishful thinking. Development economics remains an area in which our uncertainties are profound, and the fact that China has been for two decades the world's fastest growing large economy must give any defender of E3 or E4 serious pause at the very least.

However, everyone committed to the modern social and political project agrees that organization of incentives — so, market structures in the broadest sense — are importantly *relevant to* all aspects of that project. This seems very clearly to be a *fact*, not an ideological construction. To the extent that economic analysis has helped us to recognize this fact, economics has achieved goal (iv) on one reasonable interpretation of it. If there are facts about the way in which E3 and E4 could be confirmed or refuted, then study of the contributions of markets to liberty and democracy can be science rather than (political) ideology.

## BIBLIOGRAPHY


[Addleson, 1997] M. Addleson. *Equilibrium Versus Understanding.* London: Routledge, 1997.

[Albin, 1998] P. Albin. *Barriers and Bounds to Rationality.* Princeton: Princeton University Press, 1998.

[Allen, 2004] J. Allen. The tiresome second best. *US News and World Report* 11/01/2004.

[Anderson *et al.*, 1988] P. Anderson, K. Arrow, and D. Pines. *The Economy as an Evolving Complex System.* Reading, MA: Perseus, 1988.

[Arthur *et al.*, 1997] W. B. Arthur, S. Durlauf, and D. Lane. *The Economy as an Evolving Complex System II.* Reading, MA: Addison-Wesley, 1997.

[Aune, 2002] J. Aune. *Selling the Free Market.* New York: Guilford Press, 2002.

[Backhouse, 2002] R. Backhouse. *The Ordinary Business of Life.* Princeton: Princeton University Press, 2002.

[Baird *et al.*, 1994] D. Baird, R. Gertner, and R. Picker. *Game Theory and the Law.* Cambridge, MA: Harvard University Press, 1994.

[Barro, 1997] R. Barro. *Determinants of Economic Growth.* Cambridge, MA: MIT Press, 1997.

[Benhabib and Bisin, 2005] J. Benhabib and A. Bisin. Modelling internal commitment mechanisms and self-control: A neuroeconomics approach to consumption-savings decisions. *Games and Economic Behavior* 50: 460-492, 2005.

[Becker, 1976] G. Becker. *The Economic Approach to Human Behavior.* Chicago: University of Chicago Press, 1976.

[Bello, 2004] W. Bello. *Deglobalization: Ideas for a New World Economy.* London: Zed Books, 2004.

[Bhagwati, 2004] J. Bhagwati. *In Defense of Globalization.* Oxford: Oxford University Press, 2004.

[Bhorat *et al.*, 2001] H. Bhorat, M. Leibbrandt, M. Maziya, S. van den Berg, and I. Woolard. *Fighting Poverty: Labour Markets and Inequality in South Africa.* Cape Town: University of Cape Town Press, 2001.

[Binmore, 1994] K. Binmore. *Game Theory and the Social Contract, Volume One: Playing Fair.* Cambridge, MA: MIT Press, 1994.

[Binmore, 1998] K. Binmore. *Game Theory and the Social Contract, Volume Two: Just Playing.* Cambridge, MA: MIT Press, 1998.
[Blaug, 2002] M. Blaug. Ugly currents in modern economics. In U. Mäki., ed., *Fact and Fiction in Economics.* Cambridge: Cambridge University Press, pp. 35-56, 2002.
[Blume and Durlauf, 2005] L. Blume and S. Durlauf. *The Economy as an Evolving Complex System III.* Oxford: Oxford University Press, 2005.
[Bottomore, 1975] T. Bottomore. Introduction to Schumpeter, *Capitalism, Socialism and Democracy.* New York: Harper Collins, 1975.
[Bowles and Gintis, 1998] S. Bowles and H. Gintis. *Recasting Egalitarianism.* London: Verso, 1998.
[Bramwell, 1989] A. Bramwell. *Ecology in the $20^{th}$ Century: A History.* New Haven: Yale University Press, 1989.
[Brecher and Costello, 1994] J. Brecher and T. Costello. *Global Village or Global Pillage?* Cambridge, MA: South End Press, 1994.
[Brooks, 1999] R. Brooks. *Cambrian Intelligence: The Early History of the New AI.* Cambridge, MA: MIT Press, 1999.
[Bshary, 2001] R. Bshary. The cleaner fish market. In Noë, R., van Hoof, J., and Hammerstein, P., *Economics in Nature.* Cambridge: Cambridge University Press, pp. 146-172, 2001.
[Buchanan, 1985] A. Buchanan. *Ethics, Efficiency and the Market.* Totowa: Rowman and Littlefield, 1985.
[Buchanan and Tullock, 1962] J. Buchanan and G. Tullock. *The Calculus of Consent.* Ann Arbor: University of Michigan Press, 1962.
[Caldwell, 2004] B. Caldwell. *Hayek's Challenge.* Chicago: University of Chicago Press, 2004.
[Camerer, 2003] C. Camerer. *Behavioral Game Theory.* Princeton: Princeton University Press, 2003.
[Chwe, 2003] M. Chwe. *Rational Ritual: Culture, Coordination and Common Knowledge.* Princeton: Princeton University Press, 2003.
[Coase, 1960] R. Coase. The problem of social cost. *Journal of Law and Economics* 3: 1-44, 1960.
[Coleman, 2002] W. Coleman. *Economics and its Enemies.* Houndmills, Basingstoke: Palgrave Macmillan, 2002.
[Cubitt and Sugden, 2001] R. Cubitt and R. Sugden. On money pumps. *Games and Economic Behavior* 37: 121-160, 2001.
[Dasgupta, 2002] P. Dasgupta. Modern economics and its critics. In U. Mäki, ed., *Fact and Fiction in Economics.* Cambridge: Cambridge University Press, pp. 57-89, 2002.
[Dasgupta, 2005] P. Dasgupta. What do economists analyze and why? Values or facts? *Economics and Philosophy* 21: 221-278, 2005.
[Debreu, 1974] G. Debreu. Excess demand functions. *Journal of Mathematical Economics* 1: 15-23, 1974.
[Dupré, 2001] J. Dupré. *Human Nature and the Limits of Science.* Oxford: Oxford University Press, 2001.
[Edelman, 1995] S. Edelman. Representation, similarity and the chorus of prototypes. *Minds and Machines* 5: 45-68, 1995.
[Eicher and Turnovsky, 2003] T. Eicher and S. Turnovsky, eds. *Inequality and Growth: Theory and Policy Implications.* Cambridge, MA: MIT Press, 2003.
[Foster and Sonnenschein, 1970] E. Foster and H. Sonnenschein. Resource allocation and the public sector. *Econometrica* 38: 281-297, 1970.
[Frank, 2001] T. Frank. *One Market Under God.* New York: Random House, 2001.
[Freeden, 1996] M. Freeden. *Ideologies and Political Theory.* Oxford: Oxford University Press, 1996.
[Friedman, 2005] B. Friedman. *The Moral Consequences of Economic Growth.* New York: Knopf, 2005.
[Friedman, 1999] M. Friedman. *Reconsidering Logical Positivism.* Cambridge: Cambridge University Press, 1999.
[Friedman, 1953] M. Friedman. *Essays in Positive Economics.* Chicago: University of Chicago Press, 1953.
[Fullbrook, 2003] E. Fullbrook, ed. *The Crisis in Economics.* London: Routledge, 2003.
[Fuller, 2001] S. Fuller. *Thomas Kuhn: A Philosophical History for Our Times.* Chicago: University of Chicago Press, 2001.

[Galbraith, 1960] J. K. Galbraith. *The Liberal Hour.* New York: Houghton Mifflin, 1960.
[Gray, 1998] J. Gray. *False Dawn.* London: Granta, 1998.
[Hamilton, 2003] L. Hamilton. *The Political Philosophy of Needs.* Cambridge: Cambridge University Press, 2003.
[Hausman, 1992] D. Hausman. *The Inexact and Separate Science of Economics.* Cambridge: Cambridge University Press, 1992.
[Hayek, 1944] F. Hayek. *The Road to Serfdom.* Chicago: University of Chicago Press, 1944.
[Hayek, 1952] F. Hayek. *The Sensory Order.* Chicago: University of Chicago Press, 1952.
[Hayek, 1960] F. Hayek. *The Constitution of Liberty.* Chicago: University of Chicago Press, 1960.
[Heilbroner and Milberg, 1995] R. Heilbroner and W. Milberg. *The Crisis of Vision in Modern Economic Thought.* Cambridge: Cambridge University Press, 1995.
[Herrnstein, 1997] R. Herrnstein. *The Matching Law.* Cambridge, MA: Harvard University Press, 1997.
[Hodgson, 2001] G. Hodgson. *How Economics Forgot History.* London: Routledge, 2001.
[Hollis and Nell, 1975] M. Hollis and E. Nell. *Rational Economic Man: A Philosophical Critique of Neo-classical Economics.* Cambridge: Cambridge University Press, 1975.
[Ingrao and Israel, 1990] B. Ingrao and G. Israel. *The Invisible Hand.* Cambridge, MA: MIT Press, 1990.
[Jackman, 1973] R. Jackman. On the relation of economic development to democratic performance. *American Journal of Political Science* 17: 611-621, 1973.
[Keen, 2002] S. Keen. *De-bunking Economics.* New York: Zed Books, 2002.
[Kelso, 1995] S. Kelso. *Dynamic Patterns.* Cambridge, MA: MIT Press, 1995.
[Kennedy and Eberhart, 2001] J. Kennedy and R. Eberhart. *Swarm Intelligence.* San Francisco: Morgan Kauffman, 2001.
[Kenney, 1997] H. Kenney. South African economic development in the light of the new institutional economics. *The Independent Review* 2: 225-242, 1997.
[Lawson, 1997] T. Lawson. *Economics and Reality.* London: Routledge, 1997.
[Liner, 2001] G. Liner. Core authors and rankings in economics. *Atlantic Economic Journal* 29: 459-469, 2001.
[Lipsey and Lancaster, 1956] R. Lipsey and G. Lancaster. The general theory of second best. *Review of Economic Studies* 24: 11-32, 1956.
[Lowenberg, 1989] A. Lowenberg. An economic theory of apartheid. *Economic Inquiry* 27: 57-74, 1989.
[MacIntyre, 1981] A. MacIntyre. *After Virtue.* Notre Dame: University of Notre Dame Press, 1981.
[Mäki, 1986] U. Mäki. Rhetoric at the expense of coherence: a reinterpretation of Milton Friedman's methodology. In W. Samuels, ed., *Research in the History of Economic Thought and Methodology, Volume Four.* Greenwich, CT: JAI Press, pp. 127-143, 1986.
[Mäki, 1992] U. Mäki. Friedman and realism. In W. Samuels and J. Biddle, eds., *Research in the History of Economic Thought and Methodology, Volume Ten.* Greenwich, CT: JAI Press, pp. 171-195, 1992.
[Mantel, 1974] R. Mantel. On the characterization of aggregate excess demand. *Journal of Economic Theory* 7: 348-353, 1974.
[Mantel, 1976] R. Mantel. Homothetic preferences and community excess demand functions. *Journal of Economic Theory* 12: 197-201, 1976.
[McCabe, 2003] K. McCabe. Neuroeconomics. In L. Nadel et al (eds.), *The Encyclopedia of Cognitive Science.* London: Nature Publishing Group, 2003.
[Metcalf, 1980] J. Metcalf. *General Ludd.* Toronto: ECW Press, 1980.
[Mirowski, 1989] P. Mirowski. *More Heat Than Light.* New York: Cambridge University Press, 1989.
[Mirowski, 1994] P. Mirowski, ed. *Natural Images in Economic Thought: Markets Read in Tooth and Claw.* Cambridge: Cambridge University Press, 1994.
[Mirowski, 2002] P. Mirowski. *Machine Dreams: Economics Becomes a Cyborg Science.* Cambridge: Cambridge University Press, 2002.
[Montague and Berns, 2002] P. R. Montague and G. Berns. Neural economics and the biological substrates of valuation. *Neuron* 36: 265-284, 2002.
[Muller, 2002] J. Muller. *The Mind and the Market.* New York: Random House, 2002.

[Nattrass and Seekings, 2004] N. Nattrass and J. Seekings. The 'new (global) economy' and inequality in South Africa. In M. Ayogu and D. Ross, eds., *Development Dilemmas*, London: Routledge, pp. 170-189, 2004.

[Nussbaum, 1986] M. Nussbaum. *The Fragility of Goodness*. Cambridge: Cambridge University Press, 1986.

[Ormerod, 1997] P. Ormerod. *The Death of Economics*. New York: Wiley, 1997.

[Pettit, 1997] P. Pettit. *Republicanism*. Oxford: Oxford University Press, 1997.

[Polanyi, 1944] K. Polanyi. *The Great Transformation*. New York: Farrar and Rinehart, 1944.

[Posner, 1998] R. Posner. *Economic Analysis of Law*, $5^{th}$ edition. New York: Aspen, 1998.

[Przeworski *et al.*, 2000] A. Przeworski, M. Alvarez, J. Cheibub, and F. Limongi. *Democracy and Development*. Cambridge: Cambridge University Press, 2000.

[Revallion, 1994] M. Revallion. *Poverty Comparisons*. Geneva: Harwood Academic, 1994.

[Robbins, 1935] L. Robbins. *An Essay on the Nature and Significance of Economic Science*, $2^{nd}$ edition. London: Macmillan, 1935.

[Robertson, 1957] D. Robertson. *Lectures on Economic Principles, Volume One*. London: Staples Press, 1957.

[Roemer, 1996] J. Roemer. *Theories of Distributive Justice*. Cambridge, MA: Harvard University Press, 1996.

[Ross, 1998] D. Ross. Review of Addleson, *Equilibrium Versus Understanding*. *Economics and Philosophy* 14: 163-168, 1998.

[Ross, 2005] D. Ross. *Economic Theory and Cognitive Science: Microexplanation*. Cambridge, MA: MIT Press, 2005.

[Rothschild, 2002] E. Rothschild. *Economic Sentiments: Adam Smith, Condorcet and the Enlightenment*. Cambridge, MA: Harvard University Press, 2002.

[Samuelson, 1954] P. Samuelson. The pure theory of public expenditure. *Review of Economics and Statistics* 36: 387-389, 1954.

[Schumacher, 1973] E. Schumacher. *Small is Beautiful*. London: Blond and Briggs, 1973.

[Schumpeter, 1950] J. Schumpeter. *Capitalism, Socialism and Democracy*. New York: Harper and Row, 1950.

[Selfridge, 1959] O. Selfridge. Pandemonium: A paradigm for learning. In D. Blake and A. Uttley, eds. *Proceedings of the Symposium on Mechanisation of Thought Processes*. London: H. M. Stationary Office, pp. 511-529, 1959.

[Smith, 1970/1776] A. Smith. *An Inquiry into the Nature and Causes of the Wealth of Nations*. Harmondsworth: Penguin, 1776/1970.

[Sonnenschein, 1972] H. Sonnenschein. Market excess demand functions. *Econometrica* 40: 549-563, 1972.

[Sonnenschein, 1973] H. Sonnenschein. Do Walras identity and continuity characterize the class of excess demand functions? *Journal of Economic Theory* 6: 345-354, 1973.

[Sowell, 1977] T. Sowell. *Classical Economics Reconsidered*. Princeton: Princeton University Press, 1977.

[Stigler and Becker, 1977] G. Stigler and G. Becker. De gustibus non est disputandum. *American Economic Review* 67: 76-90, 1977.

[Stiglitz, 1996] J. Stiglitz. *Whither Socialism?* Cambridge MA: MIT Press, 1996.

[Stiglitz, 2002] J. Stiglitz. *Globalization and its Discontents*. London: Penguin, 2002.

[Sunstein, 2000] C. Sunstein, ed. *Behavioral Law and Economics*. New York: Cambridge University Press, 2000.

[Usher, 1981] D. Usher. *The Economic Prerequisite to Democracy*. Oxford: Blackwell, 1981.

[Van Parijs, 1995] P. Van Parijs. *Real Freedom For All*. Oxford: Oxford University Press, 1995.

[Vogel, 1996] S. Vogel. *Freer Markets, More Rules*. Ithaca: Cornell University Press, 1996.

# SOCIAL SCIENTIFIC NATURALISM AND EXPERIMENTATION IN ECONOMICS

Daniel M. Hausman

A venerable question in the philosophy of social sciences concerns "social scientific naturalism" — that is, whether studies of psychology and of society can be sciences "just like" the natural sciences (Morgenbesser 1970). This question is simultaneously pressing and obscure. No one doubts the possibility of systematic inquiries concerning psychology and society. If science is no more than systematic inquiry, then there are obviously social sciences. Nor does anyone, other than a general skeptic, doubt that these systematic inquiries have taught us something about psychology and society.

The question is instead whether there is some fundamental difference between inquiries in the natural sciences and investigations of social and psychological phenomena. The question remains obscure in part because there is no reasonably precise characterization of what constitutes a natural science. So all one can do is to examine similarities and differences among various inquiries into social and natural phenomena. Obviously there are many differences between investigations of social and psychological phenomena on the one hand, and studies of geological, chemical, or astronomical phenomena on the other. Spectrometers are of limited use in economics, while astronomers don't have to worry about grilling from human subjects committees. On the other hand, at a sufficiently high level of generality, all rational inquiry has common features. Sociologists have the same standards of logical validity as biologists. What counts as a "fundamental" similarity or difference? What would constitute evidence that the social sciences and natural sciences are fundamentally similar or fundamentally different?

The answers to these questions are implicit in specific controversies concerning whether the social sciences differ in some fundamental way from the natural sciences. These controversies have addressed many different questions. The following five have been central:

1. (Goals) If one is a realist or an instrumentalist concerning the natural sciences, does it follow that one must be a realist or an instrumentalist about the social sciences or vice versa? Although at first glance it would appear that general arguments that inquiries should or shouldn't aim to explain phenomena or to predict phenomena would apply to both social inquiries and the natural sciences, some authors have argued that social inquiries have additional goals (such as interpretative understanding — "*Verstehen*") [Weber, 1904; Schütz, 1953; Machlup 1969].

Handbook of the Philosophy of Science. Volume 13: Philosophy of Economics.
Volume editor: Uskali Mäki. General editors: Dov M. Gabbay, Paul Thagard and John Woods.

2. (Testing) Can theories in the social sciences be tested and confirmed or disconfirmed in essentially the same way that theories in the natural sciences are appraised? For example, is introspection a special source of knowledge of psychology? Is it fallible just like the evidence from voltage meters? What are the barriers to experimentation in the social sciences, and how important are they? For example, will the fact that human experimental subjects are rational and free to act as they choose permit them to frustrate the experimenter's purposes?

3. (Explanation) Do the same models of explanation apply to both the natural and social sciences? Many explanations in the social sciences involve *reasons* and *norms*. How are explanations that cite reasons or norms related to causal and theoretical explanations in the natural sciences? Does the fact that explanations in the social science may often justify or criticize what they explain establish a fundamental difference between the natural and social sciences [Davidson, 1963; Rosenberg, 1976, ch. 5; Winch, 1958; von Wright, 1971].

4. (Objectivity and values) Can the social sciences be objective or "value free" in the same way that the natural sciences are objective or value free [Weber, 1904; Myrdal, 1958; Mongin, 2006; Hausman and McPherson, 2006, appendix]? Can the social sciences neutralize the influence of values, and do they need to do so? Can they be sciences even though commitments to social outcomes, processes, institutions, cultural norms, and so forth influence the actions of social scientists?

5. (Reduction and ontology) Are social entities such as norms, cultures, institutions, tribes, or classes "real"? Are they reducible to physical things? How are minds related to bodies? Does successful explanation require reduction or at least reducibility [Churchland, 1988; Kim, 1998].

Variants of these questions are central to controversies concerning the status and distinctiveness of the social sciences. Philosophers have staked out a range of different positions. Attitudes of social scientists themselves also vary widely depending on the discipline and the school within the discipline. Most mainstream economists see their discipline as resembling the natural sciences as closely as different natural sciences resemble one another. Cultural anthropologists, on the other hand, see few resemblances between their work and the natural sciences.

Instead of attempting to survey the main arguments bearing on this multifarious controversy, I would like to focus on one line of inquiry within economics — experimentation concerning game theory — that bears in intriguing ways on the issues concerning social scientific naturalism. Through a glimpse at some experimentation in economics, I shall be able to articulate more clearly contrasts between parts of economics and most or all of the natural sciences.

Let me emphasize that *I am not making any general criticism or defense of social scientific naturalism.* Experimentation concerning game theory will turn out to resemble inquiries in the natural sciences more closely in some regards than in others. Furthermore, other inquiries in the social sciences will have different features than does experimentation concerning game theory, and those other inquiries deserve a separate examination. Not only are there, as I have suggested, many different questions concerning social scientific naturalism, so there may be many different answers with respect to different social investigations.

## 1 IS GAME THEORY TESTABLE?

Although the words, "game theory" can refer to several different things, most mathematicians, economists, and evolutionary biologists regard game theory as a branch of mathematics. A game is defined by a set of "players", a set of strategies for each player, and a set of "payoffs" for each player for each strategy combination (see for example [Osborne, 2004]). Players need not be people; they may, for example, be plants or animals, or even a rather peculiar agent called "chance." A pure strategy picks out one alternative at each node, or if there are "information sets" containing more than one node, at each information set. Information sets are characterized so abstractly that they have no necessary connection with knowledge possessed by players. Similarly, payoffs need not involve preference or utility. In some biological applications for example, payoffs might be death or survival. Game theory consists of axioms and definitions that are employed to reach conclusions concerning what strategies players will adopt given specifications concerning the number of players, their strategy sets, and the payoffs.

So, for example, figure 1 shows a simple game presented in so-called extensive form:

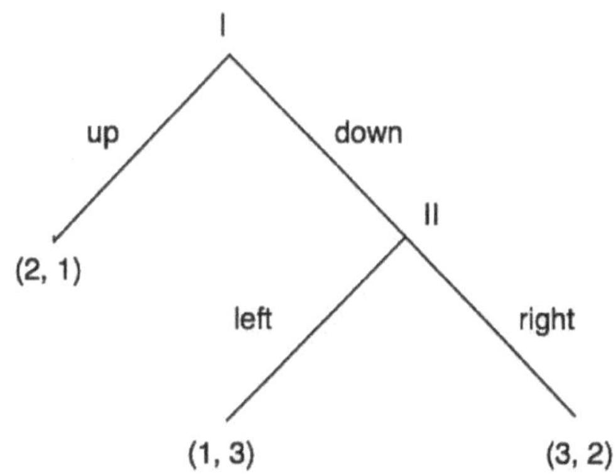


Figure 1. A simple game

At the initial node of the game at the top, player I has a choice of two strategies, which correspond to the moves labeled "*up*" and "*down*". Player II gets to move only if Player I moves *down*, and Player II has two strategies as well, which correspond to the simple moves labeled "*left*" or "*right*". The strategy combinations have payoffs, which are indicated by the numbers in parentheses. The first number in the pair indicates the payoff to Player I, and the second number the payoff to Player II. A higher number indicating a better payoff. If I plays *down*, II will play *left* because the strategy pair (*down*, *left*) has a higher payoff for Player II than (*down*, *right*). If Player I possesses the capacity to anticipate correctly what Player II will do, Player I will be able to compare the payoff from playing *up* — 2 — with the playoff from playing *down* — 1 — and Player I will play *up*. The strategy pair (*up*, *left*) is a Nash equilibrium, because *left* is at least as good a reply by Player II to *up* as is *right*, and *up* is the best reply by Player I to *left*.

Although the distinction between purely mathematical claims and contingent empirical claims is in some ways obscure, it is clear enough to justify the conclusion that there is no way to test game theory without interpreting it. Without knowing what counts as a player, a strategy, a payoff or a choice, one cannot sensibly consider the truth or falsity of claims about the number of players, what strategies they can play, what the payoffs of strategy combinations are, or which strategies will be chosen. If the players in figure 1 are ordinary people with common knowledge of everything in figure 1, and the numbers represent their preferences, then figure 1 accurately represents their circumstances and the prediction that they will play their Nash equilibrium strategies is well justified. If on the other hand, Players I and II are the pen and pencil on the desk before me, *up* and *down*, and *left* and *right* directions they respectively might propel themselves, and the numbers represent how many kisses I will give them depending on how they move, then the claims that are implicit in figure 1, including the prediction of Nash equilibrium play, are obviously false and pretty silly, too. Without some interpretation, the most one can do is to address "meta-language" questions concerning whether, for example, some sentence is syntactically well formed or whether a strategy pair is a Nash equilibrium. Without interpretations, syntactic objects such as inscriptions and utterances are not the sort of thing that could be true or false. *Game theory is not testable until it is interpreted.*

Experimental economists thus do not — and could not possibly — test game theory, full stop. They test some particular interpretation of game theory. In this interpretation, "players" are human beings, "choice nodes" are occasions when people might make choices, a player's pure strategy is a specification of a choice for each information set where the person gets to choose, payoffs are utilities (indices of preference), and so forth. Given these interpretations, Players I and II are two human agents, who, let us suppose, have common knowledge of the game. Let Player I be female and Player II male. The payoffs are indices indicating their preferences over the outcomes. Player I gets to choose first. Because the game is common knowledge, she knows that Player II prefers to play *left* if she plays *down*. Because she knows that Player II is rational, she knows that he will in fact play *left* in response to her playing *down*. Since she is rational and she prefers the outcome of playing *up* to the outcome of the strategy pair (*down*, *left*), she chooses the strategy *up*. In this way game theory justifies that prediction that Player I will choose the strategy *up*, and Player II will choose the strategy *left* (though the latter choice has of course no behavioral manifestation if Player I plays *up*).

When game theory is interpreted this way, let us call it "human premeditated game theory" — "human" because the players are human beings and "premeditated," because players rationally evaluate strategies before playing. Evolutionary game theory in contrast is typically not premeditated. Players may be completely unintelligent and unable to change their strategies. Selection weeds out unsuccessful strategies and mutation generates new strategies. When I speak of "game theory" in the rest of this paper, I shall be referring exclusively to (non-evolutionary) human premeditated game theory.

Human premeditated game theory is an interpreted theory, but it does not follow that it makes any testable claims. "If anything is a spot market for petroleum, then it is a market for petroleum" is fully interpreted, but it is not testable, and it is apparently empirically empty. This sentence is true, because any interpreted sentence with the logical form "If anything is $F$ and $G$, then it is $F$" is true. Similarly, analytic claims, such as "the substitutes for a commodity are distinct from its complements," which are true by virtue of the meaning of their terms rather than their logical form, are also (at least as a first approximation) irrefutable. Similarly (though not so simply), "If Players I and II are rational and have common knowledge of the game shown in figure 1 and of their rationality, then they will choose strategies *up* and *left* appears to follow from the definitions of rationality, common knowledge and the specification of the game. A good deal of game theory takes the form of theorems, and no matter how the terms in a theorem are interpreted, there is no point to testing a theorem (as opposed to testing its axioms or its conclusion). Nothing one could observe in a laboratory could cast any doubt on the statement just quoted.

So, for example, suppose that someone designed an experiment in which two subjects faced the interaction depicted in figure 2:

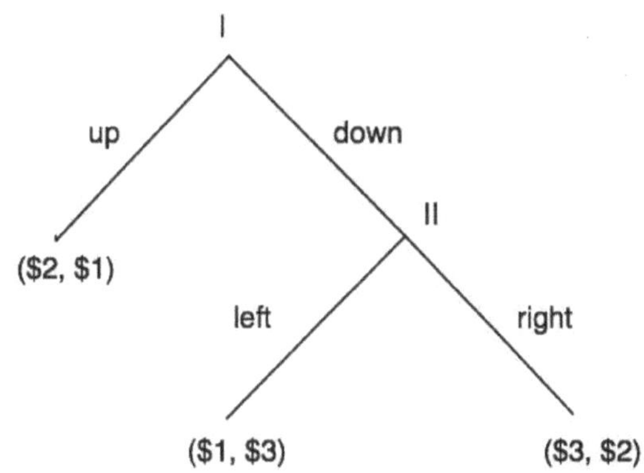


Figure 2.

Notice that figure 2 is *not* a game, since it does not specify the payoffs, which in the case of human premeditated game theory, are indices of the players' preferences. The experimental subjects, who do not know one another and do not meet, are shown figure 2 and are asked to choose what to do. If the subject in the position of Player I does not choose *up*, then at least one of the premises in the theorem predicting that Player I in the game shown in figure 1 will play *up* must be false. Here are the possibilities:

1. Player I cares about something other than her own financial payoff and so does not prefer the outcome of playing *up* to the outcome of (*down*, *left*)
2. Player I does not understand that her financial payoff will be larger if she plays *up* than if she plays *down* and Player II plays *left* in response.
3. Player I does not believe that Player II will play *left* in response to her playing *down*.

For 3 to be the case, either Player I must misunderstand the game, or Player I must believe that Player II misunderstands the game, or Player I must believe that Player II is not rational. Whatever the explanation, there is no evidence here that bears on the conditional claim, "If Players I and II are rational and have common knowledge of the game shown in figure 1 and of their rationality, then they will choose strategies *up* and *left*. It is as pointless to test this claim as it would be to test the claim the conditional claim that if bodies fall with a constant acceleration, then the distance they fall is proportional to the square of the time that they fall.

Insofar as game theory confines itself to making proven conditional claims, it is impossible to test it. Experiments such as the one sketched above do not and cannot test logical truths. All one can learn from experiments such as the one sketched above is that the antecedent conditions in the conditional claim are not all satisfied. *If game theory consists entirely of theorems, then it is not testable.* To make testable claims, game theorists must assert some of the axioms that their theorems rely on.[1]

Although empirically empty, the proven conditional claims of game theory may still be useful, because theorems can help people, who are certainly not logically omniscient, to recognize consequences and make predictions. By drawing out the implications of statements concerning the preferences, beliefs, rationality, and intelligence of players, the strategies among which they can choose, and the outcomes of those strategies, the theorems of game theory facilitate testing these statements. For example, consider experiments involving "dictator games" [Camerer and Thaler, 1995]. In these experiments, which are carried out under conditions of anonymity, one experimental subject gets to choose how money will be distributed between himself or herself and another subject. The axioms of game theory plus the assumption that experimental subjects understand the structure of the interaction they are involved in and care only about their own monetary payoffs imply

[1] I am only listing necessary conditions here. Deriving testable implications typically requires choices among solution concepts, and even then there are often multiple equilibria.

that choosers will take all the money themselves. The admittedly trivial game theoretical analysis plus the fact that choosers often share the monetary payoffs help to falsify the hypothesis that experimental subjects care only about their own dollar payoffs.

Although the point is controversial, I maintain that game theory does and should do more than make proven conditional claims. Game theorists do not and should not only explore the consequences of rationality: they also assert that humans are, to some reasonable approximation, rational. They do not only calculate what the consequences would be if humans cared only about their own monetary payoffs; some also assert that this motivational assumption is a good approximation in some circumstances. Game theorists do not only explore the consequences of salience; they also propose hypotheses concerning the importance of salience and the sorts of things that humans find salient. In my view, game theory is committed to contingent and testable assertions concerning human rationality, preferences, and beliefs. The theory is not without empirical content.

Game theory "sticks its neck out" as soon as it goes beyond proving theorems. If game theory is (as I believe) committed to claims about individual rationality and self-interest, then observing cooperation in an experiment in which subjects are supposed to be playing a prisoners' dilemma game may disconfirm game theory rather than demonstrating only that the antecedent conditions for the argument for mutual defection are not satisfied. *If game theory is interpreted and offers empirical hypotheses or asserts some of the antecedents in its theorems, then game theory is testable*, apparently just like claims in physics or chemistry.

Even in this case, game theory will not be testable *by itself.* (This claim obviously depends on distinguishing those propositions that belong to game theory from those that do not.) As Pierre Duhem famously argued [1906], significant scientific claims cannot be tested by themselves. Duhem made his point concerning the natural sciences, but it is equally applicable to the social sciences. Even a relatively superficial physical generalization such as Galileo's law does not make any categorical predictions about how bodies fall near the surface of the earth, since their fall may be influenced by other factors such as air resistance. Galileo's law can be formulated as a conditional, "If there are no other forces acting besides gravity, then bodies near the surface of the earth will fall with a constant acceleration." Unlike the conditionals I discussed above, this one is not a mathematical truth. Unlike the claim that if a body falls with a constant acceleration, then the distance it falls is proportional to the square of the time that it falls, which follows from the calculus and the definition of acceleration, to say that bodies near the surface of the earth fall with a constant acceleration in the absence of other forces is an empirical claim, which can be and has been tested. Galileo tested it using inclined planes to slow up the acceleration and thereby make the time measurement easier. Nowadays, we can build precise timers and create extremely good vacuums. Each test bears on the correctness of Galileo's law only if claims about its apparatus and circumstances are true. A test using an inclined plane might find that different bodies accelerate at different rates because Galileo failed to grease the plane between trials. A test using an evacuated chamber might find a decreasing acceleration, because the chamber was leaking. Any test of Galileo's law is simultaneously a test of other claims the experimenter has to rely on in carrying out the test. Moreover, no matter how clear cut the experiment, a failure to find the results predicted by Galileo's law can always be explained away by a failure of its antecedent — that is, by the presence of some other, non-gravitational force. This logical point does not, of course, establish that it is always reasonable or justifiable to explain away failures this way. Sometimes the only plausible explanation of an experimental result is that the hypothesis under test is false.

So even if — as I have asserted — game theory makes testable empirical claims, like the one Galileo's law makes, it can only be tested when conjoined with other propositions concerning the specific strategic interaction to which the theory is applied. This point — which is central to what is commonly called "the Quine-Duhem problem" — should be sharply distinguished from the claim that theories must be interpreted to be testable or the claim that theorems, as logical truths, cannot be refuted by observations. Each of the three claims implies that "by itself the theory cannot be tested." But the reasons are different. In the first case the theory cannot be tested, because it has no interpretation assigned to its terms and thus there is no proposition to be tested. In the second case, the theory cannot be tested, because it consists of contradictions or of logical or analytic truths. No matter what other sentences one takes to be true or false, there can be no evidence for or against logical truths or falsehoods. In the third case, one can test the theory, but only if one takes other empirical statements to be true. Since those other statements are contingent and often not testable by themselves either, it is possible to deflect the blame for experimental failures away from the theory, but not because the theory has no empirical meaning or because the theory is contradictory or logically true.

Another way of stating the same conclusions concerning the testing of game theory (when game theory is interpreted and not limited to theorems) is to maintain that what one tests are specific game theoretic *models*, rather than game *theory* itself. Game theoretic models embed the mathematical structure of game theory and its empirical claims — if there are any — in amalgams that include specific assumptions concerning features of the strategic situation to which the model will be applied. Tests of game theoretic models can bear on the empirical claims of game theory, but this bearing is not direct or unproblematic. I prefer not to make the point in this language, because doing so encourages an instrumentalist view of theories as tools for constructing models rather than as sets of testable assertions. As I have argued elsewhere, the appraisal of theories is crucial to science as we know it.[2]

None of the points considered thus far appear to mark any significant difference between testing game theory and testing theories in the natural sciences, and indeed one might construct a critique of some of the anti-naturalist's arguments.

[2]See [Hausman, 1992, pp. 81–2]. Note that I am using the term "model" here in any entirely different sense than I employed in chapter 5 of my *Inexact and Separate Science of Economics.*

Thus far we have not run across any principled barriers to experimentation of exactly the same kind that one finds in the natural sciences. The facts that the people are intelligent and rational and can reflect on what they and others — including the experimenters — are doing are all apparently accommodated within game theoretic modeling of the circumstances of the experiment. Although the choices of agents are governed by their reasons and those choices are intuitively understandable to outsiders, the generalizations concerning choices that game theorists rely on appear thus far to be subject to the same sort of testing as generalizations in the natural sciences.

## 2 DIFFICULTIES IN TESTING GAME THEORY

If one attempts to test game theory by constructing a strategic situation in the laboratory and comparing the choices of experimental subjects to those that game theory predicts players will make in some specific game, one needs to know what game experimental subjects are playing. Until one knows what the game is, there is no way to test whether the predictions of some version of game theory are correct, because until one knows what the game is, there are no predictions to test. Without knowing what game people are playing, one cannot look to game theory for advice or explanation either.

In addition, one must specify what the empirical claims of game theory are before one can consider whether they are implicated in the predictions one is testing. Accordingly, for the purposes of this discussion I shall stipulate that game theory makes empirical assertions to the effect that people are, to a reasonable degree of approximation, rational and that they are intelligent enough to figure out much of what the game theorist can. I shall not here attribute to the game theorist any further assertions about the character of preferences. One might, quite reasonably, attribute to game theorists stronger empirical generalizations concerning individual preference or belief, such as the view that people prefer more money to less money, or that they believe one another to be rational. If one took these generalizations to be a part of game theory itself, then the following discussion would have to be rephrased, but its basic points would not be changed.

On the view of game theory that I have sketched, one can think of game theory as analogous to efforts of mathematical physicists to apply classical gravitational theory to predict the trajectories of multiple interacting bodies. In both cases the central empirical generalizations are already known and relatively simple, and they are *applied* by the game theorist or the trajectory theorist rather than generated by either. Just as the game theorist relies on the standard axioms of rationality, so the trajectory theorist relies on Newton's laws of motion and his laws of gravitation. Both idealize the phenomena with which they are concerned in an effort to make them more mathematically and analytically tractable, and in both cases the hard work is mathematical. The cases are not perfectly analogous, since there are no exact mathematical solutions concerning the trajectories of three or more bodies, but the comparison nevertheless helps clarify what the empirical content of game theory is and how it might be tested.

Clever experimenters are able to control situations in the economics laboratory tightly enough that they can specify how many players there are and what strategies are open to each player. This is not as simple as it may appear. In principle, the experimenters should probably count as players along with the subjects, and special efforts must be taken to get the subjects in effect to believe that the experimenter's strategy does not depend on their choices — or at least on any of the choices they take seriously. Experimental subjects always have more choices than the experimenter specifies or the subject considers. Experimental subjects might, for example, smash their computer terminals and set the laboratory on fire, and presumably such choices would have some influence on the strategies experimenters pursue. A full specification of the possible strategies experimental subjects might adopt would have to include such possibilities. But a partial specification may be good enough. Although those who emphasize human freedom might demur, it seems to me that in fact experimenters rarely go seriously wrong in their specification of the strategic possibilities. Similarly, though with greater difficulty, experimenters can control the beliefs the players have concerning the permissible strategies, the physical outcomes of strategy combinations, and the knowledge available to other players (including their beliefs about the beliefs of each other).

There are, however, very serious difficulties in the way of determining the payoffs or, in other words, the preferences of experimental subjects. These payoffs must be determined in order for game theory to make any substantial predictions concerning laboratory behavior. Until the preferences are specified, the experimenter only knows the "game form" or "game protocol" [Weibull, 2004], not the game.

## 3 DETERMINING PREFERENCES

At first glance, determining the player's preferences might not seem that difficult. If experimenters insure that subjects never meet and cannot identify one another — thereby eliminating all sorts of extraneous motives – it might seem a reasonable first approximation to regard an experimental subject's preferences over the outcomes as tracking the monetary payoffs he or she would receive. But as I read the literature, this assumption turns out to be surprisingly unsatisfactory, even as a first approximation. People's motives are complicated and in many experiments, it is very difficult to know what they are.

To bring these points down to earth, consider a simple one-shot two-person prisoner's dilemma. In the normal form of figure 3, the numbers are utilities (indices of preference), with larger numbers indicating more preferred outcomes. The first number records Row's preferences, while the second records Column's preferences. Everything in the normal form is common knowledge. The game theoretic argument for Row choosing *Down* (or Column choosing *Right* is simple): Row's strategy choice can have no effect on Column's choice, and whatever Column chooses, Row prefers the outcome of choosing *Down*. Since rational players choose what they most prefer, Row plays *Down*. Notice that the argument requires only ordinal utilities with no interpersonal comparability. In other words the only significance the numbers have is that higher numbers are assigned to outcomes that are more preferred and equal numbers to outcomes among which an agent is indifferent. The utility indices assigned for different individuals have absolutely no relation to one another. A positive monotone transformation of either Row's or Column's payoffs changes nothing.

| | | Column | |
|---|---|---|---|
| | | Left | Right |
| Row | Up | 2,2 | 0,3 |
| | Down | 3,0 | 1,1 |

Figure 3. A Prisoner's Dilemma Game

Each player has a dominant strategy: *Down* for Row and *Right* for Column. Nothing could be simpler, and barring irrationality, confusion, or some sort of blunder in execution, Row will play *Down* and Column will play *Right.* As is common in the literature, I shall call the strategy pair (*Down*, *Right*) "mutual defection." Similarly, I shall call *Up* and *Left* "cooperative strategies" and the outcome "the cooperative solution.

Since the prediction that players will choose strongly dominant strategies rests on such simple reasoning and on nothing other than the premises that the players are rational, know the normal form, and know that their choices do not influence the choice of the other player, the prediction seems scarcely to need testing. How could anybody fail to play an obvious dominant strategy? Yet one might nevertheless perform an experiment like the following make-believe example. This example is intended merely to illustrate the points. Actual experiments resembling this illustration have been done, but contemporary experimentation in economics is a great deal more subtle and sophisticated.

*A Naive Experiment*

> Experimental subjects who do not meet and do not know each other are told:
> *You are going to have a single interaction with another subject via a computer hookup. You will never meet this other subject. Each subject can choose one of two options, A or B. The following table explains how your earnings depend on both your choice and on the choice of the other subject. The other subject receives exactly the same instruction sheet, as the one you are now reading.*

If the subjects understand their choices and if they care only about their own monetary payoffs, then they are playing a prisoner's dilemma. Since all that matters to the specification of the game are ordinal utilities, one need make no

| | | *Other subject's choice* | |
|---|---|---|---|
| | | *A* | *B* |
| *Your choice* | *A* | *\$2 for each* | *0 for you, \$3 for other* |
| | *B* | *\$3 for you; 0 for other* | *\$1 for each* |

Figure 4. Payoffs in a naive test

assumption about the utility of money — the relation between money and preferences — except that each player's utility is increasing in his or her own monetary payoffs and completely determined by them. Given this assumption, the players are playing *exactly* the game in figure 3, and game theory predicts that Row will play *Down* and Column will play *Right*. Just as an experimental chemist needs to specify accurately the composition of two solutions whose reactions he or she studies in the laboratory, as well as the conditions under which they are combined, so an experimental economist needs to specify accurately what game the subjects are playing.

Yet, as is well known, when faced with strategic situations such as the one described in this hypothetical experiment, many experimental subjects do not play their dominant strategies. One possible explanation is that the experimental subjects are inattentive and confused about the nature of their choices and the outcomes of their choices. James Andreoni has done some elegant experiments investigating how much of the anomalous behavior in related games can be attributed to confusion, and his work shows that confusion can explain only a part of the anomalous behavior [1995]. A great deal remains.

A second possibility is that people systematically misidentify what game they are playing or violate axioms of rationality. They may, for example, engage in magical thinking, supposing that choosing the cooperative strategy will somehow lead other players to choose their cooperative strategy, or subjects may accept some fallacious argument for the rationality of cooperation. Some of these explanations are cast in doubt by experimental work such as Andreoni's, which shows that repeated experience with such interactions does not make the anomalous behavior go away, but it is likely that failures in rationality or reasoning explain a good deal of the cooperation experimenters find in apparent prisoner's dilemmas.

Yet I (like many others) would emphasize a different explanation of the experimental results, which is that *other things besides monetary payoffs strongly influence the choices of experimental subjects*. My reasons are both empirical and methodological. On the one hand, there is a great deal of evidence that people's preferences respond strongly to many factors besides their own monetary payoff. On the other hand, I believe that economists can often learn more by using game theoretic anomalies to study the factors influencing preferences rather than by treating choices as disconfirming game theory. Since economists already have solid evidence showing that people do not conform perfectly to the basic axioms of game theory, and since they currently lack any serious alternatives to standard game theory, testing game theory may teach them less than employing game theory to learn about people's preferences.

The situation might be compared to tests of predicted trajectories of gravitationally interacting bodies. Though these might be used to test Newton's laws of motion and his laws of gravitation, they might instead be used to determine whether the specifications of the initial positions and momenta were accurate or to determine whether other forces are significant. I'm not supposing that the axioms of the theory of rationality have the same status as Newton's Laws — obviously they do not — but economists might already know enough about the extent to which they are reliable to be able to use the outcomes of experiments to cast light on other things, such as what the preferences of experimental subjects depend on. Consider, as a second analogy, experiments testing predictions concerning the acidity of mixtures of solutions, which may contain impurities. Chemists might use such experiments as ways to determine the level of impurities in those solutions rather than to test theories of acidity.

In addition to caring about their own monetary payoffs, subjects may be motivated by many factors. Here are five possibilities:

1. Subjects may care about the monetary payoffs that other players get. They may be altruistic or malevolent.

2. Subjects may care about "winning." They may take the interaction to be a competition, and rather than focusing exclusively on their own payoffs, they may care about how well they do, *relative to* the other subject.

3. Subjects may care about whether the outcome is in some sense fair.

4. Subjects may want to reciprocate — to repay a kindness with a kindness and a harm with a harm [Rabin, 1993].

5. Subjects may be trustworthy and concerned to do what they take other subjects to trust them to do.

This is only a partial list. There are many other possible motivations. Subjects might, for example, have a mischievous desire to mess up the experiment, or they may seek to maximize the cost to the experimenter. On the other hand, not all of the listed motives will come into play in every kind of interaction. For example, in a one-move simultaneous-play game without any prior communication, such as the prisoners' dilemma, it is impossible for subjects to signal any trust or any intention to be "kind" or "nasty." Though subjects may nevertheless believe that their partners are trusting them or that they will behave in a kind or nasty way, the scope for motives of trustworthiness or reciprocation is clearly limited.

How strong are these motives, which compete with a concern for one's own gains? Experimental results suggest that these motives are certainly not negligible. Consider, for example, the results of ultimatum game experiments. In these, one subject gets to propose how to split some sum of money, and the other subject either accepts the division or both players get nothing. The divisions that are proposed are for the most part reasonably equal. Very unequal proposed splits are regularly turned down. It seems that people are in effect willing to pay to punish those who make insulting offers. And they are willing to pay a considerable amount: These results have been replicated in experiments carried out in the Slovak Republic, where the sums were close to a month's salary [Slonim and Roth, 1998] and for similarly high stakes in Indonesia [Cameron, 1999]. Larger stakes do make people more willing to accept unequal bargains, but many still reject them. These experiments do not of course *prove* conclusively that people are not motivated only by their own financial returns. The results could, for example, be the result of confusion. But there is no way to explain the data plausibly without recognizing that people are not only concerned with their own monetary payoffs.

## 4 THE IMPLICATIONS OF PREFERENCE COMPLEXITIES

When other motives are present besides monetary self-interest, there is no easy way to read off what game subjects are playing from a monetary payoff matrix such as figure 4. Presumably, many subjects in the hypothetical prisoner's dilemma experiment sketched above are not playing a prisoner's dilemma game. So the fact that they frequently play cooperatively is no refutation of game theory.

Notice that the existence of multiple motivations is no problem for game theory itself. With few exceptions [Sen, 1974; 1987], game theorists understand the utility payoffs in figure 3 or figure 1 as already taking into account *all* factors influencing preferences. The extent to which Row cares about how an outcome affects Column is already factored into the numbers representing Row's preferences. On this interpretation, game theory does not address the problems of modeling strategic interactions as games. Instead, it supposes that they have already been solved and that the game to be analyzed is given. In some cases, all the hard work in theorizing about strategic behavior lies in modeling it as a game. What's left for the game theorist, once it has been determined what the game is, may be very simple.

Since it is difficult to know what experimental subjects prefer and hence what game they are playing, it is difficult to test game theory. One fact that complicates learning the preferences is that *preferences over outcomes of the interaction* (which Sen calls "comprehensive outcomes" [1997, p. 745]) *need not coincide with preferences over the monetary payoff pairs the outcomes involve* (which Sen calls "culmination outcomes"). Comprehensive outcomes are not identical to monetary payoff pairs. Unless people care only about the monetary payoffs (regardless of the path through the game that leads to them), their preferences over comprehensive outcomes need not coincide with their preferences over pairs of monetary payoffs. For example, an experimental subject $X$ asked to choose between ($3, $1) and ($2, $3) ($3 for $X$ and $1 for some other subject rather than $2 for $X$ and $3 for the other) might prefer ($3, $1). Yet this same subject in the role of Player II might play *right* in the interaction depicted in figure 2 to thank the first player for playing *down* rather than *up*. Or the first player in that interaction might play *down* rather than *up*, simply because it is boring to end the interaction without seeing what the second player will do. Preferences among culmination outcomes are no more than fallible evidence concerning preferences over comprehensive outcomes. One cannot read off preferences over comprehensive outcomes from preferences over simpler alternatives or preferences over culmination outcomes.

There are two main ways to respond to the difficulties in learning the preferences of experimental subjects. The first uses the opportunities that a laboratory provides to manipulate people's preferences and essentially to force subjects to play the game one wants them to play.[3] So, for example, one might have the players play for "points" rather than dollars and tell the players that each player's points will be converted to dollars according to a separate schedule that will not be revealed until the end of the game. Although more points means more money, zero points for one of the players might lead to a larger monetary reward for that player than 3 points for the other player. Not knowing how points translate into dollars would greatly diminish concerns about fairness, reciprocation, trust, and winning. There would still be room for altruism and malevolence, though they would be weakened. Though there is no guarantee that experimenters can induce subjects to have the "right" preferences, a great deal can be done; and for the purposes of testing the claims of game theory, this seems the best path to follow. This path is analogous to what physicists would do if they wanted to use observations of trajectories to test Newton's laws. They would set up a situation in which they could be sure of the initial trajectories and in which they would shield the bodies from other forces. Similarly, experimental chemists concerned to test claims about acidity would choose reagents that are known to be pure and known not to be chemically reactive in other ways, or they would purify them and treat them with chemicals that retard extraneous reactions.

But this path of heightened control is of direct little use if one is concerned with applications of game theory to explain and predict strategic behavior or to advise individuals facing strategic situations. For these purposes, one needs to be able to apply game theory to strategic situations that are not so tightly controlled. For practical purposes, one needs to know what people's preferences are and what things their preferences depend on. Which features of interactions influence preferences in which environments? Though it is important to study what people do when one forces them to have certain preferences, one will not be able to explain or predict the outcomes of interactions "in the wild" or advise people how to act unless one understands people's preferences and what they depend on. So the second response is to attempt to learn about people's preferences.

This is a very difficult task, and economists may be unwilling to tackle it, preferring a division of labor whereby psychologists and sociologists study what determine the preferences individuals have and economists then take over to investigate the consequences of those preferences. This division of labor is, I believe, unworkable, in part because game theory has so much to contribute to modeling

[3]Compare this to Vernon Smith's work on experimental markets [Smith, 2000].

strategic interactions as games and studying the determinants of preference. But if this division of labor could be carried out, it would merely change the disciplinary affiliation on the experimenter's name tag. Experimentation that employs game theory to test claims about individual preferences and hence the right way to model strategic interactions would no longer count as economics.

Whether they count as economists or some other sort of investigator, experimenters have many empirical questions to ask both about the empirical adequacy of game theory and about the character of people's preferences. Both inquiries are important. Even if the empirical difficulties with the axioms of game theory could all be resolved, empirical applications would still need accurate characterizations of people's preferences, and no matter how accurately experimenters characterize people's preferences, the predictions of game theoretic models will go astray if they do not correctly capture the principles governing individual choice, belief, preference, and reasoning.

Indeed the distinction between tests of game theory and tests that employ game theory to learn about people's preferences is by no means sharp. Consider Roth and Malouf's classic study of binary lottery games [1979].[4] In binary lottery games, two players bargain over the distribution of lottery tickets. The number of lottery tickets a player has represents the probability that the player will win a prize. On the assumption that players prefer more money to less, Nash bargaining theory asserts that players prefer one bargain to a second whenever the first has a larger monetary expectation. So players seek more lottery tickets for themselves. Furthermore, though Nash bargaining theory takes preferences to be cardinally significant, like most of its competitors, it denies that preferences are interpersonally comparable. So one can assign a utility index of one to having all the lottery tickets and zero to having none and measure utility for each player by the proportion of lottery tickets he or she has. How much money one player gets if he or she has all the lottery tickets compared to how much money the other player would get is irrelevant. What actually happens is that in experiments where the prizes to the two players are unknown, the subjects bargain to a 50–50 split of lottery tickets, which is the Nash bargaining solution. But in experiments where the prizes are known and much higher for one player than for another, some subjects split the lottery tickets evenly, but just as many bargain to an outcome that equalizes the monetary expectations.

Roth, Malouf and Murnighan argue that these results refute any descriptive theory of bargaining "whose predictions are determined exclusively by the players' preferences and strategic possibilities" [1981, p. 154]. If what people care about is how much money they get out of the bargain — period — then Roth, Malouf and Murnighan are right. But their results apparently show that lots of people care about their relative expected monetary gains. Is it part of bargaining theory itself that this information is irrelevant or is it part of how one characterizes the

[4]With regard to the division of labor, notice that this study was published in the *Psychological Review*, while the follow-up cited below appeared in the *Journal of Economic Behavior and Organization*.

preferences that go into bargaining theory? Must one revise bargaining theory and admit interpersonal comparability in order to account for these experimental results, or could one instead take preferences as depending on relative expected monetary gains and hang on to Nash bargaining theory? As this example shows, experiments can sometimes be interpreted both as tests of game theory and as investigations into the character of people's preferences.

## 5 SOME IMPLICATIONS FOR SOCIAL SCIENTIFIC NATURALISM

What conclusions does this brief foray into the testing of game theory suggest concerning the similarities or differences between the natural sciences and work in the social sciences such as game theory with respect to goals, testing, explanation, objectivity or ontology?

**Goals.** Game theory is not as purely theoretical as are some of the natural sciences. Rather than seeking general laws, it seeks to apply them to the analysis of particular strategic problems, and in addition to theoretical goals, many game theorists aim to provide advice to agents who confront these strategic problems. There have been many arguments among economists about the relative importance of explanatory and predictive goals, and following Milton Friedman [1953], many economists would insist that the ultimate goals of economics should be exclusively predictive. Although these debates differ to some extent from disputes concerning the goals of the natural sciences, mainly because economics so rarely postulates new unobservable entities or properties [Hausman, 1998], there are also natural sciences that do not postulate unobservables and which aim to give advice as well as to predict or explain.

One might argue that game theory differs from any natural science, because it advises people concerning how to play games, while the natural sciences do not of course aim to advise the objects they study, which are incapable of taking advice. But this difference is superficial. It is just happenstance that the entities studied overlap with the entities advised. Engineering and applied science investigate their subject matter in order to advise people, too.

**Testing.** As the discussion above makes clear, the logic of testing of game theory is just the same as the logic of testing claims in the natural sciences, though the practical difficulties in the way of testing game theory are serious. Yet there are clearly some details that are distinctive. First, because some human behavior is culturally specific, experimenters do not know whether experimental results will hold up when experiments are replicated in different locations with different subjects. Ultimatum game experiments, for example, have been repeated in a wide variety of cultural settings. A study found largely similar (but not identical) results in Jerusalem, Ljubljana, Pittsburgh, and Tokyo [Roth *et al.*, 1991]. Camerer and Thaler [1995, p. 217] even report on unpublished results concerning children and adolescents. Experiments in the natural sciences do not require these repetitions. But it is plausible to maintain that the difference reflects nothing more than our comparative ignorance of the factors that influence choices. This is no need to replicate in Indonesia a laser experiment that was carried out in Belgium, because physicists know that none of the many things that differ in Belgium and Indonesia are relevant to the way that lasers behave.

Second, in accord with those who emphasize the importance of "*Verstehen*" or empathic understanding, an account of the determinants of preferences needs to take the agent's point of view. Investigators must capture the discriminations that subjects make. For example, in a variant of an ultimatum game, experimenters have found that if the proposed division is known to be determined by a chance mechanism rather than by the first player, then the second player is much more likely to accept an unequal division [Blount, 1995]. Since it matters to people whether the offer is made by the first player or by a chance mechanism, those who model the situation must draw this distinction, too. But in the natural sciences, experimenters often have to attend to differential selectivity or responsiveness, too. Chemicals discriminate in the sense that they react with only certain substances, and all living things make discriminations.

A third possibly distinctive feature of experimentation concerning game theory is that the discriminations and choices that agents make are subject to *evaluation* by the agents who make them. This has two consequences. First, insofar as experimentation makes subjects aware of what they distinguish and what they treat as the same (and of course it need not), it raises for the experimental subjects the question of whether they *ought* rationally to make the discriminations that they do. And having raised such questions, agents may change their choice behavior. Some experiments concerned with patterns of irrationality in choice behavior actually teach people to avoid those mistakes [Chu and Chu, 1990]. The observation of the behavior of experimental subjects can in this way easily pass over to become the training of the subjects. But this can happen in biological experimentation on non-humans, too.

A second implication of the fact that subjects, experimenters and others *evaluate* what subjects do in experiments is that experimental outcomes can give rise to moral reflection. Human behavior poses moral problems. Consequently experiments themselves can have moral consequences for those involved and for others as well. Among other things, this means that there are serious questions about which experiments are morally permissible and about how to protect human subjects. Though some of these issues arise in medical experimentation as well, the issues are distinctive features of psychological and social scientific research.

**Explanation, reasons and causes.** In explaining and predicting choices, game theorists cite causes that are also reasons; and this clearly marks a significant difference from the natural sciences, which are not concerned with reasons. The fact that game theory cites reasons is, of course, essential to the goal of giving rational advice. All of the factors that game theorists cite, apart from purely physical constraints, influence choices via their role in rational deliberation. So the way in which they influence choices is subject to rational evaluation as well as to causal analysis. One might emphasize this difference and argue that game theory is a fundamentally different kind of science than the natural sciences, or one might instead point out that many of the natural sciences also add additional constraints on the causal factors that they take to be of interest.

**Role of values.** Though the *subjects*' moral evaluations of choices and moral reflection on their own and other's preferences are clearly important, there seems to be no reason why the moral attitudes of game theorists or experimenters toward strategies, beliefs, preferences, or outcomes need play any role. I believe that one can in fact see the influence of the moral and political values of experimenters in the questions they choose to ask and in the design of experiments, and there are, no doubt, occasional failures in the analysis of data and interpretation of results owing to biases. But I see no fundamental difference here between game theory and work on issues in the natural sciences that are of practical importance.

**Reduction and ontology.** Although not as evident in the specific experiments discussed in this paper and in the aspects I focused on, experimentation concerning game theory bears in several ways on the relations between mind and body and between social entities and properties and physical entities. Though I cannot go at all deeply into these issues, let me make three observations. First, human premeditated game theory rejects behaviorism. The task of the game theorist is to explain or predict strategies or advise agents concerning what strategies to play on the basis of subjective preferences and beliefs [Hausman, 2000]. A behaviorist approach would leave the game theorist with nothing to do. Furthermore, the strategy discussed in this paper, of using experimentation and game theory in order to determine what subjective preferences depend on, presupposes that there are such things as subjective preferences. Second, even if mental states, such as an individual's particular beliefs and preferences at some moment of time, are realized in certain physical states of the individual, it is doubtful that explanations of choices in terms of physical states and processes could enrich, let alone replace explanations in terms of beliefs and preferences. Not only is there the possibility of multiple realizability — that an agent's beliefs and preferences may be realized by different physical (brain) states at different times — but explanations of actions in terms of physical states would appear not to be reason giving. How could establishing that certain brain states have certain causal consequences resolve questions about which of two alternative choices is the more rationally defensible? Third, game theory and experimentation on game theory, has a good deal to say about the status, generation, maintenance and consequences of social norms. Although outcomes of ultimatum game experiments are similar across cultures, there are some systematic differences, which reflect cultural norms. Experiments on other games show larger effects of norms, and there are also experiments showing how conventions can arise and in turn engender or undermine social norms [Sugden,

2005, Vanderschraaf, 2001]. Any attempt to reduce norms to features of individuals (as part of a larger attempt to unify the social and natural sciences) will want to incorporate these insights.

## 6 CONCLUSIONS

Though examining a small slice of one activity in economics, this paper has addressed and clarified (though certainly not answered) some of the questions that have been asked about the differences between the social and the natural sciences. This paper has shown that conceiving of game theory as if it were a theory in the natural sciences enables one to clarify the ways in which it is and is not testable and of why it is often the case that experiments involving game theory are better understood as experiments that employ game theory to learn about preferences than as tests of game theory. Yet there are certainly some distinctive features and both social science naturalists and anti-naturalists can find some support in this discussion. But, as this essay has illustrated, social scientific naturalism, like social scientific anti-naturalism, is not a clear position and the conviction that the social sciences are sciences just like the natural sciences, like the conviction that there is something fundamentally different between social inquiries and the natural sciences, is more valuable as a hunch motivating specific inquiries than as a general thesis that can be defended or refuted.

## ACKNOWLEDGEMENTS

Parts of this essay derive from [Hausman, 2005]. An earlier version was delivered as the keynote address at the 2005 meetings of the Pittsburgh-Carnegie Mellon Graduate Student Philosophy Conference.

## BIBLIOGRAPHY

[Andreoni, 1995] J. Andreoni. Cooperation in Public-Goods Experiments: Kindness or Confusion? *American Economic Review.* 85: 891-904, 1995.

[Blount, 1995] S. Blount. When Social Outcomes Aren't Fair: The Effect of Casual Attributions on Preferences, *Organizational Behavior and Human Decision Processes*, 63:2 (August), 131-144, 1995.

[Camerer and Thaler, 1995] C. Camerer and R. Thaler. Ultimatums, Dictators and Manners. *Journal of Economic Perspectives* 9: 209-19, 1995.

[Cameron, 1999] L. A. Cameron. Raising the Stakes in the Ultimatum Game: Evidence from Indonesia, *Economic Inquiry*, 37:1 (January), 47-59, 1999.

[Chu and Chu, 1990] Y. Chu and R. Chu. The Subsidence of Preference Reversals in Simplified and Marketlike Experimental Settings: A Note. *American Economic Review* 80: 902-11, 1990.

[Churchland, 1988] P. Churchland. *Matter and Consciousness.* Cambridge, MA: MIT Press, 1988.

[Davidson, 1963] D. Davidson. Actions, Reasons, and Causes. *Journal of Philosophy* 60: 685-700, 1963.

[Duhem, 1906] P. Duhem. *The Aim and Structure of Physical Theory*, 1906. Tr. Philip Weiner. Princeton: Princeton University Press, 1954.

[Friedman, 1953] M. Friedman. The Methodology of Positive Economics, pp. 3-42 of *Essays in Positive Economics*. Chicago: University of Chicago Press, 1953.

[Hausman, 1992] D. Hausman. *The Inexact and Separate Science of Economics*. Cambridge: Cambridge University Press, 1992.

[Hausman, 1998] D. Hausman. Problems with Realism in Economics, *Economics and Philosophy* 14: 185-213, 1998.

[Hausman, 2000] D. Hausman. Revealed Preference, Belief, and Game Theory. *Economics and Philosophy* 16: 99-115, 2000.

[Hausman, 2005] D. Hausman. 'Testing' Game Theory. *Journal of Economic Methodology* 12: 211-23, 2005.

[Hausman and McPherson, 2006] D. Hausman and M. McPherson. *Economic Analysis, Moral Philosophy, and Public Policy*. Cambridge: Cambridge University Press, 2006.

[Kim, 1998] J. Kim. *Mind in a Physical World*. Cambridge, MA: MIT Press, 1998.

[Machlup, 1969] F. Machlup. If Matter Could Talk, pp. 286-305 of Sidney Morgenbesser, Patrick Suppes, and Morton White, eds. *Philosophy, Science, and Method*. New York: St. Martin's Press, 1969.

[Mongin, 2006] P. Mongin. Value Judgments and Value Neutrality in Economics. *Economica* 73, 2006.

[Morgenbesser, 1970] S. Morgenbesser. Is It a Science? pp. 20-35 of Dorothy Emmet and Alasdair MacIntyre, eds. *Sociological Theory and Philosophical Analysis*. New York: Macmillan, 1970.

[Myrdal, 1958] G. Myrdal. *Value in Social Theory*, London, Routledge (edited and introduced by Paul Streeten, 1958.

[Osborne, 2004] M. Osborne. *An Introduction to Game Theory*. Oxford: Oxford University Press, 2004.

[Rabin, 1993] M. Rabin. Incorporating Fairness into Game Theory and Economics. *American Economic Review* 83: 1281-1302, 1993.

[Rosenberg, 1976] A. Rosenberg. *Microeconomic Laws: A Philosophical Analysis*. Pittsburgh, University of Pittsburgh Press, 1976.

[Roth and Malouf, 1979] A. Roth and M. Malouf. Game theoretical Models and the Role of Information in Bargaining. *Psychological Review* 86: 574-94, 1979.

[Roth *et al.*, 1981] A. Roth, M. Malouf, and J. K. Murnighan. *Journal of Economic Behavior and Organization* 2: 153-77, 1981.

[Roth *et al.*, 1991] A. Roth, V. Prasnikar, S. Zamir, and M. Okuno-Fujiwara. Bargaining and Market Behavior in Jerusalem, Ljubljana, Pittsburgh, and Tokyo: An Experimental Study. *American Economic Review* 81: 1068-95, 1991.

[Schütz, 1953] A. Schütz. Common-Sense and Scientific Interpretation of Human Action. *Philosophy and Phenomenological Research* 14: 1-38, 1953.

[Sen, 1974] A. Sen. Choice, Orderings, and Morality. in Stephen Körner, ed. *Practical Reason*. New Haven: Yale University Press, pp. 54-67, 1974.

[Sen, 1987] A. Sen. *On Ethics and Economics*. Oxford: Blackwell, 19o87.

[Sen, 1997] A. Sen. Maximization and the Act of Choice. *Econometrica* 65: 745-79, 1997.

[Slonim and Roth, 1998] R. Slonim and A. Roth. Learning in High Stakes Ultimatum Games: An Experiment in the Slovak Republic. *Econometrica* 66: 569-96, 1998.

[Smith, 2000] V. Smith. *Bargaining and Market Behavior : Essays in Experimental Economics*. Cambridge: Cambridge University Press, 2000.

[Sugden, 2005] R. Sugden. *The Economics of Rights, Cooperation and Welfare*. 2nd ed. London: Palgrave Macmillan, 2005.

[Vanderschraff, 2001] P. Vanderschraff. *Learning and Coordination: Inductive Deliberation, Equilibrium and Convention*. London: Routledge, 2001.

[von Wright, 1971] G. von Wright. *Explanation and Understanding*. Ithaca: Cornell University Press, 1971.

[Weber, 1904] M. Weber. 'Objectivity' in Social Science and Social Policy, pp. 49-112 of *The Methodology of the Social Sciences*, 1904. Tr. and ed. E. Shils and H. Finch. New York: Macmillan, 1949.

[Weibull, 2004] J. Weibull. Testing Game Theory, in Steffen Huck, ed. *Advances in Understanding Strategic Behaviour, Game Theory, Experiments, and Bounded Rationality: Essays in Honor of Werner Güth*. London: Macmillan, pp. 85-104, 2004.

[Winch, 1958] P. Winch. *The Idea of a Social Science*. London: Routledge, 1958.

Part B

# Specific Methods, Theories, Approaches, Paradigms, Schools, Traditions

# THE PHILOSOPHY OF ECONOMIC FORECASTING

Clive W. J. Granger

## 1 INTRODUCTION

I believe that it is accurate to say that the typical economic forecaster does not ask herself questions about the underlying philosophy concerning what is being attempted. In fact, most could not define "philosophy" or would even attempt to do so. This is not necessarily a sign of intellectual weakness as even philosophers have difficulty defining philosophy and its objectives. "One might say that philosophy is what philosophers characteristically do" is a quotation from an article on Philosophy in "The Encyclopedia of Philosophy," Macmillan, (1996).

The same article stated that an earlier article on the same topic in the original version of the Encyclopedia "identified the distinctive feature of philosophy as its being a critical discussion of critical discussion." It also says that "Philosophy as a commonly characterized is a multifaceted discipline that resists simple characterization." One obvious approach is to ask a philosopher what he does but typically it will be very difficult to understand the answer as, like any other discipline, it has its own distinct terminology. However, philosophers and others will often ask interesting and penetrating questions that deserve the attention of forecasters, both to improve their understanding of what they are doing and possibly, in consequence, improve the quality of their output.

Forecasting is a very ancient occupation. The earliest groups of people who gathered together in small villages would be interesting in forecasting the seasons to know when to plant crops, when to move camp to where herds would be passing by, or when the salmon were running. Then, as now, forecasting was largely a practical process, involved with statements that could produce decisions that improved the economic well-being of the group involved.

## 2 PREREQUISITES

For convenience, it is important at this juncture to make two fundamental points that will be needed in what follows. The first is that I will consider the "economy" to consist of all the decision makers involved such as the consumers, investors, employers, and government policy makers as well as the various economic institutions,

Handbook of the Philosophy of Science. Volume 13: Philosophy of Economics.
Volume editor: Uskali Mäki. General editors: Dov M. Gabbay, Paul Thagard and John Woods.

such as the banks, corporations, trusts, and so forth. This will be called the "actual economy." In the literature prepared by philosophers the economy is usually taken to be the same as the constructs considered by economic theorists. This I will call the "theoretical economy." The economic theorists construct models based on sets of assumptions and perceived rational behavior by decision makers in an attempt to represent a simplified form of the actual economy. Sometimes these models are successful, sometimes less so according to data analysis. It is certainly true to say that philosophers in their writings about economics often confuse the theoretical economy with the actual economy. It is probably also correct to say that most decision makers in the actual economy are unaware of the results in the theoretical economy, and they do not suffer very much from this, although this could be less clear in the area of finance.

The second fundamental point is that it will be necessary to distinguish between "forecasting" and "prediction." Forecasting will be limited to the extrapolations based on empirical models or data exploration, whereas a prediction will be formed from a theoretical model. These differences are further explored in Section 3.

It will be helpful to use what has become the standardize "set-up" for forecasting in recent years. Let $X_t$ be a time series measured at equal intervals of time, such as each minute, day, or month as appropriate. The requirement that the series is recorded at equal time intervals can be relaxed but is technically more difficult. The fact that months are not strictly equal in length is merely pedantic and has been considered in the literature. It will be assumed that the series is not measured continuously in time, which is true in the actual economy, but continuous time is often assumed in the theoretical economy. This assumption will be discussed further below. $X_t$ will usually be taken to be a single series but it could be a vector, where $X_t$ is a particular economic variable such as a price, unemployment, or production.

The current moment of time is denoted $n$ indicating "now," so that $X_n$ is the current value of the $X$ series. At time $n$ there is available some empirical data including past and present values of $X_t$, which is denoted $XP_n$, so that $XP_n = \{X_n, X_{n-1}, X_{n-2}, \ldots, \}$. In practice there are only a finite number of past values available, but the impact of this fact is usually considered to be small. Other data series and their past will also be available, denoted as $WP_n$, where $W$ is usually a vector. It is usual to consider the information available at time $n$ which is used to form a forecast. An "information set" $I_n$ could consist, for example, of $XP_n$ and $WP_n$. A wider information set $J_n$ could consist of the contents of $I_n$ and also $YP_n$, where $Y_t$ is another series. We may be interested to know if the $Y$ series contains useful information that is not in the other series, as will be seen later. The information sets can also include non-numerical information, including opinions or constraints from economic theories.

When forecasting it is usual to have a specific horizon in mind, so the objective will be taken to look ahead $h$ steps, to the value of $X_{n+h}$. As the future may well be uncertain, otherwise one would not be forecasting, $X_{n+h}$ will be a random variable and thus can be described by a conditional distribution function $F_{x,n,h}(I_n) =$

Prob $(X_{n+h} < x \mid I_n)$ or its associated density function $f_{x,n,h}(I_n)$, which is the derivative of $F_x$. Here the forecast will be a density function dependent on the information set used and the horizon selected. It is important to note that even if $h$ is fixed, as $n$ changes the information set will alter and so the predictive density will also change. Thus forecasts will change with information, with horizon, and with time.

Historically, it was often too difficult to provide a predictive distribution and so simpler statistics were used instead. Typically only the forecast of the mean, denoted $m_{n,h}$, was given, such as "unemployment rate next month will be 7%" or "inflation will be 5%." Such figures only capture the middle of the predictive distribution and without some idea of the width and shape of the distribution sensible decisions are difficult to achieve. Statisticians would strongly recommend providing measures of uncertainty, such as the variance or the 95% confidence interval, although these were often difficult to interpret or were so wide that they were embarrassing!

This basic setup is quite general, as it can cover several important special cases. For example, $X_t$ can be constrained in some way, such as being positive or bounded to be between zero and one in value. It also included "event forecasts," such as a volcano will erupt, or there will be a financial crisis, or a business cycle downturn. Such events are captured with a zero-one random variable, with zero for when the event does not occur, and the predictive distribution will consist of just a probability $p_{n,h}$ of the event happening and probability $1 - p_{n,h}$ of it not occurring. The probability $p_{n,h}$ will be a function of the information set used and so will evolve over time.

It might be said that economic historians just look backwards and that some economist just look sideways, but forecasters have to look back to be able to look forward. They have to select the useful pieces of information from the past from the mass of information that is available from which to form their forecasts It is clear that many forecasts could be made and so a process of evaluation is essential to learn what seems to be helpful to decision makers and what does not.

At time $n + h$ there will exist the observed values of the series $X_{n+h}$ and a forecast of this quantity that was made at time $n$, i.e., the predictive density $f(x, n, h(I_n))$ based on the information set $I_n$. The error series, which is defined as the actual minus the forecast will have density $f(X_{n+h} - x, n, h(I_n))$. At time $n + h$ all components of this density are known and so all of the properties of the error can be obtained and the evaluation can be conducted on them. A standard measure is to record the average "likelihood" of the actual, given by the average of $f(X_{n+h}, n, h(I_n))$ over some appropriate sample.

The expectation of the error density, defined as

$$\int_{-\infty}^{\infty} x f(x, n)$$

produces the "point forecast error" = actual - point forecast, or in notation $e_{n,h} = X_{n+h} - m_{n,h}$. Traditionally, and certainly until the end of the twentieth century, forecast evaluation concentrated on these errors. If the forecast is to be used by a decision make, the cost of making an incorrect forecast might be measure by a "cost function $c_e$," so that an error of the amount $e$ results in a cost $c_e$.

Many aspects of economic forecasting, including the evaluation of forecasts, can be found in "*The Handbook of Economic Forecasting*" edited by G. Elliott, C.W.J. Granger, and A. Timmermann, Elsevier, 2006.

A critical aspect of forecasting is the choice of the information set, which will include data from the past and present, any available stated plans or policies for the future and include changes in the structure of the economy, laws and institutions. A forecast will be forward looking partially based on backward information, but not entirely so. The proposition that a society, and thus an economy, should have some stability over time and some momentum together with understandable changes, is not a very surprising one and forms the basis of many forecasts. Thus, potentially at least, we learn from the lessons of history when forecasting.

## 3 FORECASTING, PREDICTION, AND ECONOMICS

Much of the actual, as well as theoretical, economy is forward looking. Decision makers make decisions now that will have impacts in the future. Investors decide where to invest now and wait to see what return occurs; consumers buy now but consume over the net few hours or days; a house-buyer decides now and uses the purchase over several years; an employer agrees to hire a worker and makes use of his or her skill over some later period. Essentially the decision maker has to forecast the future consequences of the decision. Further, policy making is clearly about the future. It can be thought of as a number of alternative conditional forecasts. If the agency does one thing, we expect the future to be like this. But if the agency does something else, the future will be like that. The policy make chooses the better, expected future. It is thus seen that major components of both macro- and micro-economics will involve forecasting. The extensions to international economics and to finance are obvious and in fact both of the actual economies in these areas are major consumers of forecasts, sometimes called "expectations" in the media.

At this point it is important to carefully distinguish between "forecasting" as discussed in Section 2 above, and "prediction." Here prediction will mean taking a model, usually based on economic theory and assuming that it is correct, then drawing implications from it about the behavior of the economy, at least the theoretical one and possibly the actual one. Some example are given below. Prediction occurs when there is a model of the form

$$X_t = a + bY_t + e_t$$

where $X$ and $Y$ are a pair of specific economic variables, $e$ is a residual and the coefficients $a$ and $b$ have been estimated or chosen in some way. The model could be theoretical or empirical in origin. A simple example might have $Y$ a basic interest rate and $X$ inflation. A prediction of $X$ is formed by inserting a particular value for $Y$ into the equation, and then assuming that the model is correct. If, in the model $X_t$ is replaced by $X_{t+1}$ then putting an observed value for $Y_t$ into the model will provide a forecasting of the next value of $X$. This paper will usually be considering forecasts, although usually of a more sophisticated form.

A simple example of a prediction comes from price theory and says that if a company raises prices then the consequence is a reduction in sales. This is the kind of prediction that does not depend on a sophisticated theory and is observed in the actual economy to be usually true, but not always. These exceptions can be explained both using theory and empirical arguments. Blaug [1980, 2nd edition, 1992, pp. 151] suggests several other similar examples: "an increase in demand leads to a rise in both output and product prices," "a lump sum tax on business profits will have no effect on output," and "a rise in money wages causes a fall in employment." Note that all of these predictions are non-specific, the amount of the change and the timing are not given. Usually forecasts would be more specific.

On occasions a prediction from the theoretical economy about that economy can be evaluated by the actual economy. For example, Blaug [as before] states that the theory of the firm "predicts unequivocally that a profit maximizing firm in a perfectly competitive market will not advertise: it has no incentive to do so because it faces a perfectly elastic demand curve and can sell all that it can produce." As many firms do advertise their differentiated products, then the assumptions upon which the theory is based have to be incorrect.

As will be seen, prediction plays an important role in the topic of model evaluation and that forecasting becomes embroiled in the discussion.

## 4 THE PURPOSE OF ECONOMICS

It is useful to know the purpose for some body of work as it give a starting point for evaluation. For some disciplines such as medicine, psychology, and law, the purpose is to be helpful to their clients. However, for areas such as history or mathematics, which are certainly important and distinguished, being immediately helpful is unlikely to be the suggested purpose. The are a number of philosopher/economists such as Lawson [1997], Redman [1991], and Blaug [1980, 2nd edition, 1992] who consider many aspects of the interaction between the two areas, and the latter two take definite views on the purpose. Blaug [1980, 2nd edition, 1992, p. 246] states "the central aim of economics is to predict and not merely to understand" although he goes on to mix up forecasting and prediction. His statement should be taken to mean that prediction should be used to evaluate an economic theory. Redman [1992, p. 120] quotes Worswick [1972] "the idea of economics as positive science makes predictability the test of its performance, the prediction of relationships is situations not previously observed, as well as the prediction of future events, which in some ways is the acid test." This statement covers prediction in cross-sectional situations where everything occurs at the same time. In this paper only future events will be considered.

Of course, prediction is not the purpose of economics, even of theoretical economics. It is quite easy to formulate theories, one starts with a group of reasonable assumptions, adds a few generally accepted economic concepts such as a rational market, include some institutional constraints, and then prove theorems about the "economy" so derived. The theory can be simple or it can be very complicated but it usually will not be unique. The question of evaluation will have to ask if any of the models is adequate, in some fashion, and then which is the best. The evaluation can perhaps be based on prediction and on falsification.

Redman [1992, p. 24] also quotes Kuhn [1970] about a demarcation criterion without which no field is potentially a science: "(1) concrete predictions must emerge from the practice of the field; (2) for a subclass of phenomena, whatever passes for predictive success must be achieved; (3) predictive techniques must have roots in a theory which, however metaphysical, simultaneously justifies them, explains their limited success, and suggests means for their improvement in both precision and scope. Finally, the improvement of predictive technique must be a challenging task, demanding on occasions the very highest measure of talent and devotion."

Unfortunately, most of the early discussions of topics such as "the purpose of economics" and "is economics a science?" are based on viewpoints that are now generally considered outmoded. The early position taken was that physics (of a traditional form) was the standard against which one measured a field being a science. The methodology of traditional physics was the one to use for comparison. In this area the world was deterministic and not stochastic, and experiments should get the correct answer if properly conducted, or if repeated often enough the average will certainly tend to the correct value. Certainly the old theory had its clear successes, as Blaug [1992, p. 7] points out "who can deny the extraordinary predictive power of Newtonian theory particularly after the confirmation in 1758 of Edmond Halley's prediction of the return of 'Halley's comet,' topped in 1846 by Leverrier's use of the inverse-square law to predict the existence of a hitherto unknown planet, Neptune, from the observed aberrations in the orbit of Uranus." Since then the same theory has been extended to forecast the time and height of tides on virtually every beach in the world from now and for many years into the future. Of course all such forecasts are based on a set of assumptions and if the change so will the forecast, certainly a tsunami would change tides in the short run and if the Moon broke into two pieces the tide would be changed forever.

As the twentieth century evolved, with the advent of quantum physics and areas such as meteorology and oceanography, the definition of a science changed together with the appropriate methodology. The move from dealing with just inanimate objects, as with classical physics, to animate ones as with medicine and biology, greatly extends the range of the subjects being considered and of the topic "what is a science?"

The next extension is to objects (or subjects) that are individual decision makers, covered by areas such as psychology, economics, and political science, although some parts of biology will also fall into this category. As the type of objective being studied changes it is reasonable to expect that the methodology will evolve as will the objective of the subject area.

I do not think that economists have been involved in a careful enough discussion about what is the purpose of economics. My personal view comes from the observation made above that the economy consists of many types of decision makers. It follow then that the objective of economics should be to help decision makers make better decisions. It is fairly easy to understand now to do this in some parts of economics such as finance and macro-economics, but much more difficult in those areas where decisions are not emphasized, such as parts of cross-section, micro- and theoretical economics.

## 5 PHILOSOPHICAL QUESTIONS

A number of questions will now be considered that may be thought of as having philosophical origins.

### *5.1 Is the Economy Deterministic or Stochastic?*

A system, such as an economy, is deterministic if its progress can be fully described without the use of probabilities (other than zero and one). Know the past will completely determine the immediate future, and then by iteration, all of the future. The basic idea that the universe could then be deterministic comes from classical physics, which has known, simple, and unchanging laws that operate everywhere and at all times. As stated before, this allows the positions of the planets to be known exactly in the future, for example, and thus the timing of tides anywhere on earth can be determined, provided that the basic assumptions continue to hold.

Historians may also subscribe to their domain of interest being deterministic, as the past cannot be changed, although interpretations about why things happen are not constant: the reason for the decline of the Roman Empire or for the occurrence of the Black Death changes every decade or so. Although history is certainly unchanging, what we know about it is by no means constant and so interpretation can evolve. The theoretical economy is often assumed to be deterministic as results are usually easier to obtain under this assumptions.

It should be pointed out that for a theoretical economy, ANY basic assumption can be made. the only requirement is that the participants in this economy behave in an "economically sensible" fashion given these assumptions. There is no requirement that these economies be realistic and there can exist several of them about the same topic but with different assumptions.

In contrast, a stochastic system is one that has to use probabilistic concepts in describing its progress, such as "if today we are at $A$, then tomorrow we will be at $B$ with probability 0.4, and at $C$ with probability 0.6." With this definition, anything that is not deterministic must be stochastic. However, it is more convenient to consider processes that are "purely stochastic," which would rapidly collapse to a constant (or possibly a simple trend) if the stochastic component was switched off, and then to have systems which consists of both deterministic and purely stochastic components. Suppose that we could invent a measure $Q$ which takes values between zero and one, with $Q = 0$ corresponding to deterministic and $Q = 1$ to purely stochastic. Then classical physics would have $Q = 0$, quantum physics $Q = e$, where $e$ is a small positive number, $Q = 0.3$ for meteorology, and $Q = 0.6$ for macroeconomics with $Q = 0.9$ for much of finance. I suppose that history has $Q = 0$, but that is open to debate.

Only if $Q = 0$ can you assume that perfect forecasting is possible, otherwise forecast errors will occur. However, if errors do occur it may be because we are not good at forecasting rather than because of the inherent stochastics.

A complicating issue is the existence of a class of mathematical iterative processes known as "chaos" or chaotic A very simple example (known as the logistic map) is

$$X_{t+1} = a(X_t(1 - X_t))$$

with the starting value $X_1$ chosen in the region (0,1) and the parameter $a$ chosen to be in the region 3.6 to 4.0. Data generated from this map has the properties of white noise, with a constant mean and variance and all serial correlations that are zero, when estimated. However, the generated data does not have the properties of an independent series, although this is sometimes claimed in the chaos literature, as powers of the series are not serially uncorrelated. However, more complicated maps than the logistic shown above can generate series that have more of the properties of an independent series and will also be chaotic. Some of these maps are used in computer programs to generate "artificial random numbers" that are used in various statistical procedures such as the bootstrap and simulations. Provided the sample sizes used are not too large, these artificial series will usually work well and appear to be random. Nevertheless, a long enough series will fail a test of randomness and will suggest that they are generated from a deterministic map. One can then go and devise a yet more complicated map which will produce series that are more difficult to distinguish from strictly random, although with enough data they can be, in theory at least. It is seen that the division between deterministic white chaos and a truly stochastic random process is becoming very unclear. Whether there is any difference in the limit is truly a philosophical question; it is deep and difficult but its solution has little practical relevance.

If a theoretical economy is deterministic it is due to the assumptions being used. If an actual economy is deterministic, then this is a basic property of the economy. It is possible for part of an economy to be deterministic, but not other parts, just as in the actual physical world the tides could be deterministic, but the temperature of the water involved could be stochastic. An example is economics would be the month of the year with the greatest store sales in a European country (December) and the amount sold in that month. Limitations on the causal relationships between the deterministic and stochastic parts are discussed later.

It might be worth pointing out that a totally deterministic society is very boring as it is highly forecastable, at least in the short run. There will be no horse racing or gambling; there is little point in playing any sporting contest as everyone know the outcome and every political election can be very short and inexpensive. The winner is already known. These results require the generating map to be either know or well approximated by a neural network analysis. The degradation of the forecasts as the horizon increases is due to the accumulated effects of a round-off error.

A very well known economic theorist, Sir John Hicks, stated [Hicks, 1979] that economics is "on the edge of science and on the edge of history" as it tries to use the techniques of science but its subject matter behaves differently. Hicks [1986] says "If a scientific theory is good, it is good now and would have been good a thousand years ago ... but the aspects of economic life which we need to select in order to make useful theories can be different at different times." (Quotes from [Redman, 1991, p. 106].) Chaos theory is designed for a deterministic, unchanging physical world and has not performed well in the decision theoretic world of economics.

## *5.2 Can An Economic Agent Have Perfect Foresight?*

Amongst the assumptions that are sometimes made within an economic theory for the sake of simplicity is that of "perfect foresight." The purpose of such assumptions is to reach some immediate conclusions from the theory, and they are later dropped to see if the same conclusions hold in a more general situation. If an agent had perfect foresight, she could continually make optimum investments and accumulate considerable wealth. She would win every "game" situation as she would know her opponent's choices. It is doubtful if every agent could be assumed to have perfect foresight as game situations would have no solutions as no one would be able to make a choice. This is not a very interesting assumption and is a totally unrealistic one.

If everyone had perfect foresight the economy as we know it would cease to exist. There would be no markets as everyone would know the eventual price obtained, economic policies would not work as they are perfectly anticipated and everyone knows the impact, if any.

Occasionally economic theorists who are used to making a perfect foresight assumption will criticize an economic forecaster for producing imperfect forecasts. Only a little thought produces reasons why many forecasts will be imperfect such as short-term and, even more clearly, long-term weather forecasts, as well as forecasts of a horse race. There are too many things that can occur. Sen [1986] points to two particular reasons for economics: the large number of individual decision makers involved in a typical economy (a hundred million households in the United States and the European Union, with even more in China and India), and also the many interactions between these decision makers.

## *5.3 Is It Worth Making A Forecast That Is Not Perfect?*

In 1928 Oscar Morgenstern, who later became famous as a co-author of the first book on game theory, published in German a pamphlet on the irrelevance of economic forecasts. This work has become known through the attack on it by Marget [1929]. Morgenstern essentially makes the point that economic forecasts can never be perfect as they are based on an inadequate economic theory and poor data. He states that if they are not perfect, then they cannot be used for policy purposes. His arguments relate to classical, pre-quantum physics and his policy points have been largely superseded by the development of decision making under uncertainty. Marget essentially tries to weaken the arguments proposed without going to a stochastic viewpoint. It should be noted that Morgenstern makes no mention of his position in his later books on "the accuracy of economic date" and on the "forecastability of stock market prices," the second of which is written with me.

A few writers go beyond the imperfection of economic forecasts to conclude that all such forecasts are so bad that they should be disregarded. A few may even claim that economic forecasting is not possible, although there is a difficulty with semantics. Blaug [1982, p. 158] firmly disagrees saying "If prediction of human behavior were truly impossible, if none of us could predict anything about the behavior of other people, economic life itself, not to mention theories about economic life, would be unimaginable. Not only would the total incapacity to predict economic events wipe out economic theory: it would wipe out every other type of economics, as well as all pretences of offering advice to governments and business enterprises."

## *5.4 Omniscience*

Suppose there exists some entity that is omniscient. Following the philosophical literature I will call the entity "God" and use the pronoun "He," without there being any implications from these choices. The fact that if God has omniscience then there are important philosophical implications is not of immediate relevance for an essay about forecasting. I will not be concerned with policy questions at this moment and certainly not free-will.

By omniscience I take it to mean that God could forecast any component of the economy at any time in the future if He cared to do so. In particular, he could have perfect foresight about the behavior of every decision maker. It follows that if He were rational and utility maximizing He could quickly acquire immense wealth, and would soon be testing the theories about there being a satiation level for wealth. Of course, as God would have nothing to spend his wealth on, it is irrational to expect Him to have a standard utility function.

As a forecaster, should my behavior change if I am told that there exists a God who can forecast perfectly? It would imply that if I improve my technique and gather a good enough information set, then I should be able to do almost as well. Alternatively, it could imply that I would need godly abilities and resources to do so well, and so should be content with much less. If I add a small positive probability that God does not exist, I am back to a stochastic economy.

The idea that an all-knowing God with omniscience will know the future of us all with certainty is probably placing us at too high a level of importance. For Him to foresee the exact position and behavior of every living creature, from microbes up, on every planet under his control, is quite possibly within his computing abilities, but it is very unclear why He would want to ever undertake that task, even though it only has to be done once. We have no idea of His reasoning, requirements, and desires and we certainly do not know if His time scale is the same as the one with which we are involved, or if beings on other planets thinking vastly quicker or slower than us. Without more basic knowledge, or further assumptions, it is doubtful if the possibility of omniscience has any impact on everyday economic forecasting.

## 5.5 *Why Cannot We Forecast Perfectly?*

It is general knowledge that economic forecasts are not perfect, and this is the basis for many jokes. Sen [1986] states "It is, in fact, tempting to see the economist as the trapeze performer who tends to miss the cross bar, or as the jockey who keeps falling off his horse." What is not clear is why the economists should be singled out. Does a patient who is sick go to a doctor one week and then complain the following week if he is not completely cured? Are there articles in the press asking why the horse-racing correspondent did not pick all the winners yesterday or why the weather forecasts do not turn out to be perfect? Sen is obviously reflecting the traditional approach, taken by Morgenstern and based on the believe (or the assumption) that economics is a science, in the old fashioned sense. However, Sen does then go on to give at least two plausible reasons for the non-perfection: the difficulty in anticipating human behavior; and aggregation or size effect.

1. Anticipation of human behavior follows from the fact that many individual decision makers are involved (who are not automatons) and that their decisions will evolve as the learn, their tastes change, their choice sets evolve, and the institutions and society changes around them. Each person can react differently to these changes.

2. The size effect comes from the fact that there are many millions of families in the typical economy, with complicated interactions. As Sen says, there are "millions of human beings each with different values, objectives, motivations, expectations, endowments, rights, means, and circumstances." This will make aggregation difficult both for theorists and for data analysts without some simplifying assumptions. Some of these assumptions may be reasonable, but others (such as having "representative agents") are generally thought to be not useful in practice.

These are certainly important and relevant reasons that would be likely to be included in a defense by an empirical forecaster, although there, more attention would be paid to the likelihood of the economy being stochastic. If the level of stochasticity is high, forecasts will be imperfect.

Sen was concerned with the topic "Prediction and Economics Theory" and so was considering the use of a theoretical model to provide "predictions," which are not necessarily forecasts as mentioned earlier. They are based on the assumption that the theory is correct. He discusses the relevance of topics such as "equilibrium," "rationality," "maximization" and, later, the use of an assumption such as "self-choice goal" in which each act of choice of a person is the pursuit of one's own goal (such as the maximization of utility). He finds that many of these concepts are difficult to use for prediction. Currently certain equilibrium models are being used for long-term macro forecasting, but evaluation is difficult.

Of course it has to be admitted that the forecasts may be imperfect because of the incompetence of the forecasters. They may be using poor quality data sets or insufficiently sophisticated forecasting techniques, or it could just be that the computing power is insufficient for the task, as the economy is just too complicated. If these were all or some of our problems, I believe that we could expect to see improvements in forecastability, either a steady progress or a series of steps as breakthroughs occur. There has been some progress, but the variables being forecast have changed in nature and it seems that the data may have declined in quality in some important cases.

## *5.6 Differences in Forecastability*

It has been observed in the actual economy that economic variables vary in their "forecastability;" that is, the extent to which they can be forecast. For example, it is quite easy to forecast the demand for electricity at every hour tomorrow in an American city. The demand is to a very large extent determined by the particular day, by the regular pattern of activities through the day of the consumers in the city, and the forecast of the temperature for the day. Since temperature is quite easy to forecast twenty-four hours ahead, and as the use-of-electricity pattern is stable given the temperature, the forecast can be made a day ahead and will usually be very accurate. This forecast is of considerable importance to the electric utility company that supplies the electricity for the region. It is worth noting that the variable essentially consists of two components: the regular daily use patter (which changes each day); and the very complicated (possibly stochastic) weather component.

At the other extreme returns from stock market prices are very difficult to forecast, as was found empirically from very early work by Bachelier [1900] and later by various statisticians considering a model called "the random walk hypothesis," which essentially says that these returns are not forecastable. Economic theorists later stated these ideas in the "efficient market hypothesis," which notes that if you could forecast the return from any speculative asset, you would have a "money machine" which would produce unlimited amounts of money. As such a machine is impossible, the returns cannot be forecastable.

Naturally, most economic variables lay between these two extremes. It is generally true that anything that one can easily profit from, good forecasts are difficult to make. Commodity prices, interest rates, exchange rates, and commodity rates fall into this group. However, if an interest rate is used as a control variable, such as by the Federal Reserve Bank, The Australian National Bank, or the European Bank, it does become easier to forecast. Some variables from a stock market, such as daily volume traded, or the number of stocks advancing in a day, or even daily volatility of an individual stock are all somewhat forecastable. It is generally true that the levels of variables are much more forecastable than the corresponding changes or rates of return. For example, the level of unemployment rather than the change in it, or the price level rather than inflation. All such statements are observed properties of the actual economy as observed through the lens of the present forecasting methodology. They could change as the methodology improves. It might be noted that if the economy was deterministic, then the level of a variable and its change would both be perfectly forecastable.

Economic variables are included to change in value as new and relevant information accumulates. This happens very quickly in a speculative market, quite slowly for the major variables in macroeconomics, and very slowly in population economics. In general, users of forecasts prefer higher accuracy rather than lower, but not necessarily in all cases. For example, if someone offered to forecast the date of your death, most people would prefer not to have that information even though knowledge of it would lead to more rational investment decisions.

## *5.7 Should Forecasts Be Rational?*

The "rational expectations" revolution in macroeconomics took place in the 1970's, but the basis of the idea and the corresponding theory was developed a decade early by Muth in 1961. It was observed that economic decision makers were being assumed to be rational and that their decisions would be influenced by forecasts or "expectations" and so these also should be rational in the sense that they should not be obviously sub-optimum. A "rational expectation" should use all the relevant information that is available and also appropriate methods of forming a forecast. A given set of forecasts could be shown to be "irrational" if they were clearly sub-optimum, as shown by a statistical test. The theory could become complicated as some of the models used to form the expectations involved expectations, so some problem usually reflects the lack of subtlety about timing of occurrences within the model.

If better forecasts are easily available it would certainly be irrational to use inferior ones, but finding the very best may be too expensive in terms of searching for slightly better methods and a few useful but expensive last pieces of information.

An implication of the considerations of rational expectations was that the usefulness and relevance of much government policy was thrown into doubt, at least over the long run. An unexpected change in policy could still have an immediate effect, which will continue into the future.

Many countries have important survey efforts that try to measure the plans of industrialists about their future capital investment and employment and also consumer about their buying plans. the most successful of these seems to be the investment plans, which once started are less easy to stop without considerable cost. This possibility illustrates the fact that useful forecasts can come from a non-theory or model based approach.

### *5.8 How Far Can One Forecast?*

The question of how far one can successfully forecast is tied to the topic of evaluation. A forecasting model can be run out into the indefinite future, but the relevant question is: over what horizon are the forecasts of any value? The answer is also tied to the concept of the forecastability of various types of economic variables. Some variables are slow moving and are very predictable over long horizons, such as population growth, whereas others have virtually no possibility to forecast, such as speculative returns.

A deterministic variable can be (perfectly forecast) into the indefinite future without any error. In contrast, a variable with a stochastic element will steadily accumulate the stochastic, unforecastable component until no forecastable part can be detected.

In macroeconomic, the longest horizons attempted are about three years, although forecasts up to ten years are sometimes presented. In finance, the longest forecast horizons are usually much shorter.

In might be noted that evaluation is difficult for these long term forecasts as it takes many years for the actual value to become known to compare to the forecast.

Some economic series contain what may appear to be clear trends; that is, a steadily increasing central value, such as a straight line, or a quadratic or exponential curve in time. A simple example would be Real Gross National Product, Investment or Consumption. If such a variable grows steadily ti will produce an exponential curve and such a curve is occasionally found in practice, but not in every country. However, series such as unemployment, prices, and interest rates do not contain trends, and so cannot be forecast over long periods, other than naively.

## 6 CAUSALITY AND CONTROL

### *6.1 Causality and Control*

This is a very important and extensive topic that is covered in a different chapter in this Handbook prepared by Kevin Hoover. Here I will just discuss some aspects of forecasting in economic causality.

Most, but not all, economists accept the proposition that the cause occurs in time before the effect. The time distance between the two may be very small, but it has to be positive. See, for example White [2005]. There is also an extensive literature on instantaneous causality, but as it has no implications for prediction, I will not discuss it. Hume [1739] and Hicks [1979] can be included in those who specifically have the effect occurring before the effect.

This temporal order does not necessarily indicate predictability of the cause by the effect. A definition suggested by the famous mathematician, Norbert Wiener (and previously discussed by Bunge [1963] and doubtless other philosophers) is the idea that I extended and made specific in Granger [1969] and [1980]. There are two requirements:

1. that the cause precedes the effect; and

2. that the cause has information about the effect that is not available in a wide group of other variables.

In terms of distributions, where $F(X/Y)$ denotes the distribution function of the random variable $X$ conditional on $Y$, then $Y$ does not cause $X$ (with respect to $W$) if $F(X/Y(W)) = F(X/W)$, where here $W$ is a vector of variables not including $Y$ or $X$. If the equality is replaced with an inequality then causality is indicated.

An immediate implication of the definition is that causality of $X_{\bar{t}+1}$ by $Y_t$ means that $Y_t$ will help forecast $X_{t+1}$ in distribution. The definition can also be stated using just means rather than distributions and "tests for causality" can be easily constructed in this case. In economics, this has become the most commonly used definition of causality because it is easy to understand and to test. It has also been much misunderstood and misused. Due to the forecasting aspect of the definition, it is often used to help in the specification of empirical models that are to be used for forecasting.

The link between causality and control may seem to be an obvious one and to be closely related to forecasting. The usual position is that if a causal relationship is known, or believed to be known, then it can be manipulated to provide a control mechanism and thus appropriate policy methods. Economic writers strongly disagree on the relationship between cause and control, some make it the basis of their definition of causality, such as Hoover [2001] and Pearl [2000], but other claim that there is no necessary link. This is not an appropriate place to survey such a complicated topic. My personal view can be given in terms of an example. Suppose that it is observed that a particular New York newspaper has considerable influence with its readers when recommending who to vote for in local elections. A wealthy investor decides to buy the newspaper so that it will support politicians of his choosing. If this becomes widely known, the original causality/control will be lost and a new forecasting regime will begin. the example shows that the can be causality, but when it is used as a control, the causal relationship can be broken. I believe that controllability is a deeper concept that causality and thus more difficult to test for using economic data.

One topic that has received little attention is: can a deterministic process cause a stochastic one?

## *6.2 Forecasting and Ethics*

In the traditional areas of forecasting such as predicting the weather or the timing of the next high tide, it is difficult to imagine the forecast having any impact on the variable being considered. The physical process that generates rain, for example, is unaware of the statements made by the weather forecaster. However, this will not necessarily be the case in the social sciences such as economics. If a financial journalist states that a certain stock price should increase over the next week, investors may believe the forecast, invest accordingly, and induce a change in price. The resulting ethical problem is clear as investors who know the forecast early and invest immediately, as the market will adjust to the forecast price rapidly. Those who clearly have a chance of profiting from the situation are the journalist herself, her immediate family and friends, and possibly the staff of the newspaper involved.

Many economic forecasts potentially have the ability to influence the actual economy. A forecast of a turning point in the business cycle or a higher employment rate or an increase in inflation could produce a policy change by some government agency. Naturally, this will only occur if the forecaster is particularly accomplished and has a previous good performance record. However, the policy changes may ensure that the forecasts do not become correct, suggesting that the forecaster will be less successful.

A forecaster is trained to produce the best forecast possible but there is no need to produce just a single value. One can make a forecast without taking into account the possible policy change and a further forecast will indicate the likely policy change and its impact.

Ethical problems will largely arise if a forecaster produces values that represent a biased viewpoint or if the values are not released publicly immediately. Transparency of the data and methods used and to who and when they are issued become essential features. With sufficient information the question of determining ethics becomes one for the forecasting community who have to evaluate the forecasts produced. With the availability of superior computers and forecasting programs widespread, evaluation is easy to accomplish.

Some econometric models and other techniques are deliberately biased to represent the view of some political party, on the left or right for example, and will naturally produce biased forecasts. A central bank which will forecast inflation, and will also be interested in controlling inflation, will likely produce downward biased forecasts of inflation. This can be achieved by using a non-symmetric cost function when forming the forecast. There seems to be no ethical problem if this behavior is well understood, but if kept a secret it is a problem.

## *6.3 Evaluation*

The only major topic in the area of forecasting that has not been considered here is the question of how to evaluate forecasts. Evaluation is an important component in the forecasting process as it allows one to improve techniques and to discover which methods are the most satisfactory in practice. This is a wholly pragmatic subject, perhaps based on basic aspects of decision theory, and is therefore not particularly relevant to the main theme of this paper.

## BIBLIOGRAPHY

[Bachelier, 1900] L. Bachelier. "Theory of Speculation." *Ann. Sci. École Norm. Sup. (3)*, No. 1018, Gauthier-Villars, Paris, 1900.

[Baranzini and Scazzieri, 1986] M. Baranzini and R. Scazzieri, eds. "Foundations of Economics." Basil Blackwell, Oxford, 1986.

[Blaug, 1980] M. Blaug. "The Methodology of Economics: or, How Economists Explain." Cambridge University Press, New York, 1980.

[Granger, 1969] C. W. J. Granger. "Testing For Causality and Feedback." *Econometrica* 37. pp. 424–438, 1969.

[Granger, 1988] C. W. J. Granger. "Testing for Causality: A Personal Viewpoint." *Journal of Economic Dynamics and Control* 2, 329-352, 1988.

[Hicks, 1979] J. R. Hicks. "Causality in Economics." Basil Blackwell, Oxford, 1979.

[Hicks, 1986] J. R. Hicks. "Is Economics a Science?" in Baranzini and Scazziero (eds.), *Foundations of Economics*, Basil Blackwell, Oxford, 1986.

[Hoover, 2001] K. Hoover. "Causality in Macroeconomics." Cambridge University Press, New York, 2001.

[Hume, 1730] D. Hume. "A Treatise of Human Nature", 1730. Page numbers refer to the edition by L.A. Selby-Bigge, Clarendon Press, Oxford (1888).

[Lawson, 1997] T. Lawson. "Economics and Reality." Routledge, New York, 1997.

[Marget, 1929] A. W. Marget. "Morgenstern on the Methodology of Economic Forecasting." *Journal of Political Economy* 37, pp. 312-339, 1929.

[Redman, 1991] D. A. Redman. "Economics and the Philosophy of Science." Oxford University Press, New York, 1991.

[Pearl, 2000] J. Pearl. "Causality: Models, Reasoning, and Inference." Cambridge Univ. Press, New York, 2000.

[Sen, 1986] A. K. Sen. "Prediction and Economic Theory." *Proceedings of The Royal Society London A*, 407, pp. 3-23, 1986.

[White, 2005] H. White. "Causal, Predictive and Explorative Modeling in Economics." Oxford University Press, 2005.

[Worswick, 1972] G. D. N. Worswick. "Is Progress in Economic Science Possible?" *Economic Journal* 82, pp. 73-100, 1972.

# PHILOSOPHY OF ECONOMETRICS

Aris Spanos

## 1 INTRODUCTION

Philosophy of econometrics is concerned with the systematic study and appraisal of general principles, statistical procedures and modeling strategies, as well as philosophical presuppositions that underlie econometric methods, with a view to evaluate their effectiveness in achieving the primary objective of 'learning from data' about economic phenomena of interest. In philosophical jargon it is a core area of the philosophy of economics, concerned primarily with *epistemological* and *metaphysical* issues pertaining to the empirical foundations of economics. In particular, it pertains to *methodological* issues having to do with the effectiveness of statistical methods and procedures used in empirical inquiry, as well as *ontological* issues concerned with the worldview of the econometrician. Applied econometricians, grappling with the complexity of bridging the gap between theory and data, face numerous philosophical/methodological issues pertaining to transforming non-experimental, noisy and incomplete data into reliable evidence for or against a substantive hypothesis or a theory.

Discussions of econometric methodology since the late 1970s have been primarily 'local' affairs [see Granger, 1990; Hendry *et al.*, 1990; Hendry, 2000; Leamer 1978; Pagan, 1987; Sims, 1980; Spanos, 1988; 1989], where no concerted effort was made to integrate the discussions into the broader philosophy of science discourses concerning empirical modeling; some notable recent exceptions are [Hoover, 2002; 2006], [Keuzenkamp, 2000] and [Stigum, 2003]. In certain respects, other social sciences, such as psychology, sociology or even political science, have been more cognizant of methodological issues pertaining to statistical inference and modeling; see [Morrison and Henkel, 1970; Lieberman, 1971; Harlow *et al.*, 1997]. A recent exception in economics is [Ziliak and McCloskey, 2008].

The philosophy of econometrics, as an integral part of economic modeling, is currently at its infancy, with most econometricians being highly sceptical about the value of philosophical/methodological discussions. The focus of the econometric literature since the early 1960s has been primarily on technical issues concerned with extending estimation and testing procedures associated with the Classical Linear Regression (CLR) and related models in a number of different directions. These modifications/extensions are theory-dominated and driven by the objective to 'quantify theory-intimated (structural) models'. As a result, the focus has been on (a) technical problems such as endogeneity/simultaneity, dependence,

Handbook of the Philosophy of Science. Volume 13: Philosophy of Economics.
Volume editor: Uskali Mäki. General editors: Dov M. Gabbay, Paul Thagard and John Woods.

heterogeneity, heteroskedasticity and non-linearity, and (b) different types of data (time series, cross-section and panel); see [Greene, 2000; Kennedy, 2008].

The methodology of economics literature, although extensive, so far has focused primarily on issues such as the status of economic assumptions, the structure of economic theories, falsification vs. verification, Kuhnian paradigms vs. Lakatosian research programs, the sociology of scientific knowledge, realism vs. instrumentalism, 'post-modernist' philosophy, etc.; see [Backhouse, 1994; Blaug, 1992; Davis *et al.*, 1998; Mäki, 2001; 2002; 2009; Redman, 1991]. Even in methodological discussions concerning the relationship between economic theories and reality, econometrics is invariably neglected [Caldwell, 1994, p. 216] or even misrepresented [Lawson, 1997]. Indeed, one can make a case that, by ignoring the philosophical issues pertaining to *empirical* modeling, the literature on economic methodology has painted a rather lopsided picture of the relevance of the current philosophy of science in availing philosophical/methodological problems that have frustrated economics in its endeavors to achieve the status of a credible empirical science. When assessing the current state of philosophy of science and its value for economic methodology, Hands [2001] argued that philosophy of science is "currently in disarray on almost every substantive issue" and provides "no reliable tool for discussing the relationship between economics and scientific knowledge." (p. 6). I consider such admonitions unhelpful and believe that parts of current philosophy of science focusing on 'learning from data' (see [Chalmers, 1999; Hacking, 1983; Mayo, 1996]) have a lot to contribute toward redeeming the credibility of economics as an empirical science.

In recent discussions on the financial crises that burst onto the scene in September 2008, the economists participating in the debate concerning the different policies on how to deal with the deepening recession were invariably invoking *causal knowledge* between key policy variables, like government expenditure, and macro aggregates like the Gross Domestic Product (GDP). The problem was that all they had to offer as *evidence* for their claimed knowledge was a combination of strong *beliefs* in the appropriateness of their particular economic perspective (Classical, Keynesian, Neo-Keynesian, monetarist, Neo-Classical, etc.), combined with armchair empiricism based on analogical reasoning from past 'similar' episodes. Establishing causal knowledge will require a lot more than that, including securing the statistical and substantive adequacy of the models appealed to. Unfortunately, the current econometric literature seems rather oblivious to this crucial problem. Indeed, a closer look at the empirical evidence published in prestigious journals over the last half century reveals heaps of untrustworthy estimates and testing results which provide at best a tenuous, if any, connection between economic theory and observable economic phenomena, and facilitate no veritable learning from data; see [Spanos, 2006a].

The main thesis of the paper is that *without* proper philosophical/methodological foundations to guide the practitioner on how to properly use the various statistical procedures, as well as interpret the resulting inferences, *no* veritable knowledge can be accumulated using data modeling. Accretions of statistical methods with ever increasing technical sophistication to quantify one's favorite structural (estimable theory) model, without the underlying philosophy of when and how to apply such procedures in order give rise to reliable inferences, will continue to add to the mountains of untrustworthy evidence. Indeed, the increasing technical sophistication makes matters worse by giving practitioners a sense of misplaced faith in the credibility of the evidence produced by such procedures; see [Spanos, 2010c].

The main aim of this paper is to attempt a demarcation of the intended scope of a philosophy of econometrics with a view to integrate its subject matter into the broader philosophy of science discourses. An important objective is to bring out the potential value of a bidirectional relationship between philosophy of science and applied fields in the social sciences. Econometrics can benefit from the broader philosophical discussions on 'learning from data', and philosophy of science can enrich its perspective by paying more attention to the empirical modeling practices in disciplines, like econometrics, which rely primarily on observational (non-experimental) data.

In section 2, a simple empirical example is used to bring out the diversity and complexity of philosophical/methodological issues raised by such modeling attempts in applied econometrics. Section 3 attempts to provide a highly selective summary of 20th century philosophy of science, focusing primarily on aspects of that literature that pertain to empirical modeling. Section 4 brings out the foundational issues bedeviling statistical inference since the 1930s, as a prelude to section 5 which discusses the *error-statistical perspective* [Mayo and Spanos, 2010b], as providing an appropriate framework for a philosophy of econometrics. This perspective is presented as a refinement/extension of the Fisher-Neyman-Pearson (F-N-P) approach to statistical induction, which can be used to effectively address some of the inveterate foundational problems that have bedeviled frequentist statistical inference since the late 1930s. The error-statistical approach is further developed in section 6 to secure the trustworthiness of evidence for or against substantive claims. The error statistical perspective is then used in section 7 to shed new light on a number of crucial philosophical/methodological problems pertaining to econometrics.

## 2 RELEVANT PHILOSOPHICAL/METHODOLOGICAL ISSUES

To give the reader some idea as to the kind of philosophical/methodological issues raised by empirical modeling in economics, let us consider the following basic question:

When do data $\mathbf{z}_0$ provide evidence for or against a hypothesis or a theory $H$?

In econometric modeling it is often insufficiently realized how many different philosophical/methodological issues such a question raises, or how difficult it is to give satisfactory answers.

## 2.1 *Probing the different ways an inference might be in error*

To bring out some of these methodological issues let us revisit Moore's [1914, pp. 62-88] estimated 'statistical demand' curve for corn:

$$y_t = \underset{(2.175)}{7.219} - \underset{(.083)}{0.699}x_t + \widehat{u}_t,\ R^2{=}.622,\quad s{=}14.447,\quad n{=}45, \tag{1}$$

based on annual observations for the period 1866-1911: $\mathbf{z}_0{:=}\{(x_t, y_t),\ t{=}1,2,...,n\}$, where $x_t{=}\left([100(p_t{-}p_{t-1})]\,/p_t\right)$ and $y_t{=}\left([100(q_t{-}q_{t-1})]\,/q_t\right)$, $p_t$- average price per bushel, $q_t$- production in bushels; standard errors in brackets. In view of the fact that:

(i) the estimated coefficients appear to be statistically significant:

$$\tau(\widehat{\beta}_0){=}\tfrac{7.219}{2.175}{=}3.319 \Rightarrow \beta_0{\neq}0, \qquad \tau(\widehat{\beta}_1){=}\tfrac{.699}{.083}{=}8.422 \Rightarrow \beta_1{\neq}0, \tag{2}$$

(ii) they have the "correct" signs ($\widehat{\beta}_0 > 0,\ \widehat{\beta}_1 < 0$), and

(iii) and the goodness-of-fit is reasonably high ($R^2{=}.622$),

one might consider the empirical results in (1) as providing corroborating evidence *for* the 'demand schedule':

$$Q^D = \beta_0 + \beta_1 P, \quad \beta_0 > 0,\ \beta_1 < 0. \tag{3}$$

Such a claim, however, will be premature and unwarranted before one needs to assess the reliability of these inferences by probing the different ways they might be in error and ensure that such errors are absent. What errors?

**(I) Statistical Misspecification.** This source of potential error arises when the estimated model in (3) is *statistically inadequate*: a subset of the probabilistic assumptions:

$$\{1\}u_t \backsim \mathsf{N}(.,.), \{2\}E\left(u_t\right){=}0, \{3\}Var\left(u_t\right){=}\sigma^2, \{4\}E\left(u_t u_s\right){=}0,\ \ t{\neq}s, t, s{=}1, ..., n,$$

underlying the Linear Regression (LR) model, is invalid for data $\mathbf{z}_0$. A typical set of Mis-Specification (M-S) tests (see [Spanos and McGuirk, 2001]) is reported in table 1. The tiny p-values [in square brackets] indicate serious departures from assumptions {2}-{4}, rendering the inferences (i)-(iii) concerning the statistical significance, sign and the magnitude of $(\beta_0, \beta_1)$ *unwarranted.*

| **Table 1 - Mis-Specification (M-S) tests** | |
|---|---|
| **Normality**: | $D'AP = 3.252[.197]$ |
| **Linearity**: | $F(2,41){=}19.532[.000001]^*$ |
| **Homoskedasticity**: | $F(2,41){=}14.902[.000015]^*$ |
| **No-Autocorrelation**: | $F(2,41){=}18.375[.000011]^*$ |

The M-S testing results in table 1 indicate that the estimated model in (1) constitutes an *unreliable basis* for inference. The statistical unreliability stems from the fact that when any of the assumptions {1}–{4} are invalid, the relevant *nominal* and *actual error probabilities* are likely to be very different. Applying a .05 significance level t-test, when the actual type I error is .98, renders the test highly unreliable; see [Spanos and McGuirk, 2001].

The question that naturally arises at this stage is 'how many published applied econometric papers over the last 50 years are likely to pass this *statistical adequacy test*?' The astounding answer is 'very few', raising serious doubts about the trustworthiness of the mountains of evidence accumulated in econometrics journals during this period; see [Spanos, 2006a]. Indeed, in most cases the modeler is not even aware of all the probabilistic assumptions constituting the statistical premises of inference; compare assumptions {1}-{4} with [1]-[5] in table 7. What makes matters worse is that statistical inadequacy is only one of several potential sources of error that could render empirical evidence untrustworthy.

**(II) Inaccurate data.** This second source of potential error arises when data $\mathbf{z}_0$ are marred by *systematic errors* imbued by the collection/compilation process; see [Morgenstern, 1963]. Such systematic errors are likely to distort the statistical regularities and give rise to misleading inferences. The discussion of the data in [Moore, 1914] gives enough clues to suspect that inaccurate data is likely to be another serious source of error contributing to the unreliability of any inference based on (1). In particular, the averaging of different prices over time and taking proportional differences is likely to distort their probabilistic structure and introduce systematic errors into the data; see [Abadir and Talmain, 2002].

**(III) Incongruous measurement.** This third source of potential error arises when data $\mathbf{z}_0$ do not adequately quantify the concepts envisioned by the theory. This, more than the other sources of error, is likely to be the most serious one in ruining the trustworthiness of Moore 'statistical demand' in (1). Moore's contention that $x_t$ and $y_t$ provide adequate quantification for the theoretical variables 'quantify demanded' ($Q^D$) and the corresponding 'price' ($P$) is altogether unconvincing. The gap between, on one hand, the intentions to buy $Q^D_{it}$, at some point in time $t$, and the set of hypothetical prices $P_{it}$, $i$=$1, 2, ..., m$, and, on the other, the quantities transacted $q_t$ and the corresponding observed prices $p_t$, over time $t$=$1, 2, ..., n$, cannot possibly be bridged by the 'proportional change' transformation; see [Spanos, 1995].

**(IV) Substantive inadequacy.** This fourth source of potential error arises when the circumstances envisaged by the theory in question differ 'systematically' from the *actual* data generating mechanism and pertains to the realisticness of the theory in question. This inadequacy can easily arise from impractical *ceteris paribus* clauses, external invalidity, missing confounding factors, false causal claims, etc.; see [Guala, 2005; Hoover, 2001]. Substantive adequacy concerns the extent to which the estimated model accounts for all systematic aspects of the reality it purports to explain in a statistically and substantively adequate way, shedding light on the phenomenon of interest, i.e. 'learning from data'. Given the potentially grievous effects of the other sources of error on the trustworthiness of the inference based on (1), raising questions about its substantive inadequacy seems rather gratuitous.

In view of the seriousness of all these errors, taking the estimated regression in (1) at face value and drawing any inferences seems like a very bad idea. An interesting question to consider is how a textbook econometrician is likely to proceed when faced with the empirical results reported in (1).

## 2.2 The Pre-Eminence of Theory (PET) perspective

The single most important contributor to the untrustworthiness of empirical evidence in economics is the methodological framework that has dominated empirical modeling in economics since Ricardo. This framework, known as the *Pre-Eminence of Theory* (PET) perspective, asserts that empirical modeling takes the form of constructing simple idealized models which capture certain key aspects of the phenomenon of interest, with a view to shed light or even explain economic phenomena, and gain insight concerning potential alternative policies. From the PET perspective empirical modeling is strictly theory-driven with the data playing only a subordinate role in quantifying theory-models (presumed true); see [Spanos, 2010a].

The widely practiced strategy of foisting one's favorite theory on the data usually gives rise to an estimated model which is both *statistically* and *substantively misspecified*, with no way to distinguish between the two sources of misspecification and apportion blame:

is the substantive information false? or are the statistical premises mispecified? (4)

Statistical premises constitute a set of probabilistic assumptions pertaining to the stochastic process $\{\mathbf{Z}_t,\ t\in\mathbb{N}:=(1,2,...,n,...)\}$ that render data $\mathbf{z}_0$ a 'typical realization thereof'; hence statistical premises are data specific. An example of what is meant by statistical premises in given in table 7 for the Linear Regression (LR) model. The model assumptions [1]-[5] pertain exclusively to the process $\{\mathbf{Z}_t,\ t\in\mathbb{N}\}$ underlying data $\mathbf{z}_0$, without invoking any substantive information. Indeed, *ab initio* the statistical premises need to be separated from the substantive information stemming from the theory. Unfortunately, the textbook specification of the LR model blends the two sources of information and renders the problem of establishing statistical and substantive adequacy hopeless; see [Spanos, 2010c]. The statistical misspecification undermines the *reliability* of any inductive inference by rendering the *actual* error probabilities different from the *nominal* ones. This implies that any inferential claim concerning the sign, magnitude and significance of estimated coefficients, however informal, is likely to be misleading. Hence, when such inferences are drawn, despite the presence of statistical misspecification, they shed no reliable light on the underlying economic phenomena.

### 2.2.1 *Statistical misspecification vs. the 'realisticness' issue*

Criticisms concerning the devastating effects of using statistically misspecified models to draw inferences fall on deaf ears with the advocates of the PET perspective because to them such admonitions sound like a well-rehearsed complaint concerning the *unrealisticness* of their structural models, going back to Malthus who criticized the Ricardian method. Modern advocates of the PET perspective, respond by invoking the authority of Friedman [1953] to counter that such unrealisticness is inevitable, since all models involve abstraction and idealization and cannot be exact descriptions of reality; see [Mäki, 2009]. This, however, exemplifies a major confusion between statistical and substantive inadequacy. There is a crucial difference between:

(a) the *unrealisticness* of the substantive assumptions comprising the theory-model (substantive premises), vis-à-vis the phenomenon of interest, and

(b) the *invalidity* of the probabilistic assumptions comprising the statistical model (inductive premises), vis-à-vis the data in question.

The reason one needs to distinguish between the two is primarily because the kinds of errors to probe for and guard against are very different in the two cases. Unfortunately, the PET perspective ignores this distinction and often foists the theory-model on the data at the outset giving rise to both *statistically* and *substantively misspecified* models. The only way to address the Duhemian ambiguity in (4) is to secure the statistical adequacy first in order to render reliable the statistical tools for assessing the substantive adequacy.

The realisticness of the theory is an issue that pertains to the substantive adequacy of the estimated model vis-à-vis the phenomenon of interest, i.e. whether the model in question provides a veritable explanation for that phenomenon. Securing substantive adequacy calls for additional probing of (potential) errors in bridging the gap between theory and data. However, without securing statistical adequacy first, such probing is likely to be misleading because the statistical procedures employed cannot be trusted to yield reliable inferences; see [Spanos, 2009b].

The PET perspective relies on certain statistical criteria, such as goodness-of-fit and prediction statistics, as well as several subjective judgements pertaining to the model's capacity to 'shed light' and/or confirm preconceived beliefs by the modeler. What is often ignored is that, without statistical adequacy, such criteria are, at best, questionable. Indeed, this calls into question Friedman's [1953] widely quoted passage calling for 'judging a theory by it predictive power', as well as his call for using 'factual evidence in assessing the validity of a theory' (p. 8). The only way to implement such calls appositely is to secure statistical adequacy first in order to render the criteria being used reliable; see [Spanos, 2010c].

## 2.3 *Reflecting on textbook econometrics*

In practice, the methodological framework and its philosophical underpinnings adopted in traditional textbook econometric modeling do *not* include systematic probing for errors as part of the accepted rules and strategies for learning from data. To make matters worse, this methodological framework is usually implicit and is often adopted without any scrutiny as part and parcel of 'learning' econometrics.

The dominance of the PET perspective in econometric modeling ensures that statistical model specification is primarily theory-driven. Indeed, a closer look at the assumptions of statistical models like Linear Regression reveals that they constitute an amalgam of statistical and substantive assumptions, making it impossible to distinguish between statistical and substantive premises at any stage of modeling; see [Spanos, 2010c]. The emphasis in textbook econometrics is *not* placed on probing for potential errors at each stage of the modeling, but on 'quantifying a particular theoretical model'. This encourages the adoption of the weakest possible probabilistic structure that would 'justify' a method; the justification coming in the form of 'consistent' (and asymptotically Normal) estimators of the parameters of interest. In particular, the cornerstone of the textbook approach, the Gauss-Markov (G-M) theorem – as well as analogous theorems concerning the asymptotic 'optimality' of Instrumental Variables (IV), Generalized Method of Moments (GMM) and non-parametric methods – distance themselves from strong probabilistic assumptions, especially Normality, in an attempt to gain greater generality for certain inference propositions. The rationale is that the reliance on weaker probabilistic assumptions will render OLS, IV and GMM-based inferences less prone to statistical misspecifications and thus potentially more reliable; see [Greene, 2000]. This rationale raises very interesting philosophical/methodological questions that need to be discussed and appraised. For instance:

► in what sense weaker assumptions give rise to more reliable inferences?

► what does one accomplish, in terms of generality, by not assuming Normality in the Gauss-Markov (G-M) and related theorems?

► to what extent can one use the G-M theorem as a basis for reliable inferences?

► how does one ensure the reliability of an inference when the premises are not testable (vis-a-vis data $\mathbf{z}_0$), as in the case of nonparametric/semiparametric inference? and

► does reliance on consistent and asymptotically Normal estimators suffice for reliable inferences and trustworthy evidence?

The question that naturally arises is "what would a traditional econometrician do when faced with the empirical results in (1)?" An ostensible diagnostic checking that relies on a small number of traditional M-S tests, such as the skewness-kurtosis (S-K), the Durbin-Watson (D-W) and the White heteroskedasticity (W) tests:

$$S\text{-}K{=}2.186[.335],\;\; D{-}W{=}2.211,\;\; W(2,42){=}15.647[.000], \tag{5}$$

reveals a clear departure from assumption {3}. In textbook econometrics, however, when any of the error assumptions {1}-{4} are found wanting, conventional wisdom recommends a sequence of 'error-fixing' procedures which are designed to remedy the problem. A textbook econometrician faced with the results in (5) is likely to count his/her blessings because they do not seem to show devastating departures from assumptions {1}-{4}. The presence of heteroskedasticity, according to the conventional wisdom, will only affect the efficiency of $(\widehat{\beta}_0, \widehat{\beta}_1)$; unbiasedness and consistency still hold [Greene, 2000]. The departure is supposed to be 'accounted for' by employing the so-called Heteroskedasticity Consistent Standard Errors (HCSE). Hence, in view of the fact that $\mathsf{HCSE}(\widehat{\beta}_0)$=2.363, $\mathsf{HCSE}(\widehat{\beta}_1)$=.108, these inferences are usually declared 'robust' to the departure from {3}.

These conventional wisdom recommendations raise many interesting philosophical/methodological problems with a long history in philosophy of science, such as ad-hoc modifications, double-use of data, curve-fitting, pre-designation vs. post-designation, etc.; see [Mayo, 1996]. Interesting questions raised by the above textbook 'error-fixing' strategies are:

► are the 'error-fixing' procedures justifiable on statistical grounds?

► is 'error-fixing' the best way to respecify a statistically inadequate model?

► what kind of robustness/reliability does the use of HCSE bring about?

► are the various implicit or explicit specification searches justified statistically?

► how thorough should M-S testing be to avert any data mining charges?

► how does one decide what M-S tests are the most appropriate to apply in a particular case?

► how does one distinguish between legitimate and illegitimate double-use of data?

Another set of issues likely to be raised by practitioners of textbook econometrics relate to the *simultaneity* problem between $y_t$ and $x_t$. The contention is that the endogeneity of $x_t$ (arising from the demand/supply theory) calls into question the substantive validity of (1), and the only way to render the empirical results meaningful is to account for that. This amounts to bringing into the modeling additional variables $\mathbf{W}_t$, such as rainfall and the prices of complementary and substitute commodities, which could potentially influence the behavior of both $x_t$ and $y_t$. This reasoning gives rise to an implicit reduced form [Spanos, 1986]:

$$y_t = \pi_{10} + \pi_{11}^{\top}\mathbf{w}_t + \varepsilon_{1t}, \qquad x_t = \pi_{20} + \pi_{21}^{\top}\mathbf{w}_t + \varepsilon_{2t},\ t\in\mathbb{N}. \tag{6}$$

Again, this modeling strategy raises interesting methodological issues which are often neglected. For example:

► how does a mixture of statistical significance and theoretical meaningfulness renders a model "best"?

► in what sense does the IV amplification of the model in (6) alleviate the statistical inadequacy problem for (1)?

► how does the substantive information in (6) relate to the statistical information unaccounted for by (1)?

► how does one chooses the 'optimal' instruments $\mathbf{W}_t$ in (6)?

► what conditions would render the IV-based inference for $(\beta_0, \beta_1)$ any more reliable than OLS-based inference in (1)?

The above textbook arguments stem from adopting an implicit methodological framework (a paradigm) that defines the fundamental ideas and practices that demarcate econometric modeling, and determine the kind of questions that are supposed to be asked and probed, how these questions are to be structured and answered, and how the results of scientific investigations should be reported and interpreted; it establishes the 'norms' of scientific research – what meets the 'standards' of publication in learned journals and what does not. An important task of philosophy of econometrics is to make all these implicit methodological presuppositions *explicit*, as well as scrutinize their effectiveness.

## 3 PHILOSOPHY OF SCIENCE AND EMPIRICAL MODELING

From the perspective of the philosophy of econometrics, a central question in 20th century philosophy of science has been:

How do we learn about phenomena of interest in the face of uncertainty and error?

This raises several interrelated philosophical/methodological questions:

(a) Is there such a thing as a scientific method?

(b) What makes an inquiry scientific or rational?

(c) How do we appraise a theory vis-a-vis empirical data?

(d) How do we make reliable inferences from incomplete and noisy data?

(e) How do we obtain good evidence for (or against) a hypothesis or a theory?

These are some of the most crucial questions that philosophy of science has grabbled with during the 20th century; see [Mayo, 1996]. For the discussion that follows, it will be convenient to divide 20th century philosophy of science into several periods: 1918-1950s: logical positivism/empiricism (Hempel, Nagel), 1960s-1980s: the downfall of logical empiricism (Quine, Kuhn, Popper, Lakatos), 1980s-1990s: miscellaneous turns (historical, naturalistic, sociological, pragmatic, feminist, etc.), 1990s: new experimentalism and learning from error.

The following discussion is ineluctably sketchy and highly selective with the emphasis placed on philosophical/methodological issues and problems pertaining to empirical modeling. For a more balanced textbook discussion of current philosophy of science see [Chalmers, 1999; Godfrey-Smith, 2003; Machamer and Silberstein, 2002; Newton-Smith, 2000]; for a more economics-oriented perspective see [Hands, 2001; Redman, 1991].

### *3.1 Logical positivism/empiricism*

The tradition that established philosophy of science as a separate sub-field within philosophy, during the first half of the 20th century, was that of logical positivism/empiricism. Its roots can be traced back to the 19th century traditions of positivism and empiricism, but what contributed significantly in shaping logical positivism into a dominating school of thought were certain important developments in physics and mathematics in the early 20th century.

In physics the overthrow of Newtonian mechanics by Einstein's theory of relativity (special and general), as well as the predictive success of quantum mechanics, raised numerous philosophical problems and issues that were crying out for new insights and explanations concerning scientific methods and the nature of knowledge; how do we acquire attested knowledge about the world? The re-introduction of the axiomatic approach to mathematics by Hilbert and the inception and development of propositional and predicate logic by Frege, Russel, Whitehead and Wittgenstein, provided a formal logico-mathematical language that promised to bring unprecedented clarity and precision to mathematical thinking in general, and to foundational inquiry in particular. The new formal language of first order predicate logic, when combined with the exhaustive specification of the premises offered by the axiomatic approach, appeared to provide a model for precise and systematic reasoning, and thus an ideal tool for elucidating the many aspects of scientific reasoning and knowledge.

These developments called into question two of the most sanctified pillars of knowledge at the time, Newtonian mechanics and Euclidean geometry. The combination of general relativity and Hilbert's axiomatization of Euclidean geometry left no doubts that our knowledge of geometry cannot be synthetic a priori in Kant's sense.

It's no coincidence that the founding group of logical positivism (Schlick, Hahn, Waismann, Carnap, Neurath, Frank, Reichebach) were primarily mathematicians and physicists who aspired to use physics as their paradigmatic example of a real scientific field. Their aspiration was that this formal logico-mathematical language will help to formalize the structure of scientific theories as well as their relationship to experiential data in precise ways which would avoid the ambiguities and confusions of the natural language. The idea being that a philosophy of science modeled on physics could then be extended and adapted to less developed disciplines, including the social sciences. Not surprisingly, the early primary focus of logical positivism/empiricism was on the *form and structure* of scientific theories as well as *epistemology,* which is concerned with issues and problems about knowledge (meaning, nature, scope, sources, justification, limits and reliability), evidence and rationality. The strong empiricist stance adopted by this tradition marginalized *metaphysics,* which is concerned with issues and problems about the nature and structure of reality. At the same time it elevated empirical meaningfulness to a demarcation criterion between scientific and non-scientific statements and put forward a Hypothetic-Deductive (H-D) form of reasoning as the way science is grounded in observation and experiment, as well as how we acquire knowledge about the world from experience. Viewing a theory $h$ as empirically interpretable (via correspondence rules) deductive axiomatic system, H-D reasoning,in its simplest form, boils down to assessing the empirical validity of certain observational implications $\mathbf{e}$ of $h$. If $\mathbf{e}$ turns out to be true, it provides confirmatory evidence for the (probable) validity of $h$ :

$$\boxed{\begin{array}{c} \text{If } h \text{ then} \quad \mathbf{e} \\ \mathbf{e}, \\ \hline \therefore \text{ (probably) } h \text{ is true} \end{array}} \tag{7}$$

The above argument is deductively invalid (known as affirming the consequent fallacy), but it provided the basis of (inductive) confirmation for logical empiricists; see [Nagel, 1961; Hempel, 1965].

From the perspective of empirical modeling, a major weakness of the logical empiricist tradition was its failure to put forward a satisfactory explanation of how we learn from experience (induction). The tradition's simplistic confirmation reasoning in (7) as a means to assess the truth of a hypothesis $h$, in conjunction with the inadequacy of the inductive logics devised to evaluate the relative support of completing hypotheses, contributed significantly to the tradition's demise by the 1970s. Their attempts to formalize induction as primarily a logical relationship $C(\mathbf{e}, h)$ between evidence $\mathbf{e}$ and a hypothesis $h$, both taken as objectively given, failed primarily because they did not adequately capture the complexity of the relationship between $h$ and $\mathbf{e}$ in scientific practice. Indeed, an enormous amount of hard work and ingenuity go into fashioning a testable form $h$ of a hypothesis of interest, and establishing experiential facts $\mathbf{e}$ from noisy, finite and incomplete data $\mathbf{x}_0$, as well as relating the two. Their view of theory confirmation as a simple logical argument which involves two readily given statements, $h$ — the hypothesis of interest and $\mathbf{e}$ — the experiential facts, was not just overly simplistic, but misleading in so far as neither $h$ or $\mathbf{e}$ are straight forward nor readily available in actual scientific practice. Moreover, hypotheses or theories expressed as a set of sentences in an axiomatic system of first order logic are not easily amenable to empirical analysis. Not surprisingly, the inductive logics of logical empiricists were plagued by several paradoxes (ravens, grue), and they had little affinity to the ways practicing scientists learn from data. This was particularly true of learning from data in statistical induction as developed by Fisher in the early 1920s and extended by Neyman and Pearson in the early 1930s.

## *3.2 The fading of logical empiricism*

Part of the appeal of logical positivism/empiricism stemmed from the fact that there was something right-headed about their presumption that the distinguishing features of science, as opposed to other forms of human activity, can be found in observation and experiment; that knowledge about the world is secure only when it can be tested against observation and experiment; see [Glymour, 1981]. However, their answers to the above crucial questions (a)–(e) in the first half of the 20th century turned out to be inadequate and rather unconvincing. The tradition's undue reliance on formal logics, axiomatization, the analytic-synthetic and theoretical-observational distinctions, were instrumental in undermining its credibility and its dominance in philosophy of science. The view that scientific theories and research activity can be codified in terms of these idealized tools turned out to be overly optimistic. By the early 1970s there was general consensus that logical empiricism was not only inadequate but also untenable. The downfall of logical empiricism was hastened by critics such as Quine, Popper and Kuhn who pinpointed and accentuated these weaknesses.

**Quine** [1953; 1960] contributed to the downfall of logical empiricism in a number of ways, but the most influential were: (i) his undermining of the analytic-synthetic distinction, (ii) his reviving and popularizing of **Duhem**'s [1914] theses that (a) 'no hypothesis can be tested separately from an indefinite set of auxiliary hypotheses' and (b) 'crucial experiments that could decide unequivocally between competing theories do not exist', and (iii) his initiating the naturalistic turn.

His revisiting of Duhem's theses became known as the Duhem-Quine problem which gave rise to an inveterate conundrum:

(I) **The underdetermination of theory by data** – the view that there will always be more than one theory *consistent* with any body of empirical data.

*Naturalism* constitutes an epistemological perspective that emphasizes the 'continuity' between philosophy and science in the sense that the methods and strategies of the natural sciences are the best guides to inquiry in philosophy of science; there is no higher tribunal for truth and knowledge than scientific practice itself. Philosophy should study the methods and findings of scientists in their own pursuit of knowledge, while heightening its evaluative role.

**Popper** [1959; 1963] replaced the confirmation argument in (7) with a falsification argument, based on *modus tollens* (a deductively valid argument):

$$\boxed{\begin{array}{c}\text{If } h \text{ then} \quad \mathbf{e} \\ \text{not-}\mathbf{e}, \\ \hline \therefore\ \text{not-}h \text{ is true}\end{array}} \tag{8}$$

His falsificationism was an attempt to circumvent the problem of induction as posed by Hume, as well as replace confirmation as a demarcation criterion with falsifiability: a hypothesis $h$ is scientific if and only it's falsifiable by some potential evidence $\mathbf{e}$, otherwise it's non-scientific.

Popper's falsificationism was no more successful in explaining how we learn from experience than the inductive logics, it was designed to replace, for a variety of reasons, including taking $h$ and $\mathbf{e}$ as readily available. The most crucial of its problems was that raised by Duhem: the premises $h$ entailing $\mathbf{e}$ is usually a combination of a primary hypothesis $H$ of interest and certain auxiliary hypotheses, say $A_1,\ A_2, ..., A_m$. Hence, not-$h$ does not provide a way to distinguish between not-$H$ and not-$A_k$, $k$=1, ..., $m$. As a result, one cannot apportion blame for the failure to observe $\mathbf{e}$ to any particular sub-set of the premises $(H, A_1,\ A_2, ..., A_m)$. *Second*, Popper's falsification does not allow one to learn anything positive about $h$ using the data. When several 'genuine' attempts to refute $h$ fail to do so, one cannot claim that $h$ is true, or justified, or probable or even reliable. A Popperian can only claim that hypothesis $h$ is the "best tested so far" and that it is *rational to accept* it (tentatively) because it has survived 'genuine' attempts to falsify it. *Third*, any attempt to measure the degree of 'corroboration' — credibility bestowed on $h$ for surviving more and more 'genuine' attempts to refute it — brings back the vary problem of induction falsificationism was devised to circumvent.

Despite the failure of falsificationism to circumvent induction as capturing the way we learn from experience, there is something right-minded about Popper's intuition underlying some of his eye-catching slogans such as "Mere supporting instances are as a rule too cheap to be worth having", "tests are severe when they constitute genuine attempts to refute a hypothesis" and "we learn from our mistakes". This intuition was garnered and formalized by Mayo [1996] in the form of severe testing, but placed in the context of frequentist statistical induction.

**Kuhn** [1962; 1977] undermined the logical empiricist tradition by questioning the wisdom of abstracting scientific theories and the relevant experiential data from their historical and a social context, arguing that the idealized formal models did not capture the real nature and structure of science in its ever-changing complexity. Partly motivated by Duhem's problem he proposed the notion of a *scientific paradigm* to denote the set of ideas and practices that define a scientific discipline during a particular period of time, and determine what is to be observed and scrutinized, the kind of questions that are supposed to be asked and probed, how these questions are to be structured, and how the results of scientific investigations should be interpreted. Using the notion of *normal science* within a paradigm, Kuhn questioned the positivist account of cumulative growth of knowledge, arguing that old paradigms are overrun by new ones which are usually 'incommensurable' with the old.

As a result of the extended controversy that ensued, Kuhn's ideas had an important influence on the development of philosophy of science to this day, and his legacy includes a number of crucial problems such as:

**(II)** **Theory-dependence of observation.** An observation is theory-laden, if, either the statement expressing the observation employs or presupposes certain theoretical concepts or knowing the truth of the observation statement requires the truth of some theory. The theory-ladeness of data problem has to do with whether data can be considered an unbiased or neutral source of information when assessing the validity of theories, or whether data are usually 'contaminated' by theoretical information in a way which prevents them from fulfilling that role.

**(III)** **Relativism** refers to the view that what is true or a fact of nature is so only relative to some overarching conceptual framework of which the truth of fact of the matter is expressible or discoverable. The idea that the truth of justification of a claim, or the applicability of a standard or principle, depends on one's perspective.

**(IV)** **The social dimension of science.** What makes science different form other kinds of inquiry, and renders it especially successful, is its unique social structure. This unique social structure has an important role to play in establishing scientific knowledge.

Kuhn's move to 'go large' from a scientific theory to an all-encompassing scientific paradigm was followed by **Lakatos** [1970] and **Laudan** [1977] who proposed the notions of a scientific research programme and a research tradition, respectively, in their attempts to avoid the ambiguities and unclarities, as well as address some of the failings of Kuhn's original notion of a scientific paradigm.

Despite the general understanding that logical empiricism was no longer a viable philosophical tradition, by the 1980s there was no accord as to which aspects of logical empiricism were the most problematic, or how to modify/replace the basic tenets of this tradition; there was no consensus view on most of the crucial themes in philosophy of science including the form and structure of theories, the nature of explanation, confirmation , theory testing, growth of knowledge, or even if there is such a thing as a scientific method; see [Suppe, 1977]. This disagreement led to a proliferation of philosophical dictums like "anything goes", 'evidence and confirmation are grounded on rhetoric or power", which began to gain appeal in certain disciplines, but especially in the social sciences where rock-solid scientific knowledge is more difficult to establish. This was part of the broader movement of miscellaneous turns (historical, sociological, pragmatic, feminist, social constructivist, discursivist, etc.) aspiring to influence the tradition that will eventually emerge to replace logical empiricism; see [Hands, 2001].

By the 1980s, the combination of Duhem's problem, the underdetermination conundrum and the theory-dependence of observation problem, made theory appraisal using observational data seem like a hopeless task.

## *3.3 The New Experimentalism*

An important disconnect between philosophy of science and scientific practice was that practitioners have always known from experience that establishing $\mathbf{e}$ (or not-$\mathbf{e}$) as *observational facts* constitutes one of the most difficult tasks in scientific research because the raw data $\mathbf{x}_0$ contain uncertainties, noise and are never in plenitude needed. Indeed, the raw data $\mathbf{x}_0$ usually need to be perceptively modeled to separate the systematic (signal) from the non-systematic (noise) information, as well as provide a measure of the reliability of inference based on $\mathbf{x}_0$. Such modeling is often vulnerable to numerous errors that would render $\mathbf{e}$ far from being 'objectively given facts'.

The first concerted effort in philosophy of science to study the process generating the raw data $\mathbf{x}_0$ and secure observational facts $\mathbf{e}$ (or not- $\mathbf{e}$) was made by the "new experimentalist" tradition; [Hacking, 1983; Mayo, 1997] — see [Chalmers, 1999] for a summary. Using the piece-meal activities involved and the strategies used in successful experiments, Hacking [1983] argued persuasively against the theory-dominated view of experiment. He made a strong case that in scientific research an experiment can have a 'life of its own' that is independent of 'large-scale theory', and thus alleviating the theory-dependence of observation problem. Mayo [1996] argued that scientists employ a panoply of practical step-by-step strategies for eliminating error and establishing the 'factual basis of experimental effects' without any 'tainting' from large-scale theory.

## *3.4 Learning from Error*

Contrary to the Popperian and growth of knowledge traditions' call for 'going bigger' (from theories to paradigms, to scientific research programs and research traditions), in order to deal with such problems as theory-laden observation, underdetermination and Duhem-Quine, Mayo [1996, p. 58], argued for 'going smaller':

> "The fact that theory testing depends on intermediate theories of data, instruments, and experiment, and that the data are theory laden, inexact and "noisy", only underscores the necessity for numerous local experiments, shrewdly interconnected."

Her attempt to put forward an epistemology of experiment includes, not only how observational facts **e** are established using experimental controls and learning from error, but also how the hypothesis of interest $h$ is fashioned into an estimable form appropriate to face the tribunal of **e**. This comes in the form of a hierarchy of interconnected models: 'primary, experimental and data models' (p. 128).

Mayo proposed a formalization of the research activities and strategies for detecting and eliminating errors motivated by a modification/extension of the Fisher-Neyman-Pearson (F-N-P) frequentist approach to inference, she called *error statistics*. The F-N-P approach is supplemented with a post-data evaluation of inference based on severe testing reasoning, which assesses, not the degree of support for a hypothesis $H$, but rather the capacity of the testing procedure to detect discrepancies from $H$. Probability is firmly attached to the testing procedures (not $H$), to inform us of their probativeness and capacity to detect errors. Her error statistical framework includes questions about 'what data are relevant', 'how the data were generated', 'how can the relevant data be adequately summarized in the form of data models' etc. The reliability of evidence is assessed at all three levels of models by using error-statistical procedures based on learning from error reasoning.

Mayo [1996] made a strong case that there is a domain of 'experimental knowledge' that can be reliably established independent of high-level theory and the continuity of scientific progress consists in part of the steady build up of claims that pass severe tests. She provided answers to the philosophical/methodological questions (a)–(e) posed above that are distinctly different from those of logical empiricism as well as the other post received-view 'large-scale theory' traditions.

What makes the error-statistical account highly promising as a methodological framework for empirical modeling are the following features:

(i) it focuses on 'learning from error' procedures that underlie the fashioning of a testable form of a hypothesis of interest $H$, as well as establishing experiential facts (trustworthy evidence) $\mathbf{e}$ from noisy, finite and incomplete data $\mathbf{x}_0$,

(ii) it provides an account based on a chain of complecting models (primary, experimental, data), that can potentially capture the complexity of bridging the gap between theory and data in scientific practice, and

(iii) it harnesses the power of modern statistical inference and modeling to bear upon the problems and issues raised by our attempt to come to grips with learning from experience.

The fundamental intuition underlying the error statistical perspective can be formally captured in the context of the F-N-P frequentist approach whose premises are clearly delineated by a statistical model $\mathcal{M}_\theta(\mathbf{x})$, and hypotheses are formulated in terms of the unknown parameters $\theta$. The primary difficulty in implementing this principle was that, since the 1930s, the frequentist approach had been bedeviled by its own inveterate foundational problems, which remained largely unresolved.

Mayo [1996] argued that the mid 20th century crises in philosophy of science and statistics are linked, and tackling the foundations problems in statistics helps to formulate a general account of inductive inference that sheds very different light on the philosopher's problems of induction, objective evidence and underdetermination.

## 4 STATISTICAL INFERENCE AND ITS FOUNDATIONAL PROBLEMS

### 4.1 *Frequentist statistics and its foundational problems*

R. A. Fisher [1922] pioneered modern frequentist statistics as a model-based approach to statistical induction anchored on the notion of a *statistical model*, formalized by:

$$\mathcal{M}_\theta(\mathbf{x})=\{f(\mathbf{x};\theta),\ \theta\in\Theta\},\ \mathbf{x}\in\mathbb{R}^n_X,\ \Theta\subset\mathbb{R}^m,\ m<n, \tag{9}$$

where the distribution of the sample $f(\mathbf{x};\theta)$ 'encapsulates' the probabilistic information in the statistical model. He was able to recast statistical inference by turning Karl Pearson's [1920] *induction by enumeration*, proceeding from data $\mathbf{z}_0{:=}(z_1,...,z_n)$ in search of a frequency curve $f(z;\vartheta)$ to describe its histogram, on its head. Fisher proposed to begin with a prespecified $\mathcal{M}_\theta(\mathbf{z})$ (a 'hypothetical infinite population'), and view $\mathbf{z}_0$ as a realization thereof. He envisaged the specification of $\mathcal{M}_\theta(\mathbf{z})$ as a response to the question:

> "Of what population is this a random sample?"(ibid., p. 313)

underscoring that:

"the adequacy of our choice may be tested a posteriori."(p. 314)

Fisher identified the 'problems of statistics' to be: (1) specification, (2) estimation and (3) distribution and emphasized that addressing (2)-(3) depended crucially on dealing with (1) successfully first.

Frequentist statistical inference was largely in place by the late 1930s. Fisher [1922; 1925; 1934], almost single-handedly, created the current theory of 'optimal' point estimation and formalized significance testing based on the p-value reasoning. Neyman and Pearson [1933] proposed an 'optimal' theory for hypothesis testing, by modifying/extending Fisher's significance testing; see [Pearson, 1966]. Neyman [1937] proposed an 'optimal' theory for interval estimation analogous to N-P testing. Broadly speaking, the formal apparatus of frequentist statistics were largely in place by the late 1930s, but its philosophical foundations concerned with the proper form of the underlying inductive reasoning were in a confused state. Fisher [1935a; 1935b] was arguing for 'inductive inference', spearheaded by his significance testing in conjunction with p-values and his fiducial probability for interval estimation. Neyman [1957] was arguing for 'inductive behavior' based on N-P testing and confidence interval estimation firmly grounded on pre-data error probabilities; see [Mayo, 2006].

The last exchange between these pioneers took place in the mid 1950s (see [Fisher, 1955; 1956; Neyman, 1956; Pearson, 1955]) and left the philosophical foundations of the field in a state of confusion with many more questions than answers.

▶ What is the correct interpretation of the p-value? Can high p-values be interpreted as providing evidence for the null?

▶ In N-P testing, does accept/reject the null imply that there is evidence for the null/alternative?

▶ What are the differences between a Fisher significance test and an N-P test?

▶ Does a proper test require an alternative hypothesis? What about goodness-of-fit tests like Pearson's?

▶ Are the notions of type II error probability and power applicable (or relevant) to Fisher-type tests?

▶ Are error probabilities meaningful and relevant post-data? Is the p-value a legitimate post-data error probability?

▶ Is there an intrinsic relationship between p-values and posterior probabilities?

▶ Does Fisher's fiducial distribution yield legitimate error probabilities?

▶ Can one distinguish between different values of the unknown parameter within an observed Confidence Interval (CI)?

▶ Can one infer substantive significance from an observed CI?

▶ In what sense does conditioning on an ancillary statistic enhance the precision and data-specificity of inference?

These questions were primarily concerned with:

(a) the proper form of inductive reasoning underlying frequentist inference,

(b) the role of pre-data vs. post-data error probabilities (Hacking, 1965),

(c) safeguarding the p-value and the N-P coarse accept/reject decisions against:

(i) the fallacy of acceptance: interpreting accept $H_0$ [no evidence against $H_0$] as evidence for $H_0$; e.g. the test had low power to detect existing discrepancy,

(ii) the fallacy of rejection: interpreting reject $H_0$ [evidence against $H_0$] as evidence for a particular $H_1$; e.g. conflating statistical with substantive significance; [Mayo, 1996].

It has been long-familiar that the N-P coarse 'accept/reject' rules were susceptible to the fallacies of acceptance and rejection. Fisher's interpretation of the p-value as reflecting discordance with the null, was equally susceptible to the fallacy of rejection since the p-value often goes to zero as the sample size $n \to \infty$. Moreover, interpreting a 'large' p-value as evidence for $H_0$ would render it vulnerable to the fallacy of acceptance. Hacking [1965, p. 99] criticized the Neyman-Pearson approach to testing for its incompleteness. The *pre-data* (before-trial) error probabilistic account of inference, although adequate for assessing optimality, is inadequate for a *post-data* (after-trial) evaluation of the inference reached.

By the early 1960s the confused state of the philosophical underpinnings of frequentist inference, especially as it relates to its underlying inductive reasoning, began to be used as evidence for its philosophical destitution and the superiority of Bayesian inference whose reasoning seemed clear cut in comparison; see [Savage, 1962].

The subsequent literature on frequentist statistics shed very little (if any) additional light on these philosophical/foundational issues. Not surprisingly, due to the absence of any guidance from statistics or philosophy of science, the practitioners in several disciplines came up with their own 'pragmatic' ways to deal with the philosophical puzzles bedeviling the frequentist approach. Indeed, the above questions gave rise to a numerous debates (see [Harper and Hooker, 1976]), which were especially heated in the social sciences like psychology, sociology and education [Morrison and Henkel, 1971; Lieberman, 1971], and more recently re-discovered in economics [McCloskey, 1985]. This resulted in a hybrid of the Fisher and N-P inference accounts which is "inconsistent from both perspectives and burdened with conceptual confusion." [Gigerenzer, 1993, p. 323]. This inconsistent hybrid eventually acquired a life of its own in these separate fields and led to widespread abuses of these methods that continue unabated to this day; see [Harlow *et al.*, 1997].

The literature in philosophy of science, apart from a few notable exceptions (e.g. [Godambe and Sprott, 1971; Giere, 1984]), largely ignored important developments in frequentist statistics. In direct contrast to the practitioners' extensive use of statistics in almost all scientific fields, by the early 1950s logical empiricism had adopted a largely Bayesian perspective on inductive inference with Carnap's [1950] confirmatory logics (logical relations between statements and evidence —

going back to [Keynes, 1921]) dominating the evidential accounts in philosophy of science; see [Neyman, 1957].

Despite the obvious weaknesses in its philosophical foundations and the criticisms from the Bayesian perspective, the frequentist approach to statistical inference continued to dominate applied research in most scientific fields during the 1970s and 1980s. Indeed, its extensive application, especially in the social sciences, raised additional philosophical/methodological problems, the most important of which are:

(d) the role of substantive subject matter information in statistical modeling,

(e) how one could narrow down a (possibly) infinite set $\mathcal{P}(\mathbf{x})$, of all possible models that could have given rise to data $\mathbf{x}_0$, to a single statistical model $\mathcal{M}_\theta(\mathbf{x})$,

(f) how could one assess the adequacy a statistical model $\mathcal{M}_\theta(\mathbf{x})$ *a posteriori*? and

(g) how could one address issues like double-use of data, data mining, pre-test bias, circularity and infinite regress?

These outstanding issues created endless confusions in the minds of practitioners concerning the appropriate use and proper interpretation of the frequentist approach to inference. This muddiness was compounded by advocates of the Bayesian approach to inference who introduced further confusion by misinterpreting certain frequentist inference notions and procedures; see [Berger and Wolpert, 1988; Ghosh *et al.*, 2006].

## *4.2 Bayesianism and its criticisms of the frequentist approach*

The Bayesian approach to inference supplements a statistical model $\mathcal{M}_\theta(\mathbf{x})$ with a *prior* distribution, $\pi(\theta)$, $\theta \in \Theta$, which, loosely speaking, assigns probabilities $\pi(\theta)d\theta$ (interpreted as *degrees of belief*) to each individual model (corresponding to a particular value of $\theta$) in $\mathcal{M}_\theta(\mathbf{x})$. For inference purposes Bayesian procedures do away with error probabilities altogether by focusing exclusively on the likelihood function $L(\theta;\mathbf{x}_0) \propto f(\mathbf{x}_0;\theta)$, $\theta \in \Theta$, which depends only on $f(\mathbf{x}_0;\theta)$, and ignoring all $\mathbf{x} \neq \mathbf{x}_0$, for $\mathbf{x} \in \mathbb{R}^n_X$ -the sample space; see [Jeffreys, 1961; Savage, 1962; Pratt, 1961]. Bayesian inference is based primarily on the posterior distribution (see [Poirier, 1995]):

$$\pi(\theta \mid \mathbf{x}_0) \propto \pi(\theta) \cdot L(\theta;\mathbf{x}_0),\ \theta \in \Theta, \tag{10}$$

which assigns revised (in light of the data $\mathbf{x}_0$) probabilities $\pi(\theta \mid \mathbf{x}_0)d\theta$ in the context of $\mathcal{M}_\theta(\mathbf{x})$. The underlying reasoning is *across-the-board* in nature because inferences are evaluated in terms of all possible values of $\theta \in \Theta$. In this context, *learning from data* takes the form of revising one's *prior beliefs,* represented by $\pi(\theta)$, in light of the sample information in $L(\theta;\mathbf{x}_0)$, $\theta \in \Theta$. Moreover, evidence for or against a hypothesis or a claim $H$ formulated in terms of $\theta$, comes in the form of revised degrees of belief associated with different values of $\theta \in\Theta$. Whose degrees of belief do the prior and posterior distributions represent is an inveterate problem, which along with the notion of non-informative priors (see [Kass and Wasserman, 1996]), rank very high on the list of contentious issues in Bayesian inference.

EXAMPLE 1. Consider the simple Bernoulli model (table 3), where $\pi(\theta)=1$ is uniform over $[0,1]$. The combination of this prior and the likelihood function gives rise to a Beta *posterior* distribution of the form:

$$\pi(\theta \mid \mathbf{x}_0) \propto \pi(\theta)\cdot L(\theta;\mathbf{x}_0) = \left[\theta^{n\overline{x}_n}(1-\theta)^{n(1-\overline{x}_n)}\right].$$

A natural *Bayesian estimator* of $\theta$ is $\widehat{\theta}=\overline{x}_n=\left(\frac{m}{n}\right)$, which represents the *mode* of $\pi(\theta|\,\mathbf{x}_0)$. Another possible Bayesian estimator is the *mean* of $\pi(\theta \mid \mathbf{x}_0)$ which takes the form $\widetilde{\theta}=\frac{m+1}{n+2}=\lambda\overline{x}_n+(1-\lambda)\overline{\theta}$, where $\lambda=[n/(n+2)]$, $\overline{\theta}=E(\theta)=\int_0^1\theta\pi(\theta)d\theta=.5$ is the mean of the prior distribution. How does one choose between these estimators on optimality grounds? The answer is based on the chosen loss function $\mathcal{L}(\widehat{\theta}(\mathbf{X}),\theta)$ which determines the appropriate Bayes estimator by minimizing the posterior risk:

$$R(\widehat{\theta}(\mathbf{X}),\theta) = \int_{\theta\in\Theta}\mathcal{L}(\widehat{\theta}(\mathbf{X}),\theta)\pi(\theta|\,\mathbf{x}_0)d\theta.$$

(i) When $\mathcal{L}(\widehat{\theta},\theta)=(\widehat{\theta}-\theta)^2$ the resulting Bayes estimator is the mean of $\pi(\theta \mid \mathbf{x}_0)$,

(ii) when $\mathcal{L}(\widetilde{\theta},\theta)=|\widetilde{\theta}-\theta|$ the Bayes estimator is the mode of $\pi(\theta|\,\mathbf{x}_0)$, and

(iii) when $\mathcal{L}(\overline{\theta},\theta)=\delta(\overline{\theta},\theta)$, where $\delta(.)=0$ when $\overline{\theta}=\theta$ and $\delta(.)=1$ when $\overline{\theta}\neq\theta$, the Bayes estimator $\overline{\theta}$ is the median of $\pi(\theta \mid \mathbf{x}_0)$; see [Schervish, 1995].

A $(1-\alpha)$ credible interval for $\theta$ is defined in terms of $\pi(\theta|\,\mathbf{x}_0)$ by:

$$\int_a^b \pi(\theta|\,\mathbf{x}_0)d\theta = (1-\alpha).$$

In practice one can define an infinity of $(1-\alpha)$ credible intervals using the same posterior $\pi(\theta|\mathbf{x}_0)$. To avoid this indeterminancy one needs to impose additional restrictions like the interval with the *shortest length* or one with *equal tails*; see [Robert, 2007].

EXAMPLE 2. For $n=10$, and $m=2$, a .95 equal tails *credible interval* for $\theta$ yields $(.060 \leq \theta \leq .517)$, which can be interpreted as saying that data $\mathbf{x}_0$ revised one's prior .95 degree of belief from $(.025 \leq \theta \leq .975)$ to $(.060 \leq \theta \leq .517)$.

Hypothesis testing turns out to be rather complicated in the context of the Bayesian approach for both technical and methodological reasons, resulting in numerous (contrasting) proposals on how to deal with these problems; see [Robert, 2007]. The technical problems have to do with assigning posterior probabilities to individual values of $\theta \in\Theta$, since $\Theta$ is often an uncountable subset of the real line. The methodological issues stem primarily from the fact that the *across-the-board* Bayesian reasoning cannot be easily adapted to emulate the *hypothetical* reasoning underlying frequentist testing. Hence, Bayesian testing almost invariably involves the use of special types of prior distributions, such as assigning $\pi(\theta_0)=\frac{1}{2}$ to the null value $\theta_0$, and distributing the rest of the prior probability to the other values of $\theta\neq\theta_0$, which would be considered contrived for any other form of Bayesian inference; see [Schervish, 1995].

The lack of interest in the philosophical foundations of frequentist inference during the 1960s and 1970s, in both statistics and philosophy of science, created the general impression that Bayesian inference occupied the philosophical high ground because of its grounding in the axiomatic approach and its upholding of the likelihood (LP) and coherency principles, while frequentist inference violates both; see [Berger and Wolpert, 1988]. This impression continues to be reiterated, largely unchallenged, to this day in both statistics (see [Berger, 1985; Schervish, 1995; Ghosh *et al.*, 2006]), and philosophy of science (see [Howson and Urbach, 2005]).

A crucial argument for the Bayesian case was based on Birnbaum's [1962] result that the *Conditionality Principle* (CP) and the *Sufficiency Principle* (SP), when combined, give rise to the *Likelihood principle* (LP). This result was broadly interpreted by Bayesians to imply that recognizing the need for conditional inference leads inevitably to adopting the Bayesian perspective; see [Poirer, 1995]. Moreover, the Bayesian case against the frequentist approach was built primarily by availing the confusions bedeviling this approach since the 1930s, including the misuse of the p-value and the observed confidence intervals. Bayesians claim that the source of confusion is that the practitioner "really" wants to attach probabilities to hypotheses, and to different values of $\theta$ in an observed CI, but the frequentist approach does not provide that. In contrast, Bayesianism furnishes exactly what the practitioner wants in the form of posterior probabilities; see [Ghosh *et al.*, 2006; Howson and Urbach, 2005]). In addition, several examples are employed, including the mixture of Normals and Welch uniform example, to make their case that the 'optimal' N-P test often gives rise to absurd results; see [Berger and Wolpert, 1988, examples 1–5; Berger, 1985].

## 5 ERROR-STATISTICS (E-S) AND INDUCTIVE INFERENCE

Error Statistics (see [Mayo and Spanos, 2010b]) has a dual dimension involving both: (1) a general philosophy of inductive inference based on frequentist probability, and (2) a cluster of statistical tools, together with their interpretation and justification. It is unified by a general attitude to a fundamental question of interest to both statisticians and philosophers of science:

> *How do we obtain reliable knowledge about the real world despite uncertainty, limited data and error?*

The main thesis of this paper is that most of the philosophical/methodological issues in the previous section can be addressed in the context of the *error-statistical* framework. It is important to emphasize at the outset that the error-statistical perspective provides a broader *methodology of error inquiry* that encourages detecting and identifying the different ways an inductive inference could be in error by applying effective methods and procedures which would detect such errors when present with very high probability. Indeed, it is argued that this perspective offers a philosophy of econometrics that can address numerous philosophical/methodological issues currently bedevilling econometric modeling.

The error statistical approach, viewed narrowly at the statistical level, blends in the Fisher and Neyman-Pearson (N-P) testing perspectives to weave a coherent frequentist inductive reasoning anchored firmly on *error probabilities*, both pre and post data. The key to this coalescing is provided by recognizing that Fisher's p-value reasoning is based on a *post-data* error probability, and Neyman-Pearson's type I and II errors reasoning is based on *pre-data* error probabilities, and they fulfill crucial complementary roles. The post-data component of this coalescing was proposed by Mayo [1991] in the form of *severe testing reasoning.*

The Error-Statistical (E-S) framework adopts a frequentist model-based approach to inductive inference, where a statistical model $\mathcal{M}_\theta(\mathbf{x})$ plays a pivotal role because:

(i) it specifies the inductive premises of inference,

(ii) it determines what constitutes *a legitimate* event,

(iii) it assigns probabilities to all legitimate events via $f(\mathbf{x};\theta),\ \mathbf{x}\in\mathbb{R}^n_X$,

(iv) it defines what are legitimate hypotheses and/or inferential claims,

(v) it determines the relevant error probabilities in terms of which the optimality and reliability of inference methods is assessed, and

(vi) it designates what constitute legitimate data $\mathbf{x}_0$ for inference purposes.

The simple Normal provides the quintessential statistical model, given in table 2 in terms of a statistical Generating Mechanism (GM) and assumptions [1]–[4].

**Table 2 - Simple Normal Model**

| | | |
|---|---|---|
| Statistical GM: | $X_k=\mu+u_k,\quad k\in\mathbb{N}=\{1,2,...\}$ | |
| [1] Normality: | $X_k \backsim \mathsf{N}(.,.),\ x_k\in\mathbb{R},$ | $k\in\mathbb{N}.$ |
| [2] Constant mean: | $E(X_k)=\mu,$ | |
| [3] Constant variance: | $Var(X_k)=\sigma^2,$ | |
| [4] Independence: | $\{X_k,\ k\in\mathbb{N}\}$ independent process | |

E-S emphasizes the reliability and precision of inference in order to enhance learning from data. One can secure statistical reliability by establishing the *statistical adequacy* of $\mathcal{M}_\theta(\mathbf{x})$: its assumptions are valid for data $\mathbf{x}_0$. *Precision* is assured by using the most effective (optimal) inference methods. In modern frequentist statistics, the *optimality* of estimators, tests and predictors is grounded in a *deductive argument* of the basic form: **if** $\mathcal{M}_\theta(\mathbf{x})$ is true, **then** $\mathbb{Q}(\mathbf{x})$ [a set of *inference propositions*] follows.

EXAMPLE 3. Inference propositions in the context of the simple Normal model:

(a) $\overline{X}_n=\frac{1}{n}\sum_{k=1}^{n}X_k$ is a *strongly consistent* and *fully efficient* estimator of $\mu$.

(b) $\{\tau(\mathbf{X}),\ C_1(\alpha)\}$, where $\tau(\mathbf{X})=\frac{\sqrt{n}(\overline{X}_n-\mu_0)}{s}$ and $C_1(\alpha)=\{\mathbf{x}:\tau(\mathbf{x})>c_\alpha\}$ defines a Uniformly, Most Powerful (UMP) test for: $H_0{:}\mu=\mu_0$ vs. $H_1{:}\mu>\mu_0$.

(c) $\mathbb{P}(\overline{X}_n-c_\alpha\frac{s}{\sqrt{n}}\leq\mu\leq\overline{X}_n+c_\alpha\frac{s}{\sqrt{n}})=1-\alpha$ defines a CI with shortest width.

The *deductive component,* $\mathcal{M}_\theta(\mathbf{x})\rightarrow\mathbb{Q}(\mathbf{x})$, is then embedded into a broader *inductive understructure* which relates data $\mathbf{x}_0$, via $\mathcal{M}_\theta(\mathbf{x})$, to inference results $\mathbb{Q}(\mathbf{x}_0)$, as they pertain to the phenomenon of interest. The literature on the frequentist approach since the 1930s has paid insufficient attention to the reliability and pertinence of inference results $\mathbb{Q}(\mathbf{x}_0)$.

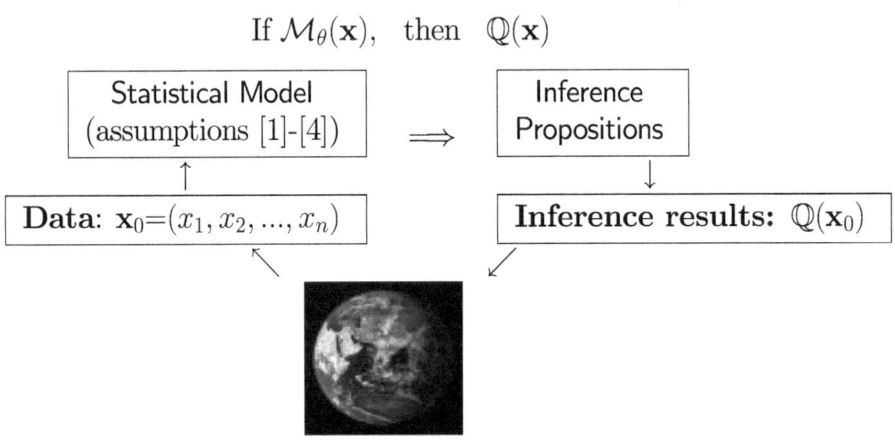


Figure 1. Model-based frequentist statistical induction

The key refinement/extensions of the F-N-P approach by the error statistical perspective can be summed up in placing due emphasis on probing for and eliminating potential errors at the two points of nexus with reality (fig. 1):

(A) From the phenomenon of interest to an adequate statistical model $\mathcal{M}_\theta(\mathbf{x})$,

(B) From inference results $\mathbb{Q}(\mathbf{x}_0)$ to evidence for (or against) substantive claims.

This is in contrast to statistics (and econometrics) textbooks which give insufficient attention to (A)-(B) by focusing almost exclusively on the deductive component, if $\mathcal{M}_\theta(\mathbf{x})$ then $\mathbb{Q}(\mathbf{x})$.

In a nutshell, the error statistical framework addresses the philosophical/ methodological issues [d]-[g], by distinguishing, *ab initio*, between *substantive* and *statistical* information and devising a purely probabilistic construal of a statistical model $\mathcal{M}_\theta(\mathbf{x})$ by viewing it as a parameterization of the stochastic process $\{\mathbf{X}_k, k\in\mathbb{N}:=(1,...,n,...)\}$ whose probabilistic structure is chosen so as to render data $\mathbf{x}_0$ a *truly typical realization* thereof; see [Spanos, 1986]. The specification of $\mathcal{M}_\theta(\mathbf{x})$ in $\mathcal{P}(\mathbf{x})$ is guided solely by *statistical adequacy*: the probabilistic assumptions making up the model are valid for data $\mathbf{x}_0$. Securing the statistical adequacy of $\mathcal{M}_\theta(\mathbf{x})$ enables one to deal with problems [a]-[c], by employing ascertainable error probabilities (pre-data and post-data) to evaluate the reliability and pertinence of inductive inferences, including the evidential appraisal of substantive claims; see [Mayo and Spanos, 2006].

The crucial features of the E-S perspective are:

(i) Emphasizing the *learning from data* (about the phenomenon of interest) objective of empirical modeling.

(ii) Paying due attention to the validity of the premises of induction via *statistical adequacy*, using thorough misspecification testing and respecification.

(iii) Emphasizing the central role of *error probabilities* in assessing the reliability (capacity) of inference, both *pre-data* as well as *post-data*.

(iv) Supplementing the original framework with a post-data assessment of inference in the form of *severity evaluations* in order the provide an evidential interpretation of test results.

(v) Bridging the gap between theory and data using a sequence of interconnected models, *theory* (primary), *structural* (experimental), *statistical* (data) built on two different, but related, sources of information: substantive subject matter and statistical information (chance regularity patterns).

(vi) Actively encouraging the thorough probing of the different ways an inductive inference might be *in error*, by localizing the error probing in the context of the different models (theory, structural, statistical and empirical).

The next few sub-sections elaborate on these key features as a prelude to using the error-statistical perspective to elucidate a number of philosophical/methodological issues pertaining to statistical modeling in general and to econometrics in particular.

## *5.1 Induction by enumeration vs. model-based induction*

*Induction by enumeration* seeks to generalize observed *events*, such as '80% of A's are B's', beyond the data in hand. In particular, the form of inference based on it takes the form (see [Salmon, 1967, p. 50]):

> "*Straight-rule:* if the proportion of red marbles from a sample of size $n$ is $(m/n)$, infer that approximately a proportion $(m/n)$ of all marbles in the urn are red."

The reliability of this inference is thought to depend on the *a priori* stipulations of (i) the 'uniformity' of *nature* and (ii) the 'representativeness' of the sample [Mills, 1924, pp. 550-2]. In addition, an emphasis was placed on 'large enough samples' stemming from the fact that under (i)–(ii) one can show that, as $n \to \infty$, the observed proportion $(m/n)$ converges in probability to the true proportion $\theta$; see [Pearson, 1920].

Fisher's model-based statistical induction extends the intended scope of induction-by-enumeration by replacing its focus on *events* and associated probabilities with modeling the stochastic *mechanism* that could have given rise to data $\mathbf{x}_0$. For example, the statistical model $\mathcal{M}_\theta(\mathbf{x})$ underlying the above straight-rule is the *simple Bernoulli model* (table 3). The inference concerning the proportion $\theta$ of red marbles in the urn amounts to choosing the point estimator $\widehat{\theta}_n(\mathbf{X})=\frac{1}{n}\sum_{k=1}^{n} X_k$; note that the estimate is $\widehat{\theta}_n(\mathbf{x}_0)=\frac{m}{n}$. The intuitive claim that $(m/n)$ converges to $\theta$ is more formally stated in terms of $\widehat{\theta}_n(\mathbf{X})$ being a *strongly consistent* estimator of $\theta: \ \mathbb{P}(\lim_{n\to\infty} \widehat{\theta}_n(\mathbf{X}) = \theta) = 1$.

**Table 3 - Simple Bernoulli Model**

| | | |
|---|---|---|
| Statistical GM: | $X_k = \theta + u_k, \ t\in\mathbb{N}.$ | |
| [1] Bernoulli: | $X_k \backsim \mathsf{Ber}(.,.), \ x_k=0,1,$ | $t\in\mathbb{N}.$ |
| [2] constant mean: | $E(X_k) = \theta,$ | $t\in\mathbb{N}.$ |
| [3] constant variance: | $Var(X_k) = \theta(1-\theta),$ | $t\in\mathbb{N}.$ |
| [4] Independence: | $\{X_k, \ k\in\mathbb{N}\}$ is an independent process | |

(11)

Viewed from the E-S perspective the straight-rule inference is fraught with potential unreliability problems. *First*, the inference in the form of a point estimate is rather weak without some measure of reliability; one needs to calibrate the qualifier 'approximately'. Using the *sampling distribution* $f(\widehat{\theta}_n(\mathbf{x}))$ under assumptions [1]–[4]:

$$\widehat{\theta}_n(\mathbf{X}) \backsim \mathsf{Bin}(\theta, \tfrac{\theta(1-\theta)}{n}), \quad \text{for any } n > 1, \tag{12}$$

where '$\mathsf{Bin}$' stands for a 'Binomial' distribution, gives a complete description of the probabilistic structure of $\widehat{\theta}_n(\mathbf{X})$, and furnishes the *error probabilities* needed to assess the reliability of any inference concerning $\theta$. *Second,* reliance on consistency alone provides no assurance for reliable inference for a given sample size $n$. *Third,* the soundness of the premises of inference, upon which the reliability of inference depends, relies on the validity of the priori stipulations (i)–(ii). In contrast, one can establish the soundness of the premises in the E-S set up by securing the validity of assumptions [1]–[4]; see [Spanos, 2009b] for further discussion.

## 5.2 *The frequentist interpretation of probability*

The frequentist interpretation of probability is gounded on the *Strong Law of Large Numbers (SLLN)*, which asserts that *under certain restrictions on the probabilistic structure of the process* $\{X_k,\ k\in\mathbb{N}\}$, the most restrictive being IID, it follows that:

$$\mathbb{P}(\lim_{n\to\infty}(\tfrac{1}{n}\textstyle\sum_{k=1}^{n}X_k)=p)=1. \tag{13}$$

The first SLLN was proved by Borel in 1909 in the case of a Bernoulli, IID process, but since then the result in (13) has been extended to hold with much less restrictive probabilistic structure, including $\{X_k,\ k\in\mathbb{N}\}$ being a *martingale difference* process; see [Spanos, 1999].

The *frequentist interpretation* identifies the probability of an event $A$ with the *limit* of the relative frequency of its occurrence:

$$P(A):=\lim_{n\to\infty}(\tfrac{1}{n}\textstyle\sum_{k=1}^{n}X_k)=p, \tag{14}$$

viewed in the context of a well-defined stochastic mechanism $\mathcal{M}_{\theta}(\mathbf{x})$. This aims to formalize the relationship between probability and 'stable long-run frequencies' that has been instinctively perceived by humans since the dawn of history. This suggests that from a modeling perspective, the SLLN is essentially an *existence* result for stable relative frequencies ($\frac{1}{n}\sum_{k=1}^{n}X_k\overset{a.s.}{\to}p$-constant) in the sense that it specifies sufficient conditions for the process $\{X_k,\ k\in\mathbb{N}\}$ to be amenable to statistical modeling and inference.

The common sense intuition underlying the SLLN in (13) is that the relative frequency of occurrence of event $A$ converges to $\mathbb{P}(A)=p$. This intuition is often the source of the charge that the justification of the frequentist interpretation of probability in (14) is *circular*: it uses *probability* to define *probability*; see [Lindley, 1965; Keuzenkamp, 2000; Howson and Urbach, 2005]. This is denied by some notable mathematicians including Renyi [1970, p. 159] who draws a clear distinction between the intuitive description in (14), and the purely a mathematical result in (13), dismissing the circularity charge as based on conflating the two. Indeed, a closer look at (13) reveals that it relies solely on measure theoretic results; see [Spanos, 2009c].

## 5.3 *Statistical induction: factual vs. hypothetical reasoning*

The difference in the nature of reasoning between estimation and testing has caused numerous confusions in the literature, especially as it relates to the relevant error probabilities of different inference procedures (estimation, testing, prediction and policy analysis), as well as the interpretation of the inference results.

Returning to simple Normal model (table 2), it is well known that the statistics:

$$\overline{X}_n=\tfrac{1}{n}\sum_{k=1}^{n}X_k\backsim\mathsf{N}\left(\mu,\tfrac{\sigma^2}{n}\right),\ s^2=\tfrac{1}{(n-1)}\textstyle\sum_{k=1}^{n}(X_k-\overline{X})^2\backsim\tfrac{\sigma^2}{(n-1)}\chi^2(n-1), \tag{15}$$

constitute 'optimal' estimators of $(\mu, \sigma^2)$, where $\chi^2(n-1)$ denotes the chi-square distribution with $(n-1)$ degrees of freedom; see [Cox and Hinkley, 1974]. To the sampling distributions in (15), one should add Gosset's [1908] famous result:

$$\frac{\sqrt{n}(\overline{X}_n-\mu)}{s} \backsim \mathsf{St}(n-1), \tag{16}$$

where $\mathsf{St}(n-1)$ denotes the Student's t distribution with $(n-1)$ degrees of freedom. This result, more than any other, inspired Fisher [1922] to pioneer the model-based frequentist approach to statistical inference. What is often not appreciate enough is that these sampling distributions are interpreted very differently in inference, depending on the nature of the underlying form of reasoning employed in each case.

The reasoning used in estimation and prediction is known as *factual* because it concerns evaluation of $\mathcal{M}_\theta(\mathbf{x})$ under the True State of Nature (TSN), but the reasoning underlying hypothesis testing is known as *hypothetical* because it is based on conjectural scenarios concerning $\mathcal{M}_\theta(\mathbf{x})$. To illustrate this, let us focus on (16). As (16) stands it constitutes a *pivot* — a function which depends on both the sample and parameter spaces — whose interpretation demands to be spelled out under the different forms of reasoning.

## *5.4 Factual reasoning: estimation and prediction*

*Factual reasoning* relies on evaluating the sampling distribution of a statistic under the TSN; the 'true' values of $(\mu, \sigma^2)$, say $(\mu_*, \sigma_*^2)$, whatever those happen to be. Gosset's result takes the form:

$$\tau(\mathbf{X}; \mu_*) = \frac{\sqrt{n}(\overline{X}_n-\mu_*)}{s} \overset{\mathsf{TSN}}{\backsim} \mathsf{St}(n-1). \tag{17}$$

In contrast, for a given value of $\mu$, say $\mu_1$ :

$$\tau_1(\mathbf{X}) = \frac{\sqrt{n}(\overline{X}_n-\mu_1)}{s} \overset{\mathsf{TSN}}{\backsim} \mathsf{St}(\delta_1; n-1), \;\; \delta_1 = \frac{\sqrt{n}(\mu_*-\mu_1)}{\sigma_*}, \tag{18}$$

where $\delta_1$ denotes the non-centrality parameter.

The difficulty with this form of inductive reasoning is that to render the error probabilities ascertainable one needs to know $(\mu_*, \sigma_*^2)$ . In this sense, point estimators and their optimal properties do *not* provide sufficient information to evaluate the *reliability* of a particular point estimate for a given $n$.

*Confidence Intervals* (CI) (interval estimation) attempts to rectify this deficiency by providing a way to evaluate the probability of 'covering' the true value $\theta^*$ of $\theta$, without knowing $\theta^*$. In the case of the simple Normal model:

$$\mathbb{P}\left(\overline{X}_n - c_{\frac{\alpha}{2}}(\tfrac{s}{\sqrt{n}}) \leq \mu \leq \overline{X}_n + c_{\frac{\alpha}{2}}(\tfrac{s}{\sqrt{n}}); \mu=\mu^*\right) = 1-\alpha, \tag{19}$$

where '$\mu=\mu^*$' indicates evaluation under the TSN. This result stems from (17), and evaluation of (19) under $\mu \neq \mu^*$ yields $\alpha$ - the *coverage error* probability.

Another attempt to circumvent the lack of error probabilities for point estimators is the use of the expected loss, such as the minimum *Mean Square Error (MSE),* defined by:

$$\mathsf{MSE}(\widehat{\theta}) = E(\widehat{\theta} - \theta)^2, \quad \text{for all } \theta \in \Theta. \tag{20}$$

The underlying reasoning in (20) is *not* factual is the sense used above, but *across-the-board* in the sense that the evaluation is based on the expected loss based on the function $L(\widehat{\theta};\theta) = (\widehat{\theta} - \theta)^2$, which considers all possible values of $\theta$. Indeed, the underlying reasoning does not even need the existence of a true $\theta^*$. Instead, it evaluates the decision-theoretic risk associated with all different values of $\theta$. In this sense, the reasoning is akeen to the Bayesian reasoning, where a prior $\pi(\theta)$ for all $\theta \in \Theta$, is used to bestow probabilities to all the different values of $\theta$. A moment's reflection, however, suggests that there is something wrong-headed about the use of the quantifier 'for all possible values of $\theta$' in (20) because it gives rise to dubious results.

EXAMPLE 4. In the case of the simple Normal model (table 2), the MSE evaluation suggests that $\overline{X}_n$ is *not* better than $\widetilde{\mu}$=7405926 (an arbitrary number which ignores the data completely), as an estimator of $\mu$, since for certain values of $\mu$ close to $\widetilde{\mu}$, the latter is better:

$$MSE(\overline{X}_n) = \tfrac{\sigma^2}{n} > MSE(\widetilde{\mu}) \text{ for values of } \mu \in \left(7405926 - \tfrac{\sigma^2}{n},\ 7405926 + \tfrac{\sigma^2}{n}\right),$$

The question that naturally arises is why would one care about the expected loss for values of $\theta \neq \theta^*$. The commonly used answer that in practice ones does not know $\theta^*$, is unconvincing because, despite that, one can still use factual reasoning, as in (17), or hypothetical reasoning as in (23), to draw frequentist inferences!

*Prediction* takes the estimated model $\mathcal{M}_{\widehat{\theta}}(\mathbf{x})$ as given and seeks a best guesstimate for observable *events* beyond the observation period, say $X_{n+1}=x_{n+1}$, in the form of a predictor $\widehat{X}_{n+1} = h(\mathbf{X})$. The prediction error is defined by $e_{n+1} = (X_{n+1} - \widehat{X}_{n+1})$, and its sampling distribution is evaluated under the *true state of nature* (TSN).

EXAMPLE 5. In the case of the simple Normal model (table 2):

$$e_{n+1} = (X_{n+1} - \overline{X}_n) \overset{\text{TSN}}{\backsim} \mathsf{N}\left(0,\ \sigma_*^2(1+\tfrac{1}{n})\right) \Rightarrow \frac{e_{n+1}}{s\sqrt{(1+\frac{1}{n})}} \overset{\text{TSN}}{\backsim} \mathsf{St}\,(n-1).$$

This can be used to construct a prediction CI of the form:

$$\mathbb{P}\left(\overline{X} - c_{\frac{\alpha}{2}} s\sqrt{(1+\tfrac{1}{n})} \leq x_{n+1} \leq c_{\frac{\alpha}{2}} s\sqrt{(1+\tfrac{1}{n})};\, \mu=\mu^*, \sigma^2=\sigma_*^2\right) = 1-\alpha, \tag{21}$$

where $(1-\alpha)$ denotes the coverage probability for the value $X_{n+1}$.

## 5.5 Hypothetical reasoning: testing

*Hypothetical reasoning* relies on comparing the sampling distribution of a statistic under different hypothetical scenarios with what actually happened, i.e. data $\mathbf{x}_0$. Returning to the simple Normal model (table 2), in testing the *hypotheses*:

$$H_0 : \mu = \mu_0 \quad \text{vs.} \quad H_1 : \mu \neq \mu_0, \tag{22}$$

the test statistic $\tau(\mathbf{X}){=}\frac{\sqrt{n}(\overline{X}_n-\mu_0)}{s}$ is evaluated under numerous hypothetical scenarios:

$$\text{(i) } \tau(\mathbf{X}) \overset{H_0}{\backsim} \mathsf{St}(n{-}1), \qquad \text{(ii) } \tau(\mathbf{X}) \overset{H_1(\mu_1)}{\backsim} \mathsf{St}(\delta; n{-}1), \text{ for } \mu_1{\neq}\mu_0,\ \delta{=}\frac{\sqrt{n}(\mu_1-\mu_0)}{\sigma}, \tag{23}$$

where (23)(i)-(ii) can be used to define the *type I & II error probabilities*:

$$\mathbb{P}\left(|\tau(\mathbf{X})| > c_{\frac{\alpha}{2}};\ H_0\right){=}\alpha, \quad \mathbb{P}\left(|\tau(\mathbf{X})| \leq c_{\frac{\alpha}{2}};\ H_1(\mu_1)\right){=}\beta(\mu_1), \text{ for } \mu_1{>}\mu_0. \tag{24}$$

as well as the *power* of the test:

$$\mathfrak{P}(\mu_1) = \mathbb{P}(\tau(\mathbf{X}) > c_\alpha;\ H_1(\mu_1)){=}1{-}\beta(\mu_1), \text{ for all } \mu_1 > \mu_0.$$

It can be shown that the above test is UMP, Unbiased; see [Lehmann, 1986].

Notwithstanding the well-known (mathematical) duality between hypothesis testing and *interval estimation:*

$$C_0(\alpha){=}\{\mathbf{x}\text{: } |\tau(\mathbf{x})| \leq c_{\frac{\alpha}{2}}\} \Leftrightarrow CI(\mathbf{X};\alpha){=}\{\mu\text{: } |\tau(\mathbf{X};\mu)| \leq c_{\frac{\alpha}{2}}\},$$

there is a crucial difference in the interpretation of the two types of inference, stemming from their underlying reasoning. In factual reasoning that there is only *one* scenario, but in hypothetical reasoning there is an *infinite* number of possible scenarios.

This has two important implications. *First*, due to the legion of hypothetical scenarios, testing poses sharper questions and often elicits more precise answers. *Second*, the error probabilities associated with hypothetical reasoning are properly defined *post-data* as well, but those associated with factual reasoning become *degenerate.* This is because factual reasoning inevitably involves the TSN, and thus post-data the inference is either true or false; the relevant probabilities are either *one* (1) or *zero* (0). Which situation is instantiated in a particular case can only be assessed when the true value $\mu^*$ is known.

This crucial difference between pre and post-data error probabilities can be used to shed light on several philosophical/methodological issues mentioned above.

## 5.6 Post-data error probabilities in confidence intervals

The post-data degeneracy of the factual error probabilities is the reason why one cannot distinguish between different values of $\mu$ within the *observed* CI:

$$[\overline{x}_n - c_{\frac{\alpha}{2}}(s/\sqrt{n}),\ \overline{x}_n + c_{\frac{\alpha}{2}}(s/\sqrt{n})], \tag{25}$$

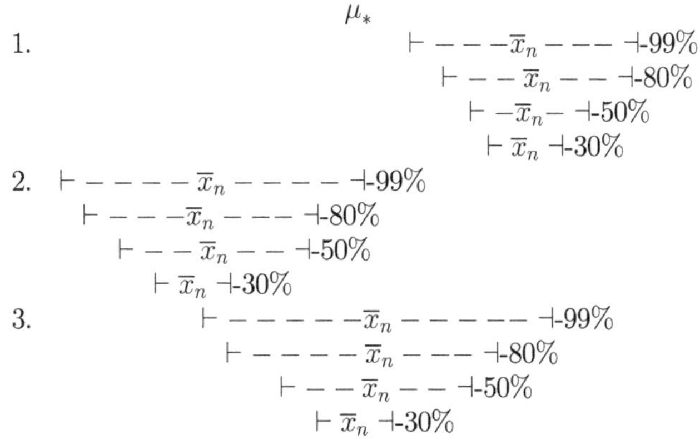


Figure 2. A sequence of observed confidence intervals

using probabilistic arguments; $\overline{x}_n$ denotes the observed value of $\overline{X}_n$. This is because, post-data the observed CI covers the true $\mu$ with probabilities 0 or 1. This brings out the fallacy in often made claims like:

> "... the [parameter] is much more likely to be near the middle of the confidence interval than towards the extremes." [Altman *et al.*, 2000, p. 22]

In general, one cannot provide proper post-data *coverage probabilities* for inferential claims like:

$$\mu \geq \overline{x}_n - c_{\frac{\alpha}{2}}(s/\sqrt{n}) \text{ or } \mu \leq \overline{x}_n + c_{\frac{\alpha}{2}}(s/\sqrt{n}), \tag{26}$$

beyond the uninformative degenerate ones. Any attempt to transfer the pre-data error probability to the observed CI commits the *fallacy of probabilistic instantiation.*

Equally fallacious is the often invoked argument that one can evaluate proper post-data coverage error probabilities for CIs when using a sequence of CIs by changing $\alpha$. This misconception can be seen in fig. 2 below where 3 typical observed CIs are shown for different coverage probabilities, and it's clear that, for a given true $\mu_*$, there is no general probabilistic statement relating to (26) one can make which will be consistent with all three cases.

## *5.7 Severity: a post-data evaluation of inference*

Practitioners in several disciplines have long felt that the smaller the p-value the better the accord of $\mathbf{x}_0$ *with* $H_1$, but the dependence of $p(\mathbf{x}_0)$ on the sample size made that intuition very difficult to flesh out correctly. A way to formalize this intuition and bridge the gap between the coarse accept/reject rule and the evidence for or against a hypothesis warranted by the data was proposed by Mayo [1991] in the form of a post-data evaluation of inference using the notion of severity.

### 5.7.1 *Severity reasoning*

A hypothesis $H$ passes a *severe test* $T$ with data $\mathbf{x}_0$ if,

(S-1) $\mathbf{x}_0$ agrees with $H$, and

(S-2) with very high probability, test $T$ would have produced a result that accords less well with $H$ than $\mathbf{x}_0$ does, if $H$ were false.

The evidential interpretation stems from the fact that $H$ passing test $T$ provides good evidence for inferring $H$ (is correct) to the extent that $T$ severely passes $H$ with data $\mathbf{x}_0$. Severity takes the pre-data error probabilities as determining the generic capacity of the test procedure, and custom-tailors that to the particular case of data $\mathbf{x}_0$ and the relevant inferential claim $H$, rendering the post-data evaluation test-specific, data-specific and claim-specific. Thus, from the thesis of *learning from error*, it follows that a severity assessment allows one to determine whether there is evidence for (or against) $H$; see [Mayo, 1996].

EXAMPLE 6. In the case of the simple Normal model (table 2), let the *hypotheses* of interest be:

$$H_0\colon\ \mu = \mu_0 \quad \text{vs.} \quad H_1\colon\ \mu > \mu_0. \tag{27}$$

The t-test defined by: $T_\alpha := \left\{\tau(\mathbf{X}) = \frac{\sqrt{n}(\overline{X}_n - \mu_0)}{s},\ C_1(\alpha) = \{\mathbf{x}\colon\ \tau(\mathbf{x}) > c_\alpha\}\right\}$, is UMP; see [Lehmann 1986]. Depending on whether this test has given rise to accept or reject $H_0$ with data $\mathbf{x}_0$, the post-data evaluation of that inference takes the form of:

$$\begin{aligned} \mathsf{Sev}(T_\alpha; \mathbf{x}_0; \mu \leq \mu_1) &= \mathbb{P}(\tau(\mathbf{X}) > \tau(\mathbf{x}_0); \mu > \mu_1), \\ \mathsf{Sev}(T_\alpha; \mathbf{x}_0; \mu > \mu_1) &= \mathbb{P}(\tau(\mathbf{X}) \leq \tau(\mathbf{x}_0); \mu \leq \mu_1), \end{aligned} \tag{28}$$

respectively, where $\mu_1 = \mu_0 + \gamma$, for $\gamma \geq 0$. Severity introduces a *discrepancy parameter* $\gamma \geq 0$ in order to evaluate the relevant *inferential claims* associated when $H_0$ is accepted ($\mu \leq \mu_1$) or rejected ($\mu > \mu_1$). This amounts to establishing the smallest (largest) discrepancy $\gamma \geq 0$ from $H_0$ warranted by data $\mathbf{x}_0$, associated with the N-P decision to accept (reject) $H_0$. When the severity evaluation of a particular inferential claim, say $\mu \leq \mu_0 + \gamma$, is very high (close to one), it can be interpreted as indicating that this claim is warranted to the extent that the test has ruled out discrepancies larger than $\gamma$; the underlying test would have detected a departure from the null as large as $\gamma$ almost surely, and the fact that it didn't suggests that no such departures were present. This evaluation can be applied to the result of any (properly defined) N-P test to address the fallacies of acceptance and rejection; see [Mayo and Spanos, 2006].

### 5.7.2 *Severe testing and the p-value*

A small p-value, say $p(\mathbf{x}_0)$=.01, indicates that $\mathbf{x}_0$ *accords with* $H_1$, and the question is whether it provides evidence for $H_1$. Using the severe-testing interpretation one can argue that $H_1$ has passed a severe test because the probability that test $T_\alpha$ would have produced a result that accords less well with $H_1$ than $\mathbf{x}_0$ does (values of $\tau(\mathbf{x})$ less than $\tau(\mathbf{x}_0)$), if $H_1$ were false ($H_0$ true) is very high:

$$\mathsf{Sev}(T_\alpha;\mathbf{x}_0;\mu{>}\mu_0){=}\mathbb{P}(\tau(\mathbf{X}){\leq}\tau(\mathbf{x}_0);\mu{\leq}\mu_0){=}1{-}\mathbb{P}(\tau(\mathbf{X}){>}\tau(\mathbf{x}_0);\mu{=}\mu_0){=}.99.$$

The severity construal of the p-value brings out its most crucial weakness: it establishes the existence of *some* discrepancy $\gamma \geq 0$, but provides no information concerning the *magnitude* warranted by data $\mathbf{x}_0$. Moreover, the dependence of the p-value on the sample size can belie the warranted discrepancy. The severity evaluation addresses both of these problems [Mayo and Spanos, 2006].

### 5.7.3 *The fallacies of acceptance and rejection*

Fallacy of acceptance: *no* evidence against $H_0$ is misinterpreted as evidence *for* $H_0$.
Fallacy of rejection: evidence *against* $H_0$ is misinterpreted as evidence *for* a particular $H_1$.

Hence, in general, accepting $H_0$ should not be interpreted as evidence for it because the discrepancy $\gamma \geq 0$ warranted with data $\mathbf{x}_0$ might be sizeable (in substantive terms). Similarly, rejecting $H_0$ should not be interpreted as evidence for $H_1$ because the warranted discrepancy $\gamma \geq 0$ from the $H_0$ could be tiny (in substantive terms).

The best example of the fallacy of rejection is the case of statistical significance being misinterpreted as substantive significance. In the case of the hypotheses in (27), rejecting $H_0$ only establishes the presence of *some* discrepancy from $\mu_0$, say $\delta > 0$, but it does not provide any information concerning its magnitude.

The severity evaluation $\mathsf{Sev}(T_\alpha;\mathbf{x}_0;\mu > \mu_1)$ [$\mathsf{Sev}(T_\alpha;\mathbf{x}_0;\mu \leq \mu_1)$] of the claim that $\mu > \mu_1{=}\mu_0{+}\gamma$ [$\mu \leq \mu_1{=}\mu_0{+}\gamma$] for some $\gamma \geq 0$, can be used to establish the warranted discrepancy $\gamma^*$, which can be used, in conjunction with substantive information, to settle the issue of substantive significance; see [Mayo and Spanos, 2006].

The severity assessment can be used to address an important instance of the fallacy of rejection known as conflating statistical and substantive significance; see [Spanos, 2008c].

### 5.7.4 *Revisiting observed Confidence Intervals (CI)*

As argued above, the post-data error probabilities associated with a CI are degenerate. In contrast, testing reasoning gives rise to well-defined error probabilities post-data because it compares what actually happened to what it is expected under different scenarios (hypothetical values of $\mu$), since it does *not* involve TSN.

In view of that, it is evident that one can evaluate the probability of claims of the form given in (26) by relating $\mu_1$ to whatever values one is interested in, including $\overline{x}_n \pm c_{\frac{\alpha}{2}}(s/\sqrt{n})$ for different $\alpha$, using hypothetical (not factual) reasoning. Indeed, this is exactly how the severity assessment circumvents the problem facing observed CIs, whose own post-data error probabilities are zero or one, and provides an effective way to evaluate inferential claims of the form:

$$\mu \geq \mu_1 = \mu_0 + \gamma, \text{ for } \gamma \leq 0, \text{ or } \mu \leq \mu_1 = \mu_0 + \gamma, \text{ for } \gamma \geq 0,$$

using well-defined post data error probabilities by relating $\gamma$ to different values of $c_{\frac{\alpha}{2}}(s/\sqrt{n})$; see [Mayo and Spanos, 2006]. The reasoning underlying such severity evaluations is fundamentally different from the factual reasoning underlying a sequence of CIs; section 5.4.

The severity evaluation also elucidates the comparisons between p-values and CIs and can be used to explain why the various attempts to relate p-value and observed confidence interval curves (see [Birnbaum, 1961; Kempthorne and Folks, 1971; Poole, 1987]) were unsuccessful. In addition, it can be used to shed light on the problem of evaluating 'effect sizes' (see [Rosenthal *et al.*, 1999]) sought after in some applied fields like psychology and epidemiology; see [Spanos, 2004].

## 5.8 *Revisiting Bayesian criticisms of frequentist inference*

As mentioned above, the primary Bayesian argument employed to question frequentist inference was based on circumstantial evidence stemming from several examples employed to make a case for Fisher's Conditionality Principle (CP), including the Welch [1939] uniform, the mixture of Normals and certain cannibalizations of the N-P set up; see [Berger and Wolpert, 1988; Berger, 1985]. All these examples involve some kind of 'rigging' of the statistical model or the testing set up so that it appears as though the CP provides the only way out, when in fact alternative frequentist principles allow extrication in every case.

Bayesian examples based on cannibalizing the N-P formulation often come the form of taking two arbitrary values of the unknown parameter, say $\mu_0$=-1 and $\mu_1$=1 in the context of the simple Normal model (table 2) $\mathcal{M}_\mu(\mathbf{x})$ where $\mu \in \mathbb{R}$. One then applies what seems to be an optimal N-P test with $\overline{x}_n$=0 to show that it will often lead to absurd results; see [Berger and Wolpert, 1988]. The problem here is that even though for substantive purposes only two values of $\mu$ are relevant, for statistical inference purposes the whole of the parameter space, as specified in $\mathcal{M}_\mu(\mathbf{x})$, is relevant. The proper way to handle this is to choose one of the two values as the null and consider the other value as determining the discrepancy of interest; see [Spanos, 2008b].

The examples used to illustrate how the conditional inference leads to the Bayesian approach are often chosen to have an overlap between the parameter and sample spaces. For the Welch uniform example, where the sample is IID from $X_k \backsim \mathsf{U}(\theta - \frac{1}{2}, \theta + \frac{1}{2})$, $k$=1, ..., $n$, Berger and Wolpert [1988] argue that:

> "The conditional interval is considerably more appealing than "various" optimal nonconditional intervals, as discussed by Pratt (1961)."(p. 14).

A closer scrutiny of the Welch example shows that the subtle rigging stems from the fact that this distribution is *irregular* in the sense that its support depends on the unknown parameter $\theta$. This irregularity creates a restriction between $\theta$ and the data $\mathbf{x}_0$, in the sense that post-data the feasible range of values of $\theta$ is $A(\mathbf{x}_0)=[x_{[n]}-\frac{1}{2}, x_{[1]}+\frac{1}{2}]$, where $x_{[n]}=\max(\mathbf{x}_0)$ and $x_{[1]}=\min(\mathbf{x}_0)$. The CP principle calls for replacing the unconditional distribution of $\widehat{\theta}(\mathbf{X})=[X_{[n]}+X_{[1]}]/2$, say $f(\widehat{\theta};\theta))$, which allows for values of $\theta$ outside the feasible support $\theta \in A(\mathbf{x}_0)$, with the conditional distribution $f(\widehat{\theta} \mid R=R)$ where $R=(X_{[n]}-X_{[1]})$ denotes the range, which is an ancillary statistic. However, $f(\widehat{\theta} \mid R=R)$ being uniform over $\theta \in A(\mathbf{x}_0)$, has no discriminatory capacity; see [Cox and Hinkley, 1974, p. 221]. It turns out that a more effective frequentist way to account for this post-data information is to use the truncated distribution $f(\widehat{\theta} \mid A(\mathbf{x}_0);\theta)$ which has genuine discriminatory capacity and addresses the infeasibility problem associated with $f(\widehat{\theta};\theta))$; see [Spanos, 2007d].

More recent methodological discussions in some Bayesian circles, known as 'Objective' (O) [Bernardo, 2005], shifted their focus away from the earlier foundational principles, and call instead for: (i) relying on the statistical model itself to determine a 'reference' prior viewed "as consensus priors with low information" [Ghosh *et al.*, 2006, p. 147], (ii) aligning their perspective toward a reconciliation with Fisherian conditionalism, and (iii) promoting O-Bayesian procedures with 'good' frequentist properties; see [Berger, 2004]. The problem is that the moves (i)-(iii) flout the earlier foundational principles upon which the subjective Bayesians built their original case against the frequentist approach. Indeed, numerous Bayesians quote or paraphrase (with a hint of sarcasm) Jeffreys [1961, p. 453], that frequentist procedures are absurd for "taking account of other possible realizations, $\mathbf{x} \neq \mathbf{x}_0$ for $\mathbf{x} \in \mathbb{R}^n_X$, that might have been observed but were not". A moment's reflection suggests that provides the only way a frequentist can establish the generic capacity of inference procedures.

Viewing the O-Bayesian approach from the error-statistical perspective, raises several philosophical/methodological issues.

*First*, by focusing exclusively on $\mathbf{x}_0$ the Bayesian approach leaves no room for assessing the validity of the statistical model defining the likelihood function. This is because Mis-Specification (M-S) testing requires Fisher significance testing reasoning which involves entertaining hypothetical scenarios beyond the observed data $\mathbf{x}_0$ and/or the pre-specified model. In relation to this, it is important to emphasize that any Bayesian inference is as vulnerable to misspecification as the frequentist because any departures from the statistical model assumptions will invalidate the likelihood function and result in misleading inferences based on $\pi(\theta \mid \mathbf{x}_0)$, $\theta \in \Theta$, in (10), irrespective of the choice of the prior $\pi(\theta)$, $\theta \in \Theta$.

*Second*, Cox and Mayo [2010] call into question the apparent LP dilemma facing a frequentist to either renounce sufficiency or renounce error probabilities altogether "an illusion". Indeed, Mayo [2010] goes much further than simply raise questions about the cogency of the LP for frequentist inference. She subjects Birnbaum's [1962] "proof" to a careful logical scrutiny and shows that the underlying argument is fallacious.

*Third*, the choice of the 'reference' priors by O-Bayesians, requires evaluations which involve the whole of the sample space, violating both the likelihood (LP) and the stopping rule principles — long embraced as fundamental for, and as logically entailed by, the Bayesian paradigm (see [Berger and Wolpert, 1988]). In view of these crucial foundational changes, the question one might ask is: what is there left to render the inference Bayesian, apart from the unpersuasive claim that the only way to provide an evidential account of inference is to attach probabilities to hypotheses?

# 6 STATISTICAL ADEQUACY AND THE RELIABILITY OF INFERENCE

How does the error statistical approach ensure that the link between the phenomenon of interest and an adequate statistical model $\mathcal{M}_\theta(\mathbf{x})$ is sound?

The gravity of statistical misspecification stems from the fact any departures from the probabilistic assumptions of $\mathcal{M}_\theta(\mathbf{x})$ will give rise to a *misspecified* $f(\mathbf{x};\theta)$ and will vitiate the sampling distribution $F_n(t)$ of any statistic $T_n{=}g(X_1,...,X_n)$, since:

$$F_n(t) = \mathbb{P}(T_n \leq t) = \int \cdots \int_{\{\mathbf{x}:\ g(\mathbf{x})\leq t\}} f(\mathbf{x};\theta)d\mathbf{x},\ \ t{\in}\mathbb{R}. \tag{29}$$

In particular, $F_n(t)$ will undermine the reliability of any inference based on it by yielding actual error probabilities that are *different* from the nominal ones.

## 6.1 A statistical model can have 'a life of its own'

A crucial feature of error-statistics is its reliance on error probabilities, pre-data, to evaluate the capacity of an inference procedure, and post-data to provide an evidential warrant for a claim that passed. For such evaluations to be reliable, however, one needs to ensure the validity of the underlying statistical model $\mathcal{M}_\theta(\mathbf{x})$ vis-a-vis data $\mathbf{x}_0$.*Statistical adequacy* is tantamount to affirming that data $\mathbf{x}_0$ constitute a 'truly typical realization' of the stochastic process parametrized by $\mathcal{M}_\theta(\mathbf{x})$. Statistical adequacy is assessed using thorough *Mis-Specification (M-S) testing*: probing for departures from the probabilistic assumptions comprising $\mathcal{M}_\theta(\mathbf{x})$ vis-a-vis data $\mathbf{x}_0$.

What is important for theory testing purposes is that a *statistically adequate model* needs to be built without invoking substantive information, so that it can be used to provide the broader inductive premises for evaluating substantive adequacy. The autonomy of $\mathcal{M}_\theta(\mathbf{x})$ stems from the fact that is built on purely probabilistic information by being selected to account the 'chance regularities' exhibited by data $\mathbf{x}_0$, when the latter is viewed as a realization of a generic stochastic process $\{X_k,\ k{\in}\mathbb{N}\}$. In this sense, a statistically adequate model provides a form of *statistical knowledge*, analogous to what Mayo [1996] calls *experimental knowledge*, against which the substantive information could be appraised. The notion of a statistically adequate model formalizes the sense in which data $\mathbf{x}_0$ have 'a voice of its own', separate from the one ideated by the theory in question.

The notion of *statistical information,* separate from substantive, has been disputed, not only by econometric textbooks, but by mainstream economics for centuries (see [Spanos, 2010a]). The fact of the matter is that it constitutes a crucial step in securing the reliability of inference. Indeed, in disciplines which rely primarily on observational data, a statistically adequate model provides a crucial necessary step in assessing the validity of any substantive subject matter information and offers a way: "to know precisely what there is to explain"; see [Schumpeter, 1954, p. 14]. Indeed, one can go as far as to suggest that the one thing that unites critics of textbook econometrics like Hendry [1995; 2000] and Sims [1980], is the call for allowing the data 'to have a voice of its own'.

In an attempt to dispel this myth consider the data exhibited in figures 3 and 4. Viewing the t-plot in figure 3 as a realization of a generic stochastic process $\{X_k,\ k{\in}\mathbb{N}\}$ (free from any substantive information), it is not unreasonable to conjecture that $\mathbf{x}_0$ constitutes a typical realization of a NIID process, for which the simple Normal model is a particular parameterization; it can be verified that, indeed, assumptions [1]–[4] (table 2) are valid for the data in question. On the other hand if the data are the ones shown in figure 4, it is reasonable to conjecture that the simple Normal model will be *misspecified* because the t-plot of data $\mathbf{x}_0$ exhibit cycles which indicate departures from the ID assumption; see [Spanos, 1999, ch. 5]. A more appropriate probabilistic structure for the stochastic process $\{X_k,\ k\in\mathbb{N}\}$ underlying the data in fig. 4 might be that it's Normal, Markov (M) and Stationary (S), yielding:

$$f(x_1,x_2,...,x_n;\phi)\ \overset{\text{M\&S}}{=}\ f_0(x_1;\theta_1)\prod_{t=2}^{n}f(x_t|x_{t-1};\theta),$$

where the Normality of $\{X_t,\ t{\in}\mathbb{N}\}$ implies that for $\mathbf{X}_{t-1}^0{:=}(X_{t-1},...,X_1)$:

$$(X_t\mid\mathbf{X}_{t-1}^0)\ \backsim\ \mathsf{N}\left(\alpha_0+\alpha_1X_{t-1},\ \sigma_0^2\right),\quad t{\in}\mathbb{N}.$$

This reduction gives rise to the AR(p) model in terms of complete and internally consistent set of testable [vis-à-vis data $\mathbf{x}_0$] probabilistic assumptions [1]–[5] (table 4).

**Table 4 - Normal/AutoRegressive Model**

| | | | |
|---|---|---|---|
| Statistical GM: | | $X_t=\alpha_0+\alpha_1X_{t-1}+u_t,\ t{\in}\mathbb{N}.$ | |
| [1] | Normality: | $\left(X_t\mid\mathbf{X}_{t-1}^0\right)\backsim\mathsf{N}(.,.),\ x_t{\in}\mathbb{R},$ | $t{\in}\mathbb{N}.$ |
| [2] | Linearity: | $E\left(X_t\mid\mathbf{X}_{t-1}^0\right)=\alpha_0+\alpha_1X_{t-1},$ | |
| [3] | Homoskedasticity: | $Var\left(X_t\mid\mathbf{X}_{t-1}^0\right)=\sigma_0^2,$ | |
| [4] | Markov dependence: | $\{X_t,\ t{\in}\mathbb{N}\}$ is a Markov process, | |
| [5] | t-invariance: | $(\alpha_0,\alpha_1,\sigma_0^2)$ are *not* changing with $t$, | |

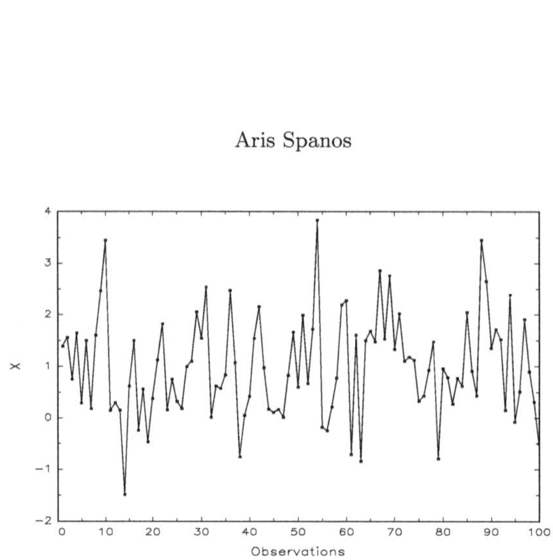


Figure 3. t-plot of $x_t$

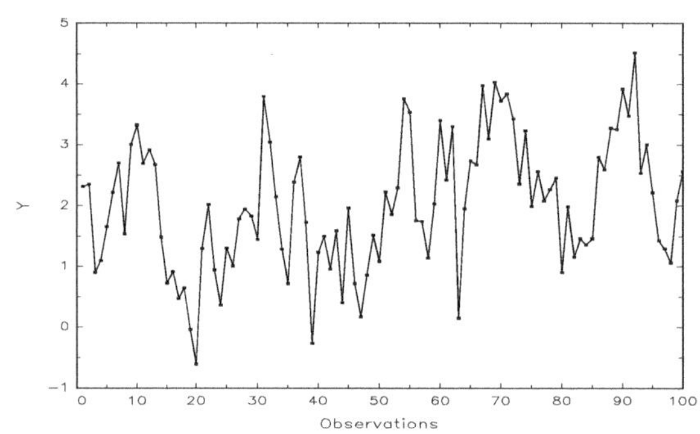


Figure 4. t-plot of $x_t$

## *6.2 Relating the substantive and the statistical information*

Another aspect of modeling that the error-statistical approach differs appreciably from other perspectives is in terms of how the *statistical* and *substantive information* are integrated without compromising the credibility of either source of information. The problem is viewed more broadly as concerned with bridging the gap between theory and data using a *chain of complecting models,* theory (primary), structural (experimental), statistical (data) built on two different, but related, sources of information: substantive subject matter and statistical information (chance regularity patterns); see [Spanos, 2006b]. Disentangling the role of the two sources of information has been a major problem in statistics (see [Lehmann, 1990; Cox, 1990]).

The error-statistical perspective provides a framework in the context of which these sources of information are treated as complementary, and the chain of interconnected models can be used to disentangle their respective roles. It proposes to distinguish, *ab initio*, between statistical and substantive information and then bridge the gap between them by a sequence of models which enable one to delineate and probe for the potential errors at different stages of modeling.

From the theory side, the substantive information is initially encapsulated by a theory model and then modified into a structural model $\mathcal{M}_{\varphi}(\mathbf{x})$ to render it estimable with data $\mathbf{x}_0$. From the data side, the statistical information is distilled by a statistical model $\mathcal{M}_{\theta}(\mathbf{x})$, whose parameterization is chosen with a view to render $\mathcal{M}_{\varphi}(\mathbf{x})$ a reparametrization/restriction thereof.

**Statistical Adequacy Principle (SAP).** The statistical adequacy of $\mathcal{M}_{\theta}(\mathbf{x})$ needs to be secured first, in order to ensure the reliability of the primary inferences concerned with appraising *substantive* claims, including the adequacy of $\mathcal{M}_{\varphi}(\mathbf{x})$.

The first step in assessing substantive information is to embed the structural $\mathcal{M}_{\varphi}(\mathbf{x})$ into a statistical model $\mathcal{M}_{\theta}(\mathbf{x})$ via reparametrization/restriction, whose generic form is the implicit function $\mathbf{G}(\varphi, \theta)= \mathbf{0}$, where $\varphi \in\Phi$, and $\theta \in\Theta$, denote the structural and statistical parameters, respectively. This provides a link between $\mathcal{M}_{\theta}(\mathbf{x})$ and the phenomenon of interest that takes the form of **identification**:

does the implicit function $\mathbf{G}(\varphi, \theta) = \mathbf{0}$ define $\varphi$ *uniquely* in terms of $\theta$?

Often, there are more statistical than structural parameters, and that enables one to test the additional substantive information using the *overidentifying restrictions*:

$$H_0\colon \mathbf{G}(\varphi, \theta)= \mathbf{0}, \text{ vs. } H_1\colon \mathbf{G}(\varphi, \theta) \neq \mathbf{0}. \tag{30}$$

This error statistical view of identification differs from the traditional textbook notion (see [Greene, 2000]) in so far as it requires that the underlying statistical model (the reduced form) be validated vis-a-vis data $\mathbf{x}_0$ for the link between structural parameters and the phenomenon of interest to be rendered trustworthy ([Spanos, 1990]).

The following example illustrates the problems raised when statistical and substantive information are intermeshed at the outset to specify a model for inferences purposes.

**Mixture of Normals.** Consider the case where data $\mathbf{x}_0$ have arisen from only one of two possible simple Normal models:

| $\mathcal{M}_{\varphi_1}(\mathbf{x})$: $X_k \backsim \mathsf{N}(\mu, \sigma_1^2)$, | $\mathcal{M}_{\varphi_2}(\mathbf{x})$: $X_k \backsim \mathsf{N}(\mu, \sigma_2^2)$, $k$=1, ..., $n$, |
|---|---|

(31)

where it is assumed that: (i) $\sigma_2^2 > \sigma_1^2$ and both variances are *known* a priori, and (ii) a priori each model could have given rise to data $\mathbf{x}_0$ with probability $\frac{1}{2}$.

Using the binary random variable: $Z$=0 if $\mathcal{M}_{\varphi_1}(\mathbf{x})$, and $Z$=1 if $\mathcal{M}_{\varphi_2}(\mathbf{x})$, their *joint* density takes the form:

$$f(x, z; \mu)=f(x|z; \mu)\cdot f(z)=\frac{1}{2}\phi(x; \mu, \sigma_1^2)^{1-z}\phi(x; \mu, \sigma_2^2)^z, z=0, 1,$$

$\phi(x; \mu, \sigma^2)$ being the density of $\mathsf{N}(\mu, \sigma^2)$. The primary hypotheses of interest are:

$$H_0 : \mu = \mu_0 \text{ vs. } H_1 : \mu \neq \mu_0. \tag{32}$$

This is a famous example that was initially introduced by Cox [1958] to illustrate Fisher's Conditionality Principle (CP), and provided the basic idea for Birnbaum's [1962] notion of a *mixed experiment*; a key element of his derivation of the Likelihood Principle (LP). It also features prominently among the examples used by Bayesians to question the frequentist approach; [Berger and Wolpert, 1988; Ghosh *et al.*, 2006].

The conventional wisdom is that, in light of the substantive information (i)–(ii), the relevant model for frequentist inference is the *mixed model*:

$$\mathcal{M}_{\varphi}(\mathbf{x}) = \tfrac{1}{2}\mathcal{M}_{\varphi_1}(\mathbf{x}) + \tfrac{1}{2}\mathcal{M}_{\varphi_2}(\mathbf{x}), \qquad (33)$$

based on the *marginal* density $f(x;\mu){=}\sum_z f(x,z;\mu){=}\frac{1}{2}\phi(x;\mu,\sigma_1^2) + \frac{1}{2}\phi(x;\mu,\sigma_2^2)$. However, when (33) is used as a basis of inference, the N-P test for (32) gives rise to several paradoxes and fallacies; see [Lehmann, 1983]. Moreover, it is claimed that the only frequentist way to avoid these problems is to use the CP which calls for conditioning on $Z{=}z$, since $Z$ is ancillary for $\mu$, and then proceed to test (32) on the basis of one of the models in (31) based on the *conditional* densities $f(x|z{=}0){=}\phi(x;\mu,\sigma_1^2)$ and $f(x|z{=}1){=}\phi(x;\mu,\sigma_2^2)$.

Viewed from the perspective of the Statistical Adequacy Principle (SAP), this conventional wisdom is called into question on two grounds.

*First*, the SAP calls for securing the statistical adequacy of the underlying statistical model:

$$\mathcal{M}_{\theta}(\mathbf{x})\colon\ X_k \backsim \mathsf{N}(\mu,\sigma^2),\ \ \theta{:=}(\mu,\sigma^2){\in}\mathbb{R}{\times}\mathbb{R}_{+},\ \ k{=}1,...,n, \qquad (34)$$

before appraising/imposing the substantive information in (i)–(ii); note that $\mathcal{M}_{\varphi_1}(\mathbf{x})$, $\mathcal{M}_{\varphi_2}(\mathbf{x})$ and $\mathcal{M}_{\varphi}(\mathbf{x})$ incorporate *untested* substantive information. As argued above, foisting the substantive information on the data at the outset constitutes an imprudent modeling strategy because one has no way to delineate between substantive and statistical misspecification.

*Second*, the probabilistic nature of (ii) belies the form of relevant information for statistical model specification grounded solely on statistical information in data $\mathbf{x}_0$. The only statistical model one can specify on the basis of data like those depicted in fig. 3 is (34), where both parameters $(\mu,\sigma^2)$ are *unknown*. Indeed, accounting for the information in (ii) results in the mixed model (33), which is clearly *statistically misspecified,* since by assumption, at least one of the two components did *not* contribute to generating $\mathbf{x}_0$. Hence, when $\mathcal{M}_{\varphi}(\mathbf{x})$ is used as the basis of inference, the nominal and actual error probabilities will be different; no wonder it leads to fallacious inferences. In frequentist inference *learning from data* can only occur when the inferential error probabilities relate directly to an adequate description of the underlying mechanism; hence the importance of the SAP.

A closer look at assumption (ii) reveals that it is equivalent to assuming a *prior*:

| $\sigma^2$ | $\sigma_1^2$ | $\sigma_2^2$ |
|---|---|---|
| $\pi(\sigma^2)$ | $\frac{1}{2}$ | $\frac{1}{2}$ |

which, when combined with (31), gives rise to a *posterior* that happens to coincide with the distribution of $\mathcal{M}_{\varphi}(\mathbf{x})$ in (33). That is, the misspecification of $\mathcal{M}_{\varphi}(\mathbf{x})$ fits nicely into the Bayesian approach as a natural consequence of using a prior distribution to represent the specification uncertainty relating to substantive information. In sharp contrast, frequentist inference separates the statistical model specification and validation facets from the inference phase, in order to ensure that specification error would not vitiate the relevant error probabilities.

The SAP suggests that the relevant statistical model for frequentist inference is not (33) since it's misspecified, but $\mathcal{M}_{\theta}(\mathbf{x})$ in (34), whose adequacy needs to be assessed (test assumptions [1]–[4] in table 2) first; ignoring the substantive information in (i)–(ii). If $\mathcal{M}_{\theta}(\mathbf{x})$ is statistically validated, one can then proceed to test the cogency of (i) to infer whether $\mathcal{M}_{\varphi_1}(\mathbf{x})$ or $\mathcal{M}_{\varphi_2}(\mathbf{x})$ or neither model could have given rise to $\mathbf{x}_0$. Assuming that one of the two models is data-cogent, say $\mathcal{M}_{\varphi_1}(\mathbf{x})$, one could then impose the substantive information $\sigma^2 = \sigma_1^2$, and proceed to test (32) on the basis of the *empirical model* $\mathcal{M}_{\widehat{\varphi}_1}(\mathbf{x})$.

Hence, from the error statistical perspective, the ability to assess the validity of the substantive information in (i), in the context of a statistically adequate model $\mathcal{M}_{\theta}(\mathbf{x})$ (34), renders the probabilistic information in (ii) — representing specification uncertainty — impertinent and potentially misleading if imposed at the outset. Indeed, this calls into question the cornerstone of Birnbaum's [1962] derivation of the LP, based on a version of the CP asserting that *the mixed experiment based on (33) provides the same evidence about $\theta$ as the model that actually gave rise to the data.* When evidence is evaluated in terms of error probabilities, this claim is patently false; the relevant error probabilities for testing (32) based on the mixed model $\mathcal{M}_{\varphi}(\mathbf{x})$ are very different from those stemming from $\mathcal{M}_{\theta}(\mathbf{x})$ or $\mathcal{M}_{\varphi_1}(\mathbf{x})$.

## *6.3 Mis-Specification (M-S) testing and Respecification*

Denoting the set of all possible models that could have given rise to data $\mathbf{x}_0$ by $\mathcal{P}(\mathbf{x})$, the generic form of M-S testing is:

$$H_0\colon\ f^*(\mathbf{x}) \in \mathcal{M}_{\theta}(\mathbf{x}), \quad \text{vs.} \quad H_1\colon\ f^*(\mathbf{x}) \in [\mathcal{P}(\mathbf{x}) - \mathcal{M}_{\theta}(\mathbf{x})], \tag{35}$$

where $f^*(\mathbf{x})$ denotes the 'true' joint distribution of the stochastic process $\{X_t,\ t\in\mathbb{N}\}$. The specification of the null and alternatives in (35) indicates that M-S testing constitutes probing outside the boundaries of $\mathcal{M}_{\theta}(\mathbf{x})$, in contrast to N-P testing which is probing within this boundary; see [Spanos, 1999].

The problem that needs to be addressed in order to render (35) implementable is to particularize $[\mathcal{P}(\mathbf{x}) - \mathcal{M}_{\theta}(\mathbf{x})]$ representing the set of all possible alternative models. This can be as specific as a broader statistical model $\mathcal{M}_{\psi}(\mathbf{x})$ that parametrically encompasses $\mathcal{M}_{\theta}(\mathbf{x}) \subset \mathcal{M}_{\psi}(\mathbf{x})$, or as vague as a direction of departure from $\mathcal{M}_{\theta}(\mathbf{x})$, which might only be implicitly determined, such as a goodness-of-fit test; see [Spanos, 2000].

The hypothetical reasoning underlying M-S tests is similar to Fisher's *significance test reasoning*: data $\mathbf{x}_0$ provide evidence for a departure from a null hypothesis $H_0$ in so far as the value of a statistic $d(\mathbf{x}_0)$ is 'improbably far' from what would have been expected if $\mathcal{M}_\theta(\mathbf{x})$ were true. In the case where the alternative is specified in terms of an encompassing model $\mathcal{M}_\psi(\mathbf{x})$, $d(\mathbf{X})$ can be chosen using power. However, in the case where $[\mathcal{P}(\mathbf{x})-\mathcal{M}_\theta(\mathbf{x})]$ is not explicitly operationalized in the form of an encompassing model, the chosen form of $d(\mathbf{X})$ defines the implicit alternative to be the direction of departure from $\mathcal{M}_\theta(\mathbf{x})$ with maximum power; see [Davidson and MacKinnon, 1987]. In an M-S test the primary role for the particularized alternative is to determine the form of the distance function, and hence the power of the test. In that sense, rejection of the null in an M-S test cannot (should not) be interpreted as evidence for that alternative because that will constitute a case of the fallacy of rejection.

The question that one might naturally pose at this stage is that, despite the apparent differences sketched above, the model specification comes down to comparing one statistical model to another to find out which one is more appropriate. Such a view represents a misleading oversimplification.

A closer look at the above specification argument for AR(p), reveals that one is *not* choosing a statistical model as such, but a probabilistic structure for the stochastic process $\{X_k,\ k{\in}\mathbb{N}\}$ that would render data $\mathbf{x}_0$, a typical realization thereof; $\mathcal{M}_\theta(\mathbf{x})$ constitutes a particular parameterization of this structure. This standpoint sheds new light on the problem of *underdetermination* in this context. There can be two statistically adequate models only when they represent two alternative parametrizations of the same probabilistic structure; see [Spanos, 2007a]. The choice between them is made using other criteria, including the substantive questions of interest.

The selected model $\mathcal{M}_\theta(\mathbf{x})$ is viewed as an element of the set $\mathcal{P}(\mathbf{x})$ of all possible statistical models that could have given rise to data $\mathbf{x}_0$. But how does one narrow down a possibly infinite set $\mathcal{P}(\mathbf{x})$ to one model $\mathcal{M}_\theta(\mathbf{x})$? The narrowing down is attained by partitioning $\mathcal{P}(\mathbf{x})$ (see fig. 5) using probabilistic assumptions from three broad categories: Distribution (D), Dependence (M) and Heterogeneity (H); see [Spanos, 1995].

EXAMPLE 7. The partitioning by reduction is illustrated in figure 3 in the case the simple Normal model which is based on the reduction assumptions that $\{X_k,\ k{\in}\mathbb{N}\}$ is NIID; a model that seems appropriate for the data in figure 4.

The tripartite partitioning also plays a crucial role in **M-S testing** based on (35), in the sense that it creates a framework wherein one can formally assess the model assumptions relating to $\{X_k,\ k{\in}\mathbb{N}\}$ because it provides an *exhaustively complete* probing strategy. Changing the original reduction assumptions in deliberative ways, in light of the information one can glean from exploratory data analysis, gives rise to effective M-S tests which can eliminate an *infinite* number of alternative models at a time; see [Spanos, 1999]. The most *inefficient* way to do this is to attempt to probe $[\mathcal{P}(\mathbf{x})-\mathcal{M}_\theta(\mathbf{x})]$ one model at a time $\mathcal{M}_{\varphi_i}(\mathbf{x})$, $i{=}1,2,..$

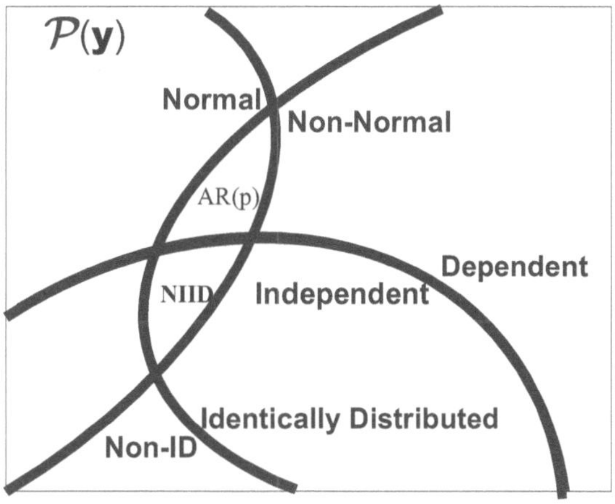


Figure 5. Specification by partitioning

since there is an infinity of models to search through. The majority of the procedures under the banner of model selection, including the Akaike-type information criteria, adopt such a strategy; see [Spanos, 2010b].

**Respecification** amounts to returning to $\mathcal{P}(\mathbf{x})$ and recasting the original reduction assumptions in an attempt to account for statistical systematic information unaccounted for by the original model. For instance, the Normal, AR(p) model in table 4 can be viewed as a respecification of the simple Normal model, where the reduction NIID assumptions have been replaced by $\{X_k,\ k\in\mathbb{N}\}$ is (D) Normal, (M) Markov and (H) Stationary; see figure 5.

This error statistical strategy of M-S testing and respecification by re-partitioning is in complete contrast to the traditional textbook approach based on ad hoc diagnostics and 'repairing' the original model using 'error-fixing' techniques. It can be shown that ad hoc and partial M-S testing can easily give rise to unreliable diagnoses, and the traditional error-fixing strategies, such as error-autocorrelation and heteroskedasticity corrections, as well as the use of heteroskedasticity consistent standard errors (see [Greene, 2000]), do *not* address the unreliability of inference problem. If anything, they often make matters worse; see [Spanos and McGuirk, 2001].

## *6.4 Methodological problems associated with M-S testing*

As argued above, statistical adequacy renders the relevant error probabilities *ascertainable* by ensuring that the *nominal* error probabilities are approximately equal to the *actual* ones. Spanos and McGuirk [2001] demonstrated that even seemingly minor departures from the assumptions of $\mathcal{M}_\theta(\mathbf{x})$ can have devastating effects on the reliability of inference; see also [Spanos, 2009b]. In light of these, why is there such unwillingness to secure statistical adequacy using M-S testing in applied econometrics?

One possible explanation is that M-S testing is invariably viewed as undefendable against several methodological charges including double-use of data, infinite regress, circularity and pre-test bias; see [Kennedy, 2008]. Let us take a closer look at these issues as they pertain to the error statistical account.

### *6.4.1 Illegitimate double-use of data*

In the context of the error statistical approach it is certainly true that the same data $\mathbf{x}_0$ are being used for two different purposes: (a) to test primary hypotheses in terms of the unknown parameter(s) $\theta$, and (b) to assess the validity of the prespecified model $\mathcal{M}_\theta(\mathbf{x})$, but 'does that constitute an illegitimate double-use of data?' The short answer is *no*, because, *first*, (a) and (b) pose very different questions to data $\mathbf{x}_0$, and *second*, the probing takes place within vs. outside $\mathcal{M}_\theta(\mathbf{x})$, respectively.

Neyman-Pearson (N-P) testing assumes that $\mathcal{M}_\theta(\mathbf{x})$ is adequate, and poses questions within its boundaries. In contrast, the question posed by M-S testing is whether or not the particular data $\mathbf{x}_0$ constitute a '*truly typical realization*' of the stochastic mechanism described by $\mathcal{M}_\theta(\mathbf{x})$, and the probing takes place outside its boundaries, i.e. in $[\mathcal{P}(\mathbf{x})-\mathcal{M}_\theta(\mathbf{x})]$; see [Spanos, 2000]. Indeed, one can go as far as to argue that the answers to the questions posed in (a) and (b) rely on distinct information in $\mathbf{x}_0$.

Spanos [2007b] has demonstrated that, for many statistical models, including the simple Normal (table 2) and the Normal/Linear Regression (table 7) models, the distribution of the sample $f(\mathbf{x};\theta)$ simplifies as follows:

$$f(\mathbf{x};\theta) = |J|\cdot f(\mathbf{s},\mathbf{r};\theta) = |J|\cdot f(\mathbf{s};\theta)\cdot f(\mathbf{r}),\ \forall\,(\mathbf{s},\mathbf{r})\in\mathbb{R}_s^m\times\mathbb{R}_r^{n-m}, \tag{36}$$

where $|J|$ denotes the Jacobian of the transformation $\mathbf{X} \rightarrow (\mathbf{S}(\mathbf{X}),\ \mathbf{R}(\mathbf{X}))$, $\mathbf{R}(\mathbf{X}){:=}(R_1,...,R_{n-m})$, is a *complete sufficient* statistic and $\mathbf{S}(\mathbf{X}){:=}(S_1,...,S_m)$ a *maximal ancillary* statistic. This reduction implies that $\mathbf{S}(\mathbf{X})$ and $\mathbf{R}(\mathbf{X})$ are independent. The separation in (36) means that all primary inferences can be based exclusively on $f(\mathbf{s};\theta)$, and $f(\mathbf{r})$ (free of $\theta$) can be used to appraise the validity of the statistical model in question. The crucial argument for relying on $f(\mathbf{r})$ for model validation purposes is that the probing for departures from $\mathcal{M}_\theta(\mathbf{x})$ is based on error probabilities that do not depend on $\theta$. Although this is not a general result, it holds 'approximately' in the case of statistical models whose inference is based on asymptotic Normality, which comprises the overwhelming majority of statistical models of interest in econometrics.

EXAMPLE 8. For the simple Normal model (table 2), (36) holds with the minimal sufficient statistic being $\mathbf{S}{:=}(\overline{X}_n, s^2)$ (see (15)), and the maximal ancillary statistics being $\mathbf{R}(\mathbf{X}){=}(\widehat{v}_3,..,\widehat{v}_n)$, where $\widehat{v}_k{=}(\sqrt{n}(X_k{-}\overline{X}_n)/s)$, $k{=}1,2,..,n$, are known as the *studentized* residuals. This result explains why it's no accident that the majority of M-S tests rely on the residuals.

### *6.4.2 The infinite regress and circularity charges against M-S testing*

The *infinite regress* charge is often articulated by claiming that each M-S test relies on a set of assumptions, and thus it assesses the assumptions of the model $\mathcal{M}_\theta(\mathbf{z})$ by invoking the validity of its own assumptions, trading one set of assumptions with another *ad infinitum*. Indeed, this reasoning is often *circular* because some M-S tests inadvertently assume the validity of the very assumption being tested!

A closer look at the reasoning underlying M-S testing reveals that both charges are misplaced. *First*, the scenario used in evaluating the type I error invokes no assumptions beyond those of $\mathcal{M}_\theta(\mathbf{z})$, since every M-S test is evaluated under:

$H_0$: *all* the probabilistic assumptions making up $\mathcal{M}_\theta(\mathbf{z})$ are valid.

EXAMPLE 9. The *runs test*, using the residuals from an AR(p) model $\{\widehat{\varepsilon}_t,\ t{=}1, 2, ..., n\}$, is an example of an omnibus M-S test for assumptions [4]-[5] (table 4) based a test statistic: $Z_R(\mathbf{Y}){=}\ [R{-}E(R)]/\sqrt{Var(R)}$; see Spanos [1999]. For $n \geq 40$, the type I error probability evaluation is based on:

$$Z_R(\mathbf{Y}) = \frac{R-([2n-1]/3)}{\sqrt{[16n-29]/90}} \overset{[1]\text{-}[5]}{\backsim} \mathsf{N}(0,1).$$

*Second*, the type II error (and power), for any M-S test, is determined by evaluating the test statistic under certain forms of departures from the assumptions being appraised [hence, no circularity], but retaining the rest of the model assumptions, or choose M-S tests which are insensitive to departures from the retained assumptions.

For the runs test, the evaluation under the alternative takes the form:

$$Z_R(\mathbf{Y}) \overset{\overline{[4]}\text{-}\overline{[5]}\&[1]-[3]}{\backsim} \mathsf{N}(\delta,\tau^2),\ \delta \neq 0,\ \tau^2 > 0,$$

where $\overline{[4]}$ and $\overline{[5]}$ denote specific departures from these assumptions considered by the test in question. It is important to note that the runs test is *insensitive* to departures from Normality; one of its virtues in practice. The type of departures implicitly or explicitly considered by the M-S test in question will affect the power of the test in a variety of ways, and one needs to apply a battery of different M-S tests to ensure broad probing capacity and self-correcting in the sense that the effect of any departures from the maintained assumptions can also detected.

In practice, potential problems such as circular reasoning, inadequate probing and erroneous diagnoses can be circumvented by employing [Mayo and Spanos, 2004]:

(a) Judicious combinations of parametric, non-parametric, omnibus and simulation-based tests, probing as broadly as possible and invoking dissimilar assumptions.

(b) Perceptive *ordering* of M-S tests so as to exploit the interrelationship among the model assumptions with a view to 'correct' each other's diagnosis.

(c) *Joint M-S tests* (testing several assumptions simultaneously) chosen to minimize the maintained assumptions and prevent 'erroneous' diagnoses.

These strategies enable one to argue with *severity* that when no departures from the model assumptions are detected, the validated model provides a reliable basis for inference, including appraising substantive claims; see [Spanos, 2000].

### 6.4.3 *Revisiting the pre-test bias argument*

In the context of the error-statistical approach, a number of modeling procedures, such as Mis-Specification (M-S) testing and respecification with a view to find a statistically adequate model, are often criticized by the textbook econometrics perspective as illegitimate data mining that induces biases into the resulting inferences. The most widely used charge is that of pre-test bias; see [Kennedy, 2008].

To discuss the merits of the *pre-test bias* charge in the case of M-S testing/respecification, consider the Durbin-Watson test, for assessing the assumption of no autocorrelation for the linear regression errors, based on (see [Greene, 2000]):

$$H_0\colon\ \rho=0,\ \text{vs.}\ H_1\colon\ \rho\neq 0,$$

*Step 1.* The pre-test bias perspective interprets this M-S test as equivalent to choosing between two models:

$$\begin{array}{ll}\mathcal{M}_\theta(\mathbf{z})\colon & y_t=\beta_0+\beta_1 x_t+u_t,\\ \mathcal{M}_\psi(\mathbf{z})\colon & y_t=\beta_0+\beta_1 x_t+u_t,\ u_t{=}\rho u_{t-1}+\varepsilon_t.\end{array} \tag{37}$$

*Step 2.* This is formalized in decision-theoretic language into a choice between two estimators of $\beta_1$, conceptualized in terms of the *pre-test estimator*:

$$\ddot{\beta}_1{=}\lambda\widehat{\beta}_1+(1{-}\lambda)\widetilde{\beta}_1,\ \lambda{=}\begin{cases}1, & \text{if } H_0 \text{ is accepted}\\ 0, & \text{if } H_0 \text{ is rejected;}\end{cases} \tag{38}$$

$\widehat{\beta}_1$ is the OLS estimator under $H_0$, and $\widetilde{\beta}_1$ is the GLS estimator under $H_1$.

*Step 3.* This perspective claims that the relevant error probabilities revolve around the Mean Square Error (MSE) of $\ddot{\beta}_1$, whose sampling distribution is usually non-Normal, biased and has a highly complicated variance structure; see [Leeb and Pötscher, 2005].

When viewed in the context of the error-statistical approach, the pre-test bias argument, based on (38), seems highly questionable on a number of different grounds.

*First,* it misinterprets M-S testing by recasting it as a decision-theoretic estimation problem. As argued discerningly by Hacking [1965, pp. 31]:

"Deciding that something *is* the case differs from deciding to *do* something."

M-S testing asks whether $\mathcal{M}_\theta(\mathbf{z})$ *is* statistically adequate, i.e. it accounts for the chance regularities in data $\mathbf{z}_0$ or not. It is not concerned with selecting one of two models come what may. Having said that, one can potentially construct an M-S test with a view to assess a subset of the model assumptions by viewing an alternative model $\mathcal{M}_\psi(\mathbf{z})$ as a result of narrowing $[\mathcal{P}(\mathbf{z})-\mathcal{M}_\theta(\mathbf{z})]$ (see (35)) down to a single alternative model which (parametrically) encompasses $\mathcal{M}_\theta(\mathbf{z})$; see [Spanos, 1999]. When the ultimate inference is concerned with whether $\mathcal{M}_\theta(\mathbf{z})$ is statistically adequate and an inference is made, the relevant errors are:

(i) the selected model is inadequate but the other model is adequate, or

(ii) both models are inadequate.

In contrast, $E(\ddot{\beta}_1-\beta_1)^2$ evaluates the expected loss resulting from the modeler's supposedly tacit intention to use $\ddot{\beta}_1$ as an estimator of $\beta_1$. Is there a connection between $E(\ddot{\beta}_1-\beta_1)^2$, for all $\beta_1\in\mathbb{R}$, and the errors (i)-(ii)? The short answer is none. The former evaluates the expected loss stemming from one's (misguided) *intentions*, but the latter pertain to the relevant error probabilities (type I & II) associated with the inference that one of the two models is statistically adequate. As argued in section 5.3, the latter errors are based on hypothetical (testing) reasoning, but the former are risk evaluations based on an arbitrary loss function.

*Second*, the case where an M-S test supposedly selects the alternative ($\mathcal{M}_\psi(\mathbf{z})$), the implicit inference is that $\mathcal{M}_\psi(\mathbf{z})$ is statistically adequate. This constitutes a classic example of *the fallacy of rejection*. The validity of $\mathcal{M}_\psi(\mathbf{z})$ needs to be established separately by thoroughly testing its own assumptions. Hence, in an M-S test one should *never* accept the alternative without further testing; see [Spanos, 2000].

*Third*, the case where an M-S test supposedly selects the null ($\mathcal{M}_\theta(\mathbf{z})$), the implicit inference is that $\mathcal{M}_\theta(\mathbf{z})$ is statistically adequate. This inference is problematic for two reasons. First, given the multitude of assumptions constituting a model, there is no single comprehensive M-S test based on a parametrically encompassing model $\mathcal{M}_\psi(\mathbf{z})$, that could, by itself, establish the statistical adequacy of $\mathcal{M}_\theta(\mathbf{z})$. Second, the inference is vulnerable to *the fallacy of acceptance*. It is possible that the particular M-S test did not reject $\mathcal{M}_\theta(\mathbf{z})$ because it had very low power to detect an existing departure. In practice this can be remedied using additional M-S tests with higher power to cross-check the results, or/and use a post-data evaluation of inference to establish the warranted discrepancies from $H_0$.

To summarize, instead of devising ways to circumvent the fallacies of rejection and acceptance to avoid erroneous inferences in M-S testing, the pre-test bias argument embraces these fallacies by recasting the original problem (in step 1), formalizes them (in step 2), and evaluates risks (in step 3) that have no bearing on erroneously inferring that the selected model is statistically adequate. The pre-test bias charge is ill-conceived because it misrepresents model validation as a choice between two models come what may.

## 7 PHILOSOPHICAL/METHODOLOGICAL ISSUES PERTAINING TO ECONOMETRICS

The error-statistical perspective has been used to shed light on a number of methodological issues relating to specification, misspecification testing, and respecification, including the role of graphical techniques, structural vs. statistical models, model specification vs. model selection, and statistical vs. substantive adequacy; see [Spanos, 2006a-c]. In addition, this perspective has been used to illuminate a number of crucial problems in statistics, such as the likelihood principle and the role of conditioning (see [Mayo and Cox, 2006; Cox and Mayo, 2009]), as well as philosophy of science including the problems of curve-fitting, underdetermination and Duhemian ambiguities; see [Mayo, 1997; Spanos, 2007a].

In this section the error-statistical perspective is used to shed some new light on a number of different philosophical/methodological issues pertaining to econometrics.

### *7.1 Statistical model specification vs. model selection*

As argued in section 4.1, from the error-statistical perspective the *problem of specification*, as originally envisaged by Fisher [1922], is one of choosing a statistical model $\mathcal{M}_\theta(\mathbf{x})$ so as to render the particular data $\mathbf{x}_0$ a *truly typical realization* of the stochastic process $\{X_k,\ k\in\mathbb{N}\}$ parameterized by $\mathcal{M}_\theta(\mathbf{x})$. This problem is addressed by evaluating $\mathcal{M}_\theta(\mathbf{x})$ in terms of whether it is statistically adequate — it accounts for the regularities in the data; its probabilistic assumptions are valid for data $\mathbf{x}_0$. In cases where the original model is found wanting one should respecify and assess model adequacy until a validated model is found; see [Spanos, 2006b].

The model validation problem is generally acknowledged in statistics:

> "The current statistical methodology is mostly model-based, without any specific rules for model selection or validating a specified model." [Rao, 2004, p. 2]

Over that last 25 years or so, Fisher's specification problem has been recast in the form of *model selection* which breaks up the problem into two stages where, a broad family of models $\{\mathcal{M}_{\theta_i}(\mathbf{x}),\ i=1,2,...m\}$ is selected first, and then a particular model within that family, say $\mathcal{M}_{\theta_k}(\mathbf{x})$, is chosen using certain normed-based (goodness-of-fit) criteria; see [Rao and Wu, 2001]. The quintessential example of such a model selection procedure is the Akaike Information Criterion (AIC) where one compares different models within a prespecified family using:

$$\mathsf{AIC}(i) = -2\ln f_i(\mathbf{x};\widehat{\theta}_i) + 2K_i,\ \ i=1,2,...,m, \tag{39}$$

where $K_i$ denotes the number of unknown parameters for model $i$. There are numerous variations/extensions of the AIC; see [Burnham and Anderson, 2002]. Such norm-based model selection encompasses several procedures motivated by mathematical approximation, such as curve-fitting by least-squares, structural estimation using GMM as well as nonparametric procedures; see [Pagan and Ullah, 1999].

Spanos [2010b] argued that Akaike-type model selection procedures invariably give rise to unreliable inferences because:

(i) they ignore the preliminary step of validating the prespecified family of models,

(ii) their selection amounts to testing comparisons among the models within the prespecified family but without 'controlling' the relevant error probabilities.

The end result is that the selected model $\mathcal{M}_{\theta_k}(\mathbf{x})$ is invariably statistically inadequate. This is is illustrated in [Spanos, 2007a] where the Kepler and Ptolemy models for the motion of the planets are compared in terms of goodness-of-fit vs. statistical adequacy. It is shown that, despite the excellent fit of the Ptolemaic model, it does not 'account for the regularities in the data', contrary to conventional wisdom; see [Laudan, 1977]. In contrast, the statistical adequacy of the Kepler model renders it a statistical model with a life of its own, regardless of its substantive adequacy which stems from Newton's law of universal gravitation.

One can argue that securing *statistical adequacy* addresses both objectives associated with the model selection procedures: selecting a prespecified family of models, and determining the 'best' model within this family, rendering these procedures superfluous and potentially misleading; see [Spanos, 2010b].

## *7.2 The reliability/precision of inference and robustness*

It is well known in statistics that the *reliability* of any inference procedure (estimation, testing and prediction) depends crucially on the validity of the *premises*: the model probabilistic assumptions.

The *trustworthiness* of a frequentist inference procedure depends on two interrelated pre-conditions:

(a) adopting optimal inference procedures, in the context of

(b) a statistically adequate model.

In frequentist statistics, the unreliability of inference is reflected in the *difference* between the *nominal* error probabilities, derived under the assumption of valid premises, and the *actual* error probabilities, derived taking into consideration the particular departure(s) from the premises. Indeed, this difference provides a measure of *robustness*: the sensitivity of the inference procedure to the particular departure from the model assumptions; see [Box, 1979].

The main argument of this paper is that *reliable* and *precise inferences* are the result of utilizing the *relevant error probabilities* obtained by ensuring (a)-(b). Condition (a) ensures the approximate equality of the nominal and actual error probabilities, hence the reliability of inference, and (b) secures the high capacity of the inference procedure. What is often not appreciated enough in practice is that without (b), (a) makes little sense. An example of this is given by the traditional textbook econometrics way of dealing with departures from the homoskedasticity assumption, by adopting the HCSE for the least squares estimators of the coefficients; see section 2.1. In contrast, in the context of the error-statistical approach the unreliability of inference problem is addressed, not by using actual error probabilities in the case of misspecification, but by *respecifying* the original statistical model and utilizing inference methods that are optimal in the context of the new (adequate) premises; see [Spanos, 2009b].

The distinctions between *nominal*, *actual* and *relevant error probabilities* is important because the traditional discussion of *robustness* compares the actual with the nominal error probabilities, but downplays the interconnection between (a) and (b) above. When the problem of statistical misspecification is raised, the response is often a variant of the following argument invoking robustness:

All models are misspecified, to 'a greater or lesser extent', because they are mere approximations. Moreover, 'slight' departures from the assumptions will only lead to 'minor' deviations from the 'optimal' inferences.

This seemingly reasonable argument is shown to be highly misleading when one attempts to *quantify* 'slight' departures and 'minor' deviations. It is argued that invoking robustness often amounts to 'glossing over' the unreliability of inference problem instead of bringing it out and addressing it; see [Spanos, 2009b].

EXAMPLE 10. Assume that data $\mathbf{x}_0$ constitute a 'truly typical realization' of the stochastic process represented by the simple Normal model (table 2), but it turns out that assumption [4] is actually invalid, in the sense that:

$$Corr(X_i, X_j) = \rho, \quad 0<\rho<1, \ i \neq j, \quad i, j = 1, ...n. \tag{40}$$

This is likely to render inferences based on this model *unreliable*. Let $\mu_0$=0, $n$=100, $\alpha$=.05, $c_\alpha$=1.66. Table 5 shows that even a tiny correlation ($\rho$=.05) will induce a sizeable discrepancy between the *nominal* ($\alpha$=.05) and *actual type I error probability* ($\alpha^*$=.25), with the discrepancy increasing as $\rho \rightarrow 1$.

**Table 5 - Type I error of t-test**

| $\rho$ | 0.0 | .05 | .10 | .30 | .50 | .75 | .90 |
|---|---|---|---|---|---|---|---|
| $\alpha^*$-actual | .05 | .249 | .309 | .383 | .408 | .425 | .431 |

| Table 6 - Power $\pi^*(\mu_1)$ of the t-test | | | | | |
|---|---|---|---|---|---|
| $\rho$ | $\pi^*(.02)$ | $\pi^*(.05)$ | $\pi^*(.1)$ | $\pi^*(.2)$ | $\pi^*(.4)$ |
| **0.0** | **.074** | **.121** | **.258** | **.637** | **.991** |
| .05 | .276 | .318 | .395 | .557 | .832 |
| .1 | .330 | .364 | .422 | .542 | .762 |
| .3 | .397 | .418 | .453 | .525 | .664 |
| .5 | .419 | .436 | .464 | .520 | .630 |
| .75 | .434 | .447 | .470 | .516 | .607 |
| .9 | .439 | .452 | .473 | .514 | .598 |

Similarly, the presence of dependence will also distort the power of the t-test. As shown in table 6, as $\rho \to 1$ the power of the t-test increases for small discrepancies from the null, but it decreases for larger discrepancies. That is, the presence of correlation would render a powerful smoke alarm into a *faulty one,* being triggered by burning toast but not sounding until the house is fully ablaze; see [Mayo, 1996].

The above example illustrates how misleading the invocation of robustness can be when one has no way of quantifying 'slight' departures and 'minor' deviations. Another widely used example of dependence is Markov where:

$$Corr(X_i, X_j) = \rho^{|i-j|}, \ |\rho| < 1,$$

which gives rise to the AR(1) model in table 4; see [Spanos, 2010b].

## *7.3 Weak assumptions and the reliability/precision of inference*

The current approbation in textbook econometrics for using the GMM [Hall, 2005] and non-parametric methods [Pagan and Ullah, 1999], is often justified in terms of the rationale that the broad premises assumed by these methods are less vulnerable to misspecification and thus often lead to more reliable inferences. Indeed, these methods are often motivated by claims that weak probabilistic assumptions provide a way to overcome unreliability. Matyas [1999, p. 1] went as far as to argue that, "the crises of econometric modeling in the seventies" ... was "precipitated by reliance on highly unrealistic strong probabilistic assumptions", and the way forward is to abandon such assumptions in favor of weaker ones. As argued in [Spanos, 2001], this rationale is highly misleading in so far as broader premises give rise to less precise inferences without any guarantee of reliability, because they invariably invoke non-tested and non-testable (differentiability of unknown density functions and boundedness conditions) assumptions, or/and asymptotic results of unknowable pertinence. Moreover, contrary to commonly used claims data plots (t-plots, scatter plots, etc.) convey a good deal of information pertaining to the underlying distributions and associated functional forms; see [Spanos, 1999, ch. 5].

The quintessential example of this perspective is the *Gauss-Markov (G-M) theorem* in the context of the Classical Linear model:

$$\begin{array}{c}\mathbf{y} = \mathbf{X}\beta + \mathbf{u}, \\ (1)\ E(\mathbf{u}) = \mathbf{0},\ (2)\ E(\mathbf{u}\mathbf{u}^\top) = \sigma^2\mathbf{I}_n,\ (3)\ rank(\mathbf{X}){=}k.\end{array} \tag{41}$$

This theorem establishes that the OLS $\widehat{\beta} = (\mathbf{X}^\top\mathbf{X})^{-1}\mathbf{X}^\top\mathbf{y}$ is Best Linear Unbiased Estimator (BLUE) of $\beta$ under the G-M assumptions (1)-(3), *without* invoking Normality: (4) $\mathbf{u} \backsim \mathsf{N}(.,.)$. In addition to being of very limited value since BLUE secures only the relative efficiency of $\widehat{\beta}$, the G-M theorem yields an unknown sampling distribution for $\widehat{\beta}$, i.e. $\widehat{\beta} \backsim \overset{?}{\mathsf{D}}(\beta, \sigma^2(\mathbf{X}^\top\mathbf{X})^{-1})$, which provides a poor basis for any form of inference that involves error probabilities. Finite sample inference can only be based on inequalities like Chebyshev's which often turn out to be very crude and imprecise; [Spanos, 1999]. As a result, practitioners usually invoke the central limit theorem in order to use the approximation $\widehat{\beta} \backsimeq \mathsf{N}(\beta,\sigma^2(\mathbf{X}^\top\mathbf{X})^{-1})$, but one has no way of knowing how good this approximation is for the particular sample size $n$; unless one is prepared to do a thorough job with probing for departures from the premises of the Linear Regression model as given in table 7; see [Spanos, 2006a].

As argued in [Spanos, 1999, ch. 10], there is a lot of scope for non-parametric inference in empirical modeling, such as in exploratory data analysis and M-S testing, but not for providing the premises of inference when reliability and precision are the primary objectives; see also [Spanos, 1999; 2001; 2009b].

## *7.4 Statistical 'Error-fixing' strategies and data mining*

A number of different activities in empirical modeling are often described as unwarranted 'data mining' when the procedures followed undermine the trustworthiness of the evidence they give rise to.

Typically a textbook econometrician begins with a theory model, more or less precisely specified, and proceeds to specify a statistical model in the context of which the quantification will take place, by viewing the theory model as its systematic component and attaching a *white noise error* as its non-systematic component. This implicitly assumes that the chosen data provide apposite observations for the concepts envisaged by the theory. Usually, the estimated model does not give rise to the "expected" results in the sense that it often yields 'wrong' signs, insignificant coefficients for crucial variables, as well as indications that some of the model assumptions, (see (41)) are invalid. What does one do next? According to Wooldridge [2006]:

> "When that happens, the natural inclination to try different models, different estimation techniques, or perhaps different subsets of data until the results correspond more closely to what was expected." (ibid., p. 688)

This describes the well-known textbook 'error-fixing' strategy which takes the form of estimating several variants of the original model by modifying the underlying assumptions (using OLS, GLS, GMM, IV), guided by a combination of diagnostic checking and significance testing of the coefficients, in the hope that one of these variants will emerge as the "best" model, and then used as a basis of inference. What is "best" is conventionally left vague, but it's understood to comprise a combination of statistical significance and theoretical meaningfulness.

The statistical 'error-fixing' strategies are based on a textbook repertoire of recommendations which arise from relaxing the G-M assumptions (1)–(3) (see (41)) one at a time, and seeking 'optimal' estimators under a particular departure. For example, when the *no-autocorrelation* assumption in (2) is invalid and instead $E(\mathbf{u}\mathbf{u}^\top) = \Omega \neq \sigma^2 \mathbf{I}_n$, the recommendation is twofold. Either to retain the OLS estimator $\widehat{\beta} = (\mathbf{X}^\top \mathbf{X})^{-1}\mathbf{X}^\top \mathbf{y}$ and utilize the HCSE for inference purposes, or to use a Feasible Generalized Least Squares (FGLS) estimator based on the autocorrelation-corrected model where: $u_t = \rho u_{t-1} + \varepsilon_t$. When the *homoskedasticity* assumption in (2) is invalid a similar twofold recommendation is prescribed where one 'fixes' the problem by either retaining the OLS estimator $\widehat{\beta}$ and uses the HCSE for inference, or estimates the heteroskedastic variances using an auxiliary regression, $\widehat{u}_t^2 = c_0 + \mathbf{c}_1^\top \mathbf{z}_t + v_t$, and applies weighted least squares. As argued by Greene [2000, p. 521]:

> "It is rarely possible to be certain about the nature of the heteroskedasticity in regression model. In one respect, the problem is only minor. The weighted least squares estimator is consistent regardless of the weights [$\mathbf{z}_t$] used, as long as the weights are uncorrelated with the disturbances."

This claim is clearly misleading when one realizes that the regression and skedastic functions are the first two moments of the same conditional distribution $f(y_t \mid \mathbf{x}_t; \psi)$, whose structure is determined by the underlying joint distribution $f(y_t, \mathbf{x}_t; \varphi)$; see [Spanos, 1994].

In practice one is encouraged to try out different forms for the weights $\mathbf{z}_t$ and pick the one with the "best" results. When such statistical 'error-fixing' recommendations are tried out, one is supposed to keep one eye on the 'theoretical meaningfulness' of the estimated variants and choose between them on the basis of what can be rationalized both statistically and substantively. It is widely acknowledged that these 'error-fixing' strategies constitute problematic forms of data mining:

> "Virtually all applied researchers search over various models before finding the "best" model. Unfortunately, this practice of data mining violates the assumptions we have made in our econometric analysis." [Wooldridge, 2006, p. 688]

The end result is that such 'error-fixing' misuses data in ways that 'appear' to provide empirical (inductive) *support* for the theory in question, when in fact the inferences are usually unwarranted. These 'error-fixing' procedures illustrate the kind of problematic use of the data to construct (ad hoc) a model to account for an apparent 'anomaly' (departures from error assumptions) that naturally gives rise to skepticism; this is known as pejorative 'double-use' of data.

**Table 7 - The Normal/Linear Regression Model**

| | |
|---|---|
| **Statistical GM:** | $y_t = \beta_0 + \beta_1^\top \mathbf{x}_t + u_t,\ t\in\mathbb{N}$, |
| [1] **Normality:** | $(y_t \mid \mathbf{X}_t = \mathbf{x}_t) \backsim \mathsf{N}(.,.)$, |
| [2] **Linearity:** | $E(y_t \mid \mathbf{X}_t = \mathbf{x}_t) = \beta_0 + \beta_1^\top \mathbf{x}_t$, linear in $\mathbf{x}_t$, |
| [3] **Homoskedasticity:** | $Var(y_t \mid \mathbf{X}_t = \mathbf{x}_t) = \sigma^2$, free of $\mathbf{x}_t$, |
| [4] **Independence:** | $\{(y_t \mid \mathbf{X}_t = \mathbf{x}_t),\ t\in\mathbb{N}\}$ is an independent process, |
| [5] **t-invariance:** | $\theta := (\beta_0, \beta_1, \sigma^2)$ do not change with $t$. |

These strategies, driven by the search for an 'optimal' estimator for each different set of error assumptions (OLS, GLS, FGLS, IV, GMM, etc.), ignore the fact that model assumptions, such as [1]–[5] (table 7), are interrelated and thus the various 'anomalies' are often misdiagnosed, and the ad hoc 'fixes' of specific error assumptions lead to exacerbating (not ameliorating) the reliability of inference (see [Spanos and McGuirk, 2001]). For instance, when autocorrelated *residuals* are interpreted as autocorrelated *errors,* any inference based on the 'autocorrelation-corrected' model' is likely to be unreliable because the latter model is often as misspecified as the original; see [McGuirk and Spanos, 2009]. As shown by Spanos and McGuirk [2001], the HCSE do very little, if anything, to ameliorate the reliability of inference is practice. The general reasoning flaw in this *respecification* strategy is that by adopting the alternative hypothesis in a misspecification test commits the fallacy of rejection. More often than not, after such 'error-fixing' takes place — by choosing the 'optimal' estimator that goes with the new set of error assumptions — one often ends up (unwittingly) with another misspecified model (see [Mayo and Spanos, 2004]). This latter model gives rise to unreliable inferences when used as a basis for deciding the sign and significance of key coefficients used to secure theoretical meaningfulness.

Viewed from the error-statistical perspective, each step in the above 'error-fixing' strategies fosters further errors, and ignores existing one (see section 2), with the modeler unwittingly worsening the overall trustworthiness of the evidence these strategies give rise to. Moreover, the modeler focuses on 'saving the theory' by retaining the systematic component and ignoring alternative theories which might fit the same data equally well or even better. By focusing the 'error-fixing' strategies the textbook perspective overlooks the ways the systematic component may be misspecified. In addition, incomplete specifications of statistical models (assumption [5] in table 7) are not conducive to securing statistical adequacy. This should be contrasted with warranted 'data mining', such as the use of graphical techniques and M-S testing, in context of the error-statistical where they enhance the reliability of the inferences reached; see [Spanos, 2000].

The error-statistical perspective suggests that once certain departures from the original model assumptions are established, the way to proceed is not to use the actual error probabilities, but to respecify the original model and construct a new optimal inference procedure based on the respecified model; see [Spanos, 2009b].

## 7.5 Unreliable strategies for 'upholding' a theory

Since the 1970s the question most often posed in seminars to any presenter of an applied econometrics paper, when discussing the estimation of any linear regression:

$$y_t = \beta_0 + \beta_1 x_t + u_t, \quad t \in \mathbb{N}, \tag{42}$$

is: 'did you account for simultaneity in your model?' The estimated model in (1) provides a perfect target for the cognoscenti of textbook econometrics. The 'right' answer is supposed to be 'yes I did and here are my Instrumental Variables (IV) estimates'. The discussion would invariably move to whether the particular set of chosen instruments, say $\mathbf{W}_t$, are 'optimal' or not, and the 'correct' answer to that is expected to be a good 'story' on why it is reasonable to assume that:

$$\text{(i) } E(X_t u_t) \neq 0 \text{ in (42), (ii) } E(\mathbf{W}_t \varepsilon_{2t}) = \mathbf{0}, \text{ (iii) } Cov(\mathbf{W}_t, X_t) \neq \mathbf{0} \text{ in (6),}$$

conditions which ensure that the IV estimator of $\beta_1$ is at least consistent. A comparison between the OLS and IV estimates is often used as an indication of how serious the simultaneity problem is, and the choice between the two estimators (models) is often made on the basis of a combination of statistical significance of key coefficients like $\beta_1$ and theoretical meaningfulness; whatever that might mean. With these criteria in mind, the cognoscenti of textbook econometrics search through several sets of instruments $\mathbf{W}_t$, and choose as 'optimal' the set that meets their expectations, and then they forge an 'explanation' for this choice. This is a textbook substantive 'doctoring' strategy which is nothing short of theory fixing that usually gives rise to unreliable inferences with probability one. This is because such a procedure is rife with potential errors and one has no way of detecting or avoiding them.

Viewed in the context of the error-statistical approach, the problem begins with conditions (i) and (ii) which are clearly unverifiable, giving the impression that the choice of 'optimal' instruments is not a matter of rhetoric! The choice of instruments is not just a matter of giving a persuasive 'story' why the set of instruments $\mathbf{W}_t$ one happens to choose satisfies (i)-(iii). Spanos [1986; 2007d] argued that the choice of optimal instruments also depends on the *statistical adequacy* of the system of equations in (6), and the validity of (iii) and (iv) $Cov(\mathbf{W}_t, y_t) \neq \mathbf{0}$.

To illustrate these problems with the textbook argument let us return to the estimated model in (1) and consider the following set of instruments: $W_{1t}$ — price of oats, $W_{2t}$ — output of oats, $W_{3t}$ - price of potatoes, $W_{4t}$ — output of potatoes, $W_{5t}$ — rainfall; all prices and output series denote per cent proportional changes. Re-estimating (1) using the IV method yields:

$$y_t = \underset{(2.179)}{7.180} - \underset{(.090)}{0.689} x_t + \widetilde{u}_t, \; R^2 = .622, \quad s = 14.450, \quad n = 45, \tag{43}$$

showing only minor differences between the OLS and IV estimates. In the textbook econometrics tradition this is interpreted as an excellent indication that the original estimates are robust to simultaneity. However, looking at the overidentifying restrictions test for (43), $F(4,39)$=13.253[.0000007], indicates that such an inference will be unwarranted; the restrictions are strongly rejected. Having said that, the truth of the matter is that none of the t-ratios, and F-statistics invoked in the above arguments is statistically meaningful unless the implicit reduced form in (6) is statistically adequate. Not surprisingly, several M-S tests for this system of equations (see [Spanos, 1986, ch. 24; Spanos, 1990]) one can easily verify that both estimated equations (1) and (43) are seriously statistically misspecified, calling into question the reliability of all inferences, including that of the overidentifying restrictions test.

Hence, the substantive 'error-fixing' strategy of invoking simultaneity and using IV estimators does is not usually remedy the initial statistical misspecification of (1) problem, but instead it enhances the unreliability of inference by bringing into the statistical analysis additional equations which are also statistically misspecified.

## *7.6 Revisiting the omitted variables bias argument*

The omitted variables problem in often discussed in terms of comparing the following two alternative models:

$$\mathcal{M}_0\text{: } y_t = \beta_0 + \beta_1 x_{1t} + u_t, \qquad \mathcal{M}_1\text{: } y_t = \alpha_0 + \alpha_1 x_{1t} + \alpha_2 x_{2t} + \varepsilon_t, \tag{44}$$

where the decision is made on the basis of the t-test for the hypotheses:

$$H_0\text{: } \alpha_2 = 0, \text{ vs. } H_1\text{: } \alpha_2 \neq 0; \tag{45}$$

see [Leeb and Potscher, 2005]. This example is different from the pre-test bias problem in (37) (section 6.4.3) in so far as the latter poses a question concerning *statistical adequacy*, but (44) poses a question concerning *substantive adequacy:*

> assuming $\mathcal{M}_1$ is statistically adequate, does model $\mathcal{M}_0$ provide a substantively adequate description of the relationship between $X_{1t}$ and $y_t$?

The hypotheses in (45) raise the crucial problem of *confounding:* whether the estimated model $\mathcal{M}_0$ has omitted a certain potentially important factor $X_{2t}$ misidentifying the influence of $X_{1t}$ on $y_t$, and thus giving rise to substantively misleading inferences. The pre-test bias argument formulates this confounding problem as a choice between the two models based on the pre-test estimator $\ddot{\beta}_1 = \lambda\widehat{\beta}_1 + (1-\lambda)\widehat{\alpha}_1$, where $\lambda$ is given in(38) and $(\widehat{\beta}_1, \widehat{\alpha}_1)$ denote the OLS estimators of $(\beta_1, \alpha_1)$, respectively. This formulation is problematic for several reasons.

*First*, and most crucially, the underlying parameterizations of $(\beta_1, \alpha_1)$ in (44) are very different. That is, one is *not* estimating the same parameter in the two cases since the implicit statistical parameterization in the two cases is (see [Spanos, 1986]):

$$\beta_1 = (\sigma_{21}/\sigma_{22}), \quad \alpha_1 = ([\sigma_{21} - \tfrac{\sigma_{23}\sigma_{31}}{\sigma_{33}}]/[\sigma_{22} - \tfrac{\sigma_{23}^2}{\sigma_{33}}]), \tag{46}$$

$\sigma_{21}=Cov(X_{1t},y_t)$, $\sigma_{22}=Var(X_{1t})$, $\sigma_{33}=Var(X_{3t})$, $\sigma_{23}=Cov(X_{1t},X_{2t})$, $\sigma_{31}=Cov(X_{2t},y_t)$. Hence, the very idea of a pre-test estimator of one unknown parameter is ill-conceived because, as $n\rightarrow\infty$, the estimators $(\widehat{\beta}_1,\widehat{\alpha}_1)$ converge to very different parameters. Even when $\sigma_{23}=0$ the two models can give rise to different inferences; see [Spanos, 2006c]. This can easily explain the 'lumpiness' of the parameter space and the convergence problems raised by Leeb and Potcher [2005].

*Second*, the framing of the problem in terms of a choice between two point estimators is inadequate for the task, because it automatically (mis-)interprets accept and reject the null as evidence for $\mathcal{M}_0$ and $\mathcal{M}_1$, respectively; committing both classic fallacies of acceptance and rejection.

*Third*, the pre-test bias is evaluated in terms of estimation error probabilities, like the Mean Square Error, and the associated sensitivity analysis can be shown to be much too crude for reliable answers to the question of confounding. When the confounding issue is posed as an N-P testing problem, one can show that there are eight alternative scenarios (different answers) in (44), depending on the non-zero values of $(\sigma_{21},\sigma_{23},\sigma_{31})$, which cannot be distinguished by the traditional estimation and any associated sensitivity analysis.

*Fourth*, the comparison in (44) gives rise to reliable inferences only to the extent that $\mathcal{M}_1$ in (44) is statistically adequate, ensuring that the N-P tests employed to distinguish between the different scenarios are reliable. Indeed, posing the confounding question as a testing issue in the context of the error-statistical approach enables one to guard against the fallacies of acceptance/rejection by supplementing the accept/reject decisions with a post-data evaluation of inference; see [Spanos, 2006c].

## 7.7 *If everything else fails, blame multicollinearity*

Another questionable modeling strategy one often encounters in applied econometrics is the appeal to multicollinearity. When in practice a variety of 'error-fixing' and theory upholding strategies fail to give rise to an estimated model with theoretically 'correct' signs and magnitudes, as well as (seemingly) statistically significant coefficients for the variables of interest, applied econometricians often invoke the presence of near-multicollinearity as the culprit for the failure to corroborate their theory.

Near-multicollinearity is understood as a departure from the G-M assumption (3) $\mathsf{rank}(\mathbf{X})=k$, see (41), where the $(\mathbf{X}^\top\mathbf{X})$ matrix is nearly singular. Greene [2000, p. 256], nicely summarizes the traditional perspective:

> "The problem faced by applied researchers is usually ... that regressors are highly, although not perfectly, correlated. In this instance, the following symptoms are typically observed:

- Small changes in the data can produce wide swings in the parameter estimates.

- Coefficients may have very high standard errors and low significance levels even though they are jointly highly significant and the $R^2$ in the regression is quite high.
- Coefficients will have the "wrong" sign or implausible magnitudes."

Despite the universal agreement among traditional econometric textbooks, it can be shown that, when one accounts for the underlying statistical parameterizations such as (46) above, none of the above symptoms stems from high correlation among the regressors. A much more plausible explanation for the wrong signs and magnitudes, as well as insignificant coefficients, is the severe statistical misspecification such estimated models often suffer from; see [Spanos and McGuirk, 2002]. Indeed, statistical misspecification renders all the invoked statistics like the standard errors, t-ratios and the $R^2$, meaningless artifacts upon which no reliable inference concerning signs and magnitudes can be drawn.

The real problem for the practioner is not high correlation among regressors as such, but the ill-conditioning of $(\mathbf{X}^\top\mathbf{X})$ — a data specific problem — which gives rise to *erratic volatility* as it relates to the sensitivity of the coefficient estimates $\widehat{\beta} = (\mathbf{X}^\top\mathbf{X})^{-1}\mathbf{X}^\top\mathbf{y}$ to (potential) changes in the data matrices $(\mathbf{X}^\top\mathbf{X}),(\mathbf{X}^\top\mathbf{y})$. To quantify such potential erratic volatility the modeler could utilize norm bounds, and then pose the question whether such volatility is likely to endanger the reliability of inference. If yes, the way to proceed is to use one of several options to enhance the sample information in an attempt to render $(\mathbf{X}^\top\mathbf{X})$ well-conditioned; see [Spanos and McGuirk, 2002].

## 8 SUMMARY AND CONCLUSIONS

The current state of applied econometrics, viewed as the empirical understructure of economics, calls for much greater attention to be paid to the philosophical foundations of empirical modeling. Like political arithmetic towards the end of the 18th century (see [Spanos, 2008a]), current econometrics runs a great risk of losing credibility as a basis for understanding economic phenomena and formulating optimal policies. The accumulation of mountains of untrustworthy empirical evidence over the last century is a symptom of several major weaknesses in the current methodological framework for empirical modeling in economics. The current textbook approach to econometric modeling pays little, if any, attention to ensuring the reliability of inference by probing for and eliminating potential errors that could lead the inference astray, including the *data inaccuracy*, *incongruous measurement* and *substantive inadequacy.* The emphasis on more and more technical procedures for 'quantifying structural models', and an ever increasing repertoire of 'error-fixing' strategies, invariably, give rise to unreliable inferences and untrustworthy empirical evidence.

It is argued that foisting the substantive information on the data by estimating a structural model $\mathcal{M}_\varphi(\mathbf{x})$ directly, is invariably an unwise modeling strategy because statistical specification errors are likely to undermine the prospect of reliably evaluating substantive hypotheses. Such a strategy often gives rise to estimated models which are both statistically and substantively inadequate, and one has no way to delineate the two sources of error.

Unfortunately, the textbook approach to econometrics leaves no room to separate the statistical and substantive information, and provides no way to secure the reliability [either statistical or substantive] of inference. A glance at the assumptions underlying the most basic of statistical assumptions in econometrics, the Linear Regression model, reveals that the two sources of information are hopelessly commingled, making it impossible to secure either statistical or substantive adequacy; see [Spanos, 2010c].

Substantive subject matter information is crucially important in learning from data about phenomena of interest, but no learning can take place in the context of statistically misspecified models, irrespective of any theoretical meaningfulness. Substantive information can potentially increase the precision of inference in cases where it is data-validated in the context of a statistically adequate model. Securing both statistical and substantive adequacy can contribute significantly to 'learning from data' and establish economics as an empirical science.

In this paper, an attempt has been made to bring out some of the weaknesses of the textbook econometrics approach and make constructive suggestions on how to improve the reliability of inductive inference in econometrics by viewing empirical modeling in a richer and more refined methodological framework known as error-statistical. This framework provides a coherent inductive reasoning for frequentist statistics and focuses on 'learning from data' about phenomena of interest by employing reliable procedures based on ascertainable error probabilities, both pre-data and post-data. The error-statistical account strongly encourages the probing of the different ways an inference might be in error, and has been used in this paper to elucidate several important methodological issues which concern the nature, interpretation, and justification of methods and strategies that are relied upon to learn from data.

## ACKNOWLEDGEMENTS

I would like to thank Deborah G. Mayo, my co-author in several philosophical papers, for numerous creative discussions and insightful comments and suggestions that helped to shape my views on several issues discussed in this chapter

## BIBLIOGRAPHY

[Abadir and Talmain, 2002] K. Abadir and G. Talmain. Aggregation, Persistence and Volatility in a Macro Model, *Review of Economic Studies*, **69**: 749-779, 2002.

[Altman, 2000] D. G. Altman, D. Machin, T. N. Bryant and M. J. Gardner. *Statistics with Confidence*, (eds), British Medical Journal Books, Bristol, 2000.

[Backhouse, 1994] R. E. Backhouse. *New Directions in Economic Methodology*, Routledge, London, 1994.

[Bernardo, 2005] J. M. Bernardo. Reference Analysis, pp. 17–90 in *Handbook of Statistics*, vol. 25: Bayesian Thinking, Modeling and Computation, D. K. Dey and C. R. Rao, (eds.), Elsevier, North-Holland, 2005.

[Berger, 1985] J. O. Berger. *Statistical Decision Theory and Bayesian Analysis*, 2nd ed., Springer, NY, 1985.

[Berger, 2004] J. O. Berger. The Case for Objective Bayesian Analysis, *Bayesian Analysis*, 1: 1–17, 2004.

[Berger and Wolpert, 1988] J. O. Berger and R. Wolpert. *The Likelihood Principle*, 2d ed., Institute of Mathematical Statistics, Hayward, CA, 1988.

[Birnbaum, 1961] A. Birnbaum. Confidence Curves: An Omnibus Technique for Estimation and Testing," *Journal of the American Statistical Association*, **294**: 246-249, 1961.

[Birnbaum, 1962] A. Birnbaum. On the Foundations of Statistical Inference (with discussion), *Journal of the American Statistical Association*, **57**: 269-306, 1962.

[Blaug, 1992] M. Blaug. The Methodology of Economics, Cambridge University Press, Cambridge, 1992.

[Box, 1979] G. E. P. Box. Robustness in the Strategy of Scientific Model Building, in *Robustness in Statistics*, ed. by Launer, R. L. and G. N. Wilkinson, Academic Press, NY, 1979.

[Burnham and Anderson, 2002] K. P. Burnham and D. R. Anderson. *Model Selection and Multimodel Inference: A Practical Information-Theoretic Approach*, 2nd ed., Springer, NY, 2002.

[Caldwell, 1994] B. Caldwell. *Beyond Positivism: Economic Methodology in the Twentieth Century*, 2nd ed., George Allen & Unwin, London 1994.

[Carnap, 1950/1962] R. Carnap. *Logical Foundations of Probability*, 2nd ed., The University of Chicago Press, Chicago, 1950/1962.

[Chalmers, 1999] A. F. Chalmers. *What is this thing called Science?*, 3rd ed., Hackett, Indianapolis, 1999.

[Cox, 1958] D. R. Cox. Some problems connected with statistical inference, *Annals of Statistics*, **29**: 357-372, 1958.

[Cox, 1990] D. R. Cox. Role of Models in Statistical Analysis, *Statistical Science*, **5**: 169-174, 1990.

[Cox and Hinkley, 1974] D. R. Cox and D. V. Hinkley. *Theoretical Statistics*, Chapman & Hall, London, 1974.

[Cox and Mayo, 2010] D. R. Cox and D. G. Mayo. Objectivity and Conditionality in Frequentist Inference, pp. 276-304 in *Error and Inference*, D. G. Mayo and A. Spanos, 2010.

[Davidson and MacKinnon, 1987] R. Davidson and J. G. MacKinnon. Implicity alternatives and the local power of test statistics, *Econometrica*, **55**: 1305-1329, 1987.

[Davis *et al.*, 1998] J. B. Davis, D. W. Hands, and U. Mäki. *The Handbook of Economic Methodology*, (eds.), Edward Elgar, Cheltenham, 1998.

[Duhem, 1914] P. Duhem. *The Aim and Structure of Physical Theory*, English translation published by Princeton University Press, Princeton, 1914.

[Fisher, 1922] R. A. Fisher. On the mathematical foundations of theoretical statistics", *Philosophical Transactions of the Royal Society A*, **222**: 309-368, 1922.

[Fisher, 1925] R. A. Fisher. Theory of Statistical Estimation, *Proceedings of the Cambridge Philosophical Society*, **22**: 700-725, 1925.

[Fisher, 1934] R. A. Fisher. Two New Properties of Maximum Likelihood, *Proceedings of the Royal Statistical Society*, A, **144**: 285-307, 1934.

[Fisher, 1935a] R. A. Fisher. The logic of inductive inference", *Journal of the Royal Statistical Society*, **98**: 39-54, with discussion pp. 55-82, 1935.

[Fisher, 1935b] R. A. Fisher. The Fiducial Argument in Statistical Inference, *Annals of Eugenics*, **6**: 391-398 1935.

[Fisher, 1955] R. A. Fisher. Statistical methods and scientific induction, *Journal of the Royal Statistical Society*, **B**, **17**: 69-78. 1955.

[Fisher, 1956] R. A. Fisher. *Statistical Methods and Scientific Inference*, Oliver and Boyd, Edinburgh, 1956.

[Friedman, 1953] M. Friedman. The Methodology of Positive Economics, pp. 3-43 in *Essays in Positive Economics*, Chicago University Press, Chicago, 1953; reprinted in Mäki, 2009.

[Giere, 1984] R. N. Giere. *Understanding Scientific Reasoning*, 2nd ed., Holt, Rinehart and Winston, NY, 1984.

[Gigerenzer, 1993] G. Gigerenzer. The superego, the ego, and the id in statistical reasoning, pp. 311-39 in Keren, G. and C. Lewis (eds.), *A Handbook of Data Analysis in the Behavioral Sciences: Methodological Issues*, Lawrence Erlbaum Associates, Hillsdale, New Jersey, 1993.

[Gosh *et al.*, 2006] J. K. Ghosh, M. Delampady and T. Samanta. *An Introduction to Bayesian Analysis: Theory and Methods*, Springer, NY, 2006.

[Glymour, 1981] C. Glymour. *Theory and Evidence*, Princeton University Press, NJ, 1981.

[Godambe and Sprott, 1971] V. P. Godambe and D. A. Sprott. *Foundations of Statistical Inference: a Symposium*, Holt, Rinehart and Winston, Toronto, 1971.

[Godfrey-Smith, 2003] P. Godfrey-Smith. *Theory and Reality: An Introduction to the Philosophy of Science*, The University of Chicago Press, Chicago, 2003.

[Gosset, 1908] W. Gossett. The probable error of the mean, *Biometrika*, **6**, 1-25, 1908.

[Granger, 1990] C. W. J. Granger, ed. *Modelling Economic Series*, Clarendon Press, Oxford. 1990.

[Greene, 2000] W. H. Greene. *Econometric Analysis*, 4th ed., Prentice Hall, NJ, 2000.

[Guala, 2005] F. Guala. *The Methodology of Experimental Economics*, Cambridge University Press, Cambridge, 2005.

[Hacking, 1965] I. Hacking. *Logic of Statistical Inference*, Cambridge University Press, Cambridge, 1965.

[Hacking, 1983] I. Hacking. *Representing and Intervening*, Cambridge University Press, Cambridge, 1983.

[Hall, 2005] A. P. Hall. *Generalized Method of Moments*, Oxford University Press, Oxford, 2005.

[Hands, 2001] W. D. Hands. *Reflection without Rules: Economic Methodology and Contemporary Science Theory*, Cambridge University Press, Cambridge, 2001.

[Harlow *et al.*, 1997] L. L. Harlow, S. A. Mulaik and J. H. Steiger. *What if there were no Significance Tests?* Mahwah, Erlbaum, NJ, 1997.

[Harper and Hooker, 1976] W. L. Harper and C. A. Hooker. *Foundations of Probability Theory, Statistical Inference, and Statistical Theories of Science, Vol. II: Foundations and Philosophy of Statistical Inference*, Reidel, Dordrecht, 1976.

[Hempel, 1965] C. G. Hempel. *Aspects of Scientific Explanation and Other Essays in the Philosophy of Science*, Mcmillan, New York, 1965.

[Hendry, 1995] D. F. Hendry. *Dynamic Econometrics*, Oxford University Press, Oxford, 1995.

[Hendry, 2000] D. F. Hendry. *Econometrics: Alchemy or Science?*, 2nd ed., Blackwell, Oxford, 2000.

[Hendry *et al.*, 1990] D. F. Hendry, E. E. Leamer and D. J. Poirier. The ET dialogue: a conversation on econometric methodology, *Econometric Theory*, **6**: 171-261, 1990.

[Hoover, 2001] K. D. Hoover. *Causality in Macroeconomics*, Cambridge University Press, Cambridge, 2001.

[Hoover, 2002] K. D. Hoover. Econometrics and Reality, in Mäki, [2002, pp. 152-177].

[Hoover, 2006] K. D. Hoover. The Methodology of Econometrics, in Mäki, [2002, pp. 152-177].

[Howson and Urbach, 2005] C. Howson and P. Urbach. *Scientific Reasoning: The Bayesian Approach*, 3rd ed., Open Court, Chicago, IL 2005.

[Jeffreys, 1939/1961] H. Jeffreys. *Theory of Probability*, 3rd ed., Oxford University Press, Oxford, 1939/1961.

[Kass and Wasserman, 1996] R. E. Kass and L. Wasserman. The Selection of Prior Distributions by Formal Rules, " *Journal of the American Statistical Association*, **91**: 1343-1370, 1996.

[Kempthorne and Folks, 1971] O. Kempthorne and L. Folks. *Probability, Statistics, and Data Analysis*, The Iowa State University Press, Ames, IA, 1971.

[Kennedy, 2008] P. Kennedy. *A Guide to Econometrics*, 6th edition, MIT Press, MA, 2008.

[Keuzenkamp, 2000] H. A. Keuzenkamp. *Probability, Econometrics and Truth*, Cambridge University Press, Cambridge, 2000.

[Keynes, 1921] J. M. Keynes. *A Treatise on Probability*, MacMillan, London, 1921.

[Kuhn, 1962] T. Kuhn. *The Structure of Scientific Revolutions*, The University of Chicago Press, Chicago, 1962.

[Kuhn, 1977] T. Kuhn. *The Essential Tension: Selected Studies in Scientific Tradition and Change*, The University of Chicago Press, Chicago, 1977.

[Lakatos, 1970] I. Lakatos. Falsification and the Methodology of Scientific Research Programms, in Lakatos and Musgrave (1970), pp. 91-196, 1970.

[Lakatos and Musgrave, 1970] I. Lakatos and A. Musgrave, eds. *Criticism and Growth of Knowledge*, Cambridge University Press, Cambridge, 1970.

[Laudan, 1977] L. Laudan. *Progress and Its Problems: Towards a Theory of Scientific Growth*, Berkeley: University of California Press, 1977.

[Lawson, 1997] T. Lawson. *Economics and Reality*, Routledge, London 1997.

[Leamer, 1978] E. E. Leamer. *Specification Searches: Ad Hoc Inference with Nonexperimental Data*, Wiley, New York, 1978.

[Leeb and Pötscher, 2005] H. Leeb and B. M. Pötscher. Model Selection and Inference: Facts and Fiction," *Econometric Theory*, **21**: 21-59, 2005.

[Lehmann, 1993] E. L. Lehmann. The Fisher and Neyman-Pearson Theories of Testing Hypotheses: One Theory or Two? *Journal of the American Statistical Association*, **88**: 1242-9, 1993.

[Lehmann, 1986] E. L. Lehmann. *Testing Statistical Hypotheses*, 2nd ed., Wiley, NY 1986.

[Lehmann, 1990] E. L. Lehmann. Model specification: the views of Fisher and Neyman, and later developments", *Statistical Science*, **5**: 160-168, 1990.

[Lieberman, 1971] B. Lieberman. *Contemporary Problems in Statistics: a Book of Readings for the Behavioral Sciences*, Oxford University Press, Oxford, 1971.

[Lindley, 1965] D. V. Lindley. *Introduction to Probability and Statistics from the Bayesian Viewpoint*, Cambridge University Press, Cambridge, 1965.

[Machamer and Silberstein, 2002] P. Machamer and M. Silberstein. *The Blackwell Guide to the Philosophy of Science*, Blackwell, Oxford, 2002.

[Mäki, 2001] U. Mäki. *The Economic World View: Studies in the Ontology of Economics*, Cambridge University Press, Cambridge, 2001.

[Mäki, 2002] U. Mäki. *Fact and Fiction in Economics*, Cambridge University Press, Cambridge, 2002.

[Mäki, 2009] U. Mäki. *The Methodology of Positive Economics: Reflections on the Milton Friedman Legacy*, Cambridge University Press, Cambridge, 2009.

[Matyas, 1999] L. Matyas, ed. *Generalized Method of Moments Estimation*, Cambridge University Press, Cambridge, 1990.

[Mayo, 1991] D. G. Mayo. Novel Evidence and Severe Tests, *Philosophy of Science*, **58**: 523-552, 1991.

[Mayo, 1996] D. G. Mayo. *Error and the Growth of Experimental Knowledge*, The University of Chicago Press, Chicago, 1996.

[Mayo, 1997] D. G. Mayo. Duhem's Problem, the Bayesian Way, and Error Statistics, or What's Belief Got to Do with It?, *Philosophy of Science*, **64**, 222-244, 1997.

[Mayo, 2005] D. G. Mayo. Philosophy of Statistics, in S. Sarkar and J. Pfeifer (eds.), *Philosophy of Science: An Encyclopedia*, London: Routledge, pp. 802–15, 2006.

[Mayo, 2010] D. G. Mayo. An Error in the Argument from Conditionality and Sufficiency to the Likelihood Principle," pp. 305-314 in Mayo, D.G. and A. Spanos, *Error and Inference*, Cambridge University Press, Cambridge, 2010.

[Mayo and Spanos, 2004] D. G. Mayo and A. Spanos. Methodology in Practice: Statistical Misspecification Testing", *Philosophy of Science*, **71**: 1007-1025, 2004.

[Mayo and Spanos, 2006] D. G. Mayo and A. Spanos. Severe Testing as a Basic Concept in a Neyman-Pearson Philosophy of Induction, *The British Journal for the Philosophy of Science*, **57**: 323-357, 2006.

[Mayo and Cox, 2006] D. G. Mayo and D. R. Cox. Frequentist statistics as a theory of inductive inference, pp. 96-123 in *The Second Erich L. Lehmann Symposium – Optimality*, Lecture Notes-Monograph Series, Volume 49, Institute of Mathematical Statistics, 2006.

[Mayo and Spanos, 1010a] D. G. Mayo and A. Spanos, eds. *Error and Inference: Recent Exchanges on Experimental Reasoning, Reliability and the Objectivity and Rationality of Science*, Cambridge University Press, Cambridge, 2010.

[Mayo and Spanos, 2010b] D. G. Mayo and A. Spanos. Error Statistics, forthcoming in *Philosophy of Statistics*, the *Handbook of Philosophy of Science*, Elsevier (editors) D. Gabbay, P. Thagard, and J. Woods, 2010.

[McCloskey, 1985] D. N. McCloskey. *The Rhetoric of Economics*, University of Wisconsin, Madison 1985.

[McGuirk and Spanos, 2009] A. McGuirk and A. Spanos. Revisiting Error Autocorrelation Correction: Common Factor Restrictions and Granger Non-Causality, *Oxford Bulletin of Economics and Statistics,* **71**: 273-294, 2009.

[Mills, 1924] F. C. Mills. *Statistical Methods*, Henry Holt and Co., NY, 1924.

[Mills and Patterson, 2006] T. C. Mills and K. Patterson. *New Palgrave Handbook of Econometrics*, vol. 1, MacMillan, London, 2006.

[Moore, 1914] H. L. Moore. *Economic Cycles - Their Laws and Cause*, McMillan, NY, 1914.

[Morgenstern, 1963] O. Morgenstern. *On the accuracy of economic observations*, 2nd edition, Princeton University Press, New Jersey, 1963.

[Morrison and Henkel, 1970] D. E. Morrison and R. E. Henkel. *The Significance Test Controversy: A Reader*, Aldine, Chicago, 1970.

[Nagel, 1961] E. Nagel. *The Structure of Science*, Hackett, Indianapolis, 1961.

[Newton-Smith, 2000] W. H. Newton-Smith, ed. *A Companion to the Philosophy of Science*, Blackwell, Oxford, 2000.

[Neyman, 1937] J. Neyman. Outline of a Theory of Statistical Estimation based on the Classical Theory of Probability, *Philosophical Transactions of the Royal Statistical Society of London*, A, **236**: 333–380, 1937.

[Neyman, 1956] J. Neyman. Note on an Article by Sir Ronald Fisher, *Journal of the Royal Statistical Society*, B, **18**: 288-294, 1956.

[Neyman, 1957] J. Neyman. Inductive Behavior as a Basic Concept of Philosophy of Science, *Revue Inst. Int. De Stat.*, **25**: 7-22, 1957.

[Neyman and Pearson, 1933] J. Neyman and E. S. Pearson. On the problem of the most efficient tests of statistical hypotheses", *Phil. Trans. of the Royal Society, A,* **231**: 289-337, 1933.

[Pagan, 1987] A. R. Pagan. Three econometric methodologies: a critical appraisal", *Journal of Economic Surveys,* **1**, 3-24, 1987. Reprinted in C. W. J. Granger (1990).

[Pagan and Ullah, 1999] A. R. Pagan and A. Ullah. *Nonparametric Econometrics*, Cambridge University Press, Cambridge, 1999.

[Pearson, 1920] K. Pearson. The Fundamental Problem of Practical Statistics, *Biometrika*, **XIII**, 1-16, 1920.

[Pearson, 1955] E. S. Pearson. Statistical Concepts in the Relation to Reality, J*ournal of the Royal Statistical Society, Series B*, **17**, 204-207, 1955.

[Pearson, 1966] E. S. Pearson. The Neyman-Pearson Story: 1926-34, in *Research Papers in Statistics: Festschrift for J. Neyman*, ed. by F. N. David, Wiley, NY, pp. 1-23, 1966.

[Poirier, 1995] D. J. Poirier. *Intermediate Statistics and Econometrics*, MIT Press, Cambridge 1995.

[Poole, 1987] C. Poole. Beyond the Confidence Interval, *The American Journal of Public Health*, **77**: 195-199, 1987.

[Popper, 1959] K. R. Popper. *The Logic of Scientific Discovery*, Hutchinson, London, 1959.

[Popper, 1963] K. R. Popper. *Conjectures and Refutations,* Routledge and Kegan Paul, London, 1963.

[Pratt, 1961] J. W. Pratt. Review of 'Testing Statistical Hypotheses' by E. L. Lehmann, *Journal of the American Statistical Association*, **56**: 163-166, 1961.

[Quine, 1953] W. V. Quine. *From the Logical Point of View*, Harvard University Press, Cambridge, 1953.

[Quine, 1960] W. V. Quine. *World and Object*, The MIT Press, Cambridge, 1960.

[Rao, 2004] C. R. Rao. Statistics: Reflections on the Past and Visions for the Future, *Amstat News*, **327**: 2-3, 2004.

[Rao and Wu, 2001] C. R. Rao and Y. Wu. On Model Selection, pp. 1-64 in *Model Selection*, ed. by P. Lahiri, Institute of Mathematical Statistics, Lecture Notes-Monograph series, vol. 38, Beachwood, OH, 2001.

[Redman, 1991] D. A. Redman. *Economics and the Philosophy of Science*, Oxford University Press, Oxford, 1991.

[Renyi, 1970] A. Renyi. *Probability Theory*, North-Holland, Amsterdam, 1970.

[Robert, 2007] C. Robert. *The Bayesian Choice*, 2nd ed., Springer, NY, 2007.

[Rosenthal *et al.*, 1999] R. Rosenthal, R. L. Rosnow, and D. B. Rubin. *Contrasts and Effect Sizes in Behavioral Research: A Correlational Approach*, Cambridge University Press, Cambridge, 1999.

[Salmon, 1967] W. Salmon. *The Foundations of Scientific Inference*, University of Pittsburgh Press, Pittsburgh, PA 1967.

[Savage, 1962] L. Savage, ed. *The Foundations of Statistical Inference: A Discussion.* London, Methuen 1962.

[Schervish, 1995] M. J. Schervish. *Theory of Statistics*, Springer-Verlag, NY, 1995.

[Schumpeter, 1954] J. A. Schumpeter. *History of Economic Analysis*, Oxford University Press, Oxford, 1954.
[Sims, 1980] C. A. Sims. Macroeconomics and Reality, *Econometrica*, **48**: 1-48. 1980.
[Spanos, 1986] A. Spanos. *Statistical Foundations of Econometric Modelling*, Cambridge University Press, Cambridge, 1986.
[Spanos, 1988] A. Spanos. Towards a Unifying Methodological Framework for Econometric Modelling, *Economic Notes*, 107-134, 1988; reprinted in Granger [1990].
[Spanos, 1989] A. Spanos. On re-reading Haavelmo: a retrospective view of econometric modeling, *Econometric Theory*, **5**: 405-429, 1989.
[Spanos, 1990] A. Spanos. The Simultaneous Equations Model revisited: statistical adequacy and identification, *Journal of Econometrics*, **44**: 87-108, 1990.
[Spanos, 1994] A. Spanos. On Modeling Heteroskedasticity: the Student's t and Elliptical Linear Regression Models, *Econometric Theory*, **10**: 286-315, 1994.
[Spanos, 1995] A. Spanos. On theory testing in Econometrics: modeling with nonexperimental data, *Journal of Econometrics*, **67**: 189-226, 1995.
[Spanos, 1999] A. Spanos. *Probability Theory and Statistical Inference: econometric modeling with observational data*, Cambridge University Press, Cambridge, 1999.
[Spanos, 2000] A. Spanos. Revisiting Data Mining: 'hunting' with or without a license, *The Journal of Economic Methodology*, **7**: 231-264, 2000.
[Spanos, 2001] A. Spanos. Parametric versus Non-parametric Inference: Statistical Models and Simplicity," pp. 181-206 in *Simplicity, Inference and Modelling*, edited by A. Zellner, H. A. Keuzenkamp and M. McAleer, Cambridge University Press, 2001.
[Spanos, 2004] A. Spanos. Confidence Curves, Consonance Intervals, P-value Functions vs. Severity Evaluations," Working Paper, Virginia Tech, 2004.
[Spanos, 2006a] A. Spanos. Econometrics in Retrospect and Prospect, pp. 3-58 in Mills, T.C. and K. Patterson, *New Palgrave Handbook of Econometrics*, vol. 1, MacMillan, London, 2006.
[Spanos, 2006b] A. Spanos. Where Do Statistical Models Come From? Revisiting the Problem of Specification, pp. 98-119 in *Optimality: The Second Erich L. Lehmann Symposium*, edited by J. Rojo, Lecture Notes-Monograph Series, vol. 49, Institute of Mathematical Statistics, 2006.
[Spanos, 2006c] A. Spanos. Revisiting the omitted variables argument: substantive vs. statistical adequacy," *Journal of Economic Methodology*, **13**: 179–218, 2006.
[Spanos, 2007a] A. Spanos. Curve-Fitting, the Reliability of Inductive Inference and the Error-Statistical Approach, *Philosophy of Science*, **74**: 1046–1066, 2007.
[Spanos, 2007b] A. Spanos. Sufficiency and Ancillarity Revisited: Testing the Validity of a Statistical Model" Working Paper, Virginia Tech, 2007.
[Spanos, 2007c] A. Spanos. The Instrumental Variables Method revisited: On the Nature and Choice of Optimal Instruments, pp. 34-59 in *Refinement of Econometric Estimation and Test Procedures*, ed. by G. D. A. Phillips and E. Tzavalis, Cambridge University Press, Cambridge, 2007.
[Spanos, 2007d] A. Spanos. Revisiting the Welch Uniform Model: A case for Conditional Inference? Working Paper, Virginia Tech, 2007.
[Spanos, 2008a] A. Spanos. Statistics and Economics, pp. 1129-1162 in the *New Palgrave Dictionary of Economics*, 2nd edition, Eds. S. N. Durlauf and L. E. Blume. Palgrave Macmillan, London, 2008.
[Spanos, 2008b] A. Spanos. Bayesian Criticisms of Neyman-Pearson Testing: the Arbitrariness of the Choice Between One-Sided vs. Two-Sided or Simple-vs-Simple Hypotheses, Working Paper, Virginia Tech, 2008.
[Spanos, 2008c] A. Spanos. Review of Stephen T. Ziliak and Deirdre N. McCloskey's The Cult of Statistical Significance, *Erasmus Journal for Philosophy and Economics*, 1:154-164, 2008. `http://ejpe.org/pdf/1-1-br-2.pdf`.
[Spanos, 2009a] A. Spanos. The Pre-Eminence of Theory versus the European CVAR Perspective in Macroeconometric Modeling, *Economics: The Open-Access, Open-Assessment E-Journal*, Vol. 3, 2009-10, 2009. `http://www.economics-ejournal.org/economics/journalarticles/2009-10`.
[Spanos, 2009b] A. Spanos. Statistical Misspecification and the Reliability of Inference: the simple t-test in the presence of Markov dependence, *Korean Economic Review*, **25**: 165-213.
[Spanos, ] Spanos, A. (2009c), Model-based Induction and the Frequentist Interpretation of Probability, Virginia Tech working paper, 2009.

[Spanos, 2010a] A. Spanos. Theory Testing in Economics and the Error Statistical Perspective, pp. 202-246 in *Error and Inference*, edited by Mayo, D. G. and A. Spanos, 2010.

[Spanos, 2010b] A. Spanos. Akaike-type Criteria and the Reliability of Inference: Model Selection vs. Statistical Model Specification, forthcoming, *Journal of Econometrics*, 2010.

[Spanos, 2010c] A. Spanos. Statistical Adequacy and the Trustworthiness of Empirical Evidence: Statistical vs. Substantive Information, forthcoming in *Economic Modelling*, 2010.

[Spanos and McGuirk, 2001] A. Spanos and A. McGuirk. The Model Specification Problem from a Probabilistic Reduction Perspective, *Journal of the American Agricultural Association*, **83**: 1168-1176, 2001.

[Spanos and McGuirk, 2002] A. Spanos and A. McGuirk. The Problem of Near-Multicollinearity Revisited: Erratic vs. Systematic Volatility, *Journal of Econometrics*, **108**: 365-393, 2002.

[Stigum, 2003] B. P. Stigum. *Econometrics and the Philosophy of Economics*, Princeton University Press, Princeton, 2003.

[Suppe, 1977] F. Suppe. *The Structure of Scientific Theories*, 2nd ed., University of Illinois Press, Urbana, 1977.

[Welch, 1939] B. L. Welch. On Confidence Limits and Sufficiency, and Particular Reference to Parameters of Location, *Annals of Mathematical Statistics*, **10**: 58-69, 1939.

[Wooldridge, 2006] M. J. Wooldridge. *Introductory Econometrics: a Modern Approach*, 3rd ed., Thomson, South-Western, 2006.

[Ziliak and McCloskey, 2008] S. T. Ziliak and D. N. McCloskey. *The Cult of Statistical Significance: How the Standard Error Costs Us Jobs, Justice, and Lives*, The University of Michigan Press, Ann Arbor, 2008.

# MEASUREMENT IN ECONOMICS

Marcel Boumans

> Measurement is the link between mathematics and science. The nature of measurement should therefore be a central concern of the philosophy of science. [Ellis, 1968, 1]

## 1 THE REPRESENTATIONAL THEORY OF MEASUREMENT

The dominant measurement theory of today is the Representational Theory of Measurement (RTM).[1] The core of this theory is that measurement is a process of assigning numbers to attributes or characteristics of the empirical world in such a way that the relevant qualitative empirical relations among these attributes or characteristics are reflected in the numbers themselves as well as in important properties of the number system.

The origins of RTM can be traced in Maxwell's method of using formal analogies. A first glimpse of it appeared in Maxwell's article 'On Faraday's lines of force [1855/1965]. In discussing his method of using analogies, the 'representational view' is made *en passant*: 'Thus all the mathematical sciences are founded on relations between physical laws and laws of numbers, so that the aim of exact science is to reduce the problems of nature to the determination of quantities by operations with numbers' (p. 156). Helmholtz took up Maxwell's view and continued to think in this direction. Usually Helmholtz [1887] is taken as the starting point of the development of the representational theory. The development since Helmholtz's seminal paper is described by Michell [1993] and Savage and Ehrlich [1992].

In the formal representational theory, measurement is defined set-theoretically as:

> Given a set of empirical relations $\mathbf{R} = \{R_1, \ldots, R_n\}$ on a set of extra-mathematical entities $\mathbf{Y}$ and a set of numerical relations $\mathbf{P} = \{P_1, \ldots, P_n\}$ on the set of numbers $\mathbf{N}$ (in general a subset of the set of real numbers), a function $\phi$ from $\mathbf{Y}$ into $\mathbf{N}$ takes each $R_i$ into $P_i, i = 1, \ldots, n$, provided that the elements $Y_1, Y_2, \ldots$ in $\mathbf{Y}$ stand in relation $R_i$ if and only if the corresponding numbers $\phi(Y_1), \phi(Y_2), \ldots$ stand in relation $P_i$.

[1] See for an early account [Suppes and Zinnes 1963].

Handbook of the Philosophy of Science. Volume 13: Philosophy of Economics.
Volume editor: Uskali Mäki. General editors: Dov M. Gabbay, Paul Thagard and John Woods.

In other words, measurement is conceived of as establishing homomorphisms from empirical relational structures $\Psi = \langle \mathbf{Y}, \mathbf{R} \rangle$ into numerical relational structures $\mathrm{N} = \langle \mathbf{N}, \mathbf{P} \rangle$. We say then that the ordered triple $\langle \Psi, \mathrm{N}, \phi \rangle$ is a *scale*. Figure 1 shows a diagrammatic representation of this set-theoretical definition of measurement.

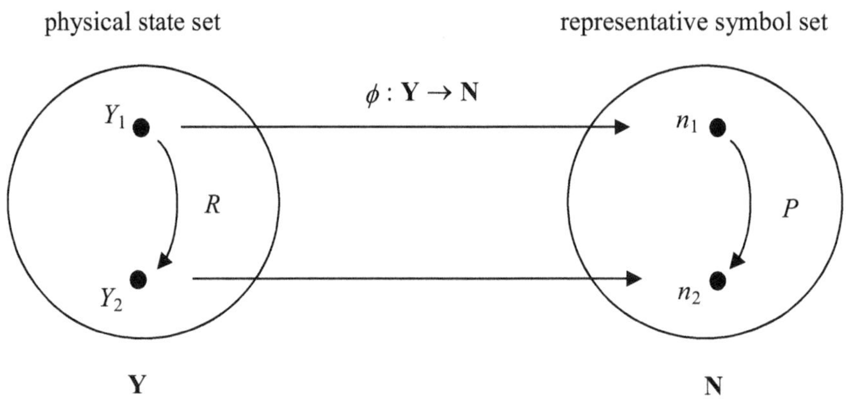


Figure 1. Representational theory of measurement

A numerical relational structure representing an empirical relational structure is also called a model, therefore RTM is sometimes called the Model Theory of Measurement.

The problem of this representational view on measurement is that when the requirements for assessing the representations or models are not further qualified, it can easily lead to an operationalist position, which is most explicitly expressed by Stevens' dictum:

> [M]easurement [is] the assignment of numerals to objects or events according to rule — any rule. Of course, the fact that numerals can be assigned under different rules leads to different kinds of scales and different kinds of measurements, not all of equal power and usefulness. Nevertheless, provided a consistent rule is followed, some form of measurement is achieved. [Stevens, 1959, 19]

A model should meet certain criteria to be considered homomorphic to an empirical relational structure. This is called the *representation problem*. In economics, there are two different foundational approaches to deal with this representation problem: an axiomatic approach (discussed in section 2) and an empirical approach (discussed in section 3).

The second fundamental problem of RTM is called the *uniqueness problem*: the determination of the scale type. The type of scale is determined by the relative uniqueness of the numerical assignment $\phi$. A scale is unique up to a permissible transformation. A transformation $\phi \rightarrow \phi'$ is permissible if and only if $\phi$ and $\phi'$ are both homomorphisms of $\langle \mathbf{Y}, \mathbf{R} \rangle$ into the same numerical structure $\langle \mathbf{N}, \mathbf{P} \rangle$. A scale type is then usually described in terms of the group of permissible transformations. Stevens [1959] distinguishes six groups of transformations: any one-to-one substitution, any strictly increasing function, any linear function $r\phi + s$ with $r > 0$, any similarity transformation $r\phi$ with $r > 0$, any power function $r\phi^n$ with $r, n > 0$, and the identity transformation. The corresponding scales are called nominal, ordinal, interval, ratio, logarithmic interval, and absolute.

## 2 AXIOMATIC REPRESENTATIONAL THEORY OF MEASUREMENT

The axiomatic theory is presented in Pfanzagl [1968], Roberts [1979], Narens [1985], Suppes [2002], and most comprehensively in a three-volume survey *Foundations of Measurement*, edited by Krantz, Luce, Suppes and Tversky [1971; 1989; 1990]. According to this literature, the foundations of measurement are established by axiomatization. Therefore, this approach will be labeled as the Axiomatic Representational Theory of Measurement (ARTM).

To view the foundations of measurement, ARTM focus on the properties of numerical assignments, rather than on the procedure for making these assignments. ARTM considers the task of the foundations of measurement as the explication and axiomatization of these properties of numerical assignments. The few explicit properties from which all others can be deduced are called axioms. The analysis into the foundations of measurement involves, for any particular empirical relation structure, the formulation of a set of axioms that is sufficient to establish two types of theorems: an *axiomatic representation theorem* and a *uniqueness theorem*. An *axiomatic representation theorem* asserts that if a given relational structure satisfies certain axioms, then a homomorphism into a certain numerical relational structure can be constructed. A *uniqueness theorem* sets forth the permissible transformations $\phi \rightarrow \phi'$, see above.

This axiomatic approach is closely linked to Suppes' [1962; 1967] semantic view of theories. In this view, a model for a theory is considered as an interpretation on which all the axioms of that theory are true. To characterize a theory, one defines the intended class of models for a particular theory. Both Suppes' semantic view as his foundational analysis of the theory of measurement are based on Tarski's theory of models [1954; 1955].

Because most of the major contributors to ARTM have been mathematicians and psychologists, ARTM has been influential in the field where economics and psychology overlap, namely the field where decision, choice and game theory flourish, and which might be more or less adequately labeled as microeconomics. Key examples will be discussed in section 2.1. Beside these often-referred applications, ARTM was also successful in index theory, which will be discussed in section 2.2.

## 2.1 Measurement of utility

Probably the first example of ARTM in economics is Frisch [1926/1971]. To establish an 'objective' definition of utility as a quantity, it introduces three axioms, where $Y_i$ indicates a position in a commodity space.

> *Axiom of choice* (connectness). One of the three cases $Y_1 \prec Y_2, Y_1 = Y_2, Y_1 \succ Y_2$ always holds.
>
> *Axiom of coordination* (transitivity). $Y_1 \succ Y_2$ and $Y_2 \succ Y_3$ imply $Y_1 \succ Y_3$.
>
> *Axiom of addition.* $Y_1 \succ Y_2$ and $Y_3 \succ Y_4, Y_1, Y_2, Y_3$, and $Y_4$ being infinitesimals, imply $Y_1 + Y_3 \succ Y_2 + Y_4$.

This first axiomatization appeared in a Norwegian journal and was written in French. Moreover, his *New Methods of Measuring Marginal Utility* [1932], which gives an extensive elaboration of the 1926 paper, does not reproduce these axioms. This is probably the reason for its neglect in the literature until 1971, when Chipman translated Frisch's paper into English and published it in *Preferences, Utility, and Demand*, a standard reference work in utility measurement.

The work which is more often referred to, as the one that introduced axiomatization to economics, is von Neumann and Morgenstern's *Theory of Games and Economic Behavior* [1944/1956]. It requires the numerical assignment (or 'correspondence', as they called it) $\phi : \mathbf{Y} \to \mathbf{N}$ to be order-preserving: $Y_1 \succ Y_2$ implies $\phi(Y_1) > \phi(Y_2)$, and linear: $\phi(\alpha Y_1 + (1-\alpha)Y_2) = \alpha\phi(Y_1) + (1-\alpha)\phi(Y_2)$, where $\alpha \in (0,1)$.

The uniqueness theorem it arrives at entails that the transformation $\phi \to \phi'$ is permissible if $\phi'$ is a linear function of $\phi$, with the corresponding scale being an interval scale. The representation theorem consists of the following list of axioms securing the homomorphism:

1. (a) Connected: One of the three cases $Y_1 \prec Y_2, Y_1 = Y_2, Y_1 \succ Y_2$ always holds.
   (b) Transitive: $Y_1 \succ Y_2$ and $Y_2 \succ Y_3$ imply $Y_1 \succ Y_3$.
2. (a) $Y_1 \succ Y_2$ implies that $Y_1 \succ \alpha Y_1 + (1-\alpha)Y_2 \succ Y_2$.
   (b) $Y_1 \succ Y_3 \succ Y_2$ implies the existence of an $\alpha$ and $\beta$ with $\alpha Y_1 + (1-\alpha)Y_2 \succ Y_3 \succ \beta Y_1 + (1-\beta)Y_2$.
3. (a) $\alpha Y_1 + (1-\alpha)Y_2 = (1-\alpha)Y_2 + \alpha Y_1$.
   (b) $\alpha(\beta Y_1 + (1-\beta)Y_2) + (1-\alpha)Y_2 = \alpha\beta Y_1 + (1-\alpha\beta)Y_2$.

## 2.2 Axiomatic index theory

Another field in economics in which the axiomatic approach has been influential is the axiomatic index theory, surveyed by Balk [1995]. This theory originates from Fisher's work on index numbers [1911/1963; 1922/1967]. Fisher evaluates in a systematic manner a very large number of indices with respect to a number of criteria. These criteria are called 'tests'. Fisher himself didn't expect that it would be possible to devise an index number that would satisfy all of these tests. Moreover, Frisch [1930] proves the impossibility of maintaining a certain set of Fisher's tests simultaneously. It is, however, Eichhorn ([1973; 1976], [1976], co-authored with Voeller), who provides a definite evaluation of Fisher's tests by his axiomatic approach.

The axiomatic approach should be distinguished from two other index theories. Within the axiomatic theory prices and quantities of commodities are considered as separate variables. There is no assumption made concerning an underlying optimizing behavior, which is central to the microeconomic theory of price and quantity indices. Secondly, price and quantity changes of commodities do not originate from an underlying probability distribution, characteristic for the statistical theory of indices.

Eichhorn looks systematically at the inconsistencies between various tests (and how to prove such inconsistencies) by means of the functional equation theory, in particular Aczél's [1966] solution of Cauchy's functional equations. Functional equation theory is transferred into index theory if the price index is defined as a positive function $P(p_s, x_s, p_t, x_t)$ that satisfies a number of axioms, where $p$ is a price vector and $x$ a commodity vector, and the subscripts are time indices. These axioms do not, however, determine a unique form of the price index function. Several additional tests are needed for assessing the quality of a potential price index. Both axioms and tests are formalized as functional equations.

Frisch [1930] discusses the following seven tests:

1. Identity test: $P(p_s, x_s, p_s, x_t) = 1$
2. Time reversal test $P(p_s, x_s, p_t, x_t) \times P(p_t, x_t, p_s, x_s) = 1$
3. Base test: $\frac{P(p_s, x_s, p_u, x_u)}{P(p_s, x_s, p_t, x_t)} = \frac{P(p_v, x_v, p_u, x_u)}{P(p_v, x_v, p_t, x_t)}$
4. Circular test: $P(p_s,\ x_s,\ p_t,\ x_t) \times P(p_t,\ x_t,\ p_u,\ x_u) = P(p_s,\ x_s,\ p_u,\ x_u)$
5. Commensurability test: $P(\lambda p_s,\ x_s/\lambda,\ \lambda p_t,\ x_t/\lambda) = P(p_s,\ x_s,\ p_t,\ x_t)$
6. Determinateness test: The index number shall not be rendered zero, infinite, or indeterminate by an individual price or quantity becoming zero.
7. Factor reversal test: $P(p_s,\ x_s,\ p_t,\ x_t) \times P(x_s,\ p_s,\ x_t,\ p_t) = p_t \cdot x_t / p_s \cdot x_s$

Note, that when assuming the identity test (1) the time reversal test (2) follows from the circular test (4), which in its turn follows from the base test. This can be seen by first substituting $t$ for $v$, which gives (4), and subsequently $s$ for $u$, which gives (2).

Frisch's approach is to consider these tests as conditions on the functional form $P$ of the index formula, and then to derive mathematically the general forms satisfying combinations of these tests. As a result, Frisch arrives at the unique index formula satisfying the circular test (4), commensurability test (5) and the factor reversal test (7). However, Frisch also shows that the base test (3) (or circular test (4)), the commensurability test (5) and the determinateness test (6) can not all be fulfilled at the same time — they are incompatible. So, one has to choose between the tests, which lead to a long discussion in the index literature on the economic meaning and significance of each of them.

An important consideration for maintaining the circular test is that, when this condition is met, an index number is freed from one base year. Another reason, crucial to a microeconomic approach, is that the circular test is considered as the property of transitivity, which is essential for any index based on choice theory, see former section.

Eichhorn's axiomatic approach is an application of the axiomatic method as practiced in mathematical logic and is based on Tarski's model theory. For an axiomatic system $\Sigma$, one of the most fundamental questions to analyze is whether $\Sigma$ is consistent. Finding an interpretation of $\Sigma$ can prove its consistency. An interpretation of $\Sigma$ is an assignment of meanings to the undefined terms of $\Sigma$ in such a way that the axioms become simultaneously true statements for all values of the variables. Such interpretation is also called a model of $\Sigma$. When the axioms are formalized as functional equations, inconsistency theorems can then be proven by showing that for the relevant combinations of functional equations, the solution space is empty.

To analyze an axiomatic system, another crucial question is whether its axioms are independent. Let $A$ denote one of the axioms of $\Sigma$, and the denial of $A$ by $\sim A$, and let $\Sigma - A$ denote system $\Sigma$ with $A$ deleted. If $S$ is any statement phrased in terms of $\Sigma$, let $\Sigma + S$ mean the axiom system containing the axioms of $\Sigma$ and the statement $S$ as a new axiom. Then, $A$ is called independent in $\Sigma$, or an independent axiom of $\Sigma$, if both $\Sigma$ and the axiom system $(\Sigma - A) + \sim A$ have an interpretation.

The power of this approach was immediately demonstrated in Eichhorn [1973]. The paper discusses five of Fisher's tests:

1. Proportionality test: $P(p_s, x_s, \lambda p_s, x_t) = \lambda$
2. Circular test
3. Commensurability test
4. Determinateness test
5. Factor reversal test

The proportionality test is more general than the identity test where $\lambda = 1$. Eichhorn obtains the same results as Frisch [1930] — namely, the functional form of an index that fulfills the commensurability test, the circular test and the factor reversal test. Eichhorn also shows that the derived index fulfills the determinateness test but not the proportionality test.

These five tests, however, are inconsistent, which requires that one test be rejected. Because the economic significance of the factor reversal test is generally considered to be controversial, Eichhorn abandons this test. He then shows that the other four are independent but still inconsistent.

Eichhorn [1976] discusses weaker versions of Fisher's system of tests. It appears that if one weakens only the circular test, by replacing it by the time reversal test, then the system of five tests is consistent. To obtain consistency, one has to give up the economic meaningful circular test.

Eichhorn's axiomatic approach, his 'art of model building' which he not only applied to index numbers but also to production functions, can be summarized as follows:

- formulate some important properties ($P_1, \ldots, P_k$, *say*) of the required functions,
- prove their consistency by presenting a function that has all these properties,
- show the independence of the properties

Then, these properties (assumptions, hypotheses, premises, desiderata, axioms) constitute a model [Stehling 1993].

## 3 EMPIRICAL REPRESENTATIONAL THEORY OF MEASUREMENT

Anderson [1981] mentions three limitations on the axiomatic approach. The first limitation is that it leaves out the question of how the mathematical structures gain their empirical significance in actual practical measurement. Secondly, the axiomatic approach lacks concrete measurement procedures, devices and methods. The representation theorem is non-constructive. Although the theorem may imply that a scale exists, it does not provide any way to get it. And thirdly, the axiomatic approach applies only to error-free data; it says nothing about handling the response variability in real data.

Influenced by the program of axiomatization, launched by Hilbert, axiomatization is considered to put theories — and thereby measurement — on firm foundations, an ambition that is explicitly indicated by the title of Krantz, Luce, Suppes and Tversky's three-volume survey. An apparent representative of this position is Roberts [1979, 3] by stating: 'We are not interested in a measuring apparatus and in the interaction between the apparatus and the objects being measured. Rather, we attempt to describe how to put measurement on a firm, well-defined foundation'. To put measurement in the social sciences on a firm foundation, axioms about individual judgments, preferences and reactions need to be developed — the so-called representational problem. And it often turns out to be that the axioms are developed more in consideration of logical requirements, like consistency, than trying to achieve empirical significance.

Because of this emphasis on axiomatization, ARTM does not provide an adequate understanding of other measurement practices based in more empirical traditions lesser dominated by axiomatization, which are mainly to be found in macroeconomics, econometrics, and its combination macro-econometrics. Measurements of important macroeconomic indicators like business cycle, unemployment and GDP are not adequately described by ARTM. For example, Chao [2002] uses a non-axiomatized RTM to give an account of consumption measurements.

These practices deal with the measurement of macroeconomic phenomena, which have a different ontology than the objects of classical theories of measurement. Measurement is assigning numbers to properties. In the classical view of measurement, which arose in the physical sciences and received its fullest exposition in the works of Campbell [1928], these numbers represents properties of *things*. Measurement in the social sciences does not necessarily have this thing-relatedness. It is not only properties of 'things' that are measured but also those of phenomena: states, events, and processes.

To arrive at an account of measurement that acknowledges Anderson's objections, Woodward's [1989], (see also [Bogen and Woodward, 1988]) distinction between phenomena and data is helpful. According to Woodward, phenomena are relatively stable and general features of the world and therefore suited as objects of explanation and prediction. Data, that is, the observations playing the role of evidence for claims about phenomena, on the other hand involve observational mistakes, are idiosyncratic and reflect the operation of many different causal factors and are therefore unsuited for any systematic and generalizing treatment. Theories are not about observations — particulars — but about phenomena — universals.

Woodward characterizes the contrast between data and phenomena in three ways. In the first place, the difference between data and phenomena can be indicated in terms of the notions of error applicable to each. In the case of data the notion of error involves observational mistakes, while in the case of phenomena one worries whether one is detecting a real fact rather than an artifact produced by the peculiarities of one's instruments or detection procedures. A second contrast between data and phenomena is that phenomena are more 'widespread' and less idiosyncratic, less closely tied to the details of a particular instrument or detection procedure. A third way of thinking about the contrast between data and phenomena is that scientific investigation is typically carried on in a noisy environment, an environment in which the observations reflect the operation of many different causal factors.

> The problem of detecting a phenomenon is the problem of detecting a signal in this sea of noise, of identifying a relatively stable and invariant pattern of some simplicity and generality with recurrent features — a pattern which is not just an artifact of the particular detection techniques we employ or the local environment in which we operate.

> Problems of experimental design, of controlling for bias or error, of selecting appropriate techniques for measurement and of data analysis are, in effect, problems of tuning, of learning how to separate signal and noise in a reliable way. [Woodward, 1989, 396-397]

Underlying the contrast between data and phenomena is the idea that theories do not explain data, which typically will reflect the presence of a great deal of noise. Rather, an investigator first subjects the data to analysis and processing, or alters the experimental design or detection technique, in an effort to separate out the phenomenon of interest from extraneous background factors. Although phenomena are investigated by using observed data, they themselves are in general not directly observable. To 'see' them we need instruments, and to obtain numerical facts about the phenomena in particular we need measuring instruments. In social science, we do not have physical instruments, like thermometers or galvanometers. Mathematical models function as measuring instruments by transforming sets of repeated observations into a measurement result [Boumans, 2005].

Theories are incomplete with respect to the quantitative facts about phenomena. Though theories explain phenomena, they often (particularly in economics) do not have built-in application rules for mathematizing the phenomena. Moreover, theories do not have built-in rules for measuring the phenomena. For example, theories tell us that metals melt at a certain temperature, but not at which temperature (Woodward's example); or they tell us that capitalist economies give rise to business cycles, but not the duration of recovery. In practice, by mediating between theories and the data, models may overcome this dual incompleteness of theories. As a result, models that function as measuring instruments mediate between theory and data by transferring observations into quantitative facts about the phenomenon under investigation:

$$\text{Data} \rightarrow \text{Model} \rightarrow \text{Facts about the phenomenon}$$

Because facts about phenomena are not directly measured but must be inferred from the observed data, we need to consider the reliability of the data. These considerations cannot be derived from theory but are based on a closer investigation of the experimental design, the equipment used, and need a statistical underpinning. This message was well laid out for econometrics by Haavelmo [1944, 7]: 'The data [the economist] actually obtains are, first of all, nearly always blurred by some plain errors of measurement, that is, by certain extra "facts" which he did not intend to "explain" by his theory'.

In this paradigm-setting paper, Haavelmo [1944] explicitly formulates what the method of econometric research should aim at, namely, 'at a conjunction of economic theory and actual measurement, using the theory and technique of statistical inference as a bridge pier' (p. iii). Morgan [1988] shows that the econometricians of the 1930s — but her observation still applies to current econometricians — 'have been primarily concerned with finding satisfactory empirical models, not with trying to prove fundamental theories true or untrue'. The ideas about assessing whether the models were 'satisfactory' depended on the purpose of the models. Morgan interprets these early econometricians' idea of testing as something like quality control testing. Criteria were applied to empirical models: Do they satisfy the theoretical criteria? Do they satisfy standard statistical criteria? Can they be used to explore policy options? Do they bring to light unexpected relationships, or help us refine relationships? A model found to exhibit desired economic-theoretical and statistical qualities might be deemed satisfactory. The empirical models were matched both with theory and with data, to bridge the gaps between both. Current econometricians are even more pragmatic in their aims. An example of this pragmatic attitude is Granger [2003]. He notes when discussing the evaluation of models that 'a theory may be required to be internally consistent, although consistency says little or nothing about relevance'.

Does this shift from an axiomatic to an empirical approach to measurement result in a foundationless measurement science? Not necessarily if one attempts to found science on empirical phenomena. In his history of how economics became a mathematical science, Weintraub [2002] emphasizes that one should not identify 'rigor' with 'axiomatics', because the late-nineteenth-century mathematics considered 'rigor' and 'axiomatization' antithetical. Rigor was then understood to mean 'based on a substrate of physical reasoning'. The opposite of 'rigorous' was not 'informal' but rather 'unconstrained', as with a mathematical argument unconstrained by instantiation in a natural science model. However, this view of science and scientific explanation, which entailed rigor in modeling in the sense of developing economic explanations from mechanical ones, was increasingly unsatisfactory as a solution to the crisis of those days in the natural sciences. The crisis was resolved by the formalist position on explanation whereby mathematical analogy replaced mechanical analogy, and mathematical models were cut loose from their physical underpinnings in mechanics. The result was that in the first decades of the twentieth century a rigorous argument was reconceptualized as a logically consistent argument instead of as an argument that connected the problematic phenomenon to a physical phenomenon by use of empirical data. This distinction between rigor as materialist-reductionist quantification and rigor as formal derivation established it self in the distinction between econometrics and mathematical economics, between applied economics and economic theory.

So, if we look at the measuring practices in macroeconomics and econometrics, we see that their aims can be formulated as: Measures are results of modeling efforts recognized as satisfactory for their goal of obtaining quantitative information about economic phenomena.

To give an account of these empirical measurement practices, the subsequent sections will explore in which directions the representational theory has to be extended. This extension will be based on accounts that deal explicitly with measuring instruments and measurement errors.

## 4 INSTRUMENT MEASUREMENT

The problem of lack of empirical significance in ARTM is discussed by Heidelberger [1994a; 1994b], who argues for giving the representational theory a 'correlative interpretation', based on Fechner's principle of mental measurement.

The disadvantage of an axiomatic approach is that it is much too liberal. As Heidelberger argues, we could not make any difference between a theoretical determination of the value of a theoretical quantity and the actual measurement. A correlative interpretation does not have this disadvantage, because it refers to the handling of a measuring instrument. This interpretation of RTM is based on Fechner's correlational theory of measurement. Fechner had argued that

> the measurement of any attribute $Y$ generally presupposes a second, directly observable attribute $X$ and a measurement apparatus $A$ that can represent variable values of $Y$ in correlation to values of $X$. The correlation is such that when the states of $A$ are arranged in the order of $Y$they are also arranged in the order of $X$. The different values of $X$ are *defined* by an intersubjective, determinate, and repeatable calibration of $A$. They do not have to be measured on their part. The function that describes the correlation between $Y$ and $X$ relative to $A$ (underlying the measurement of $Y$ by $X$ in $A$) is precisely what Fechner called the measurement formula. Normally, we try to construct (or find) a measurement apparatus which realizes a 1:1 correlation between the values of $Y$ and the values of $X$ so that we can take the values of $X$ as a direct representation of the value of $Y$. (Heidelberger [1993, 146][2])

To illustrate this, let us consider an example of temperature measurement. We can measure temperature, $Y$, by constructing a thermometer, $A$, that contains a mercury column which length, $X$, is correlated with temperature: $X = F(Y)$. The measurement formula, the function describing the correlation between the values of $Y$ and $X, x = f(y)$, is determined by choosing the shape of the function, $f$, e.g. linear, and by calibration. For example, the temperature of boiling water is fixed at 100, and of ice water at 0.

The correlative interpretation of measurement implies that the scales of measurement are a specific form of indirect scales, namely so-called associative scales. This terminology is from Ellis [1968] who adopted a conventionalist view on measurement. To see that measurement on the one side requires empirical significance — Heidelberger's point — and on the other hand is conventional, we first have a closer look at direct measurement, thereupon we will discuss Ellis' account of indirect measurements and finally explicate instrument measurement.

A *direct* measurement scale for a class of measurands is one based entirely on relations among that class and not involving the use of measurements of any other class. This type of scale is implied by the definition of RTM above, see Figure

[2] I have replaced the symbols $Q$ and $R$ in the original text by the symbols $Y$ and $X$, respectively, to make the discussion of the measurement literature uniform.

1, and is also called a *fundamental* scale. Direct measurement assumes direct observability — human perception without the aid of any instrument — of the measurand.

However, there are properties, like temperature, for which it is not possible or convenient to construct satisfactory direct scales of measurement. Scales for the measurement of such properties can, however, be constructed, based on the relation of that property, $Y$, and quantities, $X^i (i = 1, \ldots, m)$, with which it is associated and for which measurement scales have been defined. Such scales are termed *indirect*. *Associative* measurement depends on there being some quantity $X$ associated with property $Y$ to be measured, such that when things are arranged in the order of $Y$, under specific conditions, they are also arranged in the order of $X$. This association is indicated by $F$ in Figure 2. An associative scale for the measurement of $Y$ is then defined by taking $h(\phi(X))$ as the measure of $Y$, where $\phi(X)$ is the measure of $X$ on some previously defined scale, and $h$ is any strictly monotonic increasing function. Associative measurement can be pictured as an extended version of direct measurement, see Figure 2.

We have *derived* measurement if there exists an empirical law $h = h(\phi_1(X^1), \ldots, \phi_m(X^m))$ and if it is the case that whenever things are ordered in the order of $Y$, they are also arranged in the order of $h$. Then we can define $h(\phi_1(X^1), \ldots, \phi_m(X^m))$ as a derived scale for the measurement of $Y$.

The measurement problem then is the choice of the associated property $X$ and the choice of $h$, which Ellis following Mach called the 'choice of principle of correlation'.[3] For Ellis, the only kinds of considerations that should have any bearing on the choice of principle of correlation are considerations of mathematical simplicity [Ellis, 1968, 95–96]. But this is too much conventionalism, even Mach noted that whatever form one chooses, it still should have some empirical significance.

> It is imperative to notice that whenever we apply a definition to nature we must wait to see if it will correspond to it. With the exception of pure mathematics we can create our concepts at will, even in geometry and still more in physics, but we must always investigate whether and how reality correspond to these concepts. (Mach [1896/1966, 185])

This brings us back to Heidelberger.

According to Heidelberger [1993, 147], 'Mach not only defended Fechner's measurement theory, he radicalized it and extended it into physics'. To Mach, any establishment of an objective equality in science must ultimately be based on sensation because it needs the reading (or at least the gauging) of a material device by an observer. The central idea of correlative measurement, which stood in the center of Mach's philosophy of science, is that 'in measuring any attribute we always have to take into account its empirical lawful relation to (at least) another attribute. The distinction between fundamental [read: direct] and derived [read:

[3]Ellis' account of associative measurement is based on Mach's chapter 'Kritik des Temperaturbegriffes' from his book *Die Principien der Wärmelehre* (Leipizg, 1896). This chapter was translated into English and added to Ellis' 1968 book as Appendix I.

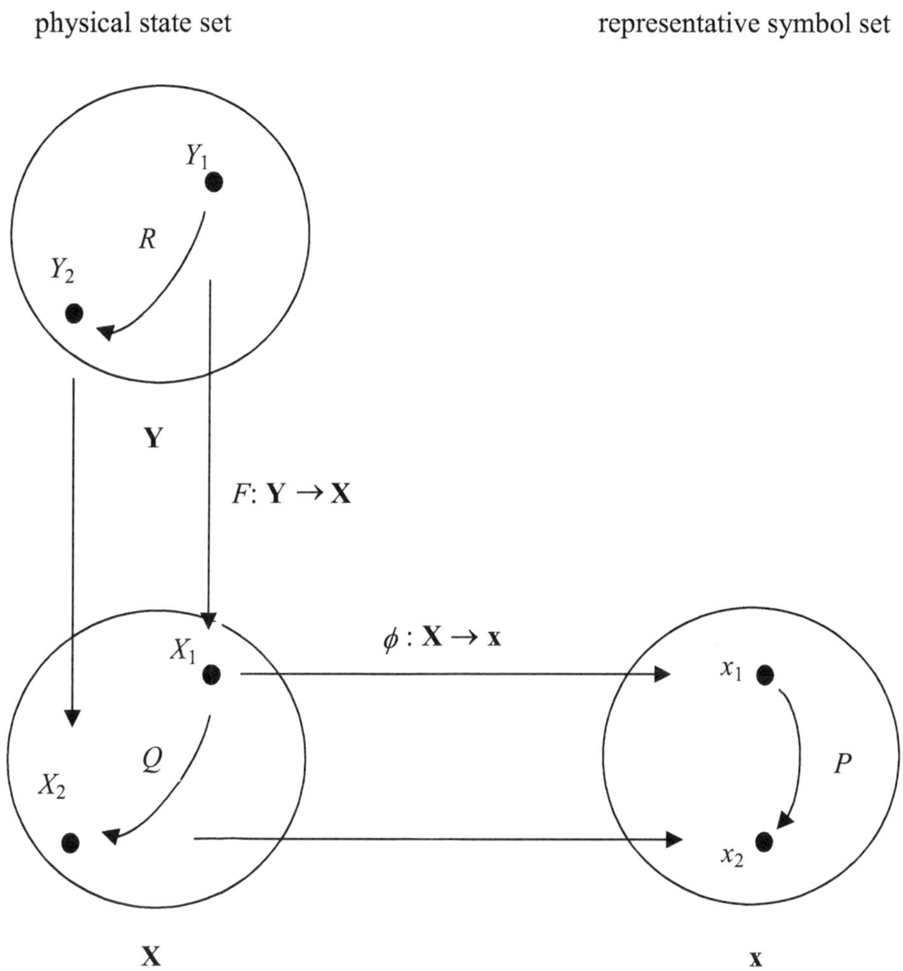


Figure 2. Associative measurement

indirect] measurement, at least in a relevant epistemological sense, is illusory' [Heidelberger, 1994b, 11].

Thus, in addition to direct (fundamental) and indirect (associative and derived), a third type, called *instrument measurement*, may be noted. This kind of measurement, involving an instrument, was also mentioned by Suppes and Zinnes [1963], where it was called 'pointer measurement', but its discussion disappeared in later accounts of RTM. Generally, by instrument measurement we mean a numerical assignment based on the direct readings of some validated instrument. A measuring instrument is validated if it has been shown to yield numerical values that correspond to those of some numerical assignments under certain standard conditions. This is called calibration. To construct a measuring instrument, it is generally necessary to utilize some established empirical law or association.

One difference between Ellis' associative measurement and Heidelberger's correlative measurement is that, according to Heidelberger, the mapping of $X$ into numbers, $\phi(X)$, is not the result of (direct) measurement but is obtained by calibration (see Heidelberger's quote above). To determine the scale of the thermometer no prior measurement of the expansion of the mercury column is required; by convention it is decided in how many equal parts the interval between two fixed points (melting point and boiling point) should be divided. In the same way, a clock continuously measures time, irrespective of its face. The face is the conventional part of time measurement and the moving of the hands the empirical determination of time.

Another difference between both accounts is that Heidelberger's account involves the crucial role of measuring devices to maintain the association between $Y$ and $X$. To represent the correlative interpretation, Figure 3 is an expansion of Figure 2 by adding the measurement apparatus $A$ to maintain the association $F$ between the observations $X \in \mathbf{X}$ and the not-directly-observable states of the measurand $Y \in \mathbf{Y}$. A correlative scale for the measurement of $Y$ is then defined by taking

(1) $x = \phi(X) = \phi(F(Y, OC))$

where $\phi(X)$ is the measure of $X$ on some previously defined scale. The correlation $F$ also involves other influences indicated by $OC$. $OC$, an acronym of 'other circumstances', is a collective noun of all other quantities that might have an influence on $X$.

The central idea of correlative measurement is that in measuring any attribute $Y$ we always have to take into account its empirical lawful relation to (at least) another attribute $X$. To establish this relation we need a measurement apparatus or experimental arrangement, $A$. In other words, a measuring instrument has to function as a nomological machine. This idea is based on Cartwright's account that a law of nature — necessary regular association between properties — hold only relative to the successful repeated operation of a 'nomological machine', which she defines as:

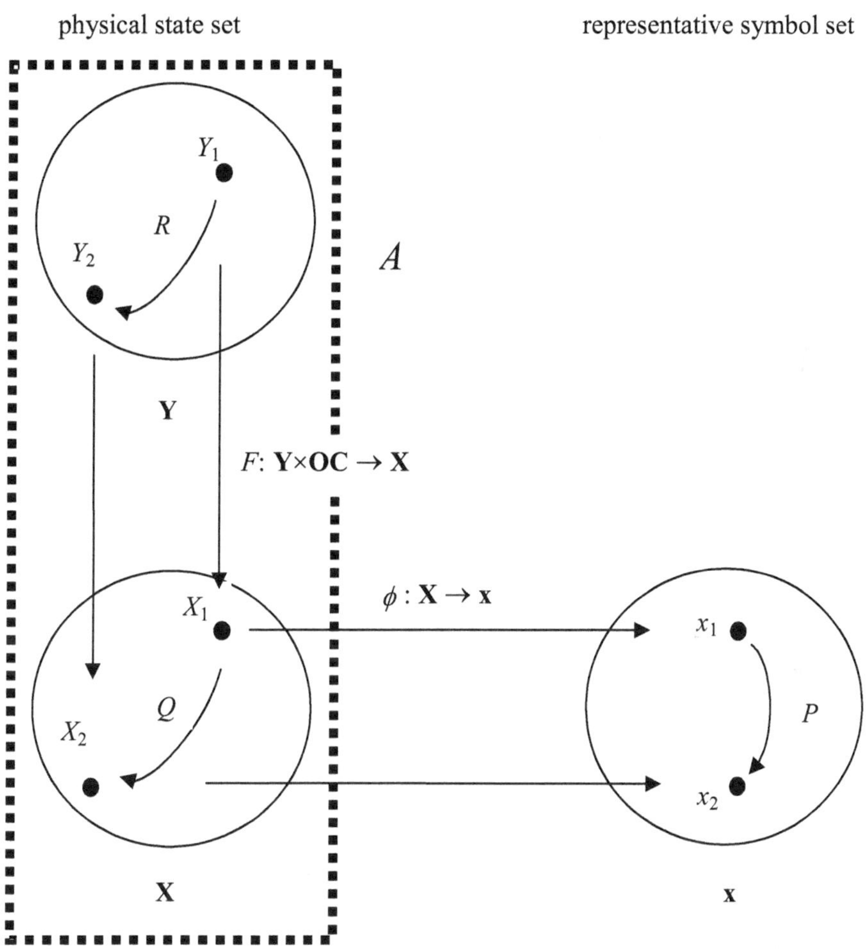


Figure 3. Correlative measurement

> a fixed (enough) arrangement of components, or factors with stable (enough) capacities that in the right sort of stable (enough) environment will, with repeated operation, give rise to the kind of regular behaviour that we represent in our scientific laws. [Cartwright, 1999, 50]

It shows why empirical lawful relations on which measurement is based and measuring instruments are two sides of the same coin. The measuring instrument must function as a nomological machine to fulfill its task. This interconnection is affirmed by Ellis' definition of lawful relation as an arrangement under specific conditions and Finkelstein's observation that the 'law of correlation' is 'not infrequently less well established and less general, in the sense that it may be the feature of specially experimental apparatus and conditions' [Finkelstein, 1975, 108].

The correlative interpretation of RTM gives back to measurement theory the idea that it concerns concrete measurement procedures and devices, taking place in the domain of the physical states as a result of an interaction between **X** and **Y**.

To understand correlatie measurement approaches, let us consider the problem of measuring a property $Y$ of an economic phenomenon. $X_i (i = 1, \ldots, k)$ are repeated observations of $Y$ to be used to determine its value. Variations in these observations are assumed to arise because influence quantities — other than the measurand itself of course — that can affect the observation, and are indicated by $OC$, might vary. In other words, each observation involves an observational error, $E_i$:

$$(2) \quad X_i = F(Y, OC_i) = F(Y, 0) + E_i \quad (i = 1, \ldots, k)$$

This error term, representing noise, reflects the operation of many different, sometimes unknown, background conditions. Now, accuracy of the observation is obtained by reducing noise as much as possible. One way of obtaining accuracy is by taking care that the other influence quantities, indicated by $OC$, are held as constant as possible, in other words, that *ceteris paribus* conditions are imposed. To show this, equation (2) is rewritten to express how $Y$ and possible other circumstances ($OC$) influence the observations:

$$(3) \quad \Delta X = \Delta F(Y, OC) = F_Y \cdot \Delta Y + F_{OC} \cdot \Delta OC = F_Y \cdot \Delta Y + \Delta E$$

Then, imposing *ceteris paribus* conditions, $\Delta OC \approx 0$, reduces noise $\Delta E \approx 0$.

Equation (3) shows that accuracy can be obtained 'in the right sort of stable (enough) environment' by imposing *ceteris paribus* conditions ($cp$), which also might include even stronger *ceteris absentibus* conditions: $OC \approx 0$. As a result the remaining factor $Y$ can be varied in a systematic way to gain knowledge about the relation between $Y$ and $X$:

$$(4) \quad F_Y = \frac{\Delta X_{cp}}{\Delta Y}$$

If the ratio of the variation of $X_{cp}$ and the variation of $Y$ appears to be stable, the correlation is an invariant relationship and can thus be used for measurement aims.

So, an observation in a controlled experiment is an accurate measurement because of the stabilization of background noise ($\Delta E = 0 \rightarrow E$ is stable: $E = S$).

$$(5) \quad x_{cp} = \phi(X_{cp}) = \phi(F(Y, S))$$

Knowledge about stable conditions $S$ is used for calibrating the instrument.

However, both kinds of conditions imply (almost) full control of the circumstances and (almost) complete knowledge about all potential influence quantities. Besides uncertainty about the observations, in both natural and social science, due to inadequate knowledge about the environmental conditions $OC$, there is an additional problem of control in economics. Fortunately, a measuring instrument can also be designed, fabricated or used such that the influences of all these uncontrollable circumstances are negligible. Using expression (3), this means that it is designed and constructed such that $F_{OC} \approx 0$. In other words, a measuring device should be constructed and used such that it is sensitive to changes in $Y$ and at the same time insensitive to changes in the other circumstances ($OC$), which is therefore called here the *ceteris neglectis* condition. In economics, the environment often cannot be furnished for measurement purposes, so, a 'natural' nomological machine $A$ have to be looked for satisfying *ceteris neglectis* requirements. If we have a system fulfilling the *ceteris neglectis* condition, we do not have to worry about the extent to which the other conditions are changing. They do not have to be controlled as is assumed by the conventional *ceteris paribus* requirements.

Observation with a natural system $A$ that we cannot control — so-called passive observation — does not, however, solve the problem of achieving accuracy. The remaining problem is that it is not possible to identify the reason for a disturbing influence, say $Z$, being negligible, $F_Z \cdot \Delta Z \approx 0$. We cannot distinguish whether its potential influence is very small, $F_Z \approx 0$, or whether the factual variation of this quantity over the period under consideration is too small, $\Delta Z \approx 0$. The variation of $Z$ is determined by other relationships within the economic system. In some cases, a virtually dormant quantity may become active because of changes in the economic system elsewhere. Each found empirical relationship is a representation of a specific data set. So, for each data set it is not clear whether potential influences are negligible or only dormant.

In practice, the difficulty in economic research does not lie in establishing simple relations, but rather in the fact that the empirically found relations, derived from observations over certain time periods, are still simpler than we expect them to be from theory, so that we are thereby led to throw away elements of a theory that would be sufficient to explain apparent 'breaks in structure' later. This is what Haavelmo [1944] called the problem of autonomy. Some of the empirical found relations have very little 'autonomy' because their existence depends upon the simultaneous fulfillment of a great many other relations. Autonomous relations are those relations that could be expected to have a great degree of invariance with respect to various changes in the economic system.

Confronted with the inability of control, social scientists deal with the problem of invariance and accuracy by using models as virtual laboratories. Morgan [2003] discusses the differences between 'material experiments' and 'mathematical models as experiments'. In a mathematical model, control is not materialized but assumed. As a result, accuracy has to be obtained in a different way. Accuracy is dealt with by the strategy of comprehensiveness and it works as follows (see [Sutton, 2000]): when a relationship appears to be inaccurate, this is an indication that a potential factor is omitted. As long as the resulting relationship is inaccurate, potential relevant factors should be added. The expectation is that this strategy will result in the fulfillment of two requirements: 1) the resulting model captures a complete list of factors that exert large and systematic influences; 2) all remaining influences can be treated as a small noise component. The problem of passive observations is solved by accumulation of data sets: the expectation is that we converge bit by bit to a closer approximation to the complete model, as all the most important factors reveal their influence. This strategy however is not applicable in cases when there are influences that we cannot measure, proxy, or control for, but which exert a large and systematic influence on the outcomes.

To connect this strategy with measurement theory, let's assume a set of observations

(6) $x_i = f(y) + \varepsilon_i \ (i = 1, \ldots, k)$

where $f$ is a representation of the correlation $F$ and $\varepsilon_i$ is a numerical representation of the observational errors $E_i$. To transform the set of observations into a measurement result the specification of a model is needed. So, to measure $Y$ a model $M$ has to be specified of which the values of the observations $x_i$ functions as input and the output estimate $\hat{y}$ as measurement result. If — and in economics this is often the case — data indicate that $M$ does not model the measurand to the degree imposed by the required accuracy of the measurement result, additional input quantities must be included in $M$ to eliminate this inaccuracy. This may require introducing input quantities to reflect incomplete knowledge of a phenomenon that affects the measurand. This means that the model has to incorporate a representation of the full nomological machine $A$, denoted by $a$, that is should represent both properties of the phenomenon to be measured as well as the background conditions influencing the observations. To take account of this aspect of measurement, Figure 3 has to be further expanded as shown in Figure 4.

When one has to deal with a natural measuring system $A$ that can only be observed passively, the measurement procedure is first to infer from the observations $X_i$ nature's design of this system to determine next the value of the measurand $Y$. So, first an adequate representation $a$ of system $A$ has to be specified before we can estimate the value of $Y$. A measurement result is thus given by

(7) $\hat{y} = M(x_i; a)$

If one substitute equation (6) into model $M$, one can derive that, assuming that $M$ is a linear operator (usually the case):

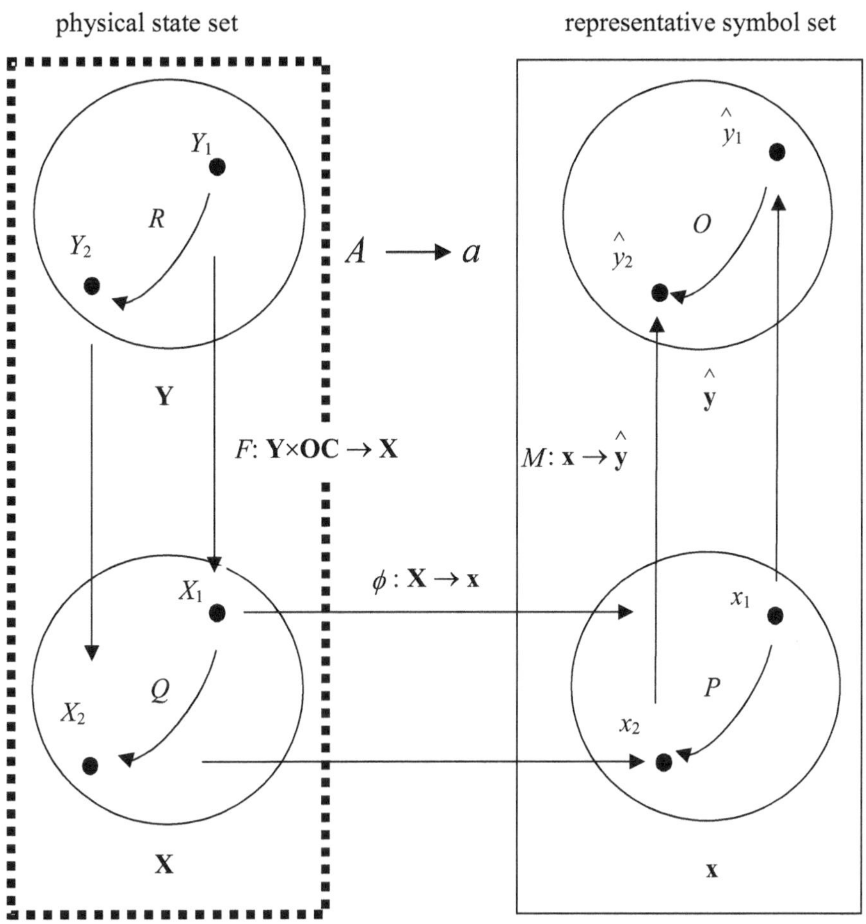


Figure 4. Instrument measurement

(8) $\hat{y} = M(f(y) + \varepsilon_i; a) = M_y(y; a) + M_\varepsilon(\varepsilon_i; a)$

A necessary condition for the measurement of $Y$ is that a model $M$ must involve a theory of the measurand as part of $M_y$, and a theory of the error term as part of $M_\varepsilon$. To obtain a reliable measurement result with an immaterial mathematical model, the model parameters have to be adjusted in a specific way. So, tuning, that is separating signal and noise, is done by adjusting the parameter values.

## 5 RELIABLE MEASUREMENT RESULTS

A true signal, that is the true value of $Y$, however, can only be obtained by a perfect measurement, and so is by nature indeterminate. The reliability of the model's outputs therefore depends on other aspects of the model's performance. To describe the performance of a model that functions as a measuring instrument the terms *accuracy* and *precision* are important. In metrology, accuracy is defined as a statement about the closeness of the mean taken from the scatter of the measurements to the value declared as the standard [Sydenham, 1979, 48]. Precision is a statement about the closeness to a particular value that the individual measurements possess, or in other words a statement about the spread of the estimated measurement errors.

For an instrument to be considered producing objective measuring results, it is essential that accuracy and precision be achieved by mechanical procedures. The usual mechanical procedure to attain precision is by minimizing the variance of errors. The 'least squares method' is an example of such an often-used mechanical procedure to obtain precision.

The mechanical procedure to obtain accuracy is *calibration*, which is the establishment of the relationship between values indicated by a measuring instrument and the corresponding values realized by standards. This means, however, that accuracy can only be assessed in terms of a standard. In this context, a standard is a representation (model) of the properties of the phenomenon as they appear under well-defined conditions.

To discuss this problem in more detail, we split the measurement error in three parts:

(9) $\hat{\varepsilon} = \hat{y} - y = M_\varepsilon + (M_y - S) + (S - y)$

where $S$ represents the standard. The error term $M_\varepsilon$ is reduced as much as possible by reducing the spread of the error terms, in other words by aiming at precision. $(M_x - S)$ is the part of the error term that is reduced by calibration. So, both errors terms are dealt with by mechanical procedures. However, the reduction of the last term $(S - y)$ can only dealt with by involving theoretical assumptions about the phenomenon and independent empirical studies. Note that the value $y$ is not known. Often the term $(S - y)$ is reduced by building as accurate representations $a$ of the economic system as possible. This third step is called standardization.

This problem of standardization is closely related to the 'problem of nomic measurement', which has been discussed by Chang [2004, 59]:[4]

1. We want to measure quantity $Y$.
2. Quantity $Y$ is not directly observable, so we infer it from another quantity $X$, which is directly observable.
3. For this inference we need a law that expresses $y$ as a function of $x$, as follows: $y = h(x)$.
4. The form of this function $h$ cannot be discovered or tested empirically, because that would involve knowing the values of both $X$ and $Y$, and $Y$ is the unknown variable that we are trying to measure.

Chang mentions this problem when discussing the thermometer. But a clock is also a nice and simple example to clarify the problem of nomic measurement. A clock measures time by assuming a functional relationship $h$ between time $t$ and the distance $d$ traveled by the arms of the clock: $t = h(d)$. The shape of this function is assumed to be linear: $t = \alpha d + \beta$. As such $h$ functions as a representation of time, and is assumed to be accurate: $S - y = h(d) - t = 0$. As a result, standardization can be defined as finding representations $h$ of the measurand such that $S - y = h(x) - y \rightarrow 0$.

To illustrate this issue of standardization, let us assume the simplest case in which we have data of a measurand $Y$ with inevitable observational errors:

$$(10) \quad x_i = y_i + \varepsilon_i$$

where $i = 1, \ldots, n$. In the case of time series, the index $i$ denotes time. A broadly applied general model in economics — indices, barometers, filters and graduation methods — to estimate the value $y_t$ is a weighted average of these observations:

$$(11) \quad \hat{y}_t = \sum_{i=-n}^{n} w_i x_{t+i}$$

which can be split into two terms:

$$(12) \quad \hat{y}_t = \sum_{i=-n}^{n} w_i y_{t+i} + \sum_{i=-n}^{n} w_i \varepsilon_{t+i}$$

To turn the observations into a reliable measurement result, one has to decide on the values of the weighting system $w_i$. Therefore, two different methods are applied. One method, the precision method, is to reduce the second, error term. The weights have to be chosen such that the spread of the errors $\varepsilon_i$ is reduced. Usually a least squares method is applied.

The criterion of precision is not sufficient to determine the weighting system. Therefore, one has to apply the method of accuracy. This means that the weights have to be chosen such that

[4]The symbols are again adopted to make the discussion uniform.

$$(13)\quad y_t = \sum_{i=-n}^{n} w_i y_{t+i}$$

is a representation of an underlying law or (aspects of) the phenomenon. As a result, the values of the weights have to meet standards of stability, smoothness or the like. For example in the case of time series, it is usually assumed that the time shape of $y$ is a polynomial of low degree (1, 2 or 3).

The issue is how we arrive at these standards. They are numerical representations of the relevant empirical relational structure. In economics, they are not given by theory. Theory tells us only that, for example, which variables are of relevance, and which is connected to or depended on which. To arrive at numerical representations is usually the result of measurement. But for measurement we need standards, which are numerical representations. The circularity which results from the empirical approach - science founded on measurement founded on the definition of measurands founded on science — is in fact not a closed circle but is better captured by the term 'epistemic iteration'. This term is coined by Chang [2004], and which he describes as follows: In epistemic iteration we start by adopting an existing system of knowledge, with some respect for it but without any firm assurance that it is correct; on the basis of that initially affirmed system we launch inquiries that result in the refinement and even correction of the original system. Chang shows that it is this self-correcting progress that justifies (retrospectively) successful courses of development in science, not any assurance by reference to some indubitable foundation.

## 6 ECONOMIC MODELING

An often-used method of evaluation in economics to verify whether the model of the economic system is accurate is to test it on its predictive performance. The modeling procedure is to add to the model a variable, suggested by theory, each time the model predictions can be improved. So, in this 'structural-equations' strategy, two models, I and II are compared with each other, and the one that provides the best predictions is chosen.

In economics, these representations are often assumed to be linear operators. From now on, therefore, $a$ denotes a matrix: $a = (\alpha_{ij})$, where $\alpha_{ij}$ are the matrix parameters, and $x$ and $y$ denote vectors. The subscript $t$ denotes time:

Model I:

$$(14)\quad \hat{x}^{I}_{it+1} = \sum_{j=1}^{k} \alpha^{I}_{ij} x_{jt} \quad (i : 1, \ldots, k)$$

Model II:

$$(15)\quad \hat{x}^{II}_{it+1} = \sum_{j=1}^{k+1} \alpha^{II}_{ij} x_{jt} \quad (i : 1, \ldots, k+1)$$

If $\left\|x_{it+1} - \hat{x}^{II}_{it+1}\right\| < \left\|x_{it+1} - \hat{x}^{I}_{it+1}\right\|$ for the majority of these error terms ($i$ : $1, \ldots, k$) and where $\|\cdot\|$ is a statistically defined norm, choose model II. Note that for each additional quantity the model is enlarged with an extra (independent) equation. As a result, the prediction errors are assumed to be reduced by taking into account more and more potential influence quantities. As long as all potential influences are indirectly measurable by the observational proxies, there is no problem, in principle. As datasets accumulate, it might reasonably be expected that the model converge bit by bit to a more accurate representation of the economic system, as all the most important $x$s reveal their potential influence. But what if there are quantities that cannot be (indirectly) measured, and which exert a large and systematic influence on outcomes? Then their presence will induce a bias in the measurement. This doubt about this strategy was enforced by empirical research that showed large-scale models failed to be better predicting devices than very simple low-order autoregressive (AR) models, or simple autoregressive moving average (ARMA) models, which are used to study time series.

In interpreting these results, Milton Friedman [1953] suggested that the programme of building large-scale models is probably faulty and needs reformulation. For him, the ability to predict is the quality of a model that should be evaluated not its realisticness. This methodological standpoint is spelled out in the among economists well-known article 'The Methodology of Positive Economics' [Friedman, 1953]. The strategy he suggests is to keep the model $a$ as small as possible by avoiding to model the 'other circumstances' $OC$ and instead to search for those systems for which $a$ is an accurate model (tested by its predictive power). In other words, try to decide by empirical research for which systems the other circumstances are negligible ($F_{OC} \approx 0$). Enlargement of the model is only justified if it is required by the phenomenon to be measured. The relevant question to ask about a model is not whether it is descriptively realistic but whether it is a sufficiently good approximation for the purpose at hand. As a consequence applied modelers shifted their interest in macro modeling away from a whole economy to parts of economic activities in which economic theories were relatively well developed. In this kind of empirical research, the strategy is to start with simple models and to investigate for which domain these models are accurate descriptions.

A very influential paper in macroeconomics [Lucas, 1976] showed that the estimated so-called structural parameters ($\alpha_{ij}$) achieved by the above 'structural-equations' strategy are not invariant under changes of policy rules. The problem is that the model equations in economics are often representations of behavioral relationships. Lucas has emphasized that economic agents form expectations of the future and that these expectations play a crucial role in the economy because they influence the behavior of economic actors. People's expectations depend on many things, including the economic policies being pursued by governments and central banks. Thus, estimating the effect of a policy change requires knowing how people's expectations will respond to policy changes. Lucas has argued that the above estimation methods do not sufficiently take into account the influence of changing expectations on the estimated parameter values. Lucas assumed that economic agents have 'rational expectations', that is the expectations based on all information available at time $t$ and they know the model, $a$, which they use to form these expectations.

Policy-invariant parameters should be obtained in an alternative way. Either they could be supplied from micro-econometric studies, accounting identities, or institutional facts, or they are chosen to secure a good match between a selected set of the characteristics of the actual observed time-series and those of the simulated model output. This latter method is a method of estimation which entails simulating a model with ranges of parameters and selecting from these ranges those elements that best match properties of the simulated data with those of the observed time series. An often-used criterion is to measure the difference between some empirical moments computed on the observed variables $x_t$ and its simulated counterpart $\hat{x}_t$. Let $m(x)$ be the vector of various sample moments, so $m(x)$ could include the sample means and variances of a selected set of observable variables. $m(\hat{x})$ is the vector of simulated moments, that is, the moments of the simulations $\hat{x}(a)$. Then the estimation of the parameters is based on:

(16) $a_{MSM} = \arg\min_{a} \|m(x) - m(\hat{x}(a))\|$

These alternative ways of obtaining parameter values are in economics all covered by the label as calibration. It is important that, whatever the source, the facts being used for calibration should be as stable as possible. However, one should note that in social science, standards or constants do not exist in the sense as they do in natural science: lesser universal, more local and of shorter duration. In general, calibration in economics works as follows: use stable facts about a phenomenon to adjust the model parameters.

As a result of Lucas' critique on structural-equations estimations, he introduced a new program for economics, labeled as 'general-equilibrium economics', in which it is no longer required for representations being homomorphic to an empirical relational structure. One should not aim at models as 'accurate descriptive representations of reality':

> A 'theory' is not a collection of assertions about the behavior of the actual economy but rather an explicit set of instructions for building a parallel or analogue system — a mechanical, imitation economy. A 'good' model, from this point of view, will not be exactly more 'real' than a poor one, but will provide better imitations. Of course, what one means by a 'better imitation' will depend on the particular questions to which one wishes answers. [Lucas, 1980, 696–7]

This approach was based on Simon's [1969] account of artifacts, which he defines as

> a meeting point — an 'interface' in today's terms — between an 'inner' environment, the substance and organization of the artifact itself, and an 'outer' environment, the surroundings in which it operates. If the

inner environment is appropriate to the outer environment, or vice versa, the artifact will serve its intended purpose. [Simon, 1969, 7]

The advantage of factoring an artificial system into goals, outer environment, and inner environment is that we can predict behavior from knowledge of the system's goals and its outer environment, with only minimal assumptions about the inner environment. It appears that different inner environments accomplish identical goals in similar outer environments, such as weight-driven clocks and spring-driven clocks. A second advantage is that, in many cases, whether a particular system will achieve a particular goal depends on only a few characteristics of the outer environment, and not on the detail of that environment, which might lead to simple models. A model is useful only if it foregoes descriptive realism and selects limited features of reality to reproduce.

Lucas' program was most explicitly implemented by Kydland and Prescott [1996]. According to them, any economic 'computational experiment' involves five major steps: *1. Pose a question*: The purpose of a computational experiment is to derive a quantitative answer to some well-posed question. *2. Use well-tested theory*: Needed is a theory that has been tested through use and found to provide reliable answers to a class of questions. A theory is not a set of assertions about the actual economy, rather, following Lucas [1980], defined to be an explicit set of instructions for building a mechanical imitation system to answer a question. *3. Construct a model economy*: An abstraction can be judged only relative to some given question. The features of a given model may be appropriate for some question (or class of questions) but not for others. *4. Calibrate the model economy*: In a sense, model economies, like thermometers, are measuring devices. Generally, some economic questions have known answers, and the model should give an approximately correct answer to them if we are to have any confidence in the answer given to the question with unknown answer. Thus, data are used to calibrate the model economy so that it mimics the world as closely as possible along a limited but clearly specified, number of dimensions. *5. Run the experiment.*

Kydland and Prescott's specific kind of assessment is similar to Lucas' idea of testing, although he didn't call it calibration. To test models as 'useful imitations of reality' we should subject them to shocks 'for which we are fairly certain how actual economies, or parts of economies, would react. The more dimensions on which the model mimics the answer actual economies give to simple questions, the more we trust its answer to harder questions' [Lucas, 1980, 696–7]. This kind of testing is similar to calibration as defined by Franklin [1997, 31]: 'the use of a surrogate signal to standardize an instrument. If an apparatus reproduces known phenomena, then we legitimately strengthen our belief that the apparatus is working properly and that the experimental results produced with that apparatus are reliable'.

The economic questions, for which we have known answers, or, the standard facts with which the model is calibrated, were most explicitly given by Cooley and Prescott [1995]. They describe calibration as a selection of the parameters values for the model economy so that it mimics the actual economy on dimensions associated with long-term growth by setting these values equal to certain 'more or less constant' ratios. These ratios were the so-called 'stylized facts' of economic growth, 'striking empirical regularities both over time and across countries', the 'benchmarks of the theory of economic growth'.

What we have seen above is that in modern macroeconomics, the assessment of models as measuring instruments is not based on the evaluation of the homomorphic correspondence between the empirical relational structure and the numerical relational structure. The assessment of these models is more like what is called *validation* in systems engineering. Validity of a model is seen as 'usefulness with respect to some purpose'. Barlas [1996] notes that for an exploration of the notion validation it is crucial to make a distinction between white-box models and black-box models. In black-box models, what matters is the output behavior of the model. The model is assessed to be valid if its output matches the 'real' output within some specified range of accuracy, without any questioning of the validity of the individual relationships that exists in the model. White-box models, on the contrary, are statements as to how real systems actually operate in some aspects. Generating an accurate output behavior is not sufficient for model validity; the validity of the internal structure of the model is crucial too. A white-box model must not only reproduce the behavior of a real system, but also explain how the behavior is generated.

Barlas [1996] discusses three stages of model validation: direct structural tests, structure-oriented behavior tests and behavior pattern tests. For white models, all three stages are equally important, for black box models only the last stage matters. Barlas emphasizes the special importance of structure-oriented behavior tests: these are strong behavior tests that can provide information on potential structure flaws. The information, however, provided by these tests does not give any direct access to the structure, in contrast to the direct structure tests.

Models that pass the structure-oriented behavior tests and behavior pattern tests — in line with the labeling of the other two types of models — could be called gray-box models. Gray-box models are validated by the kinds of tests that in the general-equilibrium literature all fall under the general heading of 'calibration', where it is defined generally enough to cover all tests which Barlas [1996] called structure-oriented behavior tests. To trust the results of a simulation for measurement purposes, the models that are run should be calibrated and need not to be accurate representations of the relevant economic systems.

## ACKNOWLEDGEMENTS

I am grateful to Hsiang-Ke Chao and Mary Morgan for their valuable comments.

# BIBLIOGRAPHY


[Aczél, 1966] J. Aczél. *Lectures on Functional Equations and Their Applications.* New York: Academic Press, 1966.

[Anderson, 1981] N. H. Anderson. *Foundations of Information Integration Theory.* New York: Academic Press, 1981.

[Balk, 1995] B. M. Balk. Axiomatic price index theory: A survey, *International Statistical Review* 63.1: 69-93, 1995.

[Barlas, 1996] Y. Barlas. Formal aspects of model validity and validation in system dynamics, *System Dynamics Review* 12.3: 183-210, 1996.

[Bogen and Woodward, 1988] J. Bogen and James Woodward. Saving the phenomena, *The Philosophical Review* 97: 303-352, 1988.

[Boumans, 2005] M. Boumans. *How Economists Model the World into Numbers*, London: Routledge, 2005.

[Campbell, 1928] N. R. Campbell. *Account of the Principles of Measurement and Calculation*, London: Longmans, Green, 1928.

[Cartwright, 1999] N. Cartwright. *The Dappled World. A Study of the Boundaries of Science.* Cambridge: Cambridge University Press, 1999.

[Chang, 2004] H. Chang. *Inventing Temperature: Measurement and Scientific Progress.* Oxford: Oxford University Press, 2004.

[Chao, 2002] H.-K.Chao. *Representation and Structure: The Methodology of Econometric Models of Consumption.* Amsterdam: Thela Thesis and Tinbergen Institute, 2002.

[Cooley and Prescott, 1995] T. F. Cooley and E. C. Prescott. Economic growth and business cycles, in *Frontiers of Business Cycle Research*, ed. T.F. Cooley, 1-38. Princeton: Princeton University Press, 1995.

[Eichhorn, 1973] W. Eichhorn. Zur axiomatischen Theorie des Preisindex, *Demonstratio Mathematica* 6: 561-573, 1973.

[Eichhorn, 1976] W. Eichhorn. Fisher's tests revisited, *Econometrica* 44: 247-255, 1976.

[Eichhorn and Woeller, 1976] W. Eichhorn and J. Voeller. *Theory of the Price Index*, Berlin, Heidelberg and New York: Springer-Verlag, 1976.

[Ellis, 1968] B. Ellis. *Basic Concepts of Measurement.* Cambridge: Cambridge University Press, 1968.

[Finkelstein, 1975] L. Finkelstein. Fundamental concepts of measurement: Definition and scales, *Measurement and Control* 8: 105-110, 1975.

[Fisher, 1911/1963] I. Fisher. *The Purchasing Power of Money; Its Determination and Relation to Credit, Interest and Crises*, 1911. 2nd rev. ed. New York: Kelley, 1963.

[Fisher, 1922/1967] I. Fisher. *The Making of Index Numbers; A Study of Their Varieties, Tests, and Reliability*, 1922. 3rd rev. ed. New York: Kelley, 1967.

[Franklin, 1997] A. Franklin. Calibration, *Perspectives on Science* 5: 31-80, 1997.

[Friedman, 1953] M. Friedman. The methodology of positive economics, in *Essays in Positive Economics*, 3-43. Chicago: University of Chicago Press, 1953.

[Frisch, 1926/1971] R. Frisch. On a problem in pure economics, in *Preferences, Utility, and Demand*, eds. John S. Chipman, Leonid Hurwicz, Marcel K. Richter, Hugo F. Sonnenschein, 386-423. New York: Harcourt Brace Jovanovich, 1926. Translation by J.S. Chipman of 'Sur un problème d'économique pure', *Norsk Matematisk Forenings Skrifter*, Serie I, Nr. 16, 1971.

[Frisch, 1930] R. Frisch. Necessary and sufficient conditions regarding the form of an index number which shall meet certain of Fisher's tests, *Journal of the American Statistical Association* 25: 397-406, 1930.

[Frisch, 1932] R. Frisch. *New Methods of Measuring Marginal Utility*, Tuebingen: Mohr, 1932.

[Granger, 2003] C. Granger. Evaluations of theory and models, in *Econometrics and the Philosophy of Economics: Theory - Data Confrontations in Economics*, ed. B. Stigum, 480-496. Oxford: Princeton University Press, 2003.

[Haavelmo, 1944] T. Haavelmo. The probability approach in econometrics, supplement to *Econometrica* 12, 1944.

[Heidelberger, 1993] M. Heidelberger. Fechner's impact for measurement theory, *Behavioral and Brain Sciences* 16.1: 146-148, 1993.

[Heidelberger, 1994a] M. Heidelberger. Alternative Interpretationen der Repräsentationstheorie der Messung, in *Proceedings of the 1st Conference "Perspectives in Analytical Philosophy"*, eds. G. Meggle and U. Wessels. Berlin and New York: Walter de Gruyter, 1994.

[Heidelberger, 1994b] M. Heidelberger. Three strands in the history of the representational theory of measurement, Working Paper, Humboldt University Berlin, 1994.

[Helmholtz, 1887] H. von Helmholtz. Zählen und Messen, erkenntnis-theoretisch betrachtet, *Philosophische Aufsätze*, Leipzig: Fues, 1887.

[Krantz *et al.*, 1971, 1989, 1990] D. H. Krantz, R. Duncan Luce, P. Suppes and A. Tversky. *Foundations of Measurement.* 3 Vols. New York: Academic Press, 1971, 1989, 1990.

[Kydland and Prescott, 1996] F. E. Kydland and E. C. Prescott. The computational experiment: An econometric tool, *Journal of Economic Perspectives* 10.1: 69-85, 1996.

[Lucas, 1976] R. E. Lucas. Econometric policy evaluation: A critique, in *The Phillips Curve and Labor Markets*, eds. Karl Brunner and Allan H. Meltzer, 19-46. North-Holland, Amsterdam, 1976.

[Lucas, 1980] R. E. Lucas. Methods and problems in business cycle theory, *Journal of Money, Credit, and Banking* 12: 696-715, 1980.

[Mach, 1896/1966] E. Mach. Critique of the concept of temperature, in *Basic Concepts of Measurement*, 1896. B. Ellis, translated by M.J. Scott-Taggart and B. Ellis, 183-196. Cambridge: Cambridge University Press, 1966.

[Maxwell, 1855/1965] J. C. Maxwell. On Faraday's lines of force, 1855. In *The Scientific Papers of James Clerk Maxwell*, ed. W.D. Niven, Vol. I, 155-229. New York: Dover, 1965.

[Michell, 1993] J. Michell. The origins of the representational theory of measurement: Helmholtz, Hölder, and Russell, *Studies in History and Philosophy of Science* 24.2, 185-206, 1993.

[Morgan, 1988] M. S. Morgan. Finding a satisfactory empirical model, in *The Popperian Legacy in Economics*, ed. Neil de Marchi, 199-211. Cambridge: Cambridge University Press, 1988.

[Morgan, 2003] M. S. Morgan. Experiments without material intervention: Model experiments, virtual experiments, and virtually experiments, in *The Philosophy of Scientific Experimentation*, ed. Hans Radder, 216-235. Pittsburgh: University of Pittsburgh Press, 2003.

[Narens, 1985] L. Narens. *Abstract Measurement Theory.* Cambridge, Mass.: MIT Press, 1985.

[Pfanzagl, 1968] J. Pfanzagl. *Theory of Measurement.* Würzburg: Physica-Verlag, 1968.

[Roberts, 1979] F. S. Roberts. *Measurement Theory with Applications to Decisionmaking, Utility, and the Social Sciences*, London: Addison-Wesley, 1979.

[Savage and Ehrlich, 1992] C. W. Savage and P. Ehrlich. A brief introduction to measurement theory and to the essays, in *Philosophical and Foundational Issues in Measurement Theory*, eds. C.W. Savage and P. Ehrlich, 1-14. Hillsdale, New Jersey: Lawrence Erlbaum Associates, 1992.

[Simon, 1969] H. A. Simon. *The Sciences of the Artificial*, Cambridge: MIT Press, 1969.

[Stehling, 1993] F. Stehling. Wolfgang Eichhorn and the art of model building, in *Mathematical Modelling in Economics; Essays in Honor of Wolfgang Eichhorn*, eds. W. Erwin Diewert, Klaus Spremann and Frank Stehling, vii-xi. Berlin: Springer-Verlag, 1993.

[Stevens, 1959] S. S. Stevens. Measurement, psychophysics, and utility, in *Measurement. Definitions and Theories*, eds. C. West Churchman and Philburn Ratoosh, 18-63. New York: Wiley, 1959.

[Suppes, 1962] P. Suppes. Models of data, in *Logic, Methodology and Philosophy of Science: Proceedings of the 1960 International Congress*, eds. Ernest Nagel, Patrick Suppes and Alfred Tarski, 252-261. Stanford: Stanford University Press, 1962.

[Suppes, 1967] P. Suppes. What is a scientific theory? in *Philosophy of Science Today*, ed. Sidney Morgenbesser, 55-67. New York: Basic Books, 1967.

[Suppes, 2002] P. Suppes. *Representation and Invariance of Scientific Structures.* Stanford: CSLI Publications, 2002.

[Suppes and Zinnes, 1963] P. Suppes and J. L. Zinnes. Basic measurement theory, in *Handbook of Mathematical Psychology*, eds. R. Duncan Luce, Robert R. Bush, and Eugene Galanter, 1-76. New York, London and Sydney: Wiley, 1963.

[Sutton, 2000] J. Sutton. *Marshall's Tendencies: What Can Economists Know?* Leuven: Leuven University Press and Cambridge and London: The MIT Press, 2000.

[Sydenham, 1979] P. H. Sydenham. *Measuring Instruments: Tools of Knowledge and Control.* London: Peter Peregrinus, 1979.

[Tarski, 1954] A. Tarski. Contributions to the theory of models. I, II, *Indagationes Mathematicae* 16: 572-581, 582-588, 1954.
[Tarski, 1955] A. Tarski. Contributions to the theory of models. III, *Indagationes Mathematicae* 17: 56-64, 1955.
[von Neumann and Morgenstern, 1944/1956] J. von Neumann and O. Morgenstern. *Theory of Games and Economic Behavior*, Princeton: Princeton University Press, 1944/1956.
[Weintraub, 2002] E. R. Weintraub. *How Economics Became a Mathematical Science*, Durham NC and London: Duke University Press, 2002.
[Woodward, 1989] J. Woodward. Data and phenomena, *Synthese* 79: 393-472, 1989.

# GEOGRAPHICAL ECONOMICS AND ITS NEIGHBOURS — FORCES TOWARDS AND AGAINST UNIFICATION

Caterina Marchionni

## 1 INTRODUCTION

The neglect of spatial issues in economics has been "one of the great puzzles about the historical development of economics" [Blaug, 1996, p. 612]. Economic activity clearly does not take place in the proverbial head of a pin: space and distance do affect economic activity in a non-trivial way. Aimed at ending the long silence of the economics discipline on the spatial economy, a new approach developed at the beginning of the 1990s. Almost by accident, Paul Krugman, at that time already well known for his contribution to new trade theory, noticed that a small modification to his new trade models would allow the endogenous derivation of spatial agglomeration: the New Economic Geography was set off. Later, partly as a reaction to the complaints of "economic geographers proper" [Martin, 1999], the New Economic Geography became also known as geographical economics [GeoEcon, henceforth], a label that more clearly underscores its disciplinary origin. Today, GeoEcon is a well-established field of economics [Fujita *et al.*, 1999; Fujita and Thisse, 2002; Brakman *et al.*, 2001; Baldwin *et al.*, 2003].[1] GeoEcon appears to have successfully brought geography back into economics.

Why did GeoEcon succeed in bringing spatial issues to the attention of mainstream economics? A complete answer to this question possibly requires appeal to a wide range of institutional, social and historical factors. Allowing a certain degree of simplification, however, the GeoEcon adherence to the scientific and methodological standards that are most cherished by economists appears to explain a great deal of its success. According to its proponents, GeoEcon's contribution, vis-à-vis extant theories dealing with the spatial distribution of economic activity, is twofold. First, GeoEcon shows that similar economic mechanisms are at work in bringing about a host of phenomena that were previously studied by separate disciplines. In doing so, it addresses Ohlin's call [1933] for the unification of trade theory and location theory. Second, GeoEcon is the only field within

[1] In 2008 Paul Krugman was awarded the Nobel Prize in Economics "for his analysis of trade patterns and location of economic activity." The Nobel Prize press release can be found at: `http://nobelprize.org/nobel_prizes/economics/laureates/2008/press.html`

Handbook of the Philosophy of Science. Volume 13: Philosophy of Economics.
Volume editor: Uskali Mäki. General editors: Dov M. Gabbay, Paul Thagard and John Woods.

economics that provides a micro-foundation in a general equilibrium framework for the spatial distribution of economic activity. Both contributions satisfy widely held scientific ideals of economists: the desire for unified theories and the search for micro-foundations.

On the face of it one would expect economists and social scientists concerned with spatial/geographical issues to have welcomed the GeoEcon appearance. Reactions have been rather mixed instead. Urban and regional economists and regional scientists claim that the theoretical ideas on which GeoEcon models rest are not new; they have just been dressed up differently. Economic geographers charge GeoEcon of several flaws: it is just another instance of imperialism on the part of economics; it subscribes to positivist ideals, which geographers rejected long ago; its models are overly unrealistic, and therefore incapable of explaining relevant aspects of real-world spatial phenomena.

In this Chapter, I examine topics arising in the context of GeoEcon and its neighbors that are of interest from a philosophy of economics perspective, namely explanatory unification; theoretical unification and inter-field integration; economics imperialism; and theoretical models, their unrealistic assumptions and their explanatory power. Two main themes run through the Chapter and knit the various topics together. The first theme concerns the web of inter- and intra- disciplinary relations in the domain at the intersection of economics and geography that have been affected by GeoEcon. The second theme concerns the role played by the pursuit of unification and the search for micro-foundations both as drivers of the GeoEcon theoretical development and as vehicles through which inter- and intra-disciplinary relations have been affected. The investigation of these themes reveals the co-existence of two sets of forces, forces towards and against unification, none of which succeeds to fully prevail over the other.

In dealing with these issues I follow recent trends in the philosophy of science and economics that appreciate the importance of looking at actual scientific practice as a means to supply a salient philosophy of economics. Although the value of general philosophical views is undeniable, the practical import of philosophy of economics is at its best when it delves into particular episodes and their specific contextual problems. In this Chapter, I show how philosophical ideas could help resolve the concrete problems faced by economists and their neighboring social scientists.

## 2 GEOGRAPHICAL ECONOMICS AND ITS NEIGHBOURS

GeoEcon seeks to explain the phenomena of spatial agglomeration and spatial dispersion as they occur at different spatial scales. The concept of agglomeration refers to seemingly very distinct empirical phenomena: the existence of the core-periphery structure corresponding to the North-South dualism; regional disparities within countries; the existence of cities and systems of cities, which are sometimes specialized in a small number of industries; industry clusters such as Silicon Valley; and finally the presence of commercial districts within cities such as Soho in London. Although each type of agglomeration could be the result of different types of agglomeration economies, geographical economists hypothesize that these apparently distinct phenomena are at least partly the result of similar mechanisms, viz. "economic mechanisms yielding agglomeration by relying on the trade-off between various forms of increasing returns and different types of mobility costs" [Fujita and Thisse, 2002, p. 1].

GeoEcon's approach to spatial issues rests on two building blocks: the presence of increasing returns at the firm level and transportation/trade costs. Increasing returns at the firm level requires dropping the assumption of perfect competition and replacing it with that of imperfect competition, which in GeoEcon is modeled according to the Dixit-Stiglitz [1977] monopolistic competition framework. At the aggregate level, increasing returns and transportation costs give rise to pecuniary externalities, or market size effects. Pecuniary externalities are transmitted through the market via price effects and, simply put, their presence implies that the more firms and workers there are in a locality, the more the locality becomes attractive as a location for further firms and workers. This creates a cumulative process whose end result might be that all economic activity turns out to be concentrated in one location. While pecuniary externalities are forces that push towards the concentration of economic activity (agglomerating or centripetal forces), the presence of immobile factors, of congestion and the like, push towards dispersion (dispersing or centrifugal forces). The models are characterized by the presence of multiple equilibria: whether or not, and where, agglomeration arises depends on the relative strength of those forces and on initial conditions, that is, on previous locational decisions. The cumulative nature of the process of agglomeration is such that a small advantage of one location due to locational chance events in the past can have snowball effects which turn that location into the centre of economic activity, even though this outcome might not be the optimal one.

The domain of phenomena GeoEcon claims as its own was not *terra incognita.* There are a number of fields both within economics and without, whose domains overlap with that of GeoEcon: urban and regional economics, trade theory and growth theory within economics, and regional science and economic geography outside economics (see Figure 1).

| | **Within economics** | **Outside Economics** |
|---|---|---|
| **Spatial fields** | Urban & regional economics | Regional science<br>Economic Geography |
| **A-spatial fields** | Trade Theory<br>Growth theory | |

Figure 1. GeoEcon's neighbouring fields

Trade and growth theory are important and well-known bodies of work in economics. I will have more to say about them and their relation to GeoEcon in Section 4. For now it suffices to note that GeoEcon is perceived to have succeeded where others have failed: GeoEcon introduced spatial considerations in these traditionally a-spatial fields. Urban and regional economics deal instead with spatial and geographical questions (at the level of cities and regions respectively) but traditionally they have been somewhat marginal to the mainstream of economics.[2] Although a number of urban and regional economists have generally downplayed the importance of the GeoEcon's novel contributions, the general attitude has been one of acceptance; some of the recent contributions to the GeoEcon literature come from urban and regional economists. What is known as *location theory* constitutes the main overlap between urban and regional economics on the one hand and GeoEcon on the other hand. Location theory is a strand of thought whose origin traces back to the works of von Thünen, Christaller, Weber and Lösch, and refers to the modeling of the determinants and consequences of the locational decisions of economic agents. Location theory, trade theory and growth theory are the theories that GeoEcon purports to unify (Section 4 below discusses this aspect).

Outside economics, regional science and economic geography lay claim on substantial parts of the domain of GeoEcon. At the beginning of the 1950s Walter Isard established regional science as a field of inquiry that studies, with a scientific approach, social and economic phenomena with regional or spatial dimensions [Isard, 1975]. Influenced by the philosophy of science dominant at that time, the scientific approach was equated with the search for laws of universal applicability and with a strong emphasis on quantitative approaches. Regional science was thought of as an interdisciplinary field, bringing together economists, geographers, regional planners, engineers etc, and its ultimate aim was to provide a unified theory of spatial phenomena. Although regional science never reached the status of an institutionalized discipline, and failed in its unifying ambitions, the field is still alive today. Location theory is one of the principal themes that fall within the purview of regional science (see for example [Isserman, 2001]), and thus it is the area where urban and regional economics, regional science, and GeoEcon mostly overlap (see Figure 2).

Finally, economic geography is a relatively recent subfield of human geography. In the 1950s many regional scientists came from human geography, which at that time had left behind its characteristic ideographic approach to embrace the sci-

[2] Urban and regional economics are separate sub-fields, but since the boundaries are hard to delineate, for simplicity I treat them as one field. It is also somewhat artificial to treat regional science as a separate field vis-à-vis urban and regional economics. Some claim that works in location theory should be regarded as regional science and that GeoEcon itself is a branch of regional science (see for example [Martin, 1999]). As I will mention below, the overlaps between urban and regional economics, regional science and GeoEcon are extensive. This makes it hard and presumably pointless to identify a given contribution as belonging to urban & regional economics, to regional science or to GeoEcon. Nevertheless, there are non-empty sets that belong to one but not to the others. Treating them as distinct fields captures the perception of scholars declaring the affiliation to one or the other.

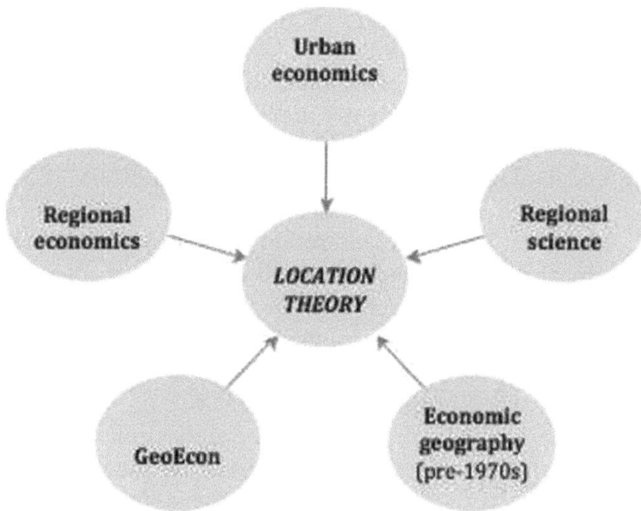


Figure 2. The area of overlap between spatial fields.
Location theory, the modeling of the determinants and consequences of the locational decisions of economic agents, constitutes the theoretical common ground between regional and urban economics, GeoEcon, regional science, and economic geography mostly before its critical turn in the 1970s.

entific ideals on which regional science was founded. In the span of twenty years, however, there was a fracture between the two fields that still lasts to these days. Geography went through its 'critical' turn, mainly inspired by Marxist ideas, and rejected altogether the philosophical and methodological commitments of regional science. The hostility towards abstract mathematical modeling based on maximization and equilibrium still characterizes contemporary economic geography. Economic geographer Allen Scott [2004, p. 483] lists, among others, an empirical turn, an interpretative turn, a normative turn, a cultural turn, a policy turn, and a relational turn that the field of economic geography undertook in recent years. Today the field is very rich both in its scope and methods. It is nevertheless common to characterize economic geography in terms of a special emphasis on the complexity of empirical reality, on place rather space, on concepts like contingency and specificity, and at the level of method, in terms of an extensive use of case studies and a discursive style of theorizing.[3] It is therefore not surprising that the harsher criticisms of GeoEcon came from economic geography ([Martin, 1999] provides a wide ranging and influential critique of GeoEcon.) Some of these criticisms will be taken up in the following sections. But first let us examine GeoEcon and its unificationist features.

[3]See [Scott, 2000] for an overview of the first half-century of economic geography.

## 3 EXPLANATORY UNIFICATION[4]

Explanatory unification broadly corresponds to the idea of 'explaining much by little', which is then cashed out differently in different proposals. The philosophical literature has almost exclusively focused on unification in the natural sciences, mainly physics and biology (exceptions are [Kincaid, 1997; Mäki, 1990; 2001]). And yet, unification is a widely held ideal shaping theoretical development in economics too. GeoEcon embraces this ideal: the unification of phenomena and theories is taken to be one of its principal contributions. Since unification in science is not a uniform phenomenon, much is to be learned about it from the way it takes place and drives theoretical development in actual practice. In what follows, guided by extant philosophical views on unification I offer a characterization of what unification amounts to in the case of GeoEcon.

I begin by distinguishing between explanatory unification and theoretical unification. Explanatory unification occurs at the level of phenomena, and it is a matter of explaining with the same, or fewer, explanantia several classes of explanandum phenomena. Theoretical unification instead occurs at the level of theories: it is a matter of unifying previously separate theories by means of a theory that possesses all (or most) of their explanatory content. In standard models of unification there is no room for such a distinction. What counts as a class of phenomena is defined by a theory, so that a theory that successfully unifies two classes of phenomena (the unifying theory) also unifies the respective theories (the unified theories). For instance, Maxwell's theory unified electromagnetism and optics by showing that electromagnetic waves and light waves were one and the same thing; similarly, Newton's theory unified Galileo's laws of terrestrial mechanics and Kepler's laws for celestial bodies by showing that the motions of celestial and terrestrial bodies could be explained by the law of universal gravitation. If the unifying theory is believed to be true (or more approximately true), then it just replaces the unified ones. The paradigmatic cases of unification in the history of science have often accomplished unification at both levels. The distinction between explanatory unification and theoretical unification nonetheless proves useful when examining actual social scientific practice where more mundane unifications take place.

The possibility of decoupling unification of phenomena and of theories arises from considerations of the following sort. Scientific theories differ on the basis of what they theoretically isolate as doing the explaining and as in need of explanation, and involve various degrees of abstraction and idealization [Mäki, 1992]. This also holds for theories that unify. Their isolations and idealizations however are likely to be different from those involved in the unified ones. Each theory, both the unifying and the unified ones, may then prove useful for different explanatory, predictive or heuristic purposes. Since social scientific theories often account for more than one aspect of a given phenomenon, a unifying theory might account for only a subset of the phenomena that the unified ones taken together explain.

[4]This section is based on work carried out jointly with Uskali Mäki (see [Mäki and Marchionni, 2010].

It can be argued that this only applies to non-genuine unifications, or at least to unifications that have not yet reached their full potential. In principle, the unifying theory, if it is truly unificatory, could be refined and extended so as to account for all the phenomena the previously separate theories accounted for. For my purposes, however, the 'in principle' issue can be left aside, so as to focus on the 'in practice' achievement of GeoEcon at the level of phenomena (this section) and at the level of theories and fields (next section).

The standard exposition of explanatory unification is Philip Kitcher's [1981; 1989]. According to Kitcher [1989, p. 432], "science advances our understanding of nature by showing us how to derive descriptions of many phenomena, using the same patterns of derivation again and again, and, in demonstrating this, it teaches us how to reduce the number of types of facts we have to accept as ultimate (or brute)." In his view, to explain is to unify, and unification (and explanation) is a matter of inference and derivation. Unification proceeds via reducing the number of argument patterns while maximizing the number of explanandum sentences that can be derived. Kitcher's account of unification seems particularly well suited to characterize theoretical development in economics (see [Mäki, 2001; Lehtinen and Kuorikoski, 2007b]). Economists do not use the vocabulary of 'argument pattern', or 'pattern of derivation'; in their stead they talk about 'models', 'derivations', 'theorems' and 'conclusions'. What we see in economics is that specific models are construed using a general type of model as template, and then derivations are performed within the model in terms of its inferential resources. This is in line with Kitcher's own view that a general argument pattern can be embodied in a "general model type". Unification in economics can then be seen to proceed via the application of a small number of similar model types to an ever-increasing number of economic and non-economic phenomena.

The way in which the GeoEcon unification has proceeded can also be largely captured by Kitcher's account of unification. In Mäki and Marchionni [2009], we identify two model types that have so far effected the unification of different classes of phenomena and we supply a rough schematization of them as general argument patterns. These are the *core-periphery* model (set out in [Krugman, 1991]; henceforth CP model) and the *vertical linkages* model (set out in [Krugman and Venables, 1996]; henceforth VL model). Both model types rest on the Dixit-Stiglitz monopolistic competition framework with transportation costs, and derive the agglomeration of economic activity between two a priori identical locations. The difference between the two types lies in the foundation they postulate for the agglomeration mechanism. In the CP model, the size of the market in each location is determined by the migration decisions of workers: a larger market is a more attractive location for firms and through a reduction in the price of the goods also for workers. In the VL model, workers are immobile, and market size is made endogenous through the presence of input-output linkages between firms: the more firms in a location, the larger the market for upstream firms and the lower the costs for downstream firms. These model types are then filled in with specific variables to explain diverse classes of agglomeration phenomena. For instance, the general model type includes the abstract term 'location.' In each instantiation of the general argument pattern, 'location' is to be replaced with 'zones within a metropolitan area', 'regions in a country', or 'regions involving more than one country.'[5] (See [Mäki and Marchionni, 2009] for a full characterization of the argument patterns.)

In spite of the fact that Kitcher's provides a good fitting model for the GeoEcon unification, it is still possible to keep, contra Kitcher, unification separate from both derivation and explanation. That is, we can ask the following questions: (1) Is GeoEcon unification achieved merely by way of deriving large numbers of explananda from a small set of patterns of derivation, or is it also a matter of revealing a shared ontology? (2) Is it the unifying component of the theory that yields explanation and understanding of the phenomena, or is it some other property of it? Geographical economists' view and practice will supply the answers to these questions.

## *3.1 A shared ontology?*

To address the first question I introduce two distinctions, which will help to characterize the kind of unification GeoEcon pursues and what it entails regarding unity among the phenomena. The first is Uskali Mäki's distinction between explanatory unification of the derivational kind and explanatory unification of the ontological kind [1990; 2001], and the second is Margaret Morrison's distinction between synthetic and reductive unification.

Derivational unification is a matter of deriving large classes of explanandum sentences from a parsimonious set of premises, theoretical structures or inferential patterns. Ontological unification instead is a matter of redescribing a large number of apparently independent phenomena as forms or manifestations of a common system of entities, capacities, or causes, thus revealing an underlying ontic unity between apparently diverse phenomena. Kitcher's account is a variant of derivational unification, for it is an explicit attempt to cash out a notion of unification detached from the metaphysics of causation. Mäki [2001] however points out that although in some cases all that unification amounts to is derivation, in many cases derivational and ontological unification can go together. A theory might be conceived as unifying in virtue of unraveling the real unity among the phenomena, which is achieved by way of applying the same pattern of derivation to the explanation of diverse phenomena. In particular, Mäki [2001] provides some evidence that in economics unification often manifests itself as derivational unification with ontological grounding. The idea of a derivational unification with ontological grounding comes close to Salmon's suggestion [1984] that the causal-mechanical and the unification views of explanation can be reconciled if scientific unity is seen as a product of delineating "pervasive causal mechanisms."[6] Skipper

[5]The VL model is thought to be more appropriate for explaining international trade where the mobility of workers is indeed lower than at the national level.

[6]Salmon [1994] put forth the view that sometimes the same phenomenon can be explained in

[1999] expands on Salmon's suggestion and proposes that on a causal-mechanical view of explanation, explanations that unify empirical phenomena proceed via the application of schematized causal mechanisms, what he calls "mechanism schema".

The analysis of GeoEcon shows that the kind of unity pursued has to do with different phenomena being governed by similar kinds of economic mechanisms [Marchionni, 2004; Mäki and Marchionni, 2009]. If this interpretation is correct, then it makes sense to see GeoEcon unification as the successive application of a mechanism schema to different kinds of agglomeration phenomena. In other words, the CP and the VL model types are not merely two similar patterns of derivation. What the CP and the VL model types lay down and successive applications retain are schematized causal mechanisms, which are fleshed out according to the specifics of each explanandum phenomenon.

The second distinction concerns more specifically the kind of unity that a given unification entails at the level of the phenomena. Reductive unity is established when two phenomena are identified as being of the same kind (e.g. electromagnetic and optical processes; [Morrison, 2000, p. 5]). Synthetic unification instead involves the integration of two separate processes or phenomena under one theory (e.g. the unification of electromagnetism and weak force; Ibid: 5). Both reductive and synthetic unifications might be merely a logical or formal achievement; in Morrison's view, the mere product of mathematical formalism. When the unifications involve more than that, however, the kind of implications regarding unity of the phenomena are different. Whereas reductive unification implies a reduction of one type of entities or processes to entities or processes of another type, synthetic unification can reveal the phenomena to be interconnected (Ibid: 177).[7] Put it otherwise, there are two kinds of unity between the phenomena, "unity as singleness" and "unity as interconnectedness" [Hacking, 1996]. Provided that they are more than just formal achievements, reductive unifications entail singleness at the level of phenomena whereas synthetic unifications entail interconnectedness.

The GeoEcon unification is not a matter of reducing one type of phenomena to another for say cities are not shown to be one and the same as industry clusters. What binds the phenomena together and permits their treatment under a unified framework is the presence of a set of common causal mechanisms, and the kind of unity at the level of the phenomena that GeoEcon entails is therefore one of interconnectedness. The unification of phenomena is not just a derivational achievement: GeoEcon applies the same mechanism schemata over and over again to explain diverse agglomeration phenomena, and by so doing it hopes to capture

two different and complementary ways, the causal-mechanical and the unificationist. This view differs from the one advanced in Salmon [1984] because the latter admits that explanation by unification can sometimes proceed independently of the delineation of pervasive causal mechanisms. In the GeoEcon case, however, unification does appear to be derivative from the description of underlying causal mechanisms.

[7]For example, in the case of Maxwell's reductive unification of magnetic and optical phenomena, light waves are shown to be just electromagnetic waves. On the other hand, Einstein's synthetic unification of electricity and magnetism reveals their "interconnectedness." Regarding electric and magnetic fields, Morrison claims that they can be isolated in a frame-dependent way, and hence are not in essence the same entity [2000, p. 179].

the ontic interconnectedness that binds these phenomena together.

## *3.2 What yields explanation?*

The second question I posed above concerns whether what makes GeoEcon explanatory is its unifying power, or some other component or feature of the theory. Answering this question is not straightforward. Scientists might not be aware that their causal and explanatory judgments are derivative from judgments about unifying power. This has roughly been Kitcher's reply to the criticism that in actual scientific practice causal talk is pervasive and often independent of unification. If Kitcher were right, actual scientific practice would be a poor arbiter to adjudicate between the primacy of unification vis-à-vis causation and vice versa. In conformity to the stand I take throughout this Chapter, however, I take seriously actual scientific practice. In this context, this means examining what geographical economists claim about explanation and identify what feature of the theory they regard as doing the explanatory work.

In economics, the widespread view is that a phenomenon is not genuinely explained if it cannot be derived from well-defined microeconomic parameters. This is roughly what is generally referred to as the thesis of methodological individualism. At the level of practice, this translates into the search for micro-foundations for theories about aggregates. GeoEcon fully embraces the economists' view of what constitutes genuine explanation. To see this, it is instructive to look at geographical economists' discussions of some of their predecessors.

A well-known theory whose origin traces back to Christaller and Lösch explains the existence of hierarchical systems of cities in terms of their efficiency in the provision of goods and services. Different locations enjoy different degrees of centrality, and places with higher locational centrality will not only offer the goods that less central places offer, but also those that the latter do not provide. The classical exposition of the theory is graphical and depicts cities as hexagons of different sizes. According to GeoEcon, central place theory is a "descriptive story, or an exercise in geometry" and not "a causal model" [Brakman *et al.*, 2001, [p . 32]; see also [Fujita *et al.*, 1999, p. 27]. The problem, so the argument goes, is that the equilibrium outcome, the hierarchy of cities, is not derived from the underlying behavior of consumers and firms. Recent regional science models seek to give central place theory a theoretical economic foundation, but still fail to deal with individual firms or consumers, so that the "central outcome is merely rationalized and *not explained* from the underlying behavior of consumers and producers, nor from their decisions and (market) interactions" [Brakman *et al.*, 2001, p. 32, my emphasis]. GeoEcon at last provides an explanation for hierarchical systems of cities by deriving them from microeconomic considerations. In a similar vein, theories that rely on technological externalities and knowledge spillovers, which are common in urban economics and economic geography, are criticized for failing to genuinely explain agglomeration. The problem with technological externalities is again that their emergence cannot be derived from the behavior of economic agents; they are a black box (see [Fujita *et al.*, 1999, p. 4]. The following quote exposes this idea quite nicely:

> The main thrust of the new geography literature has been to get inside that particular black box and derive the self-reinforcing character of spatial concentration form more fundamental considerations. The point is not just that positing agglomeration economies seems a bit like assuming one's conclusion; as a sarcastic physicist remarked after hearing one presentation on increasing returns, "So you are telling us that agglomerations form because of agglomeration economies." The larger point is that by modeling the sources of increasing returns to spatial concentration, we can learn something about how and when these returns may change, and then explore how the economy's behavior change with them. [Fujita *et al.*, 1999, p. 4]

If, as it seems, genuine explanation in GeoEcon has to do with the presence of micro-foundations, then having brought diverse phenomena under the same unified framework is not what makes the theory genuinely explanatory. And this is so, even though it is the search of micro-foundations that has helped to reveal that different classes of phenomena are governed by the same basic principles. For GeoEcon, unification is magnificent but it is not explanation (to paraphrase the title of Halonen and Hintikka's article [1999]).

In addition, Morrison [2000] notices that in many cases of unification, not only unification is different from explanation, but also explanatory power and unifying power trade off against each other:

> The more general the hypothesis one begins with, the more instances or particulars it can, in principle, account for, thereby "unifying" the phenomena under one single law or concept. However, the more general the concept or law, the fewer the details one can infer about the phenomena. Hence, the less likely it will be able to explain why particular phenomena behave as they do. If even part of the practice of giving explanation involves describing how and why particular processes occur — something that frequently requires that we know specific details about the phenomena in question—then the case for separating unification and explanation becomes not just desirable but imperative. [Morrison, 2000, p. 20]

In her view, unification typically involves less explanatory power because it occurs via a process of abstraction. More abstract and general laws may unify, but they have less explanatory power because they neglect details specific to the phenomena they are applied to. In order to explain diverse phenomena, the GeoEcon mechanism needs to be stripped down to its bare essentials. Geographical economists seem to be aware of this:

> By using highly stylized models, which no doubt neglect a lot of specifics about urban/regional/international phenomena, geographical economics

> is able to show that the same mechanisms are at work at different levels of spatial aggregation ... In order to lay the foundations for a unified approach, there is a price to be paid in terms of a neglect of institutional and geographical details... [Brakman *et al.*, 2001, p. 323]

The above quote suggests that the GeoEcon unification could not be achieved without neglecting institutional and geographical details of different classes of agglomeration phenomena. When the theory is used to explain and understand particular aspects of specific phenomena, it is indeed not the unifying mechanism alone that bears the explanatory burden, but the specific 'details' too.[8] Even so, the claim that there is a trade off between unifying power and explanatory power needs to be qualified. First, more details about the causal history of a phenomenon do not necessarily mean a better explanation. Morrison avoids committing herself to a particular view on explanation, but doing so deprives her argument of the capacity to discriminate those causal details that are explanatory from those that are not. (Mäki and Marchionni [2009] discuss this in more detail.) Second, even if one holds that explanation is not tantamount to unification, one can still maintain that the unifying power of a theory constitutes one dimension on which its explanatory power can be assessed. I will have more to say about this in Section 6.3. Now, I turn to the discussion of the kind of unification that GeoEcon achieves at the level of theories and fields within economics.

## 4 INTRA-DISCIPLINARY UNIFICATION OF LOCATION, TRADE AND GROWTH

GeoEcon has been celebrated because it promises to unify the phenomena of location, trade and growth, previously studied by separate theories, thereby paving the way for the unification of location, trade and growth theories. The development of GeoEcon is closely tied to that of contemporary theories of trade and growth in the context of the "increasing returns revolution" or "second monopolistic revolution" in economics [Brakman and Heijdra, 2004]. GeoEcon is said to be the "fourth wave of the increasing returns revolution in economics" [Fujita *et al.*, 1999, p. 3]. The revolution consists in shifting away from the constant returns to scale-perfect competition paradigm that dominated the discipline until the 1970s and 1980s to increasingly adopt the increasing returns-imperfect competition framework. Appreciating the way in which the increasing revolution has unfolded and led to GeoEcon is important in order to identify the main characteristics of the GeoEcon theoretical unification.

In what follows I briefly introduce the increasing returns revolution in economics, and the role played in it by a particular mathematical model, namely the

[8]Kitcher's account of explanatory unification does not necessarily deny this. When an argument pattern is instantiated, details specific to the explanandum to be derived are filled in. Within a unifying theory, there is not just one argument pattern but a few similar ones, which serve to explain diverse kinds of phenomena.

Dixit-Stiglitz model of monopolistic competition (D-S model henceforth). The D-S model is not only what made the increasing returns revolution successful, but also what made GeoEcon and its unificatory ambitions possible. Next, I examine the kind of unification GeoEcon achieves at the level of theories and fields of research in economics. What the discussion shows is that theoretical unification is a much more complex and heterogeneous phenomenon than it is often assumed, and that models of integration between fields might be better suited than models of theoretical unification in characterizing the relation between GeoEcon and its neighbors within economics. This also constitutes the first opportunity to observe a tension between forces towards and against unification.

## *4.1 The fourth wave of the increasing returns revolution in economics*

The first monopolistic competition revolution was triggered by the works of Chamberlin [1933] and Robinson [1933], but its impact on mainstream economics has been rather small. Johnson [1967] writes that

> ... what is required at this stage [viz. after Chamberlin and Robinson's work on monopolistic competition] is to convert the theory from an analysis of the static equilibrium conditions of a monopolistically competitive industry... into an operationally relevant analytical tool capable of facilitating the quantification of those aspects of real-life competition so elegantly comprehended and analysed by Chamberlin but excluded by assumption from the mainstream of contemporary trade theory. [Johnson, 1967, p. 218]

For many economists the D-S model provides precisely that "operationally relevant analytical tool." Its workability and analytical flexibility allows its application to a number of different areas of inquiry. Although the D-S model was originally conceived as a contribution to the literature on product differentiation, it was later applied to phenomena of international trade, growth, development and geography, all of which are taken to be the result of the presence of increasing returns. These new applications resulted in the development of "new trade theory" [Krugman, 1979; Dixit and Norman, 1980], "new growth theory" [Romer, 1987; Lucas, 1988; Grossman and Helpman, 1991] and GeoEcon. The impact of the "second monopolistic competition revolution" has therefore been much greater than that of its predecessor.

The application of the D-S model to phenomena of growth and trade largely follows a similar path. In both cases, the neoclassical variant was incapable of addressing some stylized facts and the presence of increasing returns was regarded as a possible explanation. Krugman describes the situation of trade theory around the 1970s as "a collection of highly disparate and messy approaches, standing both in contrast and in opposition to the impressive unity and clarity of the constant-returns, perfect competition trade theory" [Krugman, 1995, p. 1244]. It was thanks to the introduction of the D-S model that theories of growth and trade phenomena based on increasing returns became serious alternatives to the neoclassical ones. The result has been the development of new growth and new trade theory, which were treated as complementary to their neoclassical predecessors and in fact were later integrated with the latter.

The new trade theory enjoys a special role in the path towards unification of GeoEcon. In a sense, GeoEcon has developed out of a sequence of progressive extensions of new trade theory models. Witness the role of Paul Krugman as founding father of both new trade theory and GeoEcon. As observed by a commentator, "in stressing the relevance to regional issues of models derived from trade theory, Krugman has not so much created a new-subfield as extended the applicability of an old one" [Neary, 2001, p. 28]. Krugman [1979] shares with GeoEcon the presence of increasing returns and the D-S monopolistic competition framework, but it does not include transportation costs, an essential ingredient of the GeoEcon models. Krugman [1980], still a new trade theory model, includes transportation costs and differences in market size: together these assumptions imply that a country will produce those varieties for which the home demand is higher (market-size effect). In both Krugman [1979] and Krugman [1980] the distribution of economic activity is assumed to be even and fixed (agglomeration therefore cannot emerge). In a later work, Krugman and Venables [1990], uneven distribution of economic activity is introduced and thereby agglomeration can be shown to emerge. Yet, firms and factors of production are assumed to be immobile across countries, and differences in market size are given, not determined by the locational choices of the agents. It is the inclusion of factor mobility, which in turn endogenously determines market size, which generates the first GeoEcon model, namely Krugman [1991].

GeoEcon appears to provide a unified framework for the study of trade and location phenomena. Recent modeling efforts have also been made to integrate growth into the spatial models of GeoEcon. That geography is relevant for economic growth was clear before GeoEcon, and new growth models do allow for agglomeration of economic activity. Yet, differently from GeoEcon, "the role of location does not follow from the model itself and ... it is stipulated either theoretically or empirically that a country's rate of technological progress depends on the location of that country" [Brakman *et al.*, 2001 , p. 52]. Instead, GeoEcon models of growth aim to make the role of geography endogenous.[9] Not only is GeoEcon one of the fields partaking in the increasing returns revolution, but it can also be seen as its culmination, as it holds out the promise to unify the most prominent theories engendered by the revolution.

[9]Baldwin and Forslid [2000] combines GeoEcon core model with a dynamic framework of inter-temporal optimization to explain increases in output per capita and seems able to account for a larger number of stylised facts about growth. Fujita and Thisse [2002] extends the Baldwin and Forslid model. A new agglomerating force is added to the core model by way of modelling an R&D sector that creates positive spillovers, which are stronger when the sector is concentrated in one location. The model predicts full agglomeration of the R&D sector and partial agglomeration of manufacturing activity and the mutual reinforcement of growth and agglomeration.

## *4.2 Theoretical unification and inter-field integration*

In 1933, Bertil Ohlin, a well-known international trade theorist, claimed that the separation between international trade theory and location theory was artificial: "International trade theory cannot be understood except in relation to and as part of the general location theory, to which the lack of mobility of goods and factors has equal relevance" (p. 142). Ohlin's idea was that by allowing varying degrees of factor mobility and transportation costs, the difference between international trade, trade between regions within a country, or trade at the local level would be revealed to be just a matter of degree [Meardon, 2002, p. 221]. This unified theory of trade at different levels of geographical aggregation would naturally be a part of a general theory of the location of economic activity. Ohlin however was unable to accomplish the desired unification. As reported by Meardon [2002], the reason lied in the general equilibrium framework Ohlin was committed to. Within that framework, lacking any form of increasing returns, the introduction of factor mobility would lead to the equalization of the prices of factors, which was inconsistent with the empirical fact of persistent factor prices inequality. In 1979, Ohlin wrote:

> ... no one has yet made a serious attempt to build a general location theory and introduce national borders and their effects as modifications in order to illuminate international economic relations and their development by a method other than conventional trade theory. (Ohlin [1979, p. 6], quoted in [Meardon, 2002, p. 223]).

Only twelve years later, Paul Krugman [1991] published the seminal GeoEcon model. Thanks to the advancement in modeling techniques, Ohlin's dream of a general theory of the location of economic activity within which trade and growth phenomena find their proper place might be on the way to its realization.

On the standard view of theoretical unification, GeoEcon, the unifying theory, would eventually replace international and location theory, and possibly also growth theory. The reason is clear enough. If GeoEcon had all the explanatory content of the separate theories, then the disunified theories would just be redundant. They could be retained for heuristic purposes, but from the point of view of explanation, they would be superfluous. Unifications in actual scientific practice however do not always satisfy this model. If the GeoEcon explanatory content only overlaps with and does not fully cover that of the disunified theories, then dispensing with the latter amounts to leave unexplained some of the stylized facts that were previously accounted for. In such situations, what we are left with is a plurality of partially overlapping theories. To generalize, we can think of theoretical unification as occurring in degrees, and distinguish complete from partial unifications. When the unifying theory does not explain some of the phenomena explained by the disunified theories, then we have a partial unification. When the unifying theory can account for all the phenomena that the disunified theories could separately account for, then the unification is complete (the unifying theory could also explain facts that none of the disunified theories explains).

At least thus far, the unification in GeoEcon is at best partial: There are a number of stylized facts about location, trade and growth that GeoEcon alone cannot account for. One of the reasons is that the distinct identity of GeoEcon lies in its focus on a certain kind of economic mechanisms (pecuniary externalities), which is believed to operate in bringing about diverse classes of phenomena. But there are other mechanisms and forces specific to each class that are not part of the GeoEcon theory. The relative importance of the alternative mechanisms and forces will vary so that whereas for certain stylized facts the GeoEcon mechanism will be more important than the specific ones, in other cases the reverse will be true. Economists in fact perceive growth theory (in both its neoclassical and new variant), trade theory (again in both variants), location theory and GeoEcon as complementary. This appears to be a relatively common feature: newer theories do not always replace old ones but they often live side by side and are deployed for different explanatory and predictive purposes. In our case, the different theories postulate different kinds of economic mechanisms as being responsible for their respective phenomena. Dispensing with one theory would amount to dispensing with one kind of mechanism and one possible explanation. Depending on the phenomenon we are interested in, a different mechanism or a different combination of mechanisms acting together will be relevant. This is where the complementarity between the different theories emerges. In principle, it could be possible that further developments in GeoEcon and neighboring fields will provide a general theory that tells us when, how and which combinations of mechanisms operate in bringing about the phenomena. But as things now stand we have no reason to believe so. What we now have is a plurality of overlapping, interlocking theories in different subfields, which GeoEcon has contributed to render more coherent and integrated.

So far I have focused on relations between theories. Now I take fields as the unit of analysis. It has been noted that standard models of inter-theoretic relations, including models of theoretical unification, do a poor job in depicting actual scientific practice and the tendencies towards unity therein. In their place, models of inter- or cross-field integration have been proposed as more appropriate. Integration between fields can occur via a number of routes, of which the unification of theories is just one. Darden and Maull [1977, p. 4] characterize a field as follows:

> A central problem, a domain consisting of items taken to be facts related to that problem, general explanatory facts and goals providing expectations as to how the problem is to be solved, techniques and methods, and sometimes, but not always, concepts, laws and theories which are related to the problem and which attempt to realize the explanatory goals.

In Darden and Maull's original account, integration takes place via the development of inter-field theories, that is, theories that set out and explain the relations between fields. Their model was mainly put forward to account for vertical relations. The concept of inter-field integration however can be easily extended to apply to horizontally-related fields. Since theories are just one of the elements comprising a field, theoretical unification as well as reduction is seen as a local affair that rarely, if ever, culminates in the abandonment of one field in favor of the one where the unifying theory was originally proposed. What happens instead is that new theories that integrate insights from different fields are developed; in some cases, new fields are engendered, but never at the expense of existing ones. The crucial insight of Darden and Maull's account is to look at how fields become increasingly integrated through the development of theories that explain the relation between them.

In our case, the developments made possible by the D-S model of monopolistic competition have further increased the degree of integration between several fields in economics. The D-S model constituted a powerful vehicle of integration: the same framework/technique was employed with the appropriate modifications in different fields of economics, and for precisely the same purpose, namely to deal with increasing returns at the firm level and imperfect competition. In this perspective, GeoEcon can be looked upon as a new field, or less ambitiously as an interfield theory, which studies the relations between the phenomena of location, trade, and growth partly drawing on insights developed in separate fields. This explains why the fields continue to proceed autonomously in spite of the introduction of new unifying theories. This discussion also brings to the fore what can be thought of as opposing forces towards and against unity: on the one hand, the unifying ambitions of GeoEcon push towards various degrees of unification of phenomena, theories and fields, on the other, the presence of theories whose domains only partially overlap with that of GeoEcon and of fields that continue to proceed at least partly autonomously resist the unificationist attempts.

## 5 INTER-DISCIPLINARY UNIFICATION: ECONOMICS IMPERIALISM[10]

Abrahamsen [1987] identifies three kinds of relations between neighboring disciplines: (1) Boundary maintaining, where the two disciplines pursue their inquiries independently with no or little contact with one another; (2) Boundary breaking, where a theory developed in one discipline is extended across the disciplinary boundaries; and (3) Boundary bridging, where the two disciplines collaborate rather than compete for the same territory. The relationship between economics and geography had traditionally been one of boundary maintaining. Things have changed however with the appearance of GeoEcon. Geographers have perceived GeoEcon as an attempt to invade their own territory. For instance, economic geographers Ron Martin and Peter Sunley [2001, p. 157] confidently claim that "Fine (1999) talks of an economic imperialism colonizing the social sciences more generally, and this is certainly the case as far as the 'new economic geography'

[10]This section is largely based on work carried out jointly with Uskali Mäki (see our paper 'Is geographical economics a form of intellectual imperialism?').

is concerned."[11] GeoEcon, it is said, has broken the disciplinary boundaries, and has done so unilaterally.

Economics is notorious for its repeated attempts at colonizing the domain of neighboring disciplines. Economics-style models and principles are used to study marital choices, drug addiction, voting behavior, crime, and war, affecting disciplines such as sociology, anthropology, law and political science. The phenomenon of economics imperialism has received a great deal of attention among social scientists: while some celebrate it unconditionally, others despise it. Few philosophers of economics however have entered the debate. This is unfortunate because philosophers have something to contribute in evaluating the benefits and risks of episodes where disciplinary boundaries are broken. This is what the analysis that follows aims to accomplish. If GeoEcon constitutes an instance of economics imperialism, we should ask whether it is to be blamed or celebrated. In other words, the key issue is whether this episode of boundary breaking is beneficial or detrimental to scientific progress.

In a series of recent papers Uskali Mäki [2001; 2009, and Mäki and Marchionni, 2011] has sought to provide a general framework for appraising economics imperialism. The point of departure of Mäki's framework is to see scientific imperialism as a matter of expanding the explanatory scope of a scientific theory. This aspect of scientific imperialism he calls imperialism of scope. Imperialism of scope can be seen as a manifestation of the general ideal of explanatory unification. If we think of scientists as seeking to increase a theory's degree of unification by way of applying it to new types of phenomena, it is largely a matter of social and historical contingency whether these phenomena are studied by disciplines other than those where the theory was originally proposed. It follows that whether scope expansion turns into scientific imperialism is also a matter of social and historical contingency. A given instance of imperialism of scope promotes scientific progress only if it meets three kinds of constraints: ontological, epistemological and pragmatic. The ontological constraint can be reformulated as a methodological precept: unification in theory should be taken as far as there is unity in the world. The epistemological constraint has to do with the difficulties of theory testing and the radical epistemic uncertainty that characterizes the social sciences. Caution is therefore to be recommended when embracing a theory and rejecting its alternatives. Finally, the pragmatic constraint pertains to the assessment of the practical significance of the phenomena that a theory unifies.

GeoEcon's foray into the field of economic geography can be seen as a consequence of its pursuit of unification of location and trade phenomena. That some of these phenomena fall within the purview of economic geography should not constitute a problem. It is however doubtful that GeoEcon satisfactorily meets the three sets of constraints outlined above. The development of GeoEcon is motivated by considerations of unity among the phenomena (as discussed in the previous section), but the empirical performance of GeoEcon has not yet been determined and

[11] Fine [2006] regards GeoEcon as a manifestation of a new virulent wave of economics imperialism.

the practical significance of the insights it provides has been questioned (see [Mäki and Marchionni, 2009]).

Rather than being a peculiarity of GeoEcon, it is quite difficult for any economic or social theory to meet those constraints. The consequence is that although per se imperialism of scope is not harmful, it ought not be praised unconditionally, but carefully evaluated. This is more so given that in most cases the forays of economics into neighboring territories implicate other aspects of interdisciplinary relations. Imperialism of scope is in fact often accompanied by what Mäki [2007] calls imperialism of style and imperialism of standing. Imperialism of standing is a matter of academic status and political standing as well as societal and policy relevance: the growth in the standing of one discipline comes at the expense of that of another. Imperialism of style has to do with the transference or imposition onto other disciplines of conceptions and practices concerning what is regarded as genuinely scientific and what is not, what is viewed as more and what as less rigorous reasoning, and what is presented to be of higher or lower scientific status. As John Dupré [1994, p. 380] puts it, "scientific accounts are seldom offered as one tiny puzzle: such a modest picture is unlikely to attract graduate students, research grants, Nobel prizes, or invitations to appear on Night Line." It is in these circumstances that economics imperialism is likely to trigger the hostile reactions of the practitioners of the colonized disciplines.

A significant component of the worries of economic geographers concerns the standing of GeoEcon and economics more generally vis-à-vis economic geography. The danger, as they perceive it, is that GeoEcon might end up enjoying increasing policy influence just in virtue of the higher standing of economics, and not in virtue of the empirical support it has gained as a theory of spatial phenomena. Similarly, the alleged 'scientificity' of economics could give GeoEcon an extra edge in the academic competition, so that the GeoEcon general equilibrium models might end up colonizing economic geography entirely at the expense of the latter's varied theoretical and methodological commitments.

In the cases Abrahamsen [1987] examines, boundary breaking is typically followed by boundary bridging, namely by the mutual exchange of results and methods. In the case of GeoEcon and economic geography, a number of concrete attempts have been made to bridge the boundaries between economists and geographers. Notable initiatives have been the publication of *The Oxford Handbook of Economic Geography* [Clark *et al.*, 2000], and the launch of the *Journal of Economic Geography*, platforms explicitly designed to foster cross-fertilization. On the other hand, judged on the basis of patterns of cross-references in leading journals for economic geographers and geographical economists, mutual ignorance seems to remain the prevalent attitude between scholars of the two fields [Duranton and Rodríguez-Pose, 2005]. The presence of these contrasting tendencies makes it hard to predict whether effective bridging of boundaries will take place.

What does this discussion teach economic geographers and geographical economists? That is, how does philosophy help in resolving this heated debate and direct it through more progressive paths? There are two general lessons that are worth taking stock of. The first is that there is nothing inherently problematic in attempting to extend the scope of a theory outside its traditional domain. Disciplinary boundaries are the product of institutional and historical developments, and often have little to do with 'carving nature at the joints'. GeoEcon is thus given a chance. It is still possible that the spatial phenomena GeoEcon unifies are not in reality so unified, or that the range and significance of the explanatory and practical questions GeoEcon can meet is very limited. All this however has to be established empirically, and not ruled out a priori. Second, GeoEcon and its supporters are recommended to adopt a cautious and modest attitude. If what is exported outside the disciplinary boundaries is not so much a theory, but an allegedly superior research style and/or the higher standing of a discipline, the connection of scientific imperialism to the progress of science is remote at best. The mechanisms sustaining and reinforcing these aspects of the imperialistic endeavor can tip the balance in favor of theories whose empirical support is poor at best. As things stand now, it is not at all clear that there is any warrant for the superiority of GeoEcon vis-à-vis alternative theories in the existing domain of spatial phenomena. The worries voiced by economic geographers are therefore to be taken seriously. Here again we can see at work forces towards as well as forces against unification. On the one hand, GeoEcon pursuit of unification generates pressures on disciplinary boundaries, on the other, economic geographers have refused to accept GeoEcon, and in spite of attempts at bridging the boundaries, the two fields continue to proceed in mutual ignorance of each other's work.

## 6 UNREALISTIC ASSUMPTIONS, IDEALIZATIONS AND EXPLANATORY POWER

Economic geographers also complain that the highly stylized unrealistic models of GeoEcon cannot capture the complexity of real-world spatial and geographical phenomena, and hence cannot provide explanation and understanding of those phenomena. Although in some cases particular unrealistic assumptions are blamed, some geographers argue against the practice of theoretical model building altogether.

The role, function and structure of theoretical models in science are topics of wide philosophical interest.[12] Despite disagreements on several aspects of scientific modeling, recent philosophical literature appears to converge on the view that unrealistic models, in the social sciences and economics too, play a variety of important heuristic and epistemic functions. Here I organize the discussion around two themes that specifically arise in the context of GeoEcon models and their reception in neighboring disciplines. One concerns the problem of false assumptions in theoretical models, and the other has to do with the kind of explanations theoretical models can afford. I draw on recent philosophical literature to pro-

[12]The literature is quite vast, and a number of excellent reviews are available. Frigg and Hartman [2006] provide a nice overview of recent philosophy of science literature on the topic.

vide a qualified defense of the GeoEcon theoretical models against the criticisms that geographers have leveled against them. It is important however to bear in mind that nothing in what follows implies the truth of the GeoEcon's explanation, let alone its superiority vis-à-vis theories of economic geographers. This is an empirical issue and the empirical evidence gathered so far does neither support nor reject GeoEcon. The defense of GeoEcon has thus to be read in terms of a *potential* to generate explanations of real-world spatial phenomena. The lesson, which I take to be generalizable to analogous disputes, is that there is nothing inherently problematic with explaining the world via unrealistic theoretical models, and the parties in the dispute do better to focus on the empirical and practical performance of genuinely competing theories than on the wholesale rejection of each other's methodologies.

## *6.1 Galilean idealizations and causal backgrounds*

Disputes over the unrealisticness of models and their assumptions abound in economics and neighboring disciplines. These disputes often centre on the question of whether a given model (or a set of models) is realistic enough to explain the real-world phenomena it is supposed to represent. Economic geographers have forcefully complained that the GeoEcon models contain too many unrealistic assumptions. More pointedly, GeoEcon is held to ignore the role of technological or knowledge spillovers, to treat space as neutral and assume identical locations, to pay too little attention to the problem of spatial contingency, and to overlook the possibility that different mechanisms might be at work at different spatial scales. Critics of economics, including some geographers, typically depict economists as subscribing to the Friedmanian idea that unrealistic assumptions do not matter as long as the models yield accurate predictions, and hence typically interpret the economists' models instrumentally.[13]

Philosophers of economics have made it clear that such characterizations do a poor job in depicting the practice of model building in economics. The presence of unrealistic assumptions per se does not pose problems for a realistic interpretation of the models. Instead, it is precisely thanks to the presence of these unrealistic assumptions that models are capable to tell us something about the real world (see [Cartwright, 1989; Mäki, 1992]). One way to take this idea across is to compare theoretical models to controlled experiments [Mäki, 2005; Morgan, 2002]. Both controlled experiments and theoretical models isolate a causal mechanism by way of eliminating the effects of those factors that are presumed to interfere with its working. Whereas experiments do so by material isolations, theoretical models employ theoretical isolations [Mäki, 1992]. Theoretical isolations are effected by means of idealizations, that is, assumptions through which the effect of interfering factors is neutralized. Following McMullin [1985], let's call this species of assumptions Galilean idealizations in analogy to Galileo's method of experimentation.

[13]Marchionni [2004] shows that Paul Krugman and most geographical economists adopt a realist attitude towards their theory.

Not every unrealistic assumption is of this kind, however (see for example [Mäki, 2000; Hindriks, 2006]). A substantial portion of unrealistic assumptions of economic models is made just for mathematical tractability. Since the problems of and justifications for the latter kind of assumptions deserves a discussion of their own I will come back to them below. First I would like to spend a few words on Galilean idealizations and illustrate their role in GeoEcon models.

Both controlled experiments and theoretical models are means to acquire causal knowledge. They typically do so by inquiring into how changes in the set of causal factors and/or the mechanism that is isolated change the outcome [Woodward, 2003]. Because of this feature, contrastive accounts of explanation [Garfinkel, 1980; Lipton, 1990; Woodward, 2003; Ylikoski, 2007] fit the way in which both models and laboratory experiments are used to obtain causal and explanatory knowledge. Briefly, contrastivity has it that our causal statements and explanations have a contrastive structure of the following form: $p$ rather than $q$ because of $m$.[14] This implies that the typically long and complex causal nexus behind $p$ is irrelevant except for that portion of it that discriminates between $p$ and $\neg q$, what I referred to as $m$. The whole causal nexus except $m$ constitutes the *causal background*, which is *shared* by the fact and the foil.[15] As Lipton [1990] proposes, in order for a contrast to be sensible, the fact and the foil should have largely similar causal histories. What explains $p$ rather than $q$ is the causal difference between $p$ and $q$, which consists of the cause of $p$ and the absence of a corresponding event in the history of $\neg q$, where a corresponding event is something that would bear the same relation to $q$ as the cause of $p$ bears to $p$ [Lipton, 1990, p. 257]. In other words, to construe sensible contrasts we compare phenomena having similar causal histories or nexuses, and we explain those contrasts by citing the difference between them. It is the foil then that determines what belongs to the casual background. The choice of foils is partly pragmatic, but once the foil is picked out, what counts as the explanatory cause of $p$ rather than $q$ is objective.

In the case of theoretical models, the shared causal background is fixed by means of Galilean idealizations. That is, everything else that is part of the causal nexus of $p$ and $q$, except the explanatory factor or mechanism $m$ that we want to isolate, is made to belong to a shared causal background [Marchionni, 2006]. Once the shared causal background has been fixed via idealizations, the kind of causal and explanatory statements we can obtain from a given theoretical model becomes an objective matter. In other words, the kind of mechanism we want to isolate determines what idealizations are introduced in the model, which in turn determine the kind of contrastive questions the model can be used to explain. This means that the explanation afforded by theoretical models depends on the structure of the theoretical models themselves, that is, by what has been isolated

[14]It has recently been proposed that causation itself is contrastive (see for example [Schaffer, 2005]). Note however that here I take the contrastive theory as a theory of explanation, and not as a theory of causation. A contrastive theory of explanation is compatible with theories of causation other than the contrastive one.

[15]The foil $q$ can either be a single alternative or a list or class of alternatives. In the latter case, we talk about a contrast class.

as the explanatory mechanism and what has been idealized to generate the shared causal background.

To illustrate, consider the CP model of GeoEcon. The model focuses on the effects of the mechanism of pecuniary externalities on the emergence of a core periphery pattern. Its result is that the emergence of a core-periphery pattern depends on the level of transportation costs, economies of scale, and the share of manufacturing. As economic geographers have been ready to point out, the CP model ignores a host of determinants of real-world agglomeration. For instance, locations in the CP model are assumed to be identical, which is clearly false of the real world. Among other things, they differ in terms of first-nature geography such as resource endowments, climate, and geography. A full answer to the question of why manufacturing activity is concentrated in a few regions would include the causal role of first-nature geography (and much more, such as the effects of knowledge spillovers, thick labor markets, social and cultural institutions etc.). Geographical economists by contrast regard the assumption of identical locations as desirable: "One of the attractive features of the core model of geographical economics is the neutrality of space. Since, by construction, no location is preferred initially over other locations, agglomeration (a center-periphery structure) is not imposed but follows endogenously from the model" [Brakman *et al.*, 2001, p. 167]. By assuming identical locations, first-nature geography is fixed as causal background that is shared by the fact, agglomeration, and the foil, dispersion. Agglomeration (or dispersion) then results exclusively from the interactions of economic agents (second-nature geography).[16] The assumption of identical locations serves to create a shared causal background where the only difference in the causal nexuses of agglomeration and dispersion lies in the parameters that determine whether centrifugal or centripetal forces are stronger. The shared causal background determines the kind of explanatory questions the CP model can be used to answer. For example, it can explain agglomeration in either of two locations in contrast to uniform dispersion but not agglomeration in one location in contrast to agglomeration in another. To explain agglomeration in contrast to different foils, we must construe models that fix the shared causal background differently from the CP model and that allow us to see how the new isolated mechanism (or set of factors) explains the new contrastive explanandum.

In general the contrastive perspective on the role of unrealistic assumptions in theoretical models proves valuable for the following reasons. First, the affinity between theoretical models, causal knowledge and explanation comes out with significant clarity. The presence of a causal background is not a feature peculiar to theoretical models, but it is part and parcel of our causal and explanatory activities. It is common to all our causal and explanatory claims, independently of how they have been arrived at and how they are presented. Second, a contrastive perspective on theoretical models makes it easy to judge what a model can and cannot achieve in terms of potential explanation; misjudgments of explanatory power are

[16]GeoEcon models can be used to explain both why agglomeration rather than dispersion occurs as well as why dispersion rather than agglomeration occurs.

often due to misspecification of the contrast. One of the charges of economic geographers against the CP model is precisely that it cannot tell where agglomeration occurs. Here contrastivity helps to see why this charge is at once justified and misplaced. It is justified because in fact by assuming identical locations, GeoEcon cannot account for the contrast between agglomeration in one location rather than another. But it is also misguided because to investigate why agglomeration occurs in some locations and not in others requires the construction of a different causal background than the one featured in the CP model. Finally, contrastivity also sheds light on how and why relaxing assumptions that fix the causal background affect the kind of causal and explanatory claims a theoretical model can afford. In recent GeoEcon models, the original assumption of identical locations has been relaxed, thereby modifying the extension of the causal background. As a result, a new set of contrasts become potentially available for explanation within the GeoEcon framework. More complicated models can be seen as having narrower causal backgrounds, but we should not be misled by this into thinking that there is a continuous progression towards ever more realistic models. There is no such thing as a fully realistic model, and there is no causal or explanatory statement without a background causal field. I will have more to say about this aspect of theoretical models in Section 6.3.

## *6.2 Tractability and robustness*

Not all assumptions directly serve to theoretically isolate the mechanism of interest. Many assumptions of economic models are there to make the theoretical model tractable so as to obtain deductively valid results. Let's call them tractability assumptions (Hindriks 2006). Tractability assumptions are false, and the knowledge available at a given point in time does not say how they can be relaxed. Consider once more the CP model. A number of its assumptions are explicitly made in order to obtain a mathematically tractable model. Without them, no neat conclusion about causal and explanatory dependencies is forthcoming. For example, transportation costs in the CP model are assumed to be of the iceberg form, meaning that of each unit of the good shipped only a fraction of it arrives at destination. Tractability also determines the form of the utility and production functions. The CP model assumes constant elasticity of substitution, which is a very specific and unrealistic assumption to make. It is telling that geographical economists themselves refer to them as 'modeling tricks.' The unrealisticness of these assumptions is far more problematic than that of Galilean idealizations. The point is that at a given point in time there may be no way to substitute these assumptions with more realistic ones while keeping the rest exactly the same. In many cases, the most we can do is to construct models that include different sets of unrealistic assumptions. Cartwright [2007] claims that tractability assumptions provide the most reason for concern. But how do economists deal with them in practice?

They deal with them by checking the robustness of their modeling results with respect to changes in those modeling assumptions. Kuorikoski, Lehtinen and Marchionni [2010] propose to understand this practice as a form of robustness analysis, intended as Wimsatt [1981] does as a form of triangulation via independent means of determination (see also [Levins, 1966; Weisberg, 2006a]). On this view, the practice of economics of construing models where just one or a few assumptions are modified acquires a crucial epistemic role. The purpose of robustness analysis is in fact to increase the confidence about the reliability of a given result; in other words, that a result is robust across models with different sets of unrealistic assumptions increases the confidence that the result is not an artifact of a particular set of unrealistic assumptions. In addition, robustness analysis serves to assess the relative importance of various components of a model, or of a family of models.

Much of model refinement in GeoEcon can be seen as checking whether the main results of its core models (the CP and the VL models) are robust with respect to changes of unrealistic assumptions. Two main cases follow from this procedure. First, the results are found to be robust to different sets of unrealistic assumptions. For instance, models subsequent to the CP model find that the dependency between the level of transportation costs and agglomeration is robust to changes in specifications of functional forms and transport technology. This increases the confidence that the CP result does not crucially depend on particular false assumptions. Instead, it increases the confidence that the results depend on those elements that are common across models, that is, those elements that describe the isolated causal factors or mechanism. In GeoEcon, this is the mechanism of pecuniary externalities.

The second case is when the results of the model break down. One of the functions of robustness analysis is to help assess the relative importance of various components of the model. Thus, it is also employed to see how changes to the background causal field impact on the results of the model. In [Kuorikoski *et al.*, 2010] we discuss examples in which additional spatial costs are included in the model. If a different set of tractability assumptions yields a different result, then this can mean either of two things. It can indicate either that the particular assumption had implications for the causal background that were not recognized or that the results are artifacts of the specific modeling assumptions.

Obviously I do not want to claim that robustness analysis resolves all the epistemic difficulties that unrealistic theoretical models present us with, or that it solves all the difficulties of GeoEcon. For one, robustness analysis in GeoEcon displays conflicting results, which still needs to be reconciled. More generally, the number of unrealistic assumptions of economics models is very large, and many of these assumptions are rarely if ever checked for robustness. And even if that were done, the problem of determining the truth of a reliable result, which ought to be done empirically, would still remain.

## *6.3 The explanatory power of theoretical models*

Scientists and philosophers alike quite commonly talk about explanatory power as if it was a clear concept, but unfortunately it is not. Philosophical literature on this issue is quite scarce, and surprisingly so given the extensive use of ideas like explanatory power, explanatory depth and the like (much of what I discuss below are advancements of Marchionni [2006; 2008].[17] In clarifying the notion of explanatory power, either of two strategies can be adopted. The first is to advance a preferred account of what explanation is and to derive a notion of explanatory power from it. The second strategy is pluralistic and admits the presence of different dimensions of explanatory power that different explanations have to different degrees. I prefer this latter strategy because I believe it permits to illuminate more about the way in which scientists judge scientific theories and models. In different scientific contexts, different dimensions of explanatory power are valued more than others and this is why so many disagreements arise about the potential for explanation of models and theories. Adopting this somewhat pluralistic stance however does not mean to give up the idea that there is one particular feature that makes something an explanation. We can for instance adopt a contrastive theory of explanation and hold that adequate explanations are answers to contrastive why-questions that identify what makes a difference between the fact and its foils.

In what follows I do not pretend to offer a well-worked out theory of the dimensions of explanatory power, but rather wish to present together a few ideas that are scattered in the literature and can supply the building blocks of such a theory. In particular, I examine three dimensions of explanatory power: contrastive force, depth and breadth. Since theoretical models are the means whereby GeoEcon, and economists more generally, provide explanations, I will bring these dimensions to bear on features of theoretical models (but many of the observations I propose can easily be extended to theories).

The first dimension I consider is contrastive force. Contrastive force directly connects to the previous discussion on unrealistic assumptions, contrastive explanation and causal backgrounds. To my knowledge, Adam Morton [1990; 1993] has been the first to employ the idea of contrastive explanation to evaluate the potential explanatory power of theoretical models. Morton [1993] argues that false models have quite restricted *contrastive force*, in the sense that they address some contrastive questions about $p$ but not others. Morton's example is of a weather model, a barotropic model, which assumes wind velocity not to change with height. This model can be used to explain why the wind backs rather than veers (given suitable conditions), but cannot explain why the wind backs rather than dying away. The degree of contrastive force constitutes an obvious dimension on which to judge the explanatory power of theoretical models. Although false models in general can be expected to have very limited contrastive force, there is some room for variation (see also Marchionni 2006). As I show above, GeoEcon's exclusive focus on a certain kind of economic mechanisms (pecuniary externalities) limits

[17] Hitchcock and Woodward [2003] is a prominent exception to the generalized neglect of this issue. More recently, Kuorikoski and Ylikoski [2010] also seek to dissect the notion of explanatory power. A discussion of the differences between these and my account will have to wait for another occasion.

the range of contrastive questions about agglomeration it can address, as for example, it cannot tell where economic activity agglomerates or why firms agglomerate rather than join into a single larger firm.

*Explanatory breadth*, the second dimension of explanatory power I consider originates from the unification theory of explanation [Marchionni, 2008]. It has to do with unifying power: explanations that account for a large number of phenomena by appeal to the same or fewer explanantia are more explanatory. In order for a model to provide a unifying explanation of different phenomena, its explanantia will be described so as to abstract away from a host of details about specific phenomena and their particular instantiations. Although all theoretical models are general to some degree, they are likely to possess different degrees of explanatory breadth. Very abstract and stylized models can be applied to explain a wider range of phenomena. Using these models to explain fine-grained questions about particular occurrences, such as why a particular variable took the value it did rather than any other value, will certainly ensue in poor explanations. By contrast, models that incorporate a lot of information specific to the working of a mechanism in a particular situation have limited unifying power, but are better at answering fine-grained questions. Whether we want answers to coarse-grained or fine-grained questions depend on our interests and purposes. In turn our purposes and interests determine the amount of specific details included in a given theoretical model. The GeoEcon models possess a high degree of unifying power, but as seen above, the price to pay has been the neglect of details about specific phenomena. The explanatory power of the CP model might then fare good if we judge it in terms of the number and kinds of coarse-grained phenomena it can be used to explain, but it provides a very poor explanation of say why Silicon Valley developed when it did.

Finally, *explanatory depth* has to do with the requirement that explanations include a description of how $m$ brings about $p$ rather than $q$, that is, to include a description of the mechanism.[18] To illustrate, consider an explanation that clearly lacks depth. For example, to say that 'economic activity is agglomerated rather than dispersed because of agglomeration economies' is ostensibly a shallow explanation. The way in which depth is achieved varies from context to context because what counts as a description of a mechanism is itself context-dependent.[19] As we have seen above, for GeoEcon and economics more generally, deep explanations are those that explain the emergence of a phenomenon as the result of the interaction of consumers and firms. This provides the template for what a mechanism in economics should look like. Description of a mechanism is done by

[18]Hitchcock and Woodward [2003] provide an account of explanatory depth and distinguish it both from unifying power and amount of information. Yet the notion of explanatory depth is tied to a specific account of causation and explanation (the manipulability account) and takes depth as the only dimension of explanatory power.

[19]Achieving depth is often a matter of describing mechanisms whose component parts are at a lower level than the phenomenon to be explained. But it is not always so. Recent accounts of mechanistic explanations are for example [Bechtel and Richardson, 1993; Machamer *et al.*, 2000; Glennan, 1996].

way of building theoretical models that *analytically derive* the phenomenon from a well-defined set of micro-economic parameters. I emphasize 'analytical derivation' because economists are generally quite suspicious of derivations effected through simulations (cf. [Lehtinen and Kuorikoski, 2007a]). Early models of GeoEcon that relied on numerical methods to obtain equilibrium solutions were indeed seen with suspicion, and much effort has been put into building analytically solvable models. As the above discussion of the GeoEcon's contribution in terms of micro-foundations makes clear, on economists' standards of deep explanation GeoEcon fares quite good.

Regarding the relation between the various dimensions, it is important to dispel two possible sources of confusions. First, the depth of an explanation is sometimes equated with the amount of information about the causal nexus that is included. Irrespective of the amount of information, however, if nothing is said about how the explanatory factors are responsible for the explanandum, the explanation is shallow. Whereas deep explanations are typically more detailed than shallow ones, detailed explanations are not always deep. In the case of models whose main purpose is predictive accuracy, this can be seen clearly: they might be very detailed about the specifics of the phenomenon, but they will often provide shallow explanations or no explanation at all (see also [Weisberg, 2006b]). If we are clear that depth is not a consequence of the amount of details included in a model, then theoretical models that isolate a lot can fare very well in terms of depth. This clarification can be brought to bear on the dispute between economic geographers and geographical economists concerning the superiority of "discursive theorizing" vis-à-vis "mathematical modeling". To economic geographers, discursive theorizing "permits the construction of much richer maps or representations of reality" [Martin, 1999, p. 83]. Rich representations of reality might indeed allow us to address a wider range of contrastive questions, especially when we are interested in explaining particular occurrences. But the comparative advantage of theoretical models might lie precisely in the depth they can achieve. By their very nature, theoretical models render manifest how changing the explanatory factors changes the outcome. Although the mathematical requirements of theoretical modeling might constrain the degree of detail with which a mechanism is represented, changes in what is effectively included can be more clearly related to changes in the explanandum than it is possible with descriptions that include a lot of details.

The second clarification concerns the relation between depth and breadth. It is sometimes suggested that breadth has to be bought at the expense of depth, and vice versa. I think this is a misleading idea (I discuss it at some length in [Marchionni, 2008]).[20] Breadth is a matter of how unifying an explanatory account is. As some have claimed (e.g. [Morrison, 2000]), in order to increase unifying power and breadth, information specific to each class of phenomena or to each

[20] Recently Paul Thagard [2007] has claimed that a scientific theory is approximating the truth if it is increasing its explanatory coherence by way of explaining more phenomena (breadth) and by investigating layers of mechanisms (depth). Thus, he also appears to reject the view that breadth and depth trade off against each other.

instantiation of those phenomena is abstracted away. Information about specific phenomena however does not necessarily amount to depth. Explananda can be construed at various levels of grain and broad explanations will typically explain coarse-grained explananda. Broad explanations need not be shallow even when they are unsatisfactory as explanations of fine-grained explananda. In fact the GeoEcon case shows that breadth and depth can go together. The vehicle through which GeoEcon offers a unifying explanation of various agglomeration phenomena is the provision of micro-foundations, which is also what makes the explanation deep. We can think that enriching its models with information about psychological mechanisms could deepen further the GeoEcon explanation. Although I am not persuaded that economic theories necessarily improve their depth by including information about psychological mechanisms, I do think that their inclusion does not need to have any implication on the breadth of the GeoEcon explanation. An explanation that appeals to the psychological mechanisms underpinning the behavior of economic agents can be unifying as well if those mechanisms are described at an equally high level of abstraction.

The explanatory power of theoretical models can then be judged according to different dimensions. These dimensions will sometimes pull in different directions. When and how they do so ultimately depend on contextual factors such as the kind of phenomena explained, the types of forces that impinge on them, available modeling techniques, etc. Even so, I believe that these distinctions serve well in both diachronic and synchronic comparative assessments. Regarding different stages of development of a given theory, we can see what kind of improvement at the level of explanatory power has been achieved. I mentioned before how in GeoEcon relaxing some of the unrealistic assumptions that fix the causal background might translate into increased contrastive force.[21] Regarding different theories of the same phenomenon at a given point in time, Marchionni [2006] shows that a lack of clarity about the explanatory potential of the GeoEcon models and of the geographers' theories affects the dispute between them.

Considerations regarding explanatory power expose yet another aspect of this episode where opposing forces for and against unity can be thought to be at work. Although GeoEcon might score well both in terms of depth and unifying power, its contrastive force is rather limited. Since GeoEcon addresses only a limited number of questions about the spatial economy, alternative theories are often potential complements rather than competitors.

[21]In a recent account that builds on a contrastive theory of explanation, Hindriks [2008] interprets simplified models as explanatory engines. For instance, in Krugman [1991] either full agglomeration or uniform dispersion can result. The model functions as an explanatory engine by generating a series of models of increasing realisticness addressing the question, why is economic activity partially rather than fully clustered in a few locations? The process of relaxing unrealistic assumptions in successive models comes to be seen as a way of identifying what accounts for why economic activity is partially rather than fully agglomerated.

## 7 CONCLUDING REMARKS

Thanks to what are celebrated as its main contributions, namely a unified framework for the study of location, trade and growth phenomena explicitly built on micro-economic foundations, GeoEcon has finally succeeded to bring geography back into economics. Because the domain of phenomena GeoEcon claims as its own largely overlaps with fields both within and outside economics, its appearance has generated pressures on the status quo. These constitute the main themes that knit together the topics examined in this Chapter. These two threads have crossed each other at many junctures where two sets of opposing forces have been at work: those pushing towards higher degrees of unification and integration, and those pushing towards plurality. At some points and from certain perspectives, one set of forces might have appeared stronger than the other, but neither complete unification nor extreme disunity proved to be a stable equilibrium. Rather than being a peculiarity of GeoEcon and its neighbors, the coexistence of opposing forces for and against unity might be a characteristic of economics and of science in general. In these concluding remarks, I want to briefly sum up those junctures where the opposition between the two sets of forces showed up more clearly.

First, GeoEcon's unifying achievement at the level of theories and fields within economics is better characterized either as partial unification, or if we switch the focus from theories to fields, as a form of inter-field integration. There is no replacement of the old theories with the new one. What is involved instead is the development of a theory that allows integrating insights from different theories in different fields. It is a specific kind of integration, a piecemeal integration that follows the D-S model's application to different areas of inquiry within economics. GeoEcon can be seen as the culmination of this process of integration: it provides the location theory of urban and regional economists and of regional scientists with micro-economic foundations in a general equilibrium framework, and it brings geography to bear on the a-spatial theories of trade and growth.

Second, the phenomena of location, trade and growth are still the purview of a plurality of complementary theories in economics and outside it. The words of Alan Garfinkel, a champion of the contrastive theory of explanation, very well characterize inter-theoretic relations between GeoEcon and its neighbors

> Some of the theories may address different phenomena or different realms of phenomena. Some are genuinely competing, others can be reconciled with one another, while still others pass one another by, answering different questions. They fit together only in a very complicated and overlapping geometry". [1981, p. 1]

The contrastive approach to explanation goes some way into finding out this geometry, and does more than that. It makes clear why theories can rarely, if ever, explain all aspects of a given phenomenon but usually explain one sometimes quite narrow aspect of it, leaving room for a plurality of complementary theories of the same phenomenon, each answering different questions and serving different purposes.

Third, the GeoEcon's pursuit of unification of trade and location phenomena had the effect of breaking the boundaries between the disciplines of economics and geography. Rather than bringing geography into economics, it is economics that enters, uninvited, the field of human geography. It is here that GeoEcon has encountered the fiercest resistance: Economic geographers have rejected the standards of methods, evidence and explanation of mainstream economics that GeoEcon seems to force upon them. Today attempts at bridging boundaries between GeoEcon and economic geography coexist with the geographers' calls to arms to the effect of erecting even thicker boundaries.

Finally, we have seen that the fields that claim as their own the domain at the intersection of economics and geography overlap only partially. Where they do, often the boundaries are blurry and shifting. The point is that "questions of space and spatial relations" are "in practice open to appropriation by virtually any social science, given that space is intrinsically constitutive of all social science." [Scott, 2004, p. 481]. This explains both why the unificationist pretensions of GeoEcon (and previously of regional science) have arisen and why they have failed. GeoEcon has nevertheless yielded a higher degree of integration of fields within economics, and, to a less extent, more interaction at the boundaries with economic geography and regional science. If philosophers of science are right that plurality of independent but interacting ways of knowing is not only a feature of actual scientific practice, but also the feature of it that is more likely to lead to scientific progress (e.g. [Feyerabend, 1963; Longino, 1990; Solomon, 1994]), then the GeoEcon's entry in this populated domain might ultimately prove beneficial at least via this indirect root.

## ACKNOWLEDGEMENTS

Thanks to Jaakko Kuorikoski, Luis Mireles Flores and Julian Reiss for useful comments on earlier drafts. All remaining mistakes are obviously mine.

## BIBLIOGRAPHY

[Abrahamsen, 1987] A. Abrahamsen. Bridging boundaries versus breaking boundaries: psycholinguistics in perspective. *Synthese* 72, 355-388, 1987.

[Amin and Thrift, 2000] A. Amin and N. Thrift. What kind of economic theory for what kind of economic geography. *Antipode* 32 (1), 4-9, 2000.

[Baldwin and Forslid, 2000] R. E. Baldwin and R. Forslid. The core-periphery model and endogenous growth: stabilizing and destabilizing integration. *Economica* 67, 307-324, 2000.

[Baldwin *et al.*, 2003] R. Baldwin, R. Forslid, P. Martin, G. Ottaviano, and F. Robert-Nicoud. *Economic Geography and Public Policy.* Princeton University Press, 2003.

[Bechtel and Abrahamsen, 2005] W. Bechtel and A. A. Abrahamsen. Explanation: a mechanistic alternative. *Studies in the History and Philosophy of the Biological and Biomedical Sciences* 36, 421-441, 2005.

[Blaug, 1996] M. Blaug. *Economic Theory in Retrospect.* Cambridge: Cambridge University Press, $5^{th}$ ed, 1996.

[Brakman *et al.*, 2001] S. Brakman, H. Garretsen, and C. van Marrewijk. *An Introduction to Geographical Economics: Trade, Location and Growth.* Cambridge: Cambridge University Press, 2001.

[Brakman and Heijdra, 2004] S. Brakman and B. J. Heijdra. *The Monopolistic Competition Revolution in Retrospect.* Cambridge: Cambridge University Press, 2004.

[Cartwright, 2007] N. Cartwright. *Hunting Causes and Using Them.* Cambridge: Cambridge University Press, 2007.

[Chamberlin, 1933] E. H. Chamberlin. *The Theory of Monopolistic Competition.* Cambridge: Harvard University Press, 1933.

[Clark, 1998] G. L. Clark. Stylized facts and close dialogue: methodology in economic geography. *Annals of the Association of American Geographers* 88, 73-87, 1998.

[Clark *et al.*, 2000] G. L. Clark, M. Feldman, and M. Gertler, eds. *The Oxford Handbook of Economic Geography.* Oxford: Oxford University Press, 2000.

[Darden and Maull, 1977] L. Darden and N. Maull. Interfield theories. *Philosophy of Science* 43, 44-64, 1977.

[Dixit and Norman, 1980] A. K. Dixit and V. Norman. *Theory of International Trade.* Cambridge University Press: Cambridge, 1980.

[Dixit and Stiglitz, 1977] A. K. Dixit and J. E. Stiglitz. Monopolistic competition and optimum product diversity. *American Economic Review* 67, 297-308, 1977.

[Dupré, 1994] J. Dupré. Against scientific imperialism. *Proceedings of the Biennial Meeting of the Philosophy of Science Association* 2, 374-381, 1994.

[Duranton and Rodriguez-Pose, 2005] G. Duranton and A. Rodriguez-Pose. When economists and geographers collide, or the tale of the lions and the butterflies. *Environment and Planning A* 37, 1695-1705, 2005.

[Feyerabend, 1963] P. Feyerabend. How to be a good empiricist – a plea for tolerance in matters epistemological. In B. Baumrin, ed., *Philosophy of Science*, The Delaware Seminar, 2, 3-39m 1963.

[Fine, 1999] B. Fine. A question of economics: is it colonizing the social sciences? *Economy and Society* 28 (3), 403-425, 1999.

[Fine, 2006] B. Fine. Debating the 'new' imperialism. *Historical materialism* 14(4), 133-156, 2006.

[Frigg and Hartmann, 2006] R. Frigg and S. Hartmann. Models in science. *The Stanford Encyclopedia of Philosophy*, Edward N. Zalta (ed.). Online at `http://plato.stanford.edu/archives/spr2006/entries/models-science/`

[Fujita and Thisse, 2002] M. Fujita and J.-F. Thisse. *Economics of Agglomeration. Cities, Industrial Location and Regional Growth.* Cambridge: Cambridge University Press, 2002.

[Fujita *et al.*, 1999] M. Fujita, P. Krugman, and A. Venables. *The Spatial Economy. Cities, Regions and International Trade.* Cambridge Mass: MIT Press, 1999.

[Garfinkel, 1981] A. Garfinkel. *Forms of Explanation.* New Haven, Yale University Press, 1981.

[Glennan, 1996] S. Glennan. Mechanisms and the nature of causation. *Erknntnis* 44, 49-71, 1996.

[Grossman and Helpman, 1991] G. Grossman and E. Helpman. *Innovation and Growth in the Global Economy.* Cambridge: MIT Press, 1991.

[Hacking, 1996] I. Hacking. The disunities of the sciences. In P. Galison and D. Stamp, eds., *The Disunity of Science.* Stanford: Stanford University Press, 37-74, 1996.

[Halonen and Hintikka, 1999] I. Halonen and J. Hintikka. Unification – it is magnificent but is it explanation? *Synthese* 120, 27-47, 1999.

[Hindriks, 2006] F. Hindriks. Tractability assumptions and the Musgrave-Mäki typology. *Journal of Economic Methodology* 13 (4), 401-423, 2006.

[Hindriks, 2008] F. Hindriks. False models as explanatory engines. *Philosophy of the Social Sciences* 38, 334-360, 2008.

[Isrd, 1975] W. Isard. *An Introduction to Regional Science.* Englewood Cliffs, NJ: Prentice Hall, 1975.

[Isserman, 2001] A. Isserman. Regional science. *International Encyclopedia of the Social Sciences.* Amsterdam: Elsevier, 2001.

[Johnsn, 1967] H. G. Johnson. International trade theory and monopolistic competition theory. In R. E. Kuenne, ed., *Monopolistic Competition Theory: Studies in Impact.* John Wiley & Sons: New York, 203-218, 1967.

[Kincaid, 1997] H. Kincaid. *Individualism and the Unity of Science.* Lanham, MD: Rowman and Littlefield, 1997.

[Kitcher, 1981] P. Kitcher. Explanatory Unification. *Philosophy of Science* 48: 251-81, 1981.

[Kitcher, 1989] P. Kitcher. Explanatory unification and causal structure. *Minnesota Studies in the Philosophy of Science* 13, 410-505. Minneapolis: University of Minnesota Press, 1989.

[Krugman, 1979] P. Krugman. Increasing returns, monopolistic competition, and international trade. *Journal of International Economics* 9, 469-479, 1979.

[Krugman, 1980] P. Krugman. Scale economies, product differentiation, and the pattern of trade. *American Economic Review* 70, 950-959, 1980.

[Krugman, 1991] P. Krugman. Increasing returns and economic geography. *Journal of Political Economy* 99, 183-99, 1991.

[Krugman, 1995] P. Krugman. *Development, Geography and Economic Theory.* Cambridge and London: MIT Press, 1995.

[Krugman and Venables, 1990] P. Krugman and A. Venables. Integration and the competitiveness of peripheral industry. In C. Bliss and J. Braga de Macedo, eds., *Unity with Diversity in the European Economy.* Cambridge: Cambridge University Press, 56-75, 1990.

[Krugman and Venables, 1996] P. Krugman and A. Venables. Integration, specialization and adjustment. *European Economic Review* 40, 959-67, 1996.

[Kuorikoski and Ylikoski, 2010] J. Kuorikoski and P. Ylikoski. Dissecting explanatory power. *Philosophical Studies*, 148(2), 201–291, 2010.

[Kuorikoski *et al.*, 2010] J. Kuorikoski, A. Lehtinen, and C. Marchionni. Economic modelling as robustness analysis. Forthcoming in *British Journal for the Philosophy of Science*, 2010.

[Lehtinen and Kuorikoski, 2007a] A. Lehtinen and J. Kuorikoski. Computing the perfect model: why economists shun simulation? *Philosophy of Science* 74, 304-329, 2007.

[Lehtinen and Kuorikoski, 2007b] A. Lehtinen and J. Kuorikoski. Unrealistic assumptions in rational choice theory. *Philosophy of the Social Sciences* 37(2), 115-138, 2007.

[Levins, 1966] R. Levins. The strategy of model building in population biology. *American Scientist*, 45, 421–31, 1966.

[Lipton, 1990] P. Lipton. Contrastive explanations. In D. Knowles, ed., *Explanation and its Limits.* Cambridge University Press. Cambridge, 247-266, 1990.

[Longino, 1990] H. Longino. *Science as Social Knowledge: Values, Objectivity in Scientific Inquiry.* Princeton: Princeton University Press, 1990.

[Lucas, 1988] R. Lucas. On the mechanics of economic development. *Journal of Monetary Economics* 22 (1), 3-42, 1988.

[Machamer *et al.*, 2000] P. Machamer, L. Darden, and C. F. Craver. Thinking about mechanisms. *Philosophy of Science* 67, 1-25, 2000.

[Mäki, 1992] U. Mäki. On the method of isolation in economics. *Poznan Studies in the Philosophy of the Sciences and Humanities* 317-351, 1992.

[Mäki, 2000] U. Mäki. Kinds of assumptions and their truth. Shaking an untwisted F-twist. *Kyklos* 53(3), 303-22, 2000.

[Mäki, 2001] U. Mäki. Explanatory unification: double and doubtful. *Philosophy of the Social Sciences* 31(4), 488-506, 2001.

[Mäki, 2005] U. Mäki. Models are experiments, experiments are models. *Journal of Economic Methodology* 12(2), 303-315, 2005.

[Mäki, 2007] U. Mäki. Economics imperialism and scientific progress. *Unpublished manuscript*, 2007.

[Mäki, 2009] U. Mäki. Economics imperialism: concept and constraints. *Philosophy of the Social Sciences.* 39 (3), 351-380, 2009.

[Mäki and Marchionni, 2009] U. Mäki and C. Marchionni. On the structure of explanatory unification: the case of geographical economics. *Studies in History and Philosophy of Science* 40 (2), 185–195, 2009.

[Mäki and Marchionni, 2011] U. Mäki and C. Marchionni. Is geographical economics imperializing economic geography? *Journal of Economic Geography*, forthcoming, 2011.

[Marchionni, 2004] C. Marchionni. Geographical economics versus economic geography: towards a clarification of the dispute. *Environment and Planning A* 36, 1737-1753, 2004.

[Marchionni, 2006] C. Marchionni. Contrastive explanation and unrealistic models: The case of the new economic geography. *Journal of Economic Methodology* 13: 4, 425-446, 2006.

[Marchionni, 2008] C. Marchionni. Explanatory pluralism and complementarity: From autonomy to integration. *Philosophy of the Social Sciences* 38, 314-333, 2008.

[Martin, 1999] R. Martin. The 'new' geographical turn in economics: some critical reflections. *Cambridge Journal of Economics* 23, 65-91, 1999.

[Martin and Sunley, 2001] R. Martin and P. Sunley. Rethinking the 'economic' in economic geography: broadening our vision or losing our focus? *Antipode* 33(2), 148-161, 2001.

[McMullin, 1985] E. McMullin. Galilean idealization. *Studies in the History and Philosophy of Science* 16 (3), 247-273, 1985.

[Meardon, 2001] S. Meardon. Modeling agglomeration and dispersion in city and country: Gunnar Myrdal, Francois Perroux, and the new economic geography. *The American Journal of Economics and Sociology* 60 (1): 25-57, 2001.

[Meardon, 2002] S. Meardon. On the new economic geography and the progress of geographical economics. In S. Bohem *et al.* eds., *Is There Progress in Economics?*, Cheltenham: Edward Elgar, 217-39, 2002.

[Morgan, 2002] M. Morgan. Model experiments and models in experiments. In L. Magnani and N. Nersessian, eds., *Model-Based Reasoning: Science, Technology, Values.* New York: Kluwer Academy/Plenum, 41-58, 2002.

[Morrison, 2000] M. Morrison. *Unifying Scientific Theories. Physical Concepts and Mathematical Structures.* Cambridge: Cambridge University Press, 2000.

[Morton, 1990] A. Morton. Mathematical modeling and contrastive explanation. *Canadian Journal of Philosophy* Suppl. Vol. 16, 251-70, 1990.

[Morton, 1993] A. Morton. Mathematical models: questions of trustworthiness. *British Journal for the Philosophy of Science* 44(4), 659-674, 1993.

[Neary, 2001] J. P. Neary. On hypes and hyperbolas: introducing the new economic geography. *Journal of Economic Literature* 39, 536-561, 2001.

[Ohlin, 1933] B. Ohlin. *Interregional and International Trade.* Cambridge, Mass: Harvard University Press, 1933.

[Ohlin, 1979] B. Ohlin. Some insufficiencies in the theories of international economic relations. *Essays in International Finance*, 134, Princeton, Princeton University, 1979.

[Robinson, 1933] J. Robinson. *The Economics of Imperfect Competition.* London: MacMillan, 1933.

[Romer, 1987] P. M. Romer. Growth based on increasing returns due to specialization. *American Economic Review* 77 (2), 56-62, 1987.

[Salmon, 1984] W. Salmon. *Scientific Explanation and the Causal Structure of the World.* Princeton: Princeton University Press, 1984.

[Schaffer, 2005] J. Schaffer. Contrastive causation. *The Philosophical Review* 114 (3), 297-328, 2005.

[Scott, 2000] A. Scott. Economic geography: the great half-century. *Cambridge Journal of Economics* 24, 483-504, 2000.

[Scott, 2004] A. Scott. A perspective of economic geography. *Journal of Economic Geography* 4, 479-499, 2004.

[Skipper, 1999] R. Skipper. Selection and the extent of explanatory unification. *Philosophy of Science* 66, S196-S209, 1999.

[Solomon, 1994] M. Solomon. Social Empiricism. *Noûs* 28, 325-43, 1994.

[Thagard, 2007] P. Thagard. Coherence, truth, and the development of scientific knowledge. *Philosophy of Science* 74, 28-47, 2007.

[Weisberg, 2006] M. Weisberg. Forty years of the "The Strategy": Levins on model building and idealization. *Biology and Philosophy* 21 (5), 623-645, 2006.

[Weisberg, 2006a] M. Weisberg. Robustness analysis. *Philosophy of Science*, 73, 730–42, 2006.

[Wimsatt, 1981] W. Wimsatt. Robustness, reliability and overdetermination. In M. B. Brewer and B. E. Collins, eds., *Scientific Inquiry and the Social Sciences*, Jossey-Bass, San Francisco, 124-163, 1981.

[Woodard, 2003] J. Woodward. *Making Things Happen.* New York: Oxford University Press, 2003.

[Ylikoski, 2007] P. Ylikoski. The idea of contrastive explanandum. In J. Persson and P. Ylikoski, eds., *Rethinking Explanation*, Dordrecht: Springer, 27-42, 2007.

# THE *HOMO ECONOMICUS* CONCEPTION OF THE INDIVIDUAL: AN ONTOLOGICAL APPROACH

John B. Davis

This chapter discusses the *Homo economicus* conception of the individual in economics in its neoclassical formulation from an ontological point of view. Ontological analysis is a relatively recent area of investigation in the philosophy of economics with primary attention having been devoted to the issue of realism as a comprehensive theory of the world. However, if realism implies that the world is populated by real existents, a further issue that arises is how the existence of particular entities to be understood. Aristotle in the *Metaphysics* (1924; cf. [Ross, 1923]) originated this domain of investigation in connection with the theory of being as such which he conceived of as substance. In reaction to Plato's theory of forms that treated substances as universals, Aristotle treated substances as individual things — not the concrete things we perceive but things in their essential nature — and then advanced a 'principle of individuation' for marking off one kind individual substance from another in terms of differences in their forms. This chapter undertakes a related though different approach to explaining existents in economics by similarly setting forth a systematic basis for understanding and evaluating different conceptions of the individual economic agent as a real existent in economic theories. The approach is termed an identity criteria approach, and while only applied here to individual economic agents, it can also be applied to other types of existents in economics, including collections of individuals (such as families, firms, and governments), and states of affairs such as equilibria.

The chapter begins in Section 1 by distinguishing the ontological perspective from an epistemological one, and then proceeds in Section 2 to explain the former perspective in a systematic manner in terms of two separate existence or identity conditions that can be applied to explain the existence or identity of different kinds of things in economics. After brief discussion of how these identity conditions can be applied to different kinds of existents in economics, the chapter turns in Section 3 to its main focus: the existence of the individual in economics, and more specifically the existence of the individual as it is understood in the standard *Homo economicus* conception. This conception is evaluated using the two existence or identity conditions, and limitations in its characterization of individuals are set forth. One important thing we learn from this Section 3 investigation is that the more basic limitation of the standard *Homo economicus* conception concerns the problem of showing how individuals can be thought to be distinct and

Handbook of the Philosophy of Science. Volume 13: Philosophy of Economics.
Volume editor: Uskali Mäki. General editors: Dov M. Gabbay, Paul Thagard and John Woods.

independent from each other. This issue emerged in the literature in the 1970s in connection with the multiple selves problem, and has more recently re-appeared in the form of a closely related problem of explaining how individuals can have social identities. In Section 4, accordingly, this general subject comes in for more extended discussion in connection with the multiple selves problem. Two views of how the problem might be addressed are distinguished in this discussion. In Section 5, then, the multiple selves issue is re-approached in terms of the concept of social identity. The social identity concept creates difficulties for understanding individuals' distinctness and independence when individuals are strongly identified with social groups. The discussion in this Section begins with an examination of a set of precursor arguments in the standard literature on individuals and society which anticipates important issues in regard to social identity. Section 6 then turns to more recent work that focuses explicitly on individuals having (multiple) social identities, and reviews this literature in terms of the earlier multiple selves debate. Finally, Section 7 offers by way of a conclusion a look toward the future with a brief discussion of how the conception of the individual has changed from the traditional *Homo economicus* conception in new approaches to economics that have emerged since the 1980s.

## 1 EXISTENCE AS A CATEGORY OF INVESTIGATION

What is economics about? If we formulate this question as one that asks what *things* or *entities* concern us in economics, we suggest an ontological view of the question. Since ontology is about what exists, asking what things or entities economics is about is then a matter of asking what things or entities exist. But formulating our question ontologically in terms of existence does not guarantee that it will be investigated in an ontological manner. Often the response to the question about what things exist in economics is to provide definitions of things thought to exist. For example, one thing economics is thought to be about is *Homo economicus*, and *Homo economicus* is generally defined as a rational, 'self-interested' being. But definitions place conceptual boundaries on things rather than ontological boundaries on things, and consequently they tell us how to explain things rather than tell us how they may exist. That is, definitions provide epistemological characterizations of things. What, then, constitutes a specifically ontological characterization of a thing?

An ontological characterization of a thing, as indicated, needs to account for its existence. Suppose, then, that we look at the ontological task of accounting for the existence of things in a manner analogical to the epistemological task of defining them. Ideally, definitions give necessary and sufficient conditions for how a thing is characterized in an explanatory sense. Then an ontological characterization of a thing can also be said to give necessary and sufficient conditions for believing a thing exists. That is, we want to specify necessary and sufficient *existence conditions* for things in order to be able to say they exist. Existence conditions for things, moreover, may be understood to be those most basic conditions under which they may be said to endure or persist.

The idea of something enduring or persisting in turn involves two different conditions or dimensions of existence. First, it must endure as a single thing. Were something to endure but in the process also to become two things, the nature of its existence would be ambiguous, and we would not be able to say what exists. Aristotle thus asserted that what is true of being is true of unity. Thus one condition for being able to say something exists is that it maintain number or remain a single thing. In effect, the boundaries on the thing we wish to say exists must continue to distinguish that thing from other things. This may be termed an *individuation* condition for a thing's existence. Second, for a thing to endure and therefore exist as a thing it must also — in some sense to be determined — retain a single set of characteristics associated with its being that thing. Were something to endure but in the process change all its characteristics, we could only say that something exists but not what. Aristotle thus argued that the true nature of being also concerns that which is substantial and unchangeable. Thus, in addition to remaining one single thing, a thing that endures must also be in some way a single, selfsame thing. In contrast to the idea of boundaries that separate one single thing from another, in this instance we have the idea of boundaries on allowed change in the thing. This may be termed a *re-identification* condition for a thing's existence.

Thus the existence of things can be understood in terms of two existence conditions. Alternatively, the question of the existence of things can be assessed according to the application of two existence criteria. Or, the existence of things can be investigated by determining whether candidate existents pass two existence tests. Applying this framework to establish what things exists is then a matter of analyzing conceptions of things that are candidates for existence to determine whether those conceptions fulfill these two existence criteria formulated as existence tests. For example, should we ask whether *Homo economicus* exists, we would take the standard conception economists employ of *Homo economicus*, and evaluate it by analyzing this conception to determine whether it could be thought to pass the two existence tests.

In the discussion here, rather than use the term 'existence' when referring to these two existence conditions I use as an equivalent expression the term 'identity,' and speak of 'identity conditions,' 'identity criteria,' and 'identity tests,' in order to remain consistent with my previous usage [Davis, 2003]. Thus the existence of things is understood to be a matter of the identity of things. Nothing important turns on this change in terminology. Indeed there are advantages to using identity language rather than existence language in that the connotation of the former is readily associated with the issue of picking out *which* things exist in economics, as we commonly speak of identifying things when we are concerned with what exists.

## 2 WHAT EXISTS IN ECONOMICS?

What things or entities is economics about? There are many candidate existents, but the three things or entities most widely thought to exist in economics are individuals, collections of individuals such as families, firms, and governments, and equilibria. Note that these three things are quite different types of things. First, on the traditional view in economics dating back at least to the late nineteenth century marginalist Revolution, individuals exist as single persons. Indeed the *Homo economicus* conception is most closely associated with this type of individual. Second, families, firms, and governments exist as collections of persons. Often in economics such collections are treated as 'black boxes' so as to be more simply represented as single individuals. But there is also systematic analysis into what makes such collections single individuals. For example in the case of firms, there is a well-developed literature in economics that seeks to explain their existence in terms of the boundaries between them — thus how they count as single existents — and also literatures that investigate their persistence from birth to death — thus how they can be seen to be the selfsame firms across change in their activities and characteristics. Third, equilibria exist as states of affairs involving relations between individuals and collections of persons, as in supply-and-demand market equilibria and Nash equilibria in games. The long-standing concern in economics with the existence, uniqueness, and stability of equilibria investigates the conditions under which equilibria shown to exist are also single and distinct — the uniqueness question — and endure or persist — the stability question.

Put in terms of the two identity criteria set forth above, individuals, collections of individuals, and equilibria, though quite different kinds of existents, can all be investigated in terms of whether they may be individuated and re-identified as the kinds of things they are. Below I briefly outline how the two identity criteria operate in each case.

First, in the case of individuals seen as single persons in the standard *Homo economicus* conception, the individuation criterion comes into play when persons are said to be distinct and independent in virtue of each having his or her *own* preferences [Davis, 2003, pp. 47ff].[1] Having one's own preferences may be thought necessary and sufficient for demonstrating that single persons may be individuated as separate existents. It is necessary in that on the subjectivist understanding of individuals historically associated with this conception nothing else about them appears available for individuating them as single persons. It is sufficient in that it *prima facie* makes sense to say that one's own preferences could never belong to someone else. Second, the re-identification criterion comes into play in that on the standard view an individual's own preferences are said to be unchanging [Stigler and Becker, 1977], and unchanging preferences are argued to be necessary and sufficient for saying that persons can be re-identified as the selfsame individuals.

[1] Individuals' own preferences need not be unique to them for individuals to be distinct and independent. Two persons could have the same preferences, but those preferences still pick them out as distinct individuals in virtue of the relation of ownership.

They are necessary in that having one's own preferences, not only at a point in time but through time, is required for picking out the distinct person who is a candidate for re-identification across change. They are sufficient in that there being something unchanging about individuals directly provides a basis for saying individuals endure in terms of some single set of characteristics.

Second, in the case of the firm, a widely held view is that the individuation criterion comes into play when firms are said to be distinct and independent in virtue of patterns of transactions costs in the economy [Coase, 1937].[2] When transaction costs are low between individuals as compared to those associated with operating through the market, they rely on direct, non-market relationships by organizing themselves in firms, whereas when these transaction costs are high individuals rely on indirect, market-based relationships by trading across firms. Firms are thus distinct and independent in virtue of the market relationships that obtain between them, and also in virtue of the non-market relationships internal to them that constitute them as single things. In a world in which firms are defined as areas of (productive) economic activity where market relationships are absent, high levels of transaction costs associated with market relations (as compared to the costs of internal organization) are necessary and sufficient to individuate firms, because they function as the only boundaries there are between firms. The re-identification criterion comes into play in a related way. Firms can be regarded as the selfsame, re-identifiable firms if the pattern of transaction costs between them is sustained. But when those patterns change, firms may cease to exist and new firms may emerge.

Third, the framework in which equilibria conceptions are investigated in economics is that of existence, uniqueness, and stability. Whether equilibria exist is obviously an ontological concern, but whether they are unique and stable is not always immediately seen in this light. On the one hand, however, the question of the uniqueness of a given equilibrium is simply the question of whether that equilibrium can be shown to be single state of affairs distinct from other equilibrium states representing the same set of underlying economic activities. That is, if a particular set of economic activities is consistent with more than one equilibrium, neither is individuated with respect to that set of activities, violating the necessary and sufficient number requirement inherent in the idea of something enduring, namely, for something to endure it must do so as a single thing. On the other hand, the question of stability of a given equilibrium is simply the question of whether that equilibrium can be shown to endure as a single, selfsame state of affairs through a process of change. Generally whether equilibria are stable is thought of in terms of whether an economy can be shown to return to its equilibrium state after some disturbance that displaces it from that state. That an economy returns to its original, single equilibrium state, is a necessary and

[2]Here, since there are alternative views of what explains the existence of the firm, I put aside whether the transactions costs explanation of the firm in terms of individuation and reidentification criteria can be represented in terms of necessary and sufficient conditions.

sufficient condition for re-identifying it as the same state of affairs preceding the process of change operating upon it via those disturbing forces.

There are other candidate existents in economics that could also be examined within the identity conditions framework employed here. For example, economists have developed a variety of explanations of institutions, and these different conceptions could be compared and evaluated according to whether they succeed in showing that institutions thus understood are distinct and independent states of affairs that endure through change.[3] The example of institutions also suggests a related topic of investigation concerning what exists in economics, namely, how arguments for the existence of one type of thing or entity in economics bear on or are related to arguments for other types of things or entities in economics. Thus, since the particular conception of institutions in the 'new institutional economics' approach broadly explains institutions as resulting from the behavior of individuals, it can then be asked whether institutions exist independently or individuals. However, since the main focus of this chapter is the existence of the individual in economics, further attention to other candidate existents and issues such as this one is put aside in what follows.

## 3 THE *HOMO ECONOMICUS* CONCEPTION OF THE INDIVIDUAL

The *Homo economicus* conception of the individual has a long history in economics and consequently also a variety of interpretations. Indeed as a conception possessing a number of philosophical dimensions it has been the subject of extensive debate in economics and the social sciences for many years. The discussion here, however, isolates the main features of the microeconomics version of that conception that has been the workhorse in both theoretical and econometric research in the postwar period. This version of the *Homo economicus* conception is also a reasonably determinate one in that it has been standardized by means of its formal representation in terms of the idea of an individual utility function. While some economists dispute the utility function representation of the individual, the great majority of economists accept it. In any event, its formal representation offers the advantage of making the contents of the conception clear.

The principal feature of the utility function conception is its explanation of the individual in terms of preferences. Formally, the utility function has as arguments or independent variables various kinds of objects or characteristics of objects whose consumption increases utility. These objects can be market commodities, leisure, or things that individuals produce themselves using time and other resources, but the way in which these objects generate utility for individuals is a matter of what their preferences are over these objects or their characteristics. From psychological perspective, preferences are mental states, but in the revealed preference approach to choice that has been dominant in postwar economics this psychological side is

[3]An application of the identity conditions method of evaluating institutions' existence is [Dolfsma *et al.*, 2005].

de-emphasized.[4] In its place preferences have been given a logical characterization in terms of a set of axioms thought to apply to them and ensure that individual choice can be represented as rational. Applying these axiomatic conditions to preferences also makes it possible to say that an individual's preferences can be represented by a single utility function, which effectively singles the individual out as distinct and independent being, and one moreover that endures through time in virtue of the unchanging nature of those preferences. It is this utility function idea, then, that needs to be examined in explaining and evaluating the ontological account of individuals in the standard *Homo economicus* conception in economics.

Employing the two identity conditions or tests described above, consider first the individuation test that requires that for a thing to exist it must be shown to be a single thing separate and distinct from other things. On the understanding of *Homo economicus* just set out, the individual is represented as a single distinct thing in virtue of having a single utility function. But the unitary character of the utility function produced by the axiomatic representation of preferences does not preclude individuals having identical preferences. Thus that individuals can be argued to have but one utility function does not guarantee that it is unique to them, or show that individuals can be distinguished from one another as separate existents. To draw this stronger conclusion it must also be argued that each individual's utility function is in some way unique to that individual. The basis for this claim is that the preferences underlying the individual's utility function are unique to the individual, implying that the utility function representation of the individual is both unitary and unique. That is, that an individual's preferences are own preferences is the basis for individuating one person from another. Unfortunately, using own preferences to show uniqueness involves a circularity in reasoning whereby what is to be shown is presupposed. Thus by the individuation criterion the standard microeconomic conception of *Homo economicus* fails to provide a means of individuating persons as distinct existents.[5]

That the *Homo economicus* conception of the individual fails the individuation test makes it unnecessary to apply the second re-identification condition or test, because that test determines whether something already shown to be distinct and independent in some particular way can also be shown to be distinct and independent in that same way through a process of change, and this has in this case not been done. But it may be nonetheless be valuable in terms of understanding the ontological analysis of the individual to still apply the re-identification test to the *Homo economicus* conception, bracketing its failing the individuation test, in order to see what further can be learned about the preference basis for that conception when examining whether individuals thus understood might endure through a process of change. Here, then, we take one application of the conception that

[4]The originator of revealed preference theory, Paul Samuelson, recommended his approach as a means of removing the "vestigial traces of the utility concept" from economics [Samuelson, 1938, p. 61].

[5]In [Davis, 2003, pp. 53ff] this circularity problem is traced back to John Locke's attempted explanation of individual in terms of a memory criterion for personal identity. Locke's account was shown to be circular by Bishop Butler.

explicitly involves a process of change, namely, an individual's investment in human capital, and ask whether individuals assumed to be distinct and independent in terms of having their own preferences can be re-identified as such when making such investments.

Note that investments in human capital presuppose that individuals endure through change, because the investor expects to be the same individual who benefits from the investment. How, then, does investment in human capital affect the individual? A paradigmatic example in the economics literature is investment in music appreciation [Stigler and Becker, 1977].[6] Individuals invest in stocks of music listening capital by listening to and studying music, and these acquired stocks subsequently enhance their enjoyment or utility in further listening to and study of music. The standard view of this is that larger capital stocks lower the price of listening to music, and cause individuals to substitute towards higher consumption of music. But empirically in terms of observable behavior there is nothing to distinguish this interpretation from one that explains investments in listening to music as changing individuals' preferences for music vis-à-vis other types of consumption. Were this indeed the correct explanation, then individuals could not be re-identified in terms of a single set of own preferences (supposing that the meaning of 'own preferences' could be established in a non-circular manner), and thus could not be said to endure or persist through change thus understood. Thus, the standard *Homo economicus* conception of the individual is not shown to pass the second of the two identity test, though in this instance for a reason independent of its failure in the case of the individuation test, namely, that preferences cannot be shown to be unchanging.[7]

What, then, does this ontological analysis tell us? If we compare an epistemological analysis of the *Homo economicus* conception with an ontological one, we see that we learn quite different things about that conception. An epistemological analysis asks how we know that individuals defined as rational, 'self-interested' beings behave in such a way. But grounds for believing that they do can be both conceptual and empirical, and the availability of two types of epistemic criteria has historically meant that judgments regarding the satisfactoriness of the standard definition have received conflicting answers according to the different weights that can be placed upon the two criteria. Note, then, that this epistemological analysis is motivated at least in part by the idea that individuals thus defined are real existents.[8] Thus if being a rational, 'self-interested' being is further understood to include the utility function ideas discussed above, a prior concern with the standard conception becomes whether there are good reasons to suppose such beings exist. That is, we might ask whether we are entitled to suppose that a particular conception of the individual successfully refers to a real existent, where successful

[6]For a fuller treatment, see [Davis, 2003, pp. 55ff].

[7]A related problem is that acquiring music capital injects others' preferences into the individual's preference set. This problem concerns the individuation criterion directly, or the idea that preferences are own preferences.

[8]One might also be interested in the behavior of such beings in an ideal world, as elaborated in abstract axiomatic general equilibrium models.

reference involves successfully passing existence or identity tests as set out above. This is not to say that ontological analysis is always prior to epistemological analysis, but rather to emphasize that it is complementary to it. In philosophy of economics research until recently, however, ontological analysis has been largely neglected, and this argues for greater attention to what it offers both apart from and in combination with epistemological analysis.

## 4 THE PROBLEM OF MULTIPLE SELVES

Here we turn to a more extended focus on the problem of individuation as especially fundamental to ontologically explaining individuals as real existents. The problem of individuation is prior in importance to the re-identification problem in that, as seen above, the analysis of the second problem essentially presupposes the first has been successfully addressed. Indeed, were one to solve the individuation problem, one might still find that individuals seen as distinct and independent are nonetheless short-lived and not re-identifiable through change. The individuation problem is also particularly important in connection with the *Homo economicus* conception, because the distinctness and independence of individuals has been so widely assumed in connection with it. Thus in what follows in this section we turn to the first of two important challenges to the assumption that individuals are distinct and independent as has been investigated in the literature: the multiple selves problem.

On the surface, the idea that individuals could have multiple selves, or multiple utility functions as the problem was originally understood, does not link up in an obvious way to the question of what makes an individual a distinct being. The connection, however, may be understood in terms of Aristotle's principle of individuation. For him, saying that something exists implies it is a single thing, or that what is true of being must be true of unity. From this perspective, if something lacks a unity, such as an 'individual' with multiple selves, it cannot be an individual. This might be understood as saying that if the candidate single thing is internally divided, it is not possible to draw boundaries around it that distinguish it from other things. Note that this ontological characterization of the multiple selves problem is somewhat different than the more epistemological view of the problem associated with supposing that individuals might have multiple utility functions, since there emphasis rests on how one might explain the individual as having a single choice when there are different choice sets over which an individual can maximize utility. That is, from this latter perspective the problem is how are we to explain individual behavior when the basis for doing permits multiple inferences.

The multiple utility-multiple selves problem has as its source a difficulty in the utility function already encountered above: the idea that it must be an own utility function or the relation of ownership as a means of associating different utility functions with different individuals. Thus, since ownership is a contingent relationship, there is no way in principle of excluding the possibility that a single individual might 'own' more than one utility function. Different authors have adopted this view for various reasons. For example, Harsanyi [1955] hypothesized that individuals might have both subjective and ethical preferences, where the latter express what the individual prefers "only in those possibly rare moments when he forces a special impartial and impersonal attitude upon himself" [Harsanyi, 1955, pp. 315-16]. Margolis subsequently argued that the individual is a "divided self" with two utility functions, one for self-interested utility and a second for group-interested utility [Margolis, 1982]. This logic was subsequently extended to its natural conclusion by Steedman and Krause [1986] who argued that individuals might have any number of utility functions, since just as self-interest and group-interest constituted points of view, so individuals might have many points of view on life. On this analysis, the idea that individuals might have a single utility ranking rather than many becomes a special case within a general theory of individuals as having multiple selves. But by Aristotle's standard of being that general theory in fact cannot be a theory of an individual existent!

Thus much of the response to the multiple utility-multiple selves problem in the literature involved different strategies for creating a unity out of the disunity of the individual. One route by which this occurred involved efforts to create some sort of structural hierarchy within the individual. Sen [1977] suggested individuals might have meta-preferences which ranked different preference sets. Schelling [1978] argued that an individual's 'authentic self' emerged in efforts the individual undertakes to exert self-control or command over alternative, competing selves. Thaler and Shefrin [1981] applied principal-agent reasoning from the economics of the firm to model individual efforts at self-control. But all these explanations possessed an *ad hoc* and functionalist quality to them in that they injected some principle of unity into the account of the individual not immediately motivated by any characterization of the individual, but rather motivated by the assumption that the individual needed to be seen as a unity.

A second more promising route for addressing the multiple utility-multiple selves problem identified a principle that was thought to be characteristic of the individual — choice — and then attempted to show how it could be used to explain the unity of the individual. Here, Elster [1979] offered the most sophisticated analysis in his account of the myopic or shortsighted individual. For Elster, the multiple selves problem concerned a relationship between the self in the present and the self in the future. The two phenomena that he then investigated were myopia and weakness of will, or the consequent inclination individuals had to revise their earlier (myopic) plans upon encountering their later consequences. A revision of plans created the multiple selves problem, because then individuals would be inconsistent in their choice over time. However, were it argued that individuals did not revise their plans upon encountering their consequences, they would still be myopic but at least consistent. As he, put it, individuals would be consistently irrational, where irrationality was associated with myopia. How, then, could it be argued that individuals did not regularly revise their plans over time, and demonstrate themselves to be inconsistently irrational? Elster argued that individuals were aware of their myopia, and, just as Ulysses had himself bound to the mast of his ship when sailing past the Sirens, they adopt precommitment strategies that require them to remain consistent across time, so as to live with the consequences of their choices. Precommitment strategies are essentially binding agreements with others that place others in a position of monitoring individual consistency. Yet while this is an interesting and perhaps realistic description of how individuals deal with weakness of will, it makes social relationships ultimately the determinant of individual unity, not some principle strictly internal to the individual. Thus we are essentially left with the conclusion that individuals in themselves are divided across their multiple selves.

In a particularly important paper, Kavka [1991] built on the choice-based approach to the multiple selves problem in two ways. First, he recognized that the problem of explaining choice for individuals with multiple selves was analogous to the problem of explaining choice social choice for multiple individuals. That is, *intra*personal collective choice problems are essentially the same kinds of problems as *inter*personal collective choice problems, since in each case what is at stake is identifying "the aggregation rule that integrates the various dimensional evaluations into an overall decision" [Kavka, 1991, p. 158]. Second, he demonstrated by means of this homology that there were serious obstacles to resolving the multiple selves problem in a choice framework, since the social choice literature — ranging from Arrow's impossibility theorem to majority voting paradoxes to prisoner's dilemma games — has enjoyed an uneven success at best in demonstrating that multiple individuals successfully function as a social unity.

Kavka's conclusions about multiple selves and the choice framework, together with the relatively unsatisfactory character of earlier structural approaches, meant that the multiple selves problem largely ceased to be a subject of sustained investigation by the 1990s.[9] But it may be argued to have re-appeared in somewhat different form in the following decade in connection with the investigation of social identity. Just as individuals having different points of view could be seen as a way of representing their having multiple selves, so their having different social identities could also be seen as a way of representing their having multiple selves. However, whereas the points of view representation of multiple selves is largely silent about why individuals might have multiple selves, the idea that multiple selves could be understood to be a matter of individuals having different social identities explicitly linked the problem to the individual's relations to others and, as we will see, particularly to collections of other individuals in social groups. The question this association thus raised is how were individuals to be seen as both distinct and social at the same time.

[9]Multiple selves are investigated in Ainslie's [2001] picoeconomics approach in terms of individuals' short-term and long-terms interests and Glimcher's [2003] neuroeconomics approach in terms of individuals' different brain modules, but neither Ainslie nor Glimcher are economists.

## 5 THREE PRECURSOR SOCIAL IDENTITY ARGUMENTS

The concept of social identity possesses at least two main meanings, only one of which creates difficulties for explaining individuals as being distinct from one another. Thus, if an individual's social identity is understood to mean something which that individual possesses, it can be considered a characteristic of the individual in a way not essentially different from many other characteristics which the individual might be said to possess. Just as a person might be tall in height or resident of some location, so other characteristics a person might possess that would contribute to his or her social identity might include his or her gender, national origin, religion, political affiliation, occupation, etc. This understanding of the concept of social identity as a characteristic or characteristics of the individual, in fact, is entirely compatible with the concept of an individual that Aristotle advanced in opposition to Plato, where universals or forms were attributes of individuals rather than substances themselves of which individuals were instantiations. However, the concept of social identity has the additional meaning as being something that results from some activity the individual engages in whereby the individual identifies *with* some social group or collective. This meaning of the concept, moreover, contains a significant ambiguity regarding the extent to which this identification undermines or even eliminates individuality. Thus on a strong view of the idea of 'identifying with,' the individual ceases to exist as a separate being, and becomes an essentially indistinguishable part of a social group or collective. In contrast, a more moderate understanding of the idea of 'identifying with' maintains the idea of the individual as a independent being, but allows that this independence is somehow conditioned by the act of social identification. Since the stronger sense of the meaning of 'identifying with' is incompatible with seeing individuals as distinct beings, the challenge that the concept of social identity creates for seeing individuals as distinct — if we are to successfully maintain this view of individuals at all — is to explain in terms of the latter, more moderate sense of 'identifying with' just how individuals can identify with others and yet still remain individual over and above this identification.

Social identification, it should be noted, is generally understood to concern how individuals identify with others in specific social groups rather than simply with others as individuals. For example, one might identify with others by gender or religion (very large social groups) or with others in one's workplace or neighborhood (intermediate size social groups) or with sets of friends or those in one's immediate family (small social groups). In each case, there is an identification both with particular people in a group who have certain group characteristics and also an identification with the group itself. Social identification, moreover, is not an exclusive relationship in that individuals identify with multiple social groups at the same time. This multiple social identification provides the strongest connection between the social identity literature and the earlier multiple selves issue, and links the focus in the latter on attempting to explain the individual as a unity amidst disunity with the added focus of seeking to explain the individual as both distinct and social at the same time.

In what follows, attention is first directed to three well known, landmark contributions to the literature on individuals and society which prefigure in important ways the basic idea of social identification, though without actually using this concept *per se*. The goal here is to examine early attempts to explain how individuals might identify with or be identified with other individuals taken as a single group where the group is simply all other individuals. Attention then turns in Section 6 to the more recent social identity literature proper in which individuals are explicitly seen as identifying with others in social groups and also as simultaneously having multiple social identities. Both sets of literatures are evaluated in terms of how individual distinctness is understood when strong social associations come into play in explaining individual behavior.

First, then, consider Arrow's famous impossibility theory theorem or Arrow's paradox [Arrow, 1963/1951]. Arrow took individuals to be fully represented in terms of their individual preference functions, and then asked whether it was somehow possible to aggregate these preferences to produce a representation of social preference or a social welfare function. He assumed there to be five criteria that a social welfare function needed to observe: unrestricted domain or universality, non-imposition or citizen sovereignty, non-dictatorship, positive association of social and individual values or monotonicity, and independence of irrelevant alternatives.[10] Arrow's theorem is that for at least two individuals and at least three options to decide among, it is impossible to construct a social welfare function that satisfies all five criteria at once. Though the theorem is a mathematical result, it has been interpreted as showing that no voting system can meet such criteria. The paradoxical quality of the theorem rests on the plausibility of the five criteria or their fairness as Arrow put it. Alternatively, the theorem is paradoxical because the one way in which a voting system can escape the impossibility conclusion to produce a social welfare function is to allow for dictatorship, or the idea that the social welfare function is identical with that one individual's preference function. However, dictatorship of course essentially violates the idea that there is a voting system.

What is of interest in Arrow's theorem for the discussion here, then, is what may be understood as an implicit social identity argument regarding alignment of the social welfare function with the dictator's individual preference function. Using the stronger sense of the 'identifying with' interpretation of the social identity concept, the issue that arises is how individuals can identify with others in some social group, and yet still be distinct and independent. In the case of Arrow's theorem, others would be all other individuals and the social group would be represented as their social welfare function. From this perspective, Arrow's conclusion both solves and fails to solve the challenge presented by the social identity concept. On the one hand, by assumption the dictator remains a distinct individual, despite identifying with others through the matching of the dictator's individual preference function

[10]An additional version of Arrow's theorem replaces the monotonicity criterion with that of unanimity or Pareto efficiency, but this does not change the basic result.

and the social preference function. On the other hand, individual distinctness is only preserved by ignoring the individual preference functions of all other individuals in determining the social preference function. A fair response, then, would be that Arrow's theorem is not a proper exhibition of the social concept, because it elides the tension in the idea of the individual 'identifying with' others in a social group. But the theorem nonetheless is about individuals' relations to groups, and indeed explains the matching of dictator's individual preference function and the social welfare functions as an identity. Thus it may be regarded as a precursor social identity argument, particularly as the dilemma is raises is replicated in subsequent arguments that have a similar precursor quality.

The second such instance is Harsanyi's [1953; 1955; 1977] impartial observer theorem of social ethics.[11] Harsanyi was interested in using the cardinal utility concept to interpret the concept of social welfare, and wished to demonstrate that value judgments concerning income distribution were objective if they involved "nonegoistic impersonal judgments of preference" [1953, 434]. Such judgments were those that were taken from the perspective of an impartial observer defined as an individual completely ignorant of his or her own relative position, or as one having an equal chance of being anyone in the population. Put in terms of the idea of giving equal weights to all individuals, Harsanyi's theorem implies that individuals are to receive equal treatment in judgments of social welfare. From this perspective, then, Harsanyi shows that were such an impartial observer to exercise an impartiality of this kind, the only decision rule possible is the utilitarian one of maximizing the average sum of (von Neumann and Morgenstern) individual utility functions. Later formal representations of the theorem, including Harsanyi's [1977], have adopted Arrow's [1963/1951] treatment of interpersonal comparisons in terms of the concept of 'extended preference,' where in contrast to individuals' actual preferences over social states, extended preferences concern an individual's preferences over social states in the position of others. Intuitively, the idea of extended preference involves the idea that impartial observers somehow empathize with others in the sense of being able to imagine trading places with them.

Mongin develops a causal account of extended preferences seen as most consistent with Harsanyi's arguments and as the most defensible interpretation of the concept, but then shows that "a genuinely utilitarian formula, that is, with equal weights and no observer-dependence, is out of reach," because "observer-dependence follows from the observer's implicit reliance on a subjective probability and the weights are unequal because they are determined by this subjective probability" [Mongin, 2001, 174]. For our purposes, it is worth noting an alternative account of extended preferences which Mongin recognizes as inherently problematic. That is, one might also consider that the impartial observer with extended preferences identifies with others. But as Mongin notes, this route would raise difficult personal identity issues involved in trying to main a distinction between the observer and the observed: "how much of the observer's identity is preserved by sympathetic identification or empathetic identification of the non-deductive sort?

[11]See [Mongin, 2001] for a full discussion. Vickery [1945] anticipates Harsanyi.

Is there enough left, as it were, to warrant the claim that it is the observer who makes the preference judgment? (*Ibid.*, p. 161). Here, then, we have a problem not unlike that in the case of Arrow's theorem. If the extended preference concept involves empathy with others, then the impartial observer's making a social welfare judgment is comparable to the individual identifying with a social group. But the failure of Harsanyi's argument runs parallel to Arrow's impossibility result. Only in the case in which the impartial observer is able to truly identify with others is there a possibility of overcoming the observer's implicit reliance on making a subjective probability judgment. However, there is nothing in Harsanyi's account to assure us that, as Mongin sees it, enough of the observer's identity is left to still regard that individual as distinct and independent.

The third social identity precursor argument is Lucas' representative individual analysis in macroeconomics.[12] Real world economies, of course, contain very large numbers of individual agents, and thus modeling them involves challenges that go significantly beyond modeling particular markets. To simplify the analysis, New Classical macroeconomic models represent the choices of an economy's many real world agents as if they were the choices of one single utility maximizing individual: the representative individual. One rationale for this was that since macro models were thought to require microfoundations, and since microeconomic models treat individuals as utility maximizing agents, it seemed reasonable to say in the case of macro models that a single utility maximizing agent represented all an economy's many actual economic agents. A second rationale was to provide a framework in which macroeconomic equilibria could be said to be unique and stable. Thus, since individual excess demand curves do have unique and stable equilibria, modeling the macroeconomy as if it were occupied by a single representative individual guaranteed these properties. A third rationale was that differences between individuals, while important in individual markets, averaged out at the level of the economy as a whole. Individuals differed in terms of their preferences and endowments, but all nonetheless had preferences and endowments, and thus might be represented by a single utility maximizing individual.[13]

Note, then, that the representative individual assumption resembles Arrow's dictator solution to problem of constructing a social welfare function. In Arrow's analysis, it is impossible to aggregate individual preference functions into a social preference function under reasonable assumptions about preferences unless one lets the preferences of one individual dictate the social welfare function. That is, both the dictator and the representative individual need to be identified with all particular individuals to achieve the goals of the analysis. But there are a variety of reasons to suppose that this identification is problematic. A series of general equilibrium theory results going back to Sonnenschein [1972] and Debreu

[12]The first representative agent model is Lucas and Rapping [1970], though as Rapping subsequently abandoned the framework Lucas is generally seen as its key original proponent. Other important proponents are Sargent [1979] and Kydland and Prescott [1982].

[13]For further discussion of New Classical representative agent models and their earlier antecedents, see Hoover [1988] and Hartley [1997].

[1974] show that in multi-agent models equilibria which exist are neither unique nor stable.[14] This undercuts the second and third rationales above, since the representative individual cannot be said to represent many individuals in this regard. Kirman [1992], however, infers from this that one cannot then generate aggregate relationships from the standard assumptions on individuals in general equilibrium models, and thus that the entire microfoundations project is misguided as well. It makes no sense, consequently, to identify one typical individual as being representative of many diverse, heterogeneous individuals within the rational maximizing framework.

In light of this review of Arrow, Harsanyi, and Lucas on individuals and society, then, note that in all three cases the strong sense of the meaning of 'identifying with' incompatible with seeing individuals as distinct beings is involved in their accounts. For Arrow, the dictator's preferences are identified with the social welfare function. But since the social welfare function is identified with the preferences of all other individuals, the dictator's preferences are effectively identified, if not 'with,' even more strongly, *as* their preferences. For Harsanyi, the impartial observer identifies with all other individuals in virtue of being completely ignorant of his or her own relative position, or as having an equal chance of being anyone in the population. As Mongin comments, on this view the separate identity of the impartial observer is not easy to sustain. And for Lucas, the preferences of the representative individual, like Arrow's dictator, are simply identified as the preferences of all the individuals in the macroeconomy, though in contrast to Arrow's dictator, the representative individual is a constructed individual not any particular individual. Thus in all three accounts one individual is identified with all other individuals.

At the same time, there is also an interesting difference between the three accounts. For Arrow and Lucas the dictator and representative individuals respectively are preserved as independent agents, and all other individuals effectively disappear, whereas for Harsanyi it is the impartial observer that effectively disappears and all other individuals that are preserved. These opposed slants on the individual-society relationship suggest that the social identification concept, as an interpretation of the three accounts, is ambiguous with regard to how individuals actually identify with others. In effect, there is insufficient social structure on the society side of the individual-society relationship to pin down how social identification works.

This reflects the fact that, as social identification involves individuals identifying with groups rather than with other individuals (especially all other individuals), the Arrow, Harsanyi, and Lucas arguments are not quite social identity arguments. All three are indeed rather interested in the relationship between individuals and society *per se*, and not in the relationship between individuals and social groups as subsets of society (though a case could be made for considering society the largest of all social groups). This makes their arguments precursor rather than

[14]These results are now generally known as the Sonnenschein-Mantel-Debreu results (cf. [Rizvi, 2006])

actual social identity arguments in that they concern an important element in the social identity relationship, namely whether the relationship of individuals to others is compatible with individuals retaining their status as distinct individuals, without investigating the role that social structure plays in that relationship. The subsequent social identity literature in economics, then, can be distinguished from these precursor arguments in virtue of the attention it devotes to social structure in explaining social identification.

## 6 RECENT SOCIAL IDENTITY ARGUMENTS

When social structure is introduced into social identification analysis, it becomes necessary to ask what aspects of that structure enter into individuals' identification with others. Alternatively, it needs to be asked what aspects of social structure mediate individuals' social identification with other individuals. The widely held answer to this question is that individuals identify with others through the medium of social groups. That is, individuals identify with social groups that have characteristics which reflect their membership. This understanding, however, is also the source of the chief problem facing the social identity literature in economics. Since there are many social groups, and since there is considerable evidence that individuals identify with different social groups at the same time, what explains the individual's own identity? That is, what is it that explains the unity of the individual over and above his or her multiple social identities? This is essentially the multiple selves problem discussed in Section 4 in new guise. The problem here is different, however, in that there is no explicit connection in the multiple selves literature to individuals' location in a social space. That earlier literature allows individuals might logically have multiple selves, but either does not consider why this might be so, or associates an individual having multiple selves with matters specific to the isolated individual, such as having short term and long term interests. In contrast, the social identity literature ties individuals' multiple selves directly to their relationships to others. This provides a more tangible sense of the individual's possible fragmentation, since individuals' being involved in different social groups with which they identify is typically associated with their occupying different roles in different social groups.

There are thus two aspects to recent arguments about individuals' social identity. One concerns the nature of the social identification relationship or the connection that individuals have to others; the second concerns how the individual who identifies with others is to be modeled and re-interpreted as compared to the standard *Homo economicus* conception. The discussion that follows reviews three important explanations of individuals and social identity in terms of these two concerns: Akerlof and Kranton's neoclassical model, Sen's commitment approach, and Kirman *et al.*'s complexity analysis.

Akerlof and Kranton [2000] explain social identity as a set of self-images individuals have in virtue of seeing themselves as members of certain social categories.[15] As they put it, an individual's "identity is bound to social categories; and individuals *identify with* people in some categories and differentiate themselves from those in others" ([Akerlof and Kranton, 2000, p. 720]; emphasis added). Self-image is accordingly incorporated as an argument (or more accurately as a vector of arguments, one for each self-image) in the individual's utility function, such that maximizing utility involves individuals strategically interacting with other individuals to maintain their different self-images. Akerlof and Kranton explain individuals' interaction with others as often challenging their sense of what they ought to do when seeing themselves as falling into a certain social category, and this then causes them anxiety or cognitive dissonance, which they seek to reduce. That is, maximizing utility is a matter of minimizing anxiety. Or, individuals maximize utility by in effect maintaining their different self-image stocks through the operation of an unconscious psychodynamic feedback mechanism. The literature on which they draw for their analysis is known as the 'social identity' approach in social psychology, and was originated by Tajfel [1972; 1981] and further developed as 'self-categorization theory' by Turner [1985; 1987].[16] Akerlof and Kranton's innovation is thus to combine this approach with neoclassical utility function reasoning.

Regarding the first of the two main concerns in the economics social identity literature — the nature of the social identification relationship or the connection that individuals have to others — Akerlof and Kranton can be said to employ a matching or correspondence rule for explaining why individuals have certain social identities. This reflects the emphasis placed on the concept of a social category in the 'social identity' approach and 'self-categorization theory.' Social categories are broad social science classifications used in academic research and by government agencies to describe widely recognized social aggregates. The main focus in the 'social identity' approach is on individuals' behavior, given their perceiving themselves as falling into certain social categories. Little attention is devoted to asking how individuals might come to fall into certain social categories. This latter issue is important, however, since people with characteristics associated with certain social categories often do not understand themselves in those terms. Thus the matching or correspondence view of the social identity relationship abstracts in important ways from how individuals act toward their social identities.

This is relevant to the second of the two main concerns in the economics social identity literature — the modeling of the individual who identifies with others. Here the issue, as in the earlier multiple selves literature, is how is the individual to still constitute a unity when possessing many social identities. For Akerlof and Kranton, the implicit answer is that all the individual's social identities are arguments in one utility function identified with the individual, and thus the utility function provides the unity of the individual. But, as argued above in Section 3 and at more length elsewhere [Davis, 2003], the argument that the utility function

[15]The discussion here is drawn from Davis [2007].

[16]See [Hogg, Terry, and White, 1995].

explains the identity of the individual is circular, and thus cannot account for the unity of the individual. This problem re-manifests itself in the context of Akerlof and Kranton's reliance on a matching or correspondence concept of social identity. That concept does not explain how individuals come to have certain social identities but simply takes them as given. But if any number of social identities can be attributed to an individual, there do not seem to be any boundaries on the individual as one single entity. That is, without a way of saying how the individual has a particular set of social identities it does not seem possible to say that the individual is a unity of his or her social identities. Thus, while offering an interesting account of how individuals maintain their given social identities, Akerlof and Kranton's analysis does not succeed in providing a viable new account of *Homo economicus*.

The second social identity analysis considered here, Sen's commitment approach, is based on Sen's distinction between sympathy and commitment [1977].[17] Sen argues [Sen, 2002; 2005] that individuals' ability to form commitments cannot be explained in the utility maximizing framework, and that one of the most important forms of commitment that individuals make is to social groups of which they are members. He also understands individuals' involvement in social groups through commitment-making as generating social identities for those individuals [Sen, 2004]. But at the same time Sen argues (against some communitarians) that individuals are not captive to their identifications with others in social groups in the sense that they can reason about their social affiliations, and decide whether and the extent to which they will act according to the rules that operate in those groups. As he puts it, an individual is able to engage in a process of "reasoning and self-scrutiny" [Sen, 2002, p. 36], and thereby effectively determine what weight if any is to be placed on any given social identity. This can be understood as a form of reflexive behavior in which the individual takes him or herself as an object of consideration as opposed to objects independent of him or herself (such as other individuals). Identifying with others in social groups accordingly involves at one and the same time an orientation toward others and an orientation toward oneself. Additionally, Sen recognizes that individuals can identify simultaneously with many different social groups.

Regarding the nature of the social identification relationship or the connection that individuals have to others, Sen explicitly rejects the matching or correspondence view since he opposes the view of some communitarians that individuals 'discover' they have certain social identities. Rather, given his emphasis on individuals' "reasoning and self-scrutiny" in determining their social group affiliations, his concept of social identification can be characterized as interactionist, thus reflecting how the interaction between individuals and groups produces social identities. In this respect, his view can be associated with another social psychology approach to social identity known as the 'sociological approach.'[18] On the 'sociological approach' there is an interactive reciprocal relation between the self and

[17] The discussion here is drawn from Davis [2006b].

[18] See [Stets and Burke, 2000].

society in the sense that each influences the other. Individuals always act in social contexts, and influence society through its groups, organizations, and institutions, while society influences individuals through shared language meanings and other inherited social structures that enable individuals to interact and take on social roles. Sen does not make reference to the 'sociological approach,' but his view of social identity fits it reasonably well.

As with Akerlof and Kranton, then, we may use Sen's particular understanding of the social identity concept to say something about his view of the second of the two main concerns in the economics social identity literature — the modeling of the individual who identifies with others. What, then, does an interactionist view of individuals having different social identities imply about the nature of the individual? Sen's rejection of the utility function framework and subsequent adoption of the capability framework suggests that individuals being able to form commitments to others in social groups and engage in a process of "reasoning and self-scrutiny" about their different social affiliations should be understood as one capability among many individuals can develop. Though he does not explain what is involved for individuals in their exercising such a capability, supposing individuals to have such a capability gives the individual an identity apart from their involvement in social groups. That is, individuals would have both many social identities and also a personal identity that is to be understood in terms of the way the individual manages his or her particular collection of social identities. Since such a capability is individuating, in principle the conception of the individual thus understood passes the individuation test set out above in Section 3. Sen's view, then, goes some considerable distance toward solving the multiple selves/social identity problem in providing the basis for an account of the individual as a unity.

The third social identity account to be considered here is the complexity analysis of individuals and their social identities developed by Horst, Kirman, and Teschl [2005]. One source of complexity theory in economics lies in the critique of standard general equilibrium theory particularly as it pertains to the atomistic individual conception (cf. [Davis, 2006a]). Kirman has repeatedly emphasized this connection, and argued that individuals are better conceptualized as directly interacting with one another in social contexts rather than indirectly through markets [Kirman, 1992; 1997]. In more recent work, Kirman and his colleagues have argued that individuals form self-images through their interaction with others in social groups (rather than in terms of social categories). They do so by matching what they believe to be their own personal characteristics to those social characteristics they believe particular groups exhibit. But recalling the 'sociological approach' to identity, they see the individual-social interaction as a two-way street in which individuals are not only influenced by their social contexts and membership in social groups, but also influence social contexts and these social groups by their actions, thus creating recursive feedback relations between self-image and social context as individuals join groups, groups thereby change, changing what groups individuals wish to join, and so on. This brings "into question immediately the notion of a utility function which is unchanging over time" [Horst, Kirman, and

Teschl, 2005, p. 12], and also leads to the conclusion that both the personal identities of individuals and the identities of social groups are in a continual state of change relative to one another.

The understanding of the social identification relationship or the connection that individuals have to others that we find in this complexity analysis of individuals and social identities, then, combines the Akerlof and Kranton matching or correspondence strategy and Sen's interactionist strategy, since individuals match personal and social group characteristics but find the basis on which they do so continually transformed by their changing patterns of social interaction. Indeed on the matching side, Akerlof and Kranton's cognitive dissonance motivation is adopted to account for individuals' matching of personal and social group characteristics. On the interactionist side, Sen's view that individuals reflexively evaluate themselves is approximated in the complexity framework by the idea that change in personal and social characteristics leads individuals to regularly re-determine which groups provide a match with their own characteristics.

Regarding the second of the two main concerns in the economics social identity literature — the modeling of the individual who identifies with others — the complexity approach takes a radical position. Since individuals' characteristics are always changing due to continual change in social group affiliations, Horst, Kirman, and Teschl assert that there is no single unchanging, re-identifiable self. Indeed, they argue that the idea that re-identification is required for understanding individual is mistaken, and that a chain-linking concept tying together a succession of related but non-identical selves is preferred. This, however, naturally invites us to ask why we should not consider a 'chain' of related but non-identical selves an individual identity concept, since a 'chain' is a type of entity, and in fact nicely represents the idea of an individual having many related but different selves. One might then individuate and re-identify a chain in terms of its complete pattern of sequential interconnectedness. Horst, Kirman, and Teschl, in fact, have an interpretation of the interconnectedness principle as cognitive dissonance reduction. Individuals always move to and from groups — thus creating links in the chain and moving down the chain — by matching their personal and social characteristics so as to reduce cognitive dissonance. That is, they can always be individuated and re-identified as socially interactive cognitive dissonance reducers.

## 7 THE CONCEPTION OF THE INDIVIDUAL IN RECENT ECONOMICS

In the last two decades the economics research frontier has been significantly transformed by the emergence of a collection of new approaches which criticize traditional neoclassical assumptions, and whose origins lie largely in other sciences and disciplines [Davis, 2006c]. These 'post-neoclassical' research approaches include: classical game theory, evolutionary game theory, behavioral game theory, evolutionary economics, behavioral economics, experimental economics, neuroeconomics, and agent-based computational or complexity economics. They can be shown to collectively share the idea that human individuals are not isolated, atomistic beings, though they differ significantly in how they understand this critique. The idea that human individuals are not isolated, atomistic beings can be explained by saying they are socially embedded [Davis, 2003]. Generally, that is, individuality arises out of relations to others rather than isolation from others. Thus, at issue in the new approaches in economics is how individuality arises out of social interaction, or how individual behavior depends upon aggregate behavior. Here I cannot do more than introduce a sample of the new views of the individual, and select one example from a more static type of approach and one from a more dynamic type of approach.

As an instance of the first, behavioral economics, particularly as it has emerged from the work of Kahneman and Tversky, has made abandonment of the rational choice theory's independence axiom central to a new view of the individual by adding a procedural element to choice behavior in supposing that individuals rely on a variety of decision heuristics or rules sensitive to context to frame their choices. Thus in Kahneman and Tversky's prospect theory (e.g., [1979]), choice is a two-phase process with prospects 'edited' in the first phase using different decision heuristics, such that choices are then made in the second phase from a restricted or reformulated class of prospects. This casts doubt on the traditional idea that individuals possess stable and coherent preferences, and implies that preferences are malleable and dependent on the context in which they are elicited [Camerer and Loewenstein, 2003]. But if individuals' preferences depend on context, social influences and interaction with other individuals presumably are involved, and individuals can no longer be seen to be atomistic as in the *Homo economicus* conception.

As an instance of a more dynamic type of approach, we might consider evolutionary game theory. The central assumption of this approach is that players adapt their behaviors in terms of the strategies they play over the course of repeated games. Payoffs represent "fitness" in some selection process that players achieve by adapting their strategies to the dynamics of competition. One of the more interesting aspects of this approach concerns how the players of games are to be understood. If we see evolutionary game theory as simply an extension of classical game theory, players are the human individuals whose choices reflect beliefs about which strategies are the best replies to the strategies of others. But if we suppose that the selection process determines which strategies produce fitness, strategies themselves are the players, and individuals "are simply passive vehicles for these strategies, coming to play their brief hands and then dying off to be replaced by others who inherit their dispositions with modifications induced by mutation and, at the population level, by selection" [Ross, 2005, p. 198]. In this case, individuals are so highly embedded in the games they play that they cease to be autonomous individuals.

Further examples of the embedded individual conception can be found in the other new research approaches in economics. In general, all such conceptions can be evaluated in a systematic manner in terms of two separate existence or identity conditions that were set forth above to evaluate the *Homo economicus* conception. Again, the rationale behind such evaluations is to compare and judge the ontological credentials of different ways of explaining individuals in economics. More generally, the goal of examining the status of different kinds of existents in economics is to make ontological analysis more central to economic methodology. This in turn is then a part of a wider program of developing comprehensive theory of the world, as exhibited in economic science.

## BIBLIOGRAPHY

[Ainslie, 2001] G. Ainslie. *Picoeconomics*, Cambridge: Cambridge University Press, 2001.

[Akerlof and Kranton, 2000] G. Akerlof and R. Kranton. Economics and Identity, *Quarterly Journal of Economics*, 115, 3: 715-753, 2000.

[Aristotle, 1924] Aristotle. *Metaphysics*, rev. with an introduction and commentary by W.D. Ross, Oxford: Clarendon Press, 1924.

[Arrow, 1963/1951] K. Arrow. *Social Choice and Individual Values*, 1951. $2^{nd}$ ed., New Haven and London: Yale University Press, 1963.

[Camerer and Loewenstein, 2003] C. Camerer and G. Loewenstein. Behavioral Economics: Past, Present, Future, *Advances in Behavioral Economics*, Camerer, Loewenstein, and M. Rabin, eds., Princeton: Princeton University Press, 2003.

[Coase, 1937] R. Coase. The Nature of the Firm, *Economica*, 4: pp. 386-405, 1937.

[Davis, 2003] J. Davis. *The Theory of the Individual in Economics*, London: Routledge, 2003.

[Davis, 2006a] J. Davis. Complexity theory's network conception of the individual, in *Money and Markets*, Alberto Giacomin and Cristina Marcuzzo, eds., Cheltenham: Elgar, 2006.

[Davis, 2006b] J. Davis. Identity and Commitment: Sen's Fourth Aspect of the Self, in Bernhard Schmid and Fabienne Peters, eds., *Rationality and Commitment*, Oxford: Oxford University Press, 2006.

[Davis, 2006c] J. Davis. The Turn in Economics: Neoclassical Dominance to Mainstream Pluralism? *Journal of Institutional Economics*, Vol. 2, no. 1: pp. 1-20, 2006.

[Davis, 2007] J. Davis. Akerlof and Kranton on Identity in Economics, *Cambridge Journal of Economics*, 31(3): 349–362, 2007.

[Debreu, 1974] G. Debreu. Excess Demand Functions, *Journal of Mathematical Economics*, 1 (March): 15-23, 1974.

[Dolfsma *et al.*, 2005] W. Dolfsma, J. Finch, and R. McMaster. Market and society: how do they relate, and how do they contribute to welfare? *Journal of Economic Issues*, 39: 347-356, 2005.

[Elster, 1979] J. Elster. *Ulysses and the Sirens*. Cambridge: Cambridge University Press, 1979.

[Glimcher, 2003] P. Glimcher. *Decisions, Uncertainty, and the Brain*, Cambridge, MA: MIT Press, 2003.

[Harsanyi, 1953] J. Harsanyi. Cardinal utility in welfare economics and in the theory of risk-taking, *Journal of Political Economy*, 61: 434-35, 1953.

[Harsanyi, 1955] J. Harsanyi. Cardinal welfare, individualistic ethics and interpersonal comparisons of utility, *Journal of Political Economy*, 63: 309-21, 1955.

[Harsanyi, 1977] J. Harsanyi. *Rational Behavior and Bargaining Equilbrium in Games and Social Situations*, Cambridge: Cambridge University Press, 1977.

[Hartley, 1997] J. Hartley. *The Representative Agent in Macroeconomics*, London: Routledge, 1997.

[Hogg *et al.*, 1995] M. Hogg, D. Terry, and K. White. A Tale of Two Theories: A Critical Comparison of Identity Theory with Social Identity Theory, *Social Psychology Quarterly*, 58: 255-269, 1995.

[Horst *et al.*, 2005] U. Horst, A. Kirman, and M. Teschl. Searching for Identity, *Journal of Economic Methodology*, 13 (3), 2005.

[Hoover, 1988] K. Hoover. *The New Classical Macroeconomics: A Sceptical Inquiry*, Oxford: Blackwell, 1988.

[Kavka, 1991] G. Kavka. Is Individual Choice Less Problematic than Collective Choice? *Economics and Philosophy*, 7(1): 143-165, 1991.

[Kahneman and Tversky, 1979] D. Kahneman and A. Tversky. Prospect Theory: An Analysis of Decision under Risk, *Econometrica*, 47 (2): 263-91, 1979.

[Kirman, 1992] A. Kirman. Whom or What Does the Representative Individual Represent? *Journal of Economic Perspectives*, 6 (2): 117-136, 1992.

[Kirman, 1997] A. Kirman. The Economy as an Interactive System, in W. B. Arthur, S. Durlauf, and D. Lane, eds., *The Economy as an Evolving Complex System II*, Reading, Mass: Addison-Wesley, 1997.

[Kydland and Prescott, 1982] F. Kydland and E. Prescott. Time to Build and Aggregate Fluctuations, *Econometrica* 50, (6): 1345-70, 1982.

[Lucas and Rapping, 1970] R. Lucas and L. Rapping. Real Wages, Employment and Inflation, in E. Phelps, ed., *Microeconomic Foundations of Employment and Inflation Theory*, New York: Norton: 257-305, 1970.

[Margolis, 1982] H. Margolis. *Selfishness, Altruism and Rationality,* Cambridge: Cambridge University Press, 1982.

[Mongin, 2001] P. Mongin. The Impartial Observer Theorem of Social Economics, *Economics and Philosophy* 17 (2): 147-79, 2001.

[Rizvi, 2006] A. Rizvi. The Sonnenschein-Mantel-Debreu Results after 30 Years, forthcoming in D. W. Hands and P. Mirowski, eds, *Agreement on Demand*, Durham: Duke University Press, 2006.

[Ross, 2005] D. Ross. *Economic Theory and Cognitive Science*, Cambridge: MIT Press, 2005.

[Ross, 1923] W. D. Ross. *Aristotle*, London: Methuen, 1923.

[Samuelson, 1938] P. Samuelson. A Note on the Pure Theory of Consumer's Behaviour, *Economica*, 5: pp. 61-71, 1938.

[Sargent, 1979] T. Sargent. *Macroeconomic Theory*, New York: Academic Press, 1979.

[Sen, 1977] A. Sen. Rational Fools, *Philosophy and Public Affairs*, 6: 317-44, 1977.

[Sen, 2002] A. Sen. *Rationality and Freedom*, Cambridge, MA: Belknap Press, 2002.

[Sen, 2004] A. Sen. Social Identity, *Revue de Philosophique économique*, 9 (1): 7-27, 2004.

[Sen, 2005] A. Sen. Why Exactly is Commitment Important for Rationality? *Economics and Philosophy*, 21 (1): 5-14, 2005.

[Schelling, 1978] T. Schelling. Egonomics, or the art of self-management, *American Economic Review: Papers and Proceedings*, 68: 290-4, 1978.

[Sonnenschein, 1972] H. Sonnenschein. Market Excess Demand Functions, *Econometrica*, 40 (3): 549-63, 1972.

[Steedman and Krause, 1986] I. Steedman and U. Krause. Goethe's *Faust,* Arrow's Possibility Theorem and the individual decision-taker, in *The Multiple Self*, J. Elster (ed.), Cambridge: Cambridge University Press: 197-231, 1986.

[Stets and Burke, 2000] J. Stets and P. Burke. Identity theory and social identity theory, *Social Psychological Quarterly*, 63: 283-295, 2000.

[Stigler and Becker, 1977] G. Stigler and G. Becker. De gustibus non est disputandum, *American Economic Review,* 67: 76-90, 1977.

[Tajfel, 1972] H. Tajfel. Social categorization, in S. Moscovici, ed., *Introduction à la psychologie sociale*, Vol. 1, Paris: Larousse: 272-302, 1972.

[Tajfel, 1981] H. Tajfel. *Human Groups and social categories: Studies in Social Psychology*, Cambridge: Cambridge University Press, 1981.

[Thaler and Shefrin, 1981] R. Thaler and M. Shefrin. An economic theory of self-control, *Journal of Political Economy,* 89: 392-406, 1981.

[Turner, 1985] J. Turner. Social Categorization and the Self-Concept: A Social Cognitive Theory of Group Behavior, in E. Lawler, ed., *Advances in Group Processes: Theory and Research*, Vol. 2, Greenwich, CT: JAI: 77-122, 1985.

[Turner *et al.*, 1987] J. Turner, M. Hogg, P. Oakes, S. Reicher, and M. Wetherell. *Rediscovering the Social Group: A Self-Categorization Theory*, Oxford: Blackwell, 1987.

[Vickery, 1945] W. Vickery. Measuring marginal utility by reaction to risk, *Econometrica*, 13: 319-33, 1945.

# RATIONAL CHOICE AND SOME DIFFICULTIES FOR CONSEQUENTIALISM*

Paul Anand

## 1 INTRODUCTION

Rational choice constitutes a field in which philosophers share interests particularly with economists but also with political theorists, sociologists, psychologists. Theory, over the past century, has been dominated by the axiomatic approach which offers a distinctive contribution to our understanding of deliberation and choice and one that contains some heavy-weight theories that have been highly influential. Within both the programme of research and its intellectual *disaspora*, two theories stand out as demanding our attention — expected utility theory, previously the main workhorse for the analysis of decision-making and Arrow's impossibility theorem — a theorem that suggests reasonable social choice mechanisms are destined to being undemocratic. Both theories are axiomatic and share the fact that they were taken to identify reasonable behaviour in individual or group settings.

However, our ideas about both theories have changed since they first emerged and they continue to evolve in ways that are quite dramatic. So far as utility theory is concerned, there is widespread acceptance that subjective expected utility theory is false in significant respects, growing recognition that it is technically possible to construct more general theories and acceptance that rationality does not require transitivity (a view I have argued for and which Rabinowicz [2000] calls 'the modern view'[1]). The issues surrounding Arrow's Theorem are slightly different but it can similarly be seen as a theory that heralded a body of research that is coming to take radically different perspectives on concepts like democracy, social choice and the nature of human welfare. Of course there are differences between the contributions made by expected utility to decision theory, and by Arrow's impossibility theorem to social choice, but there are some common issues that arise from the fact that both are axiomatic approaches to decision science and it some of these themes that I wish to focus on in this chapter.

*I am grateful to many colleagues for discussions of these issues but I particularly wish to acknowledge discussions with Wlodez Rabinowicz, Cristian List and Kenneth Arrow concerning the philosophical foundations of the latter's famous theorem. The usual caveat applies.

[1]See also Gendin [1996] and Putnam [1995].

Handbook of the Philosophy of Science. Volume 13: Philosophy of Economics.
Volume editor: Uskali Mäki. General editors: Dov M. Gabbay, Paul Thagard and John Woods.

Specifically, I want to argue that whilst axiomatic arguments concerning the nature of rational and social choice are important, intellectually impressive and even aesthetically pleasing, they are also prone to certain weaknesses. These weaknesses are often logical or methodological but they are also intimately related to the doctrine of consequentialism which I view as being poorly designed for picking out some key structures and intuitions to do with reasonable choice in individual or social settings (even if it is well suited to do this for some issues). This chapter is therefore in some ways a potted summary of a theme which I have been exploring for some time and which I hope will help readers come to grips with some of the transformations that have gone on in the field over the past 25 years.

To this end, I shall review the interpretation and justification of three assumptions (transitivity, independence and non-dictatorship) that sit at the heart of the theories mentioned above. In each case, I try to offer a critical assessment of each assumption, on its own terms and show that neither transitivity nor independence should be taken as canons of rational choice and that Arrow's characterisation of dictatorship is questionable in a number of respects. I shall not be arguing against the use of axiomatic method or even against the view that both theories under consideration are not the intellectual giants worthy of our attention that they are widely taken to be. Rather my conclusion will be that whilst we need and benefit from such theories, their 'take-home message' is rarely as decisive as the formal representation theorems might lead one to suppose. The rest of the chapter is structured as follows. Sections 2 and 3 provide an overview of arguments why rational agents might wish to violate the transitivity and independence axioms respectively whilst section 4 focuses on some difficulties with Arrow's characterisation of dictatorship. Section 5 discusses the identification problem in the context of the transitivity assumption (common to both theories though arguably in a way that is most relevant to its application in decision theory) whilst section 6 provides a short summary that offers some thoughts about the consequences for future research. I focus on transitivity, not simply because its simplicity belies the existence of some unsuspected difficulties but also because it is a shared cornerstone of decision theory and social choice under the assumption of consequentialism. A theme that I hope will begin to emerge is that the reasons for rejecting particular axioms, in philosophical terms at least, are often related to a common concern about consequentialism's lack of comprehensiveness.

## 2 TRANSITIVITY

The assumption that agents have transitive preferences (if $Pab$ and $Pbc$ then $Pac$ where $P$ is the preference relation and $a, b$ and $c$ are objects that could be chosen) was, at one time, inextricably linked to formalisation. It appears both in von Neumann and Morgenstern's axiomatisation of utility and in Arrow's 'impossibility' theorem so it was core both to decision theory and social choice. For a long time it was thought that formal results would be difficult to obtain without until demonstrations to the contrary started to emerge in the 1970s in the work of Mas-Collel

[1974] and Kim and Richter [1986]. By this time the idea that there could be a formal theory of rational choice which imposed formal constraints on preference and choice had taken hold though as many were beginning to argue (see Anand [1986], Sugden [1985]) none of the arguments that try to demonstrate why rational agents should have transitive preferences are logically valid. It also seems possible to find plausible examples which show that rational agents could have intransitive preferences (see also Bar-Hillel and Margalit [1988] for an early review). In what follows, I illustrate both kinds of criticisms.

The attempt to ground transitivity in logic is perhaps one of the most basic methods of defending the assumption. It relies on a feeling that there is something illogical about having intransitive preferences as the title of Georg von Wright's *The Logic of Preference* [1963] suggests. A similar view is articulated by John Broome [1991] and Gordon Tullock [1964, p. 403] who writes:

> The proof of intransitivity is a simple example of reductio ad absurdum. If the individual is alleged to prefer $A$ to $B$, $B$ to $C$ and $C$ to $A$, we can enquire which he would prefer from the collection of $A$ $B$ and $C$. *Ex-hypothesi* he must prefer one: say he prefers $A$ to $B$ or $C$. This however contradicts the statement that he prefers $C$ to $A$, and hence the alleged intransitivity must be false.

Despite its air of plausibility, Tullock's argument lacks validity. The problem is just that the argument equates, without further defense, an elision between binary preference relations and ternary ones. We are offered a statement about three binary preferences which can be represented by the set $\{Bab, Bbc, Bca\}$ though strictly any choice from the threesome either gives rise to a ternary relation (or choice function). Without loss of generality let us write the ternary preference Tullock proposes as $Ta\{b, c\}$ (read $a$ is preferred to $b$ or $c$ when all three are available). Unfortunately this does not yield the desired contradiction as that would require that we are able to generate an element of the set $\{\neg Bab, \neg Bbc, \neg Bca\}$ which none out of $Ta\{b, c\}, Tb\{a, c\}$ and $Tc(a, b\}$ is. The difficulty with this elision stands out if one comes to transitivity from logic but is less obvious if one has in mind a comparative greater than ($>$) relation. Greater than is so deeply transitive that it encourages one to think of similar relations as being transitive whereas for logical relations the property is much more open-ended.

A device that could be used to complete Tullock's proof is Sen's alpha condition which would, given a ternary preference ranking, say $Tabc$, allow one to infer the relevant set of binary relations $Bab, Bbc$ and $Bac$. So if we have a ternary preference relation and we accept that contraction consistency is logically required, then we could argue that intransitive binary preferences contradict ternary ranking combined with contraction consistency. But Tullock offers no such argument and therefore his logical case for transitive preference remains unproven.

Although capturing an intuition which seems to be incorrect, there is a case which has taken to be much more persuasive, known as the money pump argument. In essence the view is that if a person has intransitive preferences, they can be made, by some cunning trader, to participate in a series of exchanges that bring the person back to where they started but at a less preferred wealth level. So if you prefer $a$ to $b$, $b$ to $c$ and $c$ to $a$, you would be willing to trade $a$ for $c$, $c$ for $b$ and $b$ for $a$ paying a small, strictly positive amount each time thereby having given three small positive sums of money for the privilege. This is sometimes described as a pragmatic argument and on the surface it seems sensible enough though if one looks more carefully things are not so straightforward.

To better understand the money pump we might ask what exactly it means to say that a person prefers $a$ to $b$, $b$ to $c$ and so on. We could begin by thinking of these relations as constraining a constellation of preferences at a particular point in time, a reading that suggests a counter-factual interpretation. To say that a person has transitive binary preferences under the counter-factual interpretation means that were it the case the feasible set were $\{a, b\}$, then the decision-maker would prefer $a$ over $b$. Similarly if the feasible set were $\{b, c\}$ then she would prefer $b$ over $c$, and so on. We could write our preference relations using counterfactual notation thus: $\{a, b\} \Box\!\!\rightarrow a, \{b, c\} \Box\!\!\rightarrow b$, and $\{a, c\} \Box\!\!\rightarrow c$. However if we do this, although we capture the simultaneous sense in which we might think, as theorists, of transitivity, we have a problem in that the setting is one in which the chain of trades described by bilking does not appear. Either the feasible set is $\{a, b\}$ in which case the choice set is the singleton $a$, or the feasible set is $\{b, c\}$ in which case the choice is $b$, or the feasible set is $\{a, c\}$, in which case the choice is $c$. In every possible case we have a trade, a choice and a stopping point. The counterfactual interpretation, whilst appealing as an interpretation of what it is to have transitive preferences, leaves no room for bilking.

A natural conclusion to draw from this is that we must chain the feasible sets in some way to get the pump going. We can achieve the effect by turning the counterfactual conditional relation into a material conditional and indexing the feasible sets with different time subscripts (a device that Debreu uses in his account of general equilibrium). We then obtain $\{a, b\}_t \rightarrow a, \{b, c\}_{t+1} \rightarrow b$, and $\{a, c\}_{t+2} \rightarrow c$ and this evidently describes a bilking process of the kind that advocates of the money pump seem to be looking for. However, in this case there is a cost and it comes from the fact that we expect subjects to be given full information about their options at the start and are not surprised if subjects make a sub-optimal choice if not fully informed. Rationality, whatever elsewhere it requires, does not require a decision-maker to be omniscient, just that they make full use of the information they do have. So a person with intransitive preferences who was duped could point out that they were not properly informed about the sequence of choices to follow when offered $\{a, b\}$ at time $t$. Indeed they could go a step further and point out that if the feasible set were completely and properly described, $F = \{\{a, b\}_t, \{b, c\}_{t+1}, \{a, c\}_{t+2}\}$, then they would use higher order preferences appropriate to such composite choice sets. One could imagine this happening in an experimental setting. The experimenter offers a subject three choice sets sequentially, detects an intransitive pattern and confronts the subject with evidence of their irrationality. The subject counters by pointing out that in

Table 1.

| | s1 | s2 | s3 | s4 | s5 | s6 |
|---|---|---|---|---|---|---|
| Dice | | | | | | |
| a | 1 | 1 | 4 | 4 | 4 | 4 |
| b | 3 | 3 | 3 | 3 | 3 | 3 |
| c | 5 | 5 | 2 | 2 | 2 | 2 |

an experiment where the sequence of feasible sets is known in advance, there is no need to use binary preferences over choice 'windows' which are at best only local approximations — a point made both by Anand [1993] and Lavalle and Fishburn [1988].

There are numerous variations on these themes (see also Anand, Pattanaik and Puppe [2009]) but none of which I am aware, stand up to scrutiny and, in a sense, that is where the argument should finish. However, it is reasonable to ask whether there are any cases where the violation of preference transitivity is positively appealing and there are indeed a number of arguments and examples to this effect.

One that many find particularly appealing depends on thinking how you might choose in the following setting. There are three possible dice each of which has six faces and a number on each face as indicated in Table 1.

The choice problem is this. A third party selects two dice and you have to choose one and your opponent gets the other. You then both throw your die and the player with the highest number wins a prize. The die are independent and each side has a 1/6 chance of landing face-up. How should you choose in such a scenario?

Assuming you wish to maximise your chances of winning you would prefer die $a$ if the choice were from $\{a, b\}$ as this gives a two-thirds chance of winning and you would prefer $b$ if the choice were from $\{a, c\}$ as there is only a one-third chance of winning on $c$. However, if you were to choose from $a$ and $c$ the only way you could win with $a$ is by getting a 4 in the event that your opponent does not get a five and the probability of that conjunction is $2/3 \times 2/3$ or $4/9$. So a maximiser would be better off choosing c[2]. The example seems to underline the point that Phillipe Mongin [2000] makes, namely that optimisation does not require transitivity.

There are many other instances of example based defences of intransitive preference[3] but the die example is of interest because it serves to emphasise the importance of context. The object of choice may not be a complete specification of the thing you are choosing though it is a *sine qua non* of consequentialist rationality that it should be. One might be tempted to throw any phenomena into the consequentialist bag but as I shall suggest later on, there are some logical limits to how far one can go. In any case, in the following section, I want to consider

[2]This example derives from work by Packard [1982] and Blythe [1972].

[3]Which I have discussed extensively in references cited at the end of chapter.

a similar kind of evaluation of a mathematically and conceptually distinct axiom, namely independence.

## 3 INDEPENDENCE

There are many independence axioms in the literature but the one of primary interest to decision theorists is a version that requires utility to be linearly weighted with respect to its probability. In a review of arguments that purport to demonstrate why rational agents should adhere to independence in the linearity sense, Ned McClennen [1989; 2009] argues against the claim and I find his arguments both to be persuasive and, on occasion, closely related to the reasons one might reject transitivity. This section covers one of McClennen's static arguments and an argument related to dynamic consistency due to Mark Machina.

We might begin by asking why would anyone think that utility should be linear with respect to probabilities? Historically, expected utility maximisation emerges as a way of resolving a problem associated with the expected value maximisation rule, but the resolution doesn't, in fact, speak to the constraint issue. Bernouilli was concerned by the fact the expected value of participating in the St Petersberg Paradox is infinite and yet people seemed willing to pay only very small amounts to participate in such games. The paradox turns around a game in which a coin is tossed and you win \$1 if the coin comes up heads on the first round at which point the game terminates. If the game goes on, you win \$2 on termination at round two, or \$4 on termination at round three and so on. Such a game has an infinite expected value but typically attracts very low valuations and this was something that puzzled Bernouilli who proposed that one reason was that people were maximising not expected value but expected utility and that their utility of money functions were logarithmic (ie increasing but at a very slow rate). People take Bernoulli's solution to be a justification of conventional decision theory whereas in reality it is just one way of resolving the paradox. The fact that it does so successfully need not be taken to be an argument that utility must be linear in probabilities as this just happens to be a by-product of Bernouilli's particular proposal.

Much later on, the mathematical economist and philosopher Frank Ramsey [1931] declined to be explicit about the linearity axiom (or any others for that matter) on the grounds that he believed linearity to be approximate, but both Allais [1953] and Ellsberg [1961] go a step further by devising thought-experiments which aim to show that rational preferences could certainly violate linearity. Ellsberg's version of the problem introduces the problem of uncertainty as ill-defined or unknown probabilities and raises a range of issues so for current purposes I shall confine my attention here to Allais's Paradox which focuses attention clearly on the independence axiom.

Consider two choice situations I and II. In I, you can select $A$ or $B$ which have payoffs as indicated in Table 2 which materialise depending on states of the world with externally and fairly determined probabilities as given. In choice setting II,

Table 2. The Allais Paradox

| | States of the World | | |
|---|---|---|---|
| | S1 (p=0.89) | S2(p=0.10) | S3(p=0.01) |
| Choice Situation I | | | |
| *A* | £1m | £5m | |
| *B* | £1m | £1m | £1m |
| Choice Situation II | | | |
| *A'* | | £5m | |
| *B'* | | £1m | £1m |

the payoffs are modified by removing a common £1m from the payoff schedule to give rise to a choice between *A*' and *B*'. The independence axiom says that if you prefer *A* then you should prefer *A*' and if you prefer *B*, then you should prefer *B*'. However, Allais noted that there was a strong tendency for people to prefer *B* and *A*'.

In the Allais version of this paradox, what drives our preferences for particular gambles seems to be some kind of preference for certainty suggesting that there is either a discontinuity at $p = 1$ or a non-linearity in utility as $\lim p \to 1$. In a one shot setting the preference constellation satisfies intelligibility. We certainly understand why a person might have such preferences. In I, *B* represents a sure payoff whereas in II the chances of winning are rather similar so one might be swayed by the significantly higher payoff.

Choice problems where the number of repetitions is very high are, of course, a different matter because the law of large numbers suggests that the valuation of small gambles repeated frequently will tend to expected value. The fact that we may have such repeated choices at the back of our minds can help to explain the existence of pro-linear intuitions but it does not serve to ground choice in single choice problems with significant payoffs though these are precisely the ones that lie at the heart of decision theory as Savage's [1954] and Raiffa's [1967] accounts demonstrate.

This issue is not so different to the way in which attitudes to risk are thought to vary with wealth. The wealthier one is, the less risk-averse one need be. The one shot attitude could legitimately be risk averse or risk preferring and will with repetition (again for small gambles) tend to an expected valuation. A more comprehensive treatment would be relevant for other purposes (for example allowing for risk-aversion in the gains domain and risk-preference in the loss domain) but these points serve to underline the importance of one-offness and largeness for understanding the role that probability should play in a utility function and in turn this further questions whether capturing risk-attitude exclusively in terms of the concavity of a riskless utility of money function is a justified modelling strategy.

Beyond the Allais and Ellsberg paradoxes it might be questioned whether there are relevant principles on which we can draw to adjudicate the rationality of preferences that violate linearity. As it happens, Samuelson [1952] suggested that the concept of complementarity provides such an argument. In the analysis of (consumer) choice under certainty, goods that are consumed conjointly can thereby exhibit complementarities in utility but there is no room for this to happen in gambles as only one outcome materialises by construction. The opportunity for complementarity does not, therefore, exist, so the argument goes.

This view can be challenged. McClennen [1988, p. 170] suggests that the absence of complementary goods only removes one reason for non-independence but fails to make any positive, let alone conclusive, case for independence. Anand [1986; 1987] agrees and argues further that whilst the ex post outcome is only a singleton, it is the ex ante set-up that determines the choices made (in conventional decision theory) and in this case, it is clear that a gamble does comprise a set of simultaneously enjoyed chances of experiencing particular outcomes. McClennen (op cit) supports the point indirectly by noting that results in Becker *et al.* [1963], Coombs [1975] and Ellsberg (*op cit.*) suggest that their results provide behavioural evidence of just this complementarity.

A quite different approach in the literature tries to argue that independence is required by dynamic consistency. Dynamic consistency has become an important topic in the analysis of choice over time and in dynamic choice problems, some uncertainty is resolved after the decision-maker has chosen. Machina's [1989] argument against the imposition of independence on rational agents in such contexts is wide-ranging and, again in my view, persuasive, though here I shall focus on one aspect of his treatment of his dynamic case.[4]

The standard argument for linearity as rationality can be seen with the help of the following decision problem. In this case, we consider two opportunity sets of lotteries given by the decision trees in Figure 1.

Someone who violates independence with behaviour that exhibits a preference for certainty might plausibly, in the left-hand tree of Figure 1, choose the down branch $B$ and in the right-hand tree the up branch $A$'. Note that in this case there are two points in time when a decision maker can elect how to move along the tree — initially before nature moves (at the first circle) and then subsequently when and if the person actually arrives at the choice node within the tree. The dynamic consistency argument for someone who starts off with an Allais plan runs as follows. If the decision-maker prefers the lottery to which the upper branch leads, then a person who gets to the decision tree with an Allais plan will have to ditch the plan in order to access the most preferred option which is the lottery in choice situation I. On the other hand, if the decision-maker prefers the certain outcome, £1m, then an Allais plan will pick out the best option if the decision-maker gets to the internal decision-node. However, in that case there is a corresponding problem in choice situation II as the Allais plan picks out the lottery whereas the agent prefers the £1m option. So in general, decision-makers who violate independence

[4]Machina ultimately concludes that imposition of independence on agents with non-linear preferences is unacceptable though he says little if anything about the direct parallels with arguments against the imposition of transitivity on agents with intransitive preferences.

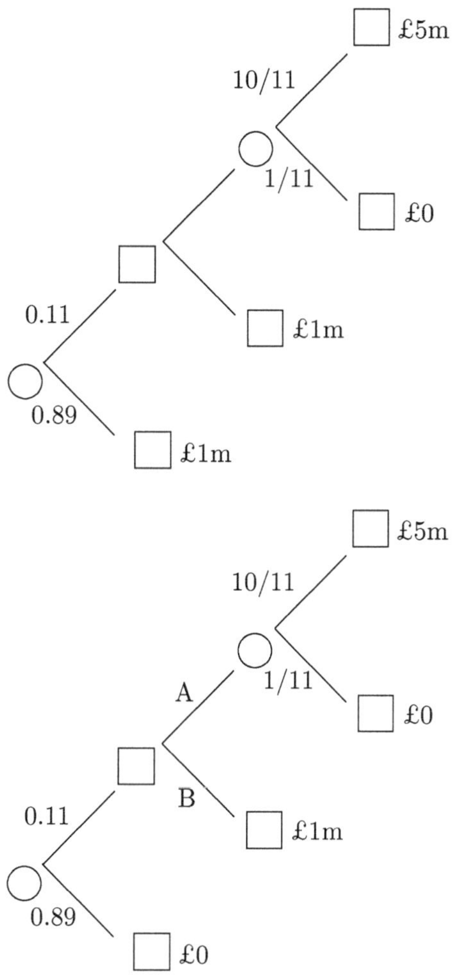


Figure 1. Allais Paradox as a Dynamic Choice Problem

have to make off-plan choices if they wish to maximise utility.

Machina's counter-argument turns on the view that independence tacitly assumes consequentialism which is precisely the doctrine that non-linearity challenges. The conventional approach to decision-making requires one to determine the opportunity set implied by a situation, identify the most preferred element of this set and then adopt a strategy that leads to the most preferred element. Furthermore, the consequentialist approach to option evaluation in decision trees allows one to snip parts of the tree off whilst leaving the ordering of remaining options unchanged.[5] So any preferences that are identified by a complete plan for all eventualities in a tree will be acted on if the relevant nodes are reached. To illustrate why one might not want to agree such pruning techniques, Machina offers a fairness example[6] in which Mom wishes to divide a treat between two offspring, Ann and Ben. The treat cannot be divided and Mom is indifferent as to which child gets it and strictly prefers, contrary to precepts of expected utility, that the treat be divided on the basis of a random coin flip.

Mom flips a coin, Ann wins and Ben objects. Ben argues that Mom actually prefers to flip a coin and asks her to flip the coin again. Mom declines, and most people would say, rightly so. Mom prefers a simple decision problem in which nature moves (heads or tails) and the outcome is a treat for Ann or Ben. But Ben wants Mom to substitute this for a tree which she disprefers, one in which when 'treat to Ann' is the outcome, she flips again. But once Mom has flipped the coin, she does in fact prefer to allocate the treat to a particular child and the reason is that nature has made a particular move. So Mom's preferences when she gets to make the allocation are, intrinsically related to an earlier move by nature. She doesn't wish to snip off earlier parts of the tree because her preferences are conditioned on this history. So runs Machina's argument and I suggest that if we allow that there could be counter-examples to axioms such as these, then this is as good a counter-example as one is likely to find. The only point of departure with Machina that I find is that his arguments at time seem to apply equally to violations of transitivity whereas he seems to believe that his case is only limited to justifying violations of independence.

## 4 DIFFICULTIES WITH THE FORMALISATION OF NON-DICTATORSHIP

Social choice shares some axioms with decision theory — transitivity being the obvious example — but it also shares a strong association with consequentialism which is now being reconsidered. Assumptions in social choice have a strongly normative character but perhaps because there are more considerations, assump-

[5]For this reason, I claim that rejection of transitivity, independence, Sen's expansion and contraction axiom and Arrow's independence of irrelevant alternatives axioms are all, potentially, intimately related.

[6]The example is a distillation of literature on interpersonal fairness and equity under uncertainty including, particularly, discussions by Strotz [1958], Harsanyi [1978], Broome [1982] and Sen [1985].

tions in social choice procedures are never quite as canonical as they might be in decision theory. Nonetheless both decision theory and social choice share an interest in the development of theories that help to characterise good decision-making by reasonable or rational agents.

Like decision theory, social choice finds itself spread across disciplines (more so in politics and less in psychology) and any reading of the relevant literatures would find it hard not to conclude that particular significance is still given to the requirement that social choice procedures be non-dictatorial. The formal literature, including relatively recent work that offers simpler proofs of Arrow's results (see for instance Barbera [1980], Dardanoni [2001], Geanakopolos [2001] and Suzumura [1988]), accepts that the avoidance of dictatorship is an important consideration for designers of social choice mechanisms. Indeed, it is difficult to imagine the grounds on which any reasonable person might object. Of course, and as Arrow reminds us, his contribution deals predominantly with formal issues, which may not exactly mirror the concept of dictatorship in natural language but even then, his characterisation of dictatorship raises some interesting difficulties that further help us understand the limits that axiomatic arguments.

To see the force of these questions, I begin with Arrow's [1963, p. 30] definition of a dictatorial SWF which holds if $\exists i \in \mathrm{S} : \forall xy \in \mathrm{O}, xP_iy \rightarrow xPy$ (1) where $i$ is an individual in some set or society, S, of $(m)$ individuals, $x$ and $y$ are social options from a set, O, of $n$ options, $P_i$ is $i$'s preference relation and $P$, society's preference relation.[7] The existence of a situation in which a single individual can determine the social ordering for all possible pair-wise choices regardless of the wishes of others, certainly seems, *prima facie*, to be something to be avoided. But the question I wish to pose concerns the extent to which (1) is an adequate formalisation of this constraint on the social choice process.

A little reflection indicates why it might not be obvious that (1) must be true even if a person with dictatorial powers, particularly ones exercised, belongs to S. It may be, for instance, that there is a relatively large sub-set of O, say $\{p, q, \ldots, x, y\} = L$, for which the implication in (1) is true even if it fails to hold for *all* possible choices. Some dictators might not want their way on absolutely everything for which they have a preference, so the universal quantifier in (1) is too strong and therefore unwarranted. Conversely, an individual might exert disproportionate influence on a subset of all possible pair-wise choices in a manner that we would find unacceptable though such a person would not be dictatorial in the sense of (1).

One possible response is to point out, as some have[8] that if, in the context of Arrow's theorem, the formal statement of what it is to be a dictator could be weaker, then Arrow's insight is even stronger than his theorem states. The

---

[7]None of the points made here turn on the distinction between strict and weak preference although they are more transparently made using the strict preference relations. Arrow defines strict preference in terms of weak preference in the customary manner: however, his characterisation of dictatorship only involves individual preferences which are strict.

[8]I am grateful to Philippe Mongin and a seminar participant in Basel for this observation.

observation is a reasonable one to make though it does nothing to rebut the view that the failure of necessity suggests that the formalisation is further away from the natural language concept than we might suppose or that this gap calls for further probing, particularly concerning questions of sufficiency.[9]

If the formal statement in (1) is not a necessary condition for the existence of at least one person with dictatorial powers, might we at least regard this an evidential or diagnostic condition i.e. one the satisfaction of which can be taken as suggestive that something is awry? It is tempting to think that we can give a positive answer to this question even if it appears to change the significance we attach to the presence of an Arrowvian dictator. If there were a single person who had the capacity to assert his or her will and did so in every possible choice where s/he had a strong preference, then (1) would be satisfied. But even from an evidential perspective, there are difficulties.

To see the point about sufficiency, suppose we rewrite the implication part of (1), suppressing the quantifiers, as a conditional probability thus: $p(xPy/xP_iy) = 1$ (2). This re-formulation brings different considerations to mind. Even if there is an individual whose preferences we can use to predict the social ordering with perfect accuracy, which is one thing (2) suggests, correlation is not the same as causation.[10] So we need to consider the possible causes that would give rise to the satisfaction of (2). One view is that the equation in (2) holds true for one individual because it is true for all $i \in$ S. In that case, for all pairs of options, if any person had a strong preference, then society would exhibit the same strong preference. The reason is as follows. If at least one person had a strong preference with respect to a pair of options, then anyone else who had a strong preference would have to have the same strong preference. This is true for all pairs of options so there would be unanimity over all strong preferences: weak preference and indifference are symmetric relations so unanimity over options for which there are strong preferences implies unanimity over all options. (If there were a pair of options where no one had a strong preference, then the dictatorship axiom, *taken on its own*, allows society to hold any preference). So (2) could be true if there were unanimity, which is hardly a disturbing cause, and certainly not a state of affairs one would always want to rule out as the Arrowvian formalisation encourages. Indeed Arrow [1963] acknowledges this problem as a difficulty though the tendency would be to rule such situations out on grounds of triviality. This ruling out may be reasonable in terms of analysis but it does not remove the fact that (1) is deficient *qua* formalisation of dictatorship because there are situations where it is met and for reasons that have nothing to do with dictatorship and not

[9]One further point that could be made concerns the extent to which dictators might manipulate other people's preferences. In general we want to limit the shaping of other people's preferences but the Arrowvian framework deals with fixed preferences so this issue cannot be discussed without further work. As it stands, the framework needs to be elaborated if it is to provide a substantially correct account of the constraints that operate on social choice mechanisms. It might be that such accounts have not been developed as they appear to be redundant from the view point of generating impossibility results.

[10]See also Brown [1975] on issues that relate to causality.

worrying in terms either of welfare or social choice. So the formalisation seems not to be sufficient.

When Arrow [1963, p. 30, definition 6] motivates (1), he stipulates that a dictator is a person who can have reflected all their strong preferences in the social ordering, 'regardless' of other people's preferences. Some people take this to be a counter to the point just made because the state of unanimity on which it relies fails to address the 'regardless' aspect of the formalisation. However, this is not quite right as Arrow, in his discussions of the unanimity issue, implicitly accepts. Arrow's Theorem holds that a conjunctive set of assumptions implies the truth of (1): the fact that (1) gives cause for concern in some situations means that we can only infer the existence of a problem for social choice in just those circumstances. Put another way, it is true that the Theorem establishes, for its assumptions, the existence of at least one individual who will always see their strong preferences mirrored in the social ordering but we cannot assume that this is, in every situation, something about which we should be distraught, as already noted.

A related difficulty arises from the observation that the conditional relationship in (1) is logically equivalent to the following holding true for all elements of $O, \neg xPy \rightarrow \neg xP_iy$ (3). (3) tells us that whenever society does not strongly prefer $x$ over $y$, there will be an individual who also does not strongly prefer $x$ to $y$, which is hardly surprising. What is surprising is that there is at least one particular individual who makes this statement true for all option pairs. The fact is hardly obvious — if not quite paradoxical — but nor is it obviously worrying. Indeed, it is difficult to think of a way in which a person *must* be worried by (3) despite its logical relation to dictatorship as formalised in the Theorem.[11]

Logic aside, one might challenge sufficiency not just abstractly but on more concrete grounds. One possibility, to be more explicit about one theme that has underpinned this discussion, is that the Theorem just points to the inevitable existence of someone who is 'lucky'; if a SWF exists which satisfies the other axioms of Arrow's theorem, then we know that *at least one person would see their binary preference mirrored in the social ordering* whatever choice was being considered. This description of dictatorship is consistent with the formalisation and the Theorem but reinforces the point that (1) is neutral with respect to causality, though causality is an inextricable part of any definition of and concern about undue influence. Such a description we might use to conclude that what Arrow shows is this: if his other conditions are satisfied, then any SWF will always guarantee that (at least) *one* person will get their way in any choice between two options. This, too, is not an obvious result as, intuitively, it would have been reasonable to conjecture that a SWF satisfying Arrow type conditions might yield the result that no one could expect to get their way in all possible choices.[12] So in this positive light,

[11]We suggest this poses a serious challenge for philosophers the resolution of which would be invaluable to economic theory. The challenge is to say what should we make of consequences that clearly have different normative implications even if they are logically equivalent.

[12]Indeed, one can still conjecture that this is true for a particular set of assumptions similar,

we could take Arrow's result to be more optimistic than the usual interpretation suggests. The worrying consequence for practice, as opposed to theory, has to do with equity — the difficulty being that a SWF which satisfies the other Arrowvian conditions guarantees perfect efficiency — but only for *one* person.

Ultimately, it would be best if social choices gave everyone what they wanted but this is only possible trivially, as we have seen, in the situation where individuals are unanimous in their orderings of social options. Such a situation might be taken as contrary in spirit to the assumption of unrestricted domain, an extreme assumption perhaps, but one that reflects the need to exclude the trivial decision problem in which everyone agrees. Yet from an efficiency view point alone, there is no reason why we should not treat preference satisfaction for as many people, in as many choices, as an asymptotic ideal for which we should aim. That this amounts to proposing that desirable SWFs should maximise, *inter alia*, the number of Arrowvian dictators constitutes a substantial reason for rejecting the conventional interpretation and significance attributed to (1), a point to which we return below.

Difficulties in the formalisation of axioms or conditions like dictatorship can arise from the context in which they are proposed and in this case that particularly includes the other principles they are designed to accompany. Although Arrow himself discusses the implications of unanimity for his formalisation of dictatorship, it is worth noting that the opposite (complete diversity) can give rise to dictatorship — Arrowvian style. To see this, suppose we have a set of six individuals, $i$ to $n$, who collectively exhibit all the possible strict preference rankings over three social options, $a, b$ and $c$ — a situation we might label the 'full realisation' of Arrow's unrestricted domain assumption for three options. For ease of exposition (see below), the orderings are written out as ternary relations from which binary preferences can be derived in the obvious way.[13]

| Six Individual Preferences | Possible Social Ordering of Three Options |
|---|---|
| $aP_ibP_ic$ | $aPbPc$ |
| $aP_jcP_jb$ | $aPcPb$ |
| $bP_kaP_kc$ | $bPaPc$ |
| $bP_lcP_la$ | $bPcPa$ |
| $cP_maP_mb$ | $cPaPb$ |
| $cP_nbP_na$ | $cPaPb$ |

In this example, it follows that if there is a SWF which maps the electorate space to social ordering element, in the manner described earlier, then it must be dictatorial because for any social ordering there is always an individual who orders the options in the same way. We might put the point more generally in the form of a proposition about the minimum of individuals required to ensure that (1) all possible SWFs are dictatorial.

but different, to those that appear in Arrow's seminal work. However, we are unaware of such results at present.

[13]Binary preferences are derived from ternary preferences simply by dropping the unavailable alternative.

If individuals are uniformly distributed over the domain of possible preference orderings, the ratio of individuals to options, $m/n$, required for the existence of at least one Arrowvian dictator $= n!/n = (n-1)!$. The example above illustrates this proposition simply — because there are three options, we need to have a minimum of 3! (6) individuals to be sure that all possible social orderings are dictatorial. So where the number of individuals is large relative to the number of social options, or more exactly where unrestricted domain is fully *realised* because every possible ranking can be found to be held by someone, satisfaction of (1) cannot be regarded as evidence of dictatorship. This shows that $U$ combined with a sufficiently large number of voters is enough to make satisfaction of (1) unsurprising, almost inevitable and certainly unworrying. Exit routes would be to constrain $U$, which might be arbitrary, expand the number of alternatives which is often desirable, or reduce the number of voters which in many cases would be absurd. From this perspective, the impact of PO and IIA is to reduce the number of voters and preference profiles that give rise to contradiction or dictatorship. The consequence for the formalisation of ND is that we have another example which shows that ND can be violated for reasons that have nothing to do with the existence of a dictator. Indeed the example demonstrates the extent to which the term 'regardless' in the motivation for the formalisation of ND, can be misleading.[14] When there are enough voters with sufficiently dispersed orderings, then for a social ranking, there will be one person whose preferences determine the social ordering, 'regardless' of the orderings held by other people.[15] Though the term regardless is not incorrect in a sense, its use here is misleading.[16] Where the number of options is small relative to the number of voters this fact alone might make (1) likely though for each dictatorial social welfare function, a different voter might have the preferences that make the function appear dictatorial.[17]

There is a final problem that goes beyond sufficiency or necessity and concerns the extent to which (1), even if we took it just to be an indicator rather than a necessary or sufficient condition, points in the correct direction. I suggest it might not for the following reason. Begin by noting that the desirability (des) of a SWF is positively related to the extent to which it can meet people's preferences. In Arrow's framework, the idea, or something very much like it, appears twice — first

[14]From Arrow [1963, p. 30] 'A social welfare function is said to be dictatorial if there exists an individual such that for all [pairwise preferences a strong individual preference implies a strong social preference]... regardless of all individuals other than i.'

[15]This is hardly an academic point. In situations where millions of voters are ranking a small number of political candidates, the existence of Arrowvian dictators seems inevitable. National elections are surely one of the first areas of application of Arrow's Theorem.

[16]Tanguiane [1994] seems to explore a similar line of thought when he shows that an agent with preferences *representative* of society's preferences always exist under Arrow's assumptions.

[17]It is interesting to compare this results due to Tangian [2000] which show that Condorcet's paradox becomes less likely as the number of voters gets larger. On the face of it his and our conclusions related to population size might seem to pull in opposite directions. However, recall that our point is that because satisfaction of the formal characterisation of dictatorship becomes more likely as population increases simply by virtue of the preference profile space being covered, so we should be less concerned about satisfaction of the formal characterisation *per se.*

as something called positive association, and second in the idea that social choice is about preference aggregation. Although we shall question this view subsequently, it should not be controversial for theories that hold social choice to be, at root, a matter of preference aggregation as Arrow's Theorem does. We might formalise this idea by saying that $des(SWF) = f(d)$ (4), where $d$ is a distance function (and its value when there is no confusion) defined over the pair $(P, (P_1, P_2, \ldots, P_m))$, bounded from below by 0 at the point where all the $P$s are the same, and where $f$ is a strictly decreasing function of $d$, (i.e. $\partial f/\partial \mathrm{d} < 0$). (4), combined with this last inequality says that the desirability of a SWF is a decreasing function of the difference between the social ordering and the profile of individual orderings.[18]

Now consider a sequence of states characterised by the number of Arrowvian dictators in a society:

$$\begin{aligned} &For\ 0\ i\ in\ S : \forall xy, xP_iy \rightarrow xPy \\ &For\ 1\ i\ in\ S : \forall xy, xP_iy \rightarrow xPy \\ &For 2\ i\ in\ S : \forall xy, xP_iy \rightarrow xPy \\ &\vdots \\ &For\ all\ m\ i\ in\ S : \forall xy, xP_iy \rightarrow xPy \end{aligned}$$

Moving from a situation in which there are $l$ dictators to $l-1$ dictators, involves, at least changing the social ordering for one pair so that, for a person who was previously dictatorial, there now exists a pair of alternatives, $x$ and $y$, such that $xP_iy \wedge \neg xPy$. This indicates an increase in d and therefore a SWF that has a lower des value.

Of course the net effect of such a change will depend on the numbers of other members in society with similar or opposed preferences and the exact nature of the metric used. Nonetheless, situations exist where this is an unambigously poor move. For example, suppose we have a unanimous population in which the final statement in the above list is true, i.e. that (1) is true because each individual is an Arrowvian dictator. In that case we could only reduce the number of individuals whose preferences satisfied (1), keeping tastes constant, by changing the social ordering so that it fails to reflect preferences in some respect where before, it did not. This is nonsensical (Pareto inferior) but as we have suggested, reflects a larger problem, namely that the formalisation of dictatorship is fundamentally at odds with the idea that better social rankings, and therefore social welfare functions, are ones which find a tighter, rather than a looser, fit between the social ordering and the profile of individual preferences.[19] In a rough, but nonetheless fundamental sense, we think of most social choice processes as needing to avoid allowing undue influence so understanding problems in the formulation of a special case,

[18]Of course, desirability might be a function of other things but this possibility could be represented with a little additional notation.

[19]The idea that social choice involves increasing the correlation (fit) between a social ordering and the preference profile is discussed at length, perhaps in one of the first such discussions, by Craven [1996]. Cardinality has come to be used in social choice though in the different context of measuring freedom and diversity.

namely dictatorship, should help us understand something about how to specify the problem of social choice itself. These considerations lead to two ideas which can summed up jointly — social choice within a preference maximisation framework might be thought of as maximising fit between social choice and individual preferences whereas dictatorship reduction — a cardinal counterpart to (1) leads in the opposite direction.

## 5 THE IDENTIFICATION PROBLEM

Mathematics has had a profound impact in the 20th century on the development of philosophical thinking about the nature of rational choice (social choice and political theory included). In some ways, the approach which can be traced back to correspondence between Bernoulli and Cramer; the methods and approach are mature but they continue to evolve and there are still a number of important paradoxes that call for resolution and here I want to discuss two issues which suggest the existence of serious identification problems in the decision theory and possibly also social choice. Within econometric and statistical systems, whether an equation is identified (estimable) can be checked using rank and order tests. Identification plays an increasingly significant role in econometric theory and practice though it is only sporadically recognised as a significant issue in the decision sciences. Here I want to illustrate two kinds identification problems, one predominantly associated with theory and the other with the search for 'true' generalisations of expected utility theory. In her assessment of economic theory, Nancy Cartwright [1999] claims that a surprising amount of work is done, not by fundamental theory, but by auxiliary assumptions that are made after theory and with the aim of making it work.[20] This section deals roughly with the same issue but by relocating it within the framework of identification problems, I aim to sketch the basis of a position that would, if extended in more depth, lead to recognising the addressing of the identification problem as a central aspect of theory development and assessment in decision sciences.

For a long time, a favoured response by defenders of assumptions like transitivity and independence to evidence of axiom violation was to argue for a more sophisticated interpretation of theory. In particular, it was claimed that if one were more detailed about the way in which primitives were individuated, then apparent violations could be made to disappear. This 'move' was attractive to those who were theoretically conservative but it raises a number of questions. Is such a move always possible? Could the move backfire by working in reverse? And if and when such redescription does work are there any scientific costs? The translation theorem, Anand [1990] addresses these questions and demonstrates how it is possible to describe any intransitive sets of behaviours in a manner in which transitivity is not violated and also to give transitive behaviours an intransitive description. The theorem is quite general and is proved as follows.

[20] See also Mäki's [2000] work on assumptions in economics.

Suppose we observe a set of intransitive choice behaviours denoted $Pab, Pbc$ and $Pac$. Rewrite the constellation with primitive descriptions that distinguish the different feasible sets thus: $P$($a$ out $a$ and $b$)($b$ out of $a$ and $b$), $P$($b$ out $b$ and $c$)($c$ out of $b$ and $c$) and $P$($a$ out of $ac$)($c$ out of $a$ and $c$). Then further redescribe these choices by mapping the refined primitives onto a new linguistic convention thus:

| Refined Primitive Descriptions | New Linguistic Convention |
|---|---|
| $a$ out of $a$ and $b$ | $l$ |
| $b$ out $a$ and $b$ | $m$ |
| $b$ out $b$ and $c$ | $n$ |
| $c$ out of $b$ and $c$ | $o$ |
| $a$ out $a$ and $c$ | $p$ |
| $c$ out $a$ and $c$ | $q$ |

It is now possible to write the initially intransitive behaviour: $Plm, Pno$ and $Ppq$ — i.e. the intransitivity has disappeared.

To travel in reverse, consider the intransitive behaviours $Pab, Pbc$ and $Pca$. Refine the description as before to obtain: $P$($a$ out $a$ and $b$)($b$ out of $a$ and $b$), $P$($b$ out $b$ and $c$)($c$ out of $b$ and $c$) and $P$($c$ out of $ac$)($a$ out of $a$ and $c$) and then follow the new linguistic convention below:

| Refined Primitive Descriptions | New Linguistic Convention |
|---|---|
| $a$ out of $a$ and $b$, $c$ out $a$ and $c$ | $l$ |
| $b$ out $a$ and $b$, $b$ out of $b$ and $c$ | $m$ |
| $c$ out $b$ and $c$, $a$ out of $a$ and $c$ | $n$ |

In this case we can now rewrite the initially 'intransitive' behaviours as $Plm, Pmn$ and $Pln$. QED.

One might argue that in many situations the relevant linguistic conventions are fixed so the argument doesn't arise but this fails to recognise that forming a set of procedures for describing units of analysis is a key element in the formalisation of any science. This is particularly true in physics, mathematics and chemistry and I would suggest that we are at a surprisingly early stage in this process in decision theory particularly. Formally, there are two conventions available to decision theorists for identifying relations and neither is terribly satisfactory. Savage's approach requires that we work with materially complete descriptions of options but then what is materially complete for one person may not be materially complete for the next, and we need these descriptions to be materially complete if subjective expected utility is to be applied. Furthermore, expected utility is recursively limited i.e. does in fact make certain assumptions about parts of the decision problem which must always stay outside the materially complete description. If this is not the case, then assumptions like transitivity in reality would have no actual behavioural content as the translation theorem above demonstrates.

The alternative approach is to use the natural language descriptors of the choice setting and within such a framework I suggest the practical examples in section 2 two and others reviewed elsewhere, it can surely be reasonable for agents to have intransitive preferences. However, the natural language examples tend mostly to work by putting important decision relevant information into the choice setting which according to Savage should be in the description of the choice options and so is unlikely to move those who want to stick with expected utility. Perhaps the only thing that one can definitively say is that there has been something of a sea-change within decision-theory after which many now recognise the theoretical and conceptual limits of expected utility and work with more general models and/or models with more detailed structures.

Generality has been a driving force in economic analysis for a long time but perhaps we are now beginning to see that other considerations are important too. Typically analysis is partial rather comprehensive and in this case we need theories that have structures relevant to the focal phenomena. The most general theories may not have the most appropriately nuanced theoretical structures for such exercises. Nor may they provide the most efficient methods for studying the phenomenological structures that are of interest.

## 6 SUMMARY

Consequentialism does not come off well from the foundational analyses that have emerged over the past twenty to thirty years. The extent of this about-turn could barely be broader but it is both a useful stepping stone and we should be careful about what we choose to discard and what we keep. The position I take here is informed by a sense that the early axiomatisations of decision theory and social choice were both essentially characterisations of consequentialism in individual and group choice. Anything can be defined as a consequence but for any of the theories we have (especially in decision theory) there are *logical* limits to how far this strategy can be applied to save a theory in the face of contrary intuitions, examples or evidence. Furthermore, and in the grand sweep of intellectual history possibly more important, there are pragmatic limits concerning the extent to which consequentialist theories are efficient ways of understanding the structures of decision-making. These considerations pose real challenges to those who might argue, as Broome does, that the good has a transitive structure. The nature, function and role of reasons is potentially an important area for development (I agree with Levi on this) though I find Scanlon's account unpersuasive in parts and his view that welfare is not a master value (because there are no master values) is somewhat chilling. What survives of the preference pattern based approaches, I suggest, is the concept of dominance but thus far the formal specifications seem not to be appealing in all settings.

## BIBLIOGRAPHY

[Allais, 1953] M. Allais. Le Comportment de l'homme rationale devant le risqué, critiques des postulates et axioms de l'ecole Americaine, *Econometrica,* **21**, 503-46, 1953.

[Anand, 1986] P. Anand. Axiomatic Choice Theory, Oxford University DPhil Thesis, Bodleian Library Oxford, 1986.

[Anand, 1987] P. Anand. Are the Preference Axioms Really Rational? Theory and Decision, **23**, 189-214, 1987

[Anand, 1990] P. Anand. Interpreting Axiomatic (Decision) Theory, *Annals of Operations Research,* **23**, 91-101, 1990.

[Anand, 1993] P. Anand. *Foundations of Rational Choice Under Risk*, Oxford, Oxford University Press, 1993

[Anand *et al.*, 2009] P. Anand, P. Pattanaik and C. Puppe. *Handbook of Rational and Social Choice*, Oxford, Oxford University Press, 2009.

[Arrow, 1963] K. Arrow. *Social Choice and Individual Values*, New Haven, Yale University Press ($2^{nd}$ edition), 1963.

[Barbera, 1980] S. Barbera. Pivotal Voters: A New Proof of Arrow's Theorem, *Economic Letters,* **6,** 13-6, 1980.

[Becker *et al.*, 1963] G. M. Becker, M. H. De Groot, and J. Marshak. An Experimental Study of Some Stochastic Models for Wagers, *Behavioural Science*, **8**, 199-202, 1963.

[Blythe, 1972] C. Blythe. Some Probability Paradoxes in Choice from among Random Alternatives, *Journal of the American Statistical Association,* **67**, 366-73, 1972.

[Broome, 1982] J. Broome. Equity in Risk Bearing, *Operations Research,* **30**, 412-14, 1982.

[Broome, 1991] J. Broome. *Weighing Goods,* Basil Blackwell, Oxford, 1991.

[Brown, 1975] D. J. Brown. Aggregation of Preferences, *Quarterly Journal of Economics,* **89**, 456-69, 1975.

[Cartwright, 1999] N. Cartwright. The limits of exact science: from Economics to Physics, *Perspectives on Science,* **7**, 318-36, 1999.

[Coombs, 1975] C. H. Coombs. Portfolio Theory and Measurement of Risk. In *Human Judgement and Decision Processes*, M. F. Kaplan and S. Schwartz, eds., pp. 63–85. Academic Press, New York, 1975.

[Craven, 1996] J. Craven. Best Fit Social Choices: An Alternative to Arrow, *Economic Journal,* **106,** 1161-74, 1996.

[Dardanoni, 2001] V. Dardanoni. A Pedagogical Proof of Arrow's Impossibility Theorem, *Social Choice and Welfare,* **18**, 107-12, 2001.

[Dowding, 1997] K. Dowding. Equity and Voting: Why Democracy Needs Dictators, *L'Annee Sociologique*, **447**, 39–53, 1997.

[Ellsberg, 1961] D. Ellsberg. Risk Ambiguity and the Savage Axioms, *Quarterly Journal of Economics,* **75,** 528-556, 1961.

[Geanakopolos, 2001] J. Geanakopolos. Three Brief Proofs of Arrow's Impossibility Theorem, New Haven, Cowles Foundation Discussion Paper 1123RRR, Yale University, 2001.

[Gendin, 1996] S. Gendin. Why Preference is Not Transitive, *The Philosophical Quarterly,* **54**, 482-88, 1996.

[Harsanyi, 1978] J. Harsanyi. Bayesian Decision Theory and Utilitarian Ethics, *American Economic Review,* **68**, 223-8, 1978.

[Kim and Richter, 1986] T. Kim and M. K. Richter. Non-transitive Non-total Consumer Theory, *Journal of Economic Theory,* **38**, 324-68, 1986.

[Kirchsteiger and Puppe, 1996] G. Kirchsteiger and C. Puppe. Intransitive Choices Based on Transitive Preferences: The Case of Menu Dependent Information, *Theory and Decision,* **41**, 37-58, 1996.

[Lavalle and Fishburn, 1988] I. Lavalle and P. C. Fishburn. Context Dependent Choice with Nonlinear and Nontransitive Preferences, *Econometrica,* **56**, 1221-39, 1988.

[Machina, 1989] M. Machina. Dynamic Consistency and Non-Expected Utility Models of Choice Under Uncertainty, *Journal of Economic Literature*, **XXVII**, 1622-1668, 1989.

[Mäki, 2000] U. Mäki. Kinds of Assumptions and Their Truth, *Kyklos,* **53**, 317-35, 2000.

[Mas-Collel, 1974] A. Mas-Collel. An Equilibrium Existence Theorem without Complete or Transitive Preferences, *Journal of Mathematical Economics,* **1**, 237-46, 1974.

[May, 1954] K. O. May. Intransitivity Utility and Aggregation of Preference Patterns, *Econometrica,* **XXII,** 1-13, 1954.

[McClennen, 1989] E. F. McClennen. Sure-thing Doubts. In *Decision Probability and Utility,* P. Gärdenfors and N.-E. Sahlin, eds. Cambridge, Cambridge University Press, 1989.

[McClennen, 2009] E. F. McClennen. The Normative Status of the Independence Axiom. In *Handbook of Rational and Social Choice*, P. Anand *et al.*, eds. Oxford, Oxford University Press, 2009.

[Mongin, 2000] P. Mongin. Does Optimisation Imply Rationality? *Synthese,* **124**, 73-111, 2000.

[von Neumann and Morgenstern, 1944] J. von Neumann and O. Morgenstern. *Theory of Games and Economic Behavior,* Princeton, Princeton University Press, 1944.

[Packard, 1982] D. J. Packard. Cyclical Preference Logic, *Theory and Decision*, **14**, 415-26, 1982.

[Putnam, 1995] H. Putnam. On the Rationality of Preferences, Santa Clara University Conference, March 4 (mimeo), 1995.

[Rabinowicz, 2000] W. Rabinowicz. Money Pump with Foresight. In *Imperceptible Harms and Benefits*, M. Almeida, ed., pp. 123–143. Dordrecht, Kluwer, 2000.

[Raiffa, 1968] H. Raiffa. *Decision Analysis,* Reading Ma, Addison-Wesley, 1968.

[Ramsey, 1931] F. P. Ramsey. *The Foundations of Mathematics and Other Logical Essays,* Kegan Paul, London, 1931.

[Rachels, 1998] S. Rachels. Counterexamples to the Transitivity of Better Than, *The Australian Journal of Philosophy,* **76,** 71-83, 1998.

[Savage, 1954] L. J. Savage. *The Foundations of Statistics,* New York, John Wiley. 1954.

[Sen, 1970] A. K. Sen. *Collective Choice and Social Welfare,* San Francisco, Holden-Day, 1970.

[Sen, 1985] A. K. Sen. Rationality and Uncertainty, *Theory and Decision,* **18**, 109-27, 1985.

[Strotz, 1956] R. H. Strotz. Myopia and Inconsistency in Dynamic Utility Maximisation, *Review of Economic Studies,* **23**, 165-80, 1956.

[Sugden, 1985] R. Sugden. Why Be Consistent? *Economica,* **52**, 167-84, 1985.

[Suzumura and Xu, 2009] K. Suzumura and Y. Xu. Consequentialism and Non-Consequentialism: The Axiomatic Approach. In *Handbook of Rational and Social Choice,* Anand *et al.*, eds. Oxford, Oxford University Press, 2009.

[Tangiane, 1994] A. S. Tangiane. Arrow's Paradox and Mathematical Theory of Democracy, *Social Choice and Welfare,* **11**, 1-82, 1994.

[Tangiane, 2000] A. S. Tangiane. Unlikelihood of Condorcet's paradox in a large society, *Social Choice and Welfare,* **17**, 337-65, 2000.

[Tempkin, 1986] L. Tempkin. A Continuum Argument for Intransitivity, *Philosophy and Public Affairs,* **25**, 175-210, 1986.

[Tullock, 1964] G. Tullock. The Irrationality of Intransitivity, *Oxford Economic Papers,* **16**, 401-6, 1964.

[von Wright, 1963] G. von Wright. *The Logic of Preference,* Edinburgh, Edinburgh University Press, 1963; ($2^{nd}$ edition 1991).

[Walsh, 1996] V. Walsh. *Rationality Allocation and Reproduction,* Oxford, Oxford University Press, 1996.

# RATIONAL CHOICE, PREFERENCES OVER ACTIONS AND RULE-FOLLOWING BEHAVIOR

Viktor J. Vanberg

"Man is as much a rule-following animal as a purpose-seeking one." [Hayek, 1973, p. 11]

## 1 INTRODUCTION

Economists' seemingly unshakable loyalty to rational choice theory is presumably due in no small part to the fact that, in its most general version, it is of considerable intuitive appeal. Its claim that in going about their lives people do what, in the situations they are confronted with, they consider most preferable, in terms of their own standards of evaluation, is not only extremely plausible, it seems impossible to even think of human action in any other way. How could we make sense of each other's actions if we were not to assume that people behave in ways that, in their own judgment, are preferable to the alternatives that they consider? In fact, it seems outright impossible for us even to imagine someone acting differently from what, among his available options, appears to him preferable.[1]

A theory for which we cannot even imagine contradicting evidence, that is compatible with everything that might conceivably happen, has a drawback, though. It can be of no help whatsoever in explaining real world events. It is irrefutable because it has no empirical content and, hence, no explanatory power [Popper, 1980, 119ff.]. If rational choice theory is to be able to explain real world phenomena, empirical content must somehow be infused into it in the form of assumptions that go beyond the irrefutable claim that people choose what they prefer, assumptions that rule out events as factually impossible that are conceivable. Implicitly and explicitly economists who wanted to offer more than exercises in pure tautological transformation have always included such assumptions in their rational choice accounts. The purpose of this paper is to discuss some of the content-enriching strategies employed in economic versions of rational choice theory and their shortcomings with a particular focus on the role of rule following in human conduct.

[1]This observation prompted Ludwig von Mises [1949, p. 18] to conclude: "Human action is necessarily rational. The term 'rational action' is therefore pleonastic and must be rejected as such."

Handbook of the Philosophy of Science. Volume 13: Philosophy of Economics.
Volume editor: Uskali Mäki. General editors: Dov M. Gabbay, Paul Thagard and John Woods.

## 2 RATIONALITY PRINCIPLE AND RATIONALITY HYPOTHESES IN ECONOMICS

What I have referred to above as the most general form of rational choice theory may be called the *rationality principle* [Vanberg, 2004a]. It essentially claims that individuals act in ways that are consistent with their beliefs about how the world works and their preferences over the states of the world that they expect to result from the different courses of action available to them. What courses of action individuals perceive as available options, what they believe to result from these options, and which outcome they prefer over all others, are all subjective matters, present in a person's mind and not observable from the outside. In the absence of independent evidence an observer who infers a person's beliefs and preferences from her behavior can 'explain' every conceivable action, including the most absurd, by hypothesizing beliefs and preferences that are consistent with the action. To the extent that action-independent evidence of a person's beliefs and preference is available such 'explanations' may be refutable. Yet, the refutation concerns only the specific assumptions made about the content of a person's beliefs and preferences in the particular instance. The rationality principle itself, i.e. the general claim that people act in subjectively consistent ways, remains totally unaffected by such refutation.

If one wants to turn the rationality principle itself into a refutable conjecture, into an empirically refutable *rationality hypothesis* [Vanberg, 2004a], one has to place *general bounds* on the assumptions about people's beliefs and preferences that are admitted in explanations. In other words, one has to rule out — if not the existence at least the explanatory relevance of — certain kinds of beliefs and preferences. Neoclassical economics has responded to this challenge by modeling humans as maximizers of their utility function,[2] where the latter reflects their preferences and the 'maximizing' is meant to imply that they act on adequate theories about what are efficient ways to accomplish their goals. While there may still be room for interpretation what 'adequate beliefs' is exactly meant to entail and how utility functions are to be specified, a standard assumption in neoclassical theorizing has been that economic agents act on perfect knowledge of the relevant aspects of their environment, and that their utility function is essentially about the (material) payoffs that they expect from their actions for themselves.

It is this model of *perfectly rational* and *self-interested* behavior[3] that has long

[2]The founding father of the neoclassical paradigm, Léon Walras, noted: "In our theory each trader may be assumed to determine his own utility or want function as he pleases. Once these curves have been determined, we show how prices result from them under a hypothetical régime of absolutely free competition" [Walras, 1954, p. 256]. Nicholas Georgescu-Roegen [1971, p. 343] points out that Walras' s successor on the Lausanne chair, Vilfredo Pareto, "overtly claimed, (that) once we have determined the means at the disposal of the individual and obtained 'a photograph' of his tastes ... the individual may disappear."

[3]The term 'self-interested behavior' is more appropriate in this context than the often used term 'selfish behavior' because the attribute 'selfish' carries with it certain (negative) connotations that bias the issue. It implies assumptions about *the ways in which* persons go about seeking to 'maximize their utility' that need not be entailed at all in a theory that supposes

since been, and continues to be, the principal target of criticism.[4] From Thorsten Veblen's early biting critique[5] to the more recent critique coming from the behavioral and experimental camps within economics,[6] fundamental doubts have always been voiced about the realism of the view of human behavior that this model embodies. To such critique economists have responded essentially in one of two ways. They have either insisted that its lack of 'realism' does not prevent the maximization model from serving its explanatory purposes quite well. Or they have sought to add realism to their theories by revising the core assumptions of traditional neoclassical theory. In the remainder of this section I shall look at the most prominent example of the first kind of response, namely Milton Friedman's [1953] defense of unrealistic 'as if' assumptions. As an example of the second kind of response I shall discuss in section 3 arguments that have more recently gained prominence in behavioral and experimental economics.

There are surely few arguments in modern economics that have been more intensely debated than Milton Friedman's claim, put forward in his 1953 essay on "The Methodology of Positive Economics," that unrealistic 'as if' assumptions are legitimate scientific tools as long as they yield workable predictions [Mäki, 2009a]. I shall concentrate my comments on a few aspects of the issue that are of direct relevance in the present context.

To be noted first is the ambiguity inherent in Friedman's use of the term 'assumption.' If one accepts, as Friedman presumably would have, the argument — made by K.R. Popper [1972, p. 351] and others — that to provide a scientific explanation means to logically derive an *explicandum* from an *explanans*, it should be obvious that the explanans must include two different kinds of 'assumptions,' namely general conjectures or hypotheses (assumptions of type 1) and assumptions about the specific initial and boundary conditions that characterize the case under examination (assumptions of type 2). Whether a deliberate use of 'unrealistic assumptions' can be a legitimate strategy in the enterprise of science is a question that must surely be answered differently, depending on whether assumptions of type 1 or type 2 are concerned.[7] The three examples that Friedman draws on in

---

humans to rationally pursue their self-interest. While a selfish person may indeed be a "rational fool" [Sen, 1977], a self-interested person need not be.

[4]For a review of critiques of the rationality assumption see [Vanberg, 2002; 2004a].

[5]Veblen [1993, p. 138f.]: "The hedonistic conception of man is that of a lightning calculator of pleasures and pains, who oscillates like a homogeneous globule of desire of happiness under the impulse of stimuli that shift him about the area, but leave him intact. ... Self-imposed in elemental space, he spins symmetrically about his own spiritual axis until the parallelogram of forces bears down upon him, whereupon he follows the line of the resultant. ... Spiritually, the hedonistic man is not a prime mover."

[6]V. Smith [2003, p. 480] noted in his Nobel lecture: "Psychologists and 'behavioral economists' who study decision behavior almost uniformly report results contrary to rational theory. ... (T)he focus on 'anomalies,' beginning in the 1970's, converted the emerging discovery enterprise into a search for contradictions between reports of behavior and the caricatures of mainstream theory that constitute so much of its core." — For references to research findings that "contradict the neoclassical model of rational choice" see e.g. McFadden [1999] and [2005, 12ff.].

[7]U. Mäki [2009] appears to argue along similar lines even if not in the same terms.

support of the "maximization-of-returns hypothesis" [Friedman, 1953, p. 22] in economics are critically different in this regard.

The first example is about the claim that in many instances we can explain the fall of bodies in actual atmosphere quite well in terms of the law of gravity, even though that law is stated for conditions of vacuum (ibid., 18). The 'unrealism' in this example clearly does not concern the conjectures employed (assumption type 1), as we surely consider the law of gravity to be realistic. What is unrealistic is the assumption that the particular conditions under which the law is applied are equivalent to a vacuum (assumption type 2).

In Friedman's second example, concerning the density of leaves around a tree (ibid., 19f.), the situation is quite different. In this case the 'unrealism' does not concern the initial or boundary conditions (assumption type 2) but the general hypothesis (assumption type 1) that is employed in the explanation, namely "the hypothesis that the leaves are positioned as if each leaf deliberately sought to maximize the amount of sunlight it receives" (ibid., 19). The question of whether in science we can afford to work with 'unrealistic assumptions' must, however, surely be answered differently when we talk about assumptions of type 1, i.e. the general conjectures that we employ, rather than assumptions of type 2. The pragmatic reasons that may justify unrealistic assumptions about initial and boundary conditions cannot be used to justify unrealistic hypotheses, at least not as long as we consider it the principal aim of science to develop 'true' theories of how the world works. Even though in many instances it may well be possible to derive, and in this sense to 'explain,' an explicandum from an explicans that includes an unrealistic as-if hypothesis (or to derive a predicandum from such a predicans), we would hardly consider an explanation satisfactory that is based on knowingly unrealistic, i.e. false conjectures. Though knowingly unrealistic hypotheses may suffice for predicting (or, in the sense specified, 'explaining') *what* happens they do not provide us with any insight into *why* it happens.

The same objections apply to Friedman's third example, the expert billard player (ibid., 21). Here, again, the 'unrealism' does not, as in the 'gravity' example, concern the assumptions about initial or boundary conditions but the general conjecture that is supposed to do the explaining, namely "the hypothesis that the billard player made his shots *as if* he knew the complicated mathematical formulas ... and could then make the ball travel in the direction indicated by the formulas" (ibid., 21). Even though in this case, as in the leaves example, the as-if hypothesis may suffice for pragmatic predictive and 'explanatory' purposes, it does not inform us about what actually accounts for the expert billard player's skills[8] and, therefore, does not give an answer to the "why" question. And that means that as-if hypotheses cannot be part of a scientific theory that aims at answering "why" questions.

[8]F.A. Hayek [1967, p. 44] notes in reference to Friedman's example: "So far we are able to describe the character of such skills we must do so by stating the rules governing the actions of which the actors will usually be unaware."

The objections raised above against the use of *as-if hypotheses* (by contrast to as-if assumptions about initial or boundary conditions) apply with equal force to Friedman's principal case, his defense of the "maximization-of-returns hypothesis," the hypothesis that businessmen "behave *as if* they were seeking rationally to maximize their expected returns ... and had full knowledge of the data needed to succeed in this attempt" (ibid., 21). There is, however, an additional issue involved here. So far, I have neglected the fact that the use of as-if hypotheses raises two separate issues. Namely, first, whether the behavior asserted by the hypothesis actually occurs, and, second, whether it occurs for the reasons specified. In the cases of the leaves and the expert billard players the 'as if' is about the latter, not the first issue. It is not meant to doubt that leaves and billard players actually behave as they would if the respective as-if hypothesis were true. What is unrealistic is the assumption that they so act for the reasons the as-if hypotheses state. In economics the controversy about the rational maximization hypothesis is, however, not only about whether economic agents maximize for the reasons the hypothesis asserts. Rather, it is also about the realism of the assumption that they actually behave as they would behave if the as-if hypothesis were true.

While readily admitting that what the maximization hypothesis assumes about *the reasons* for businessmen's behavior is unrealistic, Friedman insists that it is realistic in what it assumes about *how* they behave, employing an evolutionary selection argument in support of his claim: "Let the apparent immediate determinant of business behavior be anything at all — habitual reaction, random chance, or whatnot. Whenever this determinant happens to lead to behavior consistent with rational and informed maximization of returns, the business will prosper and acquire resources with which to expand; whenever it does not, the business will tend to lose resources ... . The process of 'natural selection' thus helps to validate the hypothesis" (ibid., 22). There are two problems with the 'evolutionary' defense of the as-if hypothesis. First, there is the issue of whether the selective forces that work in real world markets — rather than in the hypothetical world of perfect competition — exhibit sufficient strength to produce the de-facto maximizing behavior that Friedman claims they produce. Doubts about this are voiced by Kenneth J. Arrow [1987, p. 69], surely an unbiased witness, when he argues that "we need not merely pure but perfect competition before the rationality hypotheses have their full power."[9] If, however, as Friedman's argument implies, the maximization assumption is more a claim about the working properties of markets than about human behavior as such,[10] its applicability "to all of human behavior" [Becker,

[9]What is rational for an agent to do depends, of course, not only on his preferences but also on his beliefs 'about the world.' What is at issue, therefore, is under what conditions different beliefs can survive and guide agents' actions. Under conditions of 'perfect competition' mistaken beliefs about the world will be quickly corrected by learning, leading all agents to act on the same, true beliefs [Vanberg, 2004a, p. 18ff.].

[10]Friedman's claim is that markets work in ways that make market participants act as if they maximize returns. This claim must be distinguished from the tenet that markets work as if they were populated by rational maximizers. The difference between the two claims has been illuminated by experimental economists who have pointed out that the results of market

1976, p. 8] appears even more doubtful than its general applicability to market behavior.[11] As Arrow (ibid.) notes, to the extent that one moves away from the context of competitive markets "the rationality assumptions become strained and possibly even self-contradictory."

The second problem with an evolutionary defense of the as-if hypothesis concerns the already addressed issue of the actual explanatory contribution that as-if hypotheses can make. Even if the selective forces of evolution could justly be assumed to have brought about the kind of behavior the as-if hypotheses describe, a theoretical science could not be satisfied with explaining actual behavior in as-if terms.[12] Even though biological evolution has 'made' organisms capable of coping successfully with the problems they face in their typical environments, biologists would surely consider it most unsatisfactory to confine themselves in their explanations of animal behavior to the 'unrealistic' assumption that animals act as if they had perfect knowledge of the relevant laws of nature and acted upon them in a purposeful manner, no matter how well such as-if assumption might work for pragmatic purposes. They would rather want to give a more 'realistic' account of what the actual mechanism are that allow animals to act in such ways. This is, for instance, what Ernst Mayr [1988; 1992] does with his theory of program-based behavior, a theory that explains adapted, purposeful behavior in terms of 'programs' that — as a result of evolution and individual learning — are stored in an organism and that incorporate knowledge about the world.[13] What makes biology a progressive science is that it provides ever deeper insights into the principles that govern the living world, searching for realistic assumptions about the actual forces at work. Had biologists been satisfied with taking Darwin's theory as an excuse to work with as-if hypotheses their capacity to illuminate our understanding of the varieties of animal behavior would surely be less than it is today. Reversely, had economists not comforted themselves with the 'as if' excuse they might have arrived at more satisfactory accounts of economic and other social behavior than the maximization-of-returns hypothesis is able to provide.

## 3 ADJUSTING THE UTILITY FUNCTION

The alternative to Friedman's as-if response to the realism issue is for economists to seek to add realism to their behavioral model by modifying its components.

experiments are in accord with standard competitive models even if the agents do not make decisions systematically or are even — in the extreme — 'zero' intelligence robot agents [Smith, 2003, p. 468, 475].

[11]See Vanberg [2004, p. 5ff.] for a discussion of G.S. Becker's defense of the rationality postulate.

[12]V. Smith [2003, p. 475]: "And the claim that it is 'as if' agents had complete information, helps not a wit to understand the wellspring of behavior. What is missing are models of the process whereby agents go from their initial circumstances, and dispersed information, using the algorithms of the institution to update their status, and converge (or not) to the predicted equilibrium."

[13]See Vanberg [2002, p. 11ff.] for a summary of Mayr's argument.

There are two candidates for revising the notion that humans act so as to rationally maximize their utility. One can modify the assumption made about the content of the utility function and/or one can re-interpret what is precisely meant by "rational maximization." It is quite apparent that economists are much more reluctant to do the latter than the former. To be sure, they often emphasize that their models "do not necessarily presume anything in the way of reasoning ability, beyond that required to understand and perform in everyday social context" [Henrich *et al.*, 2005], and certain modifications of the perfect rationality assumption, such as the concept of 'Baysian rationality' [Albert, 2003], have been suggested. Yet, systematic efforts to add 'realism' to the economic model of man have been typically confined to modifications in the utility function, allowing for a broader variety of preferences than pure material self-interest, while maintaining the notion that agents maximize their utility, whatever it is they derive utility from. A programmatic statement of this 'revisionist' strategy is, for instance, Gary S. Becker's [1996 , p. 4] comment on the purpose of his *Accounting for Tastes*: "This book retains the assumption that individuals behave so as to maximize utility while extending the definition of individual preferences to include ... love and sympathy, and other neglected behavior."

My purpose in this section is to draw attention to what, as I suppose, is a fundamental inconsistency in some of the more recent attempts in behavioral and experimental economics to account for observed behavioral 'anomalies' by manipulating the content of the utility function. My interest here is not in the often raised issue whether adjusting the utility function to accommodate observed behavior does not result in mere ad hoc explanations. What I am concerned with is the fact that these 'revisionist' approaches are claimed to remain within the scope of the rational choice paradigm while in truth they imply, as I submit and explain below, a tacit paradigmatic shift from a rational choice perspective to a systematically different perspective.[14]

The issue that is at stake here is hinted at in K.J. Arrow's [1996, p. xiii] statement: "Choice is over sets of actions, but preference orderings are over consequences." The very point of rational choice theory — by contrast to alternative behavioral paradigms — is to explain actions exclusively in terms of the consequences the actor expects to result from them. Actions are seen as pure means or instruments by which the actor seeks to bring about desired outcomes. His preferences over expected outcomes totally determine which course of action he will choose. According to the logic of rational choice theory, there can be no other reasons for choosing action A over action B than the agent's expectation that A will result in more preferable outcomes than B. This explanatory logic allows one to speak of a person's 'preferences over actions' as long as such preferences are understood as pure derivatives of her preferences over outcomes. It does not permit one, however, to introduce as explanatory variables preferences over actions '*as such*,' i.e. preferences for acting in certain ways that a person harbors for reasons that are prior to and independent of her preferences for the consequences she may

[14]On this issue see also [Vanberg, 2006].

expect to result from her actions in particular instances.

The above argument has straightforward implications for the kind of entries that are admissible for inclusion in the utility function if an explanation is still to qualify as a rational choice account. It is precisely in this regard that, as I submit, revisionist proposals for a more realistically defined utility function, such as the one prominently advocated by Ernst Fehr, have become ambiguous if not outright inconsistent. In a number of (co-authored) articles[15] Fehr has argued that the deviations from rational choice predictions that have been observed in a variety of experiments, in particular in ultimatum games, can be systematically accounted for if one relaxes the assumption of self interest. The explanatory power of the rational choice paradigm, so he asserts, can be restored if one allows for "other-regarding" or "social" preferences to be included in individuals' utility functions, "in particular preferences for reciprocal fairness" [Fehr and Fischbacher, 2000, C1f.], while maintaining the assumption that agents are fully rational maximizers given their utility functions. Leaving aside the details of Fehr's arguments, what I want to draw attention to is the ambiguity inherent in the notion of "preferences for reciprocal fairness" and the issue of whether including such preferences is consistent with the claim of providing a *rational choice account.*

Of particular relevance in the present context is the fact that there is a significant difference between describing 'social' preferences, such as "preferences for reciprocal fairness" as concerns "about the material resources allocated to relevant reference agents" (ibid.) and interpreting them as a "predisposition to reward others for cooperative, norm-abiding behaviors, and ... a propensity to impose sanctions on others for norm violations" [Fehr and Fischbacher, 2003, p. 785]. In the first interpretation "preferences for reciprocal fairness" are clearly *preferences for outcomes*, even if they are more broadly interpreted to include outcomes that affect the welfare of others. It is equally clear, though, that in the second interpretation "preferences for reciprocal fairness" must be considered *preferences for actions as such.* After all, it is difficult to see what having a "predisposition" or a "propensity" to act in certain ways can mean if not that a person will act for reasons that are separate from the consequences to be expected in the particular instance.

There is a paradigmatic difference between explaining actions in terms of how agents evaluate their expected outcomes and explaining them in terms of their predispositions to act in certain ways in certain kinds of situations. The first explanatory mode is within the domain of rational choice theory, the second is not. As I shall argue in more detail below, to explain actions in terms of behavioral dispositions is equivalent to invoking, in one form or another, the notion of rule-following behavior, i.e. the notion that actions are carried out not for the consequences they are expected to bring about in the particular instance but because they are in accordance with rules that the agent is inclined to follow. To include such "predispositions" or "propensities" in the utility function means to tacitly shift from one explanatory paradigm to an entirely different paradigm, namely

[15] See e.g. [Fehr and Schmidt, 1999; 2003; Fehr and Falk, 2003; Fehr and Fischbacher, 2000].

from rational choice theory to a theory of rule-following behavior.

E. Fehr is surely not alone in committing the tacit paradigm shift that is at stake here.[16] A particularly instructive example is a recent, extensive report — coauthored by a number of economists, including Fehr, psychologists and researchers from other fields — on "a cross-cultural study of behavior in Ultimatum, Public Goods, and Dictator Games in fifteen small-scale societies" [Henrich, *et al.*, 2005, p. 795]. The purpose of the article is to add cultural variety to previous experimental studies, mostly done with students in modern societies, that "have uncovered large, consistent deviations from the textbook predictions of Homo economicus" (ibid., 797). The authors' principal claim is that a theoretical account of the observed 'deviations' can be provided by combining a rational choice approach — they call it the "preferences, beliefs and constraints approach" (ibid., 812) — with "insights on human motivation and reasoning from psychology and neuroscience ... under the ultimate-level evolutionary umbrella created by culture-gene coevolutionary theory" (ibid.). This claim supposes that combining the different perspectives renders an internally consistent theoretical account. In fact, however, the arguments presented in the article reflect the same kind of tacit paradigm shift that I have identified above in Ernst Fehr's argument.

The "preferences, beliefs and constraints approach" is said to be "rooted in the notion that individuals will select among alternatives by weighing how well the possible outcomes of each option meet their goals and desires. Theoretically, this is operationalized by assuming agents to maximize a *preference function* subject to informational and material *constraints*" (ibid.). Even though this statement clearly seems to imply that the "preferences" included as explanatory variables are *preferences over outcomes*, the authors do, in fact, tacitly invoke *preferences over actions as such* when they note that "such considerations as fairness, sympathy, and equity are critical for understanding the preference functions of many people" (ibid.), and when they speak of "inclinations towards fairness (equity) and 'tastes' for punishing unfairness" (ibid., 797). They tacitly shift from a rational choice outlook to a different paradigm when they speak of "the development of differing *generalized behavioral dispositions*" (ibid., 814), when they argue that "norms, such as 'treat strangers equitably' ... become goals in themselves" (ibid., 813), or when they refer to "socialization theory" as a source for understanding the "details of how norms get internalized" (ibid.). While including behavioral dispositions and norms surely adds explanatory power, it is misleading to pretend that they can be included in a rational choice framework while still maintaining the distinctive nature of its outlook at human action. As noted before, explaining actions in terms of how individuals weigh the possible outcomes of alternative options is categorically different from explaining them in terms of their *predispositions* to act in certain ways or their inclinations to follow *internalized norms.* It means to gloss over this fundamental difference when the authors speak of "behavioral rules (or sets of preferences)" (ibid., 814) as if *preferences* (over outcomes) and *behavioral rules* were the same thing.

[16]For further references see [Vanberg, 2006].

## 4 PREFERENCES OVER ACTIONS AND RULE FOLLOWING

According to its inherent logic a rational choice approach that seeks to explain human behavior as the maximization of a utility or preference function has its focus on single acts of choice, and it accounts for these acts of choice exclusively in terms of the consequences that potential alternative courses of actions are expected to bring about in the particular instance. Rational agents are assumed to decide each choice situation that they encounter 'on its own merits.' In each instance, they are predicted to choose from among available options the action that is predicted to result in the most preferred consequences. A rational choice theory, so defined, may allow for 'altruistic' or 'other-regarding' preferences, as long as these preferences are interpreted as *preferences over outcomes.* In its purely instrumental outlook at actions it can, however, not allow for actions to be chosen in terms of criteria that are different from, and independent of, the agent's preferences over outcomes, i.e. in terms of *preferences over actions per se.* Yet, such criteria or preferences over actions are inevitably — if only implicitly — invoked when "generalized behavioral dispositions" are argued to guide human behavior. The very point of invoking "predispositions" is to suppose that agents do not act merely in response to the consequences expected in particular instances, but according to *pre*conceived notions of what kind of behavior is 'appropriate' in the type of situations they are facing.

In a number of contributions Amartya Sen has addressed the very issue that is at stake here, and it is instructive to take a look at his arguments. In reference to suggestions for how the rational choice model may be revised in order to account for observed behavior that appears to contradict the assumption of rational self-interest Sen argues that a distinction must be drawn between accounting for *sympathy* and accounting for *commitment.* According to Sen, sympathy can without difficulty be accounted for within a rational choice framework, by broadening the concept of self interest. "Indeed," he argues, "being self-interested does not require one to be self-centered in any way, since one can get joys and pains from sympathy to others, and these joys and pains are quintessentially one's own" [Sen, 2002a, p. 31]. Not only can concern for others be easily accommodated "within the utility function of the persons involved" (ibid.). Concerns for any kind of 'goal' or 'value' that a person may be supposed to pursue can be accounted for in a rational choice framework, if 'rational choice' is defined in the minimal sense of maximizing an identifiable maximand. This is categorically different, though, so Sen insists, with commitment.[17] While our everyday experience as well as many empirical studies "indicate that committed behavior has its actual domain" [Sen, 2002a , p. 9], it cannot be accounted for by standard rational choice theory, even in its minimal version.[18] Accounting for committed behavior requires one, so Sen

[17]Sen [2002c, p. 214]: "Sympathy — including antipathy when it is negative — refers to one person's welfare being affected by the position of others..., whereas 'commitment' is concerned with breaking the tight link between individual welfare (with or without sympathy) and the choice of action."

[18]Sen [2005a, p. 8]: "A reason for the importance of taking note of commitment is that it can

argues, even to relax the assumption of "self-goal choice", i.e. the assumption that a person's choices reflect her own goals, and to allow for the pursuit of private goals to "be compromised by the consideration of the goals of others" [Sen, 2002c, p. 215].

As commentators like Philip Pettit have noted, Sen's claim that "people may become the executors of a goal-system that outruns the private goals that they endorse in their own name ... is highly implausible" [Pettit, 2005, p. 19]. After all, it is difficult to see in what sense human choice can be anything other than — in Sen's terminology — "self-goal choice." The difficulties inherent in Sen's notion of 'non-self-goal choice' can be easily avoided, however, if one restates his arguments on the nature of "committed behavior" in terms of the theoretical perspective that I have outlined above, a perspective that emphasizes the distinction between preferences over outcomes and preferences over actions, drawing attention to the intimate link between preferences over actions and rule-following behavior. In fact, Sen [2002c, p. 214] himself invites such restatement when he notes that "the violation of self-goal choice" involved in commitment may "arise from self-imposed restrictions on the pursuit of one's own goals (in favor of, say, following particular rules of conduct)."[19] Apparently it is, in particular, accounting for commitment to rules of behavior that Sen considers a "more fundamental" challenge to standard rational choice accounts than accommodating other-regarding preferences or non-self-welfare goals or values [Sen, 1973, p. 249ff.]. Accepting "certain rules of conduct as part of obligatory behavior" is, as he [Sen, 2002c, p. 216f.] puts it, "not a matter of asking each time, What do I get out of it? How are my own goals furthered in this way?, but of taking for granted the case for certain patterns of behavior towards others."[20]

Explaining actions in terms of pre-existing dispositions to follow rules rather than in terms of expected consequences does not mean to ignore that there are feed-back effects of consequences on behavior. It means to redirect attention from the effects of *expected* consequences on *present* behavior to the effects that the *actual* consequences of *past* behavior have on *current* choices and on the effects that the actual consequences of *current* choices will have on *future* behavior. The behavioral dispositions that guide behavior at any moment in time are themselves the product of past behavioral consequences. They have been shaped by what agents have learned in the past — from direct and indirect experience — about what outcomes different kinds of behavior tend to produce under various kinds of

help to explain many patterns of behavior that we actually observe which are hard to fit into the narrow format of contemporary rational choice theory."

[19]See also Sen [2002a, p. 7]: "[A] person's choice behavior may be constrained or influenced by the goals of others, or by rules of conduct..., thereby violating the self-goal choice." — Sen [2002c, p. 219f.]: "[A] rejection of self-goal choice reflects a type of commitment that is not able to be captured by the broadening of the goals to be pursued. It calls for behavior norms that depart from the pursuit of goals in certain systematic ways ... and it has close links with the case for rule-based conduct, discussed by Adam Smith."

[20]Sen [2002b, p. 178] "However, in following rules... the motivating factor need not be any concern about the well-being of others..., but simply following an established rule."

circumstances. Nor does a theory of rule-following behavior take issue with the notion, central to rational choice theory, that human action is based on a 'calculus of advantage.' It only asserts that we must distinguish between different levels at which such calculus of advantage occurs, namely the level of single actions and the level of rules of action. It insists that, in addition to the situational calculus on which rational choice theory focuses, human action is governed by a calculus of advantage that operates at the level at which behavioral dispositions are shaped in light of accumulated direct and indirect experiences.[21] Like rational choice theory a rule-oriented approach is 'utilitarian' in the sense of explaining human behavior in 'instrumental' terms, as a means for achieving desired outcomes. The difference between the two approaches parallels the distinction between act utilitarianism and rule utilitarianism. Rational choice theory looks at single actions as instruments for bringing about preferred outcomes. It explains actions in terms of the agent's *forward-looking* calculation of expected payoffs. By contrast, a rule-oriented approach looks at rules of actions as instruments or 'tools' for bringing about preferred *patterns* of outcomes. It explains single actions in terms of an agent's behavioral dispositions, and it explains these dispositions in turn in a *backward-looking* manner, i.e. in terms of past experiences, both direct and indirect.

As agents adopt dispositions to follow rules of action they will presumably experience *emotional consequences* from complying with or going against their behavioral inclinations. They may, for instance, feel uneasy if they 'deviate' from rules they are disposed to act on. Since these emotional consequences may appear to be like other consequences agents consider in their choice of actions, one might be inclined to conclude that behavioral dispositions can, after all, be accounted for by rational choice analysis, as components in agents' utility functions. Such conclusion would disregard, however, the essential fact that the very point of being disposed to follow rules is to act in certain ways in certain types of situation *without* considering the expected consequences in each instance. To be sure, agents may on occasion deliberately act against their rule-following inclinations, giving less weight to the 'bad conscience' from rule violation than to the benefits it promises. And there are surely cases of calculated rule compliance where agents consider the benefits to be had from rule violation insufficient to compensate for the uneasiness felt from acting against their dispositions. Yet these cases are the very instances in which agents shift from a rule-following mode to situational, case-by-case choice, even if their situational calculus includes the emotional implications of their behavioral dispositions. They do definitely not represent the 'standard' cases of rule following, i.e. the cases in which behavioral dispositions induce agents to act on preconceived notions of appropriate behavior without calculating the expected payoffs from potential alternative courses of action. It is these cases, however, that do not fit the rational choice model.

[21] I shall return below (section 6) to the issue of how the 'calculus of advantage' at the level of behavioral rules operates.

## 5 THE RATIONALE OF RULE-FOLLOWING BEHAVIOR

At the heart of Friedrich A. Hayek's theoretical contributions is the argument that the inherent limitations of our knowledge and our powers of reason require us to rely on the guidance of rules if we are successfully to live our lives and to coordinate our actions with others in a complex world. The "whole rationale of the phenomenon of rule-guided action" is, as he submits, to be found in our "inescapable ignorance of most of the particular circumstances which determine the effects of our actions" [Hayek, 1976, p. 20]. Faced with the "the inexhaustible totality of everything,", so Hayek [1979, p. 121] argues, we would soon be incapacitated if we were to decide each case on its own merits, as rational choice theory would have it.[22] Due to "our constitutional ignorance" (ibid., 8) we cannot but rely on rules that in the past have proven — in our own experience or the experience of others, including our ancestors' — to be helpful in dealing with recurrent problems of the kind we are likely to encounter in the environments in which we operate.

Rules facilitate, Hayek explains, the making of decisions in complex situations. They "limit our range of choice" [1967, p. 90] by abbreviating the "list of circumstances which we need to take into account in the particular instances, singling out certain classes of facts as alone determining the general kind of action which we should take" [Hayek, 1964, p. 11]. The fact that rules *abbreviate* what we need to take into account and *limit* our range of choice means, of course, that they lead us to *disregard* facts which we may well know and to leave potential courses of action *unconsidered.* As Hayek notes, why such disregarding of facts and limiting of choice should help us make better decisions is far from being intuitively obvious. Yet this seeming paradox can be explained, he states, by the very "necessity of coming to terms with our unalterable ignorance of much that would be relevant if we knew it" [1964, p. 12].[23]

Because we can impossibly act "in full consideration of all the facts of a particular situation" [1973, p. 30], so he reasons, we cannot but act on the basis of *selective knowledge*, i.e. considering only a fraction of the innumerable potentially relevant facts. The issue is, therefore, which *mode of selection* promises to render overall more preferable outcomes: The selectivity inherent in situational, case-by-case choices, or the selectivity of rules? And, as Hayek argues, the latter may well be superior to the former [1964. p. 12] insofar as acting on suitable rules

[22]V. L. Smith [2003, p. 468[: "It is necessary to constantly remind ourselves that human activity is diffused and dominated by unconscious, automatic, neuropsychological systems that enable people to function effectively without always calling upon the brain's scarcest resource — attentional and reasoning circuitry. This is an important economizing property of how the brain works. If it were otherwise, no one could get through the day under the burden of the self-conscious monitoring and planning of every trivial action in detail."

[23]F.A. Hayek [1960, p. 66] "Though it sounds paradoxical to say that in order to make ourselves act rationally we often find it necessary to be guided by habit rather than reflection, or to say that to prevent ourselves from making the wrong decision we must deliberately reduce the range of choice before us, we all know that this is often necessary in practice if we are to achieve our long range aims."

may, on balance, result in a more favorable pattern outcomes than discretionary case-by-case choice.[24]

In a somewhat more formal manner Ronald A. Heiner [1983] has essentially made the same argument as Hayek concerning the rationale of rule-following behavior. Heiner takes as benchmark the notion of a *perfect* agent, i.e. an agent who is able to determine with perfect reliability what, considering all circumstances, is the maximizing choice in each and every situation. For such an agent, Heiner argues, case-by-case maximization would obviously be the best policy. To the extent, however, that an agent is *not perfect*, in the sense defined, he may possibly fare better overall by adopting rules for how to behave in recurring problem situations, even though rule following will inevitably on occasion result in less than optimal outcomes. The relevant comparison here is, of course, between, on the one side, the risk of — and the expected damage from — choosing a 'wrong' alternative while attempting to maximize case by case, and, on the other side, the risk of — and the expected damage from — missing out on 'preferred exceptions' when following a rule. The first risk is correlated with what Heiner calls the 'competence' of the agent, where competence is defined relative to the difficulty or complexity of the decision problem. The second risk is a function of the nature or 'quality' of the rule in question. Accordingly, whether rule following may in fact be superior to attempted case-by-case maximization will depend on the combined effects of i) the complexity of the problem situation, ii) the competence of the agent and, iii) the nature or 'quality' of the behavioral rule.

An imperfect agent apparently faces the problem of finding a proper balance between two 'imperfections': The imperfectness of his own choice, and the imperfectness of the decision rules which he applies. The maxim 'always choose the best alternative' would obviously generate optimal outcomes, if it could be reliably administered. But it need not be the best strategy for an imperfect agent who is unable to optimally choose with perfect reliability. He may fare better with an imperfect rule, but one which he can apply more reliably. The degree of 'imperfectness' of a rule can be defined in terms of the frequency of cases in which deviating from the rule would be preferable to the agent or — stated differently — in terms of the rate of *preferred exceptions*. It will in general be the case that *simpler* rules are more *imperfect*, have a higher rate of 'preferred exceptions' than more complex rules.[25] But for the same reason, namely their simplicity, they can be applied more reliably. And what matters to imperfect agents is the combined product of the two aspects.

Hayek's and Heiner's arguments are about the rationale of rule-following behavior. They identify reasons why it may be 'rational' — in the sense of serving

[24]Where the 'balance of advantage' is in favor of following a rule, "an apparent striving after rationality in the sense of fuller taking into account all the foreseeable consequences" may, as Hayek [1964, p. 12] argues, result in "greater irrationality, less effective taking into account of remote effects and an altogether less coherent result."

[25]Since rules can be translated into "if ... then"-statements their complexity can be interpreted as a function of the specifications or qualifications enumerated in their "if"-clauses and / or their "then"-clauses.

their interests — for imperfect agents to follow rules instead of acting in a discretionary case-by-case manner. Whether rule following will in fact result in patterns of outcomes that are preferable to what discretionary case-by-case choice would generate depends, of course, on the nature of the rules that are followed. Rules will differ in their 'quality' and one can easily imagine rules which would be clearly inferior to case-by-case choice. Furthermore, among the rules which 'work better' some will tend to generate more advantageous patterns of outcomes than others. This raises the question of how agents come to adopt rules at all, and how they come to adopt certain kinds of rules rather than others.

## 6 THE EXPLANATION OF RULE-FOLLOWING BEHAVIOR

Explaining the *rationale* of rule following is, of course, not the same as explaining why it is that agents actually do follow rules and why they follow certain rules rather than others. Human agents cannot choose to adopt rules in the same manner in which they can choose among alternative courses of action. They cannot simply 'switch off' their capacity for discretionary choice, nor would they have the cognitive abilities to reliably choose the rules that may serve their interests best. The disposition that defines rule-following behavior — namely not to calculate in a case-by-case manner — is a matter of habit formation and not a trait one can simply decide to adopt because one recognizes its advantages.[26] The very limits of knowledge and reason that require imperfect agents to rely on rules deprive them likewise from the ability to reliably anticipate the relative merits of potential alternative rules of action. In fact, predicting which rules from the unlimited universe of conceivable alternatives will produce more advantageous outcome patterns over time than others presents imperfect agents with an even more daunting challenge than anticipating and comparing the prospective payoffs from the limited set of choice options they confront on a particular occasion.

Accordingly, when I said above that behavioral dispositions are based on a 'calculus of advantage' this is, of course, not meant to imply that they are the product of deliberate calculation. It is meant to say that the process in which dispositions are formed must include some 'method of accounting' that keeps track of the comparative performance of different behavioral practices in different types of situations, i.e. of how well they work in helping agents to cope with recurrent problems of the kind they are likely to encounter in the type of environment in which they operate. In the remainder of this section I shall take a look at a research perspective the common thrust of which is that such 'method of accounting' can in fact be identified at three levels, the level of biological evolution, the level of cultural evolution, and the level of individual learning. The processes of learning or 'accumulation of knowledge' that operate at these three levels are seen to be

[26] David Gauthier's [1986] concept of "constrained maximization" and Edward F. McClennen's [2004] concept of "resolute choice" entail the claim that rational agents can *choose* to become rule followers on account of their insight into the advantages to be expected thereof. For a critical examination of this claim see e.g. J. Dreier [2004, p. 164ff.] and Vanberg [1994, p. 54ff.].

governed by the same general evolutionary principle, the principle of trial and error elimination or variation and selective retention, even if the specific modes of their operation may be quite different.

Rules can assist agents in dealing with recurrent problems because they incorporate knowledge about relevant contingencies in the agents' typical environment. The issue of how the acquisition of such knowledge can be explained is the subject of Karl R. Popper's evolutionary theory of the growth of knowledge. All behavior, so Popper [1982, p. 150] argues, is about problem solving, and all problem solving is guided by pre-existing expectations or conjectural knowledge about the world, knowledge that is incorporated in agents' "action programmes" [Popper and Eccles, 1983, p. 134]: or their "dispositions to act" (ibid., 130).[27] It is, as Popper stresses, only in light of its repertoire of expectations that a living being can perceive problems, and it is only on the basis of its conjectural knowledge or dispositions that it can act or respond to the problems it faces [Popper, 1976, p. 139].[28] Since, in this sense, all perception and action occurs on the basis of pre-existing conjectural knowledge or dispositions, an agent's *acquisition of knowledge* or *learning* can only consist in the modification or correction of pre-existing expectations, dispositions or action programs.[29] In Popper's [1972, p. 71] terms: "All acquired knowledge, all learning, consists of the modification ... of some form of knowledge, or disposition, which was there previously, and in the last instance of inborn expectations."[30] Learning consists in the "tentative variation of theories or action programmes and their critical testing, by using them in our actions" [Popper and Eccles, 1983, p. 134]. As Popper emphasizes, his suggested outlook at the acquisition of knowledge can be viewed as a "Darwinian theory of the growth of knowledge" [Popper, 1972, p. 262].[31] It is an approach that he regards as equally

[27]Popper and Eccles [1983, p. 130] "Our unconscious knowledge can well be described as a set of dispositions to act, or to behave, or to expect." — "We act on the basis of action programmes" (ibid., 132).

[28]Popper and Eccles [1983, p. 134f.]: "All observations ... are interpretations in the light of theories. ... *There is no sense organ in which anticipatory theories are not genetically incorporated.* ... Thus our sense organs are products of adaptation — they can be said to be theories, or to incorporate theories."

[29]Popper and Eccles [1983, p. 132] "Learning by experience consists in modifying our expectations and theories and our action programmes. It is a process of modification and of selection, especially by the refutation of our expectations. ... We learn by modifying our theories or our action programmes by selection, that is to say, by trial and by the elimination of error."

[30]Popper and Eccles [1983, p. 121]: "There are two great sources of our information: that which is acquired through genetic inheritance and that which is acquired throughout our life. Moreover all knowledge, whether inherited or acquired, is historically a modification of earlier knowledge; and all knowledge can be traced back, step by step, to modifications of inborn or instinctive knowledge." — Popper [1972, p. 347]: "Ontogenetically (that is, with respect to the development of the individual organism) we thus regress to the state of the expectations of a newborn child; phylogenetically (with respect to the evolution of the race, the phylum) we get to the state of expectations of unicellular organisms. ... There is, as it were, only one step from the amoeba to Einstein."

[31]Popper [1972, p. 142]: "Epistemology becomes ... the theory of the growth of knowledge. It becomes the theory of problem solving or, in other words, of the construction ... and critical testing of competing conjectural theories."

applicable "to animal knowledge, pre-scientific knowledge, and to scientific knowledge" [Popper, 1972, p. 261], notwithstanding the obvious differences that may otherwise set these quite distinct levels of knowledge apart.[32]

Popper's theory of the growth of knowledge is counted among the founding contributions to the research paradigm of *evolutionary epistemology*,[33] along with contributions by F.A. Hayek and Ernst Mayr that also deserve to be briefly considered here.[34] In his *The Sensory Order — An Inquiry into the Foundations of Theoretical Psychology* (1952) as well as in some of his other writings on epistemological issues [1967a; b; c; d; 1978; 1979, p. 31ff.] Hayek has outlined a theory of the human mind that is very much compatible with Popper's evolutionary account. In Hayek's account it is through the mind's "internal representations" of the outer world — through models, rules or dispositions[35] — that all human *perception* as well as human *action* is guided, from our pre- or sub-conscious adaptations to our most deliberate and reflected responses to problems [Hayek, 1952, p. 86f., 145f.; 1967c, p. 45]. Like Popper, Hayek views the conjectural knowledge that the "internal representations" embody as the product of a process of trial-and-error elimination. More specifically, he interprets the process through which mental models, rules or dispositions become better adapted to the problem environment as a process of classification and reclassification that is controlled by success and failure [Hayek, 1952, p. 147].[36] In Hayek's account, the evolution of the mental order proceeds as a continuous reorganization of the classificatory apparatus in light of which external events are interpreted, at the level of biological evolution as well as at the level of behavioral learning [Hayek, 1952, p. 107f.; 1967c, p.

[32] Popper and Eccles [1983, p. 133]: "On all three levels of adaptation (the genetic level, the behavioral level, the level of scientific theory formation) adaptive changes always start from some *given structure*. ... But the new adaptive changes in the inherited structure happen on all three levels by way of natural *selection*: by way of competition, and of the elimination of unfit trials."

[33] The name "evolutionary epistemology" appears to have been coined by Donald T. Campbell [1974]. According to Campbell, the central tenet of this research program is that all processes that lead to an *expansion* of knowledge or problem-solving capacity can be interpreted as instances of the "variation and selective retention process of evolutionary adaptation" (ibid., 450f.), whether they occur at the level of genetic evolution, individual learning or cultural evolution.

[34] In his survey of the field W.W. Bartley [1987, p. 20f.] lists K.R. Popper, F.A. Hayek, D.T. Campbell, E. Mayr and K. Lorenz as "founders."

[35] Hayek uses the terms 'models,' 'rules' and 'dispositions' alternatively to describe the mental events that take place "between the input of (external and internal) stimuli and the output of action" [Hayek, 1982, p. 288]. While in *The Sensory Order* he mostly speaks of 'models,' in later publications he prefers to speak of "rules of action (or dispositions)" [Hayek, 1978, p. 43]. As he notes: "(D)ispositions toward *kinds* of movements can be regarded as adaptations to typical features of the environment, and the 'recognition' of such features as the activiation of the kind of disposition adapted to them. ... (A)ll the 'knowledge' of the external world which such an organism possesses consists in the action patterns which the stimuli tend to evoke. ... (W)hat we call knowledge is primarily a system of rules of action" (ibid., 41).

[36] About the general outlook he adopted in *The Sensory Order* Hayek has noted in retrospect that he was led "to interpret the central nervous system as an apparatus of multiple classification or, better, as a process of continuous and simultaneous classification and constant reclassification on many levels (of the legion of impulses proceeding in it at any moment), applied in the first instance to all sensory perception but in principle to all kinds of mental entities, such as emotions, concepts, images, drives, etc., that we find to occur in the mental universe" [1982, p. 289].

52]. While the 'knowledge' that has been accumulated over the evolutionary history of our species is incorporated, as genetically coded conjectures, in our sense (and other) organs, the capability of learning allows an organism to accumulate experience-based problem-solving knowledge over its lifetime that is incorporated in memory-coded models, rules or dispositions [Hayek, 1952, p. 53, 106, 108, 129ff., 166; 1967c, p. 51].

Biologist Ernst Mayr has proposed a theory of "teleonomic" or goal-directed behavior that attributes the capacity of organisms to solve the problems they face to "programs" that guide their behavior [Mayr, 1992, p. 127]. A "program" in the sense Mayr uses the term is "a set of instructions" (ibid., 128) that embodies knowledge about relevant properties of the problem environment. The focus of Mayr's theory is, in his terms, on the *encoding* and *decoding* of the internal models or *programs* on which problem-solving behavior is based. Encoding is about the processes through which programs are "recorded" in an organism. It is about the manner in which programs are stored, and about the ways in which they become adapted to the kind of problem environment in which the individual operates. It is governed by feed-back processes that establish a link between the effects of programmed instructions and their future role in guiding behavior. Since programs can be viewed as stored knowledge of the world, encoding can be seen as a process of learning: Experience is used to "improve" the program repertoire, i.e. to make it a more suitable guide to successful problem solving. Decoding is about how programs are implemented in, or applied to, particular choice situations. It is a matter of information processing: Information retrieved from the current (internal and external) situation and information stored in the program repertoire is processed and translated into action.[37] According to Mayr, all encoding processes can be said to be based on "natural selection" in the sense that all programs, genetically encoded as well as memory-encoded learned programs, are selected by their consequences.[38] Programs that generate "successful," problem-solving behavior are reinforced and retained, those that systematically lead to less conducive outcomes loose strength and are eventually abandoned. Even though the particular feed-back mechanisms that implement such "natural selection" are surely different in genetic evolution and in individual learning, the general principle, "selection by consequences," is the same.

An instructive attempt to model in a more formal manner the process of program adaptation and behavioral learning to which Popper's, Hayek's and Mayr's evolutionary accounts refer is John H. Holland's theory of "adaptive agents," i.e. agents who adapt the repertoire of rules on which they act to the contingencies of their environment "as experience accumulates" [Holland, 1995, p. 10]. By contrast to a theory that is "built around agents of perfect rationality — agents

[37] Mayr [1988, p. 51]: "The translation of programs into teleonomic behavior is greatly affected both by sensory inputs and by internal physiological (largely hormonal) states."

[38] Mayr [1988, p. 45]: "Each particular program is the result of natural selection, constantly adjusted by the selective value of the achieved end point, ... (whether) through a slow process of gradual selection, or even through individual learning or conditioning ... ."

that perfectly foresee the consequences of their actions, including the reactions of other agents" (ibid., 85) — Holland [1996, p. 282]. characterizes his theory as an "evolutionary approach to learning." Adaptive agents owe their "ability to anticipate" [Holland, 1992b, p. 20] to the rules on which they operate, "rules that anticipate the consequences of certain responses" (ibid.), and that can be "viewed as hypotheses that are undergoing testing and confirmation" [Holland, 1995, p. 53]. The principal focus of Holland's theory is on the process by which adaptive agents manage to improve their repertoire of rules and, thereby, to increase their capability to deal successfully with the kinds of problems they are confronted with. The process in which adaptive agents improve the internal models that guide their problem-solving efforts is explicitly modeled as an evolutionary process of variation and selection by consequences.[39] There always exists a set of rules upon which selection can operate and from which new rules are continuously generated, due to random mutation and, more importantly, through re-combination of components of existing rules. In order for selection to systematically favor 'beneficial,' and to work against 'inferior' rules a feedback or accounting mechanism must be in place that assigns 'credit' to behavioral practices according to the contribution they make to an agent's ability to operate successfully in the environment that he faces. The method of "credit assignment"[40] that serves this function must, in particular, be able to give proper credit to behavioral practices or rules that are not themselves followed by immediate rewards, but rather serve in a stage-setting role in the sense of being part of extended chains of actions only the last links of which are directly 'rewarded.'[41]

It is a significant achievement of Holland's approach that it specifies a model of how such credit assignment operates, called "bucket brigade algorithm" [Holland, 1995, p. 56; 1992a, p. 176ff.], a model the general thrust of which can be captured by the metaphor of a market in which not only the final sellers of products are rewarded by the price paid by consumers, but in which the revenue raised in the final product market is transferred back to the producers of inputs for these products, to the producers of inputs for the production of inputs, and so on. Thus, 'stage-setting' productive activities upon which success in the final product market depends are encouraged, while failure in the final stage translates into inability to reward suppliers of inputs. In similar ways the "bucket brigade algorithm" models the ways in which adaptive agents carry on a "calculus of advantage" at the level of rules of action that assigns credit to — and thus strengthens — rules according to

[39]Holland [1995, p. 53]: "That is, rules amount to alternative, competing hypotheses. When one hypothesis fails, competing rules are waiting in the wings to be tried."

[40]Holland [1995, p. 53]: "We want to assign each rule a strength that, over time, comes to reflect the rule's usefulness to the system. The procedure for modifying strength on the basis of experience is often called *credit assignment*."

[41]Holland *et al.* [1986, p. 16]: "Credit assignment is not particularly difficult when the system receives payoffs from the environment for a particular action — the system simply strengthens all the rules active at that time (a kind of conditioning). Credit assignment becomes difficult when credit must be assigned to early-acting rules that set the stage for a sequence of actions leading to payoff."

their respective contribution to the agents' overall success in solving the problems they encounter in their environments [Holland, 1996, p. 285f.]. As Holland (ibid.) emphasizes, the "bucket brigade algorithm" makes a task manageable that otherwise would surely be beyond the capacity of boundedly rational agents, namely the task of keeping track of the success record of a complex repertoire of rules that are activated, in varying combinations, as components of internal models of current problem situations.

Holland's concept of "credit assignment" can be related to what above I have described, somewhat informally, as *preferences over actions*. In Holland's "bucket brigade algorithm" the credits assigned to particular rules determine the strength of an agent's inclination or disposition to act on them. Conversely, the strength of an agent's dispositional 'commitment' to rules is a function of the 'credits' assigned to the respective practices over the agent's past behavioral history. What I have called an agent's "preferences over actions" can, in this sense, be interpreted as the product of learning processes — including the processes of biological and cultural evolution — in which experiences with the capacity of alternative behavioral practices to further the agent's wellbeing have been accumulated and have been 'condensed' in the agent's dispositional attachment to the respective practices, i.e. the strength of his inclination to act in certain ways in certain types of situations.

For agents to develop dispositions to follow rules does not mean, of course, that they become entirely oblivious to the overall incentive structure of the choice situations they are facing, responding only to the 'clues' that let them classify a given situation as one to which a particular rule applies. Even though human behavior, including moral conduct, is surely 'routinized' to a large extent in the sense that much of our everyday conduct is carried out semi-automatically without any involvement of conscious deliberation, we cannot, as noted before, simply 'switch off' our capacity for rational calculation, and anything unusual in the choice situations we encounter may activate this capacity. The 'function' or 'evolutionary rationale' of the fact, mentioned above, that emotional consequences tend to be associated with following or deviating from rules that one is disposed to act on may well lie exactly in the role they play in 'stabilizing' our rule-following dispositions in the face of opposing situational incentives.[42] The conflict that persons experience in such situations is not about a trade-off between different elements in the utility function as is suggested by authors who treat concerns for equity, fairness and the like as preferences over outcomes. Instead, it is a conflict between agents' preferences for acting according to rules that the above discussed 'accounting mechanism' tells them work well in situations of the type currently

[42]The role of emotions in human decision making has recently found growing attention in economics [Frank, 1988; Elster, 1996; 1998; Loewenstein, 2000; van Winden, 2001; Bosman *et al.*, 2005]. What is of particular interest in the context of the present paper is that in this literature two different interpretations of the role of emotions are discussed, namely, on the one hand, their role "as psychic costs or benefits that enter into the utility function on a par with satisfaction derived from material rewards" [Elster, 1998, p. 64] and, on the other hand, their role as "an action tendency" (ibid., 99), as a "pattern or readiness, which is the urge to execute a particular form of action or to abstain from a particular action" [Bosman *et al.*, 2005, p. 412].

encountered, and their preferences for outcomes that their situational calculation tells them they may achieve by deviating. The intensity of this conflict will depend on the strength of their dispositional commitments versus the attractiveness of the outcomes that they expect from rule violation.[43]

## 7 CONCLUSION

Contrasting, as I have done in this paper, rational choice theory and a theory of rule-following behavior raises the question of the relation between the two perspectives. Are they to be considered as fundamentally disjunct and mutually exclusive outlooks at behavior, or can they be integrated into a coherent, unified theory of human conduct? If we acknowledge, as we surely must, that both, forward-looking calculated choice as well as backward-looking dispositions to follow rules, are relevant aspects of human behavior — that, as Hayek puts it in the quotation chosen as motto for this paper, "man is as much a rule-following animal as a purpose-seeking one" — it would certainly be unsatisfactory to assign the study of these aspects to two entirely separated conceptual frameworks. The natural ambition of scientific inquiry would seem to be to come up with a unified theory of human behavior that accounts for its more calculative as well as for its more rule-guided versions in terms of one coherent set of explanatory principles.

There appear to be two principal candidates for attempts at providing such an integrated theoretical outlook. One can either seek to show that what we classify as rule-following behavior can in fact be integrated in a properly adjusted rational choice framework. Under the rubric "Adjusting the Utility-Function" I have discussed and criticized an example of this strategy in section 3. The other candidate for a strategy of theoretical integration is to show that what we classify as rational, calculated choice can in fact be accounted for by a properly interpreted theory of rule-following behavior. It is in support of this second strategy that I want to provide a few concluding comments.

Rational choice theory ascribes our capacity for forward-looking problem solving to the fact that we are *rational* beings, without bothering to explain where the knowledge that supposedly defines our 'rationality' comes from. By contrast, the common thrust of the theoretical approaches that I have discussed in the previous section is twofold. It is, first, that the knowledge that guides our problem-solving efforts can be derived from no other sources than past experiences, be it the experiences that our species accumulated over its evolutionary history, be it the experiences that we, as individuals, have accumulated over our lifetime, on the basis of our genetic inheritance and in the context of a social environment that in turn has been shaped by experiences accumulated in the process of socio-cultural evolution. And it is, second, that such experience-based knowledge can exist in no other form than as 'conjectures' or 'programs' that are stored, as encoded

[43]The function of emotions in 'stabilizing' rule-following behavior has been discussed in detail by Robert Frank [1988] under the rubric of "emotions as commitment devices."

information, in our genes and in our memories.

If, as Popper, Hayek, Mayr and Holland assert, *all* problem-solving behavior is based on pre-existing conjectures, programs or rules then — by distinguishing between rational choice and rule-following behavior — we cannot mean that only the latter is program-guided while as rational choosers we can do without the guidance of experience-based conjectural knowledge. The distinction can only be about the *degree* to which we consciously rely on the knowledge incorporated in memory-stored programs or conjectures as opposed to habitual, unreflected rule following. There surely is a significant difference between situations in which we explicitly consider the alternative choice options available to us, carefully weighing the consequences to be expected from each of them, and situations in which we solve recurrent problems in a routine manner, often without any awareness of what we are doing. Yet, even the most deliberated and calculated choices we make are 'program-based' in the sense that they employ memory-coded conjectural knowledge of relevant contingencies in the world around us. Furthermore, as Hayek [1976, p. 56] notes, "even decisions which have been carefully considered will in part be determined by rules of which the acting person is not aware."

Thus, rather than thinking of rational choice and rule-following behavior as two categorically different modes of human conduct, it is, as I submit, more appropriate to think of them as part of a continuum along which program-based problem solving can vary from entirely unconscious rule following to highly calculated conjecture-based choice.[44] This is not to deny that humans may also act in entirely novel ways, unaided by their evolved repertoires of conjectures, rules and programs. Yet, as notably D.T. Campbell [1987] has stressed, it means to recognize that, where our problem-solving efforts go beyond what the knowledge incorporated in our repertoire of programs can teach us, we cannot go but blindly. Such genuinely 'non-programmed' choices cannot be 'rational' in the sense of benefiting from pre-knowledge of what may be successful strategies for dealing with the problem that is addressed. It is worth noting in conclusion what Herbert A. Simon, whose name has figured more prominently than anybody else's in the debate on the limits of the economic model of rational choice, has commented on this issue. In the context of his theory of bounded rationality[45] he draws a distinction between "programmed" decisions[46] and "non-programmed" decisions [Simon, 1982, p. 380], but he hastens to add that, ultimately, all decisions rely on 'internal models' and are, in this sense, program-based, even if they may be "non-programmed" in the sense that "processes of innovation" (ibid., 393) and "the construction of

[44]For a critical discussion of this view see J. Vromen [2004, p. 14ff.].

[45]Simon [1984 , p. 47f.]: "In any realistic description of the environment of a human decision maker, the variables and information to which he might attend ... are innumerable. The hypothesis of bounded rationality claims that human beings handle this difficulty by attending to only a small part of the complexity about them. They make a highly simplified model of the world, and they make their decisions in terms of that model and the subset of variables that enter into it."

[46]Simon [1982, p. 389]: "We should view programmed decision-making as a process for making choices within the framework set by highly simplified models of real-world problems."

new programs" (ibid., 396) are initiated when existing programs fail to lead to successful problem solving. As Simon (ibid., 380) puts it: "Are there any decisions, then, that are *not* programmed? If we want to be literal, ... any sequence of events in which each event is determined in some way by the whole collection of its antecedents is 'programmed.' In these terms, even searching through a haystack for a needle is programmed choice — and perhaps it is."

## ACKNOWLEDGEMENTS

For support of this research I am indebted to Liberty Fund, Indianapolis, USA where I spent my 2006/2007 sabbatical as a resident scholar.

## BIBLIOGRAPHY

[Albert, 2003] M. Albert. Bayesian Rationality and Decision Making: A Critical Review, *Analyse & Kritik* 25, 101-117, 2003.

[Arrow, 1987] K. J. Arrow. Economic Theory and the Hypothesis of Rationality. In *The New Palgrave Dictionary of Economics*, Vol. 2, London: Macmillan, 69-75, 1987.

[Arrow, 1996] K. J. Arrow. Preface. In K.J. Arrow, E. Colombatto, M. Perlman and C. Schmidt, eds., *The Rational Foundations of Economic Behavior*, Proceedings of the IEA Conference held in Turin, Italy, New York: St. Martin's Press, xiii-xvii, 1996.

[Becker, 1976] G. S. Becker. *The Economic Approach to Human Behavior*, Chicago and London: The University of Chicago Press, 1976.

[Becker, 1996] G. S. Becker. *Accounting for Tastes*, Cambridge, Mass., and London: Harvard University Press, 1996.

[Bosman *et al.*, 2005] R. Bosman, M. Sutter, and F. van Winden. The impact of real effort and emotions in the power-to-take game. *Journal of Economic Psychology* 26, 407-429, 2005.

[Campbell, 1974] D. T. Campbell. Evolutionary Epistemology. In Paul A. Schipp, ed., *The Philosophy of Karl R. Popper*, La Salle, Illinois: Open Court, 413-463, 1974.

[Campbell, 1987] D. T. Campbell. Blind Variation and Selective Retention in Creative Thought as in Other Knowledge Processes. In Radnitzky, Gerard and W. W. Bartley, III, eds., *Evolutionary Epistemology, Rationality, and the Sociology of Knowledge*, La Salle, Illinois: Open Court, 91-114, 1987.

[Dreier, 2004] J. Dreier. Decision Theory and Morality. In Alfred R. Mele and Pies Rawling, eds., *The Oxford Handbook of Rationality*, New York: Oxford University Press, 156-181, 2004.

[Elster, 1996] J. Elster. Rationality and the Emotions. *The Economic Journal* 106, 1386-1397, 1996.

[Elster, 1998] J. Elster. Emotions and Economic Theory. *Journal of Economic Literature* XXXVI, 47-74, 1998.

[Fehr and Schmidt, 1999] E. Fehr and K. M. Schmidt. A Theory of Fairness, Competition and Cooperation. *Quaterly Journal of Economics* 114, 817-868, 1999.

[Fehr and Falk, 2003] E. Fehr and A. Falk. Reciprocal Fairness, Cooperation and Limits to Competition. In E. Fullbrook, ed., *Intersubjectivity in Economics, Agents and Structure*, London and New York: Routledge, 28-42, 2003.

[Fehr and Fischbacher, 2002] E. Fehr and U. Fischbacher. Why Social Preferences Matter — The Impact of Non-Selfish Motives on Competition, Cooperation and Incentives. *The Economic Journal* 112, C1-C33, 2002.

[Fehr and Fischbacher, 2003] E. Fehr and U. Fischbacher. The nature of human altruism. *Nature* 425, 785-791, 2003.

[Fehr and Schidt, 2003] E. Fehr and K. M. Schmidt. Theories of Fairness and Reciprocity: Evidence and Economic Applications, in: M. Dewatripont, L.P. Hansen, S. Turnovski, eds., *Advances in Economic Theory, Eighth World Congress of the Econometric Society*, Vol. 1, Cambridge: Cambridge University Press, 208-257, 2003.

[Frank, 1988] R. H. Frank. *Passions Within Reason. The Strategic Role of Emotions*, New York and London: W.W. Norton & Company, 1988.
[Friedman, 1953] M. Friedman. The Methodology of Positive Economics. In *Essays in Positive Economics*, Chicago and London: The University of Chicago Press, 3-43, 1953.
[Gintis and Khurana, 2006] H. Gintis and R. Khurana. Corporate Honesty and Business Education: A Behavioral Model. Paper presented at IEA Workshop on Corporate Social Responsibility (CSR) and Corporate Governance, Trento, Italy, 11-13 July, 2006.
[Georgescu-Roegen, 1971] N. Georgescu-Roegen. *The Entropy Law and the Economic Process*, Cambridge (MA) und London: Harvard University Press, 1971.
[Hayek, 1952] F. A. Hayek. *The Sensory Order — An Inquiry into the Foundations of Theoretical Psychology*, Chicago: The University of Chicago Press, 1952.
[Hayek, 1960] F. A. Hayek. *The Constitution of Liberty*, Chicago: The University of Chicago Press, 1960.
[Hayek, 1964] F. A. Hayek. Kinds of Order in Society. *New Individualist Review* 3, 3-12, 1964.
[Hayek, 1967a] F. A. Hayek. Degrees of Explanation. In *Studies in Philosophy, Politics and Economics*, Chicago: The University of Chicago Press, 3-21, 1967.
[Hayek, 1967b] F. A. Hayek. The Theory of Complex Phenomena. In *Studies in Philosophy, Politics and Economics*, Chicago: The University of Chicago Press, 22-42. 1967.
[Hayek, 1967c] F. A. Hayek. Rules, Perception and Intelligibility. In *Studies in Philosophy, Politics and Economics*, Chicago: The University of Chicago Press, 43-65, 1967.
[Hayek, 1967d] F. A. Hayek. Kinds of Rationalism. In *Studies in Philosophy, Politics and Economics*, Chicago: The University of Chicago Press, 82-95, 1967.
[Hayek, 1973] F. A. Hayek. *Law, Legislation and Liberty*, Vol. 1, *Rules and Order*, London: Routledge & Kegan Paul, 1973.
[Hayek, 1976] F. A. Hayek. *Law, Legislation and Liberty*, Vol. 2, *The Mirage of Social Justice*, London: Routledge & Kegan Paul, 1976.
[Hayek, 1978] F. A. Hayek. The Primacy of the Abstract. In *New Studies in Philosophy, Politics, Economics and the History of Ideas*, Chicago: The University of Chicago Press, 35-49, 1978.
[Hayel, 1979] F. A. Hayek. [orig. 1952]: *The Counter-Revolution of Science*, Indianapolis: Liberty Press, 1979.
[Hayek, 1982] F. A. Hayek. The Sensory Order After 25 Years. In W.B. Weimer and D.S. Palermo, eds., *Cognition and the Symbolic Processes*, Vol. 2, Hillsdale, N.J.: Lawrence Erbaum Associates, Publishers, 287-293, 1982.
[Heiner, 1983] R. A. Heiner. The Origin of Predictable Behavior. *American Economic Review* 73, 560-595, 1983.
[Heiner, 1990] R. A. Heiner. Rule-Governed Behavior in Evolution and Human Society. *Constitutional Political Economy* 1 (quoted here from typescript), 1990.
[Henrich *et al.*, 2005] J. Henrich *et al.* 'Economic Man' in cross-cultural perspective: Behavioral experiments in 15 small-scale societies. *Behavioral and Brain Science* 28, 795-855, 2005.
[Holland, 1988] J. H. Holland. The Global Economy as an Adaptive System. In P.W. Anderson, K.J. Arrow and D. Pines, eds., *The Economy as an Evolving Complex System*, Vol. V, Santa Fe Institute Studies in the Sciences of Complexity, Redwood City, Cal. et al.: Addison-Wesley Publishing Company, Inc., 117-124, 1988.
[Holland, 1992a] J. H. Holland. *Adaptation in Natural and Artificial Systems*, Cambridge, Mass., and London: The MIT Press, 1992.
[Holland, 1992b] J. H. Holland. Complex Adaptive Systems. *Daedalus — Journal of the American Academy of Arts and Sciences*, 121, 17-30, 1992.
[Holland, 1995] J. H. Holland. *Hidden Order: How Adaptation Builds Complexity*, Reading, Massachusetts: Helix Books, 1995.
[Holland, 1996] J. H. Holland. The Rationality of Adaptive Agents. In K. J. Arrow, E. Colombatto, M. Perlman and Ch. Schmidt, eds., *The Rational Foundations of Economic Behavior — Proceedings of the IEA Conference held in Turin*, Italy, New York: St. Martin's Press, 281-301, 1996.
[Holland *et al.*, 1986] J. H. Holland, K. J. Holyoak, R. E. Nisbett, and P. R. Thagard. *Induction*, Cambridge, Mass.: MIT Press, 1986.
[Loewenstein, 2000] G. Loewenstein. Emotions in Economic Theory and Economic Behavior. *The American Economic Review* 90, Papers and Proceedings, 426-432, 2000.
[Mäki, 1998] U. Mäki. As if. In J. Davis, W. Hands and U. Mäki, eds., *The Handbook of Economic Methodology*, Cheltenham: Edward Elgar, 25-27, 1998.

[Mäki, 2009] U. Mäki. Unrealistic assumptions and unnecessary confusions: Rereading and rewriting F53 as a realist statement. In U. Mäki, ed., *The Methodology of Positive Economics: Reflections on the Milton Friedman Legacy*, pp. 90–116. Cambridge: Cambridge University Press, 2009.

[Mäki, 2009a] U. Mäki, ed. *The Methodology of Positive Economics: Reflections on the Milton Friedman Legacy*, Cambridge: Cambridge University Press, 2007.

[Mayr, 1988] E. Mayr. *Toward a New Philosophy of Biology — Observations of an Evolutionist*, Cambridge, Mass., and London: Harvard University Press, 1988.

[Mayr, 1992] E. Mayr. The Idea of Teleology. *Journal of the History of Ideas*, 53, 117-135, 1992.

[McClennen, 2004] E. F. McClennen. The Rationality of Being Guided by Rules In Alfred R. Mele and Pies Rawling, eds., *The Oxford Handbook of Rationality*, New York: Oxford University Press, 222-239, 2004.

[McFadden, 1999] D. McFadden. Rationality for Economists? *Journal of Risk and Uncertainty* 19, 73-105, 1999.

[McFadden, 2005] D. McFadden. The New Science of Pleasure — Consumer Behavior and the Measurement of Well-Being. Frisch Lecture, Econometric Society World Congress, London, August 20, 2005.

[Mises, 1949] L. von Mises. *Human Action — A Treatise in Economics*, New Haven: Yale University Press, 1949.

[Pettit, 2005] P. Pettit. Construing Sen on Commitment. *Economics and Philosophy* 21, 15-32, 2005.

[Popper, 1972] K. R. Popper. *Objective Knowledge — An Evolutionary Approach*, Oxford: At the Clarendon Press, 1972.

[Popper, 1976] K. R. Popper. *Unended Quest — An Intellectual Biography*, La Salle, Ill.: Open Court, 1976.

[Popper, 1980] K. R. Popper. *The Logic of Scientific Discovery*, London and New York: Routledge, 1980.

[Popper, 1982] K. R. Popper. *The Open Universe — An Argument for Indeterminism*, London: Routledge, 1982.

[Popper and Eccles, 1983] K. R. Popper and J. C. Eccles. *The Self and Its Brain*, London and New York: Routledge, 1983.

[Sen, 1973] A. K. Sen. Behaviour and the Concept of Preference," *Economica, New Series*, 40, 241-259, 1973.

[Sen, 1977] A. K. Sen. Rational Fools: A Critique of the Behavioral Foundations of Economic Theory. *Philosophy and Public Affairs* 6, 317-344, 1977.

[Sen, 2002] A. K. Sen. *Rationality and Freedom*, Cambridge, Mass., and London: The Belknap Press of Harvard University Press, 2002.

[Sen, 2002a] A. K. Sen. Introduction: Rationality and Freedom. In A. Sen 2002, 3-64.

[Sen, 2002b] A. K. Sen. Maximization and the Act of Choice. In: A. Sen 2002, 158-205.

[Sen, 2002c] A. K. Sen. Goals, Commitments, and Identity. In: A. Sen 2002. 206-224.

[Simon, 1982] H. A. Simon. The Role of Expectations in an Adaptive or Behavioral Model. In *Models of Bounded Rationality*, Vol. 2, *Behavioral Economics and Business Organization*, Cambridge, Mass., and London: The MIT Press, 380-399, 1982.

[Simon, 1984] H. A. Simon. On the Behavioral and Rational Foundations of Economic Dynamics. *Journal of Economic Behavior and Organization*, 5, 35-55, 1984.

[Smith, 2003] V. L. Smith. Constructivist and Ecological Rationality in Economics. *The American Economic Review* 93, 465-508, 2003.

[Vanberg, 1994] V. J. Vanberg *Rules and Choice in Economics*, London and New York: Routledge, 1994.

[Vanberg, 2002] V. J. Vanberg. Rational Choice vs. Program-Based Behavior: Alternative Theoretical Approaches and their Relevance for the Study of Institutions. *Rationality and Society* 14, 7-53, 2002.

[Vanberg, 2004a] V. J. Vanberg. The Rationality Postulate in Economics: Its Ambiguity, its Deficiency and its Evolutionary Alternative. *Journal of Economic Methodology* 11, 1-29, 2004.

[Vanberg, 2004] V. J. Vanberg. Austrian Economics, Evolutionary Psychology and Methodological Dualism: Subjectivism Reconsidered. *Advances in Austrian Economics*. 7, 155-199 (Volume on *Evolutionary Psychology and Economic Theory* ed. by Roger Koppl), 2004.

[Vanberg, 2006] V. J. Vanberg. Rationality, Rule Following and Emotions: On the Economics of Moral Preferences, Paper prepared for presentation at the workshop on Naturalistic Perspectives on Economic Behavior — Are There Any Normative Correlates? Max Planck Institute of Economics, Jena, Germany, October 12-14, 2006.

[Veblen, 1993] T. Veblen. [orig. 1898]: Why Is Economics Not an Evolutionary Science? In R. Tilman, ed., *A Veblen Treasury — From Leisure Class to War, Peace, and Capitalism*, Armonk (NY): Sharpe, 129-143, 1993.

[Vromen, 2004] J. Vromen. Routines, genes and program-based behaviour. *Papers on Economics and Evolution*, Max Planck Institute of Economics, Jena, Germany, 2004.

[Walras, 1954] L. Walras. [orig. 1874]: *Elements of Pure Economics — Or the Theory of Social Wealth*, Homewood (IL): Richard D. Irwin Inc, 1954.

[Winden, 2001] F. van Winden. Emotional Hazard, exemplified by taxation-induced anger," *Kyklos* 54, 491-506, 2001.

# PHILOSOPHY OF GAME THEORY

Till Grüne-Yanoff and Aki Lehtinen

## 1 INTRODUCTION

Consider the following situation: when two hunters set out to hunt a stag and lose track of each other in the process, each hunter has to make a decision. Either she continues according to plan, hoping that her partner does likewise (because she cannot bag a deer on her own), and together they catch the deer; or she goes for a hare instead, securing a prey that does not require her partner's cooperation, and thus abandoning the common plan. Each hunter prefers a deer shared between them to a hare for herself alone. But if she decides to hunt for deer, she faces the possibility that her partner abandons her, leaving her without deer or hare. So, what should she do? And, what will she do?

Situations like this, where the outcome of an agent's action depends on the actions of all the other agents involved, are called *interactive*. Two people playing chess is the archetypical example of an interactive situation, but so are elections, wage bargaining, market transactions, arms races, international negotiations, and many more. Game theory studies these interactive situations. Its fundamental idea is that an agent in an interactive decision should and does take into account the deliberations of the other players involved, who, in turn, take her deliberations into account. A rational agent in an interactive situation should therefore not ask: "what should I do, given what is likely to happen?" but rather: "what will they do, given their beliefs about what I will do; and how should I respond to that?"

In this article, we discuss philosophical issues arising from game theory. We can only sketch the basic concepts of the theory in order to discuss some of their philosophical implications and problems. We will thus assume that our readers have some familiarity with the basic concepts. For those who are primarily looking for an introduction to the basics of game theory, we recommend Binmore [2007; 2008] or Kreps [1990], both of which also consider philosophical issues. Osborne and Rubinstein [1994] and Fudenberg and Tirole [1991] are textbooks that put more emphasis on the mathematical proofs. Hargreaves-Heap & Varoufakis [2001], Ross [2006b] and Grüne-Yanoff [2008b] provide philosophical accounts of game theory.[1]

Philosophy and game theory are connected in multiple ways. Game theory has been used as a tool in philosophical discussions, and some crucial game theoretical

[1]This paper is based on Grüne-Yanoff's earlier paper.

Handbook of the Philosophy of Science. Volume 13: Philosophy of Economics.
Volume editor: Uskali Mäki. General editors: Dov M. Gabbay, Paul Thagard and John Woods.

concepts have been developed by philosophers.[2] Game theory also has been the object of philosophical inquiry itself. Our discussion will concentrate on the latter. Since game theory relies heavily on mathematical models, the standard epistemic issues concerning modelling and unrealistic assumptions in philosophy of economics are also relevant for game theory. But since game theory transcends economics, a number of other philosophical issues also arise. Perhaps the most important of these is the interpretation of the theory: is game theory to be understood mainly as a tool for *recommending* rational choices, for *predicting* agents' behaviour, or for merely providing an abstract *framework for understanding* complex interactions (e.g., [Blackburn, 1998; Aydinonat, 2008])? If we settle for the first interpretation, the issue of whether the rationality concept employed by the theory is justifiable becomes pressing. Is it intuitively rational to choose as the theory prescribes? If the second interpretation is adopted, one must ask whether the theory can in principle be a good predictive theory of human behaviour: whether it has empirical content, whether it is testable and whether there are good reasons to believe that it is true or false. If the third interpretation is adopted, the question arises concerning which qualities of the theory contribute to this understanding, and to what extent these qualities are different from the prescriptive or predictive function discussed in the first two interpretations.

We will address this central question in sections 3 and 4. In order to do so, a number of game-theoretical concepts that are particularly important in a philosophical assessment must be discussed first, viz. payoffs, strategies, and solution concepts.

## 2 SOME BASIC CONCEPTS

Decision theory, as well as game theory, assesses the rationality of decisions in the light of preferences over outcomes and beliefs about the likelihood of these outcomes. The basic difference between the two lies in the way they view the likelihood of outcomes. Decision theory treats all outcomes as exogenous events, 'moves of nature'. Game theory, in contrast, focuses on those situations in which outcomes are determined by interactions of deliberating agents. It proposes that agents consider outcomes as determined by other agents' reasoning, and that each agent therefore assesses the likelihood of an outcome by trying to figure out how the other agents they interact with will reason. The likelihoods of outcomes therefore become "endogenous" in the sense that players take their opponents' payoffs and rationality into account when considering the consequences of their strategies.

The formal theory defines a game as consisting of a set of *players*, a set of *pure strategies* for each player, an *information set* for each player, and the players' *payoff functions*. A player's pure strategy specifies her choice for each time she has to choose in the game. If a player's strategy requires choices at more than one time,

[2] For example, David Lewis [1969] introduced the notion of common knowledge, and Allan Gibbard [1973] that of the game form.

we say that the strategy contains a number of *actions*. Games in which players choose between actions simultaneously and only once are called *static games*. In *dynamic games* players choose between actions in a determined temporal order. All players of a game together determine a consequence. Each chooses a specific strategy, and their combination (which is called a *strategy profile*) yields a specific consequence. The consequence of a strategy profile can be a material prize — for example money — but it can also be any other relevant event, like being the winner, or feeling guilt. Game theory is really only interested in the players' *evaluations* of this consequence, which are specified in each players' payoff or utility function.

The part of the theory that deals with situations in which players' choice of strategies cannot be enforced is called the theory of *non-cooperative* games. *Cooperative* game theory, in contrast, allows for pre-play agreements to be made binding (e.g. through legally enforceable contracts). This article will not discuss cooperative game theory. More specifically, it will focus — for reasons of simplicity — on non-cooperative games with two players, finite strategy sets and precisely known payoff functions. The first philosophical issue with respect to these games arises from the interpretation of their payoffs.

## *2.1 Payoffs*

Static two-person games can be represented by $m$-by-$n$ matrices, with $m$ rows and $n$ columns corresponding to the players' strategies, and the entries in the squares representing the payoffs for each player for the pair of strategies (row, column) determining the square in question. As an example, Figure 1 provides a possible representation of the stag-hunt scenario described in the introduction.

| | | Col's choice | |
|---|---|---|---|
| | | $C1$ | $C2$ |
| Row's choice | $R1$ | 2,2 | 0,1 |
| | $R2$ | 1,0 | 1,1 |

Figure 1. The stag hunt

The 2-by-2 matrix of Figure 1 determines two players, Row and Col, who each have two pure strategies: $R1$ and $C1$ (go deer hunting) and $R2$ and $C2$ (go hare hunting). Combining the players' respective strategies yields four different pure strategy profiles, each associated with a consequence relevant for both players: $(R1, C1)$ leads to them catching a deer, $(R2, C1)$ leaves Row with a hare and Col with nothing, $(R2, C2)$ gets each a hare and $(R1, C2)$ leaves Row empty-handed and Col with a hare. Both players evaluate these consequences of each profile. Put informally, players rank consequences as 'better than' or 'equally good as'. In the stag-hunt scenario, players have the following ranking:

| Row | Col |
|---|---|
| 1. $(R1, C1)$ | 1. $(R1, C1)$ |
| 2. *(R2,C1); (R2,C2)* | 2. *(R1,C2); (R2,C2)* |
| 3. $(R1, C2)$ | 3. $(R2, C1)$ |

Figure 2. The hunters' respective rankings of the strategy profiles

This ranking can be quite simply represented by a numerical function $u$, according to the following two principles:

1. For all consequences $X, Y : X$ is better than $Y$ if and only if $u(X) > u(Y)$
2. For all consequences $X, Y : X$ is equally good as $Y$ if and only if $u(X) = u(Y)$

A function that meets these two principles (and some further requirements that are not relevant here) is called an *ordinal utility function*. Utility functions are used to represent players' evaluations of consequences in games. One of the most important methodological principles of game theory is that *every* consideration that may affect a player's choice is included in the payoffs. If an agent, for example, cared about the other players' well-being, this would have to be reflected in her payoffs. The payoffs thus contain all other behaviour-relevant information except beliefs.

Convention has it that the first number represents Row's evaluation, while the second number represents Col's evaluation. It is now easy to see that the numbers of the game in Figure 1 represent the ranking of Figure 2. Note, however, that the matrix of Figure 1 is not the only way to represent the stag-hunt game. Because the utilities only represent rankings, there are many ways how one can represent the ranking of Figure 2. For example, the games in Figure 3 are identical to the game in Figure 1.

| | $C1$ | $C2$ |
|---|---|---|
| $R1$ | -5,-5 | -7,-6 |
| $R2$ | -7,-7 | -6,-6 |

(a)

| | $C1$ | $C2$ |
|---|---|---|
| $R1$ | 100,100 | 1,99 |
| $R2$ | 99,1 | 99,99 |

(b)

| | $C1$ | $C2$ |
|---|---|---|
| $R1$ | -5,100 | -7,99 |
| $R2$ | -6,1 | -6,99 |

(c)

Figure 3. Three versions of the stag hunt

In Figure 3a, all numbers are negative, but they retain the same ranking of consequences. And similarly in 3b, only that here the proportional relations between the numbers (which do not matter) are different. This should also make clear that utility numbers only express a ranking for one and the same player, and do not allow a comparison of different players' evaluations. In 3c, although the numbers are very different for the two players, they retain the same ranking as in Figure 1.

Comparing, say, Row's evaluation of $(R1, C1)$ with Col's evaluation of $(R1, C1)$ simply does not have any meaning.

Note that in the stag-hunt game, agents do not gain if others lose. Everybody is better off hunting deer, and lack of coordination leads to losses for all. Games with this property are therefore called *coordination games.* They stand in stark contrast to games in which one player's gain is the other player's loss. Most social games are of this sort: in chess, for example, the idea of coordination is wholly absent. Such games are called *zero-sum games.* They were the first games to be treated theoretically, and the pioneering work of game theory, von Neumann and Morgenstern's [1947] *The Theory of Games and Economic Behaviour* concentrates solely on them. Today, many of the games discussed are of a third kind: they combine coordination aspects with conflictual aspects, so that players may at times gain from coordinating, but at other times from competing with the other players. A famous example of such a game is the Prisoners' Dilemma, to be discussed shortly.

Players can create further strategies by *randomizing* over pure strategies. They can choose a randomization device (like a dice) and determine for each chance result which of their pure strategies they will play. The resultant probability distribution over pure strategies is called a *mixed strategy* $\sigma$. For example, Row could create a new strategy that goes as follows: toss a (fair) coin. Play $R1$ if heads, and $R2$ if tails. Because a fair coin lands heads 50% of the time, such a mixed strategy is denoted $\sigma_R = (0.5, 0.5)$. As there are no limits to the number of possible randomization devices, each player can create an infinite number of mixed strategies for herself. The players' evaluation of mixed strategies profiles is represented by the *expected values* of the corresponding pure-strategy payoffs. Such an expected value is computed as the weighted average of the pure-strategy payoffs, where the weights are given by the probabilities with which each strategy is played. For example, if Row in Figure 1 plays her mixed strategy $\sigma_R = (0.5, 0.5)$, and Col plays a strategy $\sigma_C = (0.8, 0.2)$, then Row's expected utility will be computed by:

$$u_R(\sigma_R, \sigma_C) = 0.5(0.8 \times 2 + 0.2 \times 0) + 0.5(0.8 \times 1 + 0.2 \times 1) = 1.3$$

With the same mixed strategies, Col's expected utility, $u_C(\sigma_R, \sigma_C) = 1$. For the payoffs of mixed strategy to be computable, the utility function has to carry *cardinal* information. That is, now it is also important how much a player prefers a consequence $X$ to a consequence $Y$, in comparison to another pair of consequences $X$ and $Z$. Because mixed strategies are a very important technical concept in game theory (although, as we will argue, the interpretation of this notion is often problematic), it is generally assumed that the utility functions characterizing the payoffs are cardinal.

It is important to note that the cardinal nature of utilities does not by itself allow making interpersonal comparisons. In fact, such interpersonal comparisons play no role in standard game theory at all. There are several reasons for this. The first is that the standard way how payoffs are measured does not permit interpersonal comparisons. Payoffs are usually interpreted as von Neumann-Morgenstern utility functions (NMUFs), which are constructed (in theory at least) with the so-called reference lottery technique. In this technique, an agent is asked to state probabilities $p$ with which he or she is indifferent between obtaining an intermediately preferred outcome for sure, and a lottery involving the best and the worst outcomes with probabilities $p$ and $1 - p$ (see e.g., [Hirshleifer and Riley, 1992, pp. 16-7] for a more thorough account). Both indifference judgments, and the judgments concerning what is the (overall) best and the worst outcome, are subjective assessments of one individual, and cannot be transferred to other individuals. Thus, when using NMUFs, it is meaningless to compare different persons' utility schedules. (And although we do not discuss them here, this meaninglessness verdict also applies to other standard utility measures.)

The second reason is that standard accounts of strategic thinking do not require the players to make interpersonal comparisons. They only maximise their own utility, and they predict other players' choices by supposing that they also maximise their respective utilities. Thus, comparisons are only made between one player's evaluation of outcomes, and not between evaluations of different players.

Steven Kuhn [2004], however, has argued that standard accounts of evolutionary dynamics and equilibrium in evolutionary game theory require interpersonal comparisons. Evolutionary game theory takes a population perspective, in which different strategies in a population compete for higher rates of replication. Payoffs in such evolutionary games represent proportions of replication — that is, how much more a strategy replicates in a certain population, when compared to its competitors. Such proportional payoffs obviously compare across strategies. This may be unproblematic in biological applications, where payoffs are interpreted as Darwinian fitness. But in many social applications of evolutionary game theory, strategies are linked to individuals, and strategy payoffs to individuals' preferences. Applying standard evolutionary dynamics and equilibria to these cases, under a natural selection interpretation, then implies the interpersonal comparability of these preferences [Grüne-Yanoff, 2008a].

## 2.2 Strategies

A pure strategy denotes a choice of an available action in games in strategic form. This is a relatively straightforward concept, at least insofar as the notions of availability and actions are well understood. But the concept of strategy also includes pure strategies in extensive games and mixed strategies. Both of these strategy kinds are philosophically problematic and will be discussed here.

In extensive games, a strategy specifies an action for each node in the game tree at which a player has to move. Take the following example. Player 1 is on a diet and wishes to avoid eating baked goods. When she is leaving work, she can choose whether to take the direct way home (L), which leads past a bakery, or take a detour (R). Player 2 (the bakery owner) then decides, without knowing which route player 1 intends to take, whether to spray a 'freshly baked bread aroma' in front of her bakery (l) or not (r). Deploying this aerosol is costly, but may influence player 1's preferences over cakes. If player 1 chose L, he now has to decide whether to buy a bun (b) or not (d).

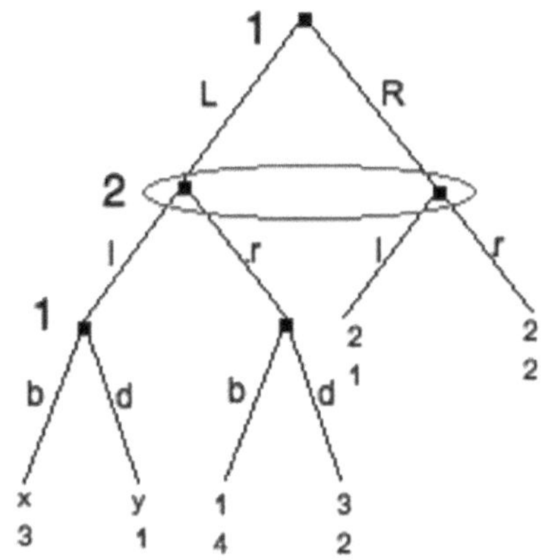


Figure 4. The baker's game

The standard strategy notion in extensive games requires that actions are specified for each of the players' decision nodes. This has two counterintuitive implications. Let us only focus on the game tree of Figure 4 to discuss the first implication (leaving the payoffs aside for a moment). Even if player 1 chooses R at the first decision node, he also has to specify what he would choose had he chosen L, and player 2 had made her choice. As Rubinstein [1991, p. 911] points out, this is not in accord with our intuition of a '*plan of action*'. Such a plan, as commonly understood, would for this game require player 1 to decide between L and R, and *only if* he chose L, to make provisional choices for when player 2 has chosen l or r. A strategy in this and other extensive form games thus goes beyond a player's 'plan of action'. Further, these unintuitive aspects of strategies are crucial for game theory. In order to assess the optimality of player 2's strategy — for the case that player 1 should deviate from his plan — we have to specify player 2's expectations regarding player 1's second choice. For this reason, Rubinstein argues, it is more plausible to interpret this part of player 1's strategy as player 2's *belief* about player 1's planned future play.

According to this interpretation, extensive game strategies comprise of a player's plan *and* of his opponent's beliefs in the event that he does not follow the plan. This has important consequences for the interpretation of game theoretic results. In many cases (for example in sequential bargaining) it is assumed that strategies are stationary — i.e. that the history of the game has no influence on players' responses to their opponents' choices. Yet under the new perspective on strategies, this means that beliefs about opponents' play are also stationary. This, Rubinstein argues, eliminates a great deal of what sequential games are intended to model, namely the changing pattern in players' behaviour and beliefs, as they accumulate experience.

In addition to this stationarity issue, this view on strategies also has a problematic uniformity consequence. If a player's strategy necessarily comprises of opponents' beliefs about her choices, then the attribution of one strategy to the agent implies that all opponents hold the same belief about that player's future behaviour. This may be an implausibly strong built-in assumption, as it in particular concerns the player's behaviour off the equilibrium path.

The second implausible implication of the standard strategy notion concerns possible preference changes during the time of play. According to the standard notion, every strategy profile has a unique payoff for each player. That implies that player 1 at the initial node knows what the payoff for each of his strategies are, given the strategies of player 2. Even under incomplete information, he knows the probability distributions over possible payoffs. Yet there are intuitively plausible cases in which players may try to influence their opponents' preferences, in order to obtain better results. This introduces a strategic element into the payoff information that cannot be adequately represented by a probability distribution.

Take the baker's game as an example. According to the standard strategy notion, player 1 knows all strategy profile payoffs at the initial node. Because he is on a diet, he will at the initial node have a preference for not consuming a bun ($d$ over $b$). Hence, independently of whether player 2 chooses $l$ or $r, y > x$, and more specifically $y = 3$ and $x = 1$. From that perspective, $(Ld, r)$ is the only sub-game perfect Nash equilibrium — the baker should never try to manipulate the dieter's preferences. Yet that is an implausible conclusion — such manipulations, after all, are often successful. Somehow, the influence of the baker's strategy on the dieter's preferences should be taken into account, that is, if player 1 chooses $L$ and player 2 chooses $l$, then $x > y$. But the standard strategy notion does not allow for such an influence of actual play on payoffs and biases standard game theory to ignore such strategic preference manipulations.

A mixed strategy is a probability distribution over all pure strategies in a strategic form game. We have already discussed their simplest interpretation, namely that players randomise their pure strategy choice. The idea is that randomisation may be a conscious decision, or may develop as an unconscious habit. Critics have objected that 'real world decision makers do not flip coins'. Such a criticism is too strong, as there are plausible cases where players randomly choose an action. Often cited examples include choices when to bluff in Poker, or how to serve in Tennis. In each of these cases, the randomising player avoids being correctly predicted — and hence outguessed — by her opponent. Yet, as Rubinstein [1991, p. 913] has pointed out, these are not mixed strategies in which actions like 'always bluff' and 'never bluff' are the pure strategies. In a mixed strategy equilibrium, the players are indifferent between the mixed strategy and a pure component of that mixed strategy. In the poker or the tennis game, in contrast, the player is not indifferent between 'always bluff' (in which case she soon will become predictable and hence exploitable) and a randomising strategy.

This feature of mixed strategy equilibria has always made them 'intuitively problematic' [Aumann, 1985, p. 43]. Why should a player choose to randomise a strategy, if she is indifferent in equilibrium between the randomisation and any pure component of the randomisation — in particular, if such randomisation is costly in terms of time or attention?

Because of these grave problems of the randomising account of mixed strategies, two alternative interpretations have been offered. The first reinterprets mixed strategies as the distribution of pure choices in a population. If populations instead of players interact in a game, a player is chosen from each population at random. The mixed strategy then specifies the probabilities with which the pure choices are drawn from the population. That is, mixed strategies are defined over sufficiently large population of players, each of which plays a pure strategy. This is an important context that we will examine in section 4, when discussing evolutionary games. But it is a rather specific one, which does not justify employing the notion of mixed strategy in a context where players are unique individuals; and it only holds in particular situations in this context anyway [Maynard Smith, 1982, pp. 183-88].

The second alternative is to reinterpret mixed strategies as the way in which games with incomplete information appear to outside observers. Each player's payoff function is subjected to a slight random perturbation, the value of which is known only to the player herself, but the other players only know the mean of her payoff function. Thus, each player will choose a pure strategy component of her mixed strategy in the resulting incomplete information game. Harsanyi [1973] showed that this incomplete information game has pure strategy equilibria that correspond to the mixed strategy equilibria of the original game. The point here is that to outside observers, the game appears as one in which players use mixed strategies, and the concept of a mixed strategy essentially represents one player's uncertainty concerning the *other* players' choice (see also Aumann 1987). This 'purification' account of mixed strategies provides an example of a game-theoretical concept, that of the mixed strategy, which is plausible only under some interpretations of game theory. The normative problem of justifying its use led to a reformulation which is sensible only if game theory is interpreted as a framework of analysis but not if it is taken to be a prescriptive theory.

## *2.3 Solution Concepts*

When interactive situations are represented as highly abstract games, the objective of game theory is to determine the outcome or possible outcomes of each game, given certain assumptions about the players. To do this is to *solve* a game. Various *solution concepts* have been proposed. The conceptually most straightforward solution concept is the *elimination of dominated strategies.* Consider the game in Figure 5. In this game, no matter what Col chooses, playing $R2$ gives Row a higher payoff. If Col plays $C1$, Row is better off playing $R2$, because she can obtain 3 utils instead of two. If Col plays $C2$, Row is also better off playing $R2$, because she can obtain 1 utils instead of zero. Similarly for Col: no matter what

Row chooses, playing $C2$ gives her a higher payoff. This is what is meant by saying that $R1$ and $C1$ are strictly dominated strategies.

| | $C1$ | $C2$ |
|---|---|---|
| $R1$ | 2,2 | 0,3 |
| $R2$ | 3,0 | 1,1 |

Figure 5. The Prisoners' Dilemma

More generally, a player $A$'s pure strategy is *strictly dominated* if there exists another (pure or mixed) strategy for $A$ that has a higher payoff for each of $A$'s opponent's strategies. Solving a game by eliminating all dominated strategies is based on the assumption that players do and should choose those strategies that are best for them, in this very straightforward sense. In cases like in that depicted in Figure 5, where each player has only one non-dominated strategy, the elimination of dominated strategies is a straightforward and plausible solution concept. Unfortunately, there are many games without dominated strategies, for example the game of Figure 6.

| | $C1$ | $C2$ | $C3$ |
|---|---|---|---|
| $R1$ | 3,4 | 2,5 | 1,3 |
| $R2$ | 4,8 | 1,2 | 0,9 |

Figure 6. A game without dominated strategies

For these kinds of games, the *Nash equilibrium* solution concept offers greater versatility than dominance or maximin (as it turns out, all maximin solutions are also Nash equilibria). In contrast to dominated strategy elimination, the Nash equilibrium applies to strategy profiles, not to individual strategies. Roughly, a strategy profile is in Nash equilibrium if none of the players can do better by *unilaterally* changing her strategy. Take the example of Figure 6. Consider the strategy profile $(R1, C1)$. If Row knew that Col would play $C1$, then she would play $R2$ because that's the best she can do against $C1$. On the other hand, if Col knew that Row would play $R1$, he would play $C2$ because that's the best he can do against $R1$. So $(R1, C1)$ is not in equilibrium, because at least one player (in this case both) is better off by unilaterally deviating from it. Similarly for $(R1, C3), (R2, C1), (R2, C2)$ and $(R2, C3)$: in all these profiles, one of the players can improve her or his lot by deviating from the profile. Only *(R1, C2)* is a pure strategy Nash equilibrium — neither player is better off by unilaterally deviating from it.

There are games without a pure strategy Nash equilibrium, as Figure 7 shows. The reader can easily verify that each player has an incentive to deviate, whichever pure strategy the other chooses.

| | $C1$ | $C2$ |
|---|---|---|
| $R1$ | 1,-1 | -1,1 |
| $R2$ | -1,1 | 1,-1 |

Figure 7. Matching pennies

However, there is an equilibrium involving mixed strategies. Randomizing between the two strategies, assigning equal probability to each, yields a payoff of $0.5(0.5 \times 1 + 0.5 \times -1) + 0.5(0.5 \times 1 + 0.5 \times -1) = 0$ for both players. As mutually best responses, these mixed strategies constitute a Nash equilibrium. As one of the fundamental results of game theory, it has been shown that *every* finite static game has a mixed-strategy equilibrium [Nash, 1950]. The interpretation of this equilibrium is problematic. If Row knew that Col plays a mixed strategy, she would be indifferent between randomising herself and playing one of the pure strategies. If randomisation came with a cost, she would prefer playing a pure strategy. So the mixed equilibrium seems unstable. If Col knew which pure strategy Row would play, he would exploit this knowledge by choosing a pure strategy himself. But that would give Row incentives again to randomise. So the mixed equilibrium would be re-installed.

Many games have several Nash equilibria. Take for example Figure 1. There, neither player has an incentive to deviate from $(R1, C1)$, nor to deviate from $(R2, C2)$. Thus both strategy profiles are pure-strategy Nash equilibria. With two or more possible outcomes, the equilibrium concept loses much of its appeal. It no longer gives an obvious answer to the normative, explanatory or predictive questions game theory sets out to answer. The assumption that one specific Nash equilibrium is played relies on there being some mechanism or process that leads all the players to expect the same equilibrium. Various *equilibrium refinements* try to rule out some of the many equilibria by capturing these underlying intuitions.

Schelling's [1960] theory of *focal points* suggests that in some "real-life" situations players may be able to coordinate on a particular equilibrium by using information that is abstracted away by the payoffs in the strategic form. Focal points are equilibria that are somehow salient. Names of strategies and past common experiences of the players provide examples of information that has such salience. It will remain very difficult to develop systematic work on the "focalness" of various strategies because what the players take to be focal depends on their cultural and personal backgrounds and salience is by definition not reflected in the payoffs. This fact makes it very hard to incorporate these concepts into the formal structure of game theory (but see [Bacharach, 1993; Sugden, 1995]).

Other refinement notions might appear to evade such context-dependence. Two prominent examples are *payoff dominance* and *risk dominance.* Consider the following coordination games:

We say that the strategy profile $(R1, C1)$ *payoff dominates* $(C2, R2)$ if and only if the payoffs of $(R1, C1)$ for each player are equal or larger than the payoffs for

| | $C1$ | $C2$ |
|---|---|---|
| $R1$ | 5,5 | 0,4 |
| $R2$ | 4,0 | 2,2 |

| | $C1$ | $C2$ |
|---|---|---|
| $R1$ | A,a | C,b |
| $R2$ | B,c | D,d |

Figure 8. A coordination game

$(R2, C2)$ and at least one of these inequalities is strict. The intuition behind this refinement idea is that players will be able to coordinate on playing a certain strategy profile if this strategy profile is Pareto-efficient for all.

In contrast to this position, it has been argued that players may not only take the payoff magnitude into account when selecting amongst multiple Nash equilibria, but that they also consider the risk of ending up in a non-equilibrium state. In other words, $(R1, C1)$ may be better for Row in Figure 8, but the possibility that Col makes a mistake and chooses $C2$ when Row chooses $R1$ bears such a risk that it is safer for Row to choose $R2$ (by symmetry, the same applies to Col). We say that $(R2, C2)$ *risk dominates* $(R1, C1)$ if and only if $(C - D)(c - d) \geq (B - A)(b - a)$ [Harsanyi and Selten, 1988, lemma 5.4.4]. Thus, in the same game of Figure 8, $(R1, C1)$ is payoff dominant, while $(R2, C2)$ is risk dominant. Cases of such possible conflicts between refinement solution concepts are exacerbated by an embarrassment of riches. More and more competing refinements were developed, some of which imposed massive demands on the agents' cognitive ability to reason (and enormous faith that other agents will follow similar reasoning paths). Some were difficult to work with and their predictions were not always consistent with intuition, common sense or experimental evidence. Even more troubling, no proper basis was found from which to interpret these refinements or to choose between them.

As it will become clearer in section 3.2, the assumptions underlying the application of the Nash concept are somewhat problematic. The most important alternative solution concept is that of *rationalizability,* which is based on weaker assumptions. Players assign a subjective probability to each of the possible strategies of their opponents, instead of postulating their opponents' choices and then finding a best response to it, as in the Nash procedure. Further, knowing their opponent's payoffs, and knowing they are rational, players expect others to use only strategies that are best responses to some belief they might have about themselves. A strategy is rationalizable for a player if it survives indefinitely repeated selections as a best response to some rational belief she might have about the strategies of her opponent. A strategy profile is rationalizable if the strategies contained in it are rationalizable for each player. It has been shown that every Nash equilibrium is rationalizable. Further, the set of rationalizable strategies is nonempty and contains at least one pure strategy for each player [Bernheim, 1984; Pearce, 1984]. Rationalizability is thus often applicable, but there are often too many rationalizable strategies, so that this solution concept often does not provide a clear answer to the advisory and predictive questions posed to game theory, and it is thus seldom actually used in real-world applications.

All solution concepts discussed so far can be applied both to strategic and extensive form games. However, the extensive form provides more information than the strategic form, and this extra information sometimes provides the basis for further refinements. Take the example of Figure 9. The game has three Nash equilibria: *(U, (L,L)); (D, (L,R))* and *(D, (R,R))*. But the first and the third equilibria are suspect, when one looks at the extensive form of the game. After all, if player 2's *right* information set was reached, the he should play *R* (given that *R* gives him 2 utils while *L* gives him only 1 util). But if player 2's *left* information set was reached, then he should play *L* (given that *L* gives him 1 util, while *R* gives him only 0 utils). Moreover, player 1 should expect player 2 to choose this way, and hence she should choose *D* (given that her choosing *D* and player 2 choosing *R* gives her 3 utils, while her choosing *U* and player 2 choosing *L* gives her only 2 utils). The equilibria *(U, (L,L))* and *(D, (R,R))* are not "credible', because they rely on an "empty threat" by player 2. The threat is empty because player 2 would never wish to carry it out. The Nash equilibrium concept neglects this sort of information, because it is insensitive to what happens off the path of play.

| | $L,L$ | $L,R$ | $R,L$ | $R,R$ |
|---|---|---|---|---|
| $U$ | 2,1 | 2,1 | 0,0 | 0,0 |
| $D$ | -1,1 | 3,2 | -1,1 | 3,2 |

(a)

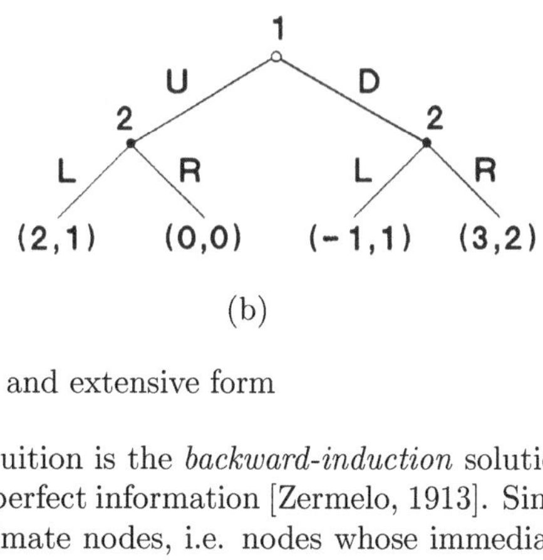


(b)

Figure 9. Strategic and extensive form

The simplest way to formalise this intuition is the *backward-induction* solution concept, which applies to finite games of perfect information [Zermelo, 1913]. Since the game is finite, it has a set of penultimate nodes, i.e. nodes whose immediate successors are terminal nodes. Specify that the player who can move at each such node chooses whichever action that leads to the successive terminal node with the highest payoff for him (in case of a tie, make an arbitrary selection). So in the game of Figure 9b, player 2's choice of *R* if player 1 chooses *U* and her choice of *L* if player 1 chooses *D* can be eliminated, so that the players act as if they were faced with the following truncated tree:

Now specify that each player at those nodes, whose immediate successors are the penultimate nodes, chooses the action that maximizes her payoff over the feasible successors, given that the players at the penultimate nodes play as we have just specified. So now player 1's choice *U* can be eliminated, as shown in Figure 11:

Then roll back through the tree, specifying actions at each node (not necessary for the given example anymore, but one gets the point). Once done, one will have specified a strategy for each player, and it is easy to check that these strategies

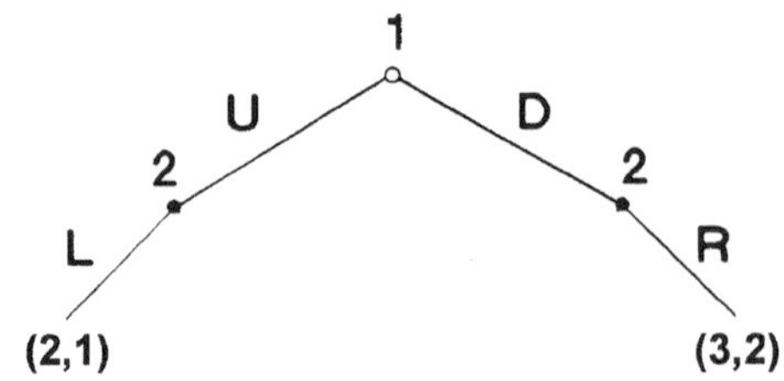


Figure 10. First step of backward induction

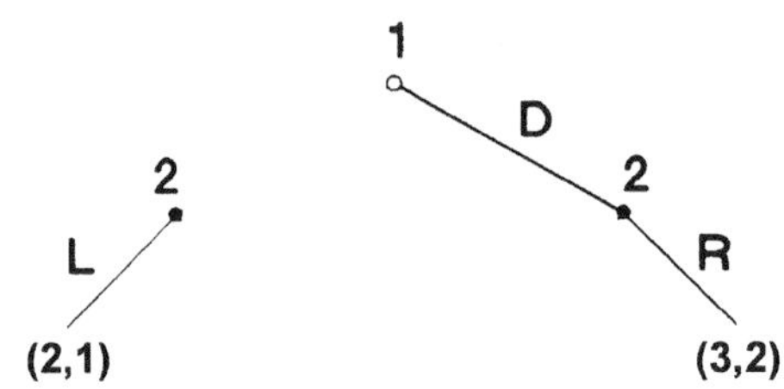


Figure 11. Second step of backward induction

form a Nash equilibrium. Thus, each finite game of perfect information has a pure-strategy Nash equilibrium.

Backward induction fails in games with imperfect information. In a game like that in Figure 11, there is no way to specify an optimal choice for player 2 in his second information set, without first specifying player 2's belief about the previous choice of player 1.

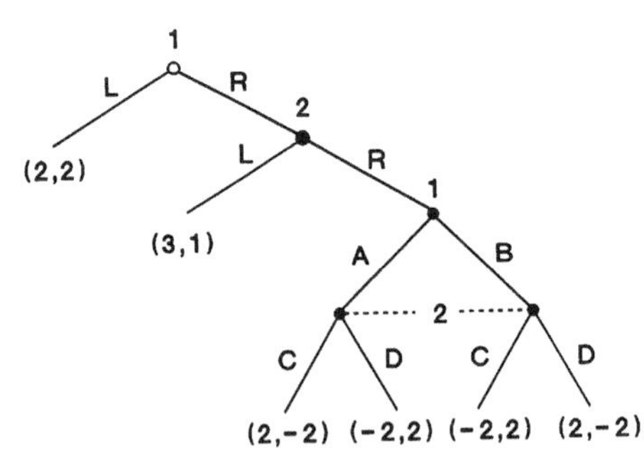


Figure 12. A game not solvable by backward induction

However, if one accepts the argument for backward induction, the following is also convincing. The game beginning at player 1's second information set is a simultaneous-move game identical to the one presented in Figure 7. The only

Nash equilibrium of this game is a mixed strategy with a payoff of 0 for both players (as noted earlier in this section when we discussed the matching pennies game). Using this equilibrium payoff as player 2's payoff from choosing $R$, it is obvious that player 2 maximizes his payoff by choosing $L$, and that player 1 maximizes her payoff by choosing $R$. More generally, an extensive form game can be analyzed into *proper subgames*, each of which satisfies the definition of extensive-form games in their own right. Games of imperfect information can thus be solved by replacing a proper subgame with one of its Nash equilibrium payoffs (if necessary, repeatedly), and performing backward induction on the reduced tree. This equilibrium refinement technique is called *subgame perfection.*

Backward induction is based on the idea that players expect other players' behaviour to be rational in future decision nodes. *Forward induction* [Kohlberg and Mertens, 1986] is the converse of this: players expect others to have been rational in their previous choices. Consider game $G$', commonly known as the 'Battle of the Sexes', which is depicted in Figure 13.

| | *LEFT* | *RIGHT* |
|---|---|---|
| *TOP* | 4,2 | 0,0 |
| *BOTTOM* | 0,0 | 2,4 |

Figure 13. Game $G'$

This game has no pure strategy equilibria, but we can compute that in a mixed strategy equilibrium (2/3, 1/3) the expected payoff is 4/3 for both players. Consider now how this game would be played if prior to playing game $G$' there was another game (depicted in Figure 14) in which playing in $G'$ was one of the possible strategies:

| | *IN* | *OUT* |
|---|---|---|
| *IN* | G', G' | 4,1 |
| *OUT* | 3,4 | 3,3 |

Figure 14. Game G

Since the expected payoff in $G'$ is 4/3>1, the column player (he) has a dominant strategy of playing *IN*. The row player (she) then has a dominant strategy of playing *OUT*, so that the solution to $G$ seems to be (*OUT*, *IN*). However, consider how she could rationalise a choice of *IN*. If she does enter the game $G$', she must be communicating her intention to obtain the best possible outcome (*TOP*, *LEFT*), and given that he understands this, he should choose *LEFT* if he were to find himself in this game. Notice that she could have secured a payoff of 3 by staying out, and that the intention of playing the (*TOP*, *LEFT*) equilibrium is the only reason for her to enter $G'$. One might object that she should simply never enter because the expected payoff in $G'$ is lower than that from playing $OUT$. The forward induction argument thus asks us to consider a counterfactual world in which something that is unimaginable from the point of view of other game-theoretic principles happens.

As we saw in the case of static games, different solution concepts, e.g. risk dominance and payoff dominance may sometimes give conflicting advice. A similar problem arises in the case of dynamic games: according to the forward induction argument, entering $G'$ seems like a perfectly rational thing to do. Indeed, the very idea of forward induction is to interpret all previous choices as rational. If the choice of $IN$ is taken as a mistake instead, it seems reasonable to continue to play the mixed strategy equilibrium. It is not very surprising that there is a fair amount of discussion on the plausibility of forward induction. As Binmore [2007, p. 426] suggests, this is because people's intuitions about how the relevant counterfactuals are to be interpreted depend on details concerning how exactly the game has been presented. If you were to find yourself in game $G'$ as a column player, would you randomise? We will continue discussing the role of counterfactuals in backward and forward induction in section 3.3.

Because of the context-dependence and possibility of contradiction, game theorists are cautious about the use of refinements. Rather, they seem to have settled for the Nash equilibrium as the 'gold standard' of game-theoretic solution concepts (see [Myerson, 1999] for a historical account). Yet as we show in section 3.2, justifications of why players should or will play equilibrium strategies are rather shaky. Instead of privileging one solution concept, one needs to take a closer look at how the choice of solution concepts is justified in the application of game theory to particular situations. This leads us to the discussion of the architecture of game theory.

## *2.4 The Architecture of Game Theory*

The structure of game theory is interesting from the perspective of the philosophy of science. Like many other theories, it employs highly stylized models, and it seeks to explain, predict and advice on real world phenomena by a theory that operates through these mathematical models. What is special about game theory, however, is that this theory does not provide a general and unified mode of dealing with all kinds of phenomena, but rather offers a 'toolbox', from which the right tools must be selected.

Ken Binmore distinguishes between *modelling* and *analysing* a game [1994, pp. 27, 161-2, 169]. Modelling means constructing a game model that corresponds to an imaginary or a real world situation. Analysing means choosing and applying a solution concept to a game model, and deriving a prediction of or a prescription for the players' choices.[3] Grüne-Yanoff and Schweinzer [2008] distinguish three main

[3]Ross [2006b, p. 24] seems to suggest, however, that choosing the solution concept is part of modelling because the choice of a refinement depends on the "underlying dynamics that equipped players with dispositions prior to commencement of a game". But Ross does not specify how the

components of game theory. The *theory proper* (on the left hand side of Figure 15) specifies the concept of a game, provides the mathematical elements that are needed for the construction of a game structure, and offers solution concepts for the thus constructed games. The *game structure* (left half of the central circle of Figure 15) is a description of a particular game that is constructed using elements of the theory proper. The *model narrative* (the right half of the central circle of Figure 15) provides an account of a real or a hypothetical economic situation. Its account of the situation interprets the game.

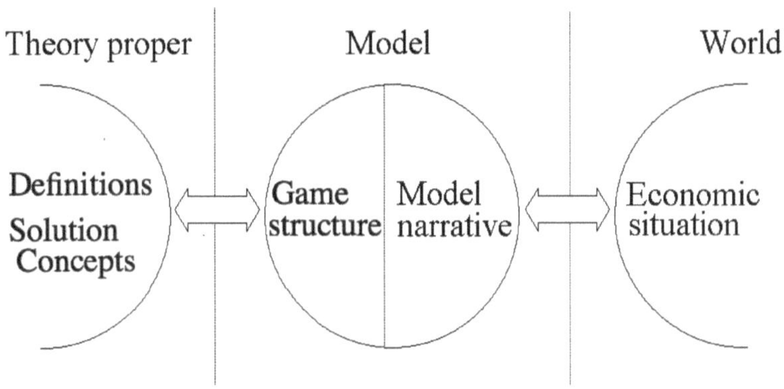


Figure 15. The architecture of game theory

A game model consists of a formal game structure and an informal model narrative. The game structure — formally characterised as a set-theoretic object — specifies the number of players, their strategies, information-sets and their payoffs.[4] The function of the theory proper is to constrain which set-theoretical structures can be considered as games, and to offer a *menu* of solution concepts for possible game structures. Game theorists often focus on the development of the formal apparatus of the theory proper. Their interest lies in proposing alternative equilibrium concepts or proving existing results with fewer assumptions, not in representing and solving particular interactive situations. "Game theory is for proving theorems, not for playing games" (Reinhard Selten, quoted in [Goeree and Holt, 2001, p. 1419]).

One reason for distinguishing between theory proper and the game structure (or between analysing and modelling) is to force the game theorist to include all possible motivating factors in the payoffs. If this is assumed, introducing new psychological variables during the analysis is ruled out. Binmore argues [1994, pp. 161-162], for example, that Sen's arguments on sympathy and commitment

choice is made in the end.

[4]The term 'game' is also used for this mathematical object, but since it is also often used to refer to the combination of the game structure *and* the accompanying narrative (think of 'Prisoner's dilemma' for example), we hope that clarity is served by distinguishing between game structures and game models.

should be written into the payoffs of a game, i.e. that they should be taken into account when it is being modelled. The point with the distinction is thus that critics of game theory should not criticise game-theoretical analyses by invoking issues that belong to modelling. This is surely a reasonable requirement. Indeed, Binmore's point is not new in the discussion. Game theorists and decision theorists have always subscribed to the idea that payoffs should be interpreted as *complete descriptions* of all possible factors that may motivate the players (see e.g., [Kohlberg and Mertens, 1986]). Furthermore, it has been recognised that if payoffs are interpreted as complete descriptions, the theory proper is empirically empty.

> In our view, game theory ... should be regarded as a purely formal theory lacking empirical content. Both theories merely state what will happen if all participants have consistent preferences and follow their own preferences in a consistent manner – whatever these preferences may be. Empirical content comes in only when we make specific assumptions about the nature of these preferences and about other factual matters [Harsanyi, 1966, pp. 413-4].

Yet not only the theory proper lacks empirical content, but the game structure does too. Although game theorists habitually employ labels like 'players', 'strategies' or 'payoffs', the game structures that the theory proper defines and helps solving are really only abstract mathematical objects. To acquire meaning, these abstract objects must be interpreted as representations of concrete situations. The interpretation is accomplished by an appropriate *model narrative* (cf. Morgan's [2005] discussion of *stories* in game theory). Such narratives are very visible in game theory — many models, like the chicken game or the prisoners' dilemma, are named after the story that comes with the model structure. The question is whether these narratives only support the use of models, or whether they are part of the model itself [Mäki, 2002, p. 14].

As regularly exemplified in textbooks, these narratives may be purely illustrative: they may describe purely fictional situations whose salient features merely help to exemplify how a particular model structure could be interpreted. Yet in other cases, narratives facilitate the relation of game structures to the real world. The narrative does this by first conceptualising a real world situation with game-theoretic notions. It identifies agents as players, possible plans as strategies, and results as payoffs. It also makes explicit the knowledge agents possess, and the cognitive abilities they have. Secondly, the narrative interprets the given game structure in terms of this re-conceptualised description of the real-world situation. Thus, model narratives fill model structures either with fictional or empirical content.

The model narrative also plays a third crucial role in game theory. As discussed in the previous sections, a specified game structure can be solved by different solution concepts. Sometimes, as in the case of minimax and Nash equilibrium for zero-sum games, the reasoning behind the solution concepts is different, but the result is the same. In other cases, however, applying different solution concepts to the same game structure yields different results. This was the case with payoff-dominance vs. risk dominance, as well as with backward and forward induction, which we discussed in section 2.3. Sometimes, information contained in the game structure alone is not sufficient for selecting between different solution concepts. Instead, the information needed is found in an appropriate account of the situation — i.e. in the model narrative. Thus, while it is true that stories (prisoner's dilemma, battle of the sexes, hawk-dove, etc.) are sometimes presented only for illustrative purposes, they take on a far more important function in these cases. They determine, together with constraints given by theory proper, the choice of the appropriate solution concept for a specific game [Grüne-Yanoff and Schweinzer, 2008]. Because model structures alone do not facilitate the choice of solution concepts, they are incomplete. Grüne-Yanoff and Schweinzer thus argue that model structure and model narrative together form the game model, and that model narratives are an essential part of game models.[5]

This conclusion raises the issue of model identity. It is quite common to hear economists identify a real-world situation with a particular game model; for example, to say that a situation $X$ 'is a Prisoners' Dilemma'. According to the above analysis, such a claim not only implies that any suitable description of $X$ can serve as an interpretation of the model structure. It also implies that this description of $X$ is appropriately similar to the model narrative of the prisoners' dilemma — for example, in terms of the knowledge of the agents, their cognitive abilities, and their absence of sympathy and altruism. Without this additional requirement of similarity of the informal background stories, identification of game model with concrete situations may lead to the unjustifiable application of certain solution concepts to that situation, and hence to incorrect results.

More generally, the observations about the architecture of game theory and the role of informal model narratives in it have two important implications. First, it becomes clear that game theory does not offer a universal notion of rationality, but rather offers a menu of tools to model specific situations at varying degrees and kinds of rationality. Ultimately, it is the modeller who judges, on the basis of her own intuitions, which kind of rationality to attribute to the interacting agents in a given situation. This opens up the discussion about the various intuitions that lie behind the solution concepts, the possibility of contravening intuitions, and the question whether a meta-theory can be constructed that unifies all these fragmentary intuitions. Some of these issues will be discussed in section 3.

The second implication of this observation concerns the status of game theory as a positive theory. Given its multi-layer architecture, any disagreement of prediction and observation can be attributed to a mistake either in the theory, the game form or the model narrative. This then raises the question how to test game theory, and whether game theory is refutable in principle. These questions will be discussed in section 4.

[5]This third function of model narratives in game theory distinguishes it from earlier accounts of stories in economic models more generally (cf. [Morgan, 2001]).

## 3 GAME THEORY AS A NORMATIVE THEORY OF RATIONALITY

Game theory has often been interpreted as a part of a general theory of rational behaviour. This interpretation was already in the minds of the founders of game theory, who wrote:

> We wish to find the mathematically complete principles which define "rational behavior" for the participants in a social economy, and to derive from them the general characteristics of that behavior. [von Neumann and Morgenstern, 1944, p. 31]

To interpret game theory as a theory of rationality means to give it a prescriptive task: it recommends what agents *should* do in specific interactive situations, given their preferences. To evaluate the success of this rational interpretation of game theory is to investigate its justification, in particular the justification of the solution concepts it proposes. That human agents ought to behave in such and such a way does not of course mean that they will do so; hence there is little sense in testing rationality claims empirically. The rational interpretation of game theory therefore needs to be distinguished from the interpretation of game theory as a predictive and explanatory theory. The solution concepts are either justified by identifying sufficient conditions for them, and showing that these conditions are already accepted as justified, or directly, by compelling intuitive arguments.

### *3.1 Is Game Theory a Generalisation of Decision Theory?*

Many game theorists have striven to develop a unifying framework for analysing games and single-person decision situations. Decision theory might provide foundations for game theory in several ways. (i) One can argue that payoffs are determined as revealed preferences in single-person decision problems (e.g., [Binmore, 2007, pp. 13-14]), or relatedly, that the payoffs are NMUFs. (ii) Another argument is to say that game-theoretical solution concepts can be reduced to the more widely accepted notion of rationality under uncertainty (e.g., [Aumann, 1987]). If such reduction is to be successful, one should be able to derive solution concepts from more primitive assumptions concerning individual rationality as in decision theory. In this section we will try to see whether this unificatory endeavour has been successful.[6]

We will point out several important differences: First, the interpretation of beliefs in decision theory is objective (vNM) or subjective (Savage), but game theoretical solution concepts imply restrictions on the players' beliefs, which in turn implies a 'logical' or 'necessitarian' interpretation (Section 3.1.1): the game determines what the relevant probabilities of rational agents ought to be. Second, the epistemic conditions for solution concepts are more stringent than those that

[6] See Mariotti [1995; 1996; 1997] for an argument that axioms of decision theory may conflict with game theoretical solution concepts. Hammond [1996; 1998; 2004] presents a thorough discussion of the role of individual utility in game theory. See also [Battigalli, 1996].

derive from the decision-theoretic axioms (Section 3.1.2). The revealed preference arguments are discussed later in Section 4.4.

### *3.1.1 Common Priors and Bayesianism*

To motivate the discussion, one may start by asking why the players do not simply maximise expected utility just as they do in single-person contexts [Kadane and Larkey, 1982; 1983]. A quick answer is that since the relevant probabilities often concern the other players' choices, those probabilities must be endogenously determined. In other words, one must analyse the whole game with a solution concept in order to determine the probabilities. This makes the interpretation of the beliefs a necessitarian one: arguments appealing to the players' rationality are used to determine constraints for the beliefs.

Bayesianism in game theory (e.g., [Aumann, 1987; Tan and Werlang, 1988]) can be characterised as the view that it is always possible to define probabilities for anything that is relevant for the players' decision-making. In addition, it is usually taken to imply that the players use Bayes' rule for updating their beliefs. If the probabilities are to be always definable, one also has to specify what players' beliefs are before the play is supposed to begin. The standard assumption is that such prior beliefs are the same for all players (see [Morris, 1995]). This *common prior assumption* (CPA) means that the players have the same prior probabilities for all those aspects of the game for which the description of the game itself does not specify different probabilities. Common priors are usually justified with the so called *Harsanyi doctrine* [Harsanyi, 1967-8], according to which all differences in probabilities are to be attributed solely to differences in the experiences that the players have had. Different priors for different players would imply that there are some factors that affect the players' beliefs even though they have not been explicitly modelled. The CPA is sometimes considered to be equivalent to the Harsanyi doctrine, but there seems to be a difference between them: the Harsanyi doctrine is best viewed as a metaphysical doctrine about the determination of beliefs, and it is hard to see why anybody would be willing to argue against it: if everything that might affect the determination of beliefs is included in the notion of 'experience', then it alone does determine the beliefs. The Harsanyi doctrine has some affinity to some convergence theorems in Bayesian statistics: if individuals are fed with similar information indefinitely, their probabilities will ultimately be the same, irrespective of the original priors.

The CPA however is a methodological injunction to include everything that may affect the players' behaviour in the game: not just everything that motivates the players, but also everything that affects the players' beliefs should be explicitly modelled by the game: if players had different priors, this would mean that the game structure would not be completely specified because there would be differences in players' behaviour that are not explained by the model. In a dispute over the status of the CPA, Faruk Gul [1998] essentially argues that the CPA does not follow from the Harsanyi doctrine. He does this by distinguishing between two different interpretations of the common prior, the 'prior view' and the 'infinite hierarchy view'. The former is a genuinely dynamic story in which it is assumed that there really is a prior stage in time. The latter framework refers to Mertens and Zamir's [1985] construction in which prior beliefs can be consistently formulated. This framework however, is static in the sense that the players do not have any information on a prior stage, indeed, the 'priors' in this framework do not even pin down a player's priors for his own types. Thus, the existence of a common prior in the latter framework does not have anything to do with the view that differences in beliefs reflect differences in information only.

It is agreed by everyone (including [Aumann, 1998]) that for most (real-world) problems there is no prior stage in which the players know each other's beliefs, let alone that they would be the same. The CPA, if understood as a modelling assumption, is clearly false. Robert Aumann [1998], however, defends the CPA by arguing that whenever there are differences in beliefs, there must have been a prior stage in which the priors were the same, and from which the current beliefs can be derived by conditioning on the differentiating events. If players differ in their present beliefs, they must have received different information at some previous point in time, and they must have processed this information correctly [1999b]; see also [Aumann, 1999a; Heifetz, 1999]. Based on this assumption, he further argues that players cannot 'agree to disagree': if a player knows that his opponents' beliefs are different from his own, he should revise his beliefs to take the opponents' information into account. The only case where the CPA would be violated, then, is when players have different beliefs, and have common knowledge about each others' different beliefs and about each others' epistemic rationality. Aumann's argument seems perfectly legitimate if it is taken as a metaphysical one, but we do not see how it could be used as a justification for using the CPA as a modelling assumption in this or that application of game theory (and Aumann does not argue that it should).

### *3.1.2 Sufficient Epistemic Conditions for Solution Concepts*

Recall that the various solution concepts presented in section 2 provide advice on how to choose an action rationally when the outcome of one's choice depends on the actions of the other players, who in turn base their choices on the expectation of how one will choose. The solution concepts thus not only require the players to choose according to *maximisation considerations*; they also require that agents maximise their expected utilities on the basis of certain beliefs. Most prominently, these beliefs include their expectations about what the other players expect of them, and their expectations about what the other players will choose on the basis of these expectations. Such epistemic conditions are not always made explicit when game theory is being discussed. However, without fulfilling them, players cannot be expected to choose in accord with specific solution concepts. To make these conditions on the agent's knowledge and beliefs explicit will thus further our understanding on what is involved in the solution concepts. In addition, if these epistemic conditions turn out to be justifiable, one would have achieved progress in justifying the solution concepts themselves. This line of thought has in fact been so prominent that the interpretation of game theory as a theory of rationality has often been called the *eductive* or the *epistemic* interpretation [Binmore, 1987]. In the following, the various solution concepts are discussed with respect to their sufficient epistemic conditions, and the conditions are investigated with regard to their acceptability.

For the solution of eliminating dominated strategies, nothing is required beyond the rationality of the players and their knowledge of their own strategies and payoffs. Each player can rule out her dominated strategies on the basis of maximization considerations alone, without knowing anything about the other player. To the extent that maximization considerations are accepted, this solution concept is therefore justified.

The case is more complex for *iterated elimination* of dominated strategies (this solution concept was not explained before, so don't be confused. It fits in most naturally here). In the game matrix of Figure 16, only Row has a dominated strategy, $R1$. Eliminating $R1$ will not yield a unique solution. Iterated elimination allows players to consecutively eliminate dominated strategies. However, it requires stronger epistemic conditions.

| | $C1$ | $C2$ | $C3$ |
|---|---|---|---|
| $R1$ | 3,2 | 1,3 | 1,1 |
| $R2$ | 5,4 | 2,1 | 4,2 |
| $R3$ | 4,3 | 3,2 | 2,4 |

Figure 16. A game allowing for iterated elimination of dominated strategies

If Col knows that Row will not play $R1$, she can eliminate $C2$ as a dominated strategy, given that $R1$ was eliminated. But to know that, Col has to know:

i. Row's strategies and payoffs

ii. That Row knows her strategies and payoffs

iii. That Row is rational

Let's assume that Col knows i.-iii., and that he thus expects Row to have spotted and eliminated $R1$ as a dominated strategy. Given that Row knows that Col did this, Row can now eliminate $R3$. But for her to know that Col eliminated $C2$, she has to know:

i. Row's (i.e. her own) strategies and payoffs

ii. That she, Row, is rational

iii. That Col knows i.-ii.

iv. Col's strategies and payoffs

v. That Col knows her strategies and payoffs

vi. That Col is rational

Let us look at the above epistemic conditions a bit more closely. i. is trivial, as she has to know her own strategies and payoffs even for simple elimination. For simple elimination, she also has to be rational, but she does not have to know it — hence ii. If Row knows i. and ii., she knows that she would eliminate $R1$. Similarly, if Col knows i. and ii., he knows that Row would eliminate $R1$. If Row knows that Col knows that she would eliminate $R1$, and if Row also knows iv.-vi., then she knows that Col would eliminate $C2$. In a similar fashion, if Col knows that Row knows i.-vi., she will know that Row would eliminate $R3$. Knowing this, he would eliminate $C3$, leaving $(R2, C1)$ as the unique solution of the game.

Generally, iterated elimination of dominated strategy requires that each player knows the structure of the game, the rationality of the players and, most importantly, that she knows that the opponent knows that she knows this. The depth of one player knowing that the other knows, etc. must be at least as high as the number of iterated eliminations necessary to arrive at a unique solution. Beyond that, no further "he knows that she knows that he knows..." is required. Depending on how long the chain of iterated eliminations becomes, the knowledge assumptions may become difficult to justify. In long chains, even small uncertainties in the players' knowledge may thus put the justification of this solution concept in doubt.

From the discussion so far, two epistemic notions can be distinguished. If all players know a proposition $p$, one says that they have *mutual knowledge* of $p$. As the discussion of iterated elimination showed, mutual knowledge is too weak for some solution concepts. For example, condition iii insists that Row not only know her own strategies, but also knows that Col knows. In the limit, this chain of one player knowing that the other knows that $p$, that she knows that he knows that she knows that $p$,etc. is continued *ad infinitum*. In this case, one says that players have *common knowledge* of the proposition $p$. When discussing common knowledge, it is important to distinguish *of what* the players have common knowledge. It is standard to assume that there is common knowledge of the structure of the game and the rationality of the players.

Analysing the epistemic conditions of other solution concepts requires more space and technical apparatus than available here. Instead of discussing the derivation, we list the results for the central solution concepts in Figure 17. As shown there, for the players to adhere to solutions provided by rationalizability, common knowledge is sufficient. Sufficient epistemic conditions for pure-strategy Nash equilibria are even stronger. Common knowledge of the game structure or rationality is neither necessary nor sufficient for the justification of Nash equilibria, not even in conjunction with epistemic rationality. Instead, it is required that all players know what the others will choose (in the pure-strategy case) or what the others

| Solution Concept | Structure of the game | Rationality | Choices or beliefs |
|---|---|---|---|
| **Simple elimination of dominated strategies** | Each player knows her payoffs | Fact of rationality | — |
| **Iterated elimination of dominated strategies** | Knowledge to the degree of iteration | Knowledge to the degree of iteration | — |
| **Rationalizability** | Common Knowledge | Common Knowledge | — |
| **Pure-strategy Nash equilibrium** | — | Fact of rationality | Mutual knowledge of choices |
| **Mixed-strategy equilibrium in two-person games** | Mutual knowledge | Mutual knowledge | Mutual knowledge of beliefs |

Figure 17. (adapted from [Brandenburger, 1992]): Epistemic requirements for solution concepts

will conjecture all players will be choosing (in the mixed-strategy case). This is rather counter-intuitive, and it shows the limitations of the epistemic interpretation of solution concepts. Alternative interpretations of the Nash equilibrium are discussed in the next section. For further discussion of epistemic conditions of solution concepts, see [Bicchieri, 1993, Chapter 2].

## *3.2 Justifying the Nash Equilibrium*

The Nash equilibrium concept is often seen as "the embodiment of the idea that economic agents are rational; that they simultaneously act to maximize their utility" [Aumann, 1985, p. 43]. Yet the previous analysis of the Nash equilibrium's sufficient epistemic conditions showed how strong these conditions are, and that they are too strong to derive the Nash equilibrium from decision theoretic principles. Claiming the Nash equilibrium to be an embodiment of rationality therefore needs further justification. We discuss three kinds of justifications in different contexts: in one-shot games, in repeated games, and in the evolutionary context of a population.

### *3.2.1 Nash Equilibria in One-Shot Games*

It seems reasonable to claim that once the players have arrived at an equilibrium pair, neither has any reason for changing his strategy choice unless the other player does too. But what reason is there to expect that they will arrive at one? Why should Row choose a best reply to the strategy chosen by Col, when Row does not know Col's choice at the time she is choosing? In these questions, the notion of equilibrium becomes somewhat dubious: when scientists say that a physical system is in equilibrium, they mean that it is in a stable state, where all causal forces internal to the system balance each other out and so leave it "at rest" unless it is disturbed by some external force. That understanding cannot be applied to the Nash equilibrium, when the equilibrium state is to be reached by rational computation alone. In a non-metaphorical sense, rational computation simply does not involve causal forces that could balance each other out. When approached from the rational interpretation of game theory, the Nash equilibrium therefore requires a different understanding and justification. In this section, two interpretations and justifications of the Nash equilibrium are discussed.

Often, the Nash equilibrium is interpreted as a *self-enforcing agreement.* This interpretation is based on situations in which agents can talk to each other, and form agreements as to how to play the game, prior to the beginning of the game, but where no enforcement mechanism providing independent incentives for compliance with agreements exists. Agreements are self-enforcing if each player has reasons to respect them in the absence of external enforcement.

It has been argued that being a self-enforcing agreement is neither necessary nor sufficient for a strategy to be in Nash equilibrium. That it is not necessary is obvious in games with many Nash equilibria: not all of the equilibria could have been self-enforcing agreements at the same time. It also has been argued that Nash equilibria are not sufficient. Risse [2000] argues that the notion of self-enforcing agreements should be understood as an agreement that provides *some* incentives for the agents to stick to it, even without external enforcement. He then goes on to argue that there are such self-enforcing agreements that are not Nash equilibria. Take for example the game in Figure 18.

| | $C1$ | $C2$ |
|---|---|---|
| $R1$ | 0,0 | 4,2 |
| $R2$ | 2,4 | 3,3 |

Figure 18.

Let us imagine the players initially agreed to play $(R2, C2)$. Now both have serious reasons to deviate, as deviating unilaterally would profit either player. Therefore, the Nash equilibria of this game are $(R1, C2)$ and $(R2, C1)$. However, in an additional step of reflection, both players may note that they risk ending up with nothing if they *both* deviate, particularly as the rational recommendation for each is to *unilaterally* deviate. Players may therefore prefer the relative security of sticking to the strategy they agreed upon. They can at least guarantee 2 utils for themselves, whatever the other player does, and this in combination with the fact that they agreed on $(R2, C2)$ may reassure them that their opponent will in fact play strategy 2. So $(R2, C2)$ may well be a self-enforcing agreement, but it nevertheless is not a Nash equilibrium.

Last, the argument from self-enforcing agreements does not account for mixed strategies. In mixed equilibria all strategies with positive probabilities are best replies to the opponent's strategy. So once a player's random mechanism has assigned an action to her, she might as well do something else. Even though the mixed strategies might have constituted a self-enforcing agreement *before* the mechanism made its assignment, it is hard to see what argument a player should have to stick to her agreement after the assignment is made [Luce and Raiffa, 1957, p. 75].

Another argument for one-shot Nash equilibria commences from the idea that agents are sufficiently similar to take their own deliberations as simulations of their opponents' deliberations.

> The most sweeping (and perhaps, historically, the most frequently invoked) case for Nash equilibrium... asserts that a player's strategy must be a best response to those selected by other players, because he can deduce what those strategies are. Player $i$ can figure out $j$'s strategic choice by merely imagining himself in $j$'s position. [Pearce, 1984, p. 1030]

Jacobsen [1996] formalizes this idea with the help of three assumptions. First, he assumes that a player in a two-person game imagines himself in both positions of the game, choosing strategies and forming conjectures about the other player's choices. Second, he assumes that the player behaves rationally in both positions. Thirdly, he assumes that a player conceives of his opponent as similar to himself; i.e. if he chooses a strategy for the opponent while simulating her deliberation, he would also choose that position if he was in her position. Jacobsen shows that on the basis of these assumptions, the player will choose his strategies so that they and his conjecture on the opponent's play constitute a Nash equilibrium. If his opponent also holds such a Nash equilibrium conjecture (which she should, given the similarity assumption), the game has a unique Nash equilibrium.

This argument has met at least two criticisms. First, Jacobsen provides an argument for Nash equilibrium conjectures, not for Nash equilibria. If each player ends up with a multiplicity of Nash equilibrium conjectures, an additional coordination problem arises over and above the coordination of which Nash equilibrium to play: now first the conjectures have to be matched *before* the equilibria can be coordinated.

Secondly, when simulating his opponent, a player has to form conjectures about his own play from the opponent's perspective. This requires that he predict his own behaviour. However, Levi [1998] raises the objection that to deliberate excludes the possibility of predicting one's own behaviour. Otherwise deliberation would be vacuous, since the outcome is determined when the relevant parameters of the choice situation are available. Since game theory models players as deliberating between which strategies to choose, they cannot, if Levi's argument is correct, also assume that players, when simulating others' deliberation, predict their own choices.

Concluding this sub-section, it seems that there is no general justification for Nash equilibria in one-shot, simultaneous-move games. This does not mean that there is no justification to apply the Nash concept to any one-shot, simultaneous-move game — for example, games solvable by iterated dominance have a Nash equilibrium as their solution. Also, this conclusion does not mean that there are no exogenous reasons that could justify the Nash concept in these games. However, the discussion here was concerned with endogenous reasons — i.e. reasons derived from the information contained in the game structure alone. And there the justification seems deficient.

### *3.2.2 Learning to Play Nash Equilibrium*

People may be unable to play Nash equilibrium in some one-shot games, yet they may *learn* to play the equilibrium strategy if they play the same game repeatedly.[7] Playing the same game repeatedly may have different learning effects, depending on the cognitive abilities of the players and the variability of the matches. *Myopic* learners observe the results of past stage games and adjust their strategy choices accordingly. They are myopic because (i) they ignore the fact that their opponents also engage in dynamic learning, and (ii) they do not care about how their deviations from equilibrium strategies may affect opponents' future play. *Sophisticated* learners take this additional information into account when choosing a strategy. Yet most game theory abstracts from the effects of type (ii) information by focussing on games in which the incentive to influence opponents' future play is small enough to be negligible.

An important example of modelling sophisticated learners is found in Kalai and Lehrer [1993]. In an $n$ player game (with a finite strategy set), each player knows her payoffs for every strategy taken by the group of players. Before making her choice of a period's strategy, the player is informed of all the previous actions taken. The player's goal is to maximise the present value of her total expected payoff.

Players are assumed to be subjectively rational: each player commences with subjective beliefs about the individual strategies used by each of her opponents. She then uses these beliefs to compute her own optimal strategy. Knowledge assumptions are remarkably weak for this result: players only need to know their own payoff matrix and discount parameters. They need not know anything about opponents' payoffs and rationality; furthermore, they need not know other players' strategies, or conjectures about strategies. Knowledge assumptions are thus weaker for learning Nash equilibria in this kind of infinite repetition than those required for Nash solutions or rationalizability in one-shot games.

[7]People may also be able to learn the equilibrium strategy in a game G from playing a game similar but not identical to G. Because similarity between games is not sufficiently conceptualised, the literature has largely eschewed this issue and focussed almost exclusively on the case of identity (for exceptions, see [LiCalzi, 1995; Rankin *et al.*, 2000]).

Players learn by updating their subjective beliefs about others' play with information about previously chosen strategy profiles. After each round, all players observe each other's choices and adjust their beliefs about the strategies of their opponents. Beliefs are adjusted by *Bayesian updating*: the prior belief is conditioned on the newly available information. Kalai and Lehrer portray Bayesian updating as a direct consequence of expected utility maximisation [Kalai and Lehrer, 1993, p. 1021]. Importantly, they do not assume common priors, but only that players' subjective beliefs do not assign zero probability to events that can occur in the play of the game. On the basis of these assumptions, Kalai and Lehrer show that (i) after repeatedly playing a game, the real probability distribution over the future play of the game is arbitrarily close to what each player believes the distribution to be, and (ii) the actual choices and beliefs of the players, when converged, are arbitrarily close to a Nash equilibrium. Nash equilibria in these situations are thus justified as potentially self-reproducing patterns of strategic expectations.

Kalai and Lehrer model sophisticated learners. Unlike myopic learners, who assume that their opponents' strategies are fixed, these sophisticated learners attempt the strategies of the infinitely repeated game. These strategies, which remain fixed, contain the reaction rules that govern all players' choices. Thus Kalai and Lehrer's model deals with the problem that players' opponents also engage in dynamic learning.

However, as Fudenberg and Levine [1998, p. 238] point out, Kalai and Lehrer's model assumes that the players' prior beliefs are such that there is a plausible model that is observationally equivalent to opponents' actual strategies — in the sense that the probability distribution over histories is the same (the so-called absolute continuity assumption). For players to 'find' these beliefs in principle requires the same kind of fixed point solution that finding a Nash equilibrium does. Thus the problem of justifying the Nash equilibrium has not been solved, but only transferred to the problem of finding appropriate beliefs.

### *3.2.3 Nash Equilibrium in a Population*

The epistemic and cognitive assumptions underlying the Nash equilibrium under the standard, individualist interpretation have led some to look for an alternative interpretation based on ideas from biology:

> Maynard Smith's book *Evolution and the Theory of Games* directed game theorists' attention away from their increasingly elaborate definitions of rationality. After all, insects can hardly be said to think at all, and so rationality cannot be so crucial if game theory somehow manages to predict their behavior under appropriate conditions. (Binmore, foreword in [Weibull, 1995, x])

Thus, the *evolutive* approach proposed that the driving force behind the arrival and maintenance of equilibrium states was a non-cognitive mechanism — a mechanism that operated in a population of interacting individuals, rather than a cognitive effort of the individual (Binmore 1987). If it is valid to model people as maximisers, this can only be because "evolutionary forces, biological, social and economic, [are] responsible for getting things maximised" [Binmore, 1994, p. 11].

This leads to an evolutionary perspective on the Nash equilibrium. Evolutionary game theory studies games that are played over and over again by players drawn from a population. These players do not have a choice between strategies, but rather are "programmed" to play only one strategy. It is thus often said that the strategies themselves are the players. Success of a strategy is defined in terms of the number of replications that a strategy will leave of itself to play in games of future generations. Rather than seeing equilibrium as the consequence of strategic reasoning by rational players, evolutionary game theory sees equilibrium as the outcome either of resistance to mutation invasions, or as the result of a dynamic process of natural selection. Its interpretation of the equilibrium concept is thus closely related to the natural scientific concept of the stable state, where different causal factors balance each other out, than that under the eductive interpretation.

Evolutionary game theory offers two ways to model this evolutionary mechanism: a static and a dynamic one. The former specifies strategies that are *evolutionary stable* against a mutant invasion. Imagine a population of players programmed to play one (mixed or pure) strategy $A$. Imagine further that a small fraction of players "mutate" — they now play a strategy $B$ different from $A$. Let the proportion of mutants in the population be $p$. Now pairs of players are repeatedly drawn to play the game, each player with equal probability. Thus, for any player that has been drawn, the probability that the opponent will play $B$ is $p$, and the probability that the opponent will play $A$ is $1\text{-}p$. A strategy $A$ is evolutionary stable if it does better when playing against some player of the invaded population than the mutant strategy itself. More generally, a strategy is an *evolutionary stable strategy* (ESS) if for every possible mutant strategy $B$ different from $A$, the payoff of playing $A$ against the mixed strategy $\sigma(1\text{-}p,p)$ is higher than the payoff of playing $B$ against $\sigma(1\text{-}p,p)$.

With these assumptions, the players' cognitive abilities are reduced to zero: they simply act according to the strategy that they are programmed to play, persevere if this strategy is stable against mutants, or perish. It has been shown that every ESS is a strategy that is in Nash equilibrium with itself [van Damme, 1991, p. 224]. However, not every strategy that is Nash equilibrium with itself is an ESS.

The dynamic approach of evolutionary game theory considers a selection mechanism that favours some strategies over others in a continuously evolving population. Imagine a population whose members are programmed to play different strategies. Pairs of players are drawn at random to play against each other. Their payoff consists in an increase or decrease in fitness, measured as the number of offspring per time unit. Each 'child' inherits the parent's strategy. Reproduction takes place continuously over time, with the birth rate depending on fitness, and the death rate being uniform for all players. Long continuations of tournaments between players then may lead to *stable states* in the population, depending on the initial population distribution. This notion of dynamic stability is wider than that of evolutionary stability: while all evolutionary stable strategies are also dynamically stable, not all dynamically stable strategies are evolutionary stable.

In the standard literature, these results have often been interpreted as a justification of the Nash equilibrium concept (e.g., [Mailath, 1998]). This was foreshadowed by Nash himself, who proposed a 'mass action interpretation' in his Ph.D. thesis [Leonard, 1994]. Yet there are at least two criticisms that can be put forward against such an interpretation. First, one can question why the Nash equilibrium, which is based on rational deliberation, should match with the evolutionary concepts, even though completely different causal mechanisms operate in the rational choice and the evolutionary scenarios. Against this criticism, game theorists have offered an 'as if defence': Although there is a more fundamental story 'behind' human behaviour, they claim, it is perfectly justifiable to treat this behaviour 'as if' it was indeed driven by cognitive maximisation efforts.

> Even if strategically interacting agents do not meet these epistemic conditions, their long-run aggregate behavior will nevertheless conform with them because of the workings of biological or social selection processes. [Weibull, 1994, p. 868]

Just as Friedman [1953] had used an evolutionary argument to defend the profit maximisation assumption, evolutionary ideas are used in game theory to prop up the classical theory - with the fine difference that formal identity proofs for results from evolutionary and classical game theory now seem to offer a much more precise foundation (cf. [Vromen, 2009]).

The second criticism of this interpretation concerns the functions of the Nash equilibrium that are thus justified. Sometimes, the claim is that the evolutionarily justified Nash equilibrium has a predictive function: it shows that people do play Nash equilibrium. This claim is somewhat dubious, however, because it is ultimately an empirical claim that cannot be established by investigating highly stylised models. It seems common practice to accept the evolutionary interpretation as a justification of the *normative* functions of the Nash equilibrium (see [Sugden, 2001] for anecdotal evidence of this claim). In the evolutionary models, players are not assumed to have preferences that they want to maximise, and for whose efficient maximisation game theory could prescribe the most efficient course of action. When it is claimed that evolutionary stability lends legitimacy to the Nash equilibrium concept, and when this concept is then used in order to prescribe efficient behaviour, the danger of committing Hume's naturalistic fallacy is obvious — an 'ought' is derived from an 'is'.

## *3.3 Backward Induction*

Backward induction is the most common Nash equilibrium refinement for non-simultaneous games. Backward induction depends on the assumption that rational players remain on the equilibrium path because of what they anticipate would happen if they were to deviate. Backward induction thus requires the players to consider out-of-equilibrium play. But out-of-equilibrium play occurs with zero probability if the players are rational. To treat out-of-equilibrium play properly, therefore, the theory needs to be expanded. Some have argued that this is best achieved by a theory of counterfactuals [Binmore, 1987; Stalnaker, 1999] which gives meaning to sentences of the sort "if a rational player found herself at a node out of equilibrium, she would choose ...". Alternatively, for models where uncertainty about payoffs is allowed, it has been suggested that such unexpected situations may be attributed to the payoffs' differing from those that were originally thought to be most likely [Fudenberg *et al.*, 1988].

The problem of counterfactuals cuts deeper, however, than a call for mere theory expansion. Consider the two-player non-simultaneous perfect information game in Figure 19, called the "centipede". For representational convenience, the game is depicted as progressing from left to right (instead of from top to bottom as is usual in extensive-form games). Player 1 starts at the leftmost node, choosing to end the game by playing *down*, or to continue the game (giving player 2 the choice) by playing *right*. The payoffs are such that at each node it is best for the player who has to move to stop the game if and only if she expects that the game will end at the next stage if she continues (by the other player stopping the game or by termination of the game). The two zigzags stand for the continuation of the payoffs along those lines. Now backward induction advises to solve the game by starting at the last node $z$, asking what player 2 would have done if he ended up here. A comparison of player 2's payoffs for his two choices implies that he would have chosen *down*, given that he is rational. Given common knowledge of rationality, the payoffs that result from player 2 choosing *down* can be substituted for node $z$. One now moves backwards to player 1's decision node. What would she have done had she ended up at node $y$? She would have chosen *down*. This line of argument then continues all the way back to the first node. Backward induction thus recommends player 1 to play *down* at the first node.

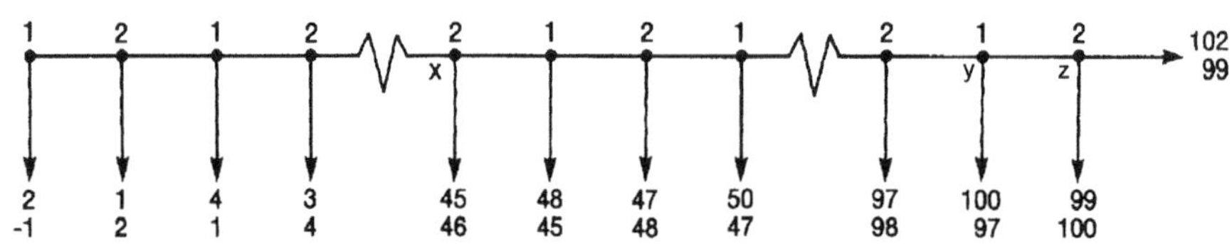


Figure 19.

So what should player 2 do if he actually found himself at node $x$? Backward induction tells him to play "down', but backward induction also tells him that if player 1 was rational, he should not be facing the actual choice at node $x$ in the first place. So either player 1 is rational, but made a mistake ('trembled' in Selten's terminology) at each node preceding $x$, or player 1 is not rational [Binmore, 1987]. But if player 1 is not rational, then player 2 may hope that she will not choose *down* at her next choice either, thus allowing for a later terminal node to be reached. This consideration becomes problematic for backward induction if it also affects the counterfactual reasoning. It may be the case that the truth of the indicative conditional "If player 2 finds himself at $x$, then player 2 is not rational" influences the truth of the counterfactual "If player 2 were to find himself at $x$, then player 2 would not be rational".

Remember that for backward induction to work, the players have to consider counterfactuals like this: "If player 2 found himself at $x$, and he was rational, he would choose *down*". Now the truth of the first counterfactual makes false the antecedent condition of the second: it can never be true that player 2 found himself at $x$ and be rational. Thus it seems that by engaging in these sorts of counterfactual considerations, the backward induction conclusion becomes conceptually impossible.

This is an intensely discussed problem in game theory and philosophy. Here only two possible solutions can be sketched. The first answer insists that common knowledge of rationality implies backward induction in games of perfect information [Aumann, 1995]. This position is correct in that it denies the connection between the indicative and the counterfactual conditional. Players have common knowledge of rationality, and they are not going to lose it regardless of the counterfactual considerations they engage in. Only if common knowledge was not immune against evidence, but would be revised in the light of the opponents' moves, then this sufficient condition for backward induction may run into the *conceptual problem* sketched above. But common knowledge by definition is not revisable, so the argument instead has to assume *common belief* of rationality. If one looks more closely at the versions of the above argument (e.g., [Pettit and Sugden, 1989]), it becomes clear that they employ the notion of common belief, and not of common knowledge.

Another solution of the above problem obtains when one shows, as Bicchieri [1993, Chapter 4] does, that limited knowledge of rationality and of the structure of the game suffice for backward induction. All that is needed is that a player, at each of her information sets, knows what the next player to move knows. This condition does not get entangled in internal inconsistency, and backward induction is justifiable without conceptual problems. Further, and in agreement with the above argument, she also shows that in a large majority of cases, this limited knowledge of rationality condition is also *necessary* for backward induction. If her argument is correct, those arguments that support the backward induction concept on the basis of common knowledge of rationality start with a flawed hypothesis, and need to be reconsidered.

## *3.4 Bounded Rationality in Game Players*

Bounded rationality is a vast field with very tentative delineations. The fundamental idea is that the rationality which mainstream cognitive models propose is in some way inappropriate. Depending on whether rationality is judged inappropriate for the task of rational advice or for predictive purposes, two approaches can be distinguished. Bounded rationality which retains a normative aspect appeals to some version of the "ought implies can" principle: people cannot be required to satisfy certain conditions if *in principle* they are not capable to do so. For game theory, questions of this kind concern computational capacity and the complexity-optimality trade-off. Bounded rationality with predictive purposes, on the other hand, provides models that purport to be better descriptions of how people actually reason, including ways of reasoning that are clearly suboptimal and mistaken. The discussion here will be restricted to normative bounded rationality.

The outmost bound of rationality is computational impossibility. Binmore [1987; 1993] discusses this topic by casting both players in a two-player game as Turing machines. A Turing machine is a theoretical model that allows for specifying the notion of computability. Very roughly, if a Turing machine receives an input, performs a finite number of computational steps (which may be very large), and gives an output, then the problem is computable. If a Turing machine is caught in an infinite regress while computing a problem, however, then the problem is not computable. The question Binmore discusses is whether Turing machines can play and solve games. The scenario is that the input received by one machine is the description of another machine (and vice versa), and the output of both machines determines the players' actions. Binmore shows that a Turing machine cannot predict its opponent's behaviour perfectly *and* simultaneously participate in the action of the game. Roughly put, when machine 1 first calculates the output of machine 2 and then takes the best response to its action, and machine 2 simultaneously calculates the output of machine 1 and then takes the best response to its action, the calculations of both machines enter an infinite regress. Perfect rationality, understood as the solution to the outguessing attempt in "I thank that you think that I think..." is not computable in this sense.

Computational impossibility, however, is very far removed from the realities of rational deliberation. Take for example the way people play chess. Zermelo [1913] showed long ago that chess has a solution. Despite this result, chess players cannot calculate the solution of the game and choose their strategies accordingly. Instead, it seems that they typically "check out" several likely scenarios and that they employ some method for evaluating the endpoint of each scenario (e.g., by counting the chess pieces). People differ in the depth of their inquiry, the quality of the "typical scenarios" they select, and the way in which they evaluate their endpoint positions.

The justification for such "piecemeal" deliberation is that computing the solution of a game can be very costly. Deliberation costs reduce the value of an outcome; it may therefore be rational to trade the potential gains from a full-blown solution with the moderate gains from "fast and frugal" deliberation procedures that are less costly (the term "fast and frugal" heuristics was coined by the ABC research group [Gigerenzer, Todd and ABC Research Group, 1999]. Rubinstein [1998] formalizes this idea by extending the analysis of a repeated game to include players' sensitivity to the *complexity* of their strategies. He restricts the set of strategies to those that can be executed by finite machines. He then defines the complexity of a strategy as the number of states of the machine that implements it. Each player's preferences over strategy profiles increase with her payoff in the repeated game, and decrease with the complexity of her strategy's complexity (He considers different ranking methods, in particular unanimity and lexicographic preferences). Rubinstein shows that the set of equilibria for complexity-sensitive games is much smaller than that of the regular repeated game.

## 4 GAME THEORY AS A PREDICTIVE THEORY

Game theory can be a good theory of human behaviour for two distinct reasons. First, it may be the case that game theory is a good theory of rationality, that agents are rational and that therefore game theory predicts their behaviour well. If game theory was correct for this reason, it could reap the additional benefit of great stability. Many social theories are inherently unstable, because agents adjust their behaviour in the light of its predictions. If game theory were a good predictive theory because it was a good theory of rationality, this would be because each player expected every other player to follow the theory's prescriptions and had no incentive to deviate from the recommended course of action. Thus, game theory would already take into account that players' knowledge of the theory has a causal effect on the actions it predicts [Bicchieri, 1993, chapter 4.4]. Such a *self-fulfilling theory* would be more stable than a theory that predicts irrational behaviour.[8] Players who know that their opponents will behave irrationally (because a theory tells them) can improve their results by deviating from what the theory predicts, while players who know that their opponents will behave rationally cannot. However, one should not pay too high a premium for the prospect that game theoretical prescriptions and predictions will coincide; evidence from laboratory experiments as well as from casual observations often cast a shadow of doubt on it.

Second, and independently of the question of whether game theory is a good theory of rationality, game theory may be a good theory because it offers the relevant tools to unify one's thought about interactive behaviour [Gintis, 2004; 2007]. This distinction may make sense when separating our intuitions about how agents behave rationally from a systematic account of our observations of how agents behave. Aumann for example suggests that

> [P]hilosophical analysis of the definition [of Nash equilibrium] itself leads to difficulties, and it has its share of counterintuitive examples. On the other hand, it is conceptually simple and attractive, and mathematically easy to work with. As a result, it has led to many important insights in the applications, and has illuminated and established relations between many different aspects of interactive decision situations. It is these applications and insights that lend it validity. [Aumann, 1985, p. 49]

[8]This was Luce and Raiffa's [1957] justification of the Nash Equilibrium.

These considerations may lead one to the view that the principles of game theory provide an approximate model of human deliberation that *sometimes* provides insights into real phenomena (this seems to be Aumann's position). Philosophy of Science discusses various ways of how approximate models can relate to real phenomena, each of which has its specific problems which cannot be discussed here.

Aumann's considerations can also lead one to seek an alternative interpretation of the Nash concept that does not refer to human rationality, but retains all the formally attractive properties. In section 3.3.3 we already discussed *evolutive* approaches to game theory as a possible way to justify the normative use of the Nash equilibrium. While this normative use was marred by a number of serious doubts, the positive use of the evolutionary stability concepts seems more promising.

## *4.1 The Evolutive Interpretation*

Evolutionary game theory was developed in biology; it studies the appearance, robustness and stability of behavioural traits in animal populations. For the history of evolutionary game theory in biology and economics, see [Grüne-Yanoff, 2010]. Biology, obviously, employs game theory only as a positive, not as a normative theory; yet there is considerable disagreement whether it has contributed to the study of particular empirical phenomena, and whether it thus has any predictive function.

Many economists seem to have subscribed to the evolutive interpretation of game theory (Binmore 1987 proposed this term in order to distinguish it from the eductive approaches discussed in Section 3), and to accept it as a theory that contributes to the prediction of human behaviour. Proponents of the evolutive interpretation claim that the economic, social and biological evolutionary pressure directs human agents to behaviour that is in accord with the solution concepts of game theory, even while they have no clear idea of what is going on.

This article cannot do justice even to the basics of this very vibrant and expanding field [Maynard Smith, 1982; Weibull, 1995; Gintis, 2000], but instead concentrates on the question of whether and how this reinterpretation may contribute to the prediction of human behaviour.

Recall from section 3.3.3 that evolutionary game theory studies games that are played over and over again by players who are drawn from a population. Players are assumed to be "programmed" to play one strategy. In the biological case, the relative fitness that strategies bestow on players leads to their differential reproduction: fitter players reproduce more, and the least fittest will eventually go extinct. Adopting this model to social settings presents a number of problems, including the incongruence of fast social change with slow biological reproduction, the problematic relation between behaviour and inheritable traits, and the difference between fitness and preference-based utility (as already discussed in section 2.1). In response to these problems, various suggestions have been made concerning how individual players could be 're-programmed', and the constitution of the population thus changed, without relying on actual player reproduction.

One important suggestion considers players' tendency to imitate more successful opponents (Schlag 1998, see also Fudenberg and Levine 1998, 66f.). The results of such models crucially depend on what is imitated, and how the imitation influences future behaviour. More or less implicitly, the imitation approach takes the notion of a meme as its basis. A meme is "a norm, an idea, a rule of thumb, a code of conduct – something that can be replicated from one head to another by imitation or education, and that determines some aspects of the behaviour of the person in whose head it is lodged" [Binmore, 1994, p. 20]. Players are mere hosts to these memes, and their behaviour is partly determined by them. Fitness is a property of the meme and its capacity to replicate itself to other players. Expected utility maximization is then interpreted as a result of evolutionary selection:

> People who are inconsistent [in their preferences] will necessarily be sometimes wrong and hence will be at a disadvantage compared to those who are always right. And evolution is not kind to memes that inhibit their own replication. [Binmore, 1994, p. 27]

The theory of the fittest memes becoming relatively more frequent is an analytic truth, as long as "fitness" is no more than high "rate of replication". But Binmore then transfers the concept of strategy fitness to player rationality. Critics have argued that the relation between memes and behaviour is ultimately an empirical question (once the concept of meme is clarified, that is), which remains largely unexplored. It therefore remains an *empirical* question whether people behave in accord with principles that game theory proposes.

Of course, the imitation/meme interpretation of strategy replication is only one possible approach among many. Alternatives include reinforcement learning [Börgers and Sarin, 1997] and fictitious play [Kandori *et al.*, 1993]. But the lesson learned from the above discussion also applies to these approaches: buried in the complex models are assumptions (mainly non-axiomatised ones like the meme-behaviour relation mentioned above), which ensure the convergence of evolutionary dynamics to classic equilibria. Until these assumptions are clearly identified, and until they are shown to be empirically supported, it is premature to hail the convergence results as support for the predictive quality of game theory, either under its eductive or its evolutive interpretation.

## *4.2 The Problem of Alternative Descriptions*

While intuitions about rational behaviour may be teased out in fictional, illustrative stories, the question of whether prediction is successful is answerable only on the basis of people's observed behaviour. *Behavioural game theory* observes how people behave in experiments in which their information and incentives are carefully controlled. With the help of these experiments, and drawing on further evidence from psychology, it hopes to test game-theoretic principles for their correctness in predicting behaviour. Further, in cases where the tests do not yield positive results, it hopes that the experiments suggest alternative principles that can be included in the theory.[9] To test game theory, the theory must be specified in such detail that it may predict particular behaviour. To construct specific experimental setups, however, particular interactive phenomena need to be modelled as games, so that the theory's solution concepts can be applied. The problem of interpretation discussed in section 2.4 then surfaces. The most contentious aspect of game modelling lies in the payoffs. The exemplary case is the disagreement over the relevant evaluations of the players in the Prisoners' Dilemma.

Some critics of the defect/defect Nash equilibrium solution have claimed that players would cooperate because they would not only follow their selfish interests, but also take into account non-selfish considerations. They may cooperate, for example, because they care about the welfare of their opponents, because they want to keep their promises out of feelings of group solidarity or because they would otherwise suffer the pangs of a bad conscience. To bring up these considerations against the prisoners' dilemma, however, would expose a grave misunderstanding of the theory. A proper game uses the players' evaluations, captured in the utility function, of the possible outcomes, not the material payoff (like e.g. money). The evaluated outcome must be described with those properties that the players find relevant. Thus either the non-selfish considerations are already included in the players' payoffs (altruistic agents, after all, also have conflicting interests — e.g. which charitable cause to benefit); or the players will *not* be playing the Prisoners' Dilemma. They will be playing some other game with different payoffs.

Incorporating non-material interests in the payoffs has been criticized for making game theory empirically empty. The critics argue that with such a broad interpretation of the payoffs, any anomaly in the prediction of the theory can be dissolved by a re-interpretation of the agents' evaluations of the consequences. Without constraints on re-interpretation, the critics claim, the theory cannot be held to any prediction.

To counter this objection, many economists and some game theorists claim to work on the basis of the *revealed preference* approach. At a minimum, this approach requires that the preferences — and hence the utility function — of an agent are *exclusively* inferred from that agent's choices.[10] This ostensibly relieves game modellers from the need to engage in "psychologising" when trying to determine the players' subjective evaluations.

However, it has been argued that the application of the revealed preference concept either trivializes game theory or makes it conceptually inconsistent. The first argument is that the revealed preference approach completely neglects the importance of beliefs in game theory. An equilibrium depends on the players' payoffs and on their beliefs of what the other players believe and what they will do.

[9]For more details on Behavioural Game Theory, their experimental methods and results, see [Camerer, 2003].

[10]For a discussion of the revealed preference account, see [Grüne, 2004]. Binmore [1994, pp. 105-6, 164, 268] discusses revealed preferences in game theory. See also [Binmore, 1998, pp. 280, 358-362] and [Ross, 2005, pp. 128-136; 2006b].

In the stag hunt game of Figure 1, for example, Row *believes* that if Col *believed* that Row would play $R2$, then he would play $C2$. But if the payoff numbers represented revealed preferences, Hausman [2000] argues, then they would say how individuals would choose, given what the other chose, period. The payoffs would already incorporate the influence of belief, and belief would play no further role. Game theory as a theory of rational deliberation would have lost its job.

The second criticism claims that it is conceptually impossible that games can be constructed on the basis of revealed preferences. Take as an example the simple game in Figure 20.

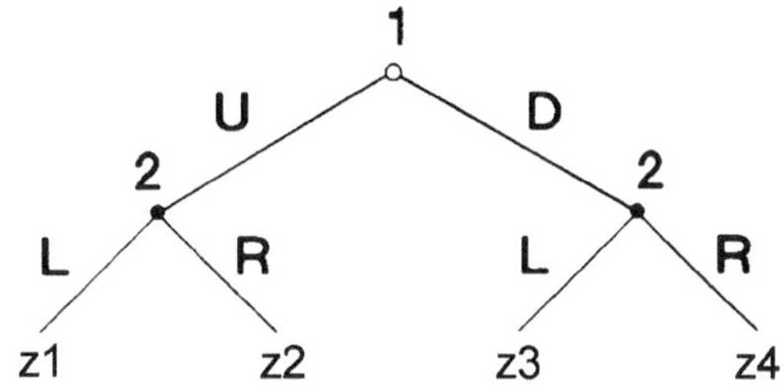


Figure 20. A game tree

How can a modeller determine the payoffs $z1 - z4$ for both players according to the revealed preference method? Let us start with player 2. Could one construct two choice situations for player 2 in which he chooses between $z1$ and $z2$ and between $z3$ and $z4$ respectively? No, argues Hausman [2000]: the two thus constructed choice situations differ from the two subgames in Figure 20 in that they are not preceded by player 1's choice. Hence it is perfectly possible that player 2 chooses $z1$ over $z2$ in the game but chooses $z2$ over $z1$ in the constructed choice situation. Assume, for example, that player 2 considers player 1's choice of $U$ unfair and chooses $L$ in the game in order to take revenge. In that case she may prefer $z1$ over $z2$, but if there is no preceding choice by player 1, she may prefer $z2$ over $z1$. Thus, her choice of $L$ merely reflects the relative desirability of $z1$ over $z2$. The problem here is that the players have state-dependent preferences: player 2 prefers $z1$ over $z2$ in one set of circumstances but $z2$ over $z1$ in another.[11] What makes this problem particularly vicious is the fact that the relevant circumstance is another player's choice in the game.

More problematically still, player 2 must be able to compare $z1$ with $z3$ and $z2$ with $z4$ if one is to assign a utility function for him over all these outcomes on the basis of his choices. But it is logically impossible that she will ever face such a choice in the game, as player 1 will choose either $U$ or $D$, and he will choose either between $z1$ and $z2$ or between $z3$ and $z4$. A similar argument applies to player 1. She never faces a choice between the final outcomes of this game at all, only

[11]See Drèze and Rustichini [2004] for an overview on state-dependence.

between $U$ and $D$. So the revealed preference theorist cannot assign preferences over outcomes to player 1 at all, and to player 2 only partially. This difficulty is clearly exposed in some recent efforts to provide revealed-preference conditions under which the players' choices rationalise various solution concepts.[12] These accounts start from the premise that preferences cannot be observed, and aim to provide conditions under which the players' choices may falsify or verify the *solution concept.*

Finally, assuming that the game has been properly modelled, what the modeller really can observe in a game are only its equilibria. Thus, by observing actual play, it would be possible to observe just that, say, player 1 chose U, and player 2 chose L.

We conclude that it seems conceptually impossible to construct players' payoffs by observing their choices in actual play. Further, preference elicitation procedures that partition the game into simpler subgames and infer revealed preferences from choices in those subgames are constrained by the required state-independence of preferences. As we showed, state-dependence prevents the success of such a elicitation procedure. As we have already seen, there are good reasons to believe that such state-independence is not likely because real people often care about how the other player has affected the outcome.

Further, determining whether or not preferences are state-dependent poses a problem itself. Even if the modeller were able to elicit preferences for 'Ling-with-revenge' and distinguish this from 'Ling-without-revenge' and 'Ling', he will not be able to elicit preferences for 'Ling-with-revenge-in-the-game-in-Figure-20-where-player-1-played-U' without assuming state-independence of some sort. The reason is that the only way of not making a state-independence assumption is to provide the game itself as the context of choice.

These problems may have contributed to a widespread neglect of the problem of preference ascription in game theoretic models. As Weibull [2004] observes:

> While experimentalists usually make efforts to carefully specify to the subject the *game form* ... they usually do not make much effort to find the subject's preferences, despite the fact that these preferences constitute an integral part of the very definition of a game. Instead, it is customary to simply hypothesize subjects' preferences. [Weibull, 2004]

Despite the problems of applying revealed preferences to game theory, the methodological rationale for the injunction to include all motivating factors into the payoffs is sound. It is just important to see its proper role in different contexts. If theoretical game theory has something to contribute, it is in providing interesting analyses of solution concepts in interesting games. For this purpose, the injunction is perfectly legitimate, and it matters little whether or not anybody is able to find some actual situation in which preferences corresponding to the game could

[12]See Sprumont [2000] for an account of normal form games, and [Ray and Zhou, 2001] for extensive form games. Carvajal *et al.* [2004] provide an overview and additional references.

be elicited. It would perhaps be best to drop reference to revealed preferences and formulate the methodological argument in terms of the distinction between modelling and analysing games. One can then interpret payoffs as *dispositions* to choose (cf. [Ross, 2006a]).

The problem of preference identification has been insufficiently addressed in rational choice theory in general and in game theory in particular. But it is not unsolvable. One solution is to find a criterion for outcome individuation. Broome offers such a criterion *by justifiers*: "outcomes should be distinguished as different if and only if they differ in a way that makes it rational to have a preference between them" [Broome, 1991, 103]. This criterion, however, requires a concept of rationality independent of the principles of rational choice. A rational choice is no longer based on preferences alone, but preferences themselves are now based on the rationality concept. This constitutes a radical departure of how most rational choice theorists, including game theorists, regard the concept of rationality. Another option that Hausman [2005] suggests is that economists can use game theoretic anomalies to study the factors influencing preferences. By altering features of the game forms and, in particular, by manipulating the precise beliefs each player has about the game and about others' conjectures, experimenters may be able to make progress in understanding what governs choices in strategic situations and hence what games people are playing.

## *4.3 Testing Game Theory*

Whether game theory can be tested depends on whether the theory makes any empirical claims, and whether it can be immunized against predictive failure.

Does the theory make testable claims? At first, it does not seem to do so. The solution concepts discussed in section 2.3 mainly take the form of *theorems*. Theorems are deductive conclusions from initial assumptions. So to test game theory, these assumptions need to be tested for their empirical adequacy. In this vein, Hausman [2005] claims that game theory is committed to contingent and testable axioms concerning human rationality, preferences, and beliefs. This claim remains controversial. Many economists believe that theories should not be tested with regard to their assumptions, but only with respect to their predictions (a widespread view that was eloquently expressed by Friedman [1953]). But the theory only makes empirical claims in conjunction with its game models.

Further, testing game theory through its predictions is difficult as such tests must operate through the mediation of models that represent an interactive situation. Here the issue of interpreting the modelled situation (see section 2.4) and of model construction drives a wedge between the predicting theory and the real world phenomena, so that predictive failures can often be attributed to model misspecification (as discussed in section 4.2).

Francesco Guala [2006] recently pointed to a specific element of game theory that seems to make an empirical claim all by itself, and independent of auxiliary hypotheses. For this purpose, he discusses the phenomenon of *reciprocity*. Agents reciprocate to other agents who have exhibited "trust" in them because they want to be kind to them. Reciprocation of an agent 1 to another agent 2 is necessarily dependent on 2 having performed an action that led 1 to reciprocate. Reciprocation is thus clearly delineated from general altruism or justice considerations.

The question that Guala raises is whether reciprocity can be accounted for in the payoff matrix of a game. The 'kindness' of an action depends on what could have been chosen: I think that you are kind to me because you could have harmed me for your benefit, but you chose not to. This would mean that the history of chosen strategies would *endogenously* modify the payoffs, a modelling move that is explicitly ruled out in standard game theory. Guala shows that the exclusion of reciprocity is connected right to the core of game theory: to the construction of the expected utility function.

All existing versions of the proofs of the existence of a utility function rely on the so-called *rectangular field assumption.* It assumes that decision makers form preferences over every act that can possibly be constructed by combining consequences with states of the world. However, if reciprocity has to be modelled in the consequences, and reciprocity depends on others' acts that in turn depend on the players' own acts, then it is *conceptually impossible* to construct acts in accord with the rectangular field assumption, because the act under question would be caught in an infinite regress. The problem is that in these cases, the Savagean distinction between consequences, states and acts cannot be consistently maintained in game theory. It follows from this that reciprocity is not the only consideration that game theory cannot put into the consequences. Things like revenge, envy, and being-suckered-in-Prisoner's-Dilemma suffer from the same problem (see also [Sugden, 1991; 1998]).

If Guala's argument is correct, it seems impossible to model reciprocity in the payoffs, and game theory is not flexible enough to accommodate reciprocity considerations into its framework. Game theory then could be interpreted as asserting that reciprocity is irrelevant for strategic interaction, or at least that reciprocity could be neatly separated from non-reciprocal strategic considerations. With this claim, game theory would be testable, and - if reciprocity were indeed an integral and non-separable factor in strategic decisions, as the evidence seems to suggest – would be refuted.

## 5 CONCLUSION

Game theory, this survey showed, does not provide a general and unified theory of interactive rationality; nor does it provide a positive theory of interactive behaviour that can easily be tested. These observations have many implications of great philosophical interest, some of which were discussed here. Many of the questions that arise in these discussions are still left unanswered, and thus continue to require the attention of philosophers.

# BIBLIOGRAPHY


[Aumann, 1999a] R. J. Aumann. Interactive Epistemology I: Knowledge, *International Journal of Game Theory,* vol. 28, no. 3, pp. 263-300, 1999.

[Aumann, 1999b] R. J. Aumann. Interactive Epistemology II: Probability, *International Journal of Game Theory,* vol. 28, no. 3, pp. 301-314, 1999.

[Aumann, 1998] R. J. Aumann. Common Priors: A Reply to Gul, *Econometrica,* vol. 66, no. 4, pp. 929-938, 2998.

[Aumann, 1995] R. J. Aumann. Backward Induction and Common Knowledge of Rationality, *Games and Economic Behavior,* vol. 8, no. 1, pp. 6-19, 1995.

[Aumann, 1987] R. J. Aumann. Correlated Equilibrium as an Expression of Bayesian Rationality, *Econometrica,* vol. 55, no. 1, pp. 1-18, 1987.

[Aumann, 1985] R. J. Aumann. What is Game Theory Trying to Accomplish? In *Frontiers of Economics*, K.J. Arrow & S. Honkapohja, eds., Basil Blackwell, Oxford, pp. 28-76, 1985.

[Aydinonat, 2008] N. E. Aydinonat. *The invisible hand in economics: how economists explain unintended social consequences*, Routledge, London, 2008.

[Bacharach, 1993] M. Bacharach. Variable Universe Games. In *Frontiers of game theory*, K. Binmore, A.P. Kirman & P. Tani, eds., MIT Press, Cambridge Mass., pp. 255-275, 1993.

[Battigalli, 1996] P. Battigalli. The Decision-Theoretic Foundations of Game Theory: Comment. In *The rational foundations of economic behaviour: Proceedings of the IEA Conference held in Turin*, K. J. Arrow *et al.*, eds., Macmillan Press, Hampshire, pp. 149-154, 1996.

[Bernheim, 1984] D. Bernheim. Rationalizable Strategic Behavior, *Econometrica,* vol. 52, no. 4, pp. 1007-1028, 1984.

[Bicchieri, 1993] C. Bicchieri. *Rationality and coordination*, Cambridge University Press, Cambridge England; New York, USA, 1993.

[Binmore, 2008] K. Binmore. *Game theory: A very short introduction*, Oxford University Press, New York, 2008.

[Binmore, 2007] K. Binmore. *Playing for Real*, Oxford University Press, New York, 2007.

[Binmore, 1998] K. Binmore. *Game theory and the social contract: Just playing*, The MIT Press, London, 1998.

[Binmore, 1994] K. Binmore. *Game theory and the social contract: Playing fair*, MIT Press, Cambridge, Mass, 1994.

[Binmore, 1993] K. Binmore. De-Bayesing Game Theory. In *Frontiers of game theory*, K. Binmore, A.P. Kirman & P. Tani, eds., MIT Press, Cambridge Mass., pp. 321-339, 1993.

[Binmore, 1987] K. Binmore. Modeling Rational Players: Part 1, *Economics and Philosophy,* vol. 3, no. 2, pp. 179-214, 1987.

[Blackburn, 1998] S. Blackburn. *Ruling passions: a theory of practical reasoning*, Clarendon Press, Oxford; New York, 1998.

[Börgers and Sarin, 1997] T. Börgers and R. Sarin. Learning through Reinforcement and Replicator Dynamics, *Journal of Economic Theory,* vol. 77, no. 1, pp. 1-14, 1997.

[Brandenburger, 1992] A. Brandenburger. Knowledge and Equilibrium in Games, *The Journal of Economic Perspectives,* vol. 6, no. 4, pp. 83-101, 1992.

[Broome, 1991] J. Broome. *Weighing goods: equality, uncertainty and time*, Basil Blackwell, Cambridge, Mass, 1991.

[Camerer, 2003] C. Camerer. *Behavioral game theory: experiments in strategic interaction*, Princeton University Press, Princeton, N.J. ; Woodstock, 2003.

[Carvajal *et al.*, 2004] A. Carvajal, I. Ray, and S. Snyder. Equilibrium Behavior in Markets and Games: Testable Restrictions and Identification, *Journal of Mathematical Economics,* vol. 40, no. 1-2, pp. 1-40.

[Dréze and Rusichini, 2004] J. H. Drèze and A. Rustichini. State-Dependent Utility and Decision Theory. In *Handbook of utility theory*, eds. S. Barberà, P.J. Hammond & C. Seidl, Kluwer Academic Publishers, Boston, pp. 839-892, 2004.

[Friedman, 1953] M. Friedman. The Methodology of Positive Economics, *in Essays in Positive Economics*, University of Chicago Press, Chicago, pp. 3-43, 1953.

[Fudenberg *et al.*, 1988] D. Fudenberg, D. M. Kreps, and D. K. Levine. On the Robustness of Equilibrium Refinements, *Journal of Economic Theory,* vol. 44, no. 2, pp. 354-380, 1988.

[Fudenberg and Levine, 1998] D. Fudenberg and D. K. Levine. *The Theory of Learning in Games*, MIT Press, Cambridge, Mass, 1998.

[Fudenberg and Tirole, 1991] D. Fudenberg and J. Tirole. *Game theory*, MIT Press, Cambridge, Mass, 1991.

[Gibbard, 1973] A. F. Gibbard. Manipulation of Voting Schemes: A General Result, *Econometrica,* vol. 41, no. 4, pp. 587-601, 1973.

[Gigerenzer *et al.*, 1999] G. Gigerenzer, P. M. Todd, and ABC Research Group. *Simple heuristics that make us smart*, Oxford University Press, Oxford ; New York, 1999.

[Gintis, 2007] H. Gintis. A Framework for the Unification of the Behavioral Sciences, *Behavioral and Brain Sciences,* vol. 30, no. 1, pp. 1-16, 2007.

[Gintis, 2004] H. Gintis. Towards the Unity of the Human Behavioral Sciences, *Politics, Philosophy and Economics,* vol. 3, no. 1, pp. 37-57, 2004.

[Gintis, 2000] H. Gintis. *Game theory evolving: A problem-centered introduction to modeling strategic behavior*, Princeton University Press, Princeton, 2000.

[Goeree and Holt, 2001] J. K. Goeree and C. A. Holt. Ten Little Treasures of Game Theory and Ten Intuitive Contradictions, *American Economic Review,* vol. 91, no. 5, pp. 1402-1422, 2001.

[Grüne, 2004] T. Grüne. The Problem of Testing Preference Axioms with Revealed Preference Theory, *Analyse & Kritik,* vol. 26, no. 2, pp. 382-397, 2004.

[Grüne-Yanoff, 2008a] T. Grüne-Yanoff. Evolutionary Game Theory, Interpersonal Comparisons and Natural Selection, mimeo, University of Helsinki, Department of Social and Moral Philosophy, 2008.

[Grüne-Yanoff, 2008b] T. Grüne-Yanoff. Game theory, *Internet encyclopedia of philosophy,* , pp. 29.4.2008. `http://www.iep.utm.edu/g/game-th.htm`.

[Grüne-Yanoff, 2020] T. Grüne-Yanoff. Models as products of interdisciplinary exchange: Evidence from evolutionary game theory. Mimeo, University of Helsinki, Collegium of Advanced Studies, 2010.

[Grüne-Yanoff and Schweinzer, 2008] T. Grüne-Yanoff and P. Schweinzer. The Role of Stories in Applying Game Theory, *Journal of Economic Methodology,* vol. 15, no. 2, pp. 131-146, 2008.

[Guala, 2006] G. Guala. Has Game Theory been Refuted?, *Journal of Philosophy,* vol. 103, pp. 239-263, 2006.

[Gul, 1998] F. Gul. A Comment on Aumann's Bayesian View, *Econometrica,* vol. 6, no. 4, pp. 923-927, 1998.

[Hammond, 1998] P. J. Hammond. Consequentialism and Bayesian Rationality in Normal Form Games. In *Game theory, experience, rationality: foundations of social sciences, economics and ethics; in honor of John C. Harsanyi*, W. Leinfellner & E. Körner , eds., Kluwer, Dordrecht, pp. 187-196, 1998.

[Hammond, 1996] P. J. Hammond. : Consequentialism, structural rationality and game theory. In *The rational foundations of economic behaviour: Proceedings of the IEA Conference held in Turin, Italy,* K.J. Arrow, E. Colombatto & M. Perlman, ed., St. Martin's Press; Macmillan Press in association with the International Economic Association, New York; London, pp. 25, 1996.

[Hargreaves-Heap and Varoufakis, 2001] S. Hargreaves-Heap and Y. Varoufakis. *Game theory: a critical introduction*, 2nd edn, Routledge, London, 2001.

[Harsanyi, 1973] J. C. Harsanyi. Games with Randomly Disturbed Payoffs: A New Rationale for Mixed Strategy Equilibrium Points, *International Journal of Game Theory,* vol. 2, pp. 1-23, 1973.

[Harsanyi, 1967-8] J. C. Harsanyi. Games with Incomplete Information Played by 'Bayesian' Players, I-III, *Management Science,* vol. 14, pp. 159-182, 320-334, 486-502, 1967-8.

[Harsanyi, 1966] J. C. Harsanyi. A General Theory of Rational Behavior in Game Situations, *Econometrica,* vol. 34, no. 3, pp. 613-634, 1966.

[Harsanyi and Selten, 1988] J. C. Harsanyi and R. Selten. *A general theory of equilibrium selection in games*, MIT Press, Cambridge, Mass, 1988.

[Hausman, 2005] D. Hausman. 'Testing' Game Theory, *Journal of Economic Methodology,* vol. 12, no. 2, pp. 211-23, 2005.

[Hausman, 2000] D. M. Hausman. Revealed Preference, Belief, and Game Theory, *Economics and Philosophy,* vol. 16, no. 1, pp. 99-115, 2000.

[Heifetz, 1999] A. Heifetz. How Canonical is the Canonical Model? A Comment on Aumann's Interactive Epistemology, *International Journal of Game Theory,* vol. 28, no. 3, pp. 435-442, 1999.

[Hirshleifer and Riley, 1992] J. Hirshleifer and J. G. Riley. *The analytics of uncertainty and information*, Cambridge University Press, Cambridge ; New York, 1992.
[Jacobsen, 1996] H. J. Jacobsen. On the Foundations of Nash Equilibrium, *Economics and Philosophy,* vol. 12, no. 1, pp. 67-88, 1996.
[Kadane and Larkey, 1983] J. B. Kadane and P. D. Larkey. The Confusion of is and Ought in Game Theoretic Contexts, *Management Science,* vol. 29, no. 12, pp. 1365-1379, 1983.
[Kadane and Larkey, 1982] J. B. Kadane and P. D. Larkey. Subjective Probability and the Theory of Games, *Management Science,* vol. 28, pp. 113-120, 1982.
[Kalai and Lehrer, 1993] E. Kalai and E. Lehrer. Rational Learning Leads to Nash Equilibrium, *Econometrica,* vol. 61, no. 5, pp. 1019-1045, 1993.
[Kandori *et al.*, 1993] M. Kandori, G. J. Mailath, and R. Rob. Learning, Mutation, and Long Run Equilibria in Games, *Econometrica,* vol. 61, no. 1, pp. 29-56, 1993.
[Kohlberg and Mertens, 1986] E. Kohlberg and J.-F. Mertens. On the Strategic Stability of Equilibria, *Econometrica,* vol. 54, no. 5, pp. 10030, 1986.
[Kreps, 1990] D. M. Kreps. *Game theory and economic modelling*, Clarendon Press; Oxford University Press, Oxford; New York, 1990.
[Kuhn, 2004] S. T. Kuhn. Reflections on Ethics and Game Theory, *Synthese,* vol. 141, no. 1, pp. 1-44, 2004.
[Leonard, 1994] R. J. Leonard. Reading Cournot, Reading Nash: The Creation and Stabilisation of Nash Equilibrium, *Economic Journal,* vol. 104, no. 424, pp. 492-511, 1994.
[Levi, 1998] I. Levi. Prediction, Bayesian Deliberation and Correlated Equilibrium. In *Game Theory, Experience, Rationality*, W. Leinfellner & E. Köhler, eds., pp. 173–185. Kluwer Academic Publishers, Dordrecht, 1998.
[Lewis, 1969] D. K. Lewis. *Convention: a philosophical study*, Harvard University Press, Cambridge, Mass, 1969.
[LiCalzi, 1995] M. LiCalzi. Fictitious Play by Cases, *Games and Economic Behavior,* vol. 11, no. 1, pp. 64-89, 1995.
[Luce and Raiffa, 1957] D. R. Luce, and H. Raiffa. *Games and decisions; introduction and critical survey*, Wiley, New York, 1957.
[Mailath, 1998] G. J. Mailath. Do People Play Nash Equilibrium? Lessons from Evolutionary. Game Theory, *Journal of Economic Literature,* vol. 36, pp. 1347-1374, 1998.
[Mäki, 2002] U. Mäki. The Dismal Queen of the Social Sciences. In *Fact and Fiction in Economics*, ed. U. Mäki, Cambridge University Press, Cambridge, pp. 3-34, 2002.
[Mariotti, 1997] M. Mariotti. Decisions in Games: Why there should be a Special Exemption from Bayesian Rationality, *Journal of Economic Methodology,* vol. 4, no. 1, pp. 43-60, 1997.
[Mariotti, 1996] M. Mariotti. The Decision-Theoretic Foundations of Game Theory. In *The rational foundations of economic behaviour: Proceedings of the IEA Conference held in Turin*, ed. Arrow, Kenneth J. et al., Macmillan Press, Hampshire, pp. 133-148, 1996.
[Mariotti, 1995] M. Mariotti. Is Bayesian Rationality Compatible with Strategic Rationality?, *Economic Journal,* vol. 105, no. 432, pp. 1099, 1995.
[Maynard Smith, 1982] J. Maynard Smith. *Evolution and the theory of games*, Cambridge University Press, Cambridge ; New York, 1982.
[Mertens and Zamir, 1985] J.-F. Mertens and S. Zamir. Formulation of Bayesian Analysis for Games with Incomplete Information, *International Journal of Game Theory,* vol. 4, no. 1, pp. 1-29, 1985.
[Morgan, 2005] M. S. Morgan. The Curious Case of the Prisoner's Dilemma: Model Situation? In *Science without laws*, A. Creager *et al.*, eds. Duke University Press, Durham, 2005.
[Morgan, 2001] M. S. Morgan. Models, Stories and the Economic World, *Journal of Economic Methodology,* vol. 8, no. 3, pp. 361, 2001.
[Morris, 1995] S. Morris. The Common Prior Assumption in Economic Theory, *Economics and Philosophy,* vol. 1, pp. 227-253, 1995.
[Myerson, 1999] R. B. Myerson. Nash Equilibrium and the History of Economic Theory, *Journal of Economic Literature,* vol. 37, no. 3, pp. 1067-1082, 1999.
[Nash, 1950] J. F. Nash. Equilibrium Points in n-Person Games, *Proceedings of the National Academy of Science,* vol. 36, pp. 48-49, 1950.
[Osborne and Rubinstein, 1994] M. J. Osborne and A. Rubinstein. *A course in game theory*, MIT Press, Cambridge, Mass, 1994.
[Pearce, 1984] D. G. Pearce. Rationalizable Strategic Behavior and the Problem of Perfection, *Econometrica,* vol. 52, no. 4, pp. 1029-1050, 1984.

[Pettit and Sugden, 1989] P. Pettit and R. Sugden. The Backward Induction Paradox, *Journal of Philosophy,* vol. 86, no. 4, pp. 169-182, 1989.

[Rankin *et al.*, 2000] F. W. Rankin, J. B. Van Huyck, and R. C. Battalio. Strategic Similarity and Emergent Conventions: Evidence from Similar Stag Hunt Games, *Games and Economic Behavior,* vol. 32, no. 2, pp. 315-337, 2000.

[Ray and Zhou, 2001] I. Ray and L. Zhou. Game Theory Via Revealed Preferences, *Games and Economic Behavior,* vol. 37, no. 2, pp. 415-24, 2001.

[Risse, 2000] M. Risse. What is Rational about Nash Equilibria?, *Synthese,* vol. 124, no. 3, pp. 361-384, 2000.

[Ross, 2006a] D. Ross. Evolutionary Game Theory and the Normative Theory of Institutional Design: Binmore and Behavioral Economics, *Politics, Philosophy & Economics,* vol. 5, no. 1, pp. 51-79, 2006.

[Ross, 2006b] D. Ross. Game theory, *Stanford Encyclopedia of Philosophy*, pp. 1-78, 2006. `http://plato.stanford.edu/entries/game-theory/`.

[Ross, 2005] D. Ross. *Economic theory and cognitive science: microexplanation*, The MIT Press, Cambridge, Mass., London, 2005.

[Rubinstein, 1998] A. Rubinstein. *Modeling bounded rationality*, MIT Press, Cambridge, Mass, 1998.

[Rubinstein, 1991] A. Rubinstein. Comments on the Interpretation of Game Theory, *Econometrica,* vol. 59, no. 4, pp. 909-924, 1991.

[Schelling, 1960] T. C. Schelling. *The strategy of conflict*, Harvard University Press, Cambridge, 1960.

[Schlag, 1998] K. Schlag. Why Imitate, and if so, how? A Boundedly Rational Approach to Multi-Armed Bandits, *Journal of Economic Theory,* vol. 78, no. 1, pp. 130-156, 1998.

[Sprumont, 2000] Y. Sprumont. On the Testable Implications of Collective Choice Theories, *Journal of Economic Theory,* vol. 93, no. 2, pp. 205-232, 2000.

[Stalnaker, 1999] R. Stalnaker. Knowledge, Belief and Counterfactual Reasoning in Games. In *The Logic of Strategy*, C. Bicchieri *et al.*, eds. Oxford University Press, Oxford, 1999.

[Sugden, 2001] R. Sugden. The Evolutionary Turn in Game Theory, *Journal of Economic Methodology,* vol. 8, no. 1, pp. 113-130, 2001.

[Sugden, 1998] R. Sugden. Difficulties in the Theory of Rational Choice [Review Article], *Journal of Economic Methodology,* vol. 5, no. 1, pp. 157-163, 1998.

[Sugden, 1995] R. Sugden. A Theory of Focal Points, *Economic Journal,* vol. 105, no. 430, pp. 533-550, 1995.

[Sugden, 1991] R. Sugden. Rational Choice: A Survey of Contributions from Economics and Philosophy, *Economic Journal,* vol. 101, no. 407, pp. 751-785, 1991.

[Tan and Werlang, 1988] T. C. Tan and S. R. da C. Werlang. The Bayesian Foundations of Solution Concepts of Games, *Journal of Economic Theory,* vol. 45, pp. 370-339, 1988.

[van Damme, 1991] E. van Damme. *Stability and Perfection of Nash Equilibria*, 2nd rev. and enlarged ed. edn, Springer, Berlin, 1991.

[von Neumann and Morgenstern, 1947] J. von Neumann and O. Morgenstern. *Theory of games and economic behavior*, 2nd edn, Princeton University Press, Princeton, 1947.

[Vromen, 2009] J. J. Vromen. Friedman's Selection Argument Revisited. In *The Methodology of Positive Economics. Reflections on the Milton Friedman Legacy*, U. Mäki, ed., pp. 257–284. Cambridge University Press, Cambridge, 2009.

[Weibull, 2004] J. W. Weibull. Testing Game Theory. In *Advances in understanding strategic behavior*, ed. S. Huck, Palgrave, New York, pp. 85-104, 2004.

[Weibull, 1995] J. W. Weibull. *Evolutionary game theory*, MIT Press, Cambridge, Mass, 1995.

[Wiebull, 1994] J. W. Weibull. The 'as if' Approach to Game Theory: Three Positive Results and Four Obstacles, *European Economic Review,* vol. 38, no. 3-4, pp. 868-881, 1994.

[Zermelo, 1913] E. Zermelo. Über Eine Anwendung Der Mengenlehre Auf Die Theorie Des Schachspiels. In *Proceedings of the Fifth International Congress on Mathematics*, E. W. Hobson & A. E. H. Love, eds., pp. 501–504. Cambridge University Press, Cambridge, 1913.

# AN EMBARRASSMENT OF RICHES: MODELING SOCIAL PREFERENCES IN ULTIMATUM GAMES

Cristina Bicchieri and Jiji Zhang

Traditional economic models presume that individuals do not take an interest in the interests of those with whom they interact. More particularly, the assumption of *non-tuism* implies that the utility function of each individual, as a measure of her preferences, is strictly independent of the utility functions of those with whom she interacts. Philip Wicksteed introduced the concept of non-tuism, stressing that an economic relationship is one entered into by two parties each of whom is intent on the furtherance of his own (not necessarily selfish) purposes, not those of the other.[1] Interestingly, this idea is quite different from the usual egoistic assumption: a non-tuist may be a caring, altruistic human being, but when involved in an economic exchange, she must necessarily regard her own interest as paramount. Thus non-tuism is important insofar as it defines the scope of economic activities. When tuism to some degree motivates one's conduct, then it ceases to be wholly economic.

There is nothing wrong in saying that exchange activities display the above kind of motivation, but it is certainly farfetched to assume that *all* activities we may model within a rational choice framework share the same, non-tuistic motivation. In fact, it is plainly untrue. Note that we are distinguishing here between non-tuism and selfishness, the latter being a more encompassing disposition that is not particularly tied with specific activities. That is, a selfish person will display a 'me first' attitude in all sorts of environments, caring just about her material well-being to the exclusion of other motives, whereas non-tuism is appropriate in all those cases in which we are expected to 'win' (as in competitive games or market interactions). Non-tuism, however, may not be appropriate at all in personal exchanges, and even in traditional economic areas such as labor economics [Fehr

[1] "He is exactly in the position of a man who is playing a game of chess or cricket. He is considering nothing except his game. It would be absurd to call a man selfish for protecting his king in a game of chess, or to say that he was actuated by purely egoistic motives in so doing. It would be equally absurd to call a cricketer selfish for protecting his wicket, or to say that in making runs he was actuated by egoistic motives qualified by a secondary concern for his eleven. The fact is that he has no conscious motive whatever, and is wholly intent on the complex feat of taking the ball. If you want to know whether he is selfish or unselfish you must consider the whole organization of his life, the place which chess-playing or cricket takes in it, and the alternatives which they open or close. At the moment the categories of egoism and altruism are irrelevant." (P. Wicksteed, *Common Sense of Political Economy*, p. 175.)

Handbook of the Philosophy of Science. Volume 13: Philosophy of Economics.
Volume editor: Uskali Mäki. General editors: Dov M. Gabbay, Paul Thagard and John Woods.

*et al.*, 1998] and public choice we know that cooperation, trust and fairness play a crucial role in smoothing interactions and producing better collective outcomes.

Experimental results in Ultimatum, Trust and Social Dilemma games have been interpreted as showing that individuals are, by and large, not driven by selfish motives. But we do not need experiments to know that. In our view, what the experiments show is that the typical economic auxiliary hypothesis of non-tuism should not be generalized to other contexts. Indeed, we know that when the experimental situation is framed as a market interaction, participants will be more inclined to keep more money, share less, and disregard other participants' welfare [Hoffman *et al.*, 1994]. When the same game is framed as a fair division one, participants overall show a much greater concern for the other parties' interests. The data thus indicate that the *context* of an interaction is of paramount importance in eliciting different motives. The challenge then is to model utility functions that are general enough to subsume a variety of motives and specific enough to allow for meaningful, interesting predictions to be made.

For the sake of simplicity (and brevity), in what follows we will concentrate upon the results of experiments that show what appears to be individuals' disposition to behave in a fair manner in a variety of circumstances [Camerer, 2003], though what we are saying can be easily applied to other research areas. Such experimental results have been variously interpreted, each interpretation being accompanied by a specific utility function. We shall consider three such functions and the underlying interpretations that support them, and assess each one on the basis of what they claim to be able to explain and predict.

## 1 SOCIAL PREFERENCES

The experiments we are going to discuss are designed in the form of strategic games, among which the Ultimatum game is one of the simplest [Guth *et al.*, 1982]. The game involves two players, a proposer and a responder. In the typical setting, the proposer is given a fixed amount of money and must decide how much to offer to the responder. The responder either accepts the offer, in which case the two players get their respective share, or rejects the offer, in which case both players get nothing. We will refer to this basic Ultimatum game as BUG henceforth. If, as usually assumed, the players simply aim at maximizing their monetary payoffs, the responder will accept as long as the offer is positive, and hence the proposer will offer the least amount allowed.[2] This prediction, however, is not confirmed by the experimental results: the modal offer is about half of the stake, and relatively mean offers are frequently rejected [Camerer, 2003]. This suggests that players' utilities are not simply increasing functions of the monetary gains.

A few utility functions have thus been developed that explicitly incorporate concerns for fairness into the preference structure. In this paper we compare

[2]We assume, throughout this paper, that the utility functions of the players are common knowledge, though particular parameter values in the functions may not be.

three such models in the context of ultimatum games — both the BUG and some variants. The three models represent very different approaches. One common explanation of the experimental data is that individuals have a *preference* for fairness in the outcome. That is, given two outcomes, individuals by and large will prefer the fairest one. The Fehr-Schmidt model is the best known example of such an approach: it is a consequentialist model, in which an agent's utility is completely determined by the final distribution of outcomes — the agent's own material payoff and others' material payoffs. By contrast, the model developed by Rabin emphasizes the role of actual actions and beliefs in determining utility. Players' utilities are not determined solely by the final distribution, but are also affected by how that distribution comes into being. This approach highlights the fact that people care about the process through which an outcome occurs, as well as the intentions of decision makers. Thus individuals will be nice to those they perceive as nice, and mean to those they believe to be mean. The alternative explanation we propose is that, in the right kind of circumstances, individuals *obey fairness norms*. To say that we obey fairness norms differs from assuming that we have a 'preference' for fairness. To conform to a fairness norm, we must have the right kind of expectations [Bicchieri, 2000; 2006]. That is, we must expect others to follow the norm, too, and also believe that there is a generalized expectation that we will obey the norm in the present circumstances. The preference to obey a norm is *conditional* upon such expectations.[3] Take away some of the expectations, and behavior will significantly change. A *conditional preference* will thus be stable under certain conditions, but a change in the relevant conditions may induce a predictable preference shift. The Bicchieri model, to a certain extent, combines the two formerly discussed approaches. On the surface it is very similar to the Fehr-Schmidt model; however, the distinguishing feature of the model — the incorporation of beliefs about (social) norms into the utility function — is closer in spirit to the Rabin model.

A norm-based theory makes testable predictions that are quite different, at least in some critical instances, from the predictions of theories that postulate a social preference for fairness. Theories that stress the importance of intentions and process over outcomes are more compatible with a norm-based scenario though, as we shall see in the next sections, the latter has greater predictive power. All the above theories, it must be noted, assume that individuals have social preferences, in that they take into consideration others' utilities when they make a choice. *How* this is done is a matter of contention, and is precisely what differentiates the three models we present.

## 2 ANALYSIS BASED ON BUG

In this section we introduce the three models and apply them to the basic ultimatum game (BUG), where the total amount of money to be divided is denoted by

[3]The conditions for following a norm are formally described in Chapter 1 of Bicchieri [2006].

$M$. The proposer will offer the responder an amount $x$ between 0 and $M$. If the responder accepts the proposal, the proposer gets $M - x$, and the responder gets $x$. Otherwise both get zero.

## 2.1 *Fairness preferences: the Fehr-Schmidt model*

The first model we consider was proposed by Fehr and Schmidt [1999]. Such model intends to capture the idea that people dislike, to a certain extent, unequal outcomes, even if they benefit from the unequal distribution. Given a group of $L$ agents, the Fehr-Schmidt utility function of agent $i$ is

$$U_i(x_1, ..., x_L) = x_i - \frac{\alpha_i}{L-1}\sum_j \max(x_j - x_i, 0) - \frac{\beta_i}{L-1}\sum_j \max(x_i - x_j, 0)$$

where $x_j$ denotes the material payoff agent $j$ gets. One constraint on the parameters is that $0 < \beta_i < \alpha_i$, which indicates that people dislike inequality against them more than they do inequality favoring them. We may think of $\alpha$ as an 'envy' weight, and $\beta$ as a 'guilt' weight. The other constraint is $\beta_i < 1$, meaning that an agent does not suffer terrible guilt when she is in a relatively good position. For example, a player would prefer getting more without affecting other people's payoff even though that results in an increase of the inequality.

Applying the model to BUG, the utility function is simplified to

$$U_i(x_1, x_2) = x_i - \begin{cases} \alpha_i(x_{3-i} - x_i) & \text{if } x_{3-i} \geq x_i \\ \beta_i(x_i - x_{3-i}) & \text{if } x_{3-i} < x_i \end{cases} \qquad i = 1, 2$$

Obviously if the responder rejects the offer, both utility functions are equal to zero, that is, $U_{1reject} = U_{2reject} = 0$. If the responder accepts an offer of $x$, the utility functions are as follows:

$$U_{1accept}(x) = \begin{cases} (1+\alpha_1)M - (1+2\alpha_1)x & \text{if } x \geq M/2 \\ (1-\beta_1)M - (1-2\beta_1)x & \text{if } x < M/2 \end{cases}$$

$$U_{2accept}(x) = \begin{cases} (1+2\alpha_2)x - \alpha_2 M & \text{if } x < M/2 \\ (1-2\beta_2)x + \beta_2 M & \text{if } x \geq M/2 \end{cases}$$

The responder should accept the offer if $U_{2accept}(x) > U_{2reject} = 0$. Solving for $x$ we get the *threshold for acceptance*: $\boldsymbol{x > \alpha_2 M/(1+2\alpha_2)}$. Evidently if $\alpha_2$ is close to zero – which indicates that player 2 (the responder) does not care much about being treated unfairly – the responder will accept very mean offers. On the other hand, if $\alpha_2$ is sufficiently large, the offer has to be close to a half to be accepted. In any event, the threshold is not higher than $M/2$, which means that hyper-fair offers (more than half) are not necessary for the sake of acceptance.

For the proposer, the utility function is monotonically decreasing in $x$ when $x \geq M/2$. Hence a rational proposer will not offer more than half of the cake. Suppose $x \leq M/2$; two cases are possible depending on the value of $\beta_1$. If $\beta_1 > 1/2$, that is, if the proposer feels sufficiently guilty about treating others unfairly, the utility is monotonically increasing in $x$, and his best choice is to offer $M/2$. On the other hand, if $\beta_1 < 1/2$, the utility is monotonically decreasing in x, and hence the best offer for the proposer is the minimum one that would be accepted, i.e. (a little bit more than) $\alpha_2 M/(1+2\alpha_2)$. Finally, if $\beta_1 = 1/2$, it does not matter how much the proposer offers, as long as it is between $\alpha_2 M/(1+2\alpha_2)$ and $M/2$. Note that the other two parameters, $\alpha_1$and $\beta_2$, are not identifiable in Ultimatum games.

As noted by Fehr and Schmidt, the model allows for the fact that individuals are heterogeneous. Different $\alpha$s and $\beta$s correspond to different types of people. Although the utility functions are common knowledge, the exact values of the parameters are not. The proposer, in most cases, is not sure what type of responder she is facing. Along the Bayesian line, her belief about the type of the responder can be formally represented by a probability distribution $P$ on $\alpha_2$ and $\beta_2$. When $\beta_1 > 1/2$, the proposer's rational choice does not depend on what $P$ is. When $\beta_1 < 1/2$, however, the proposer will seek to maximize the expected utility:

$$EU(x) = P(\alpha_2 M/(1+2\alpha_2) < x) \times ((1-\beta_1)M - (1-2\beta_1)x)$$

Therefore, the behavior of a rational proposer in UG depends on her own type ($\beta_1$) and her belief about the type of the responder. The experimental data suggest that for many proposers, either $\beta$ is large ($\beta > 1/2$) or they estimate the responder's $\alpha$ to be large. On the other side, the choice of the responder depends on his type ($\alpha_2$) and the amount of the offer.

The apparent advantages of the Fehr-Schmidt utility function are that it can rationalize both positive and negative outcomes, and that it can explain the observed variability in outcomes with heterogeneous types. One of the major weaknesses of this model, however, is that it has a consequentialist bias: players only care about final distributions of outcomes, not about how such distributions come about.[4] As we shall see, more recent experiments have established that how a situation is framed matters to an evaluation of outcomes, and that the same distribution can be accepted or rejected depending on 'irrelevant' information about the players or the circumstances of play. Another difficulty with this approach is that, if we assume the distribution of types to be constant in a given population, then we should observe, overall, the same proportion of 'fair' outcomes in Ultimatum games. Not only does this not happen, but we also observe individual inconsistencies in behavior across different situations in which the monetary outcomes are the same. If we assume, as is usually done in economics, that individual preferences are stable, then we would expect similar behaviors across Ultimatum games. If instead we conclude that preferences are context-dependent, then we should provide a mapping from contexts to preferences that indicates in a fairly predictable way how

[4]This is a *separability* of utility assumption: what matters to a player in a game is her payoff at a terminal node. The way in which that node was reached, and the possible alternative paths that were not taken are irrelevant to an assessment of her utility at that node. Utilities of terminal node payoffs are thus separable from the path through the tree, and from payoffs on unchosen branches.

and why a given context or situation changes one's preferences. Of course, different situations may change a player's expectation about another player's envy or guilt parameters, and we could thus explain why a player may change her behavior depending upon how the situation is framed. In the case of Fehr and Schmidt's utility function, however, experimental evidence that we shall discuss later implies that a player's *own* $\beta$ (or $\alpha$) changes value in different situations. Yet nothing in their theory explains why one would feel consistently more or less guilty (or envious) depending on the decision context.

## *2.2 A conditional preference for following norms: the Bicchieri model*

The norm-based utility function introduced by Bicchieri [2006] tries to capture the idea that, when a social norm exists, individuals will show different 'sensitivities' to it, and this should be reflected in their utility functions. Consider a typical n-person (normal-form) game. For the sake of formal treatment, we represent a norm as a (partial) function that maps what the player expects other players to do into what the player "ought" to do. In other words, a norm regulates behavior conditional on other people's (expected) behaviors. Denote the strategy set of player $i$ by $S_i$, and let $\boldsymbol{S}_{-i} = \prod_{j \neq i} S_j$ be the set of strategy profiles of players other than $i$. Then a norm for player $i$ is formally represented by a function $N_i$: $L_{-i} \rightarrow S_i$, where $L_{-i} \subseteq \boldsymbol{S}_{-i}$. Two points are worth noting. First, given the other players' strategies, there may or may not be a norm that prescribes how player $i$ ought to behave. So $L_{-i}$ need not be — and usually is not — equal to $\boldsymbol{S}_{-i}$. In particular, $L_{-i}$ could be empty in the situation where there is no norm whatsoever to regulate player $i$'s behavior. Second, there could be norms that regulate joint behaviors. A norm, for example, that regulates the joint behaviors of players $i$ and $j$ may be represented by $N_{i,j}$: $L_{-i,-j} \rightarrow S_i \times S_j$. Since we are concerned with a two-person game here, we will not further complicate the model in that direction.

A strategy profile $s = (s_1, \ldots, s_n)$ *instantiates* a norm for $j$ if $s_{-j} \in L_{-j}$, that is, if $N_j$ is defined at $s_{-j}$. It *violates* a norm if for some $j$, it instantiates a norm for $j$ but $s_j \neq N_j\ (s_{-j})$. Let $\pi_i$ be the payoff function for player $i$. The norm-based utility function of player $i$ depends on the strategy profile $s$, and is given by

$$U_i(s) = \pi_i(s) - k_i \max_{s_{-j} \in L_{-j}} \max_{m \neq j} \{\pi_m(s_{-j}, N_j(s_{-j})) - \pi_m(s), 0\}$$

$k_i \geq 0$ is a constant representing i's sensitivity to the relevant norm. Such sensitivity may vary with different norms; for example, a person may be very sensitive to equality and much less so to equity considerations. The first maximum operator takes care of the possibility that the norm instantiation (and violation) might be ambiguous in the sense that a strategy profile instantiates a norm for several players simultaneously. We conjecture, however, that this situation is rare, and under most situations the first maximum operator degenerates. The second maximum operator ranges over all the players other than the norm violator. In plain words, the discounting term (multiplied by $k_i$) is the maximum payoff deduction resulting from all norm violations.

In the Ultimatum game, the norm we shall consider is the norm that prescribes a fair amount the proposer ought to offer. To represent it we take the norm functions to be the following: the norm function for the proposer, $N_1$, is a constant $N$ function, and the norm function for the responder, $N_2$, is nowhere defined.[5] If the responder (player 2) rejects, the utilities of both players are zero.[6]

$$U_{1reject}(x) = U_{2reject}(x) = 0$$

Given that the proposer (player 1) offers $x$ and the responder accepts, the utilities are the following:

$$U_{1accept}(x) = M - x - k_1 \max(N - x, 0)$$
$$U_{2accept}(x) = x - k_2 \max(N - x, 0)$$

where $N$ denotes the fair offer prescribes by the norm, and $k_i$ is non-negative. Note, again, that $k_1$ measures how much the proposer dislikes to deviate from what he takes to be the norm. To obey a norm, 'sensitivity' to the norm need not be high. Fear of retaliation may make a proposer with a low $k$ behave according to what fairness dictates but, absent such risk, her disregard for the norm will lead her to be unfair.

Again, the responder should accept the offer if $U_{2accept}(x) > U_{2reject} = 0$, which implies the following *threshold for acceptance*: $\boldsymbol{x > k_2 N/(1+k_2)}$. Obviously the threshold is less than $N$: an offer more than what the norm prescribes is not necessary for the sake of acceptance.

For the proposer, the utility function is decreasing in $x$ when $x \geq N$, hence a rational proposer will not offer more than $N$. Suppose $x \leq N$. If $k_1 > 1$, the utility function is increasing in x, which means that the best choice for the proposer is to offer $N$. If $k_1 < 1$, the utility function is decreasing in $x$, which implies that the best strategy for the proposer is to offer the least amount that would result in acceptance, i.e. (a little bit more than) the threshold $k_2N/(1+k_2)$. If $k_1 = 1$, it does not matter how much the Proposer offers provided the offer is between $k_2N/(1+k_2)$ and $N$.

It should be clear at this point that $k_1$ plays a very similar role as that of $\beta_1$ in the Fehr-Schmidt model. In fact, if we take $N$ to be $M/2$ and $k_1$ to be $2\beta_1$, the two models agree on what the proposer's utility is. Similarly, $k_2$ in this model is analogous to $\alpha_2$ in the Fehr-Schmidt model. There is, however, an important difference between these formally analogous parameters. The $\alpha$'s and $\beta$'s in the Fehr-Schmidt model measure people's degree of aversion towards inequality, which is a very different disposition than the one measured by the $k$'s, i.e. people's sensitivity to various norms. The latter will usually be a stable disposition, and behavioral changes may thus be caused by changes in focus or in expectations. A theory of norms can explain such changes, whereas a theory of inequity aversion does not. We will come back to this point later.

[5]Intuitively, $N_2$ may be defined to proscribe rejection of fair (or hyper-fair) offers. The incorporation of this consideration, however, will not make a difference in the formal analysis.

[6]We assume there is no norm requiring that a responder 'ought to' reject an unfair offer.

It is also the case that the proposer's belief about the responder's type figures in her decision when $k_1 < 1$. The belief may be represented by a probability distribution over $k_2$. The proposer should choose an offer that maximizes the expected utility

$$EU(x) = P(k_2N/(1+k_2) < x) \times (M - x - k_1(N - x)).$$

As will become clear, an advantage this model has over the Fehr-Schmidt model is that it can explain some variants of BUG more naturally. However, it shares a problem with the Fehr-Schmidt model in that they both entail that if the proposer offers a close-to-fair but not exactly fair amount, the only thing that prevented her from being too mean is the fear of rejection. This prediction, however, could be easily refuted by a parallel dictator game where rejection is not an option.

## *2.3 Reciprocity and fairness equilibrium: the Rabin model*

The Fehr-Schmidt model does not consider reciprocity, a common phenomenon in human interaction, as we tend to be nice toward those who treated us well, and retaliate against those who slighted us. Matthew Rabin [1993] explicitly modeled reciprocity in the framework of psychological games [Geanakoplos *et al.*, 1989], introducing the important solution concept of *fairness equilibrium.*

The Rabin utility model is defined in a two-person game of complete information. The key idea is that a player's utility is not determined solely by the actions taken, but also depends on the player's beliefs (including second-order beliefs about first-order beliefs). Specifically, player $i$ will evaluate her "kindness" to the other player, $f_i$, by the following scheme:

$$f_i(a_i, b_j) = \begin{cases} \frac{\pi_j(b_j, a_i) - \pi_j^c(b_j)}{\pi_j^h(b_j) - \pi_j^{\min}(b_j)} & \text{if } \pi_j^h(b_j) - \pi_j^{\min}(b_j) \neq 0 \\ 0 & \text{otherwise} \end{cases}, \quad i = 1, 2; j = 3 - i$$

where $a_i$ is the strategy chosen by player $i$, and $b_j$ is the strategy that player $i$ *believes* is chosen by player $j$. $\pi_j$ is $j$'s material payoff function that depends on both players' strategies. $\pi_j^h(b_j)$ is the highest material payoff and $\pi_j^{min}(b_j)$ the lowest payoff that player $j$ can potentially get by playing $b_j$. In other words they denote, respectively, the highest and lowest payoffs player $i$ can grant player $j$ given that the latter is playing $b_j$. A key term here is $\pi_j^c(b_j)$, which is intended to represent the equitable material payoff player $j$ deserves by playing $b_j$, and is defined by Rabin as:

$$\pi_j^c(b_j) = \frac{\pi_j^h(b_j) + \pi_j^l(b_j)}{2}$$

where $\pi_j^l(b_j)$ is the worst payoff player $j$ may incur given that player $i$ does not play Pareto inefficient strategies. By definition, $\pi_j^l(b_j) \geq \pi_j^{min}(b_j)$.

Similarly, player $i$ can *estimate* player $j$'s kindness towards her, denoted by $\tilde{f}_j$:

$$\tilde{f}_j(b_j, c_i) = \begin{cases} \frac{\pi_i(c_i, b_j) - \pi_i^c(c_i)}{\pi_i^h(c_i) - \pi_i^{\min}(c_i)} & \text{if } \pi_i^h(c_i) - \pi_i^{\min}(c_i) \neq 0 \\ 0 & \text{otherwise} \end{cases}$$

where $c_i$ is the object of a second-order belief — the strategy that player $i$ believes player $j$ believes to be chosen by $i$. The meaning of other terms should be obvious given the previous explanation. Finally, the utility function of player $i$ is given by:

$$U_i(a_i, b_j, c_i) = \pi_i(a_i, b_j) + \tilde{f}_j(b_j, c_i) + \tilde{f}_j(b_j, c_i) f_i(a_i, b_j).$$

Care of reciprocity is reflected in the interaction term. Intuitively, it gives a player positive utility to be kind to (what she believes to be) kind players and tough to (what she believes to be) tough ones. An equilibrium of the game, called a *fairness equilibrium*, occurs when every belief turns out to be true, and each player's strategy maximizes her utility, relative to the other player's strategy and both players' beliefs.

In order to apply the Rabin model to the BUG, we formulate the game in the following simultaneous fashion: player 1 (the proposer) chooses an amount as her offer and player 2 (the responder) chooses an amount as his threshold for acceptance. If the offer is lower than the threshold both get nothing, otherwise the money is divided accordingly. This way of looking at the game assumes that the responder does not adopt non-monotonic strategies in which some of the offers he would accept are lower than some of the offers he would reject. It also corresponds to the game of monopoly pricing that Rabin himself analyzed in his paper.

By definition, we have at equilibrium $a_1 = b_1 = c_1$ and $a_2 = b_2 = c_2$, because all beliefs are true. Suppose $a_1 = b_1 = c_1 = x$ and $a_2 = b_2 = c_2 = y$. That is, the proposer offers $x$, believes that the responder's threshold is $y$, and believes that the responder believes she offers $x$; the responder sets the threshold at $y$, believes that the proposer offers $x$, and believes that the proposer believes that the threshold is $y$. For what values of $x$ and $y$ is this a fairness equilibrium?

Let's check. It is an equilibrium just in case $a_1 = x$ maximizes $U_1(a_1, b_2 = y, c_1 = x)$, and $a_2 = y$ maximizes $U_2(a_2, b_1 = x, c_2 = y)$. Consider $U_1(a_1, b_2 = y, c_1 = x)$ first. Given that $b_2 = y$, offers less than $y$ are Pareto inefficient options for player 1, because no player would be worse off and at least one player would be better off if player 1 chose an amount equal to or higher than $y$. It follows that $\pi_2^l(b_2) = y$ and $\pi_2^h(b_2) = M$. Hence

$$\pi_2^c(b_2) = \frac{\pi_2^h(b_2) + \pi_2^l(b_2)}{2} = \frac{y + M}{2}$$

On the other hand, because all the Pareto efficient strategies given $c_1$ result in (M-$x$, $x$) as the payoff, $\pi_1^c(c_1) =$ M-$x$. Hence

$$f_1(a_1, b_2) = \frac{\pi_2(b_2, a_1) - \pi_2^c(b_2)}{\pi_2^h(b_2) - \pi_2^{min}(b_2)} = \begin{cases} -\frac{y+m}{2M} & \text{if } a_1 < y \\ \frac{2a_1 - (y+M)}{2M} & \text{if } a_1 \geq y \end{cases}$$

$$\tilde{f}_2(b_2, c_1) = \frac{\pi_1(c_1, b_2) - \pi_1^c(c_1)}{\pi_1^h(c_1) - \pi_1^{min}(c_1)} = \begin{cases} -1 & \text{if } x < y \\ 0 & \text{if } x \geq y \end{cases}$$

From $\tilde{f}$ we see that the proposer never feels she is being treated "kindly".[7] The utility function of player 1, as a function of $a_1$, is given by the following:

$$U_1(a_1, y, x) = \begin{cases} \frac{y-M}{2M} & \text{if } a_1 < y, x < y \\ 0 & \text{if } a_1 < y, x \geq y \\ M - a_1 - \frac{2a_1+M-y}{2M} & \text{if } a_1 \geq y, x < y \\ M - a_1 & \text{if } a_1 \geq y, x \geq y \end{cases}$$

It is not hard to see that when $x < y, U_1(x, y, x) < U_1(y, y, x)$ just in case $M - y - y/M \geq 0$. The latter holds unless $y \geq M^2/(M+1)$, that is, $y \approx M$. Hence, unless the threshold is (almost) as high as the full amount, $a_1 = x$ does not maximize $U_1(a_1, b_2 = y, c_1 = x)$ if $x < y$, which means that $(x, y)$ is not a fairness equilibrium.

On the other hand, when $x \geq y, U_1(a_1, b_2 = y, c_1 = x)$ is maximized at $a_1 = y$, and it is the unique maximum except when $y = M$. So, unless $y = M$, a necessary condition for $(x, y)$ to be an equilibrium is that $x = y$.

Let's now turn to player 2, the responder. The kindness functions are:

$$f_2(a_2, b_1) = \begin{cases} -1 & \text{if } x < a_2 \\ 0 & \text{if } x \geq a_2 \end{cases}$$

$$\tilde{f}_1(b_1, c_2) = \begin{cases} -\frac{y+M}{2M} & \text{if } x < y \\ \frac{2x-(y+M)}{2M} & \text{if } x \geq y \end{cases}$$

Based on this we can calculate player 2's utility, as a function of $a_2$:

$$U_2(a_2, x, y) = \begin{cases} 0 & \text{if } x < a_2 \\ x - \frac{y+M}{2M} & \text{if } x \geq a_2, x < y \\ x + \frac{2x-(y+M)}{2M} & \text{if } x \geq a_2, x \geq y \end{cases}$$

As derived earlier, assuming $y < M$, it is necessary to have $x = y$ for $(a_1 = x, a_2 = y)$ to be an equilibrium. When $x = y$, we see that $U_2(a_2, b_1 = x, c_2 = y)$ is maximized at $a_2 = y$ just in case $x + (x - M)/(2M) \geq 0$, i.e., just in case $x \geq M/(2M+1)$. Therefore, for any $d \geq M/(2M+1)$, the following constitutes a fairness equilibrium: $a_1 = b_1 = c_1 = a_2 = b_2 = c_2 = d$.[8] If we take the unit to be one dollar, practically every offer is supported in some fairness equilibrium.

[7] This does not seem very plausible in the context of Ultimatum games, though it sounds all right when the game is phrased as monopoly pricing, as in Rabin's analysis. However, we will see later that using a kindness function that avoids this consequence does not affect the equilibria.

[8] The condition $d \geq M/(2M+1)$ is equivalent to Rabin's result about the highest price supported by fairness equilibrium in the context of monopoly pricing. The inequality $M/(2M+1) > 0$ corresponds to the fact that the highest price in Rabin's result is less than the consumer's valuation of the product, whereas the latter is the conventional monopoly price. Rabin regards this feature of the result a success of his model.

Of course, at all such equilibria the offer is accepted. When $y = M$ and $x < y$, we see that $U_2(a_2, b_1 = x, c_2 = y)$ is maximized at $a_2 = y = M$ just in case $x \leq 1$. So there is no equilibrium at which the proposer offers more than 1 unit, but the responder rejects.

To summarize, there is a fairness equilibrium for practically any amount the proposer can offer at which the responder accepts the offer, and there is no equilibrium where an offer more than one unit is rejected. The first implication is undesirable for predictive purposes, and the second is problematic in view of the empirical data. One might suspect that these implications are due to the fact that Rabin's definition of kindness is not suitable for the Ultimatum game. In particular, according to his definition, there are no "kind" responders from the proposer's perspective.

There is a natural variant to Rabin's definition of kindness that can avoid this counterintuitive consequence. Recall that all Pareto inefficient strategies are excluded in calculating the benchmark equitable material payoff $\pi_j^c(b_j)$. For extensive form games, however, one can naturally weaken the definition of Pareto efficiency: a strategy is Pareto efficient if it is not Pareto dominated in some subgames. Under this definition, given $b_2 = y$, offers lower than $y$ are still Pareto efficient because they are Pareto efficient in some subgames (though they are not Pareto efficient along the equilibrium path), so $\pi_2^l(b_2) = \pi_2^{min}(b_2) = 0$. Hence $\pi_2^c(b_2) = M/2$. This subtle change affects the kindness functions. Suppose again $a_1 = b_1 = c_1 = x$ and $a_2 = b_2 = c_2 = y$. Now the kindness functions for player 1— as functions of $a_1$ — are the following:[9]

$$f_1(a_1, b_2) = \frac{\pi_2(b_2,a_1)-\pi_2^c(b_2)}{\pi_2^h(b_2)-\pi_2^{\min}(b_2)} = \begin{cases} -\frac{1}{2} & \text{if } a_1 < y \\ \frac{2a_1-M}{2M} & \text{if } a_1 \geq y \end{cases}$$

$$\tilde{f}_2(b_2, c_1) = \frac{\pi_1(c_1,b_2)-\pi_1^c(c_0)}{\pi_1^h(c_1)-\pi_1^{\min}(c_1)} = \begin{cases} -\frac{1}{2} & \text{if } x < y \\ \frac{1}{2} & \text{if } x \geq y \end{cases}$$

(It is still the case that $\pi_1^c(c_1) = M - x$, even under the weaker condition for Pareto efficiency.) Observe that here $\tilde{f}_2$ avoids the counterintuitive consequence that the proposer never feels being "kindly" treated by the responder. The proposer's utility based on these kindness functions is given by:

$$U_1 a_1, y, x) = \begin{cases} -\frac{1}{4} & \text{if } a_1 < y, x < y \\ \frac{1}{4} & \text{if } a_1 < y, x \geq y \\ M - a_1 - \frac{M+2a_1}{4M} & \text{if } a_1 \geq y, x < y \\ M - a_1 + \frac{M+2a_1}{4M} & \text{if } a_1 \geq y, x \geq y \end{cases}$$

The implication of this utility function, however, is not different from our previous analysis. Again, if $x < y$, the utility cannot be maximized at $a_1 = x$ unless $y \approx M$. On the other hand, when $x \geq y$, the utility is maximized at $a_1 = x$ just in case

[9] Note that the kindness functions and the subsequent utility functions are still calculated according to Rabin's scheme but are based on the new idea of Pareto efficiency of strategies.

$x = y$. One can similarly recalculate the responder's utility function, and derive the same implications — that practically every offer is supported in some fairness equilibrium, and that there are no interesting equilibria in which the responder rejects an offer of more than one unit.

Therefore, the seemingly counterintuitive consequence of Rabin's kindness function is not responsible for the implications of Rabin's model. In our view, the problem lies in the fact that in Rabin's utility function, the relative importance of reciprocity/fairness versus material payoff is not well calibrated. The easiest way to fix this is to add a calibration parameter in the utility function, as used in many other utility models including the Fehr-Schmidt model and the Bicchieri model.

$$U_i(a_i, b_j, c_i) = \pi_i(a_i, b_j) + \alpha_i[\tilde{f}_j(b_j, c_i) + \tilde{f}_j(b_j, c_i)f_i(a_i, b_j)]$$

where $\alpha_i$ measures the player's attitude towards the tradeoff between reciprocity/fairness and the material payoff. Using this utility function, we can run the same analysis as before, and derive the following:

1. $a_1 = b_1 = c_1 = a_2 = b_2 = c_2 = d$ constitutes a fairness equilibrium just in case $d \geq \alpha_2 M/(2M + \alpha_2)$.
2. If $\alpha_2 < M^2/(M + \alpha_1)$, then for every $x \leq \alpha_2$ and $y \geq M^2/(M + \alpha_1)$, the following constitutes a fairness equilibrium: $a_1 = b_1 = c_1 = x, a_2 = b_2 = c_2 = y$.

From (1), we see that given a high enough $\alpha_2$, many offers are not supported in any equilibrium in which the responder accepts the offer. In other words, if the responder cares enough about fairness, then the proposer's offer has to pass a significant threshold in order to reach an equilibrium at which the responder accepts. On the flip side, we see from (2) that there may be interesting equilibria in which the responder rejects a decent offer (more than one unit), depending on the type of the players.

## 3 VARIANTS TO BUG

So far we have only considered the basic Ultimatum game, which is certainly not the whole story. There have been a number of interesting variants of the game in the literature, to some of which we now apply the models to see if they can tell reasonable stories about the data.

### 3.1 *Ultimatum Game with Asymmetric Information and Payoffs*

Kagel *et al.* [1996] designed an Ultimatum game in which the proposer is given a certain amount of chips. The chips are worth either more or less to the proposer than they are to the responder. Each player knows how much a chip is worth to her, but may or may not know that the chip is worth differently to the other. The particularly interesting setting is where the chips have higher (three times more) values for the proposer, and only the proposer knows it. It turns out that in this case the offer is (very close to) half of the chips and the rejection rate is low. A popular reading of this result is that people merely prefer to *appear* fair, as a really fair person is supposed to offer about 75% of the chips.

To analyze this variant formally, we only need a small modification of our original setting. That is, if the responder accepts an offer of $x$, the proposer actually gets $3(M-x)$ though, to the responder's knowledge, she only gets $M-x$. In the Fehr-Schmidt model, the utility function of player 1 (the proposer), given the offer is accepted, is now the following:

$$U_{1accept}(x) = \begin{cases} (3+3\alpha_1)M - (3+4\alpha_1)x & \text{if } x \geq 3M/4 \\ (3-3\beta_1)M - (3-4\beta_1)x & \text{if } x < 3M/4 \end{cases}$$

The utility function of the responder upon acceptance does not change, as to the best of his knowledge, the situation is the same as in the simple Ultimatum game. Also, if the responder rejects the offer, both utilities are again zero. It follows that the responder's threshold for acceptance remains the same: he accepts the offer if $x > \alpha_2 M/(1+2\alpha_2)$. For the proposer, if $\beta_1 > 3/4$, the best offer for her is $3M/4$, otherwise the best offer for her is the minimum amount above the threshold. An interesting implication is that even if someone offers $M/2$ in the BUG, which indicates that $\beta_1 > 1/2$, she may not offer $3M/4$ in this new condition. This prediction is consistent with the observation that almost no one offers 75% of the chips in the real game.

At this point, it seems the Fehr-Schmidt model does not entail a difference in behavior in this new game. But proposers in general do offer more in this new setting than they do in the BUG, which naturally leads to the lower rejection rate. Can the Fehr-Schmidt model explain this? One obvious way is to adjust $\alpha_2$ so that the predicted threshold increases. But there seems to be no reason in this case for the responder to change his attitude towards inequality. Another explanation might be that under this new setting, the proposer believes that the responder's distaste for inequality increases, for after all it is the proposer's belief about $\alpha_2$ that affects the offer. This move sounds as questionable as the last one, but it does point to a reasonable explanation. Suppose the proposer is uncertain about what kind of responder she is facing, and her belief about $\alpha_2$ is represented by a non-degenerate probability distribution. She should then choose an offer that maximizes the expected utility, which in this case is given by the following:

$$EU(x) = P(\alpha_2 < x/(M-2x)) \times ((3-3\beta_1)M - (3-4\beta_1)x)$$

This expected utility is slightly different from the one derived in the BUG in that it involves a bigger stake. As a result, it is likely to be maximized at a bigger $x$ unless the distribution over $\alpha_2$ is sufficiently odd. Thus the Fehr-Schmidt model can explain the phenomenon in a reasonable way.

If we apply the Bicchieri model to this new setting, again the utility function of player 2 (the responder) does not change. The utility function of player 1 (the proposer) given acceptance is changed to

$$U_{1accept}(x) = 3(M - x) - k_1 \max(N' - x, 0)$$

We use $N'$ here to indicate that the proposer's perception of the fair amount, or her interpretation of the norm, may have changed due to his awareness of the asymmetry. The model behaves pretty much in the same way as the Fehr-Schmidt one does. Specifically, the responder's threshold for acceptance is $k_2N'/(1 + k_2)$. The proposer will/should offer $N'$ only if $k_1 > 3$, so people who offer the "fair" amount in the BUG ($k_1 > 1$) may not offer the "fair" amount under the new setting. That means even if $N' = 3M/4$, the observation that few people offer that amount does not contradict the norm-based model. The best offer for most people ($k_3 < 3$) is the least amount that would be accepted. However, since the proposer is not sure about the responder's type, she will choose an offer to maximize her expected utility, and this in general leads to an increase of the offer given an increase of the stake. Although it is not particularly relevant to the analysis in this case, it is worth noting that $N'$ is probably less than $3M/4$ in the situation as thus framed. This point will become crucial in the games with obvious framing effects.

The Rabin model, as it stands, faces many difficulties. The primary trouble still centers on the kindness function. It is not hard to see that according to Rabin's definition of kindness, the function that measures the proposer's kindness to the responder does not change at all, while the function that measures the responder's kindness toward the proposer does change.[10] This does not sound plausible. Intuitively, other things being equal, the only thing that may change is the proposer's measure of her kindness to the responder. There is no reason to think that the responder's estimation of the other player's kindness toward him will change, as the responder does not have the relevant information. Strictly speaking, Rabin's original model cannot be applied to the situation where asymmetric information is present, because his framework assumes the payoffs are common knowledge. It is of course possible to adapt that framework to the new situation, but we will omit the formal details here.

It is, however, worth noting that if the kindness functions remain the same (as it is the case under our definition of kindness), the arguments available to Rabin to address the new situation are very similar to the ones available to the previous models. One move is to manipulate the $\alpha$'s, which is unreasonable as we already pointed out. Another move is to represent beliefs with more general probability distributions (than a point mass distribution), and to look for Bayesian equilibria. The latter strategy will inevitably further complicate the already complicated model, but it does seem to match the reality better.

[10]By our definition of kindness, both functions remain the same as in the simple setting.

## *3.2 Ultimatum Game with Different Alternatives*

There is also a very simple twist to the Ultimatum game, which turns out to be quite interesting. Fehr *et al.* [2000] introduced a simple Ultimatum game where the proposer has only two choices: either offer 2 (and keep 8) or make an alternative offer that varies across treatments in a way that allows the experimenter to test the effects of reciprocity and inequity aversion on rejection rates. The alternative offers in four treatments are (5,5), (8,2), (2,8) and (10,0). When the (8,2) offer is compared to the (5,5) alternative, the rejection rate is 44.4%, and it is much higher than the rejection rates in each of the three alternative treatments. In fact, it turns out that the rejection rate depends a lot on what the alternative is. The rejection rate decreases to 27% if the alternative is (2,8), and further decreases to 9% if the alternative is (10,0).[11]

Is it hard for the Fehr-Schmidt model to explain this result? In their consequentialist model there does not seem to be any role for the available alternatives to play. As the foregoing analysis shows, the best reply for the responder is acceptance if $x > \alpha_2 M/(1+2\alpha_2)$. That is, different alternatives can affect the rejection rate only through their effects on $\alpha_2$. It is not entirely implausible to say that "what could have been otherwise" affects one's attitude towards inequality. After all, one's dispositions are shaped by all kinds of environmental or situational factors, to which the 'path not taken' seem to belong. Still it sounds quite odd that one's sensitivity to fairness changes as alternatives vary.

The norm-based model, by contrast, seems better equipped to explain the data. For one thing, the model could explain the data by showing how different alternatives point the responder to different norms (or no norm at all). In particular, the way a situation is framed affects our expectations about others' behavior and what they expect from us (Bicchieri 2006). For example, when the alternative for the proposer is to offer (5,5), players are naturally focused on an equal split. The proposer who could have chosen (5,5) but did not is sending a clear message about her disregard for fairness. If the expectation of a fair share is violated, the responder can be expected to resent it, and act to punish the mean proposer. In this case, a fairness norm applies, and indeed we observe 70% of proposers to choose (5,5) over (8,2). In the (8,2) vs. (2,8) case, 70% of proposers choose (8,2), since there is no norm (at least in our culture) saying that one has to sacrifice oneself for the sake of a stranger. When the choice is between (10,0) and (8,2), 100% of proposers choose (8,2), the least damaging (for the responder) outcome, and also what responders are believed to reasonably expect. Thus a natural explanation given by the Bicchieri model is that $N$ changes (or even undefined) as the alternative varies.

A recent experiment in a similar spirit done by Dana, Weber and Kuang (2007) brings more light to this point. The basic setting is a Dictator game where the allocator has only two options. The game is played in two different situations. Under the "Known Condition" (KC), the payoffs are unambiguous, and the allo-

[11] Each player played four games, presented in random order, in the same role.

cator has to choose between (6, 1) and (5, 5), where the first number in the pair is the payoff for the allocator, and the second number is the other player's payoff. Under the "Unrevealed Condition" (UC), the allocator has to choose between (6, ?) and (5, ?), where the receiver's payoff is 1 with probability 0.5 and 5 with probability 0.5. Before the allocator makes a choice, however, she can choose to find out privately and at no cost what the receiver's payoff in fact is. It turns out that 74% of the subjects choose (5, 5) in KC, and 56% choose (6, ?) without revealing the actual payoff matrix in UC.

This result, as Dana *et al.* point out, stands strongly against the Fehr-Schmidt model. If we take the revealed preference as the actual preference, choosing (5, 5) in KC implies that $\beta_1 > 0.2$, while choosing (6, ?) without revealing in the UC condition implies that $\beta_1 < 0.2$. Hence, unless a reasonable story could be told about $\beta_1$, the model does not fit the data.[12] If a stable preference for fair outcomes is inconsistent with the above results, can a conditional preference for following a norm show greater consistency? Note that, if we were to assume that $N$ is fixed in both conditions, a similar change of $k$ would be required in the Bicchieri model in order to explain the data.[13]

However, the norm-based model can offer a more natural explanation of the data through an interpretation of $N$. In KC, subjects have only two, very clear choices. There is a 'fair' outcome (5,5) and there is an inequitable one (6,1). Choosing (6,1) entails a net loss for the receiver, and only a marginal gain for the allocator. Note that the choice framework *focuses* subjects on fairness though the usual Dictator game has no such obvious focus. Dana *et al.*'s example evokes a related situation (one that we frequently encounter) in which we may choose to give to the poor or otherwise disadvantaged: What is \$1 more to the allocator is \$4 more to the receiver, mimicking the multiplier effect that money has for a poor person. In this experiment, what is probably activated is a norm of beneficence, and subjects uniformly respond by choosing (5,5). Indeed, when receivers in Dana *et al.*'s experiment were asked what *they* would choose in the allocator's role, they unanimously chose the (5,5) split as the most appropriate.

A natural question to ask is whether we should hold the norm fixed, thus assuming a variation in people's sensitivity to the norm ($k$), or if instead what is changing here is the perception of the norm itself. We want to argue that what changes from the first to the second experiment is the perception that a norm exists and applies to the present situation, as well as expectations about other people's behavior and what their expectations about one's own behavior might be [Bicchieri, 2006]. In Bicchieri's definition of what it takes for a norm to be

[12] In KC, choosing option B implies that $U_1$ (5,5) > $U_1$ (6,1), or 5-$\alpha_1$ (0) > 6-$\beta_1$ (5). Hence, 5 > 6-5-$\beta_1$ and therefore $\beta_1 > 0.2$. In UC, not revealing and choosing option A implies that $U_1$ (6, (.5(5), .5(1))) > $U_1$ (.5(5,5), .5(6,5)), since revealing will lead to one of the two 'nice' choices with equal probability. We thus get 6 -.3($\beta_1$) > 2.5 + .5(6-$\beta_1$), which implies that $\beta_1 < 0.2$.

[13] According to the Bicchieri model, if we keep $N$ constant at 5, choosing option B in KC means that $U_1(5,5) > U_1(6,1)$. It follows that $5 > 6 - 4k_1$, i.e., that $k_1 > 0.25$. In UC, not revealing and choosing option A implies that $U_1(6,(.5(5),.5(1))) > U_1(.5(5,5),.5(6,5))$. It follows that $6 - 2k_1 > 5.5$, i.e., that $k_1 < 0.25$.

followed, a necessary condition is that a sufficient number of people expect others to follow it in the appropriate situations *and* believe they are expected to follow it by a sufficient number of other individuals. People will *prefer* to follow an existing norm *conditionally* upon entertaining such expectations. In KC, the situation is transparent, and so are the subjects' expectations. If a subject expects others to choose (5,5) and believes she is expected so to choose, she might prefer to follow the norm (provided her $k$, which measures her sensitivity to the norm, is large enough). In UC, on the contrary, there is uncertainty as to what the receiver might be getting. To pursue the analogy with charitable giving further, in UC there is uncertainty about the multiplier ("am I giving to a needy person or not?") and thus there is the opportunity for *norm evasion*: the player can avoid activating the norm by not discovering the actual payoff matrix. Though there is no cost to see the payoff matrix, people will opt to not see it in order to avoid having to adhere to a norm that could potentially be disadvantageous. So a person who chooses (5, 5) under KC may choose (6,?) under UC with the same degree of concern for norms. Choosing to reveal looks like what moral theorists call a *supererogatory* action. We are not morally obliged to perform such actions, but it is awfully nice if we do.

A very different situation would be one in which the allocator has a clear choice between (6,1) and (5,5), but she is told that the prospective receiver *does not even know* he is playing the game. In other words, the binary choice would focus the allocator, as in the KC condition, on a norm of beneficence, but she would also be cued about the absence of a crucial expectation. If the receiver does not expect the proposer to give anything, is there any reason to follow the norm? This is a good example of what has been extensively discussed in Bicchieri [2000; 2006]. A norm exists, the subject knows it and knows she is in a situation in which the norm applies, but her preference for following the norm is conditional on having certain empirical and normative expectations. In our example, the normative expectations are missing, because the receiver does not know that a Dictator game is being played, and his part in it. In this case, we would predict that a large majority of allocators will choose (6,1) with a clear conscience. This prediction is different from what a 'fairness preference' model would predict, but it is also at odds with theories of social norms as 'constraints' on action. One such theory is Rabin's [1995] model of moral constraints. Very briefly, Rabin assumes that agents maximize egoistic expected utility subject to constraints: Thus our allocator will seek to maximize her payoffs but experience disutility if her action is in violation of a social norm. However, if the probability of harming another is sufficiently low, a player may 'circumvent' the norm and act more selfishly. Because in Rabin's model the norm functions simply as a constraint, beliefs about others' expectations play no role in a player's decision to act. As the (6,1) choice does in fact 'harm' the recipient, Rabin's model should predict that the number of subject who choose (6,1) is the same as in the KC of Dana *et al.*'s experiment. In the Bicchieri model, however, the choices in the second experiment will be significantly different from the choices we have observed in Dana *et al.*'s KC condition.

### *3.3 Ultimatum Game with Framing*

Framing effects, a topic of continuing interest to psychologists and social scientists, have also been investigated in the context of Ultimatum games. Hoffman *et al.* [1985], for instance, designed an Ultimatum game in which groups of twelve participants were ranked on a scale 1-12 either randomly or by superior performance in answering questions about current events. The top six were assigned to the role of "seller" and the rest to the role of "buyer". They also ran studies with the standard Ultimatum game instructions, both with random assignments and assignment to the role of Proposer by contest. The exchange and contest manipulations elicited significantly lowered offers, but rejection rates were unchanged as compared to the standard Ultimatum game.[14]

Since, from a formal point of view, the situation is not different from that of the BUG, the previous analysis remains the same. Hence, within the Fehr-Schmidt model, one would have to argue that $\alpha_2$ is decreased by the game framing. In other words, the role of a "buyer" or the knowledge that the proposer was a superior performer dampens the responder's concern for fairness. This change does not sound intuitive, and demands some explanation. In addition, the proposer has to actually *expect* this change in order to lower her offer. It is equally, if not more difficult, to see why the framing can lead to different beliefs the proposer has about the responder.

In the Bicchieri model, the parameter $N$ plays a vital role again. Although we need more studies about how and to what extent framing affects people's expectations and perception of what norm is being followed, it is intuitively clear that framing, like the examples mentioned above, will change the players' conception of what is fair. The 'exchange' framework is likely to elicit a market script where the seller is expected to try to get as much money as possible, whereas the entitlement context has the effect of focusing subjects away from equality in favor of an equity rule. In both cases, the perception of the situation has been changed, and with it the players' expectations. An individual sensitivity to fairness may be unchanged, but what has changed is the salient division norm.

## 4 CONCLUSION

We have discussed how different utility functions try, with more or less success, to explain experimental result that clearly show that individuals take into account other parties' utilities when making a choice. Material incentives are important, but they are just one of the items agents consider: the fairness of outcomes, the intentions of other parties, and the presence or absence of social norms are other important factors that play a role in decision-making. The three utility functions we have examined highlight different reasons why, in Ultimatum games, partici-

[14]Rejections remained low throughout, about 10%. All rejections were on offers of \$2 or \$3 in the exchange instructions, there was no rejection in the contest entitlement/divide \$10, and 5% rejection of the \$3 and \$4 offers in the random assignment/divide \$10.

pants tend to favor fair outcomes. However, the cross-situational inconsistencies that we observe in many variants of the Ultimatum game put to the test these different models. We believe a norm-based utility function can better explain the variance in behavior across experiments, but much more work needs to be done to design new experiments that directly test how much expectations (both normative and descriptive) matter, and when a norm is in fact present [Bicchieri and Chavez, 2010; Bicchieri and Xiao, 2009].

## BIBLIOGRAPHY

[Bicchieri, 2000] C. Bicchieri. Words and Deeds: a Focus Theory of Norms. In *Rationality, Rules and Structure*. J. Nida-Rumelin and W. Spohn, eds., pp. 153-184. Dordecht, Kluwer Academic Publishers, 2000.

[Bicchieri, 2006] C. Bicchieri. *The Grammar of Society: The nature and Dynamics of Social Norms*. Cambridge: Cambridge University Press, 2006.

[Bicchieri and Xiao, 2009] C. Bicchieri and E. Xiao. Do the right thing: but only if others do so. *Journal of Behavioral Decision Making* **22**: 191-208, 2009.

[Bicchieri and Chavez, 2010] C. Bicchieri and A. Chavez. Behaving as Expected: Public Information and Fairness Norms. *Journal of Behavioral Decision Making* **23**(2): 161-178, 2010.

[Camerer, 2003] C. Camerer. *Behavioral Game Theory: Experiments on Strategic Interaction*. Princeton, NJ, Princeton University Press, 2003.

[Dana *et al.*, 2007] J. Dana, R. Weber, and J. X. Kuang. Exploiting Moral Wriggle Room: experiments demonstrating an illusory preference for fairness. *Economic Theory* **33**(1): 67-80, 2007.

[Fehr *et al.*, 1998] E. Fehr, E. Kirchler, A. Weichbold, and S. Gächter. When Social Norms Overpower Competition - Gift Exchange in Labor Markets, *Journal of Labor Economics* **16**, 324-351, 1998.

[Fehr, 1999] E. Fehr and K. Schmidt. A Theory of Fairness, Competition, and Cooperation. *The Quarterly Journal of Economics* **114**(3): 817-868, 1999.

[Fehr *et al.*, 2003] E. Fehr, A. Falk and U. Fischbacher. Testing Theories of Fairness - Intentions Matter. *Institute for Empirical Research in Economics, University of Zürich, Working Paper No. 63*, 2003

[Geanakopolos *et al.*, 1989] J. Geanakoplos, D. Pearce, *et al.* Psychological games and sequential rationality. *Games and Economic Behavior* **1**: 60-79, 1989.

[Guth *et al.*, 1982] W. Guth, R. Schmittberger, *et al.* An experimental analysis of ultimatum games. *Journal of Economic Behavior and Organization 3*: 367-388, 1982.

[Hoffman and Spitzer, 1985] E. Hoffman and M. Spitzer. Entitlements, rights, and fairness: An experimental examination of subjects' concept of distributive justice. *Journal of Legal Studies* **2**: 259-297, 1985.

[Hoffman *et al.*, 1994] E. Hoffman, K. A. McCabe, *et al.* Preferences, Property Rights, and Anonymity in Bargaining Games. *Games and Economic Behavior* **7**: 346-380, 1994.

[Kagel *et al.*, 1996] J. H. Kagel, C. Kim, *et al.* Fairness in ultimatum games with asymmetric information and asymmetric payoffs. *Games and Economic Behavior* **3**: 100-110, 1996.

[Rabin, 1993] M. Rabin. Incorporating Fairness into Game Theory and Economics. *American Economic Review* **83**: 1281-1302, 1993.

[Rabin, 1995] M. Rabin. Moral Preferences, Moral Constraints, and Self-Serving Biases, *Berkeley Department of Economics Working Paper No. 95-241*, August 1995.

[Wicksteed, 1910] P. H. Wicksteed. *The Common Sense of Political Economy, Including a Studyof the Human Basis of Economic Law*. London: Macmillan and Co, 1910.

# EXPERIMENTATION IN ECONOMICS

Francesco Guala

## 1 INTRODUCTION

Experimental economics has been the protagonist of one of the most stunning methodological revolutions in the history of economics. In less than three decades economics has been transformed from a discipline where laboratory experimentation was considered impossible, useless, or at any rate largely irrelevant, into a science where some of the most exciting discoveries and developments are driven by experimental data. From a historical point of view, we still lack a detailed and comprehensive account of how this revolution took place.[1] The methodological literature, in contrast, is relatively rich — partly because the founders of experimental economics were driven by serious philosophical concerns about the state of their discipline, and partly because philosophers of science are becoming increasingly interested in this new approach.

Like many other scientific disciplines, experimental economics raises a number of interesting philosophical issues. Given the limits of space, it will be impossible to cover them all. I will rather focus on the topics and problems that have attracted most attention in the literature so far, reserving some space at the end for a survey of other relevant issues. The central philosophical problem of experimental economics concerns *the validity of experiments.* Following an established tradition in psychology, the issue of validity can be analysed in at least two sub-problems, *internal* and *external* validity. Internal validity is the problem of understanding the working of a causal relation or causal mechanism within a given experimental setting. External validity is the problem of generalising from a given experimental setting to some other situation of interest.

The two validity problems however are more or less tightly related to a number of other issues in the philosophy of science and the methodology of economics in particular. Before we come to the core of this chapter, then, we will have to cover briefly important topics such as the relation between theory and empirical evidence, the role of experimentation, the notion of causation, confirmation and theory testing, and so forth. In doing that, I shall try to bridge the gap between the fairly abstract way in which such problems are addressed in the philosophy of science literature, and the way they arise concretely from the practice of experimental economics.

[1]But there are some scattered pieces: Smith [1992], Roth [1995], Leonard [1994], Moscati [2007], Guala [2008a], Lee and Mirowski [2008].

Handbook of the Philosophy of Science. Volume 13: Philosophy of Economics.
Volume editor: Uskali Mäki. General editors: Dov M. Gabbay, Paul Thagard and John Woods.

### 1.1 *The concept of experiment*

What is an experiment? Despite its prominent role in scientific practice, until recently the notion of experiment was rather peripheral in the philosophy of science literature. Traditional epistemology tended to endorse a theory-centred view of scientific knowledge, according to which what we know is encapsulated in our (best) theories, and the latter are supported by the available empirical evidence. Under the influence of logical positivism philosophers of science in the 20th century have come to represent empirical evidence as sets of *linguistic reports* of perceptual experience. Indeed, in the 1960s and 1970s, prompted by the work of Popper, Quine, Kuhn, and Feyerabend, philosophers of science even came to doubt that a sharp distinction between theoretical and observational statements could be drawn in principle. As Karl Popper puts it in an often-quoted passage, "theory dominates the experimental work from its initial planning up to its finishing touches in the laboratory" [1934, p. 107].

During the 1980s a series of studies of experimental practice challenged the theory-dominated approach.[2] However, the new studies of experiment came up with a rather patchy view of experimentation; a new consensus seemed to coalesce around the view that what constitutes an experiment — and especially a *good* experiment — may well be a context-dependent matter that cannot be settled by a priori philosophical analysis. Different disciplines and different epochs have endorsed different standards of experimental practice, thus making it very difficult to come up with a unified normative philosophical account. If this is right, a philosophical analysis of the notion of economic experiment must emerge from the study of experimental practices in economics. This approach - as a useful heuristics, rather than as a philosophical thesis — will be adopted in this chapter. At this stage, then, it will only be possible to sketch a preliminary, and admittedly vague notion of experiment.

So what is, intuitively, an experiment? The key idea is *control*: experimenting involves *observing an event or set of events in controlled circumstances.* It is useful to distinguish at least two important dimensions of control: (1) control over a variable that is changed or manipulated by the experimenter, and (2) control over other (background) conditions or variables that are set by the experimenter. Both dimensions involve the idea of design or manipulation of the experimental conditions: the experimental laboratory is in some intuitive way an "artificial" situation compared to what is likely to happen in the "natural" or "real" world.[3]

An experiment is usually designed with the aim of getting a clear-cut answer to a fairly specific scientific question. As we shall see, many different kinds of questions can be answered in the laboratory. But typically, such questions regard the mutual

[2]Hacking [1983] is widely recognized as the precursor of this "new experimentalism". Useful surveys of the literature can be found in Franklin [1998] and Morrison [1998].

[3]These terms are misleading if taken literally — of course a laboratory situation is as real or natural as anything that happens spontaneously, because scientists are part of the natural real world. Keeping this in mind, however, I'll keep using these expressions for simplicity throughout the chapter.

dependence of some variables or quantities, and in particular the *causal relations* holding between them. Consider for example a classic medical experiment: here the main question is the effect of a certain drug ($X$) on a given population of patients suffering from the symptoms of a disease ($Y$). The experimenter divides a sample of patients in two groups and gives the drug to the patients in one group (the "treatment group"). The variable $X$ (drug) is thus directly controlled or manipulated by the experimenter, who then measures the difference in recovery rates between the patients in the two groups. In order for the comparison to be useful, however, the researcher must make sure that a number of other "background conditions" (for example the other drugs taken by these patients, their age, general health, psychological conditions, etc.) are kept under control — for if the two groups are too different in other respects, we will never know whether the changes are to be attributed to the manipulated variable (the drug) or not.

The experimental method is widely accepted in the medical sciences as well as in physics, chemistry, biology, and other advanced sciences. There are, to be sure, debates concerning the importance of specific experimental procedures, and also regarding the status of experimental *vis a vis* other kinds of data (is non-experimental evidence necessarily of an inferior quality than experimental evidence, for example?).[4] But very few respectable medical researchers, say, would dare questioning the usefulness of the experimental method *in general*. In contrast, many economists and philosophers find the idea of experimenting with social phenomena dubious, if not plainly ridiculous. This was once the received view in economics, and it took many years for experimental economists to convince their peers that their project was worth pursuing.

## *1.2 Traditional objections*

Economists have generally worried about the practical hurdles that make experimentation difficult or ineffective: experimentation in economics may well be possible *in principle*, in other words, but is usually unfeasible for unfortunate contingent reasons. John Stuart Mill presents this idea in full-fledged form already in the nineteenth century:

> There is a property common to all the moral sciences, and by which they are distinguished from many of the physical; that is, that it is seldom in our power to make experiments in them. In chemistry and natural philosophy [i.e. physics], we can not only observe what happens under all combinations of circumstances which nature brings together, but we may also try an indefinite number of new combinations. This we can seldom do in ethical, and scarcely ever in political science. We cannot try forms of government and systems of national policy on a diminutive scale in our laboratories, shaping our experiments as we

[4] Cf. Worrall [2002] for a discussion of so-called "evidence-based medicine".

> think they may most conduce to the advancement of knowledge. [Mill 1836, p. 124]

This view has been dominant until at least the 1980s: there is nothing intrinsic to economics that prevents us from applying the scientific methods of the natural sciences. The limitations are only of a practical kind, for the phenomena we are interested in are typically "macro", and unfortunately economists cannot experiment with firms, markets, or entire countries in the same way as a biologist can experiment with a cell or a population of fruit flies.

The obstacles to experimentation thus have mostly to do with *size* and *lack of access* (and as a consequence, lack of control). These two obstacles of course are not unrelated, lack of access being often derivative from the big size of the object of study. One key move against practical objections consisted therefore in showing that, contrary to the received opinion, economic phenomena *can* be studied on a small scale, and that it is possible to achieve control of the most important variables of a small-scale economic system.

The study of small-scale laboratory economies became a legitimate method of inquiry only after World War II. Post-war economics was characterised by a number of important transformations. Following Morgan [2003a], we can summarise by saying that in the middle of the twentieth century economics was in the process of becoming a *"tool-based science"*: from the old, discursive "moral science" of political economy, to a scientific discipline where models, statistics, and mathematics fulfilled the role both of *instruments* and, crucially, of *objects* of investigation. In this sense, the rise of modelling is probably the most relevant phenomenon for the birth of experimental economics. Whereas from Mill to Marshall it was more or less taken for granted that economics was mainly concerned with the study of "real-world" markets, it was now possible to argue that economics was concerned with the study of *whatever could be modelled by economic theory.*

Walrasian economic theory however posed a serious obstacle to laboratory experimentation, for among the various conditions introduced to prove the existence of a unique efficient market equilibrium, the theory postulates a high (indeed, infinite) number of traders with perfect information and no transaction costs. One of the early important results of experimental economics was precisely the demonstration that in practice neither a high number of traders nor perfect information are necessary for the convergence of laboratory markets to competitive equilibria [Smith, 1962]. This result, together with the new systematization of microeconomics around expected utility and game theory, laid down the preconditions for the laboratory revolution to take place. As soon as economic theory turned to the study of small-scale systems, experimental economics became a real possibility.

Charles Plott, one of the pioneers of experimental economics, expresses this thought with great clarity: experimental economists had to remove two "constraints" that stood in the way of laboratory research:

> The first was a belief that the only relevant economies to study are those in the wild. The belief suggested that the only effective way

> to create an experiment would be to mirror in every detail, to simulate, so to speak, some ongoing natural process. [...] As a result the experiments tended to be dismissed either because as simulations the experiments were incomplete or because as experiments they were so complicated that tests of models were unconvincing. [...] Once models, as opposed to economies, became the focus of research the simplicity of an experiment and perhaps even the absence of features of more complicated economies became an asset. The experiment should be judged by the lessons it teaches about the theory and not by its similarity with what nature might have happened to have created. [Plott 1991, p. 906]

According to such an approach, experimental economics is theory-driven, just like economics as a whole. Useful experiments are always *theory-testing* experiments, in other words.

## 2 THEORY AND EXPERIMENT

It is generally agreed now that experiments have many more functions in economics than just theory-testing [Roth, 1995; Smith, 1982; 1994; Friedman and Sunder, 1994]. Plott's position however has been highly influential for many years and is worth discussing in some detail. One major advantage is that it promises to solve internal and external validity problems with a single stroke. By focusing on theory-testing one can perform the remarkable trick of generating knowledge that is automatically generalisable to non-laboratory conditions:

> The logic is as follows. General theories must apply to simple special cases. The laboratory technology can be used to create simple (but real) economies. These simple economies can then be used to test and evaluate the predictive capability of the general theories when they are applied to the special cases. In this way, a joining of the general theories with data is accomplished. [Plott, 1991, p. 902]
>
> General models, such as those applied to the very complicated economies found in the wild, must apply to simple special cases. Models that do not apply to the simple special cases are not general and thus cannot be viewed as such [ibid., p. 905].[5]

This view is strikingly similar to philosophers' Hypothetico-Deductive (HD) model of testing:

$$\begin{array}{ll} (1) & T \rightarrow O \\ (2) & \sim O \\ \hline (3) & \sim T \end{array}$$

[5]Similar claims can be found in Wilde [1981, p. 143], Smith [1982, p. 268], Loomes [1989, p. 173].

$T$ is a scientific theory or model, and must include some universal statements (laws) of the form: "For all objects $x$, if $x$ has property $P$ then it must also have property $Q$". The argument represented in (1–3) is a case of *refutation* of *falsification*, where the predicted observational statement $O$ turns out to be false, and this prompts the conclusion that the theory $T$ must also be false. Falsification of course only accounts for half of the story. Plott says nothing about the other important case, when the evidence seems to confirm the hypothesis under test.[6] It is also important to notice that we are assuming here a particularly tight relationship between the theory and the experimental claim that is being tested. In the above examples, the relation is maximally tight, i.e. deductive ($T$ implies $O$). But is this a correct representation of what goes on in real experimental practice? In order to answer this question, we must have a look at a concrete example.

## *2.1 An economic experiment*

As a matter of historical record, it is undeniable that experimental economics was initially motivated by the desire to test propositions derived from economic theory. "Gaming" — playing game-theoretic problems for real — was common practice in the small community of game theorists in the 1940s and 50s (cf. e.g. [Shubik, 1960]). Some paradigmatic experiments of this period, like the famous "Allais paradox" [Allais, 1953], were explicitly devised to test the implications of von Neumann and Morgenstern's expected utility theory. And Vernon Smith's experiments with market institutions were originally presented as testing some propositions of the neoclassical theory of competitive markets [Smith, 1962]. In this section however we shall examine a more recent experiment, as an example of productive interaction between theory and experimentation. In 1988 Jim Andreoni reported in the *American Economic Review* the results of an experiment that has become a little classic and has since been replicated several times. The experiment — known as the "Partners and Strangers" design — belongs to the family of so-called "public goods" experiments.

Public goods experiments investigate an important but disputable proposition of economic theory, namely that the absence of property rights over certain goods leads inevitably to their under-production. A so-called public good has two essential characteristics: it is (a) *nonrivalled* and (b) *nonexcludable*. This means that once it has been produced, (a) many people can consume it at the same time and (b) you cannot make individuals pay for what they consume.

We can start by representing the situation in terms of the familiar prisoner's dilemma game, as in Table 1. As customary, the first number in each cell represents

[6]The neglect of confirmation is probably due to the vague Popperianism that informs much economic rhetoric and practice. But it may also be a tactical neglect, for the case of confirmation is much more problematic for Plott's position. The observation of $O$, in fact, does not elicit any *deductive* inference to the truth of the theory $T$; we need induction. An inductive inference from $O$, however, does not necessarily warrant the conclusion that $T$ is the case. Whether it does or not, depends on the theory of inductive inference one decides to adopt. We shall come back to such issues in section 3 below.

the payoffs of the row player, the second one of the column player. Notice that *given the other player's move*, "defect" always generates a higher payoff than "cooperate." In game-theoretic jargon, "defect" is a *dominant strategy*. But then if all players play the dominant strategy, they end up with a Pareto-inferior outcome.

Table 1. A prisoner's dilemma game

| | | Other | |
|---|---|---|---|
| | | Defect | Cooperate |
| You | defect | (5,5) | (10,1) |
| | cooperate | (10,1) | (8,8) |

A public goods game is basically a prisoner's dilemma game with a higher number of players and strategies. Each player has an endowment of $x$ tokens, to be divided in two separate accounts. The first account is "private", and guarantees a unit of profit for each invested unit; the second is "public" and gives a fraction of the profits of the *total* number of tokens invested by *all* the players. For example, suppose there are five players with 50 tokens each. Suppose also that the "production function" of the public good is .5 (each player gets half of the total number of tokens invested in the public account). If everybody invests 25 tokens in the public account, their revenue will be equal to

$$25 \text{ [from the private account]} + (25 \times 5)/2 \text{ [from the public account]} = 87.5 \text{ tokens.}$$

In the standard public goods game all players play simultaneously and anonymously — at the moment of taking her decision, each subject ignores the identity of the other subjects in her group, and how much they are contributing. According to standard economic theory, the public good should not be produced, that is, there should be no contribution to the public project. This conclusion is reached by assuming that each player is indifferent to the others' payoffs, tries to maximise her own monetary gains, and is perfectly rational in the sense of Nash rationality.[7] Under these assumptions the best move — regardless of what the others do — is to contribute nothing. If the others do not contribute anything, why should one give her own tokens, given that she would get back only half of each token contributed to the project? If the others do contribute one token, it is still best not to contribute anything, and to enjoy the fruits of the others' contribution plus one's own full endowment. And so on: this reasoning can be iterated for all levels of contribution, and the moral will always be the same.

The Nash solution however is "Pareto-inferior" or sub-optimal with respect to the outcome that would be achieved if everybody were willing to cooperate by contributing to the public account. Using the previous example, in fact, it is

[7]A Nash equilibrium is such that the strategy implemented by each player is the best move given the strategies of the other players: in equilibrium, no player has an incentive to change her own strategy, in other words.

easy to calculate that the Nash solution (contribute nothing) gives each player an individual payoff of

$$50 + 0/2 = 50 \text{ tokens.}$$

The Pareto-optimal solution, instead, would have everybody contributing their full endowment to the public project, thus achieving

$$0 + (50 \times 5)/2 = 125 \text{ tokens.}$$

Despite the "irrationality" of cooperation, many experimental subjects are willing to give it a go. In a standard one-shot public goods experiment it is common to observe an average level of contribution of about fifty percent of the endowment. If you let the subjects play the game more than once, however, giving them constant feedback about the payoffs and the average contribution levels in previous rounds, their behaviour seems to change. The relatively high initial levels of contribution tend to diminish over time, converging toward the Nash equilibrium. These two phenomena are sometimes referred to in the literature as "overcontribution" and "decay" (cf. [Ledyard, 1995]).

Notice that in a finitely repeated game, according to standard economic theory, a rational *homo oeconomicus* who tries to maximise his monetary payoffs should still contribute nothing to the public account right from the start. It is a counter-intuitive result, obtained by means of "backward induction": in the last round it makes no sense to cooperate, because the game will not continue and thus there is no point in maintaining a reputation of cooperator. Whatever the others do, one is better off by free riding, just like in the one-shot game. But everybody knows this, and so at the penultimate round they will not cooperate because they know that at the last round the others will not cooperate. And so on until one reaches the first round of the game: in theory, it is never rational to cooperate.

But in reality, as we have seen, we observe overcontribution and decay. The fact that cooperation is not robust to repetition has suggested the following explanation: initially perhaps some players do not understand the logic of the game. As the game proceeds, they understand that there is a unique equilibrium and that one must always defect. This explanation has stimulated the creation of models with "error and learning", in which individuals contribute initially above the Nash equilibrium, but slowly converge towards it. Not all the observed initial cooperation however may be due to errors. If some individuals are prone to make mistakes, in fact, some free riders could try to exploit the situation by offering cooperation at the beginning of the game and defecting towards the end. This hypothesis of "strategic play" has been modelled formally by a group of game theorists (Kreps, Milgrom, Roberts and Wilson [1981] — the "Gang of Four" as it is sometimes called) and has provided material for further experimental tests.

In his experiment, Andreoni [1988] has tried to test both the "learning" and the "strategic play" hypotheses. His two main conditions are variants of the baseline public goods game, where subjects play with an endowment of fifty tokens, for ten rounds, in groups of five players. The first important variant is that there are two types of groups: "Partners" who play always with the same players (under anonymity), and "Strangers" who change group at every round. In a group of Partners it could make sense to play strategically in order to build a reputation of cooperative player. In a group of Strangers instead, to build such a reputation is pointless, and a rational player should always defect.

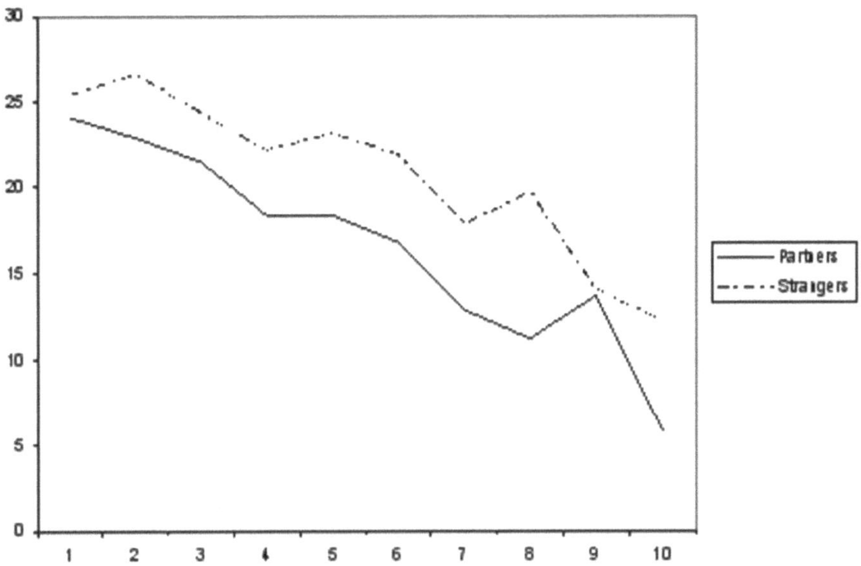


Figure 1. Partners vs. Strangers

The first interesting result reported by Andreoni is that Strangers do not contribute less than Partners, contrary to the hypothesis of strategic play. As shown in Figure 1, surprisingly, Strangers actually contribute *more*. The other interesting result concerns the learning hypothesis. Andreoni introduces a simple interruption in the middle of the game, and observes that a break of just a few minutes is sufficient to raise the average contribution to the level observed at the beginning of the game (Figure 2). The idea that decay is due to learning is therefore discredited — or, at any rate, if learning takes place it must be of a very fragile kind.

## *2.2 The Duhem–Quine problem*

In some obvious sense, Andreoni's experiment is aimed at theory-testing. The Partners/Strangers design is clearly motivated by the model of the "Gang of Four", for example. It is important to notice nevertheless that the relationship between model and experimental design is quite slack. Kreps and his colleagues for example do not model a public goods game situation explicitly. Their theoretical analysis

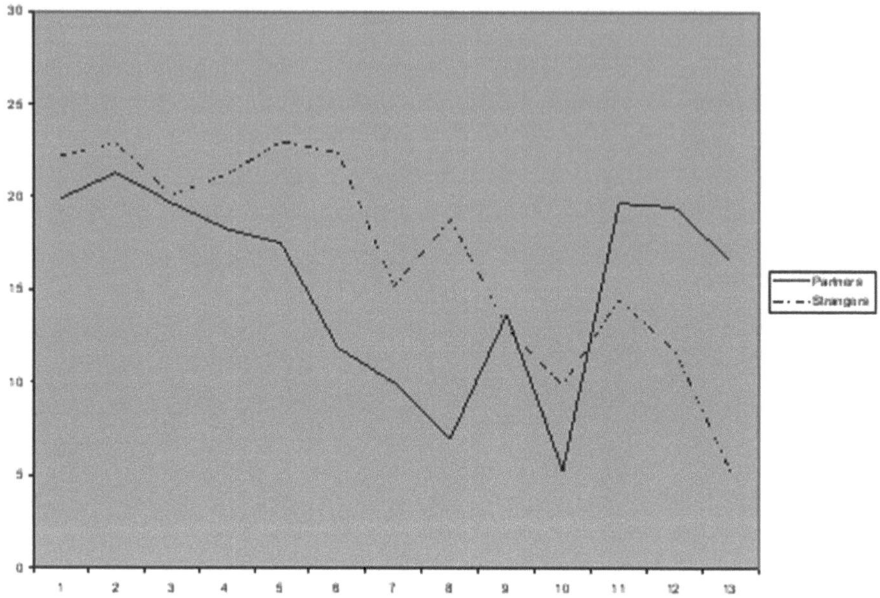


Figure 2. Effect of restart at round 10

focuses on related games like the prisoner's dilemma, and Andreoni simply assumes that it can be extended unproblematically to public goods situations. In the case of learning, similarly, Andreoni does not test specifically any of the various models that have been proposed in the literature. He focuses instead on a broad proposition (that learning is somehow robust to short interruptions) that seems to be implicitly assumed by all such theories.

Notice also that the very concept of "economic theory" under test is not so clear-cut after all. Standard microeconomics does not impose strong restrictions on the contents of individual preferences. An agent can in principle maximise all sorts of things (her income, her fun, her sleep) and still behave "economically". In order to make the theory testable, therefore, it is necessary to add several auxiliary assumptions regarding the contents of people's preferences (or, equivalently, regarding the argument of their utility functions), their constraints, their knowledge, and so forth. In our example, Andreoni is really testing only a very specific prediction obtained by adding to the basic theory some strong assumptions about people's preferences, e.g. that they are trying to maximise their monetary gains and do not care about others' payoffs.

We are of course dealing with a typical Duhem-Quine issue here. Experimental results usually do not indicate deductively the truth/falsity of a theoretical hypothesis in isolation, but rather of a whole body of knowledge or "cluster" of theoretical and auxiliary hypotheses at once.[8] Formally, the Duhem-Quine thesis can be presented as follows:

$$\begin{array}{ll} (4) & (T\&A_1\&A_2\ldots A_i) \rightarrow O \\ (5) & \sim O \\ \hline (6) & \sim T\vee \sim A_1 \vee A_2 \vee \ldots \vee A_i \end{array}$$

The argument states that from (4) and (5) we can only conclude that at least one element, among all the assumptions used to derive the prediction $O$, is false. But we cannot identify exactly which one, *from a purely logical point of view.* The last point is worth stressing because the moral of the Duhem-Quine problem has been often exaggerated in the methodological literature. The correct reading is that deductive logic is an insufficient tool for scientific inference, and hence we need to complement it by means of a theory of induction. The Duhem-Quine problem does *not* imply, as sometimes suggested, the impossibility of justifiably drawing *any* inference from an experimental result. Scientists in fact do draw such inferences all the time, and it takes a good dose of philosophical arrogance to question the possibility of doing that *in principle.* What we need is an explication of why some such inferences are considered more warranted than others. If, as pointed out by Duhem and Quine, deductive logic is insufficient, this must be a task for a theory of induction.[9]

## *2.3 Testing theoretical models*

As pointed out earlier the theory-testing position, as formulated by Plott and others, tries to solve both problems of validity at once. The Duhem-Quine problem is an obstacle for this project, to the extent that experimental results do not seem to imply deductively the truth or falsity of a particular scientific hypothesis. It is not, however, an insurmountable obstacle, provided we can define an adequate set of inductive rules to tackle Duhemian problems in a non-trivial range of situations. If this were possible, the theory-testing view would be vindicated.

Still, there are other implicit assumptions behind the Plott position that ought to be challenged. The theory-testing view assumes that theories come fully interpreted and presented in a form that makes them amenable to direct empirical testing. Remember the key passage in Plott's argument: the laboratory is a legitimate testing domain because economic models are unrestricted or universal in scope of application. So whatever situation falls in the domain of the theory (within or without the laboratory) is a legitimate testing site. But what is the domain of economic theory?

---

[8]Cf. Duhem [1905] and Quine [1953].

[9]I'm using the term "theory of induction" broadly, because such a theory does not necessarily have to be modeled on deductive logic as we know it. We could have a *sociological* theory of induction, for example, along the lines of Collins [1985], a *cognitive psychological* theory such as Giere's [1988], and so forth. There are many ways of "naturalising" the study of inductive inference, and the approach endorsed in this chapter is by no means exclusive.

Robin Cubitt [2005] distinguishes between three different relevant domains of an economic model: the *base domain*, the *intended domain*, and the *testing domain*. The base domain is a set of situations or phenomena to which the theoretical model seems to be unambiguously applicable — for example the domain of random draws from an urn, for a model of individual choice under risk. The intended domain, which does not necessarily coincide with the base domain, is instead the set of situations to which the model is expected to apply — the set of phenomena *we want* the model to explain, which is usually broader than the base domain. (We expect a theory of choice under risk to throw light on, e.g., insurance purchasing, to use Cubitt's example.) The testing domain, finally, is the set of situations where the theory can be legitimately tested, and in principle it should not necessarily be identical with any of the previous two.

Using this framework, one can read Plott as saying that the testing domain of a model *must* include its base-domain. Cubitt instead takes a more cautious stance. He argues that the base belongs in the testing domain only *prima facie*, i.e. unless there is some clearly specified reason to believe that the base and the intended domains differ in important respects. Economic models, in other words, are usually put forward with a certain target in mind — a set of phenomena or mechanisms they are intended to explain. The intended domain of a theory is often only vaguely specified, which explains why it is tempting to do away with it and simply interpret the theory literally. Interpreted literally, however, the theory applies only to a rather narrow set of phenomena (the base domain). We still need an argument showing that results obtained in the base carry over to the intended domain. Cubitt suggests that we should take this as the default case, absent a proof to the contrary.

I shall return to this argument later on. For the time being, it is important to realise that even the base domain of a model cannot always be sharply identified. In translating an abstract model into a concrete design, a series of decisions have to be made at various steps during the translation, many of which are highly arbitrary. For example, there is no particular theoretical reason why there should be four, five, or fifty subjects in each group of a public goods experiment; there could be more or less. Similarly, the theory does not say much about the production function; in theory, it should not matter, although in practice we suspect that it might. At no point the theory identifies the "right" design for experimental purposes, in other words. As Marc Isaac [1983] points out, one great virtue of laboratory work is that it forces to *operationalise* theoretical models, and in doing so the scientist is led to reflect on several aspects of the model and the experiment that wouldn't otherwise have been considered problematic.

Perhaps we should simply recognise that in empirical work we are never really testing a theoretical model, but rather one of its (many) possible interpretations or applications [Guala, 2005a, Ch.10; Hausman, 2005]. In this sense, then, an experiment in the base domain does not speak unambiguously about the truth/falsity of a theoretical model. It rather tells us something about the way it can be operationalised. But there are many ways of operationalising the model, some within and others outside the base domain. An inferential move from an experiment in the base domain to one in the intended domain requires independent justification. If this is the case, then, why has the base domain of theories become a privileged site for experimentation? In order to answer this question it will be necessary to investigate some important similarities between theoretical models and controlled experiments.

## *2.4 Models and experiments*

To operationalise, or to transform a theoretical model into an applied one, may be conceived of as a process of adding more detail to the description of a given situation. During such process, one moves progressively from *abstract* towards a *concrete* account [Cartwright, 1989, Ch. 5]. This conception is consistent with a *linguistic view* of scientific models — i.e. of models as set of propositions. Plott and Cubitt seem to have a linguistic view in mind, when they speak of theoretical models being able to specify (or not) their own domain of application. An alternative view, which has gained the status of quasi-orthodoxy in contemporary philosophy of science, in contrast sees models as *structures* — sets of entities with certain relations and properties. Under this approach — known as the "semantic view of theories" — a more concrete model is an object endowed with more realistic properties than its abstract counterpart. Speaking of models as objects or structures leads naturally to emphasise the analogies between models and experiments. In this section we discuss their relation along three important axes, namely the manipulative, the representative, and the isolative analogy.

Morrison and Morgan [1998] claim that many scientific models work as "mediators" between the abstract principles of a scientific theory and empirical reality. In a mediating model theoretical principles are combined with substantive information from the real world, to create a tool that can be used to investigate both realms: the theoretical realm by deriving interesting implications that were not obvious from an examination of the theory itself, and the real world by deriving testable predictions about observable phenomena. Morrison and Morgan's account of mediating models draws explicitly from the philosophy of experiment of the 1980s, in particular from the work of those scholars, like Ian Hacking [1983], who have emphasized the importance of intervention and manipulation in experimental science. Morrison and Morgan highlight the analogies between reasoning with models and experimental reasoning by stressing the importance of intervention and manipulation in either realm. This is the "*manipulative analogy*" between experiments and models, as I shall call it from now on.

Recent philosophical work on experimental economics has traveled the same path backwards, so to speak, from models to experiments. Economic models and experiments are both "mediating" entities, surrogate systems that can be used to study *other* entities that are too big or small in size, too complex, or too distant to be directly investigated [Guala, 1998; 2005a]. The "mediators" idea originally was meant to highlight that a laboratory experiment is rarely the final step in a research project, for experimental results must eventually be transferable to the real world systems that constituted the original target of research. Using Cubitt's terminology, the mediating metaphor highlights the gap between the testing domain and the intended domain, which ought to be bridged by a special inferential move (an external validity inference). Besides the manipulative analogy, thus, there is also a "*representative analogy*" between experiments and models: both *stand for* some other system, or set of systems, that is the ultimate target of investigation.

Finally, the "*isolative analogy*" highlights that both experiments and models derive their inferential power from their being designed so as to (1) eliminate some real-world complications, and (2) keep some potentially disturbing factors "fixed" in the background (see [Boumans and Morgan, 2001; Mäki, 2005; Morgan, 2005]). Theoretical models — especially the most abstract ones — ignore or assume away several properties of real economic systems that are potentially relevant for their behavior. This sort of abstraction or isolation[10] results in a simpler model that is more amenable to analysis, and is therefore typically justified on heuristic or pragmatic grounds. The experimental counterpart of a simple (relatively abstract) model is a relatively simple experiment in the base domain of that model. Such experiment will also be more amenable to manipulation, and interpretation. For this reason economists tend to privilege experiments in the base domain of a theory, at least at the beginning of a research program. Experimenters replicate the base domain because they try to instantiate the isolative assumptions of the model.

Uskali Mäki [2005] has formulated probably the boldest proposition regarding models and experiments. Pushing the analogy to the extreme, he has proposed to turn it into an identity: "models are experiments and experiments are models". There are reasons to resist such a move, however. One is that scientists themselves seem to find it useful to have a separate terminology to denote these scientific tools. Philosophers of course can be revisionary with respect to scientific language to a certain extent, but must also be aware that differences in language often reflect substantial differences at the level of methodology and scientific practice. What could this difference be in the case of experiments and models? Experimental economists often put it in terms of the *materials* they experiment with: "laboratory microeconomies are real live economic systems, which are certainly richer, behaviorally, than the systems parametrized in our theories" [Smith, 1982, pp. 923–5].

In order to articulate this idea, Guala [2002a] has adapted Herbert Simon's [1969] distinction between *simulating* and *experimental* devices. In a simulation one reproduces the behavior of a certain entity or system by means of a mechanism and/or material that is radically different in kind from that of the simulated entity. Paradigmatic examples may be the simulation of a historical battle by means of miniature toys, or the simulation of the propagation of light waves using a ripple tank. Although water and light waves display the same patterns and thus can be described by the same models at a relatively superficial theoretical level, the

[10] I'm using these two terms interchangeably here, although there are philosophically important differences between these procedures; see for instance Cartwright [1989, Ch. 5] and Mäki [1992].

underlying mechanisms are not the same nor obey the same fundamental laws of nature.

In this sense, *models simulate* whereas *experimental systems do not.* Theoretical models are conceptual entities, whereas experiments are made of the same "stuff" as the target entity they are exploring and aiming at understanding. The difference between models and experiments is thus *relational* rather than intrinsic — whether a mediating tool counts as a model or an experimental system depends on how it is used, and what it is used for (what its target is). Experiments are not models, in this sense, and models are not experiments — although both are mediating epistemic tools (different species of the same genus, in other words).[11]

As a consequence, modeling and experimenting have different virtues and defects. According to Morgan [2005], the advantage of experimentation over modeling is that in manipulating a model we can only be "surprised" but not "confounded". We might derive a surprising result that we had no idea was implicit in the premises/components of the model, but we rarely misinterpret the inner workings of a model, because we have built it ourselves. In contrast, an experimental system is always opaque to a certain extent, because the builder/experimenter has left some degree of freedom of expression in the system that will teach us something previously unknown. This opaqueness may be the principal source of misinterpretation of the experimental result, but is a resource for at least two reasons: (1) because it can teach us something new, as we have seen; but also (2) because it allows one to use some systems as "black boxes" that we do not understand perfectly, provided we are confident that the same basic principles (whatever they may be) are at work in the target. For example: one can use real individual agents in market experiments even though we have no general understanding of individual decision making, if we are confident that such agents are good representatives of those in the target [Guala, 2002a].

In general, it is worth keeping in mind that these conceptual distinctions probably do not reflect a sharp divide at the level of scientific tools and practices. In reality we rather find a continuum, with many "hybrid epistemic tools" that do not fall in either category neatly. In a series of papers Morgan [2002; 2003b] uses the expression "virtually experiments" to denote systems that embed a real-world material component within a predominantly simulated (model) environment.[12]

[11]Different experiments of course may deal with different "materials"; Santos [2007] provides a wider comparative discussion of the materiality of economic experiments.

[12]"Virtual experiments" in contrast are according to Morgan entirely simulating systems, which are constructed so as to generate interesting data patterns reproducing real-world features. See also Guala [2002a] for a different discussion of hybrid experiments/simulations that follows closely Simon's framework, and Parker [2009] for a critique of the materiality-based distinction between simulations and experiments.

# 3 EXPERIMENTAL INFERENCES

Economists often test models in their base domain in order to replicate the isolation assumptions of the models. But highlighting the isolative analogy exacerbates the problem of making inferences from base to intended domain. Since most experiments test theories in the base domain, and even the identification of the base domain requires some arbitrary interpretative choices, an inference from the testing or base domain to the intended domain requires independent justification.

This point underlies the crucial distinction between *internal* and *external validity*. To recall: problems of internal validity have to do with the drawing of inferences from experimental data to the causal mechanisms of a given laboratory situation. Typical internal validity questions are: Do we understand what goes on in *this* particular experimental situation? Are we drawing correct inferences *within* the experiment? External validity problems instead have to do with the drawing of inferences from experimental data to what goes on in other (laboratory or, more typically, non-laboratory) situations of interest. They involve asking questions like: Can we use experimental knowledge to understand what goes on in the "real world"? Are we drawing correct inferences *from* the experiment?[13]

So far I have said almost nothing about the inferential strategies employed to tackle the two validity problems. For various reasons it is wise to start by looking at internal validity first. The analysis of internal validity ideally should provide some basic conceptual tools to tackle the admittedly more difficult problem of external validity later on. The reasoning is as follows: both inferences within and from the experiment belong to the general category of inductive inferences. We should therefore be able to use the techniques that economists use (rather successfully) to solve internal validity problems to construct a more general theory of inductive inference. Once that has been done, the theory can be used to shed some light on external validity too.

The approach endorsed in this chapter and elsewhere (e.g. [Guala, 2005a]) is distinctively *normative* in character. This means that we shall not just look at the inferences that experimental economists as a matter of fact do draw when they interpret their results. We shall also be concerned with the *justification* of such inferences, and aim at capturing the normative core underlying experimenters' intuitive distinction between "good" and "bad", "strong and "weak", warranted and unwarranted inferences. This does not mean that descriptive approaches to inductive inference are useless or uninteresting. On the contrary, we can learn a lot by investigating the way in which psychological propensities or social conditions affect inferential performance. But just as a purely normative approach carries the risk of leading to an unrealistic theory of induction, a purely descriptive approach is unable answer the important question of the *efficacy* or adequacy of an inferential method, given certain goals. The answer surely must be a combination

[13]Experimental economists sometimes use the term "parallelism" instead of external validity (which is more common in psychology) to label the problem of generalising from laboratory to real world (see e.g. [Smith, 1982]).

of normative and descriptive investigation that is able to overcome the limitations of both.

That an intuitive distinction between good and bad inductive practices exists and is not merely a philosophical construct is of course a hypothesis, but a hypothesis that is supported by several observable facts. The birth of experimental economics for example was motivated by the desire to improve the methodological practice of economic science. I will articulate this idea by saying that the experimental method enables one to test economic hypotheses *more severely* than traditional testing with econometric data would allow. The notion of severity thus will be at the centre of the discussion. While illustrating the method of severe testing, however, it will also turn out to be useful to discuss some alternative proposals that depart in various ways from the severity approach.

## *3.1 Experiments and causal analysis*

It is interesting that Andreoni, when he illustrates the logic of his experiment, does not refer directly to theory-testing:

> The experiment reported in this paper is intended to separate learning from strategic play. The design is *subtractive*: subjects participate in a repeated-play environment, but are denied the opportunity to play strategically. Without strategic play, we can isolate the learning hypothesis. Furthermore, by comparing this group to one that *can* play strategically, we can attribute the difference, if any, to strategic play [1988, p. 294].

Andreoni says that he is trying to "isolate" some factors, by "subtracting" their influences, and studying their effects in isolation. When strategic play has been eliminated (by means of the Partner and Strangers device) all the remaining contributions to the pubic good can be attributed to learning. But should it be so attributed? This leads to the second design: "to isolate the learning hypothesis, the experiment included a 'restart"' [Andreoni, 1988, p. 295]. The answer, as we have seen, is eventually negative — there is more going on in public goods experiments than just error, learning, and strategic play.

Notice the remarkably causal flavour of Andreoni's language: there are several causal factors at work, whose effects can be separated, added, and subtracted by experimental means. Andreoni's reasoning suggests that experimental economists are not interested in testing theoretical models *per se*. Models are attempts to represent formally the working of some basic causal mechanisms in isolation. It is these mechanisms that economists are interested in understanding, and therefore their experiments sometimes depart from the letter of the theory, to "isolate" or "separate" the effects of different causal factors. In what follows we shall take this language seriously, and reconstruct the distinctive character of the experimental method as an attempt to investigate the causal influence of separate factors working in isolation.

Economists are traditionally wary of causal language (Hoover 2004), so this claim requires a bit of elaboration. Despite centuries of philosophical attempts to reduce causation to more "respectable" concepts (such as constant conjunction or statistical association), it is now generally agreed that causal relations have intrinsic properties — like asymmetry, counterfactual dependence, invariance to intervention — that cannot be fully eliminated by means of a reductive analysis. There are now several non-reductive theories of causation in the philosophical and the economic literature, which for reasons of space cannot be reviewed here (but see e.g. [Hausman, 1998; Woodward, 2003]).

Despite continuing disagreement on the central metaphysical issue of causation (its very meaning and essence), there is broad agreement that the method of the controlled experiment is a powerful tool for the discovery of causal relations. The reason, in a nutshell, is that controlled experimentation allows underlying causal relations to become manifest at the level of empirical regularities. In a competently performed experiment, single causal connections can be "read off" directly from statistical associations.

It is better to start with a homely example. Imagine you want to discover whether flipping the switch is an effective means for turning the light on (or whether "flipping the switch causes the light to turn on"). The flipping of course will have such effect only if other enabling background conditions are in place, for example if the electricity supply is in good working order. Thus first we will have to design an experimental situation where the "right" circumstances are instantiated. Then, we will have to make sure that no other extraneous variation is disturbing the experiment. Finally, we will check whether by flipping the switch on and off we are producing a regular association between the position of the switch (say, up/down) and the light (on/off). If such an association is observed, and if we are confident that every plausible source of mistake has been controlled for, we will conclude that flipping the switch is causally connected with turning the light on.

The moral, in a nutshell, is that causal discovery requires *variation, but not too much variation, and of the right kind.* In general, you want variation in one factor while keeping all the other putative causes fixed "in the background". This logic is neatly exemplified in the *model of the perfectly controlled experiment*:

Table 2. The perfectly controlled experimental design

| | Treatment (putative cause) | Putative effect | Other factors ($K_i$) |
|---|---|---|---|
| Experimental condition | $x$ | $Y_1$ | Constant |
| Control condition | — | $Y_2$ | Constant |

The $K_i$ are the background factors, or the other causes that are kept fixed across the experimental conditions. The conditions must differ with respect to just one factor ($X$, the treatment) so that any significant difference in the observed values of $Y$ ($Y_1 - Y_2$) can be attributed to the presence (or absence) of $X$. A good experimenter thus is able to discover *why* one kind of event is associated regularly with another kind of event, and not just that it does. In the model of the perfectly controlled experiment one does not simply observe that "if $X$ then $Y$", nor even that "$X$ if and only if $Y$". Both such conditionals are material implications, and their truth conditions depend on what happens to be the case, regardless of the reasons why it is so. In science in contrast — and especially in the sciences that are used regularly for policy-making, like economics — one is also interested in "what would be the case if" such and such a variable was manipulated. Scientific intervention and policy-making must rely on counterfactual conditionals. A great advantage of experimentation is that it allows to check what would happen if $X$ was *not* the case, while keeping all the other relevant conditions fixed.

We can now draw a first important contrast between the experimental method and traditional econometric inferences from field data. Econometricians apply statistical techniques to establish the strength of various correlations between economic variables. But except in some special happy conditions, the spontaneous variations found in the data do not warrant the drawing of specific causal inferences. Typically, field data display either too little or too much concomitant variation (sometimes both). Some variations of course can be artificially reconstructed post-hoc by looking at partial correlations, but the ideal conditions instantiated in a laboratory are rarely be found in the wild — except in so-called "natural experiments".[14]

This does not mean that total experimental control is always achieved in the laboratory. We must keep in mind that the perfectly controlled experiment is an idealisation, and in reality there are always going to be uncontrolled background factors, errors of measurement, and so forth. In order neutralise these imperfections, experimenters use various techniques, like for example *randomization.*[15] In a randomized experiment subjects are assigned by a chance device to the various experimental conditions, so that in the long run the potential errors and deviations are evenly distributed across them. This introduces an important element in the inference from data, i.e. *probabilities.* A well-designed randomized experiment makes it *highly likely* that the effect of the treatment be reflected in the data, but does not guarantee that this is going to be the case. Assuming for simplicity that we are dealing with bivariate variables ($X$ and $\sim X$; $Y$ and $\sim Y$), in a randomized experiment if (1) the "right" background conditions are in place, and (2) $X$ causes $Y$, then $P(Y \mid X) > P(Y \mid \sim X)$. In words: if (1) and (2) are satisfied, $X$ and $Y$ are very likely to be statistically correlated.

Some authors (notably [Cartwright, 1983]) have used this relation or some close variant thereof to define the very notion of causation. Such a definition is essentially a probabilistic equivalent of J.L. Mackie's [1974] famous INUS account, with

[14]The art of causal analysis from econometric data has received increasing attention in recent economic methodology, see for example Hoover [2001].

[15]There are other techniques that are used when the model of the perfectly controlled experiment cannot be applied for some reason, but I shall not examine them in detail here (they are illustrated in most textbooks and handbooks of experimental methodology, cf. e.g. [Christensen, 2001]).

the important addition of a "screening off" condition.[16] The latter is encapsulated in the requirement that all other causal factors in the background are kept fixed, so as to avoid problems of spurious correlation. Several interesting philosophical implications follow from choosing such a definition of causation, which however would take us too far away from our present concerns. In the following sections I shall build on the model of the perfectly controlled experimental design to articulate a more general theory of inductive inference. The perfectly controlled experiment is a "model" in a sense that should be familiar to economists: it is an idealisation that captures the essential features of a broader set of inferential strategies. Moreover, like economic models, it has also the ambition of capturing some normative truth about how we *ought* to do science, as opposed to just describing what experimenters do as a matter of fact.

## 3.2 The severity approach

The above analysis suggests an obvious way to tackle the Duhem-Quine problem, by simply asserting the truth of the background and auxiliary assumptions that are used in designing an experiment. In a competently performed controlled experiment, in other words, we are entitled to draw an inference from a set of empirical data (or evidence, $E$) and some background assumptions ($K_i$) to a causal hypothesis ($H$ = "$X$ causes $Y$"). The inference consists of the following three steps:

$$\begin{array}{ll} (7) & (H\&K_i) \rightarrow E \\ (8) & E\&K_i \\ \hline (9) & H \end{array}$$

This is an instance of the Hypothetico-Deductive model of testing. In this case the evidence indicates or supports the hypothesis. The symmetric case is the following:

$$\begin{array}{ll} (10) & (H\&K_i) \rightarrow E \\ (11) & \sim E\&K_i \\ \hline (12) & \sim H \end{array}$$

In the latter case, the inference is *deductive*. If (and sometimes this is a big "if") we are ready to assert the truth of the background assumptions $K_i$, then it logically follows that the evidence $E$ refutes or falsifies $H$. Since we are not often in the position to guarantee that the $K_i$ are instantiated in reality a refutation is usually followed by a series of experiments aimed at testing new hypotheses $H'$, $H''$, etc., each concerned with the correctness of the design and the functioning of the experimental procedures. If these hypotheses are all indicated by the evidence, then the experimenter usually feels compelled to accept the original result.

[16] INUS stands for an Insufficient Non-redundant condition within a set of jointly Unnecessary but Sufficient conditions for an effect to take place. There are several problems with such an approach, some of which are discussed by Mackie himself. The "screening-off" condition fixes some of the most obvious flaws of the INUS account.

Notice that in the first case (7–9) the conclusion of the argument is not logically implied by the premises, or in other words the inference is *inductive*. Of course many scientific inferences have this form, so the point of using the experimental method is to make sure that the inductive step is highly warranted, or that the inference is as strong as possible. The conditions for a strong inductive inference are outlined in normative theories of scientific testing. Although there is presently no generally agreed theory of inductive inference in the literature, the model of the perfectly controlled experiment suggests a few basic principles that any adequate theory should satisfy. When an experiment has been competently performed — i.e. when the experimenter has achieved a good degree of control over the background circumstances $K_i$ — the experimental data have the following, highly desirable characteristics:

(a) if $X$ causes $Y$, the observed values of the experimental variables $X$ and $Y$ turn out to be statistically correlated;

(b) if $X$ does not cause $Y$, these values are not correlated.

Another way to put it is this. In the "ideal" experiment the evidence $E$ (correlation between $X$ and $Y$) indicates the truth of $H$ ($X$ causes $Y$) unequivocally. Or, in the "ideal" experiment you are likely to get one kind of evidence ($E$) if the hypothesis under test is true, and another kind of evidence ($\sim E$) if it is false [Woodward, 2000]. Following Deborah Mayo [1996; 2005], we shall say that in such an experiment the hypothesis $H$ is *tested severely* by the evidence $E$.[17]

More precisely, severe testing implies that (i) the evidence fits the hypothesis, and (ii) that such a good fit would have been unlikely, had the hypothesis been false. One (but not the only) measure of fit is the ratio between the likelihoods $P(E \mid H)$ and $P(\sim E \mid H)$. When $P(E \mid H)/P(E \mid\sim H)$ is high, we will say that the evidence fits the hypothesis very well. A good fit however is not the end of the story: according to the second severity requirement it is necessary that such a good fit would have been highly unlikely, had $H$ been false. This second, crucial condition is established by considering not just $E$ and $H$ (and its alternatives) but the entire distribution of data-sets that *would* have been obtained if the experiment had been repeated in various circumstances.[18]

It is important to notice that we are here dealing with objective conditions or states of affair. The model of the perfectly controlled experiment does not describe an *epistemic* state. It tries to describe an ideal *testing device*: in the model of the

[17]The terminology (and, partly, the concept) of severity is Popperian. Mayo's error-probabilistic approach however departs substantially from Popper's theory of scientific testing — see Mayo [2005] for a discussion. The account of severity given below departs in some important respects from the one I defend in Guala [2005]; see Hausman [2008] for a critique of the former, and Guala [2008] for an amendment.

[18]This gives us an *error probability*, which is obtained by a very different route than likelihood reasoning. In reasoning about likelihoods, we keep $E$ fixed and consider various $H_i$; in error-probabilistic reasoning we consider various $E_i$ and reason about their distribution under different assumptions about the data-generating process.

perfectly controlled experiment there is an *objectively* high probability of obtaining $E$ if $H$ is true. The probabilities of severe testing, in other words, are *properties of the experimental set-up*, and not to be read as epistemic (logical or subjective) probabilities.

The logic of severe testing accords with the widely adopted practice of using formal statistical tests in experimental science. Suppose we are testing the hypothesis $H_1$ = "$X$ causes $Y$", by designing an experiment along the lines of the perfectly controlled model. Because of the impossibility of eliminating the influence of all disturbing factors and errors of observation, we will almost certainly observe some (perhaps quite small) difference between the values of $Y$ in the treatment (let us call them $Y_1$) and in the control condition ($Y_2$), even if $H_1$ is false. The observed frequency of $X$s and $Y$s, in other words, will be such that *some* (positive or negative) correlation will almost certainly exist between the two variables, come what may. But is such a correlation big enough to count in favour of $H_1$? The job of statistical testing is to help us determine what counts as "small" or "big" in such a context by specifying a range of values for $Y_1 - Y_2$ that we consider too unlikely to be compatible with the truth of $H_1$. Using certain statistical assumptions and the statistical properties of the data-set, experimenters can calculate the *significance levels* of the test (customarily, the 5% or 1% levels are used) and thus effectively identify what sort of evidence counts as $E$ (as indicating $H_1$) and what as $\sim E$ (as refuting $H_1$) in this particular experiment.

Suppose for example that we observe a relatively large discrepancy between $Y_1$ and $Y_2$, so large in fact that such a difference would be observed only less than 1% of the time, if $H_1$ were false (if $X$ did not cause $Y$, that is). Such a large discrepancy is our positive evidence $E$. Statistically, $E$ can be used to reject the *null* hypothesis $H_0 = \sim H$ (= "$X$ does *not* cause $Y$") at the 1% level. According to the severity approach, $E$ counts as a strong piece of evidence in favour of $H_1$, because in such circumstances $P(E; \sim H)$ is very low, and $P(E; H)$ is high.

## 3.3 *Objectivist vs. subjectivist approaches*

The first distinctive characteristic of the logic of severe testing is that it is an "objectivist" approach to inductive inference, in the sense that probabilities are used to measure the objective properties of testing devices. To appreciate the importance of such a feature, in this section I shall compare the severity approach with an alternative theory of induction (belonging to the "subjectivist" approach) that uses probabilities to measure the strength of belief or the degree of confirmation of a hypothesis in light of the evidence. This alternative theory is so-called "Personalist Bayesianism". Bayesians see the logic of science as the business of updating one's beliefs in light of the evidence, using Bayes' theorem as an engine to derive posterior subjective probabilities from prior probabilities concerning hypotheses and evidence.[19]

[19] In its simplest version, Bayes' theorem states that $P(H \mid E) = P(E \mid H)P(H)/P(E)$. $P(H)$ is the "prior probability" of $H$; $P(E)$ is the "prior probability" of $E(= P(E \mid H)P(H) + P(E \mid\sim$

As we have seen in discussing the HD model, a piece of evidence $E$ can typically be derived from a hypothesis $H$ only with the help of a series of auxiliary assumptions concerning background and boundary conditions $K_i : (H\&K_i) \rightarrow E$. It follows that from the point of view of deductive logic the observation of $E$ or $\sim E$ cannot be used to derive unambiguous conclusions regarding the truth or falsity of $H$ (Duhem-Quine thesis). The severity approach tackles the Duhem-Quine problem by identifying the conditions in which the two severity requirements (i) and (ii) are satisfied. The way of satisfying the requirements is to design a severe experimental test, i.e. to set the experimental conditions $K_i$ in such a way as to obtain the desired severity. It is important to stress that this does *not* imply the attribution of a certain (presumably high) degree of belief in a hypothesis $K_i$ = "the background assumptions are true". The severity approach is not looking for a quantitative measure of our degrees of belief as an outcome of the testing procedure, and therefore does not need a quantitative input either.

Personalist Bayesians in contrast do need such an input. Bayes' theorem is a calculative engine that transforms prior probabilities into posterior ones. The relevant inputs are the prior probability of the evidence, the prior probability of the hypothesis, and the prior probability of the background assumptions. Bayesians do not impose any restriction on the subjective degrees of belief that may be accorded to any of these (beyond some basic consistency requirements). They just impose some dynamic constraints to make sure that we can learn from the evidence, for example by stipulating that $P(H_{t+1}) = P(H_t \mid E)$.[20] This machinery ensures that the Duhem-Quine problem can be tackled dynamically, i.e. by updating the probability of a hypothesis in a series of replications.

Following Redhead [1980], Morten Søberg [2005] shows that by testing a hypothesis repeatedly in conjunction with *different* sets of auxiliary assumptions,

$$\begin{aligned}&(H\&K_1) \rightarrow E,\\&(H\&K_2) \rightarrow E,\\&(H\&K_3) \rightarrow E, \ldots\end{aligned}$$

one can reach a (subjectively) highly probable conclusion about the truth of $H$. If the series of experiments or "replications" produces consistent results (say, $E$), in fact, it is possible to show that whatever prior probability was originally assigned to $H$, it will be "washed out" by the accumulating evidence.

There are several important differences between the Bayesian and the severity approach, but one of the most striking is the diachronic character of Bayesian rationality. In the severity approach *one* competently performed experiment suffices to provide strong evidence in favor of $H$. According to Bayesianism, in contrast, it may take some time to raise (or lower) the probability of a hypothesis, because of the heavy reliance on subjective priors.

---

$H)P(\sim H))$, and $P(E \mid H)$ is the "likelihood" of $E$ given $H$. For a comprehensive defence of Bayesian inductivism see Howson and Urbach [1989].

[20]The new (prior) probability of $H$ at time $t+1$ (after the observation of $E$ at $t$) must be equal to the conditional probability of $H$at $t$ (*before* $E$ was observed) given $E$.

Bayesians at this point appeal to the distinction between *confirmation* and *support*: $H$ may not be highly confirmed (i.e. $P(H \mid E)$ may be low for all sorts of reasons, including a low subjective prior) and yet highly supported by $E$. The impact of $E$ on the probability of $H$, in fact, depends crucially on the likelihoods $P(E \mid H)$ and $P(E \mid\sim H)$, which are independent of a scientist's subjective beliefs.

Although a high $P(E \mid H)$ and a low $P(E \mid\sim H)$ imply a strong degree of support for $H$, it is important to stress again that the likelihoods differ markedly from the two severity conditions outlined above. Whereas severity measures the *objective chance* of a testing procedure to give rise to evidence $E$, under the assumption that $H$ is correct, $P(E \mid\sim H)$ is a measure of the *logical relation* between $E$ and whatever alternatives to $H$ one is able to conceive of. Suppose for example that $H$: "the coin is biased". It is always possible to create an alternative hypothesis that makes $E$ maximally likely from a logical point of view ("the coin is fair but a Cartesian devil makes the coin land tail every time I flip it"). In contrast, it is not always possible to raise severity in a similar fashion, because a given experimental procedure (e.g. flipping the coin) is not necessarily appropriate to test such alternatives. (In order to test the devil hypothesis, you need an exorcist, not a coin-flipper.)

Another way to put it is that Bayesian theories of inductive inference are happy to process *whatever piece of evidence one is able to come up with.* The impact of the evidence as well as the final posterior probability depend on various factors that do not necessarily have to do with how the evidence was generated. Severity testing is more selective: the goal is not belief updating, but rather producing a piece of evidence that is really able to speak for or against $H$. And whether this is the case depends crucially on the experimental set-up. In this sense, the severity approach seems to make better sense of the logic and practice of experimental science, where an enormous care is taken to make sure that the "right" conditions are created to generate a truly informative piece of evidence.[21]

## *3.4 "Low" vs. "high-level" hypothesis testing*

A second important characteristic of the severity approach then is that it turns hypothesis-testing into a fairly "local" business, in the sense that a given experimental design is usually appropriate for testing only a fairly precise hypothesis, but has no direct implications about the truth of broader theories. Consider the coin-flipping example in the previous section. By flipping a coin and observing that we invariably obtain "head", we can only test a hypothesis concerning the fairness of the experimental procedure, but we are not necessarily able to check the source of the bias. In order to do so, we would have to design other experiments, for example by inspecting the weight and balance of the coin itself, or the presence of a magnetic field in its vicinity. Another way to put it is that by repeatedly tossing a coin we can test a low-level hypothesis about the existence of

[21] For a more thorough comparison of the Bayesian and the severity approach, see Mayo [1996], from which many of the points of this section are taken.

a *phenomenon* (the coin's propensity to systematically land "head"), but we are not able to say much about its *explanation* (why it has got such a propensity).

To provide explanations for scientific phenomena is usually the job of scientific theories and models. The testing of complex theories however requires many years of experimentation with several different designs, each one concerned with the testing of a fairly specific or "local" aspects of the theory itself. Fortunately, experimental activity can proceed for a long time quite autonomously from high-level explanatory theory. This point has been established over many years of study of experimental practice by philosophers, historians and sociologists of science.[22] Students of experiments have long recognised that in many scientific disciplines there exists a body of experimental knowledge that is largely independent from high theory. Much of this experimental knowledge takes the form of an ability to create and replicate at will robust phenomena, which then take a "life of their own" independently of the explanations that are devised to explain their occurrence.

The severity approach can account for *both* types of experimentation — experiments devoted to theory-testing, but also of experiments devoted to the discovery and investigation of laboratory phenomena. In a recent article, Robert Sugden [2005] distinguishes between *experiments as tests* of theories and *experiments as exhibits*. An "exhibit" is an experimental design coupled with an empirical phenomenon it reliably brings about. According to Sugden, in the case of theory-testing experiments "we gain confidence in a theory by seeing it withstand those tests that, when viewed in any perspective other than that of the theory itself, seem most likely to defeat it" [2005, p. 299]. A good theory-testing experiment, in other words, maximizes the probability of obtaining a negative result, if the theory is false.

Sugden's analysis is entirely compatible with the severity approach. Remember that for a hypothesis to pass a severe test, $E$ must have a good fit with $H$, but must also be observed in an experimental set-up such that such a good fit would not be expected, had $H$ been false. In the case of theory-testing experiments Sugden clearly focuses on the second requirement (a good experiment must produce negative evidence with high probability, when viewed from the perspective of the falsity of $H$). But implicitly, he is also assuming that the initial conditions of the experiment have been designed in such a way so as to obtain a high probability of observing evidence that fits $H$. When testing a theory, in fact, one usually derives a prediction about the occurrence of a certain phenomenon, given certain assumptions about the initial and boundary conditions ($T \rightarrow E$). $T$ only issues conditional predictions and does not say what will happen when the appropriate conditions are not in place, so the conditions that make $E$ probable (if the theory is true) must be instantiated if this is to count as a genuine test of $T$.

Turning to the case of exhibits, Sugden argues that experimenters often focus on those conditions where the phenomenon is most likely to be displayed. "Is it legitimate to focus my attention on decision problems in which my intuition suggests that the kind of effect I want to display is particularly likely to be found?

[22]See e.g. Galison [1987], Gooding, Pinch and Schaffer, eds. [1989].

[...] My inclination is to answer 'Yes' [...]" [Sugden 2005, p. 300]. The search for a phenomenon is usually guided by some (possibly quite vague and informal) "hunch" about the mechanisms that may produce a certain regularity of behaviour. Because such a hunch is not precisely formulated, it is usually impossible to devise a testing situation that is able to establish the existence of a phenomenon *and* to test an explanation of why it came about. In such cases, experimenters end up designing experiments where the phenomenon is highly likely to be observed, assuming the truth of the hunch, but that do *not* minimise the probability of observing the phenomenon if that hunch was mistaken.[23]

Does this mean that the second severity requirement (that it is unlikely to observe a good fit with $H$ if $H$ were false) is violated in exhibit experiments? No. We want to distinguish between theory-testing and exhibit experiments precisely to keep in mind that a different kind of hypothesis is under test in each type of experiment. Although an exhibit experiment usually does not test severely an *explanation* of the phenomenon, it can (and should) test severely a low-level hypothesis concerning the existence of some regularity in the data (i.e. the phenomenon). The hypothesis under test is usually the null $H_0$: "the regularity is a chance effect". When this hypothesis has been rejected with a high level of significance, the second severity requirement has been satisfied.

The moral is that it is important always to ask what, if anything, has been severely tested in a given experimental set-up. Quite often, it will turn out that only low-level, fairly local claims are warranted by the evidence, whereas high-level theoretical hypotheses or explanations remain untested. The fact that one can construct a theory to explain some data does *not* mean that the theory has been tested by those data at all.

## *3.5 Novelty and construct independence*

A third distinguishing characteristic of the severity requirement is its being formulated in purely logical or synchronic terms. Whether a hypothesis has been proposed before, during or after the collection of the evidence is irrelevant in itself. It matters only if it affects the severity of the test. Severity theorists, to put it differently, deny that the temporal relation between evidence collection and theory-formation can be used to define some necessary condition for evidential support. There may well be cases of hypotheses proposed after the collection of the evidence that are nevertheless supported by that very evidence.

This indifference to temporal matters is in stark contrast with the standard methodological rule in economics — popularised by Milton Friedman [1953] — that the only relevant test of a theory is the success of its predictions. Despite paying lip-service to the Friedmanian rule, as a matter of fact economists tend to interpret the term "prediction" loosely and to allow all sorts of exceptions. This is wise, because it is easy to find episodes in the history of science where scientists

[23] I should thank Sugden for clarifying his thought on this particular point (personal correspondence).

felt no embarrassment in using some "old" evidence to argue in favour of a new theory. The fact that Einstein's relativity theory was able to account for the shifting perihelion of Mercury (a phenomenon that had been known for centuries), for example, was widely considered an important element in support of the new theory. But consider also the econometric practice of splitting a sample of data in two parts, one for estimating the parameters of a model, and one for testing the predictions (but we should say "retro-dictions") derived from the estimated model. Again, the fact that the data had been collected before the estimated model was formulated seems to be irrelevant for the issue of evidential support.

Some philosophers have tried to weaken the temporal requirement by endorsing a so-called "construct-independence" criterion that captures some intuitions behind such examples. The idea is that a piece of old evidence can legitimately speak in favour of a new theory, provided it has not been used to *construct* the theory itself — or, in other words, only if the theory had not been designed with the explicit aim of accounting for such body of evidence (cf. [Giere, 1983; Worrall, 1985]). This would rule out, for example, the malpractice of "data-snooping", or the blatant use of the same set of data to both estimate and test an econometric model.

Severity theorists argue that construct independence matters only if (or in virtue of the fact that) it helps satisfying the severity requirements. Construct independence is not a necessary condition for empirical support, and there may well be cases where the evidence can be legitimately used both to construct and to indicate the correctness of a theory (see [Mayo, 1996, Ch. 8]). Consider a simple case of picking balls of different colour (black or white) from an urn. Suppose the urn contains $n$ balls and we can pick up only $m < n$ balls. Having counted how many white balls are in our sample, we can easily construct a hypothesis regarding the proportion of white/black balls in the urn, with a certain margin of error. Such hypothesis would not only be constructed *after* the evidence has been collected, but indeed would be constructed *on the basis* of that very evidence. And yet, it would be silly to deny that the evidence supports the hypothesis so constructed.

In the context of experimental economics, Larry Samuelson [2005] has recently proposed an intriguing argument in favour of the construct independence criterion. Samuelson's article is devoted to discussing the relation between economic theory and experiments. At one point he asks "How can we use experiments to evaluate economic theories?" [2005, p. 79], and answers by outlining an evaluation procedure that resembles in many respects the one advocated by supporters of the severity criterion.

The basic elements of Samuelson's framework are an *experimental outcome* (in the form of a statistical distribution), $E$; a *predicted outcome* $E_T$ by theory $T$; and a *true distribution* $E^*$ representing the probability distribution (propensity) over the set of possible outcomes that would be obtained if we were to perform an infinitely long series of replications of the same experiment.[24] An *evaluation*

[24] I have modified Samuelson's original notation, to make it consistent with the one I have used so far. Notice that, crucially for Samuelson's proof, $E_T$ is itself a distribution that has been

*rule* $R$ combines the information provided by $E$ and $E_T$ to produce a verdict of acceptance or rejection of theory $T$ in light of $E$.

For example: imagine you are tossing a coin and you are interested in knowing whether it is biased, and if so, how. For some unfortunate circumstance, you can toss the coin only once (this is a one-shot experiment, in other words). An evaluation rule $R(E,\ E_T)$ could take for example the following form [Samuelson 2005, p. 81]:

- *Accept* if $T$ predicts *head* with $P < 1/3$, and the result is *tail*; or if $T$ predicts *head* with $P \geq 1/3$, and the result is *head.*

- *Reject* otherwise.

This evaluation rule has the property of accepting a true hypothesis with probability 1/3, and conversely rejects (does not recognise) a true hypothesis with probability 2/3. Samuelson notices that this "does not sound very impressive. By altering the evaluation rule, we could manage to boost this probability to 1/2, but could not go further in this case" [2005, p. 81] because a one-shot experiment has some obvious limitations.

But do we want to raise the probability of accepting a true theory? In principle it seems a desirable thing to do, but we must also guard ourselves from another kind of error, i.e. the mistake of accepting a false theory. Samuelson suggests (Proposition 1, p. 80) that raising the probability of accepting a true theory automatically raises the probability of making this second kind of mistake.

To understand this claim, we must define another technical term: an evaluation rule *blindly passes* a given theory if it gives a verdict of acceptance *no matter what* the experimental outcome is going to be. Samuelson proves that

PROPOSITION 1. *Any evaluation rule that accepts the truth with probability 1-$\varepsilon$ can be blindly passed with probability 1-$\varepsilon$.*

On top of a formal proof [p. 101], Samuelson provides a little game-theoretic argument to back up this result. Suppose you are playing a zero-sum game against a malevolent opponent called "Nature". Nature can choose the true distribution $E^*$, and you can choose $E_T$. You win if $T$ is accepted by whatever evaluation rule $R$ is in place, otherwise Nature wins. Assume $R$ accepts the truth with probability at least $1-\varepsilon$. If you could choose $T$after you have observed Nature's choice, you could simply choose it so that $E_T = E^*$, and guarantee a probability of success of at least 1-$\varepsilon$. Similarly, if Nature could make her move after it has observed your choice of $T$, she would try to minimize your success rate by choosing an

randomly drawn from a set of possible distributions — or, in other words, the prediction of an indeterministic theory that is made conditional on the instantiation of some indeterministic background condition or event. (Think of the prediction that tomorrow it will rain with probability $P$, a prediction made conditional on the expectation that the temperature will (probably) be quite low.) [Samuelson, 2005, p. 72]. Since this assumption is not important for my argument, I won't comment on it here.

appropriate $E^* \neq E_T$. At this point, we know from the minimax theorem of zero-sum games that your chances of succeeding in the second circumstance can be no worse than in the first one, hence that you can always win with probability at least 1-$\varepsilon$. Since in practice at the moment of choosing $T$ you don't know the truth, and fortunately Nature cannot change the truth after it has seen your move, you must be somewhere in between the best and worse scenario, which means that the theory you will choose can pass at least with probability $1 - \varepsilon$ [Samuelson 2005, p. 81].

What does this mean? Samuelson is adamant that he is providing a strong argument in favour of the criterion of construct-independence:

> Interpreting experimental evidence as supporting a theory, or offering a theory as an interpretation of experimental evidence, thus acquires bite only if the theory is clear and complete enough that it can be extended to answer new questions and confront new tests that did *not* play a role in the construction of the theory. Is the theory clear enough that others could design new tests, and is one willing to risk the theory in such tests? If not, then it is not clear that progress has been made. [2005, p. 82][25]

But in fact Samuelson does *not* prove that construct independence is a necessary condition for empirical support. His argument merely proves that it is always *possible* to construct a theory that blindly passes a test with high probability. *But why should you like to construct such a theory?* Such a theory would obviously fail to be tested severely by the evidence, as the definition of "blindly passing" makes clear. Remember that according to the severity criterion in a good test the probability of observing fitting evidence must be low; in contrast a test that blindly passes a theory has a maximally high probability of having a good fit with $H$. Thus Samuelson only proves that there is always going to be *some* theory (constructed so as to blindly pass the test) that (a) has been constructed to fit $E$, and (b) is not tested severely by $E$. Or, in other words, that being constructed to fit $E$ is not sufficient to pass a severe test with $E$.

But of course this is hardly disputable. What we want is not only a good fit but also a high severity of the test, which is denied by the definition of "blindly passing". Samuelson fails to prove that not being constructed to fit $E$ is *necessary* in order to pass a severe test with $E$. This is what construct-independence theories of scientific testing should achieve, what Samuelson falsely claims to have proven, and what is disputed by the severity approach.

[25] Samuelson also stresses that his argument is not a restatement of the view that one should commit to a theory before testing it with data; and that he is not simply repeating the common prescription to test a theory "out of sample", i.e. using new data that did not motivate the search for the theory in question [2005, p. 82].

# 4 EXTERNAL VALIDITY

There is a lot more to be said about the severity approach and alternative theories of inductive inference. For reasons of space we limit the discussion to the three features discussed in the previous sections: objectivity, locality, and a-temporality.[26] The next part of this chapter is devoted to the second issue of validity, i.e. the problem of drawing inferences from a specific experiment to other (non-experimental) circumstances of interest. Both validity issues are specific examples of what we might call the "practical" problem of induction, as opposed to Hume's well-known "logical" problem. Hume was concerned with the logical or rational justification of inductive inferences *in general*; validity, instead, has to do with the reliability of *particular* inductive moves, or in other words with the problem of distinguishing between "good" and "bad" inductive inferences. To put it differently, we are more in the realm of "Russell's chicken" than of "Hume's riddle".[27] It is worth making this distinction because it is generally recognised today that there may well not be a solution to the logical problem of induction, not at least in the form required by Hume. So it is important to stress that in asking economists to think about validity, one is not posing an unreasonable or idle philosophical challenge.

The two problems of validity have attracted very different levels of attention. Experimenters have devoted a lot of time and energy to internal validity, especially by proposing methodological rules or principles that would improve the reliability of experimental inferences within the laboratory.[28] External validity issues in contrast are often raised by the critics of experimental economics. Experimenters have sometimes dismissed such critiques as unhelpful, because they distract from other important issues of research. The general feeling was that external validity critiques must be either unanswerable because inappropriately formulated, or, if appropriately formulated, in principle answerable by means of more experimental work. In this sense, the critic is supposed to carry the burden of proving the lack of validity of economic experiments.

Philosophers also seem to have strangely neglected the external validity problem. This is due to a number of reasons, including the fact that most philosophy of science tends to be physics-based, and experimental physicists do not recognise external validity as a separate problem of inference. Be that as it may, it is a fact that, of the two validity issues, external validity is the least studied. It is also the one that raises more controversy, and where philosophers may have both something to contribute and something to learn from experimental economics.

[26]Achinstein [2005] and Taper and Lee [2004] provide useful overviews of the current debates on inductive inference and scientific testing.

[27]Russell [1912] mentions the predicament of a chicken that sees the farmer bringing food every morning at the same time, and thus runs towards him until, of course, one day the farmer comes to cut the chicken's neck. The chicken had made an unreliable generalization.

[28]See for example Smith [1976; 1982], Wilde [1981].

## 4.1 External validity and representativeness

We have seen that the logic of the perfectly controlled experiment leads quite naturally to endorse a severity approach to inductive inference. The method of the perfectly controlled experiment however is maximally useful to solve internal validity problem — when the issue is to find out what is going on within a given experimental set-up or laboratory system. Since the method relies importantly on the control of background conditions ($K_i$) in order to obtain truly informative evidence, there is usually a trade-off between internal and external validity. A simple experiment that reproduces many of the idealisations of a theoretical model is usually easier to control in the laboratory; but it also constitutes a weaker starting point for extending the experimental knowledge thus obtained to other situations of interests (where such idealisations do not hold).

So how can we tackle the external validity problem constructively? And can we indicate a solution that is consistent with the logic of the severity approach? Ideally, we would like to have a unique inductive methodology that is able to capture both types of inferential moves.

Following an old tradition in experimental psychology, Robin Hogarth [2005] argues that the problem of external validity should be framed in terms of *representativeness.* There are, more precisely, at least *two* dimensions of representativeness in an economic experiment: *subjects sample* and *design.* Whereas statistical techniques and random sampling can be used to tackle subject representativeness, the choice of the design is rarely seen as a problem of the same kind. The designs of economic and psychology experiments are often highly idiosyncratic if compared to real-world situations, and are certainly not randomly picked from the target population (e.g. the set of real-life choice-situations or real market decisions). For this reason, the "representativeness" framework might be helpful to highlight the nature of the problem, but does not do much in terms of pointing to a solution, as far as problems of design are concerned.

Why is the method of random sampling from a set of real-life situations *not* followed by experimental economists? Random sampling makes sense only if you are trying to capture a central tendency in a population of individuals with varying traits. But there may be no such central tendency in a set of, say, market exchanges. Consider bargaining: economic theory suggests that different details of the bargaining situation can influence the outcome drastically. If this is true, then an average description of different bargaining outcomes is likely to be rather uninformative and to obscure all the interesting variations in the data. What we want is instead to be able to understand how different factors or causal mechanisms interact to generate different outcomes. This is why experimenters sometimes privilege simple designs or game-situations that capture the working of just one mechanism in isolation, where somewhat "extreme" results are vividly instantiated.

## *4.2 Shifting the burden of proof*

For these reasons, external validity inferences usually do not take the form of an inference from sample to population. They rather look like inferences from a specific experimental environment to another specific real-world environment. Consider the phenomenon known as the "winner's curse", for example. In so-called "common-value sealed-bid auctions" bidders are trying to purchase an item that has approximately the same value for all the competitors, but the exact value of which is unknown to all. Each bidder makes an estimate of the value of the item, which is likely to diverge from its true value. The standard theory assumes perfect rationality; in this case, bidders are supposed to be able to anticipate that the winner of the auction will probably be the one who most *overestimates* the value of the item. To correct for this bias, the theory assumes that the bidders should revise their offers downwards.

Experimental data have shown that this revision does not take place or takes place imperfectly, and thus the winners turn out to be systematically "cursed" [Kagel and Levin, 1986]. But is this result valid outside the narrow experimental conditions where it was generated? By raising the problem of external validity, we are not necessarily asking whether the experimental design has been sampled from some relevant population of designs. We are rather asking whether the results can be transferred from the laboratory to some *specific* real-world situation of interest.

Experimental research on the winner's curse started precisely with the aim of replicating a target phenomenon, allegedly observed in the auctions of the Outer Continental Shelf, selling leases to drill oil in the Gulf of Mexico.[29] The experiments had a fairly precise intended domain of application, which makes the external validity problem tractable. If you observe a certain phenomenon in the laboratory, but you are not sure about its generalizability to real-world circumstances *in general*, it is difficult to tackle the problem constructively. You can do much better in contrast if you know exactly the sort of circumstances you want to export your results to: in this case you can look for *specific reasons* why the result may not be exportable. These reasons will usually take the form of some relevant (causal) dissimilarity between the experimental and the target system. Thus, the obvious way to proceed is by modifying the experiment to include the features of the target that could be responsible for the alleged external validity failure, and see whether they in fact make a difference or not.

Chris Starmer [1999, p. 9] defends a view of external validity inferences that is very close to the one just sketched. He points out that the putative lack of external validity *of a specific experiment* can usually be attributed to one or more "unrealistic" features of the experimental design (the lack of a potentially important factor, or the presence of an artificial condition) — where "unrealistic" here is clearly defined with reference to a target of investigation. If this is the case, whenever a potential flaw has been highlighted, it should be possible at least in principle to design a new experiment that controls for the effective causal relevance

[29]Cf. Kagel and Levin [1986].

of those factors or conditions.[30]

Starmer's position improves upon traditional defences of experimentation such as Plott's. By focusing on theory-testing, Plott is concerned with defending experimental economics *as a whole* from the charge of irrelevance, and tries to shift the burden of proof by identifying experimental economics narrowly with theory-testing. "I'm only testing theoretical models", the experimenter says. "If the model is incomplete or too simple to be applicable to a real-world system, that's a problem for the theorist, not for the experimenter". But this is disingenuous, of course. Demonstrating that experimental economics is not just a laboratory game offers little comfort, if it turns out to be just a game between theory and experiment. The critic is ultimately concerned with the real-world applicability of *both* experimental and theoretical knowledge. But even more worrying is the fact that many theoretical models are nowadays constructed with an eye to capturing robust experimental regularities. When experimental results guide theory-formation, the risk of engaging in a self-referential process of theorising and experimentation that is totally insulated from the real world becomes very high indeed [Schram, 2005, pp. 234-5].

In a recent textbook Friedman and Cassar also argue that "an honest skeptic of external validity bears the burden of guessing what makes the lab environment substantially different than the real world" [Friedman and Cassar, 2004, p. 29]. This implies that in absence of a specific critique of a given experimental design (i.e. unless one identifies a potential flaw) the external validity of an experiment should be accepted *by default*. As Deborah Mayo [2008] points out, however, this conclusion is based on a fallacy known as "argument from ignorance". The fact that I have no reason to believe that $\sim X$ is the case, is not in itself a good reason to believe that $X$ is the case. In terms of the severity approach, suppose we are dealing with two hypotheses, $H$ (= experiment $X$ has external validity) and $\sim H$ (= experiment $X$ has no external validity). To prove that $\sim H$ passes a sever test is *not* equivalent to prove that $H$ has passed such a test. The only legitimate way to argue for the external validity of an experimental result is by showing that there is good evidence ("good" according to the severity criteria) in favour of $H$.

The correct position, to sum up, is to recognise that external validity critiques have a bite only when they refer to specific experimental designs (to worry about external validity *in general* is pretty useless). But at the same time we cannot let the experimenter shift the burden onto the critic — the burden always lies with whoever is drawing the inference from laboratory to real-world circumstances, who is expected to prove the relevance of the experimental design for the investigation of a given target.[31] Whenever an inference is made, it must be warranted by the

[30]An interesting question is whether *every* property of a real-world economy can be transferred and reproduced in the laboratory. Bardsley [2005] argues that this may not be the case, and discusses two concrete cases of experimentation to back up his claim. If Bardsley is right, there may well be some economic phenomena that cannot be studied in the laboratory. How common such phenomena are is entirely an empirical matter of course.

[31]It should be stressed that experimenters are often concerned with proving the existence of certain mechanisms or phenomena in the lab only, and leave it to policy-makers or applied

data — the absence of evidence indicating the contrary does not provide positive support for the inference itself.

## *4.3 Experimental localism and economic ontology*

Dyer and Kagel [1996] have studied the winner's curse phenomenon in the context of the North-American construction industry. They identify a number of mechanisms that effectively defend bidders in that industry from the "curse" of overbidding. One of them is a rule allowing the withdrawal of winning bids in case of "arithmetical errors" in the submission of the offer. In practice the notion of arithmetical error is interpreted so broadly that almost any offer can be withdrawn without penalty if the bidder so wishes. This rule provides cover for both the contractors and their clients, because a grossly mistaken estimate can put the construction firm and the project itself at risk. Nobody wants to work with an unhappy firm that are aware of the fact that they will lose money from the contract.

Dyer and Kagel point out that traditional experiments on the winner's curse do not reproduce such rules for the withdrawal of bids. Hence, their results cannot be generalized straightforwardly to the construction industry. This is a typical case where only the detailed study of the institutional rules and practices of a specific market allows the evaluation of an external validity claim. The experimental result of course is still of some value in trying to understand what is going on in that specific market, but only as a contrast case. In principle, a new experiment could be designed which incorporates the institutional mechanisms that supposedly neutralise the effects of the winner's curse. Prior to this sort of investigation, no moral can be drawn about the applicability of the winner's curse experiments to the construction industry.

This point is of great philosophical significance. In this section we shall elaborate and investigate its implications in two directions: first, I shall look more specifically at the use of evidence in external validity arguments. Secondly, I shall examine what experimental economics can teach us about the ontology of economics and the social sciences in general.

As shown by the Dyer and Kagel article, external validity inferences require a combination of field and experimental evidence. This has been occasionally recognised by the founders of the discipline (e.g. [Smith, 1989, p. 152]), but until recently very little has been said about the specific ways in which the two sources of evidence should be combined so as to be most effective. This issue, incidentally, is by no means an exclusive concern of experimental economics. It has been discussed also in the context of experimental medicine [La Follette and Shanks, 1994; Thagard, 1999], biochemistry [Strand *et al.*, 1996], and molecular

economists to apply such knowledge in the field. There is an important division of labor in (applied and pure) science that should not be overlooked by unreasonably imposing on experimenters the task of establishing the external validity of *all* the experiments they make. See Guala [2005a, Ch. 10].

biology [Weber, 2004; Steel, 2007]. The structure of external validity inferences can be articulated as a case of *causal-analogical reasoning*. The analogical aspect of the inference can be reconstructed as follows:

(a) The target system displays phenomenon $Y$.

(b) The experimental system displays phenomenon $Y$.

(c) In the laboratory, the phenomenon is caused by factor $X$.

(d) The target phenomenon is therefore also caused by $X$.

An obvious objection can be raised at this point: the number of analogies that can be drawn between any two objects or systems is potentially infinite. So which analogies in this infinite set are "strong" or of greater epistemic significance? Analogies such as those in (a)–(d) are instructive only if we are confident that the other (background) conditions are "right". Consider the case of internal validity: a correlation between two variables is too weak a basis to infer that a causal relation exists between the two. We also need to be sure that no background variation (in the $K_i$) is confounding the inference. Similarly, the fact that $X$ causes $Y$ in $A$ does not guarantee that $X$ causes $Y$ in $B$. We must make sure that no other causal factor is confounding the inference. The second important point then is that *dis*analogies are also crucial. As in the case of the winner's curse, one must always check that no relevant causal differences exist that are able to disrupt the inferences from laboratory to target. In a nutshell, the laboratory and the target system must be made similar in all *causally relevant* respects. If we suspect there may be a causally important difference, we must check it experimentally [Guala, 2005a, Ch. 9].

Daniel Steel [2007, Ch. 8] has criticized the analogical approach for being too conservative: external validity inferences can be drawn even when we do not have the resources or the possibility to check all causally relevant disanalogies between the laboratory system and its target. Causes leave marks that are transmitted through causal mechanisms. According to the method of "comparative process tracing", it is sufficient to compare the working of an experimental and a target system by checking the presence of marks at some crucial stages of the mechanisms. Perfect identity among the systems, moreover, is no required either according to Steel. Our background knowledge of causal mechanisms sometimes allows the inference of the direction of a causal relation even when we know that some differences exist between the lab and the real world.

The analogical and the process tracing methods are both distinctively empirical approaches to the problem of external validity, and constitute sharp improvements with respect to previous discussions. External validity has too often been addressed by means of metaphysical arguments about the nature of economic and social reality, which unfortunately are of little utility. It has been argued, for example, that experimentation is impossible because there are no universal laws in economics [Economics Focus, 1999]. But there may well be no universal laws in biology, as far as we know, and yet experiments have been profitably used for decades in that discipline. Similarly, some have posited the necessity of *tendency laws* for experimentation [Siakantaris, 2000]. Following John Stuart Mill [1836], a tendency law is usually understood as a "super-causal" law of the following kind: "$A \rightarrow B$" is a tendency law if not only $A$ has the capacity of making $B$ happen in the "right" set of circumstances, but also if it *tends* to make it happen when the conditions are not right. Or, to put it slightly differently, if $A$ *contributes* to the instantiation of $B$ even when other "disturbing" or "counteracting" factors are at work [Hausman, 1992].

Of course laws of this kind *can* be tested in the laboratory. The worry is that if the (numerous) factors that are kept fixed in the background during an experiment (factors that often are not even modelled theoretically, but rather relegated in a *ceteris paribus* clause) do not combine additively but interact with the main experimental variables, then the experimental result will not be valid outside the narrow domain of its instantiation. We can still discover causal laws valid in a narrow domain, but unless they are tendency laws that are robust to changes in the boundary conditions, this knowledge will be of rather limited use.

The ontology of tendencies, then, seems to be a desideratum for the *generalizability* of experimental results, rather than a necessary requirement for the success of the experimental method itself. As a matter of fact, according to Anna Alexandrova [2006], the most successful applications of experimental economics to date do not presuppose the existence of tendencies at all. Applied economists start from the pessimistic assumption that the causal properties modelled in economic theory may be rather fragile, and then test repeatedly their robustness to changes in the boundary and background conditions (see also [Guala, 2005a, Ch. 8], for some examples).

In general, the existence of tendency laws is a post-scientific issue to be resolved by empirical evidence, rather than a pre-scientific issue to be addressed by metaphysical speculation. By combining experimental economics with field data we have got the unique chance of testing *empirically* whether the phenomena and causal relations discovered in the laboratory are "robust" and can be exported into the field. Of course we should expect different degrees of success — there may well be areas in which experimental results turn out to be more easily transferable and robust, other areas where they are less so. More tendencies are obviously preferable, but a limited degree of robustness and modularity is still preferable to nothing at all [Guala, 2002b].

## 5 THE PHILOSOPHICAL RELEVANCE OF EXPERIMENTAL ECONOMICS' RESULTS

Methodology has been at the centre of this chapter right from the start. This reflects partly my own interests, and partly the concentration of the existing literature on methodological matters. The philosophical relevance of experimental economics however is not exhausted by the problems of validity, and the related issues of causal inference, experimental design, and data-analysis. Experiments are beginning to change rather drastically the landscape of economic science, and thus carry deep implications on a number of other ontological, normative, and political issues. This is perhaps where the interaction between philosophers and economists will be most productive in the future.

Experimental economics is often perceived to have come up with two important sets of results: that neoclassical economic theory can predict remarkably well the aggregate outcome of market processes, and that the neoclassical theory of individual choice is repeatedly falsified by laboratory evidence. Although on a superficial reading these two results may appear mutually incompatible, this is in fact not the case. Both sets of results, to begin with, must be qualified by an important proviso: the neoclassical theory of markets predicts well *in the right circumstances*, and similarly the individual theory of choice suffers from robust anomalies *in specific circumstances*. In both cases, the circumstances matter.

Among the circumstances that matter, *institutions* have emerged as particularly important. Social institutions can be usefully divided in two categories, that we shall call "rules" and "norms". On the one hand we have very specific, explicitly formulated and often legally enforced *rules*, such as those regulating exchange in the stock market. On the other, we have fairly broad, informal norms such as those that govern market interactions in everyday life — norms such as "honour done deals", "do not cheat", and so forth.

Informal norms are behind some of the most robust anomalies of strategic and individual choice. There is a general agreement, for example, that norms of co-operation and especially reciprocation (cooperate only if the others do the same) cause the phenomena of overcontribution and decay in repeated public goods experiments. Other examples are the anomalous offers observed in ultimatum game experiments, dictator's games, investment games, and other similar experimental situations.[32]

Market experiments have proven that the convergence of competitive markets on efficient prices depends crucially on the institutions that govern the exchange — for example the type of auction, or the coordinating mechanism that matches buyers and sellers in a multilateral exchange [Plott and Smith, 1978]. These results fill an enormous gap in the economic literature, which until recently was occupied by an idealized fiction, the Walrasian auctioneer.

The importance of rules and norms teaches important lessons regarding the scope and character of economic theory, as well as its use in policy-making. First, it reminds us of the incompleteness of theory and of the constant need to supplement it by means of empirical investigation and insights from neighbor disciplines like psychology and sociology. Secondly, it highlights the importance of collecting local information about the context of application of a theoretical model, before policy intervention takes place. The most blatant examples of the context-sensitivity of economic knowledge are the huge failures in reforming the economies of Eastern European countries after the fall of the Soviet regimes. A common reading of these failures is that the institutional conditions that are necessary for a healthy functioning of markets simply were not in place when the transition took place.

[32]See [Bicchieri, 2006] for a survey and philosophical discussion.

However, experimental economists have also shown that when policy intervention has been carefully planned and, crucially, tested empirically, market institutions can do an egregious job at achieving certain policy goals. Examples of successful reforms of this kind are the various market design enterprises informed by game theory and experimental economics over the last couple of decades (cf. [Miller, 2002; Roth, 2002] for overviews and general discussions).[33]

All these developments have important political implications. Economics has been for much of the last two centuries dominated by the invisible hand metaphor, in its various guises. The results of experimental economics carry two messages that will probably disappoint both the enthusiasts and the radical critics of market liberalism. Experiments have shown on the one hand that markets *can* work, and not just in the abstract realm of economic theory. On the other, experiments have shown that markets are relatively delicate machines, whose smooth functioning may require a lot of careful planning, artificial design, and supervision. The interesting challenge is to learn from the institutions that have spontaneously evolved in history, while at the same time identifying their shortcomings and fixing them using the most advanced theoretical and experimental knowledge that is available.[34] The "economist as engineer" [Roth, 2002] is a character that will probably gain increasing prominence and influence in the future. Whether this is good or bad news is for all of us to decide.

## 6 OTHER ISSUES AND READINGS

The most comprehensive philosophical discussion of experimental economics to date is to be found in my book *The Methodology of Experimental Economics* [Guala, 2005a]. Bardsley *et al.* [2009] will be the second monograph on the same topic to be published in a short period. An especially valuable source of ideas and debate is a symposium recently published in the *Journal of Economic Methodology* [Sugden, 2005]. To get a sense of what experimental economics is all about, however, the novice is warmly encouraged to try a few simple experiments in his/her own class, like those illustrated in [Bergstrom and Miller, 1997] for example. Davis and Holt [1993], Friedman and Sunder [1994], and Friedman and Cassar [2004] are widely used textbooks. Excellent surveys of experimental results can be found in [Kagel and Roth, 1995; Plott and Smith, 2008]. Holt's [2000] bibliography is an extremely useful resource, and Roth's [2005] webpage is a good point of entry into the world of game theory and experimentation.

Among the issues that have not been covered in this chapter I should mention the sensitive issue of the divide between economics and psychology [Rabin, 1998;

[33]For a skeptical view of the "successes" of market design, see [Mirowski and Nik-Kah, 2006].

[34]Vernon Smith, co-recipient of the 2002 Nobel Prize, speaks of a constant interaction between "constructive" and "ecological" rationality [Smith, 2008]. Smith follows Hayek in arguing that we should trust the beneficial effects of evolutionary adaptation in the social as well as the biological realm. The postulation of an evolutionary "invisible hand" of course opens another huge and exciting area of research at the intersection between economics and philosophy.

2001; Smith, 1991], and the related issue of the importance of monetary incentives in experimental design [Hertwig and Ortmann, 2001; Read, 2005; Guala, 2005a, Ch. 11]. In relation to the issue of external validity, there is now a growing body of research carried out by means of "field experiments" — a mix of laboratory control in real-world circumstances — that is calling for methodological systematisation [Harrison and List, 2004]. Philosophers interested in normative issues will be interested in the way in which experimental results have been used to support or criticise models of normative reasoning such as Bayesian belief-updating or expected utility theory. This tradition goes back to Allais' [1953] seminal work, but has come to prominence with the so-called "human rationality debate" of the 1970s (see e.g. [Cohen, 1981; Stein, 1996]). Guala [2000] and Starmer [2005] discuss the symmetric issue of how the impact of experimental results on economic theory has been heavily influenced by normative considerations.

Finally, it seems likely that in the future the methods of experimental economics will be employed more and more frequently by naturalistically-minded philosophers interested in tackling epistemological and ontological issues using the resources of the human and social sciences (see e.g. the new "Experimental Philosophy" movement as presented by Knobe [2007]). A most fertile area or research lies at the intersection between experimental economics and social ontology: Bicchieri [2006] for example relies extensively on experimental results in economics and social psychology to develop a new formal model of social norms. Guala [2006], Mirowski and Nik-Kah [2006], and Callon and Muniesa [2006] discuss whether and in what sense the experimental practice can have a "performative" effect on economic reality — i.e. whether by experimenting one not only observes but also *creates* socio-economic entities that did not previously exist.

## ACKNOWLEDGEMENTS

Many ideas appearing in this paper were proposed and discussed at a workshop on the methodology of experimental economics held at Virginia Tech in June 2005. I must thank Deborah Mayo, Aris Spanos, Chris Starmer, Jim Woodward, Vernon Smith, Catherine Eckel, Sheryl Ball, Cristina Bicchieri and Robin Cubitt for many exchanges before, during and after the workshop. Bob Sugden also provided some useful clarifications. The remaining mistakes are of course entirely mine.

## BIBLIOGRAPHY

[Achinstein, 2005] P. Achinstein, ed. *Scientific Evidence: Philosophical Theories and Applications*. Baltimore: John Hopkins University Press, 2005.

[Alexnandrova, 2006] A. Alexandrova. Connecting Economic Models to the Real World: Game Theory and the FCC Spectrum Auctions. *Philosophy of the Social Sciences*, 36: 173-92, 2006.

[Allais, 1953] M. Allais. The Foundations of a Positive Theory of Choice Involving Risk and a Criticism of the Postulate and Axioms of the American School. In M. Allais and O. Hagen, eds., *Expected Utility Hypothesis and the Allais Paradox*. Dordrecht: Reidel, pp. 257-332, 1979.

[Andreoni, 1988] J. Andreoni. Why Free Ride? Strategies and Learning in Public Goods Experiments. *Journal of Public Economics* 37: 291-304, 1988.

[Bardsley, 2005] N. Bardsley. Experimental Economics and the Artificiality of Alteration. *Journal of Economic Methodology* 12: 239-51, 2005.

[Bardsley *et al.*, 2009] N. Bardsley, R. Cubitt, G. Loomes, P. Moffatt, C. Starmer, and R. Sugden. *Economics and the Laboratory.* Princeton: Princeton University Press, 2009.

[Bergstrom and Miller, 1997] T. C. Bergstrom and J. H. Miller. *Experiments with Economic Principles: Microeconomics.* New York: McGraw-Hill, 1997.

[Bicchieri, 2006] C. Bicchieri. *The Grammar of Society.* Cambridge: Cambridge University Press, 2006.

[Boumans and Morgan, 2001] M. Boumans and M. S. Morgan. *Ceteris Paribus* Conditions: Materiality and the Application of Economic Theory. *Journal of Economic Methodology* 8: 11-26, 2001.

[Callon and Muniesa, 2006] M. Callon and F. Muniesa. Economic Experiments and the Construction of Markets. In D. MacKenzie, F. Muniesa and L. Siu, eds., *Do Economists Make Markets? On the Performativity of Economics.* Princeton: Princeton University Press, 2006.

[Cartwright, 1983] N. Cartwright. *How the Laws of Physics Lie.* Oxford: Clarendon Press, 1983.

[Cartwright, 1989] N. Cartwright. *Nature's Capacities and Their Measurement.* Oxford: Oxford University Press, 1989.

[Christensen, 2001] L. B. Christensen. *Experimental Methodology*, 8th ed. Needham Heights, Mass.: Allyn & Bacon, 2001.

[Cohen, 1981] L. J. Cohen. Can Human Irrationality Be Experimentally Demonstrated? *Behavioral and Brain Sciences* 4: 417-70, 1981.

[Collins, 1985] H. M. Collins. *Changing Order: Replication and Induction in Scientific Practice.* London: Sage, 1985.

[Cubitt, 2005] R. Cubitt. Experiments and the Domain of Economic Theory. *Journal of Economic Methodology* 12: 297-210, 2005.

[Davis and Holt, 1993] D. D. Davis and C. H. Holt. *Experimental Economics.* Princeton: Princeton University Press, 1993.

[Duhem, 1906] P. Duhem. *La théorie physique. Son objet et sa structure.* Paris: Chevalier et Rivière, 1906; Engl. transl. *The Aim and Structure of Physical Theory.* Princeton: Princeton University Press, 1954.

[Dyer and Kagel, 1996] D. Dyer and J. H. Kagel. Bidding in Common Value Auctions: How the Commercial Construction Industry Corrects for the Winner's Curse. *Management Science* 42: 1463-75, 1996.

[Economics Focus, 1999] Economics Focus. News from the Lab. *The Economist*, May 8, p. 96, 1999.

[Franklin, 1998] A. Franklin. Experiment in Physics. In E. N. Zalta, ed., *The Stanford Encyclopaedia of Philosophy*, 1998. `http://plato.stanford.edu/entries/physics-experiment`

[Friedman and Cassar, 2004] D. Friedman and A. Cassar. *Economics Lab: An Intensive Course in Experimental Economics.* London: Routledge, 2004.

[Friedman and Sunder, 1994] D. Friedman and S. Sunder. *Experimental Methods: A Primer for Economists.* Cambridge: Cambridge University Press, 1994.

[Friedman, 1953] M. Friedman. The Methodology of Positive Economics. In *Essays in Positive Economics.* Chicago: University of Chicago Press, pp. 3-43, 1953.

[Galison, 1987] P. Galison. *How Experiments End.* Chicago: University of Chicago Press, 1987.

[Giere, 1983] R. N. Giere. Testing Theoretical Hypotheses. In J. Earman, ed., *Testing Scientific Theories.* Minneapolis: University of Minnesota Press, pp. 269-98, 1983.

[Giere, 1988] R. N. Giere. *Explaining Science.* Chicago: University of Chicago Press, 1988.

[Gooding *et al.*, 1989] D. Gooding, T. Pinch, and S. Shapin, eds. *The Uses of Experiment.* Cambridge: Cambridge University Press, 1989.

[Guala, 1998] F. Guala. Experiments as Mediators in the Non-Laboratory Sciences. *Philosophica* 62: 901–18, 1998.

[Guala, 2000] F. Guala. The Logic of Normative Falsification: Rationality and Experiments in Decision Theory. *Journal of Economic Methodology* 7: 59–93, 2000.

[Guala, 2002a] F. Guala. Models, Simulations, and Experiments. In L. Magnani and N. Nersessian, eds., *Model-Based Reasoning: Science, Technology, Values.* New York: Kluwer, pp. 59-74, 2002.

[Guala, 2002b] F. Guala. On the Scope of Experiments in Economics: Comments on Siakantaris, *Cambridge Journal of Economics* 26: 261-7, 2002.

[Guala, 2005] F. Guala. *The Methodology of Experimental Economics*. New York: Cambridge University Press, 2005.

[Guala, 2006] F. Guala. How to Do Things with Experimental Economics. In D. MacKenzie, F. Muniesa and L. Siu, eds., *Do Economists Make Markets? On the Performativity of Economics*. Princeton: Princeton University Press, 2006.

[Guala, 2008a] F. Guala. Experimental Economics, History of. In *The New Palgrave Dictionary of Economics*, London: Palgrave-MacMillan, 2008.

[Guala, 2008b] F. Guala. The Experimental Philosophy of Experimental Economics: Replies to Alexandrova, Hargreaves-Heaps, Hausman, and Hindriks, *Journal of Economic Methodology*, 15: 224-31, 2008.

[Hacking, 1983] I. Hacking. *Representing and Intervening*. Cambridge: Cambridge University Press, 1983.

[Harrison and List, 2004] G. W. Harrison and J. A. List. Field Experiments. *Journal of Economic Literature* 42: 1009-45, 2004.

[Hausman, 1992] D. M. Hausman. *The Inexact and Separate Science of Economics*. Cambridge: Cambridge University Press, 1992.

[Hausman, 1998] D. M. Hausman. *Causal Asymmetries*. Cambridge: Cambridge University Press, 1998.

[Hausman, 2005] D. M. Hausman. Testing' Game Theory. *Journal of Economic Methodology* 12: 211-23, 2005.

[Hausman, 2008] D. M. Hausman. Experimenting on Models and in the World, *Journal of Economic Methodology*, 15: 209-16, 2008.

[Hertwig and Ortmann, 2001] R. Hertwig and A. Ortmann. Experimental Practices in Economics: A Methodological Challenge for Psychologists? *Behavioral and Brain Sciences* 24: 383–451, 2001.

[Hogarth, 2005] R. M. Hogarth. The Challenge of Representative Design in Psychology and Economics. *Journal of Economic Methodology* 12: 253-263, 2005.

[Holt, 2000] C. H. Holt. The Y2K Bibliography of Experimental Economics and Social Science, 2000. `http://www.people.virginia.edu/~cah2k/y2k.htm` (29/12/1999 version)

[Hoover, 2001] K. D. Hoover. *Causality in Macroeconomics*. Cambridge: Cambridge University Press, 2001.

[Hoover, 2004] K. D. Hoover. Lost Causes. *Journal of the History of Economic Thought* 26: 149-64, 2004.

[Howson and Urbach, 1989] C. Howson and P. Urbach. *Scientific Reasoning: The Bayesian Approach*. Chicago: Open Court, 1989.

[Kagel and Levin, 1986] J. H. Kagel and D. Levin. The Winner's Curse Phenomenon and Public Information in Common Value Auctions. *American Economic Review* 76: 894–920, 1986.

[Kagel and Roth, 1995] J. H. Kagel and A. E. Roth, eds. *The Handbook of Experimental Economics*. Princeton: Princeton University Press, 1995.

[Knobe, 2007] J. Knobe. Experimental Philosophy, *Philosophy Compass* 2: 81-92, 2007.

[Kreps *et al.*, 1981] D. M. Kreps, P. Milgrom, J. Roberts, and R. Wilson. Rational Cooperation in the Finitely Repeated Prisoners Dilemma. *Journal of Economic Theory* 27: 245-52, 1981.

[Isaac, 1983] M. Isaac. Laboratory Experimental Economics as a Tool in Public Policy Analysis. *Social Science Journal* July: 45-58, 1983.

[LaFollette and Shanks, 1995] H. LaFollette and N. Shanks. Two Models of Models in Biomedical Research. *Philosophical Quarterly* 45: 141–60, 1995.

[Ledyard, 1995] J. O. Ledyard. Public Goods: A Survey of Experimental Research. In J. H. Kagel and A. E. Roth (eds.) *The Handbook of Experimental Economics*. Princeton: Princeton University Press, pp. 111-94, 1995.

[Lee and Mirowski, 2008] K. S. Lee and P. Mirowski. The Energy Behind Vernon Smith's Experimental Economics, *Cambridge Journal of Economics* 32: 257-71, 2008.

[Leonard, 1994] R. Leonard. Laboratory Strife: Higgling as Experimental Science in Economics and Social Psychology. In N. B. De Marchi and M. S. Morgan, eds., *Higgling*. History of Political Economy Supplement, Vol. 26. Durham: Duke University Press, 1994.

[Loomes, 1989] G. Loomes. Experimental Economics. In J. D. Hey (ed.) *Current Issues in Microeconomics*. New York: St. Martin's Press, pp. 152-78, 1989.

[Mackie, 1974] J. L. Mackie. *The Cement of the Universe*. Oxford: Clarendon Press 1974.

[Mäki, 1992] U. Mäki. On the Method of Isolation in Economics. *Poznan Studies in the Philosophy of the Sciences and Humanities* 26: 317-51, 1992.
[Mäki, 2005] U. Mäki. Models Are Experiments, Experiments Are Models. *Journal of Economic Methodology* 12: 303-15, 2005.
[Mayo, 1996] D. Mayo. *Error and the Growth of Experimental Knowledge*. Chicago: University of Chicago Press, 1996.
[Mayo, 2005] D. Mayo. Evidence as Passing Severe Tests: Highly Probable versus Highly Probed Hypotheses. In Peter Achinstein, ed., *Scientific Evidence: Philosophical Theories and Applications*. Baltimore: John Hopkins University Press, pp. 95-127, 2005.
[Mayo, 2008] D. Mayo. Some Methodological Issues in Experimental Economics, *Philosophy of Science*, 75: 633-45, 2008.
[Mill, 1836] J. S. Mill. On the Definition of Political Economy and the Method of Investigation Proper to It. In *Collected Works of John Stuart Mill*, Vol. 4. Toronto: University of Toronto Press, 1967, pp. 120-64, 1836.
[Miller, 2002] R. M. Miller. *Paving Wall Street: Experimental Economics and the Quest for the Perfect Market*. New York: John Wiley & Sons, 2002.
[Mirowski and Nik-Kah, 2006] P. Mirowski and E. Nik-Kah. Markets Made Flesh: Callon, Performativity, and a Crisis in Science Studies, Augmented with Consideration of the FCC Auctions. In D. MacKenzie, F. Muniesa and L. Siu, eds., *Do Economists Make Markets? On the Performativity of Economics*. Princeton: Princeton University Press, 2006.
[Morgan, 2002] M. S. Morgan. Model Experiments and Models in Experiments. In L. Magnani and N. Nersessian, eds., *Model-Based reasoning: Science, Technology, Values*. New York: Kluwer, 2002.
[Morgan, 2003a] M. S. Morgan. Economics. In *The Cambridge History of Science, Vol. 7: The Modern Social Sciences*, edited by T. Porter and D. Ross. Cambridge: Cambridge University Press, pp. 275-305, 2003.
[Morgan, 2003b] M. S. Morgan. Experiments without Material Intervention: Model Experiments, Virtual Experiments and Virtually Experiments. In H. Radder, ed., *The Philosophy of Scientific Experimentation*. Pittsburgh: Pittsburgh University Press, 2003.
[Morgan, 2005] M. S. Morgan. Experiments versus Models: New Phenomena, Inference and Surprise. *Journal of Economic Methodology* 12: 317-29, 2005.
[Morrison, 1998] M. C. Morrison. Experiment. In E. Craig, ed., *The Routledge Encyclopaedia of Philosophy*. London: Routledge, pp. 514-8, 1998.
[Morrison and Morgan, 1999] M. C. Morrison and M. S. Morgan. Models as Mediating Instruments. In M. S. Morgan and M. C. Morrison, eds., *Models as Mediators*. Cambridge: Cambridge University Press, pp. 10-37, 1999.
[Moscati, 2007] I. Moscati. Early Experiments in Consumer Demand Theory: 1930-1970, *History of Political Economy* 39: 359-401, 2007.
[Parker, 2009] W. Parker. Does Matter Really Matter? Computer Simulations, Experiments and Materiality, *Synthese*, 169: 483-96, 2009.
[Plott, 1991] C. R. Plott. Will Economics Become an Experimental Science? *Southern Economic Journal* 57: 901–19, 1991.
[Plott and Smith, 1978] C. R. Plott and V. L. Smith. An Experimental Examination of Two Exchange Institutions, *Review of Economic Studies* 45: 133-53, 1978.
[Plott and Smith, 2006] C. R. Plott and V. L. Smith, eds. *The Handbook of Results in Experimental Economics*. London: Elsevier, 2006.
[Popper, 1934] K. R. Popper. *Logik der Forschung*. Vienna: Springer, 1934; Engl. transl. *Logic of Scientific Discovery*. London: Hutchinson, 1959.
[Quine, 1953] W. O. Quine. Two Dogmas of Empiricism. In *From A Logical Point of View*. Cambridge, Mass.: Harvard University Press, pp. 20-46, 1953.
[Rabin, 1998] M. Rabin. Psychology and Economics. *Journal of Economic Literature* 35: 11–46, 1998.
[Rabin, 2002] M. Rabin. A Perspective on Psychology and Economics. *European Economic Review* 46: 657–85, 2002.
[Read, 2005] D. Read. Monetary Incentives, What Are They Good for? *Journal of Economic Methodology* 12: 265-76, 2005.
[Redhead, 1980] M. L. G. Redhead. A Bayesian Reconstruction of the Methodology of Scientific Research Programmes. *Studies in History and Philosophy of Science* 11: 341–7, 1980.

[Roth, 1995] A. E. Roth. Introduction to Experimental Economics. In J. H. Kagel and A. E. Roth, eds., *The Handbook of Experimental Economics.* Princeton: Princeton University Press, pp. 3-109, 1995.

[Roth, 2002] A. E. Roth. The Economist as Engineer: Game Theory, Experimentation, and Computation as Tools for Design Economics. *Econometrica* 70: 1341–78, 2002.

[Roth, 2005] A. E. Roth. Al Roth's Game Theory and Experimental Economics Page. `http://kuznets.fas.harvard.edu/~aroth/alroth.html` (10/10/2005 version)

[Russell, 1912] B. Russell. On Induction, 1912. In *The Problems of Philosophy.* Oxford: Oxford University Press, 1973.

[Samuelson, 2005] L. Samuelson. Economic Theory and Experimental Economics, *Journal of Economic Literature* 43: 65-107, 2005.

[Santos, 2007] A. C. Santos. The 'Materials' of Experimental Economics: Technological versus Behavioral Experiments, *Journal of Economic Methodology* 14: 311-37, 2007.

[Schram, 2005] A. Schram. Artificiality: The Tension between Internal and External Validity in Economic Experiments. *Journal of Economic Methodology* 12: 225-237, 2005.

[Shubik, 1960] M. Shubik. Bibliography on Simulation, Gaming, Artificial Intelligence and Allied Topics. *Journal of the American Statistical Association* 55: 736-51, 1960.

[Simon, 1969] H. A. Simon. *The Sciences of the Artificial.* Boston: MIT Press, 1960.

[Smith, 1962] V. L. Smith. An Experimental Study of Competitive Market Behavior. *Journal of Political Economy* 70: 111–37, 1962.

[Smith, 1976] V. L. Smith. Experimental Economics: Induced Value Theory. *American Economic Review* 66: 274–7, 1976.

[Smith, 1982] V. L. Smith. Microeconomic Systems as an Experimental Science. *American Economic Review* 72: 923–55, 1982.

[Smith, 1989] V. L. Smith. Theory, Experiment and Economics. *Journal of Economic Perspectives* 3: 151–69, 1989.

[Smith, 1991] V. L. Smith. Rational Choice: The Contrast Between Economics and Psychology. *Journal of Political Economy* 99: 877–97, 1991.

[Smith, 1992] V. L. Smith. Game Theory and Experimental Economics: Beginnings and Early Influences. In E. R. Weintraub, ed., *Towards A History of Game Theory.* Durham: Duke University Press, pp. 241-82, 1992.

[Smith, 2008] V. L. Smith. *Rationality in Economics: Constructivist and Ecological Forms.* New York: Cambridge University Press, 2008.

[Søberg, 2005] M. Søberg. The Duhem-Quine Thesis and Experimental Economics: A Reinterpretation. *Journal of Economic Methodology*12: 581-97, 2005.

[Starmer, 1999] C. Starmer. Experiments in Economics: Should We Trust the Dismal Scientists in White Coats? *Journal of Economic Methodology* 6: 1–30, 1999.

[Steel, 2007] D. Steel. *Across the Boundaries: Extrapolation in Biology and in the Social Sciences.* New York: Oxford University Press, 2007.

[Stein, 1996] E. Stein. *Without Good Reason. The Rationality Debate in Philosophy and Cognitive Science.* Oxford: Clarendon Press, 1996.

[Sugden, 2005] R. Sugden. Experiments as Exhibits and Experiments as Tests, *Journal of Economic Methodology* 12: 291-302, 2005.

[Sugden, 2005] R. Sugden, ed. Experiment, Theory, World: A Symposium on the Role of Experiments in Economics, *Journal of Economic Methodology* 12, no. 2, 2005.

[Siakantaris, 2000] N. Siakantaris. Experimental Economics under the Microscope. *Cambridge Journal of Economics* 24: 267-81, 2000.

[Strand *et al.*, 1996] R. Strand, R. Fjelland, and T. Flatmark. *In Vivo* Interpretation of *In Vitro* Effect Studies. *Acta Biotheoretica* 44: 1–21, 1996.

[Taper and Lee, 2004] M. Taper and S. Lee, eds. *The Nature of Scientific Evidence.* Chicago: University of Chicago Press, 2004.

[Thagard, 1999] P. Thagard. *How Scientists Explain Disease.* Princeton: Princeton University Press, 1999.

[Weber, 2004] M. Weber. *Philosophy of Experimental Biology.* Cambridge: Cambridge University Press, 2004.

[Wilde, 1981] L. L. Wilde. On the Use of Laboratory Experiments in Economics. In J. C. Pitt, ed., *Philosophy in Economics.* Dordrecht: Reidel, pp. 137-48, 1981.

[Woodward, 2000] J. Woodward. Data, Phenomena, and Reliability. *Philosophy of Science* 67: S163-179, 2000.

[Woodward, 2003] J. Woodward. *Making Things Happen: A Theory of Causal Explanation.* Oxford: Oxford University Press, 2003.
[Worrall, 1985] J. Worrall. Scientific Discovery and Theory-Confirmation. In J. Pitt, ed., *Change and Progress in Modern Science.* Dordrecht: Reidel, pp. 301-31, 1985.
[Worrall, 2002] J. Worrall. *What* Evidence in Evidence-Based Medicine? *Philosophy of Science*, 69: S316-30, 2002.

# BEHAVIORAL ECONOMICS

Erik Angner and George Loewenstein

## 1 INTRODUCTION

In recent years, behavioral economics has emerged as a *bona fide* subdiscipline of economics (cf. [Rabin, 2002, 657–658; Sent, 2004, 735–737]). At the time of writing, virtually all top U.S. economics departments have behavioral economists on staff. Behavioral papers appear in prime journals, and the number of doctoral dissertations, conferences, hirings, tenurings, etc. is increasing rapidly. Meanwhile, behavioral economists have been awarded the highest recognitions: MacArthur Fellowships, the John Bates Clark Medal, and most prominently, the Nobel Memorial Prize. Although a comparatively young field, it is possible to discern relatively distinct phases in the development of behavioral economics. The first phase, which we will argue began in 1980, involved identifying anomalies — commonly observed economic phenomena that were inconsistent with standard theory — and explaining them in relatively loose psychological terms. The second, which began approximately a decade later, incorporated behavioral assumptions into increasingly sophisticated, mathematically rigorous models of economic phenomena at both the micro and the macro levels [Rabin, 2002, 658]. The third phase, once again unfolding approximately a decade later, has involved the systematic application of behavioral economics to issues of public policy (see, e.g., [McCaffery and Slemrod, 2006; Diamond and Vartiainen, 2007]).

Because behavioral economics in certain ways represents a sharp departure from mainstream — that is, neoclassical — economics, it raises a number of questions of a philosophical, methodological, and historical nature. Yet, to date, it has not received the attention it deserves from historians and philosophers of science.[1] In this chapter, we take some initial steps to address this deficiency. Our purpose is to shed light on (a) the nature and historical origins of behavioral economics as a field, (b) its main results and their interpretation, (c) the methods used by its practitioners, (d) its relationship to traditional economics as well as to other emerging subdisciplines such as neuroeconomics, and (e) some of its philosophical and methodological underpinnings. We make no claim to settle or even identify all issues raised by the emergence of behavioral economics, but do want to go some way toward figuring out what those issues are.

[1]Exceptions include Brav, Heaton and Rosenberg [2004]; Sent [2004]; Motterlini and Guala [2005]; and Ross [2005; 2008].

Handbook of the Philosophy of Science. Volume 13: Philosophy of Economics.
Volume editor: Uskali Mäki. General editors: Dov M. Gabbay, Paul Thagard and John Woods.

The term "behavioral economics" was in use as early as 1958 (cf. [Johnson, 1958; Boulding, 1958/1961, 21]). These days, as it is typically employed, "behavioral economics" refers to the attempt to increase the explanatory and predictive power of economic theory by providing it with more psychologically plausible foundations.[2] By "psychologically plausible" we mean consistent with the best available psychology.[3] Notice that behavioral economics so defined has little to do with behaviorism; in fact behavioral economics can trace its roots to the cognitive revolution, which occurred in direct opposition to behaviorism (see section 2). The modifier "behavioral" — which is sometimes criticized for being redundant on the grounds that all economics is or should be about behavior — stems from the origins of behavioral economics in behavioral decision research (see section 4.1). Behavioral economists do not deny that there may be much to learn from sociology, anthropology, and other neighboring fields. However, most of the work characterized as behavioral economics these days — and virtually all the work reviewed here — is inspired by psychology. A separate subfield that draws on sociology, and which is sometimes referred to as "socioeconomics," has coalesced around a different set of researchers and journals.

Our main thesis is that the development of behavioral economics in important respects parallels the development of cognitive science. Both fields are based on a repudiation of the positivist methodological strictures that were in place at their founding and a belief in the legitimacy of making reference to unobservable entities such as emotions and heuristics. And both fields adopt an interdisciplinary approach, admitting diverse forms of evidence and using a variety of methods to generate such evidence. Moreover, the connections between the fields go beyond the parallels between them. Although behavioral economics borrows ideas from a number of different areas of psychology, the most important inputs have come from behavioral decision research, which itself can be seen as an integration of ideas from economics and cognitive science.

Because, on our reading, behavioral economics turns out to be an expression of the cognitive revolution, we are in broad agreement with Russell Sage Foundation president Eric Wanner, who helped fund research in behavioral economics since the mid-1980s and has been instrumental in the establishment of behavioral economics as an independent subdiscipline. Wanner describes behavioral economics as an application of cognitive science to the realm of economic decision-making. "The field is misnamed — it should have been called *cognitive economics*," he says. "We weren't brave enough" (quoted in Lambert [2006, 52], italics in original). There are in fact authors who use Wanner's term, at least in other languages: Matteo Motterlini and Francesco Guala [2005] use the Italian phrase *economia cognitiva* as their translation of "behavioral economics" [Motterlini and Guala, 2005, vi].

[2]Cf. Camerer [1999, 10575]; Camerer and Loewenstein [2003, 3], Weber and Dawes [2005, 91], and Bruni and Sugden [2007, 146].

[3]We do not define behavioral economics in terms of the "psychological realism" of the foundations, since the term "realism" is needlessly philosophically loaded (cf. Hansen [2006, chapter 2]).

Below, we will discuss various ways in which behavioral economics can be said to be *cognitive*; it is *economics* because it remains, as Robert H. Frank and Ben S. Bernanke [2001/2004] express the canonical view of economics, "the study of how people make choices under conditions of scarcity and of the results of those choices for society" [Frank and Bernanke, 2001/2004, 4].[4]

The parallels between behavioral economics and cognitive science are not perfect, however. Perhaps most saliently, until recently cognitive scientists have given relatively little attention to emotions, moods and feelings [Griffiths, 1998, 197; cf. Gardner, 1985/1987, 41–42]. Indeed, cognitive science is sometimes defined as the study of cognition (cf. [Bechtel *et al.*, 1998, 3]), leaving out the study of affect by definitional fiat. By contrast, behavioral economists have spent a great deal of time exploring not just the role of cognition, but also that of affective states, emotions, moods and feelings, in human judgment and decision making (see section 6.2 below). While recognizing that the parallels between cognitive science and behavioral economics break down in some domains, we will nevertheless maintain that exploring the parallels between the two is useful for understanding both the historical origins, and the nature, of behavioral economics.

## 2 THE INTELLECTUAL BACKDROP

When cognitive science emerged in the 1940s and 50s, it did so in opposition to behaviorism and a cluster of associated doctrines, including logical positivism and verificationism. Scientists of this era came to think that the methodological strictures that were fashionable at the time had become serious obstacles to scientific progress [Bechtel *et al.*, 1998, 6; Gardner, 1985/1987, 12]. This was so in large part because behaviorism and associated doctrines "eschewed entities (like concepts and ideas) that could not be readily observed and reliably measured" [Gardner, 1985/1987, 15]. Here, we will argue that something very similar is true for behavioral economics. Behavioral economics emerged in opposition to neoclassical economics, which was heavily influenced by behaviorism and associated doctrines, including verificationism and operationalism. In particular, behavioral economics emerged in reaction to the notion that social and behavioral science should avoid reference to entities (like cognitive and affective states) that cannot be directly observed.

Our examination of the origins and development of neoclassical economics serves two main purposes. First, because behavioral economics largely emerged in reaction to neoclassical economics, a historical excursion allows us to paint a fuller picture of the views against which behavioral economics reacted. Second, because most of the critics of behavioral economics have a neoclassical background, it allows us to achieve a better understanding of their criticism. In passing, this section is also intended to illustrate that the project to rid economics of its ties to psychology (a project described in section 2.2) is relatively modern; in fact,

[4]Ross [2008] takes a different view about the nature of economics.

we will argue, both classical and early neoclassical economists were deeply interested in the psychological underpinnings of economic behavior. Our exposition largely follows that of Michael Mandler [1999], who divides the history of modern economics into three main periods: *classical*, *early neoclassical*, and *postwar neoclassical* [Mandler, 1999, 3]. Like all divisions of this sort, Mandler's is imperfect — for one thing, writers characteristic of postwar economics may have published before the war — but for present purposes it is good enough.[5]

## *2.1 Classical and early neoclassical economics*

Before the emergence of behaviorism during the first decades of the twentieth century, psychologists were largely comfortable with talking about to mental states and other unobservables [Gardner, 1985/1987, 11]. Characteristic of this era was William James's statement in *Principles of Psychology* [1890]: "Psychology is the Science of Mental Life, both of its phenomena and of their conditions. The phenomena are such things as we call feelings, desires, cognitions, reasonings, decisions, and the like" [James, 1890, 1]. Similarly, as we will see, classical and early neoclassical economists made frequent reference to cognitive and affective states. Their conception of human nature — and therefore of human decision making — was often relatively sophisticated, and in many cases inspired by developments in the psychology of the time [Bruni and Sugden, 2007, 147].

These facts are important, because there are many misconceptions about the views of human nature implicit (or explicit) in classical and early neoclassical economists. This is perhaps particularly so for the classical economists of the $18^{th}$ century (including Adam Smith). These economists are often thought to have held a particularly simple psychology according to which people everywhere and always pursue their self-interest narrowly construed. The actual views of the classical economists could hardly be more different. Regarding the nature of human ends, for example, Smith wrote: "How selfish soever man may be supposed, there are evidently some principles in his nature, which interest him in the fortune of others, and render their happiness necessary to him, though he derives nothing from it except the pleasure of seeing it" [Smith, 1759/2002, 11]. Similarly, regarding people's rationality, or utility-promoting behavior, Smith wrote:

> How many people ruin themselves by laying out money on trinkets of frivolous utility? What pleases these lovers of toys is not so much the utility, as the aptness of the machines which are fitted to promote it. All their pockets are stuffed with little conveniences ... of which the whole utility is certainly not worth the fatigue of bearing the burden [Smith, 1759/2002, 211].

Whatever the exact implications of these quotes, they show rather clearly that Smith did not have the simple-minded view of human nature that some would attribute to him.

[5]For a more detailed account of this history, see, e.g. [Morgan and Rutherford, 1998; Mirowski and Hands, 2006; Moscati, 2007].

Smith did not, of course, have a theory of decision in the modern sense, but he did express a vision of human nature (and therefore human action) that is remarkably multi-faceted. As Mark Perlman and Charles McCann [1998] describe it:

> Smith's *homo economicus* ... was a man with a temporal sense, a man with loyalties, a man who clearly understood that he was part of a larger social collective. What Smith's man wanted and needed was the responsibility for making his own decisions and accepting the consequences of those decisions. This responsibility had to be understood as existing in concert with the twin principles of self-love and sympathy, for all were combined in the Smithian calculus. In brief, in modern parlance what was to be maximized by Smith's man was the right of self-determination, while still allowing a place for both moral and social sensibilities and even expressions of altruism [Perlman and McCann, 1998, 239].

The exact details of Smith's conception of human nature are contested (cf. [Otteson, 2002; Schliesser, 2005]). It should be clear, however, that Smith — like his contemporary David Hume — was deeply interested in the psychological underpinnings of human behavior. Moreover, arguably, Smith's views about human psychology were not incidental to his more purely economic work, and may have had an important impact on them (cf. [Davis, 2003, 270]).

Reading the classical economists' philosophical and economic psychology, several contemporary authors have gone as far as suggesting that Hume and Smith in fact identified and discussed some of the phenomena that now occupy behavioral economists. Thus, Ignacio Palacios-Huerta argues that both Hume and Smith analyzed dynamically inconsistent behavior and that "their analyses of this behavior remain novel" [Palacios-Huerta, 2003, 243]. Similarly, Nava Ashraf, Colin F. Camerer, and George Loewenstein [2005, 140] find that Smith's work "is not only packed with insights that presage developments in contemporary behavioral economics, but also with promising leads that have yet to be pursued."[6] These insights include the phenomena that we now call loss aversion, overconfidence, and social preferences.

Early neoclassical economics, as exemplified by the work of William Stanley Jevons, was explicitly built on a foundation of hedonic psychology — that is, an account of individual behavior according to which individuals seek to maximize pleasure and minimize pain [Bruni and Sugden, 2007, 150]. In Jevons' words: "Pleasure and pain are undoubtedly the ultimate objects of the Calculus of Economics. To satisfy our wants to the utmost with the least effort ... in other words, to *maximize pleasure*, is the problem of Economics" [Jevons, 1871/1965, 37, italics in original]. The early neoclassical economists were inspired by Bentham, who wrote: "Nature has placed mankind under the governance of two sovereign masters, *pain* and *pleasure*.... They govern us in all we do, in all we say, in all we

[6] A reference has been omitted.

think" [Bentham, 1823/1996, 11, italics in original]. These economists understood utility in terms of conscious experience like pleasure or happiness. As Jevons put it: "Utility [arising from any commodity] must be considered as measured by, or even as actually identical with, the addition made to a person's happiness" [Jevons, 1871/1965, 45].

When it came to welfare economics, early neoclassical economists were unabashed utilitarians. A. C. Pigou, author of *The Economics of Welfare* [1920/1952] and commonly considered the father of welfare economics, went to great lengths to explore and measure "total welfare" [1920/1952]. Early neoclassical economists like Pigou believed that welfare or utility could meaningfully be aggregated across individuals, and that one state was superior to another if total welfare was greater in the former than in the latter [Mandler, 1999, 4]. Of course, welfare economists of the time shared the focus on conscious experience. As Pigou put it, "the elements of welfare are states of consciousness and, perhaps, their relations" [Pigou, 1920/1952, 10].

Mandler argues that the hedonic foundations of economics — and especially the assumption that people maximize pleasure — served several purposes. First, hedonics came with an account of deliberation, according to which individuals weigh the pleasure and pain that would result from various actions and choose the one they perceive as leading to the greatest balance of pleasure over pain [Mandler, 1999, 76]. Second, hedonics provided a rationale for several critical assumptions, such as the completeness and transitivity of the preference relation, and (given the further assumptions of separability and diminishing marginal utility) the convexity of indifference curves [Mandler, 1999, 76-77]. Third, "the early neoclassical account of rational deliberation allowed for a rich description of irrational ('incorrect') behavior" [Mandler, 1999, 77]. Hedonic psychology permits people to act irrationally because, for example, they may fail to properly anticipate the pleasure resulting from certain actions, or because (in the intertemporal context) they may fail to take future pleasure properly into account in their deliberations (see, e.g., [Loewenstein, O'Donoghue and Rabin, 2003]). In sum, the assumption that people maximize pleasure could explain both why people often have transitive preferences, etc., and why they sometimes fail to do so.

The identification of utility with conscious experience had important methodological implications. Because it was assumed that individuals have direct access to their conscious experience, many economists defended the principles of hedonic psychology on the basis of their introspective self-evidence alone [Bruni and Sugden, 2007, 150-151]. Thus, John E. Cairnes wrote: "*The economist starts with a knowledge of ultimate causes.* He is already, at the outset of his enterprise, in the position which the physicist only attains after ages of laborious research" [Cairnes, 1888/1965, 87, italics in original]. The reason, Cairnes continued, is that "we have, or may have if we choose to turn our attention to the subject, direct knowledge of these causes in our consciousness of what passes in our own minds" [Cairnes, 1888/1965, 88]. Because of their belief in the power of introspection, in conjunction with the conviction that introspection supported the principles of hedonic psychology, early neoclassical economists saw little reason to use alternative methods to confirm the empirical adequacy of the foundations of their economics. The heavy reliance on introspection was not unique for the economists, but was widely shared by social and behavioral scientists [Bruni and Sugden, 2007, 151; Gardner, 1985/1987, 11].

## *2.2 Postwar neoclassical theory*

The emergence of behaviorism — marked by the appearance of John B. Watson's article 'Psychology as the Behaviorist Views it' [1913] — included an attack on both heavy reliance on introspection and references to mental states. Behaviorists like Watson argued, first, that all scientific methods should be public (thereby rejecting the use, e.g., of introspection), and second, that a science of behavior should focus on behavior only (thereby avoiding references to unobservables such as beliefs, desires, plans, and intentions) [Gardner, 1985/1987, 11]. These ideas are clearly present in the writings of the postwar neoclassical economists as well. The transition from early to postwar neoclassical theory, although inspired by earlier work (e.g., [Pareto, 1906/1971; Bruni and Sugden, 2007]), took place over the course of some 20 years, from the mid-1930s to the mid-50s [Mandler, 1999, 8]. As we will see, postwar neoclassical economists wanted to gain distance from psychology of all kinds, objected to the notion that economics should make reference to conscious states, and rejected the idea that introspection was a scientifically acceptable means to explore such states.

Postwar neoclassical economists were motivated by a variety of considerations. Many of them appear to have been directly inspired by the methodological strictures of logical positivism in philosophy, behaviorism in psychology, and operationalism in physics (cf. [Lewin, 1996]). Moreover, some economists had grown disappointed with the meager results of early neoclassicism in terms of theories with predictive power. In a tart critique of Cairnes [1888/1965], as quoted above, T. W. Hutchison [1938] remarked:

> It is possibly very encouraging for the economist to hear that compared with the natural scientist the psychological method saves him "ages of laborious research," but it is curious and a pity that this huge start has not enabled him to formulate any considerable body of reliable prognoses such as the natural sciences have managed to achieve [Hutchison, 1938, 132].

Thus, postwar neoclassical economists set out to put their discipline on firmer methodological ground, and at the same time to improve the predictive power of their theories.

According to the postwar neoclassical view, or *ordinalism* as it is often called (cf. [Hicks, 1975]), the fundamental assumption is that people have preferences. As Lionel Robbins, author of the spectacularly influential *An Essay on the Nature and Significance of Economic Science* [1932/1984] wrote, "all that is assumed ... is that different goods have different uses and that these different uses have different significances for action such that in a given situation one use will be preferred before another and one good before another" [Robbins, 1932/1984, 85–86]. Thus, a person's preference ordering just represents his or her ranking of whatever options are available, nothing more, nothing less. As Philip H. Wicksteed expressed it:

> By a man's "scale of preferences" or "relative scale," then, we must henceforth understand the whole register of the terms on which (wisely or foolishly, consistently or inconsistently, deliberately, impulsively or by inertia, to his future satisfaction or to his future regret) he will, if he gets the chance, accept or reject this or that alternative [Wicksteed, 1910/1967, 36].

In this regard, like in many others, postwar economists drew on Vilfredo Pareto [1909/1971], who had maintained that the theory of economic equilibrium in all essentials could be derived from facts about indifference [Bruni and Sugden, 2007, 155].

By using "preference" rather than "utility" as the primitive concept, postwar neoclassical economists explicitly intended to rid economics of its ties to psychological theory — hedonic and otherwise. As Robbins wrote, neoclassical economic theory "is capable of being set out and defended in absolutely non-hedonistic terms" and has no "essential connection with psychological hedonism, or for that matter with any other brand of *Fach-Psychologie*" [Robbins, 1932/1984, 85]. Again, postwar economists drew on Vilfredo Pareto, who wished economics to be a science separate from especially psychology [Bruni and Sugden, 2007, 155].

It is important to notice that postwar economists did not deny that people might be motivated by pleasure, pain, and/or other mental states. As J. R. Hicks [1939/1946] put it: "Now of course this does not mean that if any one has any other ground for supposing that there exists some suitable quantitative measure of utility, or satisfaction, or desiredness, there is anything in the above argument to set against it" [Hicks, 1939/1946, 18]. Instead, postwar economists chose to remain agnostic about questions of motivation, preference formation, and choice. Moreover, they often argued that such issues were outside the scope of economics. Thus, for example, Robbins wrote: "Why the human animal attaches particular values in this sense to particular things, is a question which we do not discuss. That is quite properly a question for psychologists or perhaps even physiologists" [Robbins, 1932/1984, 86].

Because of its agnosticism about the psychological underpinnings of human behavior, postwar neoclassical economics is often described as less committal than classical and early neoclassical economics. Hence: "Since preference orderings do not presuppose cardinal judgments of satisfaction intensity, and since agents may well form their preference rankings through entirely nonhedonistic means, ordinalism is more general than a utility- or pleasure-based approach" [Mandler, 1999, 5]. While the early neoclassical economists made assumptions about individual psychology — for instance, how feelings of pleasure and pain change as a result of consumption — and deduced the properties of preference — e.g. the claim that preferences are transitive — postwar neoclassical economists simply started treating the transitivity of preferences as axiomatic [Mandler, 1999, 5].

Ordinalist economists did not reject talk about utility, but they began using the term in a different way. They took utility to be an index or a measure of preference satisfaction [Mandler, 1999, 78]. In this view, to say that the utility of $x$ is greater than that of $y$ for person $p$, is just to say that $p$ prefers $x$ over $y$. In brief, utilities do not necessarily have anything to do with pleasure, pain, or any other psychological or motivational state. Postwar economists differed in their understanding of the concept of "preference," however. According to some accounts — like Paul Samuelson's [1948] Revealed Preference Theory — preferences are identified with observable choices. According to others — like that of Robbins — preferences are not identified with observable choices but are nevertheless closely linked to them. The link, whatever its exact nature, is such that choices mirror preferences, so that choices have the same properties as preferences and so that choice data can be used to infer preference orderings (see [Robbins, 1932/1984, 87–88]).

Ordinalism, obviously, had implications for welfare economics (see [Hicks, 1975]). First, mental state accounts of welfare (according to which welfare is a matter of happiness, pleasure, or the like) gave way to preference satisfaction accounts (according to which welfare is a matter of preference satisfaction). Moreover, the utilitarian welfare criterion was jettisoned in favor of the Pareto criterion, which says that one state is superior to another if at least one individual is better off, and nobody is worse off, in the former than in the latter. The Pareto criterion was supposed to allow economists to dispense economic advice without requiring the aggregation of utilities or interpersonal welfare comparisons [Mandler, 1999, 6]. However, realizing that few real-life changes in, e.g., economic policy are true Pareto improvements, postwar neoclassical economists often revert to criteria such as *potential* Pareto improvements, which in practice usually boil down to comparisons of total wealth regardless of distributional consequences.

Ordinalism also had methodological implications. As a result of the rejection of introspection, postwar neoclassical economists adopted the belief that the only valid method to collect information about preferences is to study market transactions or other observable choices. This belief has remained strong. As Amartya Sen [1982] points out:

> Choice is seen as solid information, whereas introspection is not open to observation.... Much of economic theory seems to be concerned with strong, silent men who never speak! One has to sneak in behind them to see what they are doing in the market, etc., and deduce from it what they prefer, what makes them better off, what they think is right, and so on [Sen, 1982, 9].

Similarly: "Much of the empirical work on preference patterns [and therefore welfare] seems to be based on the conviction that [non-verbal] behaviour is the only source of information on a person's preferences" [Sen, 1982, 71].[7] This conviction, as we have seen, was shared by the behaviorists [Gardner, 1985/1987, 11]. Typical of the attitude of behaviorists was Edward C. Tolman's famous statement that "everything important in psychology ... can be investigated in essence through the continued experimental and theoretical analysis of the determiners of rat behavior at a choice point in a maze" [Tolman, 1938, 34].

In brief, postwar neoclassical economics represents a sharp departure from the classical and early neoclassical tradition. In the process of rendering economics more consistent with contemporary methodological strictures, and to improve the predictive power of the theory, postwar theorists aspired to sever all ties with psychology, hedonic and otherwise. As a result, they developed a theory of great generality, the adequacy of which does not hinge on the plausibility of any particular account of human behavior. Meanwhile, several advantages of early neoclassical theory were lost. First, postwar theory (unlike early neoclassical theory) does not come with an account of deliberation. Thus, postwar neoclassical economists are unable to say anything about how preferences are formed. Second, and relatedly, postwar theory does not provide any theoretical basis for the assumptions on preferences. As Mandler puts it: "Lacking psychological foundations, the axioms of preference theory instead persist as primitives, unexplained and unjustified" [Mandler, 1999, 66]. Finally, and perhaps most importantly, when it comes to interactions between economics and psychology, postwar theorists lost the theoretical resources to describe irrational behavior: insofar as it is possible to interpret a person's behavior as consistent with the theory, the interpretation implies that the person is rational. Similarly, insofar as welfare or well-being is understood in terms of the satisfaction of the person's actual preferences, the theory necessarily describes any voluntary action as, at least *ex ante*, promoting his or her welfare or well-being.[8]

## 2.3 *Discussion*

In this section we have tried to paint a fuller picture of the historical background from which behavioral economics emerged: from the classical economists' multi-faceted picture of human psychology, to the early neoclassical economists' embrace of hedonism, to the postwar neoclassicals' rejection of psychological foundations. The latter is particularly important, as it remains the received view. In passing, we hope to have shown that, although behavioral economics as a subdiscipline is a rather recent development, attempts to tie economic theory to a psychologically plausible account of human judgment and decision making are as old as economics itself. In fact, both classical and early neoclassical economists were deeply interested in the psychological underpinnings of behavior.

[7]Even so, in practice, neoclassical economists often do rely on self-reports, e.g., regarding income, spending, work hours, willingness-to-pay, willingness-to-accept, etc.

[8]For more detailed discussion of this point, see Loewenstein and Haisley [2008], and Loewenstein and Ubel [2008].

A description of neoclassical economics would be incomplete if it failed to mention that there is a set of auxiliary assumptions that tend to be used in conjunction with the theory. As we have seen, in the postwar view, neoclassical economics is extraordinarily general, in the sense that it makes no assumptions about motivation, preference formation, and choice (beyond the proposition that observable choices satisfy certain axioms). For all practical purposes, therefore, the theory has to be combined with a series of auxiliary assumptions. These may take the form of assumptions about the objects of preference, the characteristics of the budget set, and the properties of the preference ordering. For instance, in the case of choice among lotteries (which is the paradigm for many decision theory problems) it is standard to assume that people's subjective probabilities correspond to limiting frequencies and that utility is some increasing concave function over wealth levels. Similarly, when it comes to intertemporal choice, it is standard to assume that individuals maximize the sum of utilities over time, discounted in the same fashion as financial markets discount cash flows. To say that such assumptions are standard does not, of course, mean that every economist adopts them, only that a large proportion of them do.

Our goal here is neither to defend nor to criticize the auxiliary assumptions, but to point out that the existence of standard auxiliary assumptions has generated some confusion about the nature of neoclassical theory. The confusion is between a weaker and a stronger conception of neoclassical economics. The weaker conception insists that the research program is defined by the bare theory alone, and that auxiliary assumptions are external and incidental. The stronger conception insists that neoclassical economics must be seen as inclusive of the standard assumptions used to generate observable predictions. Unsurprisingly, defenders of neoclassical economics tend to rely on the weaker conception, whereas critics tend to rely on the stronger one.

## 3 PSYCHOLOGICAL APPROACHES DURING THE LATE NEOCLASSICAL PERIOD

When cognitive science finally emerged as an independent discipline, it did not have to be created out of thin air, as it were, but could draw on theoretical efforts going back to the early part of the twentieth century [Gardner, 1985/1987, 16]. Something very similar is true in the case of behavioral economics. Although behavioral economics emerged as an independent subdiscipline relatively recently, it could draw upon developments that can sometimes be dated back to the beginning of the twentieth century. (This is not, of course, to say that all behavioral economists in fact draw upon this work, even when they should.) Hence, behavioral economics — like cognitive science — can be said to have "[a] long past but a relatively short history" [Gardner, 1985/1987, 9].

In this section, we discuss some of the economists who, even in the midst of the relative hegemony of postwar neoclassical economics, and in many cases apparently independently of one another, insisted that neoclassical choice theory failed to accurately describe human choice behavior, and argued that the solution may lie in foundations with greater psychological plausibility. Many of them took positive steps toward erecting economic theories on the basis of psychologically plausible foundations. The point is not that these other thinkers "anticipated" modern developments, but that behavioral economists are part of a tradition that goes back more than a century. Here, our main goal is not to identify the exact position of the various authors, or to assess how convincing those positions are, but to give a brief characterization of how, and why, they rejected the neoclassical view. As we will see, these economists refused to eschew psychological theorizing mainly because they believed psychological insights would help them do better economics.

## *3.1 The institutionalists: Veblen, Mitchell and Clark*

Some of the earliest and most vehement critics of ordinalist tendencies were the institutional economists of the early $20^{th}$ century [Lewin, 1996, 1294]. In a 1914 survey, for instance, Wesley C. Mitchell criticized "recent writers" (like [Pareto, 1909/1971]) who, he said, favored "non-intercourse with psychology" [Mitchell, 1914, 1]. In their writings, the institutionalists happily admitted that hedonist psychology is flawed. In one famous passage, for example, Thorstein Veblen [1898] dismissed it this way:

> The psychological and anthropological preconceptions of the economists have been those which were accepted by the psychological and social sciences some generations ago. The hedonistic conception of man is that of a lightning calculator of pleasures and pains, who oscillates like a homogeneous globule of desire for happiness under the impulse of stimuli that shift him about the area, but leave him intact [Veblen, 1898, 389].

However, the institutional economists also believed that it would be a mistake for economists to ignore psychology. Thus, Mitchell hoped that the failure of hedonic psychology would encourage fellow economists to look for "a sounder psychological basis for our analysis" and that "economists will find themselves not only borrowing from but also contributing to psychology" [Mitchell, 1914, 2–3]. J. M. Clark [1918] echoed these sentiments, adding that the economist cannot in the end avoid psychology. If the economist does refuse to let himself be inspired by the psychologists' conception of man, Clark argued, "he will force himself to make his own, and it will be bad psychology" [Clark, 1918, 4].

One reason why the institutionalists were interested in the psychological underpinnings of human behavior was that they thought of institutions in psychological terms. As Mitchell [1910] put it: "Institutions are themselves conceived as psychological entities — habits of thought and action prevailing among the communities under observation" [Mitchell, 1910, 112]. The institutionalists appear to have read the psychology of the day quite closely, and used the knowledge they had acquired to generate economically relevant hypotheses. Thus, for instance, Clark [1918] explored the economic implications of stimulus-response psychology, studies of attention, and phenomena like habit formation. Mitchell [1914] ended his survey in the following manner:

> It was because hedonism offered a theory of how men act that it exercised so potent an influence upon economics. It is because they are developing a sounder type of functional psychology that we may hope both to profit by and to share in the work of contemporary psychologists. But in embracing this opportunity economics will assume a new character. It will cease to be a system of pecuniary logic, a mechanical study of static equilibria under non-existent conditions, and become a science of human behavior [Mitchell, 1914, 47].

Clearly, institutionalists like Mitchell believed that the incorporation of a more plausible psychology would make for better economics.

## *3.2 The macroeconomists: Fisher and Keynes*

Other early forays into psychology appeared in the field of macroeconomics, especially in the context of monetary theory and the theory of the business cycle. Consider Irving Fisher, who is otherwise perhaps best known for his contributions to technical economics. Fisher authored the book *The Money Illusion* (1928), which aspired to explain phenomena like business-cycle fluctuations in popular terms. "Money illusion" is a concept that Fisher may have invented (cf. [Howitt, 1987, 518]), and which he used as early as 1913 [Fisher, 1913, 135]. It is defined as "the failure to perceive that the dollar, or any other unit of money, expands or shrinks in value" [Fisher, 1928, 4]. Fisher suggested that money illusion contributes to business cycle fluctuations because it conceals from view the principal cause — viz. the unstable dollar — of such fluctuations, and hence conceals the importance of stabilizing the dollar [Fisher, 1928, 60 *idem*]). At any rate, in Fisher's view, money illusion makes business cycle fluctuations vastly more harmful than they otherwise would be.

Another macroeconomist well known for his forays into psychology is John Maynard Keynes. In his 2001 Nobel Prize lecture, George A. Akerlof went so far as to assert that "Keynes' *The General Theory* (1936) was the greatest contribution to behavioral economics before the present era" [Akerlof, 2003, 37]. Indeed, Keynes departed from neoclassical orthodoxy in multiple ways. Consider the following famous passage:

> [A] large proportion of our positive activities depend on spontaneous optimism rather than on a mathematical expectation, whether moral or hedonistic or economic. Most, probably, of our decisions to do something positive, the full consequences of which will be drawn out over many days to come, can only be taken as a result of animal spirits — of a spontaneous urge to action rather than inaction, and not as the

> outcome of a weighted average of quantitative benefits multiplied by quantitative probabilities [Keynes, 1936, 161].

This passage is interesting because Keynes deviates from ordinalism in at least two ways: first, by suggesting that actual behavior is not adequately described by utility maximization, and second by speculating about the motivation of economic behavior.

## *3.3 The welfare economist: Scitovsky*

Returning to the micro level, a landmark study is Tibor Scitovsky's book *The Joyless Economy: The psychology of human satisfaction* [1976/1992]. Scitovsky, who did early work in traditional welfare economics, gradually became disillusioned with the economists' hands-off approach to the study of preferences and came to think of it as unscientific [Scitovsky, 1976/1992, xii-xiii]. He started out by writing that people's tastes and choices "are matters economists have always regarded as something they should observe, but must not poke their noses into" [Scitovsky, 1976/1992, xii]. Rejecting this perspective, Scitovsky proposed instead to follow "behavioral psychologists" and "observe behavior ... in order to find ... the foundations of a theory to explain behavior" [Scitovsky, 1976/1992, xiii]. Like these psychologists, he was not content to simply note differences in people's consumption patterns or "revealed preferences" but sought "to find the causes and explanation of the differences" [Scitovsky, 1976/1992, 28]. Scitovsky was impressed with the fact that psychologists support their theories with experimental data, and clearly believed that economists should do the same [Scitovsky, 1976/1992, xiii].

Scitovsky is particularly interesting because he made contributions to both positive and normative theory. On the positive side, Scitovsky drew on the psychology of motivation to argue that human beings (like other organisms) strive to maintain an optimal level of arousal [Scitovsky, 1976/1992, 24]. Scitovsky argued that a great deal of behavior — for instance, our desire for novelty — can be understood in terms of this search for optimum arousal. He also maintained that this process can explain the old paradox of why people would simultaneously buy insurance and lottery tickets: freely chosen uncertainty or risks (like those associated with buying lottery tickets) can help an individual approach the optimum level of arousal, Scitovsky argued, while externally imposed, prolonged uncertainty would take the individual farther away from the optimum, providing a motivation to insure against such risks [Scitovsky, 1976/1992, 57–58]. On the normative side, Scitovsky drew a distinction between comfort and pleasure. He maintained that comfort has to do with absolute levels of arousal, whereas pleasure has to do with changes in arousal levels [Scitovsky, 1976/1992, 61]. He argued that there is a tension between the pursuit of comfort and the pursuit of pleasure, in the sense that too much success at the former precludes success at the latter, and that people have a natural tendency to over-seek comfort at the expense of pleasure [Scitovsky, 1976/1992, 62]. Thirty years after Scitovsky made these observations, economists have once again become interested in hedonics and in the specific question of whether people can be relied upon to use the economic resources available to them to promote their own happiness (e.g., [Easterlin, 1974; Frey and Stutzer, 2002; Kahneman and Krueger, 2006; Clark and Oswald, 2006]).

## *3.4 The "old" behavioral economists: Simon and Katona*

In 1988, Peter E. Earl wrote: "There is no doubt that something called 'behavioural economics' has now begun to take off" [Earl, 1988]. The movement to which he referred has come to be called the "old behavioral economics," to distinguish it from the modern developments which we will discuss shortly [Sent, 2004, 740]. According to Earl, the movement emerged from four different locations: Carnegie Mellon University and the University of Michigan in the U.S., and the University of Oxford and the University of Stirling in the U.K. [Earl, 1988, 3]. Here, we will focus on the contributions of two towering individuals: Herbert A. Simon from Carnegie Mellon University — often referred to as "one of the founders of cognitive science" [Gardner, 1985/1987, 22] — and George Katona from the University of Michigan.

Simon reported that he was introduced to the social sciences by his uncle, a former student of the institutionalist economist John R. Commons [Simon, 1978/1992]. Determined to infuse into the social sciences the same kind of mathematical rigor he felt had made the physical sciences so successful, Simon entered the University of Chicago in 1933 [Simon, 1978/1992]. He ended up contributing to a range of fields, including economics, psychology and computer science, and remained fiercely anti-disciplinary. Indeed, Mie Augier and James G. March [2004] quote him as saying: "If you see any one of these disciplines dominating you ... you join the opposition and fight it for a while" [Augier and March, 2004, 4]. Simon's critique of economic man, the standard economic model of behavior, as well as the outline of an alternative conception, are already present in his doctoral dissertation, published as *Administrative Behavior* [Simon, 1947/1957]. Simon complained that economists "attribute to economic man a preposterously omniscient rationality" while psychologists following Freud tend to "reduce all cognition to affect"; as a result, he argued: "The social sciences suffer from a case of acute schizophrenia" [Simon, 1957, xxiii].

His views on the enterprise of behavioral economics are usefully developed in two entries in *The New Palgrave* dictionary of economics [Simon, 1987a; 1987b]. In his entry "Behavioural Economics," Simon [1987a] started out by identifying the assumptions of neoclassical economics. He distinguished two assumptions that tend to be explicit — that "human goals and motivations are assumed to be given a priori in the form of a utility function" and that agents choose "that one of the alternatives that yields the greatest utility" — from a range of assumptions that tend to be implicit and which "are not necessarily maintained through all the different variants of the theory" — including assumptions to the effect that agents have complete and certain knowledge or that they have a joint probability distribution [Simon, 1987a, 221].[9] Then, he added:

[9]The latter are what we called "auxiliary assumptions" above.

> Behavioural economics is concerned with the empirical validity of these neoclassical assumptions about human behaviour and, where they prove invalid, with discovering the empirical laws that describe behaviour as correctly and accurately as possible. As a second item on its agenda, behavioural economics is concerned with drawing out the implications, for the operation of the economic system and its institutions and for the public policy, of departures of actual behaviour from the neoclassical assumptions. A third item on the agenda is to supply empirical evidence about the shape and content of the utility function (or of whatever construct will replace it in a [sic] empirically valid behavioural theory) so as to strengthen the predictions that can be made about human economic behaviour [Simon, 1987a, 221].

As Simon pointed out, behavioral economics is not defined in terms of a commitment to a given theoretical framework, but "as a commitment to empirical testing of the neoclassical assumptions of human behaviour and to modifying economic theory on the basis of what is found in the testing process" [Simon, 1987a, 221].

It goes without saying that in Simon's view, neoclassical models fail to accurately describe human choice behavior. He attributed this failure to "numerous cognitive limitations" and proposed that we use the term "'bounded rationality' ... to denote the whole range of limitations on human knowledge and human computation that prevent economic actors in the real world from behaving in ways that approximate the predictions of classical and neoclassical theory" [Simon, 1987a, 222]. Simon was aware of the fact that neoclassical choice theory is not intended as a correct description of the manner in which individuals come to a decision, but only "as an apparatus for predicting choice" [Simon, 1987b, 267]. By contrast: "Theories of bounded rationality are more ambitious, in trying to capture the actual process of decision as well as the substance of the final decision itself" [Simon, 1987b, 267]. Referring to the former theories as "substantive," and the latter as "procedural," Simon suggested that procedural theories are superior both because they can better predict and explain the decisions that are actually reached, and because they alone can shed light on decision making processes, which are of independent interest [Simon, 1987b, 267].

Katona received his Ph.D. in psychology, but apparently as a result of experiencing hyperinflation in Germany in 1923 became interested in the psychological foundations of economic behavior [Katona, 1975, viii]. Drawing on his background in psychology as well as on several years experience with large-scale survey research on economic topics [Katona, 1975, ix], he published a book called *Psychological Analysis of Economic Behavior* [Katona, 1951].[10] The fundamental assumption of the book is that "economic processes stem directly from human behavior and that this simple but important fact has not received its due in modern economic analysis" [Katona, 1951, iii]. In particular, Katona was sharply critical of the use of the rationality assumption in neoclassical economics. As he wrote:

[10]The central theses of the book also appeared in an earlier paper in the *Journal of the American Statistical Association* [Katona, 1947].

> Unlike pure theorists, we shall not assume at the outset that rational behavior exists or that rational behavior constitutes the topic of economic analysis. We shall study economic behavior as we find it. In describing and classifying different reactions, as well as the circumstances that elicit them, we shall raise the question whether and in what sense certain reactions may be called "rational." After having answered that question and thus defined our terms, we shall study the fundamental problem: Under what conditions do more and under what conditions do less rational forms of behavior occur? [Katona, 1951, 16].

Katona's most fundamental critique of neoclassical economics, however, is that it fails to take proper account of the importance of intervening variables. Katona discussed statements like "consumer expenditures are a function of income" [Katona, 1975, 5] and objected that "changes in discretionary expenditures [are a] function not only of ability but also of willingness to buy" [Katona, 1975, 11]. More generally, Katona argued that "motives, attitudes, and expectations of consumers and businessmen play a significant role in determining spending, saving, and investing and that modern psychology provides conceptual as well as methodological tools for the investigation of economic behavior" [Katona, 1975, 4]. Of course willingness to buy, as well as motives, attitudes and expectations, are all examples of the intervening variables of which he spoke. In Katona's view, attention to such variables is critical: "Intervening variables are essential to psychological analysis because without them our description of economic behavior would remain incomplete, our understanding of behavior limited, and our predictions of future behavior incorrect" [Katona, 1951, 31]. When neoclassical economists fail to take proper account of intervening variables, Katona argued, they are guilty of assuming that "human beings behave mechanistically," i.e., that they "show invariably the same reactions to the same developments in the economic environment" [Katona, 1951, 6].

As we have seen in this and the previous section, "old" behavioral economics took shape during the 1950's and 60's, during the heyday of postwar neoclassical theory. While the old behavioral economists — including Simon, Katona, as well as their colleagues and collaborators — differed in many respects, they also had a great deal in common. As Sent [2004] puts it:

> Whereas mainstream economics started from a given utility function, old behavioral economics focused on discovering the empirical laws that described behavior correctly and as accurately as possible. While the neoclassical approach established a close connection between rationality and utility or profit maximization, old behavioral economics scrutinized the implications of departures of actual behavior from the neoclassical assumptions. And whereas mainstream economics started from given alternatives and known consequences, old behavioral approaches began with empirical evidence about the shape and content of the utility function [Sent, 2004, 742].

The work discussed in this section helped inspire the foundation in 1972 of the *Journal of Behavioral Economics* (*JBE*), intended to "(1) further knowledge of real world economic phenomena by integrating psychological and sociological variables into economic analysis and (2) promote interdisciplinary work" ('Introduction,' *JBE* 1972); in 1974 of the *Journal of Consumer Research;* and in 1982 of the Society for the Advancement of Behavioral Economics (SABE).

## *3.5 Discussion*

In brief, even during the relative hegemony of postwar neoclassical theory, there were economists who in various ways tried to build their economics on more psychologically plausible foundations. The above is only a brief sample. Additional work worthy of mention includes James S. Duesenberry's *Income, Saving and the Theory of Consumer Behavior* (1949), and Harvey Leibenstein's *Beyond Economic Man: A new foundation for microeconomics* (1976). Other economists joined the call for more psychologically plausible foundations, including Kenneth E. Boulding, who in a 1958 talk (published in 1961) discussed research trends in economics. Talking about development economics in particular, Boulding argued:

> In spite of the moderate usefulness of what the economist has to say on this subject ... there is a cry for a cultural anthropologist or even a psychologist when the economist runs into sacred cows, extended families, traditional motivations, levels of achievement, and social morale, all of which may be more important to economic development than any of the traditional economic variables. We still await a true synthesis of the insights of economics with those of other social sciences in the area [Boulding, 1958/1961, 19].[11]

In his paper, Boulding predicted that there would be a movement toward what he calls "behavioral economics," which in particular "involves study of those aspects of men's images, or cognitive and affective structures, which are more relevant to economic decisions" [Boulding, 1958/1961, 21]. We note that these authors do not appear to be motivated by a desire for psychological plausibility *per se.* Rather, they appear to advocate enhanced psychological plausibility as a means to an end, where the end is increased empirical adequacy. For example, none of the authors argue that the empirical adequacy of neoclassical economics is fine but that economists need to build theories with enhanced psychological plausibility anyway.

The economists discussed in this section — including the old behavioral economists — had some obvious successes. Keynes remains one of the most famous macroeconomists in the history of the discipline. The widespread reliance on consumer confidence measures reflects Katona's ideas about the importance of expectations [Curtin, 1982]. Simon was awarded the 1978 Nobel Memorial Prize for "for his pioneering research into the decision-making process within economic

[11] A footnote has been omitted.

organizations" [Bank of Sweden, 1978]. Although many of these economists were respected in the profession, however, they had little influence on the direction of economics as a whole. Insofar as they received any recognition for their work at the time, it often appears to have been in spite of, rather than because of, their efforts to provide economics with psychologically plausible foundations. More surprisingly, perhaps, these economists had only a limited impact on the development of the "new" behavioral economics. As it turns out, the rise of behavioral decision research was far more important.

## 4 THE "NEW" BEHAVIORAL ECONOMICS

The first cognitive scientists recognized that behaviorists had expressed legitimate concerns, e.g., regarding the naive reliance on introspection. As a result, they were cautious not to repeat mistakes committed by early twentieth-century psychologists and identified by the behaviorists. At the same time, early cognitive scientists came to the conclusion that it was necessary to make reference to unobservable entities like cognitive states in order to account for the phenomena. In Gardner's words:

> Cognitive science is predicated on the belief that it is legitimate — in fact, necessary — to posit a separate level of analysis which can be called the "level of representation." When working at this level, a scientist traffics in such representational entities as symbols, rules, images — the stuff of representation which is found between input and output — and in addition, explores the ways in which these representational entities are joined, transformed, or contrasted with one another [Gardner, 1985/1987, 38; cf. p. 383].

That representations are critical to cognitive science is evident, e.g., in what Paul Thagard [1996/2005] calls "the central hypothesis of cognitive science," viz. the thesis that "Thinking can best be understood in terms of representational structures in the mind and computational procedures that operate on those structures" [Thagard, 1996/2005, 10].

As we will see in this section, behavioral economists agree. Behavioral economists recognize that behaviorists were right about the uncritical reliance on introspection. However, like cognitive scientists, behavioral economists believe that it is appropriate to talk about entities such as beliefs, emotions, and heuristics, which clearly are to be found at the level of representation. Much of what they study can be understood in terms of representational structures in the mind and computational procedures on those structures. Because behavioral economists think of these entities as at least partly responsible for the production of human behavior, they believe that a deeper understanding of the former can help us better explain and predict the latter.

While cognitive scientists are fascinated by the processes that allow the human mind to accomplish complicated tasks — information processing, language acquisition, face recognition, decision making, and so on — they are also alert to the fact that it occasionally fails. And they are interested in explaining cases where thinking works poorly as well as the cases when it works well [Thagard, 1996/2005, 3]. As Keith J. Holyoak [1999] explains:

> [The] impressive power of human information processing has apparent limits. People all too often take actions that will not achieve their intended aim, and pursue short-term goals that defeat their long-term interests. Some of these mistakes arise from motivational biases, and others from computational limitations that constrain human attention, memory, and reasoning processes. Although human cognition is fundamentally adaptive, we have no reason to suppose that "all's for the best in this best of all possible minds" [Holyoak, 1999, xlviii].

Behavioral economists, as we will see, share this outlook. They acknowledge that the various mechanisms that allow us to form judgments and make decisions are fundamentally functional, but recognize that these mechanisms sometimes fail. Moreover, behavioral economics aims to develop models of human judgment and decision making that can account both for the successes and for the failures.

In this section we describe the emergence and establishment of behavioral economics as an independent subdiscipline of economics. It is not our intention to provide a survey of empirical results. Several such surveys already exist, including Matthew Rabin's 'Psychology and Economics' [1998], published in the *Journal of Economic Literature*; Colin Camerer and Loewenstein's 'Behavioral Economics: Past, present, future' [2003], published as the introduction to the book *Advances in Behavioral Economics* [Camerer, Loewenstein, and Rabin, 2003]; and the textbook treatment by Nick Wilkinson [2008]. For easy access to classical and recent articles, there are several useful collections, including Daniel Kahneman, Paul Slovic and Amos Tversky's *Judgment under Uncertainty: Heuristics and Biases* [1982]; Loewenstein, Daniel Read, and Roy Baumeister's *Time and Decision* [2003]; Kahneman and Tversky's *Choices, Values and Frames* [2000]; and the above-mentioned *Advances* [Camerer *et al.*, 2003].

## *4.1 Behavioral decision research*

From the point of view of modern — i.e. "new" — behavioral economics, the most important development was the emergence in the 1970s of a new branch of psychology called "behavioral decision making" (BDM) or "behavioral decision research" (BDR). BDR is often described as a direct consequence of the cognitive revolution. Thus, Reid Hastie and Robyn Dawes [2001] identify two insights that emerged in the cognitive revolution, and which proved critical for the development of BDR. The first insight "is that many aspects of human thinking, including judgment and decision making, can be captured with computational models," according to which we "compare, combine, and record ... mental representations" [Hastie and Dawes, 2001, 9]. The second insight is that properties of our cognitive apparatus "play major roles in our explanations for judgment and decision-making phenomena" [Hastie and Dawes, 2001, 10]. In particular, Hastie and Dawes explain many departures from optimality in terms of the limited capacity of working memory [Hastie and Dawes, 2001, 10–12].

Behavioral decision researchers, then, apply insights gleaned from the cognitive revolution to the topic of human judgment and decision making. As Hastie and Dawes summarize the take-home message of their 2001 textbook and by extension the whole field:

> The most important finding is that diverse people in very different situations often think about their decisions in the same way. We have a common set of cognitive skills that are reflected in similar decision habits. But we also bring with us a common set of limitations on our thinking skills that can make our choices far from optimal [Hastie and Dawes, 2001, 2].

As this passage makes clear, a central focus of behavioral decision researchers is to identify the common set of cognitive skills, their benefits and limitations, and to explore how they help produce observable behavior, whether optimal or not.

What truly distinguishes BDR from other approaches to human judgment and decision making, however, is that it studies judgment and decision making by taking as its starting point theories of rational decision. In Dawes' words:

> Basically, behavioral decision making is the field that studies how people make decisions. Because all types of people are making all sorts of decisions all the time, the field is potentially very broad. What has characterized the field both historically and theoretically is the comparison of actual decision making with certain principles of rationality in decision making [Dawes, 1998, 497].

The principles need not be derived from orthodox decision theory (cf. [Hastie and Dawes, 2001, 18–19]) but in actual fact they often are. Dawes [1998] adds that merely random deviations from the norm would be of little interest, but that deviations are in fact "systematic and highly replicable in experimental settings" [Dawes, 1998, 498]. Much as visual illusions can often help to identify fundamental properties of visual perception, he suggests that deviations from the ideal implicit in rational choice theory are not only interesting in their own right, but can potentially shed light on the basic mechanisms underlying human judgment and decision making.

These points are echoed by Baruch Fischhoff [1988], who writes that theories of rational decision making raise two main questions for psychologists: "(a) Do people perform the way that the models claim they should? (b) If not, how can people be helped to improve their performance?" [Fischhoff, 1988, 156]. Fischhoff goes on to explain how he sees the difference between BDR and economic approaches to decision making. He writes that "economists have traditionally taken it as self-evident that people optimize their decisions... The goal of the empirically minded economist is, therefore, not to test the hypothesis that people optimize, but to determine what it is that people are trying to optimize" [Fischhoff, 1988, 156]. To wit: since mainstream economists take for granted that people maximize utility, the only question worth exploring is what their utility function is.

As Dawes and Fischhoff make clear, BDR is radically different from mainstream economics. Yet, there is a sense in which BDR would not have existed in the absence of the models of rational choice which characterize mainstream economics. It can be said that rational choice theory gave birth to BDR by providing a "hard target" — a theory that (in conjunction with widely used auxiliary hypotheses) made clear and crisp predictions that could be explored in laboratory and other settings — for its researchers (cf. [Camerer and Loewenstein, 2003, 5–7]). BDR, incidentally, remains a highly active subfield of psychology, with organizations such as the Society for Judgment and Decision Making and the European Association for Decision Making, and journals such as *Judgment and Decision Making*. Indeed, economics is only one of many fields that behavioral decision research has influenced; others include marketing, accounting, finance, law, and medicine.

## *4.2 Tversky and Kahneman's heuristics and biases, prospect theory*

It took the work of Tversky and Kahneman to bring BDR to the attention of economists. Several factors help explain their success. As psychologists, Tversky and Kahneman were well aware of psychological approaches to the study of human judgment and decision making. Yet, they had also mastered the formalism of economic theories of decision. For one thing, Tversky was a coauthor, along with David H. Krantz, R. Duncan Luce and Patrick Suppes, of the monumental *Foundations of Measurement* [1971]. Measurement theory, as articulated in that work, had close historical and theoretical ties to economic theories of rational decision (cf. [Angner, 2009]). As Rabin puts it, Kahneman and Tversky's success resulted from the fact that "they are able and willing to address economists in standard economic language and venues" [Rabin, 1996, 111].

Here, we will focus on two of Tversky and Kahneman's research projects: first, the heuristics and biases program — which achieved prominence with their seminal 1974 *Science* paper 'Judgment under Uncertainty: Heuristics and biases' [Tversky and Kahneman, 1974] and a 1982 volume with the same title [Kahneman, Slovic and Tversky, 1982], and second, prospect theory, presented in the extraordinarily influential 1979 *Econometrica* paper 'Prospect Theory: An analysis of decision under risk' [Kahneman and Tversky, 1979] and further explored in another *Science* article titled 'The Framing of Decisions and the Psychology of Choice' [Tversky and Kahneman, 1981]. As David Laibson and Richard Zeckhauser [1998] point out: "[These] publications altered the intellectual history of economics; they brought the behavioral economics research program into the mainstream" [Laibson and Zeckhauser, 1998, 19].

The thesis of the heuristics and biases paper is that "people rely on a limited number of heuristic principles which reduce the complex tasks of assessing probabilities and predicting values to simpler judgmental operations" [Tversky and Kahneman, 1974, 1124]. Consistent with BDR in particular and cognitive science in general, Kahneman and Tversky are interested in the mechanisms underlying human judgment and decision making, and have a special interest in the conditions under which the mechanisms fail. As they put it: "In general, these heuristics are quite useful, but sometimes they lead to severe and systematic error" [Tversky and Kahneman, 1974, 1124]. Each heuristic — including representativeness, availability, and anchoring and adjustment — although generally useful, comes with characteristic biases that arise in special circumstances. By studying these biases, Kahneman and Tversky assert, we can learn something about the mechanism that generated them.

"Folk wisdom holds that 'Prospect Theory'," Laibson and Zeckhauser [1998, 8] write, "is the most-cited paper ever published in *Econometrica*." The paper "presents a critique of expected utility theory as a descriptive model of decision making under risk, and develops an alternative model, called prospect theory" [Kahneman and Tversky, 1979, 263]. Central to their critique of orthodox decision theory is the observation of what they later called "framing effects," in which "seemingly inconsequential changes in the formulation of choice problems caused significant shifts of preference" [Tversky and Kahneman, 1981, 457]. To explain framing effects and a variety of other anomalous phenomena, the two authors offer a theory in which, among other things, "value is assigned to gains and losses rather than to final assets" [Kahneman and Tversky, 1979, 263]. This theory is capable of accommodating framing effects, because what counts as a gain and what counts as a loss is relative to the frame; when going from one frame to another, the theory permits the agent to change his or her choice behavior. According to the authors, prospect theory can accommodate a range of otherwise puzzling behavior, such as the fact that many people simultaneously gamble and buy insurance [Kahneman and Tversky, 1979, 263].

## *4.3 Thaler's anomalies*

Unlike Tversky and Kahneman, Richard Thaler received his Ph.D. in economics. In addition, he received it from an institution he describes as "a University of Chicago farm club, and hardly a place to get interested in psychology" [Thaler, 1991, xi]. Apparently as a diversion from running regressions, Thaler started observing the manner in which people around him (especially, it seems, economist colleagues) made real-life decisions, and took note of the various ways in which they deviated from the ideal expressed by mainstream economic decision theory [Thaler, 1991, xii]. In the mid-1970s, he got to know Fischhoff, Slovic, Tversky, and Kahneman, whose work he felt helped explain the anomalies he had observed [Thaler, 1991, xii–xiii]. Later, through his 'Anomalies' columns published in the widely distributed *Journal of Economic Perspectives* and collected in *The Winner's Curse* [1992], Thaler helped accelerate the awareness and acceptance of behavioral economics among mainstream economists [Loewenstein, 1996b, 351].

Thaler's first major contribution to behavioral economics was his 1980 paper 'Toward a Positive Theory of Consumer Choice' [Thaler, 1980]. This paper argues that the "exclusive reliance on the normative theory [of consumer choice] leads economists to make systematic, predictable errors in describing or forecasting consumer choices" [Thaler, 1980, 39]. Drawing explicitly on Kahneman and Tversky's work [1974; 1979], Thaler offers examples of "classes of problems where consumers are particularly likely to deviate from the predictions of the normative model" [Thaler, 1980, 40]. Like Tversky and Kahneman, Thaler is interested in anomalies primarily as a means to an end, the end being the development of an empirically adequate descriptive theory of consumer choice [Thaler, 1980, 40].

Anomalies discussed in the 1980 paper include the underweighting of opportunity costs, the failure to ignore sunk costs, the influence of considerations of regret, self-control problems, and others. In a follow-up paper, 'Mental Accounting and Consumer Choice,' Thaler [1985] develops what he calls "a new model of consumer behavior ... using a hybrid of cognitive psychology and microeconomics" [Thaler, 1985, 199]. Like Tversky and Kahneman, then, Thaler uses cognitive psychology, first, to identify in what ways people's choices diverge from the predictions of rational choice theory, and second, to develop more empirically adequate theories. Thaler [1985] also proceeds to spell out the implications for economic decisions, in this case for marketing. The fact that Thaler spent so much time exploring the implications of behavioral decision research, prospect theory, and so on, certainly helped bring the relevance of these developments home to economists and other social scientists with an interest in economic decisions.

## *4.4 Later developments*

More recent behavioral economists have been inspired by, and built on, the work by Thaler, Tversky and Kahneman, and the behavioral decision researchers. This work resists easy categorization, but nevertheless falls in different clusters. To give a flavor for what sort of ideas occupy more recent behavioral economists, we discuss, in a cursory fashion, four specific themes that have been explored in recent work: other-regarding preferences, reference dependence, nonlinear probability weighting, and hyperbolic time discounting.

### *Other-regarding preferences*

One way in which behavioral economists have tried to build psychologically plausible economic models is to model people as having "other-regarding preferences." Some research has examined the nature and origin of altruistic behavior (e.g., [Andreoni, 1990; 1995]), while other research focuses on the taste for fairness [Guth *et al.*, 1982; Kahneman *et al.*, 1986]. There is extensive research on "social utility," which shows that people care about relative outcomes, and specifically have a strong distaste for situations in which their outcome falls below that of the people to whom they compare themselves [Loewenstein *et al.*, 1989; Fehr and Schmidt, 1999; Bolton and Ockenfels, 2000], and research on reciprocal altruism which addresses the common tendency to reciprocate both kind and unkind behavior directed toward the self [Rabin, 1993]. Because most of these models work by allowing agents to derive utility from the pleasure (or pain) of others, the fairness of the overall distribution of goods, and so on, they are strictly speaking consistent with neoclassical economics (which, as we know from section 2.2 above, makes no assumption about the arguments of the utility function). In this sense, then, there is not necessarily anything characteristically behavioral about models of other-regarding preferences.

New research in the area of other-regarding preferences is beginning to support a new perspective, according to which people are inherently selfish but have a desire to appear to others (and even to themselves) to be fair and generous [Dana *et al.*, 2007; Benabou and Tirole, 2006]. This perspective can help to explain a wide range of phenomena, including, perhaps most importantly, the ability of small rewards to undermine generous behaviour [Gneezy and Rustichini, 2000]. These models are obviously consistent with the traditional neoclassical approach.

*Reference-dependence*

Neoclassical theory implies that consumers' preferences are invariant with respect to their current endowment or consumption. Behavioral economists, however, object that there is evidence of "reference-dependence" — i.e., that preferences depend on an individual's "reference point," which is usually equal to his or her current endowment. The notion of "loss aversion" further specifies that people dislike negative departures from their reference point more than they like positive departures, a pattern that can be depicted as a kink in the value function, or in indifference curves, at the current endowment point [Kahneman and Tversky, 1979; 1991]. The combination of loss aversion and reference dependence has numerous implications, including a phenomenon known as the "endowment effect." The endowment effect captures the observation that people tend to become extremely attracted to objects in their possession, and averse to giving them up, even if they would not have particularly desired the object had they not possessed it (e.g., [Kahneman, Knetsch and Thaler, 1990]). Loss aversion has proved a useful concept for making sense of field data ([Camerer, 2000]; cf. section 5.3 below) and has been used to explain a wide range of empirical phenomena, including asymmetries in demand elasticities in response to price increases and decreases [Hardie *et al.*, 1993], the tendency for New York City cab drivers to quit early after reaching a daily income target, contrary to the prediction of conventional models of labor supply [Camerer *et al.*, 1997], the tendency for investors to hold on to losing stocks longer than winning ones [Odean, 1998], the "equity premium," i.e., the large gap between stock and bond returns (see [Benartzi and Thaler, 1995]), and the tendency for volume to diminish during downturns in housing markets [Genesove and Mayer, 2001].

The Achilles tendon of reference-dependence has always been its flexibility; combining reference-dependence with prospect theory allows one to "explain" almost any pattern of risk preference by assuming that the reference point is either in the domain of gains (producing risk aversion) or losses (producing risk seeking). Addressing this problem and several others, Köszegi and Rabin [2009] have proposed a model of reference-dependent preferences in which an individual's expectations serve as the single, definitive, reference point. The model has been applied successfully in a variety of contexts, including work performance [Mas, 2006] and labor supply [Farber, 2008]. However, the higher degree of precision comes at a cost. An individual's behavior is likely to be a function of her expectations, but expectations are, in turn, a function of behavior, a reciprocal interaction that suggests the introduction of the concept of a "personal equilibrium" in which expectations and behavior are mutually consistent. Tests of the model have largely ignored this problem and focused simply on the question of whether behavior can be explained by the idea that expectations serve as *the* reference point.

*Non-linear probability weighting*

The expected-utility (EU) model, which is the dominant model of risk-taking in economics, assumes that the value of a risky prospect is determined by the utility of its consequences weighted by their probabilities of occurring. Many empirical studies of decision making under risk, however, document violations of the patterns of behavior predicted by EU (see [Starmer, 2000] for a review). Some of these violations can be explained by taking account of loss aversion and reference dependence (see prior subsection), but others are well explained by assuming a specialized probability weighting function that overweights small probabilities and is insensitive to changes in probability in the midrange of probabilities. The most sophisticated of the new theories that allow for nonlinear probability weighting assume that probability weights are "rank-dependent," which means that probabilities are weighted in a way that is sensitive to how they rank within the gamble that is being considered (e.g., [Quiggin, 1982; Tversky and Kahneman, 1992]). The essential insight captured by most rank-dependent probability weighting schemes is that people often put disproportionate weight on (care disproportionately about) the best and worst outcomes of a risky prospect, as judged by the norm of expected utility theory. The non-linear probability weighting dimension of prospect theory provides another explanation for simultaneous gambling and purchase of insurance.

*Hyperbolic time discounting*

The discounted-utility (DU) model, which is the dominant economic model of intertemporal choice, assumes that people choose between intertemporal prospects by evaluating the utilities of their outcomes and discounting them according to their time of occurrence (see [Loewenstein and Prelec, 1992; Frederick, Loewenstein and O'Donoghue, 2002]). The DU model assumes that utility in each period depends only on consumption in that period, and that all forms of consumption are discounted in a similar fashion. Undoubtedly the most controversial assumption, however, and the one that has been most frequently tested (and found lacking) is the assumption that utilities are discounted exponentially, according to the formula $d(t) = \delta^t$, applying the same discount rate in each period. As it turns out, a simple quasi-hyperbolic time discounting function of $d(t) = \beta\delta^t$ tends to fit experimental data much better than exponential discounting. Hyperbolic time discounting implies that people will make relatively far-sighted decisions when planning in advance — when all costs and benefits will occur in the future — but will make relatively short-sighted decisions when some costs or benefits are immediate (cf. [Strotz, 1955; Ainslie, 1975; 1992]). Declining discount rates have been observed in experimental studies involving real money outcomes [Horowitz, 1992] and in field studies — e.g., a study in which Indian farmers made choices between amounts of rice that would be delivered at different points in time [Pender, 1996] and a study in which people made real choices between low-brow and high-brow movies that they would either be watching the same day or at times in the future [Read *et al.*, 1999].

Many authors, such as Thaler [1981], Thaler and Shefrin [1981], and Schelling [1978] have discussed issues of self-control and stressed their importance for economics. Laibson [1997] accelerated the integration of these issues into economics by incorporating a hyperbolic discount function into an otherwise standard model of lifetime consumption-savings decisions. More recent papers by Laibson *et al.* [1998] and others have demonstrated that hyperbolic discounting potentially provides a better account than does conventional exponential discounting of various savings and consumption phenomena, such as different marginal propensities to consume out of different forms of savings, and the dramatic impact of liquidity constraints on savings. Finally, in a series of papers, O'Donoghue and Rabin [1999; 2001] have demonstrated the importance for behavior of whether hyperbolic time discounters, while being impatient in the present, are naïve or sophisticated about the fact that they will also be impatient in the future — when the future becomes the present.

A final development in the economic literature on intertemporal choice is the question, raised by Daniel Read and collaborators [Read, 2001; Read and Roelofsma, 2003], of whether many of the results that have been attributed to hyperbolic time discounting can in fact be explained by what he calls "subadditive discounting," i.e., the tendency for people to show lower discount rates not for more delayed intervals but instead for longer intervals. As is true for all the areas of research summariszed herein, time discounting remains a topic of active research and continually changing perspectives.

## *4.5 Discussion*

In this section, we have argued that behavioral economics grew out of behavioral decision research (BDR) and gradually emerged as its own field. BDR, which started out as a self-conscious attempt to integrate ideas from psychology and cognitive science, examines the extent to which people's behavior conforms to the normative ideal of rational choice theory. Tversky and Kahneman, as well as Thaler, brought this line of research to the attention of economists in part by speaking a language that economists already understood and by articulating its implications for economic decisions. The discussion illustrates how behavioral economics, like BDR, "operates on the level of representation" [Gardner, 1985/1987, 38]. Indeed, both disciplines can be described as assuming "the central hypothesis of cognitive science" [Thagard, 1996/2005, 10]: the notion that judgment and decision making can be understood in terms of representational structures in the mind and operations on those structures.

It is worth noting that the authors discussed in this section criticize the orthodox theory of choice under uncertainty as a positive or descriptive theory of decision, not as normative or prescriptive one. In fact, behavioral economists for the most part have accepted the conception of rationality associated with neoclassical economics.[12] Rather than modifying their normative theory in such a way that people's behavior comes across as largely rational, behavioral economists tend to look at, e.g., framing effects as evidence that irrationality is systematic and widespread. According to Slovic, Dale Griffin, and Tversky [1990], for example, such effects "represent deep and sweeping violations of classical rationality," which implies that "it may not be possible to construct a theory of choice that is both normatively acceptable and descriptively adequate" [Slovic, Griffin, and Tversky, 1990, 26].

## 5 THE METHODS OF BEHAVIORAL ECONOMICS

One characteristic feature of cognitive science is its interdisciplinary approach. Cognitive scientists, who come from different backgrounds, believe that the interdisciplinary approach allows them to achieve insights that would be unavailable to more traditional, disciplinary approaches. The essential assumption is exemplified by the statement of Thagard [1996/2005, 10] that "The best way to grasp the complexity of human thinking is to use multiple methods, especially combining psychological and neurological experiments with computational models." As a result, research in cognitive psychology "has come to draw quite naturally on evidence from psychology, neuroscience, and artificial intelligence — so much that disciplinary lines are beginning to blur" [Gardner, 1985/1987, 42]. Behavioral economists, like cognitive scientists, are methodological eclectics: they draw on evidence of many kinds and are comfortable using different methods to generate such evidence. In particular, unlike many postwar neoclassical economists, behavioral economists do not consider choice behavior the only kind of admissible evidence (though they consider it an important one). It is often said that the commitment to the interdisciplinary approach, and the use of different kinds of evidence, is in part what has made cognitive science so successful; quite arguably,

[12]This is not to say that behavioral economists accept the additional set of assumptions incorporated into the DU model as a normative standard for intertemporal choice, however.

the same thing is true for behavioral economics.

The fact that behavioral economists use a variety of methods makes them different from experimental economists, who define themselves on the basis of their endorsement and use of experimentation as a research tool (see [Kagel and Roth, 1995]). By contrast, behavioral economists define themselves, not on the basis of the research methods that they employ, but rather on their application of psychological insights to economics. Experimental economists have made a major investment in developing novel experimental methods that are suitable for addressing economic issues, and have achieved a virtual consensus among themselves on a number of important methodological issues such as prohibitions on deceiving subjects. Although behavioral economists may not always endorse all of the methodological prescriptions of experimental economists (cf. [Loewenstein, 1999]), behavioral economists have often found it expedient to play by experimental economists' rules when conducting experiments. Outsiders' confusion of the two fields is, therefore, understandable. Recent behavioral economics, however, has relied on an increasingly diversified and sophisticated set of methods that reflect its interdisciplinary heritage.

## *5.1 Hypothetical choices*

Some of the earliest, and most important, papers in behavioral economics relied on subjects' responses to hypothetical choices — i.e., situations in which they were asked to imagine what they would do if presented with a particular decision. Consider, for example, Sarah Lichtenstein and Paul Slovic's [1971] paper on preference reversals in which subjects would price a bet with a small chance of a high payoff above a bet with a large chance of a smaller payoff, yet choose the latter over the former. One of the tasks used in that paper was described as follows: "*S* [the subject] was told he owned a ticket to play the bet and was asked to name a minimum selling price for the ticket such that he would be indifferent to playing the bet or receiving the selling price... *S*s knew their decisions were 'just imagine"' [Lichtenstein and Slovic, 1971, 47]. Similarly for Kahneman and Tversky's seminal 'Prospect Theory' [1979] paper. They wanted to demonstrate a series of violations of expected utility theory, and introduced the topic in the following way:

> The demonstrations are based on the responses of students and university faculty to hypothetical choice problems. The respondents were presented with problems of the type illustrated below.
>
> Which of the following would you prefer?
>
> A: 50% chance to win 1,000, B: 450 for sure.
> 50% chance to win nothing;
>
> ...The respondents were asked to imagine that they were actually faced with the choice described in the problem, and to indicate the decision they would have made in such a case [Kahneman and Tversky, 1979, 264].

These authors obviously assume that subjects — at least as some reasonable approximation — have an idea of how they would choose under specified counterfactual conditions.

The empirical basis of Richard Thaler's [1980; 1985] papers on mental accounting, which we contend helped kick off the field of behavioral economics, did not present empirical data at all. The evidentiary basis of these papers consisted almost exclusively of "thought experiments": hypothetical cases of economic behavior patterns that were inconsistent with standard economic theory and which were intended to have face plausibility to the reader. For example, Thaler [1985] asked the reader to consider fictional scenarios such as the following: "Mr. S. admires a $125 cashmere sweater at the department store. He declines to buy it, feeling that it is too extravagant. Later that month he receives the same sweater from his wife for a birthday present. He is very happy. Mr. and Mrs. S. have only joint bank accounts" [Thaler, 1985, 199]. Although it can be objected that the examples he provides are unpersuasive because they are not based on actual data, Thaler took the examples to be so obviously realistic as to be almost indisputable.

Over time, the use of hypothetical choice studies came under attack from experimental economists, who complained that subjects in these experiments had no incentive to provide truthful, carefully considered responses, and that some of the anomalous results uncovered by behavioral economists could be artifacts. Perhaps most famously, Grether and Plott [1979] undertook a test of the preference reversal phenomenon with the explicit intention to "discredit the psychologists' works as applied to economics" [Grether and Plott, 1979, 623]. Grether and Plott opened their paper by listing 13 different "theories" intended to explain how the results could be "artifacts of experimental methods" [Grether and Plott, 1979, 624]. The theories range from #1 "Misspecified Incentives" to #13 "The Experimenters were Psychologists" [Grether and Plott, 1979, 624–629]. Ironically, the researchers ended up not only failing to discredit the effect, but concluding rather dramatically that:

> Taken at face value the data are simply inconsistent with preference theory and have broad implications about research priorities within economics. The inconsistency is deeper than the mere lack of transitivity or even stochastic transitivity. It suggests that no optimization principles of any sort lie behind even the simplest of human choices and that the uniformities in human choice behavior which lie behind market behavior may result from principles which are of a completely different sort from those generally accepted [Grether and Plott, 1979, 623].

Subsequent research, by the way, has come to less dramatic conclusions [Tversky *et al.*, 1990]. Although Grether and Plott's effort to discredit the psychologists' work failed, worries about the validity of hypothetical choices have remained and inspired the development and use of a variety of other methods.

## *5.2 Experiments with actual outcomes*

Some behavioral decision researchers were not satisfied with hypothetical choices alone, and aspired to test their results using experiments with actual outcomes. Even in the original preference reversal paper, Lichtenstein and Slovic [1971] reported the results of an experiment designed to test "whether the predicted results would occur under conditions designed to maximize motivation and minimize indifference and carelessness," and where among other things, "[the] bets were actually played and *S*s were paid their winnings" [Lichtenstein and Slovic, 1971, 51]. Still, reversals did not go away. Subsequently, Lichtenstein and Slovic [1973] replicated the results at a Las Vegas casino, where a croupier served as experimenter, professional gamblers served as subjects, and winnings and losses were paid in real money.

Over time, experiments involving real outcomes started to replace hypothetical choices as the "gold standard" for research in behavioral economics. This shift occurred in part as psychologists were determined to show that their results would persist even in choices involving real outcomes. One prominent such study was Kahneman, Knetsch, and Thaler's [1990] investigation of the endowment effect. The three authors reported the "results from a series of experiments involving real exchanges of tokens and of various consumption goods" [Kahneman *et al.*, 1990, 1328]. Subjects traded items such as Cornell coffee mugs and folding binoculars for induced-value tokens, i.e., tokens that can be exchanged for real money at the conclusion of the experiment. The experiments allowed the authors to conclude that the endowment effect is virtually instant, in the sense that "the value that an individual assigns to such objects ... appears to increase substantially as soon as that individual is given the object," but also that "the endowment effect can persist in genuine market settings" [Kahneman *et al.*, 1990, 1342–1343].

Beyond simply switching to experiments involving real outcomes, behavioral economists have also probed whether and when, in fact, eliciting hypothetical versus real choices matters. The question of whether — or under what conditions — empirical results are robust under changes in the experimental method has generated a small literature of its own. After reviewing "74 experiments with no, low, or high performance-based financial incentives," Camerer and Robin M. Hogarth [1999] conclude: "The modal result is no effect on mean performance (though variance is usually reduced by higher payment)" [Camerer and Hogarth, 1999, 7]. However, some studies have found substantial differences between hypothetical and real outcomes. For example, Neill *et al.* [1994] elicited from subjects either real or hypothetical buying prices for a range of goods and found that hypothetical buying prices tended to be higher, as if it is easier to part with an imaginary dollar than with a real one (although, see [Johannesson *et al.*, 1997] for contrary results). Other studies have found dramatic differences in behavior as a result of the magnitude of stakes employed in an experiment [Parco *et al.*, 2002]. Still other research suggests that whether hypothetical decisions match actual decisions will depend on the situation, and specifically, that people are particularly bad at reporting on how they would behave in a situation different from their current one (e.g., [Loewenstein and Adler, 1995; VanBoven *et al.*, 2000; 2003]).

## *5.3 Field research*

During the last decade or so, behavioral economists have increasingly relied on data gathered "in the field" [Della Vigna, 2009]. Thus, Linda Babcock, Xianghong Wang, and Loewenstein [1996] studied how social comparisons influence teacher contract negotiations. The authors relied on both survey data — gathered by administering questionnaires to negotiators from 75 school districts — about social comparisons, and field data on school district and community characteristics [Babcock *et al.*, 1996, 8–10]. Camerer, Babcock, Loewenstein, and Thaler [1997] explored the labor supply of New York City cabdrivers, using data from "trip sheets" — that is, forms where drivers record the time passengers were picked up and dropped off, as well as the amount of the fares, and from the cabs' meters, which automatically record the fares [Camerer *et al.*, 1997, 412–413]. Genesove and Mayer [2001] studied patterns of sales of Boston condominiums during a downturn in prices and found, consistent with loss aversion, that those who faced the prospect of selling at a loss relative to what they had paid held out longer before selling at a particular price. Choi, Laibson, and Madrian [2005] examined the behavior of investors in the aftermath of the Enron debacle in which employees of that company invested in their own company's stock and ended up losing their retirement nest eggs along with their jobs when their company went bust. The researchers were unable to detect any impact of these events on employees' ownership of their own companies' stocks at other companies.

Behavioral economists' excursion into the field has been driven in large part by concerns about the *external validity* of laboratory experiments, that is, whether experimental findings generalize to other subjects and settings [Brewer, 2000, 4]. Because the laboratory context is inevitably different from real-world decision situations — e.g., in context, information, and stakes — there is a worry that people might make different decisions in the lab than they would make in the real world. For some types of issues, such as how people behave in internet auctions, experiments may have high external validity since all of these factors are likely to be relatively similar. For other questions, however, such as how much people save, how they invest their money, or how long or hard they work on a day, laboratory studies may not be quite as valid.

Field studies come in different, albeit often not sharply distinguished categories. The simplest studies are "observational" studies in that investigators attempt to draw inferences from observations of naturally occurring behavior, whether at the individual or market level. In this sense, both of the studies mentioned above — the one about teacher contract negotiations and the one about New York City cabdrivers — were observational. The Achilles heel of such studies derives from their correlational nature, which raises issues of *internal validity*, that is, whether empirical observations permit the inference to causal conclusions [Brewer, 2000,

4]. It is notoriously hard to definitively infer causation from correlation, so such studies are inevitably beset by problems of potential confounds and of reverse causality.

In response to worries about internal and external validity, some behavioral economists have started looking for natural experiments — situations in which it is possible to observe the impact of a quasi-exogenous change in events — or have conducted field experiments. Examples of the former are the many studies examining the impact of changes in defaults and other features of company sponsored savings plans on employee saving behavior (e.g., [Madrian and Shea, 2001]). Participants in these studies are not randomly assigned to one treatment or another, but it is often possible to measure the effect of the changes with some degree of confidence by comparing savings behavior before and after the change or by comparing the behavior of people introduced to the change at different points in their tenure at the company.

Although they are not without problems, the new gold standard for empirical evidence may be the randomized field experiment (see [Harrison and List, 2004]). Because field experiments take place under conditions highly similar or identical to those of real-life decisions, they can be argued to have high external validity. At the same time, because they involve randomized assignment to test and control groups, they make it easier to draw causal conclusions and therefore arguably have high internal validity. In one field experiment, Duflo and Saez [2002] assigned a random sample of employees in a subset of departments to be offered a $20 payment for attending an informational fair dealing with savings. Enrollment was significantly higher in departments where some individuals received the monetary inducement to attend the fair than in departments where no one received the inducement. However, increased enrollment within the treated departments was almost as high for individuals who did not receive any monetary inducement as it was for individuals who did, demonstrating the influence of social information. In another study, List [2003] assigned novice and experienced baseball card traders to conditions in which they were given the opportunity to buy or sell various sports memorabilia. The study found that inefficiently low numbers of trades occur for naive traders, but that the same effect did not occur for traders who had significant amounts of experience. Yet another field experiment, conducted by a group of economists who have been attempting to apply insights from behavioral economics to issues of economic development [Ashraf *et al.*, 2006], investigated the impact on savings behavior of offering a "deposit collection" service offered by a rural bank in the Philippines that made it easy for individuals to deposit small amounts of money in a savings account. The authors found that those offered the service saved 188 pesos more (which equates to about a 25% increase in savings stock) and were slightly less likely to borrow from the bank. Field experiments, although still relatively rare in behavioral economics, are probably the most rapidly increasing category of research.

## 5.4 *Process measures, including fMRI*

To some extent, behavioral economists also use what psychologists refer to as "process measures" — i.e., methods that provide hints about the cognitive and emotional processes underlying decision making. Although behavioral economists are acutely aware of the pitfalls of process measures, most notably the limitations of verbal accounts of the causes of one's own behavior (see [Nisbett and Wilson, 1977]), they have not rejected the use of process measures altogether. For example, several behaviorally oriented game theorists have used computerized "process tracing" software to assess what information players in games are using to make decisions — e.g., whether players in shrinking pie games choose to look at payoffs in the last round, as they would if they were solving the game using backward induction (they do not) [Camerer *et al.*, 1994; Costa Gomes *et al.*, 2001; Johnson *et al.*, 2002].

Certainly the most exotic of the process measures currently being used, however, are brain scans, typically using functional Magnetic Resonance Imaging (fMRI), which allows researchers to examine, albeit crudely, which parts of an individual's brain are activated in response to a task or decision. Although brain imaging has only been a part of behavioral economics for a few years at the time of writing this paper, imaging methods have already been applied to a diversity of economic tasks, including decision making under risk and uncertainty, intertemporal choice, buying and selling behavior and strategic behavior in games (see [Camerer *et al.*, 2005]). Moreover, even more exotic neuroscience methods are beginning to be employed. For example, Ernst Fehr and colleagues [Knoch *et al.*, 2006] studied the impact on behavior of responders in the ultimatum game of disabling a part of subjects' brains called the right dorsolateral prefrontal cortex, using a tool called Transcranial Magnetic Stimulation (TMS). Interestingly, this study produced results that were seemingly opposite to an earlier study that examined behavior in the same game using fMRI [Sanfey *et al.*, 2003], underlining ambiguities in the interpretation of neural data as well as the need to approach the same problem using multiple methods.

## 5.5 *Discussion*

In this section we have seen how behavioral economists, like cognitive scientists, draw on many kinds of evidence and are comfortable using different methods to generate such evidence. In particular, we have seen that behavioral economists do not consider choice behavior the only kind of admissible evidence (though they are suspicious of introspective data). The review of methods used by behavioral economics suggests that the field has been successful in part because it has drawn inspiration from theoretical and methodological developments in neighboring fields, and succeeded in integrating methods from these fields and in exploiting data gathered from a variety of sources. Hence, behavioral economics may have helped ensure its vibrancy by not connecting itself to any one narrow methodology, but rather exploiting new research methods as they come on line and attempting to use the best method to address whatever problem is being considered.

## 6 CURRENT DIRECTIONS

Since its emergence as an independent subdiscipline, behavioral economics has seen a remarkable expansion. In light of this fact, it would be impossible to accurately describe current research in just a few paragraphs. Nevertheless, we do want to say a few words about current developments in the field. Some of the new developments are due to the loosening of ties between behavioral economics and behavioral decision research and the importation of insights from other subdisciplines. Here we discuss two such developments: the emergence of neuroeconomics and the increased interest in the role of affect in economic behavior. The last major new development that we describe in this section is the emergence of behavioral welfare economics — including the emerging literature on "behavioral law and economics" — which attempts to draw normative conclusions and spell out policy prescriptions on the basis of the research.

### *6.1 Neuroeconomics*

As cognitive scientists have grown comfortable using methods originally developed by neuroscientists, it has become increasingly difficult to define a clear boundary between cognitive science and neuroscience. As Michael I. Posner puts it, "the combined cognitive and neuroscience methodology makes it difficult to separate mind and brain approaches to empirical issues" [Posner, 1989, xii]. Something very similar is going on in behavioral economics. As behavioral economists are growing accustomed to neuroscience methods, it is increasingly difficult to define a clear boundary between behavioral economics and neuroeconomics — "the study of how the embodied brain interacts with its external environment to produce economic behavior" (McCabe [2003, 294]; cf. [Glimcher, 2003]).

Neuroeconomics involves using the emerging array of tools developed by neuroscientists to study the neural underpinnings of economic behavior. Neuroeconomists have already conducted studies in which subjects' brains are scanned while they engage in mainstay behavioral economics tasks, such as the ultimatum game [Sanfey *et al.*, 2003], decision making under risk [Tom *et al.*, 2007] and uncertainty [Hsu *et al.*, 2005], and intertemporal choice [McClure *et al.*, 2004], as well as more traditional economic behaviors such as deciding whether to purchase consumer goods [Knutson *et al.*, 2007]. These studies have generally come to similar conclusions, namely that decision making can be understood, not as a matter of implementing existing preferences, but rather as the resolution of interaction, and often competition, between different specialized neural systems (see, e.g., [Sanfey *et al.*, 2006]).

Neuroeconomics not only encompasses empirical work using neuroscience methods, but also involves importing insights from neuroscience to refine economic models of behavior. Again, perhaps the most important of these insights is that behavior, including economic behavior, can be modeled as resulting from the interaction of multiple interacting specialized neural systems. Thus, for example, Thaler and Shefrin [1981] propose a multiple-self model in which a person's behavior is directly controlled by a series of myopic "doers" who maximize short-run satisfaction, but the behavior of the doers is itself influenced by a farsighted "planner" who maximizes the discounted sum of the doers' utilities (see [Fudenberg and Levine, 2006], for an updated version of such a model). Bernheim and Rangel [2004] build a dual-process model of addiction which assumes that the brain can operate in one of two modes, a "cold mode" or a "hot mode." In the cold mode, the person makes sound, deliberative decisions with a broad, long-term perspective. In the hot mode, the person's decision-making is influenced by emotions and motivational drives. Which mode is triggered depends (stochastically) on environmental conditions, which in turn might depend on past behavior (e.g., if you choose to go to a party tonight rather than stay home, you increase the likelihood of experiencing a craving for alcohol tonight). Benhabib and Bisin [2002] assume that a person's behavior can be determined either by "automatic processes" or by "controlled processes." In their formulation, automatic processes are initially allowed to determine behavior, but controlled processes get activated whenever the costs from letting the automatic processes carry on become too large. They apply this framework to understanding saving behavior and describe how its predictions differ from those in saving-consumption models with hyperbolic discounting.

Although neuroscience methods and ideas have up until now influenced economics in a fairly incremental fashion, it is possible that their influence will ultimately prove to be much more radical (cf. [Camerer *et al.*, 2005, 10]). Incremental approaches take as their starting point orthodox decision theory and favor piecemeal, step-wise change (cf. [Camerer and Loewenstein, 2003, 7]). Many of the most important developments in behavioral economics — like prospect theory — were the result of an incremental approach. By contrast, radical approaches try to improve the predictive power and explanatory adequacy of current theory by starting from scratch. Examples of radical approaches proposed outside of the realm of neuroeconomics include reason-based decision theory [Shafir *et al.*, 1993] and case-based decision theory [Gilboa and Schmeidler, 1995]. Though radical approaches have not yet scored any successes comparable to prospect theory, it is still too early to judge this research program. Neoclassical economics has dominated the economic scene for almost as long as classical economics dominated before it, so the time may be ripe for a new revolution. If so, behavioral economics, and perhaps its neuroeconomic variant, show promise of identifying the direction for such a transformation.

## *6.2 Affect*

Like cognitive scientists, early behavioral economists tended to emphasize cognitive processes and the biases they can generate, including judgmental biases, framing effects, hyperbolic time discounting and nonlinear probability weighting.

A number of lines of research, however, draw attention to the important role of affect in judgment and choice [Loewenstein, 1996a; Mellers *et al.*, 1997; Lerner and Keltner, 2001; Loewenstein *et al.*, 2001; Slovic *et al.*, 2002; Loewenstein and Lerner, 2003; Rick and Loewenstein, 2008]. The new research is drawing new attention to, and providing new evidence for, the idea that affect can affect decision making, e.g., that people can behave self-destructively in the "heat of the moment" (e.g., [Ariely and Loewenstein, 2005]). Indeed, the new research is also pointing to the conclusion that many biases that had earlier been viewed in cognitive terms, such as nonlinear probability weighting [Loewenstein *et al.*, 2001; Rottenstreich and Hsee, 2001] or hyperbolic time discounting [Loewenstein, 1996a; McClure *et al.*, 2004] may in fact reflect the influence of affective factors.

Parallel developments have been occurring in psychology, with a large amount of work in the field of social psychology focusing on the role of emotion in behavior (e.g., [Zajonc, 1980; 1984; Epstein *et al.*, 1992; Sloman, 1996; Wilson *et al.*, 2000]). And similar developments are occurring in decision research and neuroscience, with the latter showing signs of splitting into two subfields, one focusing on "cognitive neuroscience" and the other on "affective neuroscience" [Damasio, 1994; LeDoux, 1996; Panksepp, 1998; Rolls, 1999].

In an indication that behavioral economics is responsive to new developments in the fields it draws on, in both empirical work and in theory development, a number of behavioral economists have been incorporating insights from the new research on affect into their work (see [Rick and Loewenstein, 2008] for a recent review). Whether for the purpose of understanding problems of self-control, destructive conflict, market gyrations, or gambling behavior, there is a growing recognition among economists that large domains of economic behavior will remain outside of the range of economic models unless economists begin to get a grip on the role of emotions in behavior.

## *6.3 Behavioral welfare economics*

Although behavioral economics began as a purely descriptive enterprise, its practitioners have always been interested in how people's decision making can be improved. Thus, for example, Tversky and Kahneman closed their seminal paper on heuristics and biases by expressing the hope that a better understanding of the heuristics — that is, of the mechanism underlying people's judgments — could improve judgments and decisions under conditions of uncertainty ([Tversky and Kahneman, 1974, 1131]; see also [Fischhoff, 1988, 156], quoted in section 4.1 above). It should therefore come as no surprise that some behavioral economists have drawn normative conclusions and offered policy prescriptions. Many of the proposed interventions are motivated by the belief that people often fail to act rationally, and are intended to help people make better choices — that is, choices that better serve the chooser's interests — than they would in the absence of the interventions. In the last few years, a whole program of what has been called "light paternalism" [Loewenstein and Haisley, 2008] has gained prominence. The hope underlying this program is that it may be possible to help people make better choices — choices that better serve their own interests — with little or no restriction to their autonomy or freedom of choice (see [Camerer *et al.*, 2003; Thaler and Sunstein, 2003]).

For example, Sunstein and Thaler note that in many situations it is possible to help people make better decisions without restricting their autonomy. They illustrate the point with the hypothetical case of a company cafeteria manager who has the option of placing healthy items before unhealthy items in the food line or doing the reverse, but does not have the option of doing neither. Sunstein and Thaler argue that in such situations it is perfectly legitimate for managers to adopt the option that they believe will help employees make better choices — namely placing the healthy food ahead of the unhealthy food. Similarly, Camerer *et al.* argue that it is often possible to craft policies that will benefit people if they do make mistakes, but will not hurt people who are fully rational. For instance, if it is beneficial to invest in retirement plan, but people tend to stick with the status quo, then it may make sense to change the usual default from not contributing (with the possibility of signing up) to contributing (with the possibility of opting out). If people are, contrary to the dictates of conventional economics, influenced by the default option, then changing the default could potentially benefit them; if they are not influenced by the default, then changing it will have no effect on behavior and little if any cost.

Perhaps the most important and comprehensive "light paternalistic" intervention to promote retirement savings is the "save more tomorrow" (SMarT) program, designed and tested by Thaler and Benartzi [2004]. Employees were approached and asked if they would increase their retirement contribution rates at the time of their next pay raise. Since the contribution rate does not increase until after a raise, employees do not perceive the increased savings as a cut in take-home pay. Once employees sign up for the plan, they remain enrolled until they reach the maximum contribution rate or until they opt out, playing on the status quo effect — the reluctance of people to change patterns of behavior once they have been established. A test of this intervention found that enrollment was very high (78%), that very few who joined dropped out, and that there were dramatic increases in contribution rates (an increase from 3.5% to 11.6% over 28 months). Notice that neither one of these examples involves a reduction in the autonomy or freedom of choice of the individual. As a result, the interventions are not paternalistic at all, in the traditional sense of the word.

Some of these contributions use welfare criteria that clearly differ from those used by mainstream economists. Thus, Kahneman [1999, 15] advocates the use of "objective happiness" — the time-integral of momentary happiness – as a welfare criterion. Most contributions to behavioral welfare economics, however, are best understood as using some version of the standard preference-based criterion. As John C. Harsanyi [1982] expressed this criterion: "in deciding what is good and what is bad for an individual, the ultimate criterion can only be his own wants and his own preferences," where what counts are not necessarily the persons's "manifest" preferences — i.e., "his actual preferences as manifested by his observed behavior" — but the "true" preferences — i.e., "the preferences he *would* have if he had all the relevant factual information, always reasoned with the greatest possible care, and were in a state of mind most conducive to rational choice" ([Harsanyi, 1982, 55], italics in original).[13]

## *6.4 Discussion*

Although the cognitive revolution provided the impetus that sent behavioral economics "into orbit," the field has maintained its vibrancy by drawing on other sources of inspiration, notably, input from research on neuroscience and affect. It has also increased its broader relevance by pioneering new approaches to public policy, most notably those based on different forms of light paternalism. Finally, in a pattern much like that of rational choice theory, but compressed into a much shorter period, behavioral economics has begun to export its insights to allied fields, which have not only increased the range of applications but also thrown insights and research findings back to the core of the field.

In an essay unapologetically titled "Economic Imperialism," Edward Lazear [2000] trumpeted the expansion of neoclassical economics into such diverse fields as law, political science, history, and even demography. If neoclassical boosters such as Lazear have reason to celebrate, then behavioral economists do as well. In its relatively short lifetime, behavioral economics has influenced a wide range of subtopics of economics and allied fields, such as behavioral law and economics [Jolls *et al.*, 1998; Sunstein, 2000] to behavioral finance (e.g., [Shleifer, 2000]) behavioral development economics [Mullainathan, 2007], behavioral public finance [McCaffery and Slemrod, 2006], behavioral game theory [Camerer, 2003], and behavioral macroeconomics [Akerlof, 2003]. All of these are booming areas of research that not only extend the influence of the ideas coming out of behavioral economics, but also throw back insights and findings that enrich the foundations of the basic science core of the field.

Meanwhile, it is worth noting that behavioral economics (as we have defined it) is a research program rather than a theory. Simon ([1987a, 221], quoted above) was explicit in this regard. In this sense too, behavioral economics is like cognitive science. After pointing out that cognitive science encompasses a variety of theories of mental representations and procedures, Thagard adds:

> I believe that the different theories of mental representation now available are more complementary than competitive. The human mind is astonishingly complex, and our understanding of it can gain from considering its use of rules such as those described above as well as many other kinds of representations including some not at all familiar [Thagard, 1996/2005, 5]).

[13] Bernheim and Rangel [2008], in contrast, advocate using a choice-based approach, but limiting the range of choices that are treated as self-interested — i.e., basing judgments of welfare on a subset of choices that are deemed to be self-interested.

As a relatively young discipline, it is not surprising that behavioral economics has not developed one unified theory on which there is universal agreement. And it is at least conceivable that the multiplicity of theories about judgment and decision making are more complementary than competitive.

Finally, it should be pointed out that behavioral economics does not involve a complete rejection of neoclassical theory or methods. It is not just (as we have maintained) that understanding the neoclassical background against which behavioral economics emerged helps us better understand the latter. Behavioral economists, as we have pointed out, use experimental methods and mathematical modeling skills borrowed from neoclassical economics. They retain neoclassical theory as a normative ideal and source of null hypotheses. Moreover, very often, neoclassical theory is preserved as a special case of behavioral theories. Thus, for instance, of exponential discounting is a special case of quasi-hyperbolic discounting (when ß=1). This is what Rabin is getting at when he writes that behavioral economics "is not only built on the premise that economic *methods* are great, but also that most mainstream economic *assumptions* are great. It does not abandon the correct insights of neoclassical economics, but supplements these insights with the insights to be had from realistic new assumptions" [Rabin, 2002, 659]. It follows that behavioral economists — at least for the foreseeable future — will continue to need a solid grounding in neoclassical economics.

## 7 CONCLUSION

In this chapter, we have highlighted the parallels between behavioral economics — the attempt to increase the explanatory and predictive power of economic theory by providing it with more psychologically plausible foundations — and cognitive science. Both fields are based on a repudiation of the positivist methodological strictures that were in place at their founding and a belief in the legitimacy of working at the level of representation. And both fields adopt an interdisciplinary approach, admitting evidence of many kinds and using a variety of methods to generate such evidence. Moreover, we have argued that there are direct links between the two fields, in that behavioral economics has drawn a great deal of inspiration from behavioral decision research, which can be seen as a branch of cognitive science. So far, just as cognitive science has had a tremendous impact on psychology, behavioral economics has become a vibrant subdiscipline of economics, one that is likely to have a major impact on the face of economics over the next decades.

## ACKNOWLEDGEMENTS

The authors are grateful to Francesco Guala, Uskali Mäki, and Ivan Moscati for comments on an earlier draft.

# BIBLIOGRAPHY

[Ainslie, 1975] G. Ainslie. Specious reward: A behavioral theory of impulsiveness and impulse control. *Psychological Bulletin*, *82*, 463–496, 1975.

[Ainslie, 1992] G. Ainslie. *Picoeconomics: The Strategic Interaction of Successive Motivational States within the Person.* Cambridge: Cambridge University Press, 1992.

[Akerlof, 2003] G. A. Akerlof. Behavioral macroeconomics and macroeconomic behavior. *The American Economist*, *47*, 25–47, 2003.

[Andreoni, 1990] J. Andreoni. Impure altruism and donations to public goods: A theory of warm glow giving. *Economic Journal*, *100*, 464–477, 1990.

[Andreoni, 1995] J. Andreoni. Warm glow versus cold prickle: The effect of positive and negative framing on cooperation in experiments. *Quarterly Journal of Economics*, *110*, 1–21, 1995.

[Angner, 2009] E. Angner. Subjective measures of well-being: Philosophical perspectives. In H. Kincaid and D. Ross (Eds.), *The Oxford Handbook of Philosophy of Economics*, pp. 560–579. Oxford: Oxford University Press, 2009.

[Ariely and Loewenstein, 2004] D. Ariely and G. Loewenstein. The heat of the moment: The effect of sexual arousal on sexual decision making. *Journal of Behavioral Decision Making*, *18*, 1–12, 2004.

[Ashraf *et al.*, 2005] N. Ashraf, C. F. Camerer, and G. Loewenstein. Adam Smith, behavioral economist. *Journal of Economic Perspectives*, *19*, 131–145, 2005.

[Ashraf *et al.*, 2006] N. Ashraf, D. Karlan, and W. Yin. Deposit collectors. *Advances in Economic Analysis and Policy*, *6*, 1–22, 2006.

[Augier and March, 2004] M. Augier and J. G. March. *Models of a Man: Essays in Memory of Herbert A. Simon.* Cambridge: MIT Press, 2004.

[Babcock *et al.*, 1996] L. Babcock, X. Wang, and G. Loewenstein. Choosing the wrong pond: Social comparisons in negotiations that reflect a self-serving bias. *Quarterly Journal of Economics*, *110*, 1–19, 1996.

[Bank of Sweden, 1978] Bank of Sweden. Press Release: The Sveriges Riksbank (Bank of Sweden) Prize in Economic Sciences in Memory of Alfred Nobel for 1978. 16 October, 1978.

[Bechtel *et al.*, 1998] W. Bechtel, A. Abrahamsen, and G. Graham. The life of cognitive science. In W. Bechtel and G. Graham (Eds.), *A Companion to Cognitive Science*, pp. 1–104. Oxford: Blackwell, 1998.

[Benabou and Tirole, 2006] R. Benabou and J. Tirole. Incentives and prosocial behavior. *American Economic Review*, *96*, 1652–1678, 2006.

[Benartzi and Thaler, 1995] S. Benartzi and R. H. Thaler. Myopic loss aversion and the equity premium puzzle. *Quarterly Journal of Economics*, *110*, 73–92, 1995.

[Benhabib and Bisin, 2002] J. Benhabib and A. Bisin. Self-control and consumption-savings decisions: Cognitive perspectives. Working Paper, New York University, 2002.

[Bentham, 1823/1996] J. Bentham. *An Introduction to the Principles of Morals and Legislation.* Oxford: Clarendon, [1823] 1996.

[Bernheim and Rangel, 2004] B. D. Bernheim and A. Rangel. Addiction and cue-triggered decision processes. *American Economic Review*, *94*, 1558–1590, 2004.

[Bernheim and Rangel, 2008] B. D. Bernheim and A. Rangel. Choice-theoretic foundations for behavioral welfare economics. In A. Caplin and A. Schotter (Eds.), *The Foundations of Positive and Normative Economics: A Handbook*, pp. 155–192. Oxford: Oxford University Press, 2008.

[Bolton and Ockenfels, 2000] G. E. Bolton and A. Ockenfels. A theory of equity reciprocity and competition. *American Economic Review*, *100*, 166–193, 2000.

[Boulding, 1958/1961] K. E. Boulding. Contemporary economic research. In D. P. Ray (Ed.), *Trends in Social Science*, pp. 9–26. New York: Philosophical Library, [1958] 1961.

[Brav *et al.*, 2004] A. Brav, J. B. Heaton, and A. Rosenberg. The rational-behavioral debate in financial economics. *Journal of Economic Methodology*, *11*, 393–409, 2004.

[Brewer, 2000] M. B. Brewer. Research design and issues of validity. In H. T. Reiss and C. M. Judd (Eds.), *Handbook of Research Methods in Social and Personality Psychology*, pp. 3-16. Cambridge: Cambridge University Press, 2000.

[Bruni and Sugden, 2007] L. Bruni and R. Sugden. The road not taken: Two debates about the role of psychology in economics. *Economic Journal*, *117*, 146–173, 2007.

[Cairnes, 1888/1965] J. E. Cairnes. *The Character and Logical Method of Political Economy.* New York: A. M. Kelley, [1888] 1965.

[Camerer, 1999] C. F. Camerer. Behavioral economics: Reunifying psychology and economics. *Proceedings of the National Academy of Sciences of the United States of America, 96*, 10575–10577, 1999.

[Camerer, 2000] C. F. Camerer. Prospect theory in the wild: Evidence from the field. In D. Kahneman and A. Tversky (Eds.), *Choices, Values, and Frames*, pp. 288–300. Cambridge: Cambridge University Press, 2000.

[Camerer, 2003] C. F. Camerer. *Behavioral Game Theory: Experiments on Strategic Interaction.* Princeton: Princeton University Press, 2003.

[Camerer *et al.*, 1997] C. F. Camerer, L. Babcock, G. Loewenstein, and R. Thaler. Labor supply of New York City cabdrivers: One day at a time. *Quarterly Journal of Economics, 112*, 407–441, 1997.

[Camerer and Hogarth, 1999] C. F. Camerer and R. M. Hogarth. The effects of financial incentives in experiments: A review and capital-labor-production framework. *Journal of Risk and Uncertainty, 19*, 7–42, 1999.

[Camerer *et al.*, 1994] C. F. Camerer, E. Johnson, T. Rymon, and S. Sen. Cognition and framing in sequential bargaining for gains and losses. In K. Binmore, A. Kirman, and P. Tani (Eds.), *Frontiers of Game Theory*, pp. 27-47. Cambridge: MIT Press, 1994.

[Camerer and Loewenstein, 2003] C. F. Camerer and F. Loewenstein. Behavioral economics: Past, present, future. In C. Camerer, G. Loewenstein, and M. Rabin (Eds.), *Advances in Behavioral Economics*, pp. 3-51. New York and Princeton: Russell Sage Foundation Press and Princeton University Press, 2003.

[Camerer *et al.*, 2005] C. F. Camerer, G. Loewenstein, and D. Prelec. Neuroeconomics: How neuroscience can inform economics. *Journal of Economic Literature, 43*, 9–64, 2005.

[Camerer *et al.*, 2003] C. F. Camerer, G. Loewenstein, and M. Rabin. *Advances in Behavioral Economics.* New York and Princeton: Russell Sage Foundation Press and Princeton University Press, 2003.

[Choi *et al.*, 2005] J. J. Choi, D. Laibson, and B. C. Madrian. Are empowerment and education enough? Underdiversification in 401(k) Plans. *Brookings Papers on Economic Activity*, 151–198, 2005.

[Clark, 1918] J. M. Clark. Economics and modern psychology I. *Journal of Political Economy, 26*, 1–30, 1918.

[Clark and Oswald, 1996] A. Clark and A. Oswald. Satisfaction and comparison income. *Journal of Public Economics, 61*, 359–381, 1996.

[Costa Gomes *et al.*, 2001] M. Costa Gomes, V. Crawford, and B. Broseta. Experimental studies of strategic sophistication and cognition in normal-form games. *Econometrica, 69*, 1193–1235, 2001.

[Curtin, 1982] R. Curtin. Indicators of consumer behavior: The University of Michigan surveys of consumers. *Public Opinion Quarterly, 46*, 340–352, 1982.

[Damasio, 1994] A. R. Damasio. *Descartes' Error: Emotion, Reason, and the Human Brain.* New York: G.P. Putnam, 1994.

[Dana *et al.*, 2007] J. Dana, R. A. Weber, and J. X. Kuang. Exploiting moral wiggle room: Experiments demonstrating an illusory preference for fairness. *Economic Theory, 33*, 67–80, 2007.

[Davis, 2003] G. F. Davis. Philosophical psychology and economic psychology in David Hume and Adam Smith. *History of Political Economy, 35*, 269–304, 2003.

[Dawes, 1998] R. Dawes. Behavioral judgment and decision making. In D. T. Gilbert, S. T. Fiske, and G. Lindzey (Eds.), *The Handbook of Social Psychology, Vol. II*, pp. 497-548. Boston: McGraw-Hill, 1998.

[DellaVigna, 2009] S. DellaVigna. Psychology and economics: Evidence from the field. *Journal of Economic Literature, 47*, 315–372, 2009.

[Diamond and Vartiainen, 2007] P. Diamond and H. Vartiainen, Eds. *Behavioral Economics and Its Applications.* Princeton: Princeton University Press, 2007.

[Duflo and Saez, 2002] E. Duflo and E. Saez. Participation and investment decisions in a retirement plan. *Journal of Public Economics, 85*, 121–148, 2002.

[Duesenberry, 1949] J. S. Duesenberry. *Income, Saving, and the Theory of Consumer Behavior.* Cambridge: Harvard University Press, 2002.

[Earl, 1988] P. E. Earl, Ed. *Behavioural Economics, Vol. I.* Aldershot: Edward Elgar, 1988.

[Easterlin, 1974] R. E. Easterlin. Does economic growth improve the human lot? Some empirical evidence. In P. A. David and M. W. Reder (Eds.), *Nations and Households in Economic Growth: Essays in Honor of Moses Abramovitz*, pp. 89–125. New York: Academic Press, 1974.

[Epstein *et al.*, 1992] S. Epstein, A. Lipson, C. Holstein, and E. Huh. Irrational reactions to negative outcomes: Evidence for two conceptual systems. *Journal of Personality and Social Psychology*, *62*, 328–339, 1992.

[Farber, 2008] H. S. Farber. Reference-dependent preferences and labor supply: The case of New York City taxi drivers. *American Economic Review*, *98*, 1069–1082, 2008.

[Fehr and Schmidt, 1999] E. Fehr and K. M. Schmidt. A theory of fairness, competition and cooperation. *Quarterly Journal of Economics*, *114*, 817–868, 1999.

[Fischhoff, 1988] B. Fischhoff. Judgment and decision making. In R. J. Sternberg and E. E. Smith (Eds.), *The Psychology of Human Thought*, pp. 153–187. New York: Cambridge University Press, 1988.

[Fisher, 1913] I. Fisher. The monetary side of the cost of living problem. *The Annals of the American Academy of Political and Social Science*, *48*, 133–139, 1913.

[Fisher, 1928] I. Fisher. *The Money Illusion*. New York: Adelphi Publishers, 1928.

[Frank and Bernanke, 2001/2004] R. H. Frank and B. S. Bernanke. *Principles of Microeconomics*. Boston: Mc-Graw Hill/Irwin, [2001] 2004.

[Frederick *et al.*, 2002] S. Frederick, G. Loewenstein, and T. O'Donoghue. Time discounting and time preference: A critical review. *Journal of Economic Literature*, *40*, 351–401, 2002.

[Frey and Stutzer, 2002] B. S. Frey and A. Stutzer. What can economists learn from happiness research? *Journal of Economic Literature*. *40*, 402–435, 2002.

[Fudenberg and Levine, 2006] D. Fudenberg and D. K. Levine. A dual self model of impulse control. *American Economic Review*, *96*, 1449–1476, 2006.

[Gardner, 1985/1987] H. Gardner. *The Mind's New Science: A History of the Cognitive Revolution*. New York: Basic Books, [1985] 1987.

[Genesove and Mayer, 2001] D. Genesove and C. Mayer. Loss aversion and seller behavior: Evidence from the housing market. *Quarterly Journal of Economics*, *116*, 1233–1260, 2001.

[Gilboa and Schmeidler, 1995] I. Gilboa and D. Schmeidler. Case-based decision theory. *Quarterly Journal of Economics*, *110*, 605–639, 1995.

[Glimcher, 2003] P. W. Glimcher. *Decisions, Uncertainty and the Brain: The Science of Neuroeconomics*. Cambridge: MIT Press, 2003.

[Gneezy and Rustichini, 2000] U. Gneezy and A. Rustichini. Pay enough or don't pay at all. *Quarterly Journal of Economics*, *115*, 791–820, 2000.

[Guth *et al.*, 1982] W. Guth, R. Schmittberger, and B. Schwarze. An experimental analysis of ultimatum bargaining. *Journal of Economic Behavior and Organization*, *3*, 367–88, 1982.

[Grether and Plott, 1979] D. M. Grether and C. R. Plott. Economic theory of choice and the preference reversal phenomenon. *American Economic Review*, *69*, 623–638, 1979.

[Griffiths, 1998] P. E. Griffiths. Emotions. In W. Bechtel and G. Graham (Eds.), *A Companion to Cognitive Science*, pp. 197–203. Oxford: Blackwell, 1998.

[Hansen, 2006] F. Hansen. *Explorations in Behavioral Economics: Realism, Ontology and Experiments*. Lund University Doctoral Dissertation, 2006.

[Hardie *et al.*, 1993] B. G. S. Hardie, E. J. Johnson, and P. S. Fader. Reference dependence, loss-aversion, and brand choice. *Marketing Science*, *12*, 378–394, 1993.

[Harrison and List, 2004] G. Harrison and J. A. List. Field experiments. *Journal of Economic Literature*, *42*, 1009–1055, 2004.

[Hastie and Dawes, 2001] R. Hastie and R. Dawes. *Rational Choice in an Uncertain World: The Psychology of Judgment and Decision Making*. Thousand Oaks: Sage Publications, 2001.

[Hicks, 1939/1946] J. R. Hicks. *Value and Capital: An Inquiry into Some Fundamental Principles of Economic Theory*. Oxford: Clarendon, [1939] 1946.

[Hicks, 1975] J. R. Hicks. The scope and status of welfare economics. *Oxford Economic Papers*, *27*, 307–326, 1975.

[Holyoak, 1999] K. J. Holyoak. Psychology. In R. A. Wilson and F. C. Weil (Eds.) *The MIT Encyclopedia of the Cognitive Sciences*, pp. xxxix–l. Cambridge: MIT Press, 1999.

[Horowitz, 1992] J. Horowitz. A test of intertemporal consistency. *Journal of Economic Behavior and Organization*, *17*, 171–182, 1992.

[Howitt, 1987] P. Howitt. Money illusion. In J. Eatwell, M. Milgate, and Peter K Newman (Eds.), *The New Palgrave: A Dictionary of Economics, Vol. III*, pp. 518–519. London: Macmillan, 1987.

[Hsu *et al.*, 2005] M. Hsu, M. Bhatt, R. Adolphs, D. Tranel, and C. F. Camerer. Neural systems responding to degrees of uncertainty in human decision-making. *Science, 310*, 1680–1683, 2005.

[Hutchinson, 1938] T. W. Hutchison. *The Significance and Basic Postulates of Economic Theory*. London: Macmillan, 1938.

[James, 1890] W. James. *Principles of Psychology*. New York: H. Holt & Co, 1890.

[Jevons, 1871/1965] W. S. Jevons. *The Theory of Political Economy*. New York: A. M. Kelley, [1871] 1965.

[Johannesson *et al.*, 1997] M. Johannesson, B. Liljas, and R. M. O'Conor. Hypothetical versus real willingness to pay: Some experimental results. *Applied Economics Letters, 4*, 149–151, 1997.

[Johnson *et al.*, 2002] E. J. Johnson, C. F. Camerer, S. Sen, and T. Rymon. Detecting failures of backward induction: Monitoring information search in sequential bargaining. *Journal of Economic Theory, 104*, 16–47, 2002.

[Johnson, 1958] H. Johnson. *Exploration in Responsible Business Behavior: An Exercise in Behavioral Economics*. Georgia State College of Business Administration Research Paper No. 4, 1958.

[Jolls *et al.*, 1998] C. Jolls, C. Sunstein, and R. Thaler. A behavioral approach to law and economics. *Stanford Law Review, 50*, 1471–1550, 1998.

[Kagel and Roth, 1995] J. H. Kagel and A. E. Roth, Eds. *The Handbook of Experimental Economics*. Princeton: Princeton University Press, 1995.

[Kahneman, 1999] D. Kahneman. Objective happiness. In D. Kahneman, E. Diener, and N. Schwarz (Eds.), *Well-being: The Foundations of Hedonic Psychology*, pp. 3–25. New York: Russell Sage, 1999.

[Kahneman *et al.*, 1986] D. Kahneman, J. L. Knetsch, and R. H. Thaler. Fairness and the assumptions of economics. *Journal of Business, 59*, 285–300, 1986.

[Kahneman *et al.*, 1990] D. Kahneman, J. L. Knetsch, and R. H. Thaler. Experimental tests of the endowment effect and the Coase theorem. *Journal of Political Economy, 98*, 1325–1348, 1990.

[Kahneman and Krueger, 2006] D. Kahneman and A. B. Krueger. Developments in the measurement of subjective well-being. *Journal of Economic Perspectives, 20*, 3–24, 2006.

[Kahneman and Tversky, 1979] D. Kahneman and A. Tversky. Prospect theory: An analysis of decision under risk. *Econometrica, 47*, 263–291, 1979.

[Kahneman *et al.*, 1982] D. Kahneman, P. Slovic, and A. Tversky. *Judgment Under Uncertainty: Heuristics and Biases*. New York: Cambridge University Press, 1982.

[Kahneman and Tversky, 2000] D. Kahneman and A. Tversky. *Choices, Values, and Frames*. New York: Russell Sage Foundation and Cambridge, UK: Cambridge University Press, 2000.

[Katona, 1947] G. Katona. Contribution of psychological data to economic analysis. *Journal of the American Statistical Association, 42*, 449–459, 1947.

[Katona, 1951] G. Katona. *Psychological Analysis of Economic Behavior*. New York: McGraw-Hill, 1951.

[Katona, 1975] G. Katona. *Psychological Economics*. New York: Elsevier, 1975.

[Keynes, 1936] J. M. Keynes. *The General Theory of Employment, Interest and Money*. London: Macmillan, 1936.

[Knoch *et al.*, 2006] D. Knoch, A. Pascual-Leone, K. Meyer, V. Treyer, and E. Fehr. Diminishing reciprocal fairness by disrupting the right prefrontal cortex. *Science, 314*, 829–832, 2006.

[Knutson *et al.*, 2007] B. Knutson, S. Rick, G. E. Wimmer, D. Prelec, and G. Loewenstein. Neural predictors of purchases. *Neuron, 53*, 147–156, 2007.

[Köszegi and Rabin, 2009] B. Köszegi and M. Rabin. Reference-dependent consumption plans. *Journal of Economics, 121*, 783–821, 2009.

[Krantz *et al.*, 1971] D. H. Krantz, R. D. Luce, P. Suppes, and A. Tversky. *Foundations of Measurement*. New York, London, Academic Press, 1971.

[Laibson, 1997] D. Laibson. Golden eggs and hyperbolic discounting. *Quarterly Journal of Economics, 112*, 443–477, 1997.

[Laibson *et al.*, 1998] D. Laibson, A. Repetto, J. Tobacman, R. E. Hall, W. G. Gale, and G. A. Akerlof. Self-control and saving for retirement. *Brookings Papers on Economic Activity*, 91–196, 1998.

[Laibson and Zeckhauser, 1998] D. Laibson and R. Zeckhauser. Amos Tversky and the ascent of behavioral economics. *Journal of Risk and Uncertainty, 16*, 7–47, 1988.

[Leibenstein, 1976] H. Leibenstein. *Beyond Economic Man: A New Foundation for Microeconomics.* Cambridge: Harvard University Press, 1976.

[Lambert, 2006] C. A. Lambert. The marketplace of perceptions. *Harvard Magazine*, March-April, 50–95, 2006.

[Lazear, 2000] E. Lazear. Economic imperialism. *Quarterly Journal of Economics, 115*, 99–146, 2000.

[LeDoux, 1996] J. E. LeDoux. *The Emotional Brain: The Mysterious Underpinnings of Emotional Life.* New York: Simon and Schuster, 1996.

[Lerner and Keltner, 2001] J. S. Lerner and D. Keltner. Fear, anger, and risk. *Journal of Personality and Social Psychology, 81*, 146–159, 2001.

[Lewin, 1996] S. B. Lewin. Economics and psychology: Lessons for our own day from the early twentieth century. *Journal of Economic Literature, 34*, 1293–1323, 1996.

[Lichtenstein and Slovic, 1971] S. Lichtenstein and P. Slovic. Reversals of preference between bids and choices in gambling decisions. *Journal of Experimental Psychology, 89*, 46–55, 1971.

[Lichtenstein and Slovic, 1973] S. Lichtenstein and P. Slovic. Response-induced reversals of preference in gambling: An extended replication in Las Vegas. *Journal of Experimental Psychology, 101*, 16–20, 1973.

[List, 2003] J. A. List. Does market experience eliminate market anomalies? *Quarterly Journal of Economics, 118*, 41–71, 2003.

[Loewenstein, 1996a] G. Loewenstein. Out of control: Visceral influences on behavior. *Organizational Behavior and Human Decision Processes, 65*, 272–292, 1996.

[Loewenstein, 1996b] G. Loewenstein. Richard Thaler. In W. J. Samuels (Ed.), *American Economists of the Late Twentieth Century*, pp. 351–362. Cheltenham: Edward Elgar, 1996.

[Loewenstein, 1999] G. Loewenstein. Experimental economics from the vantage-point of behavioural economics. *Economic Journal, 109*, F25–F34, 1999.

[Loewenstein and Adler, 1995] G. Loewenstein and D. Adler. A bias in the prediction of tastes. *Economic Journal, 105*, 929–937, 1995.

[Loewenstein and Haisley, 2008] G. Loewenstein and E. Haisley. The economist as therapist: Methodological ramifications of "light" paternalism. In A. Caplin and A. Schotter (Eds.), *The Foundations of Positive and Normative Economics: A Handbook*, pp. 210–245. Oxford: Oxford University Press, 2008.

[Loewenstein and Lerner, 2003] G. Loewenstein and J. Lerner. The role of affect in decision making. In R. J. Dawson, K. R. Scherer, and H. H. Goldsmith (Eds.), *Handbook of Affective Science*, pp. 619–642. Oxford: Oxford University Press, 2003.

[Loewenstein *et al.*, 2003] G. Loewenstein, T. O'Donoghue, and M. Rabin. Projection bias in predicting future utility. *Quarterly Journal of Economics, 118*, 1209–1248, 2003.

[Loewenstein and Prelec, 1992] G. Loewenstein and D. Prelec. Anomalies in intertemporal choice: Evidence and an interpretation. *Quarterly Journal of Economics, 107*, 573–597, 1992.

[Loewenstein *et al.*, 2003] G. Loewenstein, D. Read, and R. Baumeister (Eds.), *Time and Decision.* New York: Russell Sage Foundation, 2003.

[Loewenstein *et al.*, 1989] G. Loewenstein, L. Thompson, and M. Bazerman. Social utility and decision making in interpersonal contexts. *Journal of Personality and Social Psychology, 57*, 426–441, 1989.

[Loewenstein and Ubel, 2008] G. Loewenstein and P. Ubel. Hedonic adaptation and the role of decision and experience utility in public policy. *Journal of Public Economics, 92*, 1795–1810, 2008.

[Loewenstein *et al*, 2001] G. Loewenstein, E. U. Weber, C. K. Hsee, and N. Welch. Risk as feelings. *Psychological Bulletin, 127*, 267–286, 2001.

[Madrian and Shea, 2001] B. C. Madrian and D. F. Shea. The power of suggestion: Inertia in 401(k) participation and savings behavior. *Quarterly Journal of Economics, 116*, 1149–1187, 2001.

[Mandler, 1999] M. Mandler. *Dilemmas in Economic Theory: Persisting Foundational Problems of Microeconomics.* New York: Oxford University Press, 1999.

[McCabe, 2003] K. McCabe. Neuroeconomics. In L. Nadel (Ed.), *Encyclopedia of Cognitive Science*, pp. 294–298. New York: Macmillan, 2003.
[McCaffery and Slemrod, 2006] E. McCaffery and J. Slemrod. *Behavioral Public Finance: Toward a New Agenda.* New York: Russell Sage Foundation Press, 2006.
[McClure *et al.*, 2004] S. M. McClure, D. I. Laibson, G. Loewenstein, and J. D. Cohen. Separate neural systems value immediate and delayed monetary rewards. *Science*, *304*, 503–507, 2004.
[Mas, 2006] A. Mas. Pay, reference points, and police performance. *Quarterly Journal of Economics*, *121*, 783–821, 2006.
[Mellers *et al.*, 1997] B. A. Mellers, A. Schwartz, K. Ho, and I. Ritov. Decision affect theory: Emotional reactions to the outcomes of risky options. *Psychological Science*, *8*, 423–429, 1997.
[Mirowski and Hands, 2006] P. Mirowski and D. W. Hands, Eds. *Agreement on Demand: Consumer Theory in the Twentieth Century.* Durham: Duke University Press, 2006.
[Mitchell, 1910] W. C. Mitchell. The rationality of economic activity. *The Journal of Political Economy*, *18*, 97–113, 197-216, 1910.
[Mitchell, 1914] M. Mitchell. Human behavior and economics: A survey of recent literature. *Quarterly Journal of Economics*, *29*, 1–47, 1914.
[Morgan and Rutherford, 1998] M. Morgan and M. Rutherford, Eds. *From Interwar Pluralism to Postwar Neoclassicism.* Durham: Duke University Press, 1998.
[Moscati, 2007] I. Moscati. History of consumer demand theory 1871–1971: A Neo-Kantian rational reconstruction. *European Journal of the History of Economic Thought*, *14*, 119–156, 2007.
[Motterlini and Guala, 2005] M. Motterlini and F. Guala, Eds. *Economia cognitiva e sperimentale.* Milano: University of Bocconi Press, 2005.
[Mullainathan, 2007] S. Mullainathan. Psychology and development economics. In P. Diamond and H. Vartiainen (Eds.), *Behavioral Economics and its Applications*, pp. 85–113. Princeton: Princeton University Press, 2007.
[Nisbett and Wilson, 1977] R. E. Nisbett and T. D. Wilson. Telling more than we can know: Verbal reports on mental processes. *Psychological Review*, *84*, 231–259, 1977.
[Odean, 1998] T. Odean. Are investors reluctant to realize their losses? *Journal of Finance*, *53*, 1775–1798, 1998.
[O'Donoghue and Rabin, 1999] T. O'Donoghue and M. Rabin. Doing it now or later. *American Economic Review*, *89*, 103–124, 1999.
[O'Donoghue and Rabin, 2001] T. O'Donoghue and M. Rabin. Choice and procrastination. *Quarterly Journal of Economics*, *116*, 121–160, 2001.
[Otteson, 2002] J. R. Otteson. *Adam Smith's Marketplace of Life.* Cambridge: Cambridge University Press, 2002.
[Palacios-Huerta, 2003] I. Palacios-Huerta. Time-inconsistent preferences in Adam Smith and David Hume. *History of Political Economy*, *35*, 241–268, 2003.
[Panksepp, 1998] J. Panksepp. *Affective Neuroscience.* Oxford: Oxford University Press, 1998.
[Pareto, 1906/1971] V. Pareto. *Manual of Political Economy.* New York: A. M. Kelley, [1906] 1971.
[Parco *et al.*, 2002] J. E. Parco, A. Rapoport, and W. E. Stein. Effects of financial incentives on the breakdown of mutual trust. *Psychological Science*, *13*, 292–297, 2002.
[Pender, 1996] J. L. Pender. Discount rates and credit markets: Theory and evidence from rural India. *Journal of Development Economics*, *50*, 257–296, 1996.
[Perlman and McCann, 1998] M. Perlman and C. R. McCann. *The Pillars of Economic Understanding, Vol. I: Ideas and Traditions.* Ann Arbor: University of Michigan Press, 1998.
[Pigou, 1920/1952] A. C. Pigou. *The Economics of Welfare.* London: Macmillan and Co, [1920] 1952.
[Posner, 1989] M. I. Posner. *Foundations of Cognitive Science.* Cambridge: MIT Press, 1989.
[Quiggin, 1982] J. Quiggin. A theory of anticipated utility. *Journal of Economic Behavior and Organization*, *3*, 323–343, 1982.
[Rabin, 1993] M. Rabin. Incorporating fairness into game theory and economics. *American Economic Review*, *83*, 1281–1302, 1993.
[Rabin, 1996] M. Rabin. Daniel Kahneman and Amos Tversky. In W. J. Samuels (Ed.), *American Economists of the Late Twentieth Century*, pp. 111-137. Cheltenham: Edward Elgar, 1996.
[Rabin, 1998] M. Rabin. Psychology and economics. *Journal of Economic Literature*, *36*, 11–46, 1998.

[Rabin, 2002] M. Rabin. A perspective on psychology and economics. *European Economic Review, 46*, 657–685, 2002.
[Read, 2001] D. Read. Is time-discounting hyperbolic or subadditive? *Journal of Risk and Uncertainty, 23*, 5–32, 2001.
[Read and Roelofsma, 2003] D. Read and P. H. M. P. Roelofsma. Subadditive versus hyperbolic discounting: A comparison of choice and matching. *Organizational Behavior and Human Decision Processes, 91*, 140–153, 2003.
[Read *et al.*, 1999] D. Read, G. Loewenstein, and S. Kalyanaraman. Mixing virtue and vice: Combining the immediacy effect and the diversification heuristic. *Journal of Behavioral Decision Making, 12*, 257–273, 1999.
[Rick and Loewenstein, 2008] S. Rick and G. Loewenstein. The role of emotion in economic behavior. In M. Lewis, J. M. Haviland-Jones, and L. F. Barrett, (Eds.) *The Handbook of Emotion*, pp. 138–156. New York: Guilford, 2008.
[Robbins, 1932/1984] L. Robbins. *An Essay on the Nature and Significance of Economic Science.* New York: New York University Press, [1932] 1984.
[Rolls, 1999] E. T. Rolls. *The Brain and Emotion.* New York: Oxford University Press, 1999.
[Ross, 2005] D. Ross. *Economic Theory and Cognitive Science: Microexplanation.* Cambridge: MIT Press, 2005.
[Ross, 2008] D. Ross. The economic agent: Not human, but important. This volume.
[Rottenstreich and Hsee, 2001] Y. Rottenstreich and C. K. Hsee. Money, kisses, and electric shocks: On the affective psychology of risk. *Psychological Science, 12*, 185–190, 2001.
[Samuelson, 1937] P. A. Samuelson. A note on measurement of utility. *Review of Economic Studies, 4*, 155–161, 1937.
[Samuelson, 1948] P. A. Samuelson. Consumption theory in terms of revealed preference. *Economica*, 15, 243–253, 1948.
[Sanfey *et al.*, 2003] A. G. Sanfey, J. K. Rilling, J. A. Aronson, L. E. Nystrom, and J. D. Cohen. The neural basis of economic decision-making in the ultimatum game. *Science, 300*, 1755–1757, 2003.
[Sanfey *et al.*, 2006] A. G. Sanfey, G. Loewenstein, J. D. Cohen, and S. M. McClure. Neuroeconomics: Integrating the disparate approaches of neuroscience and economics. *Trends in Cognitive Science, 10*, 108-116, 2006.
[Schelling, 1978] T. C. Schelling. Egonomics, or the art of self-management. *American Economic Review, 68*, 290–294, 1978.
[Schliesser, 2005] E. Schliesser. Some principles of Adam Smith's Newtonian methods in *The Wealth of Nations. Research in the History of Economic Thought and Methodology, 23-A*, 33–74, 2005.
[Scitovsky, 1976/1992] T. Scitovsky. *The Joyless Economy: The Psychology of Human Satisfaction.* New York: Oxford University Press, [1976] 1992.
[Sen, 1982] A. Sen. *Choice, Welfare and Measurement.* Cambridge: Harvard University Press, 1982.
[Sent, 2004] E.-M. Sent. Behavioral economics: How psychology made its (limited) way back into economics. *History of Political Economy, 36*, 735–760, 2004.
[Shafir *et al.*, 1993] E. Shafir, I. Simonson, and A. Tversky. Reason-based choice. *Cognition, 49*, 11–36, 1993.
[Shleifer, 2000] A. Shleifer. *Inefficient Markets: An Introduction to Behavioral Finance.* New York: Oxford University Press, 2000.
[Simon, 1947/1957] H. A. Simon. *Administrative Behavior: A Study of Decision-making Processes in Administrative Organizations.* New York: Macmillan, [1947] 1957.
[Simon, 1978/1992] H. A. Simon. Autobiography. In A. Lindbeck (Ed.), *Economic Sciences, 1969-1980: The Sveriges Riksbank (Bank of Sweden) Prize in Economic Sciences in Memory of Alfred Nobel*, pp. 339–342. Singapore: World Scientific, [1978] 1992.
[Simon, 1987a] H. A. Simon. Behavioural economics. In J. Eatwell, M. Milgate, and P. Newman (Eds.), *The New Palgrave: A Dictionary of Economics, Vol. I*, pp. 221–225. New York: Stockton Press, 1987.
[Simon, 1987b] H. A. Simon. Bounded rationality. In J. Eatwell, M. Milgate, and P. Newman (Eds.), *The New Palgrave: A Dictionary of Economics, Vol. I*, pp. 266–268. New York: Stockton Press, 1987.
[Sloman, 1996] S. A. Sloman. The empirical case for two systems of reasoning. *Psychological Bulletin, 119*, 3–22, 1996.

[Slovic *et al.*, 1990] P. Slovic, D. Griffin, and A. Tversky. Compatibility effects in judgment and choice. In Robin Hogarth (Ed.) *Insights in Decision Making: A Tribute to Hillel J. Einhorn*, pp. 5–27. Chicago: Chicago University Press, 1990.

[Slovic *et al.*, 2002] P. Slovic, M. Finucane, E. Peters, and D. MacGregor. The affect heuristic. In T. Gilovich, D. Griffin, and D. Kahneman (Eds.), *Heuristics and Biases: The Psychology of Intuitive Judgment*, pp. 397–420. New York: Cambridge University Press, 2002.

[Smith, 1776/1976] A. Smith. *An Inquiry into the Nature and Causes of the Wealth of Nations.* Chicago: University of Chicago Press, [1776] 1976.

[Smith, 1759/2002] A. Smith. *The Theory of Moral Sentiments.* Cambridge: University of Cambridge Press, [1759] 2002.

[Starmer, 2000] C. Starmer. Developments in non-expected utility theory: The hunt for a descriptive theory of choice under risk. *Journal of Economic Literature*, *38*, 332–382, 2000.

[Strotz, 1955] R. H. Strotz. Myopia and inconsistency in dynamic utility maximization. *Review of Economic Studies*, *23*, 165–180,1955.

[Sunstein, 2000] C. R. Sunstein. *Behavioral Law and Economics.* Cambridge: Cambridge University Press, 2000.

[Thagard, 1996/2006] P. Thagard *Mind: Introduction to Cognitive Science.* Cambridge: MIT Press, [1996] 2006.

[Thaler, 1980] R. Thaler. Toward a positive theory of consumer choice. *Journal of Economic Behavior and Organization*, *1*, 39–60, 1980.

[Thaler, 1981] R. Thaler. Some empirical evidence on dynamic inconsistency. *Economics Letters*, *8*, 201–207, 1981.

[Thaler, 1985] R. Thaler. Mental accounting and consumer choice. *Marketing Science*, *4*, 199–214, 1985.

[Thaler, 1991] R. Thaler. *Quasi Rational Economics.* New York: Russell Sage Foundation, 1991.

[Thaler, 1992] R. Thaler. *The Winner's Curse: Paradoxes and Anomalies of Economic Life.* New York: Free Press, 1992.

[Thaler and Benartzi, 2004] R. Thaler and S. Benartzi. Save more tomorrow: Using behavioral economics to increase employee savings. *Journal of Political Economy*, *112*, S164–S187, 2004.

[Thaler and Shefrin, 1981] R. Thaler and H. M. Shefrin. An economic theory of self-control. *Journal of Political Economy*, *89*, 392–406 1981.

[Thaler and Sunstein, 2003] R. Thaler and C. R. Sunstein. Libertarian paternalism. *American Economic Review*, *93*, 175–179, 2003.

[Tolman, 1938] E. C. Tolman. The determinants of behavior at a choice point. *Psychological Review*, *45*, 1–41, 1938.

[Tom *et al.*, 2007] S. M. Tom, C. R. Fox, C. Trepel, and R. A. Poldrack. The neural basis of loss aversion in decision-making under risk. *Science*, *315*, 515–518, 2007.

[Tversky and Kahneman, 1974] A. Tversky and D. Kahneman. Judgment under uncertainty: Heuristics and biases. *Science*, *185*, 1124–1131, 1974.

[Tversky and Kahneman, 1981] A. Tversky and D. Kahneman. The framing of decisions and the psychology of choice. *Science*, *211*, 453–458, 1981.

[Tversky and Kahneman, 1991] A. Tversky and D. Kahneman. Loss aversion in riskless choice: A reference-dependent model. *Quarterly Journal of Economics*, *106*, 1039–1061, 1991.

[Tversky and Kahneman, 1992] A. Tversky and D. Kahneman. Advances in prospect theory: Cumulative representation of uncertainty. *Journal of Risk and Uncertainty*, *5*, 297–323, 1992.

[Tversky *et al.*, 1990] A. Tversky, P. Slovic, and D. Kahneman. The causes of preference reversal. *American Economic Review*, *80*, 204–217, 1990.

[Van Boven *et al.*, 2000] L. Van Boven, D. Dunning, and G. Loewenstein. Egocentric empathy gaps between owners and buyers: Misperceptions of the endowment effect. *Journal of Personality and Social Psychology*, *79*, 66–76, 2000.

[Van Boven *et al.*, 2003] L. Van Boven, G. Loewenstein, and D. Dunning. Mispredicting the endowment effect: Underestimation of owners' selling prices by buyer's agents. *Journal of Economic Behavior and Organization*, *51*, 351–365, 2003.

[Veblen, 1898] T. Veblen. Why is economics not an evolutionary science? *Quarterly Journal of Economics*, *12*, 373–397, 1898.

[Watson, 1913] J. B. Watson. Psychology as the behaviorist views it. *Psychological Review*, *20*, 158–177, 1913.

[Weber and Dawes, 2005] R. Weber and R. Dawes. Behavioral economics. In N. J. Smelser and R. Swedberg (Eds.), *The Handbook of Economic Sociology*, pp. 90–108. Princeton: Princeton University Press, 2005.

[Wicksteed, 1910/1967] P. H. Wicksteed. *Common Sense of Political Economy and Selected Papers and Reviews on Economic Theory, Vol. I.* New York: A. M. Kelley, [1910] 1967.

[Wilkinson, 2008] N. Wilkinson. *An Introduction to Behavioral Economics.* Basingstoke: Palgrave Macmillan, 2008.

[Wilson *et al.*, 2000] T. D. Wilson, S. Lindsey, and T. Y. Schooler. A model of dual attitudes. *Psychological Review, 107*, 101–126, 2000.

[Zajonc, 1980] R. B. Zajonc. Feeling and thinking: Preferences need no inferences. *American Psychologist, 35*, 151–175, 1980.

[Zajonc, 1984] R. B. Zajonc. On the primacy of affect. *American Psychologist, 39*, 117–123, 1984.

# THE ECONOMIC AGENT: NOT HUMAN, BUT IMPORTANT

Don Ross

## 1 INTRODUCTION

Critics of mainstream economics typically rest important weight on the differences between people and the 'agents' that populate economic theory and economic models. Hollis and Nell [1975] is both representative of and ancestral to many more recent variations on the theme. Lately, the upgraded status of behavioral economics (BE) within the discipline's mainstream has encouraged a number of writers to use revolutionary rhetoric in promotion of a 'paradigm shift' that includes the rejection of 'rational economic man' [Ormerod, 1994; Heilbroner and Milburg, 1995; Fullbrook, 2003]. The current leading developers of BE are generally more circumspect, claiming that their approach complements standard theory rather than promising to supplant it [Camerer and Loewenstein, 2004; Angner and Loewenstein, this volume]. However, they generally join the more florid critics in supposing that microeconomics is bound to improve its empirical relevance to the extent that it substitutes the study of people for that of abstract economic agents. Another body of thought that promotes this view stems from Sen's [1977] attack on standard economic agents as 'rational fools', amplified in Davis's [2003] argument that since economic agents lack some *essential* properties of human individuals, economic theory requires fundamental reform if it is to make progress in explaining human behavior.

That economic agents and people have different properties should strike no one as surprising. Whereas people are pre-theoretical entities found in the world, economic agency is a theoretical construction elaborated as part of the development of a family of models. In philosophical terms, we might therefore describe the view that economists should forget about economic agency and directly study people instead as an expression of *normative phenomenalism*. This would be the thesis that the proper objects of scientific attention are manifest phenomena, which should be described directly rather than by way of intermediate theoretical kinds. This is not a view we find on display elsewhere in the philosophy of science. Though strong empiricists, such as Bas van Fraassen [1980; 2002], deny that we are entitled to ascribe model-independent reality to the unobservable objects of reference used in scientific theories, I have never heard anyone insist that physicists ought to stop modeling fields and manifolds and go back to generalizing directly about

Handbook of the Philosophy of Science. Volume 13: Philosophy of Economics.
Volume editor: Uskali Mäki. General editors: Dov M. Gabbay, Paul Thagard and John Woods.

rocks and tables. Elsewhere in this volume, I extensively discuss the reasons why economics has attracted a level of anti-theoretical *hostility* not encountered by other sciences (aside from evolutionary biology). I suggest that this discussion is useful background for explaining the eagerness with which revolutions in economics are promoted on grounds we don't encounter elsewhere in science. In the present essay, I will assume that normative phenomenalism, especially as applied arbitrarily to and only to economics, is not rationally motivated. This assumption does not foreclose the possibility that either current critique or the future course of economic science could reveal the idea of economic agency, either in general or in some common particular form, to be unhelpful. Use of any given agency concept in science *is* subject to requests for justification; but the mere fact that economic agency is abstractly constructed establishes *no* prima facie case against such justification.

It might be objected that normative phenomenalism is a fair standard for application to economics in particular because economic theory, unlike physical theory, generalizes only or mainly over observable types. In this connection, Mäki [1986; 1992] points out that Friedman's [1953] famous methodology isn't in fact the standard sort of instrumentalism it's typically taken to be because, unlike philosophical instrumentalists about the unobservable entities of physics, Friedman assumes the objects of economics to be manifest: consumers, firms, prices, etc. He then doubts that economic theory truly describes these objects, useful though it is for predicting their trajectories. He does not doubt, as the instrumentalist does of bosons, that the basic objects of economics exist. Though I agree with Mäki about what Friedman thought on this question, I do not think that Friedman's opinion here is correct. Because the *words* used by economists, unlike 'boson', are derived from everyday vocabulary, it is easy to forget that in their theoretical context they denote abstractions. Despite slightly quaint philosophical jargon, Stigum [1990] offers nice examples of the point: "We have knowledge by acquaintance of the salary we received last year, but we have knowledge by description only of what our income was, i.e., of the maximum amount of money we could have spent last year and been as wealthy at the end of the year as we had been at the beginning of the year ... We have knowledge by acquaintance of the price of our house, but only knowledge by description of its current market value" (p. 550). So it is with agency in economic theory: we gaze upon and shake hands with people, but not with economic agents. But, in the absence of an argument for normative phenomenalism, this fact by itself no more implies that economists should stop theorizing about agents, or equate them with people, then similar logic would rightly advise them to stop theorizing about incomes or to equate incomes with salaries. Again, this is not to deny the validity of requests for justification on grounds internal to the goals of economics (as opposed to external philosophical grounds).

The structure of the chapter is as follows. I will first sketch the standard concept of the economic agent as featured in contemporary microeconomics. I will then show why the practice of economists does not equate this agent to a person, and why economists' longstanding interests in 'individualism' and 'microfoundations' should not be interpreted as suggesting otherwise. This will show how, in detail, economists should respond to criticisms reflecting normative phenomenalism. In section 5 I will indicate why and how (some) behavioral economists propose to modify agency in light of studies of people, in cases where normative phenomenalism is *not* assumed. The core of this argument involves contesting the view held by increasingly many behavioral economists that their program collapses into the ambition of the new 'neuroeconomics' to identify and explain the processes by which brains comparatively value actual and prospective rewards. I will maintain that what I will call 'neurocellular economics' (as found in work by [Glimcher, 2003; Caplin and Dean, 2008]) is importantly different in its implicit attitude to standard economic agency from a more reductionist version of neuroeconomics that has lately been stapled to BE in would-be service of a paradigm shift [Camerer *et al.*, 2005]. Having explained why modular neuroeconomics preserves rather than challenges the standard concept of economic agency, I will defend the continued use of that concept against calls for its replacement by objects and processes identified through psychological and neuroscientific observation.

## 2 ECONOMIC AGENCY

There is a clear historical path by which the standard concept of the economic agent was developed [Mandler, 1999]. This agent first appeared in the work of the early neoclassical theorists (Jevons and Walras) as a maximizer of ceiling-less hedonic utility laboring under a finite budget, subject to diminishing marginal returns from consumption within classes of commodities he deemed to be close substitutes. I deliberately use the pronoun 'he', because at the point of his historical arrival the economic agent was both normatively male in his status as a social atom and (more importantly for present purposes) human, in that he relied on 'creature sensations' to both form his close-substitute classes and to rank them with respect to the utility they delivered. His agency revolved around his efforts, given his limited means, to create the most appealing inner environment he could, as determined by his own introspective judgment.

Although the early neoclassical agent was human, he was already not a *whole* person. In sympathy with Mill's refusal to follow Bentham in regarding all sources of satisfaction — pushpin and poetry, a foot message and an end to poverty — as lying on a single commensurable scale, Jevons [1871] took the economic agent to be the *aspect* of the person concerned with the consumption of 'lower' wants. We can fully understand what was 'lower' about these wants only by going slightly outside the frame of Jevons's text and importing some knowledge of the Victorian world-view. To some extent the lowliness of economic wants lay in their materiality. But Victorian idealism was closely bound up with the morality of social obligation: material goods were 'low' in part because, unlike 'spiritual' goods, their consumption as sources of utility was private; 'higher' wants were higher in part because attending to them expressed commitment to public civilization. Given the importance of atomism as a property of the economic agent for which he is widely rebuked by his critics (including contemporary ones), this point merits emphasis. The Victorians were pointedly and self-consciously divided amongst themselves as regards metaphysical atomism versus holism, with the scientifically minded such as Jevons inclining to the former and most philosophers defending the latter. But neither Jevons nor Walras were *moral* atomists; both rejected the idea that a person should give his highest priority to what they regarded as his economic interests.

Some readers might have jumped to the conclusion that I am calling the early neoclassical agent 'human' because he had 'feelings'. It has long been fashionable to contrast the 'cold calculator' featured in economic theory with the warm, sentimental and impulsive beings celebrated by all romantics and by most Western humanists. Though this is important for understanding sources of non-rational antipathy to economics, it seems to me ethnocentric to view emotional parochialism and impulsiveness as the core properties of the human; Western romantic humanism is a peculiar, not a globally typical, idealization of human nature. Thus I would question the long-run philosophical importance of contrasting the early agent's passions with the later agent's lack of them. Instead, I suggest, what made Jevons's economic agent human by contrast with his contemporary successor was the former's grounding in consumption within the boundaries of his *body*. The early neoclassical agent was an aspect of the human *animal*. Thus there was an implicit one-to-one mapping between these agents and human organisms, which all applications took for granted.

As recognized by many writers, and reviewed succinctly by Bruni [2005] and Bruni and Sugden [2007], Jevons's introspective agent was on the way out before the twentieth century began; Pareto, in particular, worked to reduce his defining properties to a mere disposition to consume in accordance with representation by indifference curves. Following on this lead using more powerful mathematical resources, the introspective agent was killed stone dead in the ordinalist revolution of the 1930s and 40s led by Hicks, Allen and Samuelson [Mandler, 1999]. As related by Ross [2005], however, what never disappeared from most economists' (or other people's) informal conception of the economic agent was the idea that he was still (as it were) 'ontologically grounded' in the human organism. By this I mean only that the one-to-one mapping between agents and organisms presumed by Jevons and Walras (henceforth, '$A \Leftrightarrow O$') remained the basic reference point for understanding the place of agents in the empirical interpretation of economic theory, even as the agent's human properties were steadily stripped away. There were motivations for this conservatism, as we will see; it wasn't merely a case of conceptual inertia. But, I will argue, we can make more consistent sense of the character of most economics since Samuelson by dropping the attribution to its foundations of the assumption of $A \Leftrightarrow O$.

The ordinalist revolution did not so much modify the concept of the economic agent as, to begin with, attempt to eliminate him. In the canonical ordinalist texts, Samuelson [1938; 1947] set out to derive the existence of sets of preferences mappable onto the real numbers by monotonic, complete, acyclical, and convex functions from observable schedules of aggregate demand. He would have preferred not to call these 'utility' functions, but the lure of semantic continuity turned out to be a more powerful force than his preference, and he quickly surrendered the point to convention.[1] As the label 'revealed preference theory' was intended to suggest, his utility functions were intended as descriptions of actual and hypothetical behavior, not inner evaluations of experienced relative states of satisfaction. It is common to attribute the motivation for this to the behaviorism and positivism that dominated the psychology and social science of the 1930s, 40s and 50s, and certainly this influence played its part. However, imagining it to have been the main, let alone the sole, motivation ignores the fact that Samuelson completed a process that had been underway for decades in economics, and which thus reflected a special dynamic internal to the discipline. This was the felt pressure to make economics a *social* science independent of any foundations in individual psychology. Cold war neuroses demanding adherence to 'methodological individualism' did much to obscure the point in retrospect. But as good Keynesians, Hicks and Samuelson were, in a very important sense to which we will return later, *uninterested* in individual agents, a concept of which they merely inherited from an earlier neoclassical theory they profoundly transformed. If we let Samuelson's [1947] mathematics speak for itself, as he largely though inconsistently does himself in *Foundations*, then among the short and general things we might say about the role of the agent in revealed preference theory the most accurate is that there isn't one. There is observable aggregate demand, and if this has certain testable properties then the existence of continuous preference fields is implied. What stabilizes these fields might or might not be properties of individual psychologies; the revealed preference theorist disavows professional interest in this question, a point on which Samuelson is explicit.

All this makes it easy to imagine that, and how, the agent might have disappeared altogether from economic theory had the discipline technically matured in a slightly different context. Indeed, someone might well argue that the agent *did* substantially disappear despite the fact that the *word* 'agent' soon made a comeback in the literature following on Samuelson. There are three possible interpretations to be distinguished here. By 'interpretations' I refer not to claims about what historical economists actually intended, but to attributions that might be offered by philosophical reconstructions that apply retrospective principles of charity in full knowledge of contemporary economics. The possible interpretations are:

1. The role of the agent was eliminated from microeconomic theory after World War Two.

2. Postwar microeconomic theory retained a concept of the agent, but with substantial modifications that imply abandonment of the commitment to

[1] Many economists, however, now refer to 'objective functions' rather than 'utility functions'. I hope that this becomes standard usage, but fear that the influence of behavioral economics will get in the way.

$A \Leftrightarrow O$ (whether or not many economists, who are not in the philosophy business, noticed this).

3. The absence of agents in Samuelson's version of revealed preference theory was an idiosyncratic wobble in the evolution of microeconomic theory; the reappearance of the word 'agent' in subsequent canonical texts indicates stronger continuity with early neoclassicism than Samuelson suggested, in particular, continued ontological orientation around $A \Leftrightarrow O$.

Contemporary paradigm-shifters based in BE, along with Sen and his followers, adhere to interpretation (3) and then, in rejecting social atomism, take themselves to be calling for the overthrow of a historically unified neoclassical tradition. (Thus they often refer to the contemporary mainstream as 'Walrasian'.) I will defend interpretation (2).

Let us now hoist the target of the conflicting interpretations onto the table. Again, there can be no dispute that Samuelson's avoidance of the *word* 'agent' failed to stick as a practice: the subtitle of Rubinstein's [2006] elegant formulation of the core elements of microeconomic theory, which deserves to be regarded as authoritative on matters of current convention, is "*The Economic Agent*". I will summarize the part of Rubinstein's formulation that might plausibly be taken to be *definitive* of economic agency. This is the part that can be stated independently of any assumptions about representations or computations taken to be aspects of agents' psychologies; were such assumptions to be incorporated into the definition of agency then the question distinguishing the defenders of interpretations (2) and (3) above would necessarily be begged in favor of the latter. Note that the judgment about what to regard as 'definitive' that I will express below is mine, not Rubinstein's. Note also that Rubinstein's formulation reflects the consolidation of postwar consumer theory provided by Debreu [1959], rather than the less exact version found in Samuelson [1947]; this is a point that will be important in the later discussion.

The agent is a reference point for ascription of a utility function. Utility functions are constructed from preference functions or represent preference relations. A preference function or relation generalizes a series of answers to a series of evaluative questions about elements $x$, $y$, $\ldots$, $n$ of a set $X$, with one answer per question of the form '$x$ is preferred to $y$' ($x \succ y$), '$y$ is preferred to $x$' ($y \succ x$), or '$x$ and $y$ are interchangeable in preference ranking' ($I$). Rubinstein shows that two forms of generalization are equivalent:

1. Preferences on a set $X$ are a function $f$ that assigns to any pair $(x, y)$ of distinct elements in $X$ exactly one of $x \succ y$, $y \succ x$, or $I$, restricted by two properties: (i) *no order effect*: $f(x, y) = f(y, x)$; and (ii) *transitivity*: if $f(x, y) = x \succ y$ and $f(y, z) = y \succ z$ then $f(x, z) = x \succ z$ and if $f(x, y) = I$ and $f(y, z) = I$ then $f(x, z) = I$.

2. A preference on a set $X$ is a binary relation $\succ$ on $X$ satisfying (i) *completeness*: for any $x$, $y \in X$, $x \succ y$or $y \succ x$; and (ii) *transitivity*: for any

$x, y, z \in X$ if $x \succ y$ and $y \succ z$ then $x \succ z$.

A utility function is a representation of a preference relation according to: $U : X \rightarrow \Re$ represents $\succ$ if for all $x, y \in X, x \succ y$ if and only if $U(x) \geq U(y)$.

If the foregoing is taken to restrict the conception of an agent then it follows that an agent's preferences are not lexicographic [Debreu, 1960]. This also follows from conceiving of preference relations as continuous. From Debreu [1954; 1960], any set of continuous preferences is represented by a continuous utility function.

The agent distributes her investments in alternative feasible states of the world in accordance with the weak axiom of revealed preference. I use a formulation of my own here instead of Rubinstein's: for two complete states of the world $x, y : x \neq y$, if the agent pays opportunity cost $c + y$ in exchange for $x$, then the agent will never pay opportunity cost $c + x$ in exchange for $y$. This implies that the agent's behavior will be consistent with the hypothesis that she maximizes a utility function according to which $U(x) \geq U(y)$.

When agents are located in markets where they encounter consumption problems, more is generally assumed of them. In particular, it is supposed that when they are faced with alternative investments in quantitatively measurable combinations of elements (bundles) from their utility functions, their preferences satisfy monotonicity (for any element $x \in X, x + \varepsilon \succ x$), continuity, and convexity (consumption behavior is consistent with representation by neoclassical indifference curves). Stronger assumptions, particularly that utility functions are differentiable, are typically added if we are concerned to show that a particular model of a consumer's optimization of consumption given a budget is explained by reference to her preferences. Note that economists are almost never moved by this concern except when they are engaged in explicit justification of abstract theory — that is to say, when they're not actually doing economics.

In light of the foregoing, our prior question about the ontological presumptions around agency in postwar economic theory comes down to this: what import should be attached to saying that a reference point for ascription of a utility function, as just defined, is an 'agent'? 'Reference point' here just means an element of some index constructed for a particular analytic exercise; so all the weight lies on concept of the utility function. It should be evident that what I identified earlier as the 'human' properties of Jevons's agent make no appearance in the definition. Nor, at least until the rise of BE, did they play any explicit role in interpretations of the formalism in applications. Now, there is no room for serious doubt that in the Western intellectual tradition the prototypical agent is the goal-pursuing aspect of a single person over the course of her biography from the dawn to the demise of her mature competence in practical reasoning [Ross, 2002]. The idea has a relatively clear and constant conceptual core from the work of Aristotle through Kant. From this perspective it should seem puzzling that Samuelson's avoidance of reference to agents didn't continue to be respected: reference points for ascriptions of utility functions don't seem particularly to resemble philosophers' agents. Why then is it standard practice we find Rubinstein reflecting in using 'the economic agent' as his subtitle in 2006?

In aiming to be empirical scientists, rather than members of the community of mathematicians who study constrained optimization,[2] economists necessarily suppose that their theory gives a general description of some class(es) of empirical phenomena. At the most crude level of description, there seem to be two alternatives here: the theory can be about people, or it can be about emergent systems of production, consumption and exchange, in a context of agnosticism about who or what the *ultimate* units of these activities are (*if* there need to *be* ultimate such units at all; see [Ladyman and Ross, 2007] for reasons to doubt this). Once the issue is put this way, it might be supposed that the answer to the question at the end of the previous paragraph is obvious: utility functions must be proxies for individual flesh-and-blood consumers lest we implicitly endorse mysterious 'group minds' that don't decompose into individual minds; methodological individualism follows from metaphysical atomism. If utility functions map one-to-one onto people for philosophical reasons, then in light of the same philosophical tradition according to which $A \Leftrightarrow O$, a theory of the utility function is a theory of the agent.

However, economists are usually reluctant to accept important professional doctrines simply on philosophical grounds, as they should be. One consequence of the public prominence of the Chicago School has been to greatly exaggerate the perceived commitment to methodological individualism in workaday economics. Agnosticism about microfoundations need not imply — as it certainly didn't for Keynes or Samuelson — endorsement of a transcendent Hegelian spirit which, in addition to thinking about itself and moving history along, also produces, consumes and trades. The respectable scientists who work today in complex systems theory (who are respectable as scientists regardless of whether one shares their confidence in their approach) believe in emergent processes and entities, behavior of which cannot be derived from behavior of their constituents *in vitro*, but generally do not believe that feedback-regulated dynamical systems are manifestations of Spirit. Of course, complex systems theory did not yet exist in the 1950s. But this didn't deter Samuelson from haughty indifference about the atomic material contents of the economist's structural black boxes. (For example, at one point in the *Foundations* [p. 87] he effectively implies that the firm in production theory is not a 'company' in the everyday sense, since the latter but not the former may make profits; but, he says, studying institutional contexts that allow companies to gather rents is not the economist's business. This would imply that it is also not in the economist's brief to say why people form companies in the first place.) The real liberator of economists from the ball-and-chain of microfoundations was Keynes, who enjoyed emphasizing that the concerns of the philosophers in whose company he had been intellectually trained were of no practical import in the dangerous concrete world where policy was called upon to keep revolution at bay. Keynes made economics both theoretically autonomous and professionally thrilling, and these two attractive aspects of the profession as it set about reorganizing the post-war order were closely related to one another. The conquering macroeconomists

[2]Rosenberg [1992] argues that that is in fact what economists are, whether they mean to be or not. I disagree.

of the Bretton Woods era were neither metaphysical atomists nor metaphysical holists; they were practical structuralists who left metaphysics to others.

I have already alluded, in my reference to 'Cold War neuroses', to one reason this golden moment didn't last. Opposing Stalinism obviously didn't rationally *require* that anyone swear fealty to methodological individualism; but war is no friend to subtlety (nor, as emphasized by Mirowski [2002], were the military funding sources that fueled the expansion of postwar science, including economics[3]). It cannot be rigorously demonstrated, but nevertheless seems very likely, that extra-theoretical political factors in the postwar democracies constituted the most decisive influence on economists' return to the *rhetoric* of social atomism. Because such rhetoric was also widely associated — by the loosest, Humean, kind of relation — with defense of markets against 'collectivists', and because economists are indeed appreciators of markets, Chicago School celebrities readily promoted the idea that economic theory has both descriptive and normative individualism built into its core.

Though I contend that this was indeed more a matter of rhetoric than logic, it would be seriously mistaken to suppose that the only reason economic theory didn't continue down Samuelson's agent-free path is the purely external, sociological one that its popular image was captured by cold warriors. In the first place, as I argue elsewhere in this volume, the completeness of the capture is often exaggerated. In the second place, economists were not unaware that most of their applied work continued to focus on aggregate magnitudes and relations. Economists had *reasons*, grounded in microeconomics rather than metaphysics, for thinking that agency couldn't be excised from their theoretical foundations. I will concentrate on two.

First, the invention of game theory (GT) by von Neumann and Morgenstern in 1944 allowed economists to model the interactions of idiosyncratically varying utility functions rendered interdependent by contingent distributions of scarcity. Nothing in the mathematics stipulates that these must be interpreted as the utility functions of *people*; indeed, in the most useful contemporary *economic* (as opposed to psychological) applications of GT, they represent objectives of firms rather than of humans [Ghemawat, 1998; Klemperer, 2004; Milgrom, 2004]. However, GT required the enrichment of utility theory that von Neumann and Morgenstern (and then Savage) provided in order to incorporate players' uncertainty about the valuations of and information available to other players. This enrichment was elucidated at every step by heuristics drawn from folk psychology, and thus the non-mathematical version of the vocabulary of game theory is full of psychological notions: beliefs, conjectures, aversion, attraction. Furthermore, and more substantively, GT made it possible for economists to use the core elements

[3]In echoing Mirowski here, I intend to cast no aspersion on Cold War era economists. Fully morally reasonable scientists who are passionate about their subject matter should be *expected* to make non-vicious political compromises when unprecedented resources for their work flood around them. Had economists not been influenced by the interests of the postwar military there would have been something seriously wrong with the extent of their dedication *as scientists*. Of course, some will dispute my suggestion that most of the relevant compromises were non-vicious. That discussion must be left to another occasion.

of their conceptual toolkit (constrained optimization and opportunity cost) to systematically study individual choices in strategic contexts and so, like good opportunistic scientists, they duly embarked on such study. If we are to base our views of disciplinary boundaries on what scientists actually do instead of on philosophical doctrines about how the world is objectively carved, then we must agree that the early game theorists thereby widened the scope of economics, regardless of whether a revealed-preference purist would approve.[4] Finally, GT seemed to demand progressive deepening of links between economics and psychology as it technically evolved over the past 35 years. GT *can* be given a strictly behaviorist interpretation, according to which one uses it to guide inferences about players' stable behavioral orientations through observing which vectors of possible behavioral sequences in strategic interanimation are Nash equilibria. But the power of such inferences is often limited because most games have multiple Nash equilibria. Efforts to derive stronger predictions led a majority of economic game theorists in the 1980s to interpret games as descriptions of players' *beliefs* instead of their *actions*. On this interpretation, a solution to a game is one in which all players' conjectures about one another's preferences and (conditional) expectations are mutually consistent. Such solutions are, in general, stronger than Nash equilibria, and hence more restrictive. As pointed out in criticism by Binmore [1990], the resulting 'refinement program' draws game theorists not just into psychology but deep into *philosophy*, since it requires them to study their own 'intuitions' about which chains of argument must be pursued if an agent is to count as 'rational'. In this context the idea of agency looks *fundamental* to microeconomics.

Second, the formal completion of general equilibrium theory by Arrow and Debreu [1954] required the concept of an 'economy' to be strictly regimented, and this in turn demanded imposition of strong general constraints on 'participants' in such economies [Debreu, 1959]. In particular, it was necessary to assume that the participants could rank all possible states of the world with respect to value, and that they never change their minds about these rankings. Again, nothing required that 'participants' be interpreted as coextensive with people. As argued at length in Ross [2005], if agents in general equilibrium are identified with utility functions, then the fact that changes in utility functions imply changes in agent identity is an excellent reason *not* to identify such agents with people. However, an important part of the intended point of general equilibrium theory, all the way back to Walras, has been to serve as a framework for thinking about the consequences of changes in exogenous variables, especially policy variables, for welfare. Regardless of whether descriptive individualism is persuasive as social *metaphysics* — the reader will have gathered that I think it is not — there remain the best of reasons for endorsing *normative* individualism: improvements and declines in the feelings of particular people about their well being is what most people, as a matter of fact, mainly care about, so for an economist to regard anything *else* as the appropriate topic of welfare analysis is to implicitly impose the economist's parochial value

[4]Thanks to Erik Angner for stressing this point to me.

scheme on society. Policy makers should ignore the advice of such economists.[5] Thus if the loci of preference fields in general equilibrium theory are not at least idealizations of *people*, then it is not evident why efficiency, the touchstone of general equilibrium analysis, should be important enough to *warrant* touchstone status.

Theoretical developments in the 1970s added economic substance to this philosophical concern. The 'excess demand' literature of that period, centering around the Sonnenschein-Mantel-Debreu theorem [Sonnenschein, 1972; 1973; Mantel, 1974; 1976; Debreu, 1974], showed that although all general equilibria are efficient, there is no unique one-to-one mapping between a given general equilibrium and a vector of individual demand functions. (Put more directly, for a given set of demand functions there is more than one vector of prices at which all demand is satisfied.) In tandem with the Lipsey-Lancaster [1956] theory of the second-best, Sonnenschein-Mantel-Debreu challenged the cogency of attempts by welfare economists to justify policy by reference to merely inferred (as opposed to separately and empirically observed) subjective preferences of consumers. Note that this problem arises whether one assumes an atomistic or an intersubjective (and aggregate-scale, sociological rather than psychological) theory of the basis of value. Nevertheless, the excess demand results shook the general postwar confidence that if one attended properly to the aggregate scale then specific properties of individuals could be safely ignored.

Both the theory of individual choice under uncertainty and welfare theory are *extensions* of core microeconomic theory. Therefore, the fact that both embroil economists in issues about agency is not a slam-dunk argument for interpreting that core using the standard semantic label chosen by Rubinstein. However, here it is important to remember that if the pressure to regard economics as being about agents isn't decisive, the basis for resistance to such an interpretation isn't very powerful either. As observed above, in denying that macroeconomics had necessarily to be derived from microeconomics, Keynesians expressed commitment to pragmatism, not philosophical holism: they left microeconomics behind (Keynes) or blithely cast aside its early neoclassical commitments (Hicks and Samuelson) because they thought that rigid fealty to Jevons and Walras stood in the way of exercising available capacities to control policy-relevant economic relationships and magnitudes. Therefore, if we come around to the view that psychologistic GT is relevant to policy, as all behavioral economists believe, then the same attitude that led Samuelson to drop agents from his foundations should inspire us to put it back. Furthermore, if psychologistic GT is relevant to policy because of variations in individuals' utility functions and attitudes to risk, then it seems our idea of welfare

[5] I do not mean here to just *dismiss* views of those, such as Sen [1999], who think that people's subjective preferences are often unreliable guides to their well being (though I am suspicious of such views). The intended targets of this remark are critics, such as radical environmentalists, who believe that something other than the welfare of particular human beings is the most appropriate basic standard of valuation. In my opinion this requires an unsustainable level of moral arrogance, and is especially unpalatable when promoted by materially comfortable people in a world suffering from significant levels of true poverty.

is implied to be richer than merely the vague utilitarian commitment to maximize community indifference curves that characterizes most economics applied at the scales of national and international policy.

I think that these considerations do defeat interpretation (1) of the place of agency in postwar economic theory. Economics is motivated by a broader set of empirical observations than merely noticing that ecologies of self-maintaining entities collectively demand more consumption goods than the world can provide; it is equally fundamental to the discipline as we now find it that these entities have available to them and use importantly different strategy sets and strategies for coping with specific aspects of their scarcity problems. Once we have got as far as talking about 'entities with varying utility functions and strategy sets' then it would simply be conceptually obtuse to deny that our focus is on agents. Indeed, we should arrive at this conclusion with some relief. It spares us the need to try to make general sense of preference or consumption while not being able to say that there is any kind of thing that is, in general, a possible locus for having preferences and consuming. Let me be careful in framing the significance of this point. I don't wish to make philosophy seem too important here, and I don't believe that we can aspire to close the whole conceptual system by reducing basic economic concepts to some extra-economic bedrock. Instead, preference, consumption and agency, operationalized together as a triad, plausibly constitute a collective conceptual primitive for economics, and as long as this doesn't leave economics stranded apart from other sciences this should be regarded as foundations enough. My point here is just that leaving agency in the picture doesn't seriously compromise foundational elegance *given that* preference and consumption are already admitted. Therefore, *declining* to identify utility functions with agents would give *more* weight to philosophy — refusing to 'say what comes naturally', just out of philosophical scruples — than doing so.

However, giving up the radical ambition to eliminate agency from economic theory need not carry us, with Sen and the behavioral economists, all the way to interpretation (3). I will argue over the course of the remaining sections of the chapter that although economics is about agents, it is not best regarded as staked to $A \Leftrightarrow O$.

Before I launch into this, let me deflect a potential charge that I have announced battle with a straw opponent. It might be objected that the paradigm shifters have no need to accept a generalization as strong as $A \Leftrightarrow O$, and, indeed, *do not* insist on it. They will agree that many applications of economics treat firms, households, unions and even countries as agents. Furthermore, they will note — indeed, will emphasize — that models inspired by neuroeconomics focus on sub-personal agents [Montague *et al.*, 2006, p. 438]. This idea of representing people as communities of agents — synchronic, diachronic or both at once — goes back to the very dawn of BE [Strotz, 1956], and so has some claim to being regarded as among its basic points of departure from neoclassicism.

These points are duly acknowledged. I do not claim that any economists of note maintain $A \Leftrightarrow O$ as an analytic or metaphysical necessity. They are thus open to extending the concept of agency to apply it to entities other than whole individual people, and they do regularly so extend it. However, my key point is precisely that *behavioral* economists must regard these as *extensions.* They join classical economists and early neoclassicals in regarding whole individual people as the paradigm or reference cases of agents. This is an essential assumption underlying any campaign to bring aspects of human psychology into the foundations of economic theory — as opposed to simply conjoining aspects of economics and psychology when specifically studying individual human choice. Now, if some who have employed paradigm shifting rhetoric want at this point to say that the latter idea is all they ever had in mind to promote, then disagreement dissolves. As noted above, I do not aim to tighten membership in the club of economists so as to exile the students of individual choice to another province where they must call themselves psychologists; such rigidity about disciplinary boundaries is silly. However, I claim that we dissolve the alleged basis for suggesting that economics is in theoretical crisis or would benefit from a paradigm shift if we give up the idea that the paradigmatic economic agent is a whole adult person. I will argue that the postwar practice of, and the direction of theoretical and practical progress in, economics is such that economists should be seen as venturing away from base camp whenever they turn their attention to non-aggregate phenomena. The contemporary concept of the agent is primarily a theoretical construction that facilitates modeling of aggregate phenomena; and it does a better job of this then would an agent fleshed out according to the profile of the human being furnished by psychologists.

## 3 ANIMAL AGENTS

As explained in the previous section, the agent in postwar economic theory is an abstraction. There are no manifest folk entities onto which agents need numerically map. In neuroeconomics, neurons and groups of neurons may be agents. In development economics, agents are statistically relevant households. In much macroeconomics since the 1970s, entire populations of countries are modeled as if they reflected a single 'representative' agent. By contrast, as also described above, the agent of BE is not abstract: she (no longer gendered, as in Jevons's time) is a manifest, living, breathing animal. More specifically, she is a *social* animal with a complex, multi-part control system that is too decentralized to produce the relentless consistency of the agent as previously defined.

Behavioral economists and their supporters among psychologists, philosophers and others have lately been remarkably successful in convincing other economists that in modeling agents they been neglecting important empirical considerations, and should feel chastened by discoveries coming from cognitive science generally and cognitive neuroscience particularly [Camerer *et al.*, 2005]. To cite one example, as Rubinstein [2007, p. 247] says "[t]en years ago it was difficult to publish a paper in the *QJE* which included a 'present-bias' assumption. These days it is almost impossible to publish a paper in the same journal which ignores present-bias, let alone one which criticizes the approach."

The discoveries that are supposed to chasten mainstream economists can be broadly sorted into four sets: (1) findings that people don't reason about uncertainty in accordance with sound statistical and other inductive principles; (2) findings that people behave inconsistently from one choice problem to another as a result of various kinds of framing influences; (3) findings that people systematically reverse preferences over time because they discount the future hyperbolically instead of exponentially; and (4) findings that people don't act so as to optimize their personal expected utility, but are heavily influenced by their beliefs about the prospective utility of other people, and by relations between other peoples' utility and their own. All of these are taken to threaten the supposed 'dogma' of mainstream (typically called 'neoclassical' or 'Walrasian') economics that people are rational and self-interested. The findings in sets (1)–(3) directly undermine (attributed) assumptions about peoples' practical consistency. Set (4) is often emphasized as undermining assumptions about narrow self-interest. This is an assumption which, it is quite easy to show, few economists make outside of institutionally constrained settings that specifically justify it [Cox, 2004; Weibull, 2004]. However, to the extent that people's preferences drift with those they pick up from reference groups, this will further undermine intertemporal consistency. Of course, none of these putative discoveries undermine the standard model of economic agency unless it is supposed that the paradigmatic economic agent is a natural (including socially constructed) person.

Rebel flags would not be flying from the battlements of top journals if many economists did not find the call for self-chastening persuasive. In aiming to resist it, I owe an account of this disposition to be humbled. The main part of the explanation, I believe, lies in the simplified history of their discipline that most economists imbibe from textbooks. Philosophers, whose discipline largely *consists* in its history, are apt to under-appreciate the extent to which economists, like most scientists preoccupied with achieving strikes into new terrain rather than consolidation behind the lines, typically get by with shallow narratives about the development of their paradigms. Any history of economics that gathers all 'neoclassicals', from Jevons through Samuelson to Chicago, into a single relatively homogenous doctrine is bound to be a caricature. So then working economists, highly alert to what works and doesn't work in the practice of modeling, can be readily brought to admit that the caricatured picture needs a fundamental makeover if they are to have a conceptual and methodological framework that is truly adequate to their knowledge and judgment. In addition, in my experience, no small number of economists suffer from an analogue to post-colonial guilt over their discipline's perceived arrogance as self-nominated 'queen of the social sciences'. The less nuanced BE manifestos tend to have a populist air; allowing that psychology might partly re-write basic economic theory is an obvious way to send a clear signal that economists have put imperialism behind them.

In the simplified history of thought that often frames casual (and some not-so-casual) methodological reflections in economics, it is acknowledged that economists have a long history of ignoring psychologists. This, it is then frequently supposed, has stemmed from a conviction on economists' part that, in regarding people as narrowly selfish and materially motivated, they operated with a more realistic understanding of at least the *rational* parts of behavior than psychologists. But now, it is thought, BE empirically vindicates the psychologists, while still allowing an indispensable role for economists because of their training in formal modeling. In embracing the call for paradigm change inspired by BE, then, economists can refute the charge that their minds are closed to theoretical change motivated empirically and by non-economists, particularly the oft and unfairly neglected psychologists.

This impressionistic history of interdisciplinary relations isn't entirely false, of course; economists *do* have an established tradition of distancing themselves from psychology. As alluded to in the previous section, in the late 1930s and 1940s two threads in economic theory that had been developing separately were tied together. One thread was Keynes's focus on aggregate structural features of large economies without regard to the kinds of individual agents or actions that compose them[6] — that is, the then-new macroeconomics. The other was the attempt, clearly set in play by second-generation neoclassicists (Pareto and Fisher) near the turn of the century, to squeeze the psychological assumptions about economic agents down to a minimal core — ultimately, to *nothing but* consistency of preference rankings plus the idea that no agent would be content to consume only one type of good, no matter how cheap it became ('non-monomania'). Note that the second assumption is a substantial psychological hypothesis, and much more plausibly true of human beings than the first. Then, with Samuelson, as we saw, the need for even this final plausible human property was eliminated; we don't need to hypothesize non-monomania if we can use properties of observed demand to yield downward-sloping marginal utility functions empirically. This has frequently been interpreted, following the lead of Robbins [1935; 1938], as at last making a clean break between economics and psychology.

Despite their shared rejection of interpersonal comparisons of utility as unscientific, there is an important difference between the attitudes of Robbins and Samuelson toward scientific psychology. Whereas Robbins rejected the behaviorism then prevailing in psychology,[7] revealed preference theorists considered it to be a virtue of RPT — albeit, as I said earlier, a secondary one — that it was consistent with the up-to-date psychology of their time. They thus took it that ideas about how people internally represent their own preferences — most importantly for previous economists, their supposedly not subjectively liking each additional increment to their stock of a good as much as they subjectively liked the previous increment — are unscientific claims not just as economics but *as psychology*.

[6]Keynes is sometimes cited (e.g., by [Angner and Loewenstein, this volume]) as a precursor to psychologistic economics because he attributed business cycles to contagious emotions. However, this suggestion plays no direct role in his theory, which requires only that high-unemployment states be disequilibria. As later economists made much of, it *is* important that his theory assumes incomplete expectations on the part of consumers, producers and investors. But this was more of an oversight than an insight.

[7]He referred to it as a "queer cult" [Robbins, 1935, p. 87].

This point can be used to smooth the narrative that supports the self-chastening attitude. One can say: at least some important postwar economists *meant* to remain responsible members of a partnership with psychology, but then the profession missed the bus at the cognitive revolution in the 1960s. Fortunately, the paradigm shifters can continue, thanks to findings in experimental economics, to the undermining of aggregate welfare measures by Sonnenschein-Mantel-Debreu, and to the way in which game theory evolved, the bus eventually came around again and economists could redeem the earlier error by this time climbing aboard.

In Section 2 I referred to the fact that the rise of the refinement program in game theory plunged economists deep into modeling of belief profiles and other objects conceptualized using the language of psychological states. This encouraged interpretations of agency consistent with A $\Leftrightarrow$ O. But it simultaneously introduced a tension into this commitment by inflating the computational demands on agents. The players of many refined games — e.g., those that find so-called 'sequential equilibria' [Kreps and Wilson, 1982] — are computational prodigies, instantly updating all their beliefs, using all valid principles of Bayesian probability, upon receipt of any information. The capacities such refinements imply for agents are not plausible capacities of finite human beings whose inboard computational hardware was built by natural selection's incremental tinkering. And, sure enough, experimental economists duly showed that when people play the games analyzed by game theorists in laboratories, they often do not appear to behave like the agents in the models and they converge on vectors of strategies that are often not Nash equilibria (let alone subgame-perfect or sequential equilibria) according to the models [Camerer, 2003]. Thus, it seems to paradigm shifters, the 'assumptions' about agency of standard microeconomics need correction by the empirical facts of cognitive science.

The correction in question, according to the revolutionary manifestos, turns out to be drastic. People approximate traditional economic agency *behaviorally* in that they often accomplish their projects at bearable costs; but they don't exhibit *any* of the core *computational* properties attributed to economic agents by general equilibrium theory, rational-expectations macroeconomics, or game theory with refinement. 'Their' behavioral rationality typically turns out to really be natural selection's rationality, evolution having supposedly built rough situational rules of thumb ('heuristics') into people that serve them well as long as their environments are not too strange by comparison with their ancestral ones [Gigerenzer *et al.*, 1999]. This critique then appears to be reinforced by cognitive neuroscience, which musters evidence for biases, heuristics and framing effects operating directly in the processing systems of the brain [Camerer *et al.*, 2005]. Thus, it is concluded, economics collapses not just into abstract computational psychology, but all the way into computational neuroscience. That the word 'collapse' is not too strong is indicated by the sorts of things some neuroeconomists claim to discover. Recently, a team reported having determined from inspection of dopamine neurons that people do not value rewards by reference to their opportunity cost [Knutson *et al.*, 2007]; they infer from this that economic theory requires revision. Openness to chastening from extra-disciplinary sources has gone remarkably far for any economist who admits that studies of the brain might imply revision in her view of opportunity cost as the basic state variable in microeconomics.

Once economics is taken to collapse into psychology, then discoveries in sets (1)–(4) above are naturally interpreted as tearing its standard theory apart. Furthermore, the news seems to have been getting worse since the early days of BE. Findings in sets (1)–(3) can, at least in principle, be accommodated by constructing new kinds of valuation functions. For example, people / agents can be taken to maximize *within* frames, even if not across them. Hyperbolic discount curves can be approximated by composing exponential ones of different slopes [Laibson, 1997; 1998]. However, cognitive science has lately been shaking free of a hyper-rationalistic and atomistic legacy of its own. The past decade has seen enormous upgrading of the significance attached to affect in explaining both mentation and behavior in people [Damasio, 1994; Panksepp, 1998]. Furthermore, affect itself is increasingly understood as both responding to and conditioning dynamic social interaction, an approach to modeling that seems to be borne out by the discovery of mirror neurons [Frith and Wolpert, 2004]. As individual people appear less and less to be autonomous bearers and computers of valuations, whose preferences explain their exchanges but are unchanged by them, and come instead to be seen as resembling adaptive nodes in social colonies where valuations continuously modulate one another in interacting cascades,[8] the more hopelessly inaccurate it is thought to be to model people, or aspects of them, as traditional economic agents.

Instead, it is suggested, the agent must cease to be 'bloodless'. This metaphor is apt, as we saw: the agent of classical economics (Sen's preferred model), and that of early neoclassicism, were not abstractions but organisms (or aspects of organisms). This will seem to be a banal observation if it is read simply as pointing out, with so many others, that BE aims to put emotions and lapses of rationality — failings of the flesh, as it were — back into economics. It is an equally familiar point that BE replaces the narrowly selfish agent with a socially concerned (both altruistic and envious) creature, though commentaries that make much of this often exaggerate, sometimes outrageously, the extent to which neoclassicism presupposes narrow selfishness. I want to emphasize something much less remarked upon in contrasting the (human) animal agent with the agent as characterized in Section 1. The former objects are, as it were, made by nature and 'found' in it by scientists, even if in modeling them they abstract away from all but a few of their properties; whereas the latter are not natural objects but constructed artifacts used to build models of phenomena that are, at least in the first place, social (in economists' jargon, either competitive or interactive/strategic).

Quite obviously, it could hardly be of greater importance or interest that we study the human organism. That study is, furthermore, sometimes crucial to applications of economic theory, especially when groups to which it is applied are small. However, I will now argue, study of the human organism is not *a part of* economics

[8]Such cascades are simulated in so-called 'swarm intelligence' models; see [Kennedy and Eberhart, 2001].

in a sense continuous with the core activity of postwar neoclassicism; whereas it is (of course) strongly continuous with psychology as practiced by Helmholtz and other founders of that discipline. There would be slightly less confusion abroad in the land, I suggest, if BE had instead been carried out under the label 'the psychology of valuation'. In saying this I am *not* asserting a normative claim about the 'proper' business of each discipline, or about how researchers ought to sort themselves among academic departments or about which journals should publish whose articles. On the contrary, I personally find it pleasing when the institutions of academe are allowed to become riots of methodological and conceptual diversity, at least insofar as this does not undermine the value attached to modeling rigor. Rather, what I mean to argue is that with respect to two substantively different scientific subject matters, which have historically been called 'psychology' and 'economics', BE is much more in the tradition of the former than the latter. Furthermore, BE no more implies that standard economic theory should undergo a revolutionary transformation than does any other part of psychology. I make this point by reference to ontology rather than methodology. BE, like psychology, studies the properties of people, whereas economics studies markets and networks, employing for this purpose an idea of 'agency' that is related to the concept of the person only by historical semantic tradition.

## 4 THE HEARTLAND OF ECONOMICS

To someone who both thinks that microeconomics is directly about individual human choice and behavior, and who also thinks that people are paradigmatic agents, the reason that agency is conceptually central to microeconomics needs little elaboration. As discussed in Section 2, if one is doubtful of the first two claims then the basis for the third is less obvious. In Section 2 I argued *that* agency indeed *is* central to microeconomics, given the sorts of modeling activities and analyses in which microeconomists in fact engage. However, I defended this claim strictly historically and pragmatically. Although I think that pragmatic considerations *are* highly relevant to ontology, I don't think that circumscribing the significance of philosophy should lead us to regard logic as irrelevant. The place of agency in economics should also partly be understood by reference to the logical structure of current theory.

The central objects of economic study are investment allocation, competition and strategic interaction. Economists investigate these processes by building models of their operations under different circumstances which are often, though not exclusively, inspired by real institutional environments. It is something like an analytic truth that competition and interaction must go on amongst distinct units; the economic agent is then whatever turns out to be the most serviceable concept of the competing or interacting unit. What mainly constrains this concept are features of the target explananda — which are, again, not the agents themselves, as in BE, but the competitive markets and interactive networks (which together largely determine the investment environment). Thus the properties of economic agents, as captured in the analysis derived from Rubinstein in Section 1, are those that facilitate modeling of competition and strategic interaction.

A system is competitive (is a market) to the extent that agents have isomorphic utility functions and identical strategy sets given identical budget constraints. By 'isomorphic' I mean that if all goods are tradable and there is a fully fungible and liquid medium of exchange then agents can be modeled as if their utility functions differ only in index permutations: one utility function is designated as '$i$'s' and another as '$j$'s', where the claim that $i \neq j$ is primitive and entirely open to interpretation before a model is mapped onto an empirical subsystem of reality.[9] In a competitive setting, $i$ and $j$ aim at the same sort of end — e.g., maximization of expected monetary profits — except that $i$ aims to maximize $i$'s profits and $j$ aims to maximize $j$'s. If a market is *perfectly* competitive then, because no agents face special costs of capital or transaction costs, budget constraints are strictly functions of exogenous initial endowments and will converge if fluctuations in asset values are random walks. However, markets are imperfect if they include opportunities for earning rents or generating externalities, which may arise from asymmetries of information, from regulatory constraints, or from the existence of nonexcludable and/or non-rival goods. If agent $i$'s utility maximization is constrained by $j$'s maximizing behavior, then wherever these constraints are not fully captured by perfect market relationships $i$ and $j$ are members of an interactive network to be modeled as a game. Games in extensive form may be indefinitely embedded in one another, with terminal nodes of any one game assigned as initial nodes of others, and with payoff sets of outcomes expanded accordingly as agents are added by concatenation of new games. Since markets can be modeled without loss as games (trivial games in the case of perfectly competitive markets), game theory generalizes economics. This is important philosophically because it spares us any need to try to draw a crisp line between imperfectly competitive markets, systems that don't 'feel like' markets because many prices are shadow prices, and interactive networks where non-parametric factors dominate.

Which empirical substructures of models are identified by economists with agents is thus derivative on which empirical substructures they identify with markets and strategically interactive networks. The kinds of phenomena most often modeled as agents in economic applications are firms and households. In international economics, the agents are often countries. Typically, however, when firms, households and countries fail to behave as agents (e.g., exhibit cyclical preferences), we explain their behavior by 'breaking them up' into sub-agents, recognizing that CEOs and shareholders have different utility functions of their own, that treating husbands and their wives as unitary consumers often makes for misguided welfare policy, and that trade and exchange rate policies are temporary equilibria in dynamic games amongst producer lobbies and groups of politicians. Nevertheless, only in BE and in experimental economics are the phenomena identified with

[9]This phrase refers to standard model-theoretic semantic interpretation of scientific theory construction; see Ruttkamp [2002] for the formulation that, in my opinion, ideally equilibrates between explicitness and useful generality.

agents *usually* individual people.

This is of course not news to economists who nevertheless think that people are the paradigmatic agents (though I fear it *does* sometimes come as news to some philosophers who scarcely distinguish between microeconomics and decision theory). They may shrug it off precisely on the basis of emphasizing the previous point above. Even if the agents in most applied economics are aggregate, the standing pattern of disaggregating down to people when aggregate agency hits trouble shows that the *exemplary* agents still have the same identity they did for Jevons.

I think this is the strongest argument the advocate of $A \Leftrightarrow O$ has available. I am unpersuaded by it, however. A first part of the reason for this is a certain general view of the relationship between special sciences and philosophical ontology. I do not think that philosophers are entitled to suppose that where a science is inexplicit in practice about how its fundamental objects are related to those in other sciences or in metaphysics, philosophers perform a service when they infer the most parsimonious such set of relations they can and call this 'rational reconstruction'. This attitude rests on the idea that sciences have, as it were, background 'philosophical intentions' that transcend what their practitioners actually do, so that where scientific practice is silent or equivocal on metaphysics, philosophers may pipe up on its behalf. I don't see any evident justification for this attitude other than a very general belief that metaphysical commitment — any metaphysical commitment — is preferable to metaphysical agnosticism. And *that* belief, in turn, seems to me to have no justification at all.[10]

In light of this, I suggest that we should accept that economics is committed to $A \Leftrightarrow O$ *only* if we find applied economists actually making use of it in practice. A mere general tendency to decompose complex systems that exhibit imperfect agency into sub-agents falls short of this. What we would instead need to see is a working tendency to regard well-performing models in which the agents are individual people being regarded as authoritative over models in which the agents map onto some other sort of entity. Many readers will think this tendency is exhibited in economists' regularly manifest preference for models that can be given 'microfoundations'. Philosophers typically refer by microfoundations *either* to grounding compatible with an atomistic or individualist ontology *or* with grounding explanations in distinct physical objects with well-behaved boundaries (such as people) and concrete causal mechanisms (such as supposedly 'realistic' computations in people's brains). Economists generally mean by microfoundations something much more specific and *sui generis*: equilibria among sets of optimization functions. This is indeed a preference for agent-based models (and thus for interpretation (2) over (1)). Philosophers are apt to think that this economists' preference is merely a specific expression of *their* preference for decompositional reduction because they take for granted, contrary to what I have been arguing — and begging the question with respect to what is presently at issue — that a

[10]Davies [2009] argues that most contemporary philosophy is infected to its core with residues of theology. I agree.

preference for agent-based models necessarily indicates a commitment to $A \Leftrightarrow O$.

The hasty assumption I attribute to some philosophers readily arises from supposing that agent-based explanations get their 'grounding' (or at least purport to get it) from the idea that agents represent the targets of their optimizing behavior as goals, and that their 'rationality' consists in their literally computing plans of action to realize them. I do not doubt that organisms with brains represent and compute (though I certainly do doubt, following Clark [1997],[11] that representation and computation of the sorts of abstract relationships studied by economists are carried out entirely 'in organisms' heads'). However, what is important about agency for economists is consistent correlation of agents' behavioral responses with changes in relative scarcities (and hence in imputed opportunity costs), not — at least before the coming of the refinement program in GT — to any putative mechanistic basis for such responses. On a sufficiently abstract conception of computation, all responses to changes in relative scarcities are computed. But starfish, which are perfectly respectable agents, do not perform the relevant computations with their brains, because they do not have brains; dynamical coupling between naturally selected dispositions in their motor systems and environmental contingencies 'realize' the computations (as cognitive scientists say) and lead them to pursue prey and flee from predators in highly rational ways. A similar point can be made about a large firm: that strategy $X$, distributed over the aggregated behavioral tendencies of many branch offices, tends to maximize profits (or something else, like share value) in response to changes in supply or demand parameters does *not* entail that *any* individual person's brain, or any individual machine consulted by a person, explicitly represented or computed the relevant relationships. They may instead by stabilized by environmental constraints that no agents directly represent [Satz and Ferejohn, 1994].

Becker [1962] shows that the fundamental property of the standard model of the market — downward sloping demand for any good given constant real income — depends on no claim about the *computational* rationality of any agent; it depends only on the assumption that households with smaller budgets and therefore smaller opportunity sets consume less. Thus even the majority of applications in the area of economics most directly related in principle to the theory of choice, consumer theory, make no necessary working use of the supposed identity of economic agents and biological / psychological people. This fact should be taken at least as seriously as anything said about 'individual consumers' in opening chapters of introductory micro texts. I claim that a practical, philosophically fuzzy-minded, attitude about whether they are committed to a view on $A \Leftrightarrow O$ is what most economists *prefer* to any more explicit thesis that the philosophically motivated attempt to thrust upon them. Any claim to the effect that such a preference is feckless because metaphysical completion is a virtue of a scientific theory begs the question at issue. Pressed on the issue of just what their agents are, economists are quite entitled to say: anything in an empirical substructure of a model that, interpreted in light of the analysis of agency given in Section 1, yields predictive leverage and

[11]See especially Chapter 11.

explanation through integration with other established models.

Obviously, though, a significant number of important economists — BE polemicists, Sen, others — do *not* say this. Behavioral and experimental economists who resist this claim in a non-question-begging way (i.e., do not merely assume its denial in regarding their activity as economics instead of as psychology) may appeal to empirical discoveries about the way in which the brain computes reward values. I will deal with this basis for defense of A $\Leftrightarrow$ O in the next section. For the moment let us remain in the heartland where neuroeconomic exotica are still unremarked. There, the two main developments in postwar theory discussed in Section 2 that blocked Samuelsonian elimination of agency from microeconomics altogether (the emergence of the refinement program in game theory and the attempt to derive welfare implications from general equilibrium theory) are sometimes conjoined with a largely *thoughtless* assumption of $A \Leftrightarrow O$ that is merely inherited from earlier neoclassicism. As a residual, philosophical, commitment to $A \Leftrightarrow O$, this is *not* what I have in mind by a *practical, working* commitment to it — a commitment that influences applied modeling.

When philosophers talk about 'practice' in a science they generally mean to refer to experimental protocols and accepted standards of evidence. This is still somewhat closer to epistemological norms than what I have in mind by 'practice' when considering a discipline that is as driven by engineering concerns as economics. Just as the de-psychologization of economics began before Samuelson, so did its increasing concentration on policy guidance, which in turn led to steady improvement in techniques for measuring and studying relations among aggregate variables — relations that are, or are at least widely thought to be, under the control of governments and central banks. The Keynesian revolution of the 1930s was an overnight triumph among economists because, as I mentioned in Section 3, in abandoning microeconomic modeling of macroeconomic phenomena Keynes was perceived as *liberating* the profession, exploiting his status as an all-around intellectual to give his more diffident colleagues license to dismiss ontological scruples they had maintained in deference to philosophical tradition. In the everyday practice of economics, *despite* the excitement over microfoundations that arose in the 1970s, there has been no looking back on this liberation. The overwhelming majority of working economists never estimate the utility function of an individual person. They measure elasticity coefficients of aggregate demand and production functions from changes in prices, interest rates, income distributions, national savings rates, and other index quantities. Most applied economists pay lip service to the idea that all of these things somehow 'boil down to' decisions by individual people. But by the weight of behavioral evidence this interest is usually perfunctory and the lip service is typically conventional. For example, textbooks in international economics admit that so-called 'community indifference curves' used to represent national welfare *cannot* be disaggregated into individual indifference curves without destroying the point of using them; most books cheerfully note this as a cautionary note and move on without further ado, assuming that the idea of 'national welfare' makes sense in its own right.

This is not to deny the clear fact that much economic theorizing in the mid-range between foundation building and specific applications consists in constructing microfoundations for models of aggregate-scale phenomena. However, the 'micro' here refers to the distinctive explanatory *logic* of microeconomic *theory*, not to decomposition of markets or networks into atoms. Let us consider an example. Going back to Tinbergen [1962], economists have represented trade flows between pairs of countries using so-called 'gravity models'. The original version of the gravity equation takes the form

$$M_{ij} = \alpha_k Y_i^{\beta_k} Y_j^{\gamma_k} N_i^{\zeta_k} N_j^{\upsilon_k} D_{ij}^{\sigma_k} \cup_{ijk}$$

where $M_{ijk}$ is the value of the flow of good or factor $k$ from country $i$ to country $j, Y_i$ and $Y_j$ are income in country $i$ and $j$ respectively, $N_i$ and $N_j$ are populations of countries $i$ and $j, D_{ij}$ is the distance between countries $i$ and $j$, and $U_{ij}$ is a lognormally distributed error term with $E(U_{ijk}) = 0$ [Baldwin and Taglioni, 2006]. The name 'gravity model' derives from the fact that the equation represents a 'strength of attraction' based on countries' relative sizes and distances. Its original basis was intuitive and its justification in policy applications was for many years strictly empirical. It was not deemed fit to be regarded as a proper part of trade theory until it could be derived from a model of rational behavior by countries aiming to maximize returns on factors of production. An early effort by Anderson [1979], based on the assumption that goods produced in different countries are at best imperfect substitutes, was criticized for being *ad hoc* (but see [Anderson and van Wincoop, 2003; Baldwin and Taglioni, 2006]. More recently, Feenstra *et al.* [2001] proposed and empirically tested a microfoundational explanation widely thought to suffice, based on monopolistic competition that results from countries producing surplus differentiation of goods in consequence of optimizing inframarginal production efficiencies, and then engaging in mutually advantageous reciprocal dumping. Now, the point of this example in the present context is that among economists who think that Feenstra's account is empirically persuasive, it provides *sufficient* microfoundations for the gravity model because it shows why rational agents, which in this case happen to be countries, would produce and trade in accordance with the model's description. There is no further methodological requirement that the countries be disaggregated so that production of differentiated output can be attributed to particular models of firms; it is enough that the trade behavior optimizes inframarginal efficiencies and is a self-enforcing equilibrium. Thus 'microfoundations' here, as generally, refers not to ontological 'grounding out' in behavior of people as ultimate units, but to closing the model of an economic phenomenon in strictly *economic* terms, where 'economic' is defined by reference to an axiomatic theoretical system for identifying equilibria among behavioral dispositions or strategies of agents. Any requirement that these agents be individual people requires an extra-economic motivation.

Even in the realm of high theory, where microfoundations involve explanation by reference to agents learning to forecast monetary and fiscal policy, the agents in question are 'representative' optimizers whose ontological status is indeterminate.

In some canonical models whole economies are modeled as though they are single ('infinitely lived') agents whose business cycles result from the schedules on which they invest and take profits [Kydland and Prescott, 1982; Long and Plosser, 1983]. The underlying justification for this is the assumption that what are being modeled are markets in which utility functions differ only indexically. For this reason it doesn't *matter* to the formal analysis what sorts of extra-economic entities the utility functions map onto; all that matters is that econometric tests, based on measuring aggregate variables, can distinguish between one model and another. These tests require agents in the technical sense I have discussed; they do not require that the agents in question be people.

I advance a speculative counterfactual hypothesis about the sustaining motivation for concern with microfoundations in high theory. This speculation is that the devotion to constructing such foundations would not have been remotely as strong as it has been if the mathematics of microeconomic theory were not far more powerful and elegant than those of macroeconomics. Imagine for a moment a possible world in which this did not hold. In that world, if the mandarins of economic theory nevertheless put some of their best efforts into looking for microfoundations, this would have to be because they shared a driving philosophical conviction that sound explanations of phenomena must resemble those of an idealized version of classical physics, in which all principles boil down to mechanistic relationships among atoms. Mirowski [1989] argues persuasively that this was true of the early neoclassical economists; but, I contend, this is precisely the prison that Keynes unlocked. The possible world in which economic theorists are lashed forward by firmly maintained philosophical convictions seems very far from the one inhabited by actual current economists; an excellent way to persuade a typical economist to *drop* an opinion is to convince her it derives from a philosophical hunch. And there is in any case no pressing call to attribute philosophical faith to economists because a much more plausible account of the centrality of attention to microfoundations is readily available: economists want to deploy their most powerful technical toolkit, that of microeconomics, wherever they possibly can. This expresses a highly rational general principle. If application of a model of an infinitely lived representative agent allocating his future self-payments in an atomless measure space survives econometric testing then it would be foolish not to use the model in question. Infinitely lived agents and atomless measure spaces are hardly less *metaphysically* peculiar than flows of information and exchanged assets in complex systems that stabilize some such systems into markets. Metaphysical peculiarity or comfort simply have nothing to do with the matter.

Failure to appreciate that microfoundations means equilibrium dynamics rather than thoughts experienced by people has contributed to confused interpretations of what is politically and even morally at stake in macroeconomic policy debates. Consider, for example, the controversy between new classical macroeconomists and Keynesians over business cycles. Popular commentators frequently assert that the former show ideologically inspired callousness when they deny that there is 'involuntary' unemployment. However, as Lucas [1978] stresses in tones of justified exasperation, a new classical theorist's microfoundational claim that all unemployment is voluntary is not about any aspect of any worker's psychological state, and thus does not possibly imply denial of the sincerity of anyone's misery or frustration; it is merely denial of the Keynesian claim that there are competitive equilibria in which human capital is wasted.[12] Microfoundational though it is, the macroeconomic dispute is about properties of markets, not about any properties of people.

So much for interest in microfoundations as a possible direct indicator of commitment to $A \Leftrightarrow O$. What about the possible indirect motivators identified earlier? In Section 2 I reviewed the two main developments in postwar economic theory that blocked Samuelsonian elimination of agency altogether. These were the emergence of the refinement program in game theory and the attempt to derive welfare implications from general equilibrium theory. Now I will say why I do not think that game theory provides a justified basis for doing economics according to the assumption that $A \Leftrightarrow O$. I will defer consideration of why we treat people as the proper objects of welfare concern to the very end of the essay.

In game theory, the refinement program largely expired by the turn of the century, mainly choking on a problem of its own rather than being smothered by the activities of economists turning into psychologists. The problem in question has a striking character in the present context: different possible refinements, applied separately or together, pulled economists' intuitions about rationality in conflicting directions. In consequence, game theory began increasingly to converge with, and become as unscientific as, the philosophy of ideal practical reason. Whether such philosophy is or is not a potential contributor to psychology — I here take no stand on that question — engagement with it has clearly seemed to most economists to be leading them away from their core business. The obvious way to reverse this drift into philosophy is the one that has mainly institutionally prevailed among economists: implement a stronger and cleaner distinction between 'rationality' in the thin sense — that is, Samuelsonian consistency of behavior with representation by preference orderings — and 'rationality' in the psychological sense of boundless in-board computational capacity.

In keeping with this, three main lines of research have taken centre stage among game theorists over the past ten years. One line applies classical game theory to contexts, such as auctions among highly capitalized players bidding for very valuable assets, in which institutional forces incentivize consortia to indeed behave like computational prodigies [Klemperer, 2004; Milgrom, 2004]. These consortia are not biological or psychological entities. Of course their representatives are such entities; but they are not imagined as doing their own computations, nor as choosing strategies using native, in-board cognitive resources. They have external computing equipment, including game theorist consultants with fancy software of their own. Second, game theorists have explored investment patterns in distributed markets by modeling them as games involving large numbers of players

[12] I do not intend here to imply preference for either side in this major and long-running theoretical controversy.

facing common uncertainty where all know that all know about the extent of uncertainty, and all know what technologies can be used to manage it (e.g., [Morris and Shin, 2003]). Here again is a use of game theory that eschews any appeal to psychological idiosyncrasies: players essentially use their models of the game situation to stabilize their expectations about one another, and they are embedded in institutional settings that are taken to constrain their utility functions, eliminating any special personal properties. Finally, the leading approach to multiple equilibria that has far overtaken appeal to refinements in popularity is application of evolutionary game theory [Weibull, 1995; Samuelson, 1998; Cressman, 2003]. This replaces the hyper-sophisticated agents of the refinement program with thoughtless players who simply inherit or copy strategies from others, with the probability of a strategy's getting inherited or copied being correlated with the strategy's success in previous rounds of iterated games. In this approach, strategies themselves, rather than agents, are the players of the games, with agents merely standing in to play their brief turns in a competitive process that continues beyond their individual lifespans. Agents must remain 'rational' in the thin sense — which is to say no more than that they remain agents — but much, most or all strategic and inferential computational demands are offloaded onto the selection process itself; thicker rationality 'goes virtual'. Young [1998] remains an exemplary set of applications.

Consideration of evolutionary game theory brings us to the edge of another kind of modeling that is rising in popularity in the more faddish precincts of economics, based on complex system theory [Anderson *et al.*, 1988; Arthur, 1994; Arthur *et al.*, 1997; Blume and Durlauf, 2005] It is noteworthy that many of the same people who advocate increased 'psychological realism' in economics are also fans of applying complex systems theory to social science (e.g. [Ormerod, 1999; Gintis, 2000; Beinhocker, 2006]). Denial of what philosophers call 'ontological reductionism'[13] — that is, atomism — is part of the very point of complex systems theory, with its emphasis on 'emergent' structures. These are properties and relations which are stabilized by bi-directional (that is, 'bottom-up' *plus* 'top-down) feedback relations and which cannot be decomposed into properties and relations of their parts. This new emergentism should, in my view, be approached with caution due to worries over stability of state variables across models. However, the simultaneous popularity, often in the same breasts, of extreme anti-reductionism *and* the view that economic theory ought to apply directly to individual objects with manifest boundaries is *prima facie* surprising. The odd conjunction suggests two things at once: tendencies in some quarters to favor ideas simply *because* they rebel against neoclassicism, and relatively reflexive assumption of $A \Leftrightarrow O$ that flies under theorists' radar because it is implicit, thereby sometimes capturing even those who are avowedly opposed to the intellectual tradition from which it is inherited.

[13]This locution is required to distinguish between reducing composite objects into parts, and reducing so-called 'high-level' theories to less abstract theories ('intertheoretical reduction'). Philosophers of science have generally been more interested in the latter than the former.

## 5 BEHAVIORAL ECONOMICS AND NEUROECONOMICS: THE MOLAR AND THE MOLECULAR

The argument of Section 4 was directed against interpreting recent trends in economic theory through the lens of ontological reductionism — more specifically, against interpreting economists' widespread interest in microfoundations as reflecting commitment to such reductionism. The most prominent current defenders of $A \Leftrightarrow O$ split into two camps in their attitudes to reductionism. Sen-style humanists oppose *psychological* reduction of $O$ to $A$, preferring instead that $A \Leftrightarrow O$ be preserved by *inflating* $A$. Their motivations are largely grounded in normative considerations, upon which I will touch in my concluding remarks. Behavioral economists, by contrast, sometimes push for even more radical reductionism than is mandated by the $A \Leftrightarrow O$ thesis. Encountering violations of thin economic rationality in $O$-referenced behavior, they sometimes explain this by modeling people as corporate entities that emerge from the strategic interactions of sub-personal agents [Strotz, 1956].

I have elsewhere [Ross, 2005] argued for denial of $A \Leftrightarrow O$ from (as it were[14]) both 'below and above', and the idea that people are loci of — indeed are created and maintained by — strategic interaction of sub-personal agents is a concomitant of this denial that I have specifically endorsed and expanded upon [Ross *et al.*, 2008; Ross, 2009]. However, as part of the present essay's concern to resist the collapse of economics into psychology and/or neuroscience, I will here emphasize a tension within the decompositional approach. This arises over whether the sub-personal agents posited to explain economically relevant behavior of whole people are or are not identified with functional-anatomical parts of their brains.

In earlier work [Ross, 2005; 2006b] I have emphasized the contrast between *picoeconomics* and *neuroeconomics*. The term 'picoeconomics' was coined by Ainslie [1992; 2001] to denote applications of game theory to model what philosophers have traditionally called 'weakness of will' phenomena, including relapse to addiction, inconsistent financial saving, over-eating, and procrastination. Ainslie and other picoeconomists explain these common behavioral patterns as sometime equilibrium outcomes of games played amongst sub-personal interests, which arise as manifestations of hyperbolic discounting of future rewards at the personal scale. The identities of such interests are directly inferred from goals attributed at the personal scale by folk psychology. Thus, for example, a person trying to quit smoking has a short-range interest in having a cigarette and a long-range interest in not having one. The former interest might strengthen its prospects by promoting an interest in going to the bar, where a smoking lapse is more likely, while the longer-range interest might advance its cause by teaming up with an interest in going jogging. Hyperbolic discounting may give the smoking interest an advantage in short temporal ranges despite the fact that, from a longer range, the person's behavior reveals a preference for not smoking. (Typically, the most important such

[14]I add this locution to mark the fact that I elsewhere [Ladyman and Ross, 2007] am party to denial of the metaphysical image of reality as sorted into 'levels'.

behavior is voluntary suffering from restraint which would be pointless if relapse is sure; such behavior constitutes investment.) Whereas picoeconomics thus begins from the level of manifest behavior, neuroeconomics [Glimcher, 2003; Montague and Berns, 2002; Montague *et al.*, 2006] appeals to the ontology of anatomical and functional brain areas developed by neuroscience and identifies sub-personal agents, which may at times be in conflict, with functionally delineated groups of neurons (especially neurotransmitter systems). The utility functions of these units are implicit under a linear or dynamic programming interpretation of the algorithms they compute when physically healthy. Determination of these algorithms, mainly by comparing mathematical models with neuroimaging data, is the bread-and-butter work of the neuroeconomist.

People who are reluctant to acknowledge or have difficulty understanding the possible existence of anything that isn't a three (or four) dimensional hunk of matter [Heller, 1990] are apt to simply assume that if picoeconomic interests are not mere metaphors, they must ultimately reduce to neuroeconomic agents. However, this is inconsistent with Ainslie's understanding of the interests, which he identifies with their objects rather than their bearers. He is explicit that interests persist in time only for as long as the behavior they motivate is a standing possibility. Thus the procrastinator's interest in idly surfing the web while he tries to complete his tax return lasts for only as long as the task remains uncompleted or a less obviously unproductive distraction doesn't displace surfing in his attention. Of course, people have less fleeting interests such as in avoiding punishment or getting rebates from the government; willpower precisely consists in finding shorter-range interests that align with these, and by this device bringing the influence of the longer-range interests to bear on motivation in the present, where rewards are not hyperbolically discounted. Another of Ainslie's favorite examples is of an annoying interest in scratching an itch, which will fade entirely if even briefly ignored; unless the itch is caused by a foreign irritant, as most itches are not, the interest in scratching *is* the itch. Thus picoeconomic interests aren't sub-personal in the same sense as groups of neurons with specialist functions. The former are sub-personal in the sense that they have sharply limited projects that may not be endorsed by the whole person, but it is *molar* responses — behavior of a whole person at a time — with which they are associated. The agents of neuroeconomics, by contrast, are sub-personal in the sense of being molecular components of organisms.

The contrast between 'molar' and 'molecular' scales of description and explanation is a well established one in psychology, crucial to the behaviorist program from which picoeconomics descends. Molar-scale descriptions situate behavioral systems in environmental contexts, sorting their dispositions and properties by reference to equivalence classes of problems they face. These equivalence classes can be highly heterogeneous from the molecular point of view while remaining stable objects for scientific generalization due to external environmental pressures that 'capture' different molecular processes within distinctive patterns. The logic here is the same as that which explains convergence in evolution by adaptation to niches. At the level of phylogeny, the relevant external pressures are ecological; in the case of people they are mainly social, and frequently institutional.

By contrast, neuroeconomic models are computational and cognitivist in character. The 'economics' in neuroeconomics denotes a family of models of the way in which the so-called 'reward system' in the brain — roughly, the dopaminergic neurotransmitter system that projects from midbrain areas to orbitofrontal and pre-frontal cortex — comparatively values alternative allocations of attention, motor response and consumption. Such models provide algorithms by which the reward system is taken to estimate the expected opportunity costs of attending to one stimulus rather than another and of preparing one motor response rather than another. One of the current leading functional forms in the literature corresponds closely to the Black-Scholes model of portfolio option pricing [Montague and Berns, 2002]. In contrast to picoeconomic interests, which are often though not necessarily consciously accessible to people, neuroeconomic computational mechanisms never are. They are thus, to invoke a metaphor familiar to many economists, 'under-the-hood' causes of behavior. Psychologists refer to such trains of behavioral causation as 'molecular'. This talk is not intended to refer to chemistry, notwithstanding the importance of neurochemical agents to neuroeconomic applications. 'Molecular' here is intended purely as a logical contrast to 'molar', and is thus infrequent in the language of reductionists who deny the scientific validity of an autonomous molar scale.

Since molar-scale ontologies are developed by reference to organism-environment interfaces whereas molecular-scale ontologies are based on *in vitro* functions of internal computational organs, as a matter of logic molar and molecular scale models of one and the same system can vary independently. Of course logic cannot establish that they in fact *do* so vary, since this is an empirical matter. Strong reductionists expect that they don't, and thereby expect the molar scale to turn out to be redundant for psychological explanation. No one believes that they vary *completely* independently, since this would amount to denying that brains influence behavior.

Bearing in mind this contrast drawn in psychological terms, we can identify several different ways in which one might construct economic models of people and their behavior as reflecting interactions among sub-personal agents (or, in the case of the final alternative below, interactions between a unitary agent and non-agentic aspects of the organism):

**(1A)** One can model a person as *synchronically* composed of multiple sub-agents with conflicting utility functions (following the lead of Schelling [1978; 1980; 1984]. Then a pattern of personal-scale behavior might be modeled as the solution of a Nash bargaining game among these agents. (The restriction to Nash bargaining, as opposed to some other model of bargaining, might appear unmotivated. Note, however, that bargaining among synchronous sub-personal agents would have to be non-cooperative and un-governed by norms, lest the very point of so decomposing the person be lost. Under those assumptions Nash bargaining is the most general modeling framework.)

**(1B)** One can model a person as synchronically composed of multiple sub-agents with different time preferences. The reconstruction of hyperbolic personal time preference as resulting from competition between steeply exponentially discounting 'limbic'[15] regions and more patient (less steeply exponentially discounting) 'cognitive' regions [McClure *et al.*, 2004] is currently very popular with behavioral economists. In this kind of model, molecular-scale discounting with properties familiar to microeconomists is taken to explain molar-scale discounting featuring the properties emphasized by psychologists and behavioral economists.

**(2)** One can model a person as *diachronically* composed of multiple selves (each one of which controls the whole of a person's behavior for an interval of microseconds to hours) with differing utility functions and imperfect knowledge of one another, but where later agents' utility depends on investments by earlier agents. Then a pattern of personal behavior can be modeled as the subgame-perfect or sequential equilibrium of an extensive form signaling game in which agents choose actions with attention to the information this reveals about the probable preferences of their successors [Prelec and Bodner, 2003]. Since this has the effect of attaching some present utility to future rewards, it can (though of course it might not) implement willpower and correct for personal-scale intertemporal preference reversals that may otherwise arise due to hyperbolic discounting. Benabou and Tirole [2003] show in a full modeling exercise that such games can rationalize many of the suite of core picoeconomic behavioral phenomena described by Ainslie [1992; 2001] (but not one of his core explanatory targets, so-called reward building). These models of molar-scale phenomena involve no molecular-scale hypotheses at all.

**(3)** One can push the agentic aspect of the person 'deeper into the organism', in effect treating parts of a person's brain as generating exogenous environmental impacts on the agent. Allowing for important variations in details, this modeling approach is shared by Loewenstein [1996; 1999], Read [2001; 2003], and Gul and Pesendorfer [2001; 2005]. These models (of which only Gul and Pesendorfer's are fully explicit in economic terms) all explain personal-scale violations of thin economic rationality as resulting from 'visceral' temptations to immediately consume certain sorts of rewards, which the agent may or may not successfully resist. In these models, resisting temptation is expensive for agents (paid for in short-range suffering), but so is succumbing (paid for in lower longer-range utility). Thus the appearance of a temptation constitutes a negative shock along the agent's optimizing path. How agents respond to such shocks is simply a function of

[15]For years it was standard practice to refer to the older structure as the 'limbic system' and the newer brain as the 'cognitive system', based on the idea that emotional responses are primitive and rational ones are an adaptive refinement. As Paul Glimcher urges me to point out, over the past decade or so it has become clear that this is misleading; the older part of the brain performs many 'rational' calculations, and emotional judgments and motivations are crucial to the functioning of frontal cortex. However, it remains true that the older and newer parts of the brain developed under different evolutionary pressures.

relative costs, which agents minimize subject to an exponential discount function. The resulting behavioral pattern, if graphed as though it were all just discounting behavior, yields a quasi-hyperbolic curve. This sort of account straddles the molar/molecular divide, in describing and explaining rational behavior at the molar scale while explaining inconsistent consumption episodes by appeal to hypothesized molecular-scale disturbances. If this seems to reflect conflicted intuitions, a moment's reflection should render the source of the tension familiar: it simply amounts to keeping economics and psychology strongly separate. Agents remain abstract constructs, but humans in manifesting agent-like behavior are constrained by properties of their bodies. Interestingly, models of type (3) separate economics and psychology along the opposite polarity from Jevons, according to whom the economic aspects of the person pursue creature comforts while the psychological aspect can set its sights on nobler objectives.

Note that these three modeling approaches all reject $A \Leftrightarrow O$ in the *strict* sense (i.e., as analytic rather than as identification of a prototype; see Section 2), but in quite different spirits. Approaches 1A and 1B simply add isomorphic complexity to both sides of the equivalence so as to yield the following sort of picture:

$$
\begin{aligned}
&A_1 \Leftrightarrow O_1\\
&A_2 \Leftrightarrow O_2\\
&A_3 \Leftrightarrow O_3\\
&\ldots\\
&A_n \Leftrightarrow O_n
\end{aligned}
$$

where $A_1, \ldots, A_n$ compose the agent $\mathbf{A}, O_1, \ldots, O_n$ compose the (brain of) the organism $\mathbf{O}$ and $\mathbf{A}$ and $\mathbf{O}$ are coextensive.

Approach (3) continues to numerically associate each basic agent with exactly one person, while allowing that the agent is only an aspect of the person. Approach (2) makes the person a derivative and sometime agent; a person achieves agency in the limited and temporary sense that a firm or country might, to the extent that intrapersonal signaling remains on an equilibrium path.

I will offer some provisional assessment of the relative current returns being delivered by these modeling strategies. Let the reader bear in mind here that it is still very early days for neuroeconomics and even the near future may not much resemble the immediate past.

Models of type 1 are certainly the most popular with neuroeconomic researchers. This is natural: science always tries to get as far as possible with reductionist models because they are conceptually, ontologically and structurally simplest. Indeed, we typically arrive at more complex models in science only through processes of correcting first-generation reductionist ones that turn out to be too simple in revealingly specific ways. An example of a type 1B neuroeconomic model could be obtained by setting the model of the dopamine reward system proposed by Schultz [2002] in the black box of the steep 'limbic' discounter (the '$\beta$ discounter') of McClure *et al.* [2004] and developing a correspondingly detailed model of their more patient 'cognitive' discounter (the '$\delta$ discounter') to go along with it. This example — the closest to a worked out one I am aware of — leads directly to an early intimation of the usual fate of straightforwardly reductionist models in our complex world: Glimcher *et al.* [2007] and Kable and Glimcher [2007] recently report fMRI data that they take to confute the hypothesis that different parts of the brain discount future rewards at different rates. The easier testability of reductionist accounts is their noble but tragic Popperian virtue.

It is important to point out here that models of the 1A type do not *have to* be read in a reductionist light. Suppose that, following Glimcher [2003], we interpret groups of neurons as economic agents. Suppose in particular that we so interpret the dopamine reward system. But now suppose that instead of reading the computational *processing* account of that system directly as the *economic* model of it, we derive its utility function by asking what its output would be if it optimized consistently given a maximally powerful statistical representation of its input data. (That is, suppose that we modeled it axiomatically instead of inductively.) This applies the concept of economic agency to the dopamine system in the same way that (non-behavioral) economists apply the concept to firms and households. In effect, it takes the economic model of the system to be a molar-scale account of the system in isolation, with a first-order computational account such as that of Schultz [2002] being its comparatively molecular counterpart processing model. (An account at the scale of cellular mechanisms would, on this picture, be comparatively molecular relative to the first-order computational one.) In light of the genesis and long history of the molar / molecular distinction in the stricter precincts of behaviorism, where all peeking under hoods was discouraged, this suggestion that there could be a *molar* account of a part of the brain is apt to seem strange and disorienting. However, it is not merely speculative. Recently, Caplin and Dean [2008] have furnished the first 'molar economic' model of the dopamine system *in vitro*. This model could in principle be used (for example) as input to an account of personal addictive behavior by setting it into a dynamic bargaining game with the correspondingly modeled inhibitory serotonergic system as its opponent, yielding a molar-scale economic complement to some currently popular molecular-scale neuropsychological accounts of addictive processes. The value of the economic model would lie in its potential identification of consumption properties that addiction might share with other, molecularly distinct, pathologies of impulsivity, which in turn could be expected to be relevant to policy and to non-pharmacological modes of treatment. See Ross *et al.* [2008] for more details of this picture. If this nascent approach to modeling bears empirical fruit, it should undermine the 'rebel' spin currently attached to BE about as directly as can be imagined, since it will preserve the separateness of economics from psychology in the exact Paretian spirit, while at the same time equally clearly violating $A \Leftrightarrow O$ 'from below'. I refer to this possible explanatory/modeling strategy as 'nerocellular economics', in recognition of the way in which it involves conceiving of sub-personal, functionally individuated agents as both neurally implemented in specifiable ways *and* as relatively autonomous optimizers from the modeling point of view.

Next let us consider type 3 models. In general, but again emphasizing the caveat about early days, models of this type are performing well in confrontation with data [Green and Myerson, 2004]. In light of the ontological flexibility of type 3 models, in which factors influencing behavior can be sorted pragmatically into exogenous and endogenous as suits the modeler, this is not surprising; while type 3 models often make excellent experimental design tools, Popperian virtues are not among those they parade. In this respect, type 3 models will have a familiar quality for both the economist and the most common kind of philosophical critic of economics (e.g. [Rosenberg, 1992]). I think it is a safe prediction that, given economists' strong interest in engineering applications — which, in the picoeconomic and neuroeconomic domains are mainly (potential) medical applications — type 3 models will be the most frequently observed over the coming years, even if modular neuroeconomic accounts sweep the boards with respect to unifying power, explanatory generality and theoretical rigor. Note, however, that because type 3 modeling rests on taking a casual attitude to ontological commitment, successes of such models *cannot* be used to establish that economics is a mere supplementary representational language for neuropsychology (cf. [Camerer *et al.*, 2005]) unless no less relaxed modeling strategies succeed and yield progressively improving track records. Existing type 3 models draw the distinction between agentic and non-agentic aspects of brain function in a way that is essentially arbitrary: why is a typical person's urge to slop cardiovascularly disastrous butter on her toast not an expression of her preferences while her standing attraction to a sports car, for which she might save for years, *is* such an expression? Gul and Pesendorfer [2001; 2005] define an exogenous temptation as a choice option for an agent with the property that its presence in the choice set makes the agent worse off, either because this results in her making a worse choice than she would have made in the option's absence, or because to cope with the option the agent must incur a cost of 'self-control'. This basis for distinction is clear enough for their operational purposes. But its only *justification* is pragmatic: it allows us to go on applying standard consumer theory in the face of apparent hyperbolic discounting and preference reversal. Pragmatism is a thoroughly respectable motivation for any economist; but it should not be expected to reveal unifying ontological principles — for example, that neuroscience describes 'real' processes to which economics should be expected to conform. (Gul and Pesendorfer agree.)

Finally, let us consider type 2 (picoeconomic) models. Scientists with reductionist intuitions are often inclined to regard them as beset by indeterminacies, and therefore as more like philosophical stories than scientific accounts. For example, should we expect a typical person's behavior to be described on the molar scale by one hyperbolic curve or many? Only the latter answer seems plausible. As Green and Myerson [2004] note, both temporally delayed and uncertain rewards are often discounted hyperbolically. However, people's degree of future discounting (their future-respective '$k$-values', alluding to the standard equation[16]) are not good

[16] $v_i = A_i/(1+kD_i)$, where $v_i$, $A_i$, and $D_i$ represent the present value of a delayed reward, the amount of a delayed reward, and the delay of the reward, respectively. The 1 in the denominator

general predictors of their uncertainty-respective $k$-values. Gambling addicts, for example, show the low relative concern for the future typical of all addicts (high future-respective $k$-vales) [Holt *et al.*, 2003], but also unusual tolerance for risk (low uncertainty-respective $k$-values) [Petry, 2001; Dixon *et al.*, 2003]. Ainslie [1992] observes that most people discount money less steeply than specific streams of consumption. Hoch and Loewenstein [1991] and Read [2001] point out that people do not hyperbolically discount future supplies of purely utilitarian (in their conceptual system, 'non-visceral') rewards such as petrol or computer paper; but we should not infer from this fact that they would not hyperbolically discount risk associated with the petrol supply. All of these points arise *despite* the fact that it is difficult to operationally disentangle intertemporal and uncertainty-based contingencies in economic models, since delay implies uncertainty outside of contexts where strict determinacy and perfect knowledge obtain, and (given instantaneous consumption) there can be no uncertainty about consumption without at least minimal delay. Finally, there is strong evidence that interval variance has some degree of influence on valuation of future rewards [Green and Myerson, 2004]; but, as Read [2001; 2003] objects, the picoeconomic framework abstracts away from this.

These indeterminacies would constitute embarrassments to picoeconomics only given a molecular interpretation of it. Ainslie and other advocates of picoeconomics (including me) have invited this interpretation by usually assuming that the picoeconomic model concerns delay discounting *rather than* probability discounting. This would invite a critic to suppose that the evidence of Glimcher, Kable and Louie [2007] and Glimcher and Kable [2007] mentioned earlier counter-indicates the picoeconomic model along with its molecular-scale counterpart, the McClure *et al.* [2004] opponent brain-system model. A more careful interpretation of this evidence would have it as showing that the brain *does* implement computation of future discounting at a specific rate, while the behavioral phenomena discussed in the preceding paragraph are molar-scale generalities that hold *despite* the brain's discounting dispositions. Picoeconomic models should be regarded not as proto-neuroeconomic accounts of discounting, but as molar-scale profiles of the responses of organisms to differences in reward rates under different frames of attention. Exogenous influences from environments (including, in some organisms, social and cultural environments) likely play as critical a role in cueing and regulating these frames as do neural mechanisms. Thus we should not understand the picoeconomic agent as *composed out of* neuroeconomic ones.

The general conclusion I draw from these reflections is that there is room for all three types of models in the economics of personal and sub-personal behavior, though I am doubtful about the long-run viability of reductionist versions

---

prevents the rise in reward value from going infinite when delay is zero. The $k$ parameter is a constant that is proportional to the degree of temporal discounting, with higher and lower $k$ values describing greater and lesser degrees of discounting, respectively. Thus, an agent with a higher $k$ value would discount delayed rewards more than an agent with a lower $k$ value; the former agent therefore would be more impulsive than the latter.

of type 1 models. Apparent conflicts between picoeconomic and neuroeconomic approaches arise from assuming that there is a unique way of partitioning agents into sub-agents, so that a picoeconomic ontology of interests for a person must be isomorphic to a neuroeconomic ontology of brain areas for that person. The motivation for this is reductionism: the idea that molar-scale phenomena are in principle fully explicable by reference to molecular phenomena. But this is just a piece of philosophical dogma that fits the actual history of science very poorly [Ladyman and Ross, 2007]. The only empirically justifiable motivation for holding that one domain of modeling should reduce to another is actually observing the redundancy and abandonment, in that particular instance, of molar-scale models and their replacement by molecular-scale ones. I argued in earlier parts of the present essay that no such trend is manifest as between economics in general (i.e., outside of the avowed behavioral economics movement itself) and psychology or neuroscience. This does not at all imply that psychology and neuroscience are *irrelevant* to economics. The judgments of people, and of sub-personal picoeconomic interests, depend on neural computations of reward values as crucial input.; but neuroeconomics models the brain's valuations rather than the molar person's.[17] Thus (as in general) molecular-scale processes constrain molar-scale ones without reducing them.

The key implication of this form of anti-reductionism in the present context is that we can agree that people are not identical to economic agents without this necessarily implying that economic agency as traditionally understood is a useless or confused theoretical construct for explaining aspects of individual behavior. 'Necessarily' here needs emphasis. Rejecting an *a priori* motivation for collapsing economics into psychology does not in itself answer an obvious question implied in the criticism of standard microeconomics based on cognitive and behavioral science. That question is: if economic agents are asocial computational prodigies and people are constitutively social cognitive duffers, then what *is* the relationship between economic agents and people? To answer that there is *no* relationship *would* conjure up a mystery, except to a critic of mainstream economics so radical that she doubts that it ever succeeds at predicting anything.

I will argue in the concluding section of the chapter that, far from ignoring the social constitution of people, attention to this fact about them yields the answer to the question just posed.

## 6 PEOPLE AS COORDINATING EQUILIBRIA

One portentous claim emanating from the cognitive and behavioral sciences that is widely interpreted as implying trouble for mainstream economics is that people are pervasively, sub-consciously and irresistibly sensitive to manifold social cues, pressures and signals. Thus their preferences are not exogenous with respect to their

[17]For example, a group of dopamine neurons maximizes their utility by suppressing competing serotonergic circuits. If they are too successful the result is addiction, which is a disaster for the person and which few *people* want [Ross *et al.*, forthcoming].

strategic or consumption behavior. This claim lies at the core of Sen's [1977; 1999] critique of standard preference theory and what he calls 'welfarism'. A stronger claim is often made by anthropologists, sociologists and social psychologists that people are socially *constituted*. This claim is likely to strike many economists as a fundamental challenge to their way of thinking. However, in this final section of the chapter I will outline a perspective from which it is not. The basic idea is that once we get as far as recognizing people to be molar-scale objects[18] by comparison with their brains, then we can regard them as socially constituted without having to surrender the relevance of distinctively economic (as opposed to psychological) modeling to explanation of important aspects of their behavior. The perspective I will summarize here is not new, having been extensively elaborated in Ross [2005] and elsewhere. Readers are referred there for arguments. Here I will present, for the most part, only conclusions.

Human organisms are chemically integrated in meiosis, grown in the womb and then detached from their mothers' bodies at birth — they are not socially constructed. If it is nevertheless correct to claim that *people* are constituted socially, this must reflect the fact that they are *created* from human organisms by social development. Of course this process relies on properties of their brains: humans' giant cortex, and dispositions immanent in biases in neural connections and in the architecture of neurotransmitter pathways prepare them, unlike tigers, to be socialized. But the fact that we can distinguish between a very short pre-socialized phase and a socialized phase of a human organism's life supports a distinction between, as it were, the 'raw brain' and the person as a node in a dynamic social network. Raw human brains resemble tiger brains more than they resemble people. That people are socially constituted but their brains are not is the basic reason why behaviorists were right to emphasize the molar / molecular distinction. It doesn't suggest the dualist idea that persons *transcend* their brains; brains must adapt to socialization during development, and socialization is constrained by what brains can and cannot process.

To understand *how* people are socially created, something must first be said about why such developmental trajectories have been stabilized by selection. Let us distinguish between *social* animals and *herding* animals. Whereas the latter — wildebeest, for example, or corals — gain advantage merely by staying close together and coordinating their *schedules*, the former exploit efficiencies from joint contributions to ranges of projects that individuals can't perform alone, using some degree of specialization, either merely of talent or of dedicated roles. All available evidence suggests that natural selection, given the platforms it has had to work with in terrestrial history, can produce this in two ways: by adapting animals' genetic structures to increase the value of the inclusive coefficient in fitness functions, as in social insects and naked mole rats, or by adapting animals' brains so they develop enough book-keeping capacity to strategically discriminate among conspecifics and can thereby play strategic games involving reciprocal rewards and sanctions. High intelligence (cognitive plasticity) is far from continuously dis-

[18] In fact, people are better conceived as *processes* than as objects.

tributed across species, and sociality is far from continuously distributed across clades. It is thus of powerful significance under regression analyses that the entire hyper-intelligent club, which includes apes, elephants, dogs, toothed whales, corvids and parrots along with a few others, is social.

Within this club, humans are ecologically special in navigating an effectively boundless domain of novel collaborative projects. This is made possible by signaling systems — languages — that stabilize ranges of possible signal meanings by digitalizing information. That is, human syntax enables one human to direct another's attention to a specific object of reference even when it is not present to be pointed or gazed at; I can communicatively refer to 'Napoleon' exactly, not just to an indefinite range of things sharing to various degrees Napoleon's analog blend of properties (i.e., 'napoleonishness'). Thus humans can jointly track objects over time and space even when they are not present, and coordinate on future plans involving hypothetical objects picked out by digital contrast with other members of classes into which the grammars of public languages permit them to be sorted [Ross, 2007].

Some philosophers have suggested that language plus shared perceptual saliences are sufficient to account for people's ethologically unique capacity to coordinate. This is confused: the range of projects that can be distinguished thanks to recursive grammar makes the human coordination challenge orders of magnitude *more* complex than that faced by any other species. Game theorists encourage us to underestimate the difficulty of social coordination by solving for equilibria in situations they have already modeled as definite games. They readily forget that their own chief skill is in seeing how to abstract useful strategic models of empirical situations which don't come pre-packaged in terms of utility functions or strategy sets. Real human game players must implicitly construct models of their strategic situations in real time, without benefit of explicit principles, and they must jointly coordinate on these constructions; two interacting people who don't conceptualize their situation in terms of (roughly) the same game should expect not equilibrium but unpredictable chaos. Finally, let us bear in mind that every time a person takes an action she offers a move in a game with everyone whose welfare is potentially influenced by it and who might become aware of it — directly, by observing it or through gossip, or indirectly, by inferring it from outcomes, or second-order, by being influenced by the actions of someone else who is influenced by the original action. The overwhelming majority of human actions are thus simultaneously moves in multiple games with multiple sets of players of multiple $n$.

This all implies that most human choices of actions, no matter how small in scale, amount to general equilibrium problems. For example, to determine the best strategic response to my colleague's suggestion that we nominate a third colleague for a certain committee, I should, if I want to implement full rational agency, model the entire strategic history of our species (at least to the point in the future beyond which, due to discounting, I lose interest). This game is self-evidently intractable.

It gets still worse. A person's brain has a trillion neurons and $10^{13}$ synaptic connections, organized into semi-modular sub-systems that communicate imperfectly with one another, behave semi-autonomously and can no more be micro-managed by a frontal executive system than the President of the United States can plan every postal delivery and sentry assignment. These are of course the neuroeconomic agents discussed in the previous section. Not only do I not know the exact utility functions and strategy sets of the $n$ other people with whom I'm strategically enmeshed, but I face significant uncertainty in predicting *my own* utility function and distribution of strategy sets, because much of my behavior is regulated by parts of my brain to which I have no more access than a third-person observer.

People clearly *do* coordinate, often very smoothly, over substantial stretches of time and place, and across large groups. Even more clearly, they don't do so by solving computationally impossible problems. The model of social coordination as solving for general equilibrium by solving an unbounded-$n$ game *must* be missing something important. In social embeddedness and language, the very phenomena that lead to the impasse, lie the clues to what this something is. People sensibly insist that others with whom they enter into coordination games narrate comprehensible, publicly manifest stories about themselves and conform their behavior to these stories. Thus they enforce and enable predictability, including *self*-predictability. They mutually ease the imposed burden of this task by assisting each other as co-authors of narratives, recording expectations, rewarding enrichments of each other's sub-plots, and punishing overly abrupt attempts to revise important character dispositions. Parents initially impose this regime of self-construction on their children, later handing over primary control (often involuntarily) to their offspring's peer groups. Thus people become and remain distinct. The fact that self-creation and self-maintenance are *projects* requiring *effort* is what explains prevailing *normative* individualism, even while ('metaphysical') descriptive individualism is false. Individuals are centrally important to most of us partly *because* they don't just drop out of the womb. I will return to this point at the end of the chapter.

A crucial enabling aspect of this whole edifice is that humans are biologically adapted to be highly behaviorally sensitive to very cheap rewards (e.g. smiles, laughter, raised thumbs) and punishments (e.g. frowns, eye rolling, refusal of efforts at conversation). Not only are the standard punishments very inexpensive relative to the pain they inflict, but they can be withdrawn so as to leave almost no damaged infrastructure that then requires a new infusion of capital to put right; a person says "I forgive you" and the other's misery is (typically) instantly relieved. Some leading game theorists make the social coordination problem too hard, thereby motivating extravagantly hypothesized genetic adaptations to fix it, by exaggerating the costs of everyday rewards and punishments [Gintis, 2006; Seabright, 2006]. People avoid 'cheap talk' problems, in which their threats and promises would be ignored because it's doubted that these would be followed up if ineffective, by being psychologically adapted to care a great deal about rewards and punishments that cost others almost nothing [Ross, 2006a].

The effect of everyday pressures on people to construct and maintain selves is to drastically shrink the ranges of utility functions and strategy sets over which people must coordinate their constructions of games. The structures of these self-narratives then emerge as apparent framing effects and departures from proper Bayesian reasoning when we put people into experimental games and model these games as if the players weren't constrained by their own biographical and autobiographical plots.[19] This is a ubiquitous feature of the experimental literature in behavioral economics. Researchers define their subjects' games as if they were unconstrained by socialization, show that the outcomes do not match the Nash equilibria of these games, and thereby draw two generic conclusions (as background for various more specific conclusions that give us real psychological knowledge). The first sort is unobjectionable: people *are* constrained by socialization. But that is a truism, certainly known by Jevons, Walras, Samuelson, Milton Friedman and Robert Lucas alike. The second generic conclusion is that therefore standard economic theory is refuted because that theory is necessarily about unsocialized agents. This I reject.

I argued in previous sections that nothing in economic theory requires that economic agency be identified with individual people. Economic agency is a theoretical construction. Economists use it to build abstract models of firms, nations, labor unions, consortia in auctions, lineages in evolutionary games and other feedback-sensitive, incentive-driven systems that have no psychological properties at all. The usefulness of the construction is not cast into doubt by behavioral economics or by cognitive science more generally.

It is thus open to us to ask whether economics has *any* relevance to cognitive science (and hence to cognition understood as social). If the answer were 'no', economists in the spirit of Keynes might shrug this off and leave worries about unification of the sciences to philosophers. But the answer is not, in fact, negative. I just summarized an account of the universal human disposition to construct selves and to enforce such construction in one another. The explanation of this pattern is that it allows people to achieve many of the gains possible for economic agents — gains from trade, from specialization, and from consistent investment over time — despite the fact that their brains are too large and necessarily de-centralized as control structures to pull off economic agency by themselves. Thus economics plays a direct role in explaining the basis of social cognition. Furthermore, self-construction is only the first (necessary) aspect of the achievement of large-$n$coordination. The truly heavy lifting is done by the ultimate self-maintenance engines: institutions.

Most readers of this chapter will save money for relatively comfortable retirements. You will do this despite the fact that you would, if put in a systematically unfamiliar consumption environment, discount the future hyperbolically and therefore tend to reverse your preferences for prudent investments when temptations

[19] It's possible to induce people to escape from these constraints, in which case they tend to act much more like economic agents; but this requires deliberate effort in experimental design. See [Binmore, 2007].

to immediate reward presented themselves, then spend still more resources trying to defeat your own myopia as you learned the patterns governing the novel circumstances. Most of you will avoid this in your actual lives because your behavior is hemmed in and guarded by walls of culturally evolved and collectively designed institutions. If you persistently spend more than your income, this will be reflected in a falling credit rating that will inconvenience you *now*. Perhaps a recent housing bubble has allowed you to splurge for a few years, but as of this writing (mid-2007) market institutions are busy transmitting information about you and hundreds of millions like you that, through still other institutions, will correct your lack of prudence. If you aren't corrected quickly enough, the bank manager who supervises your mortgage may act to speed up receipt of the message. If very many of you are too sluggish responding to the news, the Chairman of the Federal Reserve Bank may reinforce it with an interest rate hike. And so on.

All of these institutions press you to approximate your behavior to that of an economic agent. They can't literally transform you, biological — psychological entity that you are, into such an agent. Even while struggling to save, you may visit a casino. You will buy some items this year that you will disdain and throw away in a year's time merely because your tastes change. But you, together with your fellows in society, have *enough* in common with economic agents, especially in modern institutional settings, that non-trivial predictions about your individual behavior can be had by modeling you as if, within temporal and institutional constraints, you were such agents. Furthermore, because you live in aggregated markets with dynamics that aren't very sensitive to psychological factors, *and* because you also play $n$-person games with other agents who are incentivized to stabilize one another's preference consistency, you can improve your prospects by learning some economic theory and feeding this social knowledge back into your personal planning. Feedback loops of this sort are the very logical essence of social cognition. *Both* your person-hood *and* your approximate economic agency — which, I have argued, are not the same thing — are socially constituted.

Individualism is thus descriptively false. As explained above, that is part of the reason *why* it is *normatively* important. This insight should allow us to see that we don't need to justify concerns for aggregate welfare by disaggregating it — which we can't in general do, as Arrow's theorem makes clear. The proper normative defense of macroeconomics without microfoundations has two parts, one familiar and narrowly economic and one less familiar and broader. First, if a policy takes a society to a higher community indifference curve than it was on before, but the new allocation and the old are Pareto-noncomparable, then we should still find that winners can compensate losers using less than the whole of their winnings; the new policy should bring about a Scitovsky-Kaldor-Hicks improvement. Second, we should see this as a *normative* improvement on utilitarian grounds *because* individual preferences are not exogenous. As modeled by Binmore [1998], people will bargain to a new distribution under the new dispensation and then they will adjust their distributive norms — that this, their collectively determined concept of justice — so as to rationalize the bargaining outcome. This will not at all impress a philosopher with Kantian intuitions, since the result may fail to 'respect' any given person's prior idea of fairness — justice is de-coupled from individual autonomy. But under the perspective I have defended here, such autonomy is a myth anyway if regarded as meaningful *outside of* an institutional specification. Such a specification is a norm-governed network. (It will happen now and then to be a market. In these unusual circumstances norms of justice doesn't matter and are only applied when people get confused.) When people adjust their norms they approximate different agents.

The Kantian philosopher is unimpressed by this story because she doesn't see any touchstone against which to regard the distribution on the higher community indifference curve as necessarily *better*. But the economist has an evaluative standard: the people are materially richer. The economic agents they formerly approximated may or may not have all had their preferences optimized; this we can't tell, for both economic and philosophical reasons. The economic reason is that Scitovsky-Kaldor-Hicks improvements aren't necessarily Pareto-improvements. The philosophical reason is that non-autonomous agents before and after institutional norm-readjustment are different agents. But although economics studies such agents as its first-order objects, and although these agents are not identical to the more enduring human entities that approximate sequences of them, the ultimate *justification* of economics is that it is useful for guiding our efforts to make *material* human animals materially better off. In a world not merely of pervasive scarcity but much outright poverty, the justification for the philosophical ethicist's activities seems to me to be comparatively thin gruel.

Thus, I conclude, a defense of economics as both objective science and normatively helpful engineering is best articulated without $A \Leftrightarrow O$. Economics is not, and should not become, a kind or branch of psychology. It is about agents, in the sense that it is interactions of agents about which it makes discoveries; and the agents it is about are not people. Its discoveries are nevertheless very important to people.

## BIBLIOGRAPHY

[Anderson, 1979] J. Anderson. A theoretical foundation for the gravity equation. *American Economic Review* 69: 106-116, 1979.

[Anderson and van Wincoop, 2003] J. Anderson and E. van Wincoop. Gravity with gravitas: a solution to the border puzzle. *American Economic Review* 93: 170-192, 2003.

[Anderson *et al.*, 1988] P. Anderson, K. Arrow, and D. Pines, eds. *The Economy as an Evolving Complex System*. Boston: Addison-Wesley, 1988.

[Anger and Loewenstein, 2010] E. Angner and G. Loewenstein. (this volume). Behavioral economics.

[Arrow and Debreu, 1954] K. Arrow and G. Debreu. Existence of equilibrium for a competitive economy. *Econometrica* 22: 265-290, 1954.

[Arthur, 1994] W. B. Arthur. *Increasing Returns and Path Dependence in the Economy*. Ann Arbor: University of Michigan Press, 1994.

[Aruthur *et al.*, 1997] W. B. Arthur, S. Durlauf, and D. Lane, eds. *The Economy as an Evolving Complex System II*. Boston: Addison-Wesley, 1997.

[Baldwin and Taglioni, 2006] R. Baldwin and D. Taglioni. Gravity for dummies and dummies for gravity equations. NBER Working Papers 12516, 2006: `http://ideas.repec.org/s/nbr/nberwo.html`

[Becker, 1962] G. Becker. Irrational behavior and economic theory. *Journal of Political Economy*, 70: 1-13, 1962.

[Beinhocker, 2006] E. Beinhocker. *The Origins of Wealth.* Cambridge, MA: Harvard Business School Press, 2006.

[Benabou and Tirole, 2003] R. Benabou and J. Tirole. Willpower and personal rules. *Journal of Political Economy* 112: 848-886, 2003.

[Binmore, 1990] K. Binmore. *Essays on the Foundations of Game Theory.* Oxford: Blackwell, 1990.

[Binmore, 1998] K. Binmore. *Game Theory and the Social Contract, Volume Two: Just Playing.* Cambridge, MA: MIT Press, 1998.

[Binmore, 2007] K. Binmore. *Does Game Theory Work? The Bargaining Challenge.* Cambridge, MA: MIT Press, 2007.

[Blume and Durlauf, 2005] L. Blume and S. Durlauf, eds. *The Economy as an Evolving Complex System III.* Oxford: Oxford University Press, 2005.

[Bruni, 2005] L. Bruni. *Hic sunt leones*: interpersonal relations as unexplored territory in the tradition of economics. In B. Gui and R. Sugden (Eds.), *Economics and Social Interaction* (pp. 206-228). Cambridge: Cambridge University Press, 2005.

[Bruni and Sugden, 2007] L. Bruni and R. Sugden. The road not taken: how psychology was removed from economics and how it might be brought back. *The Economic Journal*, 117, 146-173, 2007.

[Camerer, 2003] C. Camerer. *Behavioral Game Theory.* Princeton: Princeton University Press, 2003.

[Camerer and Loewenstein, 2004] C. Camerer and G. Loewenstein. Behavioral economics: Past, present and future. In C. Camerer, G. Loewenstein and M. Rabin, eds., *Advances in Behavioral Economics*, pp. 3-51. Princeton: Princeton University Press, 2004.

[Camerer *et al.*, 2005] C. Camerer, G. Loewenstein, and D. Prelec. Neuroeconomics: how neuroscience can inform economics. *Journal of Economic Literature* 43: 9-64, 2005.

[Caplin and Dean, 2008] A. Caplin and M. Dean. Dopamine and reward prediction error: an axiomatic approach to neuroeconomics. *American Economic Review*, 97: 248–152, 2008.

[Cox, 2004] J. Cox. How to identify trust and reciprocity. *Games and Economic Behavior* 46: 260-281, 2004.

[Cressman, 2003] R. Cressman. *Extensive Form Games and Evolutionary Dynamics.* Cambridge, MA: MIT Press, 2003.

[Damasio, 1994] A. Damasio. *Descartes's Error.* New York: Putnam, 1994.

[Davies, 2009] P. S. Davies. *Subjects of the World.* Chicago: University of Chicago Press, 2009.

[Davis, 2003] J. Davis. *The Theory of the Individual in Economics.* London: Routledge, 2003.

[Debreau, 1959] G. Debreu. *Theory of Value.* New York: Wiley, 1959.

[Debreu, 1960] G. Debreu. *Mathematical Methods in the Social Sciences.* Stanford: Stanford University Press, 1960.

[Dixon *et al.*, 2003] M. Dixon, J. Marley, and E. Jacobs. Delay discounting by pathological gamblers. *Journal of Applied Behavior Analysis* 36: 449–458, 2003.

[Feenstra *et al.*, 2001] R. Feenstra, J. Markusan, and A. Rose. Using the gravity equation to differentiate among alternative theories of trade. *Canadian Journal of Economics* 34: 430-447, 2001.

[Friedman, 1953] M. Friedman. *Essays in Positive Economics.* Chicago: University of Chicago Press, 1953.

[Frith and Wolpert, 2004] C. Frith and D. Wolpert, eds. *The Neuroscience of Social Interaction.* Oxford: Oxford University Press, 2004.

[Fullbrook, 2003] E. Fullbrook, ed. *The Crisis in Economics.* London: Routledge, 2003.

[Ghemawat, 1998] P. Ghemawat. *Games Businesses Play.* Cambridge, MA: MIT Press, 1998.

[Gigerenzer *et al.*, 1999] G. Gigerenzer, P. Todd, and the ABC Research Group. *Simple Heuristics that Make Us Smart.* Oxford: Oxford University Press, 1999.

[Gintis, 2006] H. Gintis. Behavioral ethics meets natural justice. *Politics, Philosophy and Economics* 5: 5-32, 2006.

[Glimcher, 2003] P. Glimcher. *Decisions, Uncertainty and the Brain.* Cambridge, MA: MIT Press, 2003.

[Glimcher *et al.*, 2007] P. Glimcher, J. Kable, and K. Louie. Neuroeconomic studies of impulsivity: now or just as soon as possible? *American Economic Review*, 97(2): 142–147, 2007.
[Green and Myerson, 2004] L. Green and J. Myerson. A discounting framework for choice with delayed and probabilistic rewards. *Psychological Bulletin* 130: 769 — 792, 2004.
[Gul an dPesendorfer, 2001] F. Gul and W. Pesendorfer. Temptation and self control. *Econometrica* 69: 1403-1436, 2001.
[Gul and Pesendorfer, 2005] F. Gul and W. Pesendorfer. The simple theory of temptation and self-control, 2005. `http://www.princeton.edu/~pesendor/finite.pdf`
[Heller, 1990] M. Heller. *The Ontology of Physical Objects.* Cambridge: Cambridge University Press, 1990.
[Heilbroner and Milberg, 1995] R. Heilbroner and W. Milberg. *The Crisis of Vision in Modern Economic Thought.* Cambridge: Cambridge University Press, 1995.
[Hoch and Loewenstein, 1991] S. Hoch and G. Loewenstein. Time-inconsistent preferences and consumer self-control. *Journal of Consumer Research* 17: 492-507, 1991.
[Hollis and Nell, 1975] M. Hollis and E. Nell. *Rational Economic Man.* Cambridge: Cambridge University Press, 1975.
[Holt *et al.*, 2003] D. Holt, L. Green, and J. Myerson. Is discounting impulsive? Evidence from temporal and probability discounting in gambling and non-gambling college students. *Behavioural Processes* 64: 355–367, 2003.
[Jevons, 1871] W. S. Jevons. *The Theory of Political Economy.* London: Macmillan, 1871.
[Kable and Glimcher, 2007] J. Kable and P. Glimcher. The neural correlates of subjective value during intertemporal choice. *Nature Neuroscience*, 10: 1625-1633, 2007.
[Kennedy and Eberhart, 2001] J. Kennedy and R. Eberhart. *Swarm Intelligence.* San Fransisco: Morgan Kauffman, 2001.
[Klemperer, 2004] P. Klemperer. *Auctions: Theory and Practice.* Princeton: Princeton University Press, 2004.
[Knutson *et al.*, 2007] B. Knutson, S. Rick, G. E. Wimmer, D. Prelec, and G. Loewenstein. Neural predictors of purchases. *Neuron*, 53, 147-156, 2007.
[Kreps and Wilson, 1982] D. Kreps and R. Wilson. Sequential equilibrium. *Econometrica* 50: 863-894, 1982.
[Kydland and Prescott, 1982] F. Kydland and E. Prescott. Time to build and aggregate fluctuations. *Econometrica* 50: 1345-1369, 1982.
[Ladyman and Ross, 2007] J. Ladyman and D. Ross. *Every Thing Must Go.* Oxford: Oxford University Press, 2007.
[Laibson, 1997] D. Laibson. Golden eggs and hyperbolic discounting. *Quarterly Journal of Economics*, 112, 443-477, 1997.
[Laibson, 1998] D. Laibson. Life-cycle consumption and hyperbolic discount functions. *European Economic Review*, 42, 861-871, 1998.
[Lipsey and Lancaster, 1956] R. Lipsey and G. Lancaster. The general theory of second best. *Review of Economic Studies*, 24: 11-32, 1956.
[Loewenstein, 1996] G. Loewenstein. Out of control: visceral influences on behavior. *Organizational Behavior and Human Decision Processes* 65: 272-292, 1996.
[Loewenstein, 1999] G. Loewenstein. A visceral account of addiction. In J. Elster and O.-J. Skog, eds., *Getting Hooked: Rationality and Addiction*, pp. 235-264. Cambridge, MA: Cambridge University Press, 1999.
[Long and Plosser, 1983] J. Long and C. Plosser. Real business cycles. *Journal of Political Economy* 91: 39-69, 1983.
[Lucas, 1978] R. Lucas. Unemployment policy. *American Economic Review* 68: 353-357, 1978.
[Mäki, 1986] U. Mäki. Rhetoric at the expense of coherence: a reinterpretation of Milton Friedman's methodology. In W. Samuels, ed., *Research in the History of Economic Thought and Methodology, Volume Four*, pp. 127-143. Greenwich, CT: JAI Press, 1986.
[Mäki, 1992] U. Mäki. Friedman and realism. In W. Samuels and J. Biddle, eds., *Research in the History of Economic Thought and Methodology, Volume Ten*, pp. 171-195. Greenwich, CT: JAI Press, 1992.
[Mantel, 1974] R. Mantel. On the characterization of aggregate excess demand. *Journal of Economic Theory*, 7: 348-353, 1974.
[Mantel, 1976] R. Mantel. Homothetic preferences and community excess demand functions. *Journal of Economic Theory*, 12: 197-201, 1976.

[Mandler, 1999] M. Mandler. *Dilemmas in Economic Theory.* Oxford: Oxford University Press, 1999.

[McClure *et al.*, 2004] S. McClure, D. Laibson, G. Loewenstein, and J. Cohen. Separate neural systems value immediate and delayed monetary rewards. *Science* 306: 503-507, 2004.

[Milgrom, 2004] P. Milgrom. *Putting Auction Theory to Work.* Cambridge: Cambridge University Press, 2004.

[Mirowski, 1989] P. Mirowski. *More Heat Than Light.* New York: Cambridge University Press, 1989.

[Mirowski, 2002] P. Mirowski. *Machine Dreams.* Cambridge: Cambridge University Press, 2002.

[Montague and Berns, 2002] P. R. Montague and G. Berns. Neural economics and the biological substrates of valuation. *Neuron* 36: 265-284, 2002.

[Montague *et al.*, 2006] P. R. Montague, B. King-Casas, and J. Cohen. Imaging valuation models in human choice. *Annual Review of Neuroscience* 29: 417-448, 2006.

[Morris and Shin, 2003] S. Morris and H.S. Shin. Global games: theory and applications. In M. Dewatripont, L.P. Hansen and S Turnovsky, eds., *Advances in Economics and Econometrics: Theory and Applications, Eight World Congress, Volume 1*, pp. 56-114, 2003.

[Ormerod, 1994] P. Ormerod. *The Death of Economics.* New York: Wiley, 1994.

[Panksepp, 1998] J. Panksepp. *Affective Neuroscience.* Oxford: Oxford University Press. 1998.

[Petry, 2001] N. Petry. Pathological gamblers, with and without substance abuse disorders, discount delayed rewards at high rates. *Journal of Abnormal Psychology* 110: 482-487, 2001.

[Prelec and Bodner, 2003] D. Prelec and R. Bodner. Self-signaling and self-control. In G. Loewenstein, D. Read and R. Baumeister (eds.), *Time and Decision*, pp. 277-298. New York: Russell Sage Foundation, 2003.

[Read, 2001] D. Read. Is time-discounting hyperbolic or subadditive? *Journal of Risk and Uncertainty* 23: 5-32, 2001.

[Read, 2003] D. Read. Subadditive intertemporal choice. In G. Loewenstein, D. Read and R. Baumeister, eds., *Time and Decision: Economic and Psychological Perspectives on Intertemporal Choice*, pp. 301-322. New York: Russell Sage Foundation, 2003.

[Robbins, 1935] L. Robbins. *An Essay on the Nature and Significance of Economic Science,* $2^{nd}$ edition. London: Macmillan, 1935.

[Robbins, 1938] L. Robbins. Interpersonal comparisons of utility: a comment. *Economic Journal* 43: 635-641, 1938.

[Rosenberg, 1992] A. Rosenberg. *Economics: Mathematical Politics or Science of Diminishing Returns?* Chicago: University of Chicago Press, 1992.

[Ross, 2002] D. Ross. Why people are atypical agents. *Philosophical Papers* 31: 87-116, 2002.

[Ross, 2005] D. Ross. *Economic Theory and Cognitive Science: Microexplanation.* Cambridge, MA: MIT Press, 2005.

[Ross, 2006a] D. Ross. Evolutionary game theory and the normative theory of institutional design: Binmore and behavioral economics. *Politics, Philosophy and Economics* 5: 51-79, 2006.

[Ross, 2006b] D. Ross. The Economics of the sub-personal: two research programs. In B. Montero and M. White, eds. *Economics and the Mind*, pp. 41-57.London: Routledge, 2006.

[Ross, 2007] D. Ross. *H. sapiens* as ecologically special: what does language contribute? *Language Sciences*, 2007.

[Ross *et al.*, 2008] D. Ross, C. Sharp, R. Vuchinich, and D. Spurrett. *Midbrain Mutiny: The Picoeconomics and Neuroeconomics of Disordered Gambling.* Cambridge, MA: MIT Press, 2008.

[Ross, 2009] D. Ross. Integrating the dynamics of multiscale economic agency. In H. Kincaid and D. Ross, eds., *The Oxford Handbook of Philosophy of Economics*, pp. 245-279. Oxford: Oxford University Press, 2009.

[Rubinstein, 2006] A. Rubinstein. *Lecture Notes in Microeconomic Theory: The Economic Agent.* Princeton: Princeton University Press, 2006.

[Rubinstein, 2007] A. Rubinstein. Discussion of behavioral economics. In R. Blundell, W. Newey and T. Persson, eds., *Advances in Economics and Econometrics, Theory and Applications, Ninth World Congress*, pp. 246–254. Cambridge: Cambridge University Press, 2007.

[Ruttkamp, 2002] E. Ruttkamp. *A Model-Theoretic Realist Interpretation of Science.* Dordrecht: Kluwer, 2002.

[Samuelson, 1998] L. Samuelson. *Evolutionary Games and Equilibrium Selection.* Cambridge, MA: MIT Press, 1998.

[Samuelson, 1938] P. Samuelson. A note on the pure theory of consumer's behavior. *Economica* 5: 61-72, 1938.

[Samuelson, 1947] P. Samuelson. *Foundations of Economic Analysis.* Enlarged edition (1983). Cambridge, MA: Harvard University Press, 1947.

[Satz and Ferejohn, 1994] D. Satz and J. Ferejohn. Rational choice and social theory. *Journal of Philosophy* 91: 71-87, 1994.

[Schelling, 1978] T. Schelling. Economics, or the art of self-management. *American Economic Review* 68: 290-294, 1978.

[Schelling, 1980] T. Schelling. The intimate contest for self-command. *Public Interest* 60: 94-118, 1980.

[Schelling, 1984] T. Schelling. Self-command in practice, in policy, and in a theory of rational choice. *American Economic Review* 74: 1-11, 1984.

[Schultz, 2002] W. Schultz. Getting formal with dopamine and reward. *Neuron* 36: 241-263, 2002.

[Seabright, 2006] P. Seabright. The evolution of fairness norms: an essay on Ken Binmore's *Natural Justice. Politics, Philosophy and Economics* 5: 33-50, 2006.

[Sen, 1977] A. K. Sen. Rational fools. *Philosophy and Public Affairs* 6: 317-344, 1977.

[Sen, 1999] A. K. Sen. *Development as Freedom.* New York: Random House, 1999.

[Sonnenschein, 1972] H. Sonnenschein. Market excess demand functions. *Econometrica*, 40: 549-563, 1972.

[Sonnenschein, 1973] H. Sonnenschein. Do Walras identity and continuity characterize the class of excess demand functions? *Journal of Economic Theory*, 6: 345-354. 1973.

[Stigum, 1990] B. Stigum. *Toward a Formal Science of Economics.* Cambridge, MA: MIT Press, 1990.

[Strotz, 1956] R. Strotz. Myopia and inconsistency in dynamic utility maximization. *Review of Economic Studies* 23: 165-180, 1956.

[Tinbergen, 1962] J. Tinbergen. *Shaping the World Economy.* New York: The Twentieth Century Fund, 1962.

[van Fraassen, 1980] B. van Fraassen. *The Scientific Image.* Oxford: Oxford University Press, 1980.

[van Fraassen, 2002] B. van Fraassen. *The Empirical Stance.* New Haven: Yale University Press, 2002.

[Weibull, 1995] J. Weibull. *Evolutionary Game Theory.* Cambridge, MA: MIT Press, 1995.

[Weibull, 2004] J. Weibull. Testing game theory. In S. Huck, ed., *Advances in Understanding Strategic Behavior,* pp. 85-104. Houndmills, Basingstoke, Hampshire: Palgrave, 2004.

[Young, 1998] H. P. Young. *Individual Strategy and Social Structure.* Princeton: Princeton University Press, 1998.

# ONTOLOGICAL ISSUES IN EVOLUTIONARY ECONOMICS: THE DEBATE BETWEEN GENERALIZED DARWINISM AND THE CONTINUITY HYPOTHESIS

Jack Vromen

## INTRODUCTION

Recently evolutionary economists started to pay attention to ontological issues in their own subfield. Two projects dominate the discussions: Generalized Darwinism (henceforth: GD), promoted by Geoff Hodgson and Thorbjørn Knudsen, and the Continuity Hypothesis (henceforth: CH), put forward by Ulrich Witt. As a first and crude approximation (to be refined below), GD entails the view that abstract and general Darwinian principles suit the study of biological evolution and of economic evolution equally well. The CH entails the view that ongoing economic evolution proceeds on the basis of, and is still influenced by the outcomes of preceding processes of biological evolution. At present, GD and CH are vying for hegemony in the community of evolutionary economists. GD and the CH sometimes are pitted against each other as if they were mutually excluding rivals. This paper investigates to what extent (and if so, in what sense) GD and the CH are rivals.

As we shall see, part of the debate between proponents of GD and of the CH is about the very notion of ontology itself. At stake is whether the views expressed in GD are based on ontology rather than analogy. The categorization of ontological issues into three clusters that I first presented in Vromen [2004a] is taken here as a framework to organize the discussion. Again (as I already did in that paper) I will argue that we should start with recognizing not only that quite distinct issues are all deemed ontological in the literature, but also that stances taken on an issue in the one cluster often do not prejudge the stance that can be consistently taken on an issue in another cluster. For example, taking the stance that Darwinian principles are needed to explain economic evolution does not commit one to take the extreme and wildly implausible view that our genes fully determine our behavior. But I will also discuss a few cases in which the stance taken on an issue in the one cluster does narrow down the range of stances that can be consistently taken on an issue in another cluster. Thus, while I focused mainly on independencies between positions taken in different clusters of ontological issues in Vromen [2004a],

Handbook of the Philosophy of Science. Volume 13: Philosophy of Economics.
Volume editor: Uskali Mäki. General editors: Dov M. Gabbay, Paul Thagard and John Woods.

in this contribution I will discuss independencies and interdependencies between them alike.

This contribution to the Handbook has the character of an overview rather than of an ordinary paper in which a specific thesis or claim is argued for. Presenting a fair and accurate discussion of the debate and of the several issues that are at stake in it is what I aim at. No attempt is made to add something original to these discussions. Insofar as there is originality in this contribution it is in the way in which the discussion is organized and in the links that are forged with other strands of literature. Connections will be made not only with relevant literature in philosophy of science, but occasionally, when I thought this informative and useful, also with currents in economic theorizing (that do not belong to evolutionary economics) and with currents in evolutionary theorizing in other fields and disciplines.

## *Evolutionary economics in a nutshell*

Evolutionary economics is understood here quite narrowly as the branch within economics that has been developed in the wake of Nelson and Winter's seminal *An Evolutionary Theory of Economic Change* [1982].[1] Other evolutionary economists working in this tradition include, among many others,[2] Stan Metcalfe, Ulrich Witt, Geoff Hodgson, Giovanni Dosi, Kurt Dopfer, Brian Loasby, John Foster, Pier Paolo Saviotti, Esben Sloth Anderson, Steve Klepper, Andreas Pyka, Uwe Cantner, Jason Potts, Johann Peter Murmann, Thorbjørn Knudsen, Gerald Silverberg, Bart Verspagen, Bart Nooteboom and Koen Frenken. Papers written by evolutionary economists often find their way into journals like *Journal of Evolutionary Economics*, *Industrial and Corporate Change*, and *Structural Change and Economic Dynamics*.

There are several features of evolutionary economics distinguishing it from other traditions or schools of thought within economics. Two such features stand out: the level of analysis in evolutionary economics and the key assumptions in its explanatory framework. Evolutionary economics studies processes in which changes (notably technological change) are brought about at the ('population') level of industries, sectors, branches, markets or whole economies where the key players (the 'agents') are not individual persons but firms or other organizations. Note that this is not at all unlike traditional (or standard) neoclassical theory, in which households and firms are also treated as if they were unitary agents. Evolutionary economics is also quite like the neoclassical theory of the firm in another respect. In the neoclassical theory of the firm, firms are looked at from a technological perspective: firms are in fact equated with their production function. Evolutionary

[1] Which is not to say that evolutionary economists endorse and build upon the foundations Nelson and Winter laid for evolutionary economists. As we shall see later on in this paper, the two main protagonists in the paper — Hodgson and Knudsen on the one hand and Witt on the other — distance themselves from Nelson and Winter [1982] in several respects.

[2] With sincere apologies to those whose names deserve to be mentioned but are not mentioned here.

economics likewise focuses on firm-specific capabilities and routines to produce goods or services. The ways in which firm members and units are internally organized within firms get considerably less attention. Thus evolutionary economics is unlike more recent theories of the firm, in which intra-organizational issues are put centre stage. In those recent theories the agents figuring in the nexus of contracts (which, according to some theory, a firm basically is) or in governance structures are individual persons.

This raises the issue whether it is acceptable to treat firms as unitary agents (in the *explanantia*) in explanations, given that it is clear that multi-person firms in fact are not unitary agents at all. Multi-person firms house heterogeneous persons with different interests, beliefs, intentions, attitudes, perceptions and the like. One need not be a staunch defender of methodological individualism to appreciate that the behavior of a firm at least partly depends on (the success or failure of) attempts to align all these internal differences within firms (Abell, Felin and Foss 2007). One of the hallmarks of evolutionary economics is that it acknowledges heterogeneity within industries between firms. But it seems to pay considerably less attention to the heterogeneity within firms between firm members.

Thus evolutionary economics is not quite unlike the neoclassical theory of the firm *qua* its level of analysis and its technological (rather than organizational) theoretical orientation. But *qua* their key assumptions in their explanatory (or theoretical) framework they are very different. (Static) equilibrium analysis is discarded in evolutionary economics and so are strong rationality assumptions. Agents are boundedly rational at most. They satisfice rather than maximize. What is more, agents, firms in particular, differ with respect to their behavioral properties. There is heterogeneity in this respect. Thus representative agent type of theorizing is rejected. So is equilibrium theorizing. There is no presumption that economies (or industries) are in equilibrium. There is no presumption even that economies tend to move in the direction of equilibria. To the extent that the notion of equilibrium serves any analytical purpose at all (as a benchmark, for example) in models in evolutionary economics, economies may be out-of-equilibrium all of the time. And if an economy converges on an equilibrium, it need not stay there for long. Both exogenous and endogenous changes may dislodge the equilibrium. Static (or comparative-static) equilibrium analysis is replaced by dynamic process-analysis. Dynamic process-analysis need not take the form of analytically tractable models that allow for close-form solutions. Computer simulations are readily accepted. Attempts are made to make room for endogenous technological change (innovations); attempts that are taken by some to defy closed system theorizing.

Thus while evolutionary economics shares its level of analysis and technological orientation with the neoclassical theory of the firm, it seems their theoretical assumptions could not have been more different. In what respects does evolutionary economics distinguish itself from other attempts in economics to incorporate evolutionary theorizing or insights from evolutionary theorizing elsewhere? Elsewhere [Vromen, 2004b] I introduced the following typology. I ranked evolutionary economists among the *revolutionaries*, stressing that evolutionary economists plead for a theoretical approach in economics that is radically different from the one advocated and followed in 'orthodox' economics.[3] In this they differ from 'conservatives' and 'revisionists', economists who believe that taking evolution seriously in economics entails no changes or only minor changes in the standard theoretical approach in economics. Economists stressing that the main lesson of evolutionary game theory is that the use of the solution concept of Nash equilibrium is vindicated in economics (cf. [Mailath, 1998]) I call conservatives. Revisionists include economists who argue on evolutionary grounds that utility functions should make room for a taste for fairness, for example, or for altruism (cf. [Frank, 1988]).

In Vromen [2008] I stress that evolutionary economists focus on current ongoing processes of economic change, which they take to be evolutionary (in senses yet to be clarified) in kind. This is really different from economists who hold, for example, that the main service evolutionary theorizing can render to economics is that it helps with identifying our basic preferences. I do not only have in mind here economists who want to accommodate the ideas of evolutionary psychology, for example, but also bioeconomists and neuroeconomists [Vromen, 2007], proponents of the so-called Indirect Evolutionary Approach [Güth and Yaari, 1991] and protagonists of strong reciprocity [Bowles and Gintis, 2003] and altruistic punishment [Fehr and Gächter, 2002]. This latter group of economists have processes of biological (and possibly also cultural) evolution in mind that took place long time ago (but that allegedly still indirectly influence our current behavior — through our basic preferences). They need not (and actually most of the time do not) believe that current processes of economic change are evolutionary in any meaningful sense.

## *The positions: Generalized Darwinism (GD) and the Continuity Hypothesis (CH)*

Above I gave rough characterizations of GD and the CH. GD I described as entailing the view that abstract and general principles can be discerned in Darwinian evolutionary theory that suit the subject matters both of biology and of economics. The CH I described as entailing the view that ongoing economic evolution proceeds on the basis of, and is still influenced by the outcomes of preceding processes of biological evolution. In fact, both GD and the CH involve not only more substantive claims than the descriptions just given suggest, but also specific heuristics for further research.

### *Hodgson and Knudsen's version of GD*

Hodgson and Knudsen [2006] give more substance to GD by specifying the following three abstract and general Darwinian principles: *variation*, *inheritance* (or

[3]According to evolutionary economists, 'orthodox' economics is wedded to the '(individual) maximization cum (aggregate) equilibrium' framework.

*replication*) and *selection*.[4] Given the centrality of the three principles in their GD, it is remarkable how little Hodgson and Knudsen say about what these principles precisely are and what they entail. The few things they say about the principles are expressed in a loose way. Perhaps Hodgson and Knudsen simply take for granted that everyone knows what the principles mean. Anyway, the following can be extracted from their sparse remarks and comments about the principles. There is variation in a population of entities if the entities differ in relevant respects. There is inheritance (or replication) if there is a mechanism seeing to it that the properties are preserved (or retained) either in the units themselves or in their 'offspring' (to which the properties are passed on). And there is selection if the entities are mortal and degradable, if they face an omnipresent problem of scarcity and if they are therefore caught in a struggle for existence [Hodgson and Knudsen, 2006, 4].

Hodgson and Knudsen argue that in any system in which all three principles are present Darwinian evolution occurs. The three principles are present not only in biological systems, they argue, but also in economic systems.[5] Hodgson and Knudsen do not deny that biological and economic systems differ in many significant ways, but they argue that biological and economic systems have these three principles in common. Again, Hodgson and Knudsen do not spend many words on what exactly Darwinian evolution is. But from the foregoing it can be gathered that what they mean is evolution through *natural selection*: the degree to which the entities are relatively successful translates into the spread or decline of the frequency (or proportion) of their properties in the population. The frequency of the properties of relatively successful entities increases in the population, while the frequency of the properties of less successful decreases.

GD is given even more substance by Hodgson and Knudsen by arguing (following David Hull's 1982 terminology) that *replicators* and *interactors* are identifiable both in biological and in economic systems.[6] Hull argues that evolution through natural selection involves two processes rather than one: replication and interaction. Interaction causes replication to be differential. Interactors are the entities that interact with their environment and with each other and replicators are the entities that are replicated. More precisely, replicators are those entities that pass on their structure intact through successive replications (see also [Dawkins, 1976]). Interactors are those entities that interact as cohesive wholes with their environments in such a way as to make replication differential.[7] Paradigmatic examples

[4]The three principles (albeit under slightly different names) were already presented in Darwin [1859]. As Hodgson and Knudsen note, many scholars earlier noticed that the principles potentially have a wider scope than the biological domain (e.g. [Lewontin, 1970; Campbell, 1965; Popper, 1972; Hull, 1981; Dawkins, 1983; Plotkin, 1994; Cziko, 1995; Dennett, 1995].

[5]Both Hodgon and Knudsen and Witt and his group members assume that economic evolution is a subspecies of cultural evolution. They believe that all general properties of cultural evolution are shared by economic evolution.

[6]As will be argued in more detail below (see also [Vromen, 2007]), and as Hodgson and Knudsen themselves acknowledge, evolution through natural selection can occur without there being replicators.

[7]Hull [2001] argues that he introduced the distinction between replicators and interactors to

of replicators and interactors in the biological domain are genes and individual organisms, respectively. Hull's general rendering of evolution through natural selection in terms of interactors and replicators is meant to imply that there might be other replicators and interactors than genes and organisms, not just within, but possibly also outside the biological domain. Thus evolution through natural selection need not be confined to the biological domain. One of the things Hull is famous for, for example, is for arguing that there also is evolution through natural selection in scientific development [Hull, 1988].

Hodgson and Knudsen [2004] suggest that in the economic domain habits and routines are replicators and firms are interactors. Although they recognize that habits and routines are quite different than genes in several respects and that the way in which habits and routines are replicated differs from how genes are inherited, Hodgson and Knudsen argue that habits and routines meet Hull's definition of a replicator. And although firms are quite unlike individual organisms in many respects, they meet Hull's definition of an interactor. Hence, despite the differences between these economic and biological units, Darwinian evolution occurs in both domains. Hodgson and Knudsen also stress, however, that the fact that biological and economic evolution are both Darwinian at an abstract and general level of description does not imply that biological and economic evolution are similar in other respects. They argue that the processes differ profoundly at the less abstract and general and more detailed level.

Hodgson and Knudsen argue that explanations of the evolution of a system in which the three principles are present cannot be acceptable unless they invoke the three principles: "... an adequate explanation of the evolution of such a system *must* involve the three Darwinian principles of variation, inheritance and selection." (Hodgson and Knudsen, [2006, 5; *Italics* in the original]; see also Hodgson and Knudsen [2008]). Yet they also argue that explanations that invoke only the three principles are incomplete. If evolutionary processes in the economic domain are to be explained, auxiliary domain-specific explanations and hypotheses have to be added to the three generalized Darwinian principles. Thus Hodgson and Knudsen make a distinction between the three generalized Darwinian principles, which are taken to provide a general theoretical framework (also sometimes called universal metatheory) that is domain-unspecific, and auxiliary explanations and hypotheses, which are taken to be domain-specific details. Details that are specific for the economic domain are to be added to the three principles in order to get full-fledged causal explanations of economic evolutionary processes.

Thus Hodgson and Knudsen's case for GD involves not just a *description* of what Generalized Darwinism entails: the three general principles of variation, inheritance (or replication) and selection. It also involves the *claim* that these principles are not only applicable to economic evolution (and other forms of non-

disambiguate the phrase "unit of selection". Hull also makes clear that he believes that taken together replication and interaction are sufficient to characterize evolution by natural selection. Replication and interaction are not assumed to also cover other possible evolutionary forces causing evolution such as drift.

biological evolution) but are necessary in any study of complex evolving population systems. And, finally, it also involves a *program* (or project): more is needed than the application of just the three principles to have a satisfactory study of economic evolution. Domain-specific hypotheses and data have to be added to arrive at explanatory theories.

### *Witt's version of the CH*

Above I asserted that the CH entails the view that ongoing economic evolution proceeds on the basis of, and is still influenced by the outcomes of preceding processes of biological evolution. Witt gives more substance to the CH by arguing that psychological features of human beings are outcomes of antecedent processes of biological evolution that are of special importance to ongoing processes of economic evolution. In particular, ancient processes of biological evolution produced both the basic, innate wants and primitive, non-cognitive forms of learning (such as conditioning) that still constrain and influence the behavior of present-day human beings. On the basis of their basic wants, for example, people also learn new acquired wants through conditioning (or associative learning). Thus when people regularly consume food in specifically arranged settings that have certain aesthetic aspects (furniture, tableware, etc.), for example, they tend to acquire a want for such settings even in the absence of eating [Witt, 2001].

In virtue of their unique and superior intelligence, however, the behavioral repertoire of human beings has been extended vastly beyond these genetically encoded dispositions and capacities. People have devised all kinds of sophisticated tools for meeting their wants, for example. And they have developed refined communication technologies enabling them to socially transmit new information and new knowledge rapidly and widely. In short, due to processes of cultural evolution people have transcended the state their ancestors were in (and that their cousin mammals still are in) when cultural evolution took off. Witt stresses that cultural knowledge differs considerably from genetically coded knowledge [Witt, 2004].

> Genetic 'knowledge' comes in a form which *uno actu* interprets, expresses, and replicates its meaning in terms of blue prints for manipulating materials and/or triggering ad controlling processes, provided the necessary materials and free energy are available. Replication occurs with some variation between generations, and since genetic novelty originates from those variations, the emergence of novelty is a part of the programmed automatism. None of this holds in the case of cultural knowledge. The latter is coded and stored in a form lacking an automatic copying, interpreting, and self-expressing modus. The generation, storage, expression (utilization and application), and even the replication of cultural knowledge all need to be effected by human action and require at least a minimal form of intelligence. [Witt, 2004, 138–139]

Witt argues that differences between genetically coded knowledge and cultural knowledge like these are so huge that the Darwinian triple of variation, replication and selection is unsuitable for studying cultural evolution. The Darwinian fits biological but not cultural evolution. Instead, what biological and cultural evolution do have in common with each other is that they both deal with processes of *self-transformation*. They both involve the transformation of systems through the emergence and dissemination of novelty. The specific ways in which novelty is created and disseminated in biological and economic systems differ significantly. The creation of novelty in economic systems crucially involve intelligence and intentionality, for example, things that are completely lacking in biological evolution. Despite such differences, self-transformation through the emergence and dissemination of novelty is a generic formulation of evolutionary processes that fits both realms.

Witt [2007] argues that the CH is committed to monism and naturalism as specific "ontological creeds". Instead of assuming that the subject matters of evolutionary biological and evolutionary economics belong to different, disconnected spheres of reality, as non-monistic ontologies do, the CH takes them to be causally connected. The CH presumes that there is one and the same ontological basis for all evolutionary pheomena [Witt, 2004, 129]. In particular, the CH is at odds with the most (in)famous and tenacious two-tier ontology in history, namely Cartesian dualism. Witt also suggests that the CH implies a rejection of the doctrine that the humanities (*Geisteswissenschaften)*, to which economics belongs, ought to have a different method or approach (*Verstehen*) than the sciences (*Naturwissenschaften*, which are assumed to be in the business of *Erklären*). Like biology and the other natural sciences, the aim of economics is to explain phenomena and processes.

The ambitious research program of Witt and his Evolutionary Economics Group members in Jena is to build a new consumption theory and a new production theory on the basis of the CH.[8] The challenge is to develop new theories that can explain historical changes and trends in consumption and production patterns better than the rather sterile neoclassical consumption and production theories. On the basis of the CH, substantive conjectures are made not only about why there has been an explosion of new products and services even though many of the basic wants that they ultimately serve are satiable, but also about how consumers arrive at the preferences that they have and when, why and how preferences change [Witt, 2001; 2008]. Likewise, the CH can serve as a useful starting point for understanding better (than standard economic theory is able to do) how human cultural knowledge enables mankind both to steer nature's production processes in desired directions and to create ever new artificial production processes [Witt, 2004].

In short, Witt's CH links ongoing cultural and economic evolution with prior biological evolution: prior biological evolution paved the way for, and still defines the constraints for ongoing cultural and economic evolution. Where biological and

[8]Witt mentions Veblen, Georgescu-Roegen, Gowdy, Faber and Proops and the late Hayek as precursors of this ambitious project.

economic evolutionary processes meet in particular is in the genetic endowment of humans. The genetic endowment of humans is a product of antecedent biological evolution that still affects current human consumption and production behavior in various ways (through determining innate wants, for example, and programming non-cognitive learning processes). Focusing on antecedent processes of biological evolution allows one to reconstruct the conditions from which processes of cultural evolution started. And it puts what happened subsequently in processes of cultural evolution in the right perspective. This is why the CH is believed to be useful as a starting-point for developing new consumption and production theories that are better able to explain the enormous changes in consumption and production patterns over the last centuries than standard neoclassical consumption and production theory.

## *The debate: what is at stake?*

### *Analogy or ontology?*

Hodgson and Knudsen's GD has been criticized by the proponents of the CH, not only by Witt [2004; 2007] himself, but also by several members of his Evolutionary Economics Group at the Max Planck Institute of Economics in Jena (cf. [Buenstorf, 2006; Cordes, 2006; 2007]). Witt and his collaborators argue that Hodgson and Knudsen's GD is based on a *biological analogy.* The Darwinian triple was first formulated in the field of biological evolutionary theory and was only later transferred to, or taken over by other fields. Witt *et al.* recognize that Hodgson and Knudsen aim at giving a domain-general formulation of the Darwinian principles. But Witt *et al.* deny that Hodgson and Knudsen succeed in shaking off features that are specific and peculiar to biological evolution. Even in Hodgson and Knudsen's abstract and general rendering of the three principles, Witt *et al.* argue, the principles betray their origin in evolutionary biology.

Hodgson and Knudsen emphatically deny that their GD is based just on an analogy. They have trump cards on their sleeves here. Hodgson and Knudsen draw attention to the fact that Darwin himself hinted at applications of his three principles outside the biological domain (for example, to account for the evolution of language). So even Darwin already had a wider application of his three principles in mind than just biological evolution. Hodgson and Knudsen also note that in developing the three principles Darwin was inspired by the work of the political economist Thomas Robert Malthus on natural checks on population growth. Thus Hodgson and Knudsen call into question that the three Darwinian principles originated from within evolutionary biology. More importantly, Hodgson and Knudsen argue that their case for GD is based on the observation that biological and economic systems have the three rather abstract properties of variation, replication and selection in common. Even if it were the case that the Darwinian triple was first formulated in evolutionary biology, this would do nothing to either vindicate or invalidate this observation.

Hodgson and Knudsen's proposal to invoke the Darwinian triple to study cultural (and in particular economic) evolution arguably is based on an analogy. If all it takes for some idea or concept to be based on an analogy is that a connection involving more or less formal similarities is made between different domains of discourse (which is what Hodgson himself suggests; see [Hodgson, 2002, 263]), then their proposal is based on an analogy. After all, Hodgson and Knudsen did not invent the Darwinian triple themselves, but obtain it from Darwin and from Darwinism. The principles of variation, selection (or rather, the struggle for existence) and inheritance were first coined by Darwin, not by any of his precursors outside biology. But it seems that Hodgson and Knudsen are right in insisting that their case for GD is based on an ontological claim. Arguing that biological and economic systems have the three rather abstract properties of variation, replication and selection in common, as they do, is making an ontological claim. It is a claim about properties that different domains in reality (allegedly) have, not about concepts or principles in different theories or fields of enquiry. Hodgson and Knudsen also seem to be right in arguing that their case rests on the truth of this ontological claim rather than on the issue of whether or not the Darwinian triple first was formulated in evolutionary biology.

"Analogy or ontology" seems to be a false opposition here. Hodgson and Knudsen's case for GD is based on both analogy and ontology. Their Darwinian triple is an abstracted and generalized version of theories developed in another field of enquiry. Yet their assertion that the triple suits cultural (and more in particular economic) evolution is based on their ontological assessment that complex evolving cultural systems have the required properties for evolution through natural selection to occur. Those who reject Hodgson and Knudsen's GD also do so on ontological grounds. They believe that Hodgson and Knudsen's Darwinian triple do not fit the specific characteristics of evolving economic systems. In this respect, the objections of Witt *et al.* against Hodgson and Knudsen's GD are reminiscent of the objections earlier opponents of "the biological metaphor raised (Foster 1997; Witt 1999). These earlier opponents likewise argued that the biological metaphor is ill-suited to do justice to the specificities of economic evolution.

### *Different sorts of ontological issues are at stake*

In Vromen [2004a] I argued that the ontological claim made here belongs to a first cluster of ontological issues. If we confine our attention to biological and economic evolution, what is at stake in this first cluster is whether processes of biological and economic evolution have common properties. If so, it is possible to formulate a general (or generic) description of both processes by referring to the common properties. This is exactly what Hodgson and Knudsen aim to do with their GD. Witt *et al.* argue that Hodgson and Knudsen fail in their attempt because variation, replication and selection are properties of biological evolution but not of economic evolution. Witt *et al.* do not deny that processes of biological and economic evolution have common properties, however. Both processes are argued to involve the emergence and dissemination of novelty.[9] What this means is that strictly speaking Witt's generic description of evolution in terms of self-transformation rather than his CH is the real competitor of Hodgson and Knudsen's GD (as Witt [2003] himself recognizes). It is Witt's description of evolution in terms of self-transformation that is meant to be rivaling Hodgson and Knudsen's GD in giving a domain-unspecific description of evolutionary processes, based on different (allegedly) common properties of evolutionary processes in different domains in reality.

Witt's CH is not meant to give a generic description of evolutionary processes based on properties that evolutionary processes in different domains (allegedly) have in common. Instead, it is meant to describe how evolutionary processes in different domains (notably evolution in biology and evolution in culture) are *causally* connected to one another.[10] The issue that the CH addresses belongs to a different, second cluster of issues [Vromen, 2004a]. At stake in this second cluster is not whether or not biological and economic evolution have common properties (and, if so, what are these properties), but whether or not biological and economic evolution interact causally with each other (and, if so, how). Witt's CH asserts, as we saw above, that products of antecedent processes of biological evolution prepared the ground for, and still determine the constraints for, subsequent processes of cultural evolution. It is assumed that biological selection pressures on humans have faded away. Hence no systematic feedback effects of cultural evolution on biological evolution are envisaged. This reflects one particular view on how biological and economic evolution interact. There are others. An example is gene-culture co-evolution [Boyd and Richerson, 1985], which assumes that the causal interaction between biological and cultural evolution is a two-way rather than a one-way street. It is not just that products of biological evolution affect ongoing cultural evolution, as is recognized in Witt's CH, it is also possible that products of cultural evolution affect ongoing biological evolution.[11]

Note that it is presupposed in both Hodgson and Knudsen's GD and Witt's CH that biological and economic evolution are distinct processes. Only if biological and economic evolution are distinct processes we can ask whether they have common properties. And only of distinct processes we can ask whether they causally interact with each other. All parties mentioned thus far (not just Hodgson and Knudsen and Witt *et al.*, but also Boyd and Richerson) agree that biological and cultural evolution mutually exclude each other in that either genes (or possibly other biological units of replication) or that ideas, tunes, habits, routines (or pos-

[9] Witt (personal correspondence) stresses that both the emergence and the dissemination of novelty capture more than the emergence of new variants and selective retention processes respectively.

[10] As Witt correctly notes, we can say that evolutionary processes in all domains have particular properties in common without saying anything about how (if at all) they are causally connected [Witt, 2003, 282].

[11] Christian Cordes seems to be subscribe to Boyd and Richerson's gene-culture co-evolutionary theory rather than to Witt's one-directional view on the causal relation between biological and economic evolution.

sibly yet other cultural units) are transmitted from the one individual (or possibly a unit at a different level of organization, such as a firm) to another. All parties agree that the social transmission of cultural units does not involve the transmission of genes. The parties might disagree on many other issues, but they agree that the fact that non-biological entities are transmitted makes biological and cultural evolution two distinct, non-overlapping processes.

In fact, Hodgson and Knudsen on the one hand and Witt *et al.* on the other agree on many more things. Witt [2007] argues that his CH and Hodgson and Knudsen's GD find common ground also in their endorsement of monism.[12] And, indeed, Hodgson's [2004] discussion of a layered ontology indicates that here too Witt and Hodgson are in basic agreement.[13] Instead of assuming that reality is partitioned into two (or more) separate, disconnected spheres, the notion of a layered ontology suggests that the whole of reality is ultimately or in essence one. The notion of a layered ontology implies that adjacent layers (or levels) of organization exist in reality. Adjacent layers are assumed to be connected to each other as wholes are related to their parts, so that all layers are related ultimately with the layer that is addressed by elementary particles physics. Firms are composed of individual human beings, human beings are composed of their organs (such as their brains), organs are composed of their cells (such as neurons), cells are composed of their molecules (such as genes) and so on, all the way down to elementary subatomic particles.[14] Hodgson argues that at higher levels there are emergent properties, properties that are absent at lower levels and that cannot be fully reduced to lower-level entities and their properties. Witt [2007] likewise argues that he endorses a non-reductionist monism.

Issues like these belong to yet another, third cluster. At stake here is what is the basic furniture of the world. The issues belonging to the third cluster can be called metaphysical issues. That metaphysical issues are different in kind than the issues belonging to the second cluster can be nicely illustrated with the example of *intentionality*. The issue of how the capacity of intentionality evolved in the past (which belongs to the second cluster) differs from the issue of what (if any) is the material basis of the capacity of intentionality (which belongs to the third cluster). In both cases we can talk of the emergence of the capacity of intentionality, but the meaning of 'emergence' is different in each case. If we talk of the evolutionary origin of the capacity, we have a causal, diachronic sense of 'emergence' in mind. If we talk of the material basis of the capacity, we have a constitutive, synchronic sense of 'emergence' in mind [Bedau, 1997; Craver, 2007]. Similarly, if we look

[12]Witt seems to conflate ontological monism with methodological monism, however, when he argues that both the humanities and the sciences should aim at giving causal explanations of phenomena. Ontological monism does not imply such methodological monism (cf. Dennett's defense of taking the intentional stance).

[13]Hodgson [2002] calls evolution a multi-level process, suggesting that biological and economic evolution occur at different levels.

[14]This is not to suggest that the ways in which the components are organized (or arranged, or connected) may (and, indeed, presumably does) does not matter. Their organization surely do matter (cf. [Vromen, 2006]).

at the how economic and biological phenomena relate to each other from the metaphysical perspective of the third cluster, their connection is not causal, but constitutive.

Biological phenomena or the biological domain and economic phenomena and the economic domain are not seen here as mutually exclusive, which, as we saw, is presupposed by the adversaries Hodgson and Knudsen and Witt *et al.* alike, but rather as inclusive. Biological phenomena, pertaining to the levels of organs, cells and molecules, appear as parts of the phenomena that economists address, which typically are the higher levels of firms, industries, markets and whole economies.

Different sorts of ontological issues also surround the *routines* of firms. Nelson and Winter [1982] introduced routines as analogous both to the skills of individual persons and to the genes of organisms. Routines are characterized by Nelson and Winter as involving automatic rather than conscious, deliberate option selection, just as is the case with the exercise of skills, and as being durable or inert, just like genes. We saw that Hodgson and Knudsen likewise argue that routines are replicators in the economic domain, just as genes are paradigm cases of replicators in the biological domain. As will be spelled out in more detail below, Witt *et al.* disagree. The issue at stake here is one belonging to the first cluster: are there long-lived routines in the economic domain, and if so, do they have the properties in common with genes that Dawkins, Hull and others ascribe to replicators? Again, the shared presupposition is that the biological domain (with genes in them) and the economic domain (with routines, or other units, in them) are distinct, mutually exclusive domains of reality. This is quite different if we look at routines from a metaphysical (third cluster) point of view (cf. [Vromen, 2006]). Then the biological domain appears as part of the economic domain. Whether or not routines are similar to genes, all agree that if there are routines, their functioning involves the exercise by of certain skills of the individuals participating in the functioning of the routines, which in turn involves the existence and expression of certain genes in the individuals.

All the issues at stake in the three clusters can be called ontological. Yet they are different in kind. We saw that the relation between the biological and the economic domain is cast in a different light in each cluster. In the first cluster, biological and economic evolution are considered as distinct processes. Properties of biological and of economic evolution are compared with each other. Do biological and economic evolution have properties in common (and if so, what are these?), warranting a generic description of evolutionary processes? Hodgson and Knudsen's GD and Witt's CH both purport to provide such a generic description. Whether or not biological and economic evolution are connected with each, causally or otherwise, is not an issue here. This is clearly different in the second cluster. The issue of whether or not (and if so, how) biological and economic evolution are causally connected with each other takes centre stage here. Witt's CH speaks out on this issue: antecedent processes of biological evolution not only set the stage for more recent processes of cultural evolution (including economic evolution), but still constrain and influence ongoing processes of economic evolution. The issue of how the biological and economic domain are connected is also central in the third cluster. But here the connection considered is not causal, but constitutive (or componential). The entities in the biological domain appear here as being at a lower level of organization than (and hence to be parts of) the entities in the economic domain. Economic evolution is seen as a multi-level phenomenon, including rather than excluding biological phenomena.

*Are GD and the CH rivals, complements, both, or what?*

We saw that Hodgson and Knudsen's GD can be seen as a stance taken on an issue in the first cluster. Witt's CH can be seen as a stance taken on an issue in the second cluster. Thus seen, Hodgson and Knudsen's GD and Witt's CH are not direct rivals of each other. The direct rival of Hodgson and Knudsen's GD is Witt's self-transformation view on evolution, not his CH. Yet, Witt and members of his group at Jena criticize Hodgson and Knudsen's GD from the perspective of Witt's CH and present Witt's CH as a superior alternative to Hodgson and Knudsen's GD. What sort of opposition is there (if any) between Hodgson and Knudsen's GD and Witt's CH?

In Vromen [2004a] I argued that a particular stance taken on an issue in the one cluster typically does not commit one to take a particular stance on an issue in another cluster. Often there is independence between these. I suggested in particular that the CH and GD are compatible with each other. Contrary to what Witt *et al.* argue, acceptance of the CH need not imply the rejection of GD. The issue of whether there is one encompassing continuous causal chain leading to the evolution of human intelligence (belonging to cluster II), for example, seems to be orthogonal to the issue of whether the Darwinian triple is well-suited to grasp the dynamics of cultural systems (belonging to cluster I). Taking a stance on the first issue does not seem to prejudge the stance to be taken on the second issue.

This seems to be precisely the stance that Hodgson and Knudsen take. Hodgson and Knudsen do not take issue with Witt's CH. In this sense the debate between Hodgson and Knudsen and Witt *et al.* is asymmetrical. Whereas Witt et al. criticize Hodgson and Knudsen's GD, Hodgson and Knudsen do not criticize Witt's CH. In fact, Hodgson [2002; 2004] himself endorses a Darwinian doctrine of continuity.[15] This doctrine implies among other things that intentionality cannot be an uncaused cause. Hodgson argues that Darwinism implies that intentionality is caused in antecedent evolutionary processes. Intentionality can be called a proximate cause of human behavior; a cause produced by an ultimate cause such as natural selection [Mayr, 1961]. Hodgson's doctrine of continuity resembles Witt's CH in that both take as their starting-point the view that whatever exists is the product of antecedent evolutionary processes, either biological ones, cultural ones or a combination of both.

[15]Hodgson [2002] suggests that Darwinian ontology is related to Darwin's unflinching commitment to causal explanation rather than to Darwin's three principles of evolution through natural selection.

Hodgson seems to be right in arguing that the latter view does not rule out that ongoing cultural (and in particular economic) processes can be explained accurately with the Darwinian principles variation, replication and selection. In particular, the capacity to act intentionally that supposedly plays a large role in cultural evolution does not necessarily invalidate the applicability of the three Darwinian principles. Indeed, as many have argued (cf. [Hull *et al.*, 2001]), certain forms of human learning can be analyzed with the three principles at an abstract and general level. Sometimes Witt seems to suggest not only that the three principles are applicable only to biological evolution, but also that the products of biological evolution are limited to genetically programmed behavior (thereby ruling out more sophisticated forms of intentional action). To Hodgson and other proponents of GD this is question-begging. This is exactly what they deny. The whole point of GD is that the applicability of the three Darwinian principles is *not* limited to biological evolution and to genetically programmed behavior.

Yet, it would be premature to conclude that Witt's CH and Hodgson and Knudsen's GD are compatible. On closer inspection Witt's CH turns out to be richer, or more substantive in terms of ontology than Hodgson's doctrine of continuity. Hodgson's doctrine of continuity only involves the commitment to the idea that all causes acting now are the effects of causes acting previously. Witt's CH involves more than this. What Witt adds to this in his CH is the hypothesis that the genetic material that antecedent processes of biological evolution endowed us with has remained pretty much the same since processes of cultural evolution started long time ago. Witt furthermore argues that the specific cognitive and behavioral repertoire based on this genetic material has given rise to a dynamics of cultural evolution that is distinctly non-Darwinian. As Cordes puts it, "Darwinian theories of evolution are suited to explain the natural origins of, for example, human learning, intentionality and deliberative behavior, but they are ill-suited to grasp the dynamics of cultural evolution that is based on these evolved cognitive capabilities." [Cordes, 2006, 539]. The claim of Witt *et al.* is that antecedent Darwinian processes of biological evolution produced cognitive and behavioral dispositions in humans that paved the way for recent and ongoing non-Darwinian processes of cultural evolution to take off.

Witt argues among other things that our evolved cognitive and behavioral dispositions enable us to anticipate future (possibly disastrous) selection effects and to devise strategies to forestall them. Thus unlike Darwinian biological evolution, in which mechanisms for creating new variation and mechanisms for selection are assumed to work independently of each other, cultural evolution is characterized by systematic feedbacks between selection and variation. Likewise, Witt [2003] argues that the Darwinian assumption of "blindness" or "randomness" in the processes of variation does not do justice to human intuition and creativity in cultural evolution.

Cordes [2006] spells out in detail many more differences between biological and economic evolution. Cordes argues that the notions of replication and of replicator are especially problematic in the economic domain. There simply are no credible examples of replicators in the economic domain (and the same holds for generations and lineages). Furthermore, perfectly in line with the CH and also with Boyd and Richerson's work on cultural evolution [Boyd and Richerson, 1985; Richerson and Boyd, 2005], Cordes argues that social transmission in cultural evolution is biased by a host of biologically pre-evolved cognitive dispositions. Hence, high-fidelity copying, which is at the heart of the notion of replication, is the exception rather than the rule in cultural evolution. Biologically pre-evolved psychological mechanisms also play an important role in cultural selection. They might underlie the choice of whom to imitate, for example. Boyd and Richerson suggest that conformist and prestige-based biases in imitators (and, more generally, social learners) play a key role here.

Cordes seems to be right in arguing that especially the notions of replication and replicator do not fit cultural and economic evolution very well. As Hull himself argues, "Replication is inherently a copying process. Successive variations must in some sense be retained and then passed on" [Hull *et al.*, 2001, 514]. There is quite some evidence mounted suggesting that the notion of copying captures not even approximately what is going on in social learning and social transmission. The socially learning individual (or the receiver of cultural information) often has a specific interest in what he wants to learn; an interest that often differs from the senders of cultural information (teachers, e.g.). And even in cases in which the interests of senders and receivers coincide and in which the receiver (or learner) has an interest in making faithful copies, the fidelity in social transmission is often severely compromised by pre-evolved psychological mechanisms [Sperber, 1996; 2000; Wimsatt, 1999; Sterelny, 2006]. Note that Sperber's insights seem to be congenial to especially Cordes's views on the implications of Witt's CH.

Hodgson and Knudsen take over Nelson and Winter's [1982] suggestion that routines of firms are similar to the genes of organisms. Hodgson and Knudsen [2004] take this to mean that routines are similar to genes in the sense that both are replicators. With their routines as genes analogy, Nelson and Winter never wanted to suggest that routines are as faithfully copied by firms as genes are inherited by offspring, however. Nelson and Winter do not deny that firms sometimes engage in attempts to imitate routines of successful other firms. But they stress that these attempts are bound to lead to mutations rather than to faithful copies (see also [Winter and Szulanski, 2001]). What Nelson and Winter really wanted to establish with their routines as genes analogy is that just like genes routines tend to be long-lived rather than short-lived:

> While Winter and I [1982] referred to organizational routines as like the genes of an organization, what we largely meant was that they were what gave constancy and durability to organizational behavior, not that they were easily transferable to, or replicable by, other organizations. [Nelson, 2007, 90]

Nelson and Winter argue that once routines emerge in firms they tend to be stable and robust.[16] Routines tend to survive personnel turnover and sometimes even survive deliberate attempts by top management to change them.

Thus the notions of replication and replicator seem to be ill-suited to do justice to economic evolution. Hodgson and Knudsen's decision to give more substance to their Darwinian triple by requiring that replicators and interactors are to be identified is all the more remarkable given that there does not seem to be a compelling conceptual or theoretical reason to require this. Godfrey-Smith [2000] argues convincingly that replicators are not essential for evolution through natural selection to occur. There can be evolution by natural selection without entities that satisfy Hull's definition of 'replicator'. It is enough for evolution through natural selection to occur if offspring resemble (in the relevant respects) their parents more than other organisms in the population.

*Interdependencies between stances taken on issues in different clusters*

It now seems that even though Hodgson and Knudsen's GD and Witt's CH are stances taken on different issues, they do bear upon each other after all. Pre-evolved psychological mechanisms bias processes of cultural and economic evolution in such a way and to such a degree that Hodgson and Knudsen's notions of replication and replicator do not fit cultural and economic evolution. This shows that there can be interdependencies rather than independencies between stances taken on issues in different clusters.

Another example of such an interdependency is provided by the so-called major transitions in evolution [Maynard Smith and Szathmary, 1995; Michod, 1999]. Many take the existence of several layers or levels of organization in reality stipulated in the layered ontology (cluster III) simply for granted. But it has not always been like that. In evolutionary time, higher levels of organization emerged only recently. It took major transitions for higher levels to evolve. Solitary replicators first had to coalesce into networks of replicators enclosed in compartments. Subsequently unlinked genes had to evolve into chromosomes. Next prokaryotic cells had to give way to eukaryotic cells, single-celled organisms had to be transformed into multi-celled organisms until finally colonies arrived on the scene. According to Maynard Smith and Szathmary this is how new levels of organization have come into being. After each transition, entities that were capable of independent replication before the transition can replicate only as part of a larger whole. They leave open the possibility that other major transitions are yet to occur and that other major transitions in fact already occurred.

In terms of my three clusters of ontological issues, major evolutionary transitions belong to cluster II. Hypotheses about what major evolutionary transmissions already took place have implications for stances that can consistently be taken on

[16]This suggests that Campbell's [1965] 'retention' is befitting economic evolution better than 'replication'. Retention also seems to fit Vanberg's [2002] 'program-based explanation' better than replication. See also Stoelhorst and Hensgens [2007].

issues in cluster III. Only those levels of organization can be considered to be part of the layered ontology that evolved after a major transition.

As Okasha [2006] points out, major transitions also have consequences for how we think about group selection and, more generally, about multi-level selection. Okasha makes a useful distinction between two different conceptions of group selection. One conception is derived strictly analogously to individual selection. Lewontin's [1970] characterization of evolution through natural selection in terms of the three principles phenotypic difference, differential fitness and heritability is transposed to the group level. Groups must satisfy the three principles for group selection to occur. This means in particular that collective group fitness is measured in the (expected) number of offspring groups that the groups in some population leave. One would perhaps expect that this conception of group selection, which is strictly analogous to individual selection, would dominate the discussion. But this is not the case. The conception of group selection dominating the discussion is the one that is revitalized by Sober and Wilson [1998]. In Sober and Wilson's conception, the collective fitness of groups is not measured in terms of the (expected) number of their "offspring" groups, but as the aggregate fitness of their constituent particles (i.e., the individuals in them). Groups are not treated as Darwinian units in their own right, but as parts of the environments for the individuals in them. Sober and Wilson's conception of group selection can be epitomized as "population structure matters". The way in which populations are partitioned in groups (defined minimally in interactional terms as sets of individuals that interact at least once, where the interactions must have fitness consequences for the individuals) partly determines what evolves.

Okasha suggests that for major transitions to get off the ground there must be group selection in the second sense. For groups to emerge as a genuine collective,[17] competition between their parts must be suppressed. This can only happen if populations have the right structure. But once groups have emerged as cohesive and integrated wholes, group selection of the first kind comes into play. Although it might be a bit farfetched and premature to try to draw conclusions from Okasha's insightful discussion for our thinking about multi-level selection in economic systems, it seems that firms often do display the degree of cohesiveness and integration that is needed to get group selection in Okasha's first, substantive sense started. Hodgson and Knudsen seem to be right that firms often are interactors in Hull's sense. This implies that economic evolution is multi-level, with firm selection being similar to Okasha's group selection in the first sense. But it took something group selection in the second Sober and Wilson type for firms to evolve as interactors.

### *Are GD and the CH compatible after all?*

Let us now return to the debate between Hodgson and Knudsen's GD and Witt's CH. We just concluded that Witt and Cordes seem to be right in arguing that

[17] Note that this involves a more substantive notion of a group than Sober and Wilson's.

Witt's CH, which is ontologically speaking richer than Hodgson's doctrine of continuity, implies that Hodgson and Knudsen's GD does not fit economic evolution. How do Hodgson and Knudsen respond to this? One might expect Hodgson and Knudsen to reply that what Witt adds to Hodgson's doctrine of continuity (which, we saw, is compatible with Hodgson and Knudsen's GD) is mistaken. And indeed, Hodgson and Knudsen do seem to have reservations about Witt *et al.*'s hypothesis that allegedly unchanging products of antecedent biological evolution still have a large causal impact on ongoing economic evolution. The overall thrust of their response is not to deny the differences that Witt *et al.* observe between economic and biological evolution, however. They argue instead that these differences do not impair the usefulness (and , indeed, even the necessity) of invoking the three Darwinian principles in explanations of processes of economic evolution.

Perhaps somewhat surprisingly Hodgson and Knudsen subscribe to many, if not all the differences between biological and economic evolution that Witt et al. identify. They furthermore agree that the differences are significant. They recognize that intentionality, intelligence and learning processes, which are mostly absent in biological evolution, play an important role in economic evolution. Hodgson and Knudsen [2008] also note that replication in economic evolution is quite unlike replication in biological evolution. Replication in biological evolution is direct, while replication in economic evolution is indirect and inferential (i.e., it works via the observation of the behavioral consequences of replicators). Hodgson and Knudsen also agree that social transmission has lower fidelity than genetic inheritance. Yet they maintain that all these differences do not invalidate the use of their Darwinian triple. They argue that all these differences are differences in details that are irrelevant for assessing the suitability of the (allegedly) domain-unspecific Darwinian principles [Hodgson, 2007]. The differences only become relevant if one adds domain-specific to the (alleged) domain-unspecific Darwinian principles to arrive at full-fledged explanatory theories and explanations in biology and economics, respectively.

Thus in their interpretation of the three Darwinian principles, Hodgson and Knudsen are trying to get rid of many connotations that are commonly attributed to the principles. This they do to accommodate the many significant differences between biological and economic evolution. In their attempt to show that the principles are truly domain-general, they are driven to rather extreme levels of abstraction. The price they have to pay for this, however, is (as Cordes [2007] correctly notes) that the principles are emptied from virtually all of their content. It is hard to see how principles that are practically devoid of any content could give much guidance in the construction of full-fledged domain-specific theories and explanations [Vromen, 2007]. Almost all the substance that is needed to arrive at full-fledged causal explanations of concrete processes of economic evolution must come from elsewhere and the three principles are not of much help in finding or constructing this domain-specific substance.

Summing up now, in the foregoing discussion three stages can be distinguished with respect to the issue of whether Hodgson and Knudsen's GD and

Witt's CH are compatible with each other. In the first stage, we saw that Hodgson is right that his GD and his doctrine of continuity are compatible. If continuity means nothing more than that every proximate cause is the effect of an ultimate cause, then continuity does not rule out the possibility that the three Darwinian principles are well-suited to explain ongoing cultural evolution. We also saw that Witt's CH entails a richer ontology than Hodgson's doctrine of continuity, however. What Witt adds to Hodgson's doctrine of continuity is the hypothesis that antecedent processes of biological evolution have endowed humans with a cognitive and behavioral repertoire that makes cultural evolution significantly different than biological evolution. Indeed, these differences are so vast that the Darwinian principles (replication, in particular) seem to be ill-suited to explain cultural evolution. Thus in this second stage Hodgson and Knudsen's GD and Witt's CH appear to be incompatible. Yet in the third and final stage we saw that Hodgson and Knudsen agree with the differences between biological and cultural evolution that Witt *et al.* identify on the basis of Witt's CH. Accordingly, in their interpretation of the three Darwinian principles, Hodgson and Knudsen are prepared to dispense with connotations that are commonly associated with the principles but that they agree do not fit the economic domain. What is left is an even further watered-down version of GD that is compatible with Witt's CH.

## *Other possible uses of Darwinism*

Where does this leave us? It is not just that as a result Hodgson and Knudsen's GD is virtually devoid of content. It is also possible that in the end the same causal-etiological explanations are arrived at, whether we start from Hodgson and Knudsen's GD or from Witt's CH. This also calls into question that as research programs they provide different heuristics. Above I argued that Hodgson and Knudsen's GD and Witt's CH are rivals in the sense that they steer further research in different directions. Hodgson and Knudsen's GD spurs researchers to do further investigations into how processes of interaction (with firms as examples of interactors in the economic domain) and of replication (with routines and habits as examples of replicators in the economic domain) interact to produce processes of economic evolution. Witt's CH invites researchers to look more closely into how ongoing processes of economic evolution build upon and are still constrained and causally affected by the products of antecedent processes of biological evolution. But this was based on the assumption that the three principles and notions such as interactors and replicators retain their original connotations. Now that we have seen that Hodgson and Knudsen get rid of many of their original connotations, it is no longer clear whether their GD gives any direction to future research at all. All the content should come from domain-specific data and hypotheses and the watered-down principles and notions are not very useful in gathering the domain-specific data and in constructing the hypotheses.

It seems Witt's CH fares better in this respect. Witt's CH seems to give more direction to future research efforts than Hodgson and Knudsen's watered-down

GD. The professed final aim of both Hodgson and Knudsen's GD and Witt's CH is to arrive at causal explanations of actual concrete evolutionary processes in the economy. Witt's CH gives more guidance to how to reach this aim than Hodgson and Knudsen's GD. Witt's CH specifies innate wants and non-cognitive learning mechanisms on the basis of which people are assumed to build learned or acquired wants, for example. But here it is left unclear how these substantive hypotheses about the cognitive and behavioral repertoire of human beings follow from or are explained by Darwinian theories of evolution. It is unclear how much work is done by Darwinian evolutionary theorizing in either identifying or explaining the human repertoire. In their attempt to specify the cognitive and behavioral repertoire of human beings, Witt and his group members draw on many sources (in social psychology, for example). They argue that Darwinian evolutionary theory is well-suited to explain ancient processes of biological evolution in which human learning, intentionality and deliberative behavior evolved. But they do not provide such explanations. Nor do they provide references to work of others in which such Darwinian explanations are given. That Darwinian evolutionary theory is able to explain these human cognitive capacities and dispositions is a promissory note rather than something that is actually shown.

This leaves us wondering what contributions Darwinism does have or could make to evolutionary economics. Both camps put their cards on the guidance that Darwinism could give to constructing full-fledged causal theories, either about ancient processes of biological evolution, of ongoing processes of economic evolution, or of both. But both camps have been found to be lacking in this respect. This forces us to further reflect on what contribution Darwinism could possibly make to evolutionary economics. I want to finish this paper by briefly outlining two other possible roles that Darwinism could play in evolutionary economics.

Darwinian evolutionary theory could help in seeing common patterns in already existing explanations, both inside and outside of evolutionary economics. What Darwinism then contributes would be an increased unification, integration and systematization of work already done in evolutionary economics and other fields of enquiry.[18] What would be gained is increased simplicity and coherence [Hull, 1988, 402]; see also [Hull *et al.*, 2001, 527]. Darwinism could help in organizing discussions by giving them more theoretical structure [Nelson, 2006]. Thus Darwinism could also help in constructing bridges between various behavioral disciplines and in making them more compatible [Gintis, 2007]. In doing so, it would facilitate cross-disciplinary work and also enhance the Darwinian movement [Mesoudi *et al.*, 2006, 346–347].

All this, I submit, gets close to what Kitcher [1993] has in mind with explanatory unification. Kitcher argues that Darwin's three principles provide a paradigmatic example of a general explanatory pattern (or schema) that has been enormously successful in unifying seemingly disparate phenomena. Darwin's principles unify the phenomena by showing that they are all instantiations of the same general

[18]Hodgson and Knudsen seem to also hint at this when they call Darwinian theory a metatheory.

explanatory pattern. The more phenomena we can show to be instantiations of the same general pattern and the fewer the principles in the explanatory pattern, the greater the explanatory power of the pattern. Kitcher contrasts his notion of unification-as-explanation with causal-etiological explanation,[19] the sort of explanation that Hodgson, Knudsen and Witt think Darwinism should be conducive to.

Another possible use to which Darwinism can be put is to construct hypotheses about end-product of evolutionary processes. More specifically, Darwinism can be helpful in generating hypotheses about specific cognitive capacities, dispositions and heuristics. This is how Darwinism is actually used in for example evolutionary psychology [Cosmides, Tooby and Barkow, 1992]. Evolutionary psychology identifies specific evolutionary problems and pressures that our ancestors were confronted with in the so-called Environment of Evolutionary Adaptedness and then formulates hypotheses about specialized mental modules (or psychological mechanisms) in the human mind that supposedly evolved to solve them. Subsequently the hypotheses are put to empirical tests. There is a similar tradition in economics, starting with Becker [1976], that uses Darwinism to construct hypotheses about what basic preferences we have (see, for example, also [Guth and Yaari, 1991; Bolton and Ockenfels, 2000]. More recently, neuroeconomists started to take recourse to Darwinism to formulate hypotheses about the computations and firing rates of groups of neurons [Glimcher, 2003; Ross, 2005].

At first sight, this might resemble the use to which Witt wants Darwinism to be put. Witt [2007] takes the fact that evolutionary economists regard new developments in evolutionary psychology and cognitive science as a hopeful sign that there is support in the evolutionary economics community for his own CH rather than for Hodgson and Knudsen's GD. But it seems that Witt sees the role of Darwinism as limited to explaining already and independently identified cognitive dispositions. By contrast, the theoretical movements just alluded to want to use Darwinism as an engine to find out about the cognitive machinery of human beings. Furthermore, the specific sorts of cognitive dispositions that Witt ascribes to human beings might not be supported by Darwinism-as-an-engine for constructing hypotheses about the human mind and brain. Sometimes it seems Witt still works with traditional dichotomies (wants and dispositions are either innate and genetically encoded or are learned or culturally acquired) that evolutionary psychology wants to overcome [Cosmides and Tooby, 1992], for example.

In perhaps the most sustained attempt to see what implications Darwinism has for how the human cognitive machinery looks like to date, Sterelny [2003] argues that "... we have evolved wiring-and-connection features that are something like, but not perfectly like, beliefs and preferences as portrayed by intentional psychology" (10). We have evolved separate systems for representing preferences and beliefs, Sterelny argues, that are more sophisticated than just physiological drives or instincts and specific environmental triggers respectively. Furthermore,

[19]But see Darden and Cain [1989] and Skipper [1999] for a counter-argument that Darwin's principles are used in Darwinism to construct causal-mechanistic explanations.

the connections between the two systems are not fixed but flexible. Beliefs do not directly code for specific behaviour, for example. This seems to come close to how decision theory depicts human behaviour. But Sterelny does not believe that decision theory is vindicated. What he takes from various experimental findings is that our motivations are not stable across different contexts [Sterelny, 2004, 516–517]. Decision theory is not able to account for this rather radical form of context-sensitivity. It is not clear whether the views on the human cognitive machinery of Witt and his group members can accommodate the great context-sensitivity of human motivations observed and explained by Sterelny.

In short, the use that Hodgson and Knudsen and Witt *et al.* want to put Darwinism to, namely to use Darwinism as a point of departure for constructing causal-etiological explanations of economic evolutionary processes, is not the only use to which Darwinism might be put. What is more, there might be other uses to which Darwinism might be more profitably put. One such use is to use the three Darwinian principles to unify and integrate already existing explanations in various fields. Another use is to use Darwinism to construct new hypotheses about various parts of the human cognitive machinery.

## CONCLUSIONS

In the debate between Hodgson and Knudsen's GD and Witt's CH, the two positions are often regarded as rivals. It was argued that several sorts of ontological issues are at stake in the debate. One is about the properties that biological and economic evolution have in common. Hodgson and Knudsen's GD asserts that the Darwinian principles of variation, replication and selection aptly capture properties that biological and economic evolution share with each other. Witt and his Group members disagree. They argue that the Darwinian principles only fit the domain-specific properties of biological evolution. Their argument that the Darwinian principles do not fit economic evolution is based on Witt's CH. Yet, strictly speaking, Witt's CH addresses an ontological issue of a different sort than Hodgson and Knudsen's GD, namely how biological and economic evolution are causally connected. This issue is orthogonal to the issue of whether biological and economic evolution have common properties that is addressed by Hodgson and Knudsen's GD. Strictly speaking, the alternative to Hodgson and Knudsen's GD that Witt puts forward is not his CH, but his generic view on evolutionary systems as self-transforming systems.

Once we realize that Hodgson and Knudsen's GD and Witt's CH are not directly rivaling each other, the issue pops up how then we should think of the relation between them. Are they rivals nonetheless, are they rather compatible with each other or what? Witt and his group members argue that they are rivals nonetheless, while Hodgson and Knudsen believe that they are compatible. It was argued that the critical issue here is how much ontological substance and content is given to both Hodgson and Knudsen's GD and Witt's CH. If Witt's CH is taken to assert only that all the human cognitive capacities and dispositions at work in ongoing economic evolution are products of prior evolutionary processes, as Hodgson's own doctrine of continuity asserts, then Hodgson and Knudsen are right that their GD and Witt's CH are compatible. Witt and his group members argue that Witt's CH involves more than this, however. They argue that prior processes of biological evolution have endowed us humans with specific cognitive capacities and dispositions. These capacities and dispositions are argued to have given rise to a specific dynamics in economic evolution for which in particular Darwinian notions such as replication (and replicators) and selection are ill-suited. Hodgson and Knudsen do not counter this critique by dismissing the extra substance that Witt's CH adds to Hodgson's own doctrine of continuity, but by diminishing the ontological substance of their own GD. They purge the three Darwinian principles from several connotations that are commonly associated with the principles. This enables Hodgson and Knudsen to rescue their claim that their own GD and Witt's CH are compatible. But the price they have to pay for this is that it leaves their Darwinian principles with virtually no content.

The discussion culminated in a discussion of how useful the three Darwinian principles of variation, replication and selection can be for studying economic evolution. It is clear that if practically all the substance is removed from the principles, they are not of much help in collecting the substance that needs to be added to them in order to produce domain-specific causal explanations. Witt's hypotheses about the specific cognitive capacities and dispositions that natural selection allegedly has equipped us with seem to fare better in this respect. But here the problem is that Witt and his group members fail to make clear how these hypotheses are informed by Darwinism. Here again it is doubtful that Darwinism contributes a lot to studying economic evolution. The paper ended with a few suggestions about alternative uses to which Darwinism can be put in evolutionary economics.

## BIBLIOGRAPHY

[Becker, 1976] G. S. Becker. Altruism, Egoism, and Genetic Fitness: Economics and Sociobiology, *Journal of Economic Literature,* 14(3), 817-826, 1976.

[Bedau, 1997] M. Bedau. Weak Emergence. In *Philosophical Perspectives: Mind, Causation, and World, Volume 11.* J. Tomberlin, ed., pp. 375–399. Malden: Blackwell, 1997.

[Bolton and Ockenfels, 2000] G. Bolton and A. Ockenfels. ERC: A Theory of Equity, Reciprocity, and Competition, *The American Economic Review*, 90(1), 166-193, 2000.

[Bowles and Gintis, 2003] S. Bowles and H. Gintis. The origins of human cooperation. In *The Genetic and Cultural Origins of Cooperation*, P. Hammerstein, ed. Cambridge, Mass.: MIT Press, 2003.

[Boyd and Richerson, 1985] R. Boyd and P. Richerson, *Culture and the Evolutionary Process.* Chicago: University of Chicago Press, 1985.

[Buenstorf, 2006] G. Buenstorf. How useful is generalized Darwinism as a framework to study competition and industrial evolution?, *Journal of Evolutionary Economics*, 16, 511-527, 2006.

[Campbell, 1965] D. T. Campbell. Variation, Selection and Retention in Sociocultural Evolution. In *Social Change in Developing Areas: A Reinterpretation of Evolutionary Theory*, Barringer *et al.*, eds., pp. 19-49. Cambridge, MA: Schenkman, 1965. Reprinted in *General Systems*, 14, 69-85, 1969.

[Cordes, 2006] C. Cordes. Darwinism in economics: from analogy to continuity, *Journal of Evolutionary Economics, 16*(5), 529-541, 2006.

[Cordes, 2007] C. Cordes. Can a Generalized Darwinism be criticized? A Rejoinder to Geoffrey Hodgson, *Journal of Economic Issues* 41(1), 277-281, 2007.

[Cosmides and Tooby, 1992] L. Cosmides and J. Tooby. Cognitive adaptations for social exchange. In *The Adapted Mind: Evolutionary Psychology and the Generation of Culture*, Cosmides *et al.*, eds., pp. 163–228. New York, NY: Oxford University Press, 1992.

[Cosmides *et al.*, 1992] L. Cosmides, J. Tooby, and J. H. Barkow, eds. *The Adapted Mind: Evolutionary Psychology and the Generation of Culture,* New York, NY: Oxford University Press, 1992.

[Craver, 2007] C. Craver. *Explaining the Brain.* Oxford: Clarendon Press, 2007.

[Cziko, 1995] G. Cziko. *Without Miracles*: MIT Press, 1995.

[Darden and Cain, 1989] L. Darden and J. Cain. Selection type theories. *Philosophy of Science, 56*, 106-129, 1989.

[Darwin, 1859] C. Darwin. *On the Origin of Species by Means of Natural Selection, or the Preservation of Favoured Races in the Struggle for Life*, London: John Murray, 1859.

[Dawkins, 1976] R. Dawkins. *The Selfish Gene* Oxford: Oxford University Press, 1976.

[Dawkins, 1983] R. Dawkins. Universal Darwinism. In *Evolution from Molecules to Man*, D. S. Bendall, ed., pp. 403–425. Cambridge: Cambridge University Press, 1983.

[Dennett, 1995] D. C. Dennett. *Darwin's Dangerous Idea*, Penguin Press, 1995.

[Fehr and Gächter, 2002] E. Fehr and S. Gächter. Altruistic Punishment in Humans. *Nature*, 415, 137-140, 2002.

[Foster, 1997] J. Foster. The analytical foundations of evolutionary economics: from biological analogy to economic self-organisation, *Structural Change and Economic Dynamics*, 8, 427-445, 1997.

[Frank, 1988] R. H. Frank. *Passions within Reason*, New York: W.W. Norton & Company, 1988.

[Gintis, 2007] H. Gintis. A Framework for the Unification of the Behavioral Sciences, *Behavioral and Brain Sciences*, 30, 1-61, 2007.

[Glimcher, 2003] P. M. Glimcher. *Decisions, Uncertainty, and the Brain: The Science of Neuroeconomics*, MIT Press, 2003.

[Godfrey-Smith, 2000] P. Godfrey-Smith. The Replicator in Retrospect. *Biology and Philosophy, 15*, 403-423, 2000.

[Güth and Yaari, 1991] W. Güth and M. E. Yaari. Explaining Reciprocal Behavior in Simple Strategic Games: An Evolutionary Approach. In *Explaining Process and Change: Approaches to Evolutionary Economics*, U. Witt, ed., pp. 23–34. Ann Arbor: University of Michigan, 1991.

[Hodgson, 2002] G. M. Hodgson. Darwinism in economics: from analogy to ontology. *Journal of Evolutionary Economics*, 12(3), 259-281, 2002.

[Hodgson, 2004] G. M. Hodgson. Darwinism, causality and the social sciences, *Journal of Economic Methodology,* 11(2), 175-194, 2004.

[Hodgson, 2007] G. M. Hodgson. A response to Christian Cordes and Clifford Poirot, *Journal of Economic Issues,* 41(1), 265-76, 2007.

[Hodgson and Knudsen, 2004] G. M. Hodgson and T. Knudsen. The firm as an interactor: Firms as vehicles for habits and routines, *Journal of Evolutionary Economics,* 14(3), 281-307, 2004.

[Hodgson and Knudsen, 2006] G. M. Hodgson and T. Knudsen. Why we need a generalized Darwinism, and why generalized Darwinism is not enough, *Journal of Economic Behavior & Organization, 61*(1), 1-19, 2006.

[Hodgson and Knudsen, 2008] G. M. Hodgson and T. Knudsen. Information, Complexity and Generative Replication, *Biology and Philosophy* 43(1), 47-65, 2008.

[Hull, 1981] D. L. Hull. Units of Evolution: A Metaphysical Essay. In *The Philosophy of Evolution*, U. J. Jensen and R. Harré, eds., pp. 23-44, Brighton: Harvester Press, 1981.

[Hull, 1982] D. L. Hull. The naked meme. In *Learning, Development and Culture*, H. C. Plotkin, ed., pp. 273–327. New York: John Wiley & Sons Ltd., , 1982.

[Hull, 1988] D. L. Hull. *Science as a process: An Evolutionary Account of the Social and Conceptual Development of Science.* Chicago: University of Chicago Press, 1988.

[Hull, 2001] D. L. Hull. *Science and Selection: Essays in Biological Evolution and the Philosophy of Science*, New York & Cambidge, UK: Cambridge University Press, 2001.

[Hull *et al.*, 2001] D. L. Hull, R. E. Langman, and S. S. Glenn. A general account of selection: Biology, immunology, and behavior. *Behavioral and Brain Sciences, 24*, 511-573, 2001.

[Kitcher, 1993] P. Kitcher. *The Advancement of Science: Science without Legend, Objectivity without Illusions,* Oxford: Oxford University Press, 1993.

[Lewontin, 1970] R. C. Lewontin. The units of selection. *Annual Review Of Ecology And Systematics,* 1, 1-18, 1970.

[Mailath, 1998] G. J. Mailath. Do people play Nash equilibrium? Lessons from evolutionary game theory, *Journal of Economic Literature,* 36(3): 1347-1374, 1998.

[Maynard Smith and Szathmáry, 1995] J. Maynard Smith and E. Szathmáry. *The Major Transitions in Evolution,* Oxford: Oxford University Press, 1995.

[Mayr, 1961] E. Mayr. Cause and effect in biology, *Science* 134, 1501-1506, 1961.

[Mesoudi *et al.*, 2006] A. Mesoudi, A. Whiten, and K. N. Laland. Towards a Unified Science of Cultural Evolution, *Behavioral and Brain Sciences, 29*(4), 329-383, 2006.

[Michod, 1999] R. E. Michod. *Darwinian Dynamics: Evolutionary Transitions in Fitness and Individuality*, Princeton: Princeton University Press, 1999.

[Nelson, 2006] R. R. Nelson. *Economic Development from the Perspective of Evolutionary Economic Theory*: TTU Institute of Humanities and Social Sciences, 2006.

[Nelson, 2007] R. R. Nelson. Universal Darwinism and evolutionary social science. *Biology and Philosophy, 22*(1), 73-94, 2007.

[Nelson and Winter, 1982] R. R. Nelson and S. Winter. *An Evolutionary Theory of Economic Change*, Cambridge: Harvard University Press, 1982.

[Okasha, 2006] S. Okasha. *Evolution and the Level of Selection*, Oxford: Oxford University Press, 2006.

[Plotkin, 1994] H. Plotkin. *Darwin Machines and the Nature of Knowledge*, London: Penguin Books, 1994.

[Popper, 1972] K. R. Popper. *Objective Knowledge: An Evolutionary Approach*, Oxford: Clarendon Press, 1972.

[Ross, 2005] D. Ross. *Economic theory and cognitive science: microexplanantion*, the MIT Press, 2005.

[Skipper, 1999] R. Skipper. Selection and the extent of explanatory unification. *Philosophy of Science* 66 (*Suppl.*), S196-S209, 1999.

[Richerson and Boyd, 2005] P. J. Richerson and R. Boyd. *Not By Genes Alone: How Culture Transformed Human Evolution*, Chicago and London: University of Chicago Press, 2005.

[Sober and Wilson, 1998] E. Sober and D. S. Wilson. *Unto Others: The Evolution and Psychology of Unselfish Behavior*, Cambridge, Mass: Harvard University Press, 1998.

[Sperber, 1996] D. Sperber. *Explaining Culture: A Naturalistic Approach.* Oxford: Basil Blackwell, 1996.

[Sperber, 2000] D. Sperber. An objection to the memetic approach to culture. In *Darwinizing Culture*, R. Aunger, ed. Oxford: Oxford University Press, 2000.

[Sterelny, 2003] K. Sterelny. *Thought in a Hostile World: The Evolution of Human Cognition*, Oxford, Blackwell, 2003.

[Sterelny, 2004] K. Sterelny. Reply to Papineau and Stich, *Australian Journal of Philosophy* 82(3), 512-522, 2004.

[Sterelny, 2006] K. Sterelny. Memes Revisited, *British Journal for the Philosophy of Science, 57*(1), 145-165, 2006.

[Stoelhorst and Hensgens, 2007] J. W. Stoelhorst and R. Hensgens. *On the Application of Darwinism to Economics: From Generalization to Middle-Range Theories* (working paper), 2007.

[Vanberg, 2002] V. J. Vanberg. Rational choice vs. program-based behavior: alternative theoretical approaches and their relevance for the study of institutions, *Rationality and Society* 14, 7-53, 2002.

[Vromen, 2004a] J. J. Vromen. Conjectural revisionary economic ontology: Outline of an ambitious research agenda for evolutionary economics, *Journal of Economic Methodology, 11*(2), 213-247, 2004.

[Vromen, 2004b] J. J. Vromen. Taking evolution seriously — What difference does it make for economics? In *The Elgar Companion to Economics and Philosophy*, Davis *et al.*, eds., pp. 102-131. Cheltenham, UK: Edward Elgar, 2004.

[Vromen, 2006] J. J. Vromen. Routines, genes and program-based behaviour, *Journal of Evolutionary Economics* (special issue on *Evolutionary Concepts in Economics and Biology*, edited by Witt, U.), 16 (5), 543-560, 2006.

[Vromen, 2007] J. J. Vromen. Generalized Darwinism in Evolutionary Economics — The Devil is in the Details, *Papers on Economics and Evolution* #0711, Max Planck Institute of Economics, Jena, 2007.

[Vromen, 2009] J. J. Vromen. Evolutionary explanations in Economics. In *Oxford Handbook on Philosophy of Science on Economics*, H. Kincaid and D. Ross, eds. Oxford University Press, 2009.

[Wimsatt, 1999] W. C. Wimsatt. Genes, Memes and Cultural Heredity, *Biology and Philosophy,* 14, 279-310, 1999.

[Winter and Szulanski, 2001] S. G. Winter and G. Szulanski. Replication as Strategy. *Organization Science,* 12(6), 730-743, 2001.

[Witt, 1999] U. Witt. Bioeconomics as economics from Darwinian perspective, *Journal of Bioeconomics,* 1(1), 19-34, 1999.

[Witt, 2001] U. Witt. Learning to consume — A theory of wants and the growth of demand, *Journal of Evolutionary Economics*, 11(1), 23-36, 2001.

[Witt, 2003] U. Witt. Generic features of evolution and its continuity: A transdisciplinary perspective, *Theoria,* 48(18), 273-288, 2003.

[Witt, 2004] U. Witt. On the proper interpretation of 'evolution' in economics and its implications for production theory, *Journal of Economic Methodology*, 11(2) 125-146, 2004.

[Witt, 2007] U. Witt. Heuristic twists and ontological creeds: Road map for evolutionary economics, *Papers on Economics and Evolution* #0701. Max Planck Institute for Economics, Jena, 2007.

[Witt, 2008] U. Witt. Evolutionary economics and psychology, *Cambridge Handbook of Psychology and Economic Behavior*, Cambridge: Cambridge University Press, 493-511, 2008.

# PUBLIC CHOICE: A METHODOLOGICAL PERSPECTIVE

Hartmut Kliemt

## INTRODUCTION AND OVERVIEW

Political philosophy as a whole could be conceived as "philosophy of public choice". But traditional political philosophy should not be regarded as covering "public choice theory" as a whole. In our times "economic theories of politics", the so-called "new political economy" (for exemplary works see [Downs, 1957; Buchanan and Tullock, 1962; Olson, 1965; Brennan and Lomasky, 1993]) and more generally speaking the application of mathematical models of choice have added many insights into the "logic" and actual workings of public choice processes which go beyond those of traditional political philosophy. In the following I will discuss from a philosophical point of view analytic and explanatory theories of public choice making as well as some of the normative approaches in the constitutional political economy and social choice theory tradition. As opposed to a previous effort (see [Kliemt, 2004]) my emphasis will be more strongly on methodological and philosophy of science issues (from a critical rationalist stance as originally exposed in [Popper, 1934/2002, p. 10], summarised in [Albert, 1985] and applied paradigmatically to economics in [Albert, 1967]).

I will not introduce public choice theories in any detail (anybody interested can look that up in the authoritative survey [Mueller, 2003]). Also I will not survey the field of philosophy of science of economics (see for instance [Hausman, 1992/2003; Mäki, 2002]). As far as public choice theories are seen as economic theories applied to a specific domain the methodological considerations concerning economics in general apply. I will not present another introduction to the philosophy of science covering the more or less standard material but rather reflect philosophically on discussions that have emerged within certain "Virginian quarters" of the public choice society. In doing so the focus will be on both explanatory and normative theories of public choice processes.

The "theory of public choice" has attracted quite some interest in recent years (from now on I will use "public choice" for the thing itself while reserving capitalized "Public Choice" for the theory of public choice). But the philosophy of science of Public Choice has not been the focus of any extended specialised interest – at least none that I am aware of. Since a lack of methodological unrest is one of the signs of the maturity of a field of inquiry this is, at least in a way, a

Handbook of the Philosophy of Science. Volume 13: Philosophy of Economics.
Volume editor: Uskali Mäki. General editors: Dov M. Gabbay, Paul Thagard and John Woods.

good sign. The established "paradigm" (in the encompassing sense of that term, see [Kuhn, 1962]) or the "Denkstil" (of Kuhn's forerunner, [Fleck, 1935/1980]) is not challenged all the time and results are evaluated according to the *internal* standards of the discipline (the "do and do not" norms of the trade in the sense of [Lakatos, 1978]) which are more or less those of the "maximisation subject to constraints" framework of neo-classical economics.

Along with game theory, Public Choice has been one of the two most impressive theoretical developments in modern economics of the second half of the last century. And as an admirer of its accomplishments I do acknowledge that a firm neo-classical economics perspective was the basis of most of modern Public Choice's successes. But from a methodological point of view I remain unconvinced of the maximisation framework and other fundamental assumptions of Public Choice.

The violation of local maximisation and the sub-game perfectness requirements going along with it are pervasive (see on the original insights [Schelling, 1960/1977; Selten, 1965]). And the original ultimatum game experiments (see [Güth *et al.*, 1982]) along with other results of experimental economics dealt a lethal blow to homo oeconomicus classicus as an empirically valid explanatory hypothesis. But those working in Public Choice, though often critical themselves of certain aspects of the maximisation framework, as researchers in other fields tend to "close ranks" if they face such criticisms. And they tend to be even more firm if criticism comes from outside economics.

A particularly important and instructive case in point is the discussion of one such criticism by Dennis Mueller (see [Mueller, 2003, chap. 28]). Defending Public Choice against attacks on its core assumptions of rational choice making (see for some more recent examples of that genre [Hogart, and Reder, 1987; Green and Shapiro, 1994; Friedman, 1996]), Mueller insists that rational actor theory need not presuppose selfish motivations (nor fixed preferences as in [Stigler and Becker, 1977]) but can be open as far as the specification of the objective function is concerned (see already [Mueller, 1986]). As long as the objective function is treated as given and maximisation relative to the given ends is assumed we are still in neo-classical economics. Allegedly no fundamental reform of the explanatory basis of Public Choice is necessary. After the underlying economics has been sent through the neo-classical repair shop we can go on with the maximization under constraints business as usual.

Mueller is in good company here. Responding in particular to the evidence of experimental economics more broadly specified objective functions became increasingly popular in economics in general (see most notably [Bolton and Ockenfels, 2000; Fehr and Schmidt, 1999] and earlier, both more speculatively and daring, [Frank, 1987], see for background also, [Camerer, 2003]). These rescue operations on homo oeconomicus are intellectually impressive and partly successful. They managed to transfer homo oeconomicus from the emergency room to the intensive care unit so to say. Whether the old boy will make it out of the ICU remains to be seen, though.

According to a more radical critique the maximisation hypothesis per se is the problem (a view inspired by [Simon, 1957]). This has led some eminent economists like Reinhard Selten to a fundamental rejection of the conventional rational choice paradigm in economics as an *explanatory framework*. Though developed without a special focus on public choice the general move in economic theory towards bounded rationality as opposed to full rationality in the maximisation framework (see [Selten, 1990; Gigerenzer, 2000; Güth, 2000]) may be of particular methodological relevance for Public Choice. A universal explanatory model to explain behaviour within rules as well as when creating and maintaining rules (see on this more extensively [Kliemt, 1987b; 1993]) requires some assumptions of individual norm-boundedness that are incompatible with individually rational forward looking choice behaviour. The fundamental maximisation subject to constraints paradigm must be given up in an appropriate account of public choice.

The preceding would eventually imply a fundamental shift in the perspective of Public Choice. In view of the fact, which I have already acknowledged, that the development of Public Choice on the basis of the maximisation framework has been a great success story such a suggestion seems to require a more extended account of what has been going on so far and why it should be changed now. In the first part of the discussion I will give my own critical account of the explanatory powers, functions and failures of Public Choice. I do so within a history of thought perspective which I think is most revealing for the methodological deficits of economic theories of politics as explanatory accounts of public choice (1) In the second part I will address what may be called normative Public Choice. Without further ado I accept the means-ends paradigm of rational normative argument according to which "on ends" the theorist must "remain silent" (established for economics in [Robbins, 1935] and for philosophy in [Hume, 1739/1978] — see also [Mackie, 1980; 1977; Harman, 1977]). Against the background of the "means to given ends" justificatory constraint it is then scrutinised to what extent there can be normative Public Choice within the constraints of such normative economic argument. Special attention is devoted to the Kantian undertones of Buchanan type Constitutional Political Economy and the often neglected difference between universality of and the unanimity in judgment (2) Very brief final comments wrap things up (3).

## 1 HOMO OECONOMICUS GOES POLITICS

### *1.1 Basic rules of the game of public choice and of Public Choice*

Public choices are not something made "in public", at least not necessarily so. Nor are these choices made "by the public" in any literal sense. Literally speaking "the public" is not a choice making entity. What renders "public choices" public are their potentially wide ranging external effects which tend to concern the public at large. But that does not amount to the presumption that there is a specific choice making entity whose involvement would separate public from other kinds of choices. Quite to the contrary like on markets, in the realm of politics, results *emerge* from choices of persons (or, perhaps, agents) but are not choices made *by* any person.

On markets and in politics individuals interact with each other according to certain "rules of the game". In this wide sense the concept of a "rule of the game" is taken as comprising causal laws (natural) as well as man-made (artificial) rules. As opposed to the Hayekian usage of terms which treats spontaneously emergent rules as "natural" (see [Hayek, 1973/1993]) rules need not be deliberately enacted to qualify as "artificial". The crucial point is that they are entities that would be otherwise if men acted otherwise (see related to this [Heinimann, 1987/1945; Buchanan, 1979]). Game theoretically speaking the so-called "rules of the game" comprise everything that is beyond the causal influence of the decision making entities *in* the game (thus including preferences and artificial as well as natural features of the situation as long as they are beyond the strategic influence of the players in plays *of the game considered*).

Adopting the broad use of terms as suggested by game theory we can say that if we could take together all the rules of the game (all that is beyond the strategic influence of actors in the game) we would get a characterisation of the "game of life" in full. According to this view "public choice" is a particular "part" of "the game of life". It is the game we are playing when we "play politics".

Since the behaviour of human individuals is always what it is, human behaviour, Public Choice insists on using the same model of behaviour throughout. Whether it be political or other behaviour, its explanation should be based on a *universal* explanatory model for which the "rules of the game" are antecedent clauses while the model of individual behaviour as such must be the same across games (which of course does not rule out that some rules of a lower order game are to be explained as emergent or artificially created in a higher order game).

Beyond the requirement of universality of the basic explanatory model of individual behaviour which seems to me impervious to criticism Public Choice traditionally makes the *additional* assumption that neo-classical homo oeconomicus is in fact the empirically correct universal behavioural model. To the early theorists of Public Choice who mainly came out of economics this assumption may have seemed rather natural. But it is a much more precarious assumption than that of the universality of the behavioural model.

## *1.2 Public choice as a game*

The implications of the homo oeconomicus model began to be spelled out in more detail in non-co-operative game theory almost exactly when Public Choice started its rise. In all likelihood this is pure coincidence, yet one might argue that it makes very good methodological sense. There is one game of life with one type of rational individual populating that world. Specific results derive from the specific rules of partial or lower order specific games. Specific games like markets or voting in politics etc. are merely abstracted from the broader context to make them analytically tractable. But besides this the same methods can be applied to the various kinds of games. In short, homo oeconomicus plays all the games people play (alluding, of course, to [Maital and Maital, 1984]).

Though using the game metaphor may not seem too exciting it has stronger implications than often recognised. For, once an interaction is conceptualised as a game in non-co-operative game theoretic terms it is clear that the results of the interaction must be *emergent rather than chosen.* Single-handedly, players cannot "choose" results of a game. That this is so is the whole point of a strategic game conceptualisation of an interaction. Players in a game have full control over their individual moves but, except for special cases to which we tend to refer as "games against nature", no player has full control over results. Players therefore *cannot* "choose" *outcomes* of proper strategic games at least not in the non-metaphorical or narrow sense of *choosing* an option. In short, in the non-co-operative conceptualization of a strategic game the choice of a result is not among the options of choice — though choices of options lead to results.

For a most simple illustration consider a $2 \times 2$ matrix game. As in particular James M. Buchanan in his use of the metaphor of the $2 \times 2$ matrix game for "collective choice" has always insisted, the two players can not properly speaking "choose" a result. They can either choose a column — as column player — or a row — as row player. Each can choose one of the two moves open to each of them but none can choose one of the cells (see in particular [Buchanan, 1975/1996] and his earlier criticisms of the Social Choice paradigm as reprinted in [Buchanan, 1999]). None of the players can choose unilaterally a cell. This is impossible unless the other player were just a puppet on the strings of the choosing actor. Then the actor merely would play against "nature" rather than a strategic game against a co-player who herself is an independent centre of choice making.

In a strategic game individuals can, of course, rank collective results as might emerge for instance by means of a personal social welfare function (see below part 2.2. and also the discussion of the so called liberal paradox in the value ordering [Sen, 1996] as opposed to the game form conceptualisation as in [Buchanan, 1975/1996; Gaertner *et al.*, 1992; Sugden, 1994]). The insight that even in the most simple case of a $2 \times 2$ matrix game the results of a play of the game are not chosen but are necessarily emergent obviously extends to games with any number of players, moves, and strategies. Any conceptualisation of a social interaction in terms of non-co-operative game theory will imply it. The framework of non-co-operative game theory explicitly models all moves and thereby all causal influences of individuals on each other and their environment. It forms the most detailed and basic conceptual scheme for representing any form of social interaction.

Since public choice is a social interaction it is clear that a non-co-operative game account of it should be regarded as fundamental within Public Choice. As far as this is concerned it seems significant that Buchanan has always endorsed (non-co-operative) game theory as a conceptual tool of Public Choice (see in particular [Buchanan, 2001]). One should, however, bear in mind that classical or, to use Ken Binmore's (see [Binmore, 1987/88]) apt term, "eductive" (non-co-operative) game theory is not a behavioural theory at all but rather a "theory of reasoning about knowledge" (in the sense of [Fagin *et al.*, 1995]). The view that game theory "predicts" or "explains" what we observe in behavioural terms is, if we take these terms literally rather than merely metaphorically, quite far-fetched.

Buchanan's Constitutional Political Economy approach shares — without calling it by that name — to some extent the outlook of eductive game theory. But as he is quite well aware this stands in an uneasy relationship to explanatory science more narrowly and traditionally conceived (see [Buchanan, 1982]). Those who see Public Choice rather as an empirical behavioural science should be quite unhappy with Public Choice adopting the methods of "a logic of choice making". As far as explaining human behaviour — in a covering law sense of explanation (see [Hempel and Oppenheim, 1948]) — is concerned eductive theory has not much value. There are no behavioural laws or anything like such laws in it (or the latter must be added, see [Hempel, 1965/1970, essay 9]). The contribution of eductive game theory to forming an explanatory theory is exclusively that of a modelling tool or a language in which substantive theories can be precisely expressed ("Rational Choice Modelling" rather than "Rational Choice Theory", as defined in [Güth and Kliemt, 2007]). As opposed to that classical conceptualisations of Public Choice as formulated in Political Philosophy had some, albeit sometimes very moderate, substantive content.

## *1.3 The original economic theory of the rules of the game*

Within economics it is not sufficiently understood that there has been an economic theory of law long before the ascent of what we nowadays understand by the term "economic theory of law". The older economic theory of law originated in the works of Hobbes and Spinoza. These two early modern social theorists — and others in the same tradition — tried to explain all social phenomena in terms of the model of rational economic man or what we nowadays regard as opportunistically rational individual choice making. They were quite explicit in their requirement that not only "within rule choices" but also the existence of the rules themselves had to be explained in terms of the case-by-case rational choice making of homo oeconomicus. The following passage from Spinoza wraps this up nicely:

> "Now it is a universal law of human nature that no one ever neglects anything which he judges to be good, except with the hope of gaining a greater good, or from the fear of a greater evil; nor does anyone endure an evil except for the sake of avoiding a greater evil, or gaining a greater good. That is, everyone will, of two goods, choose that which he thinks the greatest; and of two evils, that which he thinks the least. I say advisedly that which he thinks the greatest or the least, for it does not necessarily follow that he judges right. This law is so deeply implanted in the human mind that it ought to be counted among the eternal truths and axioms.

> As a necessary consequence of the principle just enunciated, no one can honestly forego the right which he has over all things, and in general no one will abide by his promises, unless under the fear of a greater evil, or the hope of a greater good... Hence though men make promises with all the appearances of good faith, and agree that they will keep to their engagement, no one can absolutely rely on another man's promise unless there is something behind it. Everyone has by nature a right to act deceitfully, and to break his compacts, unless he be restrained by the hope of some greater good, or the fear of some greater evil." [Spinoza, 1670/1951, pp. 203-204]

As is well known such views were later challenged in particular by sociologists. They regarded all efforts to explain the existence of social order in terms of individually rational behaviour as utterly futile. Methodologically speaking the sociologists seem to have a point. Yet those who tend to think here exclusively of Talcott Parsons and what he called the Hobbesian problem of social order (see [Parsons, 1968]) should be reminded that the modern critics of the strict economic theory of law had precursors among the so-called British (see [Raphael, 1969]) and in particular the Scottish (see [Schneider, 1967]) Moralists themselves.

These precursors in fact showed the same weaknesses as their modern followers. For instance, the over-socialized model of man of some modern sociologists (see [Vanberg, 1975]) can be found in Shaftesbury already. He clearly went too far in emphasizing classical moral thinking as well as motives other than selfish ones in his reaction to the original Hobbesian approach. Nevertheless Shaftesbury had a point in his criticism of the Hobbesian model of rational expecting man (see on the latter [Meckling, 1976]). To explain the emergence of social order on the basis of the extreme assumption of case by case rational choice making seemed impossible.

David Hume (see [Hume, 1739/1978] and below 1.5) avoided the extremes and delivered what may be regarded as a kind of "new synthesis" of social thought. His approach is individualist and avoids the extreme egotism and pure case-by-case rationality. Hume's theory has room for both, norm orientation and future directed opportunism within a single model based on empirical psychological hypotheses. The model combines opportunism and commitment in a non-arbitrary way around Hume's core insight concerning "human nature".

According to this insight human beings are characterized by a "too strong" preference for what is closer than for what is more remote. This is true along the time dimension (Hume was aware of preference reversal problems due to non exponential discounting) and the social dimension (where we love our closer more than our more remote kin, friends etc.).

The natural preference for the near as compared to the more remote guides human natural responses. However, Hume had no clue, why the phenomenological brute fact that he observed prevailed. Though he, like Aristotle (see Physics, 198b), understood already the possibility of an evolutionary explanation and contrary to Aristotle thought of it as a plausible (see [Hume, 1779/1986]) rather than an absurd potential explanation of the emergence of order Hume was not Darwin.

It is the more surprising how close Hume came already to game theory and, for that matter, even evolutionary game theory.

As has been noted in particular by Michael Taylor (see [Taylor, 1976]), who was about the first to apply folk theorem logic (see for a survey of the state of the art at the time [Aumann, 1981]) explicitly to the Hobbesian problem, Hume already understood most of the game theoretic arguments without knowing any formal game theory (see also [Binmore, 1992]; my own extended defense of that claim and the Humean theory itself can be found in [Kliemt, 1985; 1987a]). Had Hume not been so clearly in favor of basing explanations of human behaviour on psychological hypotheses one could even refer to him as the first behavioural game theorist. And, after the ascent of evolutionary game theory since the 1980's social theorists almost across the board acknowledged that basic elements of their theory of the evolution of social order were anticipated to some extent in Hume's theory of conventions (see [Sugden, 1986] and later [Binmore, 1994; 1998; 2005; Skyrms, 1996]).

It may be worth re-iterating that the Humean as well as all other of the aforementioned responses to the Hobbesian problem are methodologically individualist. They use game theoretic models of interactive social situations which are based on individual choice. But all of them restrict to some extent future directed opportunism on the level of the individual. They impose a restriction on opportunism that moves them towards a bounded rationality rather than to a full rationality approach.

Even the folk theorem makes actors behave differently in view of structurally identical futures. Note, if you cut off finitely many initial rounds of an identical base game to be repeated indefinitely the remaining sequence is always still infinite and — except for "renumbering" – structurally identical. If another actor co-operated throughout *in the past* a conditional strategy may specify a co-operative response for this contingency while specifying a non-co-operative response for the other contingency of at least one non-co-operative past act. This is incompatible with strict future directedness of rational choice even in sub-game perfect super-game strategies (see [Güth *et al.*, 1991], on the stronger requirement of subgame consistency). For, if the future is structurally identical then strictly future directed behaviour should be identical.

However, even if we would disregard the preceding formal criticisms empirical ones would still stand. Even if we would concede that it is conceivable that social order might arise out of strictly opportunistic homo oeconomicus behaviour this is as a matter of fact not the way the world works. The individually rational pursuit of complicated super-game strategies may be useful to explore the realm of a conceivable possible world. However, it is empirically so far away from real human motivations that this potential explanation will always remain contrary to fact (instructively on potential explanations in a related context [Nozick, 1974]). A true explanation based on the laws that are in fact operative in human behaviour — instead of merely conceivable complicated strategies — will be "rational choice psychological" rather than "rational choice logical". It will be, so to say, "as is" rather than merely "as if".

However, economists are as reluctant when it comes to basing social science explanations on psychological hypotheses as are many sociologists. Though economists reject the methodological collectivism of the sociologists they stick to their own tradition of methodologically individualist rational choice explanations. They understand that in view of the information demands of the traditional logic of choice modeling their explanations are merely "as if". Yet they seem so afraid that their own discipline would have to become a branch of psychology should they give up on "the logic of rational decision-making" that they are willing to pay almost any methodological price for keeping psychology out and the maximization under constraints framework intact (for a forceful criticism of economics as a "logic of choice"; see [Albert, 1967/1998; 1985; 1988]).

The concerns of the economists are understandable to some extent. However the restriction of opportunism might come about, by means of introducing empirical psychological laws explicitly as foundational premises of economics or by some of the neoclassical repairs (as suggested for instance in [Bolton and Ockenfels, 2000; Rabin, 1993]) to reject the assumption of case by case optimal choice (in view of future consequences) is not a minor modification of the original economic paradigm. It is a major shift away from the core of the decision theoretic framework.

For Public Choice this shift means that we have to go against what seems the hallmark of the approach: its Spinozist streak. It forms a very serious methodological challenge for those who believe that Public Choice must be based not only on the assumption that individual behaviour is *across all contexts subject to the same empirical laws* but that it is of the homo oeconomicus type. To the extent that the "do nots" of Public Choice as a research program require not to violate the opportunism assumption of the homo oeconomicus model the most relevant methodological questions become: Can homo oeconomicus be defended against the attack of being without a behavioural foundation? Can homo oeconomicus be defended on grounds other than explanatory power? — I turn to these and related questions in the next section.

## *1.4 A role for homo oeconomicus nevertheless?*

Many economists seem still to believe that it is a sufficient defense of their "maximization subject to constraints" paradigm if individuals behave *as if* they were maximisers. However, this is convincing only if we can present the reason why we should empirically expect individuals to behave as if they were maximizing an objective function. Among several attempts to justify this as if assumption a particularly strong and elegant one is due to Armen Alchian (see [Alchian, 1950]).

In Alchian's evolutionary model firms without any foresight and understanding (in this regard they are like "zero intelligence traders" (see [Gode and Sunder, 1993]) follow fixed behavioural programs. There is a large pool of such firms all randomly endowed with one such program. Some of the programs are more successful (i.e. profitable) and thrive while others are unsuccessful and are gradually eliminated from the program-pool (it may be noted, though, that the zero intelligence traders are sufficiently intelligent already to make markets work). After sufficiently many rounds of such play only the well-adapted programs survive.

Alchian believed that surviving programs would behave as if they were opportunistically rational maximizers (for formulations in the same spirit, see [Nelson and Winter, 1982], for a fine criticism of the whole argument, [Radner, 1998; Smith, 2008, chap. 8], and for related aspects [Güth and Peleg, 2001]). Therefore, as the argument runs, it is legitimate to assume that individuals behave as if they were maximizers. Deriving predictions of human social behaviour on the basis of maximizing behaviour of homo oeconomicus seems justified ([Friedman, 1953/1966] provides a particularly distinct such methodological view).

However, note that the preceding evolutionary explanation of maximising behaviour treats this behaviour as an explanandum (the phenomenon to be explained) rather than an explanans (the explaining phenomenon). The homo oeconomicus model does not sum up empirical hypotheses that are used to explain. It is rather itself explained why the model works. To the extent that such explanations are successful they are interesting. However, they certainly do not corroborate the claim that the social world can be explained in terms of the homo oeconomicus model. They eliminate it or show how it can be eliminated from explanations.

If we give up, first, instantaneous and forward looking choice in favour of fixed programs and, second, the aim of explaining social phenomena in such terms then we get Lichtenberg's "knife without a grip that has lost its blade". Nothing is left of the original economic explanatory program. If this seems too harsh a verdict let us look at additional defenses.

### *1.4.1 Predictive instrumentalism*

Though evolutionary approaches are in themselves of great value they certainly do not have much punch in defending the assumption of rational economic man as an *explanatory* figure in economics. It might be argued, though, that the Homo oeconomicus model may be successfully applied to *predict* the outcomes of evolution. Beyond maximisation one cannot go and therefore the limit of evolutionary processes can be characterised by solving a maximisation problem. If evolution has time to run its course and if appropriate conditions prevail (see however again [Radner, 1998; Smith, 2008, chap. 8]) then the outcomes will be as if chosen by fully rational beings with unlimited computing abilities and the like. Many developments in evolutionary game theory seem to support such a view since, for instance, some of the more complicated and subtle equilibrium selection criteria can be justified in such a setting without relying on empirically outrageous assumptions about common knowledge and reasoning that have to be adopted in eductive game theory (see for instance [Damme, 1987]). But what does this exactly signify?

Since in the preceding Homo oeconomicus behaviour is used as an instrument of prediction the corresponding methodological view may be named "*predictive instrumentalism*". Schumpeter characterised the underlying basis of that kind of argument already in the following way:

> "The assumption that conduct is prompt and rational is in all cases a fiction. But it proves sufficiently near to reality, if things have time to hammer logic into men. Where this has happened, and within the limits it has happened, one may rest content with this fiction and build theories upon it ... and we can depend upon it that the peasant sells his calf just as cunningly and egoistically as the stock exchange member his portfolio of shares. But this holds good only where precedents without number have formed conduct through decades and, in fundamentals, through hundreds and thousands of years, and have eliminated unadapted behaviour. Outside of these limits our fiction loses its closeness to reality". [Schumpeter, 1959, 80]

According to this point of view the model of rational economic man cannot be used to explain. But it can be used to predict outcomes of long run evolution under sufficiently stable conditions. The assumption that such predictions as made by relying on the economists' maximisation assumption work must, however, itself be justified — i.e. explained — in terms of the evolutionary argument.

An analogous line might obviously carry over to Public Choice. If stable institutional conditions prevail for a sufficiently long time then evolutionary selection may do the trick of "hammering logic" even into political actors. Therefore under such conditions we would have good reason to assume that predictive instrumentalism may have some justification as a tool for Public Choice.

Since the evolutionary explanation of the process tells us why, it would not be a kind of miracle that such a predictive instrument based on cognitively omnipotent Homo oeconomicus works. Nevertheless, it should be noted, first, that this defence of instrumentalism is respectable only insofar as it is itself subject to a deeper explanation of why it does work in evolutionary terms. The true scientific explanation operating in the background is evolutionary and not in terms of the homo oeconomicus behaviour and strategic action. It should be noted, second, that if there is no repetition within a stable institutional framework such as to hammer the logic of rational behaviour by competitive selection into actors the previous argument seizes to be valid. If, as is most likely the case in politics, no appropriate feed back loops such as to select "as if maximizing" rational behaviour do exist the application of the model even for predictive uses loses its basis (and Lichtenberg sends his regards again).

#### *1.4.2 Low cost voting and other repairs*

That the model of *substantively egoistic* rational economic man cannot be defended on empirical grounds as applied to the realm of public choice is widely acknowledged nowadays. The perhaps most notable such acknowledgement is due to Brennan, Buchanan and Lomasky (see originally [Brennan and Buchanan, 1984] and later on in detail [Brennan and Lomasky, 1993]). They offer strong arguments why in such central concerns of Public Choice as understanding voting the assumption of maximising behaviour is particularly precarious if the objective function is substantively egoistic. Simultaneously with presenting their own criticism of substantive egotism in particular in low cost situations or behind the veil of individual insignificance [Kliemt, 1986] they try, however, to stick to the assumption of maximisation as a basic model of political behaviour. Like Mueller and many others leaning towards sending their model through the neo-classical repair shop they suggest that a broader objective function is maximised.

Now, the complaint that including factors other than the aim to increase material rewards into the objective function amounts already to "ad hocery" seems rather far fetched (pace [Stigler and Becker, 1977]). It would be just this if, for instance, for voting special motives would be assumed to operate while being assumed away in, say, market contexts. However, there is a fairly general theory of decision making in low cost situations that can be easily formulated. The behavioural model is general in that it stipulates that individuals will pursue certain aims going against material self-interest more often in low cost situations than in other situations. If their acts are rather inconsequential either due to low probabilities of having a decisive effect (see on this old theme in an exemplary way [Tullock, 1967] but also [Tullock, 1971]) or because it is only a very small effort that must be exerted against substantive self-interest then in general intrinsic motivations may prevail over extrinsic consequence based ones (on intrinsic motivation [Frey, 1997], on high and low stakes see for instance, [Slonim and Roth, 1998]).

I am quite sympathetic with such efforts and am leaning towards them myself in other contexts. The neo-classical repair shop has its own attractions (for my own sins as committed like most sins in a pair, see [Güth and Kliemt, 1994; 2000]), yet beefing up the objective functions as much as we like, in the end we will be stuck with the maximisation framework. And it is not maximisation of the satisfaction of given preferences that explains behaviour. The cognitive processes actually explaining what we observe are of a different nature.

### *1.4.3 Non-co-operative game modelling in agent forms*

The objection that nobody maximises but that everybody behaves only as if maximising is not good enough. For, it is still assuming that instead of looking at the actual psychological mechanisms we can explain behaviour referring to the so-called given preferences while leaving the processes of actual decision making in the dark, so to say. Again, this is not to deny that what is left in the dark could not be brought into the light, so to say, and be described explicitly in decision theoretic terms of the maximisation framework. If we push the modelling effort far enough we can describe whatever assumptions we want to make about human motivation by using appropriate modelling tools on the appropriate level. In particular if we are willing to split up individuals or persons into agents we can describe actions *as if* they result from the maximising behaviour of those agents.

But what these agents can and will in all likelihood do must be known to the theorist. Public Choice as an empirical theory of public choice must be done before it is cast in the basic language of non-co-operative game theory. Here non-co-operative game theory serves as a precise language to express theories about behaviour in social interaction. But what the most basic rules of games are and how they emerge must be answered by theories other than classical non-co-operative game theory. It is a tool of modelling but not a substantive theory about the world. The rules of the game including individual preferences can be *represented* in a non-co-operative game model but the content of what is modelled — including any behavioural assumptions — is *not* derived from game theory. The latter is entirely a matter of empirical findings that are represented in non-co-operative game language.

In particular the model of rational economic man and game theory stand in a much more uneasy relationship than is conventionally assumed. Since the preference representations by utility functions as the conventional game theoretic short hand can stand in for all kinds of preferences no selfishness assumption need be made in non-co-operative game modelling. Since all kinds of commitments can be explicitly modelled as *rules* of the game non-co-operative game theory does not rule out much on this end either. In short, the interactions represented in the language of games can be of all sorts.

To repeat, though game theory is called a "theory" non-co-operative game theory as rational choice modelling is in truth only a language to represent substantive theories about social interactions. As far as substantive theories are concerned practically nothing is ruled out by the structure of the language of non-co-operative game theory per se. Therefore very different substantive theories can be modelled in game theoretic language. Theories based on the Homo oeconomicus behavioural model as applied to institutional rules are one possibility. Accounts based on a model of genuine rule following behaviour form another — and as I shall argue more adequate — alternative of a substantive theory of individual behaviour and motivation.

If Public Choice is reduced to game theoretic or decision theoretic modelling of public choice then it is empirically speaking "content free". Nothing is ruled out. That may seem a devastating criticism of such Public Choice. But it is not. We all operate within the constraints of the feasible and public choice is so complex that the formation of general empirical Public Choice (theories) may be quite infeasible. In view of this it is a great merit of decision theoretic Public Choice as opposed to other forms of social theorising about public choice that it imposes its language requirements on all researchers. It is generally a great achievement once one succeeded to formulate a model of what is going on in precise decision or game theoretic terms. The explicitness requirements of the language force the theorist to make all the assumptions of his argument explicit and to state them in a transparent way. But he needs empirical propositions to create empirical content.

In this vein, coming back full circle to the theory of voting behaviour with which this discussion commenced, the assumptions about low as opposed to high cost behaviour, the perception of the situation and so on all must be made and be empirically supported. Once that is done we may try to derive testable hypotheses and also discuss the explanatory merits of the model. The latter will, however, be entirely due to the empirical input into the precise language and not to the content of the language. Using the language has instrumental value but it is not that of yielding predictions. In short, it is not instrumental to predicting something but only an instrument of formulating a prediction based on something other than the language.

Theorists like Brennan and Buchanan are in some ways admitting most of the previous (Buchanan perhaps even more so than Brennan) but they would still insist that there is a defence for making the assumption of maximisation of substantive more or less egoistic objective functions in Public Choice. It is most significant that they do so on grounds other than empirical truth. Homo oeconomicus behaviour is as Brennan and Buchanan argue (in particular in [Brennan and Buchanan, 1985]) a *contrary to fact* assumption that *should* be made for a special purpose. Let us refer to this position as "normative instrumentalism" since it justifies making the assumption of homo oeconomicus behaviour normatively.

### *1.4.4 Normative instrumentalism*

Normative instrumentalism has a long tradition that reaches back at least to – and certainly most prominently to – David Hume. Though Hume was well aware of the internal problems of a strict or Spinozist interpretation of the Hobbesian approach to social order and public choice he, like his modern followers, nevertheless went out of his way to defend some role for a strict economic behavioural model. He says "that, in contriving any system of government, and fixing the several checks and controuls of the constitution, every man ought to be supposed a knave and to have no other end, in all his actions, than private interest." [Hume, Essays, VI/I, 42]. Yet, as Hume himself observes, "it appears somewhat strange, that a maxim should be true in *politics*, which is false in *fact*." [Hume, Essays, VI/I, 42-43].

According to Hume's characterization of "normative instrumentalism" the Homo oeconomicus assumption in theory formation is an instrument to be utilised in our search for what may be called "knave proof" institutions. In theory we can get there more easily, thought Hume — and so did later Brennan and Buchanan — if we make the counter factual assumption of universal knavery. Though not all individuals are knaves in fact, to assume contrary to the facts that they are is useful. It will make it more easy to find adequate institutions that can resist behaviour of individuals who are not serving the public but only their private good.

The normative instrumentalist justification for the Homo oeconomicus model claims that the use of the model is warranted as a *pessimistic fiction* (see also [Schüssler, 1988]). It brings us to what may be regarded as the safe side in our policy prescriptions or towards proposing knave-proof social institutions and rules. We can thereby make policy prescriptions independent of assumptions about specific characteristics of the individuals who are in fact engaged in public choice.

This argument certainly has some initial plausibility and some merit. But Hume as well as his later followers do not take into account sufficiently that the greatest dangers for the common weal do not arise from selfishness but rather from unselfish behaviour in pursuit of an unworthy cause (see on this in particular [Arendt, 1951], but also Hume himself on the vices of "enthusiasm and superstition" in [Hume, 1777/1985]). In the end an empirically valid theory of human behaviour will be necessary if we intend to understand the mechanics of existing and to form better institutions. We must understand what the basic forces behind the emergence of the results of social interaction are. If this in the last resort amounts to laying psychological foundations for Public Choice (and for that matter for behavioural economics and behavioural game theory going beyond the impressive yet in the end still insufficient "repairs" in [Camerer, 2003]) what does it signify except that good old homo oeconomicus may be too imperfect to be relied upon anymore?

From a philosophy of empirical science point of view I regard the preceding criticisms as justified and therefore I do not think that I treat Public Choice unjust. It would, however, be unfair not to acknowledge that we can only work with the best theories that we have and the theories criticised before are clearly among the best. Rational choice models are extremely useful to structure our thinking about an exceedingly complex realm like public choice and they can serve as guidance in much of the empirical short range theorising by which we learn more about the actual world of public choice surrounding us. If done correctly much of the econometrics and fact finding by means of statistics is extremely helpful.

The structuring and fact finding contributions of Public Choice seem to me independent of the general theoretical behavioural model of homo oeconomicus (though it may be used for bechmarking as in experimental economics). They seem impervious to the general methodological criticisms of the "classical" paradigm of Public Choice as an explanatory discipline based on a universal application of the homo oeconomicus model. It seems, however, quite appropriate to finally compare the account of the game of public choice as given in Public Choice with the account of public choice in legal theory. From the legal theory point of view the focus is on the rules of the game of public choice rather than on within rule choices and on how the rules manage to exist. As far as I can see the model presented by legal theorists like Hume, Hart and Hayek is much superior to what is around in Public Choice. And this is so since the basic model of individual behaviour deviates in an essential aspect from opportunistically rational behaviour of homo oeconomicus (thereby developing the side of Hobbes that does not fit the bill of Spinoza's reading of Hobbes).

## *1.5 The refined theory of the rules of the public choice game*

That the economic approach to explaining public choice must be rejected becomes particularly clear if we take a closer look at the most fundamental problem of all public choice, namely that of how political power is constituted in society. As far as political power is concerned Hobbes himself noted already in his Behemoth that

"... the power of the mighty hath no foundation but in the opinion and belief of the people" [Hobbes, 1682/1990, 16]. And Hume went on to state:

> "Nothing appears more surprizing to those, who consider human affairs with a philosophical eye, than the easiness with which the many are governed by the few; and the implicit submission, with which men resign their own sentiments and passions to those of their rulers. When we enquire by what means this wonder is effected, we shall find, that, as FORCE is always on the side of the governed, the governors have nothing to support them but opinion. It is therefore, on opinion only that government is founded; and this maxim extends to the most despotic and most military governments, as well as to the most free and most popular. The soldan of EGYPT, or the emperor of ROME, might drive his harmless subjects, like brute beasts, against their sentiments and inclination: But he must, at least, have led his *mamalukes*, or *praetorian bands*, like men, by their opinion." [Hume, 1777/1985, essay iv]

The reference to opinion sounds somewhat similar to familiar sociological views on the role of internalised norms. The concept of "opinion" figures also as something akin to modern notions of commitment. In any event, as compared to the original Spinozist starting points of much of economic theory of politics and Public Choice it amounts to a major concession to allow for such aspects of individual choice making. From there on it is only a small step to introduce genuine rule following behaviour as an additional category.

Though this concession violates the classical homo oeconomicus model it can take place entirely within a methodologically individualist framework. It aims at a more adequate explanation of the existence of social and in particular legal order *within* methodologically individualist social theory. Focusing on rule following behaviour it factors in reasons other than those provided by the model of opportunistically rational behaviour. Once an appropriately enlarged psychological model of individually rational behaviour is introduced we may be in a much better position to explain and thereby to understand how power relations and political order emerge in society.

Modern political theory can provide an argument of the fundamental mechanics of power politics by relying on Herbert Hart's elaboration of Hume's theory (see also [Barry, 1981]). Hart distinguishes between two types of norms, secondary and primary ones (see [Hart, 1961]). The primary norms are those that directly require that certain things be done or omitted. Violations of such norms are enforced by sanctions, punishments and rewards. Even though norm compliant behaviour regarding primary norms will in all likelihood not be motivated in a case by case manner (as Spinoza suggested) it is clear that at least in some indirect way self-interest will enter explanations of why individuals comply with primary norms (see for a balanced account [Baurmann, 2002]). Secondary norms do not in the same way as primary norms depend on sanctions. They rather single out individuals who are *entitled (by the secondary norms)* to certain moves in the social game and due to this entitlement or the power bestowed by these secondary rules can modify the future course of the game of life in specific ways.

For illustration it may be convenient to briefly turn to the ancient issue of whether the powerful are powerful because we obey them or whether we obey them because they are powerful. It may not seem to clarify much that the right answer is: both. However, if we look in some more detail at why this is so, that answer becomes quite instructive. On the one hand, we obey the powerful because they have the means to impose sanctions. Hume's example of the Caesar of Rome who could treat his subjects like "beasts" fits here. The ordinary subjects obey their superiors because otherwise they will be punished, i.e. because the "few" in command of their legions have the power to impose punishments. But the question why the powerful are powerful in the first place is not answered by this. They are powerful because those individuals whom they have to "treat as men" and to guide "by their opinion" apply secondary norms. These norms single out the individual(s) whose signals will be followed.

It is impossible that in each and every instance all individuals will always calculate the expected costs and benefits of their "norm-compliant" or "non-compliant" behaviour. There is a disposition among sufficiently many sufficiently influential individuals (see [Marsilius, 1324/2001]) simply to apply the criteria or standards of a rule that entitles certain persons to issue certain orders. These *power conferring rules*, as they are also called, are essential in understanding the emergence of political order and in that sense of public choice. Neither their existence nor their observance can be explained fully in terms of opportunistically rational selfish choice making in a case by case manner. The *faculty* to adopt rules and to apply them from an "internal point of view" as standards guiding one's own behaviour is *not reducible* to case by case selfish choice making.

In a way, the sociologists may claim that they have said that all the time. But the details of rule following behaviour and how such behaviour enters into the constitution of a modern complex legal order require more than the rather simplistic model of norm internalisation popular among sociologists suggests. Moreover, the sociologists' claim that the existence of order is in some way proof that methodological individualism is mistaken is itself obviously mistaken since the theory proposed by Hume and Hart is purely individualist. That being said as a criticism of sociologists, the economists must be warned also that they cannot have it both ways: on the one hand, engage the pleasant task of bashing the sociologists with the economic model of case-by-case maximisation in hand and then, on the other hand, whenever it comes in handy explain rule following behaviour in terms of its advantages for the selfish actor. The latter "explanation" is only possible if individuals according to the model of individual behaviour applied *can* in fact follow rules and can commit in that sense to rules. For, only if they can do so, can they adopt rules that "overrule" case-by-case maximisation in pursuit of their selfish interests and thereby further their higher order or long term selfish interests (that individuals command that faculty is also pre-supposed in such explanations of rule following as in [Heiner, 1983]).

To illustrate this by the conventional metaphor, Ulysses can let the sailors tie him to the mast only because there is such a thing as a mast (sub-personal agents as in [Harsanyi and Selten, 1988; Elster, 1987; Ainslee, 1992; 2002] can be tied to internal masts modelling their commitments). As concepts like sub-game perfectness of promises and threats in game theory so clearly show the existence of such masts is nothing we can take for granted within a strict rational choice model (see, of course, again [Selten, 1965; 1975]). If a mast or its equivalent in a social interaction exists that must show up in the rules of the game (see on this also [Brennan and Kliemt, 1990]). Emphasising the model of opportunistically rational behaviour does not fit well with assumptions that individual commitments and individual commitment power can exist outside of the rules of the game (rules are the rules only because they are beyond individual choice making in the game characterised by the rules).

Without assuming that individuals can and will act in boundedly rational ways we cannot explain the existence of institutionally — artificially — created commitment power. Without the presence of some individual constitutional commitment power constitutional commitments on the social, the political and legal level cannot adequately be explained. The rules of the political game of public choice as endogenously created within the game of life cannot be understood adequately without the addition of some such assumptions. Here we must clearly go beyond conventional economic theory and Public Choice.

Economists like Hayek have done this all the time. In doing so Hayek did not only express the same basic truths as Hume and Hart. He joined them also in accepting the same solution of the old riddle of how power can be limited. With Hayek's own words:

> "The authority of a legislator always rests, however, on something which must be clearly distinguished from an act of will on a particular matter in hand, and can therefore also be limited by the source from which it derives its authority. This source is a prevailing opinion that the legislator is authorised only to prescribe what is right, where this opinion refers not to the particular content of the rule but to the general attributes which any rule of just conduct must possess...
>
> But the allegiance on which this sovereignty rests depends on the sovereign's satisfying certain expectations concerning the general character of those rules, and will vanish when this expectation is disappointed. In this sense all power rests on, and is limited by, opinion, as was most clearly seen by David Hume.
>
> That all power rests on opinion in this sense is no less true of the powers of an absolute dictator than of those of any other authority. As dictators themselves have known best at all times, even the most powerful dictatorship crumbles if the support of opinion is withdrawn. This is the reason why dictators are so concerned to manipulate opinion

> through that control of information which is in their power...
>
> There is thus no logical necessity that an ultimate power must be omnipotent. In fact, what everywhere is the ultimate power, namely that opinion which produces allegiance, will be a limited power, although it in turn limits the power of all legislators. This ultimate power is thus a negative power, but as a power of withholding allegiance it limits all positive power." [Hayek, 1973-79, vol.1, 92 f.]

In view of the preceding it seems entirely clear that Hayek had an adequate view of how a great, political society can work at all. It is, however, also clear that the account is not in line with the basic economic approach to human behaviour as adopted in standard Public Choice. The Hayekian account of public choice is not in terms of homo oeconomicus but rather in terms of a model of boundedly rational behaviour albeit one that is still lacking a solid foundation in empirical psychology of rule following behaviour and its limits. It is precisely in the exploration of rule following behaviour that most may be expected from experimental game theory as an empirical and experimental discipline (on the methodology of experimentalism in general see [Mayo, 1996], with specific attention to economics [Smith, 2008]). I cannot explore this strand of explanatory Public Choice any further here and turn to normative Public Choice instead.

## 2 NORMATIVE PUBLIC CHOICE

The preceding was basically a discussion of how Public Choice explains or rather fails to explain what happens in public choice. Within a methodological and philosophy of science context this clearly had to be central stage and to occupy the larger part of the discussion. But there are other parts of Public Choice that are not intended as explanatory and descriptive science but rather as normative arguments. This raises meta-theoretical questions concerning the relationship between normative ethics and normative economics of public choice.

### *2.1 Senses of normativity in Public Choice*

Much of normative Political Philosophy is nowadays inspired by decision theoretic modelling. The kind of normative argument of and in Public Choice that is relevant to my present concerns is close to this and more or less analytic. As such it is of a somewhat different nature than normative arguments of Political Philosophy. It has in recent years been conducted mainly under the rubric of Constitutional Political Economy and of (normative) Social Choice in the Arrow tradition. But before I turn to this kind of analytic normativism another sense of "normative" should be briefly sketched and side-lined for the rest of the discussion.

### 2.1.1 Normative as idealisation

Economists often use the term normative in referring to the presence of scientific idealisations. For instance the model of rational economic man as universal behavioural assumption is often described as "normative". This use of the term normative amounts basically to an acknowledgement that the assumption of rational economic behaviour is at least in part contrary to the facts.

This is not a completely mistaken use of terms since normative requirements by their very nature are "contrary to the facts". In "normative" contexts they are intended to modify or change factual courses of the world that without interventions to the contrary would emerge. But in so far as the term normative refers merely to idealisations it suggests a different relationship to basic facts: idealised theories represent the facts in a stylised way; but as far as they do represent the facts, they are descriptive rather than normative.

### 2.1.2 Embodied norms as constraints of the argument

There are other senses in which norms do play a role for Public Choice. In the Constitutional Political Economy tradition norms have been embodied in the enterprise from the outset. Buchanan defines a "game of normative Public Choice" (i.e a game of discourse or theoretical argument). In that game — the game of theory formation — a player cannot participate unless she accepts a constraint of interpersonal respect. The outlook thereby becomes different from the Hobbesian and also Robbinsian perspective. Looking at the world strictly in terms of "manipulative" means ends relationships providing guidance as how to best promote one's own particular aims is not the aim of playing that game of normative Constitutional Political Economy.

As a self-declared ethical relativist Buchanan has no compelling argument why it is so that we ultimately should be interested only in that game or, for that matter, in mutually advantageous relations (i.e. conceive of politics as mutually advantageous exchange and try to further merely that type of politics in our normative recommendations). But we must be so interested or at least act as if that were the case if we intend to participate in the Constitutional Political Economy game Buchanan style. This is the ticket so to say that we need if we want to participate. However, there is no epistemological reason why we should buy such a ticket. All that Buchanan can say is that for those who as a matter of fact do share the ideal of not imposing their on will on others have good reason to be interested in that theory of normatively constrained "Kantian" Constitutional Political Economy that he envisions.

Likewise, those who work in the Arrow tradition might want to argue that individuals who as a matter of fact do want collective choice mechanisms to have certain properties have good reason to take into account logical analyses of the implications of their desires. Work in the Arrow tradition can inform them whether their ends can consistently be pursued etc.

To be more specific, *if* you do want to evaluate the states of the world according to a social welfare function which has the property of not imposing the values of one evaluating individual (possibly yourself) on all others, no matter what, then you should look only at a specific class of functions. You might want to consider only welfare functions that happen to conform with the Arrow type non-dictatorship requirement. *If* you desire not to impose some external constraint on how to evaluate the states of the world then you might want to opt for such forms of evaluation only as are in conformity with universal domain requirements. *If* you accept the methodological norm that the intensity of desires should not enter your value judgements since there seems to be no sound empirical basis for assessing intensities then you may consider to evaluate social states only according to the ordering information contained in the representations of individual preferences that you rely on. And, of course, you must be somebody who endorses a personal commitment to forming his own personal value ranking over states of society as a function of individual preferences — not necessarily restrained to the ordering information only but allowing for, say, utilitarian such personal welfare functions judging the good of society (see for instance [Harsanyi, 1977; Broome, 1991]).

For the purposes at hand it is unnecessary to go over all the standard axioms of the Arrovian social choice tradition (for a canonical statement, see [Sen, 1970]). It should be clear from the preceding remarks already that the approach fits the bill of the means-ends framework of normative economics only if we re-interpret the role of the axioms appropriately (see on this also [Kliemt, 1987c]). That the axioms are intuitively appealing to an impartial observer or something of the kind is irrelevant. Within the normative economics framework of "means to given ends" we should rather — as in the case of the Kantian norms of mutual respect in the Buchanan framework — accept that the addressee of any such analytical argument must as a matter of fact pursue appropriate ends, aims, or values to render an Arrow type argument relevant to him.

An alternative interpretation would put the Arrow approach firmly into the analytical ethics rather than the economics camp. It would most naturally be a method for reaching a wide reflective equilibrium on personal normative convictions. Though there is also a non-cognitivist account of the Rawlsian reflective equilibrium method (see on this [Rawls, 1951; 1971; Daniels, 1979; Hahn, 2000]) relying on the intuitive appeal of axioms rather than on the instrumental value of seeing them fulfilled is akin to traditional ethical rather than to normative economic argument. Pushing on this logic it is also clear that one would look at the Arrow axioms less in terms of binary "on-off" choices (fulfilled vs. violated) but rather in terms of degrees of fulfillment allowing for adjustments at the margin (see [Baurmann and Brennan, 2006]). As in Constitutional Political Economy where in the end the norm of unanimity (in itself representing mutual respect) needs to be re-interpreted as something that can come in shades of grey (see, of course, already [Buchanan and Tullock, 1962]) so must any of the Arrow axioms according to this view be regarded as allowing for grades of fulfillment.

From a methodological point of view it is presumably right to stress that the emphasis on adjustment and grading is typical for the economic point of view. The economic outlook is that the numbers do count (in a way going beyond counting heads in the ethical discussion following [Taurek, 1977]), that opportunity costs of decisions matter across the board and that they emerge not in an "all or nothing" but rather a "more or less" way. One might note also that this methodological norm is independent of the meta-ethical normative requirement that normative argument ultimately has to be couched in terms of the means to given ends framework of justification.

Within the Humean framework of normative Public Choice value comes into the world entirely because certain desires do exist and not because reason on its own could conceivably tell us what is valuable or out of its own powers could even create value. Clearly there are meta-ethical competitors to such views but Public Choice as a sub-discipline of normative economics seems to be constrained to such means-ends arguments. As far as substantive normative arguments on specifics are concerned the meta-ethical distinction between a means-ends perspective and other more fundamental rationalist (and in particular Kantian) forms of normative argument will not be felt much anyway. Relative to given aims, ends, and some other normative presuppositions the argument of the non-cognitivist can be precisely the same as that of the cognitivist. The non-cognitivist will, however, insist that his argument ultimately rests on contigent facts (the "relatively absolute absolutes" of the Knight-Buchanan tradition, see [Buchanan, 1999]) or aims, ends, or values that must as a matter of fact be pursued or be given in that sense. The cognitivist will give some justification for the aims, ends, or values, too or treat them as known to be "right".

In sum, the difference between an on and off style of argument and a marginal adjustment argument concerning normative premises and their implications will presumably be much more significant for substantive argument than any difference ascribed to the status of the justificatory basis of premises of normative argument. But as far as the philosophy of science of normative argument — the meta-theory of the justificatory status — is concerned the distinction between what is and what is not part of the means to given ends approach is more important.

As sub-fields of Public Choice both Constitutional Political Economy and Social Choice Theory do qualify only if they are not going beyond the limits drawn in Robbins' essay on the nature and significance of economic science. Therefore I will confine my subsequent discussion of normative Public Choice to such approaches that can be viewed as falling into normative economics proper or rather I will try to interpret arguments such that they still fit in here.

## *2.2 The preference formation interpretation of the role of Constitutional Political Economy and Social Choice*

### *2.2.1 Constitutional Political Economy as preference formation*

According to Buchanan, adopting an objective explanatory attitude is not all that economists should do. Economists should go beyond delivering a purely factual account of what is. Buchanan agrees that knowledge about likely reactions of other human beings as brought about by and explained according to behavioural laws is important. Knowing what the likely behavioural proclivities of humans are is useful regardless of whether we are adopting an objective or a participant's point of view to social interaction (see on this also [Strawson, 1962]). So there is a role for a behavioural science of Public Choice as discussed in part 1. But Buchanan believes that we need to go beyond the objective attitude. The economist is always also a participant in the game of life that he tries to explain and to understand.

Buchanan is not aiming at such phenomena as the so-called self-fulfilling or self-refuting prophecies here. Neither does he intend to restate merely that the economist as a human being can adopt a participant's attitude when acting not in his role as an objective scientist. He rather tries to defend the requirement that economists *should* do economics from a participant's point of view. This is normative with respect to Public Choice but not with respect to public choice.

If we refer to economics as a behavioural science as *type one economics* we can refer to economics from the participant's point of view as *type two economics*. The descriptive and explanatory variant of type one economics has been discussed in part 1. The corresponding normative branch would develop advice from an objective behavioural point of view. It would — broadly speaking — tell the particular interests how they can "have their way". Manipulation of others rather than seeking agreement with them is the guiding principle (including "agreement seeking" as a manipulative strategy that may be used as instrument in pursuit of given ends). In Kantian terms type one economics deals with "homo phaenomenon" — subject to explanatory behavioural laws – while type two economics addresses "homo noumenon" (see [Kant, 1991]) by rational argument.

Since we have dealt with explanatory type one economics in the first part and since normative economics suggesting means to ends seems rather orthodox, I will focus on the unorthodox type two economics subsequently. Type two economics does not in the first place talk *about* other rational beings — it talks *to* them. It is part of an ongoing discourse or dialogue among addressees of rational arguments. This seems very Kantian or, for that matter, Habermasian. Concepts like that of deliberative democracy — though now in a libertarian rather than socialist spirit — come to one's mind almost immediately and certainly not without reason (regardless of the fact that Buchanan will not be too happy with these associations).

As type two normative economists we are addressing individuals rather than society at large. But we do not address individuals with the advice of how to get their ways unilaterally. We speak to them as members of a community of equals who all receive the same advice of how to reach mutual advantage – as in game theory all the actors *by assumption* receive the same "theory signal". In that spirit in particular Constitutional Political Economy tries to give advice in inventing such rules of the game that would make everybody better off as compared to the status quo game. For Buchanan this focus on what could conceivably be accepted unanimously is expressing norms of fairness and inter-personal respect which he regards as *constitutive* of normative Public Choice. Constitutional Political Economy accordingly is simply not interested in furthering particular interests at the cost of hurting other particular interests (the scholar of business administration may go on to do this).

The denial of particularism keeps Buchanan type two economics on the universalistic Kantian track (similarly Vining who explicitly argues that the economist simply is not interested in treating others as means but will always respect them as ends in themselves; [Vining, 1956]). In normative Public Choice of the Buchanan type the aim is *not* to advise the several competing rent-seeking interests how they could maximize their particular rents against the others. The aim is to show them all how it would be in their interest to avoid rent seeking altogether.

However, within the means-ends-framework in particular of type one normative economics there is no rational compelling reason why anybody should go along with Buchanan type two economics or his specific vision of Constitutional Political Economy unless he happens to share certain aims, ends, or values. Type two economics is relevant only for those who happen to endorse as their particular interests some kind of universalistic aims, ends, or values.

Moreover, since according to Buchanan there is no public choice in the narrow sense of the term "choice" the Buchanan type Constitutional Political Economy cannot give advice of how to *choose*. In this reading Constitutional Political Economy should rather be seen as a contribution to constitutional *preference* formation. The preferences induced by being exposed to Constitutional Political Economy could be influential indirectly, say, in constitutional referenda and the likes (behind the veil of individual insignificance as in [Brennan and Lomasky, 1989]). However, since Constitutional Political Economy is not about choices it cannot give an advice to act strategically in a certain manner.

The normative theory of Constitutional Political Economy would be seen in the value formation of modern welfare economics rather than in the classical decision making framework of economics. It would shape our preferences over institutions should we accept certain suitable aims, ends, or values. Though we cannot choose single handedly any of the social institutions — there are strictly speaking no such choices — we can evaluate or rank such institutions according to the evaluative theory. Such preferences — or for that matter, opinions — indirectly will support the emergence and maintenance of certain kinds of institutions. Normative Constitutional Political Economy in the spirit of type two economics has effects on choices but not by suggesting choices. If we look at Constitutional Political Economy that way we should make the same concessions to Social Choice as well.

### *2.2.2 Constitutional preference formation in Social Choice*

There have always been two views of the Arrow paradigm: an institutional and a value formation interpretation (the distinction is impressively re-iterated in [Pattanaik, 2005]). In the first reading, say, Arrow's original impossibility theorem indicates some deeper truths about the viability and stability properties of the institutions of democracy and so do theorems like May's axiomatic characterisation of the majority rule. In the value formation interpretation what is at stake are in the widest sense of that term "opinion formation" processes (using "opinion" in the broad sense introduced above).

The typical collective welfare function within the value formation interpretation of the Social Choice paradigm is a function of preference orders of individuals. It maps profiles or vectors of such preferences into a space of results or of preference orders. Since any such function — as a function – naturally treats its arguments as given the requirements of the means ends framework seem to be fulfilled. Moreover, if we accept that a value judgement must strictly speaking always be the value judgement of someone and that collectives as opposed to individuals do not qualify as "someone" then the welfare function for the collective is always expressing the value judgements of an individual judge of welfare. This individual may be either a participant of the ongoing process or an (impartial) external observer of social choice. To both, the participant as well as the external observer, Social Choice serves as a theoretical device.

Let us start with Social Choice from the perspective of the participant in social choice. The participating individual may want to incorporate preferences and possibly even judgements of other individuals into her orderings of social states. In any event there is a specific individual who intends to form a welfare function representing her personal "ethical" evaluation of the states of society.

More precisely, the ranking is a ranking of an individual who is herself part of the collective of, say, $N > 1$, actors concerned. The ranking is based on the first level orderings of the N individuals, i.e. it is the value ordering of one of the $N$ evaluators of social states based on the value orderings of the $N$ evaluators. (The personal social welfare function is always judge-relative.) The welfare function based on the N preference orders of the first order leads to a value judgement of the second order. Since by construction this welfare judgement is a second order judgement of one of the $N$ individuals it is impervious to Little's original objection against the Arrow paradigm. According to this objection it is not appropriate to speak of a welfare ordering for society, the social welfare function must rather represent the judgement of somebody (see [Little, 1952]).

But avoiding Little's objection comes at a price. The preferences taken into account cannot anymore be taken as preferences "all things considered". When introducing preferences of the second order one cannot anymore claim to start from preferences that are given and well-defined without further ado. Quite to the contrary an infinite progression of preferences based on preferences of ever higher order may emerge.

Social Choice as construed from the point of view of a participant of the social process might respond to this by assuming that only first order preferences should matter. But, though this is a viable response, Social Choice is then ruling out certain considerations (i.e. second order considerations of preferences of self-or other) that individuals may themselves include into their own preference formation process. The neutral stance of Social Choice theory as far as the nature of the preferences is concerned is given up since some considerations entering preference formation are not taken into account.

On the other hand, Social Choice may be willing to take into account second- and higher-order preferences. Social Choice might want to rely on those second- and higher-order preferences as happen to be around and stop wherever the $N$ individuals stop. Yet, at least if we operate in a setting of ideally rational individuals we might want to include some form of rational expectations and theory absorption (see [Dacey, 1976; Morgenstern and Schwödiauer, 1976; Dacey, 1976; 1981]). Then Social Choice should assume that a fully rational individual aware of Social Choice and accepting the axioms proposed in it will include second-order preferences when forming preferences. Only after all things including those of a second order have been considered the preferences emerge. But then what about third-order preferences etc.?

The preceding challenge can in principle be met by models which formulate conditions under which the progression of preferences converges against well defined limiting preferences under certain conditions (see on such models in particular [Lehrer and Wagner, 1981]). Imagine for instance that a rational individual is willing to use information other than the ordering information contained in individual preference orders. In forming her social welfare function she is willing to make intra-personal inter-personal comparisons of utility — say Harsanyi type ethical preferences (see [Harsanyi, 1977]) — and then to include these evaluations into her own evaluation with a certain weight.

To be more specific, say, each individual $i$ of the $N$ individuals allocates to the preference satisfaction of each other individual $j$ a weight $\lambda_{ij} \in [0,1], j = 1, 2, ..., N$. This leads to a matrix of weights

$$\Lambda = \begin{bmatrix} \lambda_{11} & \lambda_{12} & & \lambda_{1N} \\ & \lambda_{22} & & \lambda_{2N} \\ & & & \\ \lambda_{N1} & & \dots & \lambda_{NN} \end{bmatrix}, \quad \lambda_{ij} \in [0,1], \forall i, j \text{ } and \text{ } \forall i : \sum_{j=1}^{N} \lambda_{ij} = 1$$

If then each individual $i = 1, 2, \dots, N$, represents the preferences of each individual $j$ by the same utility function $U_j$ (the ordering information is assumed to be commonly known for simplicity's sake) the weights can be used to weigh the utilities such as to take into account interdependence. Each individual weighs others to the degree to which she sees her own preference satisfaction as dependent on the preference satisfaction of those others. *Given her own aims, ends, or values this is how she should "weigh in" the preference satisfaction of others into her own.*

After each round of weighing preferences for each individual i each such individual finds for herself a revised preference ordering of the next higher order according to $U_i' = \sum_{j=1}^{N} \lambda_{ij} U_j \quad for \text{ } all \text{ } i = 1, 2, ..., N$. Obviously this amounts to

$$\begin{bmatrix} \lambda_{11} & \lambda_{12} & & \lambda_{1N} \\ & \lambda_{22} & & \lambda_{2N} \\ & & & \\ \lambda_{N1} & & \dots & \lambda_{NN} \end{bmatrix} \begin{bmatrix} U_1 \\ U_2 \\ \\ U_N \end{bmatrix} = \begin{bmatrix} U_1' \\ U_2' \\ \\ U_N' \end{bmatrix} \Leftrightarrow \Lambda U = U'$$

and $\Lambda U = U', \Lambda\Lambda U = U'', \Lambda\Lambda\Lambda U = U''', ..., \Lambda^k U = U^k$.

For each individual to be interested in $\Lambda^k$ it is not necessary to be impartial. Each of the individuals may be partial in favour of those who are socially closer to them. Each individual may follow the Humean trias of close, closer, closest (as driving the social theory argument in book iii of [Hume, 1739/1978]) and even exclude the socially remote entirely from personal evaluations of the *first order* (setting those weights to zero). All that is needed is the willingness to assign as a matter of fact some value to the preference satisfaction of *some* other individuals.

If *as a matter of fact* the network of positive mutual respect among the participants of the social process is appropriately structured – i.e. if there are sufficiently many bridges of inter-personal respect such as to create a connected graph of such respect relationships – then the process of "weighing in" the preference satisfaction of others will converge to a state in which each and every individual implicitly should assign the same positive weights to each and every other one, or $\lim_{k\to\infty} \Lambda^k = \Lambda^*$ is a matrix with identical rows (the conditions for the matrix $\Lambda$ being fully ergodic seem rather undemanding in a social setting).

The preceding way of modelling is methodologically instructive in two ways. First, the problem of forming preferences of an ever higher order and to incorporate them into a verdict about "preferences all things considered" is solved. Letting the mathematical process run its course $\lim_{k\to\infty} \Lambda^k = \Lambda^*$ has logically considered "all" things (i.e. all weighing) in the limit. Secondly, though — at least in the simple structure proposed here — all individuals know the first order preferences of each other these first order preferences over social states may be diverging. The same holds good for the first order weights. They may be different but not completely variable. If the assumption is made that higher order weights become eventually constant or are constant from the outset then — if the graph of positive weights is appropriately connected — the weights will converge such that the implied utility function that each individual holds separately as a social welfare function for the collectivity becomes identical across individuals.

Though this result is reached by making strong assumptions it can be reached without the assumption that individuals do want to be impartial or ethical or that they respect each and every individual in society from the outset. All that is needed is that they respect some individuals who themselves respect other individuals. They must do so in a appropriate manner which assures that everybody is integrated into the social nexus of mutual respect. But given some rather undemanding conditions of overlap among the social neighborhoods such integration seems to be quite plausible. If it so happens that individuals have aims, ends, or values according to which preference satisfaction of other individuals is important then the preceding logic may apply and tell them that they are by their own given, aims, ends, or values implicitly bound to use the same weights for the preferences of each and every body. Quite in line with the basic premises of normative economics — rather than cognitivist normative or, for that matter, universalist contractarian ethics — this identical weighing is a means to the pursuit of their own *particular* given aims, ends, or values (the whole thing remains agent relative throughout, see on this in a different but related context [Scheffler, 1982; Parfit, 1984; Broome, 1991]).

Now, clearly, the Lehrer-Wagner approach to ranking social states has many weaknesses. But for the purposes at hand it has the great merit of demonstrating what kind of assumptions guarantee the emergence of an identical social welfare function for each and every individual in a setting in which the methodological constraint of starting from given individual particular preferences is respected. Moreover, in this conception of how a single inter-individually identical social welfare function may emerge under certain contingent but not unlikely circumstances the function is held by persons, namely by each and every individual $i = 1, 2, \ldots, N$ taken separately. This is important since for a methodological individualist in the true sense of the term value as represented by human preferences must always be located in an evaluating human individual (that the objects evaluated may be non-human is irrelevant as far as preference formation and social welfare functions are concerned). Higher order preferences are no exception to that. Insofar Little's original query stands but can be answered in the proposed way within Social Choice.

The mainstream of the discussion did not stick to the participant's perspective. According to a rather common view the value ordering based on the value orderings serving as the arguments of the social welfare function need not be that of one of the participants holding the N first order preferences. Instead of this it is assumed that the ordering may be that of an external (impartial) observer or an N+1 evaluator from the outset.

The requirement that the social welfare function be treated as that of a human person can be met for the external "observing" theorist. In the impartial observer interpretation Social Choice avoids the rather unsatisfactory result that there can in principle be as many social welfare functions as there are individuals. In the preceding discussion of convergence, "unanimity" was merely a contingent fact. If the evaluating individuals do not intend to include views of others in the way assumed for convergence in case of the Lehrer-Wagner models there is no way left to overcome disagreement. The impartial spectator interpretation of Social Choice avoids that. However, then Social Choice becomes a sub-branch of normative ethics. Rather than remaining within the constraints of normative economics (which, for that matter, coincides with non-cognitivist normative ethics of the Hume-Mackie type) in which all proposals are addressing the issue of how to pursue the given aims, ends, or values of the addressees of the argument it now imposes some form of social welfare function from an "objective" external point of view.

The impartial observer is an external observer as long as it is not the case that one of the individuals participating in the social process does herself as a matter of fact want to act as an impartial observer. If it so happens that one of the individuals wants to evaluate social states according to an impartial point of view then a normative theory of Social Choice formed from an external impartial observer point of view becomes internally relevant for the specific individual who desires as a matter of fact to form "moral judgements of the appropriate kind". In that case the separating line between normative economics and impartial spectator ethics becomes blurred with respect to substantive normative content. However, methodologically there is still a fundamental meta-ethical distinction. On the one hand we have theories that see all justification of normative argument as ultimately relative to given particular aims, ends, or values that happen to prevail with the addressee of the argument. On the other hand, we find theories that adopt a meta-ethically more demanding stance of universal aims, ends, or values that are to be pursued from an impartial, external or in that sense of objective point of view (relations to the philosophical discussion of agent relativity are obvious again but as before are beyond the scope of the present essay and cannot be pursued further here).

The relationship of Buchanan type Constitutional Political Economy to normative impartial observer type ethics becomes unclear as well if we accept contractarianism. Once the concept of conceivable yet fictitious unanimity is employed, the dividing line between Constitutional Political Economy and Political Philosophy ceases to exist. This is quite analogous to the fact that the dividing line between normative Social Choice and ethics ceases to exist once we interpret the axioms characterising welfare functions as ethical intuitions rather than contingent aims of someone. All the different lines of argument may be legitimately pursued. However, it seems necessary to keep them apart if confusion is to be avoided.

## CONCLUSIONS

Explanatory as well as normative Public Choice have been tremendously successful research programs. However, as the preceding discussion shows methodological foundations of both descriptive and prescriptive Public Choice seem rather precarious. Explanatory Public Choice suffers from sticking to the assumptions of the homo oecomicus model and the maximisation under constraints framework. Normative Public Choice is confronted with all the meta-ethical problems of justifying substantive value or normative judgments once it reaches beyond the "means to given ends" framework.

From a methodological point of view the development of Public Choice can rather plausibly be described in terms of the methodology of scientific research programs. It is, however, quite unclear whether it is possible to cope with all the challenges to the program without endangering its core. As in other realms of economics the model of homo oeconomicus can be used along with strict rational choice analyses to identify the most interesting explananda of social theory: Whenever phenomena agree with the predictions of the "homo oeconomicus cum rational choice" analysis we have to find a "mechanism" that explains how this astonishing result could come about.

For instance the seminal market experiments by Vernon Smith (see [Smith, 1962; 2000; Davis and Holt, 1993]) were often taken as corroborating economic theory.

However, quite the contrary is true. Though markets work as "predicted" by conventional theory under certain ideal conditions that conventional theory does not provide the explanation under real conditions. As they stand the implied law-like regularities quantify over institutions rather than individual behaviour. The fact that certain institutions like "double auctions" robustly and quite independently of the cognitive abilities and the number of participants generate efficient outcomes is surprising within the context of traditional theory. It is a challenge for the methodological individualist who has to explain in detail how the results can come about on the basis of individual cognitive processes and behaviour. Since the reasoning about knowledge approach is clearly inadequate to meet the challenge something else must be put in its place.

Likewise the status of normative Public Choice is quite unclear. If the diagnosis is correct that there are literally speaking no choices made by collectivities of individuals normative proposals cannot suggest collective choices in a literal sense. The proposals must translate somehow into suggestions for individual behaviour. For instance, in voting the theory would have to suggest specific actions to the individual voter rather than simply recommending an order of the outcomes of collective results. If we reject this strategic game view of Social Choice and stick to the evaluative version of the theory we presumably must re-interpret it in terms of preference formation. The theory forms our views of what is desirable in principle but does not tell us which choices we should make to bring about what is desirable. Quite analogously to questions of actually explaining the emergence of social results that conform with rational choice theory we have to face the necessity of providing the concrete mechanisms relating individual actions to their desired outcomes. In line with this, normative contractarianism of the Buchanan or other type should be seen as a theory shaping constitutional preferences rather than directly guiding constitutional choice. From a philosophical and methodological point of view Public Choice would be well-advised to take these observations into account. It is to a lesser extent about choice than its practitioners may assume.

## BIBLIOGRAPHY

[Ainslee, 1992] G. Ainslee. *Picoeconomics*. Cambridge, 1992.

[Ainslee, 2002] G. Ainslee. *Break Down of the Will*. Princeton, 2002.

[Albert, 1967] H. Albert. *Marktsoziologie und Entscheidungslogik*. Neuwied/Berlin, 1967.

[Albert, 1967/1998] H. Albert. *Marktsoziologie und Entscheidungslogik*. Zur Kritik der reinen Ökonomik. Tübingen, 1967/1998.

[Albert, 1985] H. Albert. *Treatise on Critical Reason*. Princeton, 1985.

[Albert, 1988] H. Albert. Hermeneutics and Economics. A Criticism of Hermeneutical Thinking in the Social Sciences. *Kyklos*, 41, 573, 1988.

[Alchian, 1950] A. A. Alchian. Uncertainty, Evolution, and Economic Theory. *Journal of Political Economy*, 58, 211-221, 1950.

[Arendt, 1951] H. Arendt. *The Origins of Totalitarianism*. New York, 1951.

[Aumann, 1981] R. J. Aumann. Survey of Repeated Games. In R. Aumann, ed., *Essays in Game Theory and Mathematical Economics*. Bibliographisches Institut BI, Mannheim, pp. 11-42, 1981.

[Barry, 1981] N. Barry. *An Introduction to Modern Political Theory.* London and Basingstoke, 1981.

[Baurmann, 2002] M. Baurmann. *The Market of Virtue*, vol. 60. Dordrecht, 2002.

[Baurmann and Brennan, 2006] M. Baurmann and G. Brennan. Majoritarian inconsistency, Arrow impossibility and the comparative interpretation. In C. Engel and L. Dalston, eds., *Is there value in inconsistency?* Nomos, Baden Baden, pp. 93-118, 2006.

[Binmore, 1987/1988] K. Binmore. Modeling rational players I&II. *Economics and Philosophy*, (3 & 4), 179-214 & 179-155, 1987/1988.

[Binmore, 1992] K. Binmore. *Fun and Games — A Text on Game Theory.* Lexington, 1992.

[Binmore, 1994] K. Binmore. *Game Theory and Social Contract Volume I – Playing Fair.* Cambridge, London, 1994.

[Binmore, 1998] K. Binmore. *Game Theory and Social Contract Volume II – Just Playing.* Cambridge, London, 1998.

[Binmore, 2005] K. Binmore. *Natural Justice.* New York, 2005.

[Bolton and Ockenfels, 2000] G. Bolton and A. Ockenfels. ERC: A Theory of Equity, Reciprocity and Competition. *American Economic Review*, 90, 166-193, 2000.

[Brennan and Buchanan, 1984] H. G. Brennan and J. M. Buchanan. Voter Choice: Evaluating Political Alternatives. *American Behavioral Scientist*, 28(No. 2, November/December), 185-201, 1984.

[Brennan and Buchanan, 1985] H. G. Brennan and J. M. Buchanan. *The Reason of Rules.* Cambridge, 1985.

[Brennan and Kliemt, 1990] H. G. Brennan and H. Kliemt. Logo Logic. *Journal of Constitutional Political Economy*, 1, No. 1, 125-127, 1990.

[Brennan and Lomasky, 1989] H. G. Brennan and L. E. Lomasky. *Large Numbers, Small Costs - Politics and Process - New Essays in Democratic Thought.* Cambridge, 1989.

[Brennan and Lomasky, 1993] H. G. Brennan and L. E. Lomasky. *Democracy and Decision.* Cambridge, 1993.

[Broome, 1991] J. Broome. *Weighing Goods. Equality, Uncertainty and Time.* Oxford, 1991.

[Buchanan, 1975/1996] J. M. Buchanan. An Ambiguity in Sen's Alleged Proof of the Impossibility of a Pareto Liberal. *Analyse & Kritik*, 18(1), 118-125, 1975/1996.

[Buchanan, 1979] J. M. Buchanan. *Natural and Artifactual Man.* Indianapolis, 1979.

[Buchanan, 1982] J. M. Buchanan. The Related but Distinct "Sciences" of Economics and of Political Economy. *British Journal of Social Psychology (Special Issue: Philosophy and Economics)*, 97-106, 1982.

[Buchanan, 1999] J. M. Buchanan. *The Logical Foundations of Constitutional Liberty, vol. 1.* Indianapolis, 1999.

[Buchanan, 2001] J. M. Buchanan. Game Theory, Mathematics, and Economics. *Journal of Economic Methodology*, 8(1), 27-32, 2001.

[Buchanan and Tullock, 1962] J. M. Buchanan and G. Tullock. *The Calculus of Consent.* Ann Arbor, 1962.

[Camerer, 2003] C. Camerer. *Behavioral Game Theory.* Princeton, 2003.

[Dacey, 1976] R. Dacey. Theory Absorption and the Testability of Economic Theory. *Zeitschrift für Nationalökonomie*, 36(3-4), 247-267, 1976.

[Dacey, 1981] R. Dacey. Some Implications of 'Theory Absorption' for Economic Theory and the Economics of Information. In J. C. Pitt, ed., *Philosophy in Economics.* D. Reidel, Dordrecht, pp. 111-136, 1981.

[Damme, 1987] E. van Damme. *Stability and Perfection of Nash Equilibria.* Berlin / Heidelberg / New York / London / Paris / Tokyo, 1987.

[Daniels, 1979] N. Daniels. Wide Reflective Equilibrium and Theory Acceptance in Ethics. *The Journal of Philosophy*, LXXVI(1), 265-282, 1979.

[Davis and Holt, 1993] D. D. Davis and C. A. Holt. *Experimental Economics.* Princeton, 1993.

[Downs, 1957] A. Downs. *An Economic Theory of Democracy.* New York, 1957.

[Elster, 1987] J. Elster, ed. *The Multiple Self.* Cambridge University Press, Cambridge, 1987.

[Fagin *et al.*, 1995] R. Fagin, J. Y. Halpern, Y. Moses, and M. Y. Vardi. *Reasoning about Knowledge.* Cambridge, MA / London, 1995.

[Fehr and Schmidt, 1999] E. Fehr and K. Schmidt. A Theory of Fairness, Competition, and Cooperation. *Quarterly Journal of Economics*, 114, 817-868, 1999.

[Fleck, 1935/1980] L. Fleck. *Entstehung und Entwicklung einer wissenschaftlichen Tatsache.* Einführung in die Lehre vom Denkstil und Denkkollektiv, vol. 312. Frankfurt, 1935/1980.

[Frank, 1987] R. Frank. If Homo Economicus Could Choose His Own Utility Function, Would He Want One with a Conscience? *The American Economic Review*, 77/4, 593-604, 1987.
[Frey, 1997] B. S. Frey. *Not Just For the Money. An Economic Theory of Personal Motivation.* Cheltenham, 1997.
[Friedman, 1996] J. Friedman, ed. *The Rational Choice Controversy.* Yale University Press, New Haven, 1996.
[Friedman, 1953/1966] M. Friedman. The Methodology of Positive Economics. In M. Friedman, ed., *Essays in Positive Economics.* Chicago University Press, Chicago, pp. 3-46, 1966.
[Gaertner *et al.*, 1992] W. Gaertner, K. Suzumura, and P. K. Pattanaik. Individual Rights Revisited. *Economica*, 59, 161-177, 1992.
[Gigerenzer, 2000] G. Gigerenzer. *Adaptive Thinking: Rationality in the Real World.* New York, 2000.
[Gode and Sunder, 1993] D. K. Gode and S. Sunder. Allocative Efficiency of Markets With Zero Intelligence Traders: Markets as a Partial Substitute for Individual Rationality. *Journal of Political Economy*, 101, 119-137, 1993.
[Green and Shapiro, 1994] D. P. Green and I. Shapiro. *Pathologies of Rational Choice Theory.* New Haven, 1994.
[Güth, 2000] W. Güth. Boundedly Rational Decision Emergence — A General Perspective and some Selective Illustrations. *Journal of Economic Psychology*, 21, 433 – 458, 2000.
[Güth and Kliemt, 1994] W. Güth and H. Kliemt. Competition or Co-operation: On the Evolutionary Economics of Trust, Exploitation and Moral Attitudes. *Metroeconomica*, 45(2), 155-187, 1994.
[Güth and Kliemt, 2000] W. Güth and H. Kliemt. Evolutionarily Stable Co-operative Commitments. *Theory and Decision*, 49, 197-221, 2000.
[Güth and Kliemt, 2007] W. Güth and H. Kliemt. The Rationality of Rational Fools. In F. Peter and H. B. Schmid, eds., *Rationality and Commitment.* Oxford University Press, Oxford, pp. 124-149, 2007.
[Güth *et al.*, 1991] W. Güth, W. Leininger, and G. Stephan. On Supergames and Folk Theorems: A Conceptual Analysis. In R. Selten, ed., *Game Equilibrium Models. Morals, Methods, and Markets.* Springer, Berlin. pp. 56-70, 1991.
[Güth and Pelet, 2001] W. Güth and B. Peleg. When Will Payoff Maximization Survive? An Indirect Evolutionary Analysis. *Evolutionary Economics*, 11, 479-499 2001.
[Güth *et al.*, 1982] W. Güth, R. Schmittberger, and B. Schwarze. An Experimental Analysis of Ultimatum Bargaining. *Journal of Economic Behavior and Organization*, 3, 367-388, 1982.
[Hahn, 2000] S. Hahn. Überlegungsgleichgewicht(e). Prüfung einer Rechtfertigungsmetapher. Freiburg i.Br, 2000.
[Harman, 1977] G. Harman. *The Nature of Morality. An Introduction to Ethics.* New York, 1977.
[Harsanyi, 1977] J. C. Harsanyi. *Rational Behavior and Bargaining Equilibrium in Games and Social Situations.* Cambridge, 1977.
[Harsanyi and Selten, 1988] J. C. Harsanyi and R. Selten. *A general theory of equilibrium selection in games.* Cambridge, Mass, 1988.
[Hart, 1961] H. L. A. Hart. *The Concept of Law.* Oxford, 1961.
[Hausmann, 1992/2003] D. M. Hausmann. *The inexact and separate science of economics.* Cambridge, 1992/2003.
[Hayek, 1973-79] F. A. van Hayek. *Law, Legislation and Liberty: A New Statement of the Liberal Principles of Justice and Political Economy.* London and Henley, 1973-79.
[Hayek, 1973-1993] F. A. van Hayek. *Law, Legislation and Liberty: A new statement of the liberal principles of justice and political economy. Rules and Order*, vol. Bd. 1. London, 1973-1993.
[Heiner, 1983] R. Heiner. The Origin of Predictable Behavior. *American Economic Review*, 73/4, 560 ff, 1983.
[Heinimann, 1987/1945] F. Heinimann. *Nomos und Physis.* Darmstadt, 1987/1945.
[Hempel, 1965/1970] C. G. Hempel. *Aspects of scientific explanation and other essays in the philosophy of science.* New York, 1965/1970.
[Hempel and Oppenheim, 1948] C. G. Hempel and P. Oppenheim. Studies in the Logic of Explanation. *Philosophy of Science*, 15(2), 135-175, 1948.
[Hobbes, 1682/1990] T. Hobbes. *Behemoth or The Long Parliament.* Chicago, 1682/1990.

[Hogart and Reder, 1987] R. M. Hogart and M. W. Reder, eds. *Rational Choice. The Contrast between Economics and Psychology.* University of Chicago Press, Chicago, 1987.
[Hume, 1739/1978] D. Hume. *A Treatise of Human Nature.* Oxford, 1739/1978.
[Hume, 1777/1985] D. Hume. *Essays. Moral, Political and Literary.* Indianapolis, 1777/1985.
[Hume, 1779/1986] D. Hume. *Dialogues concerning natural religion.* Indianapolis, 1779/1985.
[Kant, 1991] I. Kant. *Political writings. The metaphysics of morals.* Oxford, 1991.
[Kliemt, 1985] H. Kliemt. *Moralische Institutionen. Empiristische Theorien ihrer Evolution.* Freiburg, 1985.
[Kliemt, 1986] H. Kliemt. The Veil of Insignificance. *European Journal of Political Economy,* 2/3, 333-344, 1986.
[Kliemt, 1987a] H. Kliemt. *Las institutiones morales.* Barcelona, 1987.
[Kliemt, 1987b] H. Kliemt. The Reason of Rules and the Rule of Reason. *Critica,* XIX, 43-86, 1987.
[Kliemt, 1987c] H. Kliemt. Unanimous Consent, Social Contract, and the Sceptical Ethics of Economists. *Rechtstheorie,* 18, 502-515, 1987.
[Kliemt, 1993] H. Kliemt. , Constitutional commitments. In Philip *et al.* Herder Dorneich, ed., *Jahrbuch für Neuere Politische Ökonomie.* Mohr und Siebeck, pp. 145-173, 1993.
[Kliemt, 2004] H. Kliemt. Public Choice from the Perspective of Philosophy. In C. K. Rowley and F. Schneider, eds., *Encyclopedia of Public Choice.* Kluwer, Dordrecht, pp. 235-244, 2004.
[Kuhn, 1962] T. Kuhn. *The Structure of Scientific Revolutions,* 1962.
[Lakatos, 1978] I. Lakatos. *The Methodology of Scientific Research Programmes.* Cambridge, 1978.
[Lehrer and Wagner, 1981] K. Lehrer and C. Wagner. *Rational Consensus in Science and Society.* Dordrecht, 1981.
[Little, 1952] I. M. D. Little. Social Choice and Individual Values. *Journal of Political Economy,* 60, 422-433, 1952.
[Mackie, 1977] J. L. Mackie. *Ethics. Inventing Right and Wrong.* Harmondsworth, 1977.
[Mackie, 1980] J. L. Mackie. *Hume's Moral Theory.* London., 1980
[Maital andMaital, 1984] S. Maital and S. L. Maital. *Economic Games People Play.* New York, 1984.
[Mäki, 2002] U. Mäki, ed. *Fact and Fiction in Economics.* Cambridge University Press, Cambridge, UK, 2002.
[Marsiliusci, 1324/2001] Marsilius. *Defensor Pacis.* New York, 1324/2001.
[Mayo, 1996] D. G. Mayo. *Error and the Growth of Experimental Knowledge.* Chicago, 1996.
[Meckling, 1976] W. Meckling. Values and the Choice of the Model of the Individual in the Social Sciences. *Schweizerische Zeitschrift für Volkswirtschaft und Statistik,* 112/4, 545-565, 1976.
[Morgenstern and Schwödiauer, 1976] O. Morgenstern and G. Schwödiauer. Competition and Collusion in Bilateral Markets. *Zeitschrift für Nationalökonomie,* 36(3-4), 217-245, 1976.
[Mueller, 1986] D. C. Mueller. Rational Egoism Versus Adaptive Egoism as Fundamental Postulate for a Descriptive Theory of Human Behavior. *Public Choice,* 51, 3, 1986.
[Mueller, 2003] D. C. Mueller. *Public Choice III.* Cambridge, 2003.
[Nelson and Winter, 1982] R. R. Nelson and S. G. Winter. *An Evolutionary Theory of Economic Change.* Cambridge, MA, 1982.
[Nozik, 1974] R. Nozick. *Anarchy, State, and Utopia.* New York, 1974.
[Olson, 1965] M. Olson. *The Logic of Collective Action.* Cambridge, Mass, 1965.
[Parfit, 1984] D. Parfit. *Reasons and Persons.* Oxford, 1984.
[Parsons, 1968] T. Parsons. Utilitarianism. Sociological Thought. *International Encyclopedia of Social Sciences,* New York und London, 1968.
[Pattanaik, 2005] P. K. Pattanaik. Little and Bergson on Arrow's concept of social welfare. *Social Choice and Welfare,* 25, 369-379, 2005.
[Popper, 1934/2002] K. R. Popper. *Logik der Forschung.* Tübingen. 1934/2002.
[Rabin, 1993] M. Rabin. Incorporating Fairness Into Game Theory and Economics. *American Economic Review,* 83, 1281-1302, 1993.
[Radner, 1998] R. Radner. Economic Survival. In D. P. Jacobs *et al.*, eds., *Frontiers of Research in Economic Theory.* The Nancy Schwartz Memorial Lectures, 1983-1997. Cambridge University Press, Cambridge, pp. 183-209, 1998.
[Raphael, 1969] D.-D. Raphael, ed. *British Moralists.* Oxford University Press, Oxford, 1969.

[Rawls, 1951] J. Rawls. Outline of a Decision Procedure for Ethics. *Philosophical Review*, 60, 177-190, 1951.
[Rawls, 1971] J. Rawls. *A Theory of Justice*. Oxford, 1971.
[Robbins, 1935] L. Robbins. *An Essay on the Nature and Significance of Economic Science*. London, 1935.
[Scheffler, 1982] S. Scheffler. *The Rejection of Consequentialism*. Oxford. 1982.
[Schelling, 1960/1977] T. C. Schelling. *The Strategy of Conflict*. Oxford 1960/1977.
[Schneider, 1967] L. Schneider, ed. *The Scottish Moralists on Human Nature and Society*. Chicago und London, 1967.
[Schumpeter, 1959] J. A. Schumpeter. *The Theory of Economic Development*. Cambridge, MA, 1959.
[Schüssler, 1988] R. Schüssler. Der Homo Oeconomicus als skeptische Fiktion. *Kölner Zeitschrift für Soziologie*, 40, 447-463, 1988.
[Selten, 1965] R. Selten Spieltheoretische Behandlung eines Oligopolmodells mit Nachfrageträgheit. *Zeitschrift für die gesamte Staatswissenschaft*, 121, 301-324 and 667-689, 1965.
[Selten, 1975] R. Selten. Reexamination of the Perfectness Concept for Equilibrium in Extensive Games. *International Journal of Game Theory*, 4, 25-55, 1975.
[Selten, 1990] R. Selten. *Some Remarks on Bounded Rationality*, vol. 172. Bonn, 1990.
[Sen, 1970] A. K. Sen. *Collective Choice and Social Welfare*. San Francisco. 1970.
[Sen, 1996] A. K. Sen. Rights: Formulation and Consequences. *Analyse & Kritik*, 18(1), 152-170, 1996.
[Simon, 1957] H. A. Simon. *Models of Man*. New York, 1957.
[Skyrms, 1996] B. Skyrms. *Evolution of the Social Contract*. Cambridge, 1996.
[Slonim and Roth, 1998] R. Slonim and A. E. Roth. Learning in High Stakes Ultimatum Games: An Experiment in the Slovak Republic. *Econometrica*, 66, 569-596, 1998.
[Smith, 1962] V. L. Smith. An Experimental Study of Competitive Market Behavior. *The Journal of Political Economy*, 70( 2), 111-137, 1962.
[Smith, 2000] V. L. Smith, ed. *Bargaining and Market Behavior*. Cambridge University Press, Cambridge, 2000.
[Smith, 2008] V. L. Smith. *Rationality in Economics. Constructivist and Ecological Forms*. New York, 20098.
[Spinoza, 1670/1951] B. de Spinoza. *A Theologico-Political Treatise. A Political Treatise*. New York, 1670/1951.
[Stigler and Becker, 1977] G. J. Stigler and G. S. Becker. : De gustibus non est disputandum. *The American Economic Review*, 67, 76 ff, 1977.
[Strawson, 1962] P. F. Strawson. Freedom and Resentment. *Proceedings of the British Academy*, 187-211, 1962.
[Sugden, 1986] R. Sugden. *The Economics of Rights, Co-operation and Welfare*. Oxford, New York, 1986.
[Sugden, 1994] R. Sugden. The Theory of Rights. In H. Siebert, ed., *The Ethical Foundations of the Market Economy*. Mohr, Tübingen, pp. 31-53, 1994.
[Taurek, 1977] J. M. Taurek. Should the numbers count? *Philosophy and Public Affairs*, 6, 293-316, 1977.
[Taylor, 1976] M. Taylor. *Anarchy and Cooperation*. London u. a., 1976.
[Tullock, 1967] G. Tullock. *Toward a Mathematics of Politics*. Ann Arbor, 1967.
[Tullock, 1971] G. Tullock. The Charity of the Uncharitable. *Western Economic Journal*, 9, 379-392, 1971.
[Vanberg, 1975] V. Vanberg. *Die zwei Soziologien. Individualismus und Kollektivismus in der Sozialtheorie*. Tübingen, 1975.
[Vining, 1956] R. Vining. *Economics in the United States of America. A Review and Interpretation of Research*. Paris, 1956.

# JUDGMENT AGGREGATION: A SHORT INTRODUCTION

Christian List

## 1 INTRODUCTION

The aim of this article is to introduce the theory of judgment aggregation, a growing research area in economics, philosophy, political science, law and computer science. The theory addresses the following question: How can a group of individuals make consistent collective judgments on a given set of propositions on the basis of the group members' individual judgments on them? This problem is one of the fundamental problems of democratic decision-making and arises in many different settings, ranging from legislative committees to referenda, from expert panels to juries and multi-member courts, from boards of companies to the WTO and the UN Security Council, from families to large social organizations. While each real-world case deserves social-scientific attention in its own right, the theory of judgment aggregation seeks to provide a general theoretical framework for investigating some of the properties that different judgment aggregation problems have in common, abstracting from the specifics of concrete cases.

The recent interest in judgment aggregation was sparked by the observation that majority voting, perhaps the most common democratic procedure, fails to guarantee consistent collective judments whenever the decision problem in question exceeds a certain level of complexity, as explained in detail below. This observation, which has become known as the 'discursive dilemma', but which can be seen as a generalization of a classic paradox discovered by the Marquis de Condorcet in the 18th century, was subsequently shown to illustrate a deeper impossibility result, of which there are now several variants in the literature. Roughly speaking, there does not exist any method of aggregation – an 'aggregation rule' — which (i) guarantees consistent collective judgments and (ii) satisfies some other salient properties exemplified by majority voting, such as determining the collective judgment on each proposition as a function of individual judgments on that proposition and giving all individuals equal weight in the aggregation. This impossibility result, in turn, enables us to see how far we need to deviate from majority voting, and thereby from conventional democratic principles, in order to come up with workable solutions to judgment aggregation problems. In particular, the impossibility result allows us to construct a map of the 'logical space' in which different possible solutions to judgment aggregation problems can be positioned.

Handbook of the Philosophy of Science. Volume 13: Philosophy of Economics.
Volume editor: Uskali Mäki. General editors: Dov M. Gabbay, Paul Thagard and John Woods.

Just as the theory of judgment aggregation is thematically broad, so its intellectual origins are manifold. Although this article is not intended to be a comprehensive survey, a few historical remarks are useful.[1] The initial observation that sparked the recent development of the field goes back to some work in jurisprudence, on decision-making in collegial courts [Kornhauser and Sager, 1986; 1993; Kornhauser, 1992], but was later reinterpreted more generally — as a problem of majority inconsistency — by Pettit [2001], Brennan [2001] and List and Pettit [2002]. List and Pettit [2002; 2004] introduced a first formal model of judgment aggregation, combining social choice theory and propositional logic, and proved a simple impossibility theorem, which was strengthened and extended by several authors, beginning with Pauly and van Hees [2006] and Dietrich [2006]. Independently, Nehring and Puppe [2002] proved some powerful results on the theory of strategy-proof social choice which turned out to have significant corollaries for the theory of judgment aggregation [Nehring and Puppe, 2007a]. In particular, they first characterized the class of decision problems for which certain impossibility results hold, inspiring subsequent related results by Dokow and Holzman [forthcoming], Dietrich and List [2007a] and others. A very general extension of the model of judgment aggregation, from propositional logic to any logic within a large class, was developed by Dietrich [2007a]. The theory of judgment aggregation is also related to the theories of 'abstract' aggregation [Wilson, 1975; Rubinstein and Fishburn, 1986], belief merging in computer science [Konieczny and Pino Pérez, 2002; see also Pigozzi, 2006] and probability aggregation (e.g., [McConway, 1981; Genest and Zidek, 1986; Mongin, 1995], and has an informal precursor in the work of Guilbaud [1966] on what he called the 'logical problem of aggregation' and perhaps even in Condorcet's work itself. Modern axiomatic social choice theory, of course, was founded by Arrow [1951/1963]. (For a detailed discussion of the relationship between Arrovian preference aggregation and judgment aggregation, see [List and Pettit, 2004; Dietrich and List, 2007a].)

This article is structured as follows. In section 2, I explain the observation that initially sparked the theory of judgment aggregation. In section 3, I introduce the basic formal model of judgment aggregation, which then, in section 4, allows me to present some illustrative variants of the generic impossibility result. In section 5, I turn to the question of how this impossibility result can be avoided, going through several possible escape routes. In section 6, I relate the theory of judgment aggregation to other branches of aggregation theory. And in section 7, I make some concluding remarks. Rather than offering a comprehensive survey of the theory of judgment aggregation, I hope to introduce the theory in a succinct and pedagogical way, providing an illustrative rather than exhaustive coverage of some of its key ideas and results.

[1]For short technical and philosophical surveys of salient aspects of the theory of judgment aggregation, see, respectively, [List and Puppe, forthcoming; List, 2006].

## 2 A PROBLEM OF MAJORITY INCONSISTENCY

Let me begin with Kornhauser and Sager's [1986] original example from the area of jurisprudence: the so-called 'doctrinal paradox' (the name was introduced in [Kornhauser, 1992]). Suppose a collegial court consisting of three judges has to reach a verdict in a breach-of-contract case. The court is required to make judgments on three propositions:

$p$: The defendant was contractually obliged not to do a particular action.
$q$: The defendant did that action.
$r$: The defendant is liable for breach of contract.

According to legal doctrine, propositions $p$ and $q$ are jointly necessary and sufficient for proposition $r$. Suppose now that the three judges are divided in their judgments, as shown in Table 1. The first thinks that $p$ and $q$ are both true, and hence that $r$ is true as well. The second thinks that $p$ is true, but $q$ is false, and consequently $r$ is also false. The third thinks that, while $q$ is true, $p$ is false, and so $r$ must be false too. So far so good. But what does the court as a whole think?

| | $p$ | $q$ | $r$ |
|---|---|---|---|
| Judge 1 | True | True | True |
| Judge 2 | True | False | False |
| Judge 3 | False | True | False |
| Majority | True | True | False |

Table 1. A doctrinal paradox

If the judges take a majority vote on proposition $r$ — the 'conclusion' - the outcome is the rejection of this proposition: a 'not liable' verdict. But if they take majority votes on each of $p$ and $q$ instead — the 'premises' — then both of these propositions are accepted and hence the relevant legal doctrine dictates that $r$ should be accepted as well: a 'liable' verdict. The court's decision thus appears to depend on which aggregation rule it uses. If it uses the first of the two approaches outlined, the so-called 'conclusion-based procedure', it will reach a 'not liable' verdict; if it uses the second, the 'premise-based procedure', it will reach a 'liable' verdict. Kornhauser and Sager's 'doctrinal paradox' consists in the fact that the premise-based and conclusion-based procedures may yield opposite outcomes for the same combination of individual judgments.[2]

But we can also make a more general observation from this example. Relative to the given legal doctrine — which states that $r$ is true if and only if both $p$ and $q$ are true — the majority judgments across the three propositions are inconsistent. In precise terms, the set of propositions accepted by a majority, namely

[2]For recent discussions of the 'doctrinal paradox', see [Kornhauser and Sager, (2004; List and Pettit, 2005]).

{*p*, *q*,*not r*}, is logically inconsistent relative to the constraint that *r if and only if p and q*. This problem — that majority voting may lead to the acceptance of an inconsistent set of propositions — generalizes well beyond this example and does not depend on the presence of any legal doctrine or other exogenous constraint; nor does it depend on the partition of the relevant propositions into premises and conclusions.

To illustrate this more general problem, consider any set of propositions with some non-trivial logical connections; below I say more about the precise notion of 'non-triviality' required. Take, for instance, the following three propositions on which a multi-member government may seek to make collective judgments:

| | |
|---|---|
| *p*: | We can afford a budget deficit. |
| *if p then q*: | If we can afford a budget deficit, then we should increase spending on education. |
| *q*: | We should increase spending on education. |

Suppose now that one third of the government accepts all three propositions, a second third accepts *p* but rejects *if p then q* as well as *q*, and the last third accepts *if p then q* but rejects *p* as well as *q*, as shown in Table 2.

| | *p* | *if p then q* | *q* |
|---|---|---|---|
| 1/3 of individuals | True | True | True |
| 1/3 of individuals | True | False | False |
| 1/3 of individuals | False | True | False |
| Majority | True | True | False |

Table 2. A problem of majority inconsistency

Then each government member holds individually consistent judgments on the three propositions, and yet there are majorities for *p*, for *if p then q* and for *not q*, a logically inconsistent set of propositions. The fact that majority voting may generate inconsistent collective judgments is sometimes called the 'discursive dilemma' [Pettit, 2001; List and Pettit, 2002; see also Brennan, 2001], but it is perhaps best described as the problem of 'majority inconsistency'.

How general is this problem? It is easy to see that it can arise as soon as the set of propositions (and their negations) on which judgments are to be made exhibits a simple combinatorial property: it has a 'minimally inconsistent' subset of three or more propositions [Dietrich and List, 2007b; Nehring and Puppe, 2007b]. A set of propositions is called 'minimally inconsistent' if it is inconsistent and every proper subset of it is consistent. In the court example, a minimally inconsistent set with these properties is {*p*, *q*, *not r*}, where the inconsistency is relative to the constraint *r if and only if p and q*. In the government example, it is {*p*, *if p then q*, *not q*}. As soon as there exists at least one minimally inconsistent subset of three or more propositions among the proposition-negation pairs on the agenda, combinations of judgments such as the one in Table 2 become possible, for which the majority judgments are inconsistent. Indeed, as explained in section 6 below, Condorcet's classic paradox of cyclical majority preferences is an instance of this general phenomenon, which Guilbaud [1952] described as the 'Condorcet effect'.

## 3 THE BASIC MODEL OF JUDGMENT AGGREGATION

In order to go beyond the observation that majority voting may produce inconsistent collective judgments and to ask whether other aggregation rules may be immune to this problem, it is necessary to introduce a more general model, which abstracts from the specific decision problem and aggregation rule in question. My exposition of this model follows the formalism introduced in List and Pettit [2002] and extended beyond standard propositional logic by Dietrich [2007a].

There is a finite set of (two or more) individuals, who have to make judgments on some propositions.[3] Propositions are represented by sentences from propositional logic or a more expressive logical language, and they are generally denoted $p$, $q$, $r$ and so on. Propositional logic can express 'atomic propositions', which do not contain any logical connectives, such as the proposition that we can afford a budget deficit or the proposition that spending on education should be increased, as well as 'compound propositions', with the logical connectives *not*, *and*, *or*, *if-then*, *if and only if*, such as the proposition that *if* we can afford a budget deficit, *then* spending on education should be increased. Instead of propositional logic, any logic with some minimal properties can be used, including expressively richer logics such as predicate, modal, deontic and conditional logics [Dietrich, 2007a]. Crucially, the logic allows us to distinguish between 'consistent' and 'inconsistent' sets of propositions. For example, the set $\{p,\ q,\ p \textit{ and } q\}$ is consistent while the sets $\{p,\ \textit{if } p \textit{ then } q,\ \textit{not } q\}$ or $\{p,\ \textit{not } p\}$ are not.[4]

The set of propositions on which judgments are to be made in a particular decision problem is called the 'agenda'. Formally, the 'agenda' is defined as a non-empty subset of the logical language, which is closed under negation, i.e., if $p$ is on the agenda, then so is *not* $p$.[5] In the government example, the agenda contains the propositions $p$, *if* $p$ *then* $q$, $q$ and their negations. In the court example, it contains $p$, $q$, $r$ and their negations, but here there is an additional stipulation built into the logic according to which $r$ *if and only if* $p$ *and* $q$.[6]

Now each individual's 'judgment set' is the set of propositions that this individ-

[3]The agenda characterization results discussed further below require three or more individuals.

[4]In propositional logic, a set of propositions is 'consistent' if all its members can be simultaneously true, and 'inconsistent' otherwise. More generally, consistency is definable in terms of a more basic notion of 'logical entailment' [Dietrich, 2007a].

[5]For some formal results, it is necessary to exclude tautological or contradictory propositions from the agenda. Further, some results simplify when the agenda is assumed to be a finite set of propositions. In order to avoid such technicalities, I make these simplifying assumptions (i.e., no tautologies or contradictions, and a finite agenda) throughout this paper. To render finiteness compatible with negation-closure, I assume that double negations cancel each other out; more elaborate constructions can be given.

[6]The full details of this construction are given in [Dietrich and List, forthcoming].

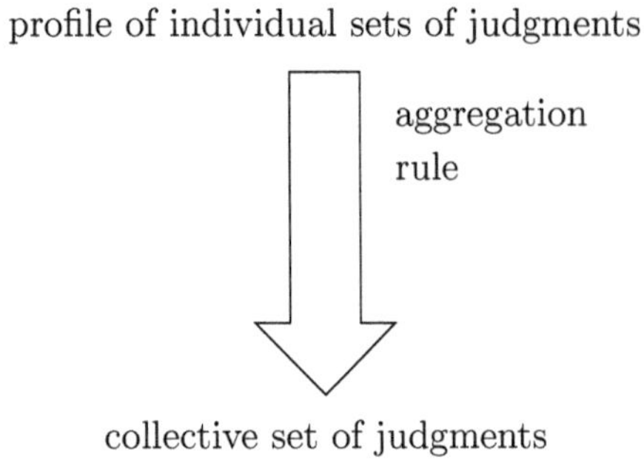


Figure 1. An aggregation rule

ual accepts; formally, it is a subset of the agenda. On the standard interpretation, to accept a proposition means to believe it to be true; on an alternative interpretation, it could mean to desire it to be true. For the present purposes, it is easiest to adopt the standard interpretation, i.e., to interpret judgments as binary cognitive attitudes rather than as binary emotive ones. A judgment set is called 'consistent' if it is a consistent set of propositions in the standard sense of the logic, and 'complete' if it contains a member of each proposition-negation pair on the agenda. A combination of judgment sets across the given individuals is called a 'profile'. Thus the first three rows of Tables 1 and 2 are examples of profiles on the agendas in question.

To complete the exposition of the basic model, it remains to define the notion of an 'aggregation rule'. As illustrated in Figure 1, an 'aggregation rule' is a function that maps each profile of individual judgment sets in some domain to a collective judgment set, interpreted as the set of propositions accepted by the collective as a whole.

Examples of aggregation rules are 'majority voting', as already introduced, where each proposition is collectively accepted if and only if it is accepted by a majority of individuals; 'supermajority' or 'unanimity rules', where each proposition is collectively accepted if and only if it is accepted by a certain qualified majority of individuals, such as two thirds, three quarters, or all of them; 'dictatorships', where the collective judgment set is always the individual judgment set of the same antecedently fixed individual; and 'premise'- and 'conclusion-based procedures', as briefly introduced in the court example above.

Although at first sight there seems to be an abundance of logically possible aggregation rules, it is surprisingly difficult to find one that guarantees consistent collective judgments. As we have already seen, majority voting notoriously fails to do so as soon as the propositions on the agenda are non-trivially logically connected. Let me therefore turn to a more general, axiomatic investigation of possible aggregation rules.

## 4 A GENERAL IMPOSSIBILITY RESULT

Are there any democratically compelling aggregation rules that guarantee consistent collective judgments? The answer to this question depends on two parameters: first, the types of decision problems — as captured by the given agenda — for which we seek to employ the aggregation rule; and second, the conditions that we expect it to meet. Before presenting some illustrative results, let me briefly explain why both parameters matter.

Suppose, for example, that we are only interested in decision problems that involve making a single binary judgment, say on whether to accept $p$ or *not* $p$. In other words, the agenda contains only a single proposition-negation pair (or, more generally, multiple logically unconnected such pairs). Obviously, we can then use majority voting without any risk of collective inconsistency. As we have already seen, the problem of majority inconsistency arises only if the agenda exceeds a certain level of complexity (i.e., it has at least one minimally inconsistent subset of three or more propositions). So the complexity of the decision problem in question is clearly relevant to the question of which aggregation rules, if any, produce consistent collective judgments.

Secondly, suppose that, instead of using an aggregation rule that satisfies strong democratic principles, we content ourselves with installing a dictatorship, i.e., we appoint one individual whose judgments are deemed always to determine the collective ones. If this individual's judgments are consistent, then, trivially, so are the resulting collective ones. The problem of aggregation will have been resolved under such a dictatorial arrangement, albeit in a degenerate way. This shows that the answer to the question of whether there exist any aggregation rules that ensure consistent collective judgments depends very much on what conditions we expect those rules to meet.

With these preliminary remarks in place, let me address the question of the existence of compelling aggregation rules in more detail. The original impossibility theorem by List and Pettit [2002] gives a simple answer to this question for a specific class of decision problems and a specific set of conditions on the aggregation rule:

THEOREM 1 List and Pettit, 2002. *Let the agenda contain at least two distinct atomic propositions (say, $p$, $q$) and either their conjunction ($p$ and $q$), or their disjunction ($p$ or $q$), or their material implication (if $p$ then $q$). Then there exists no aggregation rule satisfying the conditions of 'universal domain', 'collective rationality', 'systematicity' and 'anonymity'.*

What are these conditions? The first, universal domain, specifies the admissible *inputs* of the aggregation rule, requiring the aggregation rule to admit as input any possible profile of consistent and complete individual judgment sets on the propositions on the agenda. The second, collective rationality, constrains the *outputs* of the aggregation rule, requiring the output always to be a consistent and complete collective judgment set on the propositions on the agenda. The third and fourth, systematicity and anonymity, constrain the way the outputs are generated from the inputs and can thus be seen as *responsiveness* conditions. Systematicity is the two-part requirement that (i) the collective judgment on each proposition on the agenda depend only on individual judgments on that proposition, not on individual judgments on other propositions (the 'independence' requirement), and (ii) the criterion for determining the collective judgment on each proposition be the same across propositions (the 'neutrality' requirement). 'Anonymity' requires that the collective judgment set be invariant under permutations of the judgment sets of different individuals in a given profile; in other words, all individuals have equal weight in the aggregation.

Much can be said about these conditions — I discuss them further in the section on how to avoid the impossibility — but for the moment it is enough to note that they are inspired by key properties of majority voting. In fact, majority voting satisfies them all, with the crucial exception of the consistency part of collective rationality (for non-trivial agendas), as shown by the discursive dilemma. The fact that majority voting exhibits this violation illustrates the theorem just stated: no aggregation rule satisfies all four conditions simultaneously.

As mentioned in the introduction, this impossibility result has been significantly generalized and extended in a growing literature. Different impossibility theorems apply to different classes of agendas, and they impose different conditions on the aggregation rule. However, they share a generic form, stating that, for a particular class of agendas, the aggregation rules satisfying a particular combination of input, output and responsiveness conditions are either non-existent or otherwise degenerate. The precise class of agendas and input, output and responsiveness conditions vary from result to result. For example, Pauly and van Hees's [2006] first theorem states that if we take the same class of agendas as in List and Pettit's theorem and the same input and output conditions (universal domain and collective rationality), keep the responsiveness condition of systematicity but drop anonymity, then we are left only with dictatorial aggregation rules, as defined above. Other theorems by Pauly and van Hees [2006] and Dietrich [2006] show that, for more restrictive classes of agendas, again with the original input and output conditions and without anonymity, but this time with systematicity weakened to its first part ('independence'), we are still left only with dictatorial or constant aggregation rules. The latter are another kind of degenerate rules, which assign to every profile the same fixed collective judgment set, paying no attention to any of the individual judgment sets. Another theorem, by Mongin [forthcoming], also keeps the original input and output conditions, adds a responsiveness condition requiring the preservation of unanimous individual judgments[7] but weakens systematicity further, namely to an independence condition restricted to atomic propositions alone. The theorem then shows that, for a certain class of agendas, only dictatorial aggregation rules satisfy these conditions together.

The most general theorems in the literature are so-called 'agenda characterization theorems'. They do not merely show that for a certain class of agendas,

[7]More formally, 'unanimity preservation' is the requirement that if all individuals unanimously accept any proposition on the agenda, then that proposition be collectively accepted.

a certain combination of input, output and responsiveness conditions lead to an empty or degenerate class of aggregation rules, but they fully characterize those agendas for which this is the case and, by implication, those for which it is not. The idea underlying agenda characterizations was introduced by Nehring and Puppe [2002] in a different context, namely the theory of strategy-proof social choice. However, several of their results carry over to judgment aggregation (as discussed in [Nehring and Puppe, 2007a]) and have inspired other agenda characterization results (e.g., [Dokow and Holzman, forthcoming; Dietrich and List, 2007]).

To give a flavour of these results, recall that only agendas which have at least one minimally inconsistent subset of three or more propositions are of interest from the perspective of *im*possibility theorems; call such agendas 'non-simple'. For agendas below this level of complexity, majority voting works perfectly well.[8] Non-simple agendas may or may not have some additional properties. For example, they may or may not have a minimally inconsistent subset with the special property that, by negating some even number of propositions in it, it becomes consistent; call an agenda of this kind 'even-number-negatable'.[9]

It now turns out that, for all and only those agendas which are both non-simple and even-number-negatable, every aggregation rule satisfying universal domain, collective rationality and systematicity — i.e., the original input, output and responsiveness conditions — is either dictatorial or inversely dictatorial (the latter means that the collective judgment set is always the propositionwise negation of the judgment set of some antecedently fixed individual) [Dietrich and List, 2007a]. Further, for all and only those agendas which are just non-simple (whether or not they are even-number-negatable), every aggregation rule satisfying the same conditions and an additional 'monotonicity' condition[10] is dictatorial [Nehring and Puppe, 2002; 2007a]. If we restrict these two classes of agendas by adding a further property (called 'total blockedness' or 'path-connectedness'[11]), then similar results hold with systematicity weakened to independence and an additional responsiveness condition of 'unanimity preservation' ([Dokow and Holzman, forthcoming; Nehring and Puppe, 2002; 2007a] respectively).[12] Table 3 surveys those results.

For each of the four rows of the table, the following two things are true: first, if the agenda has the property described in the left-most column, every aggregation

[8]For such agendas, the majority judgments are always consistent and in the absence of ties also complete.

[9]This property was introduced by Dietrich [2007a] and Dietrich and List [2007a]. A logically equivalent property is the algebraic property of 'non-affineness' introduced by Dokow and Holzman [forthcoming].

[10]Roughly speaking, monotonicity is the requirement that if any proposition is collectively accepted for a given profile of individual judgment sets and we consider another profile in which an additional individual accepts that proposition (other things being equal), then this proposition remains accepted.

[11]This property, first introduced by Nehring and Puppe [2002], requires that any proposition on the agenda can be deduced from any other via a sequence of pairwise logical entailments conditional on other propositions on the agenda.

[12]A weaker variant of the result without monotonicity (specifically, an 'if' rather than 'if and only if' result) was also proved by Dietrich and List [2007a].

| Class of agendas | Input | Output | Resp'ness | Resulting agg. rules |
|---|---|---|---|---|
| Non-simple | Univ. domain | Coll. rationality | Systematicity<br>Monotonicity | Dictatorships |
| [Nehring and Puppe, 2002; 2007a] | | | | |
| Non-simple<br>Even-numb.-neg. | Univ. domain | Coll. rationality | Systematicity | Dictatorships<br>Inv. dict'ships |
| [Dietrich and List, 2007a] | | | | |
| Non-simple<br>Path-connected | Univ. domain | Coll. rationality | Independence<br>Monotonicity<br>Unanim. preserv. | Dictatorships |
| [Nehring and Puppe, 2002; 2007a] | | | | |
| Non-simple<br>Path-connected<br>Even-numb.-neg. | Univ. domain | Coll. rationality | Independence<br>Unanim. preserv. | Dictatorships |
| [Dokow and Holzman, forthcoming)] | | | | |

Table 3. Agenda characterization results

rule satisfying the specified input, output and responsiveness conditions is of the kind described in the right-most column; and second, if the agenda violates the property in the left-most column, there exist aggregation rules other than those described in the right-most column which still satisfy the specified conditions.

The theorems reviewed in this section show that *if* (i) we deal with decision problems involving agendas with some of the identified properties *and* (ii) we consider the specified input, output and responsiveness conditions to be indispensable requirements of democratic aggregation, *then* judgment aggregation problems have no non-degenerate solutions. To avoid this implication, we must therefore deny either (i) or (ii). Unless we can somehow avoid non-trivial decision problems altogether, denying (i) does not seem to be a viable option. Therefore we must obviously deny (ii). So what options do we have? Which of the conditions might we relax?

## 5 AVOIDING THE IMPOSSIBILITY

As noted, the conditions leading to an impossibility result — i.e., the non-existence of any non-degenerate aggregation rules — fall into three types: input, output and responsiveness conditions. For each type of condition, we can ask whether a suitable relaxation would enable us to avoid the impossibility.

## 5.1 *Relaxing the input conditions*

All the impossibility theorems reviewed so far impose the condition of universal domain on the aggregation rule, by which any possible profile of consistent and complete individual judgment sets on the propositions on the agenda is deemed admissible as input to the aggregation. At first sight this condition seems eminently reasonable. After all, we want the aggregation rule to work not only for some special inputs, but for all possible inputs that may be submitted to it. However, different groups may exhibit different levels of pluralism, and in some groups there may be significantly more agreement between the members' judgments than in others. Expert panels or ideologically well structured societies may be more homogeneous than some large and internally diverse electorates. Thus the profiles of individual judgment sets leading to collective inconsistencies under plausible aggregation rules such as majority voting may be more likely to occur in some heterogeneous groups than in other more homogeneous ones. Can we say something systematic about the type of 'homogeneity' that is required for the avoidance of majority inconsistencies — and by implication for the avoidance of the more general impossibility of judgment aggregation?

It turns out that there exist several combinatorial conditions with the property that, on the restricted domain of profiles of individual judgment sets satisfying those conditions, majority voting generates consistent and (absent ties) complete individual judgment sets and — of course – satisfies the various responsiveness conditions introduced in the last section. For brevity, let me here discuss just two illustrative such conditions: a very simple one and a very general one.

The first is called 'unidimensional alignment' [List, 2003]. It is similar in spirit, but not equivalent, to a much earlier condition in the theory of preference aggregation, called 'single-peakedness', which was introduced in a classic paper by Black [1948]. (Single-peakedness is a constraint on profiles of preference orderings rather than judgment sets.) A profile of individual judgment sets is 'unidimensionally aligned' if it is possible to align the individuals from left to right such that, for every proposition on the agenda, the individuals accepting the proposition are either all to the left, or all to the right, of those rejecting it, as illustrated in Table 4.

| | Ind. 1 | Ind. 2 | Ind. 3 | Ind. 4 | Ind. 5 |
|---|---|---|---|---|---|
| $p$ | True | False | False | False | False |
| *if* $p$ *then* $q$ | False | True | True | True | True |
| $q$ | False | False | False | True | True |

Table 4. A unidimensionally aligned profile of individual judgment sets

The relevant left-right alignment of the individuals may be interpreted as capturing their position on some cognitive or ideological dimension (e.g., from socio-economic left to right, or from urban to rural, or from secular to religious, or from environmentally risk-averse to environmentally risk-taking etc.), but what matters from the perspective of achieving majority consistency is not the semantic interpretation of the alignment but rather the combinatorial constraint it imposes on individual judgments.

Why is unidimensional alignment sufficient for consistent majority judgments? Since the individuals accepting each proposition are opposite those rejecting it on the given left-right alignment, a proposition cannot be accepted by a majority unless it is accepted by the middle individual on that alignment[13] – individual 3 in the example of Table 4. In particular, the majority judgments must coincide with the middle individual's judgments.[14] Hence, so long as the middle individual holds consistent judgments, the resulting majority judgments will be consistent too.[15] When restricted to the domain of unidimensionally aligned profiles of individual judgment sets,[16] majority voting therefore satisfies all the conditions introduced in the last section, except of course universal domain.

However, while unidimensional alignment is sufficient for majority consistency, it is by no means necessary. A necessary *and* sufficient condition is the following [Dietrich and List, 2007c]. A profile is called 'majority consistent' if every minimally inconsistent subset of the agenda contains at least one proposition that is not accepted by a majority. Is it easy to see that this is indeed enough to ensure consistent majority judgments. If the set of propositions accepted by a majority is inconsistent, it must have at least one minimally inconsistent subset, but not all propositions in this set can be majority-accepted if the underlying profile satisfies the combinatorial condition just defined. An important special case is given by the condition of 'value-restriction' [Dietrich and List, 2007c], which generalizes an equally named classic condition in the context of preference aggregation [Sen, 1966]. A profile of individual judgment sets is called 'value-restricted' if every minimally inconsistent subset of the agenda contains a pair of propositions $p$, $q$ not jointly accepted by any individual. Again, this is enough to rule out that any minimally inconsistent set of propositions can be majority-accepted: if it were, then, in particular, each of the propositions $p$ and $q$ from the definition of value-restriction would be majority-accepted and thus at least one individual would accept both, contradicting value-restriction. (Several other domain restriction conditions are discussed in [Dietrich and List, 2007c].)

How plausible is the strategy of avoiding the impossibility of non-degenerate judgment aggregation via restricting the domain of admissible inputs to the aggregation rule? The answer to this question depends on the group, context and decision problem at stake. As already noted, different groups exhibit different levels of pluralism, and it is clearly an empirical question whether or not any of the identified combinatorial conditions are met by the empirically occurring profiles of individual judgment sets in any given case. Some groups may be naturally homogeneous or characterized by an entrenched one-dimensional ideological or

[13]Or the middle two individuals, if the total number of individuals is odd.

[14]Or the intersection of the judgments of the two middle individuals, if the total number of individuals is even.

[15]Similarly, if the total number of individuals is even, the intersection of the individually consistent judgment sets of the two middle individuals is still a consistent set of propositions.

[16]Assuming consistency and completeness of the individual judgment sets.

cognitive spectrum in terms of which group members tend to conceptualize issues under consideration. Think, for example, of societies with a strong tradition of a conventional ideological left-right polarization. Other societies or groups may not have such an entrenched structure, and yet through group deliberation or other forms of communication they may be able to achieve sufficiently 'cohesive' individual judgments, which meet conditions such as unidimensional alignment or value-restriction. In debates on the relationship between social choice theory and the theory of deliberative democracy, the existence of mechanisms along these lines has been hypothesized [Miller, 1992; Knight and Johnson, 1994; Dryzek and List, 2003]. However, the present escape route from the impossibility is certainly no 'one size fits all' solution.

## *5.2 Relaxing the output conditions*

Like the input condition of universal domain, the output condition of collective rationality occurs in all the impossibility theorems reviewed above. Again the condition seems *prima facie* reasonable. First of all, the requirement of consistent collective judgments is important not only from a pragmatic perspective — after all, inconsistent judgments would fail to be action-guiding when it comes to making concrete decisions — but also from a more fundamental philosophical one. As argued by Pettit [2001], collective consistency is essential for the contestability and justifiability of collective decisions (for critical discussions of this point, see also [Kornhauser and Sager, 2004; List, 2006]). And secondly, the requirement of complete collective judgments is also pragmatically important. One would imagine that only those propositions will be included on the agenda that require actual adjudication; and if they do, the formation of complete collective judgments on them will be essential.

Nonetheless, the case for collective consistency is arguably stronger than that for collective completeness. There is now an entire sequence of papers in the literature that discuss relaxations of completeness (e.g., [List and Pettit, 2002; Gärdenfors, 2006; Dietrich and List, 2007b; 2007d; 2008a; Dokow and Holzman, 2006]). Gärdenfors [2006], for instance, criticizes completeness as a 'strong and unnatural assumption'. However, it turns out that not every relaxation of completeness is enough to avoid the impossibility of non-degenerate judgment aggregation. As shown by Gärdenfors [2006] for a particular class of agendas (so-called 'atomless' agendas) and subsequently generalized by Dietrich and List [2008a] and Dokow and Holzman [2006], if the collective completeness requirement is weakened to a 'deductive closure' requirement according to which propositions on the agenda that are logically entailed by other accepted propositions must also be accepted, then the other conditions reviewed above restrict the possible aggregation rules to so-called 'oligarchic' ones. An aggregation rule is 'oligarchic' if there exists an antecedently fixed non-empty subset of the individuals — the 'oligarchs' — such that the collective judgment set is always the intersection of the individual judgment sets of the oligarchs. (A dictatorial aggregation rule is the limiting case in which the set of oligarchs is singleton.) In fact, a table very similar to Table 3 above can be derived in which the output condition is relaxed to the conjunction of consistency and deductive closure and the right-most column is extended to the class of oligarchic aggregation rules (for technical details, see [Dietrich and List, 2008a]).

However, if collective rationality is weakened further, namely to consistency alone, more promising possibilities open up. In particular, groups may then use supermajority rules according to which any proposition on the agenda is collectively accepted if and only if it is accepted by a certain supermajority of individuals, such as more than two thirds, three quarters, or four fifths of them. If the supermajority threshold is chosen to be sufficiently large, such rules produce consistent (but not generally deductively closed) collective judgments [List and Pettit, 2002]. In particular, any threshold above $\frac{k-1}{k}$ is sufficient to ensure collective consistency, where $k$ is the size of the largest minimally inconsistent subset of the agenda [Dietrich and List, 2007b]. In the court and government examples above, this numer is three, and thus a supermajority threshold above two thirds would be sufficient for collective consistency. Supermajority rules, of course, satisfy all the other (input and responsiveness) conditions that I have reviewed.

Groups with a strongly consensual culture, such as the UN Security Council or the EU Council of Minister, may very well take this supermajoritarian approach to solving judgment aggregation problems. The price they have to pay for avoiding the impossibility of non-degenerate judgment aggregation in this manner is the risk of stalemate. Small minorities will be able to veto judgments on any propositions.[17] As in the case of the earlier escape route — via relaxing universal domain — the present one is no 'one size fits all' solution to the problem of judgment aggregation.

## 5.3 *Relaxing the responsiveness conditions*

Arguably, the most compelling escape-route from the impossibility of non-degenerate judgment aggregation opens up when we relax some of the responsiveness conditions used in the impossibility theorems. The key condition here is independence, i.e., the first part of the systematicity condition, which requires that the collective judgment on each proposition on the agenda depend only on individual judgments on that proposition, not on individual judgments on other propositions. The second part of systematicity, requiring that the criterion for determining the collective judgment on each proposition be the same across propositions, is already absent from several of the impossibility theorems (namely whenever the agenda is sufficiently complex), and relaxing it alone is thus insufficient for avoiding the basic impossibility result in general.

If we give up independence, however, several promising aggregation rules be-

[17] Furthermore, when *both* individual *and* collective judgment sets are only required to be consistent, a recent impossibility theorem suggests that an asymmetry in the criteria for accepting and for rejecting propositions is a necessary condition for avoiding degenerate aggregation rules [Dietrich and List, 2007d].

come possible. The simplest example of such a rule is the premise-based procedure, which I have already briefly mentioned in the context of Kornhauser and Sager's doctrinal paradox. This rule was discussed, originally under the name 'issue-by-issue voting', by Kornhauser and Sager [1986] and Kornhauser [1992], and later by Pettit [2001], List and Pettit [2002], Chapman [2002], Bovens and Rabinowicz [2006], Dietrich [2006] and many others. Abstracting from the court example, the 'premise-based procedure' involves designating some propositions on the agenda as 'premises' and others as 'conclusions' and generating the collective judgments by taking majority votes on all premises and then deriving the judgments on all conclusions from these majority judgments on the premises; by construction, the consistency of the resulting collective judgments is guaranteed, provided the premises are logically independent from each other. If these premises further constitute a 'logical basis' for the entire agenda – i.e., they are not only logically independent but any assignment of truth-values to them also settles the truth-values of all other propositions – then the premise-based procedure also ensures collective completeness.[18] (The conclusion-based procedure, by contrast, violates completeness, in so far as it only ever generates collective judgments on the conclusion(s), by taking majority votes on them alone.)

The premise-based procedure, in turn, is a special case of a 'sequential priority procedure' [List, 2004]. To define such an aggregation rule, we must specify a particular order of priority among the propositions on the agenda such that earlier propositions in that order are interpreted as epistemically (or otherwise) prior to later ones. For each profile of individual judgments sets, the propositions are then considered one-by-one in the specified order and the collective judgment on each proposition is formed as follows. If the majority judgment on the proposition is consistent with the collective judgments on propositions considered earlier, then that majority judgment becomes the collective judgment; but if the majority judgment is inconsistent with those earlier judgments, then the collective judgment is determined by the implications of those earlier judgments. In the example of Table 2 above, the multi-member government might consider the propositions in the order $p$, *if* $p$ *then* $q$, $q$ (with negations interspersed) and then accept $p$ and *if* $p$ *then* $q$ by majority voting while accepting $q$ by logical inference. The collective judgment set under such an aggregation rule is dependent on the specified order of priority among the propositions. This property of 'path-dependence' can be seen as a virtue or as a vice, depending on the perspective one takes. On the one hand, it appears to do justice to the fact that propositions can differ in their status (consider, for example, constitutional propositions versus propositions of ordinary law), as emphasized by Pettit [2001] and Chapman [2002]. But on the other hand,

[18]A first general formulation of the premise-based procedure in terms of a subset $Y$ of the agenda interpreted as the set of premises was given in List and Pettit [2002]. Furthermore, as shown by Dietrich [2006], the premise-based procedure can be axiomatically characterized in terms of the key condition of 'independence restricted to $Y$', where $Y$ is the premise-set. In some cases, an impossibility result reoccurs when the condition of unanimity preservation is imposed, as shown for certain agendas by Mongin's [forthcoming] theorem mentioned in the previous section. For recent extensions, see [Dietrich and Mongin, 2007].

it makes collective judgments manipulable by an agenda setter who can influence the order in which propositions are considered [List, 2004], which in turn echoes a much-discussed worry in social choice theory (e.g., [Riker, 1982]).

Another class of aggregation rules that give up independence — the class of 'distance-based rules' — was introduced by Pigozzi [2006], drawing on related work on the theory of belief merging in computer science [Konieczny and Pino Pérez, 2002]. Unlike premise-based or sequential priority procedures, these rules are not based on the idea of prioritizing some propositions over others. Instead, they are based on a 'distance metric' between judgment sets. We can define the 'distance' between any two judgment sets for instance by counting the number of propositions on the agenda on which they 'disagree' (i.e., the number of propositions for which it is *not* the case that the proposition is contained in the one judgment set if and only if it is contained in the other). A 'distance-based aggregation rule' now assigns to each profile of individual judgment sets the collective judgment set that minimizes the sum-total distance from the individual judgment sets (with some additional stipulation for dealing with ties). Distance-based aggregation rules have a number of interesting properties. They can be seen to capture the idea of reaching a compromise between different individuals' judgment sets. Most importantly, they give up independence while still preserving the spirit of neutrality across propositions (so long as we adopt a definition of distance that treats all propositions on the agenda equally).

What is the cost of violating independence? Arguably, the greatest cost is manipulability of the aggregation rule by the submission of insincere individual judgments [Dietrich and List, 2007e]. Call an aggregation rule 'manipulable' if there exists at least one admissible profile of individual judgment sets such that the following is true for at least one individual and at least one proposition on the agenda: (i) if the individual submits the judgment set that he/she genuinely holds, then the collective judgment on the proposition in question differs from the individual's genuine judgment on it; (ii) if he/she submits a strategically adjusted judgment set, then the collective judgment on that proposition coincides with the individual's genuine judgment on it. If an aggregation rule is manipulable in this sense, then individuals may have incentives to misrepresent their judgments.[19] To illustrate, if the court in the example of Table 1 were to use the premise-based procedure, sincere voting among the judges would lead to a 'liable' verdict, as we have seen. However, if judge 3 were sufficiently strongly opposed to this outcome, he or she could strategically manipulate it by pretending to believe that $q$ is false, contrary to his or her sincere judgment; the result would be the majority rejection of proposition $q$, and hence a 'not liable' verdict. It can be shown that an aggregation rule is *non*-manipulable if and only if it satisfies the conditions of independence and monotonicity introduced above ([Dietrich and List, 2007e]; for closely related results in a more classic social-choice-theoretic framework, see [Nehring and Puppe, 2007b]). Assuming that, other things being equal, the relax-

[19]The precise relationship between *opportunities* and *incentives* for manipulation is discussed in [Dietrich and List, 2007e].

ation of independence is the most promising way to make non-degenerate judgment aggregation possible, the impossibility theorems reviewed above can therefore be seen as pointing to a trade-off between degeneracy of judgment aggregation on the one hand (most notably, in the form of dictatorship) and its potential manipulability on the other. As in other branches of social choice theory, a perfect aggregation rule does not exist.

## 6 THE RELATIONSHIP TO OTHER AGGREGATION PROBLEMS

Before concluding, it is useful to consider the relationship between the theory of judgment aggregation and other branches of aggregation theory. Let me focus on three related aggregation problems: preference aggregation, abstract aggregation and probability aggregation.

### *6.1 Preference aggregation*

The theory of preference aggregation in the long and established tradition of Condorcet and Arrow addresses the following question: How can a group of individuals arrive at a collective preference ordering on some set of alternatives on the basis of the group members' individual preference orderings on them? Condorcet's classic paradox illustrates some of the challenges raised by this problem. Consider a group of individuals seeking to form collective preferences over three alternatives, $x$, $y$ and $z$, where the first individual prefers $x$ to $y$ to $z$, the second $y$ to $z$ to $x$, and the third $z$ to $x$ to $y$. It is then easy to see that majority voting over pairs of alternatives fails to yield a rational collective preference ordering: there are majorities for $x$ over $y$, for $y$ over $z$, and yet for $z$ over $x$ — a 'preference cycle'. Arrow's theorem [1951/1963] generalizes this observation by showing that, when there are three or more alternatives, the only aggregation rules that generally avoid such cycles and satisfy some other minimal conditions are dictatorial ones. Condorcet's paradox and Arrow's theorem have inspired a massive literature on axiomatic social choice theory, a review of which is entirely beyond the scope of this paper.

How is the theory of preference aggregation related to the theory of judgment aggregation? It turns out that preference aggregation problems can be formally represented within the model of judgment aggregation. The idea is that preference orderings can be represented as sets of accepted preference ranking propositions of the form '*$x$ is preferable to $y$*', '*$y$ is preferable to $z$*', and so on.

To construct this representation formally (following [Dietrich and List, 2007], extending [List and Pettit, 2004]), it is necessary to employ a specially devised predicate logic with two or more constants representing alternatives, denoted $x$, $y$, $z$ and so on, and a two-place predicate '*_is preferable to_*'. To capture the standard rationality conditions on preferences (such as asymmetry, transitivity and connectedness), we define a set of propositions in our predicate logic to be 'consistent' just in case this set is consistent relative to those rationality conditions. For example, the set {*$x$ is preferable to $y$*, *$y$ is preferable to $z$*} is consistent, while the set {$x$ *is preferable to* $y$, $y$ *is preferable to* $z$, $z$ *is preferable to* $x$} — representing a preference cycle — is not. The agenda is then defined as the set of all propositions of the form '$v$ *is preferable to* $w$' and their negations, where $v$ and $w$ are alternatives among $x$, $y$, $z$ and so on. Now each consistent and complete judgment set on this agenda uniquely represents a rational (i.e., asymmetric, transitive and connected) preference ordering. For instance, the judgment set {$x$ *is preferable to* $y$, $y$ *is preferable to* $z$, $x$ *is preferable to* $z$} uniquely represents the preference ordering according to which $x$ is most preferred, $y$ second-most preferred, and $z$ least preferred. Furthermore, a judgment aggregation rule on the given agenda uniquely represents an Arrovian preference aggregation rule (i.e., a function from profiles of individual preference orderings to collective preference orderings).

Under this construction, Condorcet's paradox of cyclical majority preferences becomes a special case of the problem of majority inconsistency discussed in section 2 above. To see this, notice that the judgment sets of the three individuals in the example of Condorcet's paradox are as shown in Table 5. Given these individual judgments, the majority judgments are indeed inconsistent, as the set of propositions accepted by a majority is inconsistent relative to the rationality condition of transitivity.

| | $x$ is preferable to $y$ | $y$ is preferable to $z$ | $x$ is preferable to $z$ |
|---|---|---|---|
| Individual 1 ($x \succ y \succ z$) | True | True | True |
| Individual 2 ($y \succ z \succ x$) | False | True | False |
| Individual 3 ($z \succ x \succ y$) | True | False | False |
| Majority | True | True | False |

Table 5. Condorcet's paradox translated into jugdment aggregation

More generally, it can be shown that, when there are three or more alternatives, the agenda just defined has all the complexity properties introduced in the discussion of the impossibility theorems above (i.e., non-simplicity, even-number-negatability, and total blockedness / path-connectedness), and thus those theorems apply to the case of preference aggregation. In particular, the only aggregation rules satisfying universal domain, collective rationality, independence and unanimity preservation are dictatorships [Dietrich and List, 2007; Dokow and Holzman, forthcoming]; for a similar result with an additional monotonicity condition, see [Nehring, 2003]. This is precisely Arrow's classic impossibility theorem for strict preferences: the conditions of universal domain and collective rationality correspond to Arrow's equally named conditions, independence corresponds to Arrow's so-called 'independence of irrelevant alternatives', and unanimity preservation, finally, corresponds to Arrow's 'weak Pareto principle'.

## *6.2 Abstract aggregation*

The problem of judgment aggregation is closely related to the problem of abstract aggregation first formulated by Wilson [1975] (in the binary version discussed here) and later generalized by Rubinstein and Fishburn [1986] (in a non-binary version). In recent work, the problem has been discussed by Dokow and Holzman [forthcoming] and in a slightly different formulation (the 'property space' formulation) by Nehring and Puppe [2002; 2007a]. Again let me begin by stating the key question: How can a group of individuals arrive at a collective vector of yes/no evaluations over a set of binary issues on the basis of the group members' individual evaluations over them, subject to some feasibility constraints? Suppose there are multiple binary issues on which a positive (1) or negative (0) view is to be taken. An 'evaluation vector' over these issues is an assignment of 0s and 1s to them. Let $Z \subseteq \{0,1\}^k$ be the set of evaluation vectors deemed 'feasible', where $k$ is the total number of issues. Now an 'abstract aggregation rule' is a function that maps each profile of individual evaluation vectors in a given domain of feasible ones to a collective evaluation vector. To represent Kornhauser and Sager's court example in this model, we introduce three issues, corresponding to propositions $p$, $q$ and $r$, and define the set of feasible evaluation vectors to be $Z = \{(0,0,0),(0,1,0),(1,0,0),(1,1,1)\}$, i.e., the set of 0/1 assignments that respect the doctrinal constraint whereby positive evaluations on the first two issues (corresponding to $p$ and $q$) are necessary and sufficient for a positive evaluation on the third one (corresponding to $r$). More generally, a judgment aggregation problem can be represented in the abstract aggregation model by defining the set of feasible evaluation vectors to be the set of admissible truth-value assignments to the unnegated propositions on the agenda. The problem of majoritarian inconsistency then reemerges as a failure of issue-wise majority voting to preserve feasibility from the individual to the collective level.

As discussed in List and Puppe [forthcoming], the model of abstract aggregation is informationally sparser than the logic-based model of judgment aggregation. To see that by translating judgment aggregation problems into abstract ones we lose some information, notice that the same set of feasible evaluation vectors may result from very different agendas and thus from very different decision problems. For example, the set of feasible evaluation vectors resulting from the agenda containing $p$, $p$ *if and only if* $q$, $p$ *and* $q$ (and negations), without any doctrinal constraint, coincides with that resulting from the agenda in the court example — namely $Z$ as just defined — although syntactically and interpretationally those agendas are clearly very different from each other.

The abstract aggregation model is arguably at its strongest when our primary interest lies in how the existence of non-degenerate aggregation rules depends on the nature of the feasibility constraints, as opposed to the particular syntactic structure or interpretation of the underlying propositions. Indeed, the agenda characterization theorems reviewed above have their intellectual origins in the literature on abstract aggregation (and here particularly in Nehring and Puppe's

[2002] work as well as in Dokow and Holzman's [forthcoming] subsequent paper). When the logical formulation of a decision problem is to be made explicit, or when the rationality constraints on judgments (and their possible relaxations) are to be analyzed using logical concepts, on the other hand, the logic-based model of judgment aggregation seems more natural.

## *6.3 Probability aggregation*

In the theory of probability aggregation, finally, the focus is not on making consistent acceptance/rejection judgments on the propositions of interest, but rather on arriving at a coherent probability assignment to them (e.g., [McConway, 1981; Genest and Zidek, 1986; Mongin, 1995]). Thus the central question is: How can a group of individuals arrive at a collective probability assignment to a given set of propositions on the basis of the group members' individual probability assignments, while preserving probabilistic coherence (i.e., the satisfaction of the standard axioms of probability theory)? The problem is quite a general one. In a number of decision-making settings, the aim is not so much to come up with acceptance/rejection judgments on certain propositions but rather to arrive at probabilistic information about the degree of belief we are entitled to assign to them or the likelihood of the events they refer to.

Interestingly, the move from a binary to a probabilistic setting opens up some non-degenerate possibilities of aggregation not existent in the standard case of judgment aggregation. A key insight is that probabilistic coherence is preserved under linear averaging of probability assignments. In other words, if each individual coherently assigns probabilities to a given set of propositions, then any weighted linear average of these probability assignments across individuals still constitutes an overall coherent probability assignment. Moreover, it is easy to see that this method of aggregation satisfies the analogues of all the input, output and responsiveness conditions introduced above: i.e., it accepts all possible profiles of coherent individual probability assignments as input, produces a coherent collective probability assignment as output and satisfies the analogues of systematicy and unanimity preservation; it also satisfies anonymity if all individuals are given equal weight in the averaging. A classic theorem by McConway [1981] shows that, if the agenda is isomorphic to a Boolean algebra with more than four elements, linear averaging is uniquely characterized by an independence condition, a unanimity preservation condition as well as the analogues of universal domain and collective rationality. Recently, Dietrich and List [2008b] have obtained a generalization of (a variant of) this theorem for a much larger class of agendas (essentially, the analogue of non-simple agendas). A challenge for the future is to obtain even more general theorems that yield both standard results on judgment aggregation and interesting characterizations of salient probability aggregation methods as special cases.

## 7 CONCLUDING REMARKS

The aim of this article has been to give a brief introduction to the theory of judgment aggregation. My focus has been on some of the central ideas and questions of the theory as well as a few illustrative results. Inevitably, a large number of other important results and promising research directions within the literature have been omitted (for surveys of other important results and directions, see, for example, [List and Puppe, forthcoming; List, 2006; Dietrich, 2007a; Nehring and Puppe, 2007a] as well as the online bibliography on judgment aggregation at `http://personal.lse.ac.uk/list/JA.htm`). In particular, the bulk of this article has focused on judgment aggregation in accordance with a systematicity or independence condition that forces the aggregation to take place in a proposition-by-proposition manner. Arguably, some of the most interesting *open* questions in the theory of judgment aggregation concern the relaxation of this propositionwise restriction and the move towards other, potentially more 'holistic' notions of responsiveness. Without the restriction to propositionwise aggregation, the space of possibilities suddenly grows dramatically, and I have here reviewed only a few simple examples of aggregation rules that become possible, namely premise-based, sequential priority and distance-based ones.

To provide a more systematic perspective on those possibilities, Dietrich [2007b] has recently introduced a general condition of 'independence of irrelevant information', defined in terms of a relation of informational relevance between propositions. An aggregation rule satisfies this condition just in case the collective judgment on each proposition depends only on individual judgments on propositions that are deemed relevant to it. In the classical case of propositionwise aggregation, each proposition is deemed relevant only to itself. In the case of a premise-based procedure, by contrast, premises are deemed relevant to conclusions, and in the case of a sequential priority procedure the relevance relation is given by a linear order of priority among the propositions. Important future research questions concern the precise interplay between the logical structure of the agenda, the relevance relation and the conditions on aggregation rules in determining the space of possibilities.

Another research direction considers the idea of decisiveness rights in the context of judgment aggregation, following Sen's classic work [1970] on the liberal paradox. In judgment aggregation, it is particularly interesting to investigate the role of experts and the question of whether we can arrive at consistent collective judgments when giving different individuals different weights depending on their expertise on the propositions in question. Some existing impossibility results [Dietrich and List, 2008c] highlight the difficulties that can result from such deference to experts, but many open questions remain.

Finally, as in other areas of social choice theory, there is much research to be done on the relationship between aggregative and deliberative modes of decision-making. In many realistic settings, decision-makers do not merely mechanically aggregate their votes or judgments, but they exchange and share information, communicate with each other and update their beliefs. Some authors have begun to consider possible connections between the theory of judgment aggregation and the theory of belief revision [Pettit, 2006; List, 2008; Dietrich, 2008c; Pivato, 2008]. But much of this terrain is still unexplored. My hope is that this article will contribute to stimulating further research.

## ACKNOWLEDGEMENTS

I am very grateful to Franz Dietrich and Laura Valentini for comments and suggestions on this paper.

## BIBLIOGRAPHY

[Arrow, 1951/1963] K. Arrow. *Social Choice and Individual Values.* New York (Wiley), 1951/1963.

[Black, 1948] D. Black. On the Rationale of Group Decision-making. *Journal of Political Economy* 56(1): 23-34, 1948.

[Bovens and Rabinowicz, 2006] L. Bovens and W. Rabinowicz. Democratic Answers to Complex Questions — An Epistemic Perspective. *Synthese* 150(1): 131-153, 2006.

[Brennan, 2001] G. Brennan. Collective coherence? *International Review of Law and Economics* 21(2): 197-211, 2001.

[Dietrich, 2006] F. Dietrich. Judgment Aggregation: (Im)Possibility Theorems. *Journal of Economic Theory* 126(1): 286-298, 2006.

[Dietrich, 2007a] F. Dietrich. A generalised model of judgment aggregation. *Social Choice and Welfare* 28(4): 529-565, 2007.

[Dietrich, 2007b] F. Dietrich. Aggregation theory and the relevance of some issues to others. Working paper, University of Maastricht, 2007.

[Dietrich, 2008] F. Dietrich. Bayesian group belief. Working paper, University of Maastricht, 2008.

[Dietrich and List, 2007a] F. Dietrich and C. List. Arrow's theorem in judgment aggregation. *Social Choice and Welfare* 29(1): 19-33, 2007.

[Dietrich and List, 2007b] F. Dietrich and C. List. Judgment aggregation by quota rules: majority voting generalized. *Journal of Theoretical Politics* 19(4): 391-424, 2007.

[Dietrich and List, 2007c] F. Dietrich and C. List. Majority voting on restricted domains. Working paper, London School of Economics, 2007.

[Dietrich and List, 2007d] F. Dietrich and C. List. Judgment aggregation with consistency alone. Working paper, London School of Economics, 2007.

[Dietrich and List, 2007e] F. Dietrich and C. List. Strategy-proof judgment aggregation. *Economics and Philosophy* 23: 269-300, 2007.

[Dietrich and List, 2008a] F. Dietrich and C. List. Judgment aggregation without full rationality. *Social Choice and Welfare* 31: 15-39, 2008.

[Dietrich and List, 2008b] F. Dietrich and C. List. Opinion pooling on general agendas. Working paper, London School of Economics, 2008.

[Dietrich and List, 2008c] F. Dietrich and C. List. A liberal paradox for judgment aggregation. *Social Choice and Welfare* 31: 59-78, 2008.

[Dietrich and List, forthcoming] F. Dietrich and C. List. Judgment aggregation under constraints. In T. Boylan and R. Gekker (eds.), *Economics, Rational Choice and Normative Philosophy.* London (Routledge), forthcoming.

[Dietrich and Mongin, 2007] F. Dietrich and P. Mongin. The premise-based approach to judgment aggregation. Working paper, University of Maastricht, 2007.

[Dokow and Holzman, forthcoming] E. Dokow and R. Holzman. Aggregation of binary evaluations. *Journal of Economic Theory*, forthcoming.

[Dokow and Holzman, 2006] E. Dokow and R. Holzman. Aggregation of binary evaluations with abstentions. Working paper, Technion — Israel Institute of Technology, 2006.

[Dryzek and List, 2003] J. Dryzek and C. List. Social Choice Theory and Deliberative Democracy: A Reconciliation. *British Journal of Political Science* 33(1): 1-28, 2003.

[Gärdenfors, 2006] P. Gärdenfors. An Arrow-like theorem for voting with logical consequences. *Economics and Philosophy* 22(2): 181-190, 2006.

[Genest and Zidek, 1986] C. Genest and J. V. Zidek. Combining Probability Distributions: A Critique and Annotated Bibliography. *Statistical Science* 1(1): 113-135, 1986.

[Guilbaud, 1966] G. Th. Guilbaud. Theories of the General Interest, and the Logical Problem of Aggregation. In P. F. Lazarsfeld and N. W. Henry (eds.), *Readings in Mathematical Social Science*. Cambridge/MA (MIT Press): 262-307, 1966.

[Knight and Johnson, 1994] J. Knight and J. Johnson. Aggregation and Deliberation: On the Possibility of Democratic Legitimacy. *Political Theory* 22(2): 277-296, 1994.

[Konieczny and Pino Pérez, 2002] S. Konieczny and R. Pino Pérez. Merging Information Under Constraints: A Logical Framework. *Journal of Logic and Computation* 12(5): 773-808, 2002.

[Kornhauser and Sager, 1986] L. A. Kornhauser and L. G. Sager. Unpacking the Court. *Yale Law Journal* 96(1): 82-117, 1986.

[Kornhauser and Sager, 1993] L. A. Kornhauser and L. G. Sager. The One and the Many: Adjudication in Collegial Courts. *California Law Review* 81: 1-59, 1993.

[Kornhauser, 1992] L. A. Kornhauser. Modeling Collegial Courts. II. Legal Doctrine. *Journal of Law, Economics and Organization* 8: 441-470, 1992.

[Kornhauser and Sager, 2004] L. A. Kornhauser and L. G. Sager. The Many as One: Integrity and Group Choice in Paradoxical Cases. *Philosophy and Public Affairs* 32: 249-276, 2004.

[List, 2003] C. List. A Possibility Theorem on Aggregation over Multiple Interconnected Propositions. *Mathematical Social Sciences* 45(1): 1-13 (with Corrigendum in *Mathematical Social Sciences* 52: 109-110), 2003.

[List, 2004] C. List. A Model of Path-Dependence in Decisions over Multiple Propositions. *American Political Science Review* 98(3): 495-513, 2004.

[List, 2006] C. List. The Discursive Dilemma and Public Reason. *Ethics* 116(2): 362-402, 2006.

[List, 2008] C. List. Group deliberation and the revision of judgments: an impossibility result. Working paper, London School of Economics, 2008.

[List and Pettit, 2002] C. List and P. Pettit. Aggregating Sets of Judgments: An Impossibility Result. *Economics and Philosophy* 18(1): 89-110, 2002.

[List and Pettit, 2004] C. List and P. Pettit. Aggregating Sets of Judgments: Two Impossibility Results Compared. *Synthese* 140(1-2): 207-235, 2004.

[List and Pettit, 2005] C. List and P. Pettit. On the Many as One. *Philosophy and Public Affairs* 33(4): 377-390, 2005.

[List and Puppe, forthcoming] C. List and C. Puppe. Judgment aggregation: a survey. In P. Anand, C. Puppe and P. Pattaniak (eds.), *Oxford Handbook of Rational and Social Choice*. Oxford (Oxford University Press), forthcoming.

[McConway, 1981] K. McConway. Marginalization and Linear Opinion Pools. *Journal of the American Statistical Association* 76: 410-14 1981.

[Miller, 1992] D. Miller. Deliberative Democracy and Social Choice. *Political Studies* 40(Special Issue): 54-67, 1992.

[Mongin, 1995] P. Mongin. Consistent Bayesian aggregation. *Journal of Economic Theory* 66: 313-351, 1995.

[Mongin, forthcoming] P. Mongin. Factoring Out the Impossibility of Logical Aggregation. *Journal of Economic Theory*, forthcoming.

[Nehring, 2003] K. Nehring. Arrow's theorem as a corollary. *Economics Letters* 80(3): 379-382, 2003.

[Nehring and Puppe, 2002] K. Nehring and C. Puppe. Strategyproof Social Choice on Single-Peaked Domains: Possibility, Impossibility and the Space Between. Working paper, University of California at Davis, 2002.

[Nehring and Puppe, 2007a] K. Nehring and C. Puppe. Abstract Arrovian Aggregation. Working paper, University of Karlsruhe, 2007.

[Nehring and Puppe, 2007b] K. Nehring and C. Puppe. The structure of strategy-proof social choice — Part I: General characterization and possibility results on median spaces. *Journal of Economic Theory* 135(1): 269-305, 2007.

[Pauly and van Hees, 2006] M. Pauly and M. van Hees. Logical Constraints on Judgment Aggregation. *Journal of Philosophical Logic* 35(6): 569-585, 2006.

[Pettit, 2001] P. Pettit. Deliberative Democracy and the Discursive Dilemma. *Philosophical Issues* 11: 268-299, 2001.

[Pettit, 2006] P. Pettit. When to defer to majority testimony — and when not. *Analysis* 66: 179-87, 2006.

[Pigozzi, 2006] G. Pigozzi. Belief merging and the discursive dilemma: an argument-based account to paradoxes of judgment aggregation. *Synthese* 152(2): 285-298, 2006.

[Pivato, 2008] M. Pivato. The Discursive Dilemma and Probabilistic Judgement Aggregation. Munich Personal RePEc Archive, 2008.

[Riker, 1982] W. Riker. *Liberalism Against Populism.* San Franscisco (W. H. Freeman), 1982.

[Rubinstein and Fishbur, 1986] A. Rubinstein and P. C. Fishburn. Algebraic Aggregation Theory. *Journal of Economic Theory* 38(1): 63-77, 1986.

[Sen, 1966] A. K. Sen. A Possibility Theorem on Majority Decisions. *Econometrica* 34(2): 491-499, 1966.

[Sen, 1970] A. K. Sen. The Impossibility of a Paretian Liberal. *Journal of Political Economy* 78: 152-157, 1970.

[Wilson, 1975] R. Wilson. On the Theory of Aggregation. *Journal of Economic Theory* 10(1): 89-99, 1975.

# THE ECONOMICS OF SCIENTIFIC KNOWLEDGE

Jesús P. Zamora Bonilla

## 1 THE IDEA OF AN ECONOMICS OF SCIENTIFIC KNOWLEDGE

The economics of scientific knowledge (ESK) is one of the youngest members in the heterogeneous field of 'Science Studies'. Being itself an example of the 'crossing of boundaries' movement that characterises a big part of recent academic activity, it is very difficult, if not impossible, to provide a comprehensive definition of ESK. However, for practical purposes we need in this survey some criteria which help to keep its content under reasonable limits, both in terms of extension and of coherence. So, one *prima facie* plausible definition of ESK, as including any piece of research having to do with 'the economic study of the production and diffusion of scientific knowledge', would force us to include in this paper such an enormous body of literature that at least a full book would be necessary to revise it.[1] On the other hand, the fact that this survey is part of a book on the philosophy of economics, belonging itself into a bigger *Handbook of Philosophy of Science*, suggests that we may select, from this immense literature, just those works dealing with questions more or less related to the traditional topics in the *philosophical* study of science, i.e., mainly topics of epistemological or methodological character. Hence, my working definition of ESK will be *the application of concepts and methods of economic analysis to the study of the epistemic nature and value of scientific knowledge.*

A little bit of history will be pertinent to better understand the implications of this definition. The expression 'economics of scientific knowledge' was first popularised by Wade Hands in a series of papers dating from the beginning of the nineties [Hands, 1994a; 1994b], drawing on an analogy with what defenders of the so called 'Strong Programme in the Sociology of Science' had done a couple of decades ago, i.e., to defy the traditional division of labour between sociologists of science and philosophers of science (see [Bloor, 1976]). According to that tradition, *philosophy of science* would study the *cognitive* aspects of scientific research ('methodology') and of science's epistemic outputs ('epistemology'), whereas *sociology of science* should be devoted to analyse the working of science as a social

[1]See the two volumes in Stephan and Audretsch [2000], for a good selection of papers on the economics of science falling under this comprehensive definition. Mirowski and Sent [2002a] join also a number of important papers on the economics of science, as well as on ESK.

Handbook of the Philosophy of Science. Volume 13: Philosophy of Economics.
Volume editor: Uskali Mäki. General editors: Dov M. Gabbay, Paul Thagard and John Woods.

*institution*, and its relations with other institutions, without entering into the question of what leads researchers to accept a particular method, datum, or theory as 'right'. Without much danger of confusion, we may add to the core of that tradition the thesis that the *economics of science* should be concerned just with the 'economic' problems of scientific research, i.e., how to fund it, or how is it related to economic growth through the mediation of technological progress. Little interference would exist between these three academic disciplines (philosophy-, sociology-, and economics-of-science), for no one of them put questions for which the other two might conceivably provide a relevant answer. On the contrary, the 'new' sociologists of scientific knowledge of the seventies, inspired by the work of Thomas Kuhn and of the 'second' Wittgenstein, amongst others, endorsed the view that the construction of scientific knowledge (i.e., the constitution of a consensus, or a dissensus, about any scientific item) is essentially a *social* process, in which all the agents take one decision or another on the ground of their particular *interests*. From this fact the conclusion was drawn that the creation of scientific knowledge was as legitimate a topic for social analysis as any other process of social interaction. Hence, whereas 'sociology of science' could be taken as the study of the institutional aspects of scientific activity, 'sociology of scientific knowledge' (SSK) would have amongst its legitimate objects of study those questions traditionally reserved for methodology and epistemology.

Wade Hands' suggestion was, basically, that the same argument could be applied not only to sociology, but to economics as well:

> If we mirror the distinction between the sociology of science and the sociology of scientific knowledge, then the economics of *science* would be the application of economic theory, or ideas found in economic theory, to explaining the behaviour of scientists and/or the intellectual output of the scientific community. That is, given the goals of the individual scientists or those of the scientific community (for example, the 'pursuit of truth') the economics of science might be used to explain the behaviour of those in the scientific community or to make recommendations about how those goals might be achieved in a more efficient manner. In this way the economics of science would relate to science in precisely the way that microeconomics has typically related to the firms in the market economy (...) On the other hand, the economics *of scientific knowledge* (ESK) would involve economics in a philosophically more fundamental way. The ESK would involve economics, or at least metaphors derived from economics, in the actual characterization of scientific knowledge - that is, economics would be involved fundamentally in the epistemological discourse regarding the nature of scientific knowledge. Like the SSK argues that scientific knowledge comes to be constructed out of a social process, the ESK would argue that scientific knowledge comes to be constructed out of an economic process. [Hands, 1994a, p. 87]

The main idea behind this characterisation of ESK is that it essentially deals with the 'nature' of scientific knowledge, and that the construction of this knowledge is an 'economic process', but one may suspect that many of the topics attributed to what Hands calls here 'the economics of science' (i.e., the explanation of scientists' behaviour, or the 'recommendations' about how the epistemic goals of science can be more efficiently attained) would *exactly* refer to the questions he allotted to ESK. Perhaps in order to avoid such a confusion, in a more recent work Hands draws the distinction between the economics of science and ESK in a slightly different way:

> Economics of science analyzes (explains and/or predicts) the behavior of scientists in the same way that an economist might analyze (explain and/or predict) the behavior of firms or consumers. Like the Mertonian school of sociology, the economics of science almost always *presumes* that science produces products of high cognitive quality, but investigating whether it "really" does so is not considered to be the proper subject for economic analysis (it would be like an economist investigating whether the products of a firm "really" satisfy consumer wants). By contrast, ESK, like SSK, would address the question of whether the epistemologically right stuff is being produced in the economy of science; ESK mixes economics and normative science theory. The distinction between the economics of science and ESK mirrors not only the difference between sociology of science and SSK, but also the traditional distinction between microeconomics and welfare economics. Microeconomics, it is usually argued, predicts and/or explains the behavior of economic agents, whereas welfare economics focuses on the question of whether the social configuration produced as a result of the actions of these agents is "optimal" or "efficient" (...) The economics of science predicts and/or explains the behavior of scientists and scientific institutions, whereas ESK adds the question of whether those actions and institutions produce scientific products that are cognitively efficient or optimal (or if they are not optimal, how the institutions might be changed in order to improve epistemic efficiency). [Hands, 2001, pp. 360–1]

Although I agree that normative questions are paramount in the ESK, I think the identification of ESK with something like an '(epistemically) normative branch of the economics of science' would leave too much outside. Actually, most of the works discussed by Hands in the pages following the second quotation are not only 'normative' but 'explanatory', and, what is more relevant, these works do not consist in the application to normative problems of some (merely descriptive) economic models of science *already* existing; they are, instead, explanatory models *specifically* devised to attack those normative problems. Hence, the production of models that explain the behaviour of scientists is in itself an important part of ESK (or so will it be taken in this survey), at least as long as these models refer to scientists' *epistemic* decisions, i.e., those decisions in which what is at stake is the epistemic value that must be conferred to certain theories, hypotheses, models, research programmes, data, experiments, observations, etc. Hands, however, has wisely pointed to an important difference between the sociological and the economic understanding of social phenomena: in general, economic models are constructed in such a way that they can be given a normative interpretation almost automatically, for, after all, they show transparently the evaluations made by the agents whose interaction constitutes those models' object, and these evaluations are the raw material for any normative assessment. Contrarily to some appearances, economists are proner than sociologists to offer normative guidance, at least by telling who is going to be benefited and who is going to be damaged (and how much) if things happen in such and such a way instead of otherwise; sociologists, instead, often tend to avoid anything that may sound like an evaluative claim, fearing not to look 'impartial' enough (within the fields which are closer to ours, 'science, technology and society studies' and 'social epistemology' would be the main exception; see, e.g., Fuller [1988] and [2000]). In particular, the question of the *efficiency* of scientific institutions and practices arises much more naturally in an economic research than in a sociological one, though obviously this does not entail that the latter can not deliver some important normative conclusions.

Returning to the definition of ESK offered at the beginning ('the application of concepts and methods of economic analysis to the study of the epistemic nature and value of scientific knowledge'), it entails that *ESK will be considered here more as a branch of epistemology than as a branch of economics*: economic concepts and methods are the tools, but scientific knowledge is our object. The main questions to be asked are, hence, of the following kind: how is scientific knowledge 'socially constructed'?, i.e., how does a consensus about an item of knowledge emerge within a scientific discipline?, how do scientists determine the epistemic value of that knowledge?, how can we explain and assess the norms according to which scientists make this valuation?, in particular, how can we evaluate the cognitive efficiency of the methods employed by scientists and the objectivity of their cognitive output?, and so on. Though the works that will be commented below are very heterogeneous in many aspects, they all have in common their trying to answer some of these questions by assuming that the decisions of scientists can be analysed in more or less the same way as economic models conceptualise the decisions of entrepreneurs, consumers, and other economic agents, i.e., by assuming that scientists are trying to optimise some utility function, given all the physical, psychological, and institutional constraints they face, and given that the other scientists and the other relevant agents are also trying to do the same simultaneously.

Nevertheless, as the readers of this book will have surely noticed, there is an immense diversity of approaches within economics, and this allows for a corresponding variety of brands in the ESK. In order to simplify my exposition, I will divide them according to a couple of distinctions. In the first place, two of the more general conceptual frameworks in economics are what we could call 'the optimisation paradigm' and 'the exchange paradigm' (cf. [Buchanan, 1996]): according to the former, economics is all about how to maximise some important quantities (utility, profits, social welfare...), while for the latter the essential economic phenomenon is what Adam Smith identified as our 'propensity to truck, barter, and exchange', or what the Austrian economist Ludwig von Mises called 'catallaxy'. In the second place, in some branches of economics it is assumed that the proper way of doing research is by building abstract models which try to capture, usually in a strongly idealised way, the essential aspects of the portion of reality we want to study; in other branches, however, the appropriate method is taken to be that of a discursive analysis, giving more importance to the details of economic practices than to purely formal arguments. Roughly following this classification, I will divide the main body of this survey into three parts. In the next two sectios, I will present those works that try to understand scientific research as a process of rational cost-benefit decision making (section 2) or of optimisation of an epistemic utility function (section 3). Section 4 will be devoted, instead, to analyse the idea that science is basically an institution for the exchange of items of knowledge, a 'marketplace for ideas', to use the typical expression. The last section will present those works that have tried to make a more or less systematic analysis of scientific research as a set of *social mechanisms* through which different agents interact, distinguishing between those attempts of producing mathematical models of scientists' epistemic behaviour, on the one hand, and those less formal, institutionalist approaches, on the other hand. Notwithstanding all this, if we take into account that ESK has still a very short history, one can easily draw the conclusion that many of the conceivable approaches to the economic study of the constitution of scientific knowledge are still undeveloped, or have not even been envisaged at all. I hope the realisation of this fact may encourage some readers to pursue by themselves a number of these untrodden paths.[2]

## 2 THE OPTIMISATION PARADIGM

In a certain sense, we might describe research on scientific methodology (both in its most abstract, philosophical variants, and in the most specific, field-dependent ones) as an attempt to find out what are the 'best' methodological practices, the 'most rational' ones, and so, the whole discipline would fall within the scope of an 'optimisation' approach. A sensible limitation in this survey is, of course, to circumvent it to only those works that have made an explicit use of optimisation concepts derived from economic theory. According to this limited definition, two basic ideas, not essentially in mutual contradiction, are particularly relevant: the idea of optimisation as a rational weighting of costs and benefits, and the idea of

[2]Two obvious research avenues, almost entirely open, would consist in applying social choice theory to the decisions of scientists (following the lines of research on 'judgement aggregation'; e.g., List and Pettit [2002]), as well as economic models of learning (e.g., [Brenner, 1999]). The approach developed in Goodin and Brennan [2001], in which opinions are taken as a subject for bargaining, could also be interestingly applied to the analysis of scientific consensus.

optimisation as the maximisation of a utility function. It is clear that the first concept can be reduced to the second one, since costs and benefits can be taken as the main variables of the relevant utility function, though I will use the difference just for expository reasons.

## 2.1 *Cost-benefit approaches*

Interestingly enough, the first known application of modern economic techniques to solving epistemic problems in science was very explicit in describing the value of a scientific theory as the difference between 'costs' and 'benefits'. I'm referring to Charles Sanders Peirce's 'Note of the Theory of the Economy of Research', published in 1879, less than a decade after the introduction of marginal analysis in economic theory by Carl Menger and Stanley Jevons. In that short article, Peirce considers the problem of how much time or effort to devote to several research processes, by taking into account "the relation between the exactitude of a result and the cost of attaining it" (p. 184). The solution of Peirce's model is that total benefit (the difference between the 'utility' derived from a set of experiments and the total cost of performing them, assuming this to be a constant) is maximised by devoting to each problem an amount of resources such that the 'economic urgency' of every problem, i.e., what we would now call the 'marginal utility' derived from each experiment, is exactly the same. Besides being one of the first applications of marginal utility theory, not only to problems of epistemology, but *tout court*, Peirce's 'Note' is also remarkable by connecting the idea of 'epistemic benefits' with some fundamental concepts of statistics and probability theory, and by advancing a conception statistical methods close to the modern theory of confidence intervals, specially by taking into account the relevance of costs in statistical inference. Peirce's insight about the type of theoretical and practical problems his approach could open is even more surprising when we read the last paragraph of his 'Note':

> It is to be remarked that the theory here given rests on the supposition that the object of the investigation is the ascertainment of truth. When an investigation is made for the purpose of attaining personal distinction, the economics of the problem are entirely different. But that seems to be well enough understood by those engaged in that sort of investigation. [Peirce, 1879, p. 190]

Actually, and probably to Peirce's despair, the evolution of ESK in the last decades can be described as a progressive tendency to give more importance to 'the purpose of attaining personal distinction' as an essential factor in explaining the process of knowledge construction.

Peirce's work on the economics of research, however, passed almost unnoticed by as much as a century, till it was rediscovered for the philosophical world by Nicholas Rescher, who devoted a paper to it in the mid seventies [Rescher, 1976], and who has incorporated to his pragmatist vision of science Peirce's idea that economic considerations are essential to understand the rationality of research.[3] Rescher made use of this idea in a series of books, starting by *Scientific Progress*, symptomatically subtitled 'A Philosophical Essay on the Economics of Research in Natural Science'. Although that book was written in the times when the discussion about the possibility of epistemic progress was most eager, it only contains a few references to that debate (e.g., [Rescher, 1978a, pp. 189 ff.], where he suggests that the field of practical applications of scientific knowledge can offer a common ground for 'incommensurable paradigms', in the Kuhnian sense). Instead, the book's main concern is with cultural disillusionment about science:

> Disappointment is abroad that the great promise of the first half of the century is not being kept, and there are many indications that scientists are beginning to move back towards a view of the *fin de siècle* type and to envisage an end to scientific progress. The general public is perhaps even more drastically disillusioned (...) Science has produced numerous and rapid changes in the condition of our lives, but many of them do not seem for the better. Disillusionment all too readily leads to disaffection. A great deal of sentiment is abroad that is anti-scientific and even irrationalistic in orientation (...) A realistic and dispassionate reappraisal of the future prospects of science is thus very much in order. [Rescher, 1978a, pp. 52–3]

It is in order to introduce 'realisticness' in the assessment of science that Rescher introduces the notion of costs as an essential part of his theory. This he does it by two different means. In the first place, in *Scientific Progress* he tries to show that scientific research is subject to a 'law of diminishing returns' because of the increasing cost of our 'knowledge-yielding interactions with nature' (*ibid.*, p. 16); Rescher makes a phenomenological description of the history of science, which empirically justifies this claim, and then proceeds to offer an 'economic' explanation of the phenomenon: important results grow in a diminishing way as the resources devoted to science increase, basically because of two reasons: first, there is a law according to which "when the total volume of findings of (at least) *routine* quality stands at $Q$, the volume of (at least) *important* findings stands at (...) $Q^{1/2}$" (*ibid.*, p. 98), or, in a more general way, the number of findings of merit $m$ decreases exponentially as $m$ grows; second, the increasing technical difficulties in the creation and implementation of scientific instruments and experiments makes it grow the economic cost of each *unit* of new relevant scientific information. This diagnosis allows Rescher to conclude that, on the one hand, science is going to face economic and technical limits much earlier than the limits derived from the finiteness of human ingenuity, but, on the other hand, there

[3] Joseph Sneed [1989], using the structuralist notion of a scientific theory (see Balzer, Moulines and Sneed [1987]) also provides a model analogous to Peirce's to determine the optimum research agenda in the development of a 'theory net'. In this model, the costs are resources, the benefits are specific solved problems (the 'elements' of the 'theory net'), and it is taken into account that solving a problem may modify the probability of solving further problems.

is really no end in the prospects of the quantity, quality and variety of forthcoming discoveries (see also [Rescher, 1996]).

Most important for the evolution of ESK is the second type of use Rescher makes of the Peircean insights, first in his book *Peirce's Philosophy of Science* (1978b), and more decisively in *Cognitive Economy. The Economic Dimension of the Theory of Knowledge* (1989). In the latter book, Rescher generalises the identification of rationality with cost-benefit calculation to other aspects of scientific research besides that of the selection of problems (what, as Hands [1994a, p. 87] rightly points, would belong more to the 'economics of science' than to ESK, as we defined them in the first section). In particular, Rescher employs the cost-benefit idea to argue for the following points:

a) scepticism is wrong in only considering the cost of mistakenly accepting wrong hypotheses, but does not take into account the cost or rejecting right ones (i.e., the benefits we would have had by accepting them); Cartesian rationalism commits just the opposite error; an intermediate attitude towards epistemic risks is better than both extremes;

b) scientific communication is also organised according to the principle of minimising costs, in this case, the cost of searching for relevant information;

c) rational theory choice is grounded on the principle of induction, which is given an economic interpretation: we tend to infer from our data those theories which have more simplicity, uniformity, regularity, coherence, and so on, because these virtues are cognitive labour saving; only when the most economic theory does not give us enough benefits, is it rational to look for a not so simple hypothesis;

d) from a falsifications point of view, the same applies to the decisions about what theories are going to be proposed and tested in the first place.

Another author who has tried to apply 'cost-benefit rationality' to problems in philosophy of science, and in particular to its falsificationist brand, has been Gerard Radnitzky [1986; 1987]. The problem Radnitzky initially considers is the following: according to Popper, scientists' decisions of accepting or rejecting a theory or a 'basic statement' (i.e., an empirical proposition employed to test a more general theory) are not reducible to any kind of algorithm (like deductive or inductive logic, say), but always rest on conventional decisions; Popper, however, did not explain what precise criteria scientists can or must employ in taking those decisions, in particular, what kind of arguments can be used to decide when to *stop testing* a theory or a basic statement. Radnitzky's idea is to apply Popper's 'situational logic' to that problem, reconstructing the scientist's situation as one in which account must be taken of the 'costs' and 'benefits' of every possible decision: for example, rejecting a particular basic statement can demand offering an alternative explanation of how scientific instruments work, and the latter can be 'more expensive' than the former because it not only demands to invent that explanation, but also to lose some of the *other* things which had been explained with the old theory.

Regarding the merits and demerits of Rescher's and Radnitzky's approaches, one general criticism of their 'cost-benefit' metaphor is that they hardly offer any hint about how costs and benefits can be made commensurable, and this leaves all scientific decisions basically underdetermined. In particular, I think Radnitzky's approach is still less fruitful, mainly because of the following reasons:

a) In the first place, being a true Popperian, Radnitzky attempts to separate his theory as much as he can from the 'sociologist' approaches he attempts to criticise (i.e., those according to which scientists are really moved by 'social', 'non-epistemic' interests, which usually make them more or less blind to rational arguments); this forces him to present his approach as a description of 'ideal type' researchers, motivated only by 'scientific progress', and so he does not help us to know whether *real* scientists behave according to that ideal, or, still worse, whether real human beings *can* behave that way. Rescher attaches more importance to the actual cognitive capacities of people, though without entering into many details.

b) In the second place, describing the goal of science just as 'scientific progress', as Radnitzky does, is little more than a tautology, for 'progress' means 'approximation to some goals', and this is empty until we know what the goals are. We need either a *philosophical* explanation of these goals ('certainty', 'predictive success', or 'problem solving'; but, by which criteria do we decide what problems are 'important', and what an 'interesting' solution consists in?), or we simply identify the aims of science with the goals of *real* scientists (but this seems precluded by point a). Obviously, Radnitzky's own option is the first one, and he takes the goal of science to be 'interesting truth' (but why not 'interesting' from the point of view of the 'social interests' of scientists?); unfortunately, in spite of Popper's efforts, we lack a convincing logical argument showing that falsificationism is the optimal methodology to follow in our attempt to approach to the truth. Rescher's view, on the contrary, seems to be closer to the idea that the relevant values are those of real scientists, but he does not offer a model of how these different aims are mutually interconnected or integrated.

c) In the third place, Radnitzky's use of the terms 'cost' and 'benefit' is too naive from an economic point of view. This is basically due to the fact that, having deprived himself of an operative description of the goals of science (e.g., a coherent theory about how do some methodological decisions *exactly* help in approaching the goals of science), it is always indeterminate *why* is something a 'cost' or a 'benefit', and, in a similar way, it is always unclear how can we decide that some costs are 'higher' or 'lower' than some benefits, since we lack something like a *measure* of them.

d) Lastly, we can criticise the very choice of cost-benefit analysis as an appropriate tool to understand the process of scientific research. In Radnitzky's case, this choice is probably due to his desire of going directly to an explanation of *ideal* scientists' rational decision making, without assuming that something like induction can really exist, and without giving relevance to the 'social' aspects of scientific research. An analytical tool more coherent with standard economic practice is *rational choice theory* (i.e., the hypotheses of expected utility maximisation), which Rescher does not hesitate in using, but this option requires a detailed description of the agent's goals (her 'utility function', even if it contained only epistemic factors), as well as a hypothesis about the agent's beliefs, expressed in terms of *quantitative probabilities*, and this is inconsistent with the Popperian rejection of induction. A still more appropriate analytical tool is *game theory*, which adds to rational choice considerations the idea that the results of an individual's behaviour also depend on the actions of others; but Radnitzky seems to be looking for a theory which can give methodological advises that could in principle be followed by a completely isolated researcher (a 'Robinson Crusoe', so to say), and ignores everything that could take into account the essentially *collective* nature of the scientific enterprise.

## 3 EPISTEMIC UTILITY APPROACHES

The second route that has been followed within the optimisation approach has consisted into trying to define a specific ('cognitive', or 'epistemic') utility function which rational scientific research should maximise. This has been the strategy of what is usually called *cognitive decision theory*, which is basically an adaptation of the Bayesian theory of rational choice to the case when the decisions to be made are those of accepting some propositions or hypotheses instead of others.[4] Hence, in the case of scientific research, it is assumed that scientists decide (or should decide, if we give this approach a normative interpretation) to accept a particular solution to a scientific problem, instead of an alternative solution, if and only if the expected utility they derive from accepting the former is higher than the expected utility they would attain from accepting any other solution to that problem. The expected utility of accepting the hypothesis $h$ given the 'evidence' $e$ is defined as:

$$(1) \quad EU(h,e) = \Sigma_{s \in X} u(h,s)p(s,e)$$

where the $s$'s are the possible states of the world, $u(h,s)$ is the *epistemic* utility of accepting $h$ if the true state of the world is $s$, and $p(s,e)$ is the probability of $s$ being the true state given the evidence $e$. One fundamental problem for a cognitive utility theory is, of course, that of defining an 'appropriate' epistemic utility function $u$; but, before discussing this problem, there is a still more basic conceptual difficulty that has to be mentioned: standard decision theory is a theory about what *actions* an agent will perform, given her options, her preferences, and the knowledge,

[4]See Niiniluoto [1987, ch. 12], for an exposition of the first relevant contributions to cognitive decision theory, and Weintraub [1990] for a sceptical argument.

beliefs, or information she has about how the relevant things are. It may sound even absurd to say that one can choose what to know, or what to believe. Of course, one can do things in order to gain more or less information, and one can as well allocate more effort to look for information about some topics than about others, but, once the results of this search are in front of you, you usually do not 'choose' what to believe: you just happen to have certain beliefs. Indeed, the fact that a person's beliefs have been 'chosen' by her is frequently a very strong reason to doubt of their truth, or at least, to doubt of the epistemic rationality of that person. Cognitive decision theorists counterargue that the object of an epistemic utility function is not really an agent's system of beliefs: these are represented in (1) by the (subjective) probability function $p$. The 'acts' whose cognitive utility is relevant are, rather, those of *accepting* or *rejecting* (or suspending judgement on) a given proposition (the hypothesis $h$). As it has been cogently defended by Patrick Maher [1993, pp. 133 ff.], the acceptance of a scientific hypothesis is logically independent of our belief in its truth: attaching probability 1, or any other 'high' level of probability, to a theory is neither a sufficient nor a necessary condition for its acceptance (for example, most scientific theories are accepted even though scientists actually believe they are not literally true). We may add that, as it will be evident in the next sections, scientists usually have ('social') reasons to accept a hypothesis that have nothing to do with how confident they are about its truth.

Other possible objection is that, even assuming that acceptance and belief are not the same thing, the only relevant thing from the point of view of a sound epistemology is the latter, and not the former; for example, van Fraassen [1980] made precisely this point in discussing the 'inference to the best explanation' approach: once you has concluded that $h$ has a higher probability (but less than 1) than any rival theory, accepting $h$ would entail to go further than what your evidence allows. This criticism, however, seems to be based on the assumption that accepting a theory is identical with attaching probability 1 to it, what is not the case, as Maher has argued. Nevertheless, the idea that once you have subjective probabilities you don't need acceptance may still have a point, particularly for Bayesian epistemologists. Maher's answer is to point to the fact that scientists (and ordinary people as well) do *actually* accept and reject theories and other types of propositions (an empirical phenomenon that calls for some explanation), and even more importantly:

> Much of what is recorded in the history of science is categorical assertions by scientists of one or another hypothesis, together with reasons adduced in support of those hypotheses and against competing hypotheses. It is much less common for history to record scientists' probabilities. Thus philosophers of science without a theory of acceptance lack the theoretical resources to discuss the rationality (or irrationality) or most of the judgements recorded in the history of science (...) Without a theory of acceptance, it is also impossible to infer anything about scientists' subjective probabilities from their categorical assertions. Thus for a philosophy of science without a theory of accep-

> tance, the subjective probabilities of most scientists must be largely inscrutable. This severely restricts the degree to which Bayesian confirmation theory can be shown to agree with pretheoretically correct judgements of confirmation that scientists have made. [Maher, 1993, pp. 162f.]

Once we have seen some of the reasons to take acceptance as an act scientists can perform, we can turn to the question of what is the utility function they are assumed to be maximising when they decide to accept some propositions instead of others. Cognitive decision theory is grounded on the idea that this utility function is of an epistemic nature, i.e., the utility of accepting $h$ only depends on the 'epistemic virtues' $h$ may have. Or, as the first author in using the epistemic utility concept stated:

> the utilities should reflect the value or disvalue which the outcomes have from the point of view of pure scientific research, rather than the practical advantages or disadvantages that might result from the application of an accepted hypotheses, according as the latter is true or false. Let me refer to the kind of utilities thus vaguely characterized as *purely scientific*, or *epistemic*, *utilities*. [Hempel, 1960, p. 465]

Of course, it was not assumed by Hempel, nor by other cognitive decision theorists, that a *real* scientist's utility function was affected only by epistemic factors; after all, researchers are human beings with preferences over a very wide range of things and events. But most of these authors assume that scientists, *qua* scientists, *should* base their decisions on purely epistemic considerations (and perhaps often do it). So, what are the cognitive virtues an epistemic utility function must contain as its arguments?[5] One obvious answer is 'truth': *coeteris paribus*, it is better to accept a theory if it is true, than the same theory if it is false. This does not necessarily entail that accepting a true proposition is always better than accepting a false one (although some authors have defended this, as Levi [1967]), for other qualities, which some false theories may have in a higher degree that some true theories, are also valuable for scientists, as, e.g., the informative content of a proposition (recall Rescher's argument against scepticism). So, one sensible proposal for defining the expected epistemic utility of $h$ is to take it as a weighted average of the probability $h$ has of being true, given the evidence $e$, and the amount of information $h$ provides. This leads to a measure of expected cognitive utility like the following [Levi, 1967; Hilpinen, 1968]:

$$(2) \quad EU(h,e) = p(h,e) - qp(h)$$

where the parameter $q$ is a measure of the scientist's attitude towards risk: the lower $q$ is in the epistemic utility function of a researcher, the more risk averse

[5]Thomas Kuhn's famous discussion about the fundamental values of science (precision, coherence, scope, simplicity, and fecundity), and about how they can be given different weight by different scientists [Kuhn, 1977], can easily be translated into the language of utility theory.

she is, for she will prefer theories with a higher degree of confirmation ($p(h,e)$) to theories with a high degree of content ($1 - p(h)$). If formula (2) reflects the real cognitive preferences of scientists, it entails that, in order to be accepted, a theory must be strongly confirmed by the empirical evidence, but must also be highly informative. Scientific research is a difficult task because, usually, contentful propositions become disconfirmed sooner than later, while it is easy to verify statements that convey little information. One may doubt, however, that these are the only two cognitive requisites of 'good' scientific theories. For example, (2) leads to undesirable conclusions when all the theories scientists must choose among have been empirically falsified (and hence $p(h,e)$ is zero): in this case, the cognitive value of a theory will be proportional to its content, what means that, in order to find a theory better than the already refuted $h$, you can simply join to it any proposition (it does not matter whether true or false) which does not follow from $h$. For example, Newtonian mechanics joined with the story of Greek gods would have a higher scientific value than Newtonian mechanics alone.

In order to solve this difficulty, one interesting suggestion has been to introduce as an additional epistemic virtue the notion of closeness to the truth, or verisimilitude (cf. Niiniluoto [1987] and [1998], Maher [1993]), a notion that was introduced in the philosophy of science as a technical concept in Popper [1963]: amongst false or falsified theories (and perhaps also amongst true ones) the epistemic value does not only depend on the theories' content, but also on how 'far from the full truth' they are. The main difference between Niiniluoto's and Maher's approaches is that the former is 'objective', in the sense that it assumes that there exists some objective measure of 'distance' or '(di)similarity' between the different possible states of nature, and the value of accepting a theory is then defined as an inverse function of the distance between those states of nature that make the theory true and the state which is actually the true one. Maher's proposal, instead, is 'subjective' in the sense that it starts assuming that there is an undefined epistemic utility function with the form $u(h,s)$, perhaps a different one for each individual scientists, and the verisimilitude of a hypothesis is then introduced as a normalised difference between the utility of accepting $h$ given what the true state is, and the utility of accepting a tautology. In Maher's approach, then, epistemic utility is a primitive notion, which is only assumed to obey a short list of simple axioms: (i) accepting a theory is better when it is true than when it is false, (ii) the utility of accepting a given true theory does not depend on what the true state is, (iii) accepting a true theory is better than accepting any proposition derivable from it, (iv) there is at least a true theory accepting which is better than accepting a tautology, and (v) the utility of accepting a full description of a true state of nature is a constant and higher than the utility of accepting a logical contradiction. Maher assumes that different scientists may have different cognitive utility functions, and hence, they can give different verisimilitude values to the same theories, even if the principles listed above are fulfilled. Actually, Niiniluoto's approach is not completely objective, because the definitions of distance between states depend on what factors of similarity each scientist values more or less. This is not a bad thing: after all, cognitive preferences are *preferences*, and these are always the preferences of some particular agent.

One general criticism that can be made to the proposals examined in this subsection is that the arguments their authors give in favour of one definition of cognitive utility or another, are always grounded on our 'intuitions' about what is better or worse in the epistemic sense. With the exception of Maher, they seldom discuss whether those functions do actually represent the cognitive preferences of flesh-and-bone scientists. The absence of such a discussion also deprives us of an answer to the question of what would happen if the real preferences would not coincide with the ones defended by cognitive decision theorists: should we then criticise scientists for not being 'scientific' enough?, or could we take this disagreement as an argument against the utility functions defended by those philosophers? Furthermore, from the proposed definitions it is frequently impossible to derive any behavioural prediction (besides some generalities like the ones commented in connection to formula (2)) about what decisions will be made in a minimally realistic scenario by a scientist who happend to have such cognitive preferences. A different problem is that there are too many definitions of epistemic utility, and it seems reasonable to ask whether the criteria to *prefer* one definition over the rest are also derivable from some ('higher level'?) epistemic preferences. At the very least, we should demand from a candidate definition that accepting it as an appropriate representation of the 'right' epistemic preferences is an optimum decision according to that very same definition. Regarding to this criticism, I think Maher's approach is more appropriate than the others, for, even if it could seem that by not offering an explicit definition of epistemic utility he had left this notion unexplained, I prefer to interpret his strategy as a 'liberal' one, in the sense that it allows to take *any* function that satisfies the five principles listed in the preceding paragraph as an acceptable epistemic utility. This strategy amounts to denying the philosopher the right to determine what epistemic preferences are 'appropriate', besides indicating some minimal requisites that make these preferences deserve to be called 'cognitive'.

An alternative but related approach has been defended by me in a series of papers about 'methodological truthlikeness' (e.g. Zamora Bonilla [1996; 2000]): instead of searching for a definition of cognitive utility which satisfies some intuitive requirements, or instead of just acknowledging the right of scientists to have the epistemic preferences they may have, the philosopher of science should try to *discover* what these cognitive values are. The suggested strategy is an abductive one: in the first place, we have to look for the methodological patterns scientists actually follow, i.e., their 'revealed' criteria for theory preference (patterns which are not supposed to be universal); in the second place, we must try to find a definition of cognitive utility from which those patterns could be mathematically derived as 'empirical predictions'. Both things can obviously be made with a bigger or lesser level of detail: we can look for very general methodological patterns, which would be taken as 'stylised facts' about theory choice, empirical testing, and so on, or we can alternatively inquiry about detailed methodological decisions in specific case studies; and we can also employ very simple hypothetical utility functions, with just a few arguments within them, or develop more complicated functions. My impression is that, the more we concentrate on the specificities of particular cases, the less likely it is that actual scientific decisions depend only on cognitive factors; the most general methodological patterns, on the other hand, are those defining the kind of activity scientific research is, and the type of output that society can expect to derive from it, and this allows to guess that scientific institutions and practices will have probably evolved in such a way that those patterns are coherent with scientists' more general epistemic preferences. Now that the methodology of case studies has become a kind of orthodoxy in the philosophy and the sociology of science, some may have doubts about the mere possibility of finding in the history of science any regularities regarding the scientists' methodological decisions (for, do not researchers use all methods 'opportunistically'?), and even more about the viability of deriving an explanation of these practices just from a few simplistic formulae (e.g., from the assumption that certain cognitive utility function is maximised through those decisions). To the first objection we can answer that the patterns that have to be searched are not of the type 'scientists always employ method X', but rather of the form 'under circumstances Z, scientists tend to employ method X; under circumstances Z', scientists tend to employ method X', and so on'. Regarding the second objection, the proof of the cake is obviously in the eating.

The main definition of epistemic value I have proposed in the papers mentioned above asserts that the verisimilitude of a hypothesis $h$ for a scientist given a set $E$ of empirical regularities or data, is identical to the product of the 'similarity' between $h$ and a subset $F$ of $E$ (measured as $p(h\&F)/p(hvF)$, where $p$ stands for the scientist's subjective probabilities) and the 'rigour' of $F$ (measured as $1/p(F)$), for that subset $F$ for which this product is maximum. These definitions allow to derive a wider set of 'methodological theorems' than other existing measures of epistemic utility (cf. Zamora Bonilla [1996]), but also to explain some 'stylised facts' about the development of scientific research programmes or about the differences between the role of theoretical and empirical arguments in economic theory as compared to natural science (cf. Zamora Bonilla [2003] and [1999a], respectively). I recognise that the number of 'facts' so explained is not too big, but what this indicates is not that formal models are useless (after all, other types of explanations of scientific practice haven't got a much better success record), but that they must be enriched to take into account other relevant factors in scientific decision making. This is exactly what the contributions to be examined in the next sections try to do.

## 4 THE EXCHANGE PARADIGM

### 4.1 The market metaphor

Traditionally, economics is not only about the optimisation of some magnitudes, be they utility, profits, wealth, or social welfare. Beyond the assumption that economic agents are rational beings who always try to make the best possible choice, there is the indisputable fact that the objects of economic research are *social* phenomena, that have to do with the *interrelation* between numerous agents. Classical economists introduced the idea that there is a specific realm ('the economy') the discipline they were creating dealt all about, a complex entity all of whose elements depended on the rest. Later on, more limited social fields (i.e., single markets) attracted the systematic attention of economic theorists, but the fundamental idea was still that these fields were systems composed by interdependent parts. In economics, contrarily to the majority of the other social sciences, the most fundamental type of connection existing between the elements of those systems is assumed to be that of *exchange relationships*, and economic science can then be understood as the study of those social phenomena in which the basic 'bond' consists in (more or less free) exchanges. Of course, the market is the paradigm of such social phenomena, and hence, trying to describe science as an exchange system leads us almost automatically to interpret it like something akin to a 'market'. Due to the common identification of the economic efficiency of markets with another classical metaphor (the 'invisible hand'), the thesis that 'science is like a market' has often been taken as an assumption about the working of some 'epistemic invisible hand' mechanism behind the process of scientific research. This vision of science as a 'marketplace for ideas' was not originally a technical notion in the analysis of scientific research,[6] but rather a common metaphor 'floating in the air', and probably having a basic ideological role: that of justifying the autonomy of scientific opinions from external social pressures. The following quotations, the first one by a Popperian philosopher, and the second one by a prominent economist, are illustrative of that opinion:

> I was taught as a student that the university is a marketplace of ideas where new ideas are welcome and falsehoods can be challenged without recrimination. Bartley [1990, p. xvi]

> I do not believe that (the) distinction between the market for goods and the market for ideas is valid. There is no fundamental difference between these two markets. Coase [1974, p. 389]

Nevertheless, it is one thing to express the metaphor that 'science is a market', and it is a very different thing to try to use it as an analogy to illuminate in a detailed way the essential features of scientific research (by the way, the analogy can also be used in the opposite direction, to understand the market as a knowledge generating mechanism; cf. Hayek [1948]). Once we begin to employ the metaphor as an analytical device, an obvious problem is to make it explicit what we are really understanding by the market concept, for if we take buyings and sellings as the fundamental bricks of the market, it seems clear that 'scientific ideas' or 'opinions' are not *really* bought nor sold by researchers, save in a very metaphorical

[6]Though it underlied several sociological approaches like those of R. K. Merton, W. O. Hagstrom, or J. Cole, cf. the "competition model" in Callon [1995], as well as Ziman [1968] and [2002].

sense (perhaps with the main exception of technological research; this difference between ideas researchers decide to made public — and then not sellable — and ideas kept secret — and then commodifiable — has even been proposed as the basic distinction between 'science' and 'technology', cf. Dasgupta and David [1994]). So, in order to understand ('pure') science as a market, we need to concentrate on some *abstract* features of markets, some that 'real' markets may reflect in some definite way, but that other social institutions (which can be taken as markets just by means of an analogy) materialise in different ways. As we could expect, proponents and critics of the idea of 'science as a market' have tended to concentrate on different aspects of the analogy. On the other hand, the market concept (and particularly the concept of a 'free' market) is by no means a *neutral* idea normatively speaking; the debate between pro-market and anti-market activists is longstanding, and it also reflects in the analysis of science: some authors argue that 'science is a market' and that this is a good thing both from a social and from a cognitive point of view, whereas other authors have employed the same thesis to justify scepticism about the epistemic objectivity of scientific knowledge, or to assert that, the more science 'becomes' a market, the less advantageous it is for the common citizen (cf. Fuller [2000], Mirowski and Sent [2002b]; for a more positive view, see Goldman and Cox [1996], where the idea of a 'free market for ideas' is applied to all public communication, and not only to science). In the remaining of this section, I will present in the first place Polany's pioneering understanding of science as a self-organising system; in subsection 3.3 I will discuss some of the proposals to explicitly analyse science as a kind of market, and lastly I will present some of the criticisms that these proposals have received.

## *4.2 Polany's 'Republic of Science'*

The first serious attempt to analyse the working of science by means of the market analogy was Michael Polany's classic article 'The Republic of Science. Its Political and Economic Theory' (1962), although in that paper he explicitly avoided to assimilate science with a market, but tried instead to show that both institutions are examples of self-co-ordination processes:

> (The) highest possible co-ordination of individual scientific efforts by a process of self-co-ordination may recall the self-co-ordination achieved by producers and consumers operating in a market. It was, indeed, with this in mind that I spoke of "the invisible hand" guiding the co-ordination of independent initiatives to a maximum advancement of science, just as Adam Smith invoked "the invisible hand" to describe the achievement of greatest joint material satisfaction when independent producers and consumers are guided by the prices of goods in a market. I am suggesting, in fact, that the co-ordinating functions of the market are but a special case of co-ordination by mutual adjustment. In the case of science, adjustment takes place by taking note of the published results of other scientists; while in the case of the market,

> mutual adjustment is mediated by a system of prices broadcasting current exchange relations, which make supply meet demand (...) Polany [1962, pp. 467-8].

With the help of this analogy, based on an Austrian conception of the economy as a self-regulating system, Polany's analysis proceeds by indicating the ways in which the choices of an individual scientist are constrained by the professional standards of her discipline, and how these standards emerge as a solution to the problems of co-ordination that are faced in scientific research. On the one hand, individual scientists try to attain the maximum possible 'merit' with their stock of intellectual and material resources. On the other hand, the scientific merit attached to a result depend on a number of factors, the most important ones being the result's plausibility, its accuracy, its relevance, and its originality. The three first criteria tend to enforce conformity, whereas originality encourages dissent, and this tension is essential both in guiding the decisions of individual researchers, and in explaining the tremendous cognitive success of science. Actually, Polany's claim seems to be that these are exactly the criteria employed in science *because* they have proved to be efficient in the production of knowledge: the 'invisible hand' argument refers not only to the attainment of efficient *results* in the decisions of individual researchers (who maximally exploit the gains from epistemic trade thanks to competition), but to the establishing of the most appropriate *rules* within the scientific community. Unfortunately, no detailed empirical analysis to justify these conclusions are offered in the article. In particular (and this is a problem of most of the contributions that will be surveyed in this section), Polany does not even recognise the possibility that norms which are efficient in the pursuit of knowledge may be not so efficient in the pursuit of merit, and viceversa, and it is not clear what type of efficiency has more weight in guiding the evolution of scientific standards.

Other quasi economic argument offered by Polany refers to what he calls "the uniformity of scientific standards throughout science", something which allows the commensuration of the values of very different discoveries in completely disparate parts of science:

> This possibility is of great value for the rational distribution of efforts and material resources throughout the various branches of science. If the minimum merit by which a contribution would be qualified for acceptance by journals were much lower in one branch of science than in another, this would clearly cause too much effort to be spent on the former branch as compared with the latter. Such is in fact the principle which underlies the rational distribution of grants for the pursuit of research. Subsidies should be curtailed in areas where their yields in terms of scientific merit tend to be low, and should be channelled instead to the growing points of science, where increased financial means may be expected to produce a work of higher scientific value (...) So long as each allocation follows the guidance of scientific opinion, by

> giving preference to the most promising scientists and subjects, the distribution of grants will automatically yield the maximum advantage for the advancement of science as a whole. (*ibid.*, p. 472)

Again, this is just a transposition to the case of science of the Austrian economics thesis that prices are the instrument for the co-ordination of individual decisions in the market. But, without a systematic analysis of how 'scientific value' is constituted by the interconnected decisions of different individuals, the argument lacks any logical cogency, not to talk about its *prima facie* plausibility, for, as a matter of fact, the quality standards for acceptance of contributions in different disciplines, as well as in different journals within the same discipline, are very far from uniform. A last important economic metaphor in Polany's analysis of 'the Republic of Science', also analogous to a Hayekian view of the market as an epistemic co-ordination mechanism, is his view of 'scientific opinion' as a single collective authority, what is constituted by myriads of single judgements of individual scientists, each one having competence on just a tiny fraction of all scientific knowledge overlapping more or less with the areas of competence of other colleagues:[7]

> Each scientist who is a member of a group of overlapping competences will also be a member of other groups of the same kind, so that the whole of science will be covered by chains and networks of overlapping neighbourhoods (...) Through these overlapping neighbourhoods uniform standards of scientific merit will prevail over the entire range of science (...) This network is the seat of scientific opinion. Scientific opinion is an opinion not held by any single human mid, but one which, split into thousands of fragments, is held by a multitude of individuals, each of whom endorses the others' opinion at second hand, by relying on the consensual chains which link him to all the others through a sequence of overlapping neighbourhoods. (ibid., p. 471).

I think this view of scientific opinion (which is in some sense similar to Philip Kitcher's notion of 'virtual consensus', which we will see in section 4.1) may lead in a natural way to develop analytical models and empirical studies in which scientific interactions are understood as the elements of a *network*, but this is mostly work that is still to be done.

## *4.3 Science as a market*

Curiously enough, it was not economists, but sociologists, the first ones in taking over the analogy between science and markets (an analogy that, as we have just seen, Polany explicitly presented as only working at the level of abstract mechanisms), in particular Pierre Bourdieu, in his pathbreaking article 'The Specificity

[7]For a comparison of Polany's vision of science with Hayek's general approach to mind and society, see Wible [1998, ch. 8] and Mirowski [2004, chs. 2 and 3], where the differences between both approaches are discussed.

of the Scientific Field and the Social Conditions of the Progress of Reason' (1975). According to Bourdieu, scientific research consists in the competition for scientific authority, which is a kind of monopoly power, "the socially recognised capacity to speak and act legitimately (i.e., in an authorised and authoritative way) in scientific matters" (*op.cit*, p. 31). The distribution of this authority within a scientific discipline at a given moment is what constitutes it as a 'field', in the Bourdiean sense of a structure of interrelations and capacities which determine the interests and strategies of each actor. Authority is seen as a kind of 'social capital', which can be "accumulated, transmitted, and even reconverted into other kinds of capital" (p. 34). In very explicitly economic terms, Bourdieu asserts that these 'investments'

> are organized by reference to — conscious or unconscious — anticipation of the average chances of profit (which are themselves specified in terms of the capital already held). Thus researchers' tendency to concentrate on those problems regarded as the most important ones (e.g., because they have been constituted as such by producers endowed with a high degree of legitimacy) is explained by the fact that a contribution or discovery relating to those questions will tend to yield greater symbolic profit. The intense competition which is then triggered off is likely to brig about a fall in average rates of symbolic profit, and hence the departure of a fraction of researchers towards other objects which are less prestigious but around which the competition is less intense, so that they offer profits of at least as great.
>
> [Bourdieu, 1975/1999, p. 33]

Perhaps the most characteristic feature of this type of competition as compared to others (entrepreneurial, political, artistic, and so on), is that the scientific field is highly autonomous, in the sense that "a particular producer cannot expect recognition of the value of his products (...) from anyone except other producers, who, being his competitors too, are those least inclined to grant recognition without discussion and scrutiny". Bourdieu argues that this autonomy is what has created the false impression of scientific research being a 'disinterested' activity, but he also declares that the existence of specific social interests pushing the strategies of scientists do not entail that the cognitive products of these strategies lack epistemic objectivity. Rather on the contrary, the specificity of the scientific field consists in the fact that the competition that takes place within it under an "inherent logic" which brings about, "under certain conditions, a systematic diversion of ends whereby the pursuit of private scientific interests (...) continuously operates to the advantage of the progress of science" (p. 39). This "transmutation of the anarchic antagonism of particular interests into a scientific dialectic" (i.e., one which is based on the observance of "scientific method") is effected thanks to the need of each individual scientist to fit his arguments to a set of methodological practices whose most competent performers are precisely his own competitors, a process that usually leads all competitors to a "forced agreement" (p. 41) that rarely occurs outside the natural sciences (save for the violent imposition of a dogma, as it is the case in religions and in totalitarian regimes).

Bourdieu's vision of scientific research as a market for scientific credit was transformed by Bruno Latour and Steve Woolgar [1979] into what we might call a Marxist theory of the scientific market. According to these authors, the essential aspect of the research process is that the 'capital' won by a scientists is always re-invested, generating a 'cycle of credit'. One important implication of this view is that no single element of the cycle is more fundamental than the rest, but this seems to lead Latour and Woolgar to the strange conclusion that the motivation of scientists is not the pursuit of credit, nor of any other of the elements of the cycle (access to scientific facilities, production of reliable information, publication of research results, and so on), but "the acceleration and expansion" of the cycle by itself (op.cit., p. 208), an idea which is difficult to implement in a standard economic analysis. Other important insight in Latour and Woolgar's approach is the relevance they attach to an aspect of the interdependence of researchers which is usually lacking in other sociological theories: the fact that the *value* of the information provided by a scientists depend on the *demand* of that information by other scientists, who need that information in order to produce in their turn further information who can be transformed in credibility, and so on (op. cit., p. 206). For economically oriented readers, Latour and Woolgar's avoidance to discuss an obvious question can be disappointing : to what extent the working of the credibility cycle favours the production of *reliable* information (i.e., information that *is* useful), and not only that of 'credible' information (i.e., information that is *taken to be* useful). Of course, the very same question is precluded by the fact that their chapter on the credibility cycle is a continuation of the one where they famously argue that scientific statements can not be taken as objective representations of an independent reality, for this 'external' reality is 'constructed' in the same process that leads to the collective acceptance of the statement presumably describing it. A possible answer to this unposed question is that of David Hull [1988], who asserts that the basic factor enhancing a scientist's credit is not the recognition of his results by other researchers, but the *use* they make of them, and this provides an incentive to produce results that are epistemically reliable, for, in general, wrong statements will easily lead to failed predictions and actions. Thomas Leonard [2002] also explains how some common scientific rules (particularly peer review and replication) evolved historically as mechanisms guaranteeing that individual scientists have an interest in using and producing reliable ideas.

The most systematic attempt to illuminate the process of science in terms of the market concept has been made Allan Walstad (a physicist), especially in his paper 'Science as a Market Process' [2002]. In line with Polany's contribution, Walstad develops an Austrian approach, avoiding to use mathematical models, basically because of the absence of numerical data about the relevant facts, and because of the essential instability and complexity of social interactions. Instead, he presents a list of similarities, as well as differences, between 'traditional' and 'scientific markets'. The more important similarities are the existence in both cases of a high level of *specialisation*, *exchange* ('recognition' in payment for the use of information), acquisition and *investment* of cognitive capital (but, contrarily to Latour and Woolgar, allowing for the possibility of some 'final ends', either cognitive or practical, serving as an explanation of the production cycle), *entrepreneurial activity* (both in the Schumpeterian sense of a disequilibrating force -novelty creating-, and in the Kirznerian sense of an equilibrating factor -e.g., arbitraging-), *institutional organisation* (e.g., research teams or groups, analogous to firms in traditional markets), and *self-regulation* (with evolved mechanisms that discourage inefficient activities, facilitate co-ordination, and avoid market failures; e.g., citation records performing a similar informational role, to prices in traditional markets; see also Butos and Boettke [2002]). The main differences between science and common markets is the absence of money as a means of exchange in the former; this entails that scientists can not charge different prices for citations, nor carry out indirect exchanges, nor transfer to others the right to be cited (as it is the case for patents and other property rights, for example).

## *4.4 The limits of the market metaphor*

The analysis of the scientific process in terms of market concepts can be criticised in a number of ways. For example, some may argue that the vision of researchers as 'scientific entrepreneurs' distorts the essential aspects of scientists' motivations. This criticism can be raised both by rationalist philosophers who think that scientists basically pursue epistemic goals, and by sociologists who think that scientific ideas are just rhetorical strategies to defend the power of some social classes. Fortunately, the 'entrepreneurial' character of many scientific decisions is backed enough by a huge amount of case studies (e.g., Latour [1987], Pickering [1995]), independently of whether their authors employ an 'economic' approach or not. On the other hand, the market metaphor might be criticised because it puts too much emphasis on *voluntary* exchanges, and not so much in the *institutional* mechanisms of science (e.g., Ylikoski [1995], Wray [2000]). I think this criticism is more relevant, but it surely ignores the complexity of modern economic analysis: as it will be obvious for anyone acquainted to contemporary microeconomics, there is no such a thing as 'the' market concept; what there is, instead, is a varied set of market notions linked by family resemblances, rather than united under a single definition, and this diversity reflects indeed a still wider variety of *types* of markets in the real world. One thing which is clear for almost all economists is that the differences between these types of markets essentially depend on the *institutions*, *norms*, and *habits* those markets are embedded into (although there is deep disagreement about how beneficial this institutional embedding actually is). Just to put a compelling example: any market transaction presupposes some property *rights*, as well as some *legal* mechanism to punish the infringement of those rights; it also presupposes some *procedures*: shirts in a warehouse are not bought in the same way as bonds in the stock market. So, any serious analysis of science 'as a market' must make it clear what are the institutions allowing or constraining 'scientific transactions' (cf. Polany's approach). Actually, the contributions I will examine in section 4.2 are 'institutionalist', not in the sense that they deny that the market metaphor is appropriate, but because they explicitly consider the role of institutions in the 'scientific market'. So, I think the most important criticisms to the idea that 'science is a market' are those coming from inside, i.e., those problems the very application of the idea has allowed to disclose: first, do some serious 'market failures' exist within science?, and second, is the idea of a 'scientific market' when applied to itself logically coherent?[8]

The expression 'market failure' is employed to refer to those circumstances under which the free decisions of sellers and buyers would lead to an inefficient result. Monopolies (absence of competition), externalities (decisions affecting to third parties), public goods (non divisible amongst private consumers), informational asymmetries (one party knowing more about the good than the other), and transaction costs (the ones incurred in carrying out agreements) are typical situations where suboptimal solutions to co-ordination problems may emerge if the agents are left to decide by themselves in the pursuit of their private interest (see, e.g., Salanié [2000]). The problem for market theories of science is that in the case of scientific research all these circumstances are the norm rather than the exception. For example, cognitive monopolies, i.e., the neglection of 'heterodox' theories or methods, not only arise very frequently (cf. Wible [1998, chs. 6 and 7]), but, as we saw when reporting Bourdieu's approach, the striving for the monopolisation of epistemic authority is the basic force driving scientific competition; indeed, we can interpret Thomas Kuhn's 'paradigms' as examples of scientific monopolies (cf. Oomes [1997]), and Popper's [1970] complaints about the epistemic inferiority of 'normal science' as an argument demanding more competition in research. Oomes also explain monopolies as caused by 'historical lock-in', when an idea or method becomes accepted just because of having gained a temporal advantage over its competitors.

To a high extent, epistemic competition naturally leads to monopolies because, with the exception of some relativist philosophers, it is assumed that scientific problems have only one 'right' answer, or, at least, that the more correct answers 'displace' the worse ones. Stated in economic terms, this means that knowledge is a 'public good', one that, when 'produced' for a single individual, all the other agents can freely make use of it. The public nature of knowledge was employed by many authors to justify its production through governmental funding (e.g., Nelson [1959]), although more recently it has been put into question, at least as a universal fact about scientific knowledge: Dasgupta and David [1994] explain the publicity or privacity of knowledge as an endogenous variable of the research process, and Callon [1994] argues that it is only the production of heterodox ideas what must be publicly financed. Little analysis has been done, instead, of other questions more relevant from the epistemological point of view, as whether it is scientific knowledge's being *information*, or its being *true*, or its being *collectively accepted*,

[8]See also McQuade and Butos [2003] for an Austrian explanation of science which concentrates on the *differences* between the market process and the science process.

what makes of it a public good, and what epistemic consequences each one of these options has, i.e., how does exactly the public or private nature of knowledge affect the *cognitive efficiency* of the research process. One plausible avenue for research on these questions would be to apply the ample literature about knowledge and information in non-co-operative games. Lastly, informational asymmetries and transaction costs are other phenomena that clearly manifest in the case of science. I will comment more about the former in the section 4.1. The case of transaction costs has been much less studied, the main exceptions being Mäki [1999], which will be commented below in this section, and Turner [2002], who describes science as a market system of public certification processes, which attempt to reduce the costs the evaluation of information would have for single individuals.

Finally, reflexivity can also pose problems for market theories of science, and, more generally, to the very idea of an economics of science, as it has been stated by several authors. The most obvious difficulty is that an economic analysis of science applied to economics itself *might* show that economics is not 'good enough' as a science, perhaps due to the existence of some 'market failures'. For example, Thomas Mayer [1993] argues that economics as a market for ideas fails because it is basically an activity dominated by producers: professional economists are the only agents controlling what must count as 'good' economics, whereas in other branches of science successful technological application is the final arbiter. This, according to Mayer, has lead to the dominance of mathematical over empirical research, and to putting the goal of precision before the goal of truth. A similar argument is presented in Zamora Bonilla [2002]. But, if these arguments are right, then the very intellectual tool with which they are produced might be flawed, and economics could be alright after all! This conclusion is paradoxical; in fact, it is an example of the 'Liar's paradox' ("What I'm saying is false"), that philosophers of logic have examined for centuries. Of course, this is not only a problem for an economics of science, but, in general, for any other scientific explanation of science, particularly for those approaches concluding that scientific knowledge is not 'objective' (cf. Hands [1994a, pp. 91 ff.], as well as Mäki [2004, pp. 217 ff.] for criticisms of the credibility of economics in particular). Wible [1998, chs. 11 and 12] takes this paradox as an opportunity to criticise what he calls "the architecture of economic theory and method", a criticism he hopes would justify the use of an evolutionary conception of rationality instead of classical equilibrium concepts (cf. section 4.2 below). Another possible solution to the paradox would be to argue that the particular branch (or tool within this branch) of science one is employing is not in a bad epistemic state, after all. This is what some sociologists of scientific knowledge did (e.g., Bloor [1976]), by suggesting that sociological knowledge is actually better grounded than the theories of natural science (a position advanced centuries ago by Giambattista Vico). As far as market theories of science are concerned, they have usually tended to conclude, through some kind of invisible hand argument, that science works more or less well in general, and so the paradox would not arise. But, if this were the case, a possible criticism could be made by showing that the specific strand of economics that is being used in developing such a market theory of science is actually *not* a dominant one within the economics profession (i.e., it is not very successful in the market for economic theories). Uskali Mäki [1999] has levied this criticism towards Ronald Coase's defence of a free market of ideas, but it could also be applied to the more recent, and much more developed Austrian approaches we have examined in this section. Furthermore, Mäki [2004, pp. 219–20] argues that the application of market-like models to our understanding of science might have self-destructive effects, by shaping and channelling the most selfish predispositions of scientists towards epistemically inefficient patterns of behaviour, in a similar fashion to the way exposure to neo-classical economic concepts seems to enhance the self-interestedness of economics students. Perhaps science is really a market, but it would work better if we didn't know it. Mäki's suggestion, nevertheless, is in line with that of most critics of market theories of science: we must just be careful in the application of economic concepts, being conscious of their limitations as well as of their diversity and analytical power.

## 5 SOCIAL MECHANISMS FOR KNOWLEDGE PRODUCTION

### *5.1 Mathematical models*

The most distinctive feature of modern economics is probably its reliance on the methodology of mathematical model building. As with any other powerful tool, the danger exists of people being excited by it and using it much more intensely that what would be sensible or necessary. In the case of economics, Mayer [1993] has argued that the difficulty in deciding whether economic theories are *right or wrong*, and hence in ranking economists according to their ability to discover the *truth* about economic facts, has led to take mastery in the invention and manipulation of mathematical models as a paramount criterion of scientific excellence; the mathematisation of economics would have been, hence, more an example of academic pedantry than a real epistemological virtue. Though I do not share such an extreme position, I think it can serve nevertheless to remind us that the final aim of scientific model building is that of illuminating *real* phenomena, and it has not to be carried out for its own sake. On the other hand, mathematical models are basically *logical arguments*, whose main virtue is that they allow us to see very clearly what follows, and also what does not follow, from a definite set of premises. These premises describe an imaginary world, and mathematical analysis just allows to decide in an unambiguous way what would happen in that world under some conceivable circumstances. The most important question is, hence, to what extent that imaginary world represents well enough the relevant aspects of the actual (or counterfactual) way things are, so that our conclusions are transportable to the real world (cf. Sugden [2002]), but this question is decided through a 'dialectical' process, for after all, how empirically accurate our conclusions are is usually (or it should be) the most compelling reason to judge whether our model is appropriate enough (cf. Friedman [1953]).

Mathematical models of scientific knowledge production are not common, however. This is due to a combination of circumstances: *sociologists of science* would have the main motivation to use those models, but most of them may think that it would be an example of 'economics imperialism', and that it tends to hide the qualitative complexity of social processes; most *philosophers* don't know too much about economics for even considering seriously the possibility of engaging into an economics of scientific knowledge, perhaps beyond producing some very general, qualitative arguments; *economists* have been too busy developing complicated mathematical techniques and applying them to proper 'economic' problems, for losing their time investigating such a minor question; and lastly, *philosophers and methodologists of economics* may have been the scholars where the right interests and the right resources were combined in an optimal way, but most of them are either too much critical of standard economic theory for considering worthy the effort, or fear that an economics of scientific knowledge would be dangerously close to social constructivism and relativism (cf. Davis [1998]). As a result, until now only a fistful of authors have tried to develop some formal economic analyses of the social mechanisms of scientific knowledge production.

As far as I know, the first application of an economic model to a problem clearly falling within the philosophy of science was due to Michael Blais [1987], who employed Robert Axelrod's evolutionary 'solution' to the Prisoner's Dilemma game to illustrate how *trust* in the work of scientists may emerge just as a result of self-interested behaviour, without requiring a 'moral' explanation. According to Blais, the interaction between researchers and journal editors can be represented as a Prisoner's Dilemma: the former can either 'cooperate' (i.e., perform good research) or not, and the latter can also 'cooperate' (i.e., publish good results) or not; cooperation is more costly than defection for both types of agents, although both benefit more if everyone cooperates than if everyone defects. As it is well known, Axelrod [1984] showed that, when a game like this is repeatedly played by automata which have been programmed to follow always the same strategy (although not all of them the same one), the most successful strategy amongst a high number of them which had been proposed was the one called 'tit-for-tat' (cooperate the first time, and then cooperate if and only if the other player has cooperated the last time). Using this strategy is, then, in the interest of every agent, what also makes cooperation to become the most frequent decision. Blais argues that trust in the results of scientists by part of journal editors, and in the quality of published papers by part of researchers, may have evolved in a similar way. The mechanism of interaction between scientists and editors is decisive, nevertheless, and it may lead to suboptimal 'solutions' in the Prisoner's Dilemma game, like, for example, letting pseudo-scientific papers become published (cf. Bracanovic [2002]; see also Hardwig [1991] for a criticism of Blais' thesis).

One year after the publication of Blais' paper Cristina Bicchieri published a different application of game-theoretic ideas to the understanding of scientific knowledge. In her article "Methodological Rules as Conventions" (1988), she tried to illuminate the establishment of specific scientific methods from the point of view of David Lewis' theory of conventions. Opposing both functionalist explanations of scientific rules, either epistemic (that would justify them by their ability to sustain preordained, usually cognitive goals), or sociological (that would explain the adoption of rules by individual scientists by resource to the pressure of some relevant social groups), she offers an account according to which is based on the coordination of strategic choicess of individual scientists, a coordination that can lead in principle to different sets of rules. In particular, the main element in the decision of a scientist to adopt a method, criterion, or procedure is the fact that he expects that his colleagues also obey it. In this sense, the choice of a rule or systems of rules instead of other is *arbitrary*, for individual scientists would have been equally happy if some different norms were collectively adopted. Being an equilibrium of a coordination game explains the (relative) *stability* of scientific methods, for once the individuals expect others to comply, it is costly for each agent to follow a different rule. But the rationality of the agents cannot explain why some norms *emerge* instead of others. Actually, if, as Bicchieri assumes, several norms would lead to different coordination equilibria which are exactly as good as the other for all the agents, then it is true that the 'social choice' of a rule instead of other would be arbitrary, but it is reasonable to assume that the game that individual scientists face is not a game of *pure* coordination: different rules may have more value for different and also for the samescientists, even taking into account the gains from coordination (stated differently, it is possile that in many cases the resulting game is of the 'Battle of the Sexes' type), a fact that Bicchieri marginally acknowledge in one footnote (Bicchieri [1988, p. 488]).

The most extensive and systematic application of economic modelling to the analysis of epistemological problems has been performed by the philosopher Philip Kitcher in a paper entitled "The Division of Cognitive Labour" (1990), and later extended to constitute the last chapter of his book *The Advancement of Science* (1993).[9] Kitcher's main goal in those contributions was to develop an economic branch of the field of 'social epistemology', based on a methodologically individualist conception of social processes (that sees social outcomes as deriving from the interconnected decisions of individuals) and simultaneously on a reliabilist conception of knowledge (which takes progress towards the truth as the epistemic goal of science). The role for social epistemologists would be "to identify the properties of epistemically well-designed social systems, that is, to specify the conditions under which a group of individuals, operating according to various rules for modifying their individual practices, succeed, through their interactions, in generating a progressive sequence of consensus practices" [Kitcher, 1993, p. 303]. The most idiosyncratic concept in this quotation is that of a *consensus practice*, which is one of the central ideas in Kitcher's book: by a 'practice', Kitcher refers to the collection of cognitive resources an individual or a group has, including such things as valid concepts, relevant questions, accepted answers, and exemplars of good experimental or argumentative procedures (op.cit., p. 74); a group's consensus practice will contain, so to say, the intersection of the elements included within

[9]Some early criticisms of Kitcher's game-theoretic approach were Fuller [1994], Hands [1995], Levi [1995], Mirowski [1995], and Solomon [1995].

its members' individual practices, together with the social mechanisms of deferred cognitive authority which allow to create a 'virtual' consensus, i.e., those things every member *would* accept if she happened to follow all the threads of deferred authority (op. cit., pp. 87f.). This idea of a virtual consensus represents what a scientific *community* knows (or pretends to know), in spite of no one of its single members being able of getting all that information in her own mind. A series of consensus practices is epistemically progressive if it develops an increasingly more accurate set of concepts (i.e., concepts better and better fitting real natural types) and an increasing amount of right solutions to scientific problems (i.e., objectively true descriptions of actual events and causal mechanisms). Hence, for Kitcher the task for social epistemology is, basically, to analyse those mechanisms according to which scientists interact and produce a consensus practice, in order to critically assess whether we can expect they lead to cognitive progress, or to what extent they do it.

Kitcher's strategy is divided into two stages. In the first place, he discusses how individual scientists act when taking into account their colleagues' actions, in particular, how they take their decisions about how much authority to confer those colleagues, as well as about how to compete or cooperate with them. In the second place, Kitcher analyses what epistemic consequences different distributions of researchers' efforts may have. In order to elaborate this strategy, Kitcher employs models from standard and evolutionary game theory, as well as from Bayesian decision theory. Although this strategy is grounded on methodological individualism, when it goes to normative problems it finally rests on the idea that there is some kind of collective (or 'objective') standard of epistemic value against which to measure the actual performances of a scientific community:

> There are two types of inquiry that are worth pursuing: first, we want to know what, given the range of possibilities, is the *best* approach to the problem situation in which we are interested; second, we should scrutinize which of the available combinations of individual decision procedures and sets of social relations would move the community closer to or further away from the *optimal* approach. (op. cit., p. 305; my italics).

With this way of describing the normative ambition of his project, Kitcher's models could perhaps be catalogued within the optimisation paradigm we studied in section 2; however, the relevance he gives to the interaction processes and to the decisions of individual scientists when competing against each other (what Kitcher calls 'the entrepreneurial predicament'), connects equally well his approach with the exchange paradigm. Actually, this combination is what makes of the model building approach a much more systematic way to analyse science as an economic process, as compared to the contributions discussed in the past sections. Nevertheless, in my opinion Kitcher does not explain in a satisfactory way what is the connection between the 'objective' evaluation he refers to and those of each individual scientist; for example, does the former emerge from the latter through some kind of aggregation procedure, as if it were a kind of '(cognitive) social welfare function'? The difficulty of providing such a derivation was soon indicated by Wade Hands [1995, p. 617f.]. Or is there really no connection between both types of valuation, and the former is just assumed by the philosopher while pretending to act as a (fictitious) benevolent planner of scientific research? More probably, Kitcher's view about this problem seems to be, first, that individual scientists' utility functions can be decomposed into a 'social' factor, basically related to the Bourdieu's 'credit' concept, and an 'epistemic' factor, which would basically be the pursuit of objective truth; and second, that this epistemic part of scientists' preferences will accord, in principle, with the 'objective' valuation assumed by the philosopher. Many of Kitcher's assertions substantiate this interpretation, for example:

> We can think of the problems that concern me as including those that would face a philosopher-monarch, interested in organizing the scientific work force so as to promote the collective achievement of significant truth. Science, of course, has no such benevolent dictator. In consequence, individual scientists face coordination problems. If we suppose that they internalize the (fictitious) monarch's values, how will they fare? If we assume instead that they are motivated in baser ways or that they are locked into systems of authority and deference, will they necessarily do worse than a society of unrelated individuals, each of whom is pure of heart? (op. cit., p. 305).

We can divide the models elaborated in Kitcher [1993, ch. 8] into two different groups. The first group (sections 2 to 12) relates to what the author call *'the entrepreneurial predicament'*: how do researchers pursuing scientific recognition are expected to behave in response to their colleagues' behaviour. The problems Kitcher attacks here are basically the following ones:

a) during a research process carried out by a scientist, some intermediate parts can either be directly performed by her, or she can borrow the result announced by another colleague; Kitcher analyses how this decision depends on the probability that both the scientist an her colleagues have of finding a right solution to the intermediate problem, and on the probability the former has of being the first solver of the main problem, depending on her previous choice, as well as on the different resources each researcher may have;

b) the previous discussion depends on the assumption that individual scientists may 'calibrate' the reliability of their colleagues' assertions; the next group of models Kitcher develops is directed, then, to analyse how this 'calibration' may take place, particularly when $A$ has to use $B$'s assessments of the reliability of $C$, and when $A$'s assessment of $B$ depend on $B$'s assessment of $A$; different distributions of 'authority' may also lead to different decisions about when to borrow other's result or when to do the job by oneself;

c) finally, scientists don't have to decide only whether to accept the result announced by a colleague or not: they also have the option of *replicating* it, postponing the other decision until the replication has confirmed or disconfirmed the result; here the main economic problem is that of determining the optimal number of replications (taking into account that they are costly), and of knowing whether this number can be reached by the independent decisions of individual scientists.

The second set of models relate to what Kitcher calls *'the division of cognitive labour'* (a label which could also have been applied to the former group of models, nevertheless), by which he refers not to the decisions about what problems to attack, but about what methods to employ to do it, as well as what solutions to those problems to accept (i.e., the old methodological problem of theory choice). In the latter case, by 'choosing' a theory Kitcher distinguishes two successive stages: first, scientists may choose a theory 'to work with', as a kind of exploration, so to say; and second, at some moment a consensus about what is 'the' right theory must emerge. The main question that concerns Kitcher is the difference between the distribution of efforts which is optimal from a cognitive point of view, and the distribution that would arise if each researcher were individually pursuing her own interest, and hence the problem is basically one of *coordination.* Kitcher considers several cases, according to whether individual scientists are motivated just by the pursuit of truth, or by the pursuit of success, or by a mix of both goals, and also according to whether all scientists are assumed to have the same utility preferences and estimations about the probability of each theory being right, or there is some motivational or cognitive diversity. Perhaps the most relevant conclusion Kitcher offers (pp. 364 f.) is that in a community of researchers whose members were just motivated by professional glory (i.e., they didn't mind about whether the finally accepted theory is true or false), they would always choose that theory with the highest probability of being finally accepted, and so no one would pursue other theories or methods, but, just with a slight weight attached to the goal of truth in the scientists' utility function, a distribution of efforts close to the optimum will be attained.[10]

I pass now to describe the Bayesian model offered in Goldman and Shaked [1991]. In this model, researchers gain recognition for their success in modifying the subjective probabilities that their colleagues attach to each possible solution of a scientific problem. In order to do this, researchers perform two different types of acts: investigative acts (ranging from observation to the formulation of new hypotheses), and speech acts (which can be either the presentation of evidence in favour of a solution, or the criticism of a previous speech act). The structure of the research process can be described hence as a sequential game: in the first stage, a researcher decides what investigative act to perform; second, nature 'chooses' an outcome thereof; third, the researcher decides how to interpret the outcome, i.e.,

[10]Rueger [1996] extends Kitcher's argument in order to take into account scientists' cognitive risk aversion.

what solution she thinks the outcome supports (we can understand this move as the proposal of a particular solution); fourth, the other researchers change their subjective probabilities; and lastly, the first scientist gets a recognition level determined by the application of some socially sanctioned recognition-allocating mechanism. Goldman and Shaked prove that, in a scenario like this, researchers whose utility function depends uniquely on the attainment of such a type of recognition will perform *on the average* those experiments and those speech acts more conductive to an increment in the possession of truth by the members of the scientific community (i.e., an increment in the probabilities attached to the true solutions). Some criticisms can be made to this model: in the first place, it assumes that researchers will not misrepresent their subjective probabilities (after all, if each scientist wants her own theory to be the winning one, she will not assert that she thinks another theory is better); in the second place, in the Goldman-Shaked model the proposed recognition-allocating mechanism is simply imposed to the scientists, but perhaps these would prefer to play the game according to different rules.

A couple of mathematical models of scientific knowledge production were developed by Philip Mirowski, one of them in collaboration with Steve Sklivas ([Mirowski and Sklivas, 1991; Mirowski, 1996]; both reprinted in [Mirowski, 2004]). In the first of this papers, an attempt is made of explaining the observation made by sociologists of science, according to which researchers almost never perform *exact replications* of the experiments made by others (contrarily to what positivist expositions of the scientific method prescribed), though the results of those experiments are actually *employed* in ensuing research practice (and in this sense, they are 'reproduced'). Mirowski and Sklivas develop a game theoretic account of this behaviour: the first performers of an experiment gain nothing from independent replications if these are successful, and loose if they fail, but they gain from the further use of the experiment by others; use (or 'reproduction') is costly for those researchers who perform it, though exact replication is even more costly; on the other hand, only failed replication gives a positive payoff to replicators; lastly, the more information is conveyed in the report of the original experiment, the less costly both use and replication become. From these assumptions, Mirowski and Sklivas derive the conclusion that the optimum strategy of the scientist performing an original experiment is to provide such an amount of information that is enough to incentivate use, but not enough to make replication worthwhile; replication will only have a chance if the editors of the journals command to provide still more information in the experimental reports. In the second of the models referred to above, Mirowski compares the process of measuring a physical constant to the process that determines prices in the markets: as differences in the price of the same good at different places create an opportunity to arbitrage, inconsistencies in the measured values of a constant (derivable from the use of some accepted formulae -e.g., physical laws- and the values of other constants) create an opportunity to make further relevant measurements. Graph theory is employed at this point to describe the interconnection between the measured values of several constants (the 'nodes' of the graph) and the formulae connecting them (the 'edges'), and to suggest an index measuring the degree of mutual inconsistency the existing values display. Interestingly enough, the application of this index to several branches of science shows that economics has been much less efficient in the construction of consistent sets of measures, a fact Mirowski explains by the reluctance of neo-classical economists to create an institutional mechanism capable of recognising and confronting this shortcoming (an explanation which could be tested by comparing the measures assembled by economic agencies with, say, a neo-classical or a Keynesian orientation).

Other of the authors who has contributed more to the development of an economics of scientific activity has been Paul David, partly in close collaboration with Partha Dasgupta (e.g., Dasgupta and David [1994]). Most of their work on the topic, however, fits better the category of 'economics of science' than that of 'economics of scientific knowledge' (as I defined them in sec. 1), for they have basically tried to look for an economic explanation of the social institutions of research and development. In some more recent papers, nevertheless, David has articulated some ideas which definitely belong into the ESK field, particularly in David [1998a], where he presents some models about the behaviour of reputation-seeking scientists when deciding what opinion to express (see also [David, 1994] for an analysis of cumulative advantage in science, and [1998b] for a hypothesis about the origin of peer review). In one of these models [David, 1998a, pp. 138 ff.], researchers have to adopt or reject a theory, $T$, which *in the long run* will be either accepted as right by the community, or rejected as wrong, but which it is now under discussion, so that some researchers are currently accepting it, and others rejecting it; if a scientist thinks with probability $p$ that the theory will be collectively adopted in the end (considering her own private knowledge and the opinion expressed by her neighbour colleagues), the utility she expects to get will also depend on whether now there is a majority or a minority of colleagues accepting $T$, in the following way: let $a$ be the utility of adopting $T$ if it is now majoritarily rejected, but collectively adopted in the future ('being right with the few'); let $b$ be the utility of rejecting $T$ under the same conditions ('being wrong with the crowd'); let $c$ the utility of adopting $T$ if it is now majoritarily accepted, and collectively adopted in the future ('being right with the crowd'), and let $d$ the utility of rejecting $T$ under these conditions ('being wrong with the few'); lastly, let us assume that $a > c > b > d$. It follows that the scientist will adopt the majority opinion if and only if $(1-p)/p < (c-d)/(a-b)$. This entails that, if the difference between being eventually right having defended a minority opinion, and being eventually wrong but having defended the majority opinion, is low enough in reputation terms, then conformity to the majoritarian opinion will be a dominant strategy. David also formulates a stochastic graph-theoretic model of consensus formation (*op. cit.*, pp. 145 ff.), closely related to the one just described. Imagine that at each time one single scientist is randomly selected to give her the chance of modifying her opinion about $T$; she will do it depending on the opinions that the colleagues to which she is 'connected' have expressed in the moment immediately before. This 'voting' mechanism generates a Markovian process that has unanimous acceptance of $T$ and unanimous rejection as the only absorbing states, states that are reached with a probability equal, respectively, to the proportion of individual scientists accepting or rejecting $T$ at the beginning of the process.

Other economic explanations of the 'construction' of scientific consensus were developed in the late nineties. In 1997, within a conference organised at Notre Dame by Philip Mirowski and Esther Mirjam Sent on "The Need for a New Economics of Science", a couple of papers were presented [Oomes, 1997; Brock and Durlauf, 1999] in which the choice of a theory by each individual scientist depends on two factors: an individual effect, which takes into account the researcher's 'private' assessment of the theory, and a conformity effect, which takes into account the (expected) choices of her colleagues. A similar approach, though on much weaker mathematical assumptions, was independently elaborated in Zamora Bonilla [1999b]. The main conclusions of all these models were in part related to those of David's paper, but went further than it in some respects: first, more than one social equilibrium (i.e., a distribution of individual choices such that nobody has an interest in making a different choice, given the choices of her colleagues) are possible; second, path-dependence is a significant factor in the attainment of an equilibrium (e.g., two scientific communities having *the same* empirical evidence about a couple of alternative theories might end making different choices, if their data had just been accumulated in a different *order*); but, third, contrarily to what happened in David's model, some equilibrium states can correspond to a non unanimous theory choice (i.e., diversity of individual judgements can take place in the equilibrium). Another important conclusion of these models is that, as the factors influencing the individual effects change (e.g., by finding new empirical or theoretical arguments which affect the assessment each scientist makes), the number of scientists accepting a theory can suffer a sizeable change at some point, even though those influencing factors have accumulated by small marginal increments (i.e., the dynamics of scientific consensus is not necessarily linear). Zamora Bonilla [2006a] generalises the analysis for cases where individual choices depend not only on how many colleagues are accepting a theory, but on *which ones* are doing it. The last two referred papers additionally consider the possible effects of *collective choices*, i.e., the forming of (not necessarily universal) coalitions in which every member would be interested in adopting the theory if and only if the other members did the same; the paper shows that, if coalitions are feasible, in most of the cases where two equilibria existed, only one of them becomes stable under collective choice (i.e. no other coalition can force a move to the other equilibrium), and, if it happened that one of the equilibria was Pareto-superior with respect to the other, the former one will be coalition proof. This last conclusion suggests that there is a middle ground between 'free market' and 'social planning' approaches to the economics of scientific knowledge: the epistemic efficiency of science perhaps would not mainly come from the unintended coordination of individual choices, nor from the calculations of a single planner, but from *the free constitution of groups*.

In a similar vein, Zamora Bonilla [2002] presents a model in which the members of a scientific community can choose the 'confirmation level' (or other measure of scientific quality) a theory must surpass in order to become acceptable, under the assumption that scientists are motivated not only by the quality of the theories, but mainly by being recognised as proponents of an accepted theory. The chances of getting recognition are too small both if the chosen level is very low (for then too many successful theories will exist to compete with), and if the level is very high (for then it would be very difficult to discover an acceptable theory). Zamora Bonilla [2006b] offers a game theoretic analysis of how the *interpretation* of an experimental result is chosen (in a way similar to Goldman and Shaked [1991], but taking into account strategic considerations), which illuminates the role of social mechanisms in scientific communication, understood as constraints in the way the 'game' between authors and readers is played. That the choice of scientific norms is an appropriate subject for economic analysis has being recognised in other works; for example, Kahn, Landsburg and Stockman [1996] also analyse from an economic viewpoint the choice of an empirically versus a theoretically oriented strategy by scientists; Slembeck [2000] designs a betting mechanism to compel scientists to agree on empirical facts; Michael Strevens [2003] employs optimality analysis to justify the use of the priority rule in allocating scientific resources; lastly, Max Albert [2005] offers a dynamic game model, according to which scientists select a methodological rule depending on the choices of their colleagues.

## *5.2 Institutionalist theories*

I will end this survey of the main contributions to the economics of scientific knowledge by discussing three works which attempt to offer a more or less systematic conception of the process of scientific discovery, but that abstain to employ mathematical models as their main analytical tool. The first of the contributions I will discuss is Wible [1998], which also was the first full length book on the topic. The most important parts of it in connection to ESK are its five last chapters, where Wible presents an economic view that he explicitly opposes to the idea of science as a 'market for ideas'. According to Wible (*op. cit.*, ch. 8–9), automatic self-corrective mechanisms like those assumed in 'perfect markets' do not exist, or are not too powerful, in the process of scientific knowledge production; he goes even further and considers science as an economic institution *opposite* to perfectly competitive markets, and the organisational structure of scientific decision making (research programmes, university departments, peer review, public funding, and so on) is explained in a new-institutionalist way, as ways to minimise 'transaction costs', and it is contrasted with the organisation of the market-governed aspects of science (i.e., those related to science as a consumer of economic inputs — labour, commodities... — and as a producer of commercial applications). The last three chapters are the most philosophical of the book. Here Wible offers an evolutionary account of economic and scientific rationality, understanding scientific decisions as essentially constrained by scarcity of resources, and, in general, presenting all decision making as an evolving, multidimensional and non-mechanical process of problem solving. Under this interpretation, actual scientific rationality would not be 'justificationist', in the same way that economic rationality would not really be 'maximising'. Wible also discusses the problem of self-reference (recall section 3.4): an economics of economics will necessarily be self-referential, and this may lead to detect internal inconsistencies or infinite regresses within some economic arguments; but, from an economic point of view, an infinite regress must end at some point, since our cognitive resources are limited; Wible suggests that a 'critical', 'non-justificationist' rationality, is necessary in order to handle these logical problems. This issue of reflexivity is also applied to the tacit 'economics of science' that most mainstream economists seem to assume. They tend to see their own activity (scientific research) as a competitive process similar to those which prevail in the economy, a process which tends naturally to some efficient equilibrium; but, Wible argues, the features of scientific knowledge entail that science is an imperfect and slow evolutionary process, not explainable in terms of mechanistic equilibrium concepts. One possible criticism that can be made to Wible's approach is that he gives almost no insight about how such an evolutionary account of science would look like once it were elaborated in detail, for one fears that he is not thinking in something like evolutionary *mathematical* models (e.g., those of evolutionary game theory, or those of the Nelson-Winter type). On the other hand, in the first chapters of the book Wible does not hesitate in offering some simplified equilibrium models of some types of scientists' 'misconduct' (namely, fraud and replication failure -which, according to the model by Mirowski we examined in the past subsection, needs not be consider a 'failure' at all), and so, one wonders why the same explanatory strategy would not be appropriate to analyse 'normal' research behaviour.

Another institutionalist approach to the study of scientific knowledge production has been developed by Christoph Lütge [2001] and [2004], who uses constitutional political economy as a complement to a naturalised philosophy of science (see Brennan and Buchanan [1975] for a clear exposition of constitutional economics). The main elements of this approach are the following: first, the essential object of economic analysis is not individual decision making, but *interactions*, where considerations of strategic decision arise; second, the main purpose of an economic analysis is not theoretical, but *practical*, i.e., promoting the design of institutions; and third, there are no external normative criteria, for *consensus* amongst the interacting agents is the only source of normativity. Lütge's proceeds, then, to identify *social dilemma situations* in scientific research, situations that create the opportunity for introducing institutional mechanisms allowing agents to overcome those problems. Drawing on Martin Rudwick's case study of the 'great Devonian controversy', Lütge identifies three different dilemma situations (which are not necessarily unique): the priority dilemma (i.e., how to allocate research efforts and scientific recognition), the property rights dilemma (i.e., whether, or how much, to plagiarise the works of others), and dilemma of access to objects of study (i.e., whether to 'monopolise' these objects or not). Many of these cases can lead to a Prisoner's Dilemma situation, that can only be 'solved' by collectively changing the rules according to which the interactions between researchers take place. Unfortunately, Lütge does not analyse how this collective decision could be taken. Another significant Buchanian thesis stressed by Lütge is that, though consensus is the fundamental normative criterion to evaluate scientific items, it can be applied to very different levels: scientists may agree (or disagree) about specific cognitive *achievements* (theory, data, and so on), but consensus on *norms* is much more important from a normative point of view, particularly if we distinguish amongst different *levels* of methodological or institutional rules (more on this below).

The last work I am going to discuss is surely the until now most systematic attempt to develop an economic institutionalist theory of science, Yangfei Shi's book *The Economics of Scientific Knowledge.* In the first chapters, Shi analyses the behaviour of scientists, both as a producers of scientific information, and as a *consumers* of the information produced by others, and also the *exchange* relationships which emerge between self-interested researchers, each one playing simultaneously the roles of producer and consumer. The rest of the book is devoted to analyse the *institutional structure* of science, i.e., the system of norms which regulate the behaviour of scientists (norms that are interpreted as solutions to collective action problems). These norms are classified into three different groups: 'distributive rules' (i.e., rules about the allocation of resources), 'constitutional rules' (cognitive paradigms and authority structures), and 'aggregative rules' (the mechanisms creating 'scientific order'). In spite of the fact that Shi's analysis of scientific norms is more complete than other ones, it can be subjected to several criticisms. In the first place, three very different kinds of things are conflated in his classification: individual routines, social norms, and what we could call 'equilibrating mechanisms' (more or less equivalent to Shi's 'aggregative rules'). By individual routines I mean all types of regular practices which can be observed in the behaviour of a single scientist; these practices can spread towards other scientists by imitation, but even if they are universally adopted, this does not make of them a social norm automatically, for what is characteristic of norms is that they are *taken as compulsory* by the individuals (even if everybody disobeys them). On the other hand, 'equilibrating mechanisms' are neither individual routines nor social norms, and they can even be hidden for the individuals, as in the case of an 'invisible hand mechanism', in which case they can hardly be taken as 'norms', but rather as the 'natural laws' of a social structure. In the second place, Shi's notion of 'constitutional rules' is at odds with what is ordinarily meant by these expression in standard constitutional political economy, where the idea is, first, that a sharp distinction can be made between choices made *under* rules and the choice *of* the rules themselves, and second, that social norms can be divided into 'constitutional' and 'non-constitutional' ones, the former being those which establish (ideally, by unanimity) the collective choice mechanisms by which the latter are going to be chosen (not necessarily by unanimity). On the other hand, a constitutional economists would have expected to find in Shi's discussion a distinction between cognitive norms of different *levels*, so that, in case of disagreement among scientists about a particular theory or a certain methodological practice, researchers could appeal to some 'higher level rules' to reach a common decision, if this is possible, and to rules of still a higher level if there is also disagreement about the latter, and so on. From this point of view, the 'constitutional rules' of a scientific community would only be those fundamental principles to which its members can resort in case of discursive conflict.

## ACKNOWLEDGEMENTS

This paper was prepared while its author was taking part in Spanish Government's research projects BFF2008-03607/FISO and FFI2008-01580/consolider-ingenio-CSD2009-0056. Generous support from Urrutia Elejalde Foundation is also acknowledged.

## BIBLIOGRAPHY

[Albert, 2005] M. Albert. Product Quality in Scientific Competition, mimeo, 2005.

[Axelrod, 1984] R. Axelrod. *The Evolution of Cooperation*, New York, Basic Books, 1984.

[Balzer *et al.*, 1987] W. Balzer, C. U. Moulines, and J. Sneed. *An Architectonic for Science: The Structuralist Program*, Dordrecht, D. Reidel, 1987.

[Bartley, 1990] W. W. Bartley. *Unfathomed Knowledge, Unmesured Wealth: On Universities and the World of Nations*, La Salle, Ill., Open Court, 1990.

[Bicchieri, 1988] C. Bicchieri. Methodological Rules as Conventions, *Philosophy of the Social Sciences*, 18:477-95, 1988.

[Blais, 1987] M. J. Blais. Epistemic Tit for Tat, *The Journal of Philosophy*, 84:363-75, 1987.

[Bloor, 1976] D. Bloor. *Knowledge and Social Imagery*, London, Routledge, 1976.

[Bourdieu, 1975] P. Bourdieu. The Specificity of the Scientific Field and the Social Conditions of the Progress of Reason, *Social Science Information*, 14.6:19-47 (quoted from its reprint in M. Biagioli (ed.), 1999, *The Science Studies Reader*, London, Routledge), 1975.

[Bracanovic, 2002] T. Bracanovic. The Referee's Dilemma: The Ethics of Scientific Communities and Game Theory, *Prolegomena*, 1:55-74, 2002.

[Brennan and Buchanan, 1985] G. Brennan and J. Buchanan. *The Reason of Rules*, Cambridge, Cambridge University Press, 1985.

[Brenner, 1999] Th. Brenner. *Modelling Learning in Economics*, Cheltenham, Edward Elgar, 1999.

[Brock and Durlauf, 1999] W. A. Brock and S. N. Durlauf. A Formal Model of Theory Choice in Science, *Economic Theory*, 14:113-30, 1999.

[Buchanan, 1996] J. Buchanan. *The Economics and the Ethics of Constitutional Order*, Ann Arbor, University of Michigan Press, 1996.

[Butos and Boettke, 2002] W. N. Butos and P. J. Boettke. Kirznerian Entrepreneurship and the Economics of Science, *Journal des Economistes et des Etudes Humaines*, 12:119-30, 2002.

[Callon, 1994] M. Callon. Is Science a Public Good?, *Science, Technology, and Human Values*, 19:395-424, 1994.

[Callon, 1995] M. Callon. Four Models for the Dynamics of Science, in S. Jasanoff, G. E. Markle, J. C. Petersen, and T. Pinch (eds.), *Handbook os Science and Technology Studies*, Thousand Oaks, Sage, pp. 29-63, 1995.

[Coase, 1974] R. H. Coase. The Market for Goods and the Market for Ideas, *Amercian Economic Review Papers and Proceedings*, 64:384-91, 1974.

[Dasgupta and David, 1994] P. Dasgupta and P. David. Toward a New Economics of Science, *Research Policy*, 23:487-521, 1994.

[David, 1994] P. David. Positive Feedbacks and Research Productivity in Science: Reopening Another Black Box. In G. Granstrand (ed.), *Economics of Technology*, Amsterdam, Elsevier, pp. 65-89, 1994.

[David, 1998a] P. David. Communication Norms and the Collective Cognitive Performance of 'Invisible Colleges'. In G. Barba *et al.* (eds.), *Creation and Transfer of Knowledge Institutions and Incentives*, Berlin, Springer, pp. 115-63, 1998.

[David, 1998b] P. David. Clio and the Economic Organization of Science: Common Agency Contracting and the Emergence of 'Open Science' Institutions, *American Economic Review Papers and Proceedings*, 88:15-21, 1998.

[Davis, 1998] J. B. Davis. The Fox and the Henhouses: The Economics of Scientific Knowledge, *History of Political Economy*, 29:741-6, 1998.

[Friedman, 1953] M. Friedman. The Methodology of Positive Economics. In *Essays in Positive Economics*, Chicago, The University of Chicago Press., pp. 3-43, 1953.

[Fuller, 1988] S. Fuller. *Social Epistemology*, Bloomington, Indiana University Press, 1988.

[Fuller, 1994] S. Fuller. Mortgaging the Farm to Save the (Sacred) Cow, *Studies in History and Philosophy of Science*, 25:251-61, 1994.

[Fuller, 2000] S. Fuller. *The Governance of Science*, Philadelphia, The Open University Press, 2000.

[Goldman and Cox, 1996] A. Goldman and J. C. Cox. Speech, Truth, and the Free Market for Ideas, *Legal Theory*, 2:1-32, 1996.

[Goldman an dShaked, 1991] A. Goldman and M. Shaked. An Economic Model of Scientific Activity and Truth Acquisition, *Philosophical Studies*, 63:31-55, 1991.

[Goodin and Brennan, 2001] R. E. Goodin and G. Brennan. Bargaining over Beliefs, *Ethics*, 111:256-77, 2001.

[Hands, 1994a] D. W. Hands. The Sociology of Scientific Knowledge and Economics: Some Thoughts on the Possibilities. In Robert Backhouse (ed.), *New Perspectives in Economic Methodology*, London: Routledge, pp. 75-106, 1994.

[Hands, 1994b] D. W. Hands. Blurred Boundaries: Recent Changes in teh Relationship Between Economics and The Philosophy of the Natural Science, *Studies in History and Philosophy of Science*, 25:751-72, 1994.

[Hands, 1995] D. W. Hands. Social Epistemology Meets the Invisible Hand: Kitcher on the Advancement of Science, *Dialogue*, 34:605-21, 1995.

[Hands, 2001] D. W. Hands. *Reflection without Rules. Economic Methodology and Contemporary Science Theory*, Cambridge, Cambridge University Press, 2001.

[Hardwig, 1991] J. Hardwig. The Role of Trust in Knowledge, *The Journal of Philosophy*, 88:693-700, 1991.

[Hayek, 1948] F. A. Hayek. The Use of Knoewledge in Society. In *Individualism and Economic Order*, Chicago, The University of Chicago Press, pp. 77-91, 1948.

[Hempel, 1960] C. G. Hempel. Deductive Inconsistencies, *Synthese*, 12:439-69, 1960 (reprinted in *Aspects of Scientific Explanations*, New York, The Free Press, pp. 53-79).

[Hilpinen, 1968] R. Hilpinen. *Rules of Acceptance and Inductive Logic*, Amsterdam, North-Holland, 1968.

[Hull, 1988] D. L. Hull. *Science as a Process. An Evolutionary Account of the Social and Conceptual Development of Science*, Chicago, The University of Chicago Press, 1988.

[Kahn *et al.*, 1996] J. A. Kahn, S. E. Landsburg, and A. C. Stockman. The Positive Economics of Methodology, *Journal of Economic Theory*, 68:64-76, 1996.

[Kitcher, 1990] Ph. Kitcher. The Division of Cognitive Labor, *The Journal of Philosophy*, 87:5-22, 1990.

[Kitcher, 1993] Ph. Kitcher. *The Advancement of Science: Science without Legend, Objectivity without Illusions*, Oxford, Oxford University Press, 1993.

[Kuhn, 1977] Th. S. Kuhn. Objetivity, Value Judgments, and Theory Choice. In *The essential tension*, Chicago, The University of Chicago Press, 1977.

[Latour, 1987] B. Latour. *Science in Action*, Cambridge, Ma., Harvard University Press, 1987.

[Latour and Woolgar, 1979] B. Latour and S. Woolgar. *Laboratory Life. The Social Construction of Scientific Facts*, Beverly Hills, Sage, 1979.

[Leonard, 2002] Th. C. Leonard. Reflection on Rules in Science: An Invisible-Hand Perspective, *Journal of Economic Methodology*, 9:141-168, 2002.

[Levi, 1967] I. Levi. *Gambling with Truth*, New York, Knopf, 1967.

[Levi, 1995] I. Levi. Cognitive Value and the Advancement of Science, *Philosophy and Phenomenological Research*, 55:619-625, 1995.
[List and Pettit, 2002] Ch. List and Ph. Pettit, Aggregating Sets of Judgements: An Impossibility Result, *Economics and Philosophy*, 18:89-110, 2002.
[Lütge, 2001] Ch. Lütge. *Ökonomische Wissenschaftstheorie*, Würtzburg: Königshausen & Neumann, 2001.
[Lütge, 2004] Ch. Lütge. Economics in Philosophy of Science: A Dismal Contribution?, *Synthese*, 140:279-305, 2004.
[Maher, 1993] P. Maher. *Betting on Theories*, Cambridge, Cambridge University Press, 1993.
[Mäki, 1999] U. Mäki. Science as a Free Market: A Reflexivity Test in an Economics of Economics, *Perspectives on Science*, 7:486-509, 1999.
[Mäki, 2002] U. Mäki, ed. *Fact and Fiction in Economics*, Cambridge, Cambridge University Press, 2002.
[Mäki, 2004] U. Mäki. Economic Epistemology: Hopes and Horrors, *Epistemce*, 1:211-22, 2004.
[Mayer, 1993] Th. Mayer. *Truth versus Precision in Economics*, Aldershot, Edward Elgar, 1993.
[McQuade and Butos, 2003] Th. J. McQuade and W. N. Butos. Order-Dependent Knowledge and the Eocnomics of Science, *The Review of Austrian Economics*, 16:133-152, 2003.
[Mirowski, 1995] Ph. Mirowski. Philip Kitcher's *Advancement of Science*: A Review Article, *Review of Political Economy*, 7:227-241, 1995.
[Mirowski, 1996] Ph. Mirowski. A Visible Hand in the Marketplace for Ideas. In M. Power (ed.), *Accounting and Science*, Cambridge, Cambridge University Press, 1996.
[Mirowski, 2004] Ph. Mirowski. *The Effortless Economy of Science?*, Durham, Duke University Press, 2004.
[Mirowski and Snet, 2002a] Ph. Mirowski and E.-M. Sent, eds. *Science Bought and Sold: Essays in the Economics of Science*, Chicago and London: The Chicago University Press, 2002.
[Mirowski and Sent, 2002b] Ph. Mirowski and E.-M. Sent. Introduction, in Mirowski and Sent [2002a], pp. 1-66.
[Mirowski and Sklivas, 1991] Ph. Mirowski and S. Sklivas. Why Econometricians Don't Replicate (Although They Do Reproduce)?, *Review of Political Economy*, 31:146-63, 1991.
[Mueller, 2003] D. C. Mueller. *Public Choice III*, Cambridge, Cambridge University Press, 2003.
[Nelson, 1959] R. R. Nelson. The Simple Economics of Basic Scientific Research, *Journal of Political Economy*, 67:297-306, 1959.
[Niiniluoto, 1987] I. Niiniluoto. *Truthlikeness*, Dordrecht, D. Reidel, 1987.
[Niiniluoto, 1998] I. Niiniluoto. Verisimilitude: The Third Period, *British Journal for the Philosophy of Science*, 49:1-29, 1998.
[Oomes, 1997] N. A. Oomes. Market Failures in the Economics of Science: Barriers to Entry, Increasing Returns, and Lock-In by Historical Events, paper presented to the conference on *The Need for a New Economics of Science*, Notre Dame, 1997.
[Peirce, 1879] C. S. Peirce. A Note on the Theory of the Economy of Research, *United Stated Coast Survey for the Fiscal Year Ending June 1876*, Washington D.C., 1879. (quoted from the reprint in Mirowski and Sent (2002a), pp:183-190).
[Pickering, 1995] A. Pickering. *The Mangle of Practice: Time, Agency, and Science*, Chicago, The University of Chicago Press, 1995.
[Polany, 1962] M. Polany. The Republic of Science: Its Political and Economic Theory, *Minerva*, 1:54-73, 1962. (quoted from the reprint in Mirowski and Sent (2002a), pp. 465-85.
[Popper, 1963] K. R. Popper. *Conjectures and Refutations. The Growth of Scientific Knowledge*, London, Routledge and Keagan Paul, 1963.
[Popper, 1970] K. R. Popper. Normal Science and Its Dangers, in I. Lakatos and A. Musgrave, *Criticism and the Growth of Knowledge*, Cambridge, Cambridge University Press, 1970.
[Radnitzky, 1986] G. Radnitzky. Towards an 'Economic' Theory of Methodology, *Methodology and Science*, 19:124-47, 1986.
[Radnitzky, 1987] G. Radnitzky. Cost-Benefit Thinking in the Methodology of Research: the 'Economic Approach' Applied to Key Problems of the Philosophy of Science, in G. Radnitzky and P. Bernholz (eds.) *Economic imperialism: the economic approach applied outside the field of economics*, Paragon House, New York, 1987.
[Rescher, 1976] N. Rescher. Peirce and the Economy of Research, *Philosophy of Science*, 43:71-98, 1976.

[Rescher, 1978a] N. Rescher. *Scientific Progress. A philosophical essay on the economics of research in natural science*, Pittsburg, The University of Pittsburgh Press - Basil Blackwell, 1978.

[Rescher, 1978b] N. Rescher. *Peirce's Philosophy of Science*, Notre Dame, Notre Dame University Press, 1978.

[Rescher, 1989] N. Rescher. *Cognitive Economy. The Economic Dimension of the Theory of Knowledge*, Pittsburg, The University of Pittsburgh Press, 1989.

[Rescher, 1996] N. Rescher. *Priceless Knowledge. Natural science in economic perspective*, Lanham, Rowman & Littlefield, 1996.

[Rueger, 1996] A. Rueger. Risk and Diversification in Theory Choice, *Synthese*, 109:263-80, 1996.

[Salanié, 2000] B. Salanié. *Micoreconomics of Market Failure*, Cambridge, Ma., The MIT Press, 2000.

[Schuelssler, 2000] A. A. Schuessler. *A Logic of Expressive Choice*, Princeton, Princeton University Press, 2000.

[Shi, 2001] Y. Shi. *The Economics of Scientific Knowledge: A Rational-Choice Neoinstitutionalist Theory of Science*, Cheltenham, Edward Elgar, 2001.

[Slembeck, 2000] T. Slembeck. How to Make Scientists Agree: An Evolutionary Betting Mechanism, *Kyklos*, 53:587-92, 2000.

[Sneed, 1989] J. Sneed. MicroEconomic Models of Problem Choice in Basic Science, *Erkenntnis*, 30:207-24, 1989.

[Solomon, 1995] M. Solomon. Legend Naturalism and Scientific Progress: An Essay on Philip Kitcher's *The Advancement of Science, Studies in History and Philosophy of Science*, 26:205-18, 1995.

[Stephan and Audretsch, 2000] P. Stephan and D. B. Audretsch, eds. *The Economics of Science and of Innovation* (2 vols.), Cheltenham, Edward Elgar, 2000.

[Strevens, 2003] M. Strevens. The Role of the Priority Rule in Science, *The Journal of Philosophy*, 100:55-79, 2003.

[Sugden, 2002] R. Sugden. Credible Worlds: The Status of Theoretical Models in Economics, in Mäki (2002), pp. 107-36, 2002.

[Turner, 2002] S. Turner. Scientists as Agents, in Mirowski and Sent (2002a), pp. 362-84.

[van Fraassen, 1980] B. C. van Fraassen. *The Scientific Image*, Oxford, Clarendon Press, 1980.

[Walstad, 2001] A. Walstad. On Science as a Free Market, *Perspectives on Science*, 9:324-40, 2001.

[Walstad, 2002] A. Walstad. Science as a Market Process, *The Independent Review*, 7:5-45, 2002.

[Weintraub, 1990] R. Weintraub. Decision-Theoretic Epistemology, *Synthese*, 83:159-77, 1990.

[Wible, 1998] J. R. Wible. *The Economics of Science: Methodology and Epistemology as if Economics Really Mattered*, London, Routledge, 1998.

[Wray, 2000] K. B. Wray. Invisible Hands and the Success of Science, *Philosophy of Science*, 67:163-75, 2000.

[Ylikoski, 1995] P. Ylikoski. The Invisible Hand and Science, *Science Studies*, 8:32-43, 1995.

[Zamora Bonilla, 1996] J. P. Zamora Bonilla. Verisimilitude, Structuralism and Scientific Progress, *Erkenntnis*, 44:25-47, 1996.

[Zamora Bonilla, 1999a] J. P. Zamora Bonilla. Verisimilitude and the Scientific Strategy of Economic Theory, *Journal of Economic Methodology*, 6:331-50, 1999.

[Zamora Bonilla, 1999b] J. P. Zamora Bonilla. The Elementary Economics of Scientific Consensus, *Theoria*, 14:461-88, 1999.

[Zamora Bonilla, 2000] J. P. Zamora Bonilla. Truthlikeness, Rationality and Scientific Method, *Synthese*, 122:321-35, 2000.

[Zamora Bonilla, 2002] J. P. Zamora Bonilla. Economists: Truth-Seekers or Rent-Seekers?, in U. Mäki (2002), pp. 356-75.

[Zamora Bonilla, 2006a] J. P. Zamora Bonilla. Science Studies and the Theory of Games, *Perspectives on Science*, 14:525-557, 2006.

[Zamora Bonilla, 2006b] J. P. Zamora Bonilla. Rhetoric, Induction, and the Free Speech Dilemma, *Philosophy of Science*, 73:175-93, 2006

[Ziman, 1968] J. M. Ziman. *Public Knowledge: The Social Dimension of Science*, Cambridge, Cambridge University Press, 1968.

[Ziman, 2002] J. M. Ziman. The Microeconomics of Academic Science. In Mirowski and Sent, pp. 318-40, 2002.

# INDEX OF NAMES

# GENERAL INDEX

Kolibri 360 GmbH
Ferdinand-Jühlke-Straße 7
99095 Erfurt, Deutschland
produktsicherheit@kolibri360.de